The Legal Environment of Business

JAMES L. HOUGHTELING, JR.

Carnegie Institute of Technology

and

GEORGE G. PIERCE

Northeastern University

The Legal Environment of Business

Harcourt, Brace & World, Inc.

New York / Burlingame

Library of Congress Catalog Number: 63-11409

Printed in the United States of America

Preface

This is a book about law designed primarily for students who are planning to become businessmen. As businessmen, they will need and want the advice of lawyers. And yet they should know something about the legal environment in which business operates. This environment includes the *institutions* and *processes* by which law is created, molded to meet changing needs, and applied to particular cases; it also includes the multitude of legal *rules* that serve to channel the behavior of businessmen.

We begin Part I with a consideration of the nature of legal rules and the process of adjudicating cases. We depart from the traditional coverage, however, by devoting the latter half of Chapter 3 to a critical discussion of some of the "problem areas" in the *adjudicative* process. And in Chapters 4 through 9 we examine the *lawmaking* processes: the lawmaking of judges as they build on common-law precedents and interpret statutes and constitutions; the lawmaking of legislatures and administrative agencies; and the contributions to lawmaking made by private groups (with collective bargaining between employers and unions used as an example). A brief closing chapter ventures some generalizations about the role of law in society.

In Part II we explore seven major fields of substantive law that are of particular concern to businessmen. In this part, too, we make repeated reference to legal processes and institutions and emphasize the evolutionary character of the law. Each chapter in Part II opens with a brief summary of the historical background and the economic and social context of the body of law under discussion. Then follows a statement of the general rules of law, with frequent hypothetical examples for purposes of clarification. Most of the legal principles are illustrated by actual cases that have been brought before the courts. Each chapter concludes with a summary of the rules of law that have been presented in the course of the chapter.

It has been our experience as teachers that legal principles come alive only when students read about actual cases as reported in judicial decisions. Moreover, the act of reading decisions is indispensable to an understanding of the judicial process itself. Consequently we have included numerous decisions throughout the book. We have refrained, however, from editing the decisions as extensively as is customary in books of this sort—by summarizing the facts, for example, or by omitting procedural details, or eliminating those passages that are not directly related to the principal holding of the case. Though it might be argued that extensive editing of this sort saves the student time and effort, we are convinced that the intellectual exertion involved in mastering the facts and the procedural background as explained in the official report itself is an important part of learning about the legal system. To advance the student's understanding of the legal principles embodied in the decisions, we have appended explanations of unfamiliar concepts and terms and have included many comments and questions designed to provoke reflection and discussion.

This book, we believe, can be used for courses of one, two, or three semesters. In addition, the materials can be assigned in a variety of sequences. For example, in a one-semester course that lays major stress on the legal process, the instructor might choose to concentrate on the material in Part I and use selected cases from Part II for illustration. Or, if the instructor wishes to put greater emphasis on the business-law content, he might assign some or all of Part I together with Chapter 11 on contracts or other chapters from Part II. Teachers of two- and three-semester courses might start with Chapters 1 to 3 and then turn to the chapters in Part II, interspersing later chapters from Part I among the assignments from Part II. For example: since the rules of contract and agency law are largely of judicial origin, Chapter 4 on judicial lawmaking might be assigned along with the chapter on contracts or agency. Since there has been important legislative activity in recent years in the law of sales and negotiable instruments, Chapters 5 and 6 on the enactment and interpretation of legislation might be assigned in connection with Chapters 12 and 13. Many constitutional questions and problems of administrative lawmaking are intimately associated with government regulation of business; hence it might be useful to assign Chapters 7 and 8 in conjunction with Chapter 17. Since a variety of sequences is possible, we decided to group the chapters on the legal process and those on the substantive rules in two separate sections, and to leave it to each instructor to work out the sequence that best serves his objectives.

For reference purposes, we have included a Glossary of selected legal concepts at the end of the book. In addition to the definitions, we have listed the text pages on which the concepts are discussed and on which illustrative cases are quoted. It should be emphasized that the Glossary is highly selective and that it does not include many strictly technical terms which are better left to the Index.

We are indebted to Professor Harold J. Berman of the Harvard Law School, Professor Cornelius W. Gillam of the Wharton School of Finance and Commerce at the University of Pennsylvania, and Professor Jacob Weissman of the Graduate School of Business at the University of Chicago, for their penetrating comments and criticisms of the manuscript. Mr. Houghteling, who is responsible for Part I, wishes particularly to thank Mr. Elliott Dunlap Smith, until recently Provost of the Carnegie Institute of Technology, for continuous encouragement and for many suggestions and criticisms. Colleagues and students at Carnegie and friends too numerous to mention individually raised questions and pointed out defects in particular chapters; their help is gratefully acknowledged. He also wants to thank Grace Couchman and Rose Yonge for their valuable clerical assistance. Mr. Pierce, who is responsible for Part II, wishes to thank his colleagues and students at Northeastern University for their encouragement and assistance. He also wants to thank Vera Jackson, Barbara Smith, Mary Snyder, Mary Frasca, Mary Lou Downie, and Theodore Yonge for their invaluable services in typing the manuscript. Both of us have had continuous inspiration and assistance from our wives.

J. L. H., JR.

G. G. P.

Contents

PART II
The Law of Business

PART I

The Business of Law

1 The Nature and Functions of Legal Rules

Many people have a vague feeling that they ought to know more than they do about the law. They suspect that knowledge of legal rules might help them in their jobs, or keep them out of trouble. So they read newspaper articles and watch television programs about law, and buy books with such titles as "Everyday Law for Every Man." Their questions cover a wide range of problems and situations: What formalities must be observed in buying a house? How broad is the father's duty to support his family? Are unwritten promises ever binding? Is picketing ever illegal? Under what circumstances may stockholders recover damages from an officer of the company?

This book is designed particularly for students of business who want to know something about the legal environment in which business operates. But it is not designed to enable you to be your own lawyer. Nor is it a manual of rules for you to memorize. Trying to memorize quantities of legal rules is, indeed, a waste of time—even for lawyers—for several reasons:

1. There are simply too many rules.

2. The same rules are not applied in all the states. We can make a good many generalizations that will hold good for most states, but without investigation we can never be sure that a particular generalization is true for any one state.

3. Rules are constantly being modified by legislators and judges, and to a limited extent by other officials.

4. Most rules are not simple and categorical. To state a legal rule with accuracy is likely to require a surprising number of qualifications and exceptions. (Take such an apparently simple rule as the requirement that motorists keep to the right, then think of all the circumstances in which a motorist probably is legally justified in being on the left side of the road.) Many fact-situations, we shall find, are not neatly covered by any single rule. Indeed, a lawyer—that is, an expert on legal rules—can often do no better than venture a prediction of what rule a court of law will apply to a given situation.

The proposition which underlies this book is that law must be viewed not as a body of static rules but as *a dynamic process by which rules are*

3

constantly being created, changed, and molded to fit particular situations.

In Part I of the book we shall describe and analyze the processes of the law, in the belief that no one can truly understand legal rules without understanding the processes from which they emerge. In Part II, we shall consider the rules in seven selected fields of law which are of particular importance to businessmen. In each of the seven chapters, we shall outline the basic rules and give some examples to illustrate them. But the larger portion of each chapter will consist of recorded court decisions. Rules, you will find, become meaningful only when you see them being applied to actual cases. These court decisions also illustrate the most remarkable of the lawmaking processes considered in Part I: the creation of new rules by judges as they bend old rules to make them fit novel situations.

The emphasis in Part I, then, is on what judges, legislators, and administrative officials do; while in Part II it is on contracts, agency relationships, bills and notes, corporations, and related topics. The two parts are complementary approaches to an understanding of law as a framework for business transactions.

Although most of Part I is about the *processes* by which legal rules are created and applied, we must start by considering briefly the *nature of legal rules* and some of their functions. First we shall consider these questions: Why does society need a system of legal rules? and, What are some of the essential characteristics of a successful system of rules? Then we shall try to define a little more precisely what is meant by the concept "legal rule." Finally we shall examine and distinguish between some categories of legal rules.

Why Do We Need Legal Rules?

One of the most familiar legal rules is that motorists must stop at red lights. Why do we have traffic lights at busy intersections? Because it is impossible for everyone to cross at once, and the most orderly and efficient method of handling traffic is to set up a signal which lets first one stream of cars, and then the other, move ahead.

Society itself is like a busy intersection. Individuals and groups have an infinity of wants that they seek to satisfy. Obviously, not all these wants can be wholly satisfied; indeed, some of them must be denied satisfaction altogether. Since some of these wants are more urgent, and some more socially desirable, than others, we must have a system for establishing priorities among them.

Conceivably, of course, a society could allow considerations of sheer power—physical, economic, social, political—to determine which wants should be satisfied. But civilized societies have rejected private power as the primary criterion for establishing priorities and have substituted instead such criteria as "justice" and "social utility." A major task of governments is to create and enforce rules of law based on those criteria.

What are rules of law? They may be defined as *guides to human conduct in society, established and enforced by officials acting on behalf of the whole community, and designed to achieve the best possible balancing and adjustment of the diverse interests in a society.* But the rules are not and can never be static; in societies in which new problems keep emerging, new rules are continually needed. So it is less important to know the rules than it is to understand the processes by which they are created and applied. This is why we suggested above that the best way of thinking about "law" is not as a body of rules but as a *dynamic process, a system of regularized, institutionalized procedures for the orderly decision of social questions, including the settlement of disputes.* And this is what we mean when we speak of "law and order" and of "government under law": we are referring not to the particular rules currently in effect, but to the principle of orderly, institutionalized adjustment of competing interests.

Some Requirements for an Effective Legal System

Most Rules Must Be Obeyed Voluntarily. The first objective of a legal system is to set forth guides for human conduct that will cause people to behave by choice as society wants them to behave. This is the "preventive" function of law. The most important legal rules (sometimes known as the *primary* rules) are those designed to channel the conduct of private persons and groups into patterns likely to keep conflict to a minimum. Without a large measure of voluntary compliance with the primary rules, social life would be impossible: no community could afford to employ enough officials to compel everyone to obey the law.

But inevitably some people do not comply, either deliberately or through carelessness or ignorance. So a legal system must have officials—police and judges, for instance—to apply the secondary, or *remedial,* legal rules. (These are the rules that determine what happens to people who have violated the primary rules.) But resort to officials and to remedial rules must always be exceptional. If a legal system is to be effective, most people, most of the time, must observe the speed limits, live up to their contractual commitments, pay their taxes, and in other ways comply with the law.

The Rules Must Seem Just and Reasonable. Why *do* most people comply with the rules most of the time? Partly, to be sure, because there are remedial rules: because they don't want any trouble with the officials; don't want to be arrested and prosecuted, or to be sued; and don't want to be punished, or to have to pay damages to somebody they have harmed. But we probably tend to overestimate the importance of these fears. Most people obey legal rules partly out of force of habit and partly because they feel, at least dimly, that doing so is right.

But it does not follow that people will accept just any set of rules. They must believe that the rules are relatively fair and reasonable. A rule that seems unjust or unreasonable to any considerable part of the community is sure to be difficult to enforce.

Circumstances sometimes arise, of course, in which it is desirable to establish a rule even though many people may not like it: the "anti-discrimination" laws adopted in recent years in many communities may well be examples. Such laws are designed to raise the prevailing moral standards of the community. But it is nonetheless true that a law which many people disapprove of is likely to be hard to enforce, and may even cause harm which outweighs any possible good that the law itself might have accomplished. Prohibition during the 1920's and most of our current laws against gambling are often cited as evidence to support this proposition.

The Rules Must Be Flexible.   Since the material circumstances of community life, and with them the values and attitudes of the community, are continually changing, the system of rules under which the community lives must be flexible and adaptable. There must be ways to bend existing rules to meet novel situations, and ways to make more substantial changes in the rules when such changes seem necessary. In our legal system, the task of bending the rules to meet new situations has traditionally been assigned to the courts, while the more substantial changes are usually made by legislative bodies.

The Rules Must Be Knowable.   If the community expects its members to comply with the legal rules, they must know what the rules are. It is obviously not necessary for every citizen to know all the rules, but the experts in the rules—the lawyers—must be able to advise their clients on the probable legal consequences of their acts. As a famous judge, Benjamin Nathan Cardozo, once said: "Law as a guide to conduct is reduced to the level of mere futility if it is unknown and unknowable."

Under some circumstances, though, the requirement of certainty may conflict with other requirements. The most certain and "knowable" rules tend to be those that are relatively simple, categorical, and without qualifications or exceptions. ("Thou shalt not kill.") But to make a rule seem reasonable and just, qualifications and exceptions often have to be added. (Killing in self-defense is permitted in some circumstances, as is killing in time of war, and so forth.) By the same token, flexible and changing rules are less certain in their application than inflexible and unchanging ones. One of the lawmakers' hardest tasks is trying to balance these competing requirements.

What Do We Mean by "Legal Rules"?

We have defined the term "legal rules" (or "rules of law") to cover those guides to social conduct which are created and enforced by public officials. They command or forbid or permit or encourage various kinds of behavior. This is by no means the only tenable definition, but it is a starting point.

Our definition of "legal rule" is a broad one. The term is sometimes used much more narrowly to refer to a directive prescribing that if a person does a specified act he will incur a specified consequence; for example: "If you drive over sixty miles an hour on this highway, you will be subject to arrest." But our definition is broad enough to include directives that draw the dividing line much less precisely; for example: "If you drive faster than is reasonable under all the existing circumstances, you will be subject to arrest." This sort of rule, much relied upon in our legal system, is often referred to as a *standard*. To apply such a rule to a particular motorist, someone must "measure" his driving against the standard of what sort of driving would be reasonable under the particular circumstances.

Our definition of legal rule is also broad enough to include what are commonly known as *principles* of law. A legal principle does not purport to prescribe for specific types of situation at all. It is at a higher level of abstraction. It states a *policy* of the law; for example: one of the most important of all legal principles holds that when a man acts carelessly he may have to pay for any harm he causes. This proposition is not of itself very useful in determining whether a particular motorist is liable for the harm done in a particular accident; to decide that, we need more specific rules about negligence and damages. But the difference between principles and rules defined in the narrower sense is largely one of degree, and both are developed and modified in much the same ways. Hence we are justified in including principles under our general heading of legal rules.

Legal rules are distinguishable from other rules in that public officials have created them and are supposed to enforce them. Behind legal rules stands the authority of the state. Although many of a community's customs and moral rules eventually become law, a custom or moral rule is not in itself a rule of law; it must be acknowledged as such by officials who have the power to create legal rules. By the same token, the rules that nonofficial organizations (corporations, unions, churches, clubs, schools, and so forth) impose on their members are not legal rules—though they are often taken into account by officials who are making and applying legal rules. Some writers have suggested that when two people join in a binding contract, they are "creating rules of law" for themselves, since their promises are enforceable by officials. But under our definition these promises could clearly *not* be legal rules, since officials did not create them.

Definitions of law frequently emphasize the coercive power of the state which stands behind the rules. And it is true of many rules that failure to comply with them may lead to the use of coercion by officials. Thus, if a man refuses to perform his obligations under a contract, is sued in a court for breach of contract, loses the suit, is ordered to pay damages, and refuses to do so, a sheriff may seize his property. But many rules of law merely grant permission to do certain things; the man who chooses not to do what he is permitted to do is subject to no coercion. Moreover, the government often induces people to do what it wants them to do by the lure of benefits. When the United States government wants a farmer to reduce the acreage on which he plants marketable crops, it offers him a reward for not planting on some of his land. If he ignores the offer, he is not penalized; he simply does not get the reward. Public education and information programs are another means, even more remote from any threat of ultimate coercion, which the government uses to induce people to behave in certain ways.

PROBLEM

The city council wants to compel landlords to raise the standards of safety, sanitation, and over-all habitability prevailing in apartment houses in the poorer neighborhoods. It is aware that various approaches are open to it. One of the most direct would be simply to pass a law stating that any landlord who lets his buildings fall below certain minimum standards will be subject to fine or imprisonment. What other approaches are open to the council?

Some Categories of Legal Rules

Legal rules may be classified in a variety of ways. Of these, only two need concern us at this stage.

Duties, Liberties, and Powers

One way of classifying legal rules is according to the position in which they put the people to whom they are addressed.

1. The first category imposes *duties* on people. In this class are rules that require a witness under oath to tell the truth, a husband to support his wife and children, and a person who has entered into a contract to do what he has promised. The person who fails to do what each of these rules requires may find that officials are intervening in his life.

Sometimes rules that impose duties take the form of a command. ("You are required to file an income tax return!") Sometimes they are prohibitory. ("You are forbidden to drive at more than sixty miles an hour!") The form is unimportant; what matters is that if the persons addressed do not act as the rules require, a remedial rule will apply. ("If you do drive faster than sixty miles an hour, you may be arrested and fined!") The law imposes duties on officials as well as on private persons: a policeman, for instance, is under a duty not to enter a private home without permission unless he has a search warrant.[1]

2. While rules imposing duties are probably the most familiar to us, they are neither the most numerous nor necessarily the most important type of rules. Many rules do no more than permit certain acts. These rules are said to create *privileges*, or *liberties*. In effect, they say that if a person performs a certain type of act, no other person will have any legal basis for complaint, and hence officials will not interfere.

Familiar examples of liberties established by law are freedom of speech and freedom of religion, which are guaranteed by the federal Constitution. We are required neither to speak freely nor to be silent; the law allows us to choose. Thus "liberty" simply implies the absence of a duty. Another example of a liberty is the so-called "right" of self-defense. If I am physically attacked, I am released from my usual duty to refrain from using physical force on others. But liberties invariably have their limits. "Freedom of speech" does not permit a person to slander his neighbor or to utter obscenities. "Freedom of religion" does not permit a man to have several wives at once. The "right" of self-defense merely permits one to use the minimum of force that seems reasonably necessary under the circumstances.

3. Of particular interest to the businessman is the third category: rules

---

[1] To say that one category of persons is under a legal *duty* is to say that another category of persons has a legally enforceable *right* to insist that the duty be done. If husbands have a *duty* to support their wives, wives have a *right* to be supported. If witnesses under oath have a duty to tell the truth, court officials (representing the public) have a right to insist on the truth. The word "right" is used so loosely, however, that one cannot assume that whenever a right is mentioned, a correlative duty exists.

that create *powers*. Let us suppose, for example, that BUYER is thinking about purchasing SELLER's lawnmower. BUYER, we can say, has a *power* under the law to make to SELLER what the law calls an "offer." Notice that BUYER has no *duty* to do so; he is equally free to make an offer for some other lawnmower or to make no offer at all. We could, of course, say that BUYER is at *liberty* to offer to buy SELLER's lawnmower; that would be accurate, but it would not say all that we mean when we speak of a power. A rule creating a power gives permission to do an act, but, in addition, it enables the person whose act exercises that power to create new legal duties, liberties, and powers—for himself and for others. To have a power, we might say, is to have the ability to "change the legal situation." [2]

Before BUYER makes his offer, his legal relationship to SELLER is simply the relationship that exists between any two members of the community. But once he makes the offer, a new situation prevails. As we shall see in Chapter 11, BUYER's offer "binds" him until he withdraws it or until it expires or is rejected. So long as BUYER's offer is in effect, SELLER has a *power*—which he has never had before—to accept the offer. If he does accept it (and assuming that a few other legal requirements have been met), BUYER and SELLER are from that moment linked in a binding contract, and each is subject to new legal *duties*. BUYER is under a duty to pay the agreed price, and SELLER is under a duty to deliver the lawnmower.

If one of the parties fails to honor his new obligations, the other may apply to a court for redress. Before the court can decide whether to grant the remedy asked for, it must determine whether the parties exercised their powers in the manner prescribed by the rules. In our BUYER-SELLER example, for instance, do the rules require that the offer and the acceptance had to be in writing and signed to be binding? And, if so, did they meet this requirement? Powers not exercised in the manner prescribed usually fail to achieve the desired legal result.

Most of the types of business transaction that are discussed in Part II involve the exercise of powers. The businessman is not, of course, obliged to enter into such transactions at all. But if he chooses to, he may achieve certain advantageous results if—and only if—he follows the prescribed procedures.

Officials exercise powers, too. In Part I we deal with the powers of judges to decide cases, of legislators to enact laws, and of administrators to put the laws into effect. For the acts of each type of official to be effective, certain prescribed procedures must be followed.

---

[2] Note that it would not be strictly accurate to say that BUYER has a *right* to make SELLER an offer, since that would imply that SELLER and others were under some sort of *duty* not to prevent BUYER from making it. Indeed, the distinction between a power and a right is often important. Suppose, for example, that BUYER has obtained possession of SELLER's lawnmower by fraud—perhaps by paying SELLER with a check which later "bounced." BUYER now has a *power* to sell the lawnmower to INNOCENT, in that he can transfer to INNOCENT (who did not know of the fraud) the legal ownership of the lawnmower, so that SELLER cannot get it back. Obviously, though, BUYER has no *right* to sell a lawnmower which he obtained by fraud—indeed, he has a duty not to. SELLER has a *right* to receive damages from BUYER—if he can catch up with him.

Criminal Rules and Civil Rules

The classification of legal rules and court proceedings as criminal or civil is so basic, so familiar, and yet so confusing to many people that we had better try to clarify the distinction at once.

If somebody has performed an act that probably violates some rule of law and you want to make a preliminary guess as to whether the violation is criminal or civil, ask yourself this question: What is likely to happen to the wrongdoer? If you decide that he is probably subject to official punishment—to a fine or imprisonment, for instance—then he has probably violated a criminal rule. If, on the other hand, you think that he will probably be sued and ordered to pay damages to whomever he has harmed, then he has probably violated a civil rule.

But this is only a rule of thumb; we need some definitions.

Rules of *criminal* law impose duties on people (and sometimes on associations of people) and specify that any violation of those duties is a wrong, not merely to the individuals who are harmed, but to the community at large. Since the whole community has been wronged, public officials take the initiative in bringing the wrongdoer to justice, prosecuting him before a court, and urging the judge and jury to convict and punish him. Any redress received by the individuals wronged as a result of a criminal proceeding is purely incidental. Criminal wrongs are classed as either felonies or misdemeanors, depending on their gravity. To give two examples at opposite extremes: a murder is a felony, while a parking violation is a misdemeanor.

Rules of *civil* law also impose duties on people and associations of people. (In addition, they establish liberties and powers; but in distinguishing civil from criminal rules, our concern need be only with the civil rules that impose duties.) Violation of a duty created by a civil rule is, of course, a wrong; it differs from a criminal wrong, however, in that it does *not* constitute a wrong against the community at large. When a wrongful act is merely a "civil wrong," therefore, public officials will not take the initiative in prosecuting and punishing the wrongdoer; instead, the injured person must bring a civil suit against him. Civil wrongs (excluding only breaches of contract) are more commonly known as *torts* (from the French word meaning "wrong"). Torts with which you are doubtless familiar are trespass, libel, and negligence.

The problem of definition is made more difficult because, as you may have guessed by now, a particular act may be both a criminal wrong and a civil wrong. For example: if SPEEDER, while driving recklessly and in violation of the speed limit, sideswipes FAMILYMAN and damages the latter's car, he is guilty both of a crime and of a tort. The state is likely to prosecute SPEEDER for his criminal conduct, and FAMILYMAN may sue him for the tort, asking payment for the damage done. (Under the American legal system, a criminal prosecution and a civil suit cannot be combined, even though both are based on the same act.)

Many wrongful acts, however, are *only* criminal wrongs. For instance, if SPEEDER drives recklessly and too fast, but harms no one, he is guilty only of a crime. By the same token, many wrongful acts are *only* civil wrongs, simply because the lawmakers have decided that they are not of a sort that endangers the public welfare. If HOMEOWNER carelessly leaves a rollerskate on his front porch and VISITOR steps on it and falls, injuring his back, HOMEOWNER will probably not be subject to prosecution by the state, because such negligence is usually considered tortious but not criminal. Similarly, if BUYER refuses to go through with his contract to purchase SELLER's lawnmower, he will not be prosecuted, since breach of contract is not a crime. But VISITOR and SELLER probably have grounds for bringing civil suits.

There is, unfortunately, no basis for wholly reliable prediction as to whether a particular act which appears wrongful is a crime, or a civil wrong, or both. This is because lawmakers are free (within the broad limits imposed by constitutions) to make almost any sort of act a criminal or civil wrong, just as they can "legalize" acts which have in the past been legal wrongs. For instance, nothing prevents a legislature from passing a law tomorrow which declares that failure to keep a front porch safe for visitors in certain respects shall henceforth be a misdemeanor punishable by a fine.

To recapitulate: some wrongful acts violate both criminal and civil rules of law and may result in either criminal prosecution or civil proceedings, or both. Some wrongful acts violate only criminal rules (usually because no private person can claim to have been harmed), while other wrongful acts violate only civil rules (since they are not considered to affect the public interest).[3]

Since this book is primarily concerned with the legal environment and problems of businessmen, we shall be dealing mostly with civil rules of law—mostly, indeed, with the exercise of legal powers. But every businessman is, needless to say, subject to criminal law. In a few types of transaction, knowledge of criminal rules may be of real importance to him. In any event, every businessman should be familiar with the distinctions we have been discussing.

The Creation and Application of Legal Rules: Some Introductory Remarks

The remaining chapters of Part I of this book deal with the processes and institutions by which legal rules are created and applied in particular cases. Before we move on, here is a brief overview of how we plan to cover these subjects.

When we speak of applying rules in particular cases, we are referring primarily to the process known as *adjudication*. Adjudication involves (a) deciding exactly what happened—what the facts were in the particular case —and (b) deciding what legal rules should be applied to those facts. In Chapters 2 and 3 we shall consider this process.

---

[3] Once a wrongful act has come before a court, the character of the court action can usually be identified by the label given to the proceeding. If it is something like "STATE (or PEOPLE) versus SPEEDER," it is usually criminal. But if it is "FAMILYMAN versus SPEEDER," it is civil.

When we speak of creating and modifying rules, or of *lawmaking*,[4] we are referring to several processes. The best known of these is *legislative* lawmaking, a term that refers first and foremost to the enactment of "legislation" (i.e., statutes) by popularly elected legislative bodies. Many people are aware of no other kind of lawmaking—indeed, to most of us a "law" means a legislative act.

The other great lawmaking process is *decisional* lawmaking. The notion that judges (and other case-deciders) "make law" is much less familiar than the concept of legislative lawmaking. Nonetheless it is true that law is made in the course of adjudicating cases. Whenever a question arises about the proper rule of law to apply in a particular case, the answering of that question by the judges is a creative act—an act of lawmaking. The judges make law for the future, because their decisions become potential *precedents* which are likely to influence the deciding of future cases involving similar fact-situations. Law created by judicial decisions, a by-product of the process of adjudication, is variously called "decisional law," "case law," and "judge-made law."

Chapter 4 describes how judges create new rules out of old ones by building on precedent. Chapter 5 discusses the manner in which legislators make law. Then Chapters 6 and 7 return to judicial lawmaking: Chapter 6 describes how judges interpret statutes in the course of applying them in particular cases, and Chapter 7 describes how judges interpret the federal Constitution.

Legislators and judges have been making law and adjudicating cases for hundreds of years. But the last seventy-five years have seen a vast increase in the role of administrators in the legal system. Today administrative officials and agencies are both adjudicating cases and making law. Their lawmaking is in part decisional (when they decide cases) and in part legislative (when they exercise powers delegated to them by legislatures to issue regulations which have the force of law). In Chapter 8 we shall consider the role of administrators in the legal system.

We have defined legal rules to refer only to rules created by officials. But private persons and groups make important contributions to official lawmaking, and, in addition, create rules on their own that supplement the rules of law. This contribution is considered in Chapter 9.

In Chapter 10, we shall have more to say about the role of law in a changing society.

---

[4] Since we speak continually of the creation of *rules*, we might better use the term "rule-making." But, first, because "lawmaking" is more familiar and seems more natural, and second, because "rule-making" has a somewhat special connotation among lawyers, we shall use the term "lawmaking."

2 The Courts
and the Process
of Adjudication

Only a tiny fraction of the innumerable social transactions that take place every day in our society ever come before courts of law. But the few cases that do are of peculiar importance for the legal system and for the student of law. For one thing, these cases furnish the best documentation we have of the legal system at work. Even more important, they provide the occasions on which judges make authoritative restatements of the scope and content of legal rules.

When courts decide cases, they perform two distinct, though interrelated, functions. First, they settle the controversy between the parties: they determine what the facts were and apply the appropriate rules to those facts. This is the function commonly known as *adjudication.* But whenever there is any question about what rules to apply, the courts also perform a second function: they decide what the appropriate rules are and how they fit the particular case. Deciding what rules are applicable often requires the courts to reformulate and modify the scope of existing rules. Some of these reformulations become precedents that determine the future scope and content of the rules. This second function is sometimes referred to as *judicial lawmaking.*[1] In this and the following chapter we are concerned with the first of these functions. We shall examine the second function in later chapters.

First we shall describe the categories of courts that make up a court system, and the limits placed on their jurisdiction. Then we shall go on to trace the sequence of steps that make up the adjudicative process. The following chapter will be entirely devoted to one of those steps: the trial.

Court Systems: Organization and Jurisdiction

Laymen have no need for a detailed knowledge of the numerous types of court that make up the court system of any given state, but a general

---

[1] One significant result of the precedent-creating activity of courts is to keep many disputes from coming before the courts at all. The position a court takes in Case A-1 often makes possible a relatively reliable prediction of how it would view similar Case A-2, if Case A-2 were to come before it. This predictability may deter the parties in Case A-2 from taking the time and trouble to bring their case to court.

familiarity with the structure of a typical court system is indispensable to an understanding of the adjudicative process; it is also essential to an understanding of the cases that are presented in this book.

Each of the fifty states of the United States has its own court system, and, in addition, there is the federal court system. No two are alike; indeed, the differences both in the functions and the labels given to American courts are many and bewildering, and no generalization is absolutely reliable for all states. Court systems have rarely been the product of long-range planning; nearly all represent a series of patchwork accommodations to changing needs.

Our generalized description will not cover criminal courts and proceedings, important as they are. Nor will we deal in this chapter with the many administrative agencies and tribunals—workmen's compensation boards, for example—which perform court-like functions; these will be discussed in Chapter 8.

At the outset we must recognize a basic distinction that prevails in all court systems: the distinction between trial courts and appellate courts. *Trial* courts are the courts in which cases are first heard and decided; here the opposing parties present evidence on the facts and arguments on the law. Ordinarily, a single judge hears any given trial-court proceeding. (But many trial courts are manned by more than one judge, so that several proceedings may take place simultaneously.)

The great majority of cases go no further than the trial court. But if one of the parties is dissatisfied with the outcome of the trial, the law usually provides that he may take an appeal—that is, he may ask an *appellate* court (a "court of appeal") to review the rulings of the trial court. An appellate court consists of a number of judges, several or all of whom hear each appeal.

The State Court Systems

The typical state court system consists of a considerable number of trial courts of limited jurisdiction, a smaller number of general trial courts, and a single appellate court for the whole state.

TRIAL COURTS OF LIMITED JURISDICTION. The vast majority of cases that come to our courts are tried by trial courts of limited jurisdiction. These cases are usually routine in character and of little importance except to the parties involved, while most of the important (and well-publicized) cases are tried by the general trial courts.

The trial courts of limited jurisdiction fall into three classes: minor courts, intermediate courts, and specialized courts.

The Minor Courts. (These courts are also referred to as "local," "petty," and "inferior" courts.) The lowest tier of trial courts are those manned by rural justices of the peace and their urban counterparts, often known as aldermen or magistrates. The "J.P." is heir to centuries of tradition, dating back to English knights and country squires who were commissioned by the Crown to keep the peace in rural areas. His modern namesake, who is elected to the office, has authority to try petty criminal offenses and to hear civil cases involving claims not exceeding a few hundred dollars. His remuneration consists of fees received for each case tried, and he usually has some other source of income—for example, from selling insurance. Few J.P.'s have had legal training. The traditional minor courts are often criticized for the incompetence and bias of their magistrates. But, on their behalf, it may be said that the justice they dispense is readily accessible, speedy, and relatively inexpensive.

Some states have replaced the numerous J.P. courts and their urban counterparts with a smaller number of courts manned by full-time, salaried, professionally trained judges. Even where this change has not occurred on a state-wide basis, one often finds that it has taken place in the larger towns and cities, or that at least part of the original authority of the petty magistrates has been assigned to courts with full-time, legally trained judges. In the criminal sphere, the traffic and police courts are examples of the modernized minor courts. Courts that hear civil cases (or both civil and criminal cases) often bear such labels as city, town, and municipal court.

In many ways these modernized minor courts resemble the intermediate-level trial courts (see below) more closely than they do the older type of minor court. But the trial courts in the minor court classification do have some features in common. One is that, with occasional exceptions, they do not provide for a trial before a jury. Another is that appeals from their decisions are taken to the general trial courts (or occasionally to special courts of appeal) rather than to the regular appellate courts. Furthermore, such "appeals" often consist of complete new trials rather than mere reviews of the errors alleged to have been made in the original trial.

Intermediate Trial Courts. In those states in which the modernization of the minor courts has proved constitutionally or politically impossible, an intermediate tier of trial courts has sometimes been established (particularly in urban areas) between the J.P.'s and the general trial courts. These are often called county courts. As one might expect, they usually perform functions like those of the modernized minor courts. They try the less serious criminal cases, and civil cases involving claims not in excess of a few thousand dollars. But their sphere of authority is much greater than that of the J.P.'s. Most of these intermediate courts were created to take over part of the work formerly done by the general trial courts. They provide jury trials, and appeals from their decisions go to the regular appellate courts.

Specialized Courts. On the whole there is strikingly little subject-matter specialization in the American court system. But a few subject-matter fields are frequently (particularly in urban areas) assigned to special courts.

A number of cities, for instance, have special juvenile and domestic-relations courts. Perhaps the specialized courts with the longest tradition are those (variously called probate, orphan's, and surrogate courts) which deal with such matters as the disposition of property left by deceased persons, and with guardianships and adoptions.

Why have certain kinds of case been taken away from the regular courts and assigned to specialized courts? Usually the reason has been that handling those cases required judges to perform functions markedly different from the trial judge's ordinary function of adjudication. Probate court judges, for instance, spend much of their time supervising the distribution (by executors and administrators) of property left by deceased persons—a task that involves adjudicating disputes only in exceptional cases. A major responsibility of the juvenile-court judge, once he has ascertained that a wrongful act has been done, is to search for a means of preventing the young offender from becoming a hardened criminal. An important part of the job of a domestic-relations judge is to see whether it is possible to keep estranged couples from dissolving their marriage. Performing these tasks requires knowledge and skills quite different from those required for adjudication. Hence there are important advantages to assigning such cases to judges who have, or can attain, a special competence, and whose courts can be staffed with specialized personnel—accountants, psychiatrists, and social workers, for instance.

GENERAL TRIAL COURTS (OR COURTS OF GENERAL JURISDICTION). The most important cases—those involving major crimes and large sums of money— are tried in the general trial courts. The cases you will study in this book virtually all began in general trial courts. When we speak of trial courts hereafter, we shall be referring to these courts unless we state otherwise. These courts are labeled "general" because they have authority to hear all types of case not specifically assigned to the courts of limited jurisdiction (see above). Some of the smaller states have only one general trial court for the whole state—though that court usually consists of several judges who sit separately and hear cases in different cities in the state. Most states, however, are divided into a number of judicial districts, each consisting of one or more counties, and each district has its own general trial court.

General trial courts bear such varied labels as circuit, district, superior, and common pleas. But labels can be deceptive: these same titles are used in some states to designate courts of limited jurisdiction, or even appellate courts. New York's general trial courts are called supreme courts, although this is the title usually given to final courts of appeal.

APPELLATE COURTS. Most states have only one appellate court, usually known as the supreme court. This court hears appeals from all trial-court decisions, criminal and civil, except those of minor courts. In a few states, however, the volume of appeals is so great that one or more intermediate appellate courts have been established to hear appeals in less important cases; or else the single appellate court has been subdivided into several "divisions" which hear appeals as if they were separate courts.

The accompanying chart shows the hierarchy of state courts in Pennsylvania. The two appellate courts hear appeals from the decisions of trial courts all over the state. (Appeals go to one appellate court or the other, depending on the nature of the case; appeals to the Supreme Court from Superior Court decisions are allowed only in a limited category of cases.) The trial courts shown are those in Allegheny County (in which Pittsburgh is located); they hear only cases having some connection with Allegheny County.

Supreme Court of Pennsylvania
(Highest appellate court)
Seven judges; holds sessions successively in three cities,
one of which is Pittsburgh.

Superior Court of Pennsylvania
(Intermediate appellate court)
Seven judges; holds sessions successively in four cities,
one of which is Pittsburgh.

| *Court of Common Pleas of Allegheny County* (General trial court) Sixteen judges | *Orphan's Court of Allegheny County* (Specialized court for probate cases) Four judges | *Juvenile Court of Allegheny County* (Specialized court) One judge |

County Court of Allegheny County
(Intermediate trial court)
Six judges

Minor Courts in Allegheny County, manned by
Magistrates (in police and traffic courts in the cities),
Aldermen (one in each ward in the cities), and
Justices of the Peace (one in each borough and township).

The Federal Court System

The federal court hierarchy is comparatively simple. The basic unit of jurisdiction is the *district.* Each district has a United States District Court. These are the general trial courts of the federal system. (The system has no minor courts.) There are eighty-six district courts in the fifty states, plus one in the District of Columbia and one in Puerto Rico. Many of the states constitute a single district, but some states are divided into two, three, or four districts. Each district (with one exception) forms part of a larger judicial area known as a *circuit.* There are eleven circuits, each served by a United States Court of Appeals. A major responsibility of each court of appeals is to hear appeals from the decisions of the district courts in its circuit. (The exceptional district is the District of Columbia, which not only has its own district court but also comprises the Eleventh Circuit and so has its own court of appeals. This arrangement is made necessary by the large number of cases originating in the federal administrative agencies.)

The nation's highest appellate court is the Supreme Court of the United

States, whose nine justices sit in Washington. Contrary to a widespread belief, the national Supreme Court is not available as a court of last resort for any appellant with the perseverance to take his case "all the way to the top." The truth is that the Supreme Court considers only a limited number of cases that are regarded as of particular importance to the legal system.[2]

Problems of Jurisdiction

We have already said quite a bit about the jurisdiction of courts, but without really defining "jurisdiction." Although this term is used in several somewhat different ways, the root concept has to do with the boundaries of a court's authority to hear and decide cases.

SUBJECT-MATTER JURISDICTION.   No court has unlimited jurisdiction to hear and decide all kinds of case. One type of limitation on jurisdiction is based either on the subject matter of the controversy or on the nature of the parties. Some courts, for example, deal only with cases involving property left by deceased persons; others deal only with cases involving small claims; and still others handle only those cases in which juveniles are involved.

TERRITORIAL JURISDICTION.   Every court serves some specified geographical area, which is known as its territory of jurisdiction. The territorial jurisdiction of the Supreme Court of the United States, the Court of Appeals of New York, or the Court of Common Pleas of Allegheny County, for instance, is indicated in the official title of each court. If the judges on a court are elected, the residents of the territory of jurisdiction vote to elect them. If the court is empowered to grant jury trials, the jurors are selected from among persons living within the territory. The past decisions of the court are in a sense "law" within the territory, and the cases brought before the court ordinarily have some connection with the territory.

This geographical connotation of jurisdiction accounts for the common practice of speaking of "a jurisdiction" as if it were a particular area. When we say, for instance, that a decision of the Pennsylvania Supreme Court is a binding precedent "throughout the jurisdiction," we mean that it is binding throughout Pennsylvania (or, more literally, throughout the territory of jurisdiction of the Pennsylvania Supreme Court). In general, the states are the most significant territorial units of jurisdiction in the American legal system.

JURISDICTION OVER PARTICULAR PERSONS AND PROPERTY.   Let us suppose that BUYER institutes a lawsuit against SELLER in the Court of Common Pleas of Allegheny County, asking for $10,000 in damages for breach of contract. Let us suppose, too, that the Common Pleas Court has jurisdiction over this type of controversy, and that BUYER and SELLER signed the contract now at issue in Allegheny County. It is still quite possible that the court may not have jurisdiction to try BUYER's lawsuit.

This is because another rule on jurisdiction requires that a court have

---

[2] Other federal courts include the Court of Claims, the Court of Customs and Patent Appeals, the Customs Court, and the federal courts in the Virgin Islands, Guam, and the Canal Zone.

jurisdiction over the person of the defendant who is being sued, or over some of his property. This is, first, a matter of the court's ability to exercise some control over the defendant. The officials who serve a state court never have power to act outside the state, and frequently they even lack power to act outside the court's judicial district (in our example, Allegheny County). Hence the court wants to be shown, before it hears the case and renders a decision, that there is some chance of its being able to make its decision effective. It is also important to make sure that the defendant knows he is being sued: the plaintiff's efforts to prove that the court has jurisdiction are pretty sure to make the defendant aware of what is happening.

How can BUYER demonstrate to the court that it has jurisdiction over SELLER? The most common procedure is for him to ask the court clerk to issue a "summons" (a document notifying SELLER that BUYER is suing him), and then to arrange to have the summons "served" on SELLER. There are a number of alternative methods for serving SELLER with a summons, but ordinarily it is delivered to him in person or (if he is a resident of the district) to his residence or place of business. Summonses can never be served outside the state in which they are issued, and usually they must be served within the judicial district of the issuing court. If BUYER succeeds in having a summons served on SELLER, the court will presume that a sufficient connection has been established between SELLER and the court's territory of jurisdiction to warrant it in proceeding to hear the case.

If BUYER were suing SELLER in connection with property owned by SELLER located in Allegheny County, it might under some circumstances be sufficient for BUYER to prove to the court that it has jurisdiction over the property. In that event, the court could make a decision affecting the property even though it never asserted its jurisdiction over SELLER's person.

STATE VERSUS FEDERAL JURISDICTION. The great majority of cases can be tried only in state courts, since they do not involve subject matter or parties that would bring them within the jurisdiction of the federal courts. A much smaller number of cases fall exclusively within the jurisdiction of the federal courts. And between these two groups is a sizable class of cases over which the state and federal courts have overlapping jurisdiction.

Most of the cases over which the federal courts have jurisdiction fall into one of two categories:

Cases Involving "Federal Questions." When a case involves a provision of the federal Constitution, a federal statute (that is, an act of Congress), or a treaty between the United States and a foreign country, the federal courts have jurisdiction. We have only to reflect on the wide variety of matters covered by federal legislation to realize how broad this jurisdiction is. But the jurisdiction of federal courts over these cases is not exclusive; federal and state courts have overlapping jurisdiction over cases involving "federal questions," except where Congress has indicated that it wants the federal courts to have exclusive jurisdiction. (Categories of cases over which federal jurisdiction is exclusive include: federal crimes; bankruptcy; admiralty and maritime controversies; and infringements of patents and copyrights.)

Cases Involving "Diversity of Citizenship." A large proportion of the cases in the federal district courts are there solely because the respective parties are citizens of different states. All these cases could be tried in state courts. The Founding Fathers, apprehensive of state-court bias against out-of-state parties, gave Congress authority to allow such cases to be brought to the federal courts. Congress has decided that, when the parties in a law-suit are citizens of different states and when the amount in controversy exceeds $10,000, the parties may bring their case to the federal courts. For various reasons, including the impression that federal judges are often more competent and broader in their views than their state counterparts, one party or the other in a lawsuit often chooses to take advantage of this privilege.

COMMON-LAW VERSUS EQUITY JURISDICTION. Until the present century one of the major jurisdictional distinctions was that between common-law cases and equity cases. These two terms designate two separate stems in the Anglo-American legal tradition, with entirely distinct historical origins. For centuries, cases involving equity doctrines and principles were tried in special courts of equity. Today, however, though the two stems remain distinct in a number of respects, the general trial courts and appellate courts of nearly all the states handle both kinds of case. Therefore we shall put off to a later chapter (pp. 58–60) our study of this still important dichotomy in the law.

CONFLICT OF LAWS. Once a court has decided that it has authority to hear a case, it may also have to decide whether to apply the locally applicable rules of law or those of some other jurisdiction.[3] Many people take it for granted that the courts of State x always apply the legal rules of State x in deciding cases. But this is not necessarily true. Let us suppose, for instance, that BUYER and SELLER make a contract in Illinois in which they agree that SELLER will sell to BUYER some machinery located in Indiana and that the machinery will be delivered to BUYER's plant in that state. Instead, SELLER sells the machinery to someone else, and BUYER is now preparing to sue him for breach of contract. SELLER currently lives in Pittsburgh, Pennsylvania, and BUYER decides that it will be simplest to bring his suit in the Allegheny County Court of Common Pleas.

Assume that Illinois, Indiana, and Pennsylvania have slightly different rules with respect to sales contracts. Which state's rules should be applied in this case? Although the Allegheny County court ordinarily applies Pennsylvania rules, there are perhaps reasons for not applying them in this particular case. For one thing, it seems likely that BUYER and SELLER (if they gave the matter any thought at all when they entered into the contract) contemplated that the law of Illinois (where the contract was made) or of Indiana (where it was to be performed) would apply.

For us to examine here the principles by which problems of this sort are solved would carry us far afield. The body of legal principles governing

---

[3] "Jurisdiction" is here used—as it will be frequently throughout this book—to refer to a territory of jurisdiction. See above, under "Territorial Jurisdiction."

such situations is known as "conflict of laws." You will encounter a few conflict-of-laws cases in Part II.[4]

Federal courts also have problems in deciding what set of rules to apply to a case. Suppose that, since BUYER is not a citizen of Pennsylvania but of Illinois, and since his claim exceeds $10,000, he exercises his right to sue SELLER in the federal district court in Pittsburgh. What rules of contract law will the federal court apply? Will it apply Pennsylvania, Illinois, or Indiana rules, or will it apply some sort of federal rule? In general, the federal court in Pittsburgh will try to apply the same contract rules as the state court in Pittsburgh would have applied if the case had been brought before it.[5]

The Process of Adjudication

Now that we know something about the courts and their jurisdiction, we can begin to discuss the process by which a civil suit is adjudicated in the courts.[6] First, however, we must distinguish between two classes of issue that the courts are called upon to resolve.

The Distinction Between Issues of Fact and Issues of Law

The basic tasks of courts in adjudication are (a) to appraise the *evidence* presented by the parties to support their allegations about the facts, and (b) to appraise the arguments presented by the parties to support their assertions about what rules of law should be applied to the facts. Conflicting evidence creates *questions* (or *issues*) *of fact;* conflicting arguments create *questions* (or *issues*) *of law.*[7]

Three kinds of case come before the courts. First are cases in which there is no doubt about what rules to apply once the facts have been established. Second are cases in which there is no dispute over the facts but a very real dispute over the proper rules to apply to those facts. Third are cases in which there is disagreement over both the facts and the applicable rules.

At first blush the distinction between questions of fact and questions of law seems perfectly obvious. A question of *fact* concerns "what happened" (or, in some cases, what is happening or will happen). To be more

---

[4] See, for instance, *Adamowski v. Curtiss-Wright Flying Service, Inc.*, page 270.

[5] For an example, see *Cope v. Beaumont,* page 320.

[6] Again, "adjudication" refers to the proceedings in which a controversy (which may be a civil case or a criminal prosecution) is judged. When the focus is not on the judging but on the contest between parties, we speak of "litigation." The parties are often called "litigants." This part of the chapter might equally well have been entitled "The Process of Litigation."

[7] One way of looking at the process of deciding cases is in terms of the syllogism. The major premise is supplied by answering the question(s) of law, the minor premise by answering the question(s) of fact. To use a very simple example:

All who drive over 60 m.p.h. are guilty of speeding. (*Rule.*)
John drove over 60 m.p.h. (*Fact.*)
Therefore John is guilty of speeding. (*Decision.*)

precise, it may involve an event, a relationship, a condition, or a state of mind. In the BUYER-SELLER example above, such factual questions as these might arise: What words did BUYER address to SELLER? (Event.) Had BUYER and SELLER previously been on friendly terms? (Relationship.) Was BUYER over twenty-one years old? (Condition.) Was he speaking seriously when he made his proposal? (State of mind.) To answer a pure question of fact should require no knowledge of the law.

A question of *law* involves determining what legal rule to apply to a given set of facts. Answering it clearly requires a knowledge of the law. (A convenient way of formulating a question of law is: "Given this combination of facts, what is the applicable rule?")

How a court answers a question of law is important not only to the parties concerned but to the legal system as a whole—because the court's ruling may become a precedent affecting the decision of similar cases in the future. Answers to questions of fact have no such significance. (You will not be surprised, therefore, to learn that in all the cases reported in this book the important issues in controversy were issues of law.) [8]

All this seems simple and straightforward. Unfortunately, however, some of the questions that arise in cases cannot be classified neatly as pure questions of fact or pure questions of law. Consider, for instance, these questions: "Was DRIVER driving negligently?" "Is HUSBAND still married to WIFE?" "Did BUYER make SELLER a valid offer?"

None of these questions can be characterized as purely factual or purely legal. Each contains both an element of "What happened?" and an element of "What are the rules?" Moreover, the elements must be considered together; to try to isolate out a pure question of fact would simply not be worthwhile, for in each case the factual element is stated in terms of legal concepts. We must know something about the law (of negligence, marriage, and contract) to know what facts matter. When the rule is that "All who drive over 60 m.p.h. are guilty of the offense of speeding," then the question to be answered is one of pure fact: "Was John driving over 60 m.p.h.?" No knowledge of law is needed to answer this. But when the rule is that "All who drive negligently may be liable for the harm they do," the question, "Was DRIVER driving negligently?" can be answered only by someone who knows what legal negligence is. Nor can we transform this into a pure question of fact by substituting the definition of negligence. We cannot answer the question, "Was DRIVER driving with less care than a reasonably prudent person would have shown under the same circumstances?" unless we know how a court goes about measuring DRIVER's conduct against that of "the reasonably prudent person."

Similarly, the question, "Are HUSBAND and WIFE still married?" cannot be answered without reference to the legal rules about the formation and dissolution of marriages. Nor can we say whether BUYER made SELLER a

---

[8] The facts referred to throughout this discussion are what are known as "adjudicative facts." From time to time in later chapters we shall have occasion to speak of quite a different class of facts: "legislative facts." These facts do not concern the particular parties; they are facts which the court needs to know before it can work out what is the applicable rule of law.

valid offer without knowing something about the various combinations of circumstances which the law says may constitute a valid offer, and against which the circumstances of BUYER's proposal must be compared.

In short, the factual and legal elements in these questions are inextricably intertwined. Consequently, writers about the law recognize a class of questions which they call "mixed questions of law and fact."

But, you may ask, why does it matter how a particular question is classified? It matters because questions of fact and questions of law are handled quite differently in the courts. When a case is tried before a judge and jury (as we shall see in Chapter 3), the jury's basic function is to "find the facts." Doing so is supposed to require no knowledge of law. The trial judge, on the other hand, rules on the issues of law. Moreover, courts of appeal normally accept the trial jury's findings of fact as conclusive, and they review only the answers which the trial court has given to questions of law. But no special provision is made for mixed questions. Over the years judges have put some questions that were really "mixed" into the "fact" category and others into the "law" category. Their classification has depended on tradition and on policy judgments (judgments as to what juries and judges do best, for instance) rather than on logic. The question of whether DRIVER was driving negligently is normally treated as a question of fact; in other words, it is answered by a jury, whenever a jury is hearing the case. The legal component of the question is dealt with by the judge when he explains to the jurors what the rules of negligence are and then instructs them to apply those rules to the facts they find. The classification of the question of whether BUYER made a valid offer to SELLER may depend on whether the proposal was oral or in writing. If BUYER simply made an informal oral proposal, the question of whether he intended his words to be a legal offer is usually treated as a question of fact. But if BUYER wrote SELLER a letter, the question of whether he made an offer is much more likely to be treated as a question of law. This difference in the treatment given to oral utterances and to written communications seems to be largely a matter of policy (representing perhaps a decision that jurors are well qualified to decide what a person meant by spoken words, in light of evidence as to his tone and demeanor, whereas judges should be left to interpret the more calculated intent behind a letter).[9]

Defining and Resolving the Issues

· Using an actual case for illustration, we shall now trace the steps that make up the process of adjudication.

The official report of this case begins as follows: *

---

[9] For a case involving an interesting problem as to the proper classification of a disputed question of intent, see *Embry v. Hargadine,* page 227.

* To assure legibility and to emphasize that the cases quoted are an integral part of the text, all case material has been set in the same size type as the text itself. To enable the reader to distinguish case material from text material, the symbol ► is used to signal the beginning of a case quotation, and the symbol ◄ to signal the end of a case quotation. These symbols also appear at the top of pages that carry continuing case quotations.

HURLEY v. EDDINGFIELD
Supreme Court of Indiana, 1901
156 Ind. 416, 59 N.E. 1058

► Appeal from circuit court, Montgomery County; Jere West, Judge.

Action by George D. Hurley, as administrator, against George W. Eddingfield. From a judgment in favor of the defendant, the plaintiff appeals.

Hurley & Van Cleave and Dumont Kennedy, for appellant. Clodfelter & Fine, for appellee. . . .

Hurley and Eddingfield, of course, were the adversaries. Hurley was the *plaintiff* (the party who sued) in the Montgomery County Circuit Court, while Eddingfield was the *defendant* (the person who was being sued). (The plaintiff's name is not always listed first, however; the first name is often that of the person who appeals—the *appellant*—who may originally have been either the plaintiff or the defendant.)

The decision here is that of the Supreme Court of Indiana. (Nearly all the decisions you will read in this book are decisions of appellate courts— for reasons that will be explained shortly.) The report of the decision is taken from the official reports of that court. The state of Indiana publishes the reports of its Supreme Court's decisions, as do all the states. In addition, these reports are published by the West Publishing Company, which has organized its "Reporter system" by regions; Indiana is in the "North Eastern" region.[10]

Mr. Hurley, we are told, was not suing on his own behalf but as the "administrator" of property left at death by a man who is identified in the report only as the "decedent" and the "intestate." (This latter term means simply that he died leaving no will.) One of the jobs of an administrator is to protect the rights of the deceased and his heirs.

Having lost in the trial court, Hurley appealed. He thus became the *appellant* in the state Supreme Court, while Eddingfield became the *appellee*. Their respective attorneys are listed.

The remainder of the report consists of the *opinion* written by Judge Baker on behalf of all the appellate judges who heard the case. An opinion not only announces the court's decision but presents a justification of it.[11]

► BAKER, J. The appellant sued the appellee for $10,000 damages for wrongfully causing the death of his intestate. The court sustained appellee's demurrer to the complaint, and this ruling is assigned as error.

---

[10] "156 Ind. 416" in the heading of the report tells us that the report may be found in Volume 156 of the *Indiana Reports*, beginning on page 416. "59 N.E. 1058" tells us that it may also be found in Volume 59 of the *North Eastern Reporter* in the West Publishing Company's system, beginning on page 1058.

[11] Many decisions include more than one opinion. Occasionally each judge expresses his views separately, but the usual American practice is for one judge to write an opinion for the majority, and then for other judges to write separate opinions only if they wish to "dissent" or "concur." When a judge dissents, he expresses disagreement with the result reached. When he concurs, he accepts the result, but either disagrees with the reasoning presented by the majority or adds some reasons of his own.

The material facts alleged may be summarized thus: At and for years before decedent's death appellee was a practicing physician at Mace, in Montgomery county, duly licensed under the laws of the state. He held himself out to the public as a practitioner of medicine. He had been decedent's family physician. Decedent became dangerously ill, and sent for appellee. The messenger informed appellee of decedent's violent sickness, tendered him his fee for his services, and stated to him that no other physician was procurable in time, and that decedent relied on him for attention. No other physician was procurable in time to be of any use, and decedent did rely on appellee for medical assistance. Without any reason whatever, appellee refused to render aid to decedent. No other patients were requiring appellee's immediate service, and he could have gone to the relief of decedent if he had been willing to do so. Death ensued, without decedent's fault, and wholly from appellee's wrongful act.

The alleged wrongful act was appellee's refusal to enter into a contract of employment. Counsel do not contend that, before the enactment of the law regulating the practice of medicine, physicians were bound to render professional service to every one who applied. Wharton on Negligence, §731. The act regulating the practice of medicine provides for a board of examiners, standards of qualification, examinations, licenses to those found qualified and penalties for practicing without license. Acts 1897, p. 255; Acts 1899, p. 247. The act is a preventive, not a compulsive, measure. In obtaining the state's license (permission) to practice medicine, the state does not require, and the licensee does not engage, that he will practice at all or on other terms than he may choose to accept. Counsel's analogies, drawn from the obligations to the public on the part of innkeepers, common carriers, and the like, are beside the mark. *Judgment affirmed.*   ◄

COMMENTS AND QUESTIONS

1. Though you may not understand every word and phrase in this opinion, what the question of law facing the court was, and the court's answer to that question, should be clear enough. Try to state them in your own words.

   The answer to a question of law is sometimes referred to as the "rule of the case," since it is likely to affect the decision of future cases. As we shall learn in Chapter 4, however, the precise content and breadth of such a "rule" become clear only as later cases arise and the courts decide them.

2. Why did the plaintiff's lawyers seek to draw analogies with "innkeepers, common carriers, and the like"?

PRE-TRIAL EFFORTS TO DEFINE THE ISSUES. The first stage of *Hurley v. Eddingfield* took place in the trial court. What happened there? The answer to this question is nearly always to be found near the beginning of the appellate court report. Judge Baker's opinion tells us that the trial court "sustained appellee's demurrer to the complaint, and this ruling is assigned as error." The meaning of these words will be clarified as we consider the steps in a lawsuit that precede the trial.

When the plaintiff (Hurley) first decided to bring suit, he had his lawyer send the defendant (Eddingfield) a legal document known as a *complaint*. This consisted of a brief summary of Hurley's version of what had happened and stated what remedy he was asking—$10,000 in damages. The complaint normally accompanies the summons, which we discussed a few pages back. Once Eddingfield had received the summons and the complaint, he was obliged either to make some sort of response or else lose the suit by default.

A defendant's response to a complaint may take several forms:

The Answer. If the defendant thinks he can contest the plaintiff's version of the facts, he will send the plaintiff a document known as an *answer*. In his answer he may deny all the plaintiff's important allegations of fact. (For instance, Dr. Eddingfield might simply have denied that he had been called to the decedent's bedside at all.) Denying an allegation in the complaint immediately raises an issue of fact; the court will have to decide whose allegation is correct. Alternatively, the defendant may admit some of the plaintiff's allegations but go on to allege additional facts that throw a new light on the situation. (For instance, Dr. Eddingfield might have admitted that he did not go when first summoned, but then he might have gone on to explain that he was unavoidably detained and that by the time he was free it was too late.)

If the defendant alleges new facts, the plaintiff sometimes responds with a document known as a *reply*. If his reply denies the defendant's allegations, an issue of fact is raised. If the reply admits any or all of the defendant's allegations, further exchanges, or amendments to the original documents, may be called for.

The Counterclaim. The defendant may respond to the plaintiff's complaint by entering a *counterclaim;* in other words, he may make a claim of his own for damages against the plaintiff. (For instance, in addition to justifying his failure to come to the bedside of the deceased, Dr. Eddingfield might have claimed damages on the ground that the deceased's messenger struck and injured him when he said he could not come at once.) A counterclaim may raise issues of fact or issues of law, or both.

The Demurrer. Finally, the defendant's response may say, in effect, "Even if all the plaintiff has alleged were true, it would still not provide the basis for a legal claim." This is what is known as a *demurrer* (or a "motion to dismiss"). A demurrer raises an issue of law.[12]

In the *Hurley* case, the defendant demurred. This action is in no sense an admission that all the charges made against him by the plaintiff were

---

[12] For the sake of completeness we should note that the plaintiff may "demur" to the defendant's answer, or a portion of it, and that the defendant may likewise "demur" to the plaintiff's reply. The demurrer in each instance says, "Even if that were true, it is not a legally relevant allegation of fact."

To carry the analogy to syllogistic reasoning proposed in footnote 7 above one step further, one might say that a demurrer challenges the major premise underlying the opposing party's position, while a denial in an answer or reply challenges the opponent's minor premise.

true. A demurrer admits allegations only for the purpose of argument. It merely says, "Even if these allegations *were* true, they would not constitute a basis for legal action." (Indeed, if Dr. Eddingfield's demurrer had been overruled, either by the trial court or on appeal, he would at that point have been permitted to present an answer.) If, however, the defendant is confident that the complaint states no basis for legal action, a demurrer is the simplest way to dispose of the whole matter.

The documents exchanged by the plaintiff and the defendant—the plaintiff's complaint; the defendant's answer, demurrer, or counterclaim; and, if necessary, the plaintiff's reply—are known collectively as the *pleadings.* They have three purposes: to narrow the issues to those really in dispute, to let each party know beforehand what issues he must be prepared to deal with, and to inform the trial judge (who receives copies) what the case is about before the trial begins.

For many years the exchange of pleadings was the only means used to narrow the issues in dispute prior to the trial. Yet the pleadings were often too brief to reveal all the details of the charges and countercharges that the parties intended to make against one another in the trial. Delays were often caused, and injustice sometimes done, when some element of the allegations of fact or of the legal arguments presented by one party caught the other party by surprise during the trial. Today most courts rely on various procedures, known as "discovery" procedures, to eliminate the element of surprise from the trial of a lawsuit. One of these procedures, for instance, calls for the use of "interrogatories"—written questions which each party may send to the other with a request that he supply written answers under oath. Still another procedure for clarifying the issues before the trial is the "pre-trial conference," at which the opposing lawyers review in the judge's presence their legal arguments and the evidence they propose to produce. In many courts this procedure has proved remarkably effective not only in narrowing the issues but in bringing about out-of-court settlements before any trial takes place.

THE TRIAL STAGE.[13]   A surprisingly large proportion of the lawsuits initiated actually do get settled out of court. But what does the trial court do with those cases that come to trial?

How a case is handled in the trial court depends in part on whether or not the facts are in dispute. In cases like *Hurley v. Eddingfield,* where the only issues in dispute are issues of law raised by demurrers and other types of "motions" (for instance, motions challenging the court's jurisdiction), a relatively simple procedure can be used. No jury is needed (since jurors, being laymen, have nothing to do with interpreting the law) and no witnesses have to be heard. The judge, who has read the lawyers' written arguments about the applicable rules (known as "briefs"), conducts what is

---

[13] The actual procedure of the court trial is described in some detail in Chapter 3. This section serves merely to indicate the place of the trial in the whole adjudicative process.

often known as a "hearing on motions," in which he listens to oral arguments and sometimes asks questions. At the conclusion, or at a later date if the problem is difficult, he hands down a decision. He either grants or denies the motion. His decision is often accompanied by a short opinion (though these opinions, unlike those of appellate judges, are usually not published). Cases which may be disposed of on the basis of pre-trial motions are generally heard and decided fairly expeditiously.

When there are disputed questions of fact in a case, however, a full-dress trial must be held to give the parties a chance to present evidence in support of their respective versions of the facts. Sometimes trials are held before a judge alone, in which event the judge decides both the legal and the factual issues. But cases involving claims for damages must ordinarily be tried before a jury if either party so desires.

As we have mentioned, the jury's task is to "find the facts"—that is, to decide from the evidence presented which party's version of the facts is on the whole the more convincing. (This is not because jurors are regarded as expert fact-finders; indeed most jurors have had no previous experience in weighing the conflicting evidence introduced in a trial. Rather, it is because jurors are ordinary citizens who are presumed capable of making common-sense judgments.) In most trials the jury is also responsible for applying the rules, as outlined by the judge, to the facts it has found. (For more on the jury system, see pp. 45–48.)

The judge's task in a trial is to rule on the motions made by the opposing attorneys during the proceedings. Each motion raises an issue of law. An attorney may contend, for instance, that there has been an irregularity in the conduct of the trial; or that a particular item of evidence which his opponent wishes to present should be excluded; or that the judge's instructions to the jury are incorrect; or that, since the opposing side has failed to present a case which could conceivably be regarded as convincing, a verdict should be entered for his client at once. (Each of these motions will be considered further in Chapter 3.)

THE APPELLATE STAGE. Most of the cases that come before a trial court are never appealed. But if one of the parties is dissatisfied with the outcome, he has the right to take an appeal within a specified time.

Why is an appeal allowed? There are two reasons. First, since trial judges often have to decide questions of law rapidly and with little time for reflection, they inevitably make mistakes. So it is only fair to give the loser a chance to ask an appellate court, which is under less pressure, to review the rulings of the trial judge. If the appellate court finds an error serious enough so that it may have affected the outcome of the trial, it will reverse the decision of the trial court and send the case back to that court with instructions to take further action in accordance with the appellate decision.

The second reason is that in most jurisdictions there is more than one trial court, and different trial courts faced with cases raising essentially the same question of law may give different answers to that question. This means that the same rules are not being applied throughout the jurisdiction

—a situation that is hardly conducive to public confidence. When confusion of this sort arises, an appellate court can produce uniformity by deciding once and for all what the "correct" rule is.

What does the appellate court review? It reviews the trial court's disposition of issues of law. In the *Hurley* case, for instance, the appellant "assigned as error" the trial judge's decision to sustain the appellee's demurrer. Issues of law are also raised by the other types of motion which the lawyers may make before and during the trial.

The appellate court does *not* try to re-evaluate the evidence itself. An appellate review is not a new trial. Appellate judges do not sit with juries, nor do they rehear the testimony. All they know about the evidence is what they can read in the transcript of the trial that is submitted to them. Consequently, they are in no position to decide whether the trial court has drawn the right conclusions from the evidence. The only question about the facts that appellate judges feel at liberty to ask themselves is whether there is sufficient evidence in the record to make it possible for reasonable men to reach the conclusion that the trial jury (or judge) actually reached. Once in a while it is fairly obvious to an appellate court that a trial court has been wrong in its finding on the facts (perhaps because the jury had a strong prejudice against one of the parties). But reversals on such grounds are rare, and appellate courts nearly always accept as conclusive the trial court's finding on the facts.

Each appeal is heard by several appellate judges sitting together. The opposing lawyers submit written briefs spelling out their arguments and then usually supplement them with oral arguments before the court. The judges may, in turn, question the lawyers. The courtroom atmosphere is quite different from that at a trial: with no witnesses and no jurors, it is usually quiet and undramatic. Unlike trial judges, appellate judges are not acting as referees in a close-fought tactical contest; their function is to decide close legal questions in the light of past decisions, scholarly writings, and their own perceptions of the law's ultimate objectives. And after they have arrived at a decision, they do what most trial judges have no time to do: they write opinions spelling out at length their reasons for deciding as they have the issues of law brought before them.

Unless the parties in the case can obtain a rehearing, which is rarely granted, they are obliged to accept the appellate decision as "the last word." The so-called principle of *res judicata* ("the matter having already been judged") prevents the loser from bringing a new suit against the winner on the same set of facts, either in the same court or in another court. Even if the appellate court later comes to believe that its own decision on the issues in the case was wrong, and, indeed, even if it reverses its position on the legal issue involved in the course of deciding a similar case later on, the original decision will not be reviewed or overturned.

Appellate decisions are, of course, important to the parties involved; but they are even more important to the legal system itself. Because these decisions represent the fruits of extensive judicial study and reflection, they assume great authority as declarations of the scope and meaning of legal rules. Their usefulness as precedents is particularly enhanced by the opinions that accompany them, for there the appellate judges try to explain and justify their decisions to the judges and lawyers who may in the future be confronted with similar cases.[14]

Appendix: How to Read and Abstract an Appellate Decision

Why should anyone who is not a lawyer, or training to become one, read judicial decisions? The lawyer reads them partly so that he can prophesy for his client what the courts are likely to do, and partly so that he can try to influence judges by citing precedents in support of the arguments he presents to them. Law-school students, for whom reading cases is both an intellectual exercise and a means of learning about legal rules and the judicial process, spend a great deal of their time in an exhaustive analysis and comparison of decisions involving closely related issues of law. But even for the student who is not studying to become a lawyer, there is no better way of learning about legal rules and the judicial process than by seeing how rules emerge from the decisions of courts in actual cases.

Two general observations about reading decisions must be made at the outset. First, for our purposes, reading *recent* decisions is not important. In fact, you will find that most of the decisions quoted in this book are more than a decade old. Many continuing legal problems had to be faced by the courts a long time ago; hence it is not surprising that few of the "leading cases" (in which the courts enunciate important new rules) are recent. Yet these are the very cases that are often the most instructive for students of the judicial process.

Second, as you read the judicial decisions in the pages ahead, you will encounter many unfamiliar words and phrases. Those that are essential to your understanding of the case are explained, either in footnotes or parenthetical insertions or in the text. But the language of judges contains so many technical words that if you tried to understand every one of them before proceeding, the flow of your reading and your understanding of the whole would be needlessly impeded.

Probably the best way to understand a case is to prepare an *abstract* of it. An abstract of a case is simply a brief summary, stating what were the irreducibly essential facts, what happened in the trial court, what was the question of law that the appellate court faced, how it answered that question, and how it justified its answer. If an abstract is well prepared, anyone who reads it should be able to get a clear and accurate idea of what the case was all about without having to refer back to the original report.

There is no one "right" way to abstract a case, but the outline below suggests a useful approach.

---

[14] Trial-court decisions on legal issues lack the finality of appellate decisions and are only occasionally accompanied by published opinions. So they are seldom cited as precedents. The reputation of the particular trial judge or the cogency of his reasoning may give some of these decisions considerable influence; officially, however, their authority as precedents does not extend beyond the court in which they originated.

Suggested Outline of an Abstract

Title of Case, Name of Appellate Court, Year of Decision

1. *Facts.* What were the events leading up to this lawsuit? Leave out nonessentials: for instance, P and D are usually sufficient designations for Plaintiff and Defendant, and place names can usually be omitted. But be sure you have included every fact essential to an understanding of the legal problem.

(Important note: The facts included in the appellate court's report do not necessarily represent what *really happened.* They are merely the facts the appellate court has *assumed* to be true. If the appeal is based on the trial judge's ruling on the defendant's demurrer, for instance, then the facts before the appellate court are merely those which the plaintiff *alleged* in his complaint, since a demurrer says, in effect, "Even if these alleged facts were true, they would not be a basis for legal action." In disposing of the legal question which a demurrer raises, the trial judge and the appellate court must treat the alleged facts *as if* they were true. Appellate courts also act on the assumption that a jury's findings on the facts are correct—even though the jury might very well have misinterpreted the facts. It makes no difference; though they may not be the true facts, these are the facts on which the appellate court based its decision, and the ones that must be summarized.)

The final sentence in this first section of the abstract should indicate what remedy the plaintiff is seeking; for instance, "P then sued D to recover damages for breach of contract."

2. *What happened in trial court?* The reader of the abstract will want to know three things: What rulings, if any, were made on *motions* (for instance, on demurrers) entered by the parties either before or during the trial? Was there a jury verdict, and, if so, for which party? What judgment was finally entered by the judge? For many cases a very brief answer—for example, "Verdict and judgment for P"—will suffice.

3. *What happened in appellate court?* Usually, this question can be answered with a single word: "Affirmed" or "Reversed."

4. *Question(s) of law raised on appeal.* This is the most difficult and important item in the abstract. Here are some suggestions: (a) Always frame the questions in such a way that they can be answered *Yes* or *No.* (The appellate court itself must formulate the issues in this way in order to deal with them.) (b) Don't include any questions which the court did not have to answer in order to dispose of the case. (c) *Be sure you have not inadvertently included questions about the facts.* (d) Don't frame the question too broadly. For instance, "Did P and D make a contract?" usually does not narrow the issue sufficiently. "Did D's letter constitute a valid offer?" would probably be more useful. It is normally best to word the question so that it refers to the parties. "Must a contract be in writing?" is unlikely to be as useful as "Was the agreement between P and D invalid because not in writing?"

5. *Appellate court's answers to these questions, and its reasons.* Give the court's answer to each question asked. The first word of each answer should be *Yes* or *No*, followed by a brief summary, in your own words, of the court's reasoning. This paragraph should, in short, contain a statement of the rule of law that emerges from the case.

You may wish to add one more item:

6. *Personal observations on this decision.* Ask yourself: All things considered, does this decision seem to produce "justice"? Does the court's reasoning seem sound? Does the decision seem to fit in with related rules and decisions with which you are familiar? Does the decision seem likely to provide a useful precedent on which courts faced with similar cases can build, or is it more likely to create difficulties? Is there any reason to believe that factors not revealed in the case report—for instance, the personal beliefs of the judge, or unmentioned economic facts—may provide the best explanation for the decision?

Here is a sample abstract of the decision in *Hurley v. Eddingfield* (see page 24):

HURLEY v. EDDINGFIELD
Supreme Court of Indiana, 1901

1. [*Facts*] P was administrator of the decedent's estate. His complaint alleged: That decedent, being dangerously ill, sent for D, his family physician. That messenger told D that decedent was violently sick, that no other doctor was obtainable, and that decedent was relying on D. That these statements were all true; but that, although messenger tendered payment and although D had no reason or excuse for not going, he refused to go. That D's wrongful act, and no fault of decedent's, was the cause of decedent's ensuing death. P therefore sued for damages on behalf of the decedent's heirs.

2. [*In trial court*] D's demurrer sustained.

3. [*In appellate court*] Affirmed.

4. [*Question(s) of law raised on appeal*] Did the legislative act regulating the practice of medicine create, by implication, a legal obligation on the part of D to provide decedent with medical care upon request and tender of payment? Did the defendant violate any common-law duty analogous to those imposed on innkeepers and common carriers?

5. [*Answer(s) to question(s) raised, and reasons given*] No. The act merely permits those who obtain licenses to practice medicine; they are under no requirement to practice at all or on any terms other than those they choose to accept. Nor was any common-law duty violated; the analogies advanced are beside the mark.

3 The Trial Stage

In the last chapter we reviewed the whole adjudicative process, starting with the exchange of pleadings and ending with the disposition of the final appeal. In this chapter we will focus on the trial, which, from the viewpoint of the litigants, is by far the most important stage in the adjudicative process.

The first part of the chapter consists of a step-by-step description of a civil trial before a jury.[1] The second part consists of a critical appraisal of some problem areas in the trial process.

Trial Procedure in a Civil Case Before a Jury

The following is a generalized description of the sequence of events in a trial, from the selection of the jury to the recording of a judgment. It is generalized because there are many variations in the details of procedure from one court to another.

The Jury Is Selected

As you will remember from Chapter 2, every trial court serves a judicial district. (The district of a state trial court is often a county; a federal district court may serve a whole state.) Officials in each district maintain a list of residents who are available for jury duty. Periodically, the names of enough jurors to meet the trial court's needs for its current session are chosen by lot from this list, and the prospective jurors are then summoned to the courthouse. Some of them may be excused, if they have a good reason, but the rest must report to the courthouse every day for several weeks, standing ready to serve on whatever cases they are assigned to.

When the case is ready for trial, twelve of the prospective jurors are

---

[1] Many civil cases are tried without a jury, of course: cases which involve the rules of equity, for instance (see pp. 58–60), and any case in which the parties have agreed to waive their right to a jury trial. But a trial without a jury is not sufficiently different from a jury trial to warrant a separate description. The principal difference is that in a trial without a jury the judge is both the formulator of the legal rules (including the rules of trial procedure) and the finder of the facts.

chosen by lot to fill the jury box.[2] They are then questioned—collectively or individually, by the judge or by the lawyers, according to the local practice—on whether they have any connection with any of the participants in the trial (parties, lawyers, or witnesses), or any biases on the issues involved. (For instance, in an accident case the prospective jurors may be asked whether they have ever been involved in an accident suit.)

Each lawyer may demand the exclusion of any prospective juror for a specified cause. He may also make a limited number of "peremptory challenges," without giving any reason. This privilege enables him to exclude jurors who, he feels intuitively, may be unfriendly to his client's cause. He may, for example, have a hunch that farmers, or women, would be hostile to his client, and therefore challenge any prospective jurors in these categories. The rejected jurors go back to the jury room to await assignment to other cases. Their places are taken by other prospective jurors, chosen by lot, who are also questioned. In a case that has aroused strong public interest or emotions, selecting a jury may take days or even weeks. In civil cases, however, the jury is usually chosen with little delay.

The Plaintiff Presents His Case

The lawyer representing the plaintiff [3] now makes his opening statement to the court. He outlines the version of the facts that he expects to prove and makes clear what he is asking the court to do for his client. Next he presents his evidence in whatever order he thinks best. He calls each of his witnesses to the stand and subjects them to "direct examination," phrasing questions in a way that will elicit answers favorable to his client's case. (He will almost certainly have interviewed his witnesses beforehand in an effort to prepare them for the witness stand, but efforts to have witnesses "memorize their lines" usually backfire.) D has the right to object to any of P's questions or to any answer from P's witnesses, on the ground that the question or answer is improper under the rules of evidence; the judge must either accept or reject D's objections.

When P has finished his direct examination of each witness, D may, if he wishes, "cross-examine" the witness. D may try to bring out facts that P has preferred not to touch upon, or he may try to cast doubt on testimony by revealing the witness to be confused, forgetful, misled, self-contradictory, deliberately untruthful—or, if worse comes to worst, simply ridiculous. Cross-examination at its best is a high art.

After D's cross-examination of each witness, P has another chance to question the witness. This "redirect examination" gives P an opportunity to try to repair any weakening of the witness's original testimony caused by the cross-examination.

When P has finished presenting his evidence, he "rests his case." At this point D is likely to move that P's suit be thrown out, on the grounds

---

[2] Often as many as fourteen are chosen; two of them are alternate jurors who hear the whole case and are available to replace jurors who become incapacitated during the trial.

[3] Hereafter, we shall use P in referring to the plaintiff's lawyer, and D in referring to the defendant's lawyer.

that, even if all P's evidence were true and even if it were interpreted as favorably to P's position as possible, P has still failed to prove his case. (This is known as a motion for a "directed verdict" or for a "nonsuit.") If the judge accepts D's contention, P's suit is thrown out and the trial is over. Of course, P probably would not have brought his suit to court in the first place unless he had some basis for believing that he could establish the elements of a case; hence, the chances are that D's motion will be denied. But occasionally a plaintiff's witnesses fail to give the testimony expected, or else their testimony is completely discredited on cross-examination. Then the plaintiff's case may simply collapse, and D's motion may be granted. If, however, it is denied, the trial continues.

The Rules of Evidence

Before we go on with our trial, let us look for a moment at the rules that govern the admissibility of evidence.

Why are any restraints placed on what lawyers may introduce in evidence and on what witnesses may say? Would it not be better to let the judge and jury "get the whole story," including every bit of evidence that any participant might possibly consider relevant?

The answer is clear: first, such a procedure would mean that the trial of even a fairly simple case might drag on for weeks. And second, no "finder of fact"—least of all a jury—should have to extract the truth from the tangle of irrelevant, misleading, and unreliable evidence that such a free-wheeling procedure would produce.

Our rules of evidence have been largely shaped with the jury in mind (although judges also apply them, perhaps somewhat less meticulously, in trials without a jury). Most jurors have little experience in analyzing evidence objectively, and many of them have prejudices that are not easy to suppress. They are apt to become confused, forgetful, and, in a long trial, bored and inattentive. The rules of evidence are designed to keep the jury from hearing items of evidence that are (a) irrelevant and immaterial to the questions of fact at issue, (b) repetitious of evidence already admitted, (3) of a sort shown by experience to be of dubious reliability, (d) not readily testable by cross-examination, and (e) in violation of certain confidential relationships.

The rules of evidence have been developed piecemeal over the years, mostly by judges faced with novel problems of proof. They are numerous and complex, and we shall do no more than touch on a few of them to give some idea of their purpose and operation.

Suppose that BUMPED is suing TRUCKER (a small furniture-moving company) for damage resulting from an accident in which BUMPER, a truckdriver employed by TRUCKER, collided with BUMPED's automobile.[4] BUMPED's lawyer starts to introduce evidence designed to show that BUMPER was involved in another accident three years before, and TRUCKER's lawyer immediately objects to the evidence. The question that the judge must ask

---

[4] We shall discuss the legal rules on the liability of employers for acts of their employees in Chapter 14.

himself is whether a showing that BUMPER had an earlier accident would increase the probability that he is at fault in the accident with BUMPED, thus justifying admission of the evidence. Most courts have answered no to this question, holding that the evidence is not really relevant and that there is a risk that some jurors will jump to the unwarranted conclusion that a driver with one past accident must be "accident-prone" and therefore at fault in the present case. So the judge will probably rule that BUMPED's lawyer may not present this evidence.

May BUMPED's lawyer mention before the jury that TRUCKER carries liability insurance? Carrying insurance makes TRUCKER neither more nor less responsible for the accident, but knowledge of that fact might lead some jurors to favor passing the repair bills along to the rich insurance company, regardless of who was at fault. So the evidence is excluded. (Plaintiffs' lawyers have, however, discovered various ways of hinting to the jury that the defendant is insured.)

Should the court admit testimony from a seven-year-old boy about what he saw of the accident? The answer used to be no, but in many courts now the judge will admit the testimony if he has satisfied himself, by questioning the boy outside the courtroom, that the boy is a competent witness: that he has the ability to observe, recollect, and communicate, and that he understands the importance of telling the truth.

Should a witness be allowed to express his opinion about whether BUMPER was driving carelessly when the accident occurred? Probably not. Unless a witness is an acknowledged expert on some subject that demands expertise, the court wants to hear only his factual observations, and not the inferences he has drawn from those observations. The task of drawing inferences, and of forming opinions, is for the jury.

How about the testimony of someone who did not see the accident himself but who was told about it by an eyewitness? If the eyewitness is not available to testify, should the court hear his account at second hand? Such "hearsay" is normally excluded, because the eyewitness, whose perception of the accident is what really matters, cannot be put under oath or subjected to the acid test of cross-examination. (The reliability of the eyewitness's perception of the event cannot be tested by cross-examining the person to whom he described it.) Since a great deal of valuable evidence would be lost if the courts excluded all hearsay, however, numerous exceptions to this exclusionary rule have been made to cover particular situations in which the hearsay evidence is likely to be trustworthy.

Finally, suppose that BUMPED's lawyer has reason to believe that BUMPER told his physician shortly after the accident that he had had one of his dizzy spells at the moment the accident occurred. May the lawyer insist that BUMPER's doctor take the stand and reveal what BUMPER told him? No, unless BUMPER consents. Confidential communications of patient to doctor, client to lawyer, confessant to confessor, spouse to spouse, and in a few other relationships are "privileged"; the person to whom the communication was made cannot be compelled to testify as to its contents if the communicator raises an objection.

The Defendant Presents His Case

Now to return to our trial. P has rested his case, and D now makes his opening statement, outlining what he intends to prove. He then presents his evidence. D may concentrate on rebutting the implications of P's evidence, or he may introduce new facts that alter the legal significance of what P has proved. In BUMPED's suit against TRUCKER, for instance, TRUCKER's lawyer may try to show that BUMPER was *not* driving negligently; or that, even if he was, his negligent driving did not cause the accident; or that BUMPED was also negligent (since "contributory negligence" by the plaintiff will usually prevent his recovering damages). The examination of D's witnesses follows the usual sequence: direct examination by D, cross-examination by P, and redirect examination by D if desired.

The Plaintiff Presents His Rebuttal

After D has rested his case, P is permitted to introduce further evidence in order to rebut D's evidence.

At this point D may once again move for a directed verdict; that is, he may ask that P's suit be thrown out, on the ground that P has failed to establish a case that the jury could decide otherwise than for the defendant. P may make a similar motion, contending that he has so clearly established his client's right to a judgment that no jury could reasonably decide otherwise. Once in a great while the judge will grant one of these motions, thus taking the case away from the jury. But even if the judge himself thinks that P has failed to prove his case or D his defense, he will often let the case go to the jury.

The Lawyers Make Their Closing Statements

The lawyers (usually D first and then P) now sum up. Each reviews the evidence, stressing the strong points of his own case and the weaknesses of his adversary's case. These closing statements can be extremely important, for they may be what the jurors remember best when they retire to decide on a verdict.

The Judge Instructs the Jury

The judge's most important moment in the trial comes when he instructs the jury. He usually starts by spelling out the questions of fact that the jury must answer on the basis of the evidence presented. In the federal courts and the courts of some states, the judge may give the jury his own evaluation of the various items of evidence, but in most state trial courts the judge is not permitted to do this.

Ordinarily, the jury is instructed to decide what the facts are, to apply the rules to those facts, and to come up with a "general verdict"—that is, a decision in favor of one party or the other. If it decides for the plaintiff, its verdict will include an award of damages in a specified amount. In order for the jury to arrive at a general verdict, the judge must, of course, first explain the rules that would apply to alternative findings of fact. In our auto accident case, for instance, he would have to explain to the jury what is meant by negligence, what would be the consequence of a finding of contributory negligence, and (in case the jury finds for the plaintiff) how damages are measured under the law.[5]

After the judge has given his instructions, the lawyers may challenge their correctness, or may ask him to give the jury certain additional instructions. The judge then has to decide whether these proposed instructions correctly state the law and whether a useful purpose will be served in repeating them to the jury.

The Jury Deliberates and Brings in a Verdict

The jurors' deliberations in the jury room are secret. There is no officially sanctioned way of finding out, during or after the trial, how they went about performing their task. This means, of course, that jurors may willfully ignore the judge's instructions; they may even decide the case by flipping a coin. It would seem, however, that most juries are conscientious and do the best job they can.

The judge has told the jury that under the law of the jurisdiction all twelve jurors, or some majority of them, must agree on the verdict. He has urged them to make every effort to reach agreement. But sometimes the jurors are unable to agree, even after many hours of deliberation. Then a jury is said to be "hung." A mistrial is declared and the whole case must be tried again.

If the jurors reach a verdict, they return to the courtroom and report their decision. At this point the loser may move that the court award him the judgment despite the verdict (which, he will claim, is plainly contrary to the evidence), or that a new trial be granted because of some alleged irregularity in the trial just completed. Usually, either side may ask for a new trial on the ground that the damages awarded are excessive or insufficient.

A Judgment Is Entered on the Record

Unless the judge grants a motion for a new trial, he now orders that a *judgment* be entered on the record. In most cases this judgment is in effect a formal confirmation and recording of the jury's verdict.

A dissatisfied party has a certain number of days in which he may appeal. If no appeal is taken, or if the appellate court affirms the trial court's judgment, that judgment stands on the record as the final disposition of the case. Under the rule of *res judicata,* the matter may not be brought again before any court.[6]

---

[5] Under certain circumstances, the judge instructs the jury to bring in a set of answers to the questions of fact which he formulates for them. This is known as a "special verdict." The judge himself then applies the rules to the facts found and assesses the damages. See, for instance, *Wachovia Bank & Trust Co. v. Crafton,* on page 471.

In a trial without a jury, there is, of course, no need for instructions. But the judge's written decision contains a separate statement of his "Findings of Fact" and of his "Conclusions of Law." This facilitates the task of the appellate court, which normally accepts his findings on the facts but must review his conclusions concerning the proper rules to apply.

[6] On *res judicata,* see page 29. An exception to the rule barring a new trial is made

The Judgment Is Executed

Winning a judgment for damages is not always the end of the road for the plaintiff. If the defendant does not pay up voluntarily, the plaintiff must go to the sheriff to get his judgment "executed." The sheriff has no power to act against the defendant's person to enforce an award of damages; in order to satisfy the judgment he must seize some of the defendant's property, if any can be found within the jurisdiction. As a result, valid judgments often prove impossible to execute. However, a judgment does remain on the record and may provide the basis for a later suit in the same or another court.

If, instead of a judgment for damages in an "action at law," the plaintiff had won an equity judgment—if the judge had granted him an injunction, for instance—he would have much less difficulty in enforcing it. Equity judgments (or "decrees," as they are usually called) are addressed to the defendant personally; they order him to do something, or to stop doing something. If he fails to comply with such an order, he may be held in "contempt of court" and have to pay a fine or even go to prison.

The Adversary System

At the heart of the adjudicative process are two basic principles. The first is the belief that both sides to a controversy must have a chance to be heard—that each party must have "his day in court." Closely related to this is a second belief: that the best way to find the truth and "do justice" in a case is to make the parties themselves responsible for most of what happens at the trial. In American trials, the judge is little more than a referee throughout most of the proceedings, while the jury merely observes and listens. Each party (acting through his lawyer) must plan and execute his own strategy, must find and present his own evidence and arguments. We call this the adversary system.

What are the practical implications of this system?

1. The facts on which a trial court bases its decision are those which the parties assert and substantiate with evidence. Important witnesses may go unheard and important items of evidence remain unrevealed simply because the parties did not discover them, or chose not to introduce them. Moreover, the evidence that is presented may fail to influence the outcome, even though it is important, simply because it is ineptly presented. The court, in short, does not really base its decision on "all the true and relevant facts," but merely on those facts discovered and effectively presented to it.

Although we tend to take the concept of the party presentation of evidence for granted, there are alternative methods. For instance, the court could have a staff of its own investigate the facts and report its findings to the judge. And the judge and jurors could take a much more active part

---

when a litigant is able to satisfy a court that wholly new evidence has been discovered (a) which could not have been discovered in time for the earlier trial, and (b) which is of sufficient importance that it could have changed the verdict in the earlier trial had it been introduced then.

in initiating inquiries and in asking questions of the witnesses. But underlying our adversary system is a conviction that the court is more likely to learn all the facts it needs to know and to make a balanced appraisal of them if the initiative for producing them is left with the adversaries.

2. It is up to the parties' lawyers to object whenever they believe that an irregularity in the proceedings has occurred or is about to occur. Suppose one party tries to introduce evidence that falls into one of the categories of evidence considered inadmissible under the exclusionary rules of evidence (see above, page 35). Although the judge would readily exclude such evidence if the other party objected to it, ordinarily he will not exclude it if no objection is made. (Moreover, if the lawyer fails to object at the time the evidence is introduced, he loses the right to object to it later in appealing an unfavorable decision.)

3. Although many trial judges have had years of experience in evaluating evidence, a majority of American courts do not allow the judge to comment on the evidence when he makes his charge to the jury; and, even in those jurisdictions in which he may comment on the evidence, his discretion in doing so is more restricted than in the courts of many other countries.

4. In making up his mind about what rules of law apply to a particular case, the trial judge relies heavily on the briefs and oral arguments of the lawyers. Ordinarily a trial judge simply does not have time to search out, on his own, past decisions, statutes, or relevant passages in scholarly treatises; he is obliged to rely on the citations brought to his attention by the lawyers. (Although they have more time, appellate judges also tend to choose from among the arguments made and the precedents cited by the lawyers.)

5. The remedy the court grants to the plaintiff is never more than what he has asked for.

In the case that follows, the appellate court concluded that the trial judge had gone beyond his proper function under the adversary system; therefore it granted the plaintiff's motion for a new trial.

DREYER v. ERSHOWSKY

Supreme Court of New York, Appellate Division, 1913
156 App. Div. 27, 140 N.Y.S. 819

► RICH, J. This appeal is from a judgment in favor of the defendants, entered upon the verdict of a jury in an action to recover for negligence. It may be that upon the record here presented, and considering the method pursued in the trial of this action, a verdict for the defendants was not without justification. We are convinced, however, that the cause was so hastily disposed of that an injustice may have been done. The plaintiff was represented by skillful counsel, but was not permitted to have the facts elicited from his witnesses by the counsel employed to represent him and conduct his case. The ordinary and usual procedure in the trial of causes was disregarded. The learned justice who presided at the trial took it upon himself to conduct the examination of witnesses, and we feel that in taking from counsel, who was undoubtedly familiar with the case and knew what he expected to prove by his witnesses, the opportunity of trying his case the plaintiff has been deprived of his day in court.

The plaintiff was the first witness called upon at the trial, and, after he had stated his place of residence and the nature of his business, the learned court interrupted the examination, and proceeded to question the witness as to the nature and cause of the accident and the extent of his injuries. The next witness was a physician and surgeon, and his examination in chief was also conducted by the court. The third witness for plaintiff was in defendants' employ at the time of the accident, and, after the witness had said in response to questions by the court that he saw plaintiff that day, counsel said:

> "Would your honor permit me to conduct the examination?
> "The Court: One moment, please. Get some facts first."

And the court proceeded to interrogate the witness as to the crucial questions involved. The record shows that counsel again asked to be permitted to examine the witness.

> "Mr. Gottlieb: Won't your honor allow me to examine this witness?
> "The Court: No."

Other witnesses were called for plaintiff and questioned by the court, when finally a witness was called in rebuttal. The record follows:

> "Harry Weintraub, 102 Orchard Street, Manhattan, called as a witness in behalf of the plaintiff, being duly sworn, testified:
> "By the Court: Q. Now, Weintraub, where were you on September 6, 1907?
> "Mr. Gottlieb: Will your honor permit me to examine the witness?
> "The Court: No; I am going to examine for a while.
> "Mr. Gottlieb: I except.[7]
> "A. On the corner of Delancey and Forsyth Street. Q. What were you doing there? A. I have been sitting on Mr. Rosenberg's wagon, moving van. Q. Who else was sitting on that moving van?
> "Mr. Gottlieb: I object to your honor cross-examining the witness, if your honor please.
> "Q. Who was sitting there?
> "Mr. Gottlieb: I except.
> "The Court: Counselor, you will sit down and not rise again until the court tells you.
> "Mr. Gottlieb: I except."

We think that the conduct of the court in refusing to permit counsel the examination of his witness was highly improper. While it is true that the manner in which a witness shall be examined is largely in the discretion of the trial judge, it must be understood that we have not adopted in this

---

[7] Mr. Gottlieb here "takes an exception": he asks that it be noted in the trial record that he has objected to the judge's adverse ruling. In some jurisdictions, lawyers lose their right to raise an issue in the appellate court if they fail to "take an exception" to the ruling.

country the practice of making the presiding judge the chief inquisitor. It is better to observe our time-honored custom of orderly judicial procedure, even at the expense of occasional delays; and while we recognize the commendable zeal which prompted the learned justice to expedite the litigation, it must not be forgotten that the trial of a lawsuit is an important event to the parties, and they must not only receive justice, but must be made to know that justice is being administered. The judge is an important figure in the trial of a cause; and while he has the right, and it is often his duty, to question witnesses to the end that justice shall prevail, we can conceive of no other reason for him to take the trial of the cause out of the hands of counsel. It is better that he should conduct the trial with such deliberation that the scales may be seen to balance at every stage in the progress of the trial.

We are of the opinion that the plaintiff has not had a fair opportunity of presenting his case, and the judgment and order must therefore be reversed and a new trial granted, costs to abide the event. All concur; JENKS, P. J., in result.

Judgment and order reversed and new trial granted.   ◄

> QUESTION
>
> Notice that Judge Rich concedes that a trial judge "has the right, and it is often his duty, to question witnesses to the end that justice shall prevail." In the light of the decision in this case and of what we have said about the adversary system, under what circumstances do you think it would be proper and desirable for the judge to question a witness?

The Trial Process: Some Problem Areas

A major theme of this book is that a litigant often cannot be sure what rules of law govern his case until an appellate court has finally decided it. But we shall have little to say hereafter about another form of uncertainty, just as unsettling for the litigant: Can he actually prove his version of the facts in the trial court?

Critics of American trials and trial courts claim that the hazards of litigation are greater than they need be. They complain that the adversary system puts the trial lawyer under too great a temptation to mislead the court, that juries of untrained citizens are too easily misled, that our methods of recruiting judges too often discourage the best candidates, and that the delays in securing justice in many of our trial courts constitute a denial of justice.

Let us consider briefly each of these "problem areas" in the administration of justice in the United States.

The Role of the Lawyer

As we suggested in the preceding section, under the adversary system every trial is a contest. The contestants are the lawyers—experts in the art of advocacy (that is, in preparing and presenting evidence and arguments). The rules of the game are enforced by a referee—the judge. The jury (or the judge when there is no jury) decides who wins.

The lawyer's role is thus of crucial importance. Balzac once described the jury as "twelve men chosen to decide who has the better lawyer." And true it is that the performance of a skilled lawyer often has greater effect on the jury than the testimony of witnesses or even the instructions of the judge.

Behind the adversary system is a presupposition that each lawyer will do his best to win. The expectation is usually justified. But not all lawyers are equally skillful, and the party with the stronger case, with "justice" on his side, does not necessarily have the better lawyer. Litigants with strong cases have lost because their lawyers were inept; apparently hopeless causes have been saved by brilliant advocacy.

It is hard to see what can be done to eliminate this distortion from the administration of justice. Some critics have suggested that we could offset the advantage enjoyed by a superior lawyer by assigning a more active role to the judge, allowing him more freedom to put questions to the witnesses and to comment critically to the jury on the evidence.

The adversary system raises another problem: it subjects the lawyer to conflicting loyalties. On the one hand he is expected to fight to win. In presenting his client's case, he must be one-sided and partisan, not neutral and objective. Not only is this the presupposition behind the system, it is what the client who pays him expects him to do. And the lawyer, being human, wants to win. He knows that his reputation and his future income depend on victories.[8]

On the other hand, the lawyer can never forget that he is participating in a process whose object is to do justice. He is often described as an "officer of the court," a reflection of the degree to which the court must depend on him. And yet some of the steps he may consider taking in order to win may defeat the law's objective of arriving at a just decision.

A body of rules and principles has been developed to help the lawyer reconcile these conflicting pressures. Some are official rules, enforceable with the aid of such sanctions as judicial reprimand, forfeiture of the lawyer's case, fine or imprisonment for contempt of court, and suspension or revocation of the lawyer's license to practice. (The latter penalty is known as disbarment.) But some of the most important rules are non-official and only persuasive in their force. Most of these latter rules are embodied in the Canons of Professional Ethics of the American Bar Association.[9]

The Canons are couched in general terms. Their tone and spirit are illustrated by the following excerpts, which have to do with the conflicting loyalties we mentioned above:

---

[8] This is most nakedly evident when a lawyer takes a case on a "contingency" basis: he will be paid an agreed percentage of any damages he wins—and nothing if he loses.

[9] The original thirty-two Canons were adopted by the A.B.A. in 1908. They have been taken over in their entirety or in substance by most of the state bar associations, and have been enacted into law in a few states. Since 1908 the A.B.A. has amended some of the original Canons and has adopted fifteen new ones. Since 1922 a standing committee on ethics of the Bar Association has advised lawyers on questions involving professional conduct. Its Opinions interpreting the Canons are published from time to time.

Canon 15. How Far a Lawyer May Go in Supporting a Client's Cause.
Nothing operates more certainly to create or to foster popular prejudice
against lawyers as a class, and to deprive the profession of that full
measure of public esteem and confidence which belongs to the proper
discharge of its duties, than does the false claim, often set up by the unscrupulous in defense of questionable transactions, that it is the duty of
the lawyer to do whatever may enable him to succeed in winning his
client's cause. . . .

The lawyer owes "entire devotion to the interest of the client, warm
zeal in the maintenance and defense of his rights and the exertion of his
utmost learning and ability," to the end that nothing be taken or be
withheld from him, save by rules of law, legally applied. No fear of
judicial disfavor or public unpopularity should restrain him from the
full discharge of his duty. In the judicial forum the client is entitled to
the benefit of any and every remedy and defense that is authorized by
the law of the land, and he may expect his lawyer to assert every such
remedy or defense. But it is steadfastly to be borne in mind that the great
trust of the lawyer is to be performed within and not without the bounds
of the law. The office of attorney does not permit, much less does it demand of him for any client, violation of law or any manner of fraud or
chicane. He must obey his own conscience and not that of his client.

Canon 22. Candor and Fairness.   The conduct of the lawyer before the
Court and with other lawyers should be characterized by candor and
fairness.

It is not candid or fair for the lawyer knowingly to misquote the contents of a paper, the testimony of a witness, the language or the argument of opposing counsel, or the language of a decision or a textbook;
or with knowledge of its invalidity, to cite as authority a decision which
has been overruled, or a statute which has been repealed. . . . A lawyer
should not offer evidence which he knows the Court should reject, in
order to get the same before the jury by arguing for its admissibility. . . .
These and all kindred practices are unprofessional and unworthy of an
officer of the law charged, as is the lawyer, with the duty of aiding in
the administration of justice.

The Oath of Admission to the Bar proposed by the American Bar Association and used by most states contains these words:

I do solemnly swear: . . . I will employ for the purpose of maintaining
the causes confided to me such means only as are consistent with truth
and honor, and will never seek to mislead the Judge or jury by any artifice
or false statement of fact or law. . . .

P R O B L E M
Consider the following ethical problem in connection with Canon 22:
Suppose that, while preparing his case, a plaintiff's lawyer comes upon a
piece of evidence which, if introduced in court, would weaken his client's
position. Or suppose that he finds a strong precedent directly opposed to
the legal argument he proposes to make. Then suppose that during the
trial the defendant's lawyer fails to bring out the item of evidence, or the
strong precedent, apparently because he has not discovered it. Is it the

duty of the plaintiff's lawyer to reveal the evidence, or the precedent, to his adversary or to the court? [10]

The Role of the Jury

We would have far less cause to worry about the courtroom tactics of lawyers if the finders of fact in most civil cases were trained judges, rather than untrained, easily misled jurors. American courts try a much higher proportion of cases before juries than do the courts of any other country. Most countries that use juries limit their use to major criminal cases. Only the United States uses them extensively in civil cases.

Even in this country, as we have seen, not all civil cases go before juries: most minor-court trials and most equity cases are heard by a judge alone. But either party in an ordinary suit for damages normally has a right to insist on a jury trial. For the federal courts this right is protected by the Constitution of the United States, and some form of jury-trial right is guaranteed, constitutionally or by statute, in all the states.[11]

The reasons for this loyalty to the jury system are primarily historical. The right to a trial "by a jury of one's peers"—particularly in criminal cases —was one of the hard-won victories of the long struggle against abuses of power by the kings of England. On a number of notable occasions in the colonial period, juries stood up to oppressive royal judges. When our early constitutions were framed, therefore, the right to trial by jury was considered extremely important. In the nineteenth century, during the Jacksonian era and again later in the century, public confidence in the jury was further strengthened by the concept of "popular sovereignty," which stressed popular participation in government and discounted the importance of training and expertise (such as that possessed by judges) in government service.

The average American probably continues to think favorably of trial by jury. But among students of our legal system the institution has been a subject of controversy for years. Here are some of the criticisms often made of it, and some answers to those criticisms:

1. Most jurors, say the critics, are not trained to draw objective conclusions from a body of factual evidence. They are all too often at the mercy of their emotions and prejudices. Except in very short trials, they tend to become confused, bored, inattentive, and forgetful. Eager to finish the job, they are often willing to abandon personal convictions, or even to resort to the toss of a coin, in order to reach agreement. These well-known frailties encourage the lawyer to "put on a show" for the jury—to appeal to

---

[10] What we have said in this section about the lawyer's role in the trial court obviously has some application to his role in the appellate court. But appellate judges, free from the tensions and time pressures of the trial court, are better able than trial judges to prevent the unequal abilities of the two lawyers from distorting the outcome. They also have the time to do their own research, if they wish, which makes such tactics as misinterpretation or suppression of precedents less rewarding for the unethical lawyer.

[11] The United States Constitution, Seventh Amendment, provides: "In suits at common law [see page 58, footnote 1], where the value in controversy shall exceed twenty dollars, the right of trial by jury shall be preserved. . . ." The Constitution of Pennsylvania, Article I, Section 6, says simply: "Trial by jury shall be as heretofore, and the right thereof remain inviolate."

their emotions and biases—instead of presenting his case in an orderly, logical manner as he would if a judge were trying it. Finally, if the plaintiff's lawyer (in an accident case, for instance) can win the jury's sympathy, it is likely to grant inordinately generous damages.

The defenders of the jury insist that these allegations are greatly exaggerated, and that most juries are conscientious, serious, sensible, and sometimes even rather stingy in their awards. They point to the testimony of a number of trial judges who have written about the high proportion of cases in which jury awards have been very close to what the judges would have awarded had they been sitting alone.

2. Jurors, the critics go on, are particularly ill qualified to "apply the law to the facts." To be sure, this is not necessarily their fault. The judge is supposed to explain the relevant rules in language they can understand. But he learns from bitter experience that appellate courts scrutinize his instructions to make sure that he has stated the law correctly, and he knows that if he makes any significant error they will reverse his judgment.[12] Faced with the choice of either addressing the jury in simple, layman's language or of being impeccably correct in technical language, many judges play it safe and use well-worn verbal formulas that they know will be acceptable to the appellate court—even though by so doing they may make their instructions virtually incomprehensible to the jurors.

Once again the defenders of the jury system charge exaggeration. In the great majority of cases—and notably in the personal injury cases that take up so much of the time of our trial courts—the real controversy is over the facts; the rules are simple and jurors ordinarily have no trouble understanding them.

The defenders admit, however, that in the more complex cases involving business arrangements and transactions trial by jury does not always work particularly well. In these cases, in fact, more and more litigants are waiving their right to a jury trial.

The jury's defenders may even concede to the critics that our courts should make greater use of the "special" rather than the "general" verdict (see page 38). When a judge asks the jury for a special verdict, he requires it to give yes-or-no answers to the questions of fact he has formulated. Then he applies the law to the jury's answers. The jury does not need to understand the rules of law that he will apply to its findings of fact.

3. Even when jurors understand the rules that the judge explains, retort the critics, they sometimes choose to ignore them. Take the "contributory-negligence" rule, for example. Many states still adhere to the common-law rule that contributory negligence prevents the plaintiff from recovering any damages. In an auto accident suit, for instance, even though the defendant was obviously driving carelessly, the plaintiff will not be awarded damages if he is shown to have been in the least bit careless himself. Where

---

[12] Notice as you read the cases in Part II how many of the appeals are based on alleged errors in the trial judge's instructions to the jury. It is ironic that errors in instructions, which are often not really understood by the jury, are in general more likely to cause the reversal of a judgment than errors in the admission or exclusion of evidence, though the latter type of error is much more likely to affect the verdict.

the defendant was driving very carelessly and the plaintiff was only a little bit careless, applying the rule is apt to seem grossly unfair, and in many verdicts it is clear that the jury has chosen to ignore it. This is easy to do when only a general verdict is required; the jurors have only to announce to the court that they find for the plaintiff and award him so much in damages. They are not required to specify—as they would in a special verdict—that they found the plaintiff to have been wholly without negligence. In effect, the jurors are thus able to defy the judge.[13]

The defenders of the jury contend that the jury's power to alter the law in particular cases is a *virtue* of the system. The jury, they say, blunts the law's sharp edges and brings to the trial process the average man's sympathy with human frailty and his sense of what is "reasonable" conduct. Judges are trained professionals, in the upper-income brackets, and are likely to be somewhat insulated from the harsher realities of life; hence they are usually less qualified than the jurors to apply the community's standards of what is justifiable. Moreover, there are twelve jurors to one judge: when the task is to appraise the credibility of evidence and apply vague standards, such as the "reasonable care" standard of negligence law, the consensus of twelve persons of diverse origins and temperaments may be more valid than the decision of one man.

The judge, the defenders point out, cannot make exceptions to the rule in the "hard" cases, because his interpretations of the law create precedents. Juries can make exceptions by interpreting the facts in order to reach the desired result, because their verdicts do *not* create precedents.

The critics of the jury system concede some merit to this argument, but they point out that it raises serious questions: Can juries always be counted on to bend the law in the right direction? Are they not quite capable of being shortsighted, irrational, and even vindictive? And what happens to the goals of predictability and "equality before the law" if different juries apply a rule differently in similar cases? Finally, when a rule is really unsatisfactory, isn't public pressure on the legislature (rather than a jury's defiance of the judge's instructions) the proper way to get it changed?[14]

4. Finally, the critics argue that jury trials take too long and cost too much. As we shall see later in this chapter, the long delays in obtaining justice pose a serious problem, particularly in metropolitan areas. And it is true that trials before a jury take longer than trials held before a judge alone. No time is wasted in selecting the jury and instructing it; and presenting the facts to a trained judge normally takes considerably less time than presenting them to a jury. In short, reducing the proportion of jury trials would save time and would help eliminate the delays that now plague the administration of justice. It would also lower the costs of litigation (for

---

[13] If the judge were sure that the jury had disobeyed his instruction, he could overturn the verdict. But proof of defiance is rarely available, and most judges are reluctant to overturn jury verdicts on the ground that they are contrary to the evidence. Furthermore, it seems probable that judges often tacitly approve of the jury's refusal to apply the contributory-negligence rule.

[14] It is interesting to note that, perhaps partly because of juries' widespread defiance of instructions, a number of state legislatures have substituted a rule of "comparative negligence" for the strict "contributory-negligence-bars-liability" rule described above.

the state and also for the litigant, who pays "court costs" covering part of the actual costs), both because each trial would take less time and because jurors' fees would be eliminated.

The defenders of the jury reply, first, that if the jury system has other virtues, as they contend, the extra time and money it entails are worth putting up with. They also remind us that pairs of litigants who wish to have their case tried more speedily and at less cost may waive their right to a jury trial.

The defenders of the jury have one further argument: jury service, they insist, gives the people a chance to participate in government; it is "education in citizenship"; it increases respect for the judicial process and the law; and it makes the public share responsibility for decisions that may be difficult and unpopular.

One could be more enthusiastic about all this, retort the critics, if the obligation to serve were more rationally distributed. The lists of eligibles from which jury lists are made up are rarely complete; members of many occupational groups are automatically exempt, not always for good reasons; and many people who prefer not to serve can get excused. And unfortunately, those exempted or excused are often those who would make the best jurors.

This controversy over the merits of the jury system has been going on for a long time, and will doubtless continue. The pressure for change may lead to greater use of the special verdict, and possibly to greater popularity for the "blue-ribbon jury" (drawn from a restricted list of citizens who have achieved a certain level of education) in certain kinds of case. More promising, perhaps, are the efforts being made in many communities to speed up trials by inducing litigants to forego their right to a jury trial. (More will be said about these efforts later in this chapter.) But in view of the continued popularity of the jury system and the ample constitutional protection it enjoys, it is not likely to disappear.

The Recruitment of Trial Judges

Another controversy centers on our methods of recruiting trial judges. Many students of our legal system are convinced that we could do far more to secure the services of the best possible people for our trial bench.[15]

What qualities should a trial judge possess? He must have technical competence, a broad knowledge of many fields of law. Most important, probably, is his familiarity with the rules of trial procedure and evidence; hence some prior experience as a trial lawyer is invaluable. He must have

---

[15] Much that we say in this section relates to the recruitment of appellate as well as trial judges. But most of the dissatisfaction with judicial recruitment concerns trial judges, for such reasons as these: The greater prestige of the appellate courts makes it easier to find first-rate lawyers to man them. Many appellate vacancies are filled by promoting men who have already proved themselves as trial judges. Since appellate judges sit in groups of three or more, the shortcomings of each are to some extent checked or compensated for by the others; trial judges, on the other hand, sit singly.

a "judicial temperament": not only must he be capable of rigorous objectivity, but he must be firm, patient, and not easily flustered.

The trial judge must also be capable of independence of judgment. Central to the democratic tradition is the principle that judges should be immune to improper pressures both from private-interest groups and from other officials. In principle, the only influences that may be brought to bear on a judge are those exerted in the courtroom by the presentation of evidence and argument. But other influences are always in the background. Every judge has friends and former associates; every judge belongs to a variety of organizations; every judge knows that certain officials and party leaders played a part in placing him on the bench; every judge knows that certain acts will enhance his popularity, while others will diminish it. A judge must resist the temptation to take these influences into account in arriving at decisions.

This is not to say that a judge should be insulated from the currents of popular opinion—if, indeed, that were possible. As we shall see in later chapters, the judge frequently finds that no rule of law is clearly applicable to the case before him. He must make a choice, and his beliefs about what is "just" or what is best for the community inevitably affect his decision. If his personal philosophy and convictions are too different from those held by the community, his decisions will provoke conflict and frustration. In the 1920's, for example, anti-labor judges freely granted injunctions against strikes and picketing at a time when public sympathy was swinging toward labor. The result was the Norris-LaGuardia Act, and its state counterparts, which prohibited all labor injunctions. (See below, pp. 173, 174.) But to say that a judge must share the dominant beliefs and aspirations of his time is not to say that he must court popularity by responding to every popular whim and sentiment.

THE RECRUITMENT PROCESS

Qualifications for Eligibility. In most European countries, the judiciary is a career service. The young law-school graduate who wants to become a judge takes a special set of examinations; if he passes them, he enters the service and works his way up the ladder. Each promotion is decided upon by senior judges and other civil servants. In Great Britain, all trial judgeships (except in the minor courts) are filled by appointment from among the elite group of specialized trial lawyers known as "barristers." In the United States, the only requirement is that the would-be judge be trained in the law—and even that is not necessary for some minor judgeships.

Processes of Selection. In the early decades of the Republic most judges were appointed. Then came the era of "Jacksonian Democracy," with its distrust of appointive officials and its tendency to minimize the importance of special competence and security of tenure for public officials. From then on, nearly all the new states entering the Union adopted the practice of having judges elected by the voters. Today judges are elected in about two-thirds of our states. In most of the remaining states, and in the federal system, judges are appointed by the chief executive, usually with the concurrence of one house of the legislature. A few states have variants or combinations of these methods.

Compensation.   Compensation has a lot to do with who does, and who does not, decide to become a judge. Few jurisdictions today offer salaries so inadequate as those commonly offered in earlier times, but no judge earns an income comparable to those received by highly successful private practitioners. Prestige, a sense of power, and the opportunity for public service, rather than the level of compensation, account for the willingness of able lawyers to become judges.

Tenure.   The length of the term of office also affects the attractiveness of a judicial position. A lawyer will hesitate to abandon a flourishing private practice for a judgeship if, after a few years, he does not stand a good chance of being returned to office.

Federal judges and the judges in a few states enjoy life tenure. Most judges, however, have limited terms, frequently as short as four or six years. But in some states in recent decades, terms have been lengthened; in others, reappointment or renomination has become more or less automatic for any judge who has served honorably. And under the so-called "sitting-judge" tradition which is followed in some states, a judge who has once stood for election is able to run for re-election without opposition (in other words, he is the nominee of both parties).

One reason for the reluctance of some states to grant judges extended tenure is that there is still no effective way of getting rid of bad judges. In principle, judges can be impeached, and some states provide for their removal by popular vote; but these procedures are rarely invoked and only in extreme cases. The judge whose conduct on the bench is unworthy—because he is tyrannical, arbitrary, abusive, bigoted, or even drunk—is usually hard to get rid of and is subject to no effective discipline from the higher courts.

APPOINTMENT VERSUS ELECTION.   The respective merits of appointment and election are a subject of continuing debate. Some observers believe that in a democracy the people should play a direct part in choosing their judges; others are convinced that the best men cannot be persuaded to become judges if they have to "act like politicians" and campaign for office.

But the elective and appointive systems are not really so different as they seem, and there is no evidence that states using one system have better judges than those using the other. The truth is that under both systems the selection of judges falls pretty much to local political leaders. In filling an appointive post, the president or governor almost invariably takes the advice of the local chieftains of his party in the jurisdiction where the judge will serve. When the position is elective, party leaders pick the candidates who will appear on the party ticket. (Their choice rarely fails to be ratified in the primary or by the party convention.) Since voters are notoriously unable to appraise the professional qualifications of opposing judicial candidates, they vote by party label, and the winners are swept into office along with the rest of the ticket.

In any case, campaigning for judicial office is no longer so distasteful a chore as it once was. In jurisdictions with a "sitting-judge" tradition, for example, the would-be judge knows that he will not have to wage much of a campaign when he runs, unopposed, for re-election. And even where there is a real contest, most communities no longer expect of judicial candidates the aggressive, partisan, "pie-in-the-sky" campaigning that they expect of other candidates. Furthermore, the lengthening of judicial terms in many states has meant that campaigns are less frequent. Longer terms have also meant more mid-term vacancies, created by the death or retirement of incumbents, to be filled by interim appointments. The appointee must, of course, run for the office in the next election, but by that time his name is often well enough known to give him a clear advantage in the campaign.

POLITICS AND THE JUDICIARY. What part should partisan politics play in the recruitment of judges? Are we unwise to leave the selection of judges to the political parties, as we do under both the elective and the appointive system? Or does party politics play a necessary and desirable role in the process of selecting judges?

The judiciary must be "taken out of politics," says one group. Party leaders must not be permitted to choose the appointees and the candidates, because politicians are less concerned with finding the best man than they are with using judgeships as inducements to party loyalty and as rewards for those who have worked for the party or contributed to its treasury. These critics point out that the lawyer who has stayed out of politics or who is affiliated with the party out of power stands almost no chance of becoming a judge, no matter how well qualified he is.

The judge who owes his position to a political party, moreover, comes to the bench with an indebtedness that may imperil his independence, continue the critics. Of course, he cannot openly serve the interests of that party or favor the lawyers who belong to it, but he is able to perform a host of small favors. He can help pay his political debts, for example, by choosing party regulars when he selects some of the court's regular employees. And he has the power to make appointments to a variety of temporary jobs: receivers, trustees in bankruptcy, referees in foreclosure proceedings, administrators of estates, and special guardians, for instance. Some of these posts are quite lucrative. No judge is likely to appoint a dishonest or incompetent person, but it is customary to distribute these jobs on a "patronage" basis—that is, to give them to people who have worked for the party in power.

Those who seek to take the judiciary out of politics have suggested several reforms. One is the so-called "nonpartisan" election of judges, in which candidates run in special elections without party labels. Whether calling an election nonpartisan makes it nonpolitical is open to doubt, however. Candidates nearly always have backers—either parties or private-interest groups—and the nonpartisan election may simply conceal from the voters who those backers are.

Another proposed reform is the "Missouri Plan"—so called because it was first used in choosing some of the judges in that state. Whenever a judicial vacancy occurs, a nonpartisan nominating commission—made up of appellate judges, representatives of the bar association, and laymen—selects a panel of three candidates to fill it. The governor is obliged to appoint one of the three. The appointee serves for a year's probationary period and then stands for election to a much longer term, running unopposed on his record. (The only question before the voters is whether Judge x shall be retained in office.) This plan combines nonpartisanship, the appointive principle, and the elective principle.

Opposed to this whole approach are those who insist that, since judges are not merely technicians but wielders of power and makers of rules, their recruitment simply cannot be taken out of politics. Politics, they say, is the struggle to obtain and exercise power, and judgeships are bound to be prizes in that struggle. Efforts to make the selection process nonpolitical are doomed to failure. Whatever group chooses the appointees or candidates for judgeships will become the focus of political pressure. If the bar associations make the choice, they will be dragged into the arena of political struggle. If nominating commissions do it, pressure will be exerted on those who name the commissioners and then on the commissioners themselves. Since political influences are bound to affect the selection of judges, it is better to have those influences operate through the established political parties. The voter gives his support to the party that comes nearest to standing for what he believes in, knowing that if that party wins it will probably bring into office judges who share its general attitudes and philosophy. The public can hold the party responsible.

Those who defend present methods of recruitment recognize that each has its shortcomings. But these shortcomings have been lessened, they insist, by the adoption of longer terms and the "sitting-judge" tradition.

All the evidence shows that the great majority of American trial judges are competent, conscientious, and incorruptible. And so they will remain so long as the bar and the public hold them to a high standard of conduct —higher than that to which most other officials are held. True, voters are often confused and indifferent when they have to choose between competing candidates at the polls. But they know that they want judges of high caliber, and they are prepared to punish any party whose choices for the bench prove unsatisfactory. In addition, party leaders are not likely to risk having their selections for judgeships denied endorsement, or censured, by the local bar association.

The same forces operate on the judge himself. The high standards which the public and the bar have set for the judiciary, together with the man's natural self-esteem, his own respect for the judicial office and the tradition surrounding it, combine to impel nearly all new judges to do the best job they can—regardless of how they were chosen for the office.

Delay in the Courts

Certainly the greatest source of dissatisfaction with our trial courts is the long delay that frequently occurs between a litigant's decision to bring suit and the entry of a judgment.

Fortunately, most of the disputes in our society do not have to be settled in the courts; if they did, the burden on our courts would be intolerable. Only a tiny percentage of disputes end up in lawsuits, and only a very small percentage of the suits initiated ever go to trial. The great majority are settled out of court, often "on the courthouse steps," as the saying goes.[16]

Even so, the number of cases that do reach the trial stage is so great that many of our trial courts are unable to keep up with them. This is particularly true of courts serving large metropolitan areas, where there are sometimes delays of two or more years between the time a lawsuit is initiated and the time it is disposed of by a trial court. Recently, some of these courts have taken drastic measures that promise gradually to bring them up to date (or at least to keep the backlog constant), but others are still permitting new cases to pile up on the court calendar more rapidly than they can dispose of old ones.

Some delay between the date a lawsuit is filed and the date it comes to trial is probably desirable, for it gives time for strong feelings to subside and affords the lawyers a chance to sound out the possibilities of settlement. Delays of a few months are not serious, but delays of one or several years are. The truth of the maxim, "Justice delayed is justice denied," is most dramatically illustrated by the accident victim who is deprived of his earning power by the negligence of another, but who must wait several years before a court awards him damages; during that time he may exhaust his savings and be forced to go on relief. But there are other unfortunate consequences. For one thing, the longer the delay the higher the costs of litigation become. Moreover, long delays often penalize one or both parties by depriving them of the testimony of witnesses who cease to be available. It is sometimes possible to obtain sworn statements from such witnesses while they can still be heard. But sworn statements are likely to be less effective than live testimony, just as testimony based on fresh recollection is likely to be more persuasive than testimony relating to incidents dimly remembered from several years back.

The prospect of extended delays may, it is true, encourage the parties to reach a settlement out of court. But some can better afford to wait than others. The party who finally gives in and accepts a settlement may be a plaintiff who deserved to receive more than he settled for—or a defendant, fighting a frivolous suit, who would in all likelihood have won in court had he felt he could hold out. Delays encourage the defendant with a weak defense, or the claimant with a frivolous claim, to bluff in the hope of achieving an ill-deserved settlement. It may be that the prospect of long delays serves to discourage people from bringing lawsuits, but, assuming this to be true, how do we know that those who are discouraged are not precisely those who most deserve aid from the courts?

In the ensuing paragraphs we shall mention some proposals for dealing with delays. The proposals indicate what are believed to be some of the factors causing delay. But let us note here one partial explanation. Although the volume of civil litigation has not risen as fast as the country's population, it has grown faster than the number of courts and judges available to handle it. The most striking increase is in personal injury claims (particularly claims arising from automobile accidents), which have long been our greatest source of litigation. Not only are there more personal injuries

---

[16] Moreover, of the suits which do go to trial and on which a judgment is entered, only a small percentage are appealed.

today than there used to be, but the proportion of such injuries that lead to lawsuits is rising—perhaps because of the widespread impression that juries are prone to award very generous damages to personal injury claimants.

MEASURES TO DEAL WITH DELAYS. One way of cutting down on delays would be to increase the number of courts, or at least of judges, and many jurisdictions are adopting this solution. But officials hesitate to propose an increase in the number of judges until they are satisfied that nothing else can be done to speed up the disposition of cases. Here are some of the corrective measures that are being tried or considered.

1. *Improvements in the Court System.* The efficiency of the court system would probably be improved if all the general trial courts in a state were brought into an integrated and centrally administered system; then judges with relatively light loads could be temporarily assigned to help out in overloaded courts. The federal court system has set the example here: its central administrative office compiles statistics comparing the case-loads of the various federal districts. These comparisons help the presiding judges of the higher federal courts exercise their authority in assigning district judges to temporary duty in districts other than their own. A few states have begun to follow this example.

Another way of relieving congestion in the general trial courts would be to transfer part of their case-load down to the minor courts; this could be done by raising the maximum amount that may be sued for in the minor courts. Some states have made this change. But in others the quality of justice dispensed by the minor courts is so low—particularly in the courts manned by nonprofessional, part-time justices of the peace—that the legislatures hesitate to increase their responsibilities.

2. *More Efficient Judges.* Trial judges are sometimes criticized for not working long enough or hard enough. As a generalization the charge is certainly unjustified; but it is probably fair in some instances, and some critics feel that the appellate courts should have power to supervise the performance of trial judges. A related problem is that of retirement: how can judges with failing intellectual powers be eased from the bench with dignity and compassion? Some states have a compulsory retirement age, though such arbitrary arrangements inevitably deprive our courts of the services of some judges who are still at the height of their powers.

3. *More Efficient Trial Lawyers.* Many trial lawyers take on more cases than they can handle, and then have to ask the courts for repeated postponements. By its very nature the operation of a trial court entails some time-wasting—by lawyers, litigants, witnesses, prospective jurors, and even judges. No court can plan a daily schedule with precision, because it is impossible to predict exactly how long it will take to dispose of each case. Some cases will not be tried at all: one of the participants may be ill, or there may have been a last-minute settlement. But many of the postponements requested by poorly organized lawyers could be avoided if judges were more willing to be stern and deny their requests.

4. *Better Pre-trial Techniques.* Earlier (page 27) we noted the value of pleadings, interrogatories, and pre-trial conferences with the judge. Nar-

rowing the issues to the true areas of controversy, and letting each side know exactly what the other side expects to prove and what its evidence will be, make it more likely that the trial will be a rapid and efficient proceeding. They also improve the chances of a pre-trial settlement. While the usefulness of the pre-trial conference in the judge's chambers is widely recognized, it means that the judge has correspondingly less time to spend in trying cases; hence there is some doubt about whether it really relieves congestion in the courts.

5. *Shorter Trials.* Many trials could be shortened if the judge were willing to keep a tighter rein on the proceedings—to be more strict in excluding irrelevancies, repetition, and mere showmanship. But certainly the best way to reduce the number of courtroom hours spent on each case would be to curtail the proportion of cases tried before a jury.

As we have seen, a party in a suit for damages has a constitutionally protected right to a jury trial in the federal courts and in the courts of many states. To induce litigants to forego that right voluntarily, some states require that a case be heard in a minor court or before a special tribunal before a jury trial can be demanded.[17] Others set the court costs charged for a nonjury trial much lower than the costs charged for a jury trial, in the hope that the parties will accept the nonjury trial. But as long as plaintiffs in accident cases believe that a jury will treat them more generously than a judge would, they will probably insist on their constitutional right.

A trial judge can reduce the time he must devote to nonjury trials by appointing a member of the bar to serve as his special fact-finder, thus relieving himself of the time-consuming task of hearing evidence. These special fact-finders are variously referred to as "masters," "auditors," and "referees." They take testimony at a formal hearing, not unlike an ordinary trial, and then prepare a report to the judge, summarizing the evidence and making a finding of fact on each factual issue they have been asked to examine. If the entire case has been turned over to a master, he may also recommend how the case should be decided. Although the final judgment is the responsibility of the judge, he rarely inquires further into the factual issues examined by the master. (Masters, auditors, and referees are referred to in several of the cases in Part II.)

6. *Adjudicating Cases Outside the Court System.* Certain kinds of case have been removed from the regular courts for reasons unconnected with court congestion, but this practice has served incidentally to relieve that congestion. For example, special administrative tribunals[18] have been set up to handle the claims of employees against their employers in connection with on-the-job injuries. Every state now has one or more tribunals of this sort (often called workmen's compensation boards). They resemble ordinary courts in many ways, but they follow simplified procedures and apply quite different rules in determining and measuring liability. It has been

---

[17] In some parts of Pennsylvania, for instance, plaintiffs with small claims must first have them heard by a panel of three lawyers. If a party is dissatisfied with the panel's award, however, and if he is prepared to pay the additional costs, he may insist on a regular jury trial.

[18] Administrative tribunals will be discussed in Chapter 8.

suggested that the automobile accident cases which now swamp our courts might be tried before tribunals modeled on these workmen's compensation boards. But since the suggestion has provoked a great deal of opposition from lawyers' organizations, it is not likely to be adopted in the near future.

Many business firms include an "arbitration clause" in their commercial contracts, specifying that, if a dispute should arise under the contract, it will be settled by arbitration rather than in the courts. Arbitration is nearly always speedier and less expensive than litigation. Moreover, the dispute can be settled by arbitrators who have expert knowledge of the subject matter of the disputed contract—a knowledge that trial judges are unlikely to possess.[19]

These, then, are some of the measures that are being taken, or proposed, to lessen the delays in our courts. Although some jurisdictions are making progress, the problem of court congestion remains a serious one.

---

[19] We shall have more to say about arbitration in Chapter 9, in our discussion of labor-management agreements.

4 Judicial Lawmaking I: Law Built on Precedents

When do judges "make law"? They do so every time they decide a case that no existing rule quite fits. They make law when, in order to determine what rule applies to a case, they interpret a statute or a constitutional provision. (We shall discuss these forms of judicial lawmaking in Chapters 6 and 7.) They also make law when, in the absence of either an applicable legislative rule or a directly controlling precedent, they have to create a rule by building on the precedents established in analogous cases. The present chapter is about judicial lawmaking by building on precedents.

Nowadays most of the major innovations in legal rules are introduced by legislatures, and much of the work of judges is interpreting legislative rules. But this has not always been so. In the early centuries of the legal tradition we share with England, legislative lawmaking was comparatively unimportant; most lawmaking was the work of judges building on precedents. Indeed, in some fields—contracts, for instance—the rules even to this day are primarily of judicial origin.

The Common-Law Tradition

English Origins

When the Normans conquered England in the eleventh century, they found a land with no nationwide, systematized body of law. Such law as existed was essentially a formalization of local custom. In an effort to unite the country under their rule, the early Norman kings sent royal judges out into the land to adjudicate the disputes and accusations brought before them by the people. The royal justice dispensed by these judges was firm but fair, inexpensive and expeditious. By the beginning of the thirteenth century it had wholly displaced the miscellany of Anglo-Saxon institutions that had prevailed before the Norman Conquest.

Since the royal judges had no body of generally accepted rules on which to base their decisions, they had to create rules as they went along. Understandably they drew heavily on the traditions, customs, business usages, and moral standards of the people. But they also relied on their own judgment, their "sense of justice," and their notions of the community's needs. The

body of rules which thus evolved came to be known as the *common law*—
"common" simply because it was common to all of England. For well over
a century, the process of judicial lawmaking provided England with virtually all the legal rules it had for the channeling of private conduct; it was
not until the late thirteenth century that enacted law—first royal edicts and
then acts of Parliament—became a significant element in English law.

The Emergence of Equity

By the fourteenth century, certain deficiencies had begun to appear in
the justice that was being dispensed by the royal courts. Would-be plaintiffs found themselves increasingly baffled and thwarted by the rigidly and
highly technical procedural requirements. Moreover, the royal courts tended
to confine themselves to redressing wrongs by awarding money damages
to the person wronged. Little by little, plaintiffs dissatisfied with the treatment they received from the royal courts began to petition the king for
some other form of redress. The king adopted the practice of turning these
petitions over to the Lord Chancellor, a high official in the king's court. By
the latter part of the fifteenth century this practice had become institutionalized, and the Chancellor (now presiding over a new Court of Chancery)
was issuing decrees on his own authority. The body of principles and
remedies which the Court of Chancery developed came to be known as
equity (from the Latin *aequitas*, meaning justice or fairness).

In effect, England now had two bodies of judge-made law—the traditional common law [1] of the older courts, and the newer equity. Equity
brought to English law some important new principles. (One such principle, for example, held that a plaintiff must come to equity "with clean
hands"—meaning that his own role in the affair at issue must have been
wholly without fault.) Perhaps even more important were equity's new
remedies. If a plaintiff could show that the common-law remedy of money
damages would not be adequate in his case, he might persuade the Court
of Chancery to grant him an injunction or a decree of specific performance.
These are two kinds of order addressed to the defendant and requiring him,
on pain of a fine or imprisonment for contempt of court, to do or to refrain
from doing specified acts.

---

[1] The term *common law,* you will discover, is used in several slightly different senses:

a. Most broadly, it is used to designate the Anglo-American legal tradition, which
also prevails in most other English-speaking countries. This tradition is often contrasted
with the "Civil Law" tradition, which derives from Roman law and prevails today in
the countries of continental Europe and some others.

b. "Common law" is used, as here, to distinguish the body of rules originally administered by the royal courts of law from the rules of equity, administered by the Court
of Chancery. (Sometimes the word "law" alone is also used in this sense.)

c. "Common law" is often used to refer to all judge-made rules built on precedents,
as distinguished from legislative enactments and the decisions in which these enactments
are interpreted. One often encounters the phrase, "At common law, the rule was
that . . ."; here the reference is to the decisional rule that prevailed before the passage
of some statute.

d. Lastly, "common law" occasionally refers to the body of English rules that was
transplanted to the American colonies and was in force in 1776 when the colonies
claimed their independence.

The English Legal Tradition in North America

When the English colonists settled in North America, they established a legal system modeled on what they had known in England. Though the demands of a new society in a new environment called for some changes in the old system, many English legal principles and institutions had become firmly rooted in the colonies by 1776. Despite the strong anti-British revulsion that followed the Revolution, the states of the new nation preserved intact a large part of their legal heritage. And the new states that were admitted to the Union as the years passed borrowed heavily from the same tradition.[2] Only Louisiana had a legal system that was not based on the common-law tradition; its legal institutions were inherited from France and Spain, both of which belonged to the Civil Law tradition.[3]

The Fusion of the Law Courts and the Equity Courts

Among the legal institutions transplanted to America were the rules and procedures of equity. In some colonies (and later in some of the states), separate courts of equity were established; in others, equity was administered by the regular courts of law. But in the nineteenth century, movements to reform court systems and to simplify judicial procedures led to the elimination of most separate equity courts. Today only four states have such courts; in the others, original jurisdiction over equity cases is in the trial courts of general jurisdiction (see page 16), and appeals go to the regular appellate courts.

Although the two court systems have been fused, there is still a significant distinction between a "law" case and an "equity" case. In some states, for instance, a plaintiff must indicate at the outset whether he is bringing an "action at law" or a "suit in equity." Even when no such designation is required, the judge may have to classify the case if one of the parties asks for a trial by jury. This is because the constitutional guarantees of a jury trial extend only to those cases which are essentially "legal" in character. (A plaintiff seeking an injunction or a decree of divorce cannot claim the right to a jury trial.) The procedures in the two kinds of case are essentially the same, but some of the terms used are different: a "complaint" at law is called a "bill" in equity, and a "judgment" is called a "decree."

The fusion of courts has, on the other hand, had some important con-

---

[2] A number of states have constitutional provisions or statutes incorporating the English common law into their legal systems. The following Arkansas statutory provision is representative: "The common law of England, so far as the same is applicable and of a general nature, and all the statutes of the British Parliament in aid of [it] . . . made prior to the fourth year of James the First [1607] that are applicable to our form of government, of a general nature and not local to that kingdom, and not inconsistent with the Constitution and laws of the United States or . . . of this State, shall be the rule of decision in this State unless altered or repealed by the General Assembly. . . ."

[3] The most significant difference between the Civil Law tradition and our own is that, in Civil Law countries, comprehensive legislative enactments known as *codes* have always been the main repository of legal rules. (The first code, on which all modern codes are based, was drawn up under the Roman Emperor Justinian.) Judicial lawmaking built on precedents has thus never been a part of the Civil Law tradition.

sequences for litigants. It is now possible, for instance, for a litigant in an "action at law" to introduce arguments based on equity principles, and vice versa.[4]

Over the centuries, equitable principles and remedies have undergone gradual change as judges have had to decide new cases involving novel situations. In addition, legislatures from time to time have broadened the scope and flexibility of equitable remedies and have even created some new remedies modeled on the traditional ones.

The Role of Precedents

Stare Decisis: The Doctrine and Its Rationale

The power of judges to formulate legal rules in dealing with the cases brought before them is limited by the duty, imposed on them by our legal tradition, to seek guidance by looking back at past decisions in similar cases. The principle that judges should build on the precedents established by past decisions is known as the doctrine of *stare decisis* (from the Latin phrase, *stare decisis et non quieta movere,* which means "to adhere to precedents and not unsettle things that are settled").

Observance of *stare decisis* is more than a deeply rooted tradition, however; it is a logical way for judges to act. Following precedents is often much easier and less time-consuming than working out all over again solutions to problems that have already been faced. It enables the judge to take advantage of the accumulated wisdom of successive generations. It is a curb to arbitrariness and a prop to weakness and inexperience. It conforms to the community's instinctive belief that "like wrongs deserve like remedies," and to the desire for "equal justice under law." But above all, the practice of following precedents enables citizens (with the expert assistance of lawyers) to plan their conduct in the expectation that past decisions will be honored in the future. Certainty, predictability, and continuity are not the only objectives of law, but they are important ones. Many disputes are avoided, and others are settled without litigation, simply because people have a good notion of how the courts will respond to certain types of behavior.

Precedents: The Range of Their Influence

In Chapter 2 (page 24) we examined the case of *Hurley v. Eddingfield,* which, you will remember, was decided in 1901 by the Supreme Court of Indiana. There the court held that neither the decisional law of the state nor a recently passed statute placed physicians under any legal duty to go to the aid of a sick patient when summoned.

Let's assume that the *Hurley* decision has not been overturned by a

---

[4] In *Geremia v. Boyarsky* (see page 239), the plaintiff brought an action at law to recover damages for breach of contract. The defendant's answer asked that the contract be rescinded (i.e., annulled). Rescission is an equitable remedy. The defendant's contention was based on the equitable principle that when one contracting party becomes aware of a mistake by the other, he may not take an "unconscionable" advantage of it. The case is worth reading at this point for its references to equity.

higher court or superseded by a later statute. What precisely is its influence in determining the outcome of a later case involving closely similar facts?

First, suppose that such a case were to come before an Indiana trial court any time after 1901. The answer here is clear: the Indiana trial judge would be obliged under the *stare decisis* principle to apply the rule laid down in *Hurley*, no matter what he himself thought of that rule. Within each jurisdiction, lower courts must follow the precedents established by higher courts.

But suppose that the unsuccessful plaintiff in this case was dissatisfied with the trial court judgment against him and decided to take an appeal to the Indiana Supreme Court. Under the *stare decisis* principle the appellate judges would normally feel obliged to follow the court's own earlier decision even though they themselves might have doubts concerning its correctness and wisdom. From time to time, however, appellate courts do overrule their past decisions. (We shall have more to say on this point later in the chapter.)

Finally, suppose a case very similar to *Hurley* were to come before a trial or appellate court in another jurisdiction—in Illinois, let us say. The Illinois court would be under no obligation to follow the rule laid down in *Hurley*. Properly speaking, *Hurley* is only an interpretation of the decisional and statutory law of Indiana and has no controlling effect on courts in other states. But judges normally do give consideration to decisions from other jurisdictions. If the Illinois judges found no Illinois decisions covering the point at issue, they would almost certainly look at cases decided elsewhere. After all, the American states—and, for that matter, Britain and the British Commonwealth—share a common legal tradition; moreover, their institutions and the problems they face are often similar. So it is sometimes said that decisions from other jurisdictions, though not binding, are persuasive. The persuasiveness of a given decision depends on such factors as the cogency of the supporting opinion, the prestige of the deciding court, and the unanimity of the judges. And any given decision will obviously have greater weight as a precedent if it coincides with decisions in other jurisdictions.

Building on Precedents

By simply describing our fictitious case in the preceding section as "closely similar" to *Hurley v. Eddingfield*, we put off answering some difficult questions: How similar must earlier Case A be to later Case B before it is considered a precedent? (After all, no two cases are identical.) And once the requisite similarity has been established, how do judges go about determining precisely what rule Case A stands for and just how that rule applies to Case B?

If an Indiana court were faced with a case that was exactly like *Hurley v. Eddingfield* except that the parties' names and the date and locale of the events were different, the *Hurley* decision would certainly be controlling. Any competent and scrupulous Indiana lawyer would tell a would-be plaintiff in such a controversy that his chances of winning were too slim to justify his bringing suit. Hence such cases are not likely to come up.

Litigation occurs because either the facts or the applicable legal rule is in dispute. When a court finds itself faced with a case in which *Hurley* is cited by one of the parties as a precedent, it is pretty sure to be a case resembling *Hurley* only in some respects, so that while one party is insisting on the similarities, the other party is emphasizing the dissimilarities. Imagine, for instance, a case arising in Indiana in which a patient sues his dentist for refusing to see him at once to extract an abscessed tooth; and in which the dentist demurs on the ground that under the *Hurley* decision he has violated no duty owed to the patient. The trial judge sustains the demurrer, and the patient appeals. The patient's lawyer argues in the appellate court that the cases are not analogous. How does the court go about deciding whether *Hurley* has established a precedent which must be followed?

Actually, the court has three questions to answer: First, is the earlier case essentially similar in its significant facts to the later one? Second (if it is found to be similar), what legal rule is inherent in the earlier case? Third, how does that rule apply to the later case?

Shortly, in the famous case of *MacPherson v. Buick Motor Co.*, we shall see how a new rule is built on old decisions. But a few preliminary observations will help you understand what the judges who wrote the opinions in that case were doing.

First of all, remember what we said in Chapter 3 about the role of lawyers under the adversary system. The judges depend heavily on the lawyers, not only to identify the relevant prior cases but to present arguments demonstrating the similarity or dissimilarity of those earlier cases to the current case. In a very real sense, therefore, the skill (or lack of skill) of the opposing lawyers plays a role in shaping the law.[5]

Next, remember that the judges who decided each earlier case now being cited as a precedent were preoccupied with disposing of the case before them, and only secondarily concerned with the future influence of their decision. No appellate judge is unaware that his decisions are likely to become precedents. But he can foresee only to a very limited extent what sorts of future case his decision will influence. Knowing that his opinion will probably be read by judges and lawyers for years to come, he still must concern himself primarily with justifying the court's decision to the litigants and their attorneys.

The most important implication of the foregoing observation is that what the judges said in their opinions in Case A does not crystallize for eternity the significance of that case. They could not have foreseen all the problems that would later arise in somewhat similar cases, such as Case B; hence the judges who must decide Case B should feel free to re-evaluate the facts in Case A when they review it as a possible precedent. A fact to which the earlier judges attached little importance may very well strike the later judges as crucially significant. Their re-evaluation of Case A may lead

---

[5] The litigants themselves also help shape the law. People who bring lawsuits are not always well thought of in our society, but we should recall that, if there had not been plaintiffs in the past ready to assert their rights, and defendants ready to resist those assertions, many of the decisional rules which today protect us would not exist.

them, for instance, to conclude that the rule inherent in it is much narrower in scope than the earlier judges seemed to think, and therefore that it would not apply to Case B. On the other hand, they may see similarities between Cases A and B that the earlier judges would never have acknowledged—in other words, they may find a broader rule in Case A than the earlier judges had in mind. Nor does this re-evaluation occur only once: each time Case A is re-examined in the course of deciding a later case, its significance as a precedent is likely to undergo some modification.

To illustrate, let us suppose that the opinion in *Hurley v. Eddingfield* contained (as it did not in fact) a full discussion of why a physician in the defendant's position should not be legally obliged to go to the aid of a patient—a discussion couched in terms so general as to make it clear that, in the Indiana court's opinion, the same rule was applicable to dentists, veterinarians, lawyers, and other professional people. When our imaginary case involving a dentist came up later, the judges who decided it would not be bound by anything the *Hurley* judges had said or implied about dentists. After all, the *Hurley* case in no way involved dentists, and its judges had no occasion to dwell at length on the similarities and dissimilarities between physicians and dentists. Any comments the *Hurley* judges made about dentists would be what lawyers call *dicta*—that is, remarks made in passing about hypothetical questions which do not have to be answered in order to decide the case before the court. The judges in the later case would be quite free to decide for themselves whether, for the purposes of the case before them, dentists were similar to physicians. Indeed, they would be free to reappraise the *Hurley* case in its entirety and to conclude that other facts mentioned in the report, even though virtually ignored in the *Hurley* opinion, made *Hurley* significantly similar to, or different from, the case before them.

The point of all this is not that judicial opinions are of no importance. They are enormously valuable. An opinion is essentially a brief essay—or sometimes several brief essays—in which judges discuss the relevance of the principles and doctrines gleaned from earlier opinions and from scholarly treatises and other writings. What the judges say in their opinions is extremely useful to other judges and to lawyers; the words reveal the thinking of the decision-makers. But these opinions are not in themselves binding and final interpretations of the decisions they accompany. Later judges are likely to rely heavily on what the earlier judges have written, but nonetheless they are free to find new meanings in the old cases—meanings not envisaged by the earlier judges.[6]

Clearly, then, the act of the appellate judge in building on precedents involves much more than following the rules of logic. Indeed, whenever we speak (as we repeatedly do in this book) of "applying rules to cases," we must remember that the phrase does not mean that the rules are all fixed and ready to be applied. The truth is that rules emerge during the process of deciding a case, and the judges have a considerable range of discretion

---

[6] The doctrine of precedent, after all, is known as *stare decisis*, not *stare opinionibus*. It is what the earlier court *did*, not what it *said*, that the later court must try to follow.

in determining which rules emerge. They can find that Case A contains either a rule broad enough to cover Case B or a rule narrow enough to exclude it. Indiana judges could probably hold either that the *Hurley* rule did or did not cover dentists. And their decision would probably be influenced less by the reasoning that produced the *Hurley* rule than by their own views on whether applying that rule in the later case would produce a just result.[7]

Often the appellate court must fit cases into classifications whose boundary lines are ill defined. Here the exercise of discretion—the creative act of lawmaking—is unavoidable. Consider, for instance, this problem in the law of agency (which we shall be studying in Chapter 14): Under what circumstances should an employer be held liable for harm caused by an employee who has an accident while driving a vehicle belonging to his employer? Is the employer relieved of liability if the employee has departed from the route that he was ordered to take? Broadly stated, the applicable principle is that if the employee is on a mere "detour," the employer is probably liable for any harm he causes, but that if the employee is on a "frolic of his own," the employer is not liable.[8] So far, so good. But the real problem lies in deciding whether a particular employee in a particular case is on a "detour" or on a "frolic." There are no rules of thumb for classifying the borderline case. The judges have to re-examine past decisions and decide whether the case before them is on the whole more like the "detour" cases or the "frolic" cases. But if the case is close to the line, they must also redefine a portion of the line itself. If they do a good job of explaining their decision, they may make the distinction between "detours" and "frolics" a little clearer. But the chances are slight that they will arrive at a formulation so durable that the task of classification will be easy for all future judges.

This brings us to our last point. There are two reasons why few formulations of legal rules are ever final. The first is that the number of possible fact-combinations that may occur is infinite. The formulator of rules, be he judge or scholar, is forever being surprised by unforeseen cases. The second reason is that our society is constantly producing new problems, new needs, and new community attitudes and values. Not only are truck drivers continually becoming involved in slightly different kinds of accident, but our community attitudes on the proper legal relationships between employers, employees, and injured third parties are continually changing.

Many of the major changes that must take place in our law are made by legislatures. But most of the minor adjustments are made by judges as they decide cases over the years. Judges owe a duty to the concept of certainty in the law, a duty that they fulfill by relating each new decision to

---

[7] You may be a little shocked by the thought that judges have such latitude in using precedents. What is to prevent a judge from simply making up his mind on the result he wishes to arrive at and then manipulating precedents to justify that result? We shall consider this important question in the final section of this chapter.

[8] For a case illustrating this distinction, see *Kohlman v. Hyland*, page 575.

what has gone before and by providing in their opinions a justification of each new decision based on established principles. But that duty does not oblige them to maintain fixed and unchanging rules. Rather, it obliges them to preserve continuity—to see to it that change takes place by gradual steps, with each step rationally related to preceding steps so that no single decision will ever come as a total surprise to lawyers who have studied the pattern of the judges' decisions.

An Illustrative Case: MacPherson v. Buick Motor Co.

Now let us look at a notable example of judicial lawmaking in action. The case that follows is a classic among judicial decisions, partly because the rule that emerged from it was an important one but also because of the superb judicial craftsmanship exhibited by the great judge [9] who wrote the majority opinion.

MacPherson v. Buick Motor Co. involved injuries suffered by an automobile owner when his car broke down because of a defective wheel. The trial jury, in awarding the plaintiff $5000 in damages, had determined that the accident was caused by the defective wheel. It had also determined that the defendant, the Buick Motor Company, had been negligent in failing to test sufficiently the wheel it put on the car. But a major issue of law remained: *To whom* did Buick owe a duty to test the wheel? It was reasonably clear that Buick had violated a duty of care which it owed to the dealer to whom it sold the car. It was also probable that the dealer was liable to MacPherson for a breach of warranty (see page 391). But had Buick violated any duty of care owed to MacPherson? There had been no dealings between them; indeed, Buick had never heard of MacPherson until he brought the suit. Throughout the nineteenth century, the courts had held, with only a few exceptions, that manufacturers were liable solely to those with whom they had contractual relations. The decisions involving vehicles seemed wholly unfavorable to MacPherson, from the leading case of *Winterbottom v. Wright* in 1842 right down to a 1915 case decided in a federal court the year before *MacPherson* came before the New York Court of Appeals.

This case is particularly useful for our purposes because the majority opinion and the dissenting opinion review the same group of cases but interpret them quite differently. The writer of each opinion is thus able to establish a reasoned justification for his conclusions by basing them on established precedents and principles. But the majority opinion seeks to justify a new rule, a step forward in response to new needs, while the dissent argues that the new rule favored by the majority entails an unwarranted break with the past.

---

[9] Benjamin Nathan Cardozo (1870–1938). Cardozo was named to the United States Supreme Court in 1932, after serving for eighteen years on the Court of Appeals of New York, the highest court of that state, which decided the case given here. A book by Cardozo, *The Nature of the Judicial Process,* is still widely regarded as the best description ever written of how appellate judges decide cases.

(Both opinions are quite long, and each has been somewhat abridged. To point up the techniques of analysis used by the two opinion-writers, we have interpolated a few explanatory notes and italicized certain key passages.)

MacPHERSON v. BUICK MOTOR CO.

Court of Appeals of New York, 1916
217 N.Y. 382, 111 N.E. 1050

► Appeal, by permission, from a judgment of the Appellate Division of the Supreme Court affirming a judgment in favor of plaintiff entered upon a verdict.

CARDOZO, J.   The defendant is a manufacturer of automobiles. It sold an automobile to a retail dealer. The retail dealer resold to the plaintiff. While the plaintiff was in the car, it suddenly collapsed. He was thrown out and injured. One of the wheels was made of defective wood, and its spokes crumbled into fragments. The wheel was not made by the defendant; it was bought from another manufacturer. There is evidence, however, that its defects could have been discovered by reasonable inspection, and that inspection was omitted. There is no claim that the defendant knew of the defect and wilfully concealed it. The case, in other words, is not brought within the rule of Kuelling v. Lean Mfg. Co., 183 N.Y. 78. The charge is one, not of fraud, but of negligence. The question to be determined is whether the defendant owed a duty of care and vigilance to any one but the immediate purchaser.

[Here Judge Cardozo introduces the "leading case" in New York on the manufacturer's liability to persons other than the immediate purchaser:]

The foundations of this branch of the law, at least in this state, were laid in Thomas v. Winchester, 6 N.Y. 397 [1853]. A poison was falsely labeled. The sale was made to a druggist, who in turn sold to a customer. The customer recovered damages from the seller who affixed the label. "The defendant's negligence," it was said, "put human life in imminent danger." A poison falsely labeled is likely to injure any one who gets it. Because the danger is to be foreseen, there is a duty to avoid the injury. Cases were cited by way of illustration in which manufacturers were not subject to any duty irrespective of contract. The distinction was said to be that their conduct, though negligent, was not likely to result in injury to any one except the purchaser. We are not required to say whether the chance of injury was always as remote as the distinction assumes. Some of the illustrations might be rejected today. The principle of the distinction is for present purposes the important thing.

[Cardozo now goes on to discuss some later New York cases. The first two seemed to set narrow limits to manufacturers' liability, but two later decisions extended the scope of what might be called "the Thomas rule." The opinion points out certain factors that might account for the different results in the two groups of cases:]

Thomas v. Winchester became quickly a landmark of the law. *In the application of its principle there may at times have been uncertainty or even error. There has never in this state been doubt or disavowal of the principle itself. The chief cases are well known,* yet to recall some of them will be helpful. Loop v. Litchfield, 42 N.Y. 351 [1870], is the earliest. It was the case of a defect in a small balance wheel used on a circular saw. The manufacturer pointed out the defect to the buyer, who wished a cheap article and was ready to assume the risk. The risk can hardly have been an imminent one, for the wheel lasted five years before it broke. In the meanwhile the buyer had made a lease of the machinery. It was held that the manufacturer was not answerable to the lessee. Loop v. Litchfield was followed in Losee v. Clute, 51 N.Y. 494 [1873], the case of the explosion of a steam boiler. That decision has been criticised (Thompson on Negligence, 233; Shearman & Redfield on Negligence, 117); but *it must be confined to its special facts. It was put upon the ground* that the risk of injury was too remote. The buyer in that case had not only accepted the boiler, but had tested it. The manufacturer knew that his own test was not the final one. The finality of the test has a bearing on the measure of diligence owing to persons other than the purchaser.

These early cases suggest a narrow construction of the rule. Later cases, however, evince a more liberal spirit. First in importance is Devlin v. Smith, 89 N.Y. 470 [1882]. The defendant, a contractor, built a scaffold for a painter. The painter's servants were injured. The contractor was held liable. He knew that the scaffold, if improperly constructed, was a most dangerous trap. He knew that it was to be used by the workmen. He was building it for that very purpose. Building it for their use, he owed them a duty, irrespective of his contract with their master, to build it with care.

From Devlin v. Smith we pass over intermediate cases and turn to the latest case in this court in which Thomas v. Winchester was followed. That case is Statler v. Ray Mfg. Co., 195 N.Y. 478 [1909]. The defendant manufactured a large coffee urn. It was installed in a restaurant. When heated the urn exploded and injured the plaintiff. We held that the manufacturer was liable. We said that the urn "was of such a character inherently that, when applied to the purposes for which it was designed, it was liable to become a source of great danger to many people if not carefully and properly constructed."

It may be that Devlin v. Smith and Statler v. Ray Mfg. Co. have *extended the rule of* Thomas v. Winchester. *If so, this court is committed to the extension.* The defendant argues that things imminently dangerous to life are poisons, explosives, deadly weapons—things whose normal function it is to injure or destroy. *But whatever the rule in Thomas v. Winchester may once have been, it has no longer that restricted meaning.* A scaffold is not inherently a destructive instrument. It becomes destructive only if imperfectly constructed. A large coffee urn may have within itself, if negligently made, the potency of danger, yet no one thinks of it as an implement whose normal function is destruction. What is true of the coffee urn is equally true of bottles of aerated water, Torgeson v. Schultz, 192 N.Y. 156 [1908]. . . .

[Judge Cardozo then quotes with approval the opinion of an English judge in a case similar to *Devlin* decided by the Court of Appeals of England in 1883. He sums up:]

What was said by Lord Esher in that case did not command the full assent of his associates. It may not be an accurate exposition of the law of England. Perhaps it may need some qualification even in our own state. *Like most attempts at comprehensive definition, it may involve errors of inclusion and of exclusion. But its tests and standards, at least in their underlying principles, with whatever qualification may be called for as they are applied to varying conditions, are the tests and standards of our law.*

[The *Thomas v. Winchester* "principle" is now reformulated:]

We hold, then, that *the principle of Thomas v. Winchester is not limited to poisons, explosives, and things of like nature*, to things which in their normal operation are implements of destruction. If the nature of a thing is such that it is reasonably certain to place life and limb in peril when negligently made, it is then a thing of danger. Its nature gives warning of the consequences to be expected. If to the element of danger there is added knowledge that the thing will be used by persons other than the purchaser, and used without new tests, then, irrespective of contract, the manufacturer of this thing of danger is under a duty to make it carefully. That is as far as we are required to go for the decision of this case. There must be knowledge of a danger, not merely possible, but probable. It is *possible* to use almost anything in a way that will make it dangerous if defective. That is not enough to charge the manufacturer with a duty independent of his contract. Whether a given thing is dangerous may be sometimes a question for the court and sometimes a question for the jury. There must also be knowledge that in the usual course of events the danger will be shared by others than the buyer. . . . We are not required at this time to say that it is legitimate to go back of the manufacturer of the finished product and hold the manufacturer of the component parts. . . . *We leave that question open. We shall have to deal with it when it arises.* The difficulty which it suggests is not present in this case. . . .

[The rule as reformulated is now applied to automobiles:]

From this survey of the decisions, *there thus emerges a definition of the duty of a manufacturer which enables us to measure this defendant's liability*. Beyond all question, the nature of an automobile gives warning of probable danger if its construction is defective. This automobile was designed to go fifty miles an hour. Unless its wheels were sound and strong, injury was almost certain. It was as much a thing of danger as a defective engine for a railroad. The defendant knew the danger. It knew also that the car would be used by persons other than the buyer. This was apparent from its size; there were seats for three persons. It was apparent also from the fact that the buyer was a dealer in cars who bought to resell. The maker of this car supplied it for the use of purchasers from the dealer just as plainly as the contractor in Devlin v. Smith supplied the scaffold for use by the servant of the owner. The dealer was indeed the one person of whom it might be said with some approach to certainty that by him the car would *not* be used. Yet the defendant would have us say that he was the one person whom it was under a legal duty to protect. The law does not lead us to so inconsequent a conclusion. *Precedents drawn from the days of travel by stagecoach do not fit the conditions of travel today. The principle that the danger must be imminent does not change, but the things subject to the principle do change. They are whatever the needs of life in a developing civilization require them to be.*

[Contrary decisions from other jurisdictions are noted:]

In reaching this conclusion, *we do not ignore the decisions to the contrary in other jurisdictions.* It was held in Cadillac M. C. Co. v. Johnson, 221 F. 801 [1915], that an automobile is not within the rule of Thomas v. Winchester. There was, however, a vigorous dissent. Opposed to that decision is one of the Court of Appeals of Kentucky. Olds Motor Works v. Shaffer, 145 Ky. 616 [1911]. The earlier cases are summarized by Judge Sanborn in Huset v. J. I. Case Threshing Machine Co., 120 F. 865 [1903]. *Some of them, at first sight inconsistent with our conclusion, may be reconciled* upon the ground that the negligence was too remote, and that another cause had intervened. *But even when they cannot be reconciled, the difference is rather in the application of the principle than in the principle itself.* Judge Sanborn says, for example, that the contractor who builds a bridge, or the manufacturer who builds a car, cannot ordinarily foresee injury to other persons than the owner as a probable result. We take a different view. We think that injury to others is to be foreseen not merely as a possible, but as an almost inevitable result. Indeed, Judge Sanborn concedes that his view is not to be reconciled with our decision in Devlin v. Smith. *The doctrine of that decision has now become the settled law of this state, and we have no desire to depart from it.*

[Judge Cardozo goes on to discuss the principal English cases. Some of these he finds "distinguishable"; in others he finds statements of principle which he views as supporting his formulation of the rule. In the final paragraphs of his opinion, he notes an analogous rule in the law governing the duties of landlords to tenants, discusses the issues raised by the trial judge's instructions to the jury, and rules that the defendant was not absolved from its duty to inspect merely because it had bought the defective wheel from a reputable wheel manufacturer.]

One judge dissented. In his dissenting opinion, Chief Judge Willard Bartlett reviews most of the cases already discussed by Cardozo. But he finds no justification in them for Cardozo's view that "the *Thomas* rule" had been broadened so that it covered articles not "inherently" dangerous, such as automobiles.

Bartlett's opinion, excerpts from which follow, leans heavily on *Winterbottom v. Wright,* the English case decided in 1842, which Cardozo mentions only briefly. The relevance of *Winterbottom* lies partly in the fact that it involved an injury occurring in a defectively constructed stagecoach.

(The defendant was not, however, the maker of the coach, as Cardozo's opinion points out.) Wrote Bartlett:]

The *doctrine of that decision* [*Winterbottom*] was recognized as the *law of this state by the leading New York case* of Thomas v. Winchester, which, however, involved an exception to the general rule. . . .

The case of Devlin v. Smith is cited as an *authority in conflict with the view* that the liability of the manufacturer and vendor extends to third parties only when the article manufactured and sold is inherently dangerous. . . . It is said that the scaffold, if properly constructed, was not inherently dangerous, and hence that this decision affirms the existence of liability in the case of an article not dangerous in itself, but made so only in consequence of negligent construction. Whatever logical force there may be in this view it seems to me clear from the language of Judge Rapallo, who wrote the opinion of the court, that the scaffold was deemed to be an inherently dangerous structure, and that the case was decided as it was because the court entertained that view. Otherwise he would hardly have said, as he did, that the circumstances *seemed to bring the case fairly within the principle of* Thomas v. Winchester.

I do not see how we can uphold the judgment in the present case *without overruling what has been so often said by this court and other courts of like authority* in reference to the absence of any liability for negligence on the part of the original vendor of an ordinary carriage to any one except his immediate vendee. The absence of such liability was the very point decided in the English case of Winterbottom v. Wright. . . . In the case at bar, the defective wheel on an automobile, moving only eight miles an hour, was not any more dangerous to the occupants of the car than a similarly defective wheel would be to the occupants of a carriage drawn by a horse at the same speed, and yet, unless the courts have been all wrong on this question up to the present time, there would be no liability to strangers to the original sale in the case of the horse-drawn carriage.

The rule upon which, in my judgment, the determination of this case depends, and the recognized exceptions thereto, were discussed by Circuit Judge Sanborn, of the United States Circuit Court of Appeals in the Eighth Circuit, in Huset v. J. I. Case Threshing Machine Co., in an opinion which reviews all the leading American and English decisions on the subject up to the time when it was rendered (1903). I have already discussed the leading New York cases, but as to the rest I feel that I can add nothing to the learning of that opinion or the cogency of its reasoning. I have examined the cases to which Judge Sanborn refers, but if I were to discuss them at length, I should be forced merely to paraphrase his language, as a study of the authorities he cites has led me to the same conclusions; and the *repetition of what has already been so well said would contribute nothing to the advantage of the bench, the bar, or the individual litigants whose case is before us.*

A few cases decided since his opinion was written, however, may be noticed. In Earl v. Lubbock, the Court of Appeal [of England] in 1904 considered and approved the *propositions of law* laid down by the Court of Exchequer in Winterbottom v. Wright, declaring that the decision in that case, since the year 1842, *had stood the test of repeated discussion.* The Master of the Rolls approved the principles laid down by Lord Abinger as based upon sound reasoning; and all the members of the court agreed that his decision was a *controlling authority which must be followed.* That the federal courts still adhere to the general rule, as I have stated it, appears by the decision of the Circuit Court of Appeal in the Second Circuit, in March, 1915, in the case of Cadillac Motor Car Co. v. Johnson. That case, like this, was an action by a subvendee against a manufacturer of automobiles for negligence in failing to discover that one of its wheels was defective, the court holding that such an action could not be maintained. It is true there was a dissenting opinion in that case, *but it was based chiefly upon the proposition that rules applicable to stagecoaches are archaic when applied to automobiles, and that if the law did not afford a remedy to strangers to the contract, the law should be changed. If this be true, the change should be effected by the Legislature and not by the courts.* A perusal of the opinion in that case and in the Huset Case will disclose *how uniformly the courts throughout this country have adhered to the rule and how consistently they have refused to broaden the scope of the exceptions.* I think we should *adhere to it in the case at bar,* and therefore I vote for a reversal of this judgment.

HISCOCK, CHASE, and CUDDEBACK, JJ., concur with CARDOZO, J., and HOGAN, J., concurs in result. WILLARD BARTLETT, C. J., reads dissenting opinion. POUND, J., not voting.

Judgment affirmed.   ◄

It has been suggested that legal standards—such as the "inherently dangerous" test for manufacturers' liability discussed in *MacPherson*—have a life span marked by three stages. In the first stage, the courts are groping toward a new verbal formula that will aid them in their task of drawing fine distinctions. Eventually they arrive at a standard that seems to do the job. In the second stage, the standard is pretty well accepted, though it is still being tested and refined. In the third stage, cases are arising which show that the standard is no longer satisfactory. Eventually it crumbles, whereupon the search begins for a new standard. The *MacPherson* case marked the decline and fall of the "inherently dangerous" standard. As a result of the decision, what had once been an exception to the general rule (that manufacturers were liable only to those who purchased from them) swallowed the rule itself. Today manufacturers are normally held liable for foreseeable harm resulting from defects in their products.[10]

Deciding Truly Novel Cases

What happens, you may wonder, when a case arises for which there simply are no precedents, a case that is in no way similar to anything that can be found in the court reports?

---

[10] Another case involving a manufacturer's liability for an accident caused by a defective automobile part, in which traditional doctrines were handled with a boldness equal to Cardozo's in *MacPherson*, is *Henningsen v. Bloomfield Motors, Inc.,* page 401.

During the centuries after the Norman Conquest of England, when the common-law tradition was being established, courts frequently had to cope with just this problem. As we have seen, the judges of those days drew heavily for their rules on prevailing customs, traditions, business usages, and moral standards, as well as on their own "sense of justice." These extra-legal sources of social rules continue to influence the growth of law today. But as more and more cases are decided over the years, and as more and more laws are enacted, the network of legal rules becomes ever more closely woven. An increasing number of fact-situations have been directly ruled upon by the courts, and many other situations are sufficiently similar to decided cases to make it possible to predict the probable rule with some assurance. Moreover, legal scholars are continually publishing treatises, articles, and "restatements" of the law full of speculative generalizations about the probable rules governing situations not yet ruled upon. These writings do not have the authority of judicial opinions, but they are none-theless of great value to judges and lawyers dealing with difficult cases.

In short, the truly novel case is harder to find than one might think. Indeed, it is impossible to imagine a case for which no precedents or es-tablished principles would have any relevance whatever. But while novelty is relative, cases do arise for which there are no close and obvious analogies in previous decisions.

Consider, for example, a problem that judges first had to face during the 1920's, when farmers began to complain that airplanes were disturbing the peace and frightening livestock by flying over their land. For a while there were no statutes concerning the respective rights and duties of landowners and of persons who flew aircraft over their land, nor were there any prece-dents. Yet the courts could not simply tell the plaintiffs to come back later; some decision on their complaints had to be reached.

What the judges did, essentially, was to search through the property-law cases for any analogies that seemed suggestive. For example: Were a landowner's rights with respect to overflying planes similar to the rights that enabled him to prohibit people from shooting bullets or stringing wires over his land? Or were they more like the rights of the beach-owner who objects to boats passing in front of his property? Since a landowner can do much more about wires and bullets passing over his property than he can about boats sailing past his beach, the judges' choice of an analogy had a great deal to do with how much relief the landowners would get from the airplane nuisance.

This power to choose between competing analogies (neither of which is very close to the case at hand) is obviously an instance of the judicial freedom of choice that we discussed in the preceding section. The question before the judges is not really, "Which of these analogies is the closer?" but rather, "Which analogy will lead to the more desirable result?" Judge Cardozo's opinion in the *MacPherson* case makes it clear that he believed the public interest would best be served by holding automobile manufac-turers liable to final purchasers who were injured because of defects in the cars they bought. Nor is there any doubt that the judges who decided that farmers had no legal right to forbid all plane flights over their land did so after reflecting that to grant such a right would probably strangle the infant aviation industry. Although, in their opinions, judges traditionally stress the foundations of precedent and principle more heavily than they stress considerations of public policy, the latter unquestionably play an important part in their thinking.[11]

Let us look now at another illustrative case. The situation presented by *Tuttle v. Buck* may not seem nearly so unusual as overflying airplanes were in the 1920's, but the Minnesota Supreme Court could find no case directly in point. It found in the past cases an abundance of broad statements of principle, but these pointed toward a result that the judges did not wish to reach. Notice how Judge Elliott justified their refusal to be bound by these statements of principle, and how candidly he acknowledged the relevance of changing economic conditions and beliefs. (Once again we have italicized some of the significant passages in the opinion.)

TUTTLE v. BUCK

Supreme Court of Minnesota, 1909
107 Minn. 145, 119 N.W. 946

▶ Verdict for plaintiff. From an order denying a new trial, defendant appeals.

This appeal was from an order overruling a general demurrer[12] to a complaint in which the plaintiff agreed: That for more than 10 years last past he has been and still is a barber by trade, and engaged in business as such in the village of Howard Lake, Minn., where he resides, owning and operating a shop for the purpose of his said trade. That until the injury hereinafter complained of his said business was prosperous, and plaintiff was enabled thereby to comfortably maintain himself and family out of the income and profits thereof, and also to save a considerable sum per annum, to wit, about $800. That the defendant, during the period of about 12 months last past, has wrongfully, unlawfully, and maliciously endeavored to destroy plaintiff's said business and compel plaintiff to abandon the same. That to that end he has persistently and systematically sought, by false and malicious reports and accusations of and concerning the plaintiff, by personally soliciting and urging plaintiff's patrons no longer to employ plaintiff, by threats of his personal displeasure, and by various other unlawful means and devices, to induce, and has thereby induced, many of said patrons to withhold from plaintiff the employment by them formerly given. That defendant is possessed of large means, and is engaged in the business of a banker, and is nowise interested in the occupation of a barber: yet in pursuance of the wicked, malicious, and unlawful purpose

---

[11] Note how the two types of consideration are combined in Cardozo's words in *MacPherson:* "Precedents drawn from the days of travel by stagecoach do not fit the conditions of travel today. The principle that the danger must be imminent does not change, but the things subject to the principle do change. They are whatever the needs of life in a developing civilization require them to be."

[12] What is the significance of the fact that this case came before the court on a demurrer?

aforesaid, and for the sole and only purpose of injuring the trade of the plaintiff, and of accomplishing his purpose and threats of ruining the said plaintiff's business and driving him out of said village, the defendant fitted up and furnished a barber shop in said village for conducting the trade of barbering. That failing to induce any barber to occupy said shop on his own account, though offered at nominal rent, said defendant has during the time herein stated hired two barbers in succession for a stated salary, paid by him, to occupy said shop, and to serve so many of the plaintiff's patrons as said defendant has been or may be able by the means aforesaid to direct from plaintiff's shop. That at the present time a barber so employed and paid by the defendant is occupying and nominally conducting the shop thus fitted and furnished by the defendant, without paying any rent therefor, and under an agreement with the defendant whereby the income of said shop is required to be paid to said defendant, and is so paid in partial return for his wages. That all of said things were and are done by defendant with the sole design of injuring the plaintiff, and of destroying his said business, and not for the purpose of serving any legitimate interest of his own. That by reason of the great wealth and prominence of the defendant, and the personal and financial influence consequent thereon, he has by the means aforesaid materially injured the business of the plaintiff, has largely reduced the income and profits thereof, and intends and threatens to destroy the same altogether, to the plaintiff's damage in the sum of $10,000.

ELLIOTT, J. (after stating the facts above). It has been said that the law deals only with externals, and that a lawful act cannot be made the foundation of an action because it was done with an evil motive. In Allen v. Flood, [1898] A. C. 151, Lord Watson said that, except with regard to crimes, the law does not take into account motives as constituting an element of civil wrong. In Mayor v. Pickles, [1895] A. C. 587, Lord Halsbury stated that if the act was lawful, "however ill the motive might be, he had a right to do it." In Raycroft v. Tayntor, 68 Vt. 219, the court said that, "where one exercises a legal right only, the motive which actuates him is immaterial." In Jenkens v. Fowler, 24 Pa. 318, Mr. Justice Black said that "mischievous motives make a bad case worse, but they cannot make that wrong which in its own essence is lawful." This language was quoted in Bohn Mfg. Co. v. Hillis, 54 Minn. 233, and in substance in Ertz v. Produce Exchange, 79 Minn. 143. See, also, Cooley, Torts (3d Ed.), p. 1505; Auburn & Co. v. Douglass, 9 N.Y. 444. *Such generalizations are of little value in determining concrete cases. They may state the truth, but not the whole truth.* Each word and phrase used therein may require definition and limitation. Thus, before we can apply Judge Black's language to a particular case, we must determine what act is "in its own essence lawful." What did Lord Halsbury mean by the words "lawful act"? What is meant by "exercising a legal right"? Is it not at all [Is it entirely?] correct to say that the motive with which an act is done is always immaterial, providing the act itself is not unlawful? Numerous illustrations of the contrary will be found in the civil as well as the criminal law.

We do not intend to enter upon an elaborate discussion of the subject, or become entangled in the subtleties connected with the words "malice" and "malicious." We are not able to accept without limitations the doctrine above referred to, but at this time content ourselves with a brief reference to some general principles. *It must be remembered that the common law is the result of growth, and that its development has been determined by the social needs of the community which it governs. It is the resultant of conflicting social forces, and those forces which are for the time dominant leave their impress upon the law. It is of judicial origin, and seeks to establish doctrines and rules for the determination, protection, and enforcement of legal rights. Manifestly it must change as society changes and new rights are recognized. To be an efficient instrument, and not a mere abstraction, it must gradually adapt itself to changed conditions. Necessarily its form and substance has been greatly affected by prevalent economic theories. For generations there has been a practical agreement upon the proposition that competition in trade and business is desirable, and this idea has found expression in the decisions of the courts as well as in statutes. But it has led to grievous and manifold wrongs to individuals, and many courts have manifested an earnest desire to protect the individuals from the evils which result from unrestrained business competition. The problem has been to so adjust matters as to preserve the principle of competition and yet guard against its abuse to the unnecessary injury to the individual.* So the principle that a man may use his own property according to his own needs and desires, while true in abstract, is subject to many limitations in the concrete. Men cannot always, in civilized society, be allowed to use their own property as their interests or desires may dictate without reference to the fact that they have neighbors whose rights are as sacred as their own. The existence and well-being of society require that each and every person shall conduct himself consistently with the fact that he is a social and reasonable person. The purpose for which a man is using his own property may thus sometimes determine his rights, and applications of this idea are found in Stillwater Water Co. v. Farmer, 89 Minn. 58; *Id.,* 92 Minn. 230, and Barclay v. Abraham, 121 Iowa 619.

Many of the restrictions which should be recognized and enforced result from a tacit recognition of principles which are not often stated in the decisions in express terms. Sir Frederick Pollock notes that not many years ago it was difficult to find any definite authority for stating as a general proposition of English law that it is wrong to do a willful wrong to one's neighbor without lawful justification or excuse. But neither is there any express authority for the general proposition that men must perform their contracts. Both principles, in this generality of form and conception, are modern and there was a time when neither was true. After developing the idea that *law begins, not with authentic general principles, but with the enumeration of particular remedies,* the learned writer continues: "If there exists, then, a positive duty to avoid harm, much more, then, exists the negative duty of not doing willful harm, subject, as all general duties must be subject, to the necessary exceptions." Pollock, Torts, (8th Ed.) p. 21.

It is freely conceded that there are many decisions contrary to this view; but when carried to the extent contended for by the appellant, we think they are unsafe, unsound and illy adapted to modern conditions. To divert to one's self the customers of a business rival by the offer of goods at lower prices is in general a legitimate mode of serving one's own interest, and justifiable as fair competition. But when a man starts an opposition place of business, but regardless of loss to himself, and for the sole purpose of driving his competitor out of business, and with the intention of himself retiring upon the accomplishment of his malevolent purpose, he is guilty of a wanton wrong and an actionable tort. In such a case he would not be exercising his legal right, or doing an act which can be judged separately from the motive which actuated him. To call such conduct competition is a perversion of terms. It is simply the application of force without legal justification, which in its moral quality may be no better than highway robbery.

Affirmed. JAGGARD, J. dissents.   ◀

In *Tuttle v. Buck*, the court had no real precedents on which to build. In *Pettit v. Liston*, which follows, the court's problem was quite different: although the Supreme Court of Oregon found no Oregon precedents, there was an abundance of precedents from other states. But they were about equally divided between two contrary results. Faced with such a division of authority, should a court simply adopt the rule with the larger number of decisions supporting it? The court in *Pettit* refused to take that approach. (Once again we have italicized some key passages.)

PETTIT v. LISTON

Supreme Court of Oregon, 1920
97 Ore. 464, 191 Pac. 660

▶ Plaintiff, a minor, brings this action by his guardian to recover $125, paid by him upon the purchase of a certain motorcycle purchased from the defendants.

The case involves the question of whether or not a minor, who has purchased an article of this kind, and taken and used the same, after paying part or all of the purchase price, can return the article and recover the money paid without making good to the vendors the wear and tear and depreciation of the same while in his hands.

The plaintiff purchased from [the defendants] a motorcycle at the agreed price of $325. He paid $125 down, and was to pay $25 per month upon the purchase price until the payments were completed. He took and used the motorcycle for a little over a month and finally returned the same to the defendants and demanded the return of his money. The defendants answer and allege that plaintiff used the machine, and in so doing damaged it to the amount of $156.25.

There was a demurrer to the answer, which was overruled by the court, and the plaintiff refusing to reply or plead further and standing upon his demurrer, a judgment and order were entered dismissing the cause, from which the plaintiff appeals.

BENNETT, J. (after stating the facts above). The amount involved in this proceeding is not large, but the question of law presented is a very important one, and one which has been much disputed in the courts, and about which there is a *great and irreconcilable conflict in the authorities,* and we have therefore given the matter careful attention.

The courts, in an attempt to protect the minor upon the one hand, and to prevent wrong or injustice to persons who have dealt fairly and reasonably with such minor upon the other, have indulged in many fine distinctions and recognized various slight shades of difference.

In dealing with the right of the minor to rescind his contract and the conditions under which he may do so, the decisions of the courts in the different states have not only conflicted upon the main questions involved, but *many of the decisions of the same court, in the same state, seem to be inconsistent with each other; and oftentimes one court has made its decision turn upon a distinction or difference not recognized by the courts of other states as a distinguishing feature.*

The result has been that *there are not only two general lines of decisions directly upon the question involved, but there are many others, which diverge more or less from the main line, and make particular cases turn upon real or fancied differences and distinctions,* depending upon whether the contract was executory or partly or wholly executed, whether it was for necessaries, whether it was beneficial to the minor, whether it was fair and reasonable, whether the minor still had the property purchased in his possession, whether he has received any beneficial use of the same, etc.

Many courts have held broadly that a minor may so purchase property and keep it for an indefinite time, if he chooses, until it is worn out and destroyed, and then recover the payments made on the purchase price, without allowing the seller anything whatever for the use and depreciation of the property.

Many other authorities hold that where the transaction is fair and reasonable, and the minor was not overcharged or taken advantage of in any way, and he takes and keeps the property and uses or destroys it, he cannot recover the payments made on the purchase price, without allowing the seller for the wear and tear and depreciation of the article while in his hands.

The plaintiff contends for the former rule, and supports his contention with citations from the courts of last resort of Maine, Connecticut, Indiana, Massachusetts, Vermont, Nebraska, Virginia, Iowa, Mississippi, and West Virginia, most of which (although not all) support his contention. On the contrary, the courts of New York, Maryland, Montana, Illinois, Kentucky, New Hampshire, and Minnesota, with some others, support the latter rule, which seems to be also the English rule.

Some of the cyclopedias and some of the different series of selected cases state the rule contended for by plaintiff, as supported by the strong weight of authority; but *we find the decisions rather equally balanced, both in number and respectability.* . . . [A number of decisions are here discussed, and the opinions quoted.]

Our attention has not been called to an Oregon case bearing upon the question, and as far as our investigation has disclosed, there is none.

In this condition of the authorities, we feel that we are in a position to pass upon the question as one of first impression, and announce the rule which seems to us to be the better one, upon considerations of principle and public policy.

We think, where the minor has not been overreached in any way, and there has been no undue influence, and the contract is a fair and reasonable one, and the minor has actually paid money on the purchase price, and taken and used the article, that he ought not to be permitted to recover the amount actually paid, without allowing the vendor of the goods the reasonable compensation for the use and depreciation of the article, while in his hands.

We think this rule will fully and fairly protect the minor against injustice or imposition, and at the same time it will be fair to the business man who has dealt with such minor in good faith. *This rule is best adapted to modern conditions, and especially to the conditions in our far western states.*

Here, minors are permitted to and do in fact transact a great deal of business for themselves, long before they have reached the age of legal majority. Most young men have their own time long before reaching that age. They work and earn money and collect it and spend it oftentimes without any oversight or restriction.

Again, it will not exert any good moral influence upon boys and young men, and will not tend to encourage honesty and integrity, or lead them to a good and useful business future, if they are taught that they can make purchases with their own money, for their own benefit, and after paying for them in this way, and using them until they are worn out and destroyed, go back and compel the business man to return to them what they have paid upon the purchase price. Such a doctrine, as it seems to us, can only lead to the corruption of young men's principles and encourage them in habits of trickery and dishonesty.

In view of all these considerations, we think that the rule we have indicated, and which is substantially the rule adopted in New York, is the better rule, and we adopt the same in this state.

It follows that the judgment of the court below should be affirmed.

Affirmed. Rehearing denied.   ◀

COMMENT

As the opinion itself suggests, a number of courts in other jurisdictions have taken a completely different attitude on the contractual duties of minors. (See the cases below, pp. 266, 270.) The *Pettit* case is included here solely to exemplify one kind of judicial approach to the task of lawmaking when a court has to choose between two lines of precedents.

Refusal to Follow Precedents

Some decisions meet the test of time better than others. Some become valuable precedents on which judges can build; others become barriers to progress.

Let us suppose that the highest court of State x, in trying to decide a case, comes upon its own decision in an earlier case entitled "Smith v. Jones." Although "Smith v. Jones" appears to be a controlling precedent, the court is reluctant to follow it. Perhaps the court perceives that the reasoning in the opinion is faulty. Perhaps it realizes that the facts in the case were peculiar—not really typical of the fact-combinations usually found in such cases. But the judges who decided it did not recognize this peculiarity and therefore stated "the rule of the case" in too broad a form, giving it a scope which made it appear to cover future situations for which it was ill-suited. Or perhaps the present court realizes that since the time when "Smith v. Jones" was decided changes in social arrangements or in community attitudes have undermined the appropriateness of the rule of this case for cases with apparently similar facts.

Cardozo's *MacPherson* opinion has shown us a number of ways in which the inconvenient precedent can be dealt with. It is often possible, for instance, to emphasize dissimilarities between the previous case and the present one, sometimes relying on facts in the earlier case to which the earlier judges attached little importance. This is known as "distinguishing" the earlier case, or "reconciling" the two decisions.

But this technique has its limits. Some precedents are so obviously relevant that it would be intellectually dishonest to distinguish them or to ignore them. In such a situation, judges usually feel obliged to follow the precedent. They may justify doing so with words like these: "The decision in "Smith v. Jones" is at variance with what now seems to be the more reasonable view. If the question which the present case raises were now before us for the first time, we might well answer it differently. But "Smith v. Jones" has long been a part of our law, and under the principle of *stare decisis* we have no alternative but to follow it." [13] They may go on to point out that, after all, primary responsibility for making changes in the law belongs to the legislature.[14]

As we have seen, there are excellent reasons for following precedents. But occasionally courts find themselves faced with cases in which the value of continuity is clearly outweighed by the injustice, or the plain absurdity, of blindly following the old rule. In such cases, the possibility that the legislature may some day take note of the undesirable effects of the rule does not seem to justify doing a present injustice, and the court concludes that the precedent must be swept out of the way once and for all. Such

---

[13] There are a number of cases in Part II of this book in which the judges have clearly indicated that they are following precedent reluctantly. In *Mabardy v. McHugh,* page 243, the court stated that, if the point at issue had been presented for the first time in the *Mabardy* case, it might have reached a different result. The opinion then spelled out the rationale of the *stare decisis* principle. It might be worth your while to read these paragraphs in the *Mabardy* opinion while you are still studying the present chapter.

In *Sternlieb v. Normandie,* page 266, the New York Court of Appeals was so unenthusiastic about the decisional rule it felt obliged to apply that it quoted in its opinion an Iowa statutory provision establishing a rule which it obviously considered greatly preferable. This could be taken as a hint to the New York legislature that it would do well to imitate Iowa.

[14] We shall consider the relation between decisional lawmaking and legislative lawmaking in Chapter 5.

overrulings must be exceptional, of course, or *stare decisis* would become meaningless. In some of the fields of law in which continuity and predictability are particularly important—in property law, for instance—precedents are almost never overruled. But in other fields decisional rules can be changed by new decisions with less danger of defeating legitimate expectations.

Consider, for instance, the situation that prevailed in those states in which judge-made rules once held that the driver of a vehicle had a duty to dismount and look up and down the railroad tracks before proceeding over a grade crossing. If he failed to do so and was hit by a train, his "contributory negligence" prevented him from recovering damages. As the normal speeds of trains and automobiles increased, the obligation to dismount became absurd. In the states in which the rule had not already been changed by statute, the courts usually felt free to overrule the early cases.

Let us now examine another New York case in which Judge Cardozo spoke for the majority. In *Hynes v. New York Central Railroad Co.*, the court's problem was not whether it must follow a particular precedent, but whether it had to apply literally the traditional definition of a legal concept. In four lower-court decisions in this case (two by trial judges, each of which was appealed to the intermediate appellate court), judges had ruled that, since the plaintiff's son was a "trespasser" when the defendant's negligence caused his death, the mother could not recover damages. But the result was a harsh one; the Hynes boy had trespassed only in a technical sense. His act did not fall within the reason for the rule holding that no duty of care is owed by a property-owner to a trespasser on his property. Could the highest court arrive at a result that would be just and yet would not create doubt and confusion about the continuing validity of established principles? Judge Cardozo was able to persuade only three of the six other judges who heard the case to join in his bold—and superbly written—opinion.[15]

HYNES v. NEW YORK CENTRAL RAILROAD CO.

Court of Appeals of New York, 1921
231 N.Y. 229, 131 N.E. 898

▶ Appeal from a judgment of the Appellate Division of the Supreme Court in the second judicial department, entered January 12, 1920, affirming a judgment in favor of defendant entered upon a dismissal of the complaint by the court at a Trial Term.

CARDOZO, J. On July 8, 1916, Harvey Hynes, a lad of sixteen, swam with two companions from the Manhattan to the Bronx side of the Harlem River or United States Ship Canal, a navigable stream. Along the Bronx side of the river was the right of way of the defendant, the New York Central Railroad, which operated its trains at that point by high tension

---

[15] For another case in which Judge Cardozo, speaking for the New York Court of Appeals, boldly stretched a traditional legal concept to achieve a result deemed socially desirable, see *Allegheny College v. National Chautauqua County Bank*, page 259.

wires, strung on poles and crossarms. Projecting from the defendant's bulkhead above the waters of the river was a plank or springboard from which boys of the neighborhood used to dive. One end of the board had been placed under a rock on the defendant's land, and nails had been driven at its point of contact with the bulkhead. Measured from this point of contact the length behind was five feet; the length in front eleven. The bulkhead itself was about three and a half feet back of the pier line as located by the government. From this it follows that for seven and a half feet the springboard was beyond the line of the defendant's property, and above the public waterway. Its height measured from the stream was three feet at the bulkhead, and five feet at its outermost extremity. For more than five years swimmers had used it as a diving board without protest or obstruction.

On this day Hynes and his companions climbed on top of the bulkhead intending to leap into the water. One of them made the plunge in safety. Hynes followed to the front of the springboard, and stood poised for his dive. At that moment a crossarm with electric wires fell from the defendant's pole. The wires struck the diver, flung him from the shattered board, and plunged him to his death below. His mother, suing as administratrix, brings this action for her damages. Thus far the courts have held that Hynes at the end of the springboard above the public waters was a trespasser on the defendant's land. They have thought it immaterial that the board itself was a trespass, an encroachment on the public ways. They have thought it of no significance that Hynes would have met the same fate if he had been below the board and not above it. The board, they have said, was annexed to the defendant's bulkhead. By force of such annexation, it was to be reckoned as a fixture, and thus constructively, if not actually, an extension of the land. The defendant was under a duty to use reasonable care that bathers swimming or standing in the water should not be electrocuted by wires falling from its right of way. But to bathers diving from the springboard, there was no duty, we are told, unless the injury was the product of mere willfulness or wantonness, no duty of active vigilance to safeguard the impending structure. Without wrong to them, crossarms might be left to rot; wires highly charged with electricity might sweep them from their stand, and bury them in the subjacent waters. In climbing on the board, they became trespassers and outlaws. The conclusion is defended with much subtlety of reasoning, with much insistence upon its inevitableness as a merely logical deduction. A majority of the court are unable to accept it as the conclusion of the law.

We assume, without deciding, that the springboard was a fixture, a permanent improvement of the defendant's right of way. Much might be said in favor of another view. We do not press the inquiry, for we are persuaded that the rights of bathers do not depend upon these nice distinctions. Liability would not be doubtful, we are told, had the boy been diving from a pole, if the pole had been vertical. The diver in such a situation would have been separated from the defendant's freehold. Liability, it is said, has been escaped because the pole was horizontal. The plank when projected lengthwise was an extension of the soil. We are to concentrate our gaze on the private ownership of the board. We are to ignore the public ownership of the circumambient spaces of water and of air. Jumping from a boat or a barrel, the boy would have been a bather in the river. Jumping from the end of a springboard, he was no longer, it is said, a bather, but a trespasser on a right of way.

Rights and duties in systems of living law are not built upon such quicksands.

Bathers in the Harlem River on the day of this disaster were in the enjoyment of a public highway, entitled to reasonable protection against destruction by the defendant's wires. They did not cease to be bathers entitled to the same protection while they were diving from encroaching objects or engaging in the sports that are common among swimmers. Such acts were not equivalent to an abandonment of the highway, a departure from its proper uses, a withdrawal from the waters, and an entry upon land. A plane of private right had been interposed between the river and the air, but public ownership was unchanged in the space below it and above. The defendant does not deny that it would have owed a duty to this boy if he had been leaning against the springboard with his feet upon the ground. He is said to have forfeited protection as he put his feet upon the plank. Presumably the same result would follow if the plank had been a few inches above the surface of the water instead of a few feet. Duties are thus supposed to arise and to be extinguished in alternate zones or strata. Two boys walking in the country or swimming in a river stop to rest for a moment along the side of the road or the margin of the stream. One of them throws himself beneath the overhanging branches of a tree. The other perches himself on a bough a foot or so above the ground. Both are killed by falling wires. The defendant would have us say that there is a remedy for the representatives of one, and none for the representatives of the other. We may be permitted to distrust the logic that leads to such conclusions.

The truth is that every act of Hynes, from his first plunge into the river until the moment of his death, was in the enjoyment of the public waters, and under cover of the protection which his presence in those waters gave him. The use of the springboard was not an abandonment of his rights as bather. It was a mere by-play, an incident, subordinate and ancillary to the execution of his primary purpose, the enjoyment of the highway. The by-play, the incident, was not the cause of the disaster. Hynes would have gone to his death if he had been below the springboard or beside it. The wires were not stayed by the presence of the plank. They followed the boy in his fall, and overwhelmed him in the waters. The defendant assumes that the identification of ownership of a fixture with ownership of land is complete in every incident. But there are important elements of difference. Title to the fixture, unlike title to the land, does not carry with it rights of ownership *usque ad coelum* [up to the sky]. There will hardly be denial that a cause of action would have arisen if the wires had fallen on an aeroplane proceeding above the river, though the location of the impact could be identified as the space above the springboard. The most that the defendant can fairly ask is exemption from liability where the use of the fixture is itself the efficient peril. That would be the situation, for example, if the weight of the boy upon the board had caused it to break and thereby throw him into the river. There is no such causal connection here between his position and his injuries. We think there was no moment when he was beyond the pale of the defendant's duty—the duty of care and vigilance in the storage of destructive forces.

This case is a striking instance of the dangers of "a jurisprudence of conceptions" (Pound, Mechanical Jurisprudence, 8 *Columbia Law Review* 605, 608, 610), the extension of a maxim or a definition with relentless disregard of consequences to a "dryly logical extreme." The approximate and relative become the definite and absolute. Landowners are not bound to regulate their conduct in contemplation of the presence of trespassers intruding upon private structures. Landowners *are* bound to regulate their conduct in contemplation of the presence of trouble in marking off the field of exemption and immunity from that of liability and duty. Here structures and ways are so united and commingled, super-imposed upon each other, that the fields are brought together. In such circumstances, there is little help in pursuing general maxims to ultimate conclusions. They have been framed *alio intuitu* [from another point of view]. They must be reformulated and readapted to meet exceptional conditions. Rules appropriate to spheres which are conceived of as separate and distinct cannot, both, be enforced when the spheres become concentric. There must then be readjustment or collision. In one sense, and that a highly technical and artificial one, the diver at the end of the springboard is an intruder on the adjoining lands. In another sense, and one that realists will accept more readily, he is still on public waters in the exercise of public rights. The law must say whether it will subject him to the rule of the one field or of the other, of this sphere or of that. We think that considerations of analogy, of convenience, of policy, and of justice, exclude him from the field of the defendant's immunity and exemption, and place him in the field of liability and duty.

The judgment of the Appellate Division and that of the Trial Term should be reversed, and a new trial granted, with costs to abide the event.

HOGAN, POUND and CRANE, JJ., concur; HISCOCK, C. J., CHASE and McLAUGHLIN, JJ., dissent [without opinion].

Judgments reversed, etc. ◄

QUESTIONS

If you had been one of the judges hearing this case, would you have joined in the majority opinion? Do you think Cardozo avoided creating doubt and confusion about established legal principles?

Restraints on Judicial Lawmaking

Whenever appellate judges make a choice among alternative rules in deciding a case, they are "making law." They are also making a decision about public policy. In every case we have studied in this chapter, the judges took into account not only legal precedents and principles but the community's changing needs, desires, and notions of what is fair.

Students of the law used to be reluctant to acknowledge the influence of such considerations on judicial decisions. The writings of Oliver Wendell Holmes, onetime law teacher, state appellate judge, and finally Justice of the United States Supreme Court from 1902 to 1932, helped bring about a more realistic understanding of what judges think about when they decide cases. At the beginning of his book, *The Common Law* (1881), he said:

> The life of the law has not been logic: it has been experience. The felt necessities of the time, the prevalent moral and political theories, intuitions of public policy, avowed or unconscious, even the prejudices which judges share with their fellowmen, have had a good deal more to do than the syllogism in determining the rules by which men should be governed.

Some years later, Holmes wrote:

> . . . [T]he logical method and form flatter that longing for certainty and for repose which is in every human mind. But certainty generally is illusion, and repose is not the destiny of man. Behind the logical form lies a judgment as to the relative worth and importance of competing legislative grounds. . . . I think that the judges themselves have failed adequately to recognize their duty of weighing considerations of social advantage. . . .

But the notion that judges weigh "considerations of social advantage" inevitably raises a question: What is to prevent them from simply deciding cases in accordance with their whims and prejudices and with what they conceive to be the best interests of their social class, political party, or religious group?

This question can perhaps best be answered by recalling three pertinent facts. First, appellate judges do not sit singly; three or more judges hear each appeal. Thus each judge's peculiar biases are to some extent canceled out by those of his colleagues. Second, appellate judges have no power to create the situations in which they make law; they must decide the cases brought before them. Nor can they ignore the legal contentions presented by the lawyers for each party. Third, they must explain their decisions in carefully reasoned opinions, which are subsequently published. These obligations—to convince their colleagues on the bench, to decide each case on the basis of the facts and of the contentions in the lawyers' briefs and oral arguments, and finally to explain to the world in a published opinion how they arrived at their decision—impose important constraints on judges.

But the most important constraint on the freedom of judges is a more subtle one. They are heirs to a judicial tradition of individual self-restraint and objectivity that goes back to the twelfth century, a tradition that stresses the continuity of the law and requires that each new decision be related to established principles and precedents. However prone to bias, however ardent a partisan a man may have been before becoming a judge, he is likely to find it well-nigh impossible to violate this tradition.

In one of his opinions, Justice Holmes made this comment on the limits of judicial lawmaking:

> Judges do and must legislate, but they do so only interstitially. . . . A common-law judge could not say, "I think the doctrine of consideration a bit of historical nonsense and shall not enforce it in my court."

Here is how Canon 20 of the Canons of Judicial Ethics drawn up by the American Bar Association states the argument against unrestricted judicial lawmaking:

> . . . [O]urs is a government of laws and not of men, and [the judge] violates his duty as a minister of justice under such a system if he seeks to do what he may personally consider substantial justice in a particular case and disregards the general law as he knows it to be binding on him. Such action may become a precedent unsettling accepted principles and may have detrimental results beyond the immediate controversy.

The evidence is plentiful that judges, with rare exceptions, accept the restraints imposed by the judicial tradition. If anything, they are perhaps too cautious at times. Deciding where justice and the public interest lie is often difficult. Criteria are likely to be few and uncertain. Moreover, cases rarely present whole problems; they tend rather to present fragments of problems. Judges are therefore hesitant to build bold new rules on the inadequate base provided by a single case; they tend rather to stick pretty close to the rules indicated by established precedents and principles whenever these can be found. They make choices between what Holmes candidly called "competing legislative grounds" only when precedents and clearly relevant analogies are absent. And when they do make such choices, they do their best to maintain continuity with the past and to articulate not their own views but the "felt necessities of the time"—the shared purposes of the community.

5 Lawmaking
by Legislatures

In the last chapter we saw how courts create new legal rules by building on judge-made precedents and principles. This was once the only type of lawmaking, and it remains extremely important. In the fields of contract and agency, for example, most of the basic rules are still to be found in judicial decisions rather than in statutes. But in the past century or so, legislatures have become the primary makers of new law. And in many of the fields that concern business—sales, negotiable instruments, partnerships and corporations, for instance—even the long-standing rules that were originally established by courts have now been embodied in statutes.[1]

First, let us see how statutes are enacted. Then we shall examine some of the differences between statute law and decisional law. Finally, we shall consider some of the problems that must be faced in deciding what to put into statutes.

The Legislative Process

Before a draft proposal for legislation is actually enacted into law, it must clear a series of hurdles. Some have been erected by constitutions, federal or state; others have been set up by the legislatures themselves, by rule or tradition. Although the legislative process is not the same in every legislature, the following brief description of how a bill moves through the United States Congress will give you a good idea of the procedures followed in most of the state legislatures.

Preparation and Introduction of the Bill

A draft proposal, or "bill," must first be introduced in one house or the other of the legislature.[2] Let's assume that our bill is introduced in the House of Representatives. Although the bill must be presented by a mem-

---

[1] We will use the word "statutes" as a generic term; it covers, for instance, the "acts" of Congress and the "ordinances" of local governments. The common characteristic is that all are enacted by elected legislative bodies.

[2] The United States Congress and all the state legislatures except Nebraska's consist of two houses.

ber of Congress, it may have been conceived and drafted by someone else: by the congressman's staff, by the staff of one of the House committees, by the House's Office of the Legislative Counsel, by a bureau in the executive branch, or by a private interest group.

The Committee Stage

Once the bill has been introduced, it is referred to one of the standing committees of the House. Most bills never get any further. Since it is almost impossible to compel a committee to send a bill back to the House, many proposals simply die in committee. If, however, the committee chairman, whose power is great, decides that a bill is worthy of consideration, he usually schedules a public hearing at which interested groups and individuals have an opportunity to testify on it. The committee may end up by approving the bill as originally written, or amend it, or completely redraft it, or decline to act favorably on it.

Modern legislative bodies are faced with such onerous workloads that they are obliged to rely heavily on their committees. No legislator can hope to familiarize himself with more than a fraction of the legislative proposals that are introduced. Each legislator realizes that he must trust the judgment of committee members, many of whom have become intimately familiar with a particular subject and have studied hundreds of bills related to it. So when the majority of a committee refuse to act favorably on a bill, their fellow lawmakers can rarely be induced to override the committee's decision. Nor are they likely to oppose the revisions that the committee has suggested, or to propose further amendments of their own.

In a very real sense, then, the committees determine what bills become law and what those bills contain. This is why special-interest groups, in their efforts to push a bill, try so hard to influence committee members. And it is also why the committee's report on a bill, and the committee chairman's remarks on the bill when it comes up for debate, are taken as the most authoritative interpretation of what the final enactment is intended to accomplish. We shall see that when judges attempt to interpret a statute they often rely on these items of "legislative history" in their search for the legislative intent; the assumption is that the purposes that motivated the legislature as a whole to enact a law are likely to be the same purposes that prompted the committee to recommend passage. For the great majority of bills, then, the House does little more than review and ratify the decisions of its committees.

Action by the Whole House

Responsibility for deciding when each of the bills reported out of committee should be brought before the House of Representatives rests with the House Rules Committee. This practice gives the Rules Committee almost a life-or-death power over the fate of each bill, and makes it probably the most influential committee of the House.

Some of the House members usually want to speak on the floor about a newly introduced bill. In the House (unlike the Senate) the total time allowed for discussion of any bill is severely restricted, and a member who wishes to speak must arrange for speaking time with the leaders of his party. Often the purpose of these speeches is to impress the member's constituents at home rather than to influence fellow legislators.

While most of the bills that pass the House are little changed from the versions recommended by the committees, amendments are sometimes offered. The supporters of a bill must then decide whether or not to resist each proposed amendment. If opposition to the bill is strong, they may decide to accept certain amendments, in the hope of assuring the bill's adoption.

Passage Through the Other House

After a bill has been passed by the House of Representatives, it must clear a similar set of hurdles in the Senate. If the Senate fails to approve it before the current two-year term of Congress comes to an end, the bill is dead; it must start all over again through a new Congress.

Reconciliation of Differences

If the Senate passes a bill whose text is identical to that passed by the House, the bill goes at once to the President for his signature. But if the versions are different, further action is necessary to secure agreement on a version acceptable to both houses. Sometimes the house which first passed the bill will accept the changes later made by the other house. Or else a conference committee made up of representatives of each house will try to work out a compromise version, which each house must then approve. But bills which have cleared all the earlier stages have been known to fail of passage even at this late stage.

Action by the President

Before a bill can become law, it must be brought before the chief executive, the President of the United States. He has the choice of signing the bill, letting it become law without his signature, or vetoing it. A veto can be overriden by a two-thirds vote in each house, but vetoes are not often overridden.

When a bill has passed through all these stages, it becomes a law of the United States, an act of Congress, and in due course is published in several official compilations of federal statutes.

Differences Between Decisional and Legislative Lawmaking

The two lawmaking processes, and the two forms of law which they produce, are obviously quite different. Let us consider exactly what some of the differences are.

Big Steps and Little Ones

We saw in the last chapter that the judicial tradition sharply restricts the freedom of courts to create new legal rules. Judges do make law, but, since they must build on principles and precedents, they are essentially limited to "interstitial" lawmaking: to filling gaps and making small adjustments in the rules. Rarely do they take bold strides. When they do, it is usually because a truly novel case has come before them for decision, though occasionally they bring about an abrupt shift in legal rules by over-ruling (either explicitly or implicitly) a well-established but outmoded precedent.

Legislators are much less confined. They are quite free, for instance, to repeal tomorrow a law that they passed today. They can, and quite often do, pass laws that annul long-established decisional rules. They and they alone can establish those arbitrary dividing-lines so essential to any system of laws. For example, a legislature can pass a law stating that contracts to sell personal property for a price exceeding $500 are not enforceable unless certain formal requirements have been met (see page 299). Judges can apply such a rule, of course, but they could not have originated it. The rules that judges make must be reasoned extensions of established principles, and an arbitrary dividing-line like $500, however useful, cannot be justified in terms of principle. Finally, legislators have the power to establish new government agencies and to alter the authority of existing ones. This makes possible the adoption of far-reaching legal solutions that no court could attempt, since judges have no comparable power to create and alter institutional arrangements.

This is not to say, of course, that legislatures can do anything they choose. For one thing, constitutions impose various limitations on legislative action, some of which we shall discuss in Chapter 7. More important, the need to reconcile change with continuity, progress with tradition, limits legislatures as well as courts. It is true that legislators have no formal obligation to relate what they do to what has gone before. Nonetheless, considerations of what is politically prudent and administratively feasible effectively prevent bold innovations most of the time. More often than not, legislation is a belated and insufficient response to needs that have finally become too urgent to ignore. And when legislators do take action, even when they are dealing with a really new problem (such as that raised by the advent of jet propulsion), they are likely to build on existing rules, to adapt old and tested models to new uses, or to copy effective solutions worked out in other jurisdictions. Legislators are like judges, then, in preferring small steps to large ones.

Yet the difference remains: legislatures have much more freedom to make major changes and innovations in the law than do the courts. Most people would agree, moreover, that this is both inevitable and desirable. The accumulation of precedents and the growth of an ever more complex body of principles have inevitably narrowed the scope of judicial innovation. Meanwhile, with the strengthening of democratic traditions and institutions, legislatures have become the governmental bodies most immediately responsive to the popular will and hence the most appropriate makers of major changes in the law. Finally, and perhaps most important, the swift social, economic, and technological changes of the last hundred years have necessitated the creation of new rules and new techniques of regulation at a rate which the slow judicial process of case-by-case accretion simply could not achieve.

General Problems and Particular Instances

One reason for limiting the freedom of judges to make bold policy innovations is that they do not encounter problems whole but in fragments. The first responsibility of a court is to decide the case before it. It cannot ignore the significance of its decision for future cases, of course, but its perception of the future situations that its decision will affect must always be imperfect. The court has limited means of investigating the broader problem area of which the case before it is a part. It has neither a mandate nor the apparatus for conducting a general investigation.[3]

Courts are well equipped to fit rules to cases, to fill in the gaps, and to adjust existing rules; the opposing lawyers can normally be counted on to supply the needed information. But the courts are less well equipped to work out solutions covering whole problem areas.

A legislature, on the other hand, spends far more time dealing with problem areas, with whole classes of related situations, than with particular instances. Sometimes the legislature's attention is drawn to a problem by a particular incident, but the law it eventually passes is designed for general applicability. Thus, when the members of Congress passed the federal kidnaping law of 1932, the kidnaping and death of the Lindbergh baby were fresh in their minds; but the law they enacted was designed to deal with a whole class of possible occurrences. This is not to deny that legislatures often base their efforts on what proves to be a distorted and fragmentary picture of the problem area. But at least their attention is focused on the general problem rather than on the single case. And their traditionally broad investigatory powers enable them to make a much more thorough study of the problem than can the courts.

The Opportunity and the Obligation to Act

What we have been saying suggests a relatively simple division of functions. The legislators, we might conclude, are solely responsible for formulating broad new rules and for creating and revising the institutions necessary to put them into effect. The judges, limited to the function of disposing of the cases that others have brought before them, decide how the rules apply to the cases, and in the course of doing so they make such interstitial adjustments in the rules as are needed to meet new situations.

In practice, the division of functions is not so neat. For, while legislatures are certainly in a better position than judges to take major steps—to deal with whole problems—it does not follow that they always assume responsi-

---

[3] Appellate judges are not, of course, wholly unable to inform themselves concerning the legislative facts (that is, the background facts needed for lawmaking, as distinguished from the adjudicative facts concerning the events in the particular case). The opposing lawyers may include legislative facts—statistical data, for instance—in the briefs and oral arguments, and the judges may do a certain amount of reserch on their own. Before deciding the famous school desegregation cases in 1954, for example, the Supreme Court of the United States received an enormous amount of evidence on the social and psychological consequences of school segregation. Still, nobody would seriously contend that a court is as well equipped as a legislature to undertake extensive investigations.

bility for doing so. When a court is presented with a case that falls within its jurisdiction, it must make some decision.[4] That decision may be bold and creative or it may be narrowly confined. Legislatures also may choose between broad and restricted action, but they have a third alternative: they may refrain from acting at all.

The statute books are full of outmoded laws which are no longer appropriate to the situations they were designed to cover, but which are still in force because legislatures have not amended or repealed them. And all states have numerous outmoded decisional rules which their courts feel compelled to apply because legislatures have not got around to passing laws superseding them. (One example is the "contributory negligence" rule —discussed above, page 46—which has been changed by legislation to a "comparative negligence" rule in only a minority of states. Another example, many people think, is the rule of contract law that enables minors to disaffirm their contracts; see below, pp. 265–72.)

Nearly all legislatures have more work than they can handle during their regular sessions. Only a small fraction of their time is spent in enacting laws affecting private transactions and relationships. Legislators spend much more time, for instance, in discharging their responsibility for the operation and financing of government, and in keeping in touch with their constituents. If they are to be induced to revise an existing rule, strong, persuasive, and articulate pressure must be exerted on them. If those who favor change are unable to organize and give voice to their views, or if any strong opposition to the change is expressed, busy legislators are likely to avoid taking any action.

Some forty years ago Judge Cardozo wrote an article proposing, as a means of counteracting this inertia, that each state should establish a commission for law revision. These commissions, manned by experts, would have no power of their own. They would simply carry on a continuing study of the state's legal rules, both decisional and statutory, and from time to time would submit to the state legislature draft legislation embodying needed changes in the law. New York adopted this proposal, and its commission has done valuable work. The need for revision and modernization in most states is too great, however, for any commission, even if it were working with the most conscientious and energetic of legislatures, to do much more than scratch the surface.

Under the *stare decisis* principle, primary responsibility for changing well-established but unsatisfactory decisional rules may be said to lie with the legislatures, not with the courts. But the persistent failure of legislatures to meet this responsibility puts the courts under pressure to change the unsatisfactory rules themselves by overruling the offending precedents. Some critics believe that the courts have not been sufficiently willing to take this responsibility for keeping decisional rules up to date.

---

[4] With a few exceptions: The United States Supreme Court and some other top appellate courts have the power to choose which cases they will hear; when these courts refuse to hear a case, the decision of the lower court of appeals is final.

Influencing the Lawmakers

The foregoing remarks about legislative inertia suggest another difference between the two types of lawmaking: the difference in the methods by which private persons seek to influence judges and legislators.

Assume for the moment that you are a member of a group in Indiana which is extremely dissatisfied with the rule laid down by the Indiana Supreme Court in *Hurley v. Eddingfield*.[5] Your group wants to get the rule changed. What can it do?

One possibility is to arrange for a lawsuit in the Indiana courts in which the issues of the *Hurley* case will again be raised. Arranging for such a "test case" is not always easy, but let us assume it can be done. Presumably the lower court will feel obliged to follow the *Hurley* precedent and to decide against the party your group is backing. The stage will now be set for an appeal to the Indiana Supreme Court, which will be urged to overrule its decision in *Hurley*.

Knowing how reluctant courts are to overrule their earlier decisions, your group may ask itself whether it can supplement the briefs and oral arguments of the appellant's lawyer by bringing other pressure to bear on the judges. For instance, how about sending a delegation to explain to them why the *Hurley* rule is so bad? How about persuading as many citizens as possible to write letters to the judges urging them to overrule *Hurley*? If other pressures seem insufficient, how about sending pickets with placards to parade around the courthouse?

As you know, these are not proper ways to influence judges. Picketing a court is illegal in many states, and the other proposed methods, if tried, would certainly be ignored or rebuffed by the judges. The only permissible method for trying to influence a judicial decision is through the formal presentation of evidence and arguments, with each party having an opportunity to refute the evidence and arguments of the other. This is the essence of the adversary system.

Judges are supposed to be immune to private pressures of the sort traditionally exerted on political leaders. Nor should their decisions be affected by concern for their personal popularity and career advancement. Lastly, their religious beliefs, personal associations, and political affiliations should not determine their decisions.

(This is not to say, of course, that improper pressures, biases, and calculations of advantage have never been known to affect a judge's decision. But such influences are repugnant to the whole judicial tradition. Certainly no competent attorney would even hint at such considerations in his argument.)

Suppose now that your group decides that the chances of persuading the Indiana Supreme Court to overrule *Hurley* are slim. The alternative, of course, is to try to persuade the Indiana legislature to pass a law superseding and modifying the *Hurley* rule.

Influencing a legislature is completely different from influencing a

---

[5] See above, page 24. The court held, you will remember, that a physician had no legal obligation to go to a patient's bedside when summoned.

court. The freedom of choice of legislators, as we have seen, is relatively unconfined. No "adversary principle" limits the permissible methods of influencing them. Legislators are openly and avowedly makers of policy decisions, and consequently the legislatures have always been the main arena of debate over policy. Indeed, the pressure of interest groups has always been an essential part of the legislative process. Where legislation affecting private transactions and relationships is concerned, legislators have more often been arbiters between competing groups than originators of law. In short, a group of Indiana citizens who wished to persuade Indiana legislators to change the *Hurley* rule could expect at least a respectful hearing from them.

Moreover, the legislators would be willing to listen to arguments that could not be presented to a court. The legislators would want to know whether the change would be popular, whether it would please more voters than it would displease. The citizens' group could quite openly argue that the change would bring about social and economic advantages for the community—a type of persuasion that could be of only marginal importance in arguments presented to a court.

"Written" and "Unwritten" Law

So far we have been talking about differences between two *processes* of lawmaking. There is also a difference between the *products*. Laws passed by legislatures are often referred to as "written" law, in contrast to the "unwritten" decisional law produced by courts. Actually, of course, the decisions which embody decisional rules are reported and published. But statutes and other enactments—constitutions, executive orders, and administrative regulations—are "written" in the sense that they have an exclusive, official text; whereas decisional rules are "unwritten" in the sense that, although they can be extracted from what happened in decided cases, they have no official text.

While the words of a statute often have to be interpreted, the words themselves may not be ignored. The words *are* the law. As we shall see in Chapter 6, they set limits to the meanings that can be attributed to the statute. If, for instance, a law provides that no male under the age of sixteen may marry, no amount of interpreting will make it permissible for a boy of fifteen to get married.

The language of the opinion that accompanies a judicial decision has no comparable force. As we saw in Chapter 4, the precedent is established by what the court did, not by what it said. An opinion is an authoritative discussion of rules relating to the problem at hand, but it is not the official text of a rule or rules. To put it differently: an opinion announcing an appellate decision could be phrased in a number of different ways without changing the rule of the case.

Convenience, Uniformity, and Codification

A final basis of comparison concerns the relative convenience of the decisional and statutory forms of law for the lawyers and judges who have to work with them. On the whole it is easier to determine the applicable rule in a particular case when the basic rules are statutory than when they are purely decisional. Even with all the modern aids to case research—treatises, digests, encyclopedias, and the like—finding controlling precedents is usually a much more arduous task than finding relevant statutory provisions.[6]

The greater convenience of working with statutes is one of several reasons why, over the past century, our legislatures have enacted a considerable part of American decisional law into statutory form. The process of assembling scattered decisional rules in an orderly statutory code is known as *codification*. Sometimes the transformation has taken place without change in the rules themselves; sometimes the codification has been in response to pressure for substantive change, and the legislators have modified the rules in the course of codifying them.

The drive for codification has also been stimulated by the need for greater uniformity among the rules of the several states. This has been particularly true in the commercial law fields, where conflicting state decisional rules have seriously interfered with the conduct of interstate business. In 1890 the states set up a Conference of Commissioners on Uniform State Laws. The commissioners were to be specialists in the major fields of commercial law, appointed by the state governors. Over the years the Conference has drafted a number of legislative proposals for submission to the state legislatures. Some of these proposals—for example, the Negotiable Instruments Law, the Uniform Warehouse Receipts Act, and the Uniform Sales Act—have been adopted by all or most of the states; others have been less well received. You will be studying the provisions of some of these uniform acts in Part II of this book.

The extent to which decisional law has been codified differs from state to state. Many states have, for instance, codified their criminal law and now have no purely "common-law" crimes (that is, acts made criminal solely by judicial decision). But there is still a great deal of uncodified decisional law in every one of the states; nowhere do we find the comprehensive codification which characterizes the Civil Law tradition (see page 59).

Codification was a fighting cause in the nineteenth century. Its proponents insisted that modernizing and clarifying the law would make it certain and understandable to every intelligent man. Clarity and certainty, they promised, would greatly reduce the work of the courts. Today few students of the law have such high hopes; they realize that the law is uncertain not because so many rules are embodied in scattered judicial decisions but because so many of the cases that arise involve fact-situations

---

[6] The searcher's work is not always finished, however, when he finds the statute; he may still have to look up cases. (a) The statute is likely to include concepts and subordinate rules taken from decisional law. To understand these, it may be necessary to look up cases antedating the statute. (b) Once a statute has been applied and interpreted by a court, the court's interpretation becomes in effect a part of the statute; in the future, lawyers and judges must look at the interpretation as well as the statute itself. This is why many statute-books are "annotated": following each provision is a brief summary of the decisions interpreting it.

to which existing rules—regardless of whether they are decisional or statutory—cannot be neatly fitted.[7]

Some Problems of Legislative Drafting

Some day you may be asked to collaborate with a lawyer in preparing a draft proposal for legislation in some field in which you are an expert. It is more likely, however, that your contacts with legislation will be confined to figuring out with a lawyer how some already-enacted statute affects transactions that concern you. Even if you never have anything to do with the actual drafting of legislation, you will find it useful to have some conception of the problems of draftsmanship.

Before setting to work, the drafter of a statute must ask himself certain broad questions:

What Technique of Channeling Conduct Is Most Likely to Achieve the Desired Results?

As an example, let's imagine that the framer's object is to prevent the public sale of a certain drug except in very small quantities. Should he write the law in such a way as to forbid all sales except on prescription? Or should customers be allowed to buy a small quantity without a prescription on condition that they sign the pharmacist's register? Should a pharmacist who violates the law's restrictions be subject to criminal penalties? Should he instead be subject to the forfeiture or suspension of his license? Or would it be enough to provide that any customer who claims to have suffered injury traceable to an illegally sold quantity of the drug have the right to sue the pharmacist for damages? Should customers who knowingly evade the law's restrictions suffer any penalty? Could the aim be achieved by simply requiring the pharmacist to label each bottle of the drug with a clear warning of its noxious qualities? Perhaps officials should make periodic inspections of the medicine chests in all homes, penalizing householders with excessive quantities of the drug in their possession. Or might the best approach be to launch a major educational campaign to inform the public of the drug's dangers?

Nowadays the drafter of legislation is likely to be, not a legislator, but a trained specialist in draftsmanship. Answering the foregoing questions requires the making of policy decisions which are probably beyond the authority of the draftsman. But he must be familiar with the alternative techniques of channeling private conduct, and he must know what experiences his own and other jurisdictions have had in applying these techniques to similar problems in the past. Only then will he be able to outline the alternatives and suggest what their respective advantages and shortcomings are likely to be.

---

[7] The whole process of searching for and applying legal rules promises to be revolutionized in the coming years as we develop computers capable of performing more and more data-processing and even decision-making functions.

How Precise and Detailed Should the Statute Be?

How far should the legislative draftsman go in trying to devise specific provisions to cover future situations? The ideal statute would specify all the possible situations to which it should apply. Its words, moreover, would convey precisely the same meaning to everyone who read them. Obviously no legislative draftsman could ever realize these goals. Human foresight is limited; he could never hope to anticipate all the possible situations to which his statute might conceivably apply. And words are at best imperfect symbols for communicating intent.

Most people believe that, while perfect clarity and precision are impossible, they must always be the ideals toward which the statute-writer should strive. There are circumstances, however, in which the framers of a statute are justified in being *deliberately imprecise*. Sometimes legislators realize that some sort of action must be taken to deal with a certain problem, but they realize too that the scope of the problem and of the remedies needed are not yet clear and will be revealed only as the future unfolds. They may therefore decide to enact a statute which merely identifies the problem, outlines in relatively broad terms the primary and remedial rules to be applied, and leaves the details to be filled in through successive applications of the statute to particular cases.

This is, of course, the typical approach of the framers of constitutional provisions, for they realize that constitutions must last a long time and usually are hard to amend. What phrase could be more deliberately imprecise, for instance, than "No State shall . . . deprive any person of life, liberty, or property, without due process of law"?

The key provision of the Sherman Antitrust Act of 1890 is embodied in a single sentence: "Every contract, combination in the form of trust or otherwise, or conspiracy, in restraint of trade or commerce among the several states or with foreign nations, is hereby declared to be illegal." Another sentence of about equal length and imprecision makes it illegal to "monopolize or attempt to monopolize." The rest of the brief statute consists of remedial provisions. No attempt is made to define the broad terms used in the key sentence.[8]

A statute is a sort of communication, addressed to the various categories of people who will be affected by its enactment. It requires (or forbids, or permits, or enables) private persons to do certain things; it tells enforcement officials what they must or may do; and it provides judges with a new set of rules to apply and interpret in disposing of cases. A broad, general statute in effect "passes the buck" to the addressees; it delegates to them the task of elaborating its meaning, progressively, case by case. A private person is likely to be the first to test it, by doing something which causes another private person, or an official, to react. Each of them is "inter-

---

[8] Terms like "contract," "combination," "conspiracy," "restraint of trade," and "monopolize" are not quite so empty of specific content as they may seem to the layman. They had been used before 1890 in judicial opinions and statutes, and had taken on meaning from such uses. Even so, judges had, and still have, a large measure of discretion when they apply the Sherman Act provisions to particular cases. For further comments on the Sherman Act, see pages 810 and 811.

preting" the statute. The ultimate and authoritative interpretation, however, must come from the courts, when controversies engendered by conduct with which the statute is concerned are brought before them.[9]

A broad, general statute starts out, then, as a somewhat cryptic communication. It takes on precision as its addressees test it out by adopting their successive interpretations. But the uncertainty produced initially by an imprecise law is often preferable to the crippling certainty of a highly specific law ill-adapted to the situations that arise after its enactment. Premature, excessive precision may deny enforcement officials and judges all latitude of interpretation, and may make it impossible for them to administer justice in an orderly and reasonable way. When a "hard" case arises, of a sort not foreseen by the lawmakers, the judge who must decide it finds his hands tied; he has no choice but to apply a rule that he knows will produce an inappropriate result.[10]

We must not make too strong a case for vagueness and imprecision in statute-writing, however. More often than not, imprecision is inappropriate and troublesome. Statute-writers usually fall into vague language not because they decide to do so, but because their thinking is fuzzy or because they are in a hurry. Sometimes, too, vague words are used with the hope of lulling potentially antagonistic legislators into voting for what seems to be a harmless bill.

Should the Underlying Purposes Be Spelled Out in the Statute?

When legislators vote for a statute, it is unlikely that they all have the same idea about exactly how it will work and precisely to what situations it will apply; but they have probably agreed on certain basic purposes and policies.

The drafter of a statute must ask himself whether he should try to include in the statute an explicit statement of its underlying purposes. One would certainly suppose that such a statement would simplify the task of the statute's addressees. To the layman it may seem obvious, therefore, that every statute should contain some sort of preamble in which its purposes are set forth.

Experience indicates, however, that securing agreement among the legislators on a statement of purpose precise enough to be useful is often as difficult as securing agreement on the body of the statute. And no backer of a bill wants to risk defeat merely for the sake of putting through an explicit statement of purpose. As a result, if any statement is included it is frequently so vague that it is of little value.

The experienced draftsman realizes, however, that those who must

---

[9] We traditionally employ the word "interpret" to describe what a court does when it applies a statute, even though it is obvious, when the statute is deliberately imprecise, that the judges are doing much more than determining what the words of the statute mean. We shall say more about this in the next chapter.

[10] When you read *Smith v. Hiatt* in the next chapter (page 110), ask yourself whether the statutory provision involved need have been so specific, and whether a more general statute might have prevented the absurd outcome of the case—and thus made the subsequent amendment of the statute unnecessary.

interpret the statute can often learn a great deal about its purposes by studying the reports and other pronouncements of the legislative committees that worked on the bill. It is usually safe to assume that the majority which passed the bill was ratifying the purposes and policies of the responsible committees. Carefully prepared committee reports may give interpreters of a statute more guidance concerning purposes than they could ever hope to get from a preamble.

What Vocabulary Is Appropriate?

The legislative draftsman must first try to identify the sort of people who will probably be reading the statute, and then choose a vocabulary that will be appropriate to them. He must ask himself such questions as these: Are the private addressees members of the general public, or are they a restricted group familiar with a technical vocabulary (for example, the vocabulary of pharmacology)? Are the officials who must read the statute likely to be familiar with a technical vocabulary? Must the statute be made understandable to persons without legal training?

Anyone who has read statutes must realize that the typical drafter assumes that the principal readers will be lawyers, experienced administrative officials, and judges. He makes little effort to use language intelligible to the layman. His aim rather is to avoid ambiguity at all costs, and so he tends to choose words and phrases with sharply delimited meanings familiar to persons trained in the law. Hence the unlovely style sometimes known as "legal English," which some laymen assume is designed to confuse and mystify them. Among its characteristics are the repetition of the same words or phrases, strings of near-synonyms, and awkward words like "aforesaid" and "heretofore." [11] Inelegant though they may seem, such words and phrases have a precise scope and content firmly established by judicial interpretation. Under most circumstances, drafters are justified in their decision to concentrate on speaking clearly and unambiguously to the reader trained in law.

PROBLEM

Suppose the group of citizens aroused by the *Hurley* decision in Indiana asked you to help draft a statute to supersede the *Hurley* rule. Their plan is to present a draft proposal to the state legislature. They are convinced that in a case with facts like those alleged in *Hurley*, a doctor should be under a legal duty to attend to his patient. They have not, however, thought through the whole problem. They want you to do that for them, and to embody your conclusions in a draft statute which they will discuss at their next meeting.

---

[11] A sample: "Be it enacted . . . that from and after the passage of this act it shall be unlawful for any person, company, partnership or corporation, in any manner whatsoever, to prepay the transportation, or in any way assist or encourage the immigration or migration of any alien or aliens, any foreigner or foreigners, into the United States, its Territories, or the District of Columbia, under contract or ageement, parol or special, express or implied, made previous to the importation or migration of such alien or aliens, foreigner or foreigners, to perform labor or service of any kind in the United States, its Territories, or the District of Columbia."

Prepare a short draft statute for them, together with notes explaining your inclusions and exclusions.

As a starting point, you might consider a statute that reads simply: "The decision of the Supreme Court of Indiana in the case of *Hurley v. Eddingfield,* 156 Ind. 416, is hereby disapproved, and is declared to represent no longer the applicable rule of law for cases similar to that case." Would this enunciation of the new rule answer with reasonable clarity every question that is likely to arise in the minds of the addressees of the statute?

6 Judicial Lawmaking II: The Interpretation of Statutes

What a statutory provision means, and what types of situation it covers and does not cover, are matters that are ultimately determined by the courts. The citizen who wishes to understand his legal environment should know something about this process of interpretation and application. He does not, of course, need a detailed knowledge of the many rules of statutory construction which judges have developed, but he should have some idea of the main problems which judges encounter.

This is not to say that cases arising under statutes normally present difficult problems of interpretation. Part II of this book, for instance, contains a number of cases in which the applicable rules were statutory, but in only a very few of them did the court have any trouble determining what the statutory rule was.[1] But a significant minority of cases do present such problems.

Difficulties of interpretation are created in several ways. Some statutes contain unintentional errors and ambiguities because of bad draftsmanship. Other statutes are unclear because those who pushed them through the legislature sought to avoid opposition by being vague or silent on potentially controversial matters. But the most important reason for the lack of absolute clarity and preciseness in many statutes is that their framers have not been able to foresee and provide for all possible future situations. Realizing their inability to do this, the wisest legislators have usually preferred to be deliberately imprecise; by the generality of their language they have in effect delegated to others the task of filling in the details. The principal recipients of this authority are administrative officials [2] and judges. The more imprecise the statute, the greater the delegated authority; under so broad and general a statute as the Sherman Act, the "interpreter" becomes in effect the true lawmaker.

---

[1] In most of these cases, the court had to answer a "mixed question of law and fact" (see above, page 22–23); in other words, the court's problem was to characterize the conduct of the parties so that it could be measured against the standards which the statute had established. What those standards were was fairly clear.

People v. Ford, page 690, is one of several cases included in Part II in which the meaning and scope of the statutory standard was itself at issue.

[2] On the lawmaking and adjudicative functions of administrators, see Chapter 8,

Problems of statutory interpretation typically fall into one of the following categories:

1. A legislature passes a statute which states that it applies to a designated class of persons or objects but fails to specify the precise boundaries of the class. *Examples:* In a statute that applies to "vehicles," the question is whether "vehicles" as a class includes, for instance: an airplane, a tricycle, and an ancient carriage mounted on a pedestal. Or a statute refers to "persons," and a case arises involving a corporation: is a corporation a "person"?

2. From its language alone, a statute seems pretty clearly to apply to a particular situation, but common sense suggests that it really should not. *Example:* A federal statute makes it a crime to detain a postal employee while on duty. Does this statute apply to a local sheriff who serves an arrest warrant on a postman charged with murder?

3. From its language alone, a statute seems pretty clearly *not* to apply to a particular situation, but common sense suggests that it really *should*. *Example:* An old act of Congress providing for the sale of public land at a low price to settlers specified the amount of land that single men and married men might buy. A widow sought to buy some land. Was she a "single man" or a "married man," or was she not qualified under the law to buy land?

4. An old statute remains on the books long after the immediate problems it was designed to deal with have changed. *Example:* A statute passed in 1880 refers to "vehicles." A case arising in 1962 involves an automobile. Automobiles were unknown in 1880. Does the statute apply? Is it reasonable to assume that any vehicle unknown to the statute-writers in 1880 should be excluded from its coverage? Or that any object to which the designation "vehicle" could reasonably be applied at any later date should automatically be covered? Or is some intermediate interpretation preferable?

The Intention of the Legislature

When a judge writes an opinion in a case requiring statutory construction, he usually indicates at the outset that the court's object is to carry out as best it can the intention of the legislature. There is no disagreement over this objective, but difficulties arise in trying to achieve it. Here are some of them:

Finding a Collective Intention

Determining what a group of legislators—sometimes several hundred of them—"intended" when they voted for a bill is not easy. Although they all voted for the same set of words, it does not follow that they all did so with the same intention. What they thought is, indeed, largely unrecorded, but we can be sure that they did not all favor the law for precisely the same reasons or with the same expectations as to what it would accomplish. Many of them unquestionably voted for it merely because they trusted or were beholden to its sponsors; or because they expected those sponsors to reciprocate on some later occasion; or because they were pressed to do so by the leaders of their party. Some legislators, particularly the bill's sponsors and the members of the committees that worked on it, certainly had definite views on what the bill was designed to accomplish. As we have already suggested, it is usually assumed that in voting for the bill the legislative majorities were in effect ratifying the policies enunciated by their committees. This assumption is usually justified, but one of the reasons for adopting it is the impossibility of making any better generalization about the legislative intention.

Finding an Intention with Respect to Specific Situations

Hard as it is to identify a general legislative intention, it is harder still to surmise what the legislature "intended" with respect to particular situations not explicitly provided for. Few legislators give much thought to the detailed application of a statute. And even those who are most concerned with its passage inevitably fail to foresee some of the situations which later arise and to which, consequently, its applicability is uncertain. In short, talking about the legislative intent with reference to specific fact-situations is likely to be wholly unrealistic.

Finding an Underlying Purpose

Judges have tended to conclude that the only sensible solution to this problem of identifying the "intention of the legislature" is not to look for a specific intent shared by all those who voted for the law, but to search instead for the broad purposes and policies that probably motivated those who actively favored the bill. The judges ask themselves such questions as these: What were the legal rules channeling conduct in this area of activity before this statute was enacted? How does the statute seem to change those rules? What seem to have been the ills that the statute was designed to cure? Then, having identified as best they can the general purposes underlying the statute, the judges go on to ask themselves: What interpretation of the specific statutory provisions apparently applicable to the fact-situation before us will best serve the purposes of the statute as a whole? [3]

Not only is this the only realistic way to use the legislative intent; it is the way in which legislators almost certainly expect judges to behave. Having done their best to embody their collective objectives in a final enactment, legislators do not expect judges to try to figure out precisely what their thoughts were with respect to particular fact-situations—or what their thoughts *would have been* if the situations had occurred to them. Legislators are aware that the applicability of their statute to particular cases will not always be clear. They expect judges to decide cases by accepting the authority delegated to them to elaborate the statute's meanings—that is, to work out sensible applications of the statute's identified purposes. As we have noted many times before, our legal system bestows on judges a limited power to make law.

---

[3] For an example of a purpose-oriented interpretation, see *United States v. Aluminum Co. of America*, at pp. 835–37.

Where do judges look in their search for the purposes underlying a statute? Since the legislators have agreed on a particular set of words that has become the official text of the statute, obviously the first place to look is at the text itself. And if the statutory language is carefully examined for evidence of a general purpose or purposes, an answer can usually be found in the text. It is only when the language yields no satisfactory evidence of purpose that judges sometimes turn to the statute's "legislative history."

The Interpretation of Statutory Language

The "Plain Meaning" Concept

Anybody who has to read many judicial opinions in which statutes are construed soon comes to realize that judges do not all agree on how to go about interpreting statutory language. In the light of what we have just said about the importance of searching for underlying purposes, consider, for example, the view of statutory construction expressed in the following opinion.

TEMPLE v. CITY OF PETERSBURG

Supreme Court of Appeals of Virginia, 1944
182 Va. 418, 29 S.E. 2d 357

► GREGORY, JUSTICE. The appellants, who were the complainants in the court below, filed their bill in equity against the city of Petersburg, praying that it be restrained and enjoined from using a tract of 1.01 acres of land acquired by it in 1942 for cemetery purposes. This plot of land adjoined Peoples Memorial Cemetery, which had been established and used as a cemetery for more than one hundred years. [It was acquired by the city with the intention of re-interring in it bodies which had to be exhumed in order that a road on another side of the cemetery could be widened. The tract lies directly across St. Andrews Street from the front of appellants' residence.]

The court below temporarily restrained the city from using the 1.01-acre tract as an addition to the cemetery. Later the city filed its answer to the bill and, by consent, the cause was set for hearing upon the bill, the answer, and a stipulation of counsel. The court dissolved the injunction and refused the prayer for relief.

Code, sec. 56 (Michie 1942), provides in part as follows:

> "No cemetery shall be hereafter established within the corporate limits of any city or town; nor shall any cemetery be established within two hundred and fifty yards of any residence without the consent of the owner of the legal and equitable title of such residence. . . ."

We are called upon to ascertain the proper meaning of the statute, and to decide whether or not it has been violated by the city. Specifically the controversy concerns the meaning to be given to the word, "established," used therein. The appellants maintain that under the statute the enlargement of an existing cemetery, such as is sought here, in reality is the establishment

of a cemetery, while the appellee contends that to enlarge an existing cemetery is not the establishment of a cemetery and, therefore, constitutes no
violation of the statute. . . .

The principal and determinative issue to be determined in this cause
is whether or not the proposed enlargement of Peoples Memorial Cemetery,
by the additional 1.01-acre tract, is prohibited by section 56 of the Code.

The appellants most strongly contend that the word, "established," as
used in the statute, means "located," and that the evil intended to be in-
hibited is the location of a cemetery in a city or town upon ground not
previously dedicated for cemetery purposes, or the location of a cemetery
within 250 yards of a residence, whether by enlargement or otherwise. They
contend that the purpose of the statute is to protect residences and lands
from the ill effects growing out of close proximity to a cemetery. They further contend that it is unreasonable to say that residences and lands are to
be protected against the "establishment" of cemeteries, but are not to be
protected against the encroachment or enlargement of existing cemeteries;
that the evil created by one is equally as real as that created by the other.

The position of the appellee is that the word "established" has such a
clear and precise meaning that no question of statutory construction arises.
That the statute provides that no cemetery shall be "hereafter established"
in a city or town, and that this language does not mean that a cemetery
already established shall not be hereafter enlarged. To hold otherwise would
be not to construe the statute, but in effect to amend it.

It is elementary that the ultimate aim of rules of interpretation is to
ascertain the intention of the legislature in the enactment of a statute, and
that intention, when discovered, must prevail. If, however, the intention of
the legislature is perfectly clear from the language used, rules of construction are not to be applied. We are not allowed to construe that which has
no need of construction. If the language of a statute is plain and unambiguous, and its meaning perfectly clear and definite, effect must be given to
it regardless of what courts think of its wisdom or policy. In such cases
courts must find the meaning within the statute itself.

In Commonwealth v. Sanderson, 170 Va. 33, we quoted with approval
from Saville v. Virginia Ry. and Power Co., 114 Va. 444, this statement of
the rule:

> " 'It is contended that the construction insisted upon by the plaintiff
> in error is violative of the spirit or reason of the law. The argument would
> seem to concede that the contention is within the letter of the law. We
> hear a great deal about the spirit of the law, but the duty of this court
> is not to make law, but to construe it; not to wrest its letter from its
> plain meaning in order to conform to what is conceived to be its spirit,
> in order to subserve and promote some principle of justice and equality
> which it is claimed the letter of the law has violated. It is our duty to
> take the words which the legislature has seen fit to employ and give
> to them their usual and ordinary signification, and, having thus ascer-
> tained the legislative intent, to give effect to it, unless it transcends the
> legislative power as limited by the Constitution.' "

The word "established" is defined in Webster's New International Dictionary, 2d Ed., 1936, thus: "To originate and secure the permanent existence of; to found; to institute; to create and regulate;—said of a colony, a State or other institutions."

Just why the Legislature, in its wisdom, saw fit to prohibit the establishment of cemeteries in cities and towns, and did not see fit to prohibit enlargements or additions, is no concern of ours. Certain it is that language could not be plainer than that employed to express the legislative will. From it we can see with certainty that while a cemetery may not be established in a city or town, it may be added to or enlarged without running counter to the inhibition found in section 56. We are not permitted to read into the statute an inhibition which the Legislature, perhaps advisedly, omitted. Our duty is to construe the statute as written.

If construction of the statute were necessary and proper in this case, we would be forced to the same conclusion. Even if it be assumed that there is ambiguity in the language in section 56, the legislative history of its enactment and a consideration of Code, sec. 53, a related statute, would remove all doubt as to what the legislature intended by its language in section 56.

Code, sec. 53, affords a complete answer to the question of legislative intent in the use of the word "established" in section 56, for the former section makes a distinction between "establish" and "enlarge" in these words: "If it be desired at any time to establish a cemetery, for the use of a city, town, county, or magisterial district, or to enlarge any such already established, and the title to land needed cannot be otherwise acquired, land sufficient for the purpose may be condemned. . . ."

The foregoing language, taken from section 53, completely demonstrates that the Legislature did not intend the words "establish" and "enlarge" to be used interchangeably, but that the use of one excluded any idea that it embraced or meant the other. As used, they are mutually exclusive. To enlarge or add to a cemetery is not to establish one within the meaning of section 56.

The language of the statute being so plain and unambiguous, and the intention and meaning of the Legislature so clear, we hold that the city of Petersburg has not violated Code, sec. 56, and the decree accordingly should be affirmed.

Affirmed.   ◄

Justice Gregory has two arguments to support his conclusion that the restrictions on cemeteries "hereafter established" do not apply to enlargements of existing cemeteries. The first concerns the "plain meaning" of the words of section 56 of the Virginia Code; the second involves an interpretation of section 56 in the light of the wording of section 53, a related statute. Let us confine ourselves for the present to the first argument.

The justice starts out with the familiar statement that the court's aim must be to discover and carry out the intention of the legislature, and that that intention must be looked for first in the statutory language. But he makes it clear that he has *not* looked for the *purpose* of the statute. Perhaps if he had considered the language ambiguous, he would have looked for an underlying purpose. But "rules of construction," he says, become relevant only when language is ambiguous. When it is unambiguous, no interpretation is necessary. Since the court finds the meaning of "established" perfectly plain, its only task is to apply the plain meaning, with no regard to the policy behind it.

At first blush this seems to be a sensible argument. If words are plain, why waste time applying rules of construction to them? If judges are allowed to "interpret" plain words, what is to prevent them from nullifying or distorting statutes to suit their own predilections? This "plain meaning rule" would seem to be a useful curb on judicial usurpations of the legislative function, of which there have been some notorious examples.[4]

But what are the criteria for deciding whether or not a word or phrase is "plain and unambiguous"? And what should a judge do when he realizes that to give effect to the apparently clear meaning of a statutory provision would produce a result which seems absurd, or harsh and unreasonable, or at least surprising?[5] Should he say, as Justice Gregory does, that "effect must be given to [the language] regardless of what courts think of its wisdom or policy," and let it go at that? Or should he perhaps take a second look at the statute to see whether it cannot be interpreted in another way?

When, as sometimes happens, a statute is passed which obviously contains a clerical error—the omission of the word "not," for instance—judges are always willing to give the provision its corrected meaning in order to arrive at the obviously intended result. A statutory clause reading "Unfair competitive practices are hereby declared to be lawful" makes sense of a sort; it is not gibberish. But we must assume that legislators are reasonable men, pursuing reasonable objectives by reasonable methods, and that they could not have meant to legalize at one stroke all "unfair" competitive practices. If one reads the phrase in the context of surrounding provisions, moreover, it will doubtless become clear that the final word should have been "unlawful," and judges will so assume in applying the statute.

But when giving a phrase its literal meaning would produce a result which was not downright absurd but merely surprising and seemingly unreasonable, the court's problem is more difficult. After all, judges have no

---

[4] A traditional argument for literalism in statutory interpretation is that, since the legislature presumably chose its words carefully, the best way to carry out its intentions is to give those words their natural meaning. The argument clearly has merit. On the other hand, the case reports are full of instances where judges have resorted to literal, strict, narrow interpretations not because of a scrupulous desire to carry out the legislative intent but as a means to avoid carrying out legislative policies of which they disapproved. In short, judges bent on usurping the legislative function may resort to either a too-liberal or a too-literal policy of interpretation.

[5] The perils of interpreting words too literally are illustrated by a simple story. The mistress of the house calls to the nursemaid, "Drop what you're doing and come here as fast as you can!" The nurse is giving the baby a bath. Should she obey? If she is reasonably intelligent, she will realize that her mistress does not want the baby dropped into the bath, plain though her words are.

general mandate to rewrite legislative enactments to make them more fair and reasonable.

The United States Supreme Court once interpreted an immigration law in such a way as to deny to the alien wife of a native-born American citizen a privilege which, it held, the law granted only to alien wives of naturalized citizens. "The words of the statute being clear," the Court concluded, "if it unjustly discriminates against the native-born citizen, or is cruel and inhuman in its results, as is forcefully contended, the remedy lies with Congress and not with the courts. Their duty is simply to enforce the law as it is written. . . ." But if the result reached was obviously cruel and inhuman, should not the Court have asked itself whether the meaning of the words was really as plain as it appeared to be?

Justice Gregory's interpretation of "established" raises a similar question. The result reached is not, to be sure, cruel or inhuman, but it is certainly hard to explain. Why should the Virginia legislature have wished to protect property-owners against the establishment of new cemeteries but not against the extension of old ones? Maybe the legislators had a reason for making such a distinction, but surely some effort should have been made to find it.

Justice Gregory's opinion suggests that he may have lost sight of two important truths about words:

1. *Words rarely have only a single meaning.* A few words have perfectly specific referents, but most words have a range of meanings. Indeed, they have a slightly different meaning each time they are used in a new sentence. The proper question to ask about a word, then, is not just: "What does it mean?" but "What can it mean? *What are the limits of permissible meaning that can be attributed to it?*"

"A word," Justice Holmes once wrote, "is not a crystal, transparent and unchanged; it is the skin of a living thought, and may vary greatly in color and context according to the circumstances and the time in which it is used."

To support his position, Justice Gregory cites a dictionary definition of "establish." His implication seems to be that, since the dictionary does not list "enlarge" or "extend" as a synonym of "establish," "established" may not be interpreted as including "enlarged." But the function of dictionaries is simply to report the usual meanings of words. The failure to report a particular meaning is not proof that the word can never have that meaning in any context. True, the rules of etymology (the science of word meanings) prevent "black" from being used to mean "white"; "white" is beyond the limits of permissible meaning of "black." But no such etymological limitation prevents "establish" from including the notion of enlarging something that already exists.

2. *Words cannot really be understood apart from their contexts.* Context first of all means *textual* context. Textual context includes not only the sentence in which the word or phrase appears but also the successively larger units into which the statute is divided: the paragraph, section, chapter or article, and the whole statute. "Established" in a statute dealing with

cemeteries obviously means something different from what it means in statutes dealing with the founding of colonies or banks.

In the final portion of the *Temple* opinion, Justice Gregory turns to his second argument, which is based on textual context. Here he considers the word "established" in the broad context of the Virginia Code, which includes a Section 53 (described as "a related statute," since it also concerns cemeteries but was apparently not a part of the same piece of legislation as Section 56). In Section 53 a clear distinction is drawn between the establishment and enlargement of cemeteries. Justice Gregory argues that the legislature could not have intended that "established" in Section 56 should have a broader meaning than it had in Section 53. This argument is much more persuasive than that based on "plain meaning." (It is perhaps less conclusive, however, than Justice Gregory suggests. After all, the framers of Section 56 may have ascribed to the "established" in that section a meaning broad enough to include enlargements, without remembering that the same word had been used in a more restricted sense in Section 53.)

Much broader than textual context is what is sometimes called *circumstantial* context. The circumstantial context of a statutory provision embraces such relevant matters as the sources of dissatisfaction which gave rise to the new act (e.g., the decline of land values in the vicinity of cemeteries), and the legal rules in effect prior to the new enactment (e.g., rules on the use of urban land for burials). Circumstantial context may even include the relevant aspects of the social, economic, and technological circumstances that prevailed at the time the statute was passed.

A consideration of a statute's circumstantial context is indispensable to a search for purpose. To discover what legislators intended to include under the concept "vehicle" in a statute passed in 1880, for instance, a judge will probably want to know what types of vehicle existed in 1880.[6] He will also want to identify the particular problem to which the legislators were addressing themselves. Whether the term "vehicles" in a statute enacted in 1880 should be construed today as covering automobiles and airplanes will depend on what the statute is trying to accomplish. If it concerns safety on the roads, for instance, it presumably covers automobiles (even though they did not exist in 1880) but not airplanes. If, on the other hand, it is a tax statute designed to offset local government expenditures in aid of transportation, perhaps airplanes are also covered. Whether a statute referring to "persons" covers corporations again depends on the reasons that led to its enactment. If it was designed to regulate marriages, obviously corporations are not "persons"; but if its purpose was to regulate the use of property, perhaps they are.

It is important that you understand what we are *not* saying. We are *not* saying that judges are free to give to statutory words a meaning which is outside their range of etymologically permissible meanings just to produce a more reasonable result in a particular case. Judges have no authority

---

[6] On the other hand, it is not necessarily true that the legislators intended to limit the scope of their enactment to vehicles they knew about; they may have intended that the legislation should cover new types of vehicle as they appeared.

to rewrite statutes merely because they think that the indicated meaning of the language would lead to an undesirable result, or because they suspect that the legislators have overlooked some important policy consideration. The words used *do* limit the judges' freedom of interpretation; judges may not assign a wholly unnatural meaning to words in order to carry out some surmised purpose.[7]

All we are saying is that when, to give effect to an apparently clear meaning would produce a surprising result, a judge should look again to see whether the meaning is really as clear as it seems. He should make sure that he has read the provision in relation to its underlying purpose as indicated by the textual and circumstantial contexts. If, after doing this, however, he remains convinced that no other meaning can reasonably be attributed to the words, then he must give effect to that meaning and leave to the legislature the responsibility for amending the statute if it so desires.

Suppose, for instance, that a legislature has passed a law saying that certain occupational categories are subject to a special tax, but has inadvertently omitted one category from the list. That category could not be made subject to the tax no matter how overwhelming the evidence that it should have been included. Or suppose a law specifies that "no male under the age of sixteen may marry." No judge could so construe the provision as to permit the marriage of a particular fifteen-year-old boy, whatever the peculiar circumstances of the case or the evidence that the legislature had overlooked the need for exceptions to this rule.

But "perfectly clear" statutory words are much rarer than many judges have intimated. "Established" in Section 56 of the Virginia Code did not have a single, perfectly plain meaning. The trouble with Justice Gregory's opinion in *Temple* is not that it leads him to a result that is necessarily wrong, but that it represents an inadequate approach to interpreting the meaning of words. Further examination of the statute—and perhaps of its legislative history, if necessary—might or might not have revealed whether the Virginia legislature meant to distinguish between the establishing of new urban cemeteries and the extension of old ones. But no such examination was made.

The Failure to Search for Purpose: Another Example

We have suggested that in *Temple v. City of Petersburg* a word used by the legislature may have deserved a broader and more inclusive interpretation than the court was willing to give it. Often the court is faced with the opposite problem: one of the parties contends that the statutory lan-

---

[7] We have been stressing the importance of carrying out the legislature's purpose. Another reason for limiting the freedom of judges to interpret is that private addressees of a statute may have assumed that the statutory words mean what they appear to mean. If a judge is too free to interpret, he may defeat the legitimate expectations of these addressees.

The courts are particularly careful in construing criminal statutes to make sure that those who are subject to them have had fair warning. Such statutes are construed strictly: courts try not to attribute to their words any but the clearest and most obvious meanings, lest the charge be made that a defendant was not given fair warning and has therefore been denied due process of law.

guage should not be interpreted as inclusively as its literal meaning seems to require. Instead of arguing that the legislators intended to cover situations which the words taken literally do not seem to cover, the party argues that the legislators would have used more restrictive language, or introduced qualifications or exceptions, had they realized how broad was the coverage of the words they chose.

The following case illustrates this problem.

SMITH v. HIATT

Supreme Judicial Court of Massachusetts, 1952
329 Mass. 488, 109 N.E. 2d 133

▶ JUSTICE WILLIAMS stated the facts and issues of the case as follows:

This is an action of tort to recover compensation for personal injuries. After the return of a jury verdict for the plaintiff, the judge denied, subject to their exception, a motion of the defendants for the entry of a verdict in their favor.

There was evidence that the plaintiff was employed by the defendants, who were husband and wife, in their home in Worcester as a practical nurse to care for their newborn baby. On the morning of July 17, 1946, the plaintiff went to the kitchen to prepare milk for the baby. She there found the defendant Mrs. Hiatt who had been defrosting the refrigerator. There was ice on the floor which Mrs. Hiatt either had dropped or had failed to remove after it had fallen from the refrigerator. The plaintiff slipped on the ice and was injured. We assume that the evidence was sufficient to warrant a finding that the plaintiff was in the exercise of due care and that Mrs. Hiatt was negligent. No written notice of the time, place, and cause of the injury under G. L. (Ter. Ed.) c. 84, § 21, was given by the plaintiff to either of the defendants.

The only question presented is whether in the circumstances such notice was required and was a condition precedent to the right to maintain this common law action for negligence. . . .   ◀

The statutory provision referred to is given below, together with portions of the textual context.

General Laws of Massachusetts (Tercentenary Edition)
Title XIV—Public Ways and Works
Chapter 84—Repair of Ways and Bridges

(*Section 15 to 26* of Chapter 84 concern the damages which under some circumstances can be recovered by persons injured as a result of defects on public ways.)

(*Section 17* introduces the subject of the possible liability of a county, city, or town for injuries "sustained upon a public way by reason of snow or ice thereon.")

Section 18 then provides that "A person so injured shall, within ten days thereafter, if such defect or want of repair is caused by or consists in part of snow or ice, or both . . . give to the county, city, town or person by law obliged to keep said way in repair, notice of the name and place of residence of the person injured, and the time, place and cause of such injury or damage; and if the said county, city, town or person does not pay the amount thereof, he may recover the same in an action of tort if brought within two years after the date of such injury or damage." (Two further sentences give more details about the sufficiency of the notice.)

Section 19 begins: "Such notice shall be in writing, signed by the person injured or by some one on his behalf. . . ." (Further details follow about the serving of notice.)

Section 20 deals with the effects of omissions in the notice.

Section 21 is entitled "Notice to Owners of Private Property." This is the first and only section in Chapter 84 which has to do with accidents occurring on private property. It reads:

> The three preceding sections, so far as they relate to notices of injuries resulting from snow and ice, shall apply to actions against persons founded upon the defective condition of their premises, or of adjoining ways, when caused by or consisting in part of snow or ice; provided, that notice within thirty days after the injury shall be sufficient, and that if by reason of physical or mental incapacity it is impossible for the injured person to give the notice within thirty days after the injury, he may give it within thirty days after such incapacity has been removed, and in case of his death . . . his executor or administrator may give the notice within thirty days after his appointment. Such notice may be given by posting it in a conspicuous place on such premises and by leaving it with any person occupying the whole or any part of such premises, if there be such a person, and no notice shall be invalid by reason of any inaccuracy or misstatement in respect to the owner's name if it appears that the mistake was made in good faith and did not prevent or unreasonably delay the owner from receiving actual notice of the injury and of the contention that it occurred from the defective condition of his premises or of a way adjoining the same.

Now for the rest of Justice Williams' very brief opinion for the court:

► . . . In *DePrizio v. F. W. Woolworth Co.*, 291 Mass. 143, it was decided that the statutory notice must be given where a personal injury was caused by a defective condition within the defendant's building created by snow which had been tracked in from the outside. It was there said that the statute "applies to all snow and ice made the basis of action, whether inside or outside the building and whether of natural or artificial origin." See also *Walsh v. Riverway Drug Store Inc.*, 311 Mass. 326, 328. *Whalen v. Railway Express Agency, Inc.*, 321 Mass. 382. The injury to the plaintiff was caused not by the tortious act of either of the defendants in throwing ice which struck the plaintiff, as in *Mallen v. James A. Houston Co.*, 211 Mass. 298, but by the defective condition of the floor. The plaintiff's action is founded upon this condition and she is not relieved from giving the written notice required by the statute either by the fact that Mrs. Hiatt's negligence caused the defective condition or that Mrs. Hiatt was personally present and knew of the plaintiff's fall.

Exceptions sustained. Judgment for the defendants.   ◄

If the court had any difficulty deciding this case, the short and unrevealing opinion gives no hint of it. Yet the result is surely surprising. An employee slips on a piece of ice that her employer has allowed to remain on the kitchen floor. The accident, the jury finds, was caused entirely by her employer's negligence, not at all by her own. If she had slipped on a child's toy, a spoon, or a banana peel under similar circumstances, she would undoubtedly have recovered damages from her employer. But having slipped instead on a piece of refrigerator ice, she recovered no damages at all. The defendants' lawyer had the inspiration to argue that under Section 21 of Chapter 84—the chapter in the Massachusetts General Laws that deals with "Repair of Ways and Bridges"—the plaintiff could recover damages from the defendants only if she gave them written notice within thirty days of the accident. Since she had not given such notice, the court held that she could not recover.

Of course, a literal, "plain meaning" reading of the statute makes the result seem unavoidable. After all, Section 21 refers to the "premises" of property-owners (and a kitchen is certainly a part of the premises), and to "snow and ice" (which would seem to include all ice, natural and artificial—as the court had earlier noted in the *DePrizio* case, which is cited). Nor does the statute say that it is unnecessary for the plaintiff to give written notice in instances where the property-owner witnessed the accident.

If the result in the *Smith* case is unsatisfactory, who is to blame? The plaintiff's lawyer, for not having advised his client to give timely written notice of her accident? Maybe so, but you might ask yourself whether, if you were a lawyer and a woman came to you for legal advice after suffering an accident like Mrs. Smith's, you would have thought of the possible applicability of a section of the "Repair of Ways and Bridges" chapter of the state statutes.

Shall we blame the legislators? The fault is certainly theirs, in part. As we noted in Chapter 5, statutory provisions are sometimes *too* specific and detailed. These sections in Chapter 84 of the Massachusetts Laws are a good example. When an unusual case arises that seems to be covered by the words of a very detailed statute, many judges feel obliged to interpret the words literally, even though they may wonder whether the legislators really foresaw the particular situation. The use of very detailed language inevitably suggests to the judges that the drafters chose their words with great care and intended them to be taken literally. Such language seems to deny the judges any implied authority to fill in the gaps. The absence of deliberately imprecise, general words in Section 21 or the sections that immediately precede it militates against a common-sense, purpose-oriented interpretation on the part of the judges.

Are the judges, then, free from blame? Surely not. Although the opinion in the *Smith* case does not refer to the "plain meaning" rule, the court clearly felt that the words were so plain that they must be applied literally, with no regard for purpose or policy. Yet if the key words had been read in context, the shocking result would have been avoided.

Section 21 is one of a series of sections in Chapter 84 ("Repair of Ways and Bridges") of Title XIV ("Public Ways and Works") which deals with liability for accidents caused by snow and ice produced by cold weather. In an earlier case, the Supreme Judicial Court of Massachusetts had described the underlying purpose of the statute as follows:

> In our climate defects so far as caused by ice or snow may be very transient; the manifest purpose of this and similar statutes is to give to the person charged with neglect prompt notice, so that he may have a reasonable chance to examine into the cause of complaint and collect evidence of the facts.

Having once determined that this was the statutory purpose, how could the court in a later case find Section 21 to be applicable to an accident caused by refrigerator ice on a kitchen floor? How could it read "premises" and "snow and ice" as isolated words, disregarding their textual context? No doubt the legislators realized that their enactment would be applied to situations they had not foreseen. But is there any possible justification for the court's assumption that the legislature's purposes extended to a situation so completely different from those originally contemplated? [8]

In general practice, the attitudes of legislators have a powerful influence on the manner in which judges interpret statutes, and the attitudes of judges, in turn, have a powerful influence on the way in which legislators frame statutes. When, for example, legislators draft laws that are very specific and detailed, judges conclude that they must read the laws literally, with little or no concern for the underlying purpose of the legislation. And when judges make a practice of interpreting statutes in a literal, word-oriented fashion, the legislators often feel obliged to write detailed and specific statutes covering all the fact-situations they can think of, in the belief that the judges are unwilling to accept the responsibility for making sensible, purposive interpretations of the statutory language.

PROBLEM

Suppose a state legislature has recently enacted a statute designed to prohibit price-fixing agreements among sellers of goods and services. The provisions of the new law cover business firms and "all self-employed persons engaged in business or trade."

Now suppose that somebody brings a lawsuit under the new act against several physicians who, he says, have caused him injury by their price-fixing activities. The defendants demur: regardless of whether the facts alleged are true, the law does not apply to them, they say, because

---

[8] Our surmise that the legislature's purpose in enacting the statutory provisions in question was not broad enough to cover the accident in the *Smith* case receives some indirect support from the legislature's action three years after the case was decided. In 1955 it amended Section 21 by inserting (after the first appearance of the words "snow and ice") the words "resulting from rain or snow and weather conditions."

It may be argued, of course, that literal interpretations by judges are valuable precisely because they compel legislatures to amend defective statutes. But this is a weak defense of unimaginative decision-making. Legislatures cannot be counted on to make all the needed revisions in the law, as we have seen—partly because they are so busy. In any event, why should people like the plaintiff in *Smith v. Hiatt* have to suffer just so that the court can discipline the legislature? If an unjust result can be avoided by adopting a sensible, purpose-oriented interpretation that limits the scope of words like "premises" and "snow and ice," surely the court should adopt that interpretation.

they are *not* "engaged in business or trade." The trial judge's judgment overruling this demurrer has been appealed to the state supreme court.

Several years earlier, the state legislature adopted a statute imposing a special tax on certain classes of persons and organizations, but specifically exempting (presumably because they were thought to be sufficiently taxed under existing levies) "all self-employed persons engaged in business or trade." Thus, the phrases in the two statutes were identical. For understandable reasons, physicians were eager to be classified as persons "engaged in business or trade" under this earlier statute, and rejoiced when the state supreme court so classified them in a case in which it interpreted the provision.

The question now before the supreme court is whether its decision that physicians *were* "engaged in business or trade" under the tax statute obliges it to classify them similarly under the anti-price-fixing law. What do you think? Give reasons for your answer.

The Use of Legislative History

Since the text of a statute is the final, official embodiment of the legislature's efforts, it is obviously the first place that judges must look in their search for purpose. More often than not, they can find the purpose or policy behind the statute by reading it, bearing in mind what they know of its circumstantial context. But sometimes this is not enough; sometimes the most careful reading of the language will reveal no underlying purpose that is readily applicable to the problem before the court. Faced with this situation, the judges may turn to other sources of evidence of the legislative purpose. Of these the most important is the statute's "legislative history"—the proceedings in the legislature which led to its enactment.

The most significant items of evidence in the legislative history, as we have already suggested, are undoubtedly the reports of the committees that worked on the bill and the statements made for the record by the chairmen or spokesmen of those committees. This is because legislatures ordinarily accept the work of their committees on matters of detail and merely vote to ratify the purposes that the committees have announced. Where different bills have been voted by the two houses and have had to be reconciled (see page 88), the reports of the members of the conference committee to their respective houses are also valuable. Also consulted, though less reliable, are speeches made during debate on the bill, testimony received in committee hearings, and recorded votes on amendments.

Judges have not always been willing to hear evidence of a statute's legislative history; indeed, in many jurisdictions such evidence is not considered even today. In many states the use of legislative history is effectively prevented by the absence or inadequacy of records of legislative proceedings.

For many years the United States Supreme Court was reluctant to consider evidence of legislative history. Its opinions echoed the "plain meaning" approach that we encountered in the *Temple* opinion. Only if the language of the statute before it was "of doubtful meaning and susceptible on its face of two constructions" (to quote one of its opinions) would the Court consider evidence of legislative history. If the language was plain, it would look no farther even though the result produced by applying the "plain meaning" might seem questionable. In 1940, however, a majority of the Court joined in expressing a much more receptive view: whenever there could be any doubt about the legislature's purpose—even though the literal meaning of the language was clear—a consideration of legislative history might be appropriate. This 1940 opinion is worth quoting at some length; it probably represents the present position of the Supreme Court, and of many other judges today.

> There is, of course, no more persuasive evidence of the purpose of a statute than the words by which the legislature undertook to give expression to its wishes. Often these words are sufficient in and of themselves to determine the purpose of the legislation. In such cases we have followed their plain meaning. When that meaning has led to absurd or futile results, however, this Court has looked beyond the words to the purpose of the act. Frequently, however, even when the plain meaning did not produce absurd results but merely an unreasonable one "plainly at variance with the policy of the legislation as a whole" this Court has followed that purpose, rather than the literal words. When aid to construction of the meaning of words, as used in the statute, is available, there certainly can be no "rule of law" which forbids its use, however clear the words may appear on "superficial examination." The interpretation of the meaning of statutes, as applied to justiciable controversies, is exclusively a judicial function. This duty requires one body of public servants, the judges, to construe the meaning of what another body, the legislators, has said. Obviously there is danger that the courts' conclusion as to legislative purpose will be unconsciously influenced by the judges' own views or by factors not considered by the enacting body. A lively appreciation of the danger is the best assurance of escape from its threat but hardly justifies an acceptance of a literal interpretation dogma which withholds from the courts available information for reaching a correct conclusion. . . .
>
> (*United States v. American Trucking Associations*, 310 U.S. 534 [1940].)

Many judges are still reluctant, however, to open the door to legislative history. This is not just a sign of judicial conservatism. The evidence provided by legislative history is often meager, contradictory, and hard to appraise. Much of what legislators say and do while they are acting on a bill cannot be trusted as an indication of the collective intention. Morevoer, now that legislators know that courts will look at the legislative record, they are occasionally tempted to try to "manufacture" legislative history.[9] Finally,

---

[9] Senator Mugwump, who represents a widget-manufacturing community, rises during debate on a tax bill to remark: "Naturally the excise tax which this bill establishes does not fall on widgets." Nobody contradicts him—possibly because nobody is listening. Later, when the widget manufacturers are claiming exemption from the tax, they point to Senator Mugwump's uncontradicted statement as evidence of the legislative purpose. (Competent judges would presumably not accept this assertion by a single legislator as proof of a legislative intention to exempt widgets.)

We are not suggesting that statements inserted into the record for the purpose of creating evidence of legislative intention are always unreliable. Normally, committee reports and statements by committee members are prompted, at least in part, by a desire to help addressees to interpret a piece of legislation.

the practice of reviewing evidence of legislative history may be burdensome for litigants. Once they know that the courts will look at this kind of evidence, lawyers may feel that in all cases involving problems of statutory interpretation they must pore over the legislative records for evidence to put in their briefs. But often these records are not readily accessible in local law libraries, and searching through them is a time-consuming job that may prove a waste of time in the end.

To illustrate the courts' use of legislative history, we have chosen the case of *Schwegmann Brothers v. Calvert Distilleries Corporation,* which was decided by the United States Supreme Court in 1952. The issue of interpretation in this case was relatively complex, and a few background facts may help you to understand it.

The object of Section 1 of the Sherman Act, which Congress enacted in 1890,[10] was to prohibit all agreements designed to fix the prices of goods and services. The primary aim was to prevent agreements between competing sellers of competing products, but in 1911 the Supreme Court held that the act also applied to minimum-price agreements between the manufacturer of a product and retailers selling the product. (Such agreements are sometimes known as "fair trade" agreements.) In 1936 Congress passed the Miller-Tydings Act, which was designed to supersede this 1911 ruling. The Miller-Tydings Act, the interpretation of which was at issue in the *Schwegmann* case, provided that, in any state in which local "fair trade" agreements were legalized by state law, such agreements should also be considered legal under federal law. In other words, the states could remove such agreements from the federal ban on price-fixing imposed by the Sherman Act.

By 1952, Louisiana—like most of the other states—had a law on its books that legalized fair trade agreements. Like most other state laws, Louisiana's contained a clause (known as a "nonsigner clause") which provided that, once a producer and a single retailer within the state had signed a fair trade agreement, any other retailer knowing of the agreement who thereafter sold the producer's product for less than the price stipulated in the agreement would be guilty of "unfair competition" and could be sued by the producer—even though the retailer had not himself signed an agreement.

The plaintiffs in *Schwegmann* were liquor distributors. They went to court for an injunction to prevent a "nonsigner" retailer from selling their product at less than the "fair trade" price established by agreements signed with other Louisiana retailers. The issue raised in the Supreme Court, to which the defendant appealed from adverse decisions in the lower courts, was whether the Miller-Tydings Act, which clearly permitted state legislatures to exempt voluntary fair trade agreements from the federal law against price-fixing, also permitted the states by their "nonsigner clauses" to give those agreements a much greater scope than they would otherwise have.

(The opinions are long, and we have omitted most of the paragraphs which do not concern legislative history. We have also omitted numerous

---

[10] Section 1 is quoted on page 96.

footnotes and two appendices. As you read this case, notice what kinds of evidence of legislative history judges look at, and what kinds of inference they are prepared to draw from that evidence. Note particularly that Justice Douglas for the majority and Justice Frankfurter for the dissenters draw opposite conclusions from the same evidence. And pay special attention to the arguments against all but the most restricted use of legislative history which Justice Jackson advances in his concurring opinion.)

SCHWEGMANN BROTHERS v. CALVERT DISTILLERIES CORPORATION

Supreme Court of the United States, 1952
341 U.S. 384, 71 S.Ct. 745

► Mr. Justice Douglas delivered the opinion of the Court.

Respondents [appellees], Maryland and Delaware corporations, are distributors of gin and whiskey. They sell their products to wholesalers in Louisiana, who in turn sell to retailers. Respondents have a price-fixing scheme whereby they try to maintain uniform retail prices for their products. They endeavor to make retailers sign price-fixing contracts under which the buyers promise to sell at not less than the prices stated in respondents' schedules. They have indeed succeeded in getting over one hundred Louisiana retailers to sign these agreements. Petitioner [appellant], a retailer in New Orleans, refused to agree to the price-fixing scheme and sold respondents' products at a cut-rate price. Respondents thereupon brought this suit in the District Court to enjoin petitioner from selling the products at less than the minimum prices fixed by their schedules. [The District Court granted the injunction, and its decision was sustained by the Court of Appeals.]

It is clear from our decisions under the Sherman Act that this interstate marketing arrangement would be illegal, that it would be enjoined, that it would draw civil and criminal penalties, and that no court would enforce it. Fixing minimum prices, like other types of price fixing, is illegal *per se.* Resale price maintenance was indeed struck down in Dr. Miles Medical Co. v. John D. Park & Sons Co., 220 U.S. 373 [1911]. The fact that a state authorizes the price fixing does not, of course, give immunity to the scheme, absent approval by Congress.

Respondents, however, seek to find legality for this marketing arrangement in the Miller-Tydings Act enacted in 1937 as an amendment to § 1 of the Sherman Act. That amendment provides in material part that "nothing herein contained shall render illegal *contracts or agreements* prescribing minimum prices for the resale" of specified commodities when *"contracts or agreements of that description* are lawful as applied to intrastate transactions" under local law. [Italics added by the Court.]

Louisiana has such a law. It permits a "contract" for the sale or resale of a commodity to provide that the buyer will not resell "except at the price stipulated by the vendor." The Louisiana statute goes further. It not only allows a distributor and retailer to make a "contract" fixing the resale price; but once there is a price-fixing "contract," known to a seller, with any retailer in the state, it also condemns as unfair competition a sale at less than the price stipulated even though the seller is not a party to the "contract." In other words, the Louisiana statute enforces price fixing not only against parties to a "contract" but also against nonsigners. So far as Louisiana law is concerned, price fixing can be enforced against all retailers once any single retailer agrees with a distributor on the resale price. And the argument is that the Miller-Tydings Act permits the same range of price fixing. . . .

We note to begin with that there are critical differences between Louisiana's law and the Miller-Tydings Act. . . . We start then with a federal act which does not, as respondents suggest, turn over to the states the handling of the whole problem of resale price maintenance on this type of commodity. What is granted is a limited immunity—a limitation that is further emphasized by the inclusion in the state law and the exclusion from the federal law of the nonsigner provision. The omission of the nonsigner provision from the federal law is fatal to respondents' position unless we are to perform a distinct legislative function by reading into the Act a provision that was meticulously omitted from it. . . .

The contrary conclusion would have a vast and devastating effect on Sherman Act policies. If it were adopted, once a distributor executed a contract with a single retailer setting the minimum resale price for a commodity in the state, all other retailers could be forced into line. Had Congress desired to eliminate the consensual element from the arrangement and to permit blanketing a state with resale price fixing if only one retailer wanted it, we feel that different measures would have been adopted—either a nonsigner provision would have been included or resale price fixing would have been authorized without more. Certainly the words used connote a voluntary scheme. Contracts or agreements convey the idea of a cooperative arrangement, not a program whereby recalcitrants are dragged in by the heels and compelled to submit to price fixing.

The history of the Act supports this construction. The efforts to override the rule of Dr. Miles Medical Co. v. Park & Sons Co., *supra*, were long and persistent. Many bills had been introduced on this subject before Senator Tydings introduced his. Thus in 1929, in the Seventy-First Congress, the Capper-Kelly fair trade bill was offered. It had no nonsigner provision. It merely permitted resale price maintenance as respects specified classes of commodities by declaring that no such "contract relating to the sale or resale" shall be unlawful. As stated in the House Report, that bill merely legalized an agreement "that the vendee will not resell the commodity specified in the contract except at a stipulated price." That bill became the model for the California act passed in 1931—the first state act permitting resale price maintenance. The California act contained no nonsigner clause. Neither did the Capper-Kelly bill that was introduced in the Seventy-Second Congress. So far as material here it was identical with its predecessor.

The Capper-Kelly bill did not pass. And by the time the next bill was introduced—three years later—the California act had been changed by the addition of the nonsigner provision. That was in 1933. Yet when in 1936 Senator Tydings introduced his first bill in the Seventy-Fourth Congress he followed substantially the Capper-Kelly bills and wrote no nonsigner provision into it. His bill merely legalized "contracts or agreements prescribing minimum prices or other conditions for the resale" of a commodity. By this date several additional states had resale price maintenance laws with nonsigner provisions. Even though the state laws were the models for the federal bills, the nonsigner provision was never added. That was true of the bill introduced in the Seventy-Fifth Congress as well as the subsequent one. They all followed in this respect the pattern of the Capper-Kelly bill as it appeared before the first nonsigner provision was written into state law. The "contract" concept utilized by Capper-Kelly before there was a nonsigner provision in state law was thus continued even after the nonsigner provision appeared. The inference, therefore, is strong that there was continuity between the first Tydings bill and the preceding Capper-Kelly bills. The Tydings bills built on the same foundation; they were no more concerned with nonsigner provisions than were their predecessors. In view of this history we can only conclude that, if the draftsman intended that the nonsigning retailer was to be coerced, it was strange indeed that he omitted the one clear provision that would have accomplished that result.

An argument is made from the reports and debates to the effect that "contracts or agreements" nevertheless includes the nonsigner provisions of state law. The Senate Report on the first Tydings bill, after stating that the California law authorized a distributor "to make a contract that the purchaser will not resell" except at the stipulated price, said that the proposed federal law "does no more than to remove Federal obstacles to the enforcement of contracts which the States themselves have declared lawful." The Senate Report on the second Tydings bill, which was introduced in the Seventy-Fifth Congress, did little more than reprint the earlier report. The House Report, heavily relied on here, gave a more extended analysis.

The House Report referred to the state fair trade acts as authorizing the maintenance of resale prices by contract and as providing that "third parties with notice are bound by the terms of such a contract regardless of whether they are parties to it;" and the Report also stated that the objective of the Act was to permit the public policy of the states having such acts to operate with respect to interstate contracts for the sale of goods. *This Report is the strongest statement for respondents' position which is found in the legislative history.*[11] The bill which that Report endorsed, however, did not pass. The bill which became the law was attached by the Senate Committee on the District of Columbia as a rider to the District of Columbia revenue bill. In that form it was debated and passed.

It is true that the *House Report quoted above was referred to when the Senate amendment to the revenue measure was before the House. And one Congressman in the debate said that the nonsigner provision of state laws was validated by the federal law.*

But we do not take these remarks at face value. In the first place, the House Report, while referring to the nonsigner provision when describing

---

[11] Where not otherwise indicated, italics have been added by the authors.

a typical state fair trade act, is so drafted that the voluntary contract is the core of the argument for the bill. Hence, the General Statement in the Report states that the sole objective of the Act was to "permit the public policy of States having 'fair trade acts' to operate with respect to interstate *contracts* for the resale of goods;" and the fair trade acts are referred to as legalizing "the maintenance, *by contracts,* of resale prices of branded or trade-marked goods." [Italics added by the Court.]

In the second place, the remarks relied on were not only about a bill on which no vote was taken; they were about a bill which sanctioned "contracts or agreements" prescribing not only "minimum prices" but "other conditions" as well. The words "other conditions" were dropped from the amendment that was made to the revenue bill. Why they were deleted does not appear. . . . It might well be argued that one of the "conditions" attaching to a contract fixing a minimum price would be the liability of a nonsigner. We do no more than stir the doubt, for the doubt alone is enough to make us skeptical of the full implications of the old report as applied to a new and different bill.

We look for more definite clues; and we find the following statement made on the floor by Senator Tydings: "What does the amendment do? It permits a man who manufactures an article to state the minimum resale price of the article in a contract with the man who buys it for ultimate resale to the public. . . ." *Not once did Senator Tydings refer to the non- signer provisions of state law.* Not once did he suggest that the amendment would affect anyone but the retailer who signs the contract. *We search the words of the sponsors for a clear indication that coercive as well as voluntary schemes or arrangements are permissible. We find none.* What we do find is the expression of fear in the minority report of the Senate Committee that the nonsigner provisions of the state laws would be made effective if the law passed. These fears were presented in the Senate de- bate by Senator King in opposition to the amendment. But the Senate Re- port emphasized the "permissive" nature of the state laws, not once point- ing to their coercive features.

The fears and doubts of the opposition are no authoritative guide to the construction of legislation. It is the sponsors that we look to when the meaning of the statutory words is in doubt. And when we read what the sponsors wrote and said about the amendment, we cannot find that the distributors were to have the right to use not only a *contract* to fix retail prices but a *club* as well. The words they used—"contracts or agreements"— suggest just the contrary. [Italics by the Court.]

It should be remembered that it was the state laws that the federal law was designed to accommodate. Federal regulation was to give way to state regulation. When state regulation provided for resale price maintenance by both those who contracted and those who did not, and the federal regu- lation was relaxed only as respects "contracts or agreements," *the inference is strong that Congress left the noncontracting group to be governed by pre-existing law.* In other words, since Congress was writing a law to meet the specifications of state law, it would seem that if the nonsigner pro- vision as well as the "contract" provision of state law were to be written into federal law, the pattern of the legislation would have been different.

We could conclude that Congress carved out the vast exception from the Sherman Act now claimed only if we were willing to assume that it took a devious route and yet failed to make its purpose plain.

Reversed.

MR. JUSTICE JACKSON, whom MR. JUSTICE MINTON joins, concurring.

I agree with the Court's judgment and with its opinion insofar as it rests upon the language of the Miller-Tydings Act. But it does not appear that there is either necessity or propriety in going back of it into legislative history.

Resort to legislative history is only justified where the face of the Act is inescapably ambiguous, and then I think we should not go beyond Committee reports, which presumably are well considered and carefully prepared. I cannot deny that I have sometimes offended against that rule. *But to select casual statements from floor debates, not always distinguished for candor or accuracy,* as a basis for making up our minds what law Congress intended to enact is to substitute ourselves for the Congress in one of its important functions. The Rules of the House and Senate, with the sanction of the Constitution, require three readings of an Act in each House before final enactment. That is intended, I take it, to make sure that each House knows what it is passing and passes what it wants, and that what is enacted was formally reduced to writing. *It is the business of Congress to sum up its own debates in its legislation. Moreover, it is only the words of the bill that have presidential approval, where that approval is given. It is not to be supposed that, in signing a bill, the President endorses the whole Congressional Record.* For us to undertake to reconstruct an enactment from legislative history is merely to involve the Court in political controversies which are quite proper in the enactment of a bill but should have no place in its interpretation.

Moreover, there are practical reasons why we should accept whenever possible the meaning which an enactment reveals on its face. Laws are intended for all of our people to live by; and the people go to law offices to learn what their rights under those laws are. *Here is a controversy which affects every little merchant in many States. Aside from a few offices in the larger cities, the materials of legislative history are not available to the lawyer* who can afford neither the cost of acquisition, the cost of housing, or the cost of repeatedly examining the whole congressional history. Moreover, if he could, he would not know any way of anticipating what would impress enough members of the Court to be controlling. To accept legislative debates to modify statutory provisions is to make the law inaccessible to a large part of the country.

By and large, I think our function was well stated by Mr. Justice Holmes: "We do not inquire what the legislature meant; we ask only what the statute means." And I can think of no better example of legislative history that is unedifying and unilluminating than that of the Act before us.

MR. JUSTICE FRANKFURTER, whom MR. JUSTICE BLACK and MR. JUSTICE BURTON join, dissenting.

. . . It would appear that, insofar as the Sherman Law made maintenance of minimum resale prices illegal, the Miller-Tydings Amendment made it legal to the extent that State law legalized it. "Contracts or agreements" immunized by the Miller-Tydings Amendment surely cannot have a narrower scope than "contract, combination . . . or conspiracy" in the Sherman Law. The Miller-Tydings Amendment is an amendment to § 1 of the Sherman Law. The category of contract cannot be given different content in the very same section of the same act, and every combination or conspiracy implies an agreement.

The setting of the Miller-Tydings Amendment and its legislative history remove any lingering doubts. The depression following 1929 gave impetus to the movement for legislation which would allow the fixing of minimum resale prices. In 1931, California passed a statute allowing a manufacturer to establish resale prices binding only upon retailers who voluntarily entered into a contract with him. This proved completely ineffective, and in in 1933 California amended her statute to provide that such a contract established a minimum price binding upon any person who had notice of the contract. This amendment was the so-called "non-signer" clause which, in effect, allowed a manufacturer or wholesaler to fix a minimum resale price for his product. Every "fair trade" law thereafter passed by any State contained this "non-signer" clause. By the close of 1936, 14 States had passed such laws. In 1937, 28 more States passed them. Today, 45 out of 48 States have "fair trade" laws.

A substantial obstacle remained in the path of the "fair trade" movement. In 1911, we had decided Dr. Miles Medical Co. v. Park & Sons Co., 220 U.S. 373. There, in a suit brought against a "non-signer," we held that an agreement to maintain resale prices was a "contract . . . in restraint of trade" which was contrary to the Sherman Law. To remove this block, the Miller-Tydings Amendment was enacted. It is said, however, that thereby Congress meant only to remove the bar of the Sherman Law from agreements between the manufacturer and retailer, that Congress did not mean to make valid the "non-signer" clause which formed an integral part of each of the 42 State statutes in effect when the Amendment was passed.

The Miller-Tydings Amendment was passed as a rider to a Revenue Bill for the District of Columbia. The Senate Committee which attached the rider referred the Senate to S. Rep. No. 2053, 74th Cong., 2d Sess. The House Conference Report contains only five lines concerning the rider. But the rider was not a new measure. It came as no surprise to the House, which already had before it practically the same language in the Miller Bill, reported favorably by the Committee on the Judiciary. H.R. Rep. No. 382, 75th Cong., 1st Sess. Both the House and Senate, therefore, had before them reports dealing with the substance of the Miller-Tydings Amendment. These reports speak for themselves, and I attach them as appendices to this opinion.[12] *Every State act referred to in these reports contained a "non-signer" provision. I cannot see how, in view of these reports, we can*

---

[12] These appendices, containing the reports of the House and Senate Judiciary Committees recommending the Miller and Tydings bills, respectively, to the two houses, provide further support for Justice Frankfurter's interpretation of the legislative history.

conclude that Congress meant the "non-signer" provisions to be invalid under the Sherman Law—unless, that is, we are to depart from the respect we have accorded authoritative legislative history in scores of cases during the last decade. . . . In many of these cases the purpose of Congress was far less clearly revealed than here. It has never been questioned in this Court that committee reports, as well as statements by those in charge of a bill or of a report, are authoritative elucidations of the scope of a measure.

It is suggested that we go to the words of the sponsors of the Miller-Tydings Amendment. We have done so. Their words confirm the plain meaning of the words of the statute and of the congressional reports. Senator Tydings made the following statement: "What we have attempted to do is what 42 States have already written on their statute books. It is simply to back up these acts, that is all; to have a code of fair trade practices written not by a national board such as the N.R.A. but by each State, so that the people may go to the State legislature and correct immediately any abuses that may develop."

Representative Dirksen made a statement to the House as a member of its Conference Committee. He referred to the case of Old Dearborn Co. v. Seagram Corp., 299 U.S. 183, in which this Court had held that the "non-signer" provision of the Illinois "fair trade" statute did not violate the Due Process Clause. Mr. Dirksen continued: "A question then arose as to whether or not maintenance of such resale prices under a State fair trade act might not be in violation of the Sherman Anti-Trust Law of 1890 insofar as these transactions sprang from a contract in interstate commerce. This question was presented to the House Judiciary Committee and there determined by the reporting of the Miller bill. It was essentially nothing more than an enabling act which placed the stamp of approval upon price maintenance transactions under State acts, notwithstanding the Sherman Act of 1890."

Every one of the 42 State acts which the Miller-Tydings Amendment was to "back up"—the acts on which the Miller-Tydings Amendment was to place a "stamp of approval"—contained a "non-signer" provision. As demonstrated by experience in California, *the State acts would have been futile without the "non-signer" clause. The Court now holds that the Miller-Tydings Amendment does not cover these "non-signer" provisions.* Not only is the view of the Court contrary to the words of the statute and to legislative history. It is also *in conflict with the interpretation given the Miller-Tydings Amendment by the Federal Trade Commission, by the Department of Justice, and by practically all persons adversely affected by the "fair trade" laws.* The "fair trade" laws may well be unsound as a matter of economics. Perhaps Congress should not pass an important measure dealing with an extraneous subject as a rider to a revenue bill, with the coercive influence it exerts in avoiding a veto; perhaps it should restrict legislation to a single relevant subject, as required by the constitutions of three-fourths of the States. These are matters beyond the Court's concern. *Where both the words of a statute and its legislative history clearly indicate the purpose of Congress, it should be respected.* We should not substitute our own notions of what Congress should have done.   ◄

COMMENTS AND QUESTIONS

1. What types of evidence of legislative history are referred to in these three opinions? What are the only types of evidence that Justice Jackson thought should be used?
2. Which interpretation of the legislative history do you find more convincing, Justice Douglas's or Justice Frankfurter's? Do you agree with Justice Jackson that the legislative history of the Miller-Tydings Act is "unedifying and unilluminating," or do you think that it supplies a pretty clear answer to the question of legislative purpose that was before the Court?
3. You may find it useful at this point to read *United States v. McKesson & Robbins, Inc.* (page 850), a 1956 case in which the United States Supreme Court again interpreted the Miller-Tydings Act. Once again the majority adopted a restrictive interpretation, over protests from three dissenters that the majority view ignored Congress's obvious purpose in passing the act. In both cases the dissenting opinions suggested that the majority justices were influenced by their disapproval of the legislation.

Other Aids to Statutory Interpretation

Private and Administrative Interpretations

We have said that when the courts cannot discover the purpose underlying a statutory provision by examining the statute itself, they may turn to other sources of evidence. Since it is the legislature's purpose that they are seeking, the most important of these sources is the legislative history of the statute. But judges are aware that legislatures often count on the primary addressees of a statute, both private and official, to fill in some of the gaps themselves. Hence they may sometimes be influenced by the interpretations which these addressees adopt.[13]

Private persons and organizations have to work out their own tentative interpretations of a new statute long before any case arising under it comes before the courts. If their interpretations seem to be relatively uniform, and to be motivated by a desire to comply with the law rather than by a search for loopholes in it, they may influence the interpretations adopted by the court. Likewise, the interpretations which administrative officials adopt in the course of administering a statute may be taken into account by the judges who later must work out a definitive interpretation. The administrators usually have specialized experience in the area regulated, and their interpretations are likely to be molded to fit the practical problems of administration. Judges should normally hesitate to adopt an interpretation at variance with a well-established administrative interpretation.[14]

---

[13] For an example, look back at the final paragraph of Justice Frankfurter's dissent in *Schwegmann*, in which he referred to interpretations of the Miller-Tydings Act adopted by two government agencies and by affected private parties.

[14] We are speaking here of the less formal interpretations adopted by administrators, not of the regulations that some agencies issue under authority expressly delegated to them by legislatures. These formal, published regulations are treated by the courts as having the force of law. See Chapter 8.

Prior Judicial Interpretations

When a court must apply a statutory provision in a case, what weight should it give to earlier judicial interpretations of the provision? Does the *stare decisis* principle oblige a court to follow prior interpretations even if they seem wrong? Or is the court free to return to the language and legislative history of the statute in search of a better interpretation?

One view is that, when a court is convinced that an earlier interpretation is wrong, it should adopt a new interpretation in order to give proper effect to the legislative purpose. This is particularly necessary, it is argued, because legislatures so often fail to exercise their power to pass new laws correcting erroneous interpretations. If courts are unwilling to get rid of bad interpretations, the interpretations are likely to remain in effect indefinitely.

The prevailing view, probably, is that decisions interpreting statutes should exert approximately the same control over the future as do decisions interpreting common-law rules, and for essentially the same reason. People should be able to plan their conduct on the assumption that, once an appellate court has interpreted a statutory provision, it will normally adhere to that interpretation in later cases. Most judges refuse to accept the view that the inability of legislatures to review and revise decisional rules is sufficient reason for courts to ignore the precedents they have established.

The Occasional Need for Creative Judicial Lawmaking

In a large majority of cases involving the application of statutory provisions, the meaning of the statute is so clear that no real problems of interpretation arise. In a smaller number of cases, interpretation is more difficult. But even in most of these, the judges can reach a satisfactory solution by examining the language of the statutory provision in its textual and circumstantial context. Occasionally they find it useful to look also at the legislative history, or at private or administrative interpretations. Sometimes the provision has already been interpreted by a court.

Once in a while, however, judges find that all their efforts to discover the legislative purpose of a statute are in vain. It simply is not clear how the statute applies to the case before them. In those cases the judges must do just what they do when faced with a case for which there are no precedents. They must perform a creative act of lawmaking. In all likelihood this is exactly what the legislature, unwilling to prescribe details for an unknown future, counted on them to do. It is the duty of judges to infer a purpose that is applicable to a particular case from what they know of the legislature's broader purposes and of the shared purposes and aims of the community. So long as they forward these broad purposes and not private purposes of their own, they are acting within the limits of the judicial function.

7 Judicial Lawmaking III: Interpreting the Constitution

In the last five chapters we have been speaking about how the courts and legislatures make and apply the rules that channel private conduct. We have taken for granted the authority of those bodies to make and apply legal rules. But think for a moment of a citizen who finds his activities thwarted by a statute or a decision or an administrative ruling that he considers outrageous. Such a citizen might well begin to wonder about the source of the authority that is being exercised by those whose actions have proved so annoying. If he explored the matter, he would learn that the ultimate source of all official authority in the American system are the constitutions, and that the rules about official authority stated in those constitutions or developed through judicial interpretation are known collectively as "constitutional law."

The present chapter describes how constitutional rules are created, and how they evolve as new cases involving constitutional issues are decided. Although the United States has fifty-one constitutions, we shall speak only about the federal Constitution, since it is far more important in the lives of most of us than any of the fifty state constitutions. Much of what we have to say about the federal Constitution, however, is applicable to the state constitutions as well.

Some Examples of Constitutional Issues

Here are a few examples of constitutional controversies, based on actual cases brought before the Supreme Court of the United States by parties challenging as "unconstitutional" the action of governmental officials or bodies:

1. Seeking to avert a threatened strike, the President of the United States orders federal officials to seize and operate the nation's steel mills. The steel companies challenge his power to do so under Article II of the Constitution, which deals with the powers and duties of the President.

2. Congress enacts a heavy tax on the sale of colored oleomargarine and a much lighter tax on uncolored oleomargarine, with the avowed object of restricting the sale of oleomargarine colored to resemble butter.

A dealer refuses to pay the tax, claiming that Congress's power to tax under Article I cannot be used to achieve a regulatory objective unrelated to the raising of revenue.

3. An overzealous sheriff in a small town breaks into the offices of a business firm and searches for evidence of illegal sales, even though he has no search warrant. When the firm's owners are brought to trial for unlawful operations, they challenge the admission of the evidence offered against them, on the ground that it has been illegally obtained and that admitting it would violate the "due process" clause of the Fourteenth Amendment, which is supposed to protect individuals against irregular official procedures.

4. A state legislature enacts a "privilege" tax on all persons or corporations not regularly doing business in the state who display samples in hotel rooms for the purpose of securing retail orders. An out-of-state firm pays the tax under protest and then sues for a refund, contending that the tax, by discriminating in favor of intrastate firms, places an unconstitutional burden on interstate commerce.

5. A group of homeowners sign an agreement that none of them will sell their homes to persons "not of the Caucasian race." When one of the signers later sells his home to a Negro, another signer asks a court for an injunction restraining the buyer from taking possession and divesting him of his title. The buyer resists on the ground that for a court to lend its coercive power to the enforcement of a restrictive agreement based on race would be a denial of the "equal protection of the laws" guaranteed by the Fourteenth Amendment.

American Constitutions

When an American thinks of a constitution, he thinks of a written document adopted by some sort of representative body.[1] The fifty states and the federal Union each have such a document. Constitutions typically perform three functions: They prescribe the structure, organization, and major duties of the legislative, executive, and judicial branches of government. They allocate power between the respective levels of government—that is, between the central and local authorities. Finally, having established and allocated power, constitutions place restrictions on the exercise of that power, specifying what governments may *not* do.

New constitutions (and major revisions of existing ones) are usually *adopted* initially by constitutional conventions—representative bodies especially convened for the purpose. Ordinarily the convention writes into the constitution a procedure under which the constitution must be *ratified* after being adopted by the convention. Ratification is either by popular vote or by the vote of designated representative bodies.[2]

---

[1] In contrast, when the English speak of their constitution, they have no single document in mind; they are referring to the sum of the basic laws and traditions which determine the form and functioning of their government. But the difference is more apparent than real, since American "constitutional law" is by no means limited to the rules explicitly enunciated in constitutional documents.

[2] The federal Constitution provided that ratification by conventions in nine of the

Constitutional *amendments* are normally adopted by legislatures, and then have to be ratified.[3] The amending process is customarily made rather cumbersome, in order to discourage frequent and ill-considered tampering with the fundamental law.

But, as we shall see, the process of formal amendment is not the most important means by which our constitutional law is modified. The federal Constitution has been in effect almost 175 years. In that period—during which the infant nation of 1789 was transformed into the enormously powerful and wealthy giant of today—only twenty-three amendments have been added to the Constitution. (Moreover, ten of those—the so-called "Bill of Rights"—were adopted by the first Congress in 1789, so that realistically they must be considered as a part of the original Constitution.) Some of the amendments have been important, but certainly no more important than the many changes that Americans have made in their constitutional rules without bothering to amend the Constitution. Sometimes they have created and modified institutions in order to bring about these changes: witness the development of the two-party system and of the powerful congressional committees, and the greatly reduced importance of the Electoral College. Many changes, however, are the result of the Supreme Court's reinterpretation of key constitutional phrases.

The Supreme Court as the Final Constitutional Arbiter

Challenges to the constitutionality of an official act may be raised either in a state court or in a lower federal court. Although these courts must rule on such challenges, their decisions have weight only as tentative interpretations, for the definitive interpretations of the Constitution are made by the Supreme Court of the United States.

This is not to say that the Supreme Court hears only cases that raise constitutional issues. Many of its decisions, for instance, involve the interpretation of federal statutes. (The *Schwegmann* case in the preceding chapter is an example, and there are several others in this book.) But the Court's best-known and on the whole its most important cases have involved constitutional questions.

The United States Supreme Court differs from most other appellate courts in one important respect: it has extremely wide discretion in deciding which cases it will hear. For most types of case, the only way to secure a hearing before the Court is to persuade it to grant a "writ of certiorari."[4] Out of the great number of cases that are urged upon it, it accepts only a hundred or so a year for a full hearing. For the cases it refuses to hear, the decision of the lower court becomes final. This arrangement enables the

---

original thirteen states would be sufficient to bring it into effect. Eleven of the states had ratified it before it went into effect in March 1789.

[3] A two-thirds vote by each house of Congress, followed by ratification by three-quarters of the states, is required for amendments to the federal Constitution.

[4] A writ of certiorari is an order from a higher court to a lower court directing it to send up the record of a case for review.

Court to focus its attention on cases that raise novel and important legal issues.

One might expect to find the task of interpreting the words of a constitution not too different from that of interpreting a statute. But the two processes are actually quite different, mainly because of the generality of constitutional language. We have spoken of the "deliberate imprecision" of some statutory provisions, but few statutes are as imprecise as the key phrases in the federal Constitution. The Constitution was designed to endure for centuries; it is difficult to amend and therefore infrequently amended. Consequently, the framers found it advisable to enunciate broad directives in terse and general terms. In effect, the framers delegated to the Supreme Court the responsibility for giving meaning to these provisions by relating them to the particular situations that came before it. Justice Felix Frankfurter has commented that the major constitutional phrases have been "purposely left to gather meaning from experience." Chief Justice Charles Evans Hughes once put the matter even more baldly: "The Constitution is what the Judges say it is."

Take, for instance, the power granted to Congress in Article I to "regulate commerce . . . among the several states." Again and again the Court has had to interpret this broad and imprecise provision. What is the scope of the power to "regulate"? What is "commerce"? What brings an activity into the category of "among the several states"? At different times the Court has given different answers to each of these questions. There have been periods when the Court has acted as if the commerce clause granted almost unlimited regulatory power to the federal government. During other periods it has interpreted the clause restrictively, invalidating federal statutes for exceeding the power granted to Congress.

The two most important clauses in the Fourteenth Amendment are equally imprecise: ". . . [N]or shall any State deprive any person of life, liberty, or property, without due process of law; nor deny to any person within its jurisdiction the equal protection of the laws." The framers of the amendment probably intended the words "due process of law" as a guarantee of fair treatment in police, prosecuting, and trial procedures. But between the 1890's and the early 1930's the justices of the Supreme Court used the due-process clause to strike down various state statutes regulating business which they considered arbitrary and unreasonable. During the next twenty-five years, however, the Court abandoned this broad interpretation of the due-process clause. Similarly, for many years the Court held that the clause guaranteeing "equal protection of the laws" did not stand in the way of officially ordained segregation of the races, so long as the minority races were provided "equal" (though separate) facilities. But more recently the Court has held that the "equal protection" clause makes such segregation unconstitutional.

Examples could be multiplied indefinitely. What is important to recognize is that the Court, guided by its own perception of society's changing needs and values, has been able to forge vague constitutional phrases into effective instruments for expanding or limiting official power. This arrangement imposes a heavy responsibility on the justices, but on the whole they have discharged it admirably. With comparatively few amendments, the Constitution has served as our organic law throughout an era that has seen changes in the nation's size, wealth, and world position, in the conditions of living, and in the role of government, which have far exceeded anything the Founding Fathers could possibly have foreseen.[5]

The Power of Judicial Review

The Supreme Court's power to decide constitutional issues includes the power to decide whether or not the act of another agency of government is permitted by the Constitution. This is often called the power of *judicial review*.

Suppose that an administrative official, at the federal, state, or local level, performs an act which is challenged in court as being in violation of the federal Constitution. Or suppose that a state court renders a decision which is challenged as being in conflict with the federal Constitution. Or suppose that Congress, or a state or local legislative body, passes a law which is said to be unconstitutional. In all these situations, the Supreme Court of the United States has jurisdiction and may be called upon to decide on the constitutionality of the act, decision, or law in question. If it is found to be unconstitutional, it is invalid.

In a federal system of government like ours, there must be some way of assuring that the officials, courts, and legislatures of the states do not exceed the powers permitted by the federal Constitution. The constitutional compact which the original states adopted in 1787 makes it clear that, if the act of any branch of a state or local government ever comes in conflict with the federal Constitution (or with any federal statute or treaty), the latter shall prevail. In the words of Article VI:

> This Constitution, and the laws of the United States which shall be made in pursuance thereof; and all treaties made, or which shall be made, under the authority of the United States, shall be the supreme law of the land; and the judges in every state shall be bound thereby, any thing in the Constitution or laws of any state to the contrary notwithstanding.

Although the state and lower federal courts have authority to decide constitutional issues, their decisions are not necessarily final; ever since the Judiciary Act of 1789, the Supreme Court of the United States has had the ultimate authority to decide whether or not the act of a state official or agency is constitutional. The Supreme Court has exercised this power over state acts since the early days of the Republic, and few people today

---

[5] Some of our state constitutions provide excellent examples of what happens when constitutional documents are *not* deliberately imprecise. They are lengthy and detailed; often they contain provisions concerning matters too transitory in importance to justify inclusion in a constitution at all. Constitutional provisions which are detailed and specific cannot readily be reinterpreted by a court as the need for change becomes apparent. The needed change is therefore thwarted unless it is possible to amend the constitution. As a result, these state constitutions have had to be amended much more often than has the federal Constitution—but, since amending is usually difficult, many desirable amendments have come about slowly or not at all.

seriously question its legitimacy—although particular exercises of that power have aroused great resentment and hostility to the Court.

The constitutional underpinnings of the Court's power to invalidate the acts of the other two branches of the federal government—that is, of Congress and the President—are somewhat less firm. Nowhere does the Constitution state that the Supreme Court has the final say in deciding what limits the Constitution imposes on Congress or the President. There is some evidence to suggest that most of the Founding Fathers assumed that if, in the course of deciding a case duly brought before it, the Court believed that an act of one of the other branches was contrary to the Constitution, it could deny legal effect to that act. But if this is indeed what the framers had in mind, they never spelled it out.

The argument that each branch of the federal government should be the final interpreter of its own powers is not without merit. It is the position taken in a number of other countries. But the issue was settled otherwise in 1803 when Chief Justice John Marshall, in the famous case of *Marbury v. Madison*, declared that the Court was empowered under the Constitution to invalidate an act of Congress. The Court has continued to exercise this power (and the related power to invalidate acts of the Executive). It has used the power sparingly and, on the whole, with a wise caution. On a few occasions, however, it has seriously impaired its own prestige and effectiveness by unwise invalidations of acts of Congress. The *Dred Scott* decision of 1857, for instance, unquestionably hurt the Court, as did the striking down of much of the New Deal legislation in 1935 and 1936.

It is clear today that conflicts over the extent and limits of governmental power were bound to arise, both between federal and state authorities and between the respective branches of the federal government. These conflicts had to be resolved somehow, and the Supreme Court is probably better able to do the job than any other agency. Judges have always had to interpret and apply the provisions of legal documents; interpreting constitutional provisions differs from other tasks of interpretation performed by appellate courts principally in the remarkably broad discretion granted to the judges and in the unusual importance of the issues at stake.

In one respect the Supreme Court is uniquely suited to act as final arbiter on constitutional issues. In our democratic system, Congress and the President are elected by popular majorities and can be expected to respond to majority desires. But one of the unspoken premises of the Constitution is that the majority must not be allowed to deprive racial, religious, ideological, and other minority groups of their rights. Since Supreme Court justices are appointed for life, they are relatively insulated from majority pressures. Consequently they are in a relatively good position to withstand popular opposition when they strike down arbitrary, undemocratic legislation designed to curb or penalize minority groups.

Restraints on the Exercise of Judicial Review

The power to invalidate the legislative and executive acts of popularly elected officials, lodged in the hands of nine justices who are neither chosen by nor subject to removal by the people, would be intolerable if it were not subject to restraints. In the absence of restraints, nothing would prevent the Court from striking down legislation or executive acts simply because a majority of the justices considered them unfair or unwise.

The restraints are of two sorts: (a) "external" restraints imposed by the political environment in which the Court operates; and (b) "internal" restraints which the justices have traditionally imposed on themselves.

THE EXTERNAL RESTRAINTS. The effectiveness of the Court's authority depends in large measure on how much prestige it enjoys in the eyes of the American people. In recent years, the Court's prestige has been remarkably high—even when the Court was under strong attack from certain quarters. But there have been periods when its prestige was low: in the years before 1800, for instance, and in the period following the disastrous *Dred Scott* decision of 1857. The Court has no enforcement arm of its own, and the effectiveness of its decisions depends primarily on the voluntary compliance of the officials concerned (although the executive branch may, if it is willing, aid in their enforcement). A highly unpopular decision may be resisted or ignored. This has not happened often in our history, but on a number of occasions compliance has been far from complete, and the Court's prestige has suffered. So, although the justices have no obligation to respond to every shift in popular sentiment, they cannot afford to get too far out of step with the nation's mood and desires.

Congress has certain powers that could be used to influence or restrict the Court. For example, it has the power to impeach, and it might impeach a justice of whose philosophy it violently disapproved. No justice has ever been removed by impeachment, however (though an attempt was made in 1804), and the prospect of its ever happening seems remote. But a sharp decline in the Court's prestige might bring this extreme measure within the realm of possibility.

Congress also has the power to decide what types of case the Court may hear on appeal. If the Court's decisions became irksome to enough congressmen, Congress might be induced to curtail its jurisdiction in certain areas. Indeed, several bills designed to exclude the Court from hearing certain kinds of case have been introduced in Congress within the past decade; however, the Court's prestige is currently high enough so that the passage of such legislation seems unlikely. But it has happened before,[6] and it could happen again.

Congress also has the power to increase the number of seats on the Court, and if it became sufficiently dissatisfied with the Court's performance, it could authorize the President to appoint enough additional justices to assure a more favorable line of decisions. Since 1869, however, Congress has left the Court's number of justices at nine. In 1937, President Franklin

---

[6] In 1868—when the Court's prestige was still at a low ebb following the *Dred Scott* decision—Congress, fearful lest the Court in deciding on the appeal of one McCardle should invalidate some Reconstruction legislation, passed a law which in effect withdrew the Court's appellate jurisdiction in cases such as McCardle's. Although the justices had already heard arguments in the *McCardle* case, they held (in *Ex parte McCardle*, 1869) that they no longer had jurisdiction to decide the case.

D. Roosevelt proposed that the Court be enlarged. In the preceding two years the justices had struck down a dozen major New Deal laws, and Roosevelt, fresh from his overwhelming re-election in 1936, was convinced that the justices were using the Constitution to thwart policies that the nation needed and wanted. The Roosevelt "court-packing plan," as it was called, aroused violent opposition, however, and in the end was soundly defeated in Congress.

Yet it is worth noting that, even though President Roosevelt's proposal was defeated, the Court from 1937 on stopped declaring federal economic legislation unconstitutional. One explanation may be that Chief Justice Hughes and Justice Roberts, one or both of whom had voted to strike down each of the invalidated New Deal laws, came to realize that the Court had put itself in the untenable position of standing in the way of policies and programs that most Americans favored, and for that reason changed sides. Within the following few years, too, retirement and death removed three of the justices most firmly opposed to the New Deal philosophy of government, and the President was able to replace them with justices more sympathetic to his policies.

THE INTERNAL RESTRAINTS. More important than these "external" restraints are the "internal" restraints imposed by the judicial tradition generally, and more particularly by the Supreme Court's own tradition. It was to this tradition that Justice (later Chief Justice) Harlan Fiske Stone was alluding in 1936 when he said, in a dissenting opinion: ". . . [W]hile unconstitutional exercise of power by the executive and legislative branches of the government is subject to judicial restraint, the only check upon our exercise of power is our own sense of self-restraint."

The Traditional Restraints on Judicial Lawmaking. Much of what we have said in Chapters 4 and 6 about judicial lawmaking is relevant here. The Constitution is a special sort of enactment, and judges, as we saw in Chapter 6, have rules about how enactments should be interpreted. Many constitutional rules are today embodied in decisional precedents, and judges, as we saw in Chapter 4, have rules about building on—and occasionally overruling—precedents.

One of the most basic rules of interpretation is that statutory words whose meaning is plain cannot be ignored. For example, the Constitution provides that "the Senate of the United States shall be composed of two Senators from each State"—regardless of the state's size. Under no circumstance could the Court allow a state to elect a third senator.

But the constitutional phrases around which most controversies have turned are not so precise. Phrases like "due process of law" do not *in themselves* give the Court much guidance; consequently they impose no real restraint on the justices' freedom to interpret.

Another basic rule of interpretation is that courts must try to ascertain what those who adopted an enactment meant by the language they used, what general purposes they had in mind. When we study Supreme Court opinions, we find that the Court has tried to answer these questions whenever it could. In many opinions the justices have referred back to the recorded deliberations of the Constitutional Convention of 1787 or to the deliberations of the Congresses which adopted the various amendments.

But the older a constitutional provision becomes, the less useful the guidance provided by its "legislative history" is. Those who adopted and ratified a provision a century or more ago did not and could not have anticipated our modern problems. But it seems reasonable to assume that they intended the officials, judges, and lawyers of future generations to accept responsibility for giving the original words a new and more precise meaning suited to current needs.

Thus neither the actual words of constitutional provisions nor the context of circumstances surrounding their enactment is usually the most important source of restraint on the Court's freedom of interpretation. Far more important are the restraints imposed by previous Court decisions interpreting the provision in question, for these decisions are precedents, and the Court normally feels constrained to follow its own precedents. All the important constitutional phrases have by now been interpreted in many cases, and most modern Supreme Court opinions are discussions, not of the meaning of the constitutional phrases or of the framers' presumed intention, but of the scope and applicability of prior decisions.

As we saw in Chapter 4, no appellate court invariably adheres to precedents, and the Supreme Court is no exception. The Court, in fact, has felt somewhat freer to reverse itself in constitutional cases than would a court applying common-law rules or judicial interpretations of statutes. When an ordinary appellate decision proves to be unwise or becomes outmoded, the legislature can, after all, supersede it by passing a statute. But, unless the Supreme Court is willing to overrule itself, the only way to nullify a constitutional decision is by the long and uncertain process of constitutional amendment.

Nevertheless, the Supreme Court avoids overruling its precedents directly whenever it can. It prefers to narrow the scope of the unsatisfactory decisions gradually by "distinguishing" later cases. As it holds that more and more later cases are not covered by the rule of a particular decision, that decision eventually ceases to be significant as a precedent. And when the Court does announce that it is overruling an earlier decision, the reversal is rarely unexpected; investigation will usually reveal that the Court has given warning in one or more earlier opinions that it is moving away from the original decision.

As an illustration, let us look at the overruling of *Hammer v. Dagenhart.* This was a 1918 case in which the Court held that Congress had no power to prohibit the use of child labor in the manufacture of goods to be sold in interstate commerce. It was one of a number of decisions in which the Court restricted the power of legislatures to enact economic regulations. After 1937, the year of President Roosevelt's court-packing proposal, this trend came to an end, and in the next few years an unusually large number of precedents were overruled. The decision that explicitly overruled *Hammer v. Dagenhart* was *United States v. Darby* (1941), which involved a challenge to the constitutionality of the Fair Labor Standards Act of 1938. Speaking for a unanimous Court in the *Darby* case, Justice Stone said:

. . . The motive and purpose of a regulation of interstate commerce are matters for the legislative judgment upon the exercise of which the Constitution places no restriction and over which the courts are given no control. . . .

. . . [T]hese principles of constitutional interpretation have been so long and repeatedly recognized by this Court as applicable to the Commerce Clause that there would be little occasion for repeating them now were it not for the decision of this Court twenty-two years ago in *Hammer v. Dagenhart*, 247 U.S. 251. In that case it was held by a bare majority of the Court over the powerful and now classic dissent of Mr. Justice Holmes setting forth the fundamental issues involved, that Congress was without power to exclude the products of child labor from interstate commerce. The reasoning and conclusion of the Court's opinion there cannot be reconciled with the conclusion which we have reached. . . .

Hammer v. Dagenhart has not been followed. The distinction on which the decision was rested . . . a distinction which was novel when made and unsupported by any provision of the Constitution—has long since been abandoned. . . .

The conclusion is inescapable that *Hammer v. Dagenhart* was a departure from the principles which have prevailed in the interpretation of the Commerce Clause both before and since the decision and that such vitality, as a precedent, as it then had has long since been exhausted. It should be and now is overruled.

(*United States v. Darby*, 312 U.S. 100 [1941].)

As we have remarked before, judicial lawmaking provides both for a degree of certainty and for the possibility of change when change becomes necessary. The Court's normal adherence to precedent creates a large measure of predictability. The more closely woven the web of interpretations becomes, the more unlikely it is that the Court will adopt bold new interpretations. Yet the Court retains the power to distinguish and, if necessary, to overrule undesirable precedents if that proves to be the only way to achieve essential changes in the law.[7]

Other Internal Restraints.   In addition to the traditional restraints acting on all appellate judges, there are certain special restraints which the Supreme Court has imposed on itself in dealing with constitutional issues.

In the first place, the Court has supplemented the constitutional and statutory rules defining its jurisdiction with some self-limiting jurisdictional rules of its own. For example, to implement the constitutional declaration in Article III that the Court's jurisdiction extends to "cases" and "controversies," the justices have spelled out specific standards designed to assure that the cases which it hears are true contests between parties each of whom has a genuine interest to protect.

The Court has also refused to decide certain cases because they presented "political questions." It has used this term to describe questions

---

[7] See *Connecticut General Life Insurance Co. v. Johnson* (1938), page 682, in which, in a dissenting opinion, Justice Black argues for the overruling of a long line of decisions extending the guarantees of the Fourteenth Amendment to corporations. The opinion is worth reading at this point as an example of constitutional interpretation based on history, and for its bold assertion that "the doctrine of *stare decisis* . . . has only a limited application in the field of constitutional law."

which it considered to be within the special competence of the elected branches of the government, questions which judges are not particularly well equipped to decide or which might bring the Court into open conflict with the other branches. The Court was once asked, for instance, to rule that one of the states did not have "a republican form of government," as required by the Constitution. It ruled instead that the question was one which only the executive and legislative branches could decide, that no judicial intervention was warranted. Until 1962 the Court took a similar position in refusing to rule on the persistent failure of many state legislatures to redraw the boundaries of legislative districts to take account of population shifts, but in that year it ruled that courts may adjudicate this issue. More than once in its history, the Court has lost prestige by rashly involving itself in controversies that brought it into conflict with the other branches of government, and so it has learned to shun situations in which it can perform no useful function.

Sometimes the Court avoids deciding a constitutional issue by disposing of the case before it on nonconstitutional grounds. This practice often disappoints lawyers who hope to get a definitive answer to an unresolved constitutional problem, but the Court has nearly always taken the position that when a case turns on several questions of law, the constitutional questions must be decided last—or not at all, if the case can be disposed of on other grounds.

Suppose, for instance, that an administrative official notifies John Jones that he must pay a certain tax. Jones takes the matter to court, arguing that he is exempt from the tax, and, moreover, that if the relevant provision in the tax statute were construed to cover him, the provision would be unconstitutional. The justices believe that Jones is probably right: if they interpret the provision broadly enough to make Jones taxable, then the statute probably is unconstitutional. If, however, they interpret it narrowly enough to exclude Jones, it will pass muster. In such a situation, even if the broad interpretation seems more natural, and even if it is the one that the legislature probably intended, the Court is likely to adopt the narrow interpretation in order to avoid invalidating the provision. So the Court rules that the official has misinterpreted the tax law, and that it does not apply to Jones. What the justices have done, in effect, is to refer the question of the statute's meaning back to the legislature, with this implicit message: "We, the Supreme Court, presume that you, the legislature, intended to write a constitutionally valid statute. If we were to give this provision a broad interpretation, its constitutionality would be doubtful. To avoid the possibility of having to declare it unconstitutional, we have decided to interpret it narrowly. Now this may not be what you had in mind, but it is up to you either to let our interpretation stand or else to amend the provision to achieve your purpose. If you amend it, we will decide any constitutional issues raised by your amendment when and if they are brought before us."

Even when the Court is willing to consider a constitutional question, it starts from a strong presumption that the challenged official action is constitutional and throws the burden of demonstrating its unconstitutionality on the challenging party. And when the Court does feel compelled to invalidate an official act, it usually does so on the narrowest possible grounds. If, for instance, it can dispose of a case by invalidating only a single statutory section, it will normally say nothing at all about the constitutionality of the other sections.

The Supreme Court as Policy-Maker

There was a time when judges and legal scholars spoke of constitutional interpretation as though it were entirely a matter of defining words, discovering original intentions, identifying controlling precedents, and applying the rules of logic. Some Supreme Court opinions written as late as the 1930's suggest that the Court's task is simply to put the official act in question side by side with the Constitution and to see whether the former squares with the latter. The judge, under this view, exercises no real freedom of choice; if he works hard and thinks straight, he will find the right answer.

In the 1930's a group of legal scholars, who came to be known as "legal realists," went to the other extreme. They argued that judges are just as much policy-making officials as are officials in other branches of government. They were convinced that judges reach decisions which produce results they deem socially desirable and then look for precedents and principles to justify those decisions. Some of the "realists" went on to assert that a judge's prejudices, whims, moods—even the state of his digestion—play a major part in determining how he decides cases.

The truth undoubtedly lies somewhere between these two extremes. The truth, certainly, is that with rare exceptions judges resist the temptation to decide cases according to their personal predilections. The whole judicial tradition militates against such conduct; it requires a conscientious weighing of the principles and precedents cited by the adversary parties *before* a decision is reached. On the other hand, it would be futile to pretend that judges—and particularly Supreme Court justices, given the imprecision of the Constitution—have no freedom to choose among alternative interpretations, or that their personal convictions are of no significance whatever.

When, in the early days of the Republic, Chief Justice Marshall had to interpret the scope of the federal power to regulate interstate commerce, he found little guidance in the sixteen words of the Constitution which make up the "commerce clause." Essentially, he had to make a policy decision: Would a broad or narrow interpretation of the federal power best suit the needs of the country? When the Court today has to decide whether the conduct of a certain sheriff or policeman or jailer meets the requirement of "due process of law," the constitutional phrase is of no use in itself as a standard of measurement. Past decisions may be of some use in suggesting criteria against which the official's conduct can be measured, but the Court's job is essentially to decide whether the official's conduct was within the limits of what is "fair" or "just" under the standards we set for an agent of government in our democratic society.[8] *This is a policy-making, lawmaking function.*

Sometimes an official act seems valid with reference to one constitutional principle, but invalid with reference to another. Then the Court is compelled to establish a priority between the two principles. Some of the statutes designed to restrict picketing by labor unions have raised this problem. Viewed as a potential interference with property rights, picketing would seem to be subject to regulation under the states' "police power"; but viewed as an exercise of free speech by the unions, it would seem to be protected from legislative interference by the First and Fourteenth Amendments (which together restrict the power of the states to interfere with freedom of expression). Sometimes the Court has given priority to one of these competing values, and sometimes to the other, depending on the form of regulation and the purpose of the picketing. It should be clear that the Court can take no position on a question of this sort without making a "policy" decision—without, that is, making a choice between conflicting social aims and values.

But when a Supreme Court justice acts as a policy-maker, he must display infinitely more objectivity and self-restraint than is demanded of legislative or executive policy-makers. No matter how broad the discretion granted him, his task is never to ask himself: How do *I* feel about the wisdom of this statute, the fairness of this official act? He must ask only: Is this official act—however unwise it may seem to me—within the limits of what the Constitution permits? And since, as we have seen, the words of the Constitution usually provide no direct answer, his task is to interpret the *spirit* of the Constitution and to relate that spirit to the changing needs and values of an evolving society. Finally, he may have to explain and justify his conclusions in a written opinion which, when published, should clarify and illuminate the constitutional principles in question.

Needless to say, the justices of the Supreme Court have not always practiced such perfect self-restraint. On occasion, both "conservative" and "liberal" members of the Court have confused their personal convictions with the law of the land. But some of our greatest justices have resisted this temptation. In the first half of the present century, Justices Holmes and Stone stood as outstanding examples of judicial self-restraint. Neither was enthusiastic about many of the laws regulating business that came before the Court during his tenure, yet each dissented again and again when his colleagues voted to strike down those laws. Although they each believed that many of the enactments were ill conceived and futile, they

---

[8] According to Justice Frankfurter, the concept of "due process" in matters of procedure "expresses a demand for civilized standards of law. It is thus not a stagnant formulation of what has been achieved in the past but a standard for judgment in the progressive evolution of the institutions of society." The judgment "must move within the limits of accepted notions of justice." The Court, then, must decide what are the currently accepted notions of justice.

could find nothing in the Constitution to justify the assumption that judges were better qualified than the people's elected representatives to decide what was good for a state or for the nation. Unless a legislature has clearly exceeded the express or implied powers granted to it by the Constitution, they insisted, the Court must not override its enactments, however unwise they may seem. As Justice Stone once put it: "For the removal of unwise laws from the statute books, appeal lies not to the courts but to the ballot and to the processes of democratic government. . . . Courts are not the only agency of government that must be assumed to have capacity to govern."

From time to time the Court has misused its power by acting as a sort of super-legislature. But not every attack made on the Court for abuse of power has been justified. The underlying cause of most of the attacks on the Court has been acute disappointment over the outcome of particular cases. It is not surprising that in 1935–36, when so many of the New Deal programs were being struck down, the Court's most vocal critics tended to be those who favored the New Deal programs. Today a different set of issues is being brought before the Court; many of the groups which in the 1930's deplored the Court's decisions are today its most ardent defenders, while its former friends are now among its critics.

Like other democratic institutions, the Supreme Court is not exempt from criticism. And constructive criticism (as distinguished from personal attacks on particular justices) can serve a useful purpose. Even the intemperate attacks on the Court made during the late 1950's may have encouraged people to reflect on the values and limitations of the Court as an American political institution, and on the moral issues implicit in the cases it was deciding. Indeed, the Court's decisions on such major issues as equal rights for minorities, limits of free speech, and separation of church and state do not achieve their fullest effect until they have been studied and understood by the nation's citizens. Only when they have been accepted, not just as "the law," but as just and right, are they truly effective.

The Justices

So far we have mostly spoken of the Supreme Court as a unit. But we must never forget that the Court is made up of justices who die or retire and are replaced by others, who have personal philosophies and prejudices, religious affiliations, and political, social, and economic backgrounds which inevitably influence their appraisals of "the felt necessities of the time."

Vacancies on the Court are filled by the President, "with the advice and consent of the Senate." Understandably, he is likely to appoint men whose political and economic views are not too different from his own. He is certain to nominate men with legal training, but there is no tradition requiring that his appointees have prior judicial experience, and some of our greatest justices had never previously been judges.

Once appointed, a justice has indefinite tenure and is virtually irremovable. As we have noted, this immunity insulates the justices from direct political pressure [9] and enables them to hand down decisions that they know will be unpopular in some quarters. Immunity has its disadvantages as well. Some justices have remained on the bench long after their intellectual powers have declined, or their ability to accept new ideas has vanished. But for every justice who has sought to stand in the way of change, there have been others who have kept their judicial philosophies superbly attuned to the needs of the times. Some of the most memorable justices have been persistent dissenters from the majority view in their time, only to have history prove them right; thus their dissenting views have later become the law of the land.

The Decline of "Economic Due Process": An Example of Constitutional Evolution

The constitutional interpretations which have most closely affected businessmen have been those that concerned the limits of permissible government regulation of private enterprise. The past half-century has seen a notable shift in this area of the law. In the years before 1937, the Supreme Court developed an arsenal of doctrines, concepts, and categories which in effect enabled it to act as the censor of economic legislation. The Court upheld those enactments whose ends and means a majority of the justices considered reasonable; it struck down those which a majority thought were unwarranted restrictions on economic freedom. This meant that the justices were setting their own convictions on what was reasonable against the convictions of the legislatures. As we have seen, a crisis was reached in 1937, after some of the major New Deal enactments had been invalidated. Although President Roosevelt's "court-packing" proposal of 1937 was defeated, since that time the Court has virtually ceased to strike down economic legislation on constitutional grounds.

When businessmen were challenging the constitutionality of federal regulatory legislation, the cases usually turned on the scope of Congress's power to regulate interstate commerce. Since 1937 the Court has treated that power as virtually unlimited. (Witness, for instance, the words of the unanimous opinion in *United States v. Darby*, the 1941 decision quoted above on page 135.) When state legislation was being challenged, the issue was likely to be whether the enactment was within the so-called "police power" of the states or whether it violated the requirement of the Fourteenth Amendment: ". . . [N]or shall any state deprive any person of life, liberty, or property, without due process of law."

In this final section we shall consider two cases in which state statutes were challenged as exceeding the limits imposed by the due-process clause. The challenged statute in each case had been designed to restrict the freedom of employers to make certain kinds of agreement with their employees. The first case, decided in 1915, illustrates the willingness of the Court at that time to nullify statutes which the justices considered unreasonable

---

[9] Their immunity is accompanied by a disability, however: tradition bars them from defending themselves publicly against criticism, however misguided and unfair it may be.

interferences with "liberty of contract." The second case, decided in 1949, illustrates the modern view that the Court has no authority to invalidate a state's economic legislation unless it runs afoul of some specific constitutional provision or some valid federal law.

The 1915 case is *Coppage v. Kansas.* The legislature of Kansas had passed a statute designed to protect the right of workers to organize into unions, by making it unlawful for an employer to "coerce, require, demand, or influence any person or persons to enter into any agreement . . . not to join or become or remain a member of any labor organization or association, as a condition of . . . securing employment, or of continuing in the employment" of the employer. Coppage, a superintendent for a railway company, demanded that a certain switchman sign such an agreement (popularly known as a "yellow-dog contract") or else lose his job. The switchman refused to sign and was fired. Coppage was brought to trial and convicted for violating the Kansas law. After the Supreme Court of Kansas had affirmed the judgment, Coppage appealed to the United States Supreme Court, challenging the constitutionality of the statute. In essence, his contention was that, in the absence of some overriding public interest, the due-process clause protects "liberty of contract" from government interference. No such overriding public interest was present here to justify the state's interference, he argued.

Behind the *Coppage* case is the age-old problem of how to balance the competing claims of liberty and social justice. (How much may A's liberty be restricted in order to lessen B's economic weakness?) But the immediate question that *Coppage* raised was whether the Kansas legislature was free to strike the balance as it saw fit, or whether its decision was subject to review and possible nullification by the Court.

The Supreme Court, with three justices dissenting, held that the Kansas law was unconstitutional. The majority opinion first declared that the statute interfered with freedom of contract. The employer had a "constitutional" right to hire whom he wanted and to refuse employment to a union member. The employee had a parallel right to work for the employer or not, and to choose between keeping his job and remaining a union member. Since the parties had these rights, they had the right to make bargains respecting them.

The Court went on to point out that it had a precedent in *Adair v. United States* (1908). In that case the Court had invalidated a federal statute designed to outlaw "yellow-dog contracts" in interstate railways, on the ground that the statute violated the due-process clause in the Fifth Amendment (which restricts the acts of the federal government). The *Adair* opinion had said:

> While . . . the right of liberty and property guaranteed by the Constitution against deprivation without due process of law is subject to such reasonable restraints as the common good or the general welfare may require, it is not within the functions of government . . . to compel any person in the course of his business or against his will to accept or retain the personal services of another. . . . In all such particulars the employer and the employee have equality of right, and any legislation

that disturbs that equality is an arbitrary interference with the liberty of contract, which no government can legally justify in a free land.

Although the Court might just have rested its decision on the precedent of *Adair*, it preferred to spell out again its reasons for striking down statutes that banned yellow-dog contracts:

> . . . Included in the right of personal liberty and the right of private property—partaking of the nature of each—is the right to make contracts for the acquisition of property. Chief among such contracts is that of personal employment, by which labor and other services are exchanged for money or other forms of property. If this right be struck down or arbitrarily interfered with, there is a substantial impairment of liberty in the long-established constitutional sense. The right is as essential to the laborer as to the capitalist, to the poor as to the rich; for the vast majority of persons have no other honest way to begin to acquire property, save by working for money.
>
> An interference with this liberty so serious as that now under consideration, and so disturbing of equality of right, must be deemed to be arbitrary, unless it be supportable as a reasonable exercise of the police power of the state. But, notwithstanding the strong general presumption in favor of the validity of state laws, we do not think the statute in question, as construed and applied in this case, can be sustained as a legitimate exercise of that power. . . .
>
> Upon both principle and authority, therefore, we are constrained to hold that the Kansas act of March 13, 1903, as construed and applied so as to punish with fine or imprisonment an employer or his agent for merely prescribing, as a condition upon which one may secure employment under or remain in the service of such employer, that the employee shall enter into an agreement not to become or remain a member of any labor organization while so employed, is repugnant to the "due process" clause of the Fourteenth Amendment, and therefore void. . . .

Justice Holmes, who had already dissented in *Adair*, dissented again in *Coppage*. Holmes's position had always been that, so long as reasonable men could believe that a piece of legislation might help to solve a problem, the legislation could not be so wholly arbitrary as to be unconstitutional under the due process clause. In contrast to the majority, Holmes made no assumptions concerning the comparative importance of liberty and social justice, nor did he express any personal view concerning the wisdom of the Kansas statute. He simply believed that the legislature, not the courts, must resolve these issues. His brief opinion, echoing views that he had expressed many times before, foreshadowed the Court's modern view of its proper role:

> . . . In present conditions a workman not unnaturally may believe that only by belonging to a union can he secure a contract that shall be fair to him. If that belief, whether right or wrong, may be held by a reasonable man, it seems to me that it may be enforced by law in order to establish the equality of position between the parties in which liberty of contract begins. Whether in the long run it is wise for the workingmen to enact legislation of this sort is not my concern, but I am strongly of opinion that there is nothing in the Constitution of the United States

to prevent it, and that *Adair v. United States* . . . should be over-ruled. . . .
(*Coppage v. Kansas,* 236 U.S. 1 [1915].)

By 1949, many things had changed. First of all, the balance of power in industrial relations had shifted. With the rise of powerful labor unions, legislatures were less preoccupied with the need for protecting individual workers from their employers. Some legislatures were, however, concerned with protecting individual workers against labor unions; and had enacted statutes, known as "right-to-work" laws, prohibiting employers and unions from signing "closed-shop" or "union-shop" contracts barring nonunion workers from employment.

This time the opposition to the legislation came from unions, which found themselves relying on the same "due process" arguments they had so strongly opposed when employers had used them in earlier cases. But by 1949 the Court had long ceased to strike down legislation regulating business on the ground that it was a denial of "due process." Could the unions persuade the Court to revive the doctrine of the *Coppage* case and invalidate the state "right-to-work" laws? [10]

LINCOLN FEDERAL LABOR UNION
v. NORTHWESTERN IRON & METAL CO.

Supreme Court of the United States, 1949
335 U.S. 525, 69 S.Ct. 251

► MR. JUSTICE BLACK delivered the opinion of the Court.

Under employment practices in the United States, employers have sometimes limited work opportunities to members of unions, sometimes to non-union members, and at other times have employed and kept their workers without regard to whether they were or were not members of a union. Employers are commanded to follow this latter employment practice in the states of North Carolina and Nebraska. A North Carolina statute and a Nebraska constitutional amendment provide that no person in those states shall be denied an opportunity to obtain or retain employment because he is or is not a member of a labor organization. To enforce this policy North Carolina and Nebraska employers are also forbidden to enter into contracts or agreements obligating themselves to exclude persons from employment because they are or are not labor union members.

These state laws were given timely challenge in North Carolina and Nebraska courts on the ground that insofar as they attempt to protect non-union members from discrimination, the laws are in violation of rights guaranteed employers, unions, and their members by the United States Constitution. . . . It was further contended that the state laws . . . deprived the appellant unions and employers of equal protection and due process of law guaranteed against state invasion by the Fourteenth Amendment. . . . [T]hese contentions were rejected by the State Supreme Courts

---

[10] The italics in the opinions have been added.

and the cases are here on appeal. . . . The substantial identity of the questions raised in the two cases prompted us to set them for argument together and for the same reason we now consider the cases in a single opinion. . . .

It is contended that these state laws deprive appellants of their liberty without due process of law in violation of the Fourteenth Amendment. Appellants argue that the laws are specifically designed to deprive all persons within the two states of "liberty" (1) to refuse to hire or retain any person in employment because he is or is not a union member, and (2) to make a contract or agreement to engage in such employment discrimination against union or non-union members.

Much of appellants' argument here seeks to establish that due process of law is denied employees and union men by that part of these state laws that forbids them to make contracts with the employer obligating him to refuse to hire or retain non-union workers. But that part of these laws does no more than provide a method to aid enforcement of the heart of the laws, namely, their command that employers must not discriminate against either union or non-union members because they are such. If the states have constitutional power to ban such discrimination by law, they also have power to ban contracts which if performed would bring about the prohibited discrimination.

Many cases are cited by appellants in which this Court has said that in some instances the due process clause protects the liberty of persons to make contracts. But none of these cases, even those according the broadest constitutional protection to the making of contracts, ever went so far as to indicate that the due process clause bars a state from prohibiting contracts to engage in conduct banned by a valid state law. So here, if the provisions in the state laws against employer discrimination are valid, it follows that the contract prohibition also is valid. . . . We therefore turn to the decisive question under the due process contention, which is: Does the due process clause forbid a state to pass laws clearly designed to safeguard the opportunity of non-union workers to get and hold jobs, free from discrimination against them because they are non-union workers?

There was a period in which labor union members who wanted to get and hold jobs were the victims of widespread employer discrimination practices. Contracts between employers and their employees were used by employers to accomplish this anti-union employment discrimination. Before hiring workers, employers required them to sign agreements stating that the workers were not and would not become labor union members. Such anti-union practices were so obnoxious to workers that they gave these required agreements the name of "yellow dog contracts." This hostility of workers also prompted passage of state and federal laws to ban employer discrimination against union members and to outlaw yellow dog contracts.

In 1907 this Court in *Adair v. United States*, 208 U.S. 161, considered the federal law which prohibited discrimination against union workers. . . . This Court there held, over the dissents of Justices McKenna and Holmes, that the railroad, because of the due process clause of the Fifth Amendment, had a constitutional right to discriminate against union members and could therefore do so through use of yellow dog contracts. The chief reliance for this holding was *Lochner v. New York,* 198 U.S. 45. . . . This Court had found support for its *Lochner* holding in what had been said in *Allgeyer v. Louisiana,* 165 U.S. 578, a case on which appellants here strongly rely. There were strong dissents in the *Adair* and *Lochner* cases.

In 1914 this Court reaffirmed the principles of the *Adair* case in *Coppage v. Kansas,* 236 U.S. 1, again over strong dissents, and held that a Kansas statute outlawing yellow dog contracts denied employers and employees a liberty to fix terms of employment. For this reason the law was held invalid under the due process clause.

The *Allgeyer-Lockner-Adair-Coppage* constitutional doctrine was for some years followed by this Court. It was used to strike down laws fixing minimum wages and maximum hours in employment, laws fixing prices, and laws regulating business activities. See cases cited in *Olsen v. Nebraska,* 313 U.S. 236, 244–246, and *Osborn v. Ozlin,* 310 U.S. 53, 66–67. And the same constitutional philosophy was faithfully adhered to in *Adams v. Tanner,* 244 U.S. 590, a case strongly pressed upon us by appellants. . . .

This Court, beginning at least as early as 1934, when the *Nebbia* case was decided, has steadily rejected the due process philosophy enunciated in the *Adair-Coppage* line of cases. In doing so it has consciously returned closer and closer to the earlier constitutional principle that *states have power to legislate against what are found to be injurious practices in their internal commercial and business affairs, so long as their laws do not run afoul of some specific federal constitutional prohibition, or of some valid federal law.* Under this constitutional doctrine the due process clause is no longer to be so broadly construed that the Congress and state legislatures are put in a strait jacket when they attempt to suppress business and in- dustrial conditions which they regard as offensive to the public welfare.

Appellants now ask us to return, at least in part, to the due process philosophy that has been deliberately discarded. Claiming that the Federal Constitution itself affords protection for union members against discrimina- tion, they nevertheless assert that the same Constitution forbids a state from providing the same protection for non-union members. Just as we have held that the due process clause erects no obstacle to block legislative protection of union members, we now hold that legislative protection can be afforded non-union workers.

Affirmed.

[In a concurring opinion, Justice Frankfurter articulated once again the view, so often expressed by Justices Holmes and Stone, that the only ques- tion before the Court in a constitutional case is whether the legislature was prohibited by the Constitution from doing what it did; the Court is not to consider whether an enactment is wise or foolish.]

MR. JUSTICE FRANKFURTER, concurring.

Arizona, Nebraska, and North Carolina have passed laws forbidding agreements to employ only union members. The United States Constitution is invoked against these laws. Since the cases bring into question the judicial process in its application to the Due Process Clause, explicit avowal of individual attitudes towards that process may elucidate and thereby strengthen adjudication. Accordingly, I set forth the steps by which I have reached concurrence with my brethren on what I deem the only substantial issue here, on all other issues joining the Court's opinion.

The coming of the machine age tended to despoil human personality. It turned men and women into "hands." The industrial history of the early Nineteenth Century demonstrated the helplessness of the individual employee to achieve human dignity in a society so largely affected by technological advances. Hence the trade union made itself increasingly felt, not only as an indispensable weapon of self-defense on the part of workers but as an aid to the well-being of a society in which work is an expression of life and not merely the means of earning subsistence. But unionization encountered the shibboleths of a pre-machine age and these were reflected in juridical assumptions that survived the facts on which they were based. Adam Smith was treated as though his generalizations had been imparted to him on Sinai and not as a thinker who addressed himself to the elimination of restrictions which had become fetters upon initiative and enterprise in his day. *Basic human rights expressed by the constitutional conception of "liberty" were equated with theories of laissez faire. The result was that economic views of confined validity were treated by lawyers and judges as though the Framers had enshrined them in the Constitution.* This misapplication of the notions of the classic economists and resulting disregard of the perduring reach of the Constitution led to Mr. Justice Holmes' famous protest in the *Lochner* case against measuring the Fourteenth Amendment by Mr. Herbert Spencer's Social Statics. 198 U.S. 45, 75. Had not Mr. Justice Holmes' awareness of the impermanence of legislation as against the permanence of the Constitution gradually prevailed, there might indeed have been "hardly any limit but the sky" to the embodiment of "our economic or moral beliefs" in that Amendment's "prohibitions." *Baldwin v. Missouri,* 281 U.S. 586, 595.

The attitude which regarded any legislative encroachment upon the existing economic order as infected with unconstitutionality led to disrespect for legislative attempts to strengthen the wage-earner's bargaining power. With that attitude as a premise, *Adair v. United States,* 208 U.S. 161, and *Coppage v. Kansas,* 236 U.S. 1, followed logically enough; not even *Truax v. Corrigan,* 257 U.S. 312, could be considered unexpected. But when the tide turned, it was not merely because circumstances had changed and there had arisen a new order with new claims to divine origin. The opinion of Mr. Justice Brandeis in *Senn v. Tile Layers Union,* 301 U.S. 468, shows the current running strongly in the new direction—*the direction not of social dogma but of increased deference to the legislative judgment.* "Whether it was wise," he said, now speaking for the Court and not in dissent, "for the State to permit the unions to [picket] is a question of its public policy—not our concern." . . .

It is urged that the compromise which this legislation embodies is no compromise at all because fatal to the survival of organized labor. But can it be said that the legislators and the people of Arizona, Nebraska, and North Carolina could not in reason be sceptical of organized labor's insistence upon the necessity to its strength of power to compel rather than to persuade the allegiance of its reluctant members? . . .

Even where the social undesirability of a law may be convincingly urged, invalidation of the law by a court debilitates popular democratic government. Most laws dealing with economic and social problems are matters of trial and error. That which before trial appears to be demonstrably bad may belie prophecy in actual operation. It may not prove good, but it may prove innocuous. *But even if a law is found wanting on trial, it is better that its defects should be demonstrated and removed than that the law should be aborted by judicial fiat. Such an assertion of judicial power deflects responsibility from those on whom in a democratic society it ultimately rests—the people.* If the proponents of union-security agreements have confidence in the arguments addressed to the Court in their "economic brief," they should address those arguments to the electorate. Its endorsement would be a vindication that the mandate of this Court could never give. That such vindication is not a vain hope has been recently demonstrated by the voters of Maine, Massachusetts, and New Mexico. And although several States in addition to those at bar now have such laws, the legislatures of as many other States have, sometimes repeatedly, rejected them. What one State can refuse to do, another can undo.

But there is reason for judicial restraint in matters of policy deeper than the value of experiment: it is founded on a recognition of the gulf of difference between sustaining and nullifying legislation. This difference is theoretical in that *the function of legislating is for legislatures who have also taken oaths to support the Constitution, while the function of courts, when legislation is challenged, is merely to make sure that the legislature has exercised an allowable judgment, and not to exercise their own judgment, whether a policy is within or without "the vague contours" of due process.* Theory is reinforced by the notorious fact that lawyers predominate in American legislatures. In practice also the difference is wide. In the day-to-day working of our democracy it is vital that the power of the non-democratic organ of our Government be exercised with rigorous self-restraint. Because *the powers exercised by this Court are inherently oligarchic,* Jefferson all of his life thought of the Court as "an irresponsible body" and "independent of the nation itself." The Court is not saved from being oligarchic because it professes to act in the service of humane ends. *As history amply proves, the judiciary is prone to misconceive the public good by confounding private notions with constitutional requirements, and such misconceptions are not subject to legitimate displacement by the will of the people except at too slow a pace. Judges appointed for life whose decisions run counter to prevailing opinion cannot be voted out of office and supplanted by men of views more consonant with it.* They are even farther removed from democratic pressures by the fact that their deliberations are in secret and remain beyond disclosure either by periodic reports or by such a modern device for securing responsibility to the electorate as the "press conference." But a democracy need not rely on the courts to save it from its own unwisdom. If it is alert—and without alertness by the people there can be no enduring democracy—unwise or unfair legislation can readily be removed from the statute books. It is by such vigilance over its representatives that democracy proves itself.

Our right to pass on the validity of legislation is now too much part of our constitutional system to be brought into question. But the implications of that right and the conditions for its exercise must constantly be kept in mind and vigorously observed. Because *the Court is without power to shape measures for dealing with the problems of society but has merely the power of negation over measures shaped by others*, the indispensable judicial requisite is intellectual humility, and such humility presupposes complete disinterestedness. And so, in the end, it is right that the Court should be indifferent to public temper and popular wishes. Mr. Dooley's "th' Supreme Coort follows th' iliction returns" expressed the wit of cynicism, not the demand of principle. A court which yields to the popular will thereby licenses itself to practice despotism, for there can be no assurance that it will not on another occasion indulge its own will. Courts can fulfill their responsibility in a democratic society only to the extent that they succeed in shaping their judgments by rational standards, and rational standards are both impersonal and communicable. Matters of policy, however, are by definition matters which demand the resolution of conflicts of value, and the elements of conflicting values are largely imponderable. Assessment of their competing worth involves differences of feeling; it is also an exercise in prophecy. Obviously the proper forum for mediating a clash of feelings and rendering a prophetic judgment is the body chosen for those purposes by the people. Its functions can be assumed by this Court only in disregard of the historic limits of the Constitution. ◄

Earlier in the chapter we considered some of the reasons that from time to time impel the Supreme Court to invalidate the acts of other agencies of government. Justice Frankfurter's opinion expounds with eloquence the reasons that often cause the Court to hold back and let the processes of popular democracy take their course.

8 Lawmaking and Adjudication by Administrative Agencies

For many Americans, particularly businessmen, the influence of administrative officials seems far more pervasive than that of judges and legislators.[1] Not only do these officials execute the laws; together they create more legal rules and try more cases than all the legislatures and all the courts. The body of law that controls their activity is known as "administrative law." We shall consider some of the principles of administrative law in this chapter.

Administrators perform such a great variety of functions that it would be quite impossible to enumerate them all. The following examples of their rule-making and adjudicative functions, however, will suggest the sorts of activity with which this chapter is concerned:

1. Administrators assess the value of our taxable property. They review the declarations we make of our taxable incomes. They issue regulations defining the categories of income that must be included in our income declarations. They negotiate disputes over tax liability with particular taxpayers. They man a special federal tax court that adjudicates controversies over liability when negotiation has failed.

2. Administrators grant (and may deny, suspend, or revoke) a great variety of licenses, permits, franchises, charters, and patents.

3. Administrators establish the rates charged and supervise the services provided by transportation, communications, and public-utility companies.

4. Administrators serve as both judges and prosecutors in proceedings to determine whether laws prohibiting "unfair competition," "unfair labor practices," and racial discrimination in housing and employment have been

---

[1] When we speak of administrative officials in this chapter, we are referring to officials in the executive branch of the government. While this category includes the President, state governors, mayors, and other elective officials, we shall be mostly concerned with the activities of nonelective officials: cabinet members; heads of departments, bureaus, and offices; and the innumerable officials subordinate to them. The category specifically includes those who man the so-called regulatory commissions, even though these agencies are sometimes classified as being outside the executive branch. In short, these are "the bureaucrats."

violated. They also rule on alleged violations of laws setting standards for wages and hours, and for the quality of food and drugs.

5. Administrators determine whether certain persons should be excluded from government or defense-industry jobs, and whether others should be deported from the country.

6. Administrators hear and rule on the claims of employees who have suffered injuries while at work.

The Emergence of the Modern Administrative Agency

There have always been administrators, of course, but they have not always had the breadth of discretionary power that many of them have today. How has it happened that nonelective officials now make rules governing our conduct, and officials outside the judicial tradition hear and decide cases?

The power of modern administrators is a product of economic developments that began in the latter part of the last century. In the years following the Civil War, the United States was transformed with remarkable speed from a farming and trading nation into an industrial nation. A vigorous generation of entrepreneurs created great manufacturing, railroad, and financial empires. The resulting concentration of power in private hands brought widespread abuses, which, in turn, provoked a popular demand for government regulation of business practices deemed harmful to the general interest.

Traditionally, when a legislature decided to lay down a new set of rules regulating private conduct, it simply adopted a statute setting up standards in terms as specific or as general as the circumstances warranted, and then left it to the courts to fill in the gaps in the law as cases—criminal prosecutions or civil suits, depending on the remedies provided by the statute— were brought before them. This was the pattern of lawmaking set in 1890, for example, with the enactment of the Sherman Act (see pages 96 and 810). Our body of federal antimonopoly rules has been the joint creation of Congress and the federal courts.[2]

But this traditional lawmaking technique proved inadequate in providing the complex system of regulation which Americans felt it necessary to inaugurate during the past eighty years. Legislatures came to realize that lawmaking under the new regulatory programs would not be a "one-shot" affair: it would require continuous attention and enough flexibility so that the lawmaker could readily change the rules as new problems (including new techniques of evasion) emerged. It soon became clear that legislatures had neither the time nor the knowledge to undertake this large and continuing responsibility for making and modifying the rules. Equally important, it became clear that the courts could not be saddled with primary responsibility for filling in the gaps in the new regulatory statutes. The judges were little better equipped than the legislators to acquire the knowl-

---

[2] A third participant was the Antitrust Division of the Department of Justice, which influenced the growth of antitrust law by deciding which violators to prosecute and by choosing which legal arguments to present to the judges. In this limited sense, administrators participated in lawmaking even under the traditional arrangements.

edge and experience, and to give the continuous attention, necessary for dealing with complex and rapidly changing problems.

Hence a new pattern of regulation emerged. Administrative officials began to receive much larger discretionary powers and to perform a variety of functions previously reserved to the legislatures and the courts.

The new pattern emerged at the federal level in 1887, with the enactment of the Interstate Commerce Act. The original purpose of this statute was to eliminate inequities in rate-setting and other practices in interstate rail transportation. It resembled the Sherman Act in that it provided for criminal prosecutions and civil suits against practices declared to be unlawful. But it also established a new agency, the Interstate Commerce Commission, and gave it general responsibility for making day-to-day policy decisions pertaining to the regulation of railroads. The Commission had authority, among other things, to investigate complaints by shippers against the railroads, to hold hearings at which witnesses could be compelled to testify, and, if necessary, to issue formal orders which the courts were expected to enforce.

For almost twenty years, hostile courts interpreted the assigned powers of the new agency so restrictively as to deny it any real authority. For a while, the state railway commissions, created at about the same time for similar purposes, were blocked by similar obstacles. Eventually these obstacles were overcome, however, by new legislation designed to strengthen the ICC and by an abatement of judicial hostility. Thereafter the new technique of regulating economic activities by administrative agencies came to be relied on more and more at both the federal and state levels. Among the best known of the federal regulatory agencies, all created in the twentieth century, are the Federal Trade Commission, the Federal Communications Commission, the Securities and Exchange Commission, the Civil Aeronautics Board, and the National Labor Relations Board.[3] Perhaps the best-known state regulatory agencies are the public utilities commissions.

The powers of modern regulatory agencies tend to be greater than those of nineteenth-century administrators in three respects:

First, their purely "executive" powers are greater. They have broader authority to investigate, to insist that private concerns keep certain kinds of records, to negotiate "settlements" with regulated parties, and to initiate enforcement action.

Second, many of them have expressly delegated authority to issue regulations which serve to elaborate the meaning of statutes couched in general terms. Many of the enabling statutes do no more than indicate a policy objective, defining a set of abuses to be dealt with, and prescribing in broad terms the standards against which private or official acts are to be measured. In these circumstances, the agency is the real lawmaker.

---

[3] These agencies, along with a few others, are sometimes called the "independent regulatory commissions," since they are in some ways less subject to the President's control than the agencies that make up the executive branch. The reasons for this limited grant of independence are as much historical as functional, and a number of agencies in the executive branch perform functions much like those performed by the independent commissions.

Third, many of them have authority to hold trial-like hearings to determine the facts in particular controversies. The decisions that result from these hearings are subject to review by a court, but the scope of that review is limited; it is more like an appeal than a new trial.

It is with these last two types of authority that we shall be concerned in the rest of this chapter.

Legislative Rule-Making by Administrators

In Chapter 1 we mentioned that legal rules are either *legislative* or *decisional* in origin. A "legislative" rule, you will remember, is embodied in an authoritative, official text. A "decisional" rule is a precedent, the by-product of the decision handed down in a particular case.

The statutes passed by legislatures are the most familiar embodiments of *legislative* rules. But the executive orders issued by Presidents and governors and the detailed regulations issued by administrative agencies are also examples of legislative rules. The most familiar *decisional* rules are the precedents established by appellate courts, but the decisions of administrative agencies adjudicating cases also establish precedents and hence are decisional rules.

Let us first consider the process of legislative rule-making by agencies. An administrative agency supplements the general policies enunciated in the statutes it administers by issuing a variety of pronouncements of its own. The most formal and important of these are usually known as "regulations." If an agency has explicit authority to issue such regulations, and if it exercises that authority in a valid manner, its regulations are just as much "law," just as likely to be honored in the courts, as any statute.

Regulations are normally published, so that affected parties (or at least their lawyers) may have an opportunity to learn about them. The agency is free to amend its regulations after publishing them, of course, but they remain binding on it so long as they have not been formally amended.[4]

Challenges to the Validity of Regulations

Under what circumstances might a court hold a regulation to be invalid and hence not entitled to enforcement?

Judges do *not* ask themselves whether they consider the regulation wise, fair, and likely to produce the desired result. Doing that would make the judges the ultimate legislators. Legislative power has been delegated to the administrators, presumably, because of their technical knowledge and specialized experience; and their exercise of judgment is no more an issue before the court than would be the judgment of the legislature in passing a statute.

---

[4] To have legal force, all regulations of federal agencies must be published in a daily journal called the *Federal Register* (which also publishes presidential proclamations and executive orders, as well as certain other documents). Periodically, federal regulations are codified and republished in the *Code of Federal Regulations*. A number of states have similar arrangements.

The first question the judges must ask in deciding on the validity of a regulation is whether the authority delegated to the agency is broad enough to cover the particular regulation. Has the agency done what it was told to do? Is there a reasonable correspondence between the regulation and the policies and standards enunciated in the statute? If the answer to these questions is negative, then the agency has acted *ultra vires* (beyond its powers), and its act is invalid.

The degree of discretion delegated to administrators varies; as we have already remarked, enabling statutes frequently state policies and prescribe standards in extremely general terms. Often, for instance, the legislature will instruct an agency to establish standards that are "fair and equitable," or are "in the public interest," or "serve the public convenience and necessity," or "effectuate the purposes of this Act." Obviously such general phrases leave great discretion to the agency.

These broad delegations of authority raise a constitutional issue. After all, American constitutions assign to the legislative branch the basic responsibility for legislating. (The federal Constitution says: "All legislative Powers herein granted shall be vested in a Congress of the United States. . . .") Are there no limits to the power of legislatures to delegate this responsibility?

A few judicial decisions, mostly by state courts, have invalidated executive and administrative acts on the ground that they were based on delegations of authority deemed to be excessive. (The best-known federal decision of this sort is the one that struck down the New Deal's National Industrial Recovery Act in 1935.) But most courts today seem willing to uphold laws that contain extremely general statements of policy and standards.

One of the issues in the case of *Yakus v. United States* was whether Congress had made an unconstitutional delegation of power to a federal administrative agency. The following excerpts from the Supreme Court's majority opinion are worth reading with care, both as a statement of the Court's position on the delegation-of-authority issue and as an example of the modern regulatory statute and the type of regulations that are often issued under it.

Under wartime laws designed to check inflation, the Office of Price Administration was empowered to set maximum price levels for specified commodities and services. When administrators fix maximum prices or rates they are making rules, because they are establishing standards, enforceable by the courts, for the future conduct of a class of persons. Unlike some regulatory statutes, the price-control law did not provide for administrative adjudication of alleged violations; instead, those charged with violations were criminally prosecuted. The defendants in *Yakus* were tried and convicted of selling beef at prices above the levels prescribed in the OPA's regulations. In their appeal to the United States Supreme Court, they challenged the constitutionality of the basic statute. (The authors have italicized a few phrases in the opinion and interpolated some explanatory comments.)

YAKUS v. UNITED STATES

Supreme Court of the United States, 1944
321 U.S. 414, 64 S.Ct. 660

▶ MR. CHIEF JUSTICE STONE delivered the opinion of the Court.

. . .

[The Chief Justice first identified the basic statutes and the policies underlying them:]

The Emergency Price Control Act provides for the establishment of the Office of Price Administration under the direction of a Price Administrator appointed by the President, and sets up a comprehensive scheme for the promulgation by the Administrator of regulations or orders fixing such maximum prices of commodities and rents as will effectuate the purpose of the Act and conform to the standards which it prescribes. The Act was adopted as a temporary wartime measure and provides in §1(b) for its termination on June 30, 1943, unless sooner terminated by Presidential proclamation or concurrent resolution of Congress. By the amendatory act of October 2, 1942, it was extended to June 30, 1944.

Section 1(a) declares that the Act is "in the interest of the national defense and security and necessary to the effective prosecution of the present war," and that its purposes are:

> "to stabilize prices and to prevent speculative, unwarranted, and abnormal increases in prices and rents; to eliminate and prevent profiteering, hoarding, manipulation, speculation, and other disruptive practices resulting from abnormal market conditions or scarcities caused by or contributing to the national emergency; to assure that defense appropriations are not dissipated by excessive prices; to protect persons with relatively fixed and limited incomes, consumers, wage earners, investors, and persons dependent on life insurance, annuities, and pensions, from undue impairment of their standard of living; to prevent hardships to persons engaged in business, . . . and to the Federal, State, and local governments, which would result from abnormal increases in prices; to assist in securing adequate production of commodities and facilities; to prevent a post-emergency collapse of values. . . ."

[The Court then identified the standards prescribed in the two statutes and in a presidential executive order:]

The standards which are to guide the Administrator's exercise of his authority to fix prices, so far as now relevant, are prescribed by § 2(a) and by § 1 of the amendatory Act of October 2, 1942, and Executive Order 9250. . . . By § 2(a) the Administrator is authorized, after consultation with representative members of the industry so far as practicable, to promulgate regulations fixing prices of commodities which "in his judgment will be generally fair and equitable and will effectuate the purposes of this Act" when, in his judgment, their prices "have risen or threaten to rise to an extent or in a manner inconsistent with the purposes of this Act."

The section also directs that

"So far as practicable, in establishing any maximum price, the Administrator shall ascertain and give due consideration to the prices prevailing between October 1 and October 15, 1941 (or if, in the case of any commodity, there are no prevailing prices between such dates, or the prevailing prices between such dates are not generally representative because of abnormal or seasonal market conditions or other cause, then to the prices prevailing during the nearest two-week period in which, in the judgment of the Administrator, the prices for such commodity are generally representative) . . . and shall make adjustments for such relevant factors as he may determine and deem to be of general applicability, including . . . [s]peculative fluctuations, general increases or decreases in costs of production, distribution, and transportation, and general increases or decreases in profits earned by sellers of the commodity or commodities, during and subsequent to the year ended October 1, 1941."

By the Act of October 2, 1942, the President is directed to stabilize prices, wages and salaries "so far as practicable" on the basis of the levels which existed on September 15, 1942, except as otherwise provided in the Act. By Title I, § 4 of Executive Order No. 9250, he has directed "all departments and agencies of the Government" "to stabilize the cost of living in accordance with the Act of October 2, 1942."

[The relevant administrative regulation was then summarized:]

Revised Maximum Price Regulation No. 169 was issued December 10, 1942, under authority of the Emergency Price Control Act as amended and Executive Order No. 9250. The Regulation established specific maximum prices for the sale at wholesale of specified cuts of beef and veal. As is required by § 2(a) of the Act, it was accompanied by a "statement of the considerations involved" in prescribing it. From the preamble to the Regulation and from the Statement of Considerations accompanying it, it appears that the prices fixed for sales at wholesale were slightly in excess of those prevailing between March 16 and March 28, 1942, and approximated those prevailing on September 15, 1942. Findings that the Regulation was necessary, that the prices which it fixed were fair and equitable, and that it otherwise conformed to the standards prescribed by the Act, appear in the Statement of Considerations.

. . .

[The Court then explained why the delegation of legislative power to the agency was not unconstitutional:]

Congress enacted the Emergency Price Control Act in pursuance of a defined policy and required that the prices fixed by the Administrator should further that policy and conform to standards prescribed by the Act. The boundaries of the field of the Administrator's permissible action are marked by the statute. It directs that the prices fixed shall effectuate the declared policy of the Act to stabilize commodity prices so as to prevent war-time inflation and its enumerated disruptive causes and effects. In addition the prices established must be fair and equitable, and in fixing them the Administrator is directed to give due consideration, so far as practicable, to prevailing prices during the designated base period, with prescribed administrative adjustments to compensate for enumerated disturbing factors affecting prices. . . .

The Act is thus an exercise by Congress of its legislative power. In it Congress has stated the legislative objective, has prescribed the method of achieving that objective—maximum price fixing—and has laid down standards to guide the administrative determination of both the occasions for the exercise of the price-fixing power, and the particular prices to be established. . . .

The Constitution as a continuously operative charter of government does not demand the impossible or the impracticable. It does not require that Congress find for itself every fact upon which it desires to base legislative action, or that it make for itself detailed determinations which it has declared to be prerequisite to the application of the legislative policy to particular facts and circumstances impossible for Congress itself properly to investigate. *The essentials of the legislative function are the determination of the legislative policy and its formulation and promulgation as a defined and binding rule of conduct*—here the rule, with penal sanctions, that prices shall not be greater than those fixed by maximum price regulations which conform to standards and will tend to further the policy which Congress has established. These essentials are preserved when Congress has specified the basic conditions of fact upon whose existence or occurrence, ascertained from relevant data by a designated administrative agency, it directs that its statutory command shall be effective. It is no objection that the determination of facts and the inferences to be drawn from them in the light of the statutory standards and declaration of policy call for the exercise of judgment, and for the formulation of subsidiary administrative policy within the prescribed statutory framework. . . .

Nor does the doctrine of separation of powers deny to Congress power to direct that an administrative officer properly designated for that purpose have ample latitude within which he is to ascertain the conditions which Congress has made prerequisite to the operation of its legislative command. Acting within its constitutional power to fix prices, it is for Congress to say whether the data on the basis of which prices are to be fixed are to be confined within a narrow or a broad range. In either case the only concern of courts is to ascertain whether the will of Congress has been obeyed. . . .

. . . Congress is not confined to that method of executing its policy which involves the least possible delegation of discretion to administrative officers. . . . It is free to avoid the rigidity of such a system, which might well result in serious hardship, and to choose instead the flexibility attainable by the use of less restrictive standards. . . . *Only if we could say that there is an absence of standards for the guidance of the Administrator's action, so that it would be impossible in a proper proceeding to ascertain whether the will of Congress has been obeyed, would we be justified in overriding its choice of means for effecting its declared purpose of preventing inflation.*

[Finally, the Court compared the standards of the price-control statutes with those prescribed in other laws which had been upheld by the Court in earlier decisions:]

The standards prescribed by the present Act, with the aid of the "statement of the considerations" required to be made by the Administrator, are sufficiently definite and precise to enable Congress, the courts and the public to ascertain whether the Administrator, in fixing the designated prices, has conformed to those standards. . . . Hence we are unable to find in them an unauthorized delegation of legislative power. The authority to fix prices only when prices have risen or threaten to rise to an extent or in a manner inconsistent with the purpose of the Act to prevent inflation is no broader than the authority to fix maximum prices when deemed necessary to protect consumers against unreasonably high prices . . . or the authority to take possession of and operate telegraph lines whenever deemed necessary for the national security or defense . . . or the authority to suspend tariff provisions upon findings that the duties imposed by a foreign state are "reciprocally unequal and unreasonable." . . .

The directions that the prices fixed shall be fair and equitable, that in addition they shall tend to promote the purposes of the Act, and that in promulgating them consideration shall be given to prices prevailing in a stated base period, confer no greater reach for administrative determination than the power to fix just and reasonable rates . . . or the power to approve consolidations in the "public interest" . . . or the power to regulate radio stations engaged in chain broadcasting "as public interest, convenience or necessity requires" . . . or the power to prohibit "unfair methods of competition" not defined or forbidden by the common law . . . or the direction that in allotting marketing quotas among states and producers due consideration be given to a variety of economic factors . . . or the similar direction that in adjusting tariffs to meet differences in costs of production the President "take into consideration" "in so far as he finds practicable" a variety of economic matters . . . or the similar authority, in making classifications within an industry, to consider various named and unnamed "relevant factors" and determine the respective weights attributable to each.

• • •

Affirmed.   ◄

Although the courts rarely invalidate administrative regulations on the ground that they have been issued under unconstitutional delegations of power, regulations are sometimes invalidated because they fail to satisfy other constitutional standards. Regardless of how much authority the legislature grants to an agency, the agency may not issue a regulation that represents an unconstitutional exercise of government power. For example, a federal agency whose regulatory authority is constitutionally based on the "commerce clause" may not attempt to regulate purely *intrastate* commerce. Nor may any agency issue a regulation that serves to "deprive any person of life, liberty, or property without due process of law." Several early efforts by railroad commissions to establish rates foundered on the due-process restriction in the Fourteenth Amendment; the Supreme Court decided that the rates set were so low that they deprived the railroads of property without due process. Similarly, an administrative rule establishing a discriminatory classification might be invalidated under the Fourteenth Amendment's "equal protection" clause.

Finally, in deciding on the validity of administrative regulations, the courts ask whether the agency followed proper procedures in adopting the regulations. A major purpose of procedural requirements is to assure fair treatment to the private persons who are likely to be affected by the agency's rules. Are such persons entitled, for example, to receive notice that a new rule is under consideration and to have an opportunity to express themselves on its contents? Ordinarily, an agency's failure to give notice and to hold a hearing before issuing a regulation is not considered a denial of constitutional rights.[5] Still, many of the statutes under which administrative agencies operate require the agency to publish notice of the proposed regulations and to give interested parties an opportunity to express their views.

Less Formal Administrative Pronouncements

Administrative agencies issue a variety of pronouncements, less formal and binding than their "legislative" regulations, which are designed to clarify the laws they are administering. Some of these are described as "interpretive regulations." Moreover, in response to inquiries, agencies sometimes issue advisory "rulings" which interpret the law with reference to particular types of situation. In addition, some agencies also publish instructions, guides, explanatory pamphlets, and so forth.

In approaching a federal income tax problem, for instance, a lawyer will look first at the Internal Revenue Code and at the voluminous regulations of the Treasury Department and the Internal Revenue Service. But he will also look at the other interpretations and guides that the IRS publishes. These have some of the qualities of legal rules. They indicate how the agency interprets the law it is administering, and hence they form a basis for predicting its position in particular cases. The courts, too, accord considerable respect to these informal pronouncements, particularly if they seem to be reasonable elaborations of the policies and standards of the statute.

---

[5] Nor are legislatures constitutionally required to give advance notice and to hold a hearing when they are studying a legislative proposal. But most of them try to give affected parties a chance to be heard.

Adjudication [6] and Decisional Rule-Making by Administrators

So far we have been talking about how administrators *create* rules (that is, directives designed to influence the future conduct of whole categories of persons). Now let us consider how administrators *apply* rules to particular cases.[7]

Administrative Adjudication

Administrators have always engaged in fact-finding. In order to determine whether a law was being complied with, for example, or whether an applicant was entitled to a license or a franchise, they have always had to investigate, inspect, ask questions, and insist that their questions be answered. But only with the emergence of the modern regulatory agency has the trial-like hearing, at which testimony and documents may be presented and challenged with the aid of counsel, come into widespread use.

One of the most important categories of administrative adjudication is the so-called "enforcement proceeding," which resembles a criminal prosecution in some respects. This is a proceeding to adjudicate charges that the standards established by a particular law have not been complied with. The National Labor Relations Board, for example, conducts enforcement proceedings to determine whether an "unfair labor practice" has been committed. And the state fair employment practices commissions hold enforcement proceedings to determine whether an employer's hiring and promoting practices have involved racial or religious discrimination.

The agency's enforcement officials, acting either on their own initiative or in response to a private complaint (depending on what the statute provides), inquire into possible violations. If they find evidence of wrongdoing, they usually try first to negotiate a settlement with the violator under which he agrees to comply with the law. Many violations are brought to an end by negotiation, and administrative intervention goes no further. But if negotiation proves fruitless, the agency files a formal "complaint" and holds a public hearing.

Many of the procedures of the court trial have been taken over for the administrative hearing (perhaps partly because the officials who participate in the hearings are usually lawyers). But one difference is noteworthy: in administrative hearings the functions of both "prosecutor" and "judge" are normally performed by officials of the same agency, and occasionally by the same official. In the larger agencies, cases are generally heard by a

---

[6] Used broadly, "adjudication" refers to any proceeding in which, after an examination of evidence and arguments, a finding of facts is made and a decision is reached by applying rules to the facts found. The court trial is the best-known example.

[7] Often the distinction between making general rules and deciding particular cases is merely a matter of degree. For example, when an administrative agency prescribes the freight rate to be charged by a particular railroad for transporting a particular commodity between two named points, is it establishing a rule or dealing with a particular case? Rate-setting, because it channels future conduct, is classified as rule-making; but, since the setting of a particular rate usually affects only a few private parties, it closely resembles case-deciding. Consequently, the parties affected usually get the same sort of hearing they would have if their rights were being adjudicated.

"trial examiner," whose decision is later reviewed by the top officials of the agency (usually referred to collectively as "the commission" or "the board").[8] If the commission sustains the enforcement official's contentions, it usually issues an agency order to the accused party. If this order is not voluntarily obeyed, the agency must obtain a court order to enforce it.

Other types of administrative hearing are held to determine whether a license should be revoked, or which of several parties should be awarded a franchise, or whether a person accused of past wrongdoing should be discharged from government service or deported from the country. Some hearings, in which one private party presses a claim against another, are very similar to civil proceedings—as, for example, when an employee comes before a workmen's compensation board to claim damages from his employer for an injury sustained while at work.

Judicial Review

In many situations the law does not require administrators to hold hearings before reaching a decision. After all, hearings take time and cost money, and the legislature may decide that the need for administrative efficiency is more compelling than a full hearing for those individuals who desire it. Some administrative decisions, indeed, are declared by law to be final and unreviewable. (When an American consul refuses a visa to a would-be visitor to this country, for instance, there is no legal recourse from his decision.)

But under most circumstances the individual has the right to contest an administrator's decision in the courts. This is known as "the right to judicial review." The court may not be empowered to re-examine the evidence, and it may be unwilling to overturn the administrator's interpretation of the statute under which he operates. But the individual can always ask a court to rule on such issues as the statute's constitutionality, the administrator's jurisdiction, and the regularity of the procedures followed in reaching the decision. And he can always persuade a court to reverse an administrative decision if he can prove prejudice or corruption. To cut the individual off from access to the courts would be a denial of constitutional "due process."

---

[8] This combination of the functions of prosecutor and judge has long been an object of criticism. After years of controversy, a compromise between the proponents and the critics of the "integrated" agency was incorporated into the federal Administrative Procedures Act of 1946. Proposals for a completely autonomous corps of trial examiners and for a special administrative court were rejected. Briefly, the objects of the provisions adopted were: (a) to insulate the trial examiner from intra-agency pressures by giving the Civil Service Commission a special role in decisions concerning his salary and tenure; (b) to prevent the trial examiner from discussing any case before him with outsiders or with other agency officials unless all interested parties could take part in the discussions; and (c) to deny the enforcement officials of an agency any role in making the final agency decision. In 1947 Congress responded to criticisms of the National Labor Relations Board by going one step further: it took the Board's Office of General Counsel completely out of the agency, making it an independent entity charged with investigating complaints and acting as prosecutor in enforcement proceedings heard by the Board.

Over the centuries judges and legislators have devised a variety of procedures by which the individual may challenge administrative acts in the courts. We need not enumerate them here. It is not always necessary, moreover, for the individual to take the initiative. Since, with a few exceptions, administrators have no power to enforce their own decisions (that is, to compel private persons to obey their orders or to punish them for not complying), the individual is often able to contest a decision simply by defying it and forcing the administrator to take the case to court.

Having the right to an administrative hearing does not deprive a person of his right to judicial review. But as administrative fact-finding procedures have improved, the scope of judicial review has narrowed. As legislators and judges have gained confidence in the fairness of administrative procedures, they have abandoned their earlier insistence on a judicial re-examination of the agency's findings of fact. The reviewing court may be either a trial court or an appellate court (depending on what the relevant statute provides), but in either event the review proceeding resembles an appeal rather than a new trial. The court ordinarily does not rehear the evidence; it merely reviews the record of the agency proceedings, and if there appears to be "substantial evidence in the whole record" to support the agency's finding, the judges do not reject it even though they might have drawn different conclusions from the evidence if they themselves had heard the case. The judges do, of course, review all the agency's conclusions of law. But they often acknowledge that the agency, through its knowledge and experience, is far better equipped than they to work out the implications of the statutory policy. Hence, if an agency's conclusions of law seem to be a reasoned and reasonable elaboration of the statute's objectives, most courts are inclined to accept them.

The availability of judicial review undoubtedly makes administrators less arbitrary in their decisions and more careful in construing their legal powers. But only a small percentage of each year's administrative decisions are actually reviewed in the courts. The administrator's decision is almost always the final decision.

Decisional Rule-Making by Administrators

To decide cases, then, agencies must interpret the law as well as determine the facts. Their interpretations appear in the opinions that accompany agency decisions, many of which are published. Most agencies, though they do not feel rigidly bound by *stare decisis*, still tend to follow their own precedents—for the same reasons that courts do (see page 60). Hence adjudicative decisions give interested parties a fairly reliable basis on which to predict an agency's future position. Of course, an agency ruling ceases to be controlling once it is appealed and a court reverses it. But, as we have just seen, most agency decisions are not appealed, and, of those few that are, most are upheld.

In short, agency decisions become in effect decisional rules: they channel future conduct. If, for instance, a company wishes to know how far it must go in bargaining with a union in order to satisfy the statutory requirement of "bargaining in good faith" (to be discussed below), it can do no better than to study the National Labor Relations Board's decisions (plus the relatively few court decisions) in which the requirement has been interpreted.

Since many agencies have both the power to issue regulations and the power to adjudicate cases, they can choose between the two methods of rule-making. When an agency believes that the time has come to formulate a policy decision in an official text, it can draft and issue a regulation. But when an agency prefers to wait until the contours of a problem become clearer, it can continue to deal with the problem on a case-by-case basis, formulating a series of decisional rules couched in terms that insure continuing flexibility. Furthermore, an agency, unlike a court, does not have to wait passively for cases to be brought before it. Its enforcement officials can go out looking for cases that will raise the issues its adjudicating officials want to rule on. And, since the agency can pretty much decide for itself what enforcement proceedings to initiate, it can choose cases that present the issues in such a way that the courts will be likely to uphold the agency's ruling if an appeal is taken.

An Illustrative Case

The case of the Truitt Manufacturing Company was decided by the National Labor Relations Board and then appealed first to a federal court of appeals and later to the United States Supreme Court. It exemplifies three quite different types of judicial reaction to an administrative decision.

The issue in the case was whether the Truitt Company was guilty of the "unfair labor practice" of refusing to "bargain in good faith" as required by the National Labor Relations Act. The union had filed "unfair labor practice" charges with the National Labor Relations Board, and the Board's officers—after having presumably tried and failed to settle the controversy without resorting to formal proceedings—had filed a complaint against the company. The first hearing was before one of the Board's trial examiners; his decision was then reviewed by the five-member Board itself. The specific issue was whether the company, which had rejected a requested wage increase on economic grounds but had refused to provide information demanded by the union as proof of the company's alleged inability to pay more, was refusing to "bargain in good faith." (The italics have been added by the authors.)

MATTER OF TRUITT MANUFACTURING CO.

National Labor Relations Board, 1955. 110 NLRB 856
United States Court of Appeals, Fourth Circuit, 1955. 224 F.2d 869
Supreme Court of the United States, 1956
351 U.S. 149, 76 S.Ct. 753

[*Excerpts from the Board's decision and order:*]

► We agree with the Trial Examiner that the Respondent failed to bargain in good faith with respect to wages in violation of Section 8(a)(5) of the Act. We do not, however, mean to imply, nor do we adopt the statement of the Trial Examiner, that the Respondent's failure to substantiate its economic position as to wages obligates the Respondent to accede to the Union's wage demands. On the other hand, it is settled law, that when an employer seeks to justify the refusal of a wage increase upon an economic basis, as did the Respondent herein, good-faith bargaining under the Act requires that upon request the employer attempt to substantiate its economic position by reasonable proof. In the present case, we are satisfied that the Respondent has failed to submit such reasonable proof. We shall, therefore, order that the Respondent bargain collectively with the Union.

Upon the entire record in the case, and pursuant to Section 10(c) of the National Labor Relations Act, the National Labor Relations Board hereby orders that the Respondent, Truitt Manufacturing Co., of Greensboro, North Carolina, its officers, agents, successors, and assigns, shall:

. . .

(b) Upon request furnish Shopmen's Local 729, International Association of Bridge, Structural and Ornamental Iron Workers of America, A.F.L., with such statistical and other information as will substantiate the Respondent's position of its economic inability to pay the requested wage increase and will enable the Shopmen's Local No. 729 . . . to discharge its functions as the statutory collective bargaining representative of the employees in the unit found appropriate by the Board.   ◄

[Excerpts from the opinion of the Court of Appeals:]

► PARKER, C. J. . . . It is to be noted that the statute expressly provides that neither party is under obligation to make any "concession" in connection with the bargaining; but if the position of the Board here is sustained, it will result that every employer who resists a wage increase on economic grounds must make the concession of opening up his books and disclosing to the union not only his general financial condition, but such highly confidential matters as manufacturing costs. We feel sure that it was never intended that the employer be required to disclose such information to its employees as an incident of collective bargaining; and we feel equally sure that Congress never would have passed a statute which it thought could have been given such interpretation. . . .

There is nothing in our decision in N.L.R.B. v. Whitin Machine Works which supports the order of the Board. . . . The decision of the Court of Appeals of the 2d Circuit in N.L.R.B. v. Yawman & Erbe Mfg. Co., is distinguishable on the same ground. . . .

Our conclusion is that failure to comply with the demand to furnish to the bargaining union the information here demanded did not establish bad faith in the bargaining, in which the employer here was admittedly engaged, and that there was no basis for the Board's finding of an unfair labor practice. The [Board's] petition for enforcement must accordingly be denied and the order of the Board set aside.   ◄

[*Excerpts from the opinions of the Supreme Court:*]

▶ MR. JUSTICE BLACK delivered the opinion of the Court. . . .

We think that in determining whether the obligation of good-faith bargaining has been met the Board has a right to consider an employer's refusal to give information about its financial status. While Congress did not compel agreement between employers and bargaining representatives, it did require collective bargaining in the hope that agreements would result. . . .

Good-faith bargaining necessarily requires that claims made by either bargainer should be honest claims. This is true about an asserted inability to pay an increase in wages. If such an argument is important enough to present in the give and take of bargaining, it is important enough to require some sort of proof of its accuracy. And *it would certainly not be far-fetched for a trier of fact to reach the conclusion* that bargaining lacks good faith when an employer mechanically repeats a claim of inability to pay without making the slightest effort to substantiate the claim. Such has been the holding of the Labor Board since shortly after the passage of the Wagner Act. . . . This was the position of the Board when the Taft-Hartley Act was passed in 1947 and has been its position ever since. We agree with the Board that a refusal to attempt to substantiate a claim of inability to pay increased wages *may support a finding* of a failure to bargain in good faith.

The Board concluded that under the facts and circumstances of this case the respondent was guilty of an unfair labor practice in failing to bargain in good faith. *We see no reason to disturb the findings of the Board.* We do not hold, however, that in every case in which economic inability is raised as an argument against increased wages it automatically follows that the employees are entitled to substantiating evidence. Each case must turn upon its particular facts. The inquiry must always be whether or not under the circumstances of the particular case the statutory obligation has been met. Since we conclude that *there is support in the record for the conclusion of the Board* here that respondent did not bargain in good faith, it was error for the Court of Appeals to set aside the Board's order and deny enforcement.

MR. JUSTICE FRANKFURTER, whom MR. JUSTICE CLARK and MR. JUSTICE HARLAN join, concurring in part and dissenting in part.

. . . A determination of good faith or of want of good faith normally can rest only on an inference based upon more or less persuasive manifestations of another's state of mind. The previous relations of the parties, antecedent events explaining behavior at the bargaining table, and the course of negotiations constitute the raw facts for reaching such a determination. The appropriate inferences to be drawn from what is often confused and tangled testimony about all this *makes a finding of absence of good faith one for the judgment of the Labor Board, unless the record as a whole leaves such judgment without reasonable foundation.*

An examination of the Board's opinion and the position taken by its counsel here disclose that the Board did not so conceive the issue of good-faith bargaining in this case. The totality of the conduct of the negotiation was apparently deemed irrelevant to the question; one fact alone disposed of the case. "[I]t is settled law [the Board concluded], that when an employer seeks to justify the refusal of a wage increase upon an economic basis, as did the Respondent herein, good-faith bargaining under the Act requires that upon request the employer attempt to substantiate its economic position by reasonable proof."

This is to make a rule of law out of one item—even if a weighty item— of the evidence. . . . *Since the Board applied the wrong standard here,* by ruling that Truitt's failure to supply financial information to the union constituted *per se* a refusal to bargain in good faith, the case should be returned to the Board. There is substantial evidence in the record which indicates that Truitt tried to reach an agreement. . . .

Because the record is not conclusive as a matter of law, one way or the other, I cannot join in the Court's disposition of the case. To reverse the Court of Appeals without remanding the case to the Board for further proceedings *implies that the Board would have reached the same conclusion in applying the right rule of law that it did in applying a wrong one.* I cannot make such a forecast. I would return the case to the Board so that it may apply the relevant standard for determining "good faith."   ◀

The issue before these three tribunals was a mixed question of law and fact (see pp. 22–23). The question—Was there good-faith bargaining here?— requires not only a general definition of good-faith bargaining (law), and a determination of what happened in these particular negotiations (fact), but also a decision on which facts were relevant in deciding whether there was good-faith bargaining in this case (mixed). The majority of the Supreme Court seems to have been content to let the "triers of fact" (the Board) decide this mixed question—that is, decide which facts were relevant in determining whether the company had bargained in good faith. So long as there seemed to be substantial evidence in the record to support the Board's conclusion, the majority was prepared to accept that conclusion.

The dissenters, on the other hand, believed that the Board's determination of which facts were relevant was subject to review by the Court; and they believed the Court should rule that the Board's view of the relevant facts was too narrow. The Board has thus applied the wrong standard, said Justice Frankfurter, and since we cannot assume that it would have reached the same decision if it had applied the correct standard, we should send the case back to the Board for further proceedings.[9]

---

[9] For another case raising a similar issue concerning the respective roles of the agency and the courts, see *Federal Trade Commission v. Motion Picture Advertising Service Co., Inc.,* page 864. The majority of the Supreme Court in that case upheld the Commission's order and accepted its finding that the respondent's acts constituted "unfair methods of competition," since it was "supported by substantial evidence." But Justice Frankfurter dissented; he would have sent the case back to the Commission for further findings. In his view, the Commission had merely stated its conclusions without justifying them or indicating the criteria it was applying. "[T]he scope of the prohibition of 'unfair methods of competition,' " he said, "has not been left to the administrative agency as part of its fact-finding authority but is a matter of law to be defined by the courts."

Achievements and Disappointments

Ever since the end of the nineteenth century, legislatures in the United States have been adopting policies for the regulation of a multitude of economic activities. Since the legislatures had neither the time nor the knowledge to create detailed rules, however, it was soon clear that new governmental arrangements would be needed to handle the job of rule-making. The courts, moreover, many of them already congested, would have been swamped if they had had to adjudicate all the controversies that the new legislation was bound to create; and the judges, already obliged to handle a great diversity of cases, would have been hard pressed to acquire the knowledge they needed to deal intelligently with all the new types of controversy.

So the decision was made to create a large number of specialized administrative agencies and to give them broader powers than administrators had traditionally exercised. These included the power to issue regulations having the force of law, and the power to hear and decide cases—powers that had previously been reserved to the legislatures and the courts.

It was recognized that the granting of these powers held some dangers. The "bureaucrats" who received the new rule-making power did not have to face the salutary test of standing for election every few years. And the new adjudicators were not heirs to a long and honorable professional tradition. But various safeguards existed—particularly judicial review, which, it was hoped, would curb arbitrariness, oppression, and corruption on the part of officials.

The regulatory agencies have had a mixed record of performance. Some of the hopes of those who framed the original legislation have been disappointed. For one thing, few of the regulatory agencies have become effective formulators of long-range policy. We have learned that establishing a specialized agency with broad authority to create new rules is only a beginning. The agency must be manned by officials who are bold and imaginative, farsighted in their planning and yet ready to renounce policy formulations which changing economic conditions have made obsolete, and capable of running an efficient agency without letting daily routine obscure the needs of the future. Such men have always been in short supply, and their absence has made the agencies only partially effective.

Over the past twenty-five years, the criticisms leveled against administrative agencies have changed. In the 1930's, when some of the most important agencies were still young, critics complained that the administrators were high-handed zealots, often suspicious or downright hostile toward the economic group whose practices they were supposed to regulate. In those days the main focus of criticism was on the assignment to some agencies of both enforcement and adjudicative functions. Some of these earlier criticisms have been met over the years. But a new generation of critics complains that today's administrators too often lack zeal, and are mediocre and inefficient; that they have often become so sympathetic with the problems of those they regulate that they have lost sight of the broader "public interest"; that too many top administrators have been shown to be susceptible to improper and even corrupt influences; and finally that most agencies have failed to develop coherent, long-range objectives and policies.

In conclusion we must acknowledge, however, that although some expectations have been disappointed, many have been realized. And it is difficult to see how more of the original objectives could have been achieved, within the limitations imposed by our democratic principles, the federal system, and long-standing constitutional arrangements, by any governmental arrangement substantially different from the one that was adopted.

9 Some Private Contributions to the Legal System

In this book, "law" and "legal rule" are defined as including only those guides to conduct which are created by officials; hence "lawmaking" is defined to cover only the creation of rules by officials. Some scholars use a broader definition, and speak also of "private lawmaking." They point out that many of the arrangements that private individuals and groups work out among themselves—contracts are a notable example—impose legally enforceable obligations on the negotiating parties and others; since these arrangements control future conduct, they have the same effect as legal rules.

We have adopted a narrower definition of "lawmaking," a definition which corresponds more closely to what most people understand by the term. But we cannot on that account ignore the contributions which private persons make to the legal system. These contributions are discussed in this chapter. First, we shall consider very briefly the contributions of private persons and groups to the legal fabric that is continuously being woven by legislators, judges, and administrators. Then we shall consider at much greater length the contributions that private groups make to social ordering by creating their own systems of private rules (sometimes described as "quasi-law"). As an example of such "quasi-law" systems, we shall study the "government under law" that has been developed in industry by employers and organized labor under collective-bargaining agreements.

Private Contributions to Lawmaking

In a democratic society, the major aim of government and law is to provide a setting in which the individual can pursue his own objectives. For example, we continue to rely largely on the decisions of private producers and consumers to determine what gets produced, and how, and by whom. Law establishes the framework within which such private decision-making takes place. But the reverse relationship is equally important: patterns of private conduct play a part in forming law. What the rules permit largely determines what people do, but what people do (and aspire to do) largely determines what problems officials must deal with, and thus the content of the rules they make.

How, specifically, does private conduct affect the content of legal rules?

Private Controversies Produce Decisional Rules. In the last chapter, we noted how officials who prosecute cases in the courts or in administrative hearings influence the shaping of decisional rules by their choice of which cases to bring, and of which legal arguments to present in those cases. Private parties, both plaintiffs and defendants, perform a comparable function. The character of the decisional rules that emerge from court and agency adjudications is largely determined by the way in which the legal issues are presented for decision, which in turn depends on the facts of the particular case and the arguments advanced by the parties. In short, how private persons go about settling their disputes plays a part in creating law.

Group Pressures Produce Legislative Rules. Legislative rules are enacted because of a felt need for legislative action. This felt need is usually stimulated by the actions of private persons and the political pressures of organized interest groups. In a free society such pressures are inevitable and desirable. Often an interest group will not only point out the need but propose a remedy. It may even come up with a draft bill for enactment, and where the subject matter is technical, legislators tend to rely heavily on such drafts. Clearly what private groups do about creating the need for legislative action and then pushing for specific enactments plays a part in creating law.

Private Arrangements Become Legal Standards. In Chapter 13 we will read about how the privately enforced rules and usages that merchants had been developing ever since the Middle Ages were absorbed into English law in the eighteenth century. English judges had long been willing to accept evidence of merchants' usages as aids in interpreting commercial contracts, but the eighteenth-century judges went further and declared these nonofficial arrangements to be a part of the law of England. Many of the rules that you will read about in Part II, particularly in the chapters on sales and negotiable instruments, had their origins in this privately developed body of rules: the so-called "law merchant."

This process continues in modern times. Suppose a man wishes to exercise a legal power [1] in such a way as to secure certain results while avoiding certain other results. (Perhaps he wants to complete a certain transaction while incurring the minimum possible tax liability. Or he may want to make an airtight contract with someone he does not wholly trust. Or he may want to create an ownership interest in a business with only a limited right of control.) He goes to a lawyer and presents his problem. The lawyer discovers that none of the usual tools in his kit is exactly what

---

[1] See pp. 8–9 on *powers.* Briefly, a rule of law that establishes a power says in effect that if a person acts in a prescribed fashion the law will attribute to his act a certain legal consequence. If I make out a will in the manner prescribed by law, officials will see to it that my designated heirs get my property when I die. If I sign a valid contract, I assure myself of the aid of the courts if the other party defaults.

is needed. So he invents a solution: a new arrangement, a new type of document or a new combination of words especially designed to achieve the desired result. His invention is eventually challenged and tested in a court. If it survives, and if it is shown to accomplish what the client wanted, other lawyers will learn of it and copy it. Before long the new device is likely to be given a standardized form and a label. Judges will acknowledge it as an approved method of exercising a legal power. Drafters of legislation—of uniform state commercial codes, for instance, or of tax laws—will take it into account and make provisions for it. And finally it will take its place among the tools in the kit of every competent lawyer.

The terms of standardized sales contracts, deeds, mortgages, leases, and corporate charters and bylaws were largely created by lawyers, as were such arrangements of relatively recent origin as the employee pension trust and the stock option for corporate executives.[2]

Private Supplements to Lawmaking: "Quasi-law" Systems

From time to time, as we have just observed, novel methods of solving private legal problems produce arrangements of such obvious merit that they eventually become a part of the legal fabric itself. Mostly, however, the acts of private persons and groups exercising legal powers merely impose rights and duties on the parties immediately concerned. Although the duties created by the terms of a valid contract may be enforced by a court against either party to the contract, they normally have little significance for the rest of the community. Not having been created by officials and lacking in general applicability, they are not "law" as we have defined that term.

Yet when a power is exercised by private persons in such a way as to determine the rights and duties of a large number of people, the process has much in common with lawmaking; hence we are justified in saying that such an exercise of power creates "quasi-law." Take, for example, the Major League Agreement that controls the activities of the baseball teams forming the two major leagues. In form, this agreement is a contract drawn up by the club-owners and subscribed to by all the major-league players. But it might also be described as the constitution of a system of private self-government in which the club-owners are the legislators, the league presidents the executives, and the Commissioner the judge. (The actual division of functions is not quite so neat, of course. Yet it is interesting to note that the first Commissioner of Baseball was a former federal judge.)

It would be most undesirable, if not impossible, for the state to try to

---

[2] It may be well to note here that many customs and usages which have no status as authoritative rules are regularly taken into account by courts in deciding cases. A trade practice may illuminate the probable intentions of the parties to a commercial contract, for instance. For an example, see *Chastain v. Bowman*, page 538. Moreover, when a court must decide whether a businessman or a professional person has acted with "due care," it has to measure that person's act against the traditional standards and practices of the trade or profession.

prescribe all the rules governing private conduct. Our innumerable private associations—corporations, labor unions, clubs, schools, churches, and families (to name only a few)—all have their own rules, and the state relies on these private "quasi-law" rules to do much of the conduct-channeling which our society requires. Essentially, the legal system provides a framework, a backstop, for the operation of these private rules.

A particularly interesting illustration of a "quasi-law" system is the labor-management relationship established under a collective-bargaining agreement. Such agreements have some of the characteristics of contracts, but in many ways they resemble constitutions. When the United Steelworkers of America and the major steel companies sign an agreement, their act puts into effect a set of basic rules governing the relationship of hundreds of thousands of employees with their employers. The agreement contains not only rules governing the conduct of the parties, but rules establishing institutions and procedures under which disputes arising between the parties will be handled while the agreement is in force. This type of "quasi-law" system will be the subject of the remainder of this chapter.

Industrial Self-government
Under the Collective-Bargaining Agreement

The Legal Framework of Industrial Relations

FROM THE CIVIL WAR TO 1935. American workingmen made their first efforts to organize and bargain collectively during the eighteenth century, but the modern growth of unions dates from the last three decades of the nineteenth. The rapid industrialization that followed the Civil War, the development of larger and larger enterprises, and the vast influx of immigrants swelled the ranks of the wage-earning class and accelerated the drive for worker organization. But there was no corresponding increase during this period in the willingness of employers to bargain with unions. From the 1880's well into the 1930's, the use of professional strike-breakers, company spies, "yellow-dog" contracts (which made nonmembership in a union a condition of employment), and a variety of other means of combating unions was commonplace. The workers, in turn, resorted to strikes, picketing, and boycotts to win better pay and working conditions and to compel recognition of their unions. Bitter outbreaks of violence during these years resulted in severe losses of life, property, and production.

The evolution of legal rules in this field is an interesting example of the manner in which changes in legal rules are prompted by the displacement of one theory of social ordering by another. It is also a good illustration of the relation between judicial lawmaking and legislative lawmaking.

The social theory that prevailed in the latter part of the nineteenth century has been given the label "laissez faire." Its first principle was that the community's welfare is generally best served by letting people go about their business with a minimum of government interference. According to this theory, allowing individuals to pursue their own self-interest in free markets, relying on the "invisible hand" of competition within producer groups and on free bargaining between those groups, will do a better job of achieving the greatest good for the greatest number than the most enlightened government could ever do. The proper levels of prices and wages, and the proper allocation of resources, are those ordained by the market. A related concept, extracted from the biological researches of Darwin, was that there has always been a struggle for existence in human society, a struggle in which the fittest survive. That A has prospered while B lives in poverty is simply proof that A was the fitter.

Free competition implies, of course, not only that the government does not interfere with the operation of free markets, but that producers and sellers do not get together to stifle competition. This notion had long been recognized; indeed, a common-law rule had held "conspiracies in restraint of trade" to be illegal. (In 1890 this rule was given teeth by the passage of the Sherman Act.) The rule against "restraint of trade" was thought of as applying to workers as well as to businesses; indeed, in the first part of the nineteenth century worker organizations had on a number of occasions been prosecuted for "conspiring" for the purpose of raising wages. The prevailing belief was that, just as prices should be determined by the competition of many firms for the consumer's dollar, so wages should be determined by the competition of many workers (bargaining individually with employers) for jobs and pay.

The "laissez faire" doctrines of the nineteenth century no longer dominate American economic thinking. Gradually we have come to recognize that there are situations in which government intervention is unavoidable, in which competition is unable to perform the function of automatic regulation traditionally expected of it, and in which it is unrealistic to expect genuine bargaining to take place. Neither competition nor bargaining produces the desired results if the parties are too unevenly matched. When a giant firm "competes" with a tiny one, the tiny firm goes under, and there is less competition thereafter. When a large company "bargains" with an individual employee, it usually imposes its own terms, and they may be harsh. This is perhaps what "the survival of the fittest" implies. But it is not really bargaining.

By 1900 it was clear that many employers were in fact not bargaining with their workers, but merely imposing their own terms on them. The disadvantages experienced by unorganized employees were great: few could afford to be without work for more than a brief period, and few could move to another locality where working conditions were better. Only a small proportion of workers had skills that were sufficiently scarce to give them strong bargaining power as individuals.

Historical experience in modern democratic societies suggests that when the balance between groups that must deal with each other becomes too uneven, government is likely to step in, either to regulate the terms of the transactions between the groups or to build up the strength of the weaker group. By the end of the nineteenth century, the belief was widespread that government must act, both to improve the living conditions of the workers and to reduce the losses which the community was suffering from industrial strife.

Government measures to regulate the terms of employment began to be enacted late in the nineteenth century. Early examples included laws concerning such matters as plant safety, liability for employee accidents in the plant, and maximum hours of work. Soon after came the first tentative efforts to protect the ability of employees to organize. Underlying these latter enactments was the hope that if the parties carrying on private negotiations were made more nearly equal in strength, a more extensive regulation of employment terms by the government would not be necessary. It was hoped, too, that once collective bargaining had got under way, unions and management would become more aware of each other's problems and aspirations and would abandon some of their anti-social methods of exerting pressure on each other.

Throughout the nineteenth century, the legal rules concerning labor unions and their activities were largely judge-made. Given the prevailing theory of social ordering, it is not surprising that these rules impeded efforts to organize the workers. It is probably true also that, as a class, judges tended to be unsympathetic to labor's cause. The early judicial view that unions were a criminal "conspiracy in restraint of trade" dwindled in importance after 1850, but judges continued to apply standards based on principles of tort and contract law that led them to declare unlawful many strikes, picket lines, and boycotts. Employers found that one of the most effective means of breaking a union's drive to organize workers was to ask a court for an injunction. Many judges were quite willing to enjoin strikers and pickets, often without making any inquiry into the facts of the dispute, but acting, instead, on the basis of a strong presumption that union activities were disturbing "natural market forces."

The judicial process is generally ill-suited for instituting radical changes in a body of legal rules. To reverse the whole direction of the law from hostility to encouragement of worker organization, legislative and executive action was needed. In any case most judges did not readily accept the view that society might benefit from having strong, responsible unions bargaining with employers. Legislators and executive officials, on the other hand, were more responsive to shifting public sentiment. As early as 1898, Congress passed a law designed to encourage the organizing of railway employees by outlawing "yellow-dog" contracts in that industry. In 1908 the Supreme Court invalidated the law as an unconstitutional interference with "freedom of contract." [3] During World War I, the War Labor Board sought to foster and protect worker organization and collective bargaining. This position, so essential in a period of maximum employment and labor shortages, was abandoned for a time after the war. Thereupon industrial strife broke out with new bitterness as employers resumed their efforts to stamp out the unions, which had increased their power during the war years. But in 1926 Congress passed the Railway Labor Act, designed to bring peace to that industry by officially recognizing collective bargaining

---

[3] See pp. 140–43. The excerpts quoted there from the *Adair* and *Coppage* majority opinions exemplify the older judicial view of industrial relations. The emerging view is exemplified by the excerpt from Justice Holmes's dissent in *Coppage*, and by some of Holmes's other dissents in labor cases.

as the best means of setting wages and working conditions. This time the Supreme Court upheld the legislation. And in 1932, Congress enacted the Norris-LaGuardia Act, which effectively prohibited the use of injunctions by federal judges in most labor disputes.[4]

The "New Deal" Administration of President Franklin Roosevelt brought new advances for organized labor. This was partly because many of the leading figures in the new Administration were much more "pro-labor" than their predecessors had been. But, in addition, the Administration's leaders believed that recovery from the depression depended on stabilizing, if not raising, prices and wages. Higher wages would mean increased purchasing power, and encouragement of collective bargaining in all industries within the reach of federal power appeared to be a good way to achieve higher wage levels.

The New Deal's first legislative program for stabilizing prices and wages was embodied in the National Industrial Recovery Act of 1933, which contained a provision asserting that workers had a legal right to organize and bargain collectively. Little was actually accomplished in putting this assertion into effect, however; the principal result was to encourage many employers to set up "company unions," with little real independence, to justify keeping outside labor organizers away from their employees. The New Deal's main piece of labor legislation was the National Labor Relations Act, enacted in 1935. Popularly known as the Wagner Act, this legislation has also been given such extravagant labels as "Labor's Charter of Freedom." It is without doubt the most important enactment of the era in the field of labor law.[5]

THE WAGNER ACT. The policy underlying the Wagner Act was summed up in its Section 7:

> Employees shall have the right to self-organization, to form, join, or assist labor organizations, to bargain collectively through representatives of their own choosing, and to engage in concerted activities for the purpose of collective bargaining or other mutual aid or protection.

First, employees were given the right to organize. Section 8 designated as "unfair labor practices" some of the well-known employer techniques of combating organization—for instance, establishing "company unions," interfering with the activities of organizers, and intimidating employees who wished to join the union. These practices were made illegal.

---

[4] Only federal court decisions and federal legislation are referred to in this and ensuing paragraphs. It would be impossible to describe all the parallel developments in the states. In a general way, though, one can say that the law in heavily industrialized states has tended to evolve along the same lines as has federal law. (For instance, a number of states enacted "little Norris-LaGuardia Acts.") Moreover, after 1935, federal law tended to have much greater relative importance in labor relations than it had had up to then.

[5] The National Labor Relations Act as now administered covers only firms of greater than a specified size whose activities affect interstate commerce (a concept very broadly interpreted by the courts). A number of states have laws embodying some of the same principles and procedures.

Second, employees were given the right to "bargain collectively through representatives of their own choosing." Section 9(a) declared that:

> Representatives designated or selected for the purposes of collective bargaining by the majority of the employees in a unit appropriate for such purposes shall be the exclusive representatives of all the employees [in the unit]. . . .

Once these representatives were chosen, the employer had an obligation to bargain with them.

Finally, employees were given the right to "engage in concerted activities." This provision affirmed the basic right of workers to strike, boycott, and picket. (As we shall see, however, these rights are subject to various limitations.)

To administer the new law, the National Labor Relations Board was established. Its most important tasks were:

1. To investigate and if necessary adjudicate complaints of "unfair labor practices," with the power to issue remedial orders enforceable by the courts. As we noted in Chapter 8, the N.L.R.B. has become an important creator of decisional rules governing labor-management relations.

2. To decide what constitutes an "appropriate bargaining unit" in a particular enterprise, and then to determine what union, if any, is the choice of a majority of the employees in the unit to act as their bargaining representative. The Board is empowered to conduct elections, if necessary, to make this determination. If a majority is found to favor a particular union, the Board certifies that union as the exclusive bargaining representative for *all* the workers in the unit.

The purpose behind the Wagner Act was to promote the adoption of collective bargaining—a practice that had hitherto developed entirely under private initiative in a limited number of enterprises—in all those companies within the scope of federal power in which workers wished to bargain collectively. The act sought to curb the traditional anti-union practices that had impeded worker efforts to organize; moreover, it sought to assure that, once the workers had been organized, their employers would sit down at a table with the union representatives and "bargain in good faith" with them.[6] The act did *not*, however, try to tell the parties what subjects they should bargain about or what terms they should agree upon.

THE TAFT-HARTLEY AND LANDRUM-GRIFFIN ACTS. The Wagner Act was amended and supplemented in important respects by acts of Congress passed in 1947 and 1959. Both enactments were in part attempts to counterbalance what many thought to be the excessive power attained by organized labor since 1935. But neither act repealed the basic Wagner Act provisions outlined in the preceding section.

---

[6] For a case involving the requirement of "bargaining in good faith," see *Matter of Truitt Manufacturing Co.*, page 162.

The Taft-Hartley Act of 1947 reflected a widespread popular feeling that some unions had abused the rights guaranteed to them under the earlier legislation. To the Wagner Act's declaration that workers should have the right to organize and bargain collectively was now added a new declaration that employees should have the right to refrain from participating in such activities if they preferred. To the Wagner Act's list of "unfair labor practices" by employers was added a list of unfair labor practices by unions and their agents; this list included secondary boycotts, jurisdictional strikes, and the refusal to bargain with employers. For the first time a few limitations were placed on the contents of collective-bargaining agreements. (Most important, the Taft-Hartley Act prohibits "closed-shop" provisions, under which the employer agrees to hire only union members. It does permit "union-shop" provisions, under which new employees are required to join the union within thirty days from the date of their employment, but only if certain conditions are met.)

In Section 8(d), the Taft-Hartley Act attempted to define the obligation to bargain collectively:

> . . . [T]o bargain collectively is the performance of the mutual obligation of the employer and the representative of the employees to meet at reasonable times and confer in good faith with respect to wages, hours, and other terms and conditions of employment, or the negotiation of an agreement, or any question arising thereunder, and the execution of a written contract incorporating any agreement reached if requested by either party, but such obligation does not compel either party to agree to a proposal or require the making of a concession: Provided, that where there is in effect a collective-bargaining contract . . . , the duty to bargain collectively shall also mean that no party to such contract shall terminate or modify such contract, unless. . . .
>
> [The remainder of the section specifies what steps such a party must take, the aim being to minimize the danger of a breakdown of bargaining at the end of a contract term.]

The Landrum-Griffin Act of 1959 was enacted following a Senate investigating committee's exposure of scandalous mismanagement in the internal affairs of a few unions, along with revelations of the lack of "democracy" in the governing of some unions. Much of the act was concerned with those problems. The remaining provisions were mostly amendments to the Taft-Hartley Act. Some new "unfair labor practices" by unions were identified, and one new restriction was imposed on the content of collective-bargaining agreements. But the relations existing between most unions and employers were not materially affected by this act.

To sum up: in 1935, Congress passed a law designed to increase the power of organized labor, because it believed that a better power balance between management and labor would serve the national interest. In 1947 and 1959, Congress passed new laws designed to regulate labor's use of its greatly augmented power.

But one of the main presuppositions underlying all three statutes was that, once the conditions essential to collective bargaining had been created, management and labor could be left to work out the terms of the bargain among themselves, subject only to a few legislative constraints.[7] Underlying this policy has been the conviction that in a private enterprise economy, government must not assume responsibility for setting and periodically revising the employment terms of private employees all over the country, nor (except in special situations) for settling employer-employee disputes. These important and complex tasks must be left in private hands.

Industrial Self-government Within the Legal Framework

The relations between an employer and his organized employees are carried on under a system of rules that they have themselves created, acting within the framework provided by the law. The *collective-bargaining agreement* (of which more than 75,000 are now in operation in the United States) might be described as the "constitution" of an industrial community. Such communities have other "legislative" rules, too, some of them laid down by the employer alone, but most of them the product of negotiations carried on under provisions of the agreement. The agreement also establishes a procedure for settling disputes between employer and employees. The final stage in that procedure is usually arbitration, a form of adjudication. Arbitration produces decisions which come to have some of the quality of decisional rules for the industrial community.

Let us first consider the bargaining that leads up to the collective agreement, and then the agreement itself and the arrangements established under it.

THE CONDITIONS AND PRODUCTS OF BARGAINING. What conditions are essential to effective bargaining? Remember that a bargain is an exchange. First, each party must have something that the other wants, so that it will be to their mutual advantage if they can come to terms. Second, each party must be in a position to exercise the alternative of *not* exchanging what he has if the terms offered him are too unfavorable. When a party lacks either one of these prerequisites, he has no bargaining power, and there can be no real bargaining.

Bargaining between management and labor boils down to the exchange of work opportunities for manpower. The employer may make jobs available, or he may close down the plant (an act known as a lockout). Organized workers may do the employer's work, or they may refuse as a group to go on working (an act known as a strike). Although choosing the second alternative entails short-run sacrifices, this alternative in the long run is essential to each party's bargaining position. In the days when most employees had to negotiate singly with their employers, the worker usually found that he was not really able to bargain at all. His individual services were rarely indispensable to his employer, since the supply of labor for

---

[7] We have already noted that the Taft-Hartley and Landrum-Griffin Acts contain a few restrictions on what the parties may agree to. In addition, the federal Fair Labor Standards Act of 1938 sets a lower limit on the wages and overtime pay permissible for many employers. One of the reasons for enacting this law was the realization that some employees could probably not be organized at all, and that some unions might be too weak to win wage raises above a low level; hence Congress sought to supplement private negotiation by setting minimum standards.

most types of work was relatively abundant. And even if he possessed a skill that was in short supply, he could afford to quit only if he could start at once on another job, since he normally had little or no savings, and there was no union strike fund standing ready to aid him. It was only when he joined a union that he could bargain, because then others would join him in refusing to work if their terms were not met. And even a union would be unable to bargain effectively if the law prevented it from going out on strike or using other means of pressure on the employer.

To promote bargaining, modern labor law has tried to lessen the inequalities between the parties and to bring them together around the bargaining table. But it also permits employees to strike and employers to close down their plants. Both rights are subject to limitations, however, as are the other weapons in the industrial struggle: labor's picketing and boycotts, and the various techniques that management has developed to resist union pressures. The collective-bargaining agreements negotiated by employers and unions usually contain self-imposed limitations on the right of the parties to use coercive pressures on each other during the life of the agreement, and these limitations, too, are backed up by law.

The law has, of course, never sought to assure that the bargaining parties would be of exactly equal strength. To do so would be quite impossible, for the outcome of any negotiation depends on subtle and shifting factors, including the skill of the negotiating representatives and the external circumstances at the time of the negotiation. A union's bargaining position is obviously stronger, for instance, in a period when the demand for the company's product is strong and manpower is scarce than in a period of slack demand and widespread unemployment.

The first step in the bargaining process is to secure an agreement. Then, since agreements must be renewed periodically, there is likely to be further bargaining over revisions in the agreement proposed by one party or the other. Even while an agreement is in operation bargaining goes on, as new problems in the production process appear, and as disputes arise over the meaning and application of the agreement. But, contrary to the impression given by news reports, the orderly settlement of differences at all these stages is the rule, and resort to economic warfare the exception.

THE CONTENTS OF THE COLLECTIVE-BARGAINING AGREEMENT. What matters do collective-bargaining agreements deal with? The agreements have no standard form, of course. Those negotiated in small establishments are likely to be much briefer than those negotiated in giant firms. Relatively weak unions are often unable to win some of the commitments from management that strong unions have secured. But agreements are likely to cover some or all of the following subjects: management's rights, recognition and security for the union, wages, hours of work and overtime, working conditions, leaves of absence, vacations, health and accident insurance, retirement, pensions, promotions, layoffs, seniority, discipline, subcontracting, technological changes, methods for determining work loads, and procedures for presenting and settling grievances.

Only a few of the many matters covered by the agreement need any special comment here.

Management's Rights. A basic term of any agreement, regardless of whether or not it is made explicit, is the principle that the employer is responsible for managing the enterprise and directing the labor force. Many agreements contain a section specifying that management is responsible for scheduling production, making work assignments, hiring, promoting, demoting, transferring, discharging, classifying, and disciplining personnel for just cause. In all these matters, management has the initiative. Most of the other terms of the agreement may be viewed as voluntarily accepted limitations on the fundamental prerogative of management. To give two examples: The employer's power to lay off workers during a period of reduced production may be qualified by seniority provisions in the agreement, which specify the criteria to be used in deciding who is laid off first and rehired last. The employer's power to discharge workers for disciplinary reasons may be qualified by a provision that disciplinary discharges must be "for just cause." (Then, if the union believes that an employee has been fired without just cause, it may file a grievance and have the case fully aired.)

Union Security. Every union is understandably anxious to hold on to its members, to collect members' dues regularly, and to make members of as many employees as it can. Many employers actually help the unions to do these things, usually on the ground that if the union feels secure, it is more likely to be reasonable and responsible. Unless it is prohibited by the law of the state where his plant is located, the employer has the right under federal legislation to agree to a "union-shop" clause in which he promises to discharge any employee who fails to join the union within thirty days of being employed or who fails to continue as a member thereafter.

No-Strike, No-Lockout Clause. The union pledges that it will not call any strikes or instigate any slowdowns or stoppages of production while the agreement is in effect. The company in turn pledges that there will be no lockouts. The presumption is thus established that orderly and non-disruptive methods will be used in dealing with differences that arise during the life of the agreement.

Duration. Few agreements are for less than a year, and many are for two, three, four, or even five years. Some of the longer-term agreements provide that the issue of wages may be reopened at shorter intervals. Most agreements renew themselves automatically unless one of the parties gives notice a certain number of days before the expiration date that it wishes to terminate the agreement or negotiate revisions.

THE HANDLING OF DISPUTES ARISING UNDER THE AGREEMENT. No matter how good relations are between a company and its employees, events are bound to occur that produce disagreements. For example: Brown is discharged for misconduct on the job and claims that he did not do what he is accused of, that it was not misconduct, or that discharge is too severe a penalty. Jones is promoted, whereupon Smith says that the promotion should have been his because he has been with the company longer than Jones. Management lowers the classification and wage-rate on a certain job because a newly installed machine has made the job less hazardous; the affected workers protest.

The Taft-Hartley Act makes it clear in Section 8(d), quoted above, that the legal obligation to negotiate continues after an agreement has been signed. The Act established a Federal Mediation and Conciliation Service to aid companies and unions in settling their disputes, but Section 203(d) clearly indicated that Congress wanted them to settle their disputes in their own way whenever possible. "Final adjustment by a method agreed upon by the parties," it stated, "is hereby declared to be the desirable method for settlement of grievance disputes arising over the application or interpretation of an existing collective-bargaining agreement."

Nearly all agreements make some provision for a grievance procedure. In principle, employees, the union, and management all have the right to file grievances, but the procedures are usually based on the assumption that virtually all grievances will be filed by employees supported by their union representatives. Management's position is likely to be that in running the plant it may make any decision it sees fit, subject only to its commitments under the agreement, and that if an employee believes that any management decision violates the agreement, he must file a grievance. This throws the initiative for grievance-filing on the employees, though of course the employer can indirectly take the initiative by doing something that will force the union to file a grievance.

We have spoken of the grievance procedure as an alternative to industrial strife, as indeed it is. But we must also recognize that the handling of grievances is itself far from being all sweetness and light; indeed, it is better thought of as an extension of the hardheaded bargaining that produced the agreement. In negotiating the agreement, the employer probably fought to define the area falling under the grievance procedure as narrowly as possible—because he saw a strategic advantage to keeping the area of unrestricted management discretion as broad as possible. For opposite reasons, the union probably fought to have the grievance area broadly defined.[8] The outcome is to some degree a reflection of the bargaining power and skill of the two parties. And once the grievance machinery is in operation, the volume of complaints at any given time is likely to be a function not merely of what happens in the plant but of union tactics: is this a good time to press hard or to ease up? Whether management adopts a hard or a conciliatory position on complaints filed by the union is likely to be influenced by similar tactical considerations.

Grievance settlements contribute to the "law of the plant." The outcome of a grievance proceeding (particularly if the final stage, arbitration, is reached) has a significance for the law of the industrial community roughly comparable to the significance of a judicial or administrative decision. The precedent it establishes has no binding effect, but under many circumstances it will influence patterns of future conduct. The parties are well aware of this. When the negotiators of an agreement cannot agree on the wording of a provision, they often put in some vague words, counting on the grievance procedure to help fill in the gap as the area of dispute is illuminated by actual cases. The "rule" that grows out of the grievance

---

[8] A closely related source of dispute is the breadth of the arbitration clause, which will be considered in the next section.

settlement may, indeed, prove so satisfactory to both parties that they will formalize it as a new provision in the next revision of the agreement.

In agreements negotiated with larger companies, the grievance procedure consists of a series of meetings between union representatives and management representatives at successively higher levels of authority in the company. The first step is usually for the shop steward (the elected employee who speaks for the union in the basic production unit) to present the grievance to the shop foreman immediately concerned. If no settlement can be reached at that level, the union's elected grievance committee presents the grievance to the divisional superintendent. If this does not produce a settlement, one or more further appeals are carried to managers at higher levels; the final appeal is to a representative of top management. For each step (after the first) there is usually a deadline both for filing and for responding to the appeal, so that a succession of appeals up to the top-management level ordinarily does not take more than a few weeks at most.

Most grievances are disposed of (or abandoned) at one of these stages. But in a small minority of cases a final stage is reached: the union asks that the grievance be submitted to a neutral third party for arbitration.

ARBITRATION

What Is It? When two parties submit a dispute to arbitration, they are asking one or more nonofficial "outsiders" to hear and judge the controversy, on the understanding that they will accept whatever decision is reached. Arbitration is thus a special form of *adjudication*. Its procedures, and such law as exists concerning it (mostly on the enforceability of agreements to arbitrate and of arbitral awards), have developed largely as a result of its widespread use under commercial contracts. Businessmen making such contracts often include a provision binding them to arbitrate any dispute that may arise under the contract, in the belief that arbitration is cheaper, speedier, and more "private" than litigation in the courts. Arbitration has also been used in settling certain kinds of international dispute.

Arbitration, as a form of adjudication, is to be distinguished from mediation. The essential differences are two: First, a mediator seeks an acceptable compromise between the opposing positions of the parties, while an arbitrator is supposed to arrive at a decision that is based on some body of principles: applicable legal rules; the customs, practices, and understandings of the particular "community"; or some concept of what is just and reasonable. Second, the parties are free to accept or reject a mediator's proposed solution to a dispute, but they agree in advance that they will be bound by an arbitrator's award.[9]

---

[9] The conceptual distinction between arbitration and mediation is important, but in practice arbitrators sometimes act as mediators. The same is true of judges; perhaps the best example is the judge in a domestic relations court who makes a practice of trying to aid married couples to patch up their differences before considering a petition for divorce. Judges who conduct pre-trial conferences also act as mediators on occasion.

Although some mediating by adjudicators is probably inevitable, many students of our legal institutions feel that the combining of roles should be kept to a minimum. They argue that the possibility of performing both functions may cause confusion and prevent the adjudicator from performing either one properly.

Various methods have been devised for selecting an arbitrator acceptable to both parties. One method is to invite an outside agency to submit a list of three or five names to the parties, who then take turns at eliminating a name until only one is left. Lists of persons available and qualified to serve as labor arbitrators are maintained by the Federal Mediation and Conciliation Service (a government agency) and the American Arbitration Association (a private, nonprofit organization).

Most labor arbitrators are chosen to hear only a single case (although an arbitrator whose work satisfies the parties may be chosen again by them). But large companies faced with a substantial flow of grievance cases often join with the union representing their employees in hiring one or more arbitrators on a continuing basis. Sometimes arrangement is made for "tripartite" arbitration: each party names one arbitrator and then both parties jointly name a third, who acts as the neutral chairman. Under all these arrangements the costs of arbitration are shared equally by the parties.

Special Problems of the Labor Arbitrator. Although the labor arbitrator performs functions that in many ways resemble those of both the commercial arbitrator and the trial judge, in a number of respects his role is unique.

The labor arbitrator's job differs from that of the judge in that he is not a public official whose authority is imposed on the parties by the state and whose decision will be enforced by other officials. He is hired and paid by the parties to the agreement (who may discharge him if they become dissatisfied with his performance). His assigned task is not to "do justice" in any general sense, but to perform a function in the system of self-government they have created, to apply the rules established by their agreement.

His job is different from that of the commercial arbitrator because collective-bargaining agreements are not like ordinary commercial contracts, in which the parties have normally come together only to carry out a single transaction. In contrast, management and labor are bound together by the strongest of ties. However bitter may be their occasional differences, each needs the other, and each has the same ultimate concern for maintaining the flow of production. In these circumstances, the task of adjudicating one of their disputes [10] often requires rare skill. It may be particularly challenging for the temporary (one-time) arbitrator, who somehow must rapidly acquire an awareness of the "total relationship" between the parties. If, failing to acquire such an awareness, he comes up with a decision that is formally impeccable but leaves one side bitter and relations tenser than ever, his arbitration can hardly be deemed a success. After all, a major aim of the grievance procedure is to eliminate causes of tension. "Let

---

[10] We are confining ourselves here to grievance arbitration. Sometimes an employer and a union that have been unable in their negotiations to resolve their differences over a particular term of the agreement finally decide to "leave it to arbitration." This substitution of arbitration for the negotiation of terms is quite different from the arbitration of grievances under an agreement. Some commentators, indeed, insist that it is properly a job for a mediator rather than an arbitrator, since there is ordinarily no body of principles on which an arbitrator can base a decision.

justice be done though the heavens fall" is not an appropriate slogan for a labor arbitrator.

A labor arbitrator must also bear in mind that arbitration is the last step in a settlement procedure, to be taken only after all attempts at negotiated settlement have failed. If a commercial arbitrator cannot render a satisfactory decision, the dispute can be carried to the courts. But litigation is not a practical alternative to grievance arbitration. True, the law provides that parties to a collective agreement may sue in the courts for alleged breaches of contract. But such suits are, and must always be, exceptional. There are too many grievances, and litigation is too costly. Prompt settlement of most grievances is imperative, and litigation is slow. Finally, courts, being courts *of law*, have to apply doctrines of law when they are relevant; but some of these doctrines may be quite inappropriate for the handling of grievances. The labor arbitrator can never forget, then, that the alternative to an acceptable award is likely to be not a lawsuit but a strike.[11]

Identifying the "Rules" to Apply. Perhaps the greatest difference between labor arbitration and other forms of adjudication, however, stems from the unique character of the "body of principle" on which the labor arbitrator must base his decisions.

The arbitration clause in a collective-bargaining agreement usually specifies that the arbitrator is authorized to settle only those grievances that are related to "the interpretation and application of this Agreement," and that he may not add to, subtract from, or modify the agreement. But if these words make the arbitrator's job of identifying the rules to apply sound easy, they are deceptive.

We have already compared collective-bargaining agreements with constitutions. Like most other constitutional documents, agreements tend to be notably imprecise and incomplete. They are usually pounded out by negotiators working against a deadline—the expiration date of the current contract. The temptation is always strong, when accord on a particular issue seems remote as the deadline draws near, to say nothing about the issue at all, or else to include a fuzzy provision that satisfies both sides because it means so little. Nor is the agreement couched in the carefully chosen "legalistic" words characteristic of commercial contracts. (Sometimes, indeed, lawyers play no part in the drafting.) A major aim of the negotiators is to produce a relatively brief document that can be distributed to the employees with some expectation of their understanding it. Finally, even where the negotiators try to be precise, they may still stumble into the traps presented to all drafters by the undetected ambiguity of words and by the impossibility of predicting the future.

As a consequence, the arbitrator has a wide measure of discretion. Although he cannot alter the words of the agreement, he is often able to choose from among a variety of possible meanings. When the case before

---

[11] A party is sometimes able to take a dispute arising under an agreement to the National Labor Relations Board by complaining that the other party is guilty of an "unfair labor practice" (for instance, of refusing to bargain in good faith). But constant resort to administrative adjudication is no more a practical alternative to grievance proceedings than constant resort to the courts would be.

him raises the question of whether the disciplinary discharge of a certain employee was for "just cause," for instance, he will not get very far if he simply tries to define the words, "just cause." His job, rather, is to give meaning to this empty phrase by formulating a standard against which the particular discharge can be measured.

When the agreement is not clear, where does he look for help in setting up such a standard? If he has had legal training, he may turn to relevant legal doctrines. He may also try to find out what other arbitrators have done in similar cases in the past. There is no tradition that arbitral precedents must be followed, though arbitrators are understandably prone to strive for some degree of consistency in the "interpretation" of a particular agreement. But the absence of a *stare decisis* rule does not deter arbitrators from looking for ideas in the records of earlier awards.[12] Even more important than such precedents, however, may be relevant circumstances in the "legislative history" of the negotiations that produced the agreement, and relevant practices within the enterprise (sometimes referred to as the "common law of the plant"). The arbitrator is also influenced by his own views on what is consistent with sound industrial practice and with the national labor policy, and by his own notions of what is just and reasonable.

"*Arbitrability*." Occasionally one of the parties resists the submission of a grievance to arbitration. He usually argues that, under the "arbitration clause" of the agreement, the arbitrator can only hear grievances involving the interpretation and application of the agreement, and that the grievance in question is not covered by any provision. To contest the "arbitrability" of a grievance in this way is somewhat like contesting the jurisdiction of a court to hear a case.

To take an example: An agreement contains no provision on the company's right to subcontract work out to other firms. (Either it has never occurred to the parties that a dispute might arise over subcontracting, or else they tried but were unable to agree on a formula.) The company now subcontracts out some work of a sort that might have been done in the plant, even though some of its own employees are working only part time.

The union files a grievance. It claims that subcontracting is a violation of the *implied* terms of the agreement. It points out that the agreement recognizes the union as the representative of *all* the company's production and maintenance workers, and it contends that the provisions concerning layoffs and part-time labor constitute an implied promise that work will not be turned over to outsiders while employees are idle.

The company retorts that the union's arguments are farfetched, that making decisions about subcontracting is clearly management's prerogative and that the union has nothing to say about them. The company goes on to insist that, since the contract is silent about subcontracting, the arbitrator has no authority over the matter under the terms of the arbitration clause. After all, concludes the company, when we agreed to this arbitration pro-

---

[12] Note, however, that only a minority of arbitral awards are published. Indeed, awards are often not accompanied by written opinions.

cedure we didn't agree to having every little gripe the union comes up with submitted to arbitration.

Most arbitrators are reluctant to refuse to arbitrate. After all, the result of a refusal to arbitrate is that the dispute goes back to the parties, who have already found that they could not settle it in the earlier stages of the grievance procedure. And a refusal to arbitrate usually has the effect of a decision against the grievant. If, however, the arbitrator feels that the union's attempt to relate the dispute to some provision in the agreement is completely farfetched, or if he gets the impression—from the general tone of the agreement or from what he knows of its "legislative history" —that this agreement should be interpreted literally rather than liberally, he probably will refuse to arbitrate.

If one party feels strongly enough that a dispute is not arbitrable, it can try to prevent arbitration by simply refusing to participate in the hearing. But the law now provides that the party desiring arbitration may ask a court to order the other to submit to arbitration, on the ground that the refusal to do so is a breach of the contract.

One might think that such a suit would compel the court to decide for itself whether the matter in dispute was covered by the agreement. But in three cases decided in 1960 the Supreme Court of the United States made it clear that the role of the federal courts, at least, would be much more modest. The Court held that, unless the arbitration clause of an agreement makes it perfectly clear that a particular dispute could not under any possible interpretation be covered by the agreement, the lower court must order that the dispute be submitted to arbitration, thus letting the arbitrator decide for himself whether or not to arbitrate. Nor can the lower court refuse to order a reluctant party to submit to arbitration merely because it feels that the grievance in question is frivolous and certain to be rejected. The Court also ruled that, when a party that has submitted to arbitration under protest later refuses to comply with the award, and the other party asks a lower court to order compliance, the court may not refuse to do so merely because it disagrees with the arbitrator's interpretation of the contract; if his interpretation has any possible justification, the court must accept it. The parties, the Court pointed out, bargained for the arbitrator's interpretation of the contract, not for a judge's interpretation. The prestige and usefulness of labor arbitrators were unquestionably enhanced by these decisions.

The Hearing. Arbitration hearings differ greatly in character. Some hearings are relatively formal, and in many respects resemble a court trial. At the other extreme are very informal hearings which more nearly resemble a discussion around a table. The degree of formality depends on such factors as the traditions prevailing in the industry, the complexity of the particular dispute, and the personal preference of the arbitrator himself.

The great majority of hearings, however, are considerably less formal than court trials. Agreement is general that arbitration should be thought of as a co-operative effort to arrive at a reasonable result, and not as a battle of wits in which the contestants try to outdo one another by resorting to oratory and to procedural maneuvers. In many hearings, the parties are not represented by lawyers. (Moreover, many arbitrators are not lawyers.) Usually no written briefs are submitted. The rules of evidence are not enforced, and most arbitrators are willing to listen to evidence that would be excluded as hearsay or irrelevant in a court. The arbitrator establishes the course of the proceeding to a much greater extent than a trial judge would; he is likely to do much of the questioning himself. Frequently no formal record is kept of the testimony. In short, every effort is made to keep the atmosphere at the hearing as informal, relaxed, and friendly as possible.

A Sample Arbitration Case.   The arbitrator's opinion in *Matter of Nathan Manufacturing Co.*, which follows, provides an interesting illustration of an arbitrator's justification of his award. The case involves the application of a typically vague "just cause" provision

MATTER OF NATHAN MANUFACTURING CO.

Arbitration Award, 1947. 7 Lab. Arb. Rep. 3

▶ SCHEIBER, ARBITRATOR:—The parties have submitted for arbitration grievances arising out of the discharge of J. Grady Blackwell, shop steward, and Sidney Fisher, shop chairman, which submission is pursuant to Article XIII of the contract between the parties dated September 10, 1946.

The matters to be decided by the Arbitrator under the formal submission are as follows:

1. Whether J. Grady Blackwell . . . [was] discharged for just and sufficient cause;

2. If such discharges were not for just and sufficient cause, the terms on which they should be reinstated shall be left to the discretion of the arbitrator.

The company's position is that, since under the contract its power to discharge is limited to discharges "for just and sufficient cause only" and since the submission is stated in terms of the contract, the decision to discharge is subject to reversal by the arbitrator only upon finding that "just and sufficient" cause did not exist; if it does exist, he is not empowered under the terms of the contract and of the submission to reverse the determination of the company unless he finds that the action of the company was not in good faith, was arbitrary, capricious, or discriminatory.

The arbitrator is in accord with this contention since any other holding would substitute his opinion for that of management, which is charged in law and by the contract with the efficient management of the plant. It therefore becomes necessary to first determine whether the discharges were "for just and sufficient cause."

The discharge of J. Grady Blackwell is based upon his alleged "interference with workers' assignments, violations of the contract, and subnormal production."

On January 17, 1947, while the workers during their paid clean-up time were engaged in carrying out an order previously given by the foreman to sweep around their machines, Blackwell "instructed" them to drop their brooms. He has testified that, when he gave "instructions," he expected to be obeyed.

This was apparently the "precipitating cause" of his discharge or, in the language of the plant manager, "The straw that broke the camel's back."

The following are some of the other claims presented by the company of Blackwell's countermanding orders previously given by the foreman which appear in the record:

1. January 3, 1946—Blackwell prevented Operator Hill from performing set-ups, contrary to instructions from Foreman Perna. Blackwell was warned by Mr. Boggs that it was a violation of the contract for a steward to countermand a foreman's order without referring the problem to the grievance procedure.

2. Blackwell, among others, again prevented the performance of set-ups by operators in Grades 7 and 8. At the labor-management committee meeting of March 26, 1946, the union admitted the irregularity of this and stated that it would refrain in the future from so doing and would thenceforth act in an advisory capacity only so far as job structure was concerned.

3. On September 30, 1946, Blackwell again countermanded an order of supervision which this time directed a trades helper to go from one side of the floor to the other to change oil in a machine. Blackwell was again expressly told by Mr. Boggs that the assignment of trades helpers was a matter for the foreman and not his concern.

4. In October, 1946, Blackwell, despite all prior warnings, instructed the trades helper not to clean a machine on one side of the floor, thus again countermanding Dugan's direct order. Blackwell was again expressly told that the trades helpers were to obey supervision's orders, that the "agreement" on which he relied was not applicable in the situation presented by the absence of one of the helpers, that the trades helper was to be discharged if he refused to follow Dugan's orders, and that, if Blackwell continued his interference with Dugan's running of the department, he too was to be discharged.

5. Blackwell stated that, unless the company complied with his ideas as to the performance of a time study, he "would be forced to stop the time study" and demanded of Mr. Asherman "Do you want me to pull piecework out of this department altogether?"

While the top union officials, during the course of the arbitration, and the union's research director sought to give every possible favorable intendment to Blackwell's actions, it was admitted under cross-examination that they could cite no case where a shop steward is authorized to issue orders, and two of the union's top officials concurred that the issuance of orders by a shop steward countermanding those of the foreman were beyond the powers of a shop steward.

Despite this, however, Blackwell reiterated his belief at several points in the testimony that it was his duty as union representative not to permit

the employees to perform such work as he believed they were not required to do until after it had been discussed at a labor-management meeting, and, further, that he would repeat his action if such situations arose
again.

Blackwell's failure to abide by the established grievance machinery as
manifested in the various instances where he countermanded orders given
by a foreman may have created some doubt or confusion in the plant as to
the necessity and importance of the established grievance procedure.

At the sacrifice of brevity but in the hope that the following statements and decisions may clarify this phase of the labor-management relationship and, by bringing a clearer understanding, help the parties in their
future relations, attention is directed to the following decisions in point.

While the arbitrator agrees with the union's able research director that
as yet there is no settled "labor common law," that such law is in process
of evolvement, and that these decisions therefore are not binding on the
arbitrator, he feels, nevertheless, that the decisions are entitled to some
consideration since they do represent the best thought of skilled practitioners in the field of arbitration.

The grievance procedure now a part of labor-management contracts
represents an important advance in the industrial field and should therefore be zealously adhered to and carefully guarded. It is intended for
the protection of labor and, when adhered to, advances peaceful and
constructive industrial relations with resultant benefits to labor, management, and the public.

When any union leader or worker loses sight of the great gain which
a sound grievance procedure affords to labor in the protection of its rights
and disregards its provisions, a serious disservice is being done to labor.

This has been recognized by one of this nation's leaders, Robert Schrank,
in his own book, Leadership Training for Stewards, Shop Committeemen
and Lodge Officers, where seven pages are devoted to the importance of
making grievance machinery work. . . .

In Matter of Ampco Metal, Inc., 3 LA 374 (1945), Arbitrator Updegraff
sustained the company action in disciplining a union president for leaving
his job in violation of a company rule, although that rule violated the
contract. The arbitrator declared that the grievance procedure of the contract protected the union and should have been utilized. [Discussion of
two other arbitration cases omitted.]

Since a union official must not himself flout a company rule or work
assignment, it is clear that he must not countermand a foreman's order
relating to work assignment. Where the official refuses to follow instructions personally, only one person fails to perform the appointed task; where
the union official countermands an order, the result is the failure of an
entire group to carry out instructions. This unwarranted interference with
plant production and plant efficiency is a case for discharge, especially
where, as here, the contract contains a "no cessation of work" clause. [An
opinion by a well-known arbitrator is here quoted at length.]

The record also indicates that Blackwell has persisted in operating the grievance procedure under his own interpretation of the contract. The company has pointed out numerous occasions where Blackwell has countermanded foreman's instructions to operators on the floor. Although warned repeatedly by the company that such action was a violation of the contract, would not be tolerated, and would lead to his discharge, and although informed by the union that he had no power to countermand foreman's orders, Blackwell apparently operated on the theory that the contract gave him that power, and further that he would repeat his action if such situation arose again.

On January 17, 1947, the arbitrator finds that Blackwell countermanded the order of a foreman and prevented the operators in the department from performing the duties enjoined upon them by supervision.

The arbitrator finds that there existed nothing in the past relations between the parties which prevented the foreman from giving such order. However, in the arbitrator's opinion, it is immaterial whether or not the foreman had such power. There exists a detailed grievance procedure in the contract, one which has been operative for a number of years and one which is apparently effective. If supervision exceeded its rights, Blackwell should have allowed the operation to continue but filed a grievance. The arbitrator holds that a shop steward is not empowered under this contract to countermand an order of supervision unless such order involves an unusual health hazard or a criminal act. To allow such shop steward to determine for himself when a foreman's order is unauthorized and to permit him on the basis of his own opinion to prevent the functioning of the plant would lead to chaos in the plant and would be harmful to the interests of both the company and the union.

There was considerable diversity of opinion at the hearing as to whether a past practice existed by virtue of which the company was bound to submit the discharge cases to the union before it took action to discharge. The arbitrator holds that, since this contract has a special discharge procedure and contains a grievance procedure on other matters, the company has the right to discharge, subject to protest by the union after the discharge has been consummated. The arbitrator is cognizant of the fact that Blackwell is a shop steward and that no discharge of a shop steward is a matter to be considered lightly. The arbitrator also notes that the company has repeatedly put the union on notice that Blackwell's actions were objectionable to it and, unless changed, would lead to discharge. The union either was unable to or undesirous of effecting a change. . . .

Especially in passing on Blackwell's production record as grounds for his discharge, the arbitrator must take cognizance of the fact that he was a shop steward in his department, and the discharge of a shop steward should be taken only for very grave cause.

From Company Exhibit T, the schedule of all job tickets filed by Grady Blackwell in the month of October, 1946, and in the period January 2–9, 1947, it appears that Blackwell was a poor workman, did not come up to standard production, and was actually not even producing enough to justify the payment of his date rate. . . .

The arbitrator finds that, by reason of J. Grady Blackwell's repeated violation of the contract and repeated interference with plant efficiency and his demonstrated inefficiency, the discharge of J. Grady Blackwell was for "just and sufficient cause."

The arbitrator feels that the repeated notice to the union of Blackwell's precarious standing sufficiently complies with the additional consideration which is required of the company before it can discharge a shop steward. . . .   ◄

Collective Bargaining and National Policy

The national policy on labor-management relations is to allow employers and employees to work out for themselves the rules and procedures under which their relations will be carried on. The principal aim of the legal rules in this area is to foster conditions favorable to the negotiation of collective-bargaining agreements and to the settlement of disputes arising under them. There are also legal rules that restrict the use of economic weapons and the terms the parties may agree to, and each party is given the right to seek assistance in the courts if the other party breaches the agreement. But within this legal framework, labor and management are expected to work out the details of their relationship in each industrial "community."

Underlying the national policy is the presupposition that in a free society it is ordinarily desirable for private individuals and groups to work out their own contractual arrangements. They will be better citizens if they have to bear this responsibility themselves, and they are pretty sure to devise more imaginative and flexible rules and procedures to govern their affairs than would even the wisest of public officials. (This is our policy not only for labor-management relations but also for the internal affairs of such private associations as corporations, unions, churches, educational institutions, and clubs; legal rules merely establish a framework within which the complex of voluntary private relationships take their course.)

On the whole, we can say that the record of labor-management industrial communities in the past quarter-century in setting up and operating their own systems of self-government has justified our national presupposition. Thousands of arrangements have been negotiated, and under them large numbers of grievances are settled year after year. Strikes, lockouts, picketing, and boycotts are resorted to in only a tiny minority of instances in which contract negotiations or grievance procedures have failed. In many industries it is clear that labor-management relations are no longer marked by the bitterness that characterized the era before collective bargaining was introduced.

Underlying the national policy on industrial relations is another presupposition: That the occasional results of the bargaining process that seem contrary to "the public interest" are a price worth paying for industrial self-government. From time to time negotiations are bound to break down and to produce work stoppages that are often inconvenient to the public and harmful to the economy. From time to time a company and a union will sign an agreement containing provisions (most often relating to wages) that seem likely to interfere with such national goals as price stability and rapid growth. The presupposition of our national policy is that, at least in time of peace, such occurrences are worth enduring for the sake of preserving the system of collective bargaining.

Some of the strikes and inflationary wage-settlements in basic American industries in recent years have raised questions about this second presupposition. A balancing of values is involved, and some people wonder whether the government should not have more effective means to prevent these undesirable occurrences, even though government intervention would lessen the freedom to bargain collectively.

To explore further the issues raised by recent proposals for an expanded government role in industrial relations would carry us far beyond the subject of this chapter. But this proposed increase in government intervention in certain industries does raise some important questions: What would be the effect of such intervention (either to prevent a work stoppage or to prevent adoption of a particular term in a collective agreement) on the persistence with which bargaining—both agreement-negotiation and dispute-settlement—would be pursued? [13] Is there, for instance, a danger that, when the parties know that the government may step in to prevent a strike, they will stop doing their utmost to settle the differences between them? And if the possibility of government intervention *does* weaken the bargaining processes in a particular industry, may not this result be *more* undesirable in the long run than the misfortunes that government intervention was designed to prevent? We should give serious thought to these questions before making any radical changes in our national policies regarding labor-management relations.

---

[13] There is an abundance of wartime experience to guide us here. What effect did the restrictions on strikes and wage increases imposed during World War II have on the processes of bargaining?

10 Law
in Society

Now that we have studied the processes by which law is created and applied, it may be useful to return very briefly to a theme we touched on in Chapter 1: the role of the legal system in society.

Law as a Means of Achieving the Community's Ends

The legal system of a community exists to serve the purposes of that community. Law (in the sense in which we have been using the term) is not a set of restrictions imposed on the community by some mysterious external power; rather, it is a system of rules, institutions, and procedures that the community itself has established as a means of achieving its many and varied objectives.

Some people seem to think that the only purpose of the legal system is to inflict irksome restrictions on their freedom: if it weren't for the law, they grumble, we could drive as fast as we pleased, use our property exactly as we liked, and pay no taxes. Apparently what they don't realize is that legal restrictions exist only because the organized community of which we are all members wants and needs them. This is not to say, of course, that every member of the community likes and approves of every legal rule that restricts his freedom. But experience shows that in a democratic community a rule is rarely effective unless a substantial majority of those affected are willing, however reluctantly, to accept the restraints that the rule imposes. Persistent disobedience has nullified many a law, and political pressures have prompted the repeal of many others. The rules that remain in effect, though they are not always popular, are accepted because most people dimly sense that they are necessary, or recognize the difficulties involved in devising or enforcing better ones.

Law as a Framework for Voluntary Private Action

In any event, the law is much more than a set of "do's" and "don't's." True, some rules command and prohibit. But others permit us to do certain things, and some help us to achieve our objectives. These are the rules that establish liberties and powers. Rules that create liberties say: "If you choose to act in this way, public officials will not interfere with you." Rules that create powers go even further: "If you choose to act in this way, you can alter your legal position; you can create for yourself and others new rights and duties—provided only that you follow the prescribed procedures." In the normal course of affairs, a businessman is likely to be much more preoccupied with exercising powers effectively than with worrying about whether he is complying with legal commands and prohibitions.

The following questions, for example, are typical of the business problems that we shall be examining in Part II. Notice that each one involves a rule of law that puts powers in the hands of private persons. In each question the real issue is: "How can these persons be sure of achieving the result they desired?" and not: "What does the law command or forbid them to do?"

1. Under what circumstances, if any, are contracting parties justified in relying on a purely oral agreement?

2. When a businessman entrusts to an agent the task of negotiating an agreement on his behalf, may he safely assume that he cannot be bound by any agreement which his agent makes in violation of the instructions he has received?

3. A wants to borrow some money from B. He is ready to sign a note acknowledging his indebtedness and promising to pay. How should B word the note to make his own position as a creditor as safe and convenient as possible?

4. Under what circumstances do the acts of one member of a partnership change the legal position of the other partners?

5. How may an individual stockholder challenge an act of the company in which he owns stock?

6. Under what conditions may business firms agree to set a minimum retail price for a commodity without violating the antitrust laws?

The businessman must be careful not to violate the law's commands and prohibitions, of course. But once he has done that, his primary interest is in performing voluntary acts in such a way that he will achieve the legal effect he desires.

What we are saying, really, is that the legal system furnishes guides to ensure that social relations are directed into orderly channels. These guides make it possible for people to calculate the probable legal consequences of their conduct and to act accordingly.

We are most aware of the legal system when it is dealing with breakdowns in normal social relations: when it is providing for the punishment of wrongdoers, for the compensation of those who have been wronged, and for the settlement of disputes. And these are important functions of the law. But even more important is its ability to channel conduct in such a way that most clashes of competing interests will be resolved *without* resort to policemen, prosecutors, judges, and the like. In a well-ordered community, the adjustment of differences without resort to litigation or prosecution is the normal pattern of life; disruptions requiring remedial action are the exception.

Law as a Framework for Private Systems of Social Control

The legal system is the most powerful means of exercising social control, since public officials can, if necessary, apply methods of coercion that are not available to private persons. Nevertheless, the legal system relies heavily on controls exercised by private organizations. A democratic society such as ours encourages families, churches, educational institutions, social clubs, professional associations, business enterprises, and labor unions, for example, to manage their own internal affairs. And several of these organizations make a further contribution by implanting certain moral rules in their members and by disciplining those who fail to observe them.

The truth is that these private organizations are sometimes more effective than the legal system itself. It seems clear, for example, that the legal system is better suited to deal with commercial and financial transactions than with more personal relationships. In areas where the distinctions to be drawn between right and wrong are particularly subtle, where precise information on the facts is hard to obtain, where rapid remedial action is needed, and where the law's traditional remedies (damage awards, court orders, and criminal penalties) are not really applicable, the law is pretty helpless. Courts and judges can do little to make husbands kinder to their wives, to compel students to do their homework, or to induce people to be more devout or more truthful. And as we saw in Chapter 9, officials are properly reluctant to intervene in the complex relationship that exists between an employer and his employees. Social control in all these areas probably has to be exercised by private organizations (aided sometimes by the force of public opinion)—or not at all.

Democratic societies have a special reason for relying on private organizations for social control and for limiting government intervention in their affairs: a basic aim of every democratic society is to leave the private individual as free as possible to "pursue happiness" in his own way. A society with many agencies of social control is better able to protect individual freedom than a society in which all social control is concentrated in the government.

Law and Orderly Social Change

An effective legal system must provide for the continuing evolution of rules to meet changing situations, but it must do so without making the law wholly uncertain and unpredictable.

If the members of a community are unsure about whether existing rules are uniformly applicable, or whether yesterday's rules still apply today, the legal system cannot possibly serve as an effective instrument of social control. Without some stability in the law, people have no way of foreseeing the legal consequences of their acts.

On the other hand, changes in legal rules are inevitable. True, many human actions are repeated over and over again, and it is not especially difficult to devise rules that will fit most of these repetitive occurrences. (Rules about speeding on highways are an example.) But slight departures from the usual pattern keep cropping up, requiring that the rules be adjusted to make them fit. Many other acts are not at all routine or repetitive; in fact, social, economic, and technological changes are continually prompting wholly new patterns of conduct which demand the creation of new rules. Finally, the attitudes and values of a dynamic society keep changing, so that even familiar forms of conduct are governed by rules that evolve gradually in response to those changes. (Witness, for instance, the successively higher standards of honesty and candor that have been applied to sellers of goods over the years.)

Several procedural principles have been established in the United States to ensure maximum certainty and stability in the law:

1. Before statutes are enacted, and before administrative regulations are issued, parties who will be affected by the pending action are notified and given an opportunity to express their views. Statutes and regulations must be published. Ordinarily, they cannot be made retroactive. And they remain in force until they are formally amended or repealed.

2. Those who must interpret statutes and administrative regulations in the course of deciding cases may not ignore the framers' language and must do their best to discover and carry out the framers' purposes.

3. Judges (and to some extent administrative adjudicators) are governed by the doctrine of *stare decisis*. They must follow controlling precedents in all but the most unusual circumstances, and when they exercise their authority to create new decisional rules, they must explain in reasoned opinions how the new rules are related to established precedents and principles. Change is necessary, but even in change there can be continuity.

So much for stability. How does the legal system provide for the evolution of the law? Over and over again in the foregoing chapters we have seen how the lawmaking processes interact to create, adjust, and gradually modify legal rules as successive situations and needs arise. Now let us look briefly at the respective roles of those processes in the seven fields of law that we shall explore in Part II:

1. In the law of *contracts* and *agency*, where there is still very little legislation, the courts continue to bear most of the responsibility for the development of the law. These fields provide many examples of judicial lawmaking by building on precedents.

2. The law of *sales, negotiable instruments,* and *partnerships* was virtually all judge-made until the twentieth century. But in the many states that have enacted the Uniform Sales Act, the Negotiable Instruments Law, and the Uniform Partnership Act,[1] the basic rules have been significantly changed, and future lawmaking has been set on a statutory foundation. Of course, judicial lawmaking will continue to operate in these fields as the courts interpret the provisions of these statutes. Here, then, we have typical examples of the interaction between judicial and legislative lawmaking that

---

[1] On the uniform state laws, see page 94. Recently, some states have further modified the basic rules of law governing sales and negotiable instruments by passing the Uniform Commercial Code. See page 353.

prevails today in most fields of private law (that is, law governing private conduct).

3. In the law of *corporations* and in *government regulation of business,* a far larger proportion of the rules are of statutory origin. Yet the enormously important Sherman Act, the cornerstone of antitrust law, is, as we have remarked more than once, a classic example of a deliberately imprecise statute that in effect delegates the major responsibility for lawmaking to the courts (and to the public officials who decide which cases to bring before the courts). Here we have judicial lawmaking building vigorously on a base provided by legislative lawmaking.

4. *Government regulation of business* is the only field among the seven in which administrative agencies play an important role in making and changing the rules. In some areas of government regulation, we find that administrative lawmaking is the principal source of evolution in the law.

Law and Public Policy

We said at the beginning of this chapter that the legal system exists to serve the purposes of the community. This means that behind every rule lies a public policy, a purpose: someone has made a decision, a value judgment about the community's needs. As we examined the lawmaking processes in the preceding chapters, we saw how judges, legislators, and administrators were all compelled to make decisions on policy. We have seen, moreover, that the lawmaking processes are intertwined, and that the various lawmaking agencies have certain opportunities to correct what they deem to be bad decisions on public purposes by the others.

To be sure, the policy behind a rule is not always clear, either because the officials who framed it deliberately chose to be vague, leaving the details to be filled in by others, or because they did not take the time to think the policy through. But a rule founded on no policy at all is an impossibility.

Keep this point in mind as you read the rest of this book. You will not like all the rules you encounter, and some of them will seem to make no sense at all. But in your efforts to understand a troublesome rule, try to divine the probable preoccupations, values, and aims of the policy-makers who created it—be they legislators, judges, or administrators. Your search for an underlying policy will often reveal aspects of the problem being dealt with that won't have occurred to you; then, hopefully, the rule will begin to make sense. Once you have identified the policy, of course, you may decide that it is a bad policy, or that the policy is wise but that the rule does not implement it properly.

In any event, remember that legal rules embody a social purpose, that they are the product of the never-ending, trial-and-error process of translating society's aims and objectives into effective guides to conduct.

A BIBLIOGRAPHICAL NOTE

The volume of literature about legal processes and institutions is, of course, enormous. Our purpose in the present note (and in the notes that follow each chapter in Part II) is merely to list a very limited number of works that we think will be particularly useful to the student who wishes to inquire further into the subjects we have treated. *Books available in paperback editions are marked with an asterisk.*

First, here are some books which are concerned with the nature of law and its role in society. Roscoe Pound, *Social Control through Law* (Yale University Press, 1942), is one of the books in which the former dean of the Harvard Law School has discoursed on this broad subject. Among the many books written to introduce the beginning law student to the nature of law, perhaps the most penetrating is Karl N. Llewellyn, *The Bramble Bush* (Oceana Publications, 1930, 1951). Another useful book in this category is Bernard C. Gavit, *Introduction to the Study of Law* (Foundation Press, 1951). Harold J. Berman, *The Nature and Functions of Law* (Foundation Press, 1958), is an interesting collection of cases and other materials designed for use in social science courses. Professor Berman is also the editor of a small volume in which are published seventeen short talks about American law (each by a Harvard Law School professor) that were broadcast to foreign audiences by the Voice of America; the volume is Harold J. Berman, ed., *Talks on American Law* * (Vintage Books, 1961).

We list next some works in which are discussed all or most of the processes and institutions we have examined in Part I of this book. Burke Shartel, *Our Legal System and How It Operates* (University of Michigan Law School, 1951), based on a series of lectures given at the University of Michigan Law School, and Lewis Mayers, *The American Legal System* (Harper, 1955), which describes "the administration of justice by judicial, administrative, military, and arbitral tribunals," are particularly useful. J. Willard Hurst, *The Growth of the Law: The Law Makers* (Little, Brown, 1950), considers the evolution of American legal institutions from 1790 to 1940. Also helpful are two books of cases and other materials designed to introduce students to the legal processes. The first—Carl A. Auerbach and others, *The Legal Process* (Chandler, 1961)—was compiled primarily for students not training to become lawyers; the second—Noel T. Dowling and others, *Materials for Legal Method*, 2nd Ed. by Harry Jones (Foundation Press, 1952)— was prepared for first-year law students.

Among the many books about the judicial process, Benjamin N. Cardozo, *The Nature of the Judicial Process* * (Yale University Press, 1921), is a classic. Its author was one of America's great judges and legal scholars, and the student will find some of his other writings equally helpful. Justice Cardozo was the author of two of the essays, mostly reprinted from the pages of the *Harvard Law Review*, which the *Review's* editors have brought together in a valuable collection under the title, *An Introduction to Law* * (Harvard University Press, 1957); among the authors who are represented are eight who were (or later became) distinguished judges. A penetrating analysis of the reasoning process by which appellate judges arrive at decisions is found in Edward H. Levi, *An Introduction to Legal Reasoning* * (University of Chicago Press, 1949). On this subject see also William Zelermyer, *Legal Reasoning* (Prentice-Hall, 1960). Joseph N. Ulman, *A Judge Takes the Stand* (Knopf, 1933), considers the judicial process from the viewpoint of a trial judge. Jerome Frank, *Courts on Trial* (Princeton University Press, 1949), is a brilliant and at times biting analysis of the process by which cases are tried; he is particularly critical of the jury system. Another book by a judge who was interested in the reform of judicial institutions is Arthur T. Vanderbilt, *Men and Measures in the Law* (Knopf, 1949). Frank and Vanderbilt each wrote several other important books and articles of critical commentary on the administration of justice. Charles P. Curtis, *It's Your Law* (Harvard University Press, 1954), considers the role of the advocate, the lawyer (as drafter of legal documents), the trial court, and the appellate court. Finally, a stimulating collection of readings on the judicial process is found in Walter F. Murphy and C. Herman Pritchett, *Courts, Judges, and Politics* (Random House, 1961); the emphasis here is on the federal courts and the political aspect of their functioning.

We come finally to a few works discussing some special topics that are considered in Part I. On the role of the lawyer, see Albert P. Blaustein and Charles O. Porter, *The American Lawyer* (University of Chicago Press, 1954), which summarizes a survey of the legal profession. On federal constitutional law, C. Herman Pritchett, *The American Constitution* (McGraw-Hill, 1959), is a valuable study. Among the best of many recent books on the United States Supreme Court is Robert G. McCloskey, *The American Supreme Court* (University of Chicago Press, 1960). Robert L. Hale, *Freedom through Law* (Columbia University Press, 1952), is concerned with the role of law generally (but particularly the role of the Supreme Court) in broadening economic liberty. On administrative lawmaking and adjudication, see Kenneth C. Davis, *Administrative Law Text* (West Publishing Co., 1959). And on the law of labor-management relations, see Charles O. Gregory, *Labor and the Law*, 2nd Rev. Ed. (Norton, 1958).

PART II

The
Law
of
Business

Introduction

In Part I we tried to give you some idea of what law, in general, is and how it is made. Now we are ready to concentrate on how rules of law are applied to business transactions.

In each chapter we will begin with a brief introductory essay dealing with a specific area of business law. Then we will state the general rules of law that are pertinent to that area. Sprinkled through the statement of the rules will be actual case decisions that raise problems calling for the application of those rules. At the end of each case, we will list a few comments and questions to test your understanding of the court's opinion, the rules of law involved, how the court solved the problem, and why the case was decided as it was. Finally, at the end of each chapter, we will summarize the rules of law that we have discussed in the chapter.

Before starting, we would like to offer a few words of advice and caution. First, remember that the rules stated are general in nature and are not to be taken as a comprehensive or all-inclusive summary of the law in any given area. Our purpose in presenting them is merely to give you some legal background in the particular field of business under consideration and to help you understand the cases that follow. Our aim is not to have you memorize dozens of rules of law, but, rather, to acquaint you with the process by which those rules are brought to bear on typical business problems. No one expects you to become a lawyer as a result of reading the chapters ahead, but by the time you finish the book you should at least be aware of some of the legal problems that arise in business. Such an awareness will help you decide when and how to consult a lawyer and, hopefully, will make you a better client when you do.

Our attempt to summarize the rules of law is complicated by several difficulties, some of which we have already mentioned. One difficulty is that in many areas of business law there is no uniform rule that holds good in all the states. The Supreme Judicial Court of Massachusetts may apply one rule to a given situation while the New York Court of Appeals may apply an entirely different one. You may be surprised to discover that some courts hold this way, others that way, or that a majority of states have one rule while a minority have another. Except in those fields (for example, sales and negotiable instruments) where uniform legislation has been enacted by most or all of the states, some lack of consistency is bound to exist, since each state is free to formulate its own rules as it sees fit. At the same time, however, there are many well-established rules of law that are generally accepted in most states.

Another difficulty is that many rules of law are phrased in vague terms, such as what is "reasonable" or what is the "intention" of the parties. This means that some rules are not very meaningful in themselves and are extremely difficult to apply to specific fact-situations. Reasonable men may differ in their reactions and judgments, and many matters must be left to judge and jury. This point has already been discussed in Part I and you will see many illustrations of it in Part II.

As you read the rules of law, and especially the actual case decisions, keep in mind the legal institutions and processes we described in Part I. Only by referring back to the earlier discussions can you appreciate the court's problem in each case and the manner in which the court worked out a solution. Ask yourself what the court is trying to accomplish, how the rules of law affect the transaction of business, and, conversely, how the business community itself helps to determine the law that controls it.

11 Contracts

Introduction

Almost all business transactions are based on voluntary agreements between persons or firms. We are constantly making arrangements and bargains with other people to work out mutual problems. We buy groceries or gasoline, we work for or hire someone, we buy a house or pay rent.

Most people honor their agreements and live up to their word. Life goes along fairly smoothly and, even when arguments arise, they are usually settled amicably. Occasionally, however, disputes develop which the parties cannot or will not solve by themselves. Then it is that lawyers and judges are called in to put matters right. In resolving such disputes the court must decide whether the agreement in question is one that should be enforced by legal sanctions. In other words, does the agreement create a legally binding obligation between the parties who made it? If so, it is recognized as a *contract*—an agreement that the parties must abide by. If they choose not to abide by it, they must risk the penalties imposed by law—the payment of damages, for example.[1]

Not all agreements are contracts. Many agreements give rise to no legal obligations at all, and the courts will take no action to enforce them. For example, an agreement may be made in jest and not seriously intended. Or it may be strictly social in nature (someone agrees to attend a party given by a friend). Or the court may decide that the agreement is against public policy (a gambling contract).

The primary function of contract law is to protect the rights of contracting parties so that each may rely on the other's promises and commitments. In our society we expect men to honor their contracts and to be punished if they fail to do so. Any other system would be intolerable, we feel. And yet history shows that the courts have not always imposed such strict standards. In fact, these standards are the result of a slow evolution in legal thinking. A brief review of that evolution will give you some insight into the origins of contract law.

---

[1] When a contracting party fails to perform his part of the bargain, he is guilty of a *breach of contract*. This is a term that we will meet frequently in our discussion.

Generally speaking, the concept of contract law was nonexistent in early societies. Although agreements were often recognized as morally binding, they enjoyed no legal sanctions as such, and enforcement procedures were generally confined to the use of personal force or, if the Church chose to involve itself in the dispute, the power of religious sanctions. It was not until the eleventh century in England that modern contract law had its beginnings.

In the period following the Norman Conquest, the royal courts of England evolved certain rules that imposed liability for breach of contract in two limited situations: First, if one person agreed to supply goods or render services to another, who in turn promised to pay a stipulated amount, and if the goods were actually delivered or the services rendered, the first person could recover what was due him. Until he completed his performance, however, he could not claim anything; and if the other party refused to allow him to furnish the service or supply the goods, there was nothing he could do. In other words, the mere fact that an agreement had been made was of no legal significance in and of itself.

It was also during this period that the courts first gave special consideration to so-called *contracts under seal.* If a person put his obligation in writing and signed it and placed his personal seal on the document, he was legally bound to carry out the bargain. It was felt that if someone took the trouble to execute an agreement with such formality, he should be required to perform it. (We shall have more to say about sealed contracts later on in this chapter.)

Except in these two situations, the royal courts were very reluctant to enforce contractual obligations. This was not true, however, of certain special courts that European merchants had long since established for the private settlement of commercial disputes. These informal tribunals were much more willing to enforce business agreements, and they gradually evolved a system of rules and principles called the "law merchant." Much of this law was later incorporated into the common law of England and has been carried over to our present-day contract law.

In the sixteenth century an idea emerged that was to become one of the foundations of our modern law of contracts. During that period the English courts first enunciated the rule that where two parties make promises to each other in the form of a contract,[2] both are legally bound; and if one of the contracting parties fails to carry out his promise, he must pay sufficient damages to the other to put him in as good a position as he would have been in had performance been completed. In other words, once the promises had been exchanged, each side was legally committed and each was entitled to the benefits to be had from the contract. This was a new concept and a very important one. No longer was it necessary to show that goods or services had been supplied, or that the contract had been executed with the formality of a seal. Now, all that was necessary was the exchange of mutual promises.

---

[2] In a contract, the person making a promise is referred to as the "promisor," and the party to whom the promise is made is called the "promisee." Thus, if mutual promises are exchanged, each party to the contract is both a "promisor" and a "promisee."

It soon became apparent, however, that not all promises given in exchange for other promises *should* be enforced. In many cases, no true bargain was struck, in the sense that each party was either conferring some benefit on the other or giving up something of value. (For example, when a person promises to give a watch to another person and that person agrees to accept it, the recipient of the watch has given nothing in exchange.) As a result, the courts introduced the rule that a promise must be supported by *consideration* before it is enforceable. Now, before the promisee could require the promisor to carry out his commitment, he had to show that he had given some consideration in exchange. (The requirement of consideration will be discussed at greater length in Section 4 of this chapter.)

The great expansion of business and commerce that followed the Protestant Reformation hastened the development of modern contract law. More than ever before, it seemed important that men honor their agreements and that a man who broke his contract should fully compensate the other party for his loss. Naturally, this heightened insistence on the inviolability of agreements meant that the courts had to make certain that true bargains had been reached and that no fraud, or duress, or other mitigating factors were present. It was in response to these two forces that many of our present-day rules were incorporated into contract law. (We will discuss this at greater length in Sections 2 and 3 of this chapter.)

Today, the law holds contracts in high esteem, and freedom of contract is regarded as one of our great liberties. Indeed, our federal Constitution provides, in Article 1, Section 10, that "No State . . . shall pass any law impairing the obligation of contracts. . . ." Even now, however, we are not entirely free to make agreements as we choose.

The twentieth century has witnessed a tremendous increase in state and federal regulation of contracts in the United States, with the result that many of the contracts we make must meet certain requirements specified by law, and with the further result that certain types of agreement are prohibited altogether. For example: the antitrust laws forbid two competing firms from agreeing to fix the prices of the products they sell, most states limit the amount of interest a bank or lending institution may charge on a loan, certain kinds of policy issued by insurance companies must contain clauses for the benefit and protection of policyholders, and many of the rates charged by transportation companies and utilities are fixed by state or federal administrative agencies. Most people feel that such regulation is necessary if we are to preserve a healthy economy and a wholesome society. Yet there is no denying that freedom of contract has been greatly restricted in the process.

Although government regulation plays a major role in contract law, criminal penalties are rarely, if ever, imposed on a person who defaults on his contractual obligations. In some societies, a willful breach of contract is considered a criminal offense. In our system, in most cases, the courts require only the payment of money damages to the injured party.

What, then, are the functions of contract law? The first has already been stressed: to secure and protect the rights of the contracting parties so that each may rely on the performance of the other. Second, the courts are concerned that the agreement be a true bargain and that it not violate certain economic and social principles. Third, the courts try to facilitate the making of business agreements by mediating differences between contracting parties and by interpreting the meaning of contracts when doubts and conflicts arise. You will see many examples of these functions as you read through this chapter.

Our brief historical summary has given you some idea of the sources of contract law. For the most part, contract law is judge-made law based on precedents. The rules formulated by the English royal courts and by the special commercial tribunals (i.e., the law merchant) had already become part of the common law that was brought over to the American colonies. In addition, many rules of the equity courts (see pp. 58–60) have a direct bearing on contract law.

Although they have been modified to meet changing conditions, most of the rules of basic contract law are old and well established. With the notable exception of the Statute of Frauds (to be discussed at some length later in the chapter), there has been little legislation on the subject. So, in the discussions that follow, our main emphasis will be on judicial lawmaking.

The principles outlined in this chapter are fundamental to all contractual relationships in business. In subsequent chapters we shall examine the more specific rules of law applicable to special types of contract, such as agency, sales, and partnership.

SECTION 1

NATURE AND CLASSIFICATION OF CONTRACTS

Every minute of every day people are entering into contracts. Some of these contracts are very complicated and detailed—they are carefully drafted by attorneys and signed with great ceremony (for example, a long-term lease on an office building). Others are simple exchanges: a man picks up a newspaper at the corner stand and hands the dealer a coin. Very often, nothing at all is written down: the agreement is entirely oral. Sometimes, when the intentions of the parties are clear from their actions, not a single word is spoken: a housewife gets on a bus, deposits her fare in the coin box, and rides to her destination. Some contracts consist of an exchange of promises to do something later on: a contractor agrees to build a house for someone for a given price. In other situations, the contract is made and carried out in one transaction: a man buys a package of cigarettes at the corner drugstore. Contracts are entered into by individuals, by corporations and partnerships, or by agents acting on behalf of someone else.

These examples suggest some of the ways in which contracts may be classified. For example, contracts may be either written or oral. In a few situations, the law requires written evidence of a contract (see pp. 294–300), but generally an oral agreement is just as binding and just as enforceable as a written one. True, when there is nothing in writing, proof of the contract is sometimes difficult to establish; and if there was no one around to witness the agreement, any subsequent challenge may boil down to one man's word against another's. Yet many contracts are proved in court without producing any outside witnesses or written documents.

Contracts that consist of ordinary oral or written agreements, involving no unusual formalities, are called *simple contracts*. Occasionally, however, the parties "seal" their agreement either by affixing a seal to the document itself, usually next to their signatures, or by stating that the contract is to be regarded as a sealed instrument. In earlier times, as we have already noted (page 204), so-called *contracts under seal* were the only kind of agreement that could ordinarily be enforced. Today, in most states and for most purposes, a contract under seal is no different from a simple contract. A few states, however, still hold that a sealed contract is enforceable in some situations where a simple contract is not (e.g., where no consideration is present; see page 257), and in some jurisdictions the statute of limitations is longer on sealed contracts (see page 332) than on simple contracts.

When both parties to a contract have performed all the obligations imposed on them by their agreement, it is said to be an *executed contract;* if neither party has performed his obligations, it is said to be an *executory contract.*[3] If one side has performed but the other has not, the contract is said to be executed on one side and executory on the other.

EXAMPLES

1. A lease between landlord and tenant is an executory contract. *– incomplete*
2. The purchase of a newspaper is an executed contract.
3. If one person pays another a sum of money and the other person promises to deliver some merchandise to him at a future date, the contract is executed on one side and executory on the other.

The law requires that an agreement must meet certain conditions before the parties who enter into it are obliged to carry out its terms. An agreement that meets these conditions is referred to as a *valid,* or *binding, contract.* *unita*

Sometimes, special circumstances make an agreement binding on one side but not on the other. An agreement of this sort is known as a *voidable contract,* since one of the parties has the right to avoid all the obligations spelled out in the contract if he so chooses. If he does not choose to avoid them, however, both sides are bound to perform, as they would be under a valid contract.

---

[3] Once an executory contract has been arrived at, both sides are legally obligated to carry it out, of course. The person having an obligation to perform is referred to as the "obligor," and the person who is entitled to receive performance is called the "obligee."

EXAMPLE

A, an adult, enters into an otherwise valid contract with M, a minor. Because M is under age, he is not bound to carry out the contract. But if he chooses not to avoid his obligations, the contract is binding on both sides. (We shall have more to say about minors' contracts and other types of voidable contract later on.)

Finally, the term *void contract* is sometimes used to describe an agreement that has no legal effect whatsoever. Of course, our definition of a contract as a legally enforceable agreement makes the phrase "void contract" a contradiction in terms, and its use is frowned on by many authorities. Still, since it is often found in court decisions, you should be familiar with it.

To be binding, a contract must meet certain legal conditions. These may be classified roughly as follows:

1. There must be an *agreement* between the parties, with one party making an offer, or proposal, and the other accepting it.

2. Both parties must give *genuine assent* to be bound, free of any fraud, duress, or mistake.

3. There must be *consideration* on both sides—that is, both parties must give up some legal right in exchange for the performance of some service, or for the promise to perform some service, by the other.

4. There must be *legal capacity* on both sides—that is, both must be legally competent to enter into binding agreements.

5. The contract must be in the *proper form*. If, for example, the law requires that a contract must be in written form to be enforceable, a mere oral agreement is not binding.

6. The contract must have a *legal purpose*—that is, its subject matter must be proper.

We shall return to these six conditions in the following sections.

SECTION 2

THE AGREEMENT—OFFER AND ACCEPTANCE

In General

Obviously, two or more persons or parties are necessary to make a contract, and some agreement or understanding must be reached between them before a contract comes into being. First one side makes a proposal of some kind to the other, indicating that he wishes to enter into an agreement. If the other side indicates his assent to the proposal, an agreement is formed. The proposal is called an *offer;* the assent is called an *acceptance.* The party making the offer is called the *offeror;* the party to whom the offer is made is called the *offeree.*

The Offer

A proposal must meet certain requirements to be considered a legal offer. First, it must be made seriously and not in jest. Also, it must be definite enough so that the offeree will know just what obligations are being suggested. Finally, the offer must be made known to the offeree, for clearly he must be aware of it before he can accept it.

In many cases, it is difficult to tell whether a proposal is merely a preliminary inquiry or an invitation to negotiate, or whether the offeror is making a binding offer to contract. In the case that follows, the court was faced with this very problem. Let us see how the problem was resolved.

NEBRASKA SEED CO. v. HARSH
Supreme Court of Nebraska, 1915
98 Neb. 89, 152 N.W. 310

► Action by the Nebraska Seed Company, a corporation, against H. F. Harsh. From judgment for plaintiff, defendant appeals. Reversed.[4]

MORISSEY, C. J. Plaintiff, a corporation, engaged in buying and selling seed in the city of Omaha, Neb., brought this action against the defendant, a farmer residing at Lowell, Kearney county, Neb. The petition alleges:

"That on the 26th day of April, 1912, the plaintiff purchased of and from the defendant 1,800 bushels of millet seed at the agreed price of $2.25 per hundredweight, F.O.B. Lowell, Neb., which said purchase and contract was evidenced by writing and correspondence passing between the respective parties of which the following is a copy:

"'Lowell, Nebraska, 4-24-12.
"'Neb. Seed Co., Omaha, Neb.—Gentlemen: I have about 1,800 bu. or thereabouts of millet seed of which I am mailing you a sample. This millet is recleaned and was grown on sod and is good seed. I want $2.25 per cwt. for this seed f.o.b. Lowell.
"'Yours truly,   H. F. Harsh'

"Said letter was received by the plaintiff at its place of business in Omaha, Neb., on the 26th day of April, 1912, and immediately thereafter the plaintiff telegraphed to the defendant at Lowell, Neb., a copy of which is as follows:

---

[4] Frequently, the court will indicate the final result in the opening paragraph of the opinion; in this case, for example, it is stated that the judgment of the lower court was reversed. In many cases, however, the reader is kept in suspense about how the decision is going to turn out until he comes to the end of the opinion. (Editors' footnote. Unless otherwise indicated, all footnotes to cases are the editors' and not the court's.)

◀

" '4-26-12.

" 'H. F. Harsh, Lowell, Nebr. Sample and letter received. Accept your offer. Millet like sample two twenty-five per hundred. Wire how soon can load. The Nebraska Seed Co.'

"On the same day, to wit, April 26, 1912, the plaintiff, in answer to the letter of the said defendant, wrote to him a letter and deposited the same in the United States mail, directed to the said defendant at Lowell, Neb., which said letter was duly stamped, and which the plaintiff charges that the defendant in due course of mail received. That a copy of said letter is as follows:

" '4-26-12.

" 'Mr. H. F. Harsh, Lowell, Neb.—Dear Sir: We received your letter and sample of millet seed this morning and at once wired you as follows: "Sample and letter received. Accept your offer. Millet like sample two twenty-five per hundred. Wire how soon can load." We confirm this message, have booked purchase of you 1,800 bushels of millet seed to be fully equal to sample you sent us at $2.25 per cwt. your track. Please be so kind as to load this seed at once and ship to us at Omaha. We thank you in advance for prompt attention. When anything further in the line of millet to offer, let us have samples.

" 'Yours truly,   The Nebraska Seed Co.' "

It alleges that defendant refused to deliver the seed, after due demand and tender of the purchase price, and prays judgment in the sum of $900. Defendant filed a demurrer, which was overruled. He saved an exception to the ruling [5] and answered, denying that the petition stated a cause of action; that the correspondence set out constituted a contract, etc. There was a trial to a jury with verdict and judgment for plaintiff, and defendant appeals.

In our opinion the letter of defendant cannot be fairly construed into an offer to sell to the plaintiff. After describing the seed, the writer says, "I want $2.25 per cwt. for this seed f.o.b. Lowell." He does not say, "I offer to sell to you." The language used is general, and such as may be used in an advertisement, or circular addressed generally to those engaged in the seed business, and is not an offer by which he may be bound, if accepted, by any or all of the persons addressed.

"If a proposal is nothing more than an invitation to the person to whom it is made to make an offer to the proposer, it is not such an offer as can be turned into an agreement by acceptance. Proposals of this kind, although made to definite persons and not to the public generally, are merely invitation to trade; they go no further than what occurs when one asks another what he will give or take for certain goods. Such inquiries may lead to bargains, but do not make them. They ask for offers which the proposer has a right to accept or reject as he pleases." 9 Cyc. 278e.

The letter as a whole shows that it was not intended as a final proposi-

---

[5] This means that the defendant lawyer made a formal objection to the judge's ruling against him; in most states, he must take this step if he wishes to argue the point on appeal.

tion, but as a request for bids. It did not fix a time for delivery, and this seems to have been regarded as one of the essentials by plaintiff, for in his telegram he requests defendant to "wire how soon can load."

"The mere statement of the price at which property is held cannot be understood as an offer to sell." Knight v. Cooley, 34 Iowa, 218.

The letter of acceptance is not in the terms of the offer. Defendant stated that he had 1,800 bushels or thereabouts. He did not fix a definite and certain amount. It might be 1,800 bushels; it might be more; it might be less; but plaintiff undertook to make an acceptance for 1,800 bushels—no more, no less. Defendant might not have this amount, and therefore be unable to deliver, or he might have a greater amount, and, after filling plaintiff's order, have a quantity of seed left for which he might find no market. We may assume that when he wrote the letter he did not contemplate the sale of more seed than he had, and that he fixed the price on the whole lot whether it was more or less than 1,800 bushels.

We do not think the correspondence made a complete contract. To so hold where a party sends out letters to a number of dealers would subject him to a suit by each one receiving a letter, or invitation to bid, even though this supply of seed were exhausted. In Lyman v. Robinson, 14 Allen (Mass.) 242, 254, the Supreme Court of Massachusetts has sounded the warning:

"Care should always be taken not to construe as an agreement letters which the parties intended only as a preliminary negotiation."

Holding, as we do, that there was no binding contract between the parties, it is unnecessary to discuss the other questions presented.

The judgment of the district court is reversed.   ◄

COMMENTS AND QUESTIONS

1. Summarize the important facts in this case. What was the principal issue before the court?
2. What happened in the lower court? Was there a trial? If so, how did it turn out?
3. What rule of law did the appellate court adopt here? Had a binding contract been formed? Had an offer been made?
4. Summarize the reasons given by the appellate court for its decision.

There are two basic types of offer:

An Offer Leading to a Bilateral Contract

In making this kind of offer, the offeror requests the offeree to indicate his acceptance by making some sort of promise in return. Once the promise has been made, a *bilateral contract* is formed which is binding on both sides.

EXAMPLE

BUYER says to SELLER, "I would like to buy your watch. I'll give you $50 for it." SELLER replies, "O.K. It's a deal." A bilateral contract has been made. BUYER's offer invites an acceptance by SELLER in the form of a return promise.

An Offer Leading to a Unilateral Contract

Here the offeror requests the offeree to indicate his acceptance of an offer by performing some act. Neither side is bound until the offeree has actually performed the act. Once he has done so, however, a so-called *unilateral contract* is made and the offeror must carry out his part of the bargain.

EXAMPLE

OFFEROR says to x, "If you find my wallet and return it to me, I'll give you a reward of $10." If x finds and returns the wallet, OFFEROR is bound to pay him $10. Until that time, however, x is under no obligation to look for the wallet, nor is OFFEROR under any obligation to give x a reward. In other words, OFFEROR makes it perfectly clear that he does not want to be bound by his offer until x has performed the act called for.

The famous case of *Carlill v. Carbolic Smoke Ball Co.* is a splendid illustration of the latter type of offer. Although it is an English decision handed down in 1893, it has frequently been cited by American judges and legal scholars as sound precedent. Note the "flavor" of the two opinions and the manner in which the court deals with the various arguments advanced by the defendant.

CARLILL v. CARBOLIC SMOKE BALL CO.

Court of Appeal (1893) [6]
1 Q.B. 256

► Appeal from a decision of HAWKINS, J., (1892) 2 Q.B. 484.

The defendants, who were the proprietors and vendors of a medical preparation called "The Carbolic Smoke Ball," inserted in the Pall Mall Gazette of November 13, 1891, and in other newspapers, the following advertisement:

"£100 reward will be paid by the Carbolic Smoke Ball Company to any person who contracts the increasing epidemic influenza, colds or any disease caused by taking cold, after having used the ball three times daily for two weeks according to the printed directions supplied with each ball. £1,000 is deposited with the Alliance Bank, Regent Street, shewing our sincerity in the matter.

"During the last epidemic of influenza many thousand carbolic smoke balls were sold as preventives against the disease, and in no ascertained case was the disease contracted by those using the carbolic smoke ball.

"One carbolic smoke ball will last a family several months, making it the cheapest remedy in the world at the price, 10s., post free. The ball can be refilled at a cost of 5s. Address, Carbolic Smoke Ball Company, 27, Princes Street, Hanover Square, London."

The plaintiff, a lady, on the faith of this advertisement, bought one of the balls at a chemist's and used it as directed, three times a day, from

---

[6] The Court of Appeal is the chief appellate court in England.

November 20, 1891, to January 17, 1892, when she was attacked by influenza. HAWKINS, J. held that she was entitled to recover the £100. The defendants appealed.

LINDLEY, L. J. . . . We are dealing with an express promise to pay £100 in certain events. Read the advertisement how you will, and twist it about as you will, here is a distinct promise expressed in language which is perfectly unmistakable: "£100 reward will be paid by the Carbolic Smoke Ball Company to any person who contracts the influenza after having used the ball three times daily for two weeks according to the printed directions supplied with each ball."

We must first consider whether this was intended to be a promise to all, or whether it was a mere puff which meant nothing. Was it a mere puff? My answer to that question is "No," and I base my answer upon this passage: "£1000 is deposited with the Alliance Bank, shewing our sincerity in the matter." Now for what was that money deposited or that statement made except to negative the suggestion that this was a mere puff and meant nothing at all? The deposit is called aid by the advertiser as proof of his sincerity in the matter, that is, the sincerity of his promise to pay this £100 in the event which he has specified. I say this for the purpose of giving point to the observation that we are not inferring a promise; there is the promise, as plain as words can make it.

Then it is contended that it is not binding. In the first place, it is said that it is not made with anybody in particular. Now that point is common to the words of this advertisement and to the words of all other advertisements offering rewards. They are offers to anybody who performs the conditions named in the advertisement, and anybody who does perform the conditions accepts the offer. In point of law this advertisement is an offer to pay £100 to anybody who will perform these conditions, and the performance of the conditions, is the acceptance of the offer. That rests upon a string of authorities, the earliest of which is Williams vs. Carwardine, 4 Barn. & Adol. 621, which has been followed by many other decisions upon advertisements offering rewards. . . .

We therefore, find here all the elements which are necessary to form a binding contract enforceable in point of law, subject to two observations. First of all it is said that this advertisement is so vague that you can not really construe it as a promise—that the vagueness of the language shows that a legal promise was never intended or contemplated. The language is vague and uncertain in some respects, and particularly in this, that the £100 is to be paid to any person who contracts the increasing epidemic after having used the balls three times daily for two weeks. . . . I do not think that business people or reasonable people would understand the words as meaning that if you took a smoke ball and used it three times daily for two weeks you were to be guaranteed against influenza for the rest of your life, and I think it would be pushing the language of the advertisement too far to construe it as meaning that. But if it does not mean that, what does it mean? It is for the defendants to shew what it does mean; and it strikes me that there are two, and possibly three, reasonable constructions to be put on this advertisement, any one of which will answer the purpose of the plaintiff. Possibly it may be limited to persons catching the "increasing epidemic" (that is, the then prevailing epidemic), or any colds or diseases caused by taking cold, during the prevalence of the increasing epidemic. That is one suggestion; but it does not commend itself to me. Another suggested meaning is that you are warranted free from catching the epidemic, or colds or other diseases caused by taking cold, whilst you are using this remedy after using it for two weeks. If that is the meaning, the plaintiff is right, for she used the remedy for two weeks and went on using it till she got the epidemic. Another meaning, and the one which I rather prefer, is that the reward is offered to any person who contracts the epidemic or other disease within a reasonable time after having used the smoke ball. . . .

Then it is asked, what is a reasonable time? It has been suggested that there is no standard of reasonableness; that it depends upon the reasonable time for a germ to develop! I do not feel pressed by that.[7] It strikes me that a reasonable time may be ascertained in a business sense and in a sense satisfactory to a lawyer, in this way: find out from a chemist what the ingredients are; find out from a skilled physician how long the effect of such ingredients on the system could be reasonably expected to endure so as to protect a person from an epidemic or cold, and in that way you will get a standard to be laid before a jury, or a judge without a jury, by which they might exercise their judgment as to what a reasonable time would be. It strikes me, I confess, that the true construction of this advertisement is that £100 will be paid to anybody who uses this smoke ball three times daily for two weeks according to the printed directions, and who gets the influenza or cold or other diseases caused by taking cold within a reasonable time after so using it; and if that is the true construction, it is enough for the plaintiff. . . .

It appears to me, therefore, that the defendants must perform their promise, and, if they have been so unwary as to expose themselves to a great many actions, so much the worse for them.

BOWEN, L. J.   I am of the same opinion. . . .

Then it was said that there was no notification of the acceptance of the contract. One cannot doubt that, as an ordinary rule of law, an acceptance of an offer made ought to be notified to the person who makes the offer, in order that the two minds may come together. Unless this is done the two minds may be apart, and there is not that consensus which is necessary according to English law—I say nothing about the laws of other countries to make a contract. But there is this clear gloss to be made upon that doctrine, that as notification of acceptance is required for the benefit of the person who makes the offer, the person who makes the offer may dispense with notice to himself if he thinks it desirable to do so, and I suppose there can be no doubt that where a person in an offer made by him to another person, expressly or impliedly intimates a particular mode of acceptance

---

[7] One has the impression that Lord Justice Lindley would not feel "pressed" by any argument. He obviously relishes his role as defender of the general public and thoroughly enjoys the whole thing.

as sufficient to make the bargain binding, it is only necessary for the other person to whom such offer is made to follow the indicated method of acceptance; and if the person making the offer, expressly or impliedly intimates in his offer that it will be sufficient to act on the proposal without communicating acceptance of it to himself, performance of the condition is a sufficient acceptance without notification. . . .

Now, if that is the law, how are we to find out whether the person who makes the offer does intimate that notification of acceptance will not be necessary in order to constitute a binding bargain? In many cases you look to the offer itself. In many cases you extract from the character of the transaction that notification is not required, and in the advertisement cases it seems to me to follow as an inference to be drawn from the transaction itself that a person is not to notify his acceptance of the offer before he performs the condition, but that if he performs the condition notification is dispensed with. It seems to me that from the point of view of common sense no other idea could be entertained. If I advertise to the world that my dog is lost, and that anybody who brings the dog to a particular place will be paid some money, are all the police and other persons whose business it is to find lost dogs to be expected to sit down and write a note saying that they have accepted my proposal? Why, of course, they at once look after the dog, and as soon as they find the dog they have performed the condition. The essence of the transaction is that the dog should be found, and it is not necessary under such circumstances, as it seems to me, that in order to make the contract binding there should be any notification of acceptance. It follows from the nature of the thing that the performance of the condition is sufficient acceptance without the notification of it, and a person who makes an offer in an advertisement of that kind makes an offer which must be read by the light of that common sense reflection. He does, therefore, in his offer impliedly indicate that he does not require notification of the acceptance of the offer. . . .

Appeal dismissed.   ◀

COMMENTS AND QUESTIONS

1. Summarize the important facts here. What was the principal issue before the court and how was it decided?
2. Summarize the arguments used by the defendant. How did the court deal with each of them?
3. At what point did the plaintiff accept the defendant's offer? When she purchased the smoke ball? When she used it? When she caught influenza?
4. In this case, two justices rendered opinions. Was Justice Bowen's opinion a dissenting one or a concurring one?

The Acceptance

Once an offer has been made known to an offeree, he has several courses open to him. He may accept it, reject it, or simply ignore it. If he decides to accept it, he must do so before it is withdrawn by the offeror or terminated in some other way. (We will discuss termination of offers in greater detail shortly.) To accept it, he must make some promise or statement, or perform some act that shows he agrees to the terms of the offer and is willing to enter into a contract with the offeror.

To be effective, an acceptance, like an offer, must be seriously intended and clearly expressed through words or conduct. Moreover, it must meet any conditions set by the offeror concerning the time or manner of acceptance (for example, the offeror may have asked for an acceptance in writing or by a certain date). In making his acceptance, the offeree must not tamper with or change the terms of the offer; if he does, he is said to be making a *counteroffer*, which, in turn, must be accepted by the original offeror in order to complete the agreement. Before the offeree can make any effective acceptance of an offer, he must be aware of the offer itself, and no one can accept an offer except the person to whom it was originally made.

Ordinarily, if the offeree neglects to reply to an offer and simply remains silent, no acceptance is implied on his part. Few, if any, legal scholars would question the soundness of this rule, since it is generally accepted that contractual obligations should never be imposed on an unwilling party. Yet, like any rule of law, it sometimes leads to a questionable result if applied too strictly. Witness the following:

PRESCOTT v. JONES

Supreme Court of New Hampshire, 1898
69 N.H. 305, 41 Atl. 352

► The declaration alleged, in substance, that the defendants, as insurance agents, had insured the plaintiff's buildings in the Manchester Fire Insurance Company until February 1, 1897, that on January 23, 1897, they notified him that they would renew the policy and insure his buildings for a further term of one year from February 1, 1897, in the sum of $500, unless notified to the contrary, and believing, as he had a right to believe, that the buildings would be insured by the defendants for one year from February 1, 1897, gave no notice to them to insure or not to insure, that they did not insure the buildings as they had agreed and did not notify him of their intention not to do so; so that the buildings were destroyed by fire March 1, 1897, without fault on the plaintiff's part. The defendants demurred. The question of law was referred to the appellate court without prior decision on it by the trial court.[8]

BLODGETT, J. While an offer will not mature into a complete and effectual contract until it is acceded to by the party to whom it is made and notice thereof, either actual or constructive, given to the maker, it must be conceded to be within the power of the maker to prescribe a particular form or mode of acceptance; and the defendants having designated in their offer what they would recognize as notice of its acceptance, namely,

---

[8] In this, as in many cases, the facts were not in dispute and the only question raised was one of law. Since it was likely that any decision of the lower court would be appealed by the losing party anyway, the judge decided to refer the case directly to the appellate court. In most cases, the lower court will render a decision prior to appeal; thus the procedure followed in this case is rarely seen.

failure of the plaintiff to notify them to the contrary, they may properly be held to have waived the necessity of formally communicating to them the fact of its acceptance by him.

But this did not render acceptance on his part any less necessary than it would have been if no particular form of acceptance had been prescribed, for it is well settled that "a party cannot, by the wording of his offer, turn the absence of communication of acceptance into an acceptance, and compel the recipient of his offer to refuse it at the peril of being held to have accepted it." Clark, Contracts, 31. "A person is under no obligation to do or say anything concerning a proposition which he does not choose to accept. There must be actual acceptance or there is no contract." More v. Insurance Co., 130 N.Y. 537. And to constitute acceptance, "there must be words, written or spoken, or some other overt act." Bish. Contracts, s. 329 and authorities cited.

If, therefore, the defendants might and did make their offer in such a way as to dispense with the communication of its acceptance to them in a formal and direct manner, they did not and could not so frame it as to render the plaintiff liable as having accepted it merely because he did not communicate his intention not to accept it. And if the plaintiff was not bound by the offer until he accepted it, the defendants could not be, because "it takes two to make a bargain," and as contracts rest on mutual promises, both parties are bound, or neither is bound.

The inquiry as to the defendants' liability for the non-performance of their offer thus becomes restricted to the question: Did the plaintiff accept the offer so that it became by his action clothed with legal consideration and perfected with the requisite condition of mutuality? As, in morals, one who creates an expectation in another by a gratuitous promise is doubtless bound to make the expectation good, it is perhaps to be regretted that, upon the facts before us, we are constrained to answer the question in the negative. While a gratuitous undertaking is binding in honor, it does not create a legal responsibility. . . .

All the plaintiff did was merely to determine in his own mind that he would accept the offer. There was nothing whatever to indicate it by way of speech or other appropriate act. Plainly this did not create any rights in his favor as against the defendants. From the very nature of a contract this must be so; and it therefore seems superfluous to add that the universal doctrine is that an uncommunicated mental determination cannot create a binding contract. . . .

To sum it up in a few words, the case presented is, in its legal aspects, one of a party seeking to reap where he had not sown and to gather where he had not scattered.

Demurrer sustained.   ◀

COMMENTS AND QUESTIONS

1. Summarize the important facts in this case. What was the principal contention of the plaintiff? Summarize the court's reasons for deciding against him.
2. Do you consider the decision in this case fair or unfair? If you con-

sider it unfair, what assumption do you make about the plaintiff's intentions during February concerning reinsurance?

3. Suppose the plaintiff could prove that some time during February he had mailed an acceptance to the defendants and that the acceptance had been lost. Or suppose he could prove that he had told a friend that he had decided to reinsure his buildings? In view of the court's decision, would either of these acts have constituted a valid acceptance?

4. The court states, in effect, that it must follow the well-established rule of contract law that silence does not imply acceptance. Do you agree with this position, or do you feel that the court might have "distinguished" this case and held that the general rule did not apply?

An exception to the general rule regarding silence as acceptance occurs when the offeree has had past dealings of a similar nature with the offeror, or when the offeree knowingly accepts the benefit of services and is quite aware that the offeror expects to be paid for them. In such a situation, his acceptance is implied, whether he remains silent or not.

DAY v. CATON

Supreme Judicial Court of Massachusetts, 1876
119 Mass. 513, 20 Am. Rep. 347

► Contract to recover the value of one-half of a brick party wall built by the plaintiff. . . .

The defendant requested the judge to rule that: "(1) The plaintiff can recover in this case only upon an express agreement. (2) If the jury find there was no express agreement about the wall, but the defendant knew that the plaintiff was building upon land in which the defendant had an equitable interest, the defendant's right would not be affected by such knowledge, and his silence and subsequent use of the wall would raise no implied promise to pay anything for the wall."

The judge refused so to rule, but instructed the jury as follows: "A promise would not be implied from the fact that the plaintiff, with the defendant's knowledge, built the wall and the defendant used it, but it might be implied from the conduct of the parties. If the jury find that the plaintiff undertook and completed the building of the wall with the expectation that the defendant would pay him for it, and the defendant had reason to know that the plaintiff was so acting with that expectation, and allowed him so to act without objection, then the jury might infer a promise on the part of the defendant to pay the plaintiff." The jury found for the plaintiff and defendant alleged exceptions.

DEVENS, J. The ruling that a promise to pay for the wall would not be implied from the fact that the plaintiff, with the defendant's knowledge, built the wall, and that the defendant used it, was substantially in accordance with the request of the defendant, and is conceded to have been correct. [Cases cited.]

The defendant, however, contends that the presiding judge incorrectly ruled that such promise might be inferred from the fact that the plaintiff undertook and completed the building of the wall with the expectation that the defendant would pay him for it, the defendant having reason to know that the plaintiff was acting with that expectation, and allowed him thus to act without objection.

The fact that the plaintiff expected to be paid for the work would certainly not be sufficient of itself to establish the existence of a contract, when the question between the parties was whether one was made. Taft v. Dickinson, 6 Allen, Mass., 553. It must be shown that in some manner the party sought to be charged assented to it. If a party, however, voluntarily accepts and avails himself of valuable services rendered for his benefit, when he has the option whether to accept or reject them, even if there is no distinct proof that they were rendered by his authority or request, a promise to pay for them may be inferred. His knowledge that they were valuable and his exercise of the option to avail himself of them, justify this inference. [Cases cited.] And when one stands by in silence, and sees valuable services rendered upon his real estate by the erection of a structure (of which he must necessarily avail himself afterwards in his proper use thereof), such silence, accompanied with the knowledge on his part that the party rendering the services expects payment therefor, may fairly be treated as evidence of an acceptance of it, and as tending to show an agreement to pay for it.

The maxim, "*Qui tacet consentire videtur*," [9] is to be construed indeed as applying only to those cases where the circumstances are such that a party is fairly called upon either to deny or admit his liability. But, if silence may be interpreted as assent where a proposition is made to one which he is bound to deny or admit, so also it may be if he is silent in the face of facts which fairly call upon him to speak. [Cases cited.]

If a person saw day after day a laborer at work in his field doing services, which must of necessity inure to his benefit, knowing that the laborer expected pay for his work, when it was perfectly easy to notify him if his services were not wanted, even if a request were not expressly proved, such a request, either previous to or contemporaneous with the performance of the service, might fairly be inferred. But if the fact was merely brought to his attention upon a single occasion and casually, if he had little opportunity to notify the other that he did not desire the work and should not pay for it, or could only do so at the expense of much time and trouble, the same inference might not be made. The circumstance of each case would necessarily determine whether silence with a knowledge that another was doing valuable work for his benefit and with the expectation of payment, indicated that consent which would give rise to the inference of a contract. The question would be one for the jury, and to them it was properly submitted in the case before us by the presiding judge.

Exceptions overruled. ◄

COMMENTS AND QUESTIONS

1. Summarize the principal facts in this case. What rule of law is the court stating here? Outline the reasoning by which the court arrived at its decision.

---

[9] "He who is silent is considered as assenting."

2. Note the manner in which this case was appealed. The defendant's attorney asked the trial judge to give certain instructions to the jury, but the judge refused to do so. The defendant then "excepted" to the refusal of his request, and his exceptions became the basis for his appeal. What would have happened if the Supreme Judicial Court had agreed with the defendant's contention? Would it have ordered judgment for the defendant or have returned the case for a new trial?

3. Would the result in this case have been different if the defendant had been away while the wall was being built and had had no knowledge of what the plaintiff was doing?

In spite of the ruling in the preceding case, however, an acceptance is not always taken as implied just because one person has received the benefit of another's services. Notice, for example, what happened in the famous case of *Boston Ice Co. v. Potter.*

BOSTON ICE COMPANY v. POTTER

Supreme Judicial Court of Massachusetts, 1877
123 Mass. 28, 25 Am. Rep. 9

► Contract . . . for ice sold and delivered between April 1, 1874 and April 1, 1875. Answer, a general denial.

ENDICOTT, J.   To entitle the plaintiff to recover, it must show some contract with the defendant. There was no express contract, and upon the facts stated no contract is to be implied. The defendant had taken ice from the plaintiff in 1873, but, on account of some dissatisfaction with the manner of supply, he terminated his contract, and made a contract for his supply with the Citizens' Ice Company. The plaintiff afterward delivered ice to the defendant for one year without notifying the defendant, as the presiding judge has found, that it had bought out the business of the Citizens' Ice Company, until after the delivery and consumption of the ice.

The presiding judge has decided that the defendant had a right to assume that the ice in question was delivered by the Citizens' Ice Company, and has thereby necessarily found that the defendant's contract with that company covered the time of the delivery of the ice.

There was no privity [10] of contract established between the plaintiff and defendant, and without such privity the possession and use of the property will not support an implied assumpsit.[11] Hills v. Snell, 104 Mass. 173, 177. And no presumption of assent can be implied from the reception and use of the ice, because the defendant had no knowledge that it was furnished by the plaintiff, but supposed that he had received it under the contract made with the Citizens' Ice Company. Of this change he was entitled to be informed.

A party has a right to select and determine with whom he will contract, and cannot have another person thrust upon him without his consent. It may be of importance to him who performs the contract, as when he con-

---

[10] Privity is the relationship that exists between two or more contracting parties.
[11] An undertaking or promise to perform.

tracts with another to paint a picture, or write a book, or furnish articles of a particular kind, or when he relies upon the character of qualities of an individual, or has, as in this case, reasons why he does not wish to deal with a particular party. In all these cases, as he may contract with whom he pleases, the sufficiency of his reasons for so doing cannot be inquired into. If the defendant, before receiving the ice, or during its delivery, had received notice of the change, and that the Citizens' Ice Company could no longer perform its contract with him, it would then have been his undoubted right to have rescinded the contract and to decline to have it executed by the plaintiff. But this he was unable to do, because the plaintiff failed to inform him of that which he had a right to know. If he had received notice and continued to take the ice as delivered, a contract would be implied. ◄

COMMENTS AND QUESTIONS
1. Summarize the facts in this case. What was the decision of the court? Do you agree with it?
2. Do you feel that the plaintiff in this case should have recovered something in view of the fact that the defendant actually received the ice and used it?
3. The court was faced with a difficult choice here. Do you think the average businessman would approve of its decision?

Need for Communication of Acceptance

As a general rule, the acceptance of an offer leading to a *bilateral* contract does not become effective until it has been communicated to the offeror. The reason is simple: the offeror should be aware of the acceptance before he is bound by the contract.

Acceptance of an offer leading to a *unilateral* contract, however, need not be communicated, for here the performance of the act called for by the offeror in itself constitutes acceptance. Thus, the contract becomes binding when the act is completed, *regardless* of when the offeror actually receives notice that performance has occurred.

EXAMPLE
A says to B, "If you climb that flagpole, I'll give you $25." If B climbs the flagpole when A is not present, a binding unilateral contract is formed the moment B completes the act, even though B doesn't tell A about it until some time later. In other words, no communication is necessary to complete the formation of the contract, unless, of course, A makes that a condition in his offer. Obviously, at some time, B must notify A of the performance in order to collect his money.

Communication of Acceptance by Mail or Telegraph

If acceptance of an offer leading to a bilateral contract is made by mail or telegraph, exactly when does the acceptance take effect? The general rule is that if the offeror has used mail or telegraph to communicate his offer, or if it seems reasonable under the circumstances to accept the offer by mail or telegraph, then the acceptance takes effect, and the contract is formed, the moment the offeree deposits his acceptance in the mails or delivers it to the telegraph office. This is true regardless of whether the offeror actually receives the letter or the telegram, unless, of course, he has stipulated in his offer that the acceptance will not be effective until he has actually received it. In other words, when the offeror authorizes the use of mail or telegraph for the communication of an acceptance, he is in effect assuming any risk of delay or nondelivery and agrees that the acceptance will be binding on him when so posted, or when given to the telegraph company. Of course, if a letter of acceptance is never received, it is up to the offeree to prove to the court's satisfaction that it was actually deposited in the mail.

> EXAMPLE
>
> On October 1, s writes to b offering to sell his car. b gets the letter on October 3 and mails his acceptance to s on October 4. Although s may not get the acceptance until October 6 (or may never receive it), the acceptance is effective on October 4, the moment b mails the letter. From that moment on, s is bound by the contract.

If the offeror does not authorize the use of mail or telegraph for communicating the acceptance, the acceptance does not become effective until the offeror actually receives it.

Duration and Termination of Offer

Once an offer has been made, it remains open or subject to acceptance until it is either: (1) accepted, or (2) rejected, withdrawn, or terminated. If the offer is accepted, a contract exists between the offeror and the offeree. But if the offer terminates before it is accepted, no contract results. Once an offer has terminated, it cannot be revived; one of the parties must make a new proposal. Offers may terminate in any one of the following ways:

Rejection by Offeree

If the offeree rejects an offer, by statement or act, the offer is considered terminated. Even a counteroffer by the offeree is usually taken as a rejection of the original offer, unless the offeree expressly keeps the original offer open.

Sometimes the offeree may first reject an offer and then change his mind and accept it. If his acceptance reaches the offeror first, it takes effect when it is actually received. If the rejection reaches the offeror first, however, the subsequent acceptance is regarded as a counteroffer, and the original offer is considered terminated.

Revocation by Offeror

An offeror is free to withdraw, or revoke, his offer any time before it is accepted. His revocation does not become effective, however, until the offeree has actually received it. If the offeree accepts the offer before that time, the offeror is bound by the contract.

EXAMPLE

A mails an offer to x on October 1; x mails his acceptance on October 5; A receives x's acceptance on October 7. On October 4, A mails a revocation of his offer; x receives the revocation on October 6. x's acceptance is effective on October 5, when he mailed it to A. A's revocation is not effective until October 6, when x receives it. Thus a binding agreement is formed on October 5.

Once the offeree has received notice that the offeror has revoked the offer, the offer is terminated and may no longer be accepted. If the offer is made to the public at large or to a group of unknown individuals, it may be withdrawn in the same manner in which it was originally made—a reward offer, for example, published in a newspaper may be revoked by a subsequent notice published in the same paper.

The one exception to the above rules occurs when the offeror has received money or something else of value to keep an offer open for a certain period. Then he is said to have entered into an *option contract*, which remains in force until the specified period of time has elapsed.

Termination by Lapse of Time

Some offers set a time limit for acceptance. If no acceptance takes place within the time specified, the offer automatically terminates. Even when no time limit is set, an offer terminates after a "reasonable" period of time has elapsed. Just what constitutes a reasonable period of time depends pretty much on the circumstances. Consider the following case, which was tried in the Federal District Court in Minnesota.

MINNESOTA LINSEED OIL CO. v. COLLIER WHITE LEAD CO.

United States Circuit Court, D. Minnesota, 1876
4 Dill. 431, Fed. Cas. No. 9,635

▶ This action was removed from the state court and a trial by jury waived.[12] The plaintiff seeks to recover the sum of $2,151.50, with interest from September 20, 1875—a balance claimed to be due for oil sold to the defendant. The defendant, in its answer, alleges that on August 3d, 1875, a contract was entered into between the parties, whereby the plaintiff agreed to sell and deliver to the defendant, at the city of St. Louis, during the said month of August, twelve thousand four hundred and fifty (12,450) gallons of linseed oil for the price of fifty-eight (58) cents per gallon, and that the plaintiff has neglected and refused to deliver the oil according to the contract; that the market value of oil after August 3d and during the month was not less than seventy (70) cents per gallon, and therefore claims a set-off or counter-claim to plaintiff's cause of action.[13] The reply of the

---

[12] The defendant exercised his right to have this case transferred to the federal district court on the grounds of diversity of citizenship. (The plaintiff was a resident of Minnesota and the defendant was a resident of Missouri.) The parties agreed to waive their right to a jury trial, and the trial was held before a judge only.

[13] If a defendant in a suit has a claim against the plaintiff which may be used to offset the plaintiff's claim, he is usually permitted to set it forth in his answer and have it decided by the court at the same time.

plaintiff denies that any contract was entered into between it and defendant.

The plaintiff resided at Minneapolis, Minnesota, and the defendant was the resident agent of the plaintiff, at St. Louis, Missouri. The contract is alleged to have been made by telegraph.

The plaintiff sent the following dispatch to the defendant: "Minneapolis, July 29, 1875. To Alex Easton, Secretary Collier White Lead Company, St. Louis, Missouri: Account of sales not enclosed in yours of 27th. Please wire us best offer for round lot named by you—one hundred barrels shipped. Minnesota Linseed Oil Company."

The following answer was received: "St. Louis, Mo., July 30, 1875. To the Minnesota Linseed Oil Company: Three hundred barrels fifty-five cents here, thirty days, no commission, August delivery. Answer. Collier Company."

The following reply was returned: "Minneapolis, July 31, 1875. Will accept fifty-eight cents (58), on terms named in your telegram. Minnesota Linseed Oil Company."

This dispatch was transmitted Saturday, July 31, 1875, at 9:15 p.m., and was not delivered to the defendant in St. Louis, until Monday morning, August 2, between eight and nine o'clock.

On Tuesday, August 3, at 8:53 a.m., the following dispatch was deposited for transmission in the telegraph office: "St. Louis, Mo., August 3, 1875. To Minnesota Linseed Oil Company, Minneapolis: Offer accepted—ship three hundred barrels as soon as possible. Collier Company."

The following telegrams passed between the parties after the last one was deposited in the office at St. Louis: "Minneapolis, August 3, 1875. To Collier Company, St. Louis: We must withdraw our offer wired July 31st. Minnesota Linseed Oil Company."

Answered: "St. Louis, August 3, 1875. Minnesota Linseed Oil Company: Sale effected before your request to withdraw was received. When will you ship? Collier Company."

It appeared that the market was very much unsettled, and that the price of oil was subject to sudden fluctuations during the month previous and at the time of this negotiation, varying from day to day, and ranging between fifty-five and seventy-five cents per gallon. It is urged by the defendant that the dispatch of Tuesday, August 3d, 1875, accepting the offer of the plaintiff transmitted July 31st and delivered Monday morning, August 2d, concluded a contract for the sale of the twelve thousand, four hundred, and fifty gallons of oil. The plaintiff, on the contrary, claims, 1st, that the dispatch accepting the proposition made July 31st, was not received until after the offer had been withdrawn; 2d, that the acceptance of the offer was not in due time; that the delay was unreasonable, and therefore no contract was completed.

NELSON, DISTRICT JUDGE. It is well settled by the authorities in this country, and sustained by the later English decisions,[14] that there is no difference in the rules governing the negotiation of contracts by corres-

---

[14] Note the court's reliance here on English precedent as well as American. Our common legal heritage is very strong.

pondence through the post-office and by telegraph, and a contract is concluded when an acceptance of a proposition is deposited in the telegraph office for transmission. See 14 Am. Law Reg. 401, "Contracts by Telegraph," article by Judge Redfield, and authorities cited; also, Trevor v. Wood, 36 N.Y. 307, 93 Am. Dec. 511.

In the case at bar the delivery of the message at the telegraph office signified the acceptance of the offer. If any contract was entered into, the meeting of minds was at 8:53 of the clock, on Tuesday morning, August 3d, and the subsequent dispatches are out of the case. 1 Pars. Cont. 482, 483.

This rule is not strenuously dissented from on the argument, and it is substantially admitted that the acceptance of an offer by letter or telegraph completes the contract, when such acceptance is put in the proper and usual way of being communicated by the agency employed to carry it; and that when an offer is made by telegraph, an acceptance by telegraph takes effect when the dispatch containing the acceptance is deposited for transmission in the telegraph office, and not when it is received by the other party. Conceding this, there remains only one question to decide, which will determine the issue: Was the acceptance of defendant deposited in the telegraph office Tuesday, August 3d, within a reasonable time, so as to consummate a contract binding upon the plaintiff?

It is undoubtedly the rule that when a proposition is made under the circumstances in this case, an acceptance concludes the contract if the offer is still open, and the mutual consent necessary to convert the offer of one party into a binding contract by the acceptance of the other is established, if such acceptance is within a reasonable time after the offer was received.

The better opinion is, that what is, or is not a reasonable time, must depend upon the circumstances attending the negotiation, and the character of the subject matter of the contract, and in no better way can the intention of the parties be determined. If the negotiation is in respect to an article stable in price, there is not so much reason for an immediate acceptance of the offer, and the same rule would not apply as in a case where the negotiation related to an article subject to sudden and great fluctuations in the market.

The rule in regard to the length of the time an offer shall continue, and when an acceptance completes the contract, is laid down in Parsons on Contracts (volume 1, p. 482). He says: "It may be said that whether the offer be made for a time certain or not, the intention or understanding of the parties is to govern. . . . If no definite time is stated, then the inquiry as to a reasonable time resolves itself into an inquiry as to what time is rational to suppose the parties contemplated; and the law will decide this to be that time which as rational men they ought to have understood each other to have had in mind." Applying this rule, it seems clear that the intention of the plaintiff, in making the offer by telegraph, to sell an article which fluctuates so much in price, must have been upon the understanding that the acceptance, if at all, should be immediate, and as soon after the receipt of the offer as would give a fair opportunity for consideration. The delay here was too long, and manifestly unjust to the plaintiff, for it afforded the defendant an opportunity to take advantage of a change in the market, and accept or refuse the offer as would best subserve its interests.

Judgment will be entered in favor of the plaintiff for the amount claimed. The counter-claim is denied. Judgment accordingly.   ◄

COMMENTS AND QUESTIONS

1. Summarize the principal facts here.
2. Note that the main issue in this case centers around a counterclaim by the defendant against the plaintiff. What did the defendant allege? What was the plaintiff's defense?
3. For whom did the court find on the counterclaim? What was the reasoning behind the decision?
4. Had the plaintiff withdrawn his offer before the defendant wired acceptance at 8:53 A.M. on August 3? What was the effect of the plaintiff's telegram of August 3 withdrawing the offer?
5. As we pointed out in earlier discussions, many legal rules are framed in terms of what is "reasonable." In this case, the court was faced with the problem of applying just such a rule. How did it go about it? Do you feel that the rule is too vague? If so, could it be stated more precisely?

Death or Insanity of Parties

Except in the case of an option contract, an offer usually terminates immediately on the death or insanity of either party.

Subsequent Illegality

If the contract proposed in an offer becomes illegal before the offer is accepted, the offer is automatically terminated. This is true despite the fact that the parties are unaware of the illegality.

Evidence of Agreement—Intention of Parties

In most cases, the words and actions of the offeror and offeree give clear evidence of their intention to make and accept an offer. On the basis of their written or spoken words, or their actions, the court can conclude that an agreement was formed. Occasionally, however, disputes arise over whether the words or the conduct of one of the parties mean what they seem to mean. In determining whether or not an agreement was formed, most courts consider the overt acts of the parties rather than their secret intentions. If it appears to a reasonable person that an offer or acceptance has been made, the court will usually rule that it has in fact been made, even though the party may have had no intention of entering into a contract. The court was faced with just this type of problem in the following case.

EMBRY v. HARGADINE-McKITTRICK DRY GOODS CO.

St. Louis Court of Appeals, Missouri, 1907
127 Mo. App. 383, 105 S.W. 777

► Action by Charles R. Embry against the Hargadine-McKittrick Dry Goods Company. From a judgment for defendant, plaintiff appeals. Reversed and remanded.

GOODE, J. We dealt with this case on a former appeal (115 Mo. App. 130, 91 S.W. 170). It has been retried, and is again before us for the determination of questions not then reviewed. The appellant was an employee of the respondent company under a written contract to expire December 15, 1903, at a salary of $2,000 per annum. His duties were to attend to the sample department of respondent, of which he was given complete charge. It was his business to select samples for the traveling salesmen of the company, which is a wholesale dry goods concern, to use in selling goods to retail merchants.

Appellant contends that on December 23, 1903, he was re-engaged by respondent, through its president, Thos. H. McKittrick, for another year at the same compensation and for the same duties stipulated in his previous written contract. On March 1, 1904, he was discharged, having been notified in February that, on account of the necessity of retrenching expenses, his services and that of some other employees would no longer be required.

The respondent company contends that its president never re-employed appellant after the termination of his written contract, and hence that it had a right to discharge him when it chose. The point with which we are concerned requires an epitome of the testimony of appellant and the counter testimony of McKittrick, the president of the company, in reference to the alleged re-employment.

Appellant testified: That several times prior to the termination of his written contract on December 15, 1903, he had endeavored to get an understanding with McKittrick for another year, but had been put off from time to time. That on December 23d, eight days after the expiration of said contract, he called on McKittrick, in the latter's office, and said to him that as appellant's written employment had lapsed eight days before, and as there were only a few days between then and the 1st of January in which to seek employment with other firms, if respondent wished to retain his services longer he must have a contract for another year, or he would quit respondent's service then and there. That he had been put off twice before and wanted an understanding or contract at once so that he could go ahead without worry. That McKittrick asked him how he was getting along in his department, and appellant said he was very busy, as they were in the height of the season getting men out—had about 110 salesmen on the line and others in preparation. That McKittrick then said: "Go ahead, you're all right. Get your men out, and don't let that worry you." That appellant took McKittrick at his word and worked until February 15th without any question in his mind. It was on February 15th that he was notified his services would be discontinued on March 1st.

McKittrick denied this conversation as related by appellant, and said that when accosted by the latter on December 23d, he (McKittrick) was working on his books in order to get out a report for a stockholders' meeting, and when appellant said if he did not get a contract he would leave, that he (McKittrick) said: "Mr. Embry, I am just getting ready for the stockholders' meeting to-morrow. I have no time to take it up now. I have told you before I would not take it up until I had these matters out of the way. You will have to see me at a later time. I said, 'Go back upstairs and get your men out on the road.' I may have asked him one or two other questions relative to the department, I don't remember. The whole conversation did not take more than a minute."

Embry also swore that, when he was notified he would be discharged, he complained to McKittrick about it, as being a violation of their contract, and McKittrick said it was due to the action of the board of directors, and not to any personal action of his, and that others would suffer by what the board had done as well as Embry. Appellant requested an instruction to the jury setting out, in substance, the conversation between him and McKittrick according to his version, and declaring that those facts, if found to be true, constituted a contract between the parties that the defendant would pay plaintiff the sum of $2,000 for another year, provided the jury believed from the evidence that plaintiff commenced said work believing he was to have $2,000 for the year's work. This instruction was refused, but the court gave another embodying in substance appellant's version of the conversation, and declaring it made a contract "if you (the jury) find both parties thereby intended and did contract with each other for the plaintiff's employment for one year from and including December 23, 1903, at a salary of $2,000 per annum." Embry swore that, on several occasions when he spoke to McKittrick about employment for the ensuing year, he asked for a renewal of his former contract, and that on December 23d, the date of the alleged renewal, he went into Mr. McKittrick's office and told him his contract had expired, and he wanted to renew it for a year, having always worked under year contracts. Neither the refused instruction nor the one given by the court embodied facts quite as strong as appellant's testimony, because neither referred to appellant's alleged statement to McKittrick that unless he was re-employed he would stop work for respondent then and there.

Judicial opinion and elementary treatises abound in statements of the rule that to constitute a contract there must be a meeting of the minds of the parties, and both must agree to the same thing in the same sense. Generally speaking, this may be true; but it is not literally or universally true. That is to say, the inner intention of parties to a conversation subsequently alleged to create a contract cannot either make a contract of what transpired, or prevent one from arising, if the words used were sufficient to constitute a contract. In so far as their intention is an influential element, it is only such intention as the words or acts of the parties indicate; not one secretly cherished which is inconsistent with those words, or acts. . . .

In Smith v. Hughes, L.R. 6 Q.B. 597, 607, it was said,

"If, whatever a man's real intention may be, he so conducts himself that a reasonable man would believe that he was assenting to the terms proposed by the other party, and that other party upon that belief enters into the contract with him, the man thus conducting himself would be equally bound as if he had intended to agree to the other party's terms." . . .

In view of those authorities, we hold that, though McKittrick may not have intended to employ Embry by what transpired between them according to the latter's testimony, yet if what McKittrick said would have been taken by a reasonable man to be an employment, and Embry so understood it, it constituted a valid contract of employment for the ensuing year.

The next question is whether or not the language used was of that character, namely, was such that Embry, as a reasonable man, might consider that he was re-employed for the ensuing year on the previous terms, and act accordingly. We do not say that in every instance it would be for the court to pronounce on this question, because, peradventure, instances might arise in which there would be such an ambiguity in the language relied on to show an assent by the obligor to the proposal of the obligee that it would be for the jury to say whether a reasonable mind would take it to signify acceptance of the proposal. . . . Embry was demanding a renewal of his contract, saying he had been put off from time to time and that he had only a few days before the end of the year in which to seek employment from other houses, and that he would quit then and there unless he was re-employed. McKittrick inquired how he was getting along with the department, and Embry said they, i.e., the employees of the department, were very busy getting out salesmen. Whereupon McKittrick said: "Go ahead, you are all right. Get your men out, and do not let that worry you." We think no reasonable man would construe that answer to Embry's demand that he be employed for another year, otherwise than as an assent to the demand, and that Embry had the right to rely on it as an assent. . . . The answer was unambiguous, and we rule that if the conversation was according to the appellant's version, and he understood he was employed, it constituted in law a valid contract of re-employment, and the court [15] erred in making the formation of a contract depend on a finding that both parties intended to make one. . . .

The judgment is reversed, and the cause remanded.[16] All concur.   ◄

COMMENTS AND QUESTIONS

1. In this case, the court was presented with two conflicting stories. Summarize the differing versions of the facts.
2. What instructions did Embry's lawyer request the trial judge to give to the jury? Was his request granted? If not, what instructions *did* the judge give?

---

[15] In this context, the word "court" means the judge and not the jury.

[16] In other words, the case was sent back to the lower court, which was instructed to retry it in accordance with the appellate court's decision. The main difference between the first trial and the retrial lies in the instructions given to the jury.

3. What was the decision of the appellate court? Summarize the rule of law which the court enunciated in this case.

4. Do you agree that no "reasonable" man could have construed Mc-Kittrick's alleged words other than as an acceptance? Again, we have a rule of law stated in vague terms.

5. Note that this was the *second* time this case had been appealed and that the case had already been tried *twice* in the lower court. And, as a result of this decision, the case was ordered retried *again* in the lower court! Litigation is sometimes long and costly, and even the winning party may lose more than he gains.

Quasi-contracts

Sometimes one person, acting in good faith, will do something for another person even though there has been no contract between them—either express or implied. In such cases, if the court feels that it would be unjust for the other party to retain the benefit he has received, it will require him to pay back the fair value of that benefit. This obligation, which is called a *quasi-contract*, rests solely on equitable principles of justice and fairness and is not a part of regular contract law, since there is no agreement between the parties.

EXAMPLE

x has been hit by a car and is lying on the road unconscious. MD, a doctor, who is driving along, discovers him and stops to treat him. He performs an emergency operation on the spot and saves x's life. Although x is unconscious and has made no contract for MD's services, he is probably liable to MD in quasi-contract for the reasonable value of MD's services.

The Ohio case of *Sommers v. Putnam County Board of Education* is a good illustration of quasi-contract and the theory behind it.

SOMMERS v. PUTNAM COUNTY BOARD OF EDUCATION

Supreme Court of Ohio, 1925
113 Ohio St. 177, 148 N.E. 682

▶ The plaintiff, a resident and taxpayer of Riley Township, was the father of four children of compulsory school age. He lived more than four miles from the nearest high school, Riley Township High School. Though he requested both the Township Board and the Putnam County Board of Education, defendants, that they perform their statutory duty and furnish transportation for his children to said high school, they refused to do so. The plaintiff then transported his children to and from said high school at his own expense for the school year 1922–23 after which he presented his itemized bill of $397 to the defendant, which defendant refused to pay. The plaintiff now sues the defendant for said amount, alleging the foregoing facts. A demurrer to his petition was sustained and this was affirmed in the Court of Appeals. Plaintiff brings error.[17]

---

[17] In other words, the plaintiff appeals, saying the court was wrong in sustaining the demurrer. In the opinion, he is sometimes referred to as "the plaintiff in error."

ALLEN, J. . . . In the Masters case (141 N.E. 851) this court held that it was mandatory duty of the local board of education, or, in case of the failure of the local board to perform its duties, the mandatory duty of the county board of education, either to provide work in high school branches at some school within 4 miles of the plaintiff's residence, or to have such branches made accessible to the plaintiff's children by transportation to, or board and lodging within, 4 miles of the school wherein such high school branches are offered. That case, therefore, while holding that the several duties enumerated were optional with the local and with the county board of education, held specifically that it was mandatory upon the local board, and, in the case of its default, upon the county board of education, to perform one or the other of these duties.

In the instant case the record shows that both the local board of education and the county board of education have refused to perform any one of the several optional duties resting upon them. . . .

Plaintiff in error concedes that there is no contractual relationship existing between the school boards and the plaintiff in error, but contends that, under the familiar rule of quasi contracts, this action lies for the money expended in transporting his 4 minor children to a high school outside of the 4-mile limit. With this contention we are in accord. The parents had discharged the obligation first of the local school board and next of the county school board. Moreover, this duty was imposed upon the board partly for the parent's benefit, as well as for the benefit of the children and of the public. As the performance of that duty by another is a benefit to the school boards, when he performed the duty the parent conferred a benefit upon the school boards. For this benefit the school boards ought in justice to pay, and hence the intervener, that is, the parent who performed the duty, is entitled to compensation therefor.

An act of beneficial intervention in the discharge of another's legal obligation, which results in a quasi contractual obligation, must contain the following elements: The obligation must be of such a nature that actual and prompt performance thereof is of grave public concern; the person upon whom the obligation rests must have failed or refused with knowledge of the facts to perform the obligation; or it must reasonably appear that it is impossible to perform it; and the person who intervenes must, under the circumstance, be not a mere intermeddler but a proper person to perform the duty. [Cases cited.]

Passing to the question of the appropriateness of the intervention of the parent, the father was surely the proper person to perform the obligation. It is his obligation to see that his children attend school, and the fact that the transportation has not been supplied cannot be pleaded as an excuse for his failure to send such children to school or as an excuse for the failure of the children to attend school. Section 7731–4, General Code (109 Ohio Laws, p. 290).

The performance of this legal obligation was a benefit to the school boards because it saved them from the necessity of performing the duty themselves. Hence the retention of the benefit was inequitable, although there was no contract between the parties. It would be unjust to permit those who failed to perform a duty which was a matter of such public concern to retain the benefit bestowed upon them by the plaintiff in error. . . .

The demurrer will be overruled, and the judgment of the lower courts reversed.

Judgment reversed.   ◀

COMMENTS AND QUESTIONS

1. Was there an express contract to reimburse the plaintiff? Could an agreement be implied from the conduct of the parties, as in the *Day v. Caton* case? If neither, what was the rule of law behind the court's decision in this case?
2. What happened in the lower court? Was the case tried before a jury?

SECTION 3

REALITY OF ASSENT—THE EFFECT OF MISTAKE, FRAUD, OR DURESS

In General

Occasionally, what appears to be a perfectly binding contract will turn out to be no contract at all. The presence of any one of three factors is enough to convince a court that a contract is either voidable or unenforceable: (1) one or both of the parties have acted on a mistaken notion of the facts or the law involved, (2) one side has misled the other by fraud, (3) one party has coerced the other into making the agreement by means of threats.

Mistake

A mistake may be made by both parties (a *mutual* mistake) or just one (a *unilateral* mistake). It may relate to the facts surrounding the agreement (a *mistake of fact*) or to the law that applies to those facts (a *mistake of law*). The legal consequences differ from one type of mistake to another.

Mutual Mistakes

If both parties act on a mistaken notion of a fact which is an important part of the contract (called a *material* fact), such as the identity or quantity of the things they are making the agreement about, the contract is voidable by either party.

EXAMPLES

1. B agrees to buy s's house. Both B and s assume that the house exists when they make their agreement, but actually it has burned down. The agreement is unenforceable.

2. B agrees to buy a bowl from s. Both parties assume at the time that the bowl is made of sterling silver, but it turns out to be silver plate. The contract is voidable by either side.

Quite different from this last example is the situation in which the parties agree to deal with something "as is." If they are unaware of the true nature of the property and it later turns out to possess certain characteristics that neither side suspected, the contract is nevertheless binding. Very often the dividing line between these two situations is hard to draw. For example, in the case of *Sherwood v. Walker* which follows, the justices of the Michigan Supreme Court could not agree. See what you think.

SHERWOOD v. WALKER

Supreme Court of Michigan, 1887
66 Mich. 568, 33 N.W. 919

▶ MORSE, J. Replevin [18] for a cow. Suit commenced in justice's court; judgment for plaintiff; appealed to circuit court of Wayne county, and verdict and judgment for plaintiff in that court.[19] The defendants bring error, and set out 25 assignments of the same.[20]

The main controversy depends upon the construction of a contract for the sale of the cow. The plaintiff claims that the title passed, and bases his action upon such claims. The defendants contend that the contract was executory, and by its terms no title to the animal was acquired by plaintiff. The defendants reside at Detroit, but are in business at Walkerville, Ontario, and have a farm at Greenfield, in Wayne county, upon which were some blooded cattle supposed to be barren as breeders. The Walkers are importers and breeders of polled Angus cattle. The plaintiff is a banker living at Plymouth, in Wayne county. He called upon the defendants at Walkerville for the purchase of some of their stock, but found none there that suited him. Meeting one of the defendants afterwards, he was informed that they had a few head upon their Greenfield farm. He was asked to go out and look at them, with the statement at the time that they were probably barren, and would not breed. May 5, 1886, plaintiff went out to Green-

---

[18] Replevin is an action brought to recover possession of goods or personal property which have been unlawfully taken from the plaintiff—in this case, a cow.

[19] Note that this case was tried twice before it was appealed to the Michigan Supreme Court. The first trial was before a Justice of the Peace court, which found for the plaintiff. Then the case was transferred to a court of general jurisdiction and another trial was held, which again resulted in plaintiff's favor. Quite a lot of litigation over one cow!

[20] This means that on appeal the defendants contended that the lower court had committed twenty-five mistakes in its conduct of the trial. When a case is appealed, it is customary for an attorney to make every argument possible on behalf of his client—hence, the large number of errors alleged. In most cases, however, only one or two main issues are involved.

field and saw the cattle. A few days thereafter, he called upon one of the defendants with the view of purchasing a cow, known as "Rose 2d of Aberlone." After considerable talk it was agreed that defendants would telephone Sherwood at his home in Plymouth in reference to the price. The second morning after this talk he was called up by telephone, and the terms of the sale were finally agreed upon. He was to pay five and one-half cents per pound, live weight, fifty pounds shrinkage. He was asked how he intended to take the cow home, and replied that he might ship her from King's cattle-yard. He requested defendants to confirm the sale in writing, which they did by sending him the following letter:

> "WALKERVILLE, May 15, 1886
>
> "T. C. Sherwood, President, etc.—Dear Sir: We confirm sale to you of the cow Rose 2d of Aberlone, lot 56 of our catalogue, at five and a half cents per pound, less fifty pounds shrink. We inclose herewith order on Mr. Graham for the cow. You might leave check with him, or mail to us here, as you prefer.
>
> "Yours truly,   HIRAM WALKER & SONS."

The order upon Graham inclosed in the letter reads as follows:

> "WALKERVILLE, May 15, 1886
>
> "George Graham: You will please deliver at King's cattle-yard to Mr. T. C. Sherwood, Plymouth, the cow Rose 2d of Aberlone, lot 56 of our catalogue. Send halter with the cow, and have her weighed.
>
> "Yours truly,   HIRAM WALKER & SONS."

On the twenty-first of the same month the plaintiff went to defendants' farm at Greenfield, and presented the order and letter to Graham, who informed him that the defendants had instructed him not to deliver the cow. Soon after, the plaintiff tendered to Hiram Walker, one of the defendants, $80, and demanded the cow. Walker refused to take the money or deliver the cow. The plaintiff then instituted this suit. After he had secured possession of the cow under the writ of replevin, the plaintiff caused her to be weighed by the constable who served the writ, at a place other than King's cattle-yard. She weighed 1,420 pounds.

The defendants introduced evidence tending to show that at the time of the alleged sale it was believed by both the plaintiff and themselves that the cow was barren and would not breed; that she cost $80, and if not barren would be worth from $750 to $1,000; that after the date of the letter, and the order to Graham, the defendants were informed by said Graham that in his judgment the cow was with calf, and therefore they instructed him not to deliver her to plaintiff, and on the twentieth of May, 1886, telegraphed plaintiff what Graham thought about the cow being with calf, and that consequently they could not sell her. The cow had a calf in the month of October following.

The circuit judge instructed the jury that if they believed the defendants, when they sent the order and letter to plaintiff, meant to pass the title to the cow, and that the cow was intended to be delivered to plaintiff, it did not matter whether the cow was weighed at any particular place, or by any particular person; and if the cow was weighed afterwards, as Sherwood testified, such weighing would be a sufficient compliance with the order. The court also charged the jury that it was immaterial whether the cow was with calf or not. It will therefore be seen that the defendants claim that, as a matter of law, the title of this cow did not pass, and that the circuit judge erred in submitting the case to the jury, to be determined by them, upon the intent of the parties as to whether or not the title passed with the sending of the letter and order by the defendants to the plaintiff. . . .

It appears from the record that both parties supposed this cow was barren and would not breed, and she was sold by the pound for an insignificant sum as compared with her real value if a breeder. She was evidently sold and purchased on the relation of her value for beef, unless the plaintiff had learned of her true condition and concealed such knowledge from the defendants. Before the plaintiff secured the possession of the animal, the defendants learned that she was with calf, and therefore of great value, and undertook to rescind the sale by refusing to deliver her. The question arises whether they had the right to do so. The circuit judge rules that this fact did not avoid the sale and it made no difference whether she was barren or not. I am of the opinion that the court erred in this holding. I know that this is a close question, and the dividing line between the adjudicated cases is not easily discerned. But it must be considered as well settled that a party who has given apparent consent to a contract of sale may refuse to execute it, or he may avoid it after it has been completed, if the assent was founded, or the contract made, upon the mistake of a material fact,—such as the subject-matter of the sale, the price, or some collateral fact materially inducing the agreement; and this can be done when the mistake is mutual. . . .

If there is a difference or misapprehension as to the substance of the thing bargained for; if the thing actually delivered or received is different in substance from the thing bargained for, and intended to be sold,—then there is no contract; but if it be only a difference in some quality or accident, even though the mistake may have been the actuating motive to the purchaser or seller, or both of them, yet the contract remains binding. "The difficulty in every case is to determine whether the mistake or misapprehension is as to the substance of the whole contract, going, as it were, to the root of the matter, or only to some point, even though a material point, an error as to which does not affect the substance of the consideration." Kennedy v. Panama, etc., Mail Co., L.R. 2 Q.B. 580, 587. It has been held, in accordance with the principles above stated, that where a horse is bought under the belief that he is sound, and both the vendor and vendee honestly believe him to be sound, the purchaser must stand by his bargain, and pay the full price, unless there was a warranty.

It seems to me, however, in the case made by this record, that the mistake or misapprehension of the parties went to the whole substance of the agreement. If the cow was a breeder, she was worth at least $750; if barren, she was worth not over $80. The parties would not have made the contract of sale except upon the understanding and belief that she was incapable of breeding, and of no use as a cow. It is true she is now the identical

animal that they thought her to be when the contract was made; there is
no mistake as to the identity of the creature. Yet the mistake was not of
the mere quality of the animal, but went to the very nature of the thing.
A barren cow is substantially a different creature than a breeding one.
There is as much difference between them for all purposes of use as there
is between an ox and a cow that is capable of breeding and giving milk.
If the mutual mistake had simply related to the fact whether she was with
calf or not for one season, then it might have been a good sale, but the
mistake affected the character of the animal for all time, and for its present
and ultimate use. She was not in fact the animal or the kind of animal, the
defendants intended to sell or the plaintiff to buy. She was not a barren
cow, and, if this fact had been known, there would have been no contract.
The mistake affected the substance of the whole consideration, and it must
be considered that there was no contract to sell or sale of the cow as she
actually was. The thing sold and bought had in fact no existence. She was
sold as a beef creature would be sold; she is in fact a breeding cow, and
a valuable one. The court should have instructed the jury that if they
found that the cow was sold, or contracted to be sold, upon the understanding of both parties that she was barren, and useless for the purpose
of breeding, and that in fact she was not barren, but capable of breeding,
then the defendants had a right to rescind, and refuse to deliver, and the
verdict should be in their favor.

*The judgment of the court below must be reversed, and a new trial
granted, with costs of this court to defendants.*

CAMPBELL, C. J., and CHAMPLIN, J., concurred.

SHERWOOD, J. (dissenting). I do not concur in the opinion given by my
brethren in this case. . . .

. . . The record . . . shows that the defendants, when they sold the
cow, believed the cow was not with calf, and barren; that from what the
plaintiff had been told by defendants (for it does not appear he had any
other knowledge or facts from which he could form an opinion) he believed the cow was farrow, but still thought she could be made to breed.
The foregoing shows the entire interview and treaty between the parties
as to the sterility and qualities of the cow sold to the plaintiff. The cow
had a calf in the month of October.

There is no question but that the defendants sold the cow representing
her of the breed and quality they believed the cow to be, and that the
purchaser so understood it. And the buyer purchased her believing her to
be of the breed represented by the sellers, and possessing all the qualities
stated, and even more. He believed she would breed. There is no pretense
that the plaintiff bought the cow for beef, and there is nothing in the
record indicating that he would have bought her at all only that he
thought she might be made to breed. Under the foregoing facts,—and these
are all that are contained in the record material to the contract,—it is held
that because it turned out that the plaintiff was more correct in his judgment as to one quality of the cow than the defendants, and a quality, too,
which could not by any possibility be positively known at the time by

either party to exist, the contract may be annulled by the defendants at their pleasure. I know of no law, and have not been referred to any, which will justify any such holding, and I think the circuit judge was right in his construction of the contract between the parties.

It is claimed that a mutual mistake of a material fact was made by the parties when the contract of sale was made. There was no warranty in the case of the quality of the animal. When a mistaken fact is relied upon as ground for rescinding, such fact must not only exist at the time the contract is made, but must have been known to one or both of the parties. Where there is no warranty, there can be no mistake of fact when no such fact exists, or, if in existence, neither party knew of it, or could know of it; and that is precisely this case. If the owner of a Hambletonian horse had speeded him and was only able to make him go a mile in three minutes, and should sell him to another, believing that was his greatest speed, for $300, when the purchaser believed he could go much faster, and made the purchase for that sum, and a few days thereafter, under more favorable circumstances, the horse was driven a mile in 2 min. 16 sec., and was found to be worth $20,000, I hardly think it would be held, either at law or in equity,[21] by any one, that the seller in such case could rescind the contract. The same legal principles apply in each case.

In this case neither party knew the actual quality and condition of this cow at the time of the sale. The defendants say, or rather said, to the plaintiff, "they had a few head left on their farm in Greenfield, and asked plaintiff to go and see them, stating to plaintiff that in all probability they were sterile and would not breed." Plaintiff did go as requested, and found there these cows, including the one purchased, with a bull. The cow had been exposed, but neither knew she was with calf or whether she would breed. The defendants thought she would not, but the plaintiff says that he thought she could be made to breed, but believed she was not with calf. The defendants sold the cow for what they believed her to be, and the plaintiff bought her as he believed she was, after the statements made by the defendants. No conditions whatever were attached to the terms of sale by either party. It was in fact as absolute as it could well be made, and I know of no precedent as authority by which this court can alter the contract thus made by these parties in writing,—interpolate in it a condition by which, if the defendants should be mistaken in their belief that the cow was barren, she could be returned to them and their contract should be annulled. It is not the duty of courts to destroy contracts when called upon to enforce them, after they have been legally made. There was no mistake of any material fact by either of the parties in the case as would license the vendors to rescind. There was no difference between the parties, nor misapprehension, as to the substance of the thing bargained for, which was a cow supposed to be barren by one party, and believed not to be by the other. As to the quality of the animal, subsequently developed, both parties were equally ignorant, and as to this each party

---

[21] See the earlier discussion of law and equity on pp. 58–60.

took his chances. If this were not the law, there would be no safety in purchasing this kind of stock.

I entirely agree with my brethren that the right to rescind occurs whenever "the thing actually delivered or received is different in substance from the thing bargained for, and intended to be sold; but if it be only a difference in some quality or accident, even though the misapprehension may have been the actuating motive" of the parties in making the contract, yet it will remain binding. In this case the cow sold was the one delivered. What might or might not happen to her after the sale formed no element in the contract.   ◄

COMMENTS AND QUESTIONS

1. Summarize the facts that gave rise to this lawsuit.
2. The majority of the court seems to have proceeded on the assumption that both parties thought the cow was barren. The dissenting opinion stresses the fact that the plaintiff felt that the cow would breed and bought her for that purpose. If the latter version had been accepted by the court, would the mistake have been a mutual or a unilateral one? Come back to this question after reading the following section on unilateral mistakes.

If the parties to an agreement make a mutual mistake about the law that is applicable to their agreement, they are usually bound to carry out their obligations anyway. The theory is, in effect, that ignorance of the law is no excuse. A few states, however, are beginning to break away from this doctrine and allow parties to avoid their agreement if both have acted on a mistaken notion of the law.

EXAMPLE

B agrees to purchase a house from s. B plans to convert the house into apartments to rent. Both parties proceed on the erroneous assumption that apartment houses are permitted by the zoning laws of that locality. In most states the contract is binding.

Unilateral Mistakes

Ordinarily, when only one party is mistaken about a material fact he cannot avoid the agreement. Since such mistakes are usually the result of carelessness, the court will hold the mistaken party to his contract.

EXAMPLE

s owns two houses in Chicago, one on First Street and the other on First Avenue. He writes to B offering to sell his house on First Avenue. B accepts the offer, mistakenly thinking that he is buying the place on First Street. B may not avoid the contract.

There is an important exception to this rule, however: if one of the parties makes a mistake in computing or transcribing figures, and if the mistake is obvious to the other party, the law will not allow the other side knowingly to take advantage. Here, the party who makes the mistake has the right to avoid the contract. This type of situation is well illustrated by the following Connecticut case:

GEREMIA v. BOYARSKY et al.

Supreme Court of Errors of Connecticut, 1928
107 Conn. 387, 140 A. 749

► Action to recover damages for breach of building contract by Sylvester Geremia against Morris Boyarsky and others. Judgment for defendants, and plaintiff appeals. No error.[22]

BANKS, J.   The defendants are carpenters and building contractors, and in April, 1926, the plaintiff requested them to submit bids for the carpenter work and painting for a house that he was building for himself. The defendants met in the evening of April 25th for the purpose of making their estimates, but did not complete their figures, owing to the lateness of the hour. They wrote their figures on two separate pieces of paper, but did not add the figures. The next morning the plaintiff called upon the defendants, and requested the defendant Boyarsky to stop the work that he was upon and complete the estimate. Boyarsky sat down with the plaintiff at a workbench, and proceeded to add up the various items upon the two sheets. In his haste, he made an error in adding the items on the first sheet, footing them up at $99.10, when the correct footing should have been $859.10. This error, being carried to the second sheet, made the apparent cost of the work $1,450.40 instead of $2,210.40. The plaintiff thereupon awarded the contract to the defendants, and later the same day they executed a written contract to do the work for the sum of $1,450.40. The plaintiff, when the erroneous bid was given, and when he procured the signing of the contract, had good reason to believe and know that there must have been a substantial omission or error in the amount of the bid. That evening the defendants discovered their mistake, and offered to go forward with the work according to the actual prices carried out in their estimate, and as low as any responsible contractor would do it for, if less than $2,210.40. The plaintiff refused their offer, and insisted that they complete the work for $1,450.40. The sum of $2,375 was a reasonable price for the work covered by the defendants' contract, and the plaintiff thereafter let the contract for the work to other contractors for that sum. The court found that the defendants had made a material mistake in their bid, that it would be inequitable to award the plaintiff damages for a breach of the contract, and that it should be rescinded.

The finding discloses a case where the defendants, by reason of an error in computation, have obligated themselves to perform a contract for a sum substantially less than the sum which the actual figures of their estimate totaled, and less than the reasonable cost of the work contracted to be done. It is the contention of the plaintiff that equity should not relieve the defendants from the consequences of their mistake, because (a) it was a unilateral mistake; (b) it was not material to the making of the contract; and (c) it resulted from the defendants' own negligence. While the mistake of only one of the parties inducing him to sign a contract

---

[22] "No error" means the same as "judgment affirmed." In other words, the lower court was correct and its decision will stand.

cannot be a ground for a reformation of the contract, it may be ground for its cancellation. Snelling v. Merritt, 85 Conn. 83, 101, 81 A. 1039. Though the mistake was not induced by the conduct of the other party, equity will grant relief, if the latter, when he becomes aware of the mistake, seeks to take an unconscionable advantage of it. Lieberum v. Nussenbaum, 94 Conn. 276, 108 A. 662. The plaintiff, though he is found by the court not to have participated in the mistake, had good reason to believe that one had been made before the contract was signed, was notified of the mistake by the defendants before he had changed his position in any respect, and sought to take unfair advantage of it by insisting upon the performance of the contract at a price upon which the minds of the parties had never met. When the contract is still executory and the parties can be put in *statu quo*,[23] one party to the contract will not be permitted to obtain an unconscionable advantage merely because the mistake was unilateral. 3 Williston on Contract, 1578, 1580.

That a mistake through which the defendants agreed to perform the contract for a price one-third less than the total of the actual figures of their estimate was of so essential and fundamental a character that the minds of the parties never met would not seem to require discussion. . . .

It may be conceded that the error in addition made by the defendant Boyarsky, when he hastily totaled the items of his estimate at the request of the plaintiff, involved some degree of negligence. It would be inequitable under the circumstances to permit the plaintiff, who had good reason to know, before the contract was signed, that there must have been a substantial omission or error in the amount of the bid, to take advantage of such error while the contract was still executory, and he had been in no way prejudiced,[24] and to require the defendants to do the work for an amount much less than the actual cost. In similar situations when a price has been bid which, because of erroneous arithmetical processes, or by the omission of items, was based on a mistake, rescission [25] has been allowed where the contract was still executory, and it would be inequitable to permit the other party to gain an unfair advantage from a mistake which has not prejudiced him in any way.

The mistake of the defendants was of so fundamental a character that the minds of the parties did not meet. It was not, under the circumstances, the result of such culpable negligence as to bar the defendants of redress, and the plaintiff, before the contract was signed, had good reason to believe that a substantial error had been made, and, while the contract was still executory, and he had been in no way prejudiced, refused to permit the correction of the error, and attempted to take an unconscionable ad-

---

[23] That is, in the condition in which they previously were.

[24] The word "prejudiced" is often used by judges in this context to mean the same as "damaged." In other words, the plaintiff in this case had not done anything else in reliance on the mistaken agreement which would cause him loss if the court corrected the error.

[25] Rescission means that the agreement is canceled and both parties are restored to their original positions prior to making the contract.

vantage of it. The defendants were clearly entitled to a decree canceling the contract.

There is no error.

All concur.

◀

COMMENTS AND QUESTIONS

1. Summarize the important facts in this case. What was the court's decision?
2. Several times in the opinion, the court justifies the result on the ground that the plaintiff knew or should have known of the mistake while the contract was still executory and before he had been prejudiced. Do you think the result would have been different if the plaintiff, relying on the defendants' bid, had entered into a contract with a third party before he was told of the mistake?
3. What if the mistake had been a minor one—$75, for example, instead of $760—and what if the plaintiff had no reason to suspect that an error had been made? Would the court still have found for the defendants?

When one party makes a mistake of law, he is usually not permitted to avoid the contract. This is true even though the other party is aware at the time that a mistake is being made. Just because one party has superior knowledge of the law does not mean that he is obliged to speak up and call attention to the other's mistake.

EXAMPLE

B buys a store from s. B intends to set up a liquor business in his new store, taking it for granted that such a business is legal. It turns out that selling liquor is against the law, something that s knew all along. B is nevertheless bound by the contract.

Fraud and Misrepresentation

In General

Fraud occurs when one party intentionally and deliberately misrepresents a material or important fact for the purpose of inducing the other party to make an agreement with him. If the innocent party puts his faith in the misrepresentation and suffers loss because of it, he may avoid the contract or sue for damages. Misrepresentations may be written or oral statements, or else they may result from conduct alone.

EXAMPLES

1. A misrepresentation by words: s tells B he has a certain grade of leather for sale. The leather is actually of an inferior grade.
2. A misrepresentation by conduct: s shows B a basket of apples which he offers to sell. The apples on top are good; most of the apples underneath are rotten.

Before a party to a contract can be held guilty of fraud, it must be established that he realized that his representation was false or that he was recklessly indifferent to its truth. In addition, it must be evident that he intended to deceive the other party. Although the intent to deceive is sometimes hard to prove directly, it can usually be inferred from the circumstances surrounding the transaction.

Failure to Disclose a Material Fact

As a general rule, if one party asks no questions about a material fact before entering into a contract, and the other party fails to disclose the fact, there is no misrepresentation. In other words, silence in and of itself does not constitute fraud.

> EXAMPLE
>
> s sells b some land which b has never seen. b plans to build a house on it, but he does not tell s of his intentions or ask whether it will make a good building site. The land is actually marshy and flooded and unsuitable for building. But s is under no obligation to say so unless b asks, and b may not avoid the contract because of s's failure to disclose the information.

An exception to this rule exists when the parties are in a position of trust and confidence—for example, guardian and ward, or attorney and client. In such situations, the trusted or dominating party has a duty to disclose all material facts to the other. Another exception exists when one party *knows* that the other is laboring under a misapprehension and fails to set him right. Finally, if one party misrepresents the whole truth by telling only a part of the truth, his failure to disclose is fraudulent.

> EXAMPLE
>
> e applies for a job and informs his prospective boss that he was once convicted of a crime and served time in jail. Actually he has been convicted and jailed *three* times but he fails to mention the other two convictions. His silence constitutes fraud because his part truth conceals the whole truth.

Justified Reliance

Before an injured party can claim fraud, he must demonstrate that he has actually relied on the information that the other party has misrepresented to him. And even then most courts will deny him the right to sue if he could have readily discovered the falsity of the representation. He is not, however, required to go to any great trouble or expense to ascertain the true facts.

Most courts hold that exaggerated statements of opinion, advertising claims, and dealers' claims relating to the value or quality of products should not be taken at face value. Thus, a person who relies on such misrepresentations is generally not permitted to sue for fraud. Here again, however, there are many questionable situations which give rise to difficult decisions. Take, for example, the case of *Mabardy v. McHugh*, which follows. The court was faced with a hard choice and its sympathies were obvious. Note Justice Rugg's interesting discussion of the doctrine of *stare decisis*.

MICHAEL MABARDY et al. v. PATRICK McHUGH et al.

Massachusetts Supreme Judicial Court, 1909
202 Mass. 148

▶ TORT for deceit in the sale of land. Writ in the Superior Court for the county of Middlesex dated January 18, 1906.

The case was tried before Stevens, J. The facts are stated in the opinion. The jury found for the defendants; and the plaintiffs alleged exceptions.

The case was submitted on briefs.[26]

RUGG, J. . . . There was evidence tending to show that the plaintiffs went upon a certain irregularly shaped tract of land (for false representations inducing the purchase of which this action was brought) with one of the defendants, who pointed out the true boundaries and fraudulently stated that the tract contained sixty-five acres, when in fact it contained forty and three fourths acres. Upon this aspect of the evidence, the trial judge instructed the jury that "if the plaintiffs . . . were taken over the farm by the defendants . . . or (and) were shown the bounds so that the plaintiffs knew where the farm was and what was comprised within the bounds, it would not be of any consequence that representations may have been made by the defendant in relation to the acreage." The evidence being conflicting as to whether the boundaries were shown, the jury were further instructed that if the defendant, who talked with the plaintiffs, "knew that there were not sixty-five or nearly sixty-five acres, or if he did not know anything about it and stated it as a fact within his personal knowledge, then it would be a false representation for which he would be liable provided" the other elements essential to a recovery were found to exist.

The correctness of the first of these instructions is challenged. It is in exact accordance with the law as laid down in Gordon v. Parmelee, 2 Allen, 212, and Mooney v. Miller, 102 Mass. 217. The facts in the case at bar are similar in all material respects to these cases. An attempt is made to distinguish them on the ground that the present plaintiffs were Syrians, ignorant of our language, and that hence a trust relation existed between them and the defendant. But whatever else may be said of this contention, it fails because they were accompanied by two of their own countrymen, who were thoroughly familiar with our language and acted as interpreters for them. In effect, the contention of the plaintiffs amounts to a request to overrule these two cases. They have been cited with approval in Roberts v. French, 153 Mass. 60, and as supporting authorities, without criticism, in other opinions. The court, however, has refused to apply the rule of those decisions to other facts closely analogous. This court in recent years, by pointed language and by conclusions reached, has indicated a plain disposition not to extend legal immunity for the falsehood of vendors in the course of negotiations for sales beyond the bounds already established.

This judicial attitude perhaps reflects an increasingly pervasive moral

---

[26] That is, neither of the opposing lawyers appeared before the appellate court to argue the case orally. Briefs were drawn up and submitted to the court along with the record of the lower court trial, and the case was decided on that basis alone.

sense in some of the common transactions of trade. While the science of jurisprudence is not, and under present conditions cannot be, coextensive with the domain of morality, nor generally undertake to differentiate between motives which mark acts as good or bad, yet it is true, as was said by Mr. Justice Brett, in Robinson v. Mollett, L. R. 7 H. L. 802, 817, that "The courts have applied to the mercantile business brought before them what have been called legal principles, which have almost always been the fundamental ethical rules of right and wrong." This is only a concrete expression of the broader generalization that law is the manifestation of the conscience of the Commonwealth.

In many other jurisdictions the rule of Gordon v. Parmelee and Mooney v. Miller has not been followed and false representation as to area of land, even though true boundaries were pointed out, have been held actionable.

Other cases apparently opposed to the Massachusetts rule, on examination prove to go no further than to decide that misrepresentations as to area, when there is no evidence that boundaries were shown, constitute deceit. This is the substance of the latter part of the instruction given in the Superior Court, and is the law of this Commonwealth.

If the point were now presented for the first time, it is possible that we might be convinced by the argument of the plaintiffs and the great weight of persuasive authority in its support, especially in view of Lewis v. Jewell, 151 Mass. 345. But there is something to be said in support of the two earlier decisions now questioned. A purchase and a sale of real estate is a transaction of importance and cannot be treated as entered into lightly. People must use their own faculties for their protection and information, and cannot assume that the law will relieve them from the natural effects of their heedlessness or take better care of their interests than they do themselves. Thrift, foresight and self-reliance would be undermined if it was the policy of the law to attempt to afford relief for mere want of sagacity. It is an ancient and widely, if not universally, accepted principle of the law of deceit that, where representations are made respecting a subject as to which the complaining party has at hand reasonably available means for ascertaining the truth and the matter is open to inspection, if, without being fraudulently diverted therefrom, he does not take advantage of this opportunity, he cannot be heard to impeach the transaction on the ground of the falsehoods of the other party. This rule in its general statement applies to such a case as that before us. It is easy for one disappointed in the fruits of a trade to imagine, and perhaps persuade himself, that the cause of his loss is the deceit of the other party, rather than his own want of judgment.

It is highly desirable that laws for conduct in ordinary affairs, in themselves easy of comprehension and memory, when once established, should remain fast. The doctrine of *stare decisis* is as salutary as it is well recognized. While perhaps it is more important as to far-reaching juridicial principles that the court should be right, in the light of higher civilization, later and more careful examination of authorities, wider and more thorough discussion and more mature reflection upon the policy of the law, than merely in harmony with previous decisions, it nevertheless is vital that there be stability in the courts in adhering to decisions deliberately made after ample consideration. Parties should not be encouraged to seek re-examination of determined principles and speculate on a fluctuation of the law with every change in the expounders of it. As to many matters of frequent occurrence, establishment of some certain guide is of more significance than the precise form of the rule. It is likely that no positive rule of law can be laid down that will not at some time impinge with great apparent severity upon a morally innocent person. The law of gravitation acts indifferently upon the just and the unjust. A renewed declaration of law that is already in force, supported by sound reason and not plainly wrong, in the long run probably works out substantial justice, although it may seem harsh in its application to some particular case. These considerations are regarded as so weighty by the House of Lords that it cannot overrule any of its own decisions.[27] London Tramways Co. v. London County Council, (1898) A. C. 375.

The conclusion is that we do not overrule the decisions whose soundness has been debated at the bar, although we do not extend their scope, but confine them strictly to their precise point, namely, that where the seller of real estate shows upon the fact of the earth its true boundaries to the purchaser and does not fraudulently dissuade him from making full examination and measurement and the estate is not so extensive or of such character as to be reasonably incapable of inspection and estimate, and there is no relation of trust between the parties, the purchaser has no remedy for a misrepresentation as to the area alone.[28]

The instruction as to the difference between representation and expression of opinion was adequate and adapted to the testimony.

The charge is not reported in full. No requests for rulings were presented, and the only exceptions relate to the statement of the rule of Gordon v. Parmelee and Mooney v. Miller. It does not appear, therefore, that full instructions were not given as to the effect of fraudulent dissuasion by the defendants (of which there was some evidence) from a full examination of the farm by the plaintiffs.

Judgment affirmed. ◀

COMMENTS AND QUESTIONS

1. Outline the facts in this case. What was the final decision of the court?
2. Summarize Justice Rugg's discussion of the doctrine of *stare decisis* and its application to this case. Do you agree with him?
3. The court rejects the argument that, since the plaintiffs were Syrians, ignorant of our language, a trust relation existed between them and the defendant; the reason is that the plaintiffs were accompanied by

---

[27] Taken at face value, this doctrine would seem to create a tremendous roadblock to any changes in legal rules. However, since no two cases are precisely alike in their facts, the House of Lords still has the power to "distinguish" a new case from one previously decided.

[28] In this paragraph the court serves notice on future litigants that it will not be bound by the precedent of this case unless the facts are almost the same. In other words, if a future case is presented in which the facts are slightly different, the Massachusetts court will have no difficulty in distinguishing it and arriving at a different result.

two countrymen who could have interpreted for them. Do you think the result would have been different if the two countrymen had not been present when the representations were made?

Remedies for Fraud

If the innocent party has sustained damage by relying on false information and has shown that all the required conditions of fraud exist, he has a choice of remedies. He may sue for damages amounting roughly to the difference between the value of the contract as it was represented to him and its actual value. Or he may choose to avoid the agreement and make it unenforceable. In the latter case, if either party has performed all or part of the agreement, that party is entitled to get back what he has given. Lastly, the injured party may always choose to be bound by the agreement even though he knows it to be fraudulent.

Innocent Misrepresentations

Occasionally, one party will induce the other to enter into an agreement by making an innocent misrepresentation of a material fact that he honestly, but erroneously, believes to be true. If the injured party relies on the misrepresentation, he is usually entitled to *rescind* the contract—that is, both the parties are restored to their original positions and each returns any benefit he has received. No action for damages, however, is permitted since the misrepresentation is not made with any intention to deceive.

Duress

If one party forces the other to enter into an agreement under duress, the injured party may avoid the contract. The injured party, however, must be so fearful of some threatened action by the other side that he is unable to exercise free will when he makes the agreement. The duress may consist of a threat to harm the contracting party himself, or his family or a close relative; of a threat to prosecute him for a crime, regardless of his guilt or innocence; or of a threat to destroy or harm his property. A threat to bring a civil suit, however, does not constitute duress. Whether or not duress actually exists is determined by the circumstances surrounding the transaction, such as the relative strength and personalities of the parties.

Undue Influence

When two parties are in a close relationship of trust and confidence, the stronger person sometimes takes advantage of the situation to force an inequitable contract on the weaker. In such cases, even though no duress exists, the injured party may avoid the contract at his option.

EXAMPLE

The appointed guardian of a feeble old lady persuades her to sell him valuable property for a very low price on the ground that he will "protect her interests." She will probably be able to avoid the contract.

Time Limit on Right to Avoid Contract

When the existence of mistake, fraud, or duress gives one party the right to avoid a contract, he must exercise that right within a reasonable time or else be bound by the contract. What constitutes a reasonable time will, of course, depend on the circumstances.

> EXAMPLE
>
> B fraudulently induces s to sell him a tract of land. When s discovers the fraud, he does nothing. B then occupies the land for five years and makes valuable improvements on it. Having done nothing for five years, s has waited too long and has lost his right to avoid the contract and to have the land restored to him.

SECTION 4

REQUIREMENT OF CONSIDERATION

Nature of Consideration

As we mentioned in the introduction to this chapter, the requirement of consideration was introduced into the law to ensure that a true bargain is reached between contracting parties. As a general rule, one party to an agreement cannot require the other side to perform unless he can show that he has furnished consideration for the other party's promise.

Consideration is a difficult concept to define precisely. Generally, to furnish consideration, a party must do, or promise to do, something which the other side has requested as part of the bargain. Usually, the performance of this act will be of direct benefit to the other party, but this is not necessarily the case. In some situations, only a third party may be benefited or, for that matter, no one at all may receive any direct benefit. The important point is that the party furnishing consideration agrees to do something that he is otherwise not legally obligated to do.

> EXAMPLES
>
> 1. x promises to sell his watch to y, and y promises to pay x $50 for it. The agreement is binding, since both sides have furnished consideration—i.e., their mutual promises.
> 2. x promises to give his watch to y. There is no binding agreement, since y has not furnished consideration—i.e., he has neither given nor promised to give anything in return.

3. A promises to pay B $5.00 if B will cut C's lawn. If B cuts the lawn, he can collect from A. Although B's performance does not benefit A directly, it is still deemed consideration for A's promise to pay.

In a bilateral contract, each party's promise furnishes consideration for the other (see Example No. 1 immediately preceding). In a unilateral contract, where there is only one promise, the consideration furnished by the offeree is his performance of the act called for by the offeror (see Example No. 3).

In the case that follows, the New York Court of Appeals had to decide whether consideration was present. The decision will, perhaps, throw more light on the meaning of this somewhat elusive term.

HAMER v. SIDWAY

Court of Appeals of New York, 1891
124 N.Y. 538, 27 N.E. 256

► PARKER, J. The question which provoked the most discussion by counsel on this appeal, and which lies at the foundation of plaintiff's asserted right of recovery, is whether by virtue of a contract defendant's testator [29] William E. Story became indebted to his nephew William E. Story, 2d, on his twenty-first birthday in the sum of five thousand dollars. The trial court found as a fact that on the 20th day of March, 1869, . . . William E. Story agreed to and with William E. Story, 2d, that if he would refrain from drinking liquor, using tobacco, swearing, and playing cards or billiards for money until he should become 21 years of age, then he, the said William E. Story, would at that time pay him, the said William E. Story, 2d, the sum of $5,000 for such refraining, to which the said William E. Story, 2d, agreed, and "in all things fully performed his part of said agreement."

The defendant contends that the contract was without consideration to support it, and, therefore, invalid. He asserts that the promisee by refraining from the use of liquor and tobacco was not harmed but benefited; that that which he did was best for him to do independently of his uncle's promise, and insists that it follows that unless the promisor was benefited, the contract was without consideration. A contention which, if well founded, would seem to leave open for controversy in many cases whether that which the promisee did or omitted to do was, in fact, of such benefit to him as to leave no consideration to support the enforcement of the promisor's agreement. Such a rule could not be tolerated, and is without foundation in the law. The Exchequer Chamber, in 1875, defined consideration as follows: "A valuable consideration in the sense of the law may consist either in some right, interest, profit, or benefit accruing to the one party, or some forbearance, detriment, loss, or responsibility given, suffered, or undertaken

---

[29] A testator is a person who dies leaving a will. When we speak of the "defendant's testator" or "plaintiff's testator," we mean that the defendant or plaintiff is representing the estate of the dead person, usually in the capacity of an executor. If a person dies without a will, he is referred to as "the intestate," and the terms "defendant's intestate" or "plaintiff's intestate" are used.

by the other." Courts "will not ask whether the thing which forms the consideration does in fact benefit the promisee or a third party, or is of any substantial value to any one. It is enough that something is promised, done, forborne, or suffered by the party to whom the promise is made as consideration for the promise made to him." Anson's Prin. of Con. 63.

"In general, a waiver of any legal right at the request of another party is a sufficient consideration for a promise." Parsons on Contracts, 444.

Pollock, in his work on contracts, page 166, says: "Consideration means not so much that one party is profiting as that the other abandons some legal right in the present or limits his legal freedom of action in the future as an inducement for the promise of the *first*."

Now, applying this rule to the facts before us, the promisee used tobacco, occasionally drank liquor, and he had a legal right to do so. That right he abandoned for a period of years upon the strength of the promise of the testator that for such forbearance he would give him $5,000. We need not speculate on the effort which may have been required to give up the use of those stimulants. It is sufficient that he restricted his lawful freedom of action within certain prescribed limits upon the faith of his uncle's agreement, and now having fully performed the conditions imposed, it is of no moment whether such performance actually proved a benefit to the promisor, and the court will not inquire into it, but were it a proper subject of inquiry, we see nothing in this record that would permit a determination that the uncle was not benefited in a legal sense.   ◄

COMMENTS AND QUESTIONS

1. Summarize the facts that gave rise to this case. What was the court's decision?
2. This case illustrates the rule that the promisor is bound by an agreement that is properly supported by consideration even though he derives no actual benefit from that consideration.
3. The court stresses that the promisee restricted his lawful freedom of action and abandoned certain legal rights. What if the uncle's promise had been to pay the nephew a sum of money if he refrained from using opium? Or from drinking liquor during Prohibition? In other words, must the restriction relate to some activity which the promisee has a legal right to engage in?
4. What kind of contract is involved in this case? Unilateral or bilateral? If the nephew had died before reaching the age of twenty-one, could his estate have recovered the $5,000?
5. Note the court's reliance on legal textbooks (i.e., Anson, Parsons and Pollock) rather than on prior cases in support of its decision.

Situations Where Consideration Is Absent

Certain types of act and promise are not recognized as valid consideration. Consequently, agreements based on them alone are not binding.

Past Consideration

An act or a promise that has occurred in the past does not constitute consideration for a present promise. The theory is that at the time it occurred such act or promise was not meant to be in exchange for the later promise by the other side.

> EXAMPLE
>
> UNCLE promises to give NIECE a new fur coat because she took care of him during an illness last year. UNCLE's promise is not enforceable, since NIECE's act of taking care of UNCLE occurred in the past and is not deemed to be consideration.

Performance of Existing Obligations

If one side promises to do, or does, something he is already obligated to do legally, no consideration is present. The same result is reached if he promises not to do something that he has no legal right to do in the first place.

> EXAMPLES
>
> 1. O offers to pay $1,000 reward to the person who captures and arrests ARSONIST. X, a night watchman at a warehouse, discovers ARSONIST in the act of setting fire to the warehouse and takes him into custody. X is not entitled to the reward, because his act is merely the performance of an existing contractual duty and does not furnish consideration for o's promise.
> 2. A and B are neighbors. A has been in the habit of walking across B's land on his way to work and has been ruining the grass. B promises to pay A $50 if he will promise to stop this practice. B's promise is unenforceable, since A is merely promising to refrain from doing something he has no right to do.

PROMISE TO COMPLETE EXISTING CONTRACT. Often a contractor will refuse to complete a building unless the owner agrees to pay him an additional sum over and above the original contract price. If the contractor has no valid excuse for not completing performance, the owner, of course, is not obligated to agree to pay him anything more. In fact, the owner may insist that the contractor either complete performance or else pay damages. As a practical matter, however, the owner often will make such a promise to get the job done. According to the strict rules of consideration, most states (but not all) hold that the owner's promise to pay an additional sum is unenforceable, because he is not receiving any new consideration from the contractor. In other words, the contractor is merely promising to finish something he is already obligated to do legally. A good example of this type of situation follows.

ALASKA PACKERS' ASSOCIATION v. DOMENICO

Circuit Court of Appeals of the United States, Ninth Circuit, 1902
117 Fed. 99, 54 C.C.A. 485

► Appeal from the District Court of the United States for the Northern District of California.

Before GILBERT and Ross, CIRCUIT JUDGES, and HAWLEY, DISTRICT JUDGE.

Ross, Circuit Judge. The libel [30] in this case was based upon a contract alleged to have been entered into between the libelants and the appellant corporation on the 22d day of May, 1900, at Pyramid Harbor, Alaska, by which it is claimed the appellant promised to pay each of the libelants, among other things, the sum of $100 for services rendered and to be rendered. In its answer the respondent (appellant) denied the execution, on its part of the contract sued upon, [and] averred that it was without consideration. . . .

The evidence shows without conflict that on March 26, 1900, at the city and county of San Francisco, the libelants entered into a written contract with the appellant, whereby they agreed to go from San Francisco to Pyramid Harbor, Alaska, and return, on board such vessel as might be designated by the appellant, and to work for the appellant during the fishing season of 1900, at Pyramid Harbor, as sailors, and fishermen, agreeing to do "regular ship's duty both up and down, discharging and loading; and to do any other work whatsoever when requested to do so by the captain or agent of the Alaska Packers' Association." By the terms of this agreement, the appellant was to pay each of the libelants $50 for the season, and two cents for each red salmon in the catching of which he took part.

On April 15, 1900, 21 of the libelants signed articles of agreement as seamen, on the same terms except that $60 was to be paid for the season. Under these contracts, the libelants sailed on board the Two Brothers for Pyramid Harbor, where the appellant had about $150,000 invested in a salmon cannery. The libelants arrived there early in May of the year mentioned, and began to unload the vessel and fit up the cannery. A few days thereafter, to wit, May 19th, they stopped work in a body, and demanded of the company's superintendent there in charge $100 for service in operating the vessel to and from Pyramid Harbor, instead of the sums stipulated for in and by the contract; stating that unless they were paid this additional wage they would stop work entirely and return to San Francisco. The evidence showed, and the court below found, that it was impossible for the appellant to get other men to take the places of the libelants, the place being remote, the season short and just opening; so that, after endeavoring for several days without success to induce the libelants to proceed with their work in accordance with their contracts, the company's superintendent, on the 22d day of May, so far yielded to their demands as to instruct his clerk to copy the contracts executed in San Francisco, including the words "Alaska Packers' Association" at the end, substituting, for the $50 and $60 payments, respectively, of those contracts, the sum of $100, which document, so prepared, was signed by the libelants before a shipping commissioner whom they requested to be brought from Northeast

---

[30] "Libel," as used in this context, means the statement of the plaintiff's case and the relief he seeks to obtain by his suit. The term is used frequently in admiralty and divorce cases. The person bringing a libel is referred to as a "libelant," as in this case. The latter term is, for all practical purposes, synonymous with plaintiff. The person sued is called the "libelee," a term that corresponds to defendant.

Point; the superintendent, however, testifying that he at the time told the libelants that he was without authority to enter into any such contract, or to in any way alter the contracts made between them and the company in San Francisco. Upon the return of the libelants to San Francisco at the close of the fishing season, they demanded pay in accordance with the terms of the alleged contract of May 22d, when the company denied its validity, and refused to pay other than as provided for by the contracts of March 26th and April 15th, respectively. . . .

The real questions in the case as brought here are questions of law, and, in the view that we take of the case, it will be necessary to consider but one of those. Assuming that the appellant's superintendent at Pyramid Harbor was authorized to make the alleged contract of May 22d, and that he executed it on behalf of the appellant, was it supported by a sufficient consideration? From the foregoing statement of the case, it will have been seen that the libelants agreed in writing, for certain stated compensation, to render their services to the appellant in remote waters where the season for conducting fishing operations is extremely short, and in which enterprise the appellant had a large amount of money invested; and after having entered upon the discharge of their contract, and at a time when it was impossible for the appellant to secure other men in their places, the libelants, without any valid cause, absolutely refused to continue the services they were under contract to perform unless the appellant would consent to pay them more money. Consent to such a demand, under such circumstances, if given, was, in our opinion, without consideration, for the reason that it was based solely upon the libelants' agreement to render the exact services, and none other, that they were already under contract to render. The case shows that they wilfully and arbitrarily broke that obligation. As a matter of course, they were liable to the appellant in damages. . . . The circumstances of the present case bring it, we think, directly within the sound and just observations of the Supreme Court of Minnesota in the case of King v. Railway Co., 61 Minn. 482, 63 N.W. 1105:

> "No astute reasoning can change the plain fact that the party who refuses to perform, and thereby coerces a promise from the other party to the contract to pay him an increased compensation for doing that which he is legally bound to do, takes an unjustifiable advantage of the necessities of the other party. Surely it would be a travesty on justice to hold that party so making the promise for extra pay was estopped [31] from asserting that the promise was without consideration. A party cannot lay the foundation of an estoppel by his own wrong, where the promise is simply a repetition of a subsisting legal promise. There can be no consideration for the promise of the other party, and there is no warrant for inferring that the parties have voluntarily rescinded or modified their contract. The promise cannot be legally enforced, although the party has completed his contract in reliance upon it."

· · ·

---

[31] Estopped means that a party is legally barred or precluded from asserting certain facts because of his prior conduct. The doctrine of estoppel originated in equity and is used to avoid an unjust result in certain special situations.

It results from the views above expressed that the judgment must be reversed, and the cause remanded, with directions to the court below to enter judgment for the respondent, with costs. It is so ordered.   ◄

COMMENTS AND QUESTIONS

1. Summarize the principal facts in this case. What was the basis for the court's decision in favor of the defendant?
2. The court stresses the fact that the Association had invested large sums of money in the enterprise and was coerced into promising higher wages since it could not secure other men to do the job. If substitute labor had been readily available, would the decision have been different? Or would there still be no consideration for the defendant's promise?
3. If the plaintiff employees had agreed to stay on for a longer period than originally agreed, would this have furnished consideration for the Association's promise to pay higher wages?

An exception to the general rule just stated in the *Alaska Packers* case occurs when extraordinary and unforeseen difficulties arise after the original contract is made. This exception is limited strictly to *extraordinary* circumstances which are truly *unforeseeable,* however, and does not extend to such factors as bad weather or increased labor and material costs. Moreover, a contracting party does not have to promise to pay more if he chooses not to. The Maryland case of *Linz v. Schuck* sprang from this type of problem. Let us see how the court handled it.

LINZ v. SCHUCK

Court of Appeals of Maryland, 1907
106 Md. 220, 67 Atl. 286

► Action by Albinus Schuck against John Linz. From a judgment for plaintiff, defendant appeals. Affirmed.

BOYD, J.   The appellee sued the appellant on the common counts [32] for a balance claimed to be due for work done and materials provided, etc., under the following circumstances: The appellant owned a house known as "No. 3038 Elliott Street," at the corner of Canton Street in Baltimore City, which was built without a cellar, was not plastered or partitioned off on the second story, and the rear was arranged for a stable. The appellee entered into a contract in writing with the appellant which states: "Cellar to be dug under the entire store to the partition wall between kitchen and store to a depth of 7 feet, and walls to be under pinned with good hard brick laid in cement, . . . cellar to be connected with sewer and cemented" and provides for work to be done in the kitchen, and the second story of the house, and a number of other things not necessary to mention. It concludes, "I will do the work and furnish material for the sum of fifteen hundred dollars ($1,500)." The paper was drawn in the shape of an estimate or

---

[32] Common counts are general claims which are set forth in a plaintiff's complaint or declaration alleging that the defendant owes the plaintiff money.

bid, but was accepted by the appellant, and the appellee identified it as his contract.

The appellee began work in April, 1903. He gave the contract to build the cellar to a subcontractor who started to excavate. The appellee thus described the conditions of the ground: "The house stood on a hard crust about three feet thick; and the foundation of that house didn't extend through that hard crust. It was built on that crust, and the more we got through that the more we got into a swamp like—the bottom of an old creek, black muddy stuff and soft and they tried to dig and dig and it all ran into this place and finally a big lump would cave off and fall in every now and then, and they continued on that way to get a trench dug to connect the cellar with the sewer so we thought we could drain the place a little." His foreman notified him that the house was cracking, and he then got lumber and drove "lagging" in to hold the ground. He testified that he notified Mr. Preston, the building inspector of the city, who went there with one of his assistants, that they "took sticks and shoved them down in the ground about 14 feet deep, and that Mr. Linz was present upon this occasion." He also said that Mr. Preston told him no cellar could be made, and he should fill in what he had taken out, and he stopped the work. He further testified that the appellant called on him "off and on," and wanted to see "whether we couldn't make a cellar there; wouldn't it be possible in some way to overcome it even if a small cellar." They finally thought they "could make a little cellar to get some cellar in there," and he said: "Let the thing lay, and we will drain the ground into the sewer, and maybe we can overcome it, provided you pay the additional cost and stand the consequences." He demanded a writing from the appellant, and he said "his word was as good as mine, and if I put a cellar there he would see I got pay for it; that he would pay for the additional work I was compelled to do to make a cellar." In another place he stated: "He says if I was able to get a cellar under there he would reimburse or pay me the additional cost, whatever it was to get a cellar there; that the house was no good to him without a cellar." In October we went to work again, dug out eight feet, then drove poles down eight feet long, used "concrete and cement in there to form our footing," and went to great expense and trouble to make the cellar, under the new arrangement.

The appellant introduced evidence which tended to show that some of the trouble about the cellar was owing to the negligent way in which the appellee's men did the work, and that the bad condition of the soil did not extend as deep as the appellee said it was, but there can be no doubt that the conditions were altogether different from what appeared upon the surface or what was anticipated. The appellee also testified that before he made the offer he "wanted to know how the ground was, and defendant took plaintiff in the cellar of his building" (which was on the opposite side of the street), "and he showed me he had a cellar dug there and it went all right, and the soil was nice and sound there on the other corner, and when I started I wouldn't have any trouble, and I made my figures on his say so." . . .

The principal question in the case is whether the plaintiff was entitled to recover for the additional costs and expenses incurred, by reason of those conditions, on the promise of the appellant to pay him for them. The precise question for our consideration is presented by the plaintiff's fifth prayer,[33] which was granted. After referring to the written contract made in April or May, 1903, and the refusal of the plaintiff in June, 1903, to perform and complete said contract the prayer further submitted to the jury to find whether "said refusal on the part of the plaintiff was induced by substantial and unforeseen difficulties in the performance, which would cast upon the plaintiff additional burden not anticipated by the parties when the contract was made, and if they further find that after said refusal by the plaintiff the defendant, to induce the plaintiff to resume the work thus abandoned, promised to see him through and to stand the consequences, and that, relying upon said promise, the plaintiff completed the work then their verdict may be for the plaintiff," etc. That prayer seems to have followed quite closely the language used in King v. Duluth, M. & N. Ry. Co., 61 Minn. 487, 63 N.W. 1105, which case, notwithstanding unfavorable criticisms by some writers, in our opinion, announces a principle which is not only just and equitable, but is easily reconcilable with the general rule that a promise to do, or actually doing, that which a party to a contract is already under legal obligation to do, is not valid consideration to support the promise of the other party to the contract to pay additional compensation for such performance.

. . . CHIEF JUSTICE STUART of the Minnesota court, in the course of the opinion, said: "It is entirely competent for the parties to a contract to modify or waive their rights under it and ingraft new terms upon it, and in such a case the promise of one party is the consideration for that of the other; but, where the promise to the one is simply a repetition of a subsisting legal promise, there can be no consideration for the promise of the other party, and there is no warrant for inferring that the parties have voluntarily rescinded or modified their contract. But, where the party refusing to complete his contract does so by reason of some unforeseen and substantial difficulties in the performance of the contract, which were not known or anticipated by the parties when the contract was entered into, and which cast upon him an additional burden not contemplated by the parties, and the opposite party promises him extra pay or benefits if he will complete his contract, and he so promises, the promise to pay is supported by a valid consideration. . . . Cases of this character form an exception to the general rule," etc. The opinion then goes on to say that on the other hand, when there are no unforeseen additional burdens which make the refusal to perform, unless promised further pay, equitable, and such refusal and promise of extra pay are one transaction the promise is without consideration and the case is within the general rule. It then holds that what unforeseen difficulties and burdens will make the refusal to perform equitable, so as to bring it within the exception to the general rule, must depend upon the facts of each particular case.

---

[33] Prayer, as used here, merely means a request by the plaintiff. In this case, the plaintiff's fifth request was that the judge charge the jury in a certain way; the request was granted.

We have thus referred to, and quoted from, that case at unusual length, because the principles therein announced seem to us to be, not only well and clearly stated, but just, and founded on reasons that any court of justice should hesitate to reject, unless they conflict with some binding authority or established rule of law, which in our judgment, they do not. When two parties make a contract, based on supposed facts which they afterwards ascertain to be incorrect, and which would not have been entered into by the one party if he had known the actual conditions which the contract required him to meet, not only courts of justice but all right thinking people must believe the fair course for the other party to the contract to pursue is either to relieve the contractor of going on with his contract or to pay him additional compensation. . . .

Judgment affirmed.   ◀

COMMENTS AND QUESTIONS

1. Outline the facts here. Can you distinguish this case from the *Alaska Packers* case, in which the court refused to enforce a promise to pay more money?

2. Of course, Linz, like the Alaska Packers, was under no obligation to agree to pay more. Both probably could have stood on their contract rights and sued for damages for nonperformance. We will discuss this problem in more detail in Section 9 of this chapter (see pp. 322–27).

3. Do you feel that this decision is sound from a business point of view? In other words, if "substantial" and "unforeseen" difficulties arise and the parties agree to a higher price for the work, shouldn't the new agreement be enforceable? If such promises were not enforceable, would a contractor ever agree to such an arrangement?

Compromise and Release of Debts and Claims

When one party owes a debt or an obligation to another, the two parties often "compromise"—that is, they agree to settle for less than the full amount. As a general rule, a promise by a creditor to take less than the full amount of what he is owed is not supported by consideration, since the debtor is already obligated to pay the entire debt.

EXAMPLE

D owes C $100. D tells C that he has lost his job and cannot pay him the full amount of the debt. C agrees to accept $50 in full payment. In most states, C may still sue D for the remaining $50 even after accepting the $50 as agreed.

A few states, more sympathetic to debtors, hold that a creditor waives his right to collect the remainder of the debt when he accepts part payment. In all states, if some new or additional consideration is present (such as the debtor's payment of part of the debt before the due date), or if the debtor promises to perform or actually performs an additional obligation, however small it may be (for example, debtor agrees to shine creditor's shoes), the creditor's promise to accept part payment is binding.

If the amount of a claim or obligation is in dispute, any agreement by the creditor to accept some amount in compromise, even if it is less than what he claims is owing to him, is always binding on both parties.

Another exception is recognized where a group of creditors of one debtor get together and agree to accept a lesser sum (perhaps fifty cents on the dollar) in full payment. This is known as a *composition of creditors* and is generally held to be binding, even though the creditors are getting less than the true amount of the debt.

Illegal Consideration

A promise to perform an illegal act, or the actual performance of such an act, does not constitute consideration (For more on this, see pp. 273–87.)

Adequacy of Consideration

As a general rule, the courts will not review the amount of consideration. If *some* consideration is given and if the parties have freely entered into the agreement, the courts will hold that the agreement is enforceable, even though one side has clearly got the better of the bargain. If there is any question of fraud or duress, however, the adequacy or inadequacy of consideration may be considered as relevant evidence.

> EXAMPLE
>
> s agrees to sell a sailboat to B for $200. The agreement is binding on both sides even though the boat may be worth considerably more. However, if s alleges that B fraudulently induced him to enter into the agreement, the inadequacy of consideration may be considered as evidence of the alleged fraud.

Agreements That Are Binding Without Consideration

The law recognizes certain exceptions to the rules of consideration that we have outlined in this section. In the following situations, agreements are often enforceable despite the fact that no consideration, in the strict sense, is present.

Contracts Under Seal

In the early days of common law, a contract under seal was, as we have mentioned (see page 204), the only kind of agreement that could be enforced with any degree of regularity. With the advent of the doctrine of consideration, the importance of the seal diminished greatly. As a result, in most states a contract under seal is now treated just the same as a regular contract: it is not enforceable if consideration is absent. A few states, however, still hold to the old doctrine and will enforce a contract under seal even if no consideration is present.

Revival of Discharged Debt

If a creditor waits too long to sue a debtor, he may lose his right to collect the debt. In legal terminology, the statute of limitations has run out (see page 332). A debt may also be rendered uncollectible if the debtor goes through bankruptcy, the purpose of which is to cancel his debts and give him a fresh start (see page 332). In either of these situations, the debtor may make a new promise to pay his obligation even though the creditor is powerless to collect it. Since the debtor is no longer legally required to pay, such a promise is not supported by consideration. In most states, however, if the promise is in writing, it is enforceable by the creditor, though he has given no consideration for it.

Written Promises

A few jurisdictions hold that if a promise is in writing, and if the promisor clearly indicates his intention to be bound by the promise, it is enforceable even wthout consideration. Most states, however, reject this rule.

In those states that have enacted the Uniform Commercial Code (see page 353), and in a few others, another exception to the rule of consideration is made in the case of a *firm offer* to sell goods—that is, a written offer which clearly states that the offer is to remain open for a certain period of time. Although the offeror's promise to keep the offer open is not supported by consideration, these states hold that the offer is irrevocable for the period stated.

Voluntary Subscriptions

Another exception to the general rule occurs when a person promises to make a donation to a charitable or educational cause. Although, technically, such promises are not supported by consideration, most courts will find a way to enforce them. The legal "gymnastics" involved in justifying such an exception are often interesting. Let us see how Judge Cardozo accomplished this result in the New York case that follows. Note, also, the sharp dissent of Judge Kellogg.

 ALLEGHENY COLLEGE v. NATIONAL CHAUTAUQUA COUNTY BANK OF JAMESTOWN

Court of Appeals of New York, 1927
246 N.Y. 369, 159 N.E. 173

► Action by Allegheny College against the National Chautauqua County Bank of Jamestown, as executor of the last will and testament of Mary Yates Johnston, deceased. From a judgment of the Appellate Division of the Supreme Court in the Fourth Judicial Department (219 App. Div. 852, 221 N.Y.S. 784), affirming a judgment entered upon a decision of the Trial Term of the Supreme Court in favor of the defendant, a jury having been waived, plaintiff appeals.[34] Judgments of Appellate Division and Trial Term reversed, and judgment ordered for plaintiff.

CARDOZO, C. J.   The Plaintiff, Allegheny College, is an institution of liberal learning at Meadville, Pa. In June, 1921, a "drive" was in progress to secure for it an additional endowment of $1,250,000. An appeal to con-

---

[34] The Appellate Division in New York is a good example of a so-called intermediate court of appeal. This case was tried in the Supreme Court (i.e., the lower court in New York), which found for the defendant. An appeal was then taken to the Appellate Division, which affirmed the decision of the Supreme Court. The plaintiff then appealed further to the highest appellate court in New York—that is, the Court of Appeals.

tribute to this fund was made to Mary Yates Johnston, of Jamestown, New York. In response thereto, she signed and delivered on June 15, 1921, the following writing:

> "Estate Pledge, Allegheny
> College Second Century
> Endowment.
> "Jamestown, N.Y., June 15, 1921.
> "In consideration of my interest in Christian education, and in consideration of others subscribing, I hereby subscribe and will pay to the order of the treasurer of Allegheny College, Meadville, Pennsylvania, the sum of five thousand dollars, $5,000.
> "This obligation shall become due thirty days after my death, and I hereby instruct my executor, or administrator, to pay the same out of my estate. This pledge shall bear interest at the rate of . . . per cent. per annum, payable annually, till paid. The proceeds of this obligation shall be added to the Endowment of said Institution, or expended in accordance with instructions on reverse side of this pledge.
> "Name: Mary Yates Johnston,
> "Address:
>   306 East 6th. Street, Jamestown, N.Y.
> "Dayton E. McClain, Witness,
> "T. R. Courtis, Witness,
> "To authentic Signature."

On the reverse side of the writing is the following indorsement:

> "In loving memory this gift shall be known as the Mary Yates Johnston Memorial Fund, the proceeds from which shall be used to educate students preparing for the ministry, either in the United States or in the foreign field.
> "This pledge shall be valid only on the condition that the provisions of my will, now extant, shall be first met.
>
>   Mary Yates Johnston."

The subscription was not payable by its terms until 30 days after the death of the promisor. The sum of $1,000 was paid, however, upon account in December, 1923, while the promisor was alive. The college set the money aside to be held as a scholarship fund for the benefit of students preparing for the ministry. Later, in July, 1924, the promisor gave notice to the college that she repudiated the promise. Upon the expiration of 30 days following her death, this action was brought against the executor of her will to recover the unpaid balance.

The law of charitable subscriptions has been a prolific source of controversy in this state and elsewhere. We have held that a promise of that order is unenforceable like any other if made without consideration. . . . On the other hand, though professing to apply to such subscriptions the general law of contract, we have found consideration present where the general law of contract, at least as then declared, would have said that it was absent. . . .

A classic form of statement identifies consideration with detriment to the promisee sustained by virtue of the promise. Hamer v. Sidway, 124 N.Y. 538, 27 N.E. 256. So compendious a formula is little more than a half truth. There is need of many a supplementary gloss before the outline can be so

doctrine
¶4 B,

filled in as to depict the classic doctrine. "The promise and the consideration must purport to be the motive each for the other, in whole or at least
in part. It is not enough that the promise induces the detriment or that the
detriment induces the promise if the other half is wanting." Wisconsin &
Michigan R. Co. v. Powers, 191 U.S. 379, 386. . . . If A promises B to make
him a gift, consideration may be lacking, though B has renounced other
opportunities for betterment in the faith that the promise will be kept.

The half truths of one generation tend at times to perpetuate themselves in the law as the whole truth of another, when constant repetition
brings it about that qualifications, taken once for granted, are disregarded
or forgotten. The doctrine of consideration has not escaped the common
lot. As far back as 1881, Judge Holmes in his lectures on the Common Law
(page 292), separated the detriment, which is merely a consequence of the
promise from the detriment, which is in truth the motive or inducement,
and yet added that the courts "have gone far in obliterating this distinction." The tendency toward effacement has not lessened with the years. On
the contrary, there has grown up of recent days a doctrine that a substitute
for consideration or an exception to its ordinary requirements can be found
in what is styled "a promissory estoppel." [35] Williston, Contracts, secs. 139,
116. Whether the exception has made its way in this state to such an extent
as to permit us to say that the general law of consideration has been modified accordingly, we do not now attempt to say. Certain, at least, it is that
we have adopted the doctrine of promissory estoppel as the equivalent of
consideration in connection with our law of charitable subscriptions. So
long as those decisions stand, the question is not merely whether the enforcement of a charitable subscription can be squared with the doctrine of
consideration in all its ancient rigor. The question may also be whether it
can be squared with the doctrine of consideration as qualified by the doctrine of promissory estoppel.

We have said that the cases in this state have recognized this exception,
if exception it is thought to be. Thus, in Barnes v. Perine, 12 N.Y. 18, the
subscription was made without request, express or implied, that the church
do anything on the faith of it. Later, the church did incur expense to the
knowledge of the promisor, and in the reasonable belief that the promise
would be kept. We held the promise binding, though consideration there was
none except upon the theory of a promissory estoppel. In Presbyterian Society v. Beach, 74 N.Y. 72, a situation substantially the same became the basis
for a like ruling. So in Roberts v. Cobb, 103 N.Y. 600, 9 N.E. 500, and Keuka
College v. Ray, 167 N.Y. 96, 60 N.E. 325, the moulds of consideration as
fixed by the old doctrine were subjected to a like expansion. Very likely,
conceptions of public policy have shaped, more or less subconsciously, the
rulings thus made. Judges have been affected by the thought that "defenses
of that character" are "breaches of faith toward the public, and especially

---

[35] Promissory estoppel arises when one person makes a promise to another person
which induces that other person to take some substantial action. According to this doctrine, such a promise is enforceable, even though it is not supported by consideration,
if injustice or hardship will otherwise result. The doctrine is not recognized in many
states.

towards those engaged in the same enterprise, and an unwarrantable disappointment of the reasonable expectations of those interested." W. F. Allen, J., in Barnes v. Perine, *supra*, p. 24. The result speaks for itself irrespective of the motive. Decisions which have stood so long, and which are supported by so many considerations of public policy and reason, will not be overruled to save the symmetry of a concept which itself came into our law, not so much from any reasoned conviction of its justice, as from historical accidents of practice and procedure. The concept survives as one of the distinctive features of our legal system. We have no thought to suggest that it is obsolete or on the way to be abandoned. As in the case of other concepts, however, the pressure of exceptions has led to irregularities of form.

It is in this background of precedent that we are to view the problem now before us. The background helps to an understanding of the implications inherent in subscription and acceptance. This is so though we may find in the end that without recourse to the innovation of promissory estoppel the transaction can be fitted within the mould of consideration as established by tradition.[36]

The promisor wished to have a memorial to perpetuate her name. She imposed a condition that the "gift" should "be known as the Mary Yates Johnston Memorial Fund." The moment that the college accepted $1,000 as a payment on account, there was an assumption of a duty to do whatever acts were customary or reasonably necessary to maintain the memorial fairly and justly in the spirit of its creation. The college could not accept the money and hold itself free thereafter from personal responsibility to give effect to the condition. . . . More is involved in the receipt of such a fund than a mere acceptance of money to be held to a corporate use. . . . The purpose of the founder would be unfairly thwarted or at least inadequately served if the college failed to communicate to the world, or in any event to applicants for the scholarship, the title of the memorial. By implication it undertook, when it accepted a portion of the "gift," that in its circulars of information and in other customary ways when making announcement of this scholarship, it would couple with the announcement the name of the donor. The donor was not at liberty to gain the benefit of such an undertaking upon the payment of a part and disappoint the expectation that there would be payment of the residue. If the college had stated after receiving $1,000 upon account of the subscription, that it would apply the money to the prescribed use, but that in its circulars of information and when responding to prospective applicants it would deal with the fund as an anonymous donation, there is little doubt that the subscriber would have been at liberty to treat this statement as the repudiation of a duty impliedly assumed, a repudiation justifying a refusal to make payments in the future. Obligation in such circumstances is correlative and mutual. A case much in point is New Jersey Hospital v. Wright, 95 N.J.L. 462, 464; 113 Atl. 144, where a sub-

---

[36] Judge Cardozo is admitting that it is hard to find consideration, in the traditional sense, in this case. However, he indicates that he is going to find a way to achieve this result even if he has to stretch the concept a bit.

scription for the maintenance of a bed in a hospital was held to be enforceable by virtue of an implied promise by the hospital that the bed should be maintained in the name of the subscriber. A parallel situation might arise upon the endowment of a chair or a fellowship in a university by the aid of annual payments with the condition that it should commemorate the name of the founder or that of a member of his family. The university would fail to live up to the fair meaning of its promise if it were to publish in its circulars of information and elsewhere the existence of a chair or a fellowship in the prescribed subject, and omit the benefactor's name. A duty to act in ways beneficial to the promisor and beyond the application of the fund to the mere uses of the trust would be placed upon the promisee by the acceptance of the money. We do not need to measure the extent either of benefit to the promisor or of detriment to the promisee implicit in this duty. "If a person chooses to make an extravagant promise for an inadequate consideration, it is his own affair." It was long ago said that "when a thing is to be done by the plaintiff, be it ever so small, this is a sufficient consideration to ground an action." The longing for posthumous remembrance is an emotion not so weak as to justify us in saying that its gratification is a negligible good.

We think the duty assumed by the plaintiff to perpetuate the name of the founder of the memorial is sufficient in itself to give validity to the subscription within the rules that define consideration for a promise of that order. When the promisee subjected itself to such a duty at the implied request of the promisor, the result was the creation of a bilateral agreement. . . . There was a promise on the one side and on the other a return promise, made, it is true, by implication, but expressing an obligation that had been exacted as a condition of the payment. A bilateral agreement may exist though one of the mutual promises be a promise "implied in fact," an inference from conduct as opposed to an inference from words. We think the fair inference to be drawn from the acceptance of a payment on account of the subscription is a promise by the college to do what may be necessary on its part to make the scholarship effective. The plan conceived by the subscriber will be mutilated and distorted unless the sum to be accepted is adequate to the end in view. Moreover, the time to affix her name to the memorial will not arrive until the entire fund has been collected. The college may thus thwart the purpose of the payment on account if at liberty to reject a tender of the residue. It is no answer to say that a duty would then arise to make restitution of the money. If such a duty may be imposed, the only reason for its existence must be that there is then a failure of "consideration." To say that there is a failure of consideration is to concede that a consideration has been promised, since otherwise it could not fail. No doubt there are times and situations in which limitations laid upon a promisee in connection with the use of what is paid by a subscriber lack the quality of consideration, and are to be classed merely as conditions. Williston, Contracts, sec. 112.

> "It is often difficult to determine whether words of condition in a promise indicate a request for consideration or state a mere condition in a gratuitous promise. An aid, though not a conclusive test in determining which

construction of the promise is more reasonable, is an inquiry whether the happening of the condition will be a benefit to the promisor. If so, it is a fair inference that the happening was requested as a consideration." Williston, *supra*, sec. 112.

Such must be the meaning of this transaction unless we are prepared to hold that the college may keep the payment on account, and thereafter nullify the scholarship which is to preserve the memory of the subscriber. The fair implication to be gathered from the whole transaction is assent to the condition and the assumption of a duty to go forward with performance. The subscriber does not say: I hand you $1,000 and you may make up your mind later, after my death, whether you will undertake to commemorate my name. What she says in effect is this: I hand you $1,000 and if you are unwilling to commemorate me, the time to speak is now.

The conclusion thus reached makes it needless to consider whether, aside from the feature of a memorial, a promissory estoppel may result from the assumption of a duty to apply the fund, so far as already paid, to special purposes not mandatory under the provisions of the college charter (the support and education of students preparing for the ministry)—an assumption induced by the belief that other payments sufficient in amount to make the scholarship effective would be added to the fund thereafter upon the death of the subscriber. Ladies Collegiate Institute v. French, 16 Gray, Mass., 196; Barnes v. Perine, 12 N.Y. 18, and cases there cited.

The judgment of the Appellate Division and that of the Trial Term should be reversed, and judgment ordered for the plaintiff as prayed for in the complaint, with costs in all courts.

KELLOGG, J. (dissenting). The Chief Judge finds in the expression, "In loving memory this gift shall be known as the Mary Yates Johnston Memorial Fund," an offer on the part of Mary Yates Johnston to contract with Allegheny College. The expression makes no such appeal to me. Allegheny College was not requested to perform any act through which the sum offered might bear the title by which the offeror states that it shall be known. The sum offered was termed a "gift" by the offeror. Consequently, I can see no reason why we should strain ourselves to make it, not a gift, but a trade. Moreover, since the donor specified that the gift was made, "In consideration of my interest in Christian education, and in consideration of others subscribing," considerations not adequate in law, I can see no excuse for asserting that it was otherwise made in consideration of an act or promise on the part of the donee, constituting a sufficient *quid pro quo* to convert the gift into a contract obligation. To me the words used merely expressed an expectation or wish on the part of the donor and failed to exact the return of an adequate consideration. But if an offer indeed was present, then clearly it was an offer to enter into a unilateral contract. The offeror was to be bound provided the offeree performed such acts as might be necessary to make the gift offered become known under the proposed name. This is evidently the thought of the Chief Judge, for he says: "She imposed a condition that the 'gift' should be known as the Mary Yates Johnston Memorial Fund." In other words, she proposed to exchange her offer of a donation in return for acts to be performed. Even so, there was never any acceptance of the offer, and therefore no contract, for the acts requested never have been performed. The gift has never been made known as demanded. Indeed, the requested acts, under the very terms of the assumed offer, could never have been performed at a time to convert the offer into a promise. This is so for the reason that the donation was not to take effect until after the death of the donor, and by her death her offer was withdrawn. Williston on Contracts, sec. 62. Clearly, although a promise of the college to make the gift known, as requested, may be implied, that promise was not the acceptance of an offer which gave rise to a contract. The donor stipulated for acts, not promises.

> "In order to make a bargain it is necessary that the acceptor shall give in return for the offer or the promise exactly the consideration which the offeror requests. If an act is requested, that very act and no other must be given. If a promise is requested, that promise must be made absolutely and unqualifiedly." Williston on Contracts, sec. 73.
> "It does not follow that an offer becomes a promise because it is accepted; it may be, and frequently is, conditional, and then it does not become a promise until the conditions are satisfied; and in case of offers for a consideration, the performance of the consideration is always deemed a condition." Langdell, Summary of the Law of Contracts, sec. 4.

It seems clear to me that there was here no offer, no acceptance of an offer, and no contract. Neither do I agree with the Chief Judge that this court "found consideration present where the general law of contract, at least as then declared, would have said that it was absent" in the cases of Barnes v. Perine, 12 N.Y. 18, Presbyterian Society v. Beach, 74 N.Y. 72, and Keuka College v. Ray, 167 N.Y. 96, 60 N.E. 325. In the Keuka College Case an offer to contract, in consideration of the performance of certain acts by the offeree, was converted into a promise by the actual performance of those acts. This form of contract has been known to the law from time immemorial (Langdell, sec. 46), and for at least a century longer than the other type, a bilateral contract (Williston, sec. 13). It may be that the basis of the decisions in Barnes v. Perine and Presbyterian Society v. Beach, *supra*, was the same as in the Keuka College Case. However, even if the basis of the decisions be a so-called "promissory estoppel," nevertheless they initiated no new doctrine. A so-called "promissory estoppel," although not so termed, was held sufficient by Lord Mansfield and his fellow judges as far back as the year 1765. Pillans v. Van Mierop, 3 Burr. 1663. Such a doctrine may be an anomaly; it is not a novelty. Therefore I can see no ground for the suggestion that the ancient rule which makes consideration necessary to the formation of every contract is in danger of effacement through any decisions of this court. To me that is a cause for gratulation rather than regret. However, the discussion may be beside the mark, for I do not understand that the holding about to be made in this case is other than a holding that consideration was given to convert the offer into a promise. With that result I cannot agree and, accordingly, must dissent.

POUND, CRANE, LEHMAN, and O'BRIEN, JJ., concur with CARDOZO, C. J. KELLOGG, J., dissents in opinion, in which ANDREWS, J., concurs.

Judgment accordingly.   ◄

COMMENTS AND QUESTIONS

1. Summarize the facts in this case. What was the decision of the majority of the court?
2. Outline the reasons set forth by Judge Cardozo in support of the court's decision. Don't you feel that he stretched the concept of consideration to obtain the desired result here?
3. What were the main points of the dissenting opinion?

SECTION 5

LEGAL CAPACITY OF PARTIES

In General

The law makes a special effort to protect those who cannot protect themselves—young persons, for example, who are lacking in judgment, or persons who are deficient in mental ability. Such people, of course, often enter into agreements. Generally, the courts permit them to review their agreements later on, when they are more mature or better able to understand the implications of their actions, and to reject their agreements if they choose to do so.

Minors

Definition

In most states, any person under twenty-one is considered to be an infant, or a minor. A few states, however, hold that a girl ceases to be a minor when she becomes eighteen or when she marries.

Right to Avoid Contracts

As a general rule, a contract between a minor and an adult can be avoided only by the minor; it remains binding on the adult until the minor chooses to avoid it. If the minor dies, his personal representative may avoid the contract.

If the contract is wholly executory—that is, if it has been performed on neither side—no special problems arise when the minor disaffirms it, for then it becomes completely unenforceable and the adult has no right to sue for damages. When the contract has been partially or wholly performed, however, and the minor has received the benefit of some consideration, the situation becomes more complicated. Here the general rule is that the minor may still avoid the contract but only on condition that he return to the adult any benefit he has received. And the minor, of course, is entitled to the return of any consideration he has given. But what happens if, in the meantime, the minor has lost, spent, or squandered the consideration he received? In most states, he is still permitted to avoid his contract, simply returning whatever he has left of the consideration. A few states, however, will not permit a minor to avoid a contract unless he restores full consideration to the other side.

In the New York case of *Sternlieb v. Normandie National Securities Corp.*, the Court of Appeals agonized over these choices and clearly did not approve of the result it felt bound to hand down.

IRVING STERNLIEB, Respt.
v. NORMANDIE NATIONAL SECURITIES CORPORATION, Appt.

New York Court of Appeals, 1934
263 N.Y. 245, 188 N.E. 726

▶ CRANE, J., delivered the opinion of the Court:

Again we have the troublesome question arising from the repudiation by a young gentleman, just under twenty-one, of his contract of purchase. On the 21st day of September, 1929, the plaintiff purchased from the defendant five shares of the capital stock of the Bank of United States and of the Bankus Corporation, for which he paid $990. In his complaint he alleges that he was under twenty-one years of age. After the stock had dropped in value until it was worthless, this young plaintiff further alleges that on the 14th of September, 1932, he notified the defendant that he rescinded his purchase, and that he was ready to tender and return the certificates.

In its answer the defendant as a defense alleges that the plaintiff falsely and fraudulently represented and warranted to the defendant before and at the time of purchase he was over twenty-one years of age, and that the defendant relied upon these statements in parting with the stock.

The action was brought in the Municipal Court of the city of New York. The plaintiff moved to strike out the defense. The motion was denied, and affirmed, on appeal, by the Appellate Term. The Appellate Division, however, reversed this action of the two lower courts and has certified to this court the following question: "Is the separate and distinct defense set forth in the answer herein sufficient in law?"

That young men, nearly twenty-one years of age, actively engaged in business, can at will revoke any or all of their business transactions and obligations, thereby causing loss to innocent parties dealing with them, upon the assumption or even the assurance that they were of age, has not appealed to some courts, and has been adopted without much enthusiasm by others. This state from the earliest days has followed the common-law doctrine, adopted at a time when young men were not so actively engaged in trade and in lucrative occupations as at present. The opportunities for making a living by barter and sale were not so numerous for them as now.

At common law a male infant attains his majority when he becomes twenty-one years of age, and all unexecuted contracts made by him before that date, except for necessaries, while not absolutely void are voidable at his election. In an action upon a contract made by an infant he is not estopped from pleading his infancy by any representation as to his age made by him to induce another person to contract with him. International Text Book Co. v. Connelly, 206 N.Y. 188, 99 N.E. 722. Neither could the infant be sued for damages in tort by reason of any false representations made in inducing or procuring the contract. For his torts generally, where they have no basis in any contract relation, an infant is liable, just as any other person would be, but the doctrine is equally well settled that a matter arising *ex contractu*, though infected with fraud, cannot be changed into a tort,[37] in order to charge an infant by a change of the remedy. Collins v. Gifford, 203 N.Y. 465, 96 N.E. 721. The only difference between an executory and an executed contract appears to be, that in the former the infant may disaffirm at any time short of the period of the statute of limitations,[38] unless by some act he has ratified the contract, whereas in the latter, he must disaffirm within a reasonable time after becoming of age, or his silence will be considered a ratification.

This case pertains to an executed contract for the purchase of stock which the plaintiff has disaffirmed within a reasonable time. The distinction which the appellant would have us make between these well-established authorities and the present case is the fact that the infant is here the plaintiff seeking relief from the courts and should do equity [39] before obtaining relief. That is, while as a defendant the courts will protect him from further liability on his contracts, they will not aid in getting back money or property which will give him profit or gain through his fraudulent representations regarding his age. This was the view taken by the Appellate Division of the Second Department in Falk v. MacMasters, 197 App. Div. 357, 188 N.Y.S. 795.

This court however has not gone so far. The nearest approach to the point is Rice v. Butler, 160 N.Y. 578, 55 N.E. 275. In the case the infant was a plaintiff seeking to recover installments paid upon a bicycle which he offered to return. The court recognized the right of the infant to rescind his bargain and the infant got his money, insisting, however, that he must pay for the use of, or wear and tear on, the machine. The defendant was allowed to deduct this from the money paid by the infant.

That the infant is not liable in tort for false representations of age inducing a contract. . . .

Some of the state courts, however, have taken a different view, and find

---

[37] Generally speaking, legal obligations are divided into two great classes—those which arise out of a contract (i.e., *ex contractu*) and those which arise out of a tort (called *ex delicto*). A tort occurs when one party violates a duty, other than a contractual duty, to another party and thereby damages that party's person, property, or reputation.

[38] For a discussion of the statute of limitations, see page 332.

[39] There is an old legal maxim which holds that one should do equity before one is entitled to receive equity. In other words, before one party asks the equity court to grant him relief, he should treat the other party fairly. In this case, it means that the minor should be forced to return what he received before being permitted to avoid the contract.

that fraudulent representations regarding age estop an infant from maintaining an action for relief.

Like so many questions of policy, there is much to be said upon both sides, and the necessities of one period of time are not always those of another. The law, from time out of mind, has recognized that infants must be protected from their own folly and improvidence. It is not always flattering to our young men in college and in business, between the ages of eighteen and twenty-one, to refer to them as infants, and yet this is exactly what the law considers them in their mental capacities and abilities to protect themselves in ordinary transactions and business relationships. That many young people under twenty-one years of age are improvident and reckless is quite evident, but these defects in judgment are by no means confined to the young. There is another side to the question. As long as young men and women, under twenty-one years of age, having the semblance and appearance of adults, are forced to make a living and enter into business transactions, how are the persons dealing with them to be protected if the infant's word cannot be taken or recognized at law? Are business men to deal with young people at their peril? Well, the law is as it is, and the duty of this court is to give force and effect to the decisions as we find them. Some states have met the situation by legislation. (Iowa Code,— 3190 (1897),—10494 (1927)—Kan. Rev. St. 38–103 (1923); Comp. Laws of Utah, 3967 (1917) Rem. Comp. Stat. of Wash. 5830 (1922). Let us refer to the Iowa Code, as a fair example, taken from the case of Friar v. Rae-Chandler Co. 192 Iowa, 427, at page 428, 185 N.W. 32, 33.

Sec. 3189. A minor is bound, not only by contracts for necessaries, but also by his other contracts, unless he disaffirms them within a reasonable time after he attains his majority, and restores to the other party all money or property received by him by virtue of the contract and remaining within his control at any time after his attaining his majority, except as otherwise provided.

Sec. 3190. No contract can be thus disaffirmed in cases where, on account of the minor's own misrepresentations as to his majority or from his having engaged in business as an adult, the other party had good reason to believe him capable of contracting.

We, therefore, conclude that the law of this state [i.e., New York], in accordance with the trend of most of the authorities, is to the effect that the defense pleaded in the answer is insufficient and was properly stricken out by the Appellate Division.

The order should therefore, be affirmed, with costs.[40]   ◄

COMMENTS AND QUESTIONS

1. Note that the plaintiff in this case purchased his stock just before the stock-market "crash" in 1929. How did the court hold?
2. Again in this case, the opinion acknowledges a split of opinion among the state courts. Judge Crane readily admits that he dislikes the rule which the court applies, but he says, in effect, that he is powerless to change it: ". . . The law is as it is, and the duty of this court is to

---

[40] This means that the defendant not only lost the case but had to pay for the plaintiff's costs, other than his attorney's fees.

give force and effect to the decisions as we find them." Note also that he in effect invites the New York legislature to change the law by quoting the Iowa statute with approval. Could the New York Court of Appeals change the law if it wanted to?

3. On the other hand, the opinion admits that "there is much to be said on both sides." Summarize the arguments in favor of the decision.

Misrepresentation of Age

What happens when a minor induces another party to enter into a contract by fraudulently representing his age? As indicated in the Sternlieb case, the courts disagree. Some states rule that such deceit denies the infant his right to avoid the contract; others hold that he may still avoid it but that he is liable for any damages caused by his fraud. Most states permit the adult to avoid the contract, but a few states deny him this right, on the ground that the minor should be protected despite his misconduct.

Time of Avoidance

As a general rule, a minor may avoid a contract and demand return of any consideration he has given at any time during his minority and for a reasonable period after he comes of age. If he fails to disaffirm the contract after a reasonable time following his attainment of majority, he is deemed to have ratified the contract and becomes bound by it.

What Constitutes Avoidance by a Minor

Any words, actions, or conduct on the part of the minor which indicate that he intends to repudiate the contract constitute avoidance, even though he does not say so expressly. He must repudiate the entire contract, however, for he is not allowed to reject certain parts of it and retain the benefits of other parts.

necessity- food, cloth.

EXAMPLE

M, a minor, agrees to sell a car to B. Before delivering it, however, M agrees to sell the same car to C. M's second agreement constitutes an avoidance of the original contract, since it is inconsistent with that contract.

Ratification

Although a minor may avoid a contract at any time during his minority, he is not allowed to ratify or affirm a contract until he becomes an adult. After he comes of age, any words or conduct on his part that indicate a willingness or an intention to be bound constitute ratification. As we mentioned before, though, if he says or does nothing for a reasonable period of time after he attains majority, his silence is deemed to indicate affirmation and the contract becomes binding.

EXAMPLES

1. M, a minor, purchases a car from s. After M becomes 21, he sells the car to B. By taking such action, M is deemed to have ratified the contract with s.

2. M, a minor, buys some real estate from s. After reaching majority, M

accepts rent from a tenant of the property for two years. His conduct affirms the contract.

Minor's Liability for Necessaries

As we have seen, a minor is not bound by any contract he enters into unless he ratifies it. He is, however, generally held accountable for the fair value, which may be more or less than the contract price, of *necessaries* which he contracts for and which are actually supplied to him by the other party for his use. Necessaries are those items which he requires for food, shelter, clothing, health, and education, according to his station in life or social position. A purchase of some item with which he is already well supplied is not considered a necessary. Nor is money lent to a minor considered a necessary, unless the lender makes sure that the minor actually spends it for a needed item. Until a necessary is actually supplied to the minor, he has no obligation to pay for it.

> EXAMPLE
>
> M, a minor, agrees to pay T, a tailor, $100 to make a suit for him. Up to the time the suit is completed and actually delivered to M, he may elect to disaffirm the contract and recover any money he has paid to T. After the suit has been delivered to him, however, he is liable to T for the fair value of the suit. (This value may be less than $100 if it is established that T has overcharged him.) But if M already has plenty of suits, the new one is not deemed to be a necessary; M may elect to avoid the contract and recover his money even after he has received the suit and worn it.

In the following Massachusetts case, the court was faced with several of the problems relating to minors that we have just discussed. The court's decision is rather interesting in that Justice Lummus indicates some disapproval of the findings of the lower-court judge but feels that he must uphold them.

JOHN P. ADAMOWSKI
v. THE CURTISS-WRIGHT FLYING SERVICE, INC.

Massachusetts Supreme Judicial Court, 1938
300 Mass. 281, 15 N.E. 2d 467

▶ LUMMUS, J.   The plaintiff was born on July 20, 1909. On September 25, 1929, when he was two months more than twenty years old, he paid the defendant $300 for a course of instruction in elementary aviation, and received it. On May 6, 1930, he entered into a contract with the defendant for a course of instruction as a transport pilot at a cost of $3,200, but during the month withdrew from the school and paid nothing. He attained his majority on July 20, 1930. On February 28, 1931, after receiving from the defendant a bill for a balance of less than $50 which it claimed as due, the plaintiff visited its attorney and denied liability, but said nothing about minority. He took no action by way of disaffirmance until July 11, 1931, almost a year after attaining majority, when he brought this action to recover the $1,600 which he had paid, with interest, on the ground that he was a minor at the time of the making of the contracts in question and had elected to disaffirm them. The judge found for the plaintiff, but the Appellate Division ordered judgment for the defendant. The plaintiff's appeal brings the case here.

It is agreed that the contracts were made in New York, where the defendant's aviation school was located, and that the questions raised in this case are governed by the law of New York.[41]

The defendant contends that the contracts were for necessaries, and were binding upon the plaintiff even while he was a minor. The plaintiff's father was a weaver. The money which the plaintiff paid was in part saved by himself from his manual labor and in part contributed by his family from their savings. In this country, as the judge found in substance, any stratification of society is transient and shifting. Many a young man without capital or influential connections attains education and advancement in life through his own labors. It would be hard to say that education in aviation was less necessary for the plaintiff than it would have been for another more affluent. But the law still guards the interests of minors against their own assumed improvidence and want of sound judgment. The judge found that the courses in instruction were not necessaries for the plaintiff. The finding was proper, though possibly not required as a matter of law. . . .

The next question is whether as a matter of law delay for nearly a year after majority before disaffirming the contracts was ratification of them. It is to be noticed that the contracts were wholly executed, and that there is no evidence that an earlier disaffirmance would have benefited the defendant or saved it from harm. It is to be further noticed that the plaintiff has made no use of his education in aviation, which has been of no apparent benefit to him. His duty to disaffirm within a reasonable time after majority . . . does not limit him to so short a time as though the facts were different in those respects. . . . In cases where, as in the present case, the quondam minor gained no benefit by delay and the party contracting with him suffered no harm, disaffirmance has been allowed after considerably greater delay than that in this case. . . . The finding of the judge that disaffirmance was within a reasonable time must stand.

Lastly, the defendant contends that there could be no disaffirmance because the plaintiff could not return the instruction that he had received by virtue of the contracts. In New York, as in this Commonwealth, a minor who has lost or squandered what he received under the contract may nevertheless disaffirm it and recover what he paid or gave, or its value. . . .

In principle he should be in no worse position where the nature of what he received is such that it cannot be returned. There are cases in New York, however, which are difficult to reconcile with the cases just cited, and which hold that a plaintiff suing to recover money paid while a minor for tangible property which he returns must allow for its depreciation while he had the

---

[41] The court is applying a well-established rule of conflict of laws: that the interpretation of a contract will be governed by the law of the state where the contract is made. Although the Massachusetts court was deciding the case, it was bound to apply New York law even though New York might have a different rule from that of Massachusetts.

use of it. . . . Adams, J., whose views expressed in Rice v. Butler, 25 App. Div. (N.Y.) 388, 393, were substantially adopted on appeal in Rice v. Butler, 160 N.Y. 578, said in effect that the rule is that when property is returned on disaffirmance any damage to it must be made good, and that the rule does not apply where restitution is impossible. We find no case, unless it be Mutual Milk & Cream Co. v. Prigge, 112 App. Div. (N.Y.) 652, in which the quondam minor has been required to make an allowance for an intangible benefit received. On the whole, though the matter is not free from doubt, we think that under the law of New York the plaintiff is not precluded from disaffirming the contracts and recovering the consideration that he paid, by the fact that he cannot return the instruction received.

Order of Appellate Division for judgment for defendant reversed. Judgment for plaintiff on the finding.   ◄

COMMENTS AND QUESTIONS

1. Summarize the facts in this case. What was the decision of the court and what rules of law were applied?
2. The defendant contended that the lessons were "necessaries," and that the plaintiff should therefore be required to pay for them. How did the court deal with this allegation? Do you agree?
3. Do you think the result would have been different if the plaintiff had purchased a car, for example, which he still had in his possession at the time he disaffirmed the contract?

Parent's Responsibility

ON MINOR'S CONTRACTS. Contrary to popular belief, a parent is never liable for a minor's contract unless he was actually a party to the agreement, or unless the minor was clearly acting as an agent for the parent in making the contract.

FOR MINOR'S TORTS. If a minor is old enough to appreciate the consequences of his behavior, he is personally responsible for any damage or injury which he willfully or carelessly inflicts on others. The parent, however, is *not* responsible for such conduct unless:

1. He actively shares in the minor's conduct, or
2. He directs the child in his injurious activities, or
3. He stands by and fails to control the minor when he has an opportunity to do so.

Insane Persons

A contract made by an insane person is voidable at any time while he remains insane and for a reasonable period after he recovers his sanity. He may ratify a contract only after recovering sanity. An insane person is, however, liable for the fair value of necessaries furnished to him.

The courts are a bit stricter in their attitude toward executed contracts. If the insane person has received some benefit from the other side under such a contract, and if the other side has taken no undue advantage of him, most states will deny him the right to avoid the contract unless he is able and willing to restore the entire consideration he has received.

If a legal guardian has been appointed, an insane person is not permitted to make any binding contract at all. Any agreement he purports to make is void and unenforceable.

Intoxicated Persons

If a person makes a contract while he is so intoxicated that he is incapable of understanding the effect of his actions, he may disaffirm the contract within a reasonable time after he becomes sober again. And he may ratify the contract only after he returns to a sober state. The mere fact that a person is slightly intoxicated will not excuse him so long as he can still appreciate the general effects of what he is doing. A drunkard is responsible for any necessaries that are provided to him. If a guardian has been appointed for him, no contract into which he enters is enforceable.

Married Women

In the past, married women had only a very limited right to make binding contracts. Today, however, such restrictions have been eliminated in almost all the states, and, for most purposes, a married woman is just as free to contract as any other person.

Convicts

In some states, a man convicted of a serious crime is incapable of making a binding contract.

Enemy Aliens

In time of war, an enemy alien is generally denied the right to enter into a binding contract.

SECTION 6

ILLEGAL AGREEMENTS

In General

An agreement that relates to unlawful subject matter or that has an illegal objective will not be enforced by the courts. Some agreements of this type are specifically prohibited by statute and, in addition, are often classified as crimes—if performed. Others, though not outlawed by statute, are judged by the courts to be contrary to public policy. In the latter category is the case of *Little Rock and Fort Smith Ry. Co. v. Eubanks,* an illustration of the sort of situation in which the courts, in order to protect the welfare of the community, may decide to restrict the freedom of private parties to make contracts.

LITTLE ROCK AND FORT SMITH RY. CO. v. EUBANKS

Arkansas Supreme Court, 1886
48 Ark. 460, 3 S.W. 808

► By Court, SMITH, J.   Appellee, as administratrix of J. C. Eubanks, sued appellant in the Franklin circuit court, alleging that she was the mother of the deceased, and administratrix, etc.; that on the seventh day of October, 1884, her intestate was employed under a contract as brakeman on appellant's railway; that on or before that time appellant's railway, at the town of Ozark, was in a defective condition, in this: "The defendant had constructed on its said road, and as a part of it on the track thereof at said place, a switch, and a frog, which was so worn, ill-constructed, and defective as to render it unsafe and unfit for use." The complaint alleges knowledge by appellant of these defects, and that by reason thereof, and the unsafe condition of the road at that point, and appellant's negligence, her intestate, while in the performance of his duty as brakeman under his contract, was thrown from the car, run over, and killed.

The answer denies that the switch or frog was defective, ill-constructed, or unfit for use, or that plaintiff's intestate was thrown from the car and killed by reason of any such defects; denies that the deceased was free from negligence, and alleges that his death was caused by negligence on his part. The answer also sets up and relies upon the following contract, executed by the deceased before his employment by the defendant, as a release of liability.

"Clinton Eubanks, having been employed, at his request, by the Little Rock and Fort Smith Railway in the capacity of brakeman, hereby agrees with said railway, in consideration of such employment, that he will take upon himself all risks incident to his position on the road, and will in no case hold the company liable for any injury or damage he may sustain, in his person or otherwise, by accidents or collisions on the trains or road, or which may result from defective machinery, or carelessness or misconduct of himself or any other employee and servant of the company."

The issues were submitted to a jury, which returned a verdict for the plaintiff for $9,360; upon which judgment was entered. A motion for a new trial was subsequently overruled; and a bill of exceptions was signed, saving the points hereinafter noticed.[42]

---

[42] A bill of exceptions is a list of objections made by a party during the trial of a case. When a case is appealed, the bill is signed by the trial judge to verify its accuracy and is then presented to the appellate court. Its function is to create a formal record of the points that will be argued on appeal.

The execution of the contract copied above was admitted by the plaintiff. But the court refused this prayer of the defendant: "If you find that before entering the service of defendant, deceased executed the release, a copy of which is set out in defendant's answer, you are instructed that by reason of said release plaintiff will be precluded from recovering anything in this suit, and you will find for defendant."

A common carrier, or a telegraph company, cannot, by pre-contract with its customers, relieve itself from liability for its own negligent acts. This, however, may be on the grounds of its public employment [in relation to its customers]. . . .

The validity of the contract before us is not affected by such considerations. The relation existing between the parties to it is essentially a private relation,—that, namely, of master and servant.[43] And the question is, whether a servant employed in the operation of dangerous machinery can waive [44] in advance the duties and liabilities which the master owes him, and which do not depend on contract, but spring out of the relation itself. Of course, if he can waive them so as to bind himself, a waiver will also bar his personal representative for the personal representative only succeeds to the right of action which the deceased would have had but for his death.

In 1880, the English Parliament passed the "employer's liability act," the object of which was to make employers liable for injury to workmen, caused by the negligence of those having the supervision and control of them. In Griffiths v. Earl of Dudley, L.R. 9 Q.B.D. 357, it was held that a workman might contract himself and his representatives out of the benefits of this act.

An opposite conclusion has been reached by the supreme courts of Ohio and Kansas. They hold that it is not competent for a railroad company to stipulate with its employees, at the time of hiring them, and as a part of the contract, that it shall not be liable for injuries caused by the carelessness of other employees: Lake Shore & M.L.R.R. Co. v. Spangler, Sup. Ct. Ohio, 1886; Kansas Pacific R'y Co. v. Peavey, 29 Kan. 169. . . . This, however, is not precisely the same question we have to deal with. For the negligence of a fellow-servant is not in fact and in morals the negligence of the master, although by virtue of a statute it may be imputed to the master. It is impossible for the master always to be present and control the actions of his servants. Hence a stipulation not to be answerable for their negligence, beyond the selection of competent servants in the first instance, and the discharge of such as prove to be reckless or incompetent, might be upheld as reasonable, notwithstanding a statute might abolish the old rule of nonliability for the acts and omissions of a co-servant. . . .

It is an elementary principle in the law of contracts that *modus et conventio vicunt legem*,—the form of agreement and the convention of parties override the law. But the maxim is not of universal application. Parties are permitted, by contract, to make a law for themselves only in cases where

---

[43] Master and servant, for all practical purposes, mean employer and employee. This relationship is discussed in greater detail in Chapter 14.

[44] A person waives a legal right when he voluntarily relinquishes or abandons it.

their agreements do not violate the express provisions of any law, nor injuriously affect the interest of the public.

Our constitution and laws provide that all railroads operated in this state shall be responsible for all damages to persons and property done by the running of trains. This means that they shall be responsible only in cases where they have been guilty of some negligence. And it may be questionable whether it is in their power to denude themselves of such responsibility by a stipulation in advance. But we prefer to rest our decision upon the broader ground of considerations of public policy. The law requires the master to furnish his servant with a reasonably safe place to work in, and with sound and suitable tools and appliances to do his work. If he can supply an unsafe machine, or defective instruments, and then excuse himself against the consequences of his own negligence by the terms of his contract with his servant, he is enabled to evade a most salutary rule.

In the English case above cited, it is said this is not against public policy, because it does not affect all society, but only the interest of the employed. But surely the state has an interest in the lives and limbs of all its citizens. Laborers for hire constitute a numerous and meritorious class in every community. And it is for the welfare of society that their employers shall not be permitted, under the guise of enforcing contract rights, to abdicate their duties to them. The consequence would be that every railroad company, and every owner of a factory, mill, or mine, would make it a condition precedent to the employment of labor, that the laborer should release all right of action for injuries sustained in the course of the service, whether by the employer's negligence or otherwise. The natural tendency of this would be to relax the employer's carefulness in those matters of which he has the ordering and control, such as the supplying of machinery and materials, and thus increase the perils of occupations which are hazardous even when well managed. And the final outcome would be to fill the country with disabled men and paupers, whose support would become a charge upon the counties or upon public charity.

Judgment affirmed.   ◄

COMMENTS AND QUESTIONS
1. Outline the facts in this case. How did the court decide?
2. What instruction did the defendant ask the trial judge to give to the jury? Did the judge so instruct the jury?
3. Summarize the arguments set forth by the appellate court in favor of its decision.

Kinds of Illegal Contract

The states differ a good bit on what does and does not constitute an illegal contract, but there are several classes of contract that are generally held to be illegal and unenforceable.

Contracts to Commit Crimes or Civil Wrongs

A contract that calls for one (or both) of the parties to commit a crime or a civil wrong is illegal.

EXAMPLES

1. One party agrees to burn down someone's house in exchange for a payment of money by the other party.
2. One party promises to help the other party to defraud a third person.

Contracts to Obstruct Justice or Interfere with Public Service

A contract whose purpose is to obstruct justice or interfere with the proper functioning of government is illegal.

EXAMPLES

1. One party agrees to bribe a public official for the benefit of the other party.
2. x agrees to pay a witness a bonus if the witness will falsify his testimony in a lawsuit.

Wagering Contracts

A wagering contract is an agreement whereby one party is to win money from another by chance. In most states, all gambling or wagering agreements are held to be illegal except those that are expressly permitted by statute (for example, betting at horse races in a state that has legally licensed such betting).

An agreement to purchase a commodity at some future date at a price to be determined at the present time (called a "futures transaction") may be regarded as an illegal wagering contract if the parties have no intention of delivering and receiving the goods, but merely wish to gamble or speculate on the rise or fall of the market price. If the parties actually intend to transfer the goods, however, the contract is binding.

EXAMPLE

b agrees to buy 1,000 bushels of corn from s at $.50 a bushel, with the purchase and sale to take place 60 days after the contract is made. The parties agree that if in 60 days' time the market price of corn has dropped (for example, to $.40 a bushel), b will pay s the difference ($.10 a bushel, or $100); but if the market price rises (for example, to $.70 a bushel), s will pay b the difference ($.20 a bushel, or $200). If the parties have no intention of actually transferring ownership of the corn, but are interested only in speculating on its future price, the contract is illegal.

Contracts with Unlicensed Parties

Some contracts call for the services of a professional person, or of a person who is engaged in a calling that requires a license from a state or municipality. Is such a contract legal if it turns out that the person who is to provide the services does not possess a proper license to practice? Generally speaking, whether or not the contract is enforceable depends on the purpose of the licensing statute. If the statute is designed to protect the public by setting up strict standards of competence (as in the practice of medicine or law), the contract is illegal and unenforceable. If, however, the statute simply establishes a technical requirement whose only purpose is to raise revenue (a statute, for example, requiring that a money-lender pay a small fee for a license), the contract is generally held to be enforceable. (But the unlicensed party is usually subject to some fine or other criminal penalty.) Here is a typical case in which one of the parties to a contract was unlicensed.

JOHN E. ROSASCO CREAMERIES, INC. v. COHEN
Court of Appeals of New York, 1937
276 N.Y. 274, 11 N.E. 2d 908

▶ FINCH, JUDGE. The plaintiff, a milk dealer, brought this action to recover approximately $11,000 as the agreed and reasonable value of milk sold and delivered to the defendants, who are also milk dealers. The answer admits the sale and delivery of milk, the quantity thereof, and the failure to pay, but denies the allegations concerning the agreed and reasonable value of the milk. As an affirmative defense, it alleges that the plaintiff was not licensed as a milk dealer in accordance with the Agriculture and Markets Law (Consol. Laws, c. 69) during the period when it sold the milk to the defendants. The lack of license is admitted in the reply of the plaintiff. The defendants assert two counterclaims. The first is for damages for an alleged breach of an oral contract, which it is asserted, provided that the plaintiff would sell and deliver, and defendants would purchase, all milk required by the defendants in connection with their business up to a total of 10,500 forty-quart cans per month. By the second counterclaim, the defendants seek to recover a sum of money alleged to have been overpaid to the plaintiff. The reply of the plaintiff denies allegations of the counterclaims and pleads in bar the claim urged by the defendants of the illegality of the transaction. . . .

The primary issue for decision is whether a dealer in milk, which makes sales while unlicensed, may recover the agreed price or the reasonable value of milk sold to another dealer. The contention that the failure to obtain a license renders the claim unenforceable is based on section 257 of the Agriculture and Markets Law, which reads as follows:

> "Section 257. Licenses to milk dealers. No milk dealer shall buy milk from producers or others or deal in, handle, sell or distribute milk unless such dealer be duly licensed as provided in this article. It shall be unlawful for a milk dealer to buy milk from or sell milk to a milk dealer who is unlicensed, or in any way deal in or handle milk which he has reason to believe has previously been dealt in or handled in violation of the provisions of this chapter. The commissioner may by official order exempt from the license requirements provided by this article milk dealers who purchase or handle milk in a total quantity not exceeding three thousand pounds in any month, and/or milk dealers selling milk in any quantity in markets of one thousand population or less."

Illegal contracts are generally unenforceable [sic]. Where contracts which violate statutory provisions are merely *malum prohibitum*,[45] the gen-

---

[45] Literally, a wrong prohibited. In other words, an act which is wrong only *because* it is forbidden by law. This is to be contrasted with the term *malum in se*, which

eral rule does not always apply. If the statute does not provide expressly that its violation will deprive the parties of their right to sue on the contract, and the denial of relief is wholly out of proportion to the requirements of public policy or appropriate individual punishment, the right to recover will not be denied.

In Sajor v. Ampol, Inc., 275 N.Y. 125, 9 N.E. 2d 803, the lower courts held that the plaintiff could rescind his subscription to the defendant's stock on the ground that the failure to comply with the statutory requirement which prohibited the sale of securities to the public without first filing a notice with the Department of State, rendered the sale null and void. In reversing, this court, in an opinion by CHIEF JUDGE CRANE, said:

> "The notice, requiring the name of the dealer, his business or post office address, the state of incorporation and other like matters in no way affected the plaintiff's purchase. Such a statement had no relation whatever to his transaction. Its purpose was to inform the Attorney-General and the State authorities of the stock business carried on by dealers and of the place where such business was to be conducted. . . . The statute does not make sales void or voidable or unenforceable when such notice has not been filed. Such is the requirement of many of the States of the Union which have similar statutes. Our statute has an omnibus provision relating to the violation of any provision of article 23-A of the General Business Law, making the violation a misdemeanor punishable by a fine of not more than $500, or imprisonment of not more than one year, or both (sec. 359-g subd. 2). This penalty provided for the violation is the exaction which the law makes, and no other. We should not read into the provisions of the statute that which other State legislators have found necessary to insert, in order to reach the transactions between parties. Our Legislature . . . did not intend to make void or voidable any and every contract made with a corporation dealer, otherwise valid, simply because it had failed to comply with the many administrative provisions of the law. . . ."

The reasoning of these cases is applicable to the case at bar. The statute involved does not expressly provide that contracts made by unlicensed milk dealers shall be unenforceable, although it does make a violation of the so-called milk control law a misdemeanor punishable by a fine of not less than $25 nor more than $200 or by imprisonment for not less than one month nor more than six months, or both. In the case at bar, if the contract is declared unenforceable, the effect will be to punish the plaintiff to the extent of a loss of approximately $11,000 and permit the defendants to evade the payment of a legitimate debt. Nor was the statute enacted for the purpose of protecting dealers such as the defendants. The primary purpose of the statute is to protect producers and the consuming public. Little danger to the public health is involved by the sale of milk by unlicensed dealers, the statute itself providing that dealers who have less than 3,000 pounds of milk a month and those selling milk in any quantity in markets of 1,000 population or less, may be exempted from its requirements.

---

signifies an act which is illegal by its very nature, regardless of whether it is specifically prohibited by law (e.g., murder).

This distinguishes the case at bar from those involving health and morals. Adler v. Zimmerman, 223 N.Y. 431, 135 N.E. 840; Johnston v. Dahlgren, 166 N.Y. 354, 59 N.E. 987; Accetta v. Zupa, 54 App. Div. 33, 66 N.Y.S. 303.

We have here a statute which provides that milk dealers shall not sell milk unless duly licensed. The statute imposes penalties for its violation by way of fine and imprisonment, but it does not expressly provide that contracts made by milk dealers shall be unenforceable. Nothing in this statute reveals an implied intent to deprive unlicensed dealers of the right to recover the reasonable value of the milk sold by them, and where the wrong committed by the violation of the statute is merely *malum prohibitum*, and does not endanger health or morals, such additional punishment should not be imposed unless the legislative intent is expressed or appears by clear implication.

The judgment of the Appellate Division dismissing the complaint should be reversed, and the order of the Special Term striking out the separate defense affirmed, and the matter remanded, with costs to abide the event. CRANE, C. J., and LEHMAN, O'BRIEN, HUBBS, LOUGHRAN, and RIPPEY, JJ., concur. Judgment accordingly. ◄

COMMENTS AND QUESTIONS

1. Summarize the principal facts in this case. What was the court's decision?
2. If an unlicensed dealer is allowed to recover, as in this case, will not other dealers be encouraged to violate the licensing requirements? And might not this turn of events be injurious to the consuming public? How would the court answer these questions? How does this case differ from a case involving a contract for services with an unlicensed doctor?
3. Note that the plaintiff had violated the milk-control law by selling without a license and was guilty of a crime. Here we have a good illustration of the difference between civil and criminal law: although the plaintiff had committed a crime, he retained all his rights to enforce the very contract that constituted the crime.

Usurious Loans

In most states, interest rates on loans are strictly regulated by statute. If the lender charges interest over and above the permitted maximum rate, the contract is illegal. Most states deny the offending lender any interest whatsoever, although a few states permit him to recover the legal maximum. The collection of interest in advance is permissible if the parties agree on such an arrangement.

Sunday Contracts

Several states hold that any contract made on Sunday is illegal. The courts, however, usually enforce such a contract if the parties subsequently ratify it or indicate a willingness to be bound by it, or if they start to carry out its terms without raising any objection. Many courts do not look with favor on parties who seek to use the Sunday law as a way of avoiding an otherwise valid obligation, and they make every effort to enforce such contracts wherever possible. Take, for example, the Massachusetts case that follows:

WILLIAM MAHER v. WARREN E. HAYCOCK

Massachusetts Supreme Judicial Court, 1938
301 Mass. 594, 18 N.E. 348

► Qua, J. A real estate broker brings this action to recover a commission upon the sale of the defendant's house to one Craig. The finding of the trial judge for the plaintiff is now attacked solely upon the ground that the contract between the plaintiff and the defendant was void by reason of the provision in G.L. (Ter. Ed.) c. 136, 5, prohibiting the doing of "any manner of labor, business or work, except works of necessity and charity," on the Lord's day.

Decisive facts which either were admitted or could be found are these: On Sunday, October 31, 1937, the plaintiff went to the defendant's house, identified himself to the defendant as a real estate broker, stated to the defendant that he had a customer, and obtained the defendant's promise to pay the plaintiff "a commission if the house were sold." On the same day the plaintiff brought Craig into the house and introduced him to the defendant, and they all examined the house. The plaintiff told Craig that the price was $5,500. Thereafter negotiations took place directly between the defendant and Craig. During the week of November 7 "the defendant and Craig completed the arrangements for the sale of the property" for $5,000 with an agreement that Craig would reimburse the defendant, if the defendant should be held liable for a commission. On November 14 the property "was sold and conveyed," and the defendant gave a deed to Craig and his wife, dated that day. Both November 7 and November 14 were also Sundays.

The trial judge expressly found that "there was some preliminary discussion between the plaintiff and the defendant" on October 31, and that there was "an implied contract on the part of the defendant to pay to the plaintiff the customary commission if the house was sold to Craig." The word "sold" in this connection should not, in the absence of anything to indicate the contrary, be so strictly construed as to require that title should actually pass before the plaintiff should become entitled to a commission. It was enough if the plaintiff produced a purchaser ready, willing and able to buy on the defendant's terms. The ultimate finding for the plaintiff imports such subsidiary findings as are permissible on the evidence, are not inconsistent with express findings, and are necessary to support the conclusion. The judge must therefore be deemed to have found in accordance with the evidence that all "arrangements for the sale of the property" were completed "during the week of (Sunday) November 7," and hence that the plaintiff produced a purchaser ready, willing and able to buy on the defendant's terms before Sunday, November 14, and on a secular day. For these reasons nothing turns on the fact that the deed bore the date of Sunday, November 14.

The plaintiff is not barred because of what occurred on Sunday, October

31. No contract was made on that day. The plaintiff promised nothing, and he was entitled to nothing for his time and effort as such. The conversation between plaintiff and the defendant amounted to no more than an offer on the defendant's part which would ripen into a unilateral contract when the plaintiff produced a customer ready, willing and able. He produced such a customer on a secular day. Thus it appears that the contract sued upon was not made on Sunday and did not by its terms call for the doing of business or work on Sunday. We think the case falls within a class of cases in which it has been held that a contract not made on Sunday is not rendered void by reason of the fact that preliminary negotiations or even the offer which was later accepted took place on Sunday.

In our opinion the situation is not altered even if it be the fact that the plaintiff did nothing actively to induce Craig to buy other than what he did on Sunday, October 31. In Tuckerman v. Hinkley, 9 Allen, 452 at page 455, it is said that a contract not fully closed on Sunday "is not void, because some of its terms might have been fixed upon that day, or indeed because most of the business out of which the consideration for the contract arose was transacted on that day." Any other rule would seem to require the result that no party otherwise entitled to be paid for a completed performance, as distinguished from work, labor or services by the day, could recover anything if it should appear that he had performed on Sunday any one item in a long course of preliminaries placing him in a position finally to furnish the completed performance on a secular day. Such illegality seems too remote from the contract itself to constitute an infirmity in it. We have seen no case which goes as far as that.

It becomes unnecessary to discuss the defendant's requests for rulings in detail. Those which have been argued are, we think, either unsound or immaterial because of the findings.

The order of the Appellate Division that the finding for the plaintiff be vacated and judgment entered for the defendant is reversed, and judgment is to be entered for the plaintiff on the finding of the trial judge.

So ordered.   ◄

COMMENTS AND QUESTIONS
1. Outline the facts in this case. What was the decision of the court?
2. Would the result have been different if the plaintiff had found a buyer for the property on a Sunday? When was the contract made in this case?

Contracts in Restraint of Trade

As a general rule, a contract that tends to impose unreasonable restraint on trade or competition is deemed to be contrary to public policy and hence illegal. In certain cases, however, such restrictions are permitted. For example, when a businessman sells a going business, along with its good will, he may promise the buyer that he will not set up a competing business within a certain geographic area for a certain period of time. Since the seller is usually in a position to take his old customers with him, such an agreement is considered reasonable and necessary for the protection of the buyer and is regarded as binding on the seller. If, however, the court feels that an agreement of this sort places an unreasonable restriction on the seller, it will usually refuse to enforce the contract and leave the seller free to do as he pleases. A few state courts tend to modify such agreements to render the restriction more reasonable, on the assumption that both parties must have envisaged some sort of restraint when they entered into the original agreement. A good example of this situation follows:

GEORGETTE N. THOMAS et al. v. TOUFIK PAKER

Massachusetts Supreme Judicial Court, 1951
327 Mass. 339, 98 N.E. 2d 640

► COUNIHAN, J. This is a suit in equity in which the plaintiffs seek to enjoin the defendant from engaging in the bakery business in violation of a negative covenant [46] in a bill of sale of a bakery business given by the defendant to the plaintiffs. The evidence is not reported, but the judge made voluntary findings of facts which he adopted as findings of material facts. G.L. (Ter. Ed.) c. 214, 23, as amended.

Since the evidence is not reported, the findings of material facts, not being mutually inconsistent, are taken as true. Kennedy v. Shain, 288 Mass. 458, 459. Macklin v. Macklin, 315 Mass. 451, 452. Harpel v. Craig, ante, 229, 232. Facts admitted in the pleadings and those found by the judge are as follows: On October 15, 1949, the defendant by a bill of sale sold the plaintiffs the bakery business conducted by him at No. 136 Hudson Street, Boston, "together with good will and bakery machinery in said bakery." In this bill of sale the defendant "agrees that he will not engage in the baker business directly or indirectly for a period of seven years within a radius of seven miles of Boston." The defendant during the year 1950 entered the employ of the Boston Syrian Baking Co. in Boston as a baker at a weekly salary. There was then and is now only one other baker of handmade Syrian bread in Boston. The defendant has at no time interfered with customers of the plaintiffs by way of solicitation and has not actively participated in the management or control of his employer's business.

The judge found the limitations of seven years in time and of seven miles in area unreasonable. He found, however, it reasonable to restrict the defendant from engaging in the "baker business directly or indirectly," within a radius of four miles of No. 136 Hudson Street, Boston, for a period of four years from October 15, 1949. He further found that the defendant, in violation of this restriction, is and has been engaged in the "baker business directly or indirectly," and ordered the entry of a decree enjoining the defendant from continuing in such business. From a decree to this effect the defendant appeals. There was no error in the entry of the decree.

It is well settled that a covenant of the sort here in question may be enforced by injunction "if the interest to be protected is consonant with public policy and if the restraint is limited reasonably in time and space. What is reasonable depends upon the facts." Becker College of Business

---

[46] A covenant is an agreement. A negative covenant is merely an agreement not to do something. In this case there was an agreement by the defendant not to engage in the bakery business.

Administration & Secretarial Science v. Gross, 281 Mass. 355, 358. Here the judge found the original limitations to be unreasonable and modified them to the extent necessary to protect the plaintiffs. We are of opinion that the restrictions as modified are justifiable and enforceable. Metropolitan Ice Co. v. Ducas, 291 Mass. 403, 405. New England Tree Expert Co., Inc. v. Russell, 306 Mass. 504, 509. The principles controlling these negative covenants were recently discussed in Cedric G. Chase Photographic Laboratories, Inc. v. Hennessey, ante, 137. They are applicable here.   ◄

COMMENTS AND QUESTIONS

1. Note that the lower-court judge found the restraint in the contract to be unreasonable. In most states, this would mean that the agreement was illegal and unenforceable and that the defendant was free to ignore it. What happened in this case?
2. Do you agree with the decision here? Do you feel that a judge should be able to change an agreement in this way? Summarize the arguments for and against.
3. Note that the court issued an injunction prohibiting the defendant from continuing to work in the bakery business. For how long?

We shall have more to say about contracts in restraint of trade in Chapter 17, "Government Regulation of Business."

Effect of Illegal Agreements

If a contract is illegal, it is generally unenforceable by either side, regardless of whether one or both of the parties have fully or partially performed their obligations. Neither side may collect damages for nonperformance; nor may either sue for the return of any benefit he has conferred on the other party. In other words, the court leaves the parties exactly where it finds them.

Exceptions to General Rule

There are, however, certain exceptions to the general rule governing the effect of illegal agreements:

WHERE INJURED PARTY MEANT TO BE PROTECTED.   If the contract violates a law intended for the protection of the injured party, the courts may grant him relief.

EXAMPLE

A person who is charged and pays an excessive rate of interest on a loan may be permitted to sue for damages.

WHERE ONE PARTY IS INNOCENT.   If one party performs a contract in good faith, innocently unaware of its illegality, he is generally permitted either to recover any consideration he has paid or else avoid the contract. If a person is induced by fraud or coerced into entering into an illegal contract, of course, he may seek relief in the courts. An amusing illustration of this rule follows.

WEBB v. FULCHIRE

Supreme Court of North Carolina, 1843
25 N.C. 485

► This was an action of assumpsit, brought by the plaintiff to recover the sum of forty dollars. The jury found a verdict for the plaintiff, subject to the opinion of the court on the following facts. The defendant had three acorn cups and a white ball, which he placed under one of the cups in the presence of the plaintiff. The defendant proposed to bet the plaintiff twenty dollars, that he could not tell which one of the three cups the ball was under. The plaintiff bet him that he could, and thereupon staked twenty dollars. The plaintiff pointed to the cup, and bet that the ball was under that one. The defendant raised the cup and the ball was not there. The money staked was then paid over to the defendant as being won by him. In the same way the defendant won twenty dollars more, which was in like manner paid over to him. The court was of opinion that the plaintiff could not maintain this action, and set aside the verdict and entered a nonsuit.[47] From this judgment the plaintiff appealed.

RUFFIN, C. J.   It is not denied that the law gives no action to a party to an illegal contract, either to enforce it directly, or to recover back money paid on it after its execution. Nor is it doubted, that money, fairly lost at play at a forbidden game and paid, cannot be recovered back in an action for money had and received. But it is perfectly certain, that money, won by cheating at any kind of game, whether allowed or forbidden, and paid by the loser without a knowledge of the fraud, may be recovered. A wager won by such undue means is not won in the view of the law, and, therefore, the money is paid without consideration and by mistake, and may be recovered back. That, we think, was plainly this case. The bet was, that the plaintiff could not tell, which of the three cups covered the ball. Well, the case states that the defendant put the ball under a particular one of the cups, and, then, the plaintiff selected that cup, as the one under which the ball was. Thus we must understand the case, because it states as a fact, that the defendant "placed the ball under one of the cups," and that the plaintiff "pointed to the cup," that is, the one under which he had seen the ball put, as being that which still covered it. We are not told how this matter was managed, nor do we pretend to know the secret. But it is indubitable, that the ball was, by deceit, not put under the cup, as the defendant had made the plaintiff believe, and under which belief he had drawn him into the wager; or that, after it was so placed, it was privily and artfully removed either before or at the time the cup was raised. If the former be the truth of the case, there was a false practice and gross deception upon the very point, that induced the laying of the wager, namely, that the ball was actually put under the cup. For, clearly, the words and acts of the defendant amount to a representation, that such was the fact; and indeed the case

---

[47] A nonsuit, which terminates the plaintiff's action, is a judgment of the court that the plaintiff does not have a good case. Although the jury in this case found for the plaintiff, the trial judge felt that he was not legally entitled to judgment and therefore ordered a nonsuit. Then the plaintiff appealed.

states it as the fact. Hence, and because we cannot suppose the vision of the plaintiff to have been so illuded, we rather presume the truth to be, that the ball was actually placed where the defendant pretended to place it, that is to say, under the particular cup which the plaintiff designated as covering it. Then the case states that the defendant raised that cup, and the ball was not there; a physical impossibility, unless it had been removed by some contrivance and sleight of hand by the defendant. Unquestionably it was affected by some such means; for presently we find the defendant in possession of the ball, ready for a repetition of the bet and the same artifice. Such a transaction cannot for a moment be regarded as a wager, depending on a future and uncertain event; but it was only a pretended wager, to be determined by a contingency in shew only, but in fact by a trick in jugglery by one of the parties, practiced upon the unknowing and unsuspecting simplicity and credulity of the other. Surely, the artless fool, who seems to have been alike bereft of his senses and his money, is not to be deemed a partaker in the same crime, in *pari delicto*,[48] with the juggling knave, who gulled and fleeced him. The whole was a downright and undeniable cheat; and the plaintiff parted with his money under the mistaken belief, that it had been fairly won from him, and, therefore, may recover it back.

The judgment of nonsuit is reversed, and judgment for the plaintiff according to the verdict.

PER CURIAM.[49] *Judgment below reversed and judgment for the plaintiff.* ◀

COMMENTS AND QUESTIONS

1. The court in this case assumes that the defendant must have cheated and permits recovery. But it also says that if the money had been fairly won, the plaintiff could not have recovered it. What is the basis of the court's decision? Why would the court refuse recovery in the latter case?
2. If gambling is illegal, are not *both* parties culpable? Why should the court examine illegal transactions to see if they are "fair" and lend its assistance to one of the participants?
3. The court is obviously fascinated with the game and would like to know how the trick was done.
4. Is it not surprising that a case of this nature went all the way to the Supreme Court of North Carolina?

WHERE REPENTANCE OCCURS BEFORE ILLEGAL ACT IS PERFORMED. If a party pays a sum of money to another in exchange for a promise to perform an illegal act, and then repents and repudiates his contract before the act is performed, he is generally entitled to recover his money. The theory is that the law should encourage and aid such repentance.

WHERE CONTRACT IS ONLY PARTIALLY ILLEGAL. In an agreement that consists of several obligations, some legal and some illegal, the obligations may be separately treated. The courts may enforce the legal obligations and

---

48 This means that each party is equally at fault.
49 This means "by the court." In this context, it signifies that all the members of the court join in the decision.

refuse to enforce the illegal ones. In an agreement where the obligations cannot be separated easily the courts may hold that the entire contract is illegal and unenforceable. Wherever possible, however, they will strive to separate the legal obligations from the illegal and enforce them, the presumption being that the parties intended to act legally.

SECTION 7

CONTRACTS IN WRITING

In General

We have seen that a contract which is otherwise valid is generally enforceable whether it is in writing or not. In other words, an oral agreement is just as binding as a written one in most cases. A written contract, however, is more easily proved in court and, if it is properly drafted, clarifies the obligations of the parties and makes disputes unlikely. Clearly, then, it is wise to put important contracts in writing.

Finality of Written Contracts

Often, before a contract is actually set down in writing, the parties engage in discussions and negotiations during which they reach certain agreements on what its terms will be. Sometimes, however, they do not include all their preliminary understandings in the final written contract. Then, if a dispute arises later on, one side may try to show by oral testimony, or so-called *parol evidence*, that the prior agreement of the parties differed from the written contract. In most cases, however, the court will not admit such evidence so long as the contract has been written down in what seems to be complete form. In other words, the parties are strictly bound by the terms of the written contract, and no extraneous evidence may be introduced to contradict or modify those terms. This rule, which is called the *parol evidence rule,* rests on the assumption that either (1) no prior understanding was ever reached on the disputed point, or (2) that if such an understanding was reached, the contracting parties purposely decided not to include that term in the written contract. The written document is taken to be the full expression of their agreement. Let us consider a typical example of the parol evidence rule in action.

HAYDEN v. HOADLEY

Supreme Court of Vermont, 1920
94 Vt. 345, 111 A. 343

► Powers, J. The parties to this action exchanged properties, and as a part of the arrangement the defendants gave the plaintiffs the following writing, which all signed:

> "Memorandum of agreement made this 2d day of May, A.D. 1919, by and between Melvin A. Hoadley and George A. Peck, both of Montpelier, in the county of Washington and state of Vermont, and Howard G. and Georgia V. Hayden, both of Worcester, in the county of Washington and state of Vermont, witnesseth: We, the said Hoadley and Peck, in consideration of the said Haydens having this day conveyed to us their farm in Worcester, aforesaid, and whereas, we, the said Hoadley and Peck, have this day conveyed to the said Haydens certain land and premises situated on the westerly side of North Street in the city of Montpelier, as and for additional consideration for such exchange of properties, bind ourselves and agree to make, without expense to said Haydens, the following repairs upon the premises conveyed to the said Haydens as aforesaid, viz.: The said Hoadley and Peck agree to straighten up and shingle the barn on said premises; to straighten up the house; repair and paint the roof, and paint the same back of said house; to repair the cellar wall; and to install a pump in said house."

It is for the noncompliance with this agreement that suit is brought.

At the trial, the defendants offered to show that at the time the writing was signed it was agreed that they should have until October 1, 1919, in which to make the repairs, that only $60 need be expended therefor, and that No. 2 shingles were to be used on the barn. These offers were excluded, and the defendants excepted. The rulings were correct. The case calls for the application of a rule so often and so recently reaffirmed by this court that we need take no time in its discussion. A written contract which contains no latent ambiguity cannot be qualified, controlled, contradicted, enlarged, or diminished by any contemporaneous or antecedent understanding or agreement; and oral testimony can no more be received to vary or contradict the legal intendment of such a contract than to vary or contradict its express terms. Kinnear & Gager Mfg. Co. v. Miner, 88 Vt. 324, 98 Atl. 459; Wood v. James, 93 Vt. 36, 106 Atl. 566. The legal effect of the contract before us—it being silent as to the time of performance—was to require the repairs specified to be completed within a reasonable time. Reynolds v. Reynolds, 74 Vt. 463, 52 Atl. 1036. This is a provision of the contract implied by the law, and that which is so implied is as binding as that which is expressed. In legal consequence, then, this contract is just what it would be if it was therein expressly provided that the repairs were to be made within a reasonable time. Cooker v. Franklin, etc., Co., Fed. Cas. No. 2,932, 3 Sumn. 530; Strange v. Wilson, 17 Mich. 342. To admit the testimony offered by the defendants to the effect that the parties agreed upon October 1, as the limit of the time given for the repairs would be to allow the plain legal effect of the written contract to be controlled by oral evidence. That is not permissible. Cameron Coal &

Mercantile Co. v. Universal Metal Co., 26 Okl. 615, 110 Pac. 720. The contract before us is unequivocal and complete, and to say that parol evidence can be received to fix the time of performance, on the ground that the contract is incomplete, is wholly illogical and wrong, and so much of Dunnett & Slack v. Gibson, 78 Vt. 439, 63 Atl. 141, as to that effect is overruled. From this it is not to be inferred that we question the proposition that an incomplete writing may be supplemented by parol, for this is a rule of unquestioned soundness.

The evidence under discussion was not offered on the ground that it was admissible on the question of what was a reasonable time under the circumstance, so we give that question no attention. For the same reason, the questions asked Hayden in cross-examination regarding the understanding about the amount of money to be paid out in the repairs, and the kind of a wall that should be made, were properly excluded. The record does not show when the conversations referred to in this connection took place so in support of the ruling we assume that it was before the written contract was executed. . . .   ◀

COMMENTS AND QUESTIONS

1. Summarize the facts in this case. How did the court decide?
2. This case illustrates the application of the parol evidence rule. What evidence did the defendants offer to prove regarding the time limit for finishing the work? Why did the court exclude it?
3. The court hints (in the last paragraph) that the evidence might have been admitted if it had been offered for another purpose. What purpose? Would it have made any difference to the jury if the evidence had been admitted on the other ground?

Exceptions to Parol Evidence Rule

There are certain situations, however, in which the court will permit the parties to a written agreement to present evidence of other agreements that either contradict or supplement the terms of the written agreement:

1. Where such evidence tends to show fraud or other misconduct that might make the contract voidable.
2. Where such evidence explains or clarifies an ambiguity in the written agreement.
3. Where the court regards the written contract as incomplete.
4. Where the modification has been made *after* the written contract was signed, provided the subsequent agreement is supported by new consideration.

Interpretation of Written Contracts

In spite of the best efforts of the lawyers who draft written contracts, such contracts may still be open to conflicting interpretations. Consequently the courts are often called on to determine their meaning.[50] If the terms of the

---

[50] You will recall our discussion of statutory interpretation in Chapter 6. The courts are faced with very similar problems when they come to interpret written contracts.

contract are ambiguous, or if contingencies have arisen which the parties failed to anticipate, this may be an extremely difficult task. To help the courts discharge it with reasonable speed, certain general rules of interpretation and construction have been worked out:

1. The court always make a careful study of the individual clauses, in an effort to ascertain the true intent of the parties. If, because of mistakes in spelling or grammar, some words and phrases clearly do not reflect the true intent of the parties, the court will interpret those words or phrases in a common-sense way.

2. The court always tries to read the contract as a whole, giving proper emphasis to each part. If the contract is subject to two interpretations—one legal and the other illegal—the court will presume legality wherever possible.

3. Where conflicts exist between two or more forms of written expression, the court usually chooses what it considers the more reliable mode of expression. Thus, where a handwritten clause conflicts with a typewritten clause, the handwriting prevails. A typewritten clause prevails over a printed clause; numbers which are spelled out prevail over numerals. In such cases, it is presumed that, since greater care is taken in one case than in the other, mistakes are less likely to occur.

4. Where one of the parties has drafted the whole contract, especially if it is of the stock-form variety (for example, an insurance policy or a lease), the court will construe it strictly against that party in case of ambiguity or incompleteness. The theory here is that the other side has had little or no say in formulating its terms and should be given the benefit of any doubt.

5. The court will recognize certain implied terms in the contract if it feels that such terms are necessary, and if it is convinced that the parties themselves would have included them had they given the matter more thought. Also, where considerations of public policy are present, the court will construe the contract in that light. In other words, it will interpret the agreement in terms of its effect on the welfare of the public generally.

A good example of contract interpretation occurs in the California case that follows. This case had to do with a stock-form contract (i.e., an insurance policy); moreover, it raised issues of public policy, which the court discusses at some length.

RAYMOND H. JENSEN et al.
v. TRADERS AND GENERAL INSURANCE COMPANY

California Supreme Court, 1959
52 Cal. 2d 786, 345 P. 2d 1

► McCOMB, J. From a judgment in favor of defendant after trial before a jury in an action to recover upon an accident insurance policy, plaintiffs appeal.

Facts: On April 19, 1951, John DiMatteo signed a conditional sales contract for the purchase of a used car for his minor son, plaintiff Vincent

DiMatteo. The contract contained a request that the seller obtain insurance in a company acceptable to it and include the premiums therefor in the balance due under the contract.

Defendant, upon the request of the seller, issued its policy of public liability and property damage insurance, naming plaintiff Vincent DiMatteo and his father as insureds. The DiMatteos received the policy by mail and read it to check the coverage, but did not read the fine print. All premiums were paid from May 1951 through November 1951.

The policy contained, among others, this provision:

> "This policy may be canceled by the named insured by surrender thereof or by mailing to the company written notice stating when thereafter such cancellation shall be effective. This policy may be canceled by the company by mailing to the named insured at the address shown in the policy written notice stating when not less than five days thereafter such cancellation shall be effective. The mailing of notice as aforesaid shall be sufficient proof of notice and the effective date and hour of cancellation stated in the notice shall become the end of the policy period. Delivery of such written notice either by the named insured or by the company shall be equivalent to mailing."

On August 10, 1951, two separate notices of cancellation of the policy were placed in the mail, one addressed to plaintiff Vincent DiMatteo and the other to his father. Neither of these letters was ever returned to defendant's office. Both DiMatteos testified that no cancellation notices were ever received by them and that they had no knowledge of any cancellation until November 1951.

On November 15, 1951, Vincent had an automobile accident, in which plaintiffs Jensen and Morrow were injured. A few days later, Vincent and his father learned that the policy had been canceled.

Plaintiffs Jensen and Morrow filed an action against Vincent and served him with summons and complaint. The DiMatteos retained Attorney Bernard Mendel to represent them. He made demand upon defendant by telephone to defend the action and later sent a copy of the complaint and summons to defendant with a further demand to defend, which was refused. A judgment in the sum of $10,000 was entered against Vincent in favor of plaintiffs Jensen and Morrow.

The present action was then filed against defendant predicated upon the insurance policy that it had issued. After trial, a verdict was returned in favor of plaintiffs, but the judgment rendered thereon was reversed on appeal. (Jensen v. Traders & General Ins. Co., 141 Cal. App. 2d 162, 296 P. 2d 434.) After a second trial before a jury, a judgment in favor of defendant was entered. Plaintiffs appeal, urging that it was error for the trial court to give this instruction to the jury:

> "When a policy of insurance provides as in this case that the policy may be cancelled by the company by mailing to the insured at the address shown on the policy a written notice stating when, not less than five days thereafter, such cancellation shall become effective and further provides that the mailing of such notice shall be sufficient proof of notice it is not necessary that the notice so mailed shall be received

by the insured in order to be effective. If you find that the defendant Traders and General Insurance Company mailed a notice of cancellation to John and Vincent DiMatteo they have done everything which the policy and the law requires of them and the policy ceased to remain in effect after the date specified in said notice regardless of whether or not the DiMatteos or either of them ever actually received such notice."

Questions: First. Is the standard cancellation clause set forth, *supra*, which provides that cancellation may be effected by mailing notice, (a) ambiguous and/or (b) contrary to the public policy of the State of California?

It is . . . settled that in the construction of a contract, the office of the court is simply to ascertain and declare what, in terms or in substance, is contained therein, and not to insert what has been omitted or omit what has been inserted. (Code Civ. Proc. 1858)

This rule is applicable to insurance contracts, as was pointed out by Mr. Justice Spence, speaking for this court, in New York Life Ins. Co. v. Hollender, 38 Cal. 2d 73, 81 (7), (237 P. 2d 510), where he stated: "In construing life insurance policies as in the construction of other contracts, the entire contract is to be construed together for the purpose of giving force and effect to each clause. [Citations.] While it is settled law that in case of doubt the provisions of the insurance contract will be construed most strongly against the insurer [Citations], the rule is equally well established that where the terms of the policy are plain and explicit, the court will indulge in no forced construction so as to cast a liability upon the insurance company which it has not assumed. [Citations.]"

(a) The cancellation clause in the instant case is clear and unambiguous: it means exactly what it says. It provides that the company may cancel the insurance by mailing at least a five-day notice to the insured at the address he has given the company. It expressly provides that such mailing shall be sufficient proof of notice and that the effective date stated therein shall become the end of the policy period.

It is to be noted that the clause further provides that "delivery" of such cancellation notice shall be equivalent to mailing, thus making it clear that there are two methods of canceling the policy, one by mailing, and the other by delivering, notice of cancellation to the insured.

The clause is mutually available on the same terms to both parties to the policy. The unrestricted privilege of cancellation by either side exists for the benefit of the insured, whose interest in the covered property or need for protection may cease during the policy period, as well as for the benefit of the insurer.

It is, of course, conceded that the Legislature, by statute, may prescribe that receipt of the notice is required for effective cancellation of an insurance policy. No such statute has existed, or now exists, in this state. . . .

(b) The cancellation clause here involved is not opposed to the public policy of the State of California. The determination of public policy of states resides, first, with the people as expressed in their Constitution and, second, with the representatives of the people—the state legislature.

This court well expressed the rule in Stephen v. Southern Pacific Co.,

109 Cal. 86, 89; 41 P. 783, as follows: "It has been well said that public policy is an unruly horse astride of which you are carried into unknown and uncertain paths, and here that horse would be carrying us beyond all limits ever reached before, if respondent's position should meet with our approval. While contracts opposed to morality or law should not be allowed to show themselves in courts of justice, yet public policy requires and encourages the making of contracts by competent parties upon all valid and lawful considerations, and courts so recognizing have allowed parties the widest latitude in this regard; and, unless it is entirely plain that a contract is violative of sound public policy, a court will never so declare." . . .

In Spangenberg v. Spangenberg, 19 Cal. App. 439, 446, (126 P. 379), the court said: "It is to the interest of the public generally that the right to make contracts should not be unduly restricted, and no agreement will be pronounced void as being against public policy unless it clearly contravenes that which has been declared by statutory enactment or by judicial decisions to be public policy, or unless the agreement manifestly tends in some way to injure the public."

In Superior Insurance Co. v. Restituto, 124 F Supp. 392, the District Court for the Southern District of California, at page 395 (2,3), said: "Parties to a contract may contract on such method of giving notice as they desire and unless public policy is contravened, the contract should be enforced as made. The use of the mails has become too well integrated into our economic and business life for such a public policy question to concern us. We conclude the notice by mail under the clause in question effected a termination even though the notice was never received by the insured."

In other states the courts have held that the standard clause here in question has been found free from criticism on the ground that it was against public policy. . . .

The Wisconsin Supreme Court in Putman v. Deinhamer, 270 Wis. 157 (70 N.W. 2d 652, 654), said: "As far as we have discovered from a search of the authorities, the insurer has been held to a strict compliance with the policy terms of cancellation and a slight deviation invalidates the notice sent and attempted cancellation. But we do not find from such authorities that when the policy terms are as they are here, and there is no conflicting statute, and the notice and its mailing complies with the policy provisions, the courts have refused to recognize the cancellation."

A practical consideration of the problem here presented discloses that the conclusions which we have reached are fair to both the insured and the insurer, if either desires to cancel an insurance policy.

The practice and custom of granting coverage immediately upon the request of insurance agents and brokers, leaving all opportunity to examine the acceptability of the insured to a future date is an advantage to the business community and to the motoring public.

If insurers cannot cancel coverage in an equally prompt and certain manner, they will be forced to withhold this advantage. This raises the question whether more drivers would be uninsured because their financial and driving responsibility could not be investigated in time than would have been uninsured if immediate coverage were granted and cancellation ensued.

Insurance companies have endeavored to insure rapidly and provide for a concomitant prompt and certain method of cancellation. If the insured has drifted away without leaving an adequate address of his whereabouts and the insurer is compelled to accomplish delivery of notice, the insurer may have the hard choice of leaving the policy in force or of spending more to locate the insured than the premium owed or collected.

To require the insurer to prove receipt of a letter mailed or fail in its defense of cancellation would be to compel the proof of an act accomplished, under secret circumstances, all the facts of which are in the possession of a reluctant opponent. The result would be extreme commercial uncertainty if delivery were to be a *sine qua non*. The insured who moves away or leaves on vacation can arrange for the forwarding of his mail; the insurer cannot do this for him if he fails.

If actual delivery were a prerequisite, these questions would arise: When is the policy canceled if the insured receives it in due course of the mail? When is the policy canceled if he receives it after more than the 10-day period prescribed in the notice? As of what date is he entitled to proration of the premium in either instance? What if the insured receives it and does not read it? What equities exist in favor of the insurer when the insured has purposely or inadvertently failed to communicate his new address?

If it is determined that a need exists for amendment of section 651 of the Insurance Code to correct supposed abuses, the Legislature is the proper forum for the determination of the means to be adopted, not the courts. In its deliberations, the Legislature can more broadly study the public welfare. The state, through its Insurance Commission, can be heard as can the varied interests of other segments of the public and affected industries. Such sources of information are not available to the judiciary.   ◄

COMMENTS AND QUESTIONS

1. Outline the principal facts here. What was the decision of the court?
2. This decision illustrates the care with which courts interpret stock-form written contracts such as insurance policies. In this case, the court felt that the clause in question was not ambiguous and enforced it according to its plain meaning. Does this mean that any provision which is clearly stated will be enforced? What if the policy had provided that cancellation could be effected by publishing a notice in a local paper?
3. Note that this case was finally decided eight years after the accident in question!
4. Don't you feel a little sorry for the plaintiffs here? Summarize in your own words the practical and commercial considerations which the court outlined in support of this decision.

Contracts That Require a Written Memorandum

The Statute of Frauds

Long ago in legal history, lawyers and judges decided that certain types of contract were so important that they should be put in writing if they were to be binding on the parties. To make all oral contracts enforceable would be to invite fraud and perjury and expose innocent parties to irreparable harm. Consequently the Statute of Frauds was enacted in England in 1677. The general provisions of this statute were brought over to the North American colonies and were eventually incorporated into the laws of almost every one of the United States.

The statute provides that certain kinds of contract are not enforceable unless there is a written memorandum or other written document signed by the party who is being asked to carry out its terms. In other words, before one side can compel the other to perform such a contract he must produce a written memorandum of the agreement signed by the other party. As we shall see shortly, it is not necessary that *both* sides sign the memorandum.

The Statute of Frauds applies only to the enforcement of executory contracts, however (see page 207). If both parties have fully performed an agreement, the courts regard it as binding and will not undo it. Although the law differs somewhat from state to state, the following categories of contract generally come under the protection of the statute.

CONTRACTS THAT REQUIRE MORE THAN ONE YEAR TO PERFORM. If performance of a contract cannot be fully completed within one year after it is made, neither side is required to carry it out unless he has signed a written memorandum as evidence of the contract. If it is at all possible to complete performance within a year, however, even if the possibility is very unlikely, this rule does not apply. For example, if completion of performance is conditional on some event that may possibly occur within the one-year period, the contract may be enforced even in the absence of a signed memorandum. The one-year period commences at the time the contract is made rather than at the start of performance. Also, if one party fully performs an agreement that requires more than one year to complete, and if the other side accepts the benefit of his performance, the contract becomes binding.

EXAMPLES

1. On March 1, JANITOR enters into a contract to work for BOSS for one year starting March 15. This contract requires a signed memorandum before it can be enforced. If the contract is for a ten-month period starting March 15, however, it would not be within the statute and would not have to be in writing. If JANITOR agreed to work for ten months starting May 15, the contract would have to be in writing, since performance would not be completed until March 15 of the following year.

2. If H orally agrees to work as a housekeeper for E until E dies or gets married, the contract is outside the statute and is enforceable even in the absence of a written memorandum; here completion of performance is *possible* within a year, even though it may be unlikely.

CONTRACTS FOR SALE OF REAL PROPERTY. Contracts for the sale of real estate must usually be evidenced by a written memorandum. Since transactions of this sort are of vital importance to the parties, the law requires that they must be attended by certain formalities. Most states extend the protection of the Statute of Frauds not only to the actual sale of land but to mortgages and long-term leases.

An exception to the general rule is sometimes recognized where a party occupies real property under an oral agreement and makes substantial changes or alterations in the property. If the court feels that avoidance of the agreement would work a great hardship on the occupying party, it will enforce the oral contract. This exception is made only rarely, however.

CONTRACTS OF GUARANTY. In a contract of guaranty, one party promises the other that he will be responsible for the debts or obligations of a third person. Contracts of this sort usually come under the Statute of Frauds and cannot be enforced unless the party making the promise signs a written memorandum as evidence of his commitment. This rule does not apply, however, to a situation where the promisor agrees to be solely responsible for the debt in the first place and it is understood that the third party is not liable for payment of the debt.

> EXAMPLES
>
> 1. P orally promises c that if c sells a car to d on credit, he will pay c what d owes if d fails or neglects to make payment. This is a contract of guaranty and is not enforceable unless P signs a written memorandum.
> 2. P orally tells c, "Sell the car to d and send the bill to me." Such a promise is binding even though it is not in writing, since it is understood that P is to be solely responsible for payment.

In the following case, which was decided by the Vermont Supreme Court, the defendant alleged that she was not required to perform the contract of guaranty since there was nothing in writing. The plaintiff, on the other hand, argued that the defendant had made a direct promise to pay and let it be understood that she was to be solely responsible for the debt. Let us see how the controversy was resolved.

LAWRENCE v. ANDERSON

Supreme Court of Vermont, 1936
108 Vt. 176, 184 Atl. 689

► Action by A. B. Lawrence against Lillian V. Anderson, Judgment for the defendant and plaintiff excepts.

Affirmed.

POWERS, CHIEF JUSTICE. Answering an emergency call from an unknown source, the plaintiff, licensed physician, administered to John Anderson, who had suffered severe injuries in an automobile accident somewhere on the "Williston Road" outside of the city of Burlington. This was on October 1, 1933. When the plaintiff arrived at the scene of the accident, he found there the defendant, a daughter of the injured man; and when he had introduced himself to her, she directed him as he testified, to "do everything you can under the sun to see this man is taken care of." Thereupon, the plaintiff called an ambulance, in which Anderson was taken to a hospital where the plaintiff treated him until the next morning, when he was discharged by the defendant after she had conferred with her father about it. The plaintiff made his charges for services to Mr. Anderson, and sent bills to his estate. He engaged a Burlington lawyer to proceed against the estate, for the collection of his charges, and some effort in that direction was made, but nothing came of it. About a year after the accident, the plaintiff began sending bills to Anderson's widow, but nothing came from that. Finally, about a year and a half after the accident, this suit was brought. It was returnable to the Chittenden municipal court, and there tried to a jury. At the close of the plaintiff's evidence, on motion therefor, a verdict was ordered for the defendant. The plaintiff excepted.

It is apparent that the facts above stated, standing alone, did not make a case for the jury; and if nothing more had been shown the judgment would have to be affirmed. For it fully appears that the defendant's relations with her father were such that she was not liable for the plaintiff's services unless she became so by reason of what she said or did. The rule is fully established that one who merely calls a physician to render services to another is not liable therefor in the absence of an express agreement, unless he is legally bound to furnish such service, as it is a fair inference from the evidence that it was the intention of both parties that he should pay for it. The services here sued for were not, so far as the above recited facts show, beneficial, in a legal sense, to the defendant and she would not be liable therefor. Smith v. Watson, 14 Vt. 332, 337.

But in addition to what has been recited, one Charles Brown, who was at the scene of the accident when the plaintiff arrived there, testified that in his presence the defendant said to the plaintiff, "I want my father taken care of, and give him the best care you can give him, and what the charges are . . . I will pay for it."

Ordinarily, this statement might make an entirely different case for the plaintiff. It shows that the defendant not only requested the services, but also that she made a direct promise to pay the plaintiff. Such a promise is not collateral or secondary, but primary and original. It comes within the law as laid down in Pocket v. Almon, 90 Vt. 10, 96 A. 421, and Enos v. Owens Slate Co., 104 Vt. 329, 150 A. 185. To such a contract the statute of frauds (P. L. 1675) does not apply, for the simple reason that it is not a promise to pay the debt of another, but is a promise to pay the debt of the promisor—one that he makes his own by force of his engagement.

But before we can apply this rule to the case in hand, we must consider the effect of the plaintiff's conduct.

When the defendant made the promise that Brown testified to, the plaintiff was at liberty to accept it and to rely upon it. But he was not obliged to do so. He could, if he choose, treat Anderson on his own credit. But he could not hold both Anderson and the defendant. If he gave the credit to Anderson, he could not hold the defendant, though she had tendered an engagement direct, in form. The plaintiff could not turn the defendant's sole obligation into a joint obligation without her concurrence. If he gave any credit to Anderson, he elected to accept the defendant's engagement as collateral to that of Anderson. Of course it is only where the promise sued on is primary and direct that this question we are now discussing arises. 27 C.J. p. 42. But in such cases, the extension of any credit to the third party involved requires a written promise on the part of the promisor. Blodget v. Town of Lowell, 33 Vt. 174, 175, 176.

As we have seen, it appears here that the plaintiff made his original charges against Anderson. Such a fact is not always conclusive evidence of the person who is to be regarded as the original debtor. It is subject to explanation, to be sure, Greene v. Burton and Sowles, 59 Vt. 423, 425; 10 A. 575, but to rebut the inference arising from the fact that the charges were so made, the proof must be of a strong character. Hardman v. Bradley, 85 Ill. 162. As we said in Enos v. Owens Slate Co., 104 Vt. 329, 333; 160 A. 185, the quality of a defendant's promise may usually be found by ascertaining whether the third person continues to be liable after the defendant's oral promise is made. In that case, it did not appear that the original charges for the services rendered by the plaintiff were made against the third person; and the plaintiff explained why he attempted to collect his pay from such person. Here no explanation is made or attempted. No reason is given, why these charges were made against Anderson. So it must be taken that it was because the plaintiff considered him responsible therefor. Lomax v. McKinney, 61 Ind. 374; Langdon v. Richardson, 58 Iowa 610, 12 N.W. 622. Having given credit to Anderson, the plaintiff cannot collect from the defendant. There being no error in the ruling on the motion for a verdict, there is no occasion to consider the other exceptions argued.

Judgment affirmed.   ◄

COMMENTS AND QUESTIONS

1. Summarize the principal facts in this case. For whom did the court find?
2. If Dr. Lawrence had billed the defendant and had brought suit against her at the very beginning, would he have won the case?
3. What provision of the Statute of Frauds was applied here? Do you think the result was fair?
4. What happened in the lower court? Was the case actually tried before a jury?

CONTRACTS IN CONSIDERATION OF MARRIAGE. Sometimes one person promises to do something for another if the other person marries or agrees to marry some third person. Here the promisor is not required to carry out his promise unless he signs a memorandum. This rule does not apply, however, if the promise is made between the two parties who are going to be married.

EXAMPLES

1. P orally promises A that he will give A an antique clock if A marries B. The promise is not enforceable unless P signs a memorandum.
2. A orally promises B that he will give B a clock if B marries him. The promise is enforceable even though it is not in writing.

Nature of Written Memorandum

To satisfy the Statute of Frauds (that is, to make the types of contract listed above enforceable), a written note, memorandum, or other writing must be produced. This memorandum must:

1. Describe the subject matter of the contract.
2. Identify the parties.
3. Name the consideration.
4. Specify any other important terms of the contract.

As we noted previously, this written evidence makes the agreement enforceable *only* against the party, or parties, who have signed it. It may consist of several documents—a series of letters, perhaps—which can be read together as evidence of one contract. The writing need not be in existence at the time the contract is made, but it must exist before any suit can be brought to enforce the contract. The signature of the party need not be a formal one, nor need it appear at the end of the memorandum. It must simply appear somewhere in the memorandum and it must be clearly identifiable.

> **E X A M P L E**
>
> w orally agrees to work as a gardener for e for a period of two years. Before starting to work, e sends w a signed confirmatory letter outlining the terms of the agreement in full. w does not reply. The contract is enforceable by w against e but *not* by e against w, since the writing is signed only by e and since there is no memorandum signed by w.

Contracts for the Sale of Personal Property

In addition to the classes of contract outlined above, the Statute of Frauds also applies to contracts for the sale of personal property at a price beyond a certain amount. (This minimum figure ranges from $30 in one state to $2,500 in another; $500 is the most common.) If the contract price is below this minimum amount, the agreement is binding even though it does not exist in writing. If the price is higher than the minimum amount, the contract is enforceable only if:

1. There is a sufficient written memorandum signed by the party to be charged; *or*
2. The buyer consents to accept the goods and actually takes delivery of at least a part of them; *or*
3. The buyer makes part payment for the goods.

In other words, contracts of this sort, unlike the other categories covered by the Statute, are enforceable if *any one* of these three factors is present.

The part of the statute dealing with sales of personal property does not apply to articles which are to be specially manufactured by the seller for the buyer, even if the price exceeds the minimum amount. On the other hand, if the article is regularly produced or manufactured and is readily salable, the Statute of Frauds must be complied with before the contract becomes enforceable.

> **E X A M P L E**
>
> CARPENTER orally agrees to build a special dining-room table for HOMEOWNER for $3,000. The contract is enforceable. If, however, HOMEOWNER orally orders a dining-room table for the same price from a store which

carries that type of table regularly, or if the table is regularly produced by a furniture manufacturer, the contract is not enforceable unless the statute is complied with—i.e., unless one of the three factors listed above is present.

In the South Carolina case that follows, several problems arose concerning the application of the Statute of Frauds to a sales contract. The members of the court split, and there was a dissenting opinion.

LOUISVILLE ASPHALT VARNISH CO.
v. LORICK & LOWRANCE

Supreme Court of South Carolina, 1888
29 S.C. 533, 8 S.E. 8

▶ McIver, J.   This was an action to recover the sum of $83.05, the price of certain varnish and paint alleged to have been sold by plaintiff to defendants. The defense was a general denial. At the trial the plaintiff offered testimony tending to show that on the 16th October, 1885, one of its traveling salesmen, Hutchinson by name, took from Moore, a clerk of the defendants, who, it was admitted, had authority to give the order, a verbal order for the articles specified in the account sued on, which Hutchinson immediately entered in his memorandum book as follows:

> "No. 65   Columbia, S.C. Oct. 16, 1885
> "Louisville Asphalt Varnish Co., Louisville, Ky., Ship Lorick & Lowrance, Columbia, S.C.:
>
> 1. Bbl. No. 1 Turpt. Asphalt Black Varnish .... 55¢
> 1. "   D. Roof Paint C .... 50¢
> 12. 5 gall. Pails D. Roof, do .... 55¢
> "Cr. by 2¢ gal., on acct. freight.
> "60 days.
>
>   H. L. Hutchinson, Salesman."

On the same day, a copy of this order was sent by mail, by said salesman, to the plaintiff, who received it on the 19th October, 1885, and on the next day shipped the goods, by rail, to defendants. On the 17th October, 1885, the defendants wrote to plaintiff as follows: "Louisville Asphalt Varnish Co., Louisville—Gents: Don't ship paint ordered through your salesman. We have concluded not to handle it." This letter, however, was not received by plaintiff until after the goods had been shipped; and upon its receipt plaintiff wrote defendants, saying "that shipment had gone before the request to cancel was received." When the goods arrived in Columbia, the defendants declined to receive them, but what became of them the testimony does not show. At the close of plaintiff's testimony, defendants moved for a nonsuit, which was granted, upon the ground that section 2020, Gen. St., (Statute of Frauds,) was fatal to a recovery. Plaintiff appeals, upon the several grounds set out in the record which make these two questions: First, whether there was such a note or memorandum in writing of the bargain as would satisfy the requirements of section 2020 of the General Statutes; second, if not, whether there was such an acceptance and actual receipt of the goods as would take the case out of the operation of that section.

It is quite certain that there was no formal agreement in writing, signed by the parties to be charged, for the sale of the goods in question, and we think it equally certain that there was no single instrument or memorandum in writing sufficient to satisfy the requirements of the statute; for the letter of the defendants, copied above, did not specify the necessary particulars as to quantity, nature, and price of the goods which were the subjects of the alleged contract of sale, and the copy of the order sent by the salesman to the plaintiff, which did contain all the necessary particulars, was not signed by the defendants. It is plain, therefore, that neither one of these papers, standing alone, would be sufficient. But as it is well settled that the whole agreement need not appear in a single writing, but may be made out from several instruments or written memoranda referring one to the other, and which, when connected together, are found to contain all the necessary elements, the precise practical question in this case is whether the letter of defendants can be connected with the written order sent by the salesman, so that the two together may constitute a sufficient note or memorandum in writing to satisfy the requirements of the statute.

It seems to us, therefore, that the letter of defendants, taken, as it must be, in connection with the order sent to plaintiff by the salesman, to which it expressly referred, and which was in writing, and specified all the necessary particulars to price, quantity, quality, and time of payment, constituted a sufficient note or memorandum in writing of the bargain to take the case out of the statute of frauds. In the absence of any evidence that any other order was given, the language of the letter—"Don't ship paint ordered through your salesman"—must necessarily be regarded as referring to the order of which a memorandum in writing was taken at the time by the salesman, and a copy thereof immediately forwarded to the plaintiff, who at once filled the order, and shipped the goods to the defendants. . . . The only necessity for any parol evidence at all, if, indeed, there was any, was to identify the order sent by the salesman, and for this purpose, as we have seen, such evidence would be competent. Suppose the plaintiff had, on the 16th October, 1885, written a letter to defendants, proposing to sell them the articles mentioned in the salesman's order, in the quantities there stated, and at the prices and on the time there mentioned, and that defendants had replied by letter, simply saying "I accept your offer," without repeating the particulars as to quantity, price, etc., it could not be doubted that, although defendants' letter—the only paper which they signed—did not contain in itself the necessary particulars of the bargain, yet the two letters, taken together, would be held a sufficient compliance with the statute. It seems to us that the transaction here in question was in principle practically the same as that in the supposed case, and we think there was error in holding that the contract sued on was void under the statute of frauds.

We do not see how it is possible to regard the letter of the defendants as a denial of the order given to the salesman by their clerk, Moore, who, it was conceded had authority to give the order. . . . The manifest purpose of that letter was to countermand the order, and this necessarily presupposed that the order had been given. The terms used clearly show this: "Don't ship the paint ordered through your salesman. We have concluded not to handle it." This clearly means that the paint had been ordered, but that the defendants had subsequently changed their minds and "concluded not to handle it"; and we don't see how it can be construed to mean anything else. We have then an admission in writing that an order for the goods in question through the salesman, had been given, and we have the order referred to, likewise in writing, and the two together fully satisfy the requirements of the statute. Under the view which we have taken of the first question raised by this appeal, the second question becomes immaterial, and need not, therefore, be considered.

The judgment of this court is that the judgment of the circuit court be reversed, and that the case be remanded to that court for a new trial.

SIMPSON, C. J. (dissenting). . . . The rule upon this subject, as will be seen from its discussion by Mr. Chitty, 11th ed., 544 et seq., and the cases there cited in notes, seems to be this: The letter relied on must in itself contain the terms of the contract, quantity, quality, and price of the goods, etc., or it must refer to some other paper containing them in such a way as by its own terms to connect itself with said paper. Now the letter here might possibly be construed as an admission by the defendants that they had ordered certain paints from the plaintiff, and that since said order they had concluded not to take said goods. But there is nothing in this letter which points distinctly to the contract sued on. It could as well apply to any other contract as this, and therefore a most important link is wanting, which could be supplied only by verbal testimony. If the case had gone to the jury, there was no testimony by which the memorandum made by plaintiff's salesman could have been connected with defendants' letter. It was said in Waterman v. Meigs, 4 Cush. Mass. 497, "that a letter from the purchaser to the vendor, alluding to a parol agreement for the sale of goods, and inquiring whether they will be ready at the time agreed upon, but not mentioning the quantity, quality, or price of the goods, or the time of payment, is not a sufficient memorandum to take the agreement out of the statute of frauds." See, also, Salmon Falls Manufacturing Co. v. Goddard, 14 How. 446, 14 L. Ed. 493; Bailey v. Ogden, 3 Johns, N.Y. 399. We think there was an absence of all testimony connecting defendants' letter distinctly and clearly with the memorandum made by plaintiff's agent, and sent by him as an order for the goods, so that the two would constitute one memorandum in writing, signed by the defendants; and, the letter itself failing to embody the contract as to quantity, quality, and price of goods, the nonsuit was inevitable. Thus far it has been admitted that the letter of defendants, impliedly, at least, acknowledged an order for paints, but there is great doubt whether such is a proper construction of said letter. It may well be construed as a denial of the order. This view strengthens the conclusions we have reached.

Judgment reversed.

COMMENTS AND QUESTIONS

1. Outline the facts in this case. What was the principal issue before the court?
2. At the close of the plaintiff's testimony in the trial court, the defendants moved for a nonsuit. How did the trial judge rule on the motion and what was the basis for his ruling?
3. What did the majority of the Supreme Court of South Carolina decide? What was the basis of the decision? What order did the court make with respect to the case?
4. Note the opinion of the dissenting judge. Do you agree or disagree with his conclusions? Do you think a contract such as this should be enforceable between businessmen?

SECTION 8

ASSIGNMENT OF CONTRACTUAL RIGHTS AND DUTIES— THIRD-PARTY BENEFICIARIES

In General

Although most contracts are made between two persons or firms, a third party sometimes enters the picture. One party, for example, may assign his right to receive performance to some other person, or he may delegate to a third person his duty to perform. Or he may even assign the whole contract, including all his rights and duties. Some contracts are made for the benefit of a third party at the very outset. In this section, we will discuss the rights and liabilities of third persons in these situations.

Assignment of Rights and Delegation of Duties

Nature and Form of Assignment

An assignment occurs when one party transfers all, or part, of his rights under a contract to a third person. The party who makes the assignment is called the *assignor;* the party who receives the assigned rights is called the *assignee;* the party who must perform the contractual obligation is referred to as the *obligor.*

EXAMPLE

WORKER performs services for EMPLOYER under a contract and has $100 coming to him in payment for those services. WORKER assigns his right to receive the money to the bank as security for a loan.

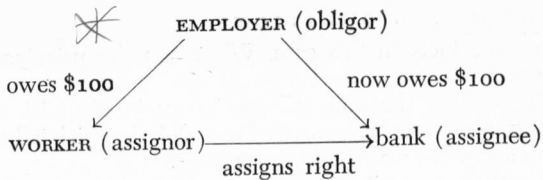

Any words or conduct that give evidence of a clear intention to transfer a contractual right constitute an assignment. Generally speaking, no written evidence is necessary, although important assignments should be put in writing. No consideration is necessary to make a binding assignment, but the assignor may usually revoke or rescind an assignment without consideration simply by giving notice to the obligor or assignee any time before the contract has been performed. If, however, the assignment is supported by consideration, it is binding on both sides and is irrevocable just like any other contract.

Rights That May Be Assigned

Almost any contract right is assignable, so long as the two contracting parties agree to the assignment. Even if the obligor objects, the assignor can go right ahead and assign his contract rights, except in the following situations:

1. Where the right involves the performance of some personal service or has to do with matters of personal credit, trust, or confidence.
2. Where performance by the obligor would be substantially changed by the assignment.
3. Where the terms of the contract or some statute expressly forbid assignment.

EXAMPLES
1. A right to the services of an employee may not be assigned.
2. The right of x, in Boston, to have a piano delivered to him by a Boston store may not be assigned to y in San Francisco, since the assignment would materially alter the store's performance. The store would not be obligated to deliver the piano to y and could refuse to honor the assignment.

Assignability of Right to Receive Money

Generally speaking, a right to receive money under an existing contract is freely assignable. This is true even though the money is not yet due. However, an assignment of a future right to money is not valid if no contract has been entered into. Many states restrict the right of an employee to assign future wages under an employment contract to a maximum percentage (often 25 per cent), and hold that any attempt to assign more than that is not enforceable.

Delegation of Duties

In certain cases, a contracting party may get someone else to perform his obligation for him. This is called a *delegation of duties*. As a general rule, any contractual duty may be delegated so long as its performance is routine in nature and may be carried out just as well by one person as another. If the obligation is personal in nature, however, or if it involves special skill, confidence, or trust, or if the contract expressly prohibits delegation, no delegation is permitted.

EXAMPLES

1. A duty to sell a certain quantity of wheat is probably delegatable, since a third person could perform the duty just as well as the original obligor.

2. A duty to serve as cook and housekeeper for someone may not be delegated, since performance involves personal skill and taste, which differ from one person to another.

A good discussion of delegation of duties is found in the English case that follows. Note the fine distinctions which the court makes and the care it takes in arriving at its decision.

THE BRITISH WAGGON CO. and the PARKGATE WAGGON CO. v. LEA & CO.

Queen's Bench Division, 1880
5 Q.B.D. 149

▶ COCKBURN, C. J. This was an action brought by the plaintiffs to recover rent for the hire of certain railway waggons, alleged to be payable by the defendants to the plaintiffs, or one of them, under the following circumstances:

By an agreement in writing of February 10, 1874, the Parkgate Waggon Company let to the defendants, who are coal merchants, fifty railway waggons for a term of seven years, at a yearly rent of £100 a year, payable by equal, quarterly payments. By a second agreement of June 13th, 1874, the company in like manner let to the defendants fifty other waggons, at a yearly rent of £625, payable quarterly like the former.

Each of these agreements contained the following clause: "The owners, their executors, or administrators, will at all times during the said term, except as herein provided, keep the said waggons in good and substantial repair and working order, and, on receiving notice from the tenant of any want of repairs, and the number or numbers of the waggons requiring to be repaired, and the place or places where it or they is or are, will, with all reasonable despatch, cause the same to be repaired and put into good working order."

On October 24th, 1874, the Parkgate Company passed a resolution, under the 129th section of the Companies Act, 1862, for the voluntary winding up of the company. Liquidators were appointed, and by an order of the Chancery Division of the High Court of Justice, it was ordered that the winding up on the company should be continued under the supervision of the court.

By an indenture of April 1st, 1878, the Parkgate Company assigned and transferred, and the liquidators confirmed to the British Company and their assigns, among other things, all sums of money, whether payable by way of rent, hire, interest, penalty, or damage, then due, or thereafter to become due, to the Parkgate Company, by virtue of the two contracts, and all the interest of the Parkgate Company and the said liquidators therein: the British Company, on the other hand covenanting with the Parkgate Company "to observe and perform such of the stipulations, conditions, provisions, and agreements contained in the said contracts, as, according to the terms thereof were stipulated to be observed and performed by the Parkgate Company." On the execution of this assignment the British Company took over from the Parkgate Company the repairing stations, which had previously been used by the Parkgate Company for the repair of the waggons let to the defendants, and also the staff of workmen employed by the latter company in executing such repairs. It was expressly found that the British Company have ever since been ready and willing to execute, and have, with all due diligence, executed all necessary repairs to the said waggons. . . .

The main contention on the part of the defendants, however, was that, as the Parkgate Company had, by assigning the contracts, and by making over their repairing stations to the British Company, incapacitated themselves to fulfil their obligation to keep the waggons in repair, that company had no right, as between themselves and the defendants, to substitute a third party to do the work they had engaged to perform, nor were the defendants bound to accept the party so substituted as the one to whom they were to look for performance of the contract; the contract was therefore at an end.

The authority principally relied on in support of this contention was the case of Robson v. Drummond, 2 B. & Ad. 303, approved by this court in Humble v. Hunter, 12 Q.B. 310. In Robson v. Drummond a carriage having been hired by the defendant of one Sharp, a coachmaker, for five years, at a yearly rent payable in advance each year, the carriage to be kept in repair and painted once a year by the maker—Robson being then a partner in the business, but unknown to the defendant—on Sharp retiring from the business after three years had expired, and making over all interest in the business and property in the goods to Robson, it was held, that the defendant could not be sued on the contract—by Lord Tenterden—on the ground that "the defendant might have been induced to enter into the contract by reason of the personal confidence which he reposed in Sharp, and therefore have agreed to pay money in advance, for which reason the defendant had a right to object to its being performed by any other person"; and by Littlefield and Parke, J. J. on the additional ground that the defendant had a right to the personal services of Sharp, and to the benefit of his judgment and taste, to the end of the contract.

In like manner, where goods are ordered of a particular manufacturer, another, who has succeeded to his business, cannot execute the order, so as to bind the customer, who has not been made aware of the transfer of the business, to accept the goods. The latter is entitled to refuse to deal with any other than the manufacturer whose goods he intended to buy. For this Boulton v. Jones, 2 H. & N. 564, is a sufficient authority. The case of Robson v. Drummond comes nearer to the present case, but is, we think, distinguishable from it. We entirely concur in the principle on which the decision in Robson v. Drummond rests, namely, that where a person contracts with another to do work or perform service, and it can be inferred that the person employed has been selected with reference to his individual skill, competency, or other personal qualification, the inability or unwillingness of the party so employed to execute the work or perform the service is a sufficient answer to any demand by a stranger to the original contract of the performance of it by the other party and entitled the latter to treat the contract as at an end, notwithstanding that the person tendered to take the place of the contracting party may be equally well qualified to do the service. Personal performance is in such a case of the essence of the contract, which, consequently, cannot in its absence be enforced against an unwilling party. But this principle appears to us inapplicable in the present instance, inasmuch as we cannot suppose that in stipulating for the repair of these waggons by the company—a rough description of work which ordinary workmen conversant with the business would be perfectly able to execute—the defendants attached any importance to whether the repairs were done by the company, or by any one with whom the company might enter into a subsidiary contract to do the work. All that the hirers, the defendants, cared for in this stipulation was that the waggons should be kept in repair; it was indifferent to them by whom the repairs should be done. Thus if, without going into liquidation, or assigning these contracts, the company had entered into a contract with any competent party to do the repairs, and so had procured them to be done, we cannot think that this would have been a departure from the terms of the contract to keep the waggons in repair. While fully acquiescing in the general principle just referred to, we must take care not to push it beyond reasonable limits. And we cannot but think that in applying the principle, the Court of Queen's Bench in Robson v. Drummond went to the utmost length to which it can be carried, as it is difficult to see how in repairing a carriage when necessary, or painting it once a year, preference would be given to one coachmaker over another. Much work is contracted for, which it is known can only be executed by means of sub-contracts; much is contracted for as to which it is indifferent to the party for whom it is to be done, whether it is done by the immediate party to the contract, or by some one on his behalf. In all these cases the maxim *Qui facit per alium facit per se* [51] applies.

In the view we take of the case, therefore, the repair of the waggons, undertaken and done by the British Company under their contract with the Parkgate Company, is a sufficient performance by the latter of their engagement to repair under their contract with the defendants. Consequently, so long as the Parkgate Company continues to exist, and, through the British Company, continues to fulfil its obligation to keep the waggons

---

[51] He who acts through another acts himself.

in repair, the defendants cannot, in our opinion, be heard to say that the former company is not entitled to the performance of the contract by them, on the ground that the company have incapacitated themselves from performing their obligations under it, or that, by transferring the performance thereof to others, they have absolved the defendants from further performance on their part. . . .

We are therefore of opinion that our judgment must be for the plaintiffs for the amount claimed. ◄

COMMENTS AND QUESTIONS

1. Summarize the facts here. What was the decision of the appellate court?
2. On what grounds did the defendant object to the delegation of the duty to repair the railway cars? Why did the court reject this argument? Is any element of skill or personal service involved in repairing railway cars?
3. What was the difference, if any, in the *Robson v. Drummond* case mentioned in the opinion, in which the same English court decided that delegation of a duty was not proper? Can you distinguish the two cases? The court here is obviously bothered somewhat by the close similarity in the fact-situations of the two cases.

OBLIGATION OF ORIGINAL PARTY. Even when the original obligor delegates certain duties, he still remains liable for performance. Thus, if the person to whom the duties are transferred fails to perform properly, the person entitled to performance may collect damages from the original obligor. In short, delegation does not relieve the assignor of responsibility for performance.

EXAMPLE

GARDENER agrees to mow HOMEOWNER's lawn for $10. GARDENER delegates his duty to x. If x fails to mow the lawn or does an unsatisfactory job, HOMEOWNER may still hold GARDENER responsible. In most states HOMEOWNER may elect to sue either x or GARDENER for breach of contract if the lawn is not mowed.

NOVATION. The person who is entitled to receive performance may agree to release the original obligor from responsibility and look only to the person to whom the duty has been delegated for performance of the contract. If all three parties agree to this arrangement, the original obligor is discharged, the old contract is abandoned, and a brand-new agreement is substituted for it. This three-sided agreement is called a *novation*. It differs from an ordinary delegation in that all the interested parties agree to release the assignor.

EXAMPLE

GARDENER contracts to mow HOMEOWNER's lawn for $10. GARDENER and HOMEOWNER agree with x to a novation whereby GARDENER is discharged from both his rights and his obligations and x is substituted in his place. HOMEOWNER may no longer look to GARDENER for performance; he may look only to x.

Effect of Assignment—Notice to Obligor

Once an assignment has been made, the assignee should notify the obligor as soon as possible, for until the obligor learns of the assignment he may simply go ahead and perform his obligation for the assignor. If this happens, the obligor is no longer liable on the contract. In such cases, of course, the assignor must account to the assignee for the value of the performance he has received. Once the obligor has been notified of the assignment, however, he is bound to perform for the assignee.

> EXAMPLE
>
> s co. sells and delivers goods to b co. on 30-day credit. s co. assigns the right to payment to x bank, but the bank neglects to notify b co. of the assignment. When the date for payment arrives, the obligor, b co., is entitled to pay the assignor, s co., and discharge its obligation. s co., of course, must turn the money over to x bank. However, the bank has no right to sue b co. for payment. If x bank notifies b co. of the assignment before b co. pays s co., then x bank can sue b, because the notice entitles the bank to receive performance.

SUCCESSIVE ASSIGNMENTS.   Once in a while, an assignor will make two successive assignments of the same right. The courts disagree on how this situation should be treated. A majority of states hold that the first assignee to *notify* the obligor is entitled to performance, but a substantial minority of states rule that the first assignee to *receive* the assignment is entitled to performance. In all jurisdictions, however, the loser may sue the assignor for any damages incurred as a result of the wrongful second assignment.

> EXAMPLE
>
> a is owed $500 for services performed for o under a contract. On August 1, a assigns the right to x. On August 5, he assigns the same right to y. On August 10, y notifies o of the assignment. On August 15, x notifies o. The majority of states hold that y is entitled to performance because he was the first to notify o. Other courts permit x to collect the $500 from o, since he was the first to receive the assignment.

Rights of Assignee and Defenses of Obligor

As a general rule, the assignee is said to stand in the assignor's shoes, and his right to demand performance from the obligor is no greater than the assignor's. If circumstances are present that would excuse the obligor from his duty to perform for the assignor, they will also excuse him from his duty to perform for the assignee. In such a situation, if the assignee suffers any loss, he must recover it from the assignor, since the latter was at fault in assigning a right that could not be enforced.

> EXAMPLES
>
> 1. c contracts to put storm windows on o's house for $500. To raise money, he assigns his right to payment to x bank as security for a loan. While c is putting up the windows, he damages shrubbery on o's land to the extent of $200. x bank's right as an assignee to recover from o now becomes subject to o's counterclaim for damages against c. Consequently x bank cannot collect the entire $500 from

o. However, x BANK can always sue c for any damage it has sustained (in this case, $200).

2. PAINTER, who is owed $700 for painting o's house, assigns his right to payment to x. x notifies o of the assignment and demands the money. o tells x that he will pay him only $400, since PAINTER owes him $300 for a car which o sold to PAINTER. x is entitled to recover only $400 from o and must look to PAINTER for the remaining $300.

Since the assignee's rights are no better than the assignor's, people are often reluctant to take an assignment unless they are sure that they will be able to enforce it. The only way an assignee can protect himself is to ask the obligor if there is any legal reason why the obligation should not be performed—in other words, could the obligor raise a valid defense if he were sued for nonperformance? If such an inquiry is made, the obligor must disclose any defenses he may have against the assignor; otherwise he loses his right to assert them. Moreover, the obligor must perform for the assignee if an assignment is made on the strength of his assurance that the assigned right is enforceable.

Obviously, it is burdensome for a prospective assignee to have to check with the obligor to make sure that a particular assignment is a good one. The consequent reluctance that many people feel about accepting assignments tends to slow business down and to restrict credit. To alleviate this situation, the doctrine of *negotiability* has been introduced into some areas of commercial law. We shall discuss this concept in detail in Chapter 13, "Negotiable Instruments." For the moment, we may say simply that the doctrine of negotiability protects an assignee from the defenses of an obligor by giving him greater rights against the obligor than those enjoyed by the assignor himself.

The following Massachusetts case illustrates some of the difficulties that arise when this doctrine is applied.

AMERICAN BRIDGE CO. v. CITY OF BOSTON

Supreme Judicial Court of Massachusetts, 1909
202 Mass. 374, 88 N.E. 1089

► Action by the American Bridge Company of New York and others against the City of Boston. Verdict for plaintiffs, and defendant excepts. Exceptions sustained.

HAMMOND, J.   This is an action of contract brought by the plaintiffs as assignees of all "the moneys now due or which may hereafter become due" to one Coburn, the assignor under two certain building contracts between him and the defendant, dated respectively July 16, 1901, and August 27, 1901. It is brought to recover the amount of two architect's certificates, one for $2,210 and the other for $3,085.50, each dated November 10, 1902. The case was heard upon the auditor's report (which was for the defendant) and certain exhibits, by a justice of the superior court, sitting without a jury, who found for the plaintiffs for the full amount claimed; and it is before us upon exceptions taken by the defendant.

These exceptions raise the general question whether in this action the defendant may recoup for the damages sustained by the default of the assignor, which occurred after the defendant had notice of the assignment.

It is contended by the plaintiffs that these sums were due and payable at the time the defendant received notice thereof, that the plaintiffs' rights were fixed at the time of notice and could not be changed by the act of the assignor or of the defendant after notice, and consequently that the damage caused to the defendant by the default of the assignor in leaving his contract unperformed, although without any fault of collusion on the part of the defendant, cannot be recouped in this action. It is contended that the only remedy open to the defendant is by way of an action against the assignor.

Even if it be conceded in favor of the plaintiffs that the sums were due and payable at the time of the notice, and that the rights of the plaintiffs were fixed at that time, still the conclusion which the plaintiffs seek to draw by no means necessarily follows.

The assignment of a chose in action [52] conveys as between the assignor and assignee, merely the right which the assignor then possesses to that thing; but as between the assignee and the debtor it does not become operative until the time of notice to the latter, and does not change the rights of the debtor against the assignor as they exist at the time of the notice.

It becomes necessary to consider the exact relation between the defendant and Coburn, the assignor, at the time of the notice. The auditor has found that written notice of the assignment was given to the defendant on November 13, 1902, before the service of any trustee process. At that time there does not seem to have been any default on the part of Coburn. At the time of the notice what were the rights between him and the defendant, so far as respects this contract? He was entitled to receive these sums, but he was also under an obligation to complete his contract. This right of the defendant to claim damages for the non-performance of the contract, existed at the making of the contract and at the time of assignment and of notice, and the assignees knew it, and they also knew that it would become available to the defendant the moment the assignor should commit a breach. Under these circumstances it must be held that the assignees took subject to that right.[53] Coburn, the assignor, abandoned the work in a few days after the notice. This action was not brought until October 30, 1906, nearly four years after the breach.

Even if the sums were due and payable in November, 1902, at the time of the notice, still if this action had been brought by the assignor after the default, there can be no doubt that the defendant would have had the right to recoup the damages suffered by his default. And the assignees who seek to enforce this claim can stand in no better position in this respect than the assignor. The defendant is simply trying to enforce a right existing under

---

[52] A chose in action is a right to recover money, damages, or property from another by suit.

[53] This means that the right to recover money which had been assigned to the plaintiffs was subordinate to the defendant's right to claim damages for the breach of contract.

the contract at the time of the notice, a right of which the assignees had knowledge, and since they have delayed suit for these sums, until after default, the defendant may recoup against them as it could have recouped against the assignor. It cannot without its own fault or consent be deprived of rights under the contract. Any other conclusion would make the contract different from that into which the defendant entered. . . .

Exceptions sustained. ◄

COMMENTS AND QUESTIONS

1. In the lower court, the case was heard by a judge alone; the parties had presumably waived their right to trial by jury. The judge found for the plaintiff assignees for the full amount of their claim. How did the lower court resolve the defendant's counterclaim for damages? What happened in the appellate court? What rule of law was applied?
2. The court points out that the action was brought nearly four years after the default of the assignor. Do you think the result would have been different if suit had been commenced for the partial payments then due under the contract before Coburn abandoned the contract? Would the defendant have had any counterclaim then?

Third-Party Beneficiaries

In General

Frequently a contract is made for the benefit of a third person who is not a party to the contract itself. An obvious example is a life insurance policy naming a beneficiary other than the policyholder. May the third-party beneficiary bring suit to enforce the obligation to perform, despite the fact he had no part in making the contract? The answer depends on the kind of benefit conferred, the intention of the parties, and the circumstances.

Donee Beneficiaries

A *donee beneficiary* is a third person to whom the promisee owes no legal obligation—that is, the benefit to be conferred on him is strictly a gift. Most states hold that such promises are enforceable. A few states limit the right to cases where the beneficiary is a close relative of the promisee, but most states do not require this. Moreover, most states hold that once the agreement has been made, the beneficiary has an absolute right to receive the benefit. Nor may that right be revoked without his consent, unless the parties expressly reserved the privilege of doing so when they entered into the contract.

EXAMPLE

GRANDFATHER promises that if FATHER will name his first son after him, he will pay the son $5,000 at the age of 21. FATHER does, in fact, name his first son after GRANDFATHER. The son is entitled to enforce the obligation when he becomes 21. Once the unilateral agreement becomes binding on GRANDFATHER (that is, once FATHER has named the boy), the son has an absolute right to receive the money when he reaches the age of 21.

Creditor Beneficiaries

A creditor beneficiary is a third person to whom the promisee already owes a legal obligation at the time the contract is made; the promisor, in effect, agrees to assume the obligation in whole or in part. In most states, such contracts are enforceable by the creditor beneficiary if it is clear that performance is expressly meant to benefit him and to discharge the promisee's obligation to him.

EXAMPLE

LAWYER, who owes X BANK $500, contracts to perform services for P for that amount. P agrees to pay the $500 directly to X BANK to discharge LAWYER's obligation to it:

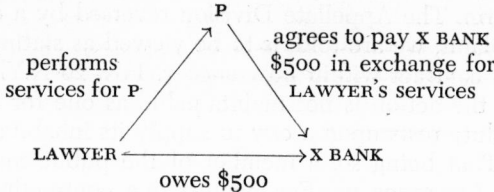

In most states, X BANK has the right to enforce the contract and collect from P.

Incidental Beneficiaries

An incidental beneficiary is a third person who is to benefit only indirectly from the performance of a contractual obligation. Generally such a beneficiary is not entitled to enforce performance. In other words, if the parties did not *expressly* intend to benefit the third person, he is not permitted to take any action. Only the original parties may sue on the contract.

Judge Cardozo, in the New York case of *Moch v. Rensselaer Water Co.*, was faced with a hard choice in deciding whether a third party could enforce a contract between a city and a waterworks company. Considerations of public policy obviously played a large role in the decision. See if you agree with the court.

MOCH v. RENSSELAER WATER CO.

Court of Appeals of New York, 1928
247 N.Y. 160, 159 N.E. 896

► CARDOZO, C. J. The defendant, a waterworks company under the laws of this state, made a contract with the city of Rensselaer for the supply of water during a term of years. Water was to be furnished to the city for sewer flushing and street sprinkling; for service to schools and public buildings; and for service at fire hydrants, the latter service at the rate of $42.50 a year for each hydrant. Water was to be furnished to private takers within the city at their homes and factories and other industries at reasonable rates, not exceeding a stated schedule. While this contract was in force, a building caught fire. The flames, spreading to the plaintiff's warehouse nearby, destroyed it and its contents. The defendant according to the complaint was promptly notified of the fire "but omitted and neglected after such notice, to supply or furnish sufficient or adequate quantity of water, with adequate pressure to stay, suppress, or extinguish the fire before it reached the warehouse of the plaintiff, although the pressure and supply which the defendant was equipped to supply and furnish, and had agreed by said contract to supply and furnish, was adequate and sufficient to prevent the spread of the fire to and the destruction of the plaintiff's warehouse and its contents." By reason of the failure of the defendant to "fulfill the provisions of the contract between it and the city of Rensselaer," the plaintiff is said to have suffered damage, for which judgment is demanded. A motion, in the nature of a demurrer, to dismiss the complaint, was denied at Special Term. The Appellate Division reversed by a divided court.

The complaint, we are told, is to be viewed as stating a cause of action for breach of contract within Lawrence v. Fox, 20 N.Y. 268.

We think the action is not maintainable as one for breach of contract.

No legal duty rests upon a city to supply its inhabitants with protection against fire. That being so, a member of the public may not maintain an action under Lawrence vs. Fox against one contracting with the city to furnish water at the hydrants, unless an intention appears that the promisor is to be answerable to individual members of the public as well as to the city for any loss ensuing from the failure to fulfill the promise. No such intention is discernible here. On the contrary, the contract is significantly divided into two branches: One a promise to the city for the benefit of the city in its corporate capacity, in which branch is included the service at the hydrants; and the other a promise to the city for the benefit of private takers, in which branch is included the services at their homes and factories. In a broad sense it is true that every city contract not improvident or wasteful is for the benefit of the public. More than this, however, must be shown to give a right of action to a member of the public not formally a party. The benefit, as it is sometimes said, must be one that is not merely incidental and secondary. It must be primary and immediate in such a sense and to such a degree as to bespeak the assumption of a duty to make reparation directly to the individual members of the public if the benefit be lost. The field of obligation would be expanded beyond reasonable limits if less than this were to be demanded as a condition of liability. A promisor undertakes to supply fuel for heating a public building. He is not liable for breach of contract to a visitor who finds the building without fuel, and thus contracts a cold. The list of illustrations can be indefinitely extended. The carrier of the mails under contract with the government is not answerable to the merchant who has lost the benefit of a bargain through negligent delay. The householder is without a remedy against manufacturers of hose and engines, though prompt performance of their contracts would have stayed the ravages of fire. "The law does not spread its protection so far."

So with the case at hand. By the vast preponderance of authority, a contract between a city and a water company to furnish water at the city hydrants has in view a benefit to the public that is incidental rather than immediate, an assumption of duty to the city and not to its inhabitants.

Such is the ruling of the Supreme Court of the United States. German Alliance Ins. Co. v. Homewater Supply Co., 226 U.S. 220, 33 S.Ct. 32. Such has been the ruling in this state . . . though the question is still open in this court. Such with few exceptions has been the ruling in other jurisdictions. Williston, Contracts, sec. 373, and cases there cited; Dillon, Municipal Corporations (5th Ed.), sec. 1340. The diligence of counsel has brought together decisions to that effect from 26 states. [Cases cited.] Only a few states have held otherwise. Page, Contracts, sec. 2401. An intention to assume an obligation of indefinite extension to every member of the public is seen to be the more improbable when we recall the crushing burden that the obligation would impose.   ◄

COMMENTS AND QUESTIONS

1. Outline the facts in this case. What was the principal issue before the court and how was it decided?

2. The plaintiff claimed to be a third-party beneficiary in this case. How did the court treat this claim? (The case of *Lawrence v. Fox*, referred to in the opinion, was a famous New York decision establishing the right of a creditor beneficiary to sue the obligor on a contract.)

3. Judge Cardozo mentions several analogies (e.g., a person obliged to furnish fuel for heating a building would not be liable to a person who catches cold from lack of heat) in which parties incidentally benefited are not allowed to sue obligors. Why shouldn't persons in such a position be allowed to sue for the harm done them? How would Judge Cardozo answer that question?

4. Note Cardozo's reference to decisions in other states, some of which had disagreed with this decision. On the other hand, the fact that defendant's counsel cited cases from twenty-six states in support of his position must have carried great weight with the court.

SECTION 9

PERFORMANCE AND DISCHARGE OF CONTRACTUAL OBLIGATIONS

In General

When two parties enter into a contract, each of them incurs a duty to perform certain obligations. Once a person properly performs his part of the contract, his obligation is said to be discharged and he has no further responsibility. However, performance is not the only way in which a party may discharge his obligation. For example, circumstances may arise that legally excuse one of the parties from performing his obligation. Or the parties may agree to discharge each other or change their obligations before performance has taken place. In this section, we will examine these various methods of discharging contractual obligations.

Discharge by Performance

Performance as a Condition

The parties to a contract are generally free to make any provision they wish about which side is obligated to perform his obligation first. Even where nothing explicit is said, however, it is usually understood that one party must first perform his obligation before he can demand payment or performance from the other.

> E X A M P L E
>
> ARTIST agrees to paint LADY's portrait for $100. If nothing is said to the contrary, ARTIST must complete performance of his obligation (i.e., painting the portrait) before he can demand performance of LADY's obligation (i.e., the payment of $100). Of course, if the contract provides that ARTIST is to receive the $100 before he does the portrait, then LADY is obligated to perform her obligation first.

If the contract makes it clear that the parties are to perform simultaneously, neither is bound to perform until the other has carried out his part of the bargain.

> E X A M P L E
>
> s agrees to convey a deed of real property to B upon the payment of $15,000. s has no duty to give B the deed until B offers the money. Nor has B any obligation to pay until s offers to hand over the deed.

If one party is obligated to perform first, he must do so before he can call on the other side to carry out his obligation. Once his obligation is performed, however, the other side must either carry out his obligation or pay damages for breach of contract. In the following sections we shall consider some of the factors that determine whether a contractual obligation has been fully and properly performed.

Performance on Time

Many contracts require that one of the parties perform by a certain date. Even if no time is stipulated, the law requires that he perform within a reasonable time. What happens if he fails to meet the deadline? Most courts are lenient and hold that even late performance discharges the obligation; at the same time, they hold that the other party may offset any damages he has sustained because of the delay. If, however, performance by a certain time is of vital importance to the other side, or if the parties clearly stipulate in their contract that "time is of the essence," late performance need not be accepted and may lead to action for breach of contract.

> E X A M P L E S
>
> 1. FLORIST agrees to furnish flowers for x's wedding on June 15 but fails to deliver them until June 16. He has no right to recover what is due

him on the contract, for his late performance does not discharge his obligation.

2. PAINTER agrees to paint x's house for $500 by June 15 but doesn't finish until June 16. Normally he is entitled to sue x for the contract price less any damages that x shows he has suffered as a result of the delay.

Incomplete Performance

Under common law, a party had to complete performance in every detail before his obligation was discharged and before he could demand payment or performance from the other side. As a general rule, this is still good law. In certain cases, however, a party who has substantially (i.e., almost completely) performed his obligation except for minor defects or omissions, and who has been acting in good faith, is permitted recovery on the contract. The other party may still, of course, offset any damage he has sustained by reason of the incomplete performance. If, however, the omission or deviation in the performance of one of the parties is significant, or if he has willfully failed to finish the job, he may not demand payment from the other party.

The case of *Bowen v. Kimbell*, which follows, gives us an example of this doctrine, known as the doctrine of substantial performance, in action.

 BOWEN v. KIMBELL

Supreme Judicial Court of Massachusetts, 1909
203 Mass. 364, 89 N.E. 542

► The facts are sufficiently stated in the opinion.

KNOWLTON, C. J.   The plaintiff Dodge made a contract in writing to erect a large building for the defendants in North Adams. He received many payments under the contract, and afterwards brought this suit to recover the balance of the contract price. Having become a bankrupt, his trustee was permitted to come into court and prosecute the suit. By agreement of parties the case was referred to a referee whose determination of all matters of fact was to be final, his decision of questions of law being subject to review by the court. He reported that the plaintiff was not entitled to recover, and judgment was ordered for the defendant, on his report. The case comes before us on an appeal by the plaintiff, which presents for our consideration all questions of the law that appear of record.

The price fixed by the contract was $96,500. It was admitted that the defendants were entitled to an allowance of $90 for a saving in the price of face brick, and that payments have been made amounting to $87,195. Nine thousand eight hundred and fifteen dollars is the balance claimed in this action.

There were many particulars in which the defendants contended that the plaintiff failed to perform his contract. But besides the plastering, of which we shall speak hereafter, there were ten different particulars in which it was found that the contract was not performed, for each of which the defendants would be entitled to an allowance, if they were obliged to pay at all. The deductions that ought to be made on account of these departures from the contract were found by the referee to amount in the aggregate to $4,071. It is not contended that any error of law entered into these findings.

The specifications in regard to the plastering provided, among other things, that the first coat for the whole building should be "good lime and hair mortar and mixed when used in with adamant plaster, two bags of adamant to one hod of lime mortar." They declared that "This mixture must be strictly adhered to without any deviation whatever." The findings on this point are as follows: "The 'adamant' referred to in these specifications is a patented composition of the class commonly called hard plasters. It contains a considerable amount of plaster of Paris. It sets more quickly than lime and mortar plastering and gives a harder surface, less liable to injury from blows of any kind, and is quite commonly used in modern office buildings. It is somewhat more expensive than lime and mortar plastering. I find that in plastering this building the plaintiff used less than half the adamant called for by the specifications. I find that this was an intentional departure from the contract in a substantial matter, which cannot be remedied afterwards without disproportionate expense. I further find that the composition of the plaster was not known to the architect until after the certificates given by him under the contract had all been issued. I therefore find that the plaintiff is not entitled to recover in this action. . . . I find that the cost of removing the plastering in the building and replastering with plaster mixed in accordance with the specifications, is eight hundred dollars ($800)."

The plaintiff contends that the conclusion of the referee in this particular is erroneous in law, and that the judgment should be reversed. This contention seems to be twofold: first, that an intentional departure from the contract in a matter of this kind will not preclude the contractor from recovering on a *quantum meruit;* [54] and secondly, that, as matter of law, the referee could not find that there was not a substantial performance of the contract. It becomes necessary to consider the law of Massachusetts in these particulars.

It is to be noticed, first, that the question whether there was a substantial performance of the contract is to be determined in reference to the entire contract, and what was done or omitted under it, and not in reference to the plastering alone. The referee might well find that the plaintiff failed to perform the contract substantially, in view of all his departures from it, even if he would not have made that finding upon the defective plastering alone. The validity of the finding must be determined in reference to all the facts of the case. But as the referee indicates that this breach is the principal reason for his decision, we will consider this branch of the case by itself.

Formerly it was generally held in this country, as it is held in England, that a contractor could not recover under a building contract, unless there was a full and complete performance of it, or a waiver as to the parts not

---

[54] This means the recovery of as much as he deserves for his work—in other words, the reasonable value of his services, not considering the contract price.

performed, and that he could not recover on a *quantum meruit* after a partial performance from which the owner had received benefit, unless there had been such subsequent dealings between the parties as would create an implied contract to pay for what had been done. Smith v. Brady, 17 N.Y. 173, 185. Ellis v. Hamlen, 3 Taunt, 52. Munroe v. Butt, 8 E. & B. 738. Sumpter v. Hedges, (1898) 1 Q.B. 673, and cases cited. But in most of the American States a more liberal doctrine has been established in favor of contractors for the construction of buildings, and it is generally held that if a contractor has attempted in good faith to perform his contract and has substantially performed it—although by inadvertence he has failed to perform it literally according to its terms—he may recover under the contract, with a proper deduction to the owner for the imperfections or omissions in the performance. . . .

It would seem that in cases of the kind, while the plaintiff recovers under the contract not the contract price, but the contract price less the deduction, he ought to aver, not absolute performance, but only substantial performance of his contract and a right to recover only the balance after allowing the owner a proper sum for the failure to do the work exactly in the way required. Spence v. Ham, 163 N.Y. 220. The rule very generally adopted is that, to entitle the plaintiff to recover, he needs to show only that he proceeded in good faith in an effort to perform the contract, and that the result was a substantial performance of it, although there may be various imperfections, or omissions that call for a considerable diminution of the contract price. The reason for this construction of such contracts is in part the difficulty of attaining perfection in the quality of the materials and workmanship, and of entirely correcting the effect of a slight inadvertence, and the injustice of allowing the owner to retain without compensation the benefit of a costly building upon his real estate, that is substantially, but not exactly, such as he agreed to pay for. In none of the courts of this country, so far as we know, is the contractor left remediless under conditions like those above stated. The recovery permitted is generally upon the basis of the contract, with a deduction for the difference between the value of the substantial performance shown and the complete performance which would be paid for at the contract price.

We think that the referee's finding of fact that the plaintiff was guilty of an intentional departure from the contract, in a substantial matter, is conclusive against his right to recover. . . . It shows a lack of good faith on the part of the plaintiff in his dealings with the defendants under the contract. We think the findings and decision of the referee, taken together, are a finding that there was not a substantial performance of the contract. On both grounds the report was rightly confirmed and judgment was rightly ordered for the defendants.

Judgment affirmed.   ◄

COMMENTS AND QUESTIONS

1. Notice that the contesting parties here agreed to have the case referred to a referee, who reported his findings of fact and law. His findings of fact were to be final, but his decisions on the law were

subject to review by the court. Referral to auditors or referees is widely used as a means of speeding up the disposition of cases.

2. The lower court ordered judgment on the referee's report. What was his decision in this case? What happened in the appellate court? Did the plaintiff recover anything?

Performance to Satisfaction of Other Party

Very often, one party to a contract will agree to perform to the personal satisfaction of the other, or else both parties will agree that performance must be approved by a third person—for example, an architect in a building contract. In such cases, most courts hold that any performance which would satisfy a reasonable man under the circumstances must be regarded as satisfactory. An exception may be made if the personal taste of the other party is obviously a controlling factor in the contract. In any case, if the party who is objecting to the performance is shown to be acting in bad faith or for the sole purpose of avoiding payment, the court will rule that performance is sufficient.

EXAMPLES

1. ARTIST contracts to paint x's portrait, "satisfaction guaranteed." If x is honestly dissatisfied with the finished portrait, ARTIST's performance will not be regarded as satisfactory. This is true even though ARTIST has done a good job, and even though most reasonable people would find the portrait acceptable.

2. CONTRACTOR agrees to build a garage "to x's satisfaction." If x has no reasonable cause for dissatisfaction with the completed building, and if a reasonable man would accept the job as satisfactory, CONTRACTOR's performance will probably be taken as adequate.

There has been much litigation in this area of the law, and each case must be decided on the basis of its own facts. Consider, for example, the New Jersey decision that follows:

COPE v. BEAUMONT

Circuit Court of Appeals of the United States
Third Circuit, 1910
181 Fed. 756, 104 C.C.A. 292

▶ In error to the Circuit Court of the United States for the District of New Jersey. Action by Wilbert Beaumont against John Purdy Cope. Judgment for plaintiff, and defendant brings error. Reversed.

LANNING, CIRCUIT JUDGE. On March 19, 1907, Wilbert Beaumont, contractor, and John Purdy Cope, owner of the Water Gap House, at Delaware Water Gap, Pa., entered into a written agreement by which Beaumont agreed to make certain alterations and additions to the Water Gap House, "under the direction and to the satisfaction of S. Hudson Vaughn, architect, acting as agent for the owner." The contract price for the work was $22,710. Seven partial payments, aggregating $12,500, were required to be made during the progress of the work. It was provided that the eighth and final payment of $10,210 should be made when the building was entirely completed. It was further provided:

> "That the final payment shall be made within thirty days after this contract is completely finished, provided that in each of the cases the architect shall certify in writing that all the work upon the performance of which the payment is to become due has been done to his satisfaction."

Beaumont has received from Cope the sum of $12,500.

In his declaration Beaumont, the plaintiff, avers generally in a special count the performance of all conditions precedent except certain alterations, which he declares Cope, the defendant, waived. He also avers that Vaughn, the architect, fraudulently neglected and refused to issue his final certificate. The claim under the special count is for $11,112.51. . . .

One of the assignments of error is that the court erred in charging the jury as follows:

> "As to the certificate, was it withheld in bad faith? Ought the architect, in the exercise of fair and reasonable judgment, to have approved the work and issued the final certificate? Was he, in fact, satisfied with it, although he professed to be dissatisfied? Does the weight of all the evidence bearing upon this question show that the certificate was rightfully withheld, or does it show that it was fraudulently withheld? That is to say, does it show that the architect acted in bad faith in withholding it? You should consider, in this connection, the acts as well as the words of the architect, and also the condition of the work, as to whether it was fully performed or not and also its character, and all other evidence tending to show whether or not the architect ought reasonably and fairly to have been satisfied with the work and approved it and issued his final certificate."

This portion of the charge related, of course, to the claim based on the special count. The contract, as we have seen, provided that the work was to be done under the direction and to the satisfaction of the architect, and that previous to each payment he should certify in writing that the work has been done "to his satisfaction." This was the contract between the parties. We cannot alter it. We cannot require that the liability of the defendant Cope shall depend upon the judgment of the jury as to whether the architect ought "reasonably and fairly to have been satisfied with the work and approved it, and issued his final certificate." Some of the language above quoted from the charge is unobjectionable, but ending as it does, with the distinct statement that the jury should consider all the evidence "tending to show whether or not the architect ought reasonably and fairly to have been satisfied with the work and approved it, and issued his final certificate," it gave to the jury an improper direction in the discharge of their duty. The jury may have been satisfied that the architect "ought reasonably and fairly to have been satisfied with the work and approved it," and yet the architect, in the exercise of his judgment, may have differed with the jury and withheld his certificate in perfect good faith and without fraud.

In Bradner v. Roffsell, 57 N.J.L. 412, 31 Atl. 387, the highest court of New Jersey said:

"But the verdict was for the whole of the unpaid price, and must obviously have rested upon the fraud of the architect in withholding a complete certificate. In presenting that subject to the jury, the trial court charged that, 'if not waived, it (the certificate of the architect) may be dispensed with only by proof that the certificate was withheld by fraud on the part of the architect. It would be prima facie evidence of fraud if the architect withheld his certificate without any substantial reason for so doing.' An exception was taken to the last sentence of this instruction, and an assignment of error is based thereon. In the Supreme Court this instruction was justly deemed open to objection, because the use of the word 'substantial' tended to substitute the judgment of the jury for the decision of the architect. In Chism v. Schipper (51 N.J.L. 1), the learned Chief Justice, who delivered the opinion of the majority of the court, carefully pointed out the need of watchful judicial supervision over the determination of juries on this question, and declared that the architect's conduct could not be impeached for want of skill or knowledge or because his judgments do not agree with those of others. To instruct a jury that they may find fraud from the withholding of such a certificate without a substantial reason is to permit them to determine what are substantial reasons, and if in their judgment there are none, then though the architect's judgment may be honestly otherwise to convict him of fraud." . . .

It is unnecessary to refer to the other assignments of error. We are forced to the conclusion that the above-quoted instruction to the jury vitiates the verdict and the judgment entered on it. *The judgment is therefore reversed and the record remanded, with direction to award a venire de novo.*[55] ◄

COMMENTS AND QUESTIONS

1. Summarize the facts in this case. What was the principal issue before the court?
2. Note the trial judge's charge to the jury. How did the trial court decide in this case? What happened on appeal?
3. This was an opinion of the Federal Court of Appeals on a case originally heard in the Federal District Court in New Jersey. How do you suppose this action happened to be tried in a federal court? Note that the cases cited in support of the opinion are New Jersey cases and that New Jersey law governs the decision.

Discharge Where Performance Excused

General Rule

As a general rule, hardships and difficulties do not excuse a party from full performance of his contractual obligations. Nor is he excused even when performance is actually impossible. For example, not even strikes, material shortages, floods, or fires are regarded as adequate excuses for failure to perform. If a party wants protection against difficulties of this sort, he must provide for it in the contract itself; otherwise, he will be forced to pay

---

[55] As used here, this phrase means that the case was sent back to the lower court with instructions to try the case over again in accordance with the appellate court's opinion.

damages. This rule often works a hardship on one of the parties, as in the Minnesota case that follows.

STEES v. LEONARD

Supreme Court of Minnesota, 1874
20 Minn. 494

▶ Appeal by defendants from an order of the district court, Ramsey county, denying a new trial.

The action was brought to recover damages for a failure of defendants to erect and complete a building on a lot of plaintiffs, on Minnesota Street, between Third and Fourth Streets, in the city of St. Paul, which by an agreement under seal between them and plaintiffs, the defendants had agreed to build, erect, and complete, according to plans and specifications annexed to and made part of the agreement. The defendants commenced the construction of the building, and had carried it to the height of three stories when it fell to the ground. The next year, 1869, they began again and carried it to the height as before, when it again fell to the ground, whereupon defendants refused to perform the contract. They claimed that in their attempts to erect the building they did the work in all respects according to the plans and specifications and that the failure to complete the building and its fall on the two occasions was due to the fact that the soil upon which it was to be constructed was composed of quicksand, and when water flowed into it, was incapable of sustaining the building. The offers of proof by defendants, and the character of the allegations in the answer, under which the court held some of the offers inadmissible, are sufficiently indicated in the opinion. . . .

Young, J. The general principle of law which underlies this case is well established. If a man bind himself, by a positive, express contract, to do an act in itself possible, he must perform his engagement, unless prevented by the act of God, the law or the other party to the contract. No hardship, no unforeseen hindrance, no difficulty short of absolute impossibility, will excuse him from doing what he has expressly agreed to do. This doctrine may sometimes seem to bear heavily upon contractors; but, in such cases, the hardship is attributable, not to the law, but to the contractor himself, who has improvidently assumed an absolute, when he might have undertaken only a qualified, liability. The law does no more than enforce the contract as the parties themselves have made it. Many cases illustrating the application of the doctrine to every variety of contract are collected in the note to Cutter v. Powell, 2 Smith, Lead. Cas. 1.

In the opinion of the court, the question is fully examined, many cases are cited, and the rule is stated

> "that where a party by his own contract creates a duty or charge upon himself he is bound to make it good, if he may, notwithstanding any accident by inevitable necessity, because he might have provided against it by his contract. . . . If, before the building is completed or accepted, it is destroyed by fire or other casualty, the loss falls upon the builder;

he must rebuild. The thing may be done, and he has contracted to do it. . . . No matter how harsh and apparently unjust in its operation the rule may occasionally be, it cannot be denied that it has its foundations in good sense and inflexible honesty. He that agrees to do an act should do it, unless absolutely impossible. He should provide against contingencies in his contract. Where one of two innocent persons must sustain a loss, the law casts it upon him who has agreed to sustain it; or, rather, the law leaves it where the agreement of the parties has put it. . . . Neither the destruction of the incomplete building by a tornado, nor its failing by a latent softness of the soil, which rendered the foundation insecure, necessarily prevented the performance of the contract to build, erect, and complete this building for the specified price. It can still be done, for aught that was opened to the jury as a defense, and overruled by the court."

Nothing can be added to the clear and cogent arguments we have quoted in vindication of the wisdom and justice of the rule which must govern this case, unless it is in some way distinguishable from the cases cited.

It is no defense to the action that the specifications directed that "footings" should be used as the foundation of the building, and that the defendants, in the construction of those footings, as well as in all other particulars, conformed to the specifications. The defendants contracted to "erect and complete the building." Whatever was necessary to be done in order to complete the building, they were bound by the contract to do. If the building could not be completed without other or stronger foundations than the footing specified, they were bound to furnish such other foundations. If the building could not be erected without draining the land, then they must drain the land, "because they have agreed to do everything necessary to erect and complete the building." 3 Dutcher, N.J. 520; and see Dermott v. Jones *supra*, where the same point was made by the contractor, but ruled against him by the court.

As the draining of the land was, in fact, necessary to the erection and completion of the building, it was a thing to be done, under the contract, by the defendants. The prior parol agreement that plaintiffs should drain the land, related therefore, to a matter embraced within the terms of the written contract, and was not, as claimed by defendants' counsel, collateral thereto. It was, accordingly under the familiar rule, inadmissible in evidence to vary the terms of the written contract, and was properly excluded.

Judgment affirmed.   ◀

COMMENTS AND QUESTIONS

1. Outline the facts here. What was the main issue in the case and how was it decided?

2. Don't you feel a little sorry for the defendants in this case? How could they have protected themselves?

3. Note that the defendants tried to introduce evidence of prior oral promises by the plaintiffs to drain the land. Why was this evidence excluded?

Exceptions to General Rule

In a few situations, the courts recognize exceptions to the general rule that difficulties and hardships do not excuse performance.

SUBSEQUENT ILLEGALITY.   If, after a contract is made, a change in the law renders performance illegal, the obligation is held to be discharged.

> E X A M P L E
>
> A contractor is hired to build a ten-story building. Before he starts work, a new zoning law is passed that prohibits the construction of such a structure. The contractor is excused from performance and his obligation is discharged.

DEATH OR DISABILITY OF PARTY.   What happens if a party to a contract dies or becomes so disabled that he is unable to perform? The answer depends on the nature of the obligation. If it requires special skill or judgment, or if it involves a personal relationship, performance is excused and the obligation terminates. On the other hand, if the obligation can be performed just as well by the party's estate or by his agent, it is not discharged.

> E X A M P L E S
>
> 1. ARCHITECT is hired by OWNER to draw up plans to remodel OWNER's house. ARCHITECT suffers a stroke and is unable to work. His obligation is discharged and the contract is terminated.
> 2. S agrees in writing to sell land to B. S dies. His executor is bound to carry out the obligation by delivering the deed to B.

DESTRUCTION OF SUBJECT MATTER.   In many contracts, the continued existence of certain property is absolutely necessary to performance. If the property is destroyed through no fault of either party, performance is excused and the obligation discharged. If, however, the destruction results from the carelessness or fault of one of the parties, he is liable for damages. And if one party has partially performed by the time the property is destroyed, he is permitted to recover the fair value of any benefit he has conferred on the other.

In the case of *Angus v. Scully,* which follows, the court was faced with just this sort of problem.

ANGUS v. SCULLY

Supreme Judicial Court of Massachusetts, 1900
176 Mass. 357, 57 N.E. 674

▶ CONTRACT, on an account annexed [56] for moving a building in Cambridge. The answer set up, among other things, nonperformance due to the destruction of the building by fire, by reason of the negligence of the plaintiffs. At the trial in the Superior Court before STEVENS, J., the jury returned a verdict for the plaintiffs; and the defendant alleged exceptions, which appear in the opinion.

HAMMOND, J.   The contract was that the plaintiffs should move a large

---

[56] This is a detailed statement of the amount claimed to be due the plaintiff; it is attached to his complaint or declaration.

building belonging to the defendant from a lot on Third Street to a lot on First Street, and also to change the location of two other buildings, of which one was on the First Street lot and one on the Third Street lot, and the defendant was to pay them $840.

In accordance with the agreement the plaintiffs began the work. "They first moved the house on the Third Street lot, and then began to move the large building from the Third Street lot across certain open lots toward the lot on First Street. When said last named building had been moved about half the distance to said lot on First Street, it was entirely consumed by fire at some time during the night, and thereupon, with the assent of the defendant, no further work was done in moving either of the other buildings."

In this action the plaintiffs seek to recover the fair value of the services rendered by them in the work done down to the time of the fire.

The court refused to rule as requested by the defendant that the plaintiffs could not recover, and submitted the case to the jury upon instructions which would authorize them to find for the plaintiffs, if they were satisfied that the fire was not attributable to any negligence of the plaintiffs.

We see no error in the rulings under which the case thus went to the jury.

Clearly one of the implied conditions of the contract was that the building should continue to exist. Upon the destruction of the building the work could not be completed according to the contract. Authorities differ as to the rights of the parties in such a case, but so far as respects this Commonwealth the rule is well settled. As stated by Knowlton, J., in Butterfield v. Byron, 153 Mass. 517, 523,

> "The principle seems to be, that when, under an implied condition of the contract, the parties are to be excused from performance if a certain event happens, and by reason of the happening of the event it becomes impossible to do that which was contemplated by the contract, there is an implied assumpsit for what has properly been done by either of them, the law dealing with it as done at the request of the other, and creating a liability to pay for its value, to be determined by the price stipulated in the contract, or in some way if the contract price cannot be made applicable."

Stated more narrowly and with particular reference to the circumstances of this case, the rule may be said to be that where one is to make repairs or do any other work on the house of another under a special contract, and his contract becomes impossible of performance on account of the destruction of the house without any fault on his part, then he may recover for what he has done.

This case comes clearly within this rule. . . .

Exceptions overruled.   ◀

COMMENTS AND QUESTIONS

1. Summarize the facts here. What was the main issue before the court?
2. Did the plaintiffs recover the contract price in this case? If not, how do you think the amount they recovered was computed?

3. Since the house burned down, the defendant certainly derived no benefit from the plaintiffs' part performance in moving the house half way to its destination. Why, then, should the defendant have to pay anything?

4. Why should the defendant be excused in a case like this and not in the *Stees v. Leonard* case (see page 323)? Distinguish the two situations.

Often a seller or a manufacturer of goods must depend on a particular source of supply in order to perform his obligation. If both parties are aware of this fact, and if the source of supply is destroyed or ceases to exist, his performance is excused. If, however, he simply promises to deliver certain goods without saying anything about their source, he must either fulfill that obligation or else pay damages.

EXAMPLES

1. FLORIST agrees to furnish special flowers for x's wedding. FLORIST and x both understand that the flowers are to come from x's greenhouse. The greenhouse is destroyed by a hurricane the day before the wedding. FLORIST's performance will be excused.

2. s agrees to supply a certain quantity of lumber to c for use on a construction job. Although s intends to furnish the lumber from his own mill, he says nothing about this source of supply when he enters into the contract. The mill is destroyed by a flood before the lumber is delivered. s is not excused from performance. He must either supply the lumber from another source or be held liable for breach of contract.

PREVENTION OF PERFORMANCE. Where one party actually prevents or substantially interferes with the other's performance, the obligation is discharged.

EXAMPLE

PAINTER is hired to paint x's house. When PAINTER comes to do the job, x refuses to allow him on the premises. PAINTER is excused from performance, his obligation is discharged, and he may sue x for damages.

Discharge by Anticipatory Breach

A breach of contract exists when one party fails to perform his contractual obligation. Normally, breaches occur only after the time for performance has arrived or during the actual period of performance. Sometimes, however, before the time for performance occurs, one party will indicate by his actions or statements that he either will not, or will not be able to, perform the obligation when it comes due. This is called an anticipatory breach. Most states hold that the other party is then entitled to treat the contract as terminated and to sue for damages or to rescind the contract immediately. He may, if he chooses, wait until the scheduled date of performance before taking any action. If he does, however, the other party may go ahead and perform as scheduled, in spite of his original repudiation. Moreover, if the promisee elects to wait until the scheduled date of performance, he may take no action on the contract that will increase the damages due him as a result of the anticipatory breach.

EXAMPLE

On September 1, GROWER agrees to sell 500 Christmas trees to DEALER, with delivery to be made on December 10. On October 1, GROWER writes to DEALER saying that he has found another customer who will pay him more and that he does not intend to carry out his contract with DEALER. DEALER is entitled to treat GROWER's letter as an anticipatory breach; he may either rescind the contract or sue for damages right away. On the other hand, DEALER may ignore the breach and wait until December 10, in which case GROWER may still deliver the trees and hold DEALER to the original contract. If DEALER waits, however, he may not add to his damages (by taking new orders from his customers between October 1 and December 10).

The rule of anticipatory breach does not apply to an obligation to pay money at a future date. In such cases, even if the debtor indicates beforehand his unwillingness or inability to pay, the creditor must wait until the due date before taking action,

A good discussion of the doctrine of anticipatory breach occurs in the following case.

PLUNKETT v. COMSTOCK, CHENEY CO.

Supreme Court of New York, Appellate Division, 1st Dept., 1925
211 App. Div. 737, 208 N.Y.S. 93

▶ Motion by the defendant, the Comstock, Cheney Company, for a new trial upon a case containing exceptions, ordered to be heard at the Appellate Division in the first instance after the direction of a verdict in favor of the plaintiffs at the close of the case upon a trial before the court and a jury at the New York Trial Term in April, 1924.

McAVOY, J.   There are two causes of action alleged on two contracts for the sale of specially selected maple and basswood lumber by plaintiffs to defendant. The making of the contracts is admitted. A portion of the lumber specified in each contract was delivered by plaintiff and paid for by defendant during the year 1920, which was the time specified for delivery under the contracts. It is admitted that at defendant's special instance and request plaintiffs withheld tender and delivery of the lumber remaining undelivered up to and including the 12th day of December, 1921. The breach alleged is that on or about December 12, 1921, the defendant notified plaintiffs that it would not accept and pay for the balance of the lumber remaining undelivered and thereby repudiated the contracts. Following the defendant's repudiation, plaintiffs on January 10, 1922, notified defendant by letter that they elected to treat the defendant's repudiation as a breach of the contracts and that plaintiffs would hold defendant for the damages suffered by them by reason of defendant's refusal to accept and pay for the lumber. Defendant offered no testimony at the trial, but rested after the close of plaintiffs' case. Both sides moved for the direction of a verdict and a verdict was directed for plaintiffs for the full amount demanded. The defendant contends on this appeal that plaintiffs failed to make out a prima facie case based upon the claim that defendant's conduct did not amount to a repudiation of the contracts.

In February, 1921, plaintiffs were urging defendant to permit the shipment of at least two or three carloads of the lumber remaining undelivered. In May of that year plaintiffs urged that defendant permit the shipment of a car or two. In September plaintiffs wrote: "We have, however, arrived at the point where we feel we must ship a few cars of this on account of our need for funds." In October plaintiffs wrote, "We have now offered shipment of your order for nearly twelve months' time, and we have nearly reached the point where much as we dislike to, we must ask you for some relief," and requested that defendant advise plaintiffs when defendant's president, Mr. Robert Comstock, would be in New York in order that a meeting might be arranged to discuss the matter.

On November 11, 1921, defendant replied that its president might be in New York in the next two or three weeks, but "if it is in regard to taking any lumber, we would say that we are not in a position, and do not intend to take in any lumber this year and probably not until next Fall."

On December 7, 1921, plaintiffs replied: "We are compelled to say that your suggestion that you do not intend to take in any lumber during 1921, and probably not until next Fall, is not at all satisfactory to us, and we cannot accede to or accept such a proposal. . . . We have now reached a point where we must have a definite understanding with you covering deliveries of the balance of our contracts within the very near future or some other plan by which we can be relieved of further carrying the burden and further loss."

Defendant replied making an appointment for its president, Mr. Comstock, to meet Mr. Webster, one of the plaintiffs, in New York on December 12, 1921. At this meeting, the conversation which was had resulted in a declaration by defendant's representative that defendant could not possibly take more than two carloads of the maple. Thereafter no communications were had between the parties excepting the plaintiffs' letter to defendant under date of January 10, 1922, which, omitting the formal parts, reads as follows:

> "Referring to your letter of November 11 and the position which you take in that letter, namely, that you do not intend to accept delivery until next fall of the balance of lumber due you under our contracts and orders with you, and to the confirmation of your position as above outlined recently given to our Mr. Ora S. Webster in conference with your Mr. Comstock, we are compelled to treat this action on your part as a breach of our contracts and orders with you. Accordingly, we hereby notify you of our election to consider these contracts and orders as rescinded, and to hold you for the damages sustained by us by reason of your refusal to accept and pay for the lumber."

No reply was ever made to this letter.

We think that it was properly determined that defendant's repudiation of the contracts was an anticipatory breach thereof giving rise to an immediate cause of action in favor of plaintiffs.

The plaintiffs in this case have adopted a remedy authorized by the rule announced in Henderson Tire & Rubber Co. v. Wilson & Son, 235 N.Y. 489. The letter of January 10, 1922, shows that they treated defendant's refusal as an abandonment and complete breach of the contracts.

It is urged by defendant that there was no breach of the contracts by it, asserting that there was no positive and unequivocal repudiation of its duty under the contract, and that the defendant as a matter of law was not in default on December twelfth, or any other time, for the reason that the original time of performance was waived and that no other time was ever fixed by notice or otherwise.

Defendant also claims that it never at any time actually repudiated the contracts and as evidence of this relies upon the statement in its letter of November 11, 1921, to the effect that it did not intend to take any lumber during that year and probably not until next fall.

At the conversation had between the parties' representatives, heretofore mentioned, a demand by Mr. Webster that defendant make up a schedule of deliveries was made. In response to this the defendant's president said: "We can't do that. We cannot possibly take more than two cars of maple." This was an unequivocal repudiation.

It is also asserted by defendant that there was no breach of the contracts by it because the defendant as a matter of law was not in default either on December 12, 1921, or at any other time for the reason that the original time for the performance was waived and that no other time was ever fixed by notice or otherwise. This would be a real point if there was no repudiation by the party against whom the default was claimed and if there had been no demand for performance or objection to the delay by the party bringing the action. In Taylor v. Goelet, 208 N.Y. 253, 259, the contention that, the time of performance having been waived, a notice fixing a time for performance is required was overruled in a like instance, the court saying: "It is to be understood, however, that the notice of intention to rescind is only necessary when the party to the contract proceeded against has merely delayed performance, not where he has abandoned the contract, or treated it as terminated, or where he has refused to perform."

A further argument is based upon the rule that as payment and delivery under the contract were to be concurrent acts, the plaintiffs were required to prove their readiness and ability to perform as to the lumber remaining undelivered. If plaintiffs had elected to disregard defendant's repudiation and to keep the contracts alive for the benefit of both parties, it would have been necessary for them to make a tender, or if a tender were waived when deliveries became due, to show readiness and willingness to make a tender. But the breach here being an anticipatory one, plaintiffs were never under any obligation to place themselves in a position of readiness or ability to perform. . . .

The plaintiffs can treat the refusal of the other party as an abandonment of the contract and sue for the profits which might have been made had the contract been performed. The plaintiffs in this case have adopted that remedy. It was, therefore, unnecessary for them to make any preparations for further performance. If the vendor has to buy instead of to manufacture, he may show what was the value of the contract by showing for what price he could have made subcontracts, just as the cost of manufacture in the case of a manufacturer may be shown.

The exceptions should be overruled and judgment should be directed for plaintiffs for the amount of the verdict, $29,929.21, with interest from the date thereof, April 17, 1924, together with costs in this court and at Trial Term.

◄

COMMENTS AND QUESTIONS

1. Outline the principal facts in this case. What was the decision of the court?
2. Note the extended correspondence between the two firms. The court was faced with the problem of determining the true intention of the parties. Do you agree with the decision?
3. Summarize the arguments raised by the defendant and the reasons for the court's rejecting them.

Discharge by Agreement of Parties

In General

Contractual obligations may be discharged or changed by agreement of the parties either before or during performance. Sometimes the contract itself contains a provision that automatically terminates the entire agreement as soon as a certain condition arises.

Mutual Rescission

The parties to a contract may call off the whole agreement any time they want to; they can restore each other to their original positions simply by returning any money or property that has changed hands. This action is known as *mutual rescission,* since each party rescinds the contract and releases the other from all obligation. The parties may ordinarily rescind a contract either orally or in writing; if the rescission involves the return or retransfer of real property, however, it must be in writing.

Substitution of New Contract

The parties may also agree to replace the original contract with a new one. If the new agreement is clearly inconsistent with the old one and is obviously intended to replace it, the original contract is automatically discharged, *provided* the new agreement is supported by adequate consideration. If adequate consideration does not exist, the new contract is not enforceable and the first agreement is still binding. Several states, however, have laws stating that a modification of an original contract is binding in spite of the lack of consideration, so long as the modification is put in writing and is signed by the party to be charged.

Novation

Another way of discharging obligations by agreement is by means of a *novation* (see page 308).

Accord and Satisfaction

Sometimes the parties to a contract disagree over exactly what obligations are called for under the original agreement. Then they may make an additional agreement that calls on one side to perform an obligation which differs somewhat from the original. This agreement is called an *accord*. When the new agreement has been fully performed, there is said to be *satisfaction* of the accord, and the original contract is thereby discharged. Until satisfaction of the accord occurs, the original agreement is still binding.

> E X A M P L E
>
> s agrees to sell a piano to B for $500. A dispute arises over the make and model to be delivered. At last the parties agree that s will deliver an organ to B instead, for the same price. Once the organ has been delivered to B, the accord is satisfied and the original contract for the sale of the piano is discharged. Until the accord has actually been satisfied, however, either party is free to repudiate it and enforce the original contract.

Discharge by Operation of Law

Statute of Limitations

If one party breaks an agreement, the other party may sue for breach of contract within a period of time specified by the *statute of limitations*. Statutes of this sort have been enacted in all the states. Generally they provide that if the injured party does not sue the other before the expiration of the time limit, he loses his right to do so. The statutory period differs from state to state and is frequently longer for written contracts than for oral. In some states the period is only three years, in many others it is six years, and in a few it is as long as fifteen or twenty years.

In most states the right to sue may be revived if after the time limit has been exceeded the party who broke the agreement makes a written promise to perform his part of the contract, or, if his obligation is to pay money, he makes a part payment of the debt.

Bankruptcy

A party who owes money under a contract may discharge his obligation by going through bankruptcy proceedings. As in the case of the statute of limitations, however, the right to sue may be revived later on if the debtor makes a written promise to pay the debt or actually pays part of it.

SECTION 10

REMEDIES AND DAMAGES
FOR BREACH OF CONTRACT

Remedies

Various remedies are open to a party who suffers a breach of contract at the hands of the other party. He may *rescind* the contract and restore each party to his original position by returning any benefits he has received. Or he may demand performance by the other side. Or he may sue for damages. The third remedy is the one most commonly resorted to.

Damages

Compensatory Damages

As a general rule, the injured party is entitled to recover enough money to put him in as good a position as he would have been in had the contract been fully performed. The money recovered is known as *compensatory damages.* How great the amount should be is a question of fact that must be decided by the jury, after it has received proper instructions from the judge. The court will accept the jury's decision unless it is clearly contrary to the evidence presented. If a judge is sitting without jury, he computes the damages himself by applying the general rule. In addition, the plaintiff is usually entitled to interest on the damages and to reimbursement for some of the cost of bringing his suit to court. Ordinarily, however, he is not permitted to recover attorney's fees, witness fees, or other legal expenses.

> EXAMPLE
>
> On October 1, B contracts to buy 100 baskets of apples from s at $1.00 a basket, to be delivered on November 1. On November 1, s fails to deliver, thereby breaking the contract. The market price of apples that day is $1.20 a basket. B has to buy the apples elsewhere, which means that he pays $20.00 more than he would have paid s under the contract. B is entitled to $20.00 damages to put him in as good a position as he would have been in had s fulfilled his obligation.

An interesting illustration of the difficulties involved in measuring damages occurred in the New Hampshire case of *Hawkins v. McGee,* which follows.

HAWKINS v. McGEE

Supreme Court of New Hampshire, 1929
84 N.H. 114, 146, Atl. 642

► This was an action by a patient against a doctor for breach of a contract by the doctor to perform a successful operation on the patient.

BRANCH, J.   The operation in question consisted in the removal of a considerable quantity of scar tissue from the palm of the plaintiff's right hand and the grafting of skin taken from the plaintiff's chest in place thereof. The scar tissue was the result of a severe burn caused by contact with an electric wire, which the plaintiff received about nine years before the time of the transactions here involved. There was evidence to the effect that before the operation was performed the plaintiff and his father went to the defendant's office, and that the defendant, in answer to the question, "How long will the boy be in the hospital?" replied, "Three or four days, not over four; then the boy can go home and it will be just a few days when he will go back to work with a good hand." Clearly this and other testimony to the same effect would not justify a finding that the doctor contracted to complete the hospital treatment in three or four days or that the plaintiff would be able to go back to work within a few days thereafter. The above statements could only be construed as expressions of opinion or predictions as to the probable duration of the treatment and plaintiff's resulting disability, and the fact that these estimates were exceeded would impose no contractual liability upon the defendant. The only substantial basis for the plaintiff's claim is the testimony that the defendant also said before the operation was decided upon, "I will guarantee to make the hand a hundred per cent perfect hand or a hundred per cent good hand." The plaintiff was present when these words were alleged to have been spoken, and, if they are to be taken at their face value, it seems obvious that proof of their utterance would establish the giving of a warranty in accordance with his contention. . . .

The substance of the charge to the jury on the question of damages appears in the following quotation: "If you find the plaintiff entitled to anything, he is entitled to recover for what pain and suffering he has been made to endure and for what injury he has sustained over and above what injury he had before." To this instruction the defendant seasonably excepted. By it, the jury was permitted to consider two elements of damage: (1) Pain and suffering due to the operation; and (2) positive ill effects of the operation upon the plaintiff's hand. Authority for any specific rule of damages in cases of this kind seems to be lacking, but, when tested by general principle and by analogy, it appears that the foregoing instruction was erroneous.

"By 'damages,' as that term is used in the law of contracts, is intended compensation for a breach, measured in the terms of the contract." Davis v. New England Cotton Yarn Co., 77 N.H. 403, 404; 92 A. 732, 733. The purpose of the law is "to put the plaintiff in as good a position as he would have been in had the defendant kept his contract." 3 Williston, Cont. 1338; Hardie-Tynes Mfg. Co. v. Easton Cotton Oil Co., 150 N.C. 150, 63 S.E. 676.

The measure of recovery "is based upon what the defendant should have given the plaintiff not what the plaintiff has given the defendant or otherwise expended." 3 Williston, Cont. 1341. "The only losses that can be said fairly to come within the terms of a contract are such as the parties must have had in mind when the contract was made, or such as they either knew or ought to have known would probably result from a failure to comply with its terms." Davis v. New England Cotton Yarn Co., 77 N.H. 403, 404; 92 A. 732, 733, Hurd v. Dunsmore, 63 N.H. 171.

The present case is closely analogous to one in which a machine is built for a certain purpose and warranted to do certain work. In such cases, the usual rule of damages for breach of warranty in the sale of chattels is applied, and it is held that the measure of damages is the difference between the value of the machine, if it had corresponded with the warranty and its actual value, together with such incidental losses as the parties knew, or ought to have known, would probably result from a failure to comply with its terms. [Citation of cases omitted.]

We therefore conclude that the true measure of the plaintiff's damage in the present case is the difference between the value to him of a perfect hand or a good hand, such as the jury found the defendant promised him and the value of his hand in its present condition, including any incidental consequences fairly within the contemplation of the parties when they made their contract. 1 Sutherland, Damages (4th Ed.) 92. Damages not thus limited, although naturally resulting, are not to be given.

The extent of the plaintiff's suffering does not measure this difference in value. The pain necessarily incident to a serious surgical operation was a part of the contribution which the plaintiff was willing to make to his joint undertaking with the defendant to produce a good hand. It was a legal detriment suffered by him which constituted a part of the consideration given by him for the contract. It represented a part of the price which he was willing to pay for a good hand, but it furnished no test of the value of a good hand, or the difference between the value of the hand which the defendant promised and the one which resulted from the operation.

It was also erroneous and misleading to submit to the jury as a separate element of damage any change for the worse in the condition of the plaintiff's hand resulting from the operation, although this error was probably more prejudicial to the plaintiff than to the defendant. Any such ill effect of the operation would be included under the true rule of damages set forth above, but damages might properly be assessed for the defendant's failure to improve the condition of the hand, even if there were no evidence that its condition was made worse as a result of the operation.

It must be assumed that the trial court, in setting aside the verdict, undertook to apply the same rule of damages which he had previously given to the jury, and since this rule was erroneous, it is unnecessary for us to consider whether there was any evidence to justify his finding that all damages awarded by the jury above $500 were excessive. Defendant's requests for instructions were loosely drawn and were properly denied. A considerable number of issues of fact were raised by the evidence, and it would have been extremely misleading to instruct the jury in accordance with defendant's request No. 2, that "the only issue on which you have to pass is whether or not there was a special contract between the plaintiff and the defendant to produce a perfect hand." Equally inaccurate was defendant's request No. 5, which reads as follows: "You would have to find, in order to hold the defendant liable in this case, that Dr. McGee and the plaintiff both understood that the doctor was guaranteeing a perfect result from this operation." If the defendant said that he would guarantee a perfect result, and the plaintiff relied upon that promise, any mental reservations which he may have had are immaterial. The standard by which his conduct is to be judged is not internal, but external. . . .

New trial.

MARBLE, J., did not sit; the others concurred.   ◄

COMMENTS AND QUESTIONS

1. Summarize the trial judge's charge to the jury in the lower court. Why was this instruction erroneous? What rule did the appellate court set forth to determine the proper measure of damages?
2. Why should members of the jury not take into account the pain and suffering which the plaintiff endured? As a practical matter, would they not have considered this factor, anyway, no matter how they had been charged?
3. What if the condition of the plaintiff's hand had been left unchanged after the operation? Would the plaintiff have been entitled to damages?
4. Note the court's derogatory comments on the defendant's requests for instructions. Such remarks are obviously embarrassing to the lawyer involved.

Unexpected and Unusual Damages

In most cases, the court will not award damages for loss or injury resulting from unexpected or unusual causes unless both parties were aware of them when they entered into the contract. In other words, a party who breaks his agreement is expected to reimburse the other party for any losses that would normally result from his failure to perform his obligation, but he is not expected to pay for losses that are out of the ordinary and are caused by conditions that he knows nothing about.

EXAMPLE

VENTRILOQUIST, who performs every Friday at a night club, leaves his dummy with REPAIRMAN on a Wednesday. REPAIRMAN agrees to repair and repaint the dummy and to have it ready by Friday noon. VENTRILOQUIST does not tell REPAIRMAN about his Friday performance, nor does he mention that he has only one dummy. REPAIRMAN delays the job and fails to have the dummy ready by Friday. He is probably not responsible for the loss of wages and profits that VENTRILOQUIST suffers as a result of being unable to perform. Unless REPAIRMAN is informed of the special circumstances, he is not liable for damages that he could not have anticipated.

Here is another famous English decision which illustrates the application of this rule of law.

HADLEY v. BAXENDALE

In the Court of Exchequer, 1854
9 Exch. 341

▶ At the trial before Crompton, J., at the last Gloucester Assizes, it appeared that the plaintiffs carried on an extensive business as millers at Gloucester; and that, on the 11th of May, their mill was stopped by a breakage of the crank shaft by which the mill was worked. The steam-engine was manufactured by Messrs. Joyce & Co., the engineers, at Greenwich, and it became necessary to send the shaft as a pattern for a new one to Greenwich. The fracture was discovered on the 12th, and on the 13th the plaintiffs sent one of their servants to the office of the defendants, who are the well-known carriers trading under the name of Pickford & Co., for the purpose of having the shaft carried to Greenwich. The plaintiffs' servant told the clerk that the mill was stopped, and that the shaft must be sent immediately; and in answer to the inquiry when the shaft would be taken, the answer was, that if it was sent up by twelve o'clock any day, it would be delivered at Greenwich on the following day. On the following day the shaft was taken by the defendants, before noon, for the purpose of being conveyed to Greenwich, and the sum of £2, 4s. was paid for its carriage for the whole distance; at the same time the defendants' clerk was told that a special entry, if required, should be made to hasten its delivery. The delivery of the shaft at Greenwich was delayed by some neglect; and the consequence was, that the plaintiffs did not receive the new shaft for several days after they would otherwise have done, and the working of their mill was thereby delayed, and they thereby lost the profits they would otherwise have received.

On the part of the defendants, it was objected that these damages were too remote, and that the defendants were not liable with respect to them. The learned Judge left the case generally to the jury, who found a verdict with £25 damages beyond the amount paid into Court.

Alderson, B. We think that there ought to be a new trial in this; but, in so doing, we deem it to be expedient and necessary to state explicitly the rule which the Judge, at the next trial, ought, in our opinion, to direct the jury to be governed by when they estimate the damages.

It is, indeed, of the last importance that we should do this; for, if the jury are left without any definite rule to guide them, it will, in such cases as these, manifestly lead to the greatest injustice. The Courts have done this on several occasions; and, in Blake v. Midland Railway Company, 18 Q.B. 93, the Court granted a new trial on this very ground, that the rule had not been definitely laid down to the jury by the learned Judge at *Nisi Prius*.[57]

Now we think the proper rule in such a case as the present is this: Where two parties have made a contract which one of them has broken, the damages which the other party ought to receive in respect of such breach of contract should be such as may fairly and reasonably be consid-

---

[57] *Nisi Prius* means the trial court.

ered either arising naturally, i.e., according to the usual course of things, from such breach of contract itself, or such as may reasonably be supposed to have been in the contemplation of both parties, at the time they made the contract, as the probable result of the breach of it. Now, if the special circumstances under which the contract was actually made were communicated by the plaintiffs to the defendants, and thus known to both parties, the damages resulting from the breach of such a contract, which they would reasonably contemplate, would be the amount of injury which would ordinarily follow from a breach of contract under these special circumstances so known and communicated. But, on the other hand, if these special circumstances were wholly unknown to the party breaking the contract, he at the most, could only be supposed to have had in his contemplation the amount of injury which would arise generally, and in the great multitude of cases not affected by any special circumstances, from such a breach of contract. For, had the special circumstances been known, the parties might have specially provided for the breach of contract by special terms as to the damages in that case; and of this advantage it would be very unjust to deprive them. Now the above principles are those by which we think the jury ought to be guided in estimating the damages arising out of any breach of contract. It is said, that other cases such as breaches of contract in the non-payment of money, or in the not making good title to land, are to be treated as exceptions from this, and as governed by a conventional rule. But as, in such cases, both parties must be supposed to be cognizant of that well-known rule, these cases may, we think, be more properly classed under the rule above enunciated as to cases under known special circumstances, because there both parties may reasonably be presumed to contemplate the estimation of the amount of damages according to the conventional rule. Now, in the present case, if we are to apply the principles above laid down, we find that the only circumstances here communicated by the plaintiffs to the defendants at the time the contract was made, were, that the article to be carried was the broken shaft of a mill, and that the plaintiffs were the millers of a mill. But how do these circumstances shew reasonably that the profits of the mill must be stopped by an unreasonable delay in the delivery of the broken shaft by the carrier to the third person? Suppose the plaintiffs had another shaft in their possession put up or putting up at the time, and that they only wished to send back the broken shaft to the engineer who made it; it is clear that this would be quite consistent with the above circumstances, and yet, the unreasonable delay in the delivery would have no effect upon the intermediate profits of the mill. Or, again, suppose that, at the time of delivery to the carrier, the machinery of the mill had been in other respects defective, then, also, the same results would follow. Here it is true that the shaft was actually sent back to serve as a model for a new one, and that the want of a new one was the only cause of the stoppage of the mill, and that the loss of profits really arose from not sending down the new shaft in proper time, and that this arose from the delay in delivering the broken one to serve as a model. But it is obvious that, in the great multitude of cases of millers sending off broken shafts to third persons by a carrier under ordinary circumstances, such consequences would not, in all probability, have occurred; and these special circumstances were here never communicated by the plaintiffs to the defendants. It follows, therefore, that the loss of profits here cannot reasonably be considered such a consequence of the breach of contract as could have been fairly and reasonably contemplated by both the parties when they made this contract. For such loss would neither have flowed naturally from the breach of this contract in the great multitude of such cases occurring under ordinary circumstances, nor were the special circumstances, which, perhaps, would have made it a reasonable and natural consequence of such breach of contract, communicated to or known by the defendants. The Judge ought, therefore, to have told the jury, that, upon the facts then before them, they ought not to take the loss of profits into consideration at all in estimating the damages. *There must therefore be a new trial in this case.* ◀

COMMENTS AND QUESTIONS

1. Outline the facts here. How did the lower court judge charge the jury? What happened on appeal?
2. Summarize the rule of law enunciated by the English court in this case. The decision is a landmark and is generally cited and followed by most American courts.

Duty to Mitigate Damages

Once a breach occurs, the injured party must do everything within reason to minimize the amount of damage he sustains. In other words, he is not allowed to increase his damages willfully, either through action or inaction.

WORKER is hired to work for BOSS for a period of one year at a monthly salary. At the end of six months he is wrongfully discharged. Unless WORKER is honestly unable to find another job of a similar nature in the same locality, he may not sit idle and collect his salary for the remaining six months. If he finds another job that pays a lower salary, he is entitled to the difference in pay between his original job and the new job during the remaining six months.

Nominal Damages

Occasionally, an injured party is unable to prove that he has suffered any loss as a result of a breach of contract. To dispose of such cases, the court may award him a very small sum, such as $1.00. Such awards are called *nominal damages.*

Liquidated Damages

Many contracts stipulate that, in the event of a breach, the damages will be fixed at a certain amount, or that they will be computed at a certain rate. Damages of this sort are known as *liquidated damages.* The courts will usually hold that they are recoverable so long as they are not excessive or purely in the nature of a penalty. Moreover, the amount must be fairly close to the damages that might reasonably have been anticipated; otherwise, the court will compute them in accordance with the general rule.

Once the court decides that the figure set for liquidated damages is reasonable, however, that will be the amount of damages awarded, *regardless* of the actual damages sustained by the injured party.

In the Wisconsin case that follows, the building contract contained a liquidated-damage clause in the event of delay in finishing the building. Notice how the court handled this situation.

SEEMAN v. BIEMANN

Supreme Court of Wisconsin, 1900
108 Wis. 365, 84 N.W. 490

► Action by the owner of a building against the contractors for $10 per day liquidated damages for delay in completing the building.

MARSHALL, J. . . . The building was to have been completed by May 22, 1897. It was not finished til July 15, 1897. There was a delay of one month and twenty-three days. There was no evidence of any claims being made for allowances of time as provided in the contract, so the contractors were clearly liable to the appellant, upon the proper rule for computing damages under the agreement.

That brings us to the necessity of determining whether the parties agreed upon $10 a day as the amount to be allowed as damages for each day's delay, or whether that clause in the contract was intended as a mere security for the completion of the building by the time agreed upon, hence should be considered as a penalty and the recoverable damages be limited to such as proof shows Farr actually sustained.

The law is too well settled to permit any reasonable controversy in regard to it at this time, that where parties stipulate in their contract for damages in the event of a breach of it, using appropriate language to indicate that the damages are agreed upon in advance, and such damages are unreasonable considered as liquidated damages, the stipulated amount will be construed to be a mere forfeiture or penalty and the recoverable damages be limited to those actually sustained. While courts adhere to the doctrine that the intention of the parties must govern in regard to whether damages mentioned in their contract are liquidated, they uniformly take such liberties in regard to the matter, based on arbitrary rules of construction, so called, as may be necessary to effect judicial notions of equity between parties, guided of course by precedents that are considered to have the force of law, sometimes calling that a penalty which the parties call stipulated damages, and that which the parties call a penalty stipulated damages, where otherwise an unconscionable advantage would be obtined by one person over another. The judicial power thus exercised cannot properly be justified under any ordinary rules of judicial construction. Such rules permit courts to go as far as possible to effect the intent of the parties where it is left obscure by their language so long as such intent can be read out of the contract without violating the rules of language or of law. But in determining whether an amount agreed upon as damages was intended as liquidated damages or as a penalty, rules of language are ignored and the expressed intent of parties is made to give way to the equity of the particular case, having due regard to precedents as before indicated. Here the damages are said by the parties to be agreed upon as $10 per day for each day's delay, to be deducted from the contract price, indicating about as clearly as language can that they intended that such damages should be considered as irrevocably stipulated damages; yet the uniform rule is that such circumstance does not absolutely control.

This court, in harmony with the weight of authority, early adopted the abitrary rule that where damages may be readily computed and the stipulated damages, so called, are largely in excess of actual damages, the court will disregard what the parties say they intended, and presume that they intended what is fair and reasonable under the circumstances, however much that may violate their language. Pierce v. Jung, 10 Wis. 30; Fitzpatrick v. Cottingham, 14 Wis. 219. In Berrinkott v. Traphagen, 39 Wis. 219, there is found quoted with approval from 3 Parsons, Cont. 156, language to the effect that parties may contract for stipulated damages at their pleasure, but such damages only as the law says are liquidated according to the artificial rules which have been adopted to justify courts in saying what the parties intended are in fact to be regarded as such damages. The most significant of such rules is the one above referred to. Applying it to the case before us, the stipulation of $10 per day for delay must be held to be a penalty merely, and not necessarily recoverable to the whole amount. The rental value of the property as found by the court was $38 per month. That is the true measure of actual damages since there were no special circumstances shown by the evidence, brought home to the knowledge of the contractor at the time of the making of the contract, from which we can say the damages which the parties then had in contemplation as the probable result of a breach of the contract as to time of completing the building were other than loss of use for the period of delay. Guetzkow Bros. Co. v. A. H. Andrews & Co., 92 Wis. 214; Kennedy v. South Shore L. Co., 102 Wis. 284.

The rental value of the building is trifling in amount as compared with the stipulated damages so called, of $10 per day. There was, in the nature of the case, at the time the contract was made, no difficulty to be apprehended in arriving at the actual damages that might arise from mere delay in completing the building. So we have the two elements recognized as controlling the language of parties respecting stipulated damages, first, the amount the parties say they agreed upon is grossly in excess of the actual damages sustained or that could have been reasonably apprehended at the time of making the contract; second the damages actually sustained are readily ascertainable.

It follows that we must hold that the parties intended the $10 per day as a mere penalty to secure the performance of the contract, and limit the recoverable damages to such as were actually sustained, to wit, $38 per month for fifty-three days, or $67.13, with six per cent. interest thereon from the date the breach of the contract was complete, July 15, 1897.

Judgment affirmed, as modified.   ◄

COMMENTS AND QUESTIONS

1. Summarize the facts in this case. What was the principal issue before the court and how was it decided?
2. If the parties freely agreed to certain liquidated damages, why should the court not enforce their contract? Summarize the court's reasons for disregarding the agreement in this case.
3. If the rental value of the property had been $380 a month instead of $38, do you think the court would have enforced the liquidated-damages clause?

Specific Performance

Ordinarily, a payment of money is regarded as adequate compensation for any damages sustained by the injured party. In special situations, however, the courts feel that a money award is insufficient and that justice requires the wrongdoer to perform his obligation. This remedy, which is known as *specific performance*, is usually reserved for cases in which a party has agreed to deliver property of unique or extraordinary value, or of special distinction, which cannot be duplicated or readily acquired elsewhere.

EXAMPLES

1. An agreement to sell real property is specifically enforceable by either party, as a general rule, on the theory that any parcel of land has a unique quality or an intrinsic worth.
2. A contract for the sale of a rare old painting is specifically enforceable.
3. An agreement to sell the controlling shares of stock in a closely held corporation is specifically enforceable.

In the case that follows, one party sought specific performance of a contract to sell land. The defendant's counsel urged the court not to follow the general rule. Did he succeed?

KITCHEN v. HERRING

Supreme Court of North Carolina, 1851
7 Ire. Eq. 190

► PEARSON, J.   In December 1846, the defendant, Herring, executed a contract in writing in these words, "Rec'd of John L. Kitchen payment in full for a certain tract of land lying on the South west side of Black River, adjoining the lands of William Haffland and Martial, for which I am to give him a good deed &c." The defendant Pridgen wrote the contract and is a subscribing witness. The plaintiff was put into possession in March 1847. Pridgen united with him; and the other defendant, Musgrove, under a contract with Pridgen, with a large number of hands, commenced cutting down the timber, which constitutes the chief value of the land. Pridgen was the surety of the plaintiff, to a note of $325, given payable at three months for the price of the land. In January, Herring executed a deed for the land to Pridgen, and under this title the plaintiff was turned out of possession.

The prayer of the Bill is for a specific performance, for an account of the profits and for an injunction. After the Bill was filed, an arrangement was made, by which Musgrove continued his operations in getting timber, and agreed to account with the successful party. . . .

It was . . . insisted, that, as it appears by the plaintiff's own showing, "the land is chiefly valuable on account of the timber," this case does not come within the principle, on which a specific performance is decreed.

The position is new, and the Counsel admitted, that there was no authority to sustain it, but he contended with earnestness, that it was so fully sustained by "the reason of the thing," as to justify a departure from a well settled rule of this Court, under the maxim, *cessante ratione cessat lex.*[58]

The argument failed wholly to prove, that "the reason of the thing" called for an exception. The principle in regard to land was adopted, not because it was fertile or rich in minerals, or valuable for timber, but simply because it was land—a favorite and favored subject in England, and every country of Anglo-Saxon origin. Our constitution gives to land pre-eminence over every other species of property; and our law, whether administered in Courts of law or of equity, gives to it the same preference. Land, whether rich or poor, cannot be taken to pay debts until the personal property is exhausted. Contracts concerning land must be in writing. Land must be sold at the Court House, must be conveyed by deeds duly registered, and other instances "too tedious to mention." The principle is, that land is assumed to have a peculiar value, so as to give an equity for a specific performance, without reference to its quality or quantity. The same is assumed as to slaves. Williams v. Howard, 3 Murph. 74, while in regard to other property, less favored, a specific performance will not be decreed, unless there be peculiar circumstances; for, if with the money, an article of the same description can be bought in the market—corn, cotton, etc., the remedy at law is adequate.

There must be a decree for the plaintiff with costs.   ◄

COMMENTS AND QUESTIONS

1. This case illustrates the special consideration that courts give to contracts for the sale of land. What were the defendant's arguments against a decree of specific performance? Note his counsel's admission that he had no authority to back his position—a difficult spot for a lawyer to be in before an appellate court.
2. Note the summary of law on specific performance of contracts for the sale of personal property. Note, too, the reference to slaves as favored property.

Specific performance of a contract to render personal services for another is never ordered by the court. However, where the services are of a special or unusual nature, the court may issue an order preventing the party from performing such services for anyone else. This, of course, is an indirect way of enforcing the original obligation.

---

58 If the reason for the law ceases, the law itself should also cease.

EXAMPLES

1. D agrees to work for o as a chauffeur for a period of one year. If D quits after six months, o's only remedy is to sue him for damages, since the court will not force D to continue working for o if he doesn't want to.
2. SINGER contracts to sing for the Neapolitan Opera Company for two years. If he quits after the first season, there is no way in which the Opera Company can force him to return for the second year. However, since his talents are unusual, the court may issue an order prohibiting SINGER from performing for any other company.

SUMMARY OF THE LAW OF CONTRACTS

Nature and Classification

A contract is an agreement between two or more parties which gives rise to legal obligations and which is enforceable in the courts. A contract may be written or oral; written contracts are sometimes under seal. When the obligations have been performed, the contract is said to be executed; if they are yet to be performed, it is said to be executory. In order for a contract to be binding, there must be: (1) an agreement between the parties; (2) genuine assent by both sides; (3) consideration; (4) legal capacity; (5) a written memorandum of the agreement if the Statute of Frauds requires it; (6) a legal purpose. If one or more of these elements is lacking, the agreement may be void, or, in some cases, unenforceable; or it may be avoided by one side but not by the other.

The Agreement

For an agreement to exist, there must be a proposal, or offer, by the offeror and an acceptance by the offeree. To constitute a legal offer, a proposal must be definite and seriously intended and must be communicated to the offeree. In addition, the proposal must be more than a preliminary inquiry or invitation to negotiate. If the offeror invites the offeree to indicate his acceptance by making a promise in return, the offeror is suggesting that a bilateral contract be formed. On the other hand, if the offeror requests the performance of an act by the offeree and makes it clear that he does not wish to be bound until that act has been performed, he is suggesting that a unilateral contract be formed.

A valid acceptance must conform to all the terms of the offer and must meet any conditions set by the offeror concerning the time or manner of acceptance. To be effective, an acceptance must occur before the offer is withdrawn or terminates in some other way. If the acceptance changes any of the terms of the offer, it is said to be a counteroffer, which, in turn, must be accepted by the original offeror before an agreement is reached. Ordinarily, silence on the part of the offeree is not construed as acceptance unless past dealings of a similar nature between the parties suggest an implied acceptance. To be effective, an acceptance of an offer leading to a bilateral contract must be communicated to the offeror. However, where acceptance is made by mail or telegraph, it is generally held to be effective when it is deposited in the mail or left at the telegraph office. An acceptance of an offer leading to a unilateral contract is not effective until the act called for has been performed, regardless of when the offeror is given notice of it.

Contracts are often implied from the circumstances even though there is no explicit agreement. In such cases, the courts consider the overt acts of the parties rather than their secret intentions. Sometimes, even though there is no contract, express or implied, if one side receives the benefit of another's services, he may be required to reimburse that person for the fair value of the benefit he has received. This is called a quasi-contract.

Reality of Assent

For a contract to exist, there must be a genuine agreement between the parties. If both parties act on a mistaken notion of a material fact, neither is bound by the agreement. However, if the mutual mistake has to do with law, neither side is excused and, in most states, the contract is binding. Where the mistake, whether of fact or law, is made by one party only (i.e., a unilateral mistake), the contract is binding unless the other party is plainly aware of the mistake and seeks to take undue advantage of it.

If one party misrepresents an important fact for the purpose of deceiving the other and inducing him to make a contract, the innocent person may sue for damages or avoid the contract. However, the other party must, in fact, rely on the misrepresentation and must investigate the facts if he has an opportunity to do so. Generally speaking, silence is not held to be a misrepresentation, since neither party has a duty to disclose information unless the other party makes an inquiry.

If one party uses duress or undue influence to force the other side to enter into a contract against his will, the innocent party usually may avoid the contract if he so chooses. However, in any case where he is given the right to avoid his obligations on account of fraud, duress, or mistake, the innocent party must take action within a reasonable period so as not to prejudice unduly the rights of the other side.

Consideration

Each party to a contract must furnish consideration before the contract is binding. Consideration usually takes the form of an act or a promise to do something which is given in exchange for an act or a promise by the other side. The performance of an act in the past does not constitute consideration for a present promise. Similarly, if one side does something or promises to do something that he is already obligated to do, no consideration is present. (A few courts make an exception to this rule, however, when an owner promises a contractor more money to complete an existing obligation.) As a general rule, the courts will not review the adequacy of consideration to make sure that each side gets a fair deal.

In the following cases, promises are held to be enforceable even though no consideration is actually present: (1) where the contract is under seal (in some states); (2) where the promise is in writing and clearly indicates an intention to be bound (in some states); (3) where a person promises to give money to a charitable or educational institution (in most states).

Legal Capacity

A contract between a minor and an adult can be avoided only by the minor; it remains binding on the adult until the minor chooses to avoid it. If the minor elects to disaffirm, he must return any benefit he has received if he still has it to give back. In most states, if he has lost or spent what he received, he may still avoid the contract and recover the consideration he has given without returning the consideration he has received. Some states deny a minor the right to avoid a contract if he has lied about his age. If he has the right to avoid, he may exercise it at any time during his minority and for a reasonable time after reaching majority. If he fails to act within that time, he is bound by the contract. If, after reaching majority, he indicates by his words or actions that he is willing to be bound, he is considered to have ratified the contract.

Although a minor is not liable for his contracts, he is responsible for the fair value of items furnished him which are necessary to his well-being and everyday life (e.g., food, clothing, and shelter).

An insane person, or a person who is so intoxicated that he is incapable of understanding the effect of his actions, may disaffirm his contracts when he regains his sanity or sobers up. However, like minors, such persons are responsible for necessaries which are furnished to them.

Illegal Agreements

An agreement that relates to unlawful subject matter or that has an illegal objective or is contrary to public policy will not be enforced by the courts. Contracts to commit crimes or civil wrongs or to obstruct justice, and wagering agreements, are generally held to be illegal. Contracts with unlicensed persons are usually enforceable unless the licensing requirement was meant to ensure a high standard of competence. Sunday contracts are not enforceable in some states unless they are later ratified or performed on a weekday. Contracts that unduly restrain trade are usually held to be illegal.

If a contract is illegal, the courts generally will not assist either party to enforce it and will leave both sides where it finds them. However, if one side is innocent or is not implicated in the illegality, he may usually recover any consideration he has paid. Also, if one side pays a sum of money to the other in exchange for a promise to perform an illegal act and then repents before the act is performed, he may recover his payment.

Written Contracts

In most cases, an oral contract is just as binding as a written contract. However, since a written contract is more easily proved in court, it is wise to put important contracts in writing.

Once an agreement has been reduced to writing, it is presumed to reflect the final understanding of the parties, and neither side may introduce evidence to contradict the written terms. In the following situations, however, the court will permit the parties to present evidence to contradict or modify the terms of a written agreement: (1) where such evidence shows fraud or other misconduct; (2) where it explains or clarifies an ambiguity in the written agreement; (3) where the written contract is not complete; (4) where the modification or change has been made *after* the written contract was entered into.

If the terms of a written contract are ambiguous, or if unanticipated contingencies arise, the court often has a difficult task in determining the meaning of the contract. In approaching this task, the court looks at the contract as a whole and attempts to ascertain the true intention of the parties. If the contract is of the stock-form variety (e.g., a lease or an insurance policy), ambiguities are resolved against the party who drafted it. In addition, when it is deemed necessary, the court will interpret a contract in terms of its effect on the public welfare.

By virtue of the Statute of Frauds, certain kinds of contract are not enforceable unless there is a written memorandum signed by the party against whom enforcement is sought. To satisfy the requirements of the statute, the memorandum must: (1) describe the subject matter of the contract; (2) identify the parties; (3) state the consideration; (4) specify any other important terms of the contract. If such a memorandum is executed, it is not necessary that the other party sign it. In most states the following kinds of contract come under the Statute of Frauds: (1) contracts that require more than one year to perform; (2) contracts for the sale of real property; (3) contracts guaranteeing the payment of another person's debt; (4) contracts in consideration of marriage.

In addition to the categories mentioned above, the Statute of Frauds also applies to sales of personal property where the price exceeds a certain minimum amount—usually $500, but varying from $30 to $2,500 from state to state. If the contract is below this minimum amount, the agreement is binding even though it is not in writing. If the price is higher than the minimum, the contract is enforceable only if: (1) there is a written memorandum signed by the party to be charged, or (2) the buyer consents to accept the goods and takes delivery of at least part of them, or (3) the buyer makes a part payment for the goods. The Statute of Frauds is not applicable to sales of personal property which is to be specially manufactured by the seller for the buyer, even if the price exceeds the minimum amount.

Assignment of Rights and Delegation of Duties

An assignment is a transfer of one party's contractual rights to a third person who was a stranger to the original contract. In most cases, an assignment need not be in writing and no consideration is necessary to make it valid. However, if it is not supported by consideration, it may be revoked before performance occurs. Generally speaking, any contractual right may be assigned except in cases where: (1) the right involves the performance of some personal service or has to do with personal trust or confidence; (2) performance is substantially changed by the assignment; (3) the contract or a statute expressly forbids an assignment.

A party may ordinarily delegate to a third party his duty to perform a contractual obligation, provided the obligation is routine in nature. However, if the obligation is personal in nature or involves special skill, confidence, or trust; or if the contract expressly prohibits an assignment, the duty may not be delegated to another. Even where delegation is permitted, the original contracting party is not relieved of his obligation to perform unless all three parties agree.

As a general rule, when a contractual right is assigned, the assignee is subject to any and all defenses which the obligor has against the assignor, and the assignee has no better rights than the assignor had.

If a contract is made expressly for the benefit of a third-party beneficiary, it is usually enforceable by him even though he was not a party to the original contract. In addition, once the contract has been made, the right to receive the benefit may not be revoked unless the contracting parties have reserved the power to do so. If, however, the original contracting parties did not *expressly* intend to benefit the third person, he is not permitted to bring suit to enforce the obligation.

Performance and Discharge of Obligations

In most cases, a party discharges his contractual obligation by performance. If one side is obligated to perform first, he must do so before he can call on the other to carry out his obligation. To satisfy his obligation, a party must prove: (1) that he performed on time, if that is an important element of the contract; (2) that he completed, or substantially completed, performance of all his obligations; (3) that his performance satisfied, or should reasonably have satisfied, the other party, if such a provision is included in the contract.

As a general rule, hardships and difficulties do not excuse performance of a contractual duty even when performance becomes impossible. However, in the following cases the courts usually make an exception and excuse performance: (1) where performance becomes illegal after the contract is made; (2) where performance of the obligation requires special skill or judgment or involves a personal relationship, and the person obliged to perform dies; (3) where certain property which is absolutely essential to performance is destroyed or damaged so that performance of the obligation becomes impossible; (4) where one party actually prevents or interferes with the other's performance.

A breach of contract exists when a party fails to perform his obligation. Normally, a breach is possible only after the time for performance has arrived. If, however, before the time for performance arrives, a party clearly indicates that he will not perform when the obligation comes due, the other side may sue for breach of contract immediately.

Contractual obligations may be discharged by agreement of the parties in one of the following ways: (1) by mutually rescinding their obligations; (2) by canceling their original contract and substituting a new one; (3) by a novation, whereby a third party is substituted for one of the contracting parties; (4) by an accord and satisfaction, whereby one side agrees to accept performance of a different obligation and the other side actually performs the new obligation.

Contractual obligations may also be discharged if the statute of limitations expires and bars an action for breach of contract, or if the party obligated to perform goes through bankruptcy proceedings.

Remedies and Damages

In most cases involving a breach of contract, the injured party sues to collect damages from the other side. As a general rule, he is entitled to recover enough money to put him in as good a position as he would have been in had the contract been fully performed. However, a court will not award damages for loss or injury resulting from unexpected or unusual causes unless both parties were aware of them when they entered into the contract. Once a breach has occurred, the injured party must do everything within reason to minimize his damages. If the parties stipulate in their contract the amount of damages to be paid in the event of breach, the provision will be enforced only if the amount is reasonably close to what might have been anticipated and only if it has not been set up merely as a penalty.

The court never orders the specific performance of a contractual obligation unless the contract involves the transfer of land or other property of unique value which cannot be acquired elsewhere.

Supplementary Reading: Contracts

Two of the best-known authorities in this field are Samuel Williston and Arthur L. Corbin, whose textbooks are highly recommended. (Williston, *A Treatise on the*

Law of Contracts, Students' Ed., Baker, Voorhis, 1938. Corbin, *Contracts,* Oxford University Press, 1952.) For case materials, see Lon L. Fuller, *Cases on the Law of Contracts* (West Publishing Co., 1947), or Edwin W. Patterson and George W. Goble, *Cases on Contracts,* 2nd Ed. (Foundation Press, 1941). For an authoritative summary of the basic rules of contract law, *The Restatement of the Law of Contracts* (American Law Institute, 1932) is extremely useful.

12 Sales

Introduction

In the preceding chapter we reviewed the basic rules of contract law. In this chapter we shall discuss the special rules of law governing the most important kind of commercial contract—the sale of goods. By "goods" we mean tangible personal property such as automobiles, groceries, clothing, appliances, and lumber.[1] In subsequent chapters, we shall deal with the sale and transfer of certain kinds of intangible personal property.[2] Although we shall not explore in any detail the special rules of law governing the sale of real property, many of the cases included deal with real estate transactions.

Sales transactions are as old as civilization. In the earliest days such transactions were very simple, generally involving just a buyer and seller who dealt with each other face to face. As trade and commerce expanded, however, the business of buying and selling became more and more complicated. Improvements in transportation meant that goods could be shipped from one section of a country to another and, eventually, from one nation to another. Since buyer and seller could no longer deal with each other in person, they turned to agents and representatives to negotiate their sales contracts.[3]

The growing complexity of sales transactions created a corresponding complexity in the contracts entered into by buyer and seller. Early sales

---

[1] Property is divided into two main classes—real and personal. Simply defined, *real property* consists of land, and the buildings and vegetation on the land. *Personal property* includes all property other than real property, and is further classified as either tangible or intangible. Roughly speaking, *tangible personal property* is property that can be touched or felt and has physical existence. *Intangible personal property* consists of legal rights to money or to other property that does not have any physical or tangible form. Examples of intangible personal property are stocks, bonds, rents, patents, and copyrights. Although these rights may sometimes be evidenced by documents (e.g., a stock certificate), generally speaking their existence does not depend on any physical form.

[2] For example, in Chapter 13 we shall discuss negotiable instruments, and in Chapter 16 we shall have something to say about stocks and bonds.

[3] The law of agency will be dealt with in Chapter 14.

contracts were usually quite simple and straightforward: they did little more than name the parties, describe the goods, and state the price. Gradually, however, as more and more sales were made on credit and through agents and middlemen, businessmen developed a great variety of contractual provisions designed to protect themselves against loss. As we shall see, this development spawned a host of legal problems for courts and legislatures.

Along with these changes in the form of sales contracts came changes in the morality of the market place. In the early stages of sales law, buyer and seller dealt with each other at arm's length, so to speak, and the slogan *caveat emptor* (let the buyer beware) was an accepted legal principle. In recent times, however, the law has taken a more enlightened attitude and has imposed certain standards of conduct on the business community. Perhaps the best example of this evolution is the doctrine of implied warranties,[4] which will be discussed in Section 3 of this chapter.

Many of the changes in sales law have resulted from the steady increase in government regulation of business practices in the last half-century. Hundreds of federal and state laws have been enacted governing such matters as the restraint of trade between competitors, unfair methods of competition, discrimination between buyers and sellers, deceptive packaging, misleading advertising and deceptive selling methods, adulterated goods, and false labeling. Since time and space do not permit a detailed discussion of all these matters, we shall concentrate in this chapter on the basic contractual relationship between buyer and seller. Some of these problems, however, particularly in the area of restraint of trade, will be dealt with in Chapter 17, "Government Regulation of Business."

Until the end of the nineteenth century, only a small portion of the law of sales had been enacted into statutory form either in England or the United States. Prior to that time, the rules had been formulated, first, in the special commercial courts (i.e., the law merchant) and, later, in the common-law and equity courts. The rules developed by these courts were often in conflict, however, and gave rise to a great divergency of opinion. In this country, the fact that the various states often applied different rules to the same problem created widespread confusion—especially as more and more sales transactions crossed state boundaries. This diversity and uncertainty led to a strong movement to codify the law of sales in an effort to make it uniform throughout the nation.

In the 1890's, in response to the combined efforts of the American Bar Association and the representatives of several state legislatures, a conference was held to discuss the possibility of drafting uniform state legislation in the law of sales and other commercial fields.[5] As a result of this and

---

[4] A *warranty* is a form of guarantee by the seller that the goods being sold meet certain standards. An *implied warranty* is one that the law, in effect, imposes on the seller regardless of whether it is stated in so many words in the contract.

[5] The same movement was also in evidence in England at this time. In 1894, Parliament passed the Sale of Goods Act, which covered a considerable portion of the law of sales. This act is still in force and has been adopted by several nations in the British Commonwealth.

succeeding conferences, a committee was appointed to draft a uniform law of sales. By 1906, the committee's work had been completed and was then submitted to the state legislatures for their consideration. The Uniform Sales Act (or U.S.A.), as it is called, was subsequently adopted by roughly three-fourths of the states, including most of the large commercial states.

The Uniform Sales Act has succeeded reasonably well in achieving its main purpose: to introduce uniformity into the law of sales. Over the years, however, many legal scholars have urged that some of its provisions be changed and that the act itself be redrafted. It is true that different courts have given quite different interpretations to a given provision, and that the act as a whole is somewhat out of harmony with certain commercial customs and practices.

As a result of such criticisms, which have been made of other uniform statutes as well, a movement was launched in the 1940's to draft and enact one comprehensive statute that would cover all the areas of commercial law. The result was the Uniform Commercial Code, or the U.C.C., which was drafted under the leadership of Professor Karl N. Llewellyn and others and was approved by the American Law Institute in 1952. The U.C.C. was first adopted by Pennsylvania in 1953 and, during the next eight years, was enacted by seventeen other states. It appears likely that many other jurisdictions will follow suit.

The Uniform Sales Act, however, was still in force in roughly half the states in 1962. Consequently, we will concentrate on its provisions and their interpretation, pointing out the principal changes introduced by the Uniform Commercial Code. Since the U.C.C. is of such recent origin, of course, very few cases have as yet arisen calling for interpretation of its provisions.

Unlike the law of contracts, most of which is judge-made law based on precedents, the law of sales consists mainly of statutes and statutory interpretations. In fact, one of the problems facing the courts in their efforts to interpret the Uniform Sales Act (and now the Uniform Commercial Code) has been deciding what effect to give to long-standing common-law precedents. The U.S.A. was intended to codify some of the common-law rules and to change others. But it does not make clear exactly how particular precedents are to be regarded. Another recurring question is just how much one appellate court should be influenced by the interpretations of a particular provision of the act by other appellate courts.

SECTION 1

THE SALES CONTRACT

In General

A *sale* is a contract whereby the seller (sometimes called the vendor) transfers ownership of goods to the buyer (or vendee) in exchange for a consideration called the price. In some cases the contract is completed in one transaction, and ownership of the goods is immediately transferred to the buyer.

> EXAMPLE
>
> B buys a dozen apples from s at the grocery store.

In other situations, however, the contract provides that ownership of the goods is to be transferred at some future time. A contract of this sort is often referred to as a *contract to sell*, to distinguish it from a present sale.

> EXAMPLE
>
> On October 1, B orders 100 Christmas trees from s for delivery on December 15. s accepts the order and agrees to deliver the trees.

A sale should be carefully distinguished from other transactions of a similar nature. Occasionally, though, the distinction is hard to draw, and reasonable men may differ in their interpretations, as the following case illustrates.

PEARLMUTTER v. BETH DAVID HOSPITAL

Court of Appeals of New York, 1954
308 N.Y. 100, 123 N.E. 2d 792

► FULD, J. This is, in effect, an action to recover damages for personal injuries sustained by plaintiff while a patient in the hospital maintained and operated by defendant. The injuries allegedly resulted from the transfusing of "bad" blood, supplied by the hospital for a price as part of the customary services rendered by the hospital to its patients. The complaint contains no allegations of negligence, but rather seeks recovery upon the theory that the supplying of blood constituted a sale within the Sales

Act [6] and that, as a consequence, there attached implied warranties imposed by that statute that the blood was "reasonably fit for (the) purpose" for which required and of "merchantable quality," Personal Property Law, McK. Consol. Laws, c. 41, 96, subds. 1, 2.

. . . Defendant moved under rules 106 and 112 of the Rules of [the New York] Civil Practice to dismiss the complaint for insufficiency. The court at Special Term denied the motion; the Appellate Division unanimously affirmed, granted defendant permission to appeal and certified the question, "Was Special Term correct in denying defendant's motion to dismiss the complaint herein?"

The answer to that question turns upon whether the transaction described in the complaint constitutes a sale under the Sales Act, whether, in other words, there was created a vendor-vendee relationship between defendant and plaintiff.

. . . The essence of the contractual relationship between hospital and patient is readily apparent; the patient bargains for, and the hospital agrees to make available, the human skill and physical material of medical science to the end that the patient's health be restored.

Such a contract is clearly one for services, and just as clearly, it is not divisible. Concepts of purchase and sale cannot separately be attached to the healing materials—such as medicines, drugs or, indeed, blood—supplied by the hospital for a price as part of the medical services it offers. That the property or title to certain items of medical material may be transferred, so to speak, from the hospital to the patient during the course of medical treatment does not serve to make each such transaction a sale. . . . Sale and transfer are not synonymous and not every transfer of personal property constitutes a sale. . . . It has long been recognized that, when service predominates, and transfer of personal property is but an incidental feature of the transaction, the transaction is not deemed a sale within the Sales Act. . . . As Benjamin put it in his work on Sales . . . , "a contract of sale is not constituted merely by reason that the property in the materials is to be transferred. . . . If they are simply accessory to work and labour, the contract is for work, labour and materials. Such is the case of medicine supplied by a medical man to a patient, or by a farrier to a horse."

Thus, a contract to paint a picture has been held to be a contract for work, labour and services rather than a sale, although the title to the canvas is actually transferred to the customer. . . . Likewise, where the contract is to construct a highway, the furnishing of gravel, even though a specific price was set for that material, was held not a sale. See Town of Saugus v. B. Perini & Sons, Inc., *supra*, 305 Mass. 403, 404–405; 26 N.E. 211. And an even more apt illustration is afforded by Babcock v. Nudelman, *supra*, 367 Ill. 626, 12 N.E. 2d 635. That case involved the question as to whether an optometrist, engaged both in prescribing and furnishing eyeglasses, was in the business of "selling tangible personal property within

---

[6] The Uniform Sales Act, as enacted in New York.

the meaning of the provisions of the Retailers' Occupation Tax Act." 367 Ill. at page 627, 12 N.E. 2d at page 636. The Illinois Supreme Court, despite the indisputable fact that eyeglasses are tangible personal property, held that furnishing them was "merely incidental to the services rendered" and not within the statute's coverage. . . .

While determination, as to whether the essence of a particular contract is for the rendition of services or for the sale of property, may at times be troublesome and vexatious, there is no doubt that the main object sought to be accomplished in this case was the care and treatment of the patient. The supplying of blood by the hospital was entirely subordinate to its paramount function of furnishing trained personnel and specialized facilities in an endeavor to restore plaintiff's health. It was not for blood— or iodine or bandages—for which plaintiff bargained, but the wherewithal of the hospital staff and the availability of hospital facilities to provide whatever medical treatment was considered advisable. The conclusion is evident that the furnishing of blood was only an incidental and very secondary adjunct to the services performed by the hospital and, therefore, was not within the provisions of the Sales Act. The fact that the treatment might have come from a physician, while the blood came from the hospital, is of no operative consequence; it is the transaction, regarded in its entirety, which must determine its nature and character. As long as it involves the medical care and treatment of a patient at a hospital, it is immaterial that it is the doctor who may diagnose and treat and the hospital which may supply facilities and material. . . .

Not at all analogous to the case before us is our decision—relied upon by plaintiff—holding that, "where a customer enters a restaurant, receives, eats and pays for food, delivered to him on his order, the transaction is a purchase of goods." Temple v. Keeler, 238 N.Y. 344, 346; 144 N.E. 635. While it has been said that a restaurant owner does not sell food, but rather renders a service, the fact is that there is "a sale of what is actually used." . . . And, indeed, semantics apart and looking at the transaction for what it actually is, there can be no doubt that, when one goes into a restaurant, he does so in order to buy what the restaurant in truth has to sell, namely, food. That is not so, though, when one enters a hospital as a patient; he goes there, not to buy medicines or pills, not to purchase bandages or iodine or serum or blood, but to obtain a course of treatment in the hope of being cured of what ails him. . . .

Our conclusion that the complaint fails to state a cause of action for breach of implied warranty under the Sales Act leaves untouched the question of defendant's liability for negligence, if any.

The order of the Appellate Division and that of Special Term should be reversed, with costs in all courts, and the matter remitted for further proceedings in accordance with this opinion. The question certified is answered in the negative. . . .

LEWIS, C. J., and DESMOND and VAN VOORHIS, JJ., concur with FULD, J. FROESSEL, J. (dissenting).

In her complaint, plaintiff . . . alleges that she "purchased" from defendant . . . blood for the purpose of transfusion . . . and that she "paid to the defendant the sum of $60.00"—an ordinary transaction of "goods supplied under a . . . sale."

It should be noted that plaintiff is not suing defendant for the service of injecting the blood into her bloodstream, but simply for the sale of "bad blood" for a separate . . . consideration over and above the consideration she was paying for "room and board and . . . service."

We have held that where a person orders food in a restaurant or ice cream in a drug store, it constitutes a sale to which the Personal Property Law annexes an implied warranty. . . . So it has been held with regard to drugs. We cannot logically differentiate those situations from the one involved here, at least as a matter of pleading.

We think the courts below were clearly correct in stating that we "may not hold as a matter of law that there was no sale without knowing any of the facts relating to the acquisition of the blood by the plaintiff" and plaintiff, under the allegations of her complaint, should be permitted to present her proofs.

The order of the Appellate Division should be affirmed. . . .

CONWAY, J. and DYE, J. concur in the dissent.   ◀

COMMENTS AND QUESTIONS

1. What was the plaintiff's principal allegation here? Did the lower courts agree with her? What happened on appeal?
2. Apparently the plaintiff could not show that the hospital was negligent. So the only possibility of recovery lay in convincing the court that the transaction was a "sale." Summarize the reasons given by the majority of the court for rejecting this contention.
3. Note the dissenting opinion by three of the seven judges. Do you feel it has merit? As a matter of law, should not the plaintiff be allowed to try to prove her allegation that there was a sale?

Formation of Sales Contracts

Since a sale is a contract, all the basic rules of contract law that we discussed in Chapter 11 (see pp. 203–350) are applicable: there must be a genuine agreement between the parties, with no mistake, fraud, or duress present; the parties must have legal capacity to act; the agreement must be supported by consideration; and the contract must have a legal purpose. If one or more of these requirements are not met, the contract is not enforceable.

The Uniform Commercial Code, in those states where it has been enacted, makes several significant changes in the application of contract law to sales transactions. Here are some of the more important changes:

1. *Definite Agreement*—Generally speaking, the courts will not enforce a contract unless it is clear that the parties have reached a definite agreement on all the important terms. The U.C.C. relaxes this strict requirement: "Even though one or more terms are left open, a contract for sale does not fail for indefiniteness if the parties have intended to make a contract and there is a reasonably certain basis for giving an appropriate remedy."

2. *Revocability of Offers*—According to the U.C.C., "An offer by a merchant to buy or sell goods in a signed writing which gives assurance that it will be held open needs no consideration to be irrevocable for a reasonable time or during a stated time, but in no event for a time exceeding three months. . . ." You will recall that in most states such offers are regarded as revocable unless they are supported by consideration.

3. *Additional Terms in Acceptance*—Basic contract law holds that for an acceptance to be binding it must be an unqualified assent to the offer, and that it must not propose additional or different terms. If such terms are proposed, the acceptance becomes a mere counteroffer. The Code, mindful of business practice, changes this rule by making the following provisions:

(1) A definite and seasonable expression of acceptance or a written confirmation which is sent within a reasonable time operates as an acceptance even though it states terms additional to or different from those offered or agreed upon.

(2) The additional terms are to be construed as proposals for additions to the contract and between merchants become part of the contract unless they materially alter it or notification of objection to them has already been given or is given within a reasonable time.

4. *Modification of Existing Sales Contracts*—Most states follow the rule that no agreement to modify an existing contract is binding unless it is supported by new consideration. The Uniform Commercial Code adopts the minority rule by providing that agreements to modify an existing sales contract *are* binding on the parties even in the absence of new consideration.

Note that the main effect of these changes is to relax the strict application of the rules of offer and acceptance and of consideration. The framers of the Uniform Commercial Code undoubtedly had in mind the widespread use of the common-law rules of contract law to avoid obligations that should be legally enforceable. Many legal and business experts feel that the changes proposed by the U.C.C. are long overdue.

Price of Goods

The parties to a sales contract may either agree on a fixed price or agree that the price will be fixed in the future on a definite basis. (E.g., they may agree that an impartial third party will set the price, or they may stipulate that the buyer will pay the market price on a given date.) On the other hand, if their contract provides that they will agree on a price at a later date, it is not binding, because there has not been a sufficient meeting of minds. However, if the contract makes no provision at all about price, it is assumed that the buyer will pay a "reasonable" price (usually the prevailing market price at the time and place of delivery). The following case illustrates some of the difficulties involved in cases where the price is not definitely fixed.

OUTLET EMBROIDERY CO., Inc.
v. DERWENT MILLS, Limited

Court of Appeals of New York, 1930
254 N.Y. 179, 172 N.E. 462

► Action by the Outlet Embroidery Company, Inc., against the Derwent Mills, Limited. From an order of the Appellate Division, First Department, 228 App. Div. 113, 239 N.Y.S. 182, affirming by a divided court an order of the Special Term denying defendant's motion to dismiss amended complaint, defendant appeals by permission.

Order affirmed, and certified question answered.

The Appellate Division, 228 App. Div. 776, 239 N.Y.S. 831, certified the following question: "Does the amended complaint herein state facts sufficient to constitute a cause of action?"

CARDOZO, C. J. The question to be determined is whether a complaint is sufficient, and this depends upon the question whether documents made part of it contain the essentials of a contract.

The defendant, by Brucks & Peyser, its agents, wrote the plaintiff as follows:

"June 15, 1929.

"Outlet Embroidery Co., 412 6th Avenue, New York City.

"Gentlemen: Enclosed please find copy of your order placed with us today, terms on same 3/10 days, delivery as soon as possible.

"We have cabled this order today to England as these goods will be made up special for you.

"Please send us your confirmation of same by return mail.

"Also note that the price of $3.10 per box on your Fil D'Angoro brand which we are to ship to you is subject to change pending tariff revision.

"Yours very truly

"Brucks & Peyser
"Morell Peyser.

"All Prices Subject to Change Pending Tariff Revision."

Accompanying this letter was an order specifying quantities and colors, and repeating the statement that the price was to be $3.10 per box. The plaintiff, on receipt of the letter and its inclosure, made answer as follows:

"June 17, 1929.

"Brucks & Peyser, 100 Fifth Avenue, New York, N.Y.

"Gentlemen: Received your letter dated June 15, 1929, enclosing copy of my order.

"We confirm the same as requested.

"We hope you will deliver the merchandise as soon as possible and avoid last season's delays.

"Very truly yours,

"Outlet Emby. Supply Co., Inc.
"Per: A. Dratler."

Three days later (June 20, 1929) the defendant canceled its acceptance, and notified the plaintiff that it would refuse to make delivery.

The plaintiff sues for the damages resulting from the refusal. The defendant insists that since the price was subject to change pending revision of the tariff, the agreement, though in other respects complete, was inchoate and abortive. . . .

The letters between plaintiff and defendant were from one merchant to another.[7] They are to be read as business men would read them, and only as a last resort are to be thrown out altogether as meaningless futilities. . . . Read the privilege of change with inflexible adherence to its form, and one turns it into nonsense. If the change of price, to be valid, must be declared while revision is still pending, no change may be permitted after the revision is accomplished, which is the very time of all when a change will be essential. To read the reservation thus is to rob it of its efficacy as an implement to be used in furtherance of a business purpose. In the transactions of business life, sanity of end and aim is at least a presumption, albeit subject to be rebutted. The defendant like the plaintiff supposed that in signing these documents it was doing something understood to be significant and serious. It not only accepted the plaintiff's order, but it asked the plaintiff to confirm the terms of the acceptance, and followed this with a cable of the order to its manufacturer abroad. Was it all sound and fury, signifying nothing?

If literalness is sheer absurdity, we are to seek some other meaning whereby reason will be instilled and absurdity avoided. In June, 1929, Congress was debating a new tariff, and the debate continued for a year. Of this we take judicial notice. During the period of suspense, an importer could not be sure whether goods previously ordered from abroad would arrive in the United States before the change or after. If they did not arrive till after, the prices would be inadequate to the extent of the new duties. In the setting of these notorious facts the reservation now in question was written and accepted.

"All prices subject to change pending tariff revision." We think there is mere fatuity in a construction of the writing that would turn this reservation into a privilege of arbitrary change, at any time or for any reason, with change of tariff or without. No seller, drafting such a writing, would expect the customer receiving it to understand it in that way. . . . No buyer would so read it. He would paraphrase the writing thus: "A change of price there may have to be if the tariff is revised. 'Pending such revision,' the buyer will have to take the risk that the price may be increased by the measure of the duty added." In the setting of the occasion, no other interpretation was possible for any reasonable mind. This being so, the court may fix the meaning, as if the inference were one of law. . . .

We find it needless to determine whether the buyer would have been at liberty, if a revision of the tariff had been followed by a change of price,

---

[7] It is interesting to note that the Uniform Commercial Code prescribes special rules of law for certain cases in which merchants are dealing with one another; these rules are not applicable to transactions between laymen. The Code defines a "merchant" as "a person who deals in goods of the kind or otherwise by his occupation holds himself out as having knowledge or skill peculiar to the practices or goods involved in the transaction. . . ."

to declare the bargain off, or would be deemed to have assented by implication to the payment of another price, the one theretofore named but augmented by the duty. If the second be the true construction, a known and established standard has fixed the price payable in every possible contingency. . . . If the first construction be preferred, there is still no failure of a contract, for revision did not follow until long after the time when performance became due. In that view of the meaning, there was a valid and perfected contract, though subject to a privilege of cancellation in a specified contingency. . . . No doubt there would be a risk in closing on such terms, yet a risk, after all not inordinate or incredible. Buyer and seller may have had faith in their ability to come together as to terms if the seller was insistent that because of tariff changes the price should be increased. The increase would not be possible unless the change was an accomplished fact. Whatever loophole was left, whatever chance that the buyer might use the privilege of cancellation harshly, was of the seller's own creation, since the form of the agreement had been drafted by its agents. Theirs, and not the buyer's, is the blame, if there was improvidence or folly.

The complaint might better have stated more precisely the pleader's construction of writings so confusing. Even if this be granted, the construction urged by the defendant is so plainly unreasonable as to justify us in holding that it is to be rejected altogether. Alternative shades of meaning may remain. There is still a true contract, whichever shade shall be accepted.

The order should be affirmed with costs, and the question certified answered "Yes." ◀

COMMENTS AND QUESTIONS

1. In the lower court, the defendant moved to dismiss the plaintiff's complaint on the ground that it failed to state a good cause of action. What was the defendant's contention? How did the New York Court of Appeals decide?
2. According to the basic rules of contract law, the parties must reach agreement on all important terms before a contract becomes binding. Had a sufficiently definite agreement been made here on the price of the goods?
3. Note the court's taking "judicial notice" of the fact that a revision of tariff rates was being debated by Congress at the time this agreement was made. This fact is important to the decision.
4. Note also the practical business view that Judge Cardozo takes of the agreement and his impatience with the defendant's arguments.

The Statute of Frauds

In the preceding chapter we discussed the application of the Statute of Frauds to contracts in general (see page 294). A special section of that statute governs the enforceability of sales contracts in which the price to be paid for the goods exceeds a certain minimum amount. This amount varies from $30 in one state to $2,500 in another, with $500 the most common. Section 17 of the statute, as it was originally enacted by the English Parliament, contains the following provision:

No contract for the sale of any goods, wares or merchandise, for the price of ten pounds sterling or upwards, shall be allowed to be good, except the buyer shall accept part of the goods so sold, and actually receive the same, or give something in earnest to bind the bargain, or in part payment, or that some note or memorandum in writing of the said bargain be made and signed by the parties to be charged by such a contract, or their agents thereinto lawfully authorized.

This provision was carried over with little or no modification by most states, except, of course, for the translation of "pounds sterling" into dollars; it was also made a part of the Uniform Sales Act.

The sales section of the Statute of Frauds says, in effect, that if the price to be paid is over the minimum amount, the sales contract may not be enforced in court unless the party seeking enforcement (which may be either the buyer or the seller) can show at least one of three things: (1) that the buyer accepted and received at least part of the goods, (2) that the buyer made at least a part payment for the goods, or (3) that the party being sued signed a note or memorandum outlining the principal terms of the contract.

There has been much litigation over the proper interpretation and application of these provisions. Typical of the cases that have arisen are the two that follow:

MAHER v. RANDOLPH

Court of Appeals of New York, 1937
275 N.Y. 80, 9 N.E. 2d 786

► LOUGHRAN, J.   As owners of 240 shares of the stock of a corporation formed under a co-operative ownership plan, plaintiffs held a lease of an apartment in a building erected by the corporation. This apartment, with its furnishings, they let to the defendant for a term to expire on May 15, 1935. The furnishings included three pairs of draperies worth about $150.

On May 5, 1935, the parties entered into an oral agreement for sale by the plaintiffs and purchase by the defendant of the 240 shares of stock for $4,000. In the course of this transaction the defendant inquired whether the plaintiffs "would consent to include the draperies in the sale," and the plaintiffs answered: "Very well, the draperies are yours." Before the time fixed for delivery of the stock and for payment of the first installment of the purchase price, the defendant withdrew from the transaction.

This is an action for breach of the contract of purchase and sale. The defense is the statute of frauds relating to personal property. . . . The question is whether there was such an acceptance and actual receipt of the curtains by the defendant as to make the contract enforceable.

"The acceptance and receipt are both necessary. The contract is not valid unless the buyer does both. These are two distinct things. There may be an actual receipt without an acceptance and an acceptance without a receipt. The receipt of the goods is the act of taking possession of them." Cooke v. Millard, 65 N.Y. 352, 367, 368; 22 Am. Rep. 619. Prior to the enactment in 1911 (Laws 1911, c. 571) of section 85 of the Personal Property Law as part of the Uniform Sales Act, it was settled for us that the mere words of the bargain are not sufficient evidence to satisfy the statute in a case where the buyer already has possession of the goods under some prior and independent transaction of the parties. Young v. Ingalsbe, 208 N.Y. 503, 102 N.E. 590. . . . Such is this case.

Plaintiffs contend that the law was changed by subdivision 3 of section 85. It is thereby provided: "There is an acceptance of goods within the meaning of this section when the buyer, either before or after delivery of the goods, expresses by words or conduct his assent to becoming the owner of those specific goods." The argument of the plaintiffs, as we understand it, is that acceptance by a buyer in independent possession includes an actual receipt; that an acceptance may now be evidenced by words without an act; and that, therefore, such a transaction, though resting in words alone is no longer condemned by the statute.

Concededly, this construction of section 85 cannot here be adopted consistently with the reasoning of the opinion of this court in a case which was the source of the decisions last cited. What was said in that case is no less true in the case in hand. "The declarations relied upon as evidence of a delivery and acceptance constitute a part of the contract, and of course are obnoxious to all the evils and every objection against which it was the policy of the law to provide." Shindler v. Houston, 1 N.Y. 261, 264; 49 Am. Dec. 316. The validity of this view of the statute, as we are aware, has been doubted and denied. But with the policy of the law as there declared in 1848 the Legislature did not see fit to interfere prior to the enactment of the foregoing subdivision 3 of section 85 of the Personal Property Law in 1911. Under the circumstances, we cannot find in section 85 sufficient expression of intention to overturn so long and so settled a course of decision.

The judgment should be affirmed, with costs.

FINCH, JUDGE (dissenting). We are no longer bound by Young v. Ingalsbe, 208 N.Y. 503, 102 N.E. 590. The rule enunciated therein has been the subject of much criticism, and is contrary to the great weight of authority. . . . In 1911 New York adopted the Uniform Sales Act which, in paragraph 3 of section 4, provides that "There is an acceptance of goods within the meaning of this section when the buyer, either before or after delivery of the goods, expresses by words or conduct his assent to becoming the owner of those specific goods." (Personal Property Law, Consol. Laws, c. 41, 85 subd. 3.) Most of the other states which have adopted the Uniform Sales Act construe this to mean that where goods are already in possession of the buyer, acceptance may be evidenced by words. . . . The statute having been amended, we are no longer bound by the earlier cases, and especially in view of our adoption of the Uniform Statute, no valid reason appears for continuing to follow a rule which seems to be counter to the new statute and is out of harmony with the rule generally adopted.[8]

---

[8] As the dissenting judge suggests, this case is a good illustration of a so-called uniform statute being interpreted in a nonuniform way. The decision points at the great

The judgment of the Appellate Division should be reversed, and the judgment of the Trial Term reinstated, with costs.

CRANE, C. J., and LEHMAN, O'BRIEN, HUBBS, and RIPPEY, JJ., concur with LOUGHRAN, J.

FINCH, J., dissents in opinion.

Judgment affirmed.   ◄

COMMENTS AND QUESTIONS

1. Since this contract involved a sale of personal property over the minimum amount, and since the contract was not in writing, the plaintiff had to show that the defendant had accepted and received at least part of the goods (i.e., the draperies) before he could enforce the contract. How did the court decide?

2. Note Judge Loughran's discussion of prior cases and his feeling that precedent should be followed. The dissenting opinion, on the other hand, takes the view that the old rule is out of date and should be discarded. Which do you feel is right?

3. The court indicates that some act by the buyer other than mere retention of goods already in his possession is necessary to take the case out of the Statute of Frauds. Does this mean that the seller must re-take possession and then retransfer the property to the buyer? Several states have adopted the rule advocated by the dissenting opinion.

DRURY v. YOUNG

Court of Appeals of Maryland, 1882
58 Md. 546, 42 Am. Rep. 343

► STONE, J., delivered the opinion of the Court.

One of the questions presented for our consideration in this case is, whether the "note or memorandum in writing" required by the seventeenth section of the Statute of Frauds, must be delivered to the other party thereto. It is apparent from the evidence that the note or memorandum in writing relied on in this case, was made by the bookkeeper, placed in their safe, among other papers, where it remained from the 27th of August, 1881, the day on which it was written, until it was produced in Court, at the trial of the case in February, 1882. There is no evidence that this note was ever seen by the appellee, or even its existence known to him until the trial; and it certainly never was delivered to him or went out of the possession of the appellants, until produced in Court. It is strongly insisted by the appellants that the Statute is not satisfied without a delivery of this note or memorandum. . . .

Now the Statute itself is entirely silent on the question of the delivery of the note or memorandum of the bargain, and its literal requirements are fulfilled by the existence of the note or memorandum of the bargain, signed

difficulties inherent in "legislating" uniformity. New York follows one rule of law (following the precedent established in this case), while other states, with identical legislation, have another rule for the same type of case.

by the party to be charged thereby. The Statute itself deals exclusively with the existence and not with the custody of the paper.

If the non-delivery of the note does not violate the letter of the Statute, would it violate its spirit and be liable to any of the mischiefs which the Statute was made to prevent?

The Statute was passed to prevent fraud practiced through the instrumentality of perjury. It was passed to prevent the defendant from suffering loss, upon the parol testimony of either a perjured or mistaken witness, speaking of a bargain different from the one in fact made. It made the defendant only liable when a note or memorandum of the bargain signed by himself was produced at the trial.

If produced from the defendant's own custody, it guards against the mischief that the Statute was passed to prevent, just as well as if produced from the custody of the plaintiff. The plaintiff is the one likely to suffer by leaving the evidence of his bargain in the hands of the defendant—not the defendant himself.

The next question which arises, is whether the note or memorandum in this case, is signed by defendant? The note is in these words:

Office of
DRURY, IJAMS & RANKIN,
Wholesale and Retail Grocers, and Dealers in Flour, Feed, and Fertilizers, Cor. Gay and High streets.
E. T. DRURY
W. H. IJAMS, JR.
S. M. RANKIN, JR.   BALTIMORE, Aug. 27th, 1881
Sold W. H. H. Young & Co., 2,500 cans, say 5,000 doz. C.C.C. tomatoes, at $1.10 p'r doz cash; cars at Phila. Depot, Balto., Md.
5,000 dozen, at $1.10 c $5,500.00

It appears that all the words, preceding the words, "Baltimore, August 27th, 1881" were printed, and that the printed part, was a letterhead, and the written portion under the heading. The names of the defendants being in print, and at the beginning of the note, the question is, whether it is a sufficient signing?

. . . It is therefore a sufficient signing, if the name be in print, and in any part of the instrument, provided that the name is recognized and appropriated by the party to be his. The note or memorandum in this case upon its face, contains all the necessary terms of a complete bargain.

The names of the vendors and purchasers, the quantity and quality of the goods contracted for, the price at which they were sold, and the terms of sale, and the place of delivery, are all clearly expressed, therein, and make a sufficiently good memorandum required by the Statute.

If the above mentioned memorandum was insufficient of itself, the following letter addressed by defendants to plaintiff, and which sufficiently refers in its terms to the former note or memorandum, would certainly be sufficient when taken in connection with it, to take this case out of the Statute:

Office of
DRURY, IJAMS & RANKIN,
Wholesale and Retail Grocers, and Dealers in Flour, Feed and Ferti-
lizers, Cor. Gay and High Streets.

E. T. DRURY,

W. H. IJAMS, JR.

S. M. RANKIN, JR.   BALTIMORE, Aug. 29th 1881

Mess. W. H. H. Young & Co.:

Gents:—We regret to say, it is impossible for the Chase's Canning Co.
to furnish the 2500 cases, 3 c. tomatoes purchased of us on 27th inst., at
1.10 per dozen. Nor do we think it possible to fill order this season, as
the fruit cannot be procured.

Hoping this may be entirely satisfactory,

We are very respectfully,

DRURY, IJAMS, & RANKIN.

There is no dispute as to the signature of the defendants to this letter,
or that it was addressed to the plaintiff, and without the aid of any parol
evidence it can easily be connected with the memorandum of 27th August,
1881.

That the letter refers to the same bargain or sale that the memorandum
does, is sufficiently shown upon the face of it, as it mentions the same sort
of goods, the same quantity and price, and refers to the same date.

The two papers can then be connected with sufficient certainty, without
the aid of any extrinsic evidence, and together make a memorandum, meeting the requirements of the Statute, even if the memorandum of sale itself
were insufficient.

We have then a sufficient note or memorandum of a bargain, provided
the jury was satisfied that an antecedent parol bargain, substantially agreeing with the said note or memorandum, had been made between plaintiff
and defendants.

Whether such antecedent parol bargain had been made or not, was
for the jury to decide, and it was also for the jury to determine the question,
whether the printed names were adopted and appropriated by the defendants as theirs, as well as the fact of the memorandum being the act of
their authorized agent. . . .

Judgment affirmed.   ◄

COMMENTS AND QUESTIONS

1. The plaintiff sued the defendant for breach of contract to deliver the
   tomatoes. The defendant contended that the action was barred by
   the Statute of Frauds in that the memorandum in writing, if any, did
   not satisfy the Statute's requirements. What arguments did the defendant use to convince the court? How did the court deal with them?

2. Apparently the plaintiff was not aware of the existence of the memorandum prior to trial but was able to produce it in court by summons-
   ing the defendant's records. Suppose, however, that the defendant
   had destroyed the memo. Would the plaintiff have been allowed to
   prove its existence by having the bookkeeper testify that he had made
   it and placed it in the safe? Probably. But suppose the bookkeeper
   could not remember its contents?

3. What about the subsequent letter of August 29? Is it not a sufficient memorandum in itself?

Goods Manufactured Specially for Buyer

As a general rule, the Statute of Frauds does not apply to contracts to sell articles that are specially manufactured for the purchaser and are not suitable for sale to other buyers in the regular course of business. Such contracts are enforceable over the minimum figure, even in the absence of a written memorandum, part payment, or acceptance and receipt. If the goods are regular stock items that can readily be sold to the general public, however, the provisions of the Statute must be satisfied.

> EXAMPLE
>
> s, a furniture manufacturer, orally agrees to build B a special, oversize bed, 12 feet long. When the bed is completed, B refuses to accept delivery and repudiates the contract. s may hold B to the contract, since the bed is not readily salable to the general public and the Statute of Frauds does not bar enforcement. If, however, the agreement was to supply an ordinary bed that could easily be disposed of, B would not be bound in the absence of a written memorandum, part payment, or acceptance and receipt.

U.C.C. Modifications of Statute of Frauds

In those states where it has been adopted, the Uniform Commercial Code makes some significant changes in the sales section of the Statute of Frauds. The more important of these changes may be summarized as follows:

1. *Contents of Written Memorandum.*   Under the Uniform Sales Act, a written memorandum must contain all the important terms of the contract in order to satisfy the Statute of Frauds. The U.C.C. relaxes this rule somewhat by requiring that there be merely "some writing sufficient to indicate that a contract for sale has been made between the parties and signed by the party against whom enforcement is sought."

2. *Who Must Sign Memorandum.*   Under the U.S.A., the written memorandum must be signed by the party against whom enforcement is being sought. Thus, if only one party signs the memorandum, the other side is not bound to carry out the contract. The Uniform Commercial Code makes an important change in this rule in cases where both parties are merchants who regularly deal in commercial transactions. The code provides that "Between merchants if within a reasonable time a writing in confirmation of the contract . . . is received and the party receiving it has reason to know its contents, it satisfies the requirements of [the Statute of Frauds] against such party unless written notice of objection to its contents is given within 10 days after it is received."

> EXAMPLE
>
> s and B, both merchants, enter into an oral contract whereby B agrees to purchase certain goods from s for $3,000. It is further agreed that s will

deliver the goods to B thirty days later. The next day, s sends a letter to B outlining the terms of the contract. B, however, does not reply to the letter or acknowledge it in any way. Under the Uniform Sales Act, s would be required to go through with the contract, since he signed a written memorandum (i.e., the letter). B, however, would not be obligated to perform, since he did not sign any memorandum and since there has been neither part payment nor acceptance and receipt. Under the U.C.C., on the other hand, B *would* be bound by the contract, since he received a written confirmation and failed to object to it within ten days. Note that this change applies only to sales contracts *between merchants;* it does not apply to any other class of persons.

SECTION 2

TRANSFER OF TITLE AND RISK OF LOSS

Introduction

As we have seen, a sale results in the transfer of the ownership of goods from seller to buyer. In other words, the title to the property passes from one party to another. Since the owner normally assumes responsibility if the goods are lost, damaged, or destroyed, it is extremely important to determine at what point in a sales transaction the ownership passes from seller to buyer. For example, if the goods are lost or destroyed before they have been delivered or while they are in transit, must the buyer still pay for them? Or does the seller bear the loss? Obviously, if the property is insured or if a third party is responsible for the loss, the risk is shifted. But even then it is important to determine who owns the goods and thus has the right to recover damages. In this section, we will review the rules of law for determining how and when title, and, with it, risk of loss, pass from seller to buyer.

Risk of Loss Generally

The general rule is that risk of loss follows ownership and passes to the buyer at the time he acquires title. So in most cases the important question is this: When did title pass to the buyer? If the parties make a specific agreement on title or risk of loss, that understanding will govern. Usually, however, no such stipulation is made, and the court must decide the question.

In some cases there is little difficulty in establishing the intent of the parties. In the usual "cash sale," for example, where delivery and payment take place almost simultaneously, title passes when the transaction is completed. A more difficult problem arises in contracts to sell, which, by definition, call for the transfer of ownership at a later date. Here the parties seldom make their intentions clear, and the courts have to fall back on certain presumptions when a controversy arises.

Rules for Determining Intention

In considering a dispute over the precise moment at which title passed from the seller to the buyer of goods, the court will first look at the terms of the contract, the conduct of the parties, the customs of the trade, and the circumstances of the case in an effort to ascertain the intention of the parties. In many situations, however, the intention either has never been expressed or else does not emerge clearly. To assist the courts in deciding such cases, the Uniform Sales Act sets forth five rules for determining when title passes from seller to buyer. These are not hard-and-fast rules, however; they are to be used only as guideposts where the parties have not made their intentions clear.

Specific Goods in Deliverable State

Rule 1.[9] Where there is an unconditional contract to sell specific goods in a deliverable state, the property [10] in the goods passes to the buyer when the contract is made and it is immaterial whether the time of payment, or the time of delivery, or both, be postponed.

EXAMPLE

s, who owns a 1955 car, agrees to sell it to B "as is" for $400. B tells s he will call for it the next day. During the night the car is destroyed by fire without the fault of either party. B must pay s and bear the risk of loss, since title passed to him when the contract was made. The car was specifically identified and ready for delivery.

Specific Goods in Nondeliverable State

Rule 2. Where there is a contract to sell specific goods and the seller is bound to do something to the goods, for the purpose of putting them into a deliverable state, the property does not pass until such thing be done.

EXAMPLE

On Monday, B agrees to buy s's car for $400. As part of the contract, s agrees to tune up the engine and fix the brakes. On Tuesday, s completes the agreed work. On Wednesday, the car is stolen, without s's fault. B must suffer the loss, since title passed to him on Tuesday as soon as the job was completed and the car was ready for delivery. If, on the other hand, s had only half finished the job when the car was stolen, he would have had to bear the risk, since the property had not yet been put into a deliverable state.

---

[9] The wording of the rules is quoted directly from the Uniform Sales Act.
[10] The term "property," as used in the rules, is roughly equivalent to "title."

This is an example of a simple case, in which the application of the rule presents no great difficulty. In other cases, however, the courts have been faced with a more perplexing situation. In the two cases that follow, notice that in one the court held that title had passed, but that in the other the opposite result was reached.

KAHN v. ROSENSTIEL et al.

District Court of the United States, S.D.N.Y., 1924
298 F. 656

► At Law. Action by Jacob J. Kahn against Lewis S. Rosenstiel and others, copartners trading under the firm name and style of the Cincinnati Distributing Company. On demurrer to the declaration. Demurrer overruled as to first count, and sustained as to second.

LEARNED HAND, DISTRICT JUDGE.   The declaration is upon the following facts: The plaintiff's assignor and the defendants made a contract on September 23, 1920, by which the plaintiff's assignor bought and the defendants sold 2,000 cases of whiskey, bottled in bond, at $26 per case f.o.b. the defendants' distillery, where it lay in the wood. The buyer agreed either to get a withdrawal permit for 1,000 cases within 30 days or to pay the balance of the price of such cases; also to do the same as to the remainder within 60 days. In the event of default in withdrawing or payment, an initial payment of $10,000 was to be treated as liquidated damages. The seller was to bottle the goods and ship them by express or freight, at buyer's option, within 30 days after arrival of the withdrawal permit.

At the time when the contract was made the seller had a permit authorizing him to sell and the buyer a permit to buy, but neither party was a wholesale manufacturer or druggist, and the permits turned out to be void. The buyer paid down $10,000, but on discovery of the illegality of the permits and before any of the liquor was delivered he declined to proceed, and demanded a return of the money paid. If the contract was not fully executed the plaintiff may recover. . . . The theory is that until the contract is performed there should be a *locus poenitentiae*.[11] Here the plaintiff alleges that, as soon as his assignor learned that the permits were void, he at once disaffirmed the bargain.

Thus the question is whether the contract was executed. Clearly not. The seller had to bottle and ship, and this brings the case within section 100, rule 2 of the New York Sales of Goods Act, Consol. Laws, c. 41, art. 5. . . . The presumption is that, while the seller has to do something more to put the goods "into a deliverable state," no title passes. The defendant's supposition is mistaken that this refers only to something done in the manufacture of the goods themselves, and does not include putting them into packages or barrels, or, as here, bottles. The first instance of the doctrine turned upon filling casks of turpentine, Rugg v. Minett, 11 East. 210, where the title passed to the filled casks and did not to the unfilled. So in the

---

[11] Literally, a place for repentance. Here, it refers to plaintiff's opportunity to withdraw from the illegal contract before it was executed (see page 286).

Elgee Cotton Cases, 22 Wall. 180, 22 L.Ed. 863, the cotton was in a warehouse, but had not been baled. It is true that some of it had apparently not been ginned either, but the court made no distinction between what was ginned and what was not. So in Robinson v. Patterson, 210 F. 839, 127 C.C.A. 389, C.C.A. 3, where pipe had only to be graded. So, too, in Noyes v. Marlott, 156 F. 753, 84 C.C.A. 409, C.C.A., 9, where the seller had only to put logs in a boom. In Schultz & Co. v. DeNood, 194 App. Div. 149, 185 N.Y.S. 785, 4th Dept., the hay had not been baled, but had been cured.

Any such distinction ignores the reason for the rule, which is that the parties do not presumptively mean to pass title till the seller has finished his part of the performance and the buyer has only to take the goods. The doctrine of section 100, rule 5, is indeed only another instance of the same notion; it provides that, when the seller must deliver at a particular place, title does not pass till delivery has been made. Normally delivery is at the seller's place of business (section 124, subd. 1) and thus the seller, as soon as the goods are in deliverable condition, has nothing further to do but allow the buyer to come and get the goods. Therefore, in the case at bar, title would not in fact pass till the defendants had "made shipment" of the bottled whiskey "f.o.b. distillery," which probably means on cars at that place. In any aspect the contract remained executory until the seller had completed his performance. . . .   ◄

COMMENTS AND QUESTIONS

1. This case involves a basic rule of law with respect to illegal contracts. What is it? How was the point decided? Did the buyer get his money back?
2. Summarize the reasons why title to the whiskey had not passed at the time the buyer disaffirmed the contract.
3. Suppose the whiskey had been bottled and shipped, and the buyer disaffirmed before he received it. Could he then have recovered his payment?

RADLOFF v. BRAGMUS

Supreme Court of Minnesota, 1943
214 Minn. 130, 7 N.W. 2d 491

► OLSON, J. Action to recover the balance of the purchase price of a flock of turkeys claimed by plaintiff to have been sold to defendants on November 9, 1940. When plaintiff rested, defendants' motion to dismiss was granted because, in the court's opinion, he had failed to make a prima facie case. He appeals from an order denying his motion for a new trial.

There is very little of dispute in the evidence. Viewing it in the light most favorable to plaintiff, the jury could have found these to be the facts: Over a period of some years plaintiff has been engaged in the business of raising and selling turkeys. Defendant Bragmus is the managing agent of defendant New Prague Product Company, which is engaged in the business of buying and processing poultry. On the day mentioned plaintiff met Bragmus at Mapleton, and there they engaged in negotiations for a sale of plaintiff's turkeys consisting of a flock of "about" 100 turkey hens and 600

Toms. After oral negotiations had reached the point of mutual assent, an instrument in writing was prepared by Mr. Bragmus reading as follows (omitting date, address, and signatures):

> "This confirms my sale to you of the following;
> About 100 Head Number 1 Hen Turkeys at 18⁵/¢ per pound.
> About 600 Head Number 1 Tom Turkeys at 13⁵/¢ per pound.
> The Number 2's to be 3¢ less in each case.
> Removal to be made Nov. 13, 1940.
> Receipt of $50.00 is hereby acknowledged."

. . . On November 11 occurred the blizzard which brought tragedy to a large section of this part of the country. Some 330 of the turkeys here involved were destroyed, and those not destroyed were damaged. It is not claimed that the loss was one for which either party is to be blamed.

As soon as the storm abated so that plaintiff could get to town, he went to the office of the produce company and demanded of Bragmus that the turkeys bargained for be taken. This demand being refused, plaintiff disposed of the live birds at a loss. The dead birds were sold to a rendering concern at four dollars per ton. The difference between the price fixed by the contract and the salvage obtained later from the sale of the remaining birds, both live and dead, as has been related, is the basis for the present action. It is therefore apparent that the question here for decision is whether the title to them passed from plaintiff to defendants on November 9. The court was of the opinion that title had not passed and for that reason dismissed the action. Counsel are in agreement that this is the decisive issue.

At the time of the making of the written agreement the jury could well find that the turkeys were in deliverable condition and that they represented plaintiff's entire flock. True, the turkeys had not been weighed or graded. But there is testimony that at least 95 per cent of them would grade No. 1 and that not to exceed five per cent would grade No. 2, both such grades being specifically covered by the written contract. Also, there is evidence from which the jury could find their fair average weight. Certainly there is no doubt that the exact weight of the turkeys killed in the storm and sold to the rendering plant was three tons. As to those not killed but sold later as live birds, it should not have been particularly difficult for a jury to ascertain their weight shortly after the storm. Plaintiff's testimony is that they lost weight because of the storm. If that was so, the extent of the loss on that account was also a jury question. . . .

We have here a simply worded contract, easily understood, which was prepared by defendants for use in their everyday business transactions. We can see nothing ambiguous about it. Plainly, by its terms there was an immediate transfer of title to the buyer. In plain language, selected and used by defendants, they confirmed the sale made to them that day by plaintiff. Upon the strength of it they paid $50 as a part of the purchase money. Defendants concede as much by their answer. They were to take the turkeys at plaintiff's farm not later than the 13th. That the turkeys were "in a deliverable state" on November 9 is not denied. There was nothing further for plaintiff to do "for the purpose of putting them into a deliverable state."

The counting, weighing, and grading of the turkeys were purely matters of routine and of simple computation, as much so, as if so many steers had been involved to be paid for at so much per pound.

In respect to grading, a matter considered by the trial judge as presenting considerable difficulty because of the possibility of a dispute over it between the parties, we think this furnishes no more opportunity for disagreement than counting or weighing. After all, grading of poultry is as well defined and established by rules and regulations as is grading of grains, hay, eggs, and many other farm products. By L. 1931, c. 394, 7, Minn. St. 1941, 27.07, the commissioner of agriculture, dairy and food is given "power to establish grades on all produce" as therein defined. And by 2 Id. (27.01 (2)), "produce" as used in this act shall mean and include "poultry and poultry products." The commissioner, instead of making and promulgating such rules, has adopted and made operative those of the Federal Agricultural Marketing Administration, effective since July 1940.

Furthermore, defendants cannot deny that they had knowledge of such rules and regulations, for in their answer they say that "plaintiff was unable to furnish or deliver to defendants any . . . turkeys, suitable for grading, and suitable for dressing, packing and resale by defendants for public use to conform with the laws of this State under which they operate."

We think the court erred when it dismissed plaintiff's cause and that it repeated the error in denying his motion for a new trial. Because defendants' attempt to alter the written memorandum by means of the allegations of their answer would have amounted to a complete change of that which was written, absent any effort to have it reformed, and because there was no suggestion of inadvertence, mutual mistake, fraud, or overreaching by any party to the contract, it must stand as made.

Order reversed.   ◄

COMMENTS AND QUESTIONS

1. When did title to the turkeys pass? Summarize the reasons given by the court for deciding as it did.

2. It appears that this was a sale of the plaintiff's entire flock. Would the result have been different if the contract had been for the sale of only a part of his flock?

3. The defendants argued that the turkeys were not yet in a deliverable condition at the time of the loss, since they had not been weighed or graded. How did the court get around this argument?

4. Justice Olson is careful to point out that the turkeys could still have been counted, weighed, and graded after the blizzard, and, therefore, that the purchase price and the damages were capable of computation. This, of course, was true in this case, since the turkeys were not totally destroyed. But suppose instead that they had been completely burned in a fire so that nothing remained to count and weigh. Would the court still hold that title passed at the time of the agreement? If so, how would it measure the damages?

5. Cases of this sort, involving weighing, measuring, and grading of goods, have given the courts a great deal of trouble. There appears to be some conflict in the decisions.

Sale with Option to Return

Rule 3. (1) When goods are delivered to the buyer "on sale or return," or on other terms indicating an intention to make a present sale, but to give the buyer an option to return the goods instead of paying the price, the property passes to the buyer on delivery, but he may revest the property in the seller by returning or tendering the goods within the time fixed in the contract, or, if no time has been fixed, within a reasonable time.

EXAMPLE

B purchases a television set from s with the agreement that he may return the set within ten days if he doesn't want to keep it. In this situation, B acquires title on delivery and must bear the risk of loss unless he returns the set within the ten-day period. If, however, B offers to return the set within that time, title and risk of loss return to s, even though s refuses to take the set back.

Sale on Trial or Approval

(2) When goods are delivered to the buyer on approval or on trial or on satisfaction, or other similar terms, the property therein passes to the buyer—

(a) When he signifies his approval or acceptance to the seller or does any other act adopting the transaction;

(b) If he does not signify his approval or acceptance to the seller, but retains the goods without giving notice of rejection, then if a time has been fixed for the return of the goods, on the expiration of such time, and, if no time has been fixed, on the expiration of a reasonable time. What is a reasonable time is a question of fact.

EXAMPLE

B purchases a vacuum cleaner from s on trial for thirty days. After fifteen days, the machine is ruined by a flood while still in B's possession. If B has not yet indicated his acceptance of the goods, the risk of loss is on s, since title has not passed to B. But if, before the flood, B had notified s that he was satisfied with the cleaner, then title would have passed to B and he would be responsible. If B had said nothing and had not returned the machine within the thirty-day period, and if the loss had occurred after thirty days, title would have passed to B and he would have to bear the risk.

Unascertained or Future Goods

Rule 4. (1) Where there is a contract to sell unascertained or future goods by description, and goods of that description and in a deliverable state are unconditionally appropriated to the contract, either by the seller with the assent of the buyer, or by the buyer with the assent of the seller, the property in the goods thereupon passes to the buyer. Such assent may be expressed or implied, and may be given either before or after the appropriation is made.

(2) Where, in pursuance of a contract to sell, the seller delivers the goods to the buyer, or to a carrier or other bailee (whether named by the buyer or not) for the purpose of transmission to or holding for the buyer,

he is presumed to have unconditionally appropriated the goods to the contract, except in the cases provided for in the next rule and in section 20. This presumption is applicable although by the terms of the contract the buyer is to pay the price before receiving delivery of the goods, and the goods are marked with the words "collect on delivery" or their equivalent.

The two sections of Rule 4 must be read together. In essence, they state that title passes to the buyer when the goods have been identified and made ready for delivery—that is, when the seller has performed his part of the contract. If the contract does not call for delivery or shipment to the buyer, title usually passes when the goods are set aside and specifically marked for the buyer, and when nothing remains to be done except for the buyer to pick them up.

EXAMPLE

B agrees to purchase from s, a dealer, a certain type of radio which is currently out of stock. s is to order the radio from the manufacturer, and B is to pick it up at the store. s acquires the radio, marks it "Hold for B," and calls B to tell him it is ready. Title passes once the radio has been marked for B and he has been notified. If it is lost or damaged before B comes to get it, the risk of loss is on B, assuming, of course, that the damage was not s's fault.

If the agreement requires the seller himself to deliver the goods to the buyer, title does not pass until they have actually been delivered; the theory here is that the property is not unconditionally appropriated so long as it is within the seller's power to recall it. If, however, the contract calls for the seller to ship the goods to the buyer by common carrier, title is usually presumed to pass when goods of the proper description have been delivered to the carrier for shipment in accordance with the agreement. In other words, once the seller has turned the goods over to the carrier and has issued proper shipping instructions, the seller has completed his obligation and risk of loss passes to the buyer. It is interesting to note that this rule applies even where the buyer is to pay for the goods before he is entitled to possess them (i.e., a "C.O.D." contract).

EXAMPLES

1. s, in New York, agrees to manufacture and ship a certain quantity of automobile parts to B in Detroit. s manufactures and crates the parts and delivers them to the New York Central Railroad for shipment to B. Title passes when the goods are delivered to the railroad, and B must bear the risk of loss while they are in transit.

2. B orders a chair C.O.D. from s, a department store. s receives the order, acknowledges it, selects a chair of that description from its stock, crates it, and delivers it to a carrier with instructions to ship C.O.D. to B. Title and risk of loss pass to B when the chair is delivered to the carrier, even though B is not entitled to receive or inspect the merchandise until he has paid for it.

The general rule that risk of loss passes to the buyer on delivery of the goods to the carrier is subject to certain exceptions. If, for example, the goods are lost or destroyed en route as a result of some fault or carelessness on the seller's part, he and not the buyer must bear the loss. Similarly, if it is customary in the particular case for the goods to be insured while in transit, the seller must either insure them himself, or, if he is not going to insure, he must notify the buyer promptly so that the buyer may procure insurance if he chooses; otherwise, the seller must bear the risk of loss until the shipment reaches its destination.

The following three cases involve the appropriation and shipment of goods. See if you can explain the results that were reached in terms of the rules given above.

WINSLOW BROS. & SMITH CO. v. UNIVERSAL COAT CO.

Supreme Judicial Court of Massachusetts, 1925
252 Mass. 7, 146 N.E. 713

▶ Action of contract by the Winslow Bros. & Smith Company against the Universal Coat Company to recover for skins delivered and refusal to accept delivery of skins sold. Report of auditor was confirmed and judgment entered for plaintiff, and defendant excepts. Exceptions overruled.

The counts of the declaration were as follows:

PIERCE, J. The case was referred to an auditor, his findings of fact to be final.[12] The auditor found in substance that the plaintiff, through the medium of letters on December 16, 1919, entered into a written contract with S. Gluck & Weingold to sell 500 dozen tanned coat leather skins in grades Nos. X, 1 and 2 "as the sorting might yield," deliveries to begin in February, 1920, at prices which varied with the grade. . . . The defendant company was substituted for S. Gluck & Weingold in the agreement, by a novation, about February 13, 1920. On February 14, 1920, the plaintiff shipped directly to the defendant 270 7/12 dozen skins at the agreed price of $12,108.30. This bill was paid in full, in part in February, 1920, and the balance on April 16, 1920. . . .

In the early part of April, 1920, the defendant notified the plaintiff that it was well stocked with these skins, and requested that no more actual shipments be made without notifying the defendant. In the latter part of May, 1920, the plaintiff had tanned and sorted out for delivery, and appropriated to the defendant under the contract, 85 1/12 dozen skins, sorted out as No. 1's. Soon thereafter an officer of the plaintiff notified the defendant of this fact. To this notice the defendant's officers said they were well stocked, did not want the leather right away, but would take it in before the latter part of June. June 25, 1920, the plaintiff sent to the defendant an invoice and bill for this leather which had been bundled ready for delivery, with a letter stating it would not actually ship the leather until the following week. June 28, 1920, the defendant returned the invoice with a letter saying it would take the matter up with the plaintiff's Mr. Whedon upon his return.

---

[12] The parties agreed to accept the auditor's finding of facts; therefore, the only question on appeal is which rules of law should be applied to the facts established by the auditor.

Whedon had a conference with the defendant in the first part of July, 1920. At this meeting the defendant's treasurer made no objection to the appropriation of the skins, acknowledged these skins were the defendant's, asked that the charge as per invoice be temporarily withdrawn, and said that the defendant would take these skins later. In reply Whedon stated that he would temporarily withdraw the charge, upon the understanding that the defendant was actually to take delivery and pay for the skins at a later date. At this time the defendant said they had a great deal of leather and would like to cancel the remainder of the contract. The plaintiff agreed that if the defendant would take and pay for the skins appropriated the plaintiff would cancel the remainder of the contract as requested.

On August 26, 1920, the plaintiff shipped to the defendant the skins above referred to as appropriated to the contract, with an invoice and bill for $3,963.76, the agreed price. The defendant refused to accept delivery and did not make any request to examine the leather. The leather was returned to the storehouse of the plaintiff. From time to time in conversations with the plaintiff the defendant "admitted the 85 1/12 dozen were the defendant's, but they would give no definite time when they would accept delivery." Under date of October 28, 1920, the defendant wrote the plaintiff:

> "In reference to our conversation regarding 85 dozen skins, we beg to advise that we cannot see our way clear to accept same as we have at this time in our stock room about $15,000 worth of leather, which is not moving, and which is more than we can afford to carry. Under these conditions we would ask you to assist us in canceling this shipment."

The 85 1/12 dozen skins exhausted or practically exhausted the leather of this kind at that time tanned by the plaintiff, and since then the plaintiff has tanned no further leather of the same description. The auditor found on the whole evidence and specifically on the agreement between Whedon and the treasurer of the defendant, *supra,* that the 85 1/12 dozen skins were unconditionally appropriated to the contract with the assent of the defendant; that the leather was appropriate for the purpose for which the defendant required it; and that the title to these skins passed to the defendant, citing . . . G.L. c. 106, 21, rule 4 (1). . . .

Damages were assessed for the agreed price of the 85 1/12 dozen skins of No. 1 leather. . . .

The several counts in the declaration are sufficient to sustain the action of the plaintiff. The finding that there was an appropriation of goods and that the title passed to the defendant was fully warranted by the recited facts and by the admissions of the defendant's officer. . . . ◀

COMMENTS AND QUESTIONS

1. At what time did title to the 85 1/12 dozen skins pass to the defendant?
2. This is a good example of a case in which appropriation takes place before the goods are shipped. Outline the reasons for the court's deciding this case as it did.
3. The important question in many of these cases, in which the buyer

repudiates the contract, is whether the seller is entitled to sue for the purchase price or whether he may sue only for damages. If title has passed, he may sue for the price, since the goods belong to the buyer. If title has not passed, the seller may sue only for damages. Obviously, the seller ordinarily prefers the former remedy.

WESTERN HAT & MFG. CO. v. BERKNER BROS., INC.

Supreme Court of Minnesota, 1927
172 Minn. 4, 214 N.W. 475

► LEES, C.   This action was brought to recover the purchase price of gloves ordered by respondent, a retailer at Sleepy Eye, from appellant, a wholesaler at Milwaukee. A recovery was denied, as was a motion for a new trial, and this appeal followed.

The court found that on April 14, 1925, respondent gave one of appellant's traveling salesmen a written order for a quantity of gloves, describing them by number, size, and name. The salesman made a memorandum, stating that the gloves were to be shipped over the Chicago & Northwestern Railway in August, and were to be paid for in November. The order was accepted and respondent notified thereof. Appellant had the gloves in stock, selected those ordered, packed them ready for shipment, set them aside in its warehouse, and attached shipping tags bearing respondent's name and address. Thereafter and on June 30, respondent countermanded the order and requested appellant to cancel it, but appellant refused. On August 12, the gloves were shipped to respondent and an invoice mailed. On receipt of the invoice, respondent notified appellant that it would refuse to receive the gloves. They were tendered to respondent by the railroad company, were refused, and have remained in the hands of the railroad company ever since. Appellant's salesmen did not carry or attempt to sell gloves after June 30. They are goods usually sold by wholesalers for the fall trade and are not readily salable after June.

The court held that these facts fell short of showing that the property in the gloves had passed to the respondent before the order was countermanded, and that appellant could not recover the purchase price. . . .

Before the uniform sales act was adopted, it was held that when one orders goods to be sent to him he makes the vendor his agent for the purpose of selecting and appropriating the specific articles to be sent to the vendee. This court has also held that, if the mode of exercising the agency is specified in the order, the vendor must observe the directions of the vendee, and, if he fails to do so, his selection and appropriation of the goods is not such an appropriation as to pass title to the vendee. . . .

In Lieb Packing Co. v. Trocke, 136 Minn. 345, 162 N.W. 449, it was held that under an executory contract for the sale of goods to be thereafter ascertained the title passes when goods conforming to the contract are appropriated thereto; that appropriation is the act of both parties, but one, by agreement, express or implied, may authorize the other to act for him in making the appropriation; and that, if the parties reside at different places and shipment of the goods is contemplated, delivery takes place when the goods are selected and received by a carrier for transportation to the buyer. . . .

Section 19 of the act begins with the words:

"Unless a different intention appears, the following are rules for ascertaining the intention of the parties as to the time at which the property in the goods is to pass to the buyer."

Then follows rule 4. . . . It thus appears that the intention of the parties controls if it is apparent, and only when it is not may resort be had to the rules. When, as here, the contract requires the seller to ship the goods to the buyer, we think it should be held, if there is nothing to show a different intention, that the parties did not intend that the property in the goods should pass prior to a delivery to a carrier for shipment. In such a case, setting the goods apart in the seller's warehouse is not an irrevocable appropriation of them to the fulfillment of the contract and will not give the seller the right to sue for the purchase price. . . .

We need not consider or discuss the question as to the seller's remedy in case of a breach of an executory contract of sale although it is referred to at some length in the briefs.

Whatever remedy appellant may have must be sought in another action. *Order affirmed.* ◄

COMMENTS AND QUESTIONS

1. What was the result here? What further action by the seller was necessary to cause title to the goods to pass to the buyer?
2. Distinguish this case from the *Winslow Bros.* case immediately preceding it. In both situations the goods were packed ready for delivery and marked for delivery to the buyer. In both cases they were to be shipped to the buyer later on. How do you explain the difference in result?

FLEMING v. COMMONWEALTH

Supreme Court of Pennsylvania, 1889
150 Pa. 138, 18 A. 622

► Error to court of quarter sessions, Mercer county.

The plaintiff in error, Joseph Fleming, being a wholesale liquor dealer, licensed and carrying on business in Allegheny county, sold and sent from his place of business, C.O.D., to Mercer county, where he had no license, liquors ordered by persons in the latter county. For this he was, at the court of quarter sessions of Mercer county, indicted, tried, convicted, and sentenced for selling liquor therein without a license. He now brings error.

GREEN, J. In the case of Garbracht v. Com., 96 Pa. St. 449, which was an indictment for selling liquor without license, we held that "the place of sale is the point at which goods ordered or purchased are set apart and delivered to the purchaser, or to a common carrier, who, for the purposes of delivery, represents him." . . . In the case now under consideration the liquor was sold upon orders sent by mail by the purchasers, living in Mercer county, to the defendant, who is a wholesale liquor dealer in Allegheny county. The goods were set apart at the defendant's place of business in Allegheny county, and were there delivered to a common carrier, consigned to the purchaser at his address in Mercer county, and by the carrier transported to Mercer county, and there delivered to the purchaser, who paid the expense of transportation. Upon these facts alone, the decision of this court in the case of Garbracht, *supra*, is directly and distinctly applicable, and requires us to reverse the judgment of the court below, unless there are other facts in the case which distinguish it from that of Garbracht.

It is claimed, and it was so held by the court below, that, because the goods were marked "C.O.D.," the sale was not complete until the delivery was made; and as that took place in Mercer county, where the defendant's license was inoperative, he was without license as to such sales, and became subject to the penalty of the criminal law. The argument by which this conclusion was reached was simply that the payment of the price was a condition precedent to the delivery, and hence there was no delivery until payment, and no title passed until delivery. The legal and criminal inference was, the sale was made in Mercer, and not in Allegheny. This reasoning ignores certain facts which require consideration. . . .

It is manifest that, when the purchaser ordered the goods to be sent to him C.O.D., he constituted the carrier his agent, both to receive the goods from the seller, and to transmit the price to the seller. When, therefore, the goods were delivered to the carrier at Pittsburgh for the purpose of transportation, the duty of the seller was performed, as we have already seen, so far as he and the purchaser were concerned, and as between them the transaction was complete. The duty of transportation devolved upon the carrier, and for it he was, in one sense, the agent of the seller, as well as of the purchaser; but, as it was to be at the expense of the purchaser, the delivery to the carrier was a delivery to the purchaser; and this was ruled in Garbracht's case. The injunction to the carrier to collect the money on delivery imposed an additional duty on the carrier, which the carrier was, of course bound to discharge. This arrangement was a matter of convenience, both to the purchaser and the seller, relative to the payment and transmission of the price; but that is all. . . . So far as the criminal law is concerned, it is only an actual sale without license that is prohibited. But there was no such sale, because all the essential facts which constitute the sale transpired in Allegheny county, where the defendant's license was operative. The carrier, being the agent of the purchaser to receive the goods, does receive them from the seller in Allegheny county, and the delivery to him for the purpose of transportation was a delivery to the purchaser. This is the legal, and certainly the common, understanding of a sale. The statute, being criminal, must be strictly construed; and only those acts which are plainly within its meaning, according to the common understanding of men, can be regarded as prohibited criminal acts. We cannot consider, therefore, that a mere undertaking on the part of the carrier to collect the price of the goods at the time of his delivery to the purchaser, though the payment of the price be a condition of the delivery, can suffice to convert the seller's delivery to the carrier for transportation and collection into a crime. We therefore hold that the sales made by the defendant upon orders, C.O.D., received from the purchasers were not in violation of the criminal statute against sales without license, and the conviction and sentence in the court below must be set aside. *The judgment of the court of quarter sessions is reversed, and the defendant is discharged from his recognizance upon this indictment.*

WILLIAMS, J. (dissenting). . . . If the defendant had taken the bottles to Mercer in person, and delivered them on receipt of the price, no one could be found to doubt that his sale was made where he took his money and delivered his goods. If he had sent a clerk in his store to do the business for him in the same manner, the character of the transaction would be equally free from doubt. Instead of sending his clerk, he employed the carrier to collect the bill and deliver the package for him; and the carrier became his agent for collection and delivery as truly as his clerk would have been. The duty of the carrier, as such, ended with the transportation of the package. Its undertaking to collect the price and make delivery of the article was outside the functions of the carrier, and made it the agent or factor of the consignor for that purpose. The transaction, taken together, was, both on principle and authority, a sale and delivery at Mercer, and not at Pittsburgh. . . .

CLARK and McCOLLUM, JJ., concur in this dissenting opinion.   ◄

COMMENTS AND QUESTIONS

1. This case involved a criminal prosecution rather than a civil suit. And yet, the court decided the case on the basis of sales law. What was the main issue here? Why did the appellate court reverse the conviction?

2. Note the sharp dissent of three members of the court. Do you agree with it? Should a case of this nature be decided on the basis of civil law, or should other considerations enter into the decision? The decision has been criticized by several legal writers.

Where Seller Obligated to Deliver Goods

Rule 5. If the contract to sell requires the seller to deliver the goods to the buyer, or at a particular place, or to pay the freight or cost of transportation to the buyer, or to a particular place, the property does not pass until the goods have been delivered to the buyer or reached the place agreed upon.

A common example of this rule is the "F.O.B." contract in which the seller agrees to transport the goods "Free On Board" to a certain place; in this case, title does not pass until the goods reach that place.

EXAMPLE

s, in Los Angeles, agrees to sell 500 airplane engines to B in New York. The contract calls for shipment F.O.B. Chicago. Title does not pass until the goods are actually delivered to the carrier in Chicago. Risk of loss is on the seller while the goods are in transit from Los Angeles to Chicago. The F.O.B. point may be either the place of shipment, the final destination, or some in-between point.

To be distinguished from the F.O.B. contract is the so-called "C.I.F." contract, in which the price of goods paid by the buyer includes the cost of the goods and the insurance and freight charges, in one lump sum. In cases involving such contracts, most courts hold that title passes to the buyer once the goods have been delivered to the carrier, since the insurance has been procured at the buyer's expense and for his own benefit. Thus risk of loss passes to the buyer as soon as the goods are in transit to him.

In the case that follows the sales contract called for an F.O.B. shipment, but circumstances were present that caused the court to disregard the general rule.

LOUIS F. DOW CO. v. BITTNER et al.

Supreme Court of Minnesota, 1932
187 Minn. 143, 244 N.W. 556

► Action by the Louis F. Dow Company against Herman Bittner and others, doing business as Bittner Bros. & Rasmussen. Decision for the plaintiff. Defendants appeal from the judgment.

Judgment affirmed.

STONE, J. Action for the purchase price of merchandise, resulting in a decision, a jury having been waived, for plaintiff. Defendants appeal from the judgment.

Defendants were copartners who, January 16, 1930, contracted with plaintiff for the purchase of 400 calendars, upon which, according to the contract, certain indicated advertising of defendants and their business was to be printed. After that printing was done, but before delivery of the calendars "f.o.b. cars, St. Paul," as the contract required, defendants attempted to repudiate. Their one defense now is that, while they might be liable for damages for breach of contract, they are not so for the contract price, their assertion being that, when repudiated, the contract was wholly executory, that the goods had not been appropriated to the contract, and so title had not passed.

1. Defendants' law is good, Sherman Nursery Co. v. Augenbaugh, 98 Minn. 201, 100 N.W. 1101, but their view of the facts all wrong. The contract had been executed to a substantial extent by plaintiff when defendants attempted to repudiate. The calendars had been printed, manufactured specially for defendants. By plaintiff's performance of the contract, they had been rendered unsuitable for the general trade, and had been set aside for shipment to defendants pursuant to the contract. Clearly, therefore, the goods had been appropriated to the contract, title had passed, and plaintiff had so far performed that defendants are liable for the purchase price. . . .

There are many cases (for example, Presley Fruit Co. v. St. Louis, I.M. & S.R. Co., 130 Minn. 121, 124, 153 N.W. 115), where goods have been sold for delivery f.o.b. cars at the shipping point, and it has been held that until such delivery the property did not pass. But that conclusion is not tenable where the process of special manufacture for the buyer has gone so far as irretrievably to allocate the goods to him under the contract. Delivery is not the essential thing, but only one, and quite a usual, way of effecting it. What is essential to the passing of title is an unconditional appropriation of the goods to the contract by one party with the assent of the other. 1 Uniform Laws Ann. (Sales) 161. "There may be appropriation without either delivery or payment." . . . Here, for example, the calendars were printed or embossed with defendants' name and their special advertising matter. That, and their setting aside for shipment to defendants, certainly made irrevocable their appropriation to the contract . . . , passed title to defendants, and made them liable for the purchase price.

2. The property passes when the parties intend that it shall pass. Section 8394, Mason's Minn. St. 1927, section 19, Uniform Sales Act, enunciates certain rules for determining the intention of the parties, "unless a different intention appears." Here, the parties could not have intended otherwise than that the property should pass not later than the moment when the calendars had put upon them the name and advertising matter of defendants, for thereafter they would be of no further use to plaintiff or anybody other than defendants.

Possibly it should be added by way of explanation that defendants attempted to cancel because of the sale of their business. Plaintiff offered to add to the printing matter on the calendar the name of the purchaser, that he was successor to defendants, and to do the work at cost. That certainly was fair enough, but defendants declined the offer.

Judgment affirmed.   ◄

COMMENTS AND QUESTIONS

1. The general rule is that when goods are to be shipped F.O.B. to a certain place, title does not pass until the goods are delivered to that place. In this case the defendants canceled the contract before the goods reached the place specified. How, then, did the court justify its holding that title passed before delivery to St. Paul? When *did* title pass?
2. Note the last paragraph of the opinion and the plaintiff's offer to fix up the calendars for the defendants' successor. Is this information material?

Situations Where Seller Retains Title but Risk Passes to Buyer

Often a seller chooses to retain title to goods as security until the buyer has paid for them. In such cases, even though title is reserved by the seller, the risk of loss passes to the buyer on shipment, delivery, or appropriation. The most common example of this situation is a conditional sale, which we shall discuss later in this chapter (pp. 429–39). Another example occurs when the seller ships goods by common carrier and has the bill of lading made out in his own name, thereby making it impossible for the buyer to procure the goods before paying for them. Here the risk of loss may pass to the buyer when the goods are delivered to the carrier for shipment, even though title technically remains with the seller. The main point to remember is that risk of loss and title do not always pass from seller to buyer at the same time.

SECTION 3

WARRANTIES IN SALES CONTRACTS

Nature and Definition

Earlier (page 241), we discussed the situation in which one party to a contract makes misrepresentations to the other concerning the subject matter of the contract. You will recall that in such cases the innocent party may either sue for damages or rescind the contract. In most sales contracts, the seller makes certain representations to the buyer concerning the nature and quality of the goods being sold. These representations, which are called *warranties,* fall into two categories: (1) express and (2) implied.

Express Warranties

An *express warranty* is an affirmative representation by the seller concerning the goods. It usually takes the form of a written or oral statement, but may sometimes result from the seller's conduct alone. No particular language or conduct is necessary so long as the seller represents certain facts to the buyer to induce him to buy the goods. Generally speaking, mere statements of opinion or estimates of the value or quality of the goods—the sort of thing that dealers commonly engage in when they are trying to make a sale—are not considered warranties.

If the buyer, by his words or conduct, indicates that he is relying on his own judgment or knowledge in purchasing the goods, no express warranty can arise. Moreover, if the seller makes the property available for inspection before a purchase is made, his express warranty is not regarded as covering obvious defects that would be apparent to a buyer who inspected the property with reasonable care. If the defect is of a sort that would not be revealed by a reasonable inspection, however, the warranty is held to be binding. Of course, if a defect is known to the buyer at the time he agrees to purchase, he may not claim the benefit of an express warranty, since he obviously has not relied on it. On the other hand, if the goods are not made available for inspection, the buyer is usually justified in relying on the seller's representation.

EXAMPLES

1. s is negotiating for the sale of a dog to b. He tells b that the dog has a pure pedigree and comes from a long line of show dogs. b relies on s's statement and agrees to purchase the dog. Later on, it becomes apparent that the dog's pedigree is anything but pure. b can probably claim the benefit of an express warranty. If, however, b knows that the warranty is false when s makes it but goes ahead and buys the dog anyway, he cannot claim a breach of express warranty, since he obviously didn't rely on it.

2. s represents to b that the dog is in good condition and is ready to be shown. b, relying on these statements, buys the dog. If the dog is available for inspection and is obviously in unsound condition, b may not sue for breach of warranty, since he has a duty to inspect before purchasing. If the unsound condition is such that it would not be revealed by inspection, however, then s is bound by the express warranty.

The following case presents an example of express warranties. It is also interesting for its discussion of the personalities involved. Note also the court's scathing denunciation of the morality of certain types of merchant.

FOOTE v. WILSON

Supreme Court of Kansas, 1919
104 Kan. 191, 178 P. 430

► BURCH, J. The action was one by a buyer to rescind a contract of sale induced by false statements of the seller, and for other relief. The seller prayed for specific performance. The plaintiff recovered, and the defendants appeal.

The transaction was typical of that form of industry which consists in assembling worthless odds and ends of stocks of goods, giving the aggregation the appearance of a "store," and selling it to a farmer. The details vary according to the ingenuity of the seller. In this instance the store was opened wide to the farmer's inspection. He was led along shelves and showcases and behind counters. Covers were removed and boxes were opened, and he saw straw hats (the sale was made in November), and narrow width, pointed toed, low shoes, and rotten rubber goods, and soiled white goods, and out of date styles. Discovering a motheaten garment, he modestly inquired if it were salable, and was assured that it was, and was told by one of the defendants that his method was not to put the price down, like some people, but always to put it up—he had been a merchant for 40 years, and always sold his goods. The plaintiff brought his wife in from the farm to look at the store. He also took to the store a merchant from a neighboring town, who spent approximately 45 minutes in examining the stock, and who gave the plaintiff little information and no advice. On three different occasions the plaintiff spent a total of 2½ or 3 hours looking, with uncomprehending eyes, at the goods, before trading his homestead and another farm for them, without an invoice. An agent of the defendants urged him to trade quickly, without an invoice, because an invoice would show so much more than the defendants claimed, they would back out. The plaintiff testified that he was without experience, that he did not make a thorough examination because of the representations of the defendants and their agent, and that when he finally made up his mind to trade, he did so, not on his own judgment, or the judgment of the merchant he called to his assistance, but because he relied on the statements of the defendants and their agent respecting the quality and quantity of goods in the store. Those statements were that the goods were salable goods, and that they would invoice from $9,000 to $11,000. The plaintiff was placed in possession. When he tried to sell the stuff, nobody would buy and when he took an inventory it amounted to about $2,500.

So-called "dealers' talk," of the kind the courts are called on to consider, is morally reprehensible because it is intended to produce the psychological effect of representation without incurring the penalties of representation. Tradesmen of the better class scorn to resort to it. They understand that what we need in business, as well as in social, political, and even international relations, is common honesty of speech, and they depend for success on serving the public needs, telling the truth about their commodities, and standing ready to make good their assertions. A few dealers still cling to the double standard of morals—one for church on Sunday, and one for business on week days. They display raucous mirth at the "sentimental" notion that men are their brothers' keepers in business, and that the Golden Rule applies to the relation between buyer and seller, and they exercise in full the privilege of trimming with luring "opinions," seductive "puffing," and shrewdly equivocal "shop talk," still permitted them by the remnant of the discredited doctrine of *caveat emptor,* "the dark age law of *caveat emptor!*" (84 Cent. Law. J. 63) which still survives. Shocking as it appears, the law of sales is still of such low-grade morality that it sends the public to its tradesmen on the basis that people should expect to meet and be deceived by the expert use of a line on an ethical par with that of horse traders, unless they be wary enough to protect themselves.

When the limits of the refined form of prevarication known as "dealers' talk" have been overstepped, and in an unguarded moment a material fact has been stated, the law does step in and protect the buyer. In this instance one deceitful representation was that the goods were salable. The representation was one of fact. Salable is the equivalent of merchantable—the sonorous bait employed in the case of Meller v. Thayer, 101 Kan. 355, 168 P. 277—which in all the dictionaries and to the common understanding means, as applied to commercial transactions, fit for sale in usual course of trade, at usual selling prices. The other representation, that the goods would invoice at from $9,000 to $11,000, was likewise a positive assertion of a definite fact, and not a mere expression of an "opinion respecting value."

The attorney for the defendants concedes, with becoming candor, that the defendants are bound by the finding of the district court relating to the representations alleged to have been made, but he directs attention to the admissions of the plaintiff that he not only had abundant opportunity for inspection, but that he inspected the goods himself as long and as often as he desired, and that he had others inspect them. Besides this, he took a bill of sale which contained no warrant, respecting salability or amount of invoice. Authorities are cited to the effect that the rule of *caveat emptor* ordinarily applies to a sale for general purposes of common articles of merchandise open to inspection, that means of knowledge is the equivalent of knowledge, that a buyer cannot be heard to say he relied on representations as to facts when the facts themselves were before his eyes, and that a buyer distrustful of his own judgment should take a warranty.

The authorities cited are either inapplicable to the facts, or else they do not represent the best modern legal thought. The defects of which the buyer complains were not obvious, that is, they were not apparent on casual observation. An examination was required. A brief examination might have been sufficient to satisfy an expert dealer, familiar with the capacity and disposition of the public to absorb such goods, but investigation was necessary. The buyer made a partial investigation. The seller might have kept silent, had he so desired, and might have allowed the buyer to improve or not, as he desired, his opportunity for investigation. The seller, however, chose not to keep silent. He not only made profert of the goods for inspection, but he made profert of his own statements of fact, for such weight as they might have. The buyer accepted the statements as true, and acted on them. Under such circumstances the seller is bound by his statements. He cannot insist that the buyer be held to the results of an inspection made, or which might have been made, because he was not content to leave the buyer to abide by such results. He induced the sale by other means, and will not be heard to say that such other means ought not to have prevailed.

In this instance the buyer was conscious of his limitations, and consequently was all the more ready to accept the seller's statements and forego full inspection and an invoice. The law does not recognize any confidential relation between buyer and seller and has no concern for gullibility as such. But the natural tendency of the uninstructed human mind, sailing off its course in strange seas, to accept expert guidance, may well have been taken into account by the trial court in determining whether or not genuine reliance was placed on the seller's representations: and the law does not permit the seller, who has influenced the navigation to his own advantage by means of his own false statements, to say that the buyer had better light to steer by. A good discussion of the subject may be found in section 208 of Williston on Sales.

Under certain circumstances, the distinction between representation and warranty may well be regarded, but in the transaction under consideration it is of no practical consequence. It affects neither the buyer's right nor the buyer's remedy. Whatever else entered into the transaction, a vital part of it was an affirmation by the seller of material facts which tended to induce the sale, and which were relied on by the buyer. When a sale has been accomplished by such means, it is purely formal and theoretical to say that the affirmation did not become an element of the contract of itself, and so constitute a warranty. Such an affirmation is a warranty (Williston on

Sales, sec. 197), and in this instance it is not material that the affirmations which the defendants made were not repeated in the bill of sale, which did not embrace the subject of warranty.

The parties entered into a preliminary written contract, which provided the manner in which the sale should later be fully consummated. The buyer was to have possession, but the money received from the sale of goods was to be kept intact, and the entire transaction was to be finally concluded within 30 days. In the preliminary contract, which was dated November 16th, the defendants agreed to give a bill of sale of the merchandise "as it is today." The bill of sale which was executed was dated November 16th, and did not contain the quoted limitation. It is suggested that the limitation was intended to exclude warranty of quality and quantity. Very clearly it had no such purpose or effect.

The judgment of the district court is affirmed.   ◄

COMMENTS AND QUESTIONS

1. What was the main issue in this case? Even if express warranties were made by the seller, did not the buyer have ample opportunity to inspect the store? Should he, then, have a right to rely on the warranties and rescind the contract? Are there not some statements made by sellers that no ordinary person relies on or takes seriously?

2. Note the manner in which the court brushes aside all the citations and authorities that were urged on it by the defendants. "The authorities cited are either inapplicable to the facts, or else they do not represent the best modern legal thought." The opinion is a real "sermon" on the morality of sales law.

In the following Illinois case, the buyer alleged that she had relied on an express warranty by the seller when she purchased mascara. Notice, however, that the circumstances were quite different from those in the Kansas case immediately preceding.

BECKETT v. F. W. WOOLWORTH CO.

Supreme Court of Illinois, 1941
376 Ill. 470, 34 N.E. 2d 427

► WILSON, J. The plaintiff, Phyllis Beckett, filed a complaint in the superior court of Cook county against the defendant, the F. W. Woolworth Co., seeking damages for breach of an express warranty alleged to have been made by the defendant incident to the sale to her of a cosmetic or toilet preparation known as "Pinaud's '612' Creamy Mascara." Plaintiff charged that the defendant warranted this preparation was pure, harmless, free from any poisonous substance or germs, and that it was fit and proper for the purpose of coloring and blackening her eyelashes. . . .

Pinaud's "612" creamy mascara is sold in tubes attached to cards along with small black brushes for applying the preparation. The card, tube and brush are made and distributed by Pinaud, Inc. of New York City. The tube of mascara is prepared by a machine which automatically mixes the mascara, fills and seals the tube. These are shipped to retailers, such as the defendant, in boxes containing one dozen cards. In 1937, it appears than

1,500,000 tubes were sold in various chain stores. On September 3, 1937, the plaintiff, a young woman thirty-five years of age, purchased at one of the defendant's retail stores in Chicago a tube of Pinaud's "612" mascara from the cosmetics counter of the "Toilet Article Department" which contained approximately seven hundred articles including four types of mascara. It appears she had patronized this store about eight years and had used the same preparation for ten or twelve years. Plaintiff testified that on the day named she engaged in conversation with the saleswoman concerning the mascara; that she picked up the card and told the clerk she would take it; that she bought the mascara, paid the purchase price, ten cents, and the saleswoman remarked, "Phyllis, don't you think you are pretty enough without it?"; that she replied, "Well, this would help," and, further, "This mascara is safe, isn't it?"; that the clerk answered, "It is on the tube, it says harmless"; that she, plaintiff, then said, "I will take it." The plaintiff then added that she had never experienced any difficulty with her previous purchases of this same product. Upon re-direct examination, plaintiff testified that at the time of the purchase in question the clerk stated that Pinaud's preparation was a "good mascara, she thought it was the nicest and no trouble with it." Upon re-cross examination, plaintiff testified that the saleswoman asked her, "Have you been using this 612 Pinaud's?" that she answered, "It is pretty good," and that the saleswoman added, "It is supposed to be the best." When plaintiff's attention was directed to her different versions of the transaction she testified that she did not say Pinaud's "612" was the best available, safe, or pure, and, further, that she did not recommend its purchase. As plaintiff was applying the mascara to her eyelashes on September 4, some of the preparation fell into her right eye. A painful and admittedly serious eye injury was suffered.

The plaintiff rests her claim solely on the ground defendant made an express warranty that the mascara was "run-proof and harmless."

. . . To obtain a reversal, defendant makes the contention, among others, that proof of an essential element of an express warranty is wanting, namely, plaintiff's purchase of the merchandise in reliance upon an affirmation of fact by the retailer having a natural tendency to induce the sale. Even if (1) the words "run-proof" and "harmless" appearing at the bottom of the small printed card to which the mascara and brush were attached and (2) the statements alleged to have been made by the saleswoman be deemed affirmations of fact by the defendant relating to the mascara purchased by plaintiff, there is no evidence tending to show that these promises induced plaintiff to purchase the mascara or that she relied upon such statements. Admittedly, plaintiff knew that the defendant was a retailer. Our examination of the card introduced in evidence discloses that it specifically sets forth that the mascara is distributed by Pinaud, Inc.; the retailer's name does not appear on the card, the tube or the brush. Plaintiff had been using this particular brand of mascara for ten or twelve years prior to her purchase on September 3, 1937, had purchased it from the defendant's store about eight years, and had experienced no previous difficulty, although she used about a tube each week. She did not profess knowledge of any statement on the card. In particular, there is no testimony in the record purporting to show that at the time of the purchase plaintiff read or saw the words "run-proof" and "harmless" on the printed card. Her own testimony discloses that she personally picked up the card, with the mascara and brush attached thereto, and handed it to the saleswoman with a dime saying she would take the article. Whether the statements attributed to the saleswoman were made prior to, concurrently with or subsequent to the consummation of the transaction, the conclusion is inescapable that plaintiff was not induced to buy the mascara in reliance upon such promises. The statements which the plaintiff claims the saleswoman made were, in fact, all made subsequent to the completion of the sale. Manifestly, acts or statements of a retailer made after a sale do not support a claim that a regular customer was induced to buy merchandise in reliance upon such statements.

The proof conclusively demonstrates that plaintiff did not rely either upon the printed words on the card containing the mascara or upon the statements attributed by her to the defendant's employee concerning the fitness for use for which the product was purchased. For the reason that there is no evidence for the plaintiff which tends to prove the essential element of reliance upon an affirmation of fact or promise relating to the mascara by the defendant with a tendency to induce her to purchase the cosmetic preparation, *the motions to direct a verdict in favor of the defendant should have been granted.*   ◄

COMMENTS AND QUESTIONS

1. What happened in the lower court? What was the decision of the Illinois Supreme Court? What rule of law is illustrated here?
2. The court found, as a matter of fact, that the saleswoman's statements were made *after* the purchase of the mascara. However, it also states that there would be no reliance on the warranties even though they were made *prior* to the sale. If the court had found as a fact that the plaintiff had had her conversation with the saleswoman *before* buying the mascara, do you feel that the court would still have decided for the defendant?

Implied Warranties

In General

In most sales contracts, certain warranties are implied by law even though the parties themselves say nothing about them. These warranties, which have come to be accepted as a necessary protection for the buyer, have been specifically incorporated into the Uniform Sales Act and, in somewhat modified form, into the Uniform Commercial Code. If the parties choose, they may exclude any or all of these implied warranties from their contract; such a provision, provided it is clear and unequivocal, will generally be enforced. Otherwise, the implied warranties automatically become part of the agreement by operation of law. In a sales transaction that contains both express and implied warranties, both will be enforced unless there is a conflict between them; in that case, the express warranty will govern.

Implied Warranty of Title

Usually, when one person sells goods to another, he impliedly warrants that he has a right to sell them and can pass good title. In addition, the seller warrants that there are no mortgages or liens on the property other than those which he tells the buyer about. These implied warranties are binding on the seller even though he may be honestly unaware of the claims of third parties.

> EXAMPLE
>
> s, honestly believing that he has good title to a boat, sells it to B. Actually, x owns the boat, and may claim possession of it. s is liable to B for breach of implied warranty of title, despite his good faith and his ignorance of x's claim of ownership.

Implied Warranty of Conformity to Description or Sample

If the subject matter of the contract is specifically described by words, numbers, grades, or other identifying symbols, there is an implied warranty that the goods delivered to the buyer will conform to the description. Similarly, if the seller furnishes a sample of the goods for the buyer to inspect, he warrants that all the property will conform to the sample.

> EXAMPLES
>
> 1. B orders a certain type and grade of seed from s, a supplier. There is an implied warranty that s will furnish B with seed of the type and grade requested, and that the goods will conform to the description.
> 2. s, a cloth merchant, shows B a sample of material. B agrees to purchase a certain quantity of it. s impliedly warrants that the cloth he delivers to B will correspond to the sample.

Implied Warranty of Merchantability

When a seller sells goods in which he customarily deals, there is an implied warranty that the goods are of merchantable quality—i.e., that they are salable in the market as goods of the kind described. To be merchantable, goods must be free from defects and reasonably fit for use for normal purposes. If the goods are available for inspection, however, this warranty does not extend to defects that a reasonably careful examination would reveal. Note, once again, that the warranty of merchantability is read into the contract *only* when the seller deals in the sort of merchandise called for in that particular contract. An occasional seller of such goods is not bound by this warranty.

> EXAMPLES
>
> 1. B purchases a lawn mower from s, a hardware dealer. The mower proves to be defective and useless for cutting grass. B may claim a breach of implied warranty of merchantability, since s customarily deals in lawn mowers. If s were not a regular dealer, however, the warranty would probably not apply.
> 2. This time, when B goes to s and says that he wants to buy a lawn mower, s invites him to inspect one with blades so dull that they are

obviously incapable of cutting grass. B goes ahead and buys it anyway. In this case, B would lose the benefit of the implied warranty of merchantability. If the defect was not readily observable, however, B could probably either sue for damages or else return the mower and get his money back.

Implied Warranty of Fitness for Particular Purpose

Although the implied warranty of merchantability requires that goods be suitable for the ordinary purposes for which they are intended, it does not require that they be suitable for unusual purposes. If, however, the buyer expressly or impliedly informs the seller that he intends to use the goods for a particular purpose, and if it is clear that he is relying on the seller's skill or judgment in deciding whether or not to buy the goods, there is an implied warranty that they will be fit for that purpose. If they are not, there has been a breach of warranty, even though the goods are fit for ordinary use.

EXAMPLE

B, a roofer, tells S, a supplier, that he needs some roof shingles that will withstand heavy snow and very cold weather. S sells B a type of shingle that is unsuited to the climate and the purpose indicated. B may claim a breach of warranty. S cannot defend his action by claiming that there is nothing wrong with the shingles and that they are suitable for ordinary use.

If a buyer orders goods by their patent name or trade name, no warranty of fitness is implied in most cases, even though the seller has been apprised of the use the buyer intends to make of the goods. The theory behind this exception is that if the buyer specifically requests a certain type or grade of merchandise, he is using his own judgment and is not relying on the seller's.

EXAMPLE

B, a roofer, orders a specific brand and grade of shingle from S, a supplier. The shingles turn out to be unsuitable for B's purposes. No warranty of fitness has been implied, even though S was aware of the intended use of the shingles.

In the case that follows, even though the buyer had ordered an article by its trade name, he argued that there was still an implied warranty of fitness.

IRON FIREMAN COAL STOKER CO. v. BROWN

Supreme Court of Minnesota, 1931
182 Minn. 399, 234 N.W. 685

▶ WILSON, C. J.   Defendants H. Rowatt and Frances M. Brown appealed from an order denying their motion for a new trial.

The action is to foreclose a mechanic's lien based on the installation of an iron fireman coal stoker. The court found, as defendants claimed, that it would not do the work for which it was sold and purchased, though reasonable efforts had been made to have it do so. The court later granted plaintiff's motion to amend the findings so as to give plaintiff the relief sought. This was upon the theory that the article was sold under a trade-name within G.S. 1923, subd. 4, and hence without an implied warranty.

G.S. 1923, sec. 8390, subd. 4, reads:

"In the case of a contract to sell or a sale of a specified article under its patent or other trade-name, there is no implied warranty as to its fitness for any particular purpose."

If a person requests a dealer to deliver to him a specifically designated article, known to the buyer and the trade by its trade-name, and it is done, it is obvious that the article would be sold under its trade-name within the meaning of the statute. Such negotiation indicates that the article is known by both parties and the buyer has designated just what he wants. He knows what he wants. The theory of the statute is that, since he knows what he wants and gets it, after having so designated it, it must be supposed that the trade-name carries such qualities as to cause the purchase.

The spirit and intent of subdivision 4 of the statute is that the seller is not held to an implied warranty because the buyer gets the distinct thing selected by him—an exact article, for which he bargains. So, acting upon his own desires, he takes his own chances as to fitness of the article, and should not be permitted to complain of the seller who has supplied him with the very thing he sought. . . . In such cases it is not important that the buyer discloses to the seller his intentions as to the use of the article. It is usually helpful to determine upon whose judgment and responsibility the purchase was made. Or, to state it another way, if the thing is itself specifically selected and ordered, the buyer takes upon himself the risk of its effecting the desired purpose. Under such circumstances, the law does not impose an implied warranty; nor should it.

The situation is quite different where the buyer yields to the trade talk of a salesman who sells something that is wholly unknown to him. Perhaps it might be said that, where the buyer selects the article, subdivision 4 applies, and where the seller selects the article suitable for the purposes needed, subdivision 1, hereinafter mentioned, applies. We are of the opinion that, where the buyer fully informs the seller of his particular needs, and the seller undertakes to select or supply an article suitable for the purpose involved, subdivision 1 applies even though the article may be described in the contract of a sale by its Trade-name. . . .

There are authorities that seem to put a strict construction upon this provision of the Uniform Sales Act and hold that, if the contract describes an article by the trade-name, there is no implied warranty, but such authorities apparently involve cases where the contract disclosed the article sold under a trade-name and the record fails to disclose any circumstances such as are involved in this case. It would seem that such a contract, in the absence of evidence of circumstances to the contrary, should be construed under the statute as if the purchaser had selected the article purchased. . . .

The mere fact that an article sold is described in the contract by its trade-name does not necessarily make the sale a sale under or by a trade-name. Whether it is so or not, depends upon the circumstances. . . .

This provision of the statute is merely a restatement of the common-law rule that, where there is a sale of a known, described, and defined article, and if that article is in fact supplied, there is no implied warranty. But we think the rule at common law and now under such a statute means articles known in the market, and among those familiar with that kind of trade, by that description. . . .

In this case it would seem that the "Iron Fireman" was not known to defendants. They were entirely ignorant as to its ability or capacity or the work which it would do. Plaintiff was in possession of all the facts. Defendants did not even know it had a trade-name. It then had a limited use in their community. Plaintiff sought to sell them the equipment, and assured them that they would not have to go to the furnace room the last thing at night nor the first thing in the morning. They were willing to buy something that would accomplish that purpose. They had no knowledge of the "Iron Fireman" by reputation or otherwise. They made their desires known to plaintiff. One of the reasons that caused them to buy was that plaintiff repeatedly told them they would take the equipment out if not satisfactory. Defendants unsuccessfully attempted to make it work. Plaintiff knew defendants had no knowledge of the equipment or its operation.

Defendants' reliance upon plaintiff's judgment as to the suitability of the equipment to meet their requirements is evident from all the circumstances.

. . . The fact that the article has a trade-name does not do away with the implied warranty arising out of the circumstances indicated. In addition to the authorities hereinbefore cited which sustained that conclusion, we believe the following authorities tend to support the same theory [cases cited].

Under the circumstances, we are of the opinion that under this subdivision of the statute there was an implied warranty that the equipment was reasonably fit for the purpose for which it was sold. . . .

Reversed.   ◄

COMMENTS AND QUESTIONS

1. What had happened in the lower court? Why did the appellate court reverse the decision?
2. How did the court get around the general rule that there is no implied warranty of fitness when an article is sold under its trade name?
3. Suppose, instead, that the defendants had known of the reputation of the "Iron Fireman" and had had some knowledge of how it operated before they purchased it from the plaintiff. Would this have changed the result?

Implied Warranties in Food and Drug Sales

In the area of food and drug sales, special problems have given rise to a great deal of litigation. The warranty of merchantability, of course, requires that regular dealers furnish products that are fit for human consumption. And yet this warranty does not generally apply to casual or occasional sellers of foodstuffs. The warranty of fitness for a particular purpose is also applicable here, but since most food products are purchased by brand or trade name, its force is considerably lessened. As a result of this gap in coverage, purchasers of impure food and drugs have occasionally been left without remedy, especially when they have dealt with someone other than a regular dealer.

Additional confusion has developed in the sale of food and drugs in packaged containers. Some states have held that, since the immediate seller is not responsible for the packaging and has no control over the contents, he is not responsible for breach of warranty if the goods prove to be unfit or improper. Most courts, however, have rejected this notion, on the ground that it is unfair to consumers.

In the New York case that follows, Judge Cardozo wrestles with some of the problems we have just outlined. Note the care he takes to distinguish between the various types of implied warranties.

RYAN v. PROGRESSIVE GROCERY STORES, INC.

Court of Appeals of New York, 1931
255 N.Y. 388, 185 N.E. 105

► Action by Patrick Ryan against the Progressive Grocery Stores, Inc. From a judgment of the Appellate Division, 230 App. Div. 792, 244 N.Y.S. 919, affirming a judgment of the City Court of the city of White Plains for plaintiff, defendant appeals by permission.

Affirmed.

CARDOZO, C. J. The action is for breach of warranty. Plaintiff through his wife, who acted as his agent, bought a loaf of bread at the defendant's grocery. The loaf had concealed in it a pin, which hurt the plaintiff's mouth. There has been a judgment for the damage.

> 1. "Where the buyer, expressly or by implication, makes known to the seller the particular purpose for which the goods are required, and it appears that the buyer relies on the seller's skill or judgment (whether he be the grower or manufacturer or not), there is an implied warranty that the goods shall be reasonably fit for such purpose." Personal Property Law; Consol. Laws, c. 41, 96, subd. 1.

The plaintiff did not rely on the seller's skill or judgment. His wife stated to the salesman that she wished to have a loaf of "Ward's bread." The salesman gave her what she asked for, wrapped in a sealed package as it had come from the Ward Baking Company, the baker. She made her own choice, and used her own judgment.

The leading case in this state as to the meaning of the statute quoted is Rinaldi v. Mohican Co., 225 N.Y. 70, 121 N.E. 471. The sale was one of pork, which turned out to be diseased. We held that reliance on the seller's skill and judgment might be gathered from the purchase as a reasonable inference. We left the question open whether a like inference would be drawn upon a sale in the original package as bought by the vendor from others.

Since Rinaldi v. Mohican Co., the scope of the implied warranty upon a sale of food in sealed containers has been discussed in other courts. There are decisions to the effect that even in such circumstances an implied war-

ranty ensues if the seller's judgment has been trusted for the selection of
the brand or make. . . . We assume for present purposes that so the rule
should be declared. Invariably, however, the limitation has been added
that there can be no inference of reliance where the buyer selects the
brand and gets what he selects. The customer will be taken to confide in
"the skill and experience of the seller in determining the kind of canned
goods which he will purchase, unless he demands goods of a definite brand
or trade-name." Ward v. Great Atlantic & Pacific Tea Co., *supra*. The
statute is then explicit. "In the case of . . . a sale of a specified article
under its patent or other trade name, there is no implied warranty as to
its fitness for any particular purpose." Personal Property Law, 96, subd. 4.
There is no room for a holding that choice shall be imputed to the seller
when the transaction shows upon its face that the judgment of the seller
was superseded, and choice determined by the buyer.

The award of damages, if it is to be upheld, must rest upon some other
basis than the imputation of reliance.

2. "Where the goods are bought by description from a seller who deals
in goods of that description (whether he be the grower or manufacturer
or not), there is an implied warranty that the goods shall be of merchantable quality." Personal Property Law, 96, subd. 2.

The facts excluding a warranty under subdivision 1, we are to inquire
whether there is a warranty under subdivision 2.

Under the common-law rule long in force in this state, the warranty
of merchantable quality was limited to sales by a manufacturer or grower.
. . . All this has been changed since the coming of the Sales Law. . . .
Dealer as well as manufacturer or grower affirms as to anything he sells,
if purchased by description, that it is of merchantable quality. The burden
may be heavy. It is one of the hazards of the business.

Most of the sales of defective foodstuffs have been dealt with by the
courts as if subdivision 1 of the section defining warranties gave the exclusive rule to be applied. In some instances the goods were not purchased
by description. In others, the courts may have been unmindful of the fact
that the warranty of merchantable quality is no longer confined to manufacturers or growers. Innovations of this order are slow to make their way.
Gradually, however, as the statute has become better known, the bearing
of subdivision 2 upon sales of food in sealed containers has been perceived
by court and counsel. The nature of the transaction must determine in each
instance the rule to be applied. There are times when a warranty of fitness
has no relation to a warranty of merchantable quality. This is so, for example, when machinery competently wrought is still inadequate for the
use to which the buyer has given notice that it is likely to be applied. There
are times, on the other hand, when the warranties co-exist, in which event
a recovery may be founded upon either. "Fitness for a particular purpose
may be merely the equivalent of merchantability." Williston, Sales, vol. 1,
235, and cases there cited.

A dual warranty is thus possible for foodstuffs as for anything else.
Both in this court and in others the possibility is recognized. . . .

Loaves baked with pins in them are not of merchantable quality. The dealer is thus charged with liability, though the buyer selects the brand, just as he would be liable for concealed defects upon a sale of wool or silk. Assume that the sale had been made by a manufacturer or a grower, and that there had been a request for a special brand. There would then be no warranty of fitness for any "particular" purpose. Would any one dispute, however, that a defect of this order, destroying value altogether, would be covered by the warranty of merchantable quality? The question carries its own answer. The rule is different, though the purchase is by description, if the goods are subject to inspection and the defects are of such a nature that inspection will reveal them. . . . Here the sale was by description, the defect was wholly latent, and inspection was impossible. In such circumstances, the law casts the burden on the seller, who may vouch in the manufacturer,[13] if the latter was to blame. The loss in its final incidence will be borne where it is placed by the initial wrong.

The argument is made that the only damage to be recovered for the breach of the warranty of merchantable quality is the price of the bread, the difference between the value of a good loaf and a bad one. The rule is not so stubborn. Undoubtedly, the difference in value supplies the ordinary measure. Personal Property 150, subds. 6 and 7, section 151. The measure is more liberal where special circumstances are present with proof of special damage. Here the dealer had notice from the nature of the transaction that the bread was to be eaten. Knowledge that it was to be eaten was knowledge that the damage would be greater than the price. . . . For damages thus foreseen, the buyer has his remedy, whether the warranty is one of fitness or of merchantable quality. . . .

The judgment should be affirmed, with costs.   ◀

COMMENTS AND QUESTIONS

1. This case contains a fine discussion of the warranties of fitness and merchantability. Which, if either, was applicable to this sale? Summarize the court's reasoning.
2. Note that it was the plaintiff's wife who actually purchased the bread. The court holds that she was acting as her husband's agent, thus giving him the right to sue for breach of warranty.

Persons Protected by Warranties

Since a sale is a contract, the general rule has long been established that the warranty obligation runs only between the two contracting parties (the seller and buyer), and that the benefit of the warranty does not extend to any other persons, even though they use or come in contact with the goods. If a third party suffers injury or damage as a result of defective goods, his only remedy is to sue the person who was responsible for the defect (usually the manufacturer), in an effort to prove that the defect was caused by that person's negligence. In most cases, such proof is very difficult to establish.

---

[13] This means that the seller may bring the manufacturer into the case; if the seller is liable to the buyer for breach of warranty, he may, in turn, recover from the manufacturer if the latter was at fault in causing the breach.

B purchases an automobile from s and lends it to x to use on a trip. x is injured when the brakes fail and the car goes off the road. x has no right to sue s for breach of warranty. His only remedy is to sue the manufacturer for negligence, and to try to prove that the defective brakes were caused by the manufacturer's fault or carelessness. If B is driving, he can sue s for breach of warranty; all he needs to show is that the brakes were defective.

Many legal authorities feel that the requirement of privity (i.e., that only the immediate buyer may sue for breach of warranty) has created a great deal of hardship and injustice. This is especially true, these critics contend, in cases related to the sale of food and drugs, which are often used by other members and guests of the buyer's household. Other critics argue that manufacturers, producers, and canners should not be immune from warranty actions merely because they are one step removed from the ultimate consumer. Consequently many states have created special rules for food and drug sales that enable the consumer to sue the seller, or permit the buyer to bring a warranty action directly against the manufacturer. The Uniform Commercial Code takes an important step in this direction by extending the seller's warranty "to any natural person who is in the family or household of his buyer or who is a guest in his home if it is reasonable to expect that such person may use, consume or be affected by the goods and who is injured in person by breach of the warranty." Some states circumvent the strict rule of privity by saying that a housewife, for example, who purchases food is acting as an agent for her husband. Thus, if the husband is injured, he may sue the grocer or dealer for breach of warranty on the theory that, since his wife bought the food for him, he is entitled to bring the action. An example of such a situation occurs in the following case, which is also interesting because of its discussion of the consumer's duty to prepare food properly before eating it.

VACCARINO v. COZZUBO

Court of Appeals of Maryland, 1943
181 Md. 614, 31 A. 2d 316

▶ DELAPLAINE, J.   Joseph Cozzubo, of Baltimore, instituted this suit on contract against Isidore Vaccarino, a retail dealer operating a grocery and meat store on South High Street in Baltimore, to recover damages caused by a breach of an alleged implied warranty that certain sausage, which was sold by the defendant and eaten by the plaintiff, was wholesome and fit for human consumption. The jury rendered a verdict in favor of the plaintiff for $2,000. Vaccarino is appealing from the judgment entered on the verdict.

On October 22, 1940, Cozzubo's wife gave some money to their daughter, Lucy, 11 years old, and told her to buy some sausage at Vaccarino's store. The little girl bought a pound of Italian-style sausage from Vaccarino, and Mrs. Cozzubo cooked it for supper. Six days later Cozzubo became ill, and several days later his wife and child also became ill. They were removed to a hospital, where their disease was diagnosed as trichinosis. Trichinosis is a disease caused by trichinae, nematodes which are occasionally found in pork and which breed in the human body causing muscular swelling, pain and fever. The disease prevented Cozzubo from returning to his employment as a stevedore, and it was not until nearly a month later that he was able to do even light work.

It was vigorously contended that there was no privity of contract between the plaintiff and the defendant. The law is well settled that an action cannot be maintained on an implied warranty where there is no privity of contract. . . . Accordingly an implied warranty of wholesomeness of food does not inure to the benefit of any consumers other than the purchaser, for any such consumers have no privity of contract with the seller. . . . But it is the clear legal duty of a husband to support his wife and supply her with necessaries suitable to her situation and his own circumstances in life. It is a fundamental rule of the common law that a wife, while living with her husband, is presumed to have authority from him to purchase the supplies which are ordinarily required for family use. Lord Abinger laid down the rule as follows: "Where a wife is living with her husband, and where, in the ordinary arrangements of the husband's household, she gives orders to tradesmen for the benefit of her husband and family, and these orders are proper and not extravagant, it is presumed that she has the authority of her husband for so doing. This rule is founded on common sense, for a wife would be of little use to her husband in their domestic arrangements, if she could not order such things as are proper for the use of a house and for her own use without the interference of her husband. The law, therefore, presumes that she does this by her husband's authority." . . . The presumption that the wife, as manager of the household and agent for her husband is authorized to purchase necessaries for the appropriate maintenance of the home arises from the fact of their living together, and the presumption may be rebutted only by proof that the purchase was made without his authority, real or apparent, and without his subsequent assent. . . . The Maryland Act, which prescribes the mutual rights and liabilities of husband and wife, declares that nothing in the Act shall be construed to relieve the husband from liability for debts or contracts which his wife may incur or enter into upon the credit of her husband or as his agent, or for necessaries for herself or for his or their children; but as to all such cases his liability shall continue as at common law. . . . In the present case the wife and daughter of Cozzubo were acting as his agents in helping him to carry out his obligation to support and maintain the family. We therefore hold that privity of contract did exist between the plaintiff and the defendant.

The principal issue presented on this appeal is whether the trial court properly instructed the jury as to the liability of the storekeeper to the purchaser. The general rule has been established in Maryland and by the weight of authority in the United States that where a retail dealer sells food for immediate domestic consumption, there is an implied warranty that the food is wholesome and fit for the purpose for which it is sold. . . .

However, no implied warranty arises either at common law or under the statute that meat, generally fit to be eaten only when properly cooked, is wholesome when eaten raw or cooked in an unusual or improper manner. It is a matter of common knowledge that pork is purchased to be eaten when cooked, not when raw. Hence, it would be unfair to impose upon a retail meat dealer an implied warranty that his pork is fit to be eaten when raw. This is especially true in view of the fact that the danger of contracting trichinosis from eating pork can be eliminated by means of proper cooking. Ferdinand A. Korff, inspector in the Bureau of Meat Inspection of the Baltimore City Health Department, testified in the Court below:

> "There are generally five ways to prevent trichinosis. The first one is to stop feeding garbage to hogs. The second is to cook the garbage. The third is to refrigerate all the pigs for a long period of time at a very cold temperature, about 5 degrees, for about 21 days. The fourth is, of course, to cook all pork products thoroughly, which every housewife should do. And the fifth is by an antigen test, which isn't such a good way. . . . The best way is, of course, cooking the pork thoroughly until all portions of the meat are heated up to 150 degrees; that isn't high, but that's enough to destroy the parasite if the meat is heated. The Federal requirements say 137 degrees; that's the killing point. But we recommend 150 degrees; so that if you cook your pork 20 minutes per pound, and are very sure to get all the redness out of the meat, the parasite will be destroyed."

It is not necessary, of course, for the plaintiff, who has been infected by eating pork, to prove that the pork was cooked at a specific temperature or for a specific length of time. It is our opinion, however, that the implied warranty in the case before us was not that the sausage was wholesome and fit to be eaten either cooked or raw, but that it was wholesome and fit to eat after ordinary domestic cooking. . . .

At the trial of this case the Court instructed the jury that if they found that the plaintiff was infected with trichinosis as a result of eating the sausage, the verdict should be for the plaintiff. The jury should have been authorized to give a verdict for the plaintiff only in case they found that the plaintiff was infected with trichinosis by eating the sausage after it was cooked in the usual or proper manner. *The judgment entered in favor of the plaintiff must therefore be reversed.*   ◄

COMMENTS AND QUESTIONS

1. The appellate court reversed the judgment for the plaintiff and ordered a new trial. How had the jury been instructed in the lower court? What was wrong with this charge? How should the new jury, in the retrial, be instructed on the issue of breach of warranty?

2. The other main question here was whether there was privity of contract between the plaintiff and the defendant. How did the court decide?

We conclude this section with a recent case that cuts across the entire field of warranties and seems to indicate a major breakthrough in this area of the law.

CLAUS H. HENNINGSEN et al.
v. BLOOMFIELD MOTORS, INC. et al.

Supreme Court of New Jersey, 1960
32 N.J. 358; 161 A. 2d 69

▶ FRANCIS, J.

Plaintiff Claus H. Henningsen purchased a Plymouth automobile, manufactured by defendant Chrysler Corporation, from defendant Bloomfield Motors, Inc. His wife, plaintiff Helen Henningsen, was injured while driving it and instituted suit against both defendants to recover damages on account of her injuries. Her husband joined in the action seeking compensation for his consequential losses. The complaint was predicated upon breach of express and implied warranties and upon negligence. At the trial the negligence counts were dismissed by the court and the cause was submitted to the jury for determination solely on the issues of implied warranty of merchantability. Verdicts were returned against both defendants and in favor of the plaintiffs. Defendants appealed. . . .

The facts are not complicated, but a general outline of them is necessary to an understanding of the case.

On May 7, 1955, Mr. and Mrs. Henningsen visited the place of business of Bloomfield Motors, Inc., an authorized De Soto and Plymouth dealer, to look at a Plymouth. They wanted to buy a car and were considering a Ford or a Chevrolet as well as a Plymouth. They were shown a Plymouth which appealed to them and the purchase followed. The record indicates that Mr. Henningsen intended the car as a Mother's Day gift to his wife. He said the intention was communicated to the dealer. When the purchase order or contract was prepared and presented, the husband executed it alone. His wife did not join as a party.

The purchase order was a printed form of one page. On the front it contained blanks to be filled in with a description of the automobile to be sold, the various accessories to be included, and the details of the financing. The particular car selected was described as a 1955 Plymouth, Plaza "6," Club Sedan. The type used in the printed parts of the form became smaller in size, different in style, and less readable toward the bottom where the line for the purchaser's signature was placed. The smallest type on the page appears in the two paragraphs, one of two and one-quarter lines and the second of one and one-half lines, on which great stress is laid by the defense in the case. These two paragraphs are the least legible and the most difficult to read in the instrument, but they are most important in the evaluation of the rights of the contesting parties. They do not attract attention and there is nothing about the format which would draw the reader's eye to them. In fact, a studied and concentrated effort would have to be made to read them. De-emphasis seems the motive rather than emphasis. More particularly, most of the printing in the body of the order appears to be 12 point block type, and easy to read. In the short paragraphs under discussion, however, the type appears to be six point script and the print is solid, that is, the lines are very close together.

The two paragraphs are:

> "The front and back of this Order comprise the entire agreement affecting this purchase and no other agreement or understanding of any nature concerning same has been made or entered into, or will be recognized. I hereby certify that no credit has been extended to me for the purchase of this motor vehicle except as appears in writing on the face of this agreement.
>
> "I have read the matter printed on the back hereof and agree to it as a part of this order the same as if it were printed above my signature. I certify that I am 21 years of age, or older, and hereby acknowledge receipt of a copy of this order."

On the right side of the form, immediately below these clauses and immediately above the signature line, and in 12 point block type, the following appears:

> "CASH OR CERTIFIED CHECK ONLY ON DELIVERY."

On the left side, just opposite and in the same style type as the two quoted clauses, but in eight point size, this statement is set out:

> "This agreement shall not become binding upon the Dealer until approved by an officer of the company."

The two latter statements are in the interest of the dealer and obviously an effort is made to draw attention to them.

The testimony of Claus Henningsen justifies the conclusion that he did not read the two fine print paragraphs referring to the back of the purchase contract. And it is uncontradicted that no one made any reference to them, or called them to his attention. With respect to the matter appearing on the back, it is likewise uncontradicted that he did not read it and that no one called it to his attention.

The reverse side of the contract contains $8\frac{1}{2}$ inches of fine print. It is not as small, however, as the two critical paragraphs described above. The page is headed "Conditions" and contains ten separate paragraphs consisting of 65 lines in all. The paragraphs do not have headnotes or margin notes denoting their particular subject, as in the case of the "Owner Service Certificate" to be referred to later. In the seventh paragraph, about two-thirds of the way down the page, the warranty, which is the focal point of the case, is set forth. It is as follows:

> "7. It is expressly agreed that there are no warranties, express or implied, made by either the dealer or the manufacturer on the motor vehicle, chassis, or parts furnished hereunder except as follows:
>
> "The manufacturer warrants each new motor vehicle (including original equipment placed thereon by the manufacturer except tires), chassis or parts manufactured by it to be free from defects in material or workmanship under normal use and service. Its obligation under this warranty being limited to making good at its factory any part or parts thereof which shall, within ninety (90) days after delivery of such vehicle to the original purchaser or before such vehicle has been driven 4,000 miles, whichever event shall first occur, be returned to it with transporta-

tion charges prepaid and which its examination shall disclose to its satisfaction to have been thus defective; this warranty being expressly in lieu of all other warranties expressed or implied, and all other obligations or liabilities on its part, and it neither assumes nor authorizes any other person to assume for it any other liability in connection with the sale of its vehicles. . . . "

After the contract had been executed, plaintiffs were told the car had to be serviced and that it would be ready in two days. According to the dealer's president, a number of cars were on hand at the time; they had come in from the factory about three or four weeks earlier and at least some of them, including the one selected by the Henningsens, were kept in the back of the shop for display purposes. When sold, plaintiffs' vehicle was not "a serviced car, ready to go." The testimony shows that Chrysler Corporation sends from the factory to the dealer a "New Car Preparation Service Guide" with each new automobile. The guide contains detailed instructions as to what has to be done to prepare the car for delivery. The dealer is told to "Use this form as a guide to inspect and prepare this new Plymouth for delivery." It specifies 66 separate items to be checked, tested, tightened or adjusted in the course of the servicing, but dismantling the vehicle or checking all of its internal parts is not prescribed. The guide also calls for delivery of the Owner Service Certificate with the car.

This Certificate, which at least by inference is authorized by Chrysler, was in the car when released to Claus Henningsen on May 9, 1955. It was not made part of the purchase contract, nor was it shown to him prior to the consummation of that agreement. The only reference to it therein is that the dealer "agrees to promptly perform and fulfill all terms and conditions of the owner service policy." The Certificate contains a warranty entitled "Automobile Manufacturers Association Uniform Warranty." The provisions thereof are the same as those set forth on the reverse side of the purchase order, except that an additional paragraph is added by which the dealer extends that warranty to the purchaser in the same manner as if the word "Dealer" appeared instead of the word "Manufacturer."

The new Plymouth was turned over to the Henningsens on May 9, 1955. No proof was adduced by the dealer to show precisely what was done in the way of mechanical or road testing beyond testimony that the manufacturer's instructions were probably followed. Mr. Henningsen drove it from the dealer's place of business in Bloomfield to their home in Keansburg. On the trip nothing unusual appeared in the way in which it operated. Thereafter, it was used for short trips on paved streets about the town. It had no servicing and no mishaps of any kind before the event of May 19. That day, Mrs. Henningsen drove to Asbury Park. On the way down and in returning the car performed in normal fashion until the accident occurred. She was proceeding north on Route 36 in Highlands, New Jersey, at 20–22 miles per hour. The highway was paved and smooth, and contained two lanes for north-bound travel. She was riding in the right-hand lane. Suddenly she heard a loud noise "from the bottom, by the hood." It "felt as if something cracked." The steering wheel spun in her hands; the car veered sharply to the right and crashed into a highway sign and a brick wall. No other vehicle was in any way involved. A bus operator driving in the left-hand lane testified that he observed plaintiffs' car approaching in normal fashion in the opposite direction; "all of a sudden (it) veered at 90 degrees . . . and right into this wall." As a result of the impact, the front of the car was so badly damaged that it was impossible to determine if any of the parts of the steering wheel mechanism or workmanship or assembly were defective or improper prior to the accident. The condition was such that the collision insurance carrier, after inspection, declared the vehicle a total loss. It had 468 miles on the speedometer at the time.

The insurance carrier's inspector and appraiser of damaged cars, with 11 years of experience, advanced the opinion, based on the history and his examination, that something definitely went "wrong from the steering wheel down to the front wheels" and that the untoward happening must have been due to mechanical defect or failure; "something down there had to drop off or break loose to cause the car" to act in the manner described.

As has been indicated, the trial court felt that the proof was not sufficient to make out a prima facie case as to the negligence of either the manufacturer or the dealer. The case was given to the jury, therefore, solely on the warranty theory, with results favorable to the plaintiffs against both defendants.

I.

The Claim of Implied Warranty
Against the Manufacturer

In the ordinary case of sale of goods by description an implied warranty of merchantability is an integral part of the transaction. . . . If the buyer, expressly or by implication, makes known to the seller the particular purpose for which the article is required and it appears that he has relied on the seller's skill or judgment, an implied warranty arises of reasonable fitness for that purpose. . . . The former type of warranty simply means that the thing sold is reasonably fit for the general purpose for which it is manufactured and sold. . . .

Of course such sales, whether oral or written, may be accompanied by an express warranty. Under the broad terms of the Uniform Sale of Goods Law any affirmation of fact relating to the goods is an express warranty if the natural tendency of the statement is to induce the buyer to make the purchase. . . . And over the years since the almost universal adoption of the act, a growing awareness of the tremendous development of modern business methods has prompted the courts to administer that provision with a liberal hand. . . . Solicitude toward the buyer plainly harmonizes with the intention of the Legislature. That fact is manifested further by the later section of the act which preserves and continues any permissible implied warranty, despite an express warranty, unless the two are inconsistent. . . .

The uniform act codified, extended and liberalized the common law of sales. The motivation in part was to ameliorate the harsh doctrine of *caveat emptor,* and in some measure to impose a reciprocal obligation on the seller to beware. The transcendent value of the legislation, particularly with respect to implied warranties, rests in the fact that obligations on the part of the seller were imposed by operation of law, and did not depend for their existence upon express agreement of the parties. And of tremendous significance in a rapidly expanding commercial society was the recognition of the right to recover damages on account of personal injuries arising from a breach of warranty. . . .

The particular importance of this advance resides in the fact that under such circumstances strict liability is imposed upon the maker or seller of the product. Recovery of damages does not depend upon proof of negligence or knowledge of the defect. . . .

As the Sales Act and its liberal interpretation by the courts threw this protective cloak about the buyer, the decisions in various jurisdictions revealed beyond doubt that many manufacturers took steps to avoid these ever increasing warranty obligations. Realizing that the act governed the relationship of buyer and seller, they undertook to withdraw from actual and direct contractual contact with the buyer. They ceased selling products to the consuming public through their own employees and making contracts of sale in their own names. Instead, a system of independent dealers was established; their products were sold to dealers who in turn dealt with the buying public, ostensibly solely in their own personal capacity as sellers. In the past in many instances, manufacturers were able to transfer to the dealers burdens imposed by the act and thus achieved a large measure of immunity for themselves. But, as will be noted in more detail hereafter, such marketing practices, coupled with the advent of large scale advertising by manufacturers to promote the purchase of these goods from dealers by members of the public, provided a basis upon which the existence of express or implied warranties was predicated, even though the manufacturer was not a party to the contract of sale.

The general observations that have been made are important largely for purposes of perspective. They are helpful in achieving a point from which to evaluate the situation now presented for solution. Primarily, they reveal a trend and a design in legislative and judicial thinking toward providing protection for the buyer. It must be noted, however, that the sections of the Sales Act, to which reference has been made, do not impose warranties in terms of unalterable absolutes. R.S. 46:30-3, N.J.S.A., provides in general terms that an applicable warranty may be negatived or varied by express agreement. As to disclaimers or limitations of the obligations that normally attend a sale, it seems sufficient at this juncture to say they are not favored, and that they are strictly construed against the seller. . . .

With these considerations in mind, we come to a study of the express warranty on the reverse side of the purchase order signed by Claus Henningsen. At the outset we take notice that it was made only by the manufacturer and that by its terms it runs directly to Claus Henningsen. . . .

The terms of the warranty are a sad commentary upon the automobile manufacturers' marketing practices. Warranties developed in the law in the interest of and to protect the ordinary consumer who cannot be expected to have the knowledge or capacity or even the opportunity to make adequate inspection of mechanical instrumentalities, like automobiles, and to decide for himself whether they are reasonably fit for the designated purpose. . . . But the ingenuity of the Automobile Manufacturers Association, by means of its standardized form, has metamorphosed the warranty into a device to limit the maker's liability. . . .

The manufacturer agrees to replace defective parts for 90 days after the sale or until the car has been driven 4,000 miles, whichever is first to occur, if the part is sent to the factory, transportation charges prepaid, and if examination discloses to its satisfaction that the part is defective. It is difficult to imagine a greater burden on the consumer, or a less satisfactory remedy. Aside from imposing on the buyer the trouble of removing and shipping the part, the maker has sought to retain the uncontrolled discretion to decide the issue of defectiveness. Some courts have removed much of the force of that reservation by declaring that the purchaser is not bound by the manufacturer's decision. Mills v. Maxwell Motor Sales Corporation, 105 Neb. 465, 181 N.W. 152. . . . In the Mills case, the court said:

> "It would nevertheless be repugnant to every conception of justice to hold that, if the parts thus returned for examination were, in point of fact, so defective as to constitute a breach of warranty, the appellee's right of action could be defeated by the appellant's arbitrary refusal to recognize that fact. Such an interpretation would substitute the appellant for the courts in passing upon the question of fact, and would be unreasonable."

Putting aside for the time being the problem of the efficacy of the disclaimer provisions contained in the express warranty, a question of first importance to be decided is whether an implied warranty of merchantability by Chrysler Corporation accompanied the sale of the automobile to Claus Henningsen.

Preliminarily, it may be said that the express warranty against defective parts and workmanship is not inconsistent with an implied warranty of merchantability. Such warranty cannot be excluded for that reason. . . .

Chrysler points out that an implied warranty of merchantability is an incident of a contract of sale. It concedes, of course, the making of the original sale to Bloomfield Motors, Inc., but maintains that this transaction marked the terminal point of its contractual connection with the car. Then Chrysler urges that since it was not a party to the sale by the dealer to Henningsen, there is no privity of contract between it and the plaintiffs, and the absence of this privity eliminates any such implied warranty.

There is no doubt that under early common-law concepts of contractual liability only those persons who were parties to the bargain could sue for a breach of it. In more recent times a noticeable disposition has appeared in a number of jurisdictions to break through the narrow barrier of privity when dealing with sales of goods in order to give realistic recognition to a universally accepted fact. The fact is that the dealer and the ordinary buyer do not, and are not expected to, buy goods, whether they be food-stuffs or automobiles, exclusively for their own consumption or use. Makers and manufacturers know this and advertise and market their products on that assumption; witness, the "family" car, the baby foods, etc. The limitations of privity in contracts for the sale of goods developed their place in the law when marketing conditions were simple, when maker and buyer frequently met face to face on an equal bargaining plane and when many of the products were relatively uncomplicated and conducive to inspection by a buyer competent to evaluate their quality. . . . With the advent of mass marketing, the manufacturer became remote from the purchaser, sales were accomplished through intermediaries, and the demand for the product was created by advertising media. In such an economy it became obvious that the consumer was the person being cultivated. Manifestly, the connotation of "consumer" was broader than that of "buyer." He signified such a person who, in the reasonable contemplation of the parties to the sale, might be expected to use the product. Thus, where the commodities sold are such that if defectively manufactured they will be dangerous to life or limb, then society's interests can only be protected by eliminating the requirement of privity between the maker and his dealers and the reasonably expected ultimate consumer. In that way the burden of losses consequent upon use of defective articles is borne by those who are in a position to either control the danger or make an equitable distribution of the losses when they do occur. . . .

Although only a minority of jurisdictions have thus far departed from the requirement of privity, the movement in that direction is most certainly gathering momentum. Liability to the ultimate consumer in the absence of direct contractual connection has been predicated upon a variety of theories. Some courts hold that the warranty runs with the article like a covenant running with land; others recognize a third-party beneficiary thesis; still others rest their decision on the ground that public policy requires recognition of a warranty made directly to the consumer. . . .

Under modern conditions the ordinary layman, on responding to the importuning of colorful advertising, has neither the opportunity nor the capacity to inspect or to determine the fitness of an automobile for use; he must rely on the manufacturer who has control of its construction, and to some degree on the dealer who, to the limited extent called for by the manufacturer's instructions, inspects and services it before delivery. In such a marketing milieu his remedies and those of persons who properly claim through him should not depend "upon the intricacies of the law of sales. The obligation of the manufacturer should not be based alone on privity of contract. It should rest, as was once said upon 'the demands of social justice.'" Mazette v. Armour & Co., 75 Wash. 622, 135 P. 633, 635; 48 L.R.A., N.S., 213 (Sup. Ct. 1913). . . .

Accordingly, we hold that under modern marketing conditions, when a manufacturer puts a new automobile in the stream of trade and promotes its purchase by the public, an implied warranty that it is reasonably suitable for use as such accompanies it into the hands of the ultimate purchaser. . . .

II.
The Effect of the Disclaimer and Limitation of Liability Clauses on the Implied Warranty of Merchantability

Judicial notice may be taken of the fact that automobile manufacturers, including Chrysler Corporation, undertake large scale advertising programs over television, radio, in newspapers, magazines and all media of communication in order to persuade the public to buy their products. As has been observed above, a number of jurisdictions, conscious of modern marketing practices, have declared that when a manufacturer engages in advertising in order to bring his goods and their quality to the attention of the public and thus to create consumer demand, the representations made constitute an express warranty running directly to a buyer who purchases in reliance thereon. The fact that the sale is consummated with an independent dealer does not obviate that warranty. . . .

These developments in the law inevitably suggest the inference that the form of express warranty made part of the Henningsen purchase contract was devised for general use in the automobile industry as a possible means of avoiding the consequences of the growing judicial acceptance of the thesis that the described express or implied warranties run directly to the consumer.

In the light of these matters, what effect should be given to the express warranty in question which seeks to limit the manufacturer's liability to replacement of defective parts, and which disclaims all other warranties, express or implied? In assessing its significance we must keep in mind the general principle that, in the absence of fraud, one who does not choose to read a contract before signing it, cannot later relieve himself of its burdens. . . . And in applying that principle, the basic tenet of freedom of competent parties to contract is a factor of importance. But in the framework of modern commercial life and business practices, such rules cannot be applied on a strict, doctrinal basis. The conflicting interests of the buyer and seller must be evaluated realistically and justly, giving due weight to the social policy evinced by the Uniform Sales Act, the progressive decisions of the courts engaged in administering it, the mass production methods of manufacture and distribution to the public, and the bargaining position occupied by the ordinary consumer in such an economy. This history of the law shows that legal doctrines, as first expounded, often prove to be inadequate under the impact of later experience. In such case, the need for justice has stimulated the necessary qualifications or adjustments. . . .

In these times, an automobile is almost as much a servant of convenience for the ordinary person as a household utensil. For a multitude of other persons it is a necessity. Crowded highways and filled parking lots are a commonplace of our existence. There is no need to look any farther than the daily newspaper to be convinced that when an automobile is defective, it has great potentiality for harm.

It is apparent that the public has an interest not only in the safe manufacture of automobiles, but also, as shown by the Sales Act, in protecting the rights and remedies of purchasers, so far as it can be accomplished consistently with our system of free enterprise. In a society such as ours, where the automobile is a common and necessary adjunct of daily life, and where its use is so fraught with danger to the driver, passengers and the public, the manufacturer is under a special obligation in connection with the construction, promotion and sale of his cars. Consequently, the courts must examine purchase agreements closely to see if consumer and public interests are treated fairly.

What influence should these circumstances have on the restrictive effect of Chrysler's express warranty in the framework of the purchase contract? As we have said, warranties originated in the law to safeguard the buyer and not to limit the liability of the seller or manufacturer. It seems obvious in this instance that the motive was to avoid the warranty obligations which are normally incidental to such sales. The language gave little and withdrew much. In return for the delusive remedy of replacement of defective parts at the factory, the buyer is said to have accepted the exclusion of the maker's liability for personal injuries arising from the breach of the warranty, and to have agreed to the elimination of any other express or implied warranty. An instinctively felt sense of justice cries out against such a sharp bargain. But does the doctrine that a person is bound by his signed agreement, in the absence of fraud, stand in the way of any relief?

The traditional contract is the result of free bargaining of parties who are brought together by the play of the market, and who meet each other on a footing of approximate economic equality. In such a society there is no danger that freedom of contract will be a threat to the social order as a whole. But in present-day commercial life the standardized mass contract has appeared. It is used primarily by enterprises with strong bargaining power and position.

> "The weaker party, in need of the goods or services, is frequently not in a position to shop around for better terms, either because the author of the standard contract has a monopoly (natural or artificial) or because all competitors use the same clauses. His contractual intention is but a subjection more or less voluntary to terms dictated by the stronger party, terms whose consequences are often understood in a vague way, if at all." Kessler, "Contracts of Adhesion—Some Thoughts about Freedom of Contract," 43 Colum. L. Rev. 629, 632 (1943). . . .

The warranty before us is a standardized form designed for mass use. It is imposed upon the automobile consumer. He takes it or leaves it, and he must take it to buy an automobile. No bargaining is engaged in with respect to it. In fact, the dealer through whom it comes to the buyer is without authority to alter it; his function is ministerial—simply to deliver it. The form warranty is not only standard with Chrysler but, as mentioned above, it is the uniform warranty of the Automobile Manufacturers Association. Members of the Association are: General Motors, Inc., Ford, Chrysler, Studebaker-Packard, American Motors (Rambler), Willys Motors, Checker Motors Corp., and International Harvester Company. Automobile Facts and Figures (1958 Ed., Automobile Manufacturers Association) 69. Of these companies the "Big Three" (General Motors, Ford, and Chrysler) represented 93.5% of the passenger-car production for 1958 and the independents 6.5%. Standard & Poor (Industrial Surveys, Autos, Basic Analysis, June 25, 1959) 4109. And for the same year the "Big Three" had 86.72% of the total passenger vehicle registrations. Automotive News, 1959 Almanac (Slocum Publishing Co., Inc.) p. 25.

The gross inequality of bargaining position occupied by the consumer in the automobile industry is thus apparent. There is no competition among the car makers in the area of the express warranty. Where can the buyer go to negotiate for better protection? Such control and limitation of his remedies are inimical to the public welfare and, at the very least, call for great care by the courts to avoid injustice through application of strict common-law principles of freedom of contract. Because there is no competition among the motor vehicle manufacturers with respect to the scope of protection guaranteed to the buyer, there is no incentive on their part to stimulate good will in that field of public relations. Thus, there is lacking a factor existing in more competitive fields, one which tends to guarantee the safe construction of the article sold. Since all competitors operate in the same way, the urge to be careful is not so pressing. . . .

The rigid scrutiny which the courts give to attempted limitations of warranties and of the liability that would normally flow from a transaction is not limited to the field of sales of goods. Clauses on baggage checks restricting the liability of common carriers for loss or damage in transit are not enforceable unless the limitation is fairly and honestly negotiated and understandingly entered into. If not called specifically to the patron's attention, it is not binding. It is not enough merely to show the form of a contract; it must appear also that the agreement was understandingly made. . . . [Cases cited.]

It is true that the rule governing the limitation of liability cases last referred to is generally applied in situations said to involve services of a public or semi-public nature. Typical, of course, are the public carrier or storage or parking lot cases. . . .

Basically, the reason a contracting party offering services of a public or quasi-public nature has been held to the requirement of fair dealing, and, when it attempts to limit its liability, of securing the understanding consent of the patron or consumer, is because members of the public generally have no other means of fulfilling the specific need represented by the contract. Having in mind the situation in the automobile industry as detailed above, and particularly the fact that the limited warranty extended by the manufacturers is a uniform one, there would appear to be no just reason why the principles of all of the cases set forth should not chart the course to be taken here.

It is undisputed that the president of the dealer with whom Henningsen dealt did not specifically call attention to the warranty on the back of the purchase order. The form and the arrangement of its face, as described above, certainly would cause the minds of reasonable men to differ as to whether notice of a yielding of basic rights stemming from the relationship with the manufacturer was adequately given. The words "warranty" or "limited warranty" did not even appear in the fine print above the place for signature, and a jury might well find that the type of print itself was such as to promote lack of attention rather than sharp scrutiny. The inference from the facts is that Chrysler placed the method of communicating its warranty to the purchaser in the hands of the dealer. If either one or both of them wished to make certain that Henningsen became aware of that agreement and its purported implications, neither the form of the document nor the method of expressing the precise nature of the obligation intended to be assumed would have presented any difficulty.

But there is more than this. Assuming that a jury might find that the fine print referred to reasonably served the objective of directing a buyer's attention to the warranty on the reverse side, and, therefore, that he should be charged with awareness of its language, can it be said that an ordinary layman would realize what he was relinquishing in return for what he was being granted? Under the law, breach of warranty against defective parts or workmanship which caused personal injuries would entitle a buyer to damages even if due care were used in the manufacturing process. Because of the great potential for harm if the vehicle was defective, that right is the most important and fundamental one arising from the relationship. Difficulties so frequently encountered in establishing negligence in manufacture in the ordinary case makes this manifest. . . . Any ordinary layman of reasonable intelligence, looking at the phraseology, might well conclude that Chrysler was agreeing to replace defective parts and perhaps replace anything that went wrong because of defective workmanship during the first 90 days or 4,000 miles of operation, but that he would not be entitled to a new car. It is not unreasonable to believe that the entire scheme being conveyed was a proposed remedy for physical deficiencies in the car. In the context of this warranty, only the abandonment of all sense of justice would permit us to hold that, as a matter of law, the phrase "its obligation under this warranty being limited to making good at its factory any part or parts thereof" signifies to an ordinary reasonable person that he is relinquishing any personal injury claim that might flow from the use of a defective automobile. Such claims are nowhere mentioned. The draftsmanship is reflective of the care and skill of the Automobile Manufacturers Association in undertaking to avoid warranty obligations without drawing too much attention to its effort in that regard. No one can doubt that if the will to do so were present, the ability to inform the buying public of the intention to disclaim liability for injury claims arising from breach of warranty would present no problem. . . .

The task of the judiciary is to administer the spirit as well as the letter of the law. On issues such as the present one, part of that burden is to protect the ordinary man against the loss of important rights through what, in effect, is the unilateral act of the manufacturer. The status of the automobile industry is unique. Manufacturers are few in number and strong in bargaining position. In the matter of warranties on the sale of their products, the Automotive Manufacturers Association has enabled them to present a united front. From the standpoint of the purchaser, there can be no arm's length negotiating on the subject. Because his capacity for bargaining is so grossly unequal, the inexorable conclusion which follows is that he is not permitted to bargain at all. He must take or leave the automobile on the warranty terms dictated by the maker. He cannot turn to a competitor for better security.

Public policy is a term not easily defined. Its significance varies as the habits and needs of a people may vary. It is not static and the field of application is an ever increasing one. A contract, or a particular provision therein, valid in one era may be wholly opposed to the public policy of another. . . . Courts keep in mind the principle that the best interests of society demand that persons should not be unnecessarily restricted in their freedom to contract. But they do not hesitate to declare void as against public policy contractual provisions which clearly tend to the injury of the public in some way. . . .

Public policy at a given time finds expression in the Constitution, the statutory law and in judicial decisions. In the area of sale of goods, the legislative will has imposed an implied warranty of merchantability as a general incident of sale of an automobile by description. The warranty does not depend upon the affirmative intention of the parties. It is a child of the law; it annexes itself to the contract because of the very nature of the transaction. . . . The judicial process has recognized a right to recover damages for personal injuries arising from a breach of that warranty. The disclaimer of the implied warranty and exclusion of all obligations except those specifically assumed by the express warranty signify a studied effort to frustrate that protection. True, the Sales Act authorizes agreements between buyer and seller qualifying the warranty obligations. But quite obviously the Legislature contemplated lawful stipulations (which are determined by the circumstances of a particular case) arrived at freely by parties of relatively equal bargaining strength. The lawmakers did not authorize the automobile manufacturer to use its grossly disproportionate bargaining power to relieve itself from liability and to impose on the ordinary buyer, who in effect has no real freedom of choice, the grave danger or injury to himself and others that attends the sale of such a dangerous instrumentality as a defectively made automobile. In the framework of this case, illuminated as it is by the facts and the many decisions noted, we are of the opinion that Chrysler's attempted disclaimer of an implied warranty of merchantability and of the obligations arising therefrom is so inimical to the public good as to compel an adjudication of its invalidity. . . .

III.
The Dealer's Implied Warranty

The principles that have been expounded as to the obligation of the manufacturer apply with equal force to separate express warranty of the dealer. This is so, irrespective of the absence of the relationship of principal and agent between these defendants, because the manufacturer and the Association establish the warranty policy for the industry. The bargaining position of the dealer is inextricably bound by practice to that of the maker and the purchaser must take or leave the automobile, accompanied and encumbered as it is by the uniform warranty.

Moreover, it must be remembered that the actual contract was between Bloomfield Motors, Inc., and Claus Henningsen, and that the description of the car sold was included in the purchase order. Therefore, R.S. 46:30-21 (2), N.J.S.A., annexed an implied warranty of merchantability to the agreement. . . . It remains operative unless the disclaimer and liability limitation clauses were competent to exclude it and the ordinary remedy for its breach. It has been said that this doctrine is harsh on retailers who generally have only a limited opportunity for inspection of the car. But as Chief Judge Cardozo said in Ryan v. Progressive Grocery Stores, 175 N.E. 105:

> "The burden may be heavy. It is one of the hazards of the business. . . . In such circumstances, the law casts the burden on the seller, who may vouch in the manufacturer, if the latter was to blame. The loss in its final incidence will be borne where it is placed by the initial wrong." 175 N.E. at pages 106 and 107.

Re-examination of the purchase contract discloses an ambiguous situation with respect to the warranty position of the dealer. Section 7, on the reverse side thereof, says no warranties, express or implied, are made by the dealer or manufacturer except the express warranty of the manufacturer discussed above. However, the last paragraph of the section says that: "The dealer also agrees to promptly perform and fulfill all terms and conditions of the owner service policy." That policy, as noted above, sets forth the same manufacturer's warranty and then adds a stipulation substituting "dealer" in the context wherever "manufacturer" appears. Presumably the intention was to incorporate the policy into the sales contract by reference. Accepting that to be the dealer's intention, the binding character of the limitation on its liability to the buyer under the warranty is even less apparent than in the case of Chrysler. The uncontradicted proof shows that the policy was not shown or given to Henningsen prior to or at the time of execution of the sales agreement; it was delivered with the car. No one suggests that the clause limiting the dealer's liability to replacement of defective parts and excluding implied warranties as well as responsibility for personal injury claims was specifically brought to Henningsen's attention, or that any attempt was made to make him understand that he was yielding his right, and that of any third person claiming in his right, to recover for such injuries.

For the reasons set forth in Part I hereof, we conclude that the disclaimer of an implied warranty of merchantability by the dealer, as well as the attempted elimination of all obligations other than replacement of defective parts, are violative of public policy and void.

IV.
Proof of Breach of the Implied Warranty of Merchantability

Both defendants argue that the proof adduced by plaintiffs as to the happening of the accident was not sufficient to demonstrate a breach of warranty. Consequently, they claim that their motion for judgment should have been granted by the trial court. We cannot agree. In our view, the total effect of the circumstances shown from purchase to accident is ade-

quate to raise an inference that the car was defective and that such condition was causally related to the mishap. . . .

V.
The Defense of Lack of Privity
Against Mrs. Henningsen

Both defendants contend that since there was no privity of contract
between them and Mrs. Henningsen, she cannot recover for breach of any
warranty made by either of them. On the facts, as they were developed, we
agree that she was not a party to the purchase agreement. . . . Her right
to maintain the action, therefore, depends upon whether she occupies such
legal status thereunder as to permit her to take advantage of a breach of
defendants' implied warranties.

For the most part the cases that have been considered dealt with the
right of the buyer or consumer to maintain an action against the manufacturer where the contract of sale was with a dealer and the buyer had
no contractual relationship with the manufacturer. In the present matter,
the basic contractual relationship is between Claus Henningsen, Chrysler,
and Bloomfield Motors, Inc. The precise issue presented is whether Mrs.
Henningsen, who is not a party to their respective warranties, may claim
under them. In our judgment, the principles of those cases and the supporting texts are just as proximately applicable to her situation. We are
convinced that the cause of justice in this area of the law can be served
only by recognizing that she is such a person who, in the reasonable contemplation of the parties to the contract, might be expected to become a user
of the automobile. Accordingly, her lack of privity does not stand in the
way of prosecution of the injury suit against the defendant Chrysler.

The context in which the problem of privity with respect to the dealer
must be considered, is much the same. Defendant Bloomfield Motors is
chargeable with an implied warranty of merchantability to Claus Henningsen. There is no need to engage in a separate or extended discussion of the
question. The legal principles which control are the same in quality. The
manufacturer establishes the network of trade and the dealer is a unit
utilized in that network to accomplish sales. He is the beneficiary of the
same express and implied warranties from the manufacturer as he extends
to the buyer of the automobile. If he is sued alone, he may implead the
manufacturer. . . . His understanding of the expected use of the car by
persons other than the buyer is the same as that of the manufacturer. And
so his claim to the doctrine of privity should rise no higher than that of
the manufacturer. . . .

It is important to express the right of Mrs. Henningsen to maintain her
action in terms of a general principle. To what extent may lack of privity
be disregarded in suits on such warranties? . . . It is our opinion that an
implied warranty of merchantability chargeable to either an automobile
manufacturer or a dealer extends to the purchaser of the car, members of
his family, and to other persons occupying or using it with his consent. It
would be wholly opposed to reality to say that use by such persons is not
within the anticipation of parties to such a warranty of reasonable suita-

bility of an automobile for ordinary highway operation. Those persons must be considered within the distributive chain.

Section 2-318 of the Uniform Commercial Code proposes that the warranty be extended to "any natural person who is in the family or household of his buyer or who is a guest in his home if it is reasonable to expect that such person may use, consume or be affected by the goods and who is injured in person by breach of the warranty." And the section provides also that "A seller may not exclude or limit the operation" of the extension. A footnote thereto says that beyond this provision "the section is neutral and is not intended to enlarge or restrict the developing case law on whether the seller's warranties, given to his buyer, who resells, extend to other persons in the distributive chain." Uniform Commercial Code, *supra*, at p. 100.

It is not necessary in this case to establish the outside limits of the warranty protection. For present purposes, with respect to automobiles, it suffices to promulgate the principle set forth above.

Defendants rely upon certain cases for the proposition that lack of privity of contract bars Mrs. Henningsen's recovery. The pertinent ones are Tomlinson v. Armour & Co., *supra*. . . . [Other cases cited.] Tomlinson v. Armour & Co. provides the foundation for the others. It was decided 52 years ago and the principle on which defendants seek support for their case is contained in a short statement which, if applied in the light of the modern marketing conditions, is not inconsistent with the basic substance of the rule we have now espoused. In discussing the legal consequences of a sale of canned ham, Chancellor Pitney said:

> "Whether a warranty be express or implied, it is a matter of contract, rendering the maker liable in case of breach, notwithstanding he used all care to prevent a breach, but rendering him liable in ordinary circumstances only to the party with whom he contracted, or to others for whose benefit the contract was made." 75 N.J.L. at pages 754–755, 70 A. at page 316.

In 1908 the need of the community for the making of distinctions growing out of the nature of the contract was not as pressing as it is in this commercial era. A common rule was applied, as indicated by the citation of Marvin Safe Co. v. Ward, 46 N.J.L. 19 (Sup.Ct. 1884), and Styles v. F. R. Long Company, 67 N.J.L. 413, 51 A. 710 (Sup.Ct. 1902), which involved agreements wholly unrelated to the sale of products for consumer use. In this day, given the present situation, it is extremely unlikely that such an enlightened jurist as Chancellor Pitney would not find his expression that "others for whose benefit the contract was made" could sue for its breach compatible in spirit with the doctrine we deem to be necessary in the interest of justice. In any event, to the extent that Tomlinson v. Armour & Co. and its cited progeny conflict with our ruling, they can no longer be considered the law of this State. . . .

Under all of the circumstances outlined above, the judgments in favor of the plaintiffs and against the defendants are affirmed.

For affirmance: CHIEF JUSTICE WEINTRAUB and JUSTICES BURLING, JACOBS, FRANCIS, PROCTOR and SCHETTINO—6.

For reversal: None   ◄

COMMENTS AND QUESTIONS

1. Summarize the various defenses raised by the dealer and the reasons given by the court for rejecting them.
2. Outline the manufacturer's defenses. How did the court deal with them?
3. Note the court's long discussion of market conditions and the relative bargaining positions of the parties.
4. There seems to be little doubt that this decision is a landmark and that many other courts will be guided by its persuasive reasoning.

SECTION 4

PERFORMANCE OF SALES CONTRACTS

In General

When two parties enter into a sales contract, each assumes a duty to perform certain acts for the other. The seller has a duty to deliver goods of the quality and quantity called for by the contract. The buyer has a duty to accept the goods and to pay for them if they conform to the specifications. As a general rule, neither side is obligated to perform his part of the bargain until the other has performed his part, or until he has offered to perform and the offer has been refused. Of course, the parties may provide in their contract that one party must perform first *regardless* of the other party's willingness to perform. Such a provision will be enforced by the courts if it is clearly stated.

EXAMPLE

s agrees to sell his car to b for $300. As a general rule, s cannot demand payment of the $300 until he delivers the car to b, or until he offers to deliver it to b and b refuses to accept it. On the other hand, b cannot demand delivery of the car until he has paid, or has offered to pay, s the money. But if the contract had provided that b was to pay s on April 1 and that s was not obligated to deliver until April 15, b would be bound to pay s before delivery.

If one party fails to carry out his obligations, the other can resort to certain rights and remedies. In this section, we shall review these rights and remedies, first from the seller's standpoint and then from the buyer's.

Seller's Rights and Remedies

When Buyer Refuses Delivery

If the buyer refuses to accept the goods and pay for them when the seller tries to make delivery, the seller is entitled to sue for damages. The amount he can recover is usually limited to the difference between the contract price and the current market price at the time and place of delivery. If there is no ready market for the goods, however, or if they have been specially manufactured for the buyer, the seller may sue for the full contract price. And if title to the goods has passed before delivery, the seller is normally entitled to recover the full contract price of the merchandise.

EXAMPLES

1. B agrees to buy ten tons of coal from s at $10.00 a ton. s agrees to deliver the coal to B's place of business. When s tries to deliver the coal, B refuses to accept it or to pay for it. s may sue B for damages. If the current market price at the time of delivery has dropped to $8.00 a ton, then s's damage will be $2.00 a ton, or $20.00. If, however, the price has risen to $12.00 a ton, s will probably be unable to recover any damages from B, since the coal can presumably be sold on the market at the higher figure.

2. Now assume that s had agreed to ship the coal to B by railroad and that title had passed to B when the coal was delivered to the carrier. In this case, s could sue B for the entire contract price—i.e., $100.00.

3. s agrees to manufacture a special piece of equipment for B and to deliver it to his factory. B refuses to accept it when it is delivered. If there is no ready market elsewhere for the equipment, B will be obligated to pay the full purchase price, since s has no way of disposing of it and covering his loss. This would be true regardless of whether title to the equipment had actually passed to B.

In the case that follows, the buyer informed the seller that it would be unable to take delivery, and the seller made claim for damages.

GARNER v. CHARLES A. KRAUSE MILLING CO.

Supreme Court of Wisconsin, 1927
193 Wis. 80, 213 N.W. 637

► C. R. Garner & Co. began an action against Charles A. Krause Milling Company to recover damages for breach of contract. From a judgment in favor of Garner & Co., the Krause Milling Company appealed.

The Krause Milling Company made three separate contracts to purchase oil meal from Garner & Co. The purchase price under these three contracts ranged from $49 to $50.50 per ton, f.o.b. cars Milwaukee, Wis. Prior to the shipment of any of the oil meal here in question, the Krause Milling Company's plant was destroyed by fire. The Krause Milling Company immediately notified Garner & Co. of the fire, and asserted that they were entirely excused from performing their contract because of such fire. Garner & Co. replied by wire:

"Since you refuse to go further under your contract we treat the same as breached and are taking the products in at the present market price."

Thereafter Garner & Co. drew upon and wrote the Krause Milling Company that this draft represented "the difference between contract price as sold you, and the market at the time of your breach of contract, per our telegram to you."

Garner & Co. took the oil meal in at what they claimed to be the market price on the date of the breach. They did not, acting as agents of the Krause Milling Company, offer the produce for sale on the open market to any other parties for the account of the Krause Milling Company. The trial court entered judgment for the full amount claimed to be the difference between the contract price and the market price on the last date on which the oil meal could have been delivered under the terms of each of the three contracts.

STEVENS, J. It is unnecessary to consider the question of what was in fact the contract entered into by these parties because it clearly appears that Garner & Co. are entitled to no recovery under the contract which they contend was made by the communications that passed between these parties.

If the contract gave the Krause Milling Company no right to cancel when its plant was destroyed by fire, Garner & Co. had the option (1) to hold the oil meal for the Krause Milling Company and sue that company for the purchase price and thus secure the profits of the bargain; or (2) to sell the oil meal as agent for the Krause Milling Company and recover the difference between the contract price and a fair market value upon resale as a liquidated amount of damages; or (3) to keep the goods and recover the difference between the contract price and the fair market value. Schuenemann v. John G. Wollaeger Co., 170 Wis. 616, 618; 176 N.W. 59.

Garner & Co., kept the meal themselves and attempted to charge the Krause Milling Company what they claimed to be the difference between the contract price and the market price at the date of the breach. They made no effort to sell the meal on the open market. The meal was not offered for sale in Milwaukee, the place of delivery. The market price claimed by Garner & Co. was based upon the price prevailing in the state of Texas. Where a seller elects to keep the article sold and attempts to collect the difference between the contract price and the market price, he is under obligation to give the defaulting buyer the advantage of the full and fair market price at the agreed delivery point in Wisconsin. Lincoln v. Charles Alshuler Mfg. Co., 142 Wis. 475, 125 N.W. 908. . . . The undisputed proof is that the market price of oil meal in Milwaukee at the time of breach was $52 a ton, which is from $1.50 to $2. a ton in excess of the prices fixed in the three contracts. It follows that Garner & Co. sustained no damage from the breach of the contract, because at the time of the breach they could have sold the meal on the open market at the place of delivery for a sum in excess of the contract price. . . .

Judgment reversed, and cause remanded, with directions to dismiss the complaint. ◄

1. How did the trial court compute the damages in this case? For what reasons did the appellate court reverse the judgment and order the complaint dismissed?

2. This is a good example of a clear breach of contract without any resulting damages. Proving damages is a very important part of any case.

If the buyer refuses to take delivery, the seller may choose just to rescind the contract rather than to sue for damages. In that case the contract is canceled, each side must return any consideration he has received, and neither side has any further obligation to the other. In the following case, the buyer argued that the seller had chosen to rescind the contract and, therefore, had given up his right to sue for damages. The case is a good illustration of the dangers involved in using legal terminology without appreciating its full meaning.

GEORGE H. FINLAY & CO. v. SWIRSKY et al.

Supreme Court of Errors of Connecticut, 1923
98 Conn. 666, 120 A. 561

► Action by George H. Finlay & Co. against Isaac Swirsky and others, for damages for breach of two contracts. Facts found and judgment for plaintiffs, and defendants appeal. No error.

On April 14, 1920, the plaintiffs and the defendants entered into two contracts for the sale by the plaintiffs to the defendants of 800 long tons of sugar at 20 cents a pound, to be shipped from Java to New York during the next July, August, or September, at the sellers' option. By one of the terms of the contracts it was stipulated that the buyers, to secure the payment of the agreed price of the sugar, should immediately open a credit in favor of the plaintiffs with an approved bank or banker for an amount sufficient to cover the invoice price of the shipments with disbursements and advances. The invoice price of both shipments was $358,400. On April 20, 1920, the defendants opened a credit of $150,000 only in a bank in New Haven, which was limited to expire on September 10, 1920. They did not at any time open credit in any other bank, although they were frequently requested, and they as often assured the plaintiffs that they were about to do so. The plaintiffs purchased in Java sufficient sugar to fill these contracts, and on August 11th and August 17th they notified the defendants that their sugar had been shipped. Shipments from Java to New York usually took from 60 to 90 days in passage. To these letters the defendants made no reply. On September 9, 1920, the plaintiffs owned and were able to deliver to the defendants 255 tons of Java sugar for $114,240, the price fixed in their contracts; but the defendants refused to accept and pay for this sugar, claiming that there was some irregularity in the papers attached to the draft presented at the New Haven bank, but they did not indicate then that they did not intend to perform their contracts. On October 9, 1920, the plaintiffs caused notice to be served on the defendants declaring that they had failed to open bank credits in accordance with the terms of the contracts, and that, unless they should do so immediately, the sugar they had bought would be disposed of elsewhere for their account, and they would be held responsible for any damages or losses. To this notice the defendants gave no attention. On October 11, 1920, the plaintiffs caused another notice to be served on the defendants, reciting the substance of the contracts and stating that they had failed to open the stipulated credits, and concluding in these words:

"Please take notice that, as you have repudiated said agreements, have manifested your inability to perform your obligations under said agreements, and have committed a material breach thereof, said G. H. Finlay & Co., hereby give you notice that they rescind both of said agreements." [14]

At the same time process in this suit was served on the defendants.

On October 7 and 29 and November 5, 1920, the plaintiffs sold all the sugar mentioned in these contracts at a fair and reasonable price under then existing market conditions, acting in good faith and judgment. Their losses in these transactions were $217,100.80, which, with interest to date of judgment, amounts to $237,735.30. The plaintiffs at all times acted in good faith, and were able, ready, and willing to perform their obligations under the contracts.

BURPEE, J. . . . In this appeal the defendants contend in the first place that the plaintiffs, by using the word "rescind" in their notice served on the defendants on October 11, 1920, then "finally put an end to both contracts as completely as if they had never existed." They argue that the unqualified meaning of the word "rescind" in this connection is to wipe out or annihilate totally, so that the contracts could not thereafter be the basis of any action whatever. We do not agree that this is the proper meaning of that word or the effect of its use in the circumstances which surrounded the parties in this case. The word "rescind" does not always and necessarily mean strictly the same as revoke, annul, or blot out. It is often employed to convey the idea of cutting off a contract and leaving the parties in the exact conditions then existing. This court has used the word with that meaning. In Trowbridge v. Jefferson Auto Co., 92 Conn. 569, 573; 103 A. 843, 844, which, like this was a suit to recover damages for breach of contract, it was said that the repudiation of the agreement by the defendant "authorized the plaintiff to rescind the contract, upon his part and bring an action for his damages." In Wetkopshy v. New Haven Gaslight Co., 90 Conn. 286, 290, 291; 96 A. 950, 952, an action similar to this, we said that it was for the jury to determine whether one party had repudiated a contract under such circumstances as to justify the other party "in rescinding it," and that, under the terms of our Sales Act . . . under the circumstances stated, "the vendor may elect to accept such repudiation as anticipatory breach by rescinding the agreement." In the present case the court was construing the language of the same statute, under which the plaintiffs are suing and which the defendants are citing

---

[14] This letter certainly *appears* to have been drafted by an attorney. Imagine his embarrassment if the case had been lost because of his use of the term "rescind" when he meant to convey another meaning.

in support of their argument. Moreover, it is evident from the facts of this case that neither the plaintiffs nor the defendants reasonably could, or in fact did, use and understand this word in the sense which the appellants would now give to it. The notices served on the defendants on October 9th and 11th, followed immediately by the summons in this suit, and considered under the light of the antecedent facts, indicate plainly the fair interpretation of the words and conduct of the parties. From all the evidence before it, the trier must determine what the intention was. Intention is an inference of fact, and the conclusion is not reviewable unless it was one which the trier could not reasonably make. . . . Here the trial court has reached the conclusion that the plaintiffs did not intend, and that the defendants did not understand, that the contracts were extinguished by the use of the word "rescind" in the notice of October 11, 1920, and that thereupon and consequently all claims for damages for their breach were abandoned. This conclusion is not questioned in this appeal. The purport and unmistakable effect of the language of the notices of October 9th and 11th was to make known to the defendants the plaintiffs' election to accept their repudiation of the contracts as putting them to an end, and to enforce their claims for damages for the breach thus made. This it was their right to do. . . . An executory contract may be terminated at some stage in its performance, or may be abandoned as a live and enforceable obligation, while the party declaring its abandonment still retains the right "to look to the contract to determine the compensation he may be entitled to under its terms for the breach which gave him the right of abandonment." Taft, J., in Hayes v. City of Nashville, 80 F. 641, 26 C.C.A. 59.

It seems to be the reasonable deduction from the decisions of the courts which have considered most logically and thoroughly the subject of the rescission of the contracts that the party not in default may, if he choose, accept the renunciation of the other party and annul the contract so that it shall be as if it had never been made, or, if he prefer, may terminate and abandon the further performance of the contract, without retroactive effect, and leaving each party under the liabilities or with the rights and remedies which have arisen from the conditions existing at the time when the contract was thus cut off. Which choice has been selected in any case must be determined by fair interpretation of the language used to indicate intention, and in the light of the conditions and circumstances present at the time the intention was distinctly and finally made known. In Hayes v. City of Nashville, 80 F. 641, 26 C.C.A. 59, the court states the rule of construction thus:

> "Courts consider not only the language of the party, but all the circumstances including the effect of a complete rescission upon the rights of the parties, and the probability or improbability that the complaining party intended such a result in reaching a conclusion as to the proper construction of the language used." . . .

There is no error.   ◄

COMMENTS AND QUESTIONS

1. Apparently the defendants did not dispute the allegation that they had broken the contract. What, then, was their defense in this case? Why did the court reject it?

Rights of Unpaid Seller

In certain cases, the seller is entitled to withhold delivery of goods to the buyer when the buyer's ability to pay is doubtful. This right to retain possession of goods as security for payment is called an *unpaid seller's lien*. It may be exercised by the seller in the following situations: (1) when the contract calls for payment on delivery—i.e., when the goods are to be shipped C.O.D.; (2) when the seller has extended credit and the credit period has expired and the seller has, for one reason or another, not yet delivered the goods to the buyer; (3) when the seller still has possession of the goods and the buyer has become insolvent—i.e., he is unable to pay his bills as they come due. In such cases, the seller may keep possession of the goods even though title may have passed to the buyer. In any case, of course, if the buyer pays, or offers to pay, the contract price, the seller is obligated to deliver. So, too, if the seller has extended credit to the buyer and the time for payment has not expired, the seller may not hold the goods unless he can show that the buyer is insolvent.

> EXAMPLE
>
> s agrees to sell some furniture to b. The terms of the contract provide that s will deliver the furniture to b and that b will be given thirty days to pay. If s discovers that b is insolvent before he delivers the furniture, he may exercise his unpaid seller's lien and keep possession of the furniture until b pays him. If, on the other hand, b is not insolvent and the thirty-day credit period has not expired, s must carry out his obligation to deliver the furniture or else risk a suit for breach of contract. If the thirty-day period *does* expire, however, and s has not yet delivered to b, s may keep the furniture until b pays him, since b was obligated to pay within the credit period and failed to perform his obligation.

RIGHT TO STOP GOODS IN TRANSIT. The unpaid seller's lien does not cease once the goods have been delivered to the carrier, even though title to the goods may pass to the buyer at that time. If the unpaid seller learns that the buyer is insolvent, he may order the merchandise stopped in transit and have the shipment returned to him at any time before it is delivered to the buyer. The seller must, of course, give the carrier time to instruct his agents to hold up the shipment; otherwise the order is ineffective. But if the order is issued in time, the carrier must comply with it. The seller must pay the cost of having the goods returned.

The right to stop goods in transit is a logical extension of the unpaid seller's lien, since a seller obviously should be allowed to recall a shipment once he realizes that the buyer will not be able to pay for it.

The Uniform Commercial Code extends the unpaid seller's lien still further: if the buyer is discovered to be insolvent, the Code permits the seller to reclaim the goods within a period of ten days after delivery. This right is subject, however, to the claims of third persons, such as creditors of the buyer who may have attached the goods after delivery.

RIGHT TO RESELL GOODS. An unpaid seller who retains possession of goods or else reclaims them by stopping them in transit is entitled to resell them if the buyer does not pay for them within a reasonable time. What is "reasonable" depends, of course, on the circumstances. As a general rule, the seller is not obligated to notify the buyer of his intention to resell, but the court may take into consideration his failure to do so in determining whether the buyer has been given a reasonable time within which to pay. In most states, the resale may be either public or private, provided the sale is conducted in good faith. If the seller receives less than the original contract price when he resells the goods, the buyer must make up the difference. But if the seller receives *more* than the original price he may keep the profit.

An interesting illustration of the exercise of an unpaid seller's lien is provided by the following case. The buyer had agreed to purchase a quantity of ale; then, after title to the ale had passed to him, he went bankrupt.

In re IRISH BEVERAGE CO., INC.

District Court of the United States, S.D. New York, 1938
24 F. Supp. 582

▶ In Bankruptcy. Proceeding in the matter of the Irish Beverage Company, Inc., bankrupt, to determine whether a certain claimant was entitled to the proceeds of sale of certain ale held by the trustee in bankruptcy. Referee's order in favor of claimant affirmed.[15]

PATTERSON, DISTRICT JUDGE. The question is whether the claimant, Johnson, should have the proceeds of sale of certain ale held by the trustee in bankruptcy.

Johnson, a merchant in Liverpool, sold the ale to the bankrupt, an importer here. The sales were f.o.b. Liverpool, the bankrupt paying ocean freight and insurance. Johnson having indicated from the outset that he was unwilling to extend credit to the bankrupt, it was arranged that he would consign the goods to a third party, Inter-Maritime Forwarding Company, and that the Inter-Maritime Company would make delivery of the goods to the bankrupt against payment of the purchase price and would forward the money to Johnson. What actually happened was that the Inter-Maritime Company would indorse the bills of lading to the bankrupt, enter the goods at the Custom House in the bankrupt's name and have

---

[15] In a bankruptcy proceeding, the *trustee* gathers all the assets of the bankrupt person or firm and holds them for safekeeping. A *referee* is appointed by the court to hold hearings and decide how the bankrupt's assets are to be distributed to the creditors. The trustee in this case claimed that the proceeds from the sale of the ale should be distributed to all the creditors. The referee, however, held that Johnson was entitled to them. This appeal followed. The main issue was Johnson's right to assert an unpaid seller's lien on the ale.

them placed in bonded warehouse in the bankrupt's name, the warehouse receiving instructions not to release them to the bankrupt except on delivery order signed by the Inter-Maritime Company. The Inter-Maritime would not issue a delivery order until the bankrupt paid the purchase price owing to Johnson. The goods were entered and stored as belonging to the bankrupt because the bankrupt was the only party with an alcohol permit. There is no proof that a negotiable warehouse receipt was issued to the bankrupt.

A quantity of the ale so purchased but not paid for by the bankrupt was in a warehouse at the time of bankruptcy. The receiver having obtained possession, the goods were sold subject to Johnson's claim, and Johnson brought a petition in the nature of reclamation for the proceeds of sale. The referee held that the proceeds belonged to Johnson. I am of the same opinion.

By the time the goods reached the warehouse, title to them was in the bankrupt. The property for most purposes had passed on delivery to the ocean carrier at Liverpool, and the seller's limited property in them for securing performance by the buyer, retained by the form of the bill of lading, passed when the bill of lading was indorsed to the bankrupt. New York Personal Property Law, Consol. Laws, c. 41, sec. 101, subd. 2. But the goods were never delivered to the bankrupt. They stood in the bankrupt's name in the warehouse, it is true, and if the bankrupt had had unfettered control over them or free access to them, the seller would have had no lien or property right good against the buyer's trustee in bankruptcy, despite an intention to reserve a lien. In re Friend, 2 Cir. 278 F. 153. It is of controlling importance, however, that the bankrupt could not lawfully get possession of the goods without production of a delivery order which could not be procured without payment of the price. In effect, the seller still had possession and thus had a lien for the unpaid purchase price. The seller's lien survives so long as the buyer has not been furnished with the means of controlling possession. This was certainly true at common law. . . . and there is no reason to doubt that it continues to be the law under the Sales Act. . . . "It is not necessary that the vendor's possession be complete or exclusive. Vendor's possession is sufficient to support a lien if the goods have not passed into the uncontrolled possession of the vendee." Poor v. American Locomotive Co., 7 Cir. 67 F. 2d 626, 630.

Any excess of the fund over the unpaid purchase price belongs to the trustee in bankruptcy, but it has not been suggested that there is any such excess.

The referee's order will be affirmed.　　　　　　　　　　　　◀

COMMENTS AND QUESTIONS

1. Note how this action arose. The buyer went bankrupt, and the trustee in bankruptcy alleged that, since title to the ale had passed to the buyer, his creditors should be entitled to the proceeds when the ale was sold. The seller disagreed. What was his theory? Who won?

2. This case is a good illustration of the extent of the unpaid seller's lien. The law recognizes that selling is sometimes a risky business and, in effect, encourages the seller to retain control of his goods until he has been paid.

Buyer's Rights and Remedies

When Seller Fails to Deliver

Sometimes a seller neglects or refuses to deliver goods after title has passed to the buyer. Then the buyer may either sue for damages or for actual possession of the merchandise. If title has not yet passed, ordinarily the buyer's only remedy is to sue for damages, which usually amount to the difference between the prevailing market price and the contract price. In other words, if the buyer would have to pay more to acquire the same goods elsewhere, he is entitled to recover the additional cost. When the goods cannot be acquired elsewhere, the court may order specific performance of the contract (i.e., actual delivery of the goods) by the seller even though title has not passed to the buyer.

Buyer's Remedies for Breach of Warranty

Depending on the circumstances, the buyer has a choice of remedies when there has been a breach of either express or implied warranty. If he has not paid for the goods, he may accept them and pay an amount consisting of the agreed price minus the extent of the breach. On the other hand, if he has already paid the contract price, he may keep the merchandise and sue the seller for damages amounting to the difference in value of the goods as they were represented to be and their value as actually delivered. If the goods have not been delivered and title has not passed, the buyer may refuse to accept them and sue for damages amounting to the difference between the contract price and the current market price. Lastly, he may rescind the contract; then he must return any goods that have been delivered and may recover any part of the purchase price he has paid. If neither side has yet performed, of course, rescission merely cancels any further obligation and denies him the right to bring any action for damages. In order to rescind, the buyer must notify the seller within a reasonable time after he discovers the breach of warranty, and he must return the goods in as good condition as when he received them; otherwise, his only remedy is an action for damages. In any case where the buyer has received the goods and has used them and has suffered injury as a result of the breach of warranty, he is entitled to sue for his damages. In the preceding section, we presented several illustrations of this rule (e.g., the *Henningsen* case on page 401).

Buyer's Right to Inspect Goods and Refuse Delivery

As a general rule, the buyer has the right to inspect goods before he accepts them. If his inspection reveals that the quality or quantity of the merchandise does not conform to contract specifications, he may reject the shipment. If the buyer accepts the goods after he has inspected them, however, he loses his right to rescind the contract and must keep the goods; his only remedy then is to bring an action for damages.

If the amount of merchandise delivered turns out to be greater than the amount specified in the contract, the buyer may (1) reject the entire shipment and rescind the contract, or (2) accept the correct amount, reject the excess, and pay the contract price, or (3) accept the entire shipment and pay for the excess merchandise at the contract rate. If the amount of merchandise delivered turns out to be *less* than what the contract calls for, the buyer may reject the whole shipment. Once the buyer accepts less than the contract amount, knowing that the seller does not intend to make full delivery, he must pay for the delivered merchandise at the contract rate. On the other hand, if the buyer is unaware that the seller does not intend to make full delivery, he is responsible only for the reasonable value of the goods actually delivered.

> E X A M P L E
>
> s, a washing-machine dealer, agrees to sell and deliver to b ten washing machines at $200 each for use in b's laundromat. If s delivers twelve machines, b may reject all of them, accept ten and reject two, or accept all of them. If s delivers only eight machines, b may accept them or reject them. If, in the latter case, b knows that s will not deliver the other two, he may accept the eight and pay $200 for each of them. If, however, he is unaware of s's intention not to deliver the other two, he is liable only for the reasonable value of the eight that have been delivered; this value might be less than $200 each.

The concluding case in this section provides an interesting illustration of the buyer's right to inspect and reject goods. Some authorities feel that the result of the case was rather harsh. See if you agree.

CREAM CITY GLASS CO. v. FRIEDLANDER

Supreme Court of Wisconsin, 1893
84 Wis. 53, 54 N.W. 28

▶ Action for money had and received. Plaintiff company manufactures glass at Milwaukee. They entered into the following contract with defendant September 4, 1890:

> "Chicago, September 4th, 1890. Cream City Glass Company: Sold to you about one hundred and fifty (150) tons Muspratt Bros. & Huntley's 48 per cent. carbonated soda ash for shipment by steamers from Liverpool, monthly, in about equal parts, during the months of October, November, and December, of the current year, (about fifty tons monthly,) at $1.65 per 100 net, invoice weights, cash on arrival, against delivery of documents, less one per cent, accidents to factory, in transit, or *force majeure* [16] excepted. Subject also to changes, if any, in United States tariff laws during pendency of this contract. L. M. Friedlander. No change in tariff impending. L.M.F."

Muspratt Bros. & Huntley were manufacturers of soda ash at Liverpool, England. In accordance with the contract, Friedlander caused to be shipped from Liverpool 63 tierces, or 113,390 pounds, of soda ash, which arrived

---

[16] Superior or irresistible force; roughly equivalent to an "act of God." In other words, the seller is excused from performance if the goods are lost or damaged as a result of some event over which the parties have no control.

on plaintiff's side track at its factory about December 13, 1890. Plaintiff paid duties and freight on the shipment, also the contract price of the goods, amounting in all to $1,698.17. The goods were unloaded by plaintiff. Upon examination the material appeared to have been damaged by water, and plaintiff caused the following letter to be sent to defendant, December 13, 1890:

> "Dear Sir: The railroad has just delivered your soda to us. On opening it, we find it absolutely unfit for use. The casks have evidently been under water until over half of the soda has soaked away. We wish you would come up and see it at once. Very truly yours, Cream City Glass Co."

On December 19, 1890, plaintiff gave to defendant personally the following notice:

> "Dear Sir: Please take notice that the shipment of soda ash made by you and received by us on or about the 10th day of December, 1890, under your contract of September 4th, 1890, amounting to about sixty-three casks, was found to be wholly unfit for the uses and purposes for which it was purchased. We therefore notify you that we hereby rescind [17] the said sale, and hereby offer to return to you the said soda ash. We further notify you that said soda ash is now at our factory, subject to your order, and that we hereby demand immediate repayment to us of the purchase price paid by us therefor. Respectfully yours, Cream City Glass Co. Richard Ogden. . . . "

Evidence was introduced tending to show that the soda ash was not suitable for the manufacture of glass, and contained but 34 per cent. of alkali, instead of 48 per cent. The evidence showed however, that the ash was of some commercial value, though not as much as it would have been worth had it contained 48 per cent. of alkali. Friedlander refused to receive the property back, and in the latter part of January or first part of February, 1891, the plaintiff made a practical test of the material, by using about 6 tierces thereof, amounting to 1,500 or 1,600 pounds, in one of its furnaces, mixing it with the other necessary materials, and endeavoring to make glass. Plaintiff claims that the test showed that glass could not be made from the ash. There was evidence tending to show that it was necessary to use this amount to make a practical test of the material. Upon the question of the effect of this test upon the plaintiff's right of rescission the trial judge charged the jury as follows:

> "If you find from the evidence that the plaintiff, in making such test, used more of the soda ash in question than was absolutely necessary to determine its merchantable quality, or whether it was fit and proper for the uses for which it was bought and sold, or whether it was in accordance with the contract, or if you find that it was unnecessary to make such test, then such act is inconsistent with such rescission, and you will find the defendant; or, if you find from all the facts and circumstances in the case that the plaintiff, after such election to rescind, did any act inconsistent with ownership of the defendant, then you will find for the defendant."

---

[17] "Rescind," as used here, has its traditional meaning.

To which charge defendant excepted. There was a verdict and judgment for plaintiff for the full amount of the purchase money, freight, and duty paid, from which defendant appeals.

WINSLOW, J. (after stating the facts). . . . We shall consider but one other question upon this appeal, and that is the question of the effect upon the rights of the parties of the use of six tierces of the soda ash by the plaintiff in January or February following the sale, for the purpose of testing its fitness for the manufacture of glass. Assuming that the evidence is sufficient to establish an implied warranty that the soda ash in question was of a quality reasonably fit to be used in the manufacture of glass, the question is, could the plaintiff, after having decided that the material was wholly unfit, and notified the defendant of its decision and its rejection of the material, proceed to use three quarters of a ton of the material in making a practical test, and still insist on its right of rejection? It seems clear that the plaintiff was entitled for a reasonable time after actual receipt of the material to exercise the right of rejection in case the goods did not conform to the contract. Benj. Sales (6th Ed.), sec. 703. If this fact could only be ascertained by a practical test, the plaintiff also had the right, within such reasonable time, to make such practical test, using only so much of the material as was reasonably necessary for the purpose, without thereby losing the right of rejection. . . . But this test is plainly for the purpose only of enabling the purchaser to decide whether the material conforms to the contract. If the fact can be determined by inspection alone, the test is not necessary, and the use of the material conforms to the contract. If the fact can be determined by inspection alone, the test is not necessary, and the use of the material, therefore, clearly unjustifiable. Now, in this case the plaintiff's officers determined at once, and upon inspection alone, that the material was unfit for their purposes, and so notified the defendant, and rejected the entire lot. They did not claim to need any test. They took their position definitely. After that act they could not deal with the property in any way inconsistent with the rejection if they proposed to insist upon their right to reject. . . . They must do no act which they would have no right to do unless they were owners of the goods. . . . Under these rules it is evident the plaintiff had no right to use up a quantity of the material several weeks after the rejection. By the rejection it became defendant's property, if such rejection was rightful. Plaintiff had no right to use any part of it. It is claimed that the use was simply for the purpose of providing evidence of unfitness for the purposes of the trial of this case; but one has no right to use his opponent's property for the purpose of making evidence. The act was an unmistakable act of ownership, and entirely inconsistent with the claim that the material had been rejected, and was owned by defendant. It follows that the judgment must be reversed. *Judgment reversed, and cause remanded for a new trial.*   ◄

COMMENTS AND QUESTIONS

1. In this case, the plaintiff paid the contract price for the goods and then sought to rescind the contract and recover his money. In the lower court, the plaintiff prevailed. Why did the Supreme Court of Wisconsin order a new trial?

2. What was the plaintiff's mistake here? The fact that he used too much of the soda ash to conduct the test? Or the fact that he used any of it at all? If you were counsel for the plaintiff, how would you advise him to proceed in future cases of this sort?

SECTION 5

CONDITIONAL SALES

Definition and Use

So far, we have been discussing the various ways in which an unpaid seller may protect himself until he has been paid. In an ordinary sales situation, it is perfectly feasible for him to withhold delivery of goods, through one device or another, until the buyer has made payment. But in long-term credit purchases the buyer takes possession of the goods immediately and then pays for them in installments over a period of time. Here the unpaid seller is ordinarily obliged to give up title to the goods when he delivers them to the buyer. And obviously he cannot refuse to deliver them. To remedy this situation, the so-called conditional sale was devised and is now widely used in business.

In a conditional sale, the buyer wins possession of the goods but the seller retains title to them until he has been paid in full. The seller may retake possession if the buyer fails to make payment, and the buyer acquires title only after he has made full payment.

EXAMPLE

B buys a washing machine for $200 from s on conditional sale, agreeing to pay $20.00 a month for ten months. After the machine has been delivered to B, he is entitled to keep it and use it as long as he meets the payments. s retains title until the purchase price has been paid in full, however, and may retake possession if B defaults on his payments.

State Regulation

Responding to the widespread use of conditional sales, many states have set up regulations to spell out the rights and duties of the parties and to protect unwary consumers. In some of these jurisdictions, the so-called Uniform Conditional Sales Act has been passed. In those states which have enacted the Uniform Commercial Code, the law of conditional sales is governed by a special provision of that statute. Still another group of states have their own special legislation governing this subject. In some jurisdictions, the law of conditional sales is still governed entirely by court decisions.

The following case illustrates the operation of the Maryland Retail Instalment Sales Act, which is typical of state regulation in this field. Note its detailed provisions for the protection of the buying public.

STRIDE v. MARTIN

Court of Appeals of Maryland, 1945
184 Md. 446, 41 A. 2d 489

▶ MARKELL, J. On February 19th, 1944, the plaintiff (appellant) bought from the defendants (appellees) a used 1936 Packard automobile for $395 cash price, plus $64.40 "finance charge," $28.50 insurance and $10.55 title, tax, and transfer charges and recording fees. At that time she made a cash payment of $71.05 (including a $10.00 deposit on February 8, 1944), and traded in a used 1936 Plymouth car, for which she was allowed $63.80, ($135.00 for the car, less a lien of $71.20), leaving a balance of $363.60, to be paid in 12 (monthly) instalments of $30.30 each. On February 21st the defendants paid the lien on the Plymouth and got the certificate of title from the lienor, and also began repairs and improvements to the Plymouth which cost about $200. . . .

The plaintiff signed a "conditional sale contract," dated February 19th, 1944, between "the undersigned Seller" and "the undersigned Buyer," on a printed form prepared by counsel for the Automobile Trade Association of Maryland in triplicate, containing "instructions to dealer" to "give pink copy to buyer, retain green copy, white copy is for record" and that the form "must be made out in triplicate, all blanks filled in." The plaintiff received a carbon copy, designated "buyer's copy," bearing her signature to the contract and also to an "acknowledgment by buyer," *viz:* "Buyer hereby acknowledges receipt of an exact, executed copy of this contract at time of execution hereof." She testified that she never received any other copy of the contract; this testimony is uncontradicted. One of the defendants testified that her copy was "a copy they usually give" the buyer. This copy does not bear the defendants' signature or their names. . . . It contains unfilled blanks for mention and description of the traded-in car . . . for the time of the instalment payments . . . for "date of signature of buyer," name and signature of seller and addresses of both . . . besides several correct figures (e.g., "finance charge" and cost of insurance) in wrong blanks. . . . There is no evidence that the plaintiff was prejudiced by the fact that the copy received by her was not "signed by the seller."

The plaintiff soon became dissatisfied with the Packard. After taking it back to the defendants several times for correction of alleged defects, on February 24th she left it with the defendants and asked for "her money back" and the Plymouth. The defendants refused to comply with her request, but did not tell her they had made repairs or improvements on the Plymouth. She did not then mention the Retail Instalment Sales Act. On February 28th they wrote her that they had "repossessed" the Packard "as of February

26th, 1944," and that "to redeem it" she "must pay off the entire balance of $363.60." As she was not then in default, they say this letter was a "mistake" —which they did nothing to correct. She consulted counsel and demanded, under the Retail Instalment Sales Act, a refund of all payments and deposits made. On March 11th the defendants' counsel wrote the plaintiff's counsel that "there has been no departure from any law which entitles your client to the action demanded"; the letter did not mention the Plymouth. On March 21st the defendants wrote the plaintiff that she had "defaulted" in her "first note payment" on the Packard. Later they sold the Packard for $395.

On April 24th the plaintiff brought suit under the Speedy Judgment Act for $134.85 (the cash payment of $71.05 plus the allowance of $63.80 for the Plymouth), claimed under the Retail Instalment Sales Act (art. 83, sec. 116, Acts of 1941, ch. 851). The defendants disputed the whole claim. Trial before the court without a jury resulted in a verdict and judgment for the defendants, from which this appeal is taken.

The Retail Instalment Sales Act provides:

"116. (Form and Delivery of Instalment Sale Agreements.)
(a) Every instalment sale agreement shall be evidenced by an instrument in writing containing all of the agreements of the parties. It shall be signed by all the parties before the seller delivers to the buyer any of the goods covered by the agreement.
"(b) At or before the time the buyer signs the instrument, the seller shall deliver to him an exact copy of it. If that copy was not executed by the seller, then unless the seller within fifteen (15) days after the buyer has signed, delivers to him a copy of the instrument signed by the seller, the agreement and the instruments signed by the buyer shall be absolutely void without any action by the buyer, and the seller shall immediately refund to the buyer all payments and deposits theretofore made.
"(c) Until the buyer signs an instalment sale agreement and receives a copy of it signed by the seller—
"(1) The buyer or prospective buyer has an unconditional right to cancel the agreement or prospective agreement and to receive immediate refund of all payments and deposits made on account of or in contemplation of the agreement; a request for such refund shall operate to cancel the agreement or prospective agreement. . . .
"(d) Any written acknowledgment of delivery of a copy of an instrument shall be printed in 12-point bold type or larger and, if contained in the agreement, shall be printed immediately below the signature to the agreement and shall be independently signed. . . .

"135. (Waivers by the Buyer.) No act, agreement, or statement of any buyer in any instalment agreement, shall constitute a valid waiver of any benefit or protection under the provisions of this sub-title.

"136. (Violations of Sections 116, 117, 118.) (a) Whenever an instalment sale agreement does not contain the material required by Sections 116 and 117 of this sub-title or the seller fails to deliver a copy to the buyer, no seller or holder of such agreement shall collect or receive any finance, delinquency or collection charge from the buyer, ex-

cept that a written acknowledgment of the delivery of the contract by
the buyer pursuant to Section 116 shall be conclusive proof of such delivery as between the buyer and any assignee of the instalment agreement, without actual knowledge to the contrary. . . ."

. . . The Retail Instalment Sales Act was enacted in 1941 after extended
consideration and investigation. Joint Resolution No. 8 of 1939 directed that
the subject be investigated by the Legislative Council, who were to report
their findings to the next regular session of the General Assembly. The
Council referred the matter to its Research Division, which made a study
and a report indicating the legislation was desirable. The Council, after a
hearing and further consideration, had a bill prepared and recommended
its passage. The Retail Instalment Sales Act is the bill submitted by the
Council, with amendments.

The Research Report (No. 6, September, 1940) reviews regulation in
other jurisdictions, especially recent legislation, generally similar but differing in details, in Indiana, Wisconsin, Massachusetts, Michigan and England. . . . This legislation reflects the view that "improvident and careless consumers who buy on the instalment plan need legal protection" . . . ,
and that without such protection "in the usual case the buyer probably is
discouraged from reading the contract and might not fully understand its
terms even if he did read it." This legislation aims to eliminate "contract
abuses" by requiring the contract to be in writing, to be delivered to the
purchaser within a definite period, to contain certain information and not
to contain certain provisions. . . . Thus the Maryland act aims not only
to prevent actual frauds . . . , but to close avenues to fraud.

The legislative history of the act, and both the similarities and the differences between such legislation in different jurisdictions, indicate that
the words of the act were chosen with care. Section 116 (b) and (c) (1)
are more explicit—more drastic perhaps—than corresponding provisions in
other jurisdictions. This Court can not mitigate these provisions by assuming a dispensing power not conferred by the act . . . or by creating exceptions or artificial estoppels which would shift upon the buyer the seller's
responsibility for neglect to comply with statutory requirements designed
for the buyer's protection.

It is not necessary to decide whether the words of the plaintiff's acknowledgment of "receipt of an exact, executed copy of this contract at time
of execution hereof" mean "executed by some party" or "executed by the
seller." Except in favor of an assignee without knowledge, the acknowledgment is not conclusive. The contract itself (on which the acknowledgment
was signed) shows that it was not executed by the seller "at time of execution" of the acknowledgment.

The defendants could not, by making repairs or improvements on the
Plymouth, prevent rescission or "cancellation" of the contract of sale of
the Packard. The plaintiff sued, not for return of the Plymouth but for "refund of all payments and deposits," including the "trade-in allowance" of
$63.80 for the Plymouth. The Act requires recital of the "down payment,
whether made in cash or represented by the agreed value of goods or both."
Section 17 (a) (4). The contract accordingly treats the "trade-in allowance"

as part of the "down payment," i.e., as cash from sale of the Plymouth. The defendants can not complain of the plaintiff's willingness to treat the sales of the Packard and the Plymouth as separable. It is not necessary to consider questions which would have been presented if the plaintiff had sued for the return of the Plymouth.

The defendants are not, by their neglect to obtain an assignment of title to the Plymouth, absolved of neglect, to comply with the Act. Presumably such an assignment is to be had for the asking; if not, the defendants (upon payment of the judgment in the instant case) will have whatever remedies they would have had if the act had not been passed.

On the facts, under the plain words of Section 116 (c) of the act, the plaintiff is entitled to recover "all payments and deposits made," including the "trade-in allowance." We leave open any questions as to the construction or application of Section 116 (a) or (b) or 117 in the instant case or on different facts. . . .

Judgment reversed and judgment entered for the appellant for $134.85 plus interest from April 24, 1944, to date of entry of judgment, with cost and a counsel fee of $50.   ◄

COMMENTS AND QUESTIONS

1. As the opinion indicates, several states have enacted similar legislation for the protection of conditional installment buyers. In what respects did the defendants fail to comply with the Maryland statute?
2. Note that last paragraph of the opinion. Not only did the court reverse the lower court and order judgment for the plaintiff; it awarded her a counsel fee of $50. Such awards are rare.

Recording—Notice to Third Parties

Serious problems often arise when innocent third parties deal with a conditional buyer. Since the conditional buyer clearly has possession of the property in question and is using it for his own benefit, he seems to be the owner, and it is extremely difficult for third parties to ascertain whether someone else actually has title. Because a conditional buyer does not yet have title to the property, he cannot, under common law, legally sell it to another. If he purports to make such a sale, the conditional seller may reclaim the property from the would-be buyer, even though the third party purchased it in good faith and without knowledge of the prior conditional sale. Moreover, at common law no creditor of the conditional buyer has any right to attach such goods or place a lien on them, since the conditional seller still holds title to them. Once the conditional buyer has paid for the goods, of course, he acquires title and may dispose of them freely.

The state laws that have been passed to protect third parties generally require the conditional seller to record the sales contract in a public place so that anyone dealing with the conditional buyer may discover where title to the property resides. (Both the Uniform Conditional Sales Act and the Uniform Commercial Code provide for the recording of conditional sales contracts.) If the conditional seller fails to record the contract, an innocent third party who purchases the property from the conditional buyer may take title to it free and clear of the conditional seller's interest. Moreover, any creditor of the conditional buyer acting in good faith may acquire a superior right to that of the conditional seller by attaching the property or placing a lien on it. If, however, the third party knows about the conditional seller's interest when he deals with the conditional buyer, he does not acquire a superior right, even though the contract has not been properly recorded.

The important point here is that recording requirements are for the protection of third parties only. They do not in any way alter the relationship between the conditional buyer and the conditional seller, who remain obligated to each other according to the terms of their contract.

EXAMPLES

1. B buys some office furniture from s on a conditional sale, agreeing to pay for it in installments over a period of three years. The transaction occurs in a state that requires the recording of conditional sales contracts. After making payments for one year, B becomes dissatisfied with the furniture and sells it to x, who buys it in good faith with no knowledge of s's interest. If s has properly recorded the contract, his right is superior to x's, and, if B defaults on the remaining payments, he may reclaim the furniture without compensating x. If the contract has not been recorded, however, s is out of luck and x gets good title to the furniture. In either case, if x is aware of s's interest when he buys the furniture from B, he is not protected.

2. If the conditional sale in the preceding example takes place in a state that does not require the recording of conditional sales contracts, x cannot acquire a superior title to s's, despite his good faith and his ignorance of s's rights.

Rights and Duties of Conditional Seller

Unless the conditional buyer falls behind in his payments, the conditional seller merely retains title, as a security measure, but he is not entitled to possession. He may, however, sell or assign his interest in the goods at any time, subject, of course, to the rights of the conditional buyer.

What happens when the conditional buyer fails to keep up his payments? Then the conditional seller may take certain steps to protect his interest.

Right to Retake Goods

A conditional seller has the right to repossess his goods if the buyer defaults. This right must be exercised peacefully, however; if the seller cannot retake the goods without resort to force, he must bring a court action. Some contracts give the seller the right to reclaim the goods, not only upon default, but when the buyer has ceased to be a good credit risk. Another common clause provides that if the buyer defaults on one installment, the entire balance becomes due; then the seller is entitled to repossess without further demand. Generally speaking, these provisions are valid and enforceable.

In most states, the seller's right to repossession is absolute and may be exercised immediately after the buyer's default. Some states, however, give the buyer a grace period in which he may "redeem" the property by performing his obligation. The Uniform Conditional Sales Act, for example, requires that the seller notify the buyer of his intention to repossess not more than forty nor less than twenty days prior to doing so. If the buyer performs his obligation before the grace period expires, the seller loses his right to reclaim the property. The Act also provides that if the seller retakes the property without giving proper notice, the buyer has ten days in which to perform; if he does perform within that time, he is entitled to recover the property from the seller.

The conditional buyer's right to redeem property was at issue in the following case, which was decided by the Alabama Supreme Court. Apparently, when this case was decided, Alabama had no statute regulating conditional sales, and the court relied on equity principles in reaching its decision.

J. D. PITTMAN TRACTOR CO. v. BOLTON

Supreme Court of Alabama, 1939
238 Ala. 300, 191 So. 360

▶ ANDERSON, C. J.   Bill in equity by buyer of personalty under conditional sale contract for equitable relief against forfeiture for nonpayment of instalment at the time stipulated. The appeal is from a final decree for complainant. . . .

The controlling facts, so found, are in substance as follows: On November 1, 1935, appellant, J. D. Pittman Tractor Co., Inc. sold to appellee, Mallie Bolton, an excavating machine, described as "one used Speeder one-half yard steam shovel, serial No. 696."

The consideration was $2,500, payable in money, and one "Byars" shovel, taken at trade in value of $1,500. The $2,500 was payable in twelve equal monthly instalments, beginning November 11, 1935, evidenced by promissory notes bearing interest from date.

The conditional sale contract, among other alternative remedies, stipulated that on default in payment of any instalment at the time specified, the seller "may take possession of said property wherever and whenever found, and, with or without notice or demand, may elect to treat buyer in default, and in such event all of the rights, titles, and equities of buyer in said property shall immediately cease and terminate, and seller shall be released from all obligations to transfer or deliver said property to the buyer, and all sums of money theretofore paid, and all sums then due and unpaid by the buyer to seller hereunder or under said promissory notes shall remain the property of seller and shall be considered compensation for the use, wear and tear and depreciation of said property, and buyer agrees forthwith to pay to seller all of said payments which are then due and unpaid."

Time was stipulated to be of the essence of the contract. Acceptance of any payment after it became due was declared not to constitute a waiver of such stipulation, or other provisions of the contract.

The sale was made in connection with an agreement between complainant, Bolton, and one Taylor whereby complainant was to buy the shovel and Taylor should pay for same from the proceeds of its operation, and payments were to be made by complainant only in case Taylor failed to meet them when due. This arrangement was known to the seller, who agreed to notify complainant when Taylor failed to pay on time.

Nine of the twelve instalments were paid. Several were paid by Taylor, some of them one to two months after maturity. In two instances, January and July, 1936, complainant made the monthly payments after notices from the seller that Taylor had failed to meet them.

The instalment due August 12th was not paid when due. On September 5th thereafter the seller wrote complainant, the buyer:

> "You have past due with us this time one note amounting to $208.33 which was due on August 12th and there is another note due on September 12th amounting to $208.33 and another one on October 12th for $208.37 all bearing interest at the rate of 6% from November 1st, 1935 to date.
>
> "We made arrangements today to repossess this machine on account of the non-payment of August 12th note, but Mr. Taylor brought Mr. Baird into Birmingham and wished us to permit he and yourselves to give us a bill of sale on the machine for your equity therein and we would in turn resell the machine to Mr. Baird, so if this is agreeable with you and if you will give us a bill of sale for the balance that is now due on this machine, we will then arrange to resell it to Mr. Baird.
>
> "For your information, the total indebtedness on this machine up to September 1st, amounts to $669.29.
>
> "Upon receipt of this bill of sale and the proper papers back from Mr. Baird we will then turn over your old papers on this machine to you."

On receipt of this letter complainant sent check to cover the principal of the note due August 12th with letter of date Sept. 9th advising that he would be in the seller's office within the next few days to see about the account.

The check was refused and returned with advice that the property had already been repossessed. It had been repossessed under date of September 1st, a bill of sale had been made to Baird in consideration of $669.29, the balance due to the seller on the sale to Bolton. In October following, and before this bill was filed, a tender was made by complainant of the full amount of the unpaid balance. . . .

The buyer under a conditional sale contract acquires a property interest of increasing value as the several instalments are paid.

Stipulations making time of the essence of the contract, empowering the seller to retake possession for condition broken,[18] all payments theretofore made being treated as rentals for the use of the property, while valid at law, are treated in equity as in the nature of a forfeiture, and not to be so enforced as to work oppression and injustice.

Dealing with such stipulations as security for the debt, though not

---

[18] That is, for failure to make payments.

strictly a mortgage, a court of equity is open to the buyer, upon tender of the amount due or, if the amount of the debt is in dispute, upon offer to do equity, to maintain a bill to set aside the forfeiture and have equitable relief appropriate to the particular case.

This case comes within this principle. The retaking of this property, and selling it to another, without notice to the buyer that the August instalment was in default, was, under the facts found by the trial court, quite inequitable, no matter what complaints had theretofore been made as to delays on the part of Taylor and insistence upon prompt payments as per contract. Some cases have stressed the waiver of the condition as to time by acceptance of payments considerably past due, lulling the buyer into the belief that such condition would not be insisted upon. This should not be extended to confer a license on the debtor to disregard his obligation to pay at the times fixed in the contract.

But equitable relief does not depend upon waiver of the conditions written into the contract. For example, if the buyer should meet every instalment on time until the greater part of the debt is paid, and then from inability or neglect fails to pay an instalment on time the seller, taking advantage of the letter of his contract, proceeds to repossess the property as his own, refusing the buyer an opportunity to pay the balance, the seller is using the forfeiture provisions of the contract oppressively. Equity, working out its own remedies, interposes to prevent injustice, provided always the buyer is ready and willing to pay the debt. The primary purpose of the contract is to secure the debt. Equity so deals with it. . . .

The tentative transaction between complainant and Taylor, never consummated by Taylor, in no way affects the equities of the case. Complainant was the sole purchaser. His equities were recognized in the letter of Sept. 5th, but ignored and repudiated when he sought to make payment.

The alternate relief granted gave respondent Tractor Company the election to pay the value of the property at the time it was repossessed less the amount of the indebtedness then unpaid. This was equitable under the circumstances. It protects Baird, the purchaser, after the property was repossessed. There is no lack of evidence to support the finding of the value of the property at that time, namely, $2,000. We need not consider the more onerous alternative relief, based on a return of the property and payment of the value of the use or hire of the property from the time it was repossessed to the date of the trial.

Affirmed.

◀

COMMENTS AND QUESTIONS

1. Summarize the court's decision in this case. Do you think the result would have been the same if only one installment had been paid instead of nine?

2. Do you think the time factor might be important in this type of case? Suppose the plaintiff had been four or five months behind in his payment and the defendant had demanded payment several times. If the defendant had then repossessed the property, do you think the court would have allowed the plaintiff to redeem it by paying the installment?

Right to Resell and Recover Deficiency

Generally speaking, the conditional seller is free to do whatever he wants to with goods that he has repossessed. He may either hold them or resell them, as he sees fit. In most states, moreover, the seller is entitled to retain any payments he has received from the buyer, and he need not make any accounting to the buyer for whatever he gets from a resale of the goods. In other words, if he sells the property for more than what the original buyer owes him, he is entitled to keep the surplus. On the other hand, unless the contract specifically gives him the right, he is not entitled to sue the buyer for any deficiency if the resale brings less than the balance due. Most conditional sellers now include such a provision in their contracts, though few contracts permit the buyer to recover any surplus resulting from a resale. The Uniform Conditional Sales Act, however, explicitly provides that the seller can recover any deficiency and that the buyer can claim any surplus, thus giving protection to both.

> EXAMPLE
>
> B purchases a car from s for $3,600 on conditional sale, agreeing to pay for it in thirty-six monthly installments of $100 each. After twelve months B fails to meet his payments and defaults, leaving a balance due of $2,400. s repossesses the car. If s resells the car for $2,000, he is not entitled to sue B for the $400 deficiency unless the contract specifically gives him that right. On the other hand, if the resale brings $2,600, he need not account to B for the $200 surplus, unless the contract requires him to. If the Uniform Conditional Sales Act is applicable, s would be entitled to sue for any deficiency so long as he observes certain procedures in reselling the car, and B would be entitled to any surplus.

Election to Sue for Unpaid Balance

After default, the seller may not wish to go to the trouble and expense of repossessing his property; he may choose instead to bring suit against the buyer for the full unpaid balance. Having made this choice, however, he often finds that he is unable to collect. Then the question arises as to whether he may still exercise his right to repossess the goods. Some courts hold that by the very act of bringing suit he waives his right to repossess. Other jurisdictions, including those that have adopted the Uniform Conditional Sales Act, permit a seller to reclaim the property even after he has brought suit.

Rights and Duties of Conditional Buyer

Although, as we have seen, the conditional seller reserves title, the conditional buyer is, for all practical purposes, the owner of the goods—assuming, of course, that he does not default on his obligation. He is entitled to full possession and use of the property, and he may sue for damages or recovery if it is damaged or wrongfully taken from him. In addition, most states permit him to sue the seller for any breach of warranty, as in an ordinary sale. Generally speaking, the conditional buyer may sell or assign his interest in the property, subject, of course, to the seller's right to repossess.

But if the conditional buyer transfers his interest to another, he still remains liable for the payment of the balance.

Once the conditional buyer has performed his obligation in full, title to the goods automatically passes to him without further ceremony. The risk of loss, however, is on the buyer from the moment the property is delivered to him. This exception to the general rule that risk follows title (see page 368) is justified on the grounds that the buyer is, in every practical respect, the owner of the property and, consequently, should bear the responsibility for any loss or damage.

EXAMPLE

B buys a television set from s on conditional sale for $240, agreeing to pay twelve installments of $20 each. After he has paid six installments, the set is destroyed by a fire. Even though B was not responsible for the fire, he must bear the loss and must pay s the remaining six installments.

SUMMARY OF THE LAW OF SALES

Definitions

A sale is a contract whereby a seller transfers ownership of goods to a buyer in exchange for a consideration. In some cases the contract is completed in one transaction and ownership is transferred to the buyer right away; in other cases the contract provides that ownership is to be transferred at some future time. The latter is sometimes called a *contract to sell*, and the former is often referred to as a *present sale*.

Formation of Sales Contracts

Generally speaking, a sales contract must satisfy the basic requirements of contract law in order to be valid (i.e., offer and acceptance, genuine agreement, legal capacity, consideration, legal purpose). However, the Uniform Commercial Code, which has been enacted by several states, makes some significant changes in these requirements:

1. The U.C.C. provides that a contract is enforceable even though one or more important terms are left open, so long as it is clear that the parties intended to make a contract. This provision relaxes the rule that a contract is not enforceable unless the parties reach a definite agreement on all important terms.

firm offer

2. The U.C.C. provides that if a merchant offers in writing to buy or sell goods and agrees to hold the offer open for a certain period, he is bound to do so up to a maximum period of three months. This provision alters the rule of contract law which holds that an offer may be revoked at any time, even if it is stated to be irrevocable, unless the offeree has given consideration.

3. The U.C.C. provides that if the offeree accepts the terms of an offer but proposes new or additional terms, a contract is formed and the new or additional terms are construed as proposals for additions or changes in the contract which the offeror is free to accept or reject. This provision modifies the rule that if the offeree proposes additional or different terms in his reply, he makes a counteroffer, rather than an acceptance.

4. The U.C.C. provides that an agreement to modify an existing contract is binding even though it is not supported by new consideration. This provision alters the rule that such agreements are not binding.

Price of Goods

If no definite price is specified for the goods in the sales contract, the buyer must pay a reasonable price; this is generally set at the prevailing market price at the time and place of delivery.

The Statute of Frauds

The sales section of the Statute of Frauds provides that where the price to be paid for goods exceeds a certain amount ($500 in many states), a sales contract may not be enforced unless the party seeking enforcement can prove at least one of three things: (1) that the buyer accepted and received at least part of the goods, (2) that the buyer made at least a part payment for the goods, or (3) that the other party signed a note or memorandum outlining the principal terms of the contract.

As a general rule, the Statute of Frauds does not apply to contracts to sell articles that have been specially manufactured for the purchaser and are not suitable for sale to other buyers in the regular course of business. Such contracts are enforceable over the minimum amount, even in the absence of acceptance and receipt, part payment, or written memorandum.

The Uniform Commercial Code makes two important changes in the rules governing the requirement of a written memorandum: (1) the rule that the memorandum must contain all the important terms of the contract is relaxed to require that there be merely "some writing sufficient to indicate that a contract for sale has been made between the parties . . . ," and (2) the rule that the memorandum must be signed by the party against whom enforcement is sought is changed to provide that, between merchants, if one party sends a written confirmation to the other and the other does not object to it in writing within ten days, the party receiving the written confirmation is bound by the contract even though he has not signed a written memorandum himself.

Transfer of Title and Risk of Loss

Since the responsibility for goods and the risk of loss or damages commonly rest with the owner, it is important to determine when title passes from seller to buyer. In some cases (e.g., a simple "cash sale"), there is little difficulty in establishing this point. In other situations, the parties may state specifically, in an agreement, when title will pass. If the parties do not make their intentions clear, however, the courts rely on certain legal presumptions to determine when title passed:

1. *Specific Goods in Deliverable State.* Title passes immediately to the buyer when the contract is made; it is immaterial whether payment or delivery is to be made later.

2. *Specific Goods in Nondeliverable State.* Title passes when the seller completes what is necessary to put the goods in deliverable state.

3. *Sale with Option to Return.* Title passes to the buyer on delivery of the goods, but he may return title to the seller by returning the goods to him within the time fixed by the contract, or, if no time has been fixed, within a reasonable time.

4. *Sale on Trial or Approval.* Title passes to the buyer when (1) he signifies his approval, or (2) he keeps the goods, without notifying the seller of his rejection, until the end of the trial period specified, or, if no definite time has been stipulated, within a reasonable period.

5. *Unascertained or Future Goods*
   a. If the contract does not call for shipment to the buyer, title passes when the goods are identified, set aside, and made ready for delivery to the buyer, with the assent of both parties.
   b. If the seller delivers the goods to a carrier for shipment to a buyer, title generally passes on delivery to the carrier. This rule applies even though the shipment is C.O.D.

6. *Where Seller Obligated to Deliver.* If the contract requires the seller to deliver the goods to the buyer, or to pay the cost of freight or transportation to a particular place, title does not pass until the goods have been delivered to the buyer or have reached the place agreed on.

An exception to the general rule that risk of loss follows title occurs when the seller retains title as security for the payment of the purchase price.

Warranties

Warranties are representations made by the seller to the buyer concerning the nature or quality of the goods being sold. Warranties are of two types: (1) express, and (2) implied.

An *express warranty* is an affirmative representation by the seller resulting from his written or oral statements or his conduct, the purpose of which is to induce the buyer to purchase the goods. Mere statements of opinion or estimates are not usually considered warranties unless the seller purposely misrepresents his true opinion and the buyer relies on that opinion. No express warranty arises if the buyer indicates that he is relying on his own judgment in purchasing the goods. Similarly, if the property is available for inspection, an express warranty does not cover obvious defects that would be apparent to a buyer who made a reasonable inspection.

In most sales contracts, certain warranties are implied by law even though the parties themselves say nothing about them. If the parties choose, however, they may exclude any or all of these implied warranties. If a sales contract contains both express and implied warranties, both will be enforced unless they conflict, in which case the express warranty governs.

Implied warranties fall into the following categories:

1. *Title.* In most situations, the seller impliedly warrants that he has good title to the goods and that he has a right to sell them free and clear of any mortgages or other claims.

2. *Conformity to Description or Sample.* If the goods are specifically described, the seller impliedly warrants that the goods delivered will conform to the description or sample.

3. *Merchantability.* A seller who customarily deals in the kind of goods being sold impliedly warrants that the goods are of merchantable quality—that is, that they are salable in the market as goods of that kind.

4. *Fitness for Particular Purpose.* If the buyer makes clear to the seller that he intends to use the goods for a particular purpose and that he is relying on the seller's skill and judgment in deciding whether or not to buy the goods, there is an implied warranty that they will be fit for that purpose. This warranty does not usually apply, however, to cases where the buyer orders goods by their patent name or trade name.

5. *Food and Drug Sales.* Generally speaking, in the sale of food and drugs there is an implied warranty that the products furnished will be fit for human consumption.

Persons Protected by Warranties

The general rule has long been established that only the immediate buyer may sue the immediate seller for breach of warranty, and that the only remedy available to others is to sue the responsible party and prove negligence. In recent years, however, there has been a noticeable tendency on the part of the courts to extend the scope of warranty protection to members and guests in the buyer's household and to others who may use or come in contact with the goods. In addition, there has been a tendency to permit the buyer to sue not only the seller but the manufacturer for breach of warranty.

Performance of Sales Contracts

The seller has a duty to the buyer to deliver the proper amount and kind of goods; the buyer has a duty to accept the goods and pay for them. Generally speaking, neither is obligated to perform his part until the other has performed his, or until he has offered to perform his part and the offer has been refused. The parties may agree, however, that one of them must perform first. If one party fails to perform, the other party may treat his failure as a breach of contract.

Seller's Rights and Remedies

If the buyer refuses to accept the goods when they are offered, the seller may sue for damages, which in most cases amount to the difference between the contract price and the market price at the time and place of delivery. If there is no ready market for the goods, or if title has passed to the buyer before delivery, the seller may recover the full contract price of the goods. If he does not choose to sue for damages, the seller may elect to rescind the contract; in that case, each side must return any consideration he has received, and neither has any further obligation to the other.

In certain cases, the seller may withhold delivery of the goods until he has been paid. This right, which is called an *unpaid seller's lien*, may be exercised (1) when the goods are shipped C.O.D., (2) when the seller has extended credit and the credit period expires before the seller delivers the goods, and (3) when the seller still has the goods and the buyer is insolvent. If, however, the buyer pays, or offers to pay, for the goods, the lien is lost and the seller must then deliver the goods to the buyer. The unpaid seller's lien is also extended to permit the seller to stop goods in transit if he learns that the buyer is insolvent. The Uniform Commercial Code goes still further and permits the seller to reclaim goods within ten days after delivery to the buyer if the latter is insolvent, subject to the rights of creditors or other third parties. In the above cases, an unpaid seller is entitled to resell the goods if the buyer does not pay within a reasonable time.

Buyer's Rights and Remedies

If the seller fails to deliver goods after title has passed to the buyer, the buyer may sue either for damages or for actual possession of the goods. If title has not yet passed, the buyer's only remedy is to sue for damages, which usually amount to the difference between the prevailing market price and the contract price. If the goods cannot be acquired elsewhere, however, the buyer may compel the seller to deliver the goods even though title has not passed to the buyer.

When there has been a breach of warranty by the seller, the buyer has a choice of remedies: (1) If he has not paid for the goods, he may accept them and pay the agreed price minus the extent of the breach. (2) If he has paid for the goods, he may keep the goods and sue the seller for damages. (3) If the goods have not been delivered and title has not passed, he may refuse to accept the goods and sue for damages. (4) He may rescind the contract. In addition, if the buyer has received the goods and has used them and has suffered injury as a result of the breach of warranty, he may sue for damages.

As a general rule, the buyer has the right to inspect goods before he accepts them; if the goods do not conform to contract specifications, he may reject them. If he accepts the goods after inspection, however, he must keep them; then his only remedy is to sue for damages if the goods do not conform to specifications. If the amount of merchandise delivered is greater than called for by the contract, the buyer may (1) reject the entire shipment, (2) accept the correct amount and reject the excess, or (3) accept the entire shipment and pay for the excess at the contract rate. If the amount delivered is less than called for by the contract, the buyer may reject the whole shipment. If he accepts the lesser amount knowing that the seller does not intend to make full delivery, he must pay at the contract rate. On the other hand, if he accepts the partial shipment and is unaware of the seller's intention not to make full delivery, he is liable only for the reasonable value of the goods delivered.

Conditional Sales

In a conditional sale, the buyer is given possession and use of the goods and agrees to pay the seller (usually in installments) at some future date. The seller retains title to the goods until he has been fully paid for them, at which time title passes to the buyer. If the buyer fails to pay for the goods, the seller may retake possession of them.

Conditional sales transactions are strictly regulated in many states. Several states require that special provisions be included in the contract for the protection of the buying public. Many states also require a conditional seller to record the sales contract in a public place so that anyone dealing with the conditional buyer may discover where title to the property resides. In those states, if the conditional seller fails to record the contract, an innocent third party who purchases the property, or attaches it as a creditor, may acquire a superior right to that of the conditional seller.

If the conditional buyer fails to keep up his payments, the seller has a right to repossess the goods. In some states the seller's right to repossession is absolute and may be exercised immediately after the buyer's default. Other states, however, give the buyer a grace period in which to pay the seller before the latter may retake the goods.

After repossession, the seller generally has a right either to hold the goods or to resell them, as he sees fit. Unless the contract provides otherwise, most states do not require the seller to account to the buyer for whatever he gets from a resale of the goods, nor do they permit the seller to sue the buyer for any deficiency if the resale brings less than the balance. The U.C.C., however, explicitly provides that the seller can recover any deficiency and that the buyer can claim any surplus.

If the seller does not wish to go to the trouble and expense of repossession when the buyer defaults, he may choose instead to sue for the full unpaid balance.

So long as he is not in default, the buyer is entitled to full possession and use of the goods. In addition, if there has been a breach of warranty, most states permit the buyer to sue the seller for damages. Once he has paid in full for the goods, title automatically passes to the buyer. Risk of loss or damage to the goods, however, is on the buyer from the moment they are delivered to him.

Supplementary Reading: Sales

Two good textbooks on the law of sales are Lawrence Vold, *Handbook of the Law of Sales* (West Publishing Co., 1931) and Samuel Williston, *The Law Governing Sales of Goods*, Rev. Ed. (Baker, Voorhis, 1948). For case materials, see Lawrence Vold, *Cases and Materials on the Law of Sales*, 2nd Ed. (West Publishing Co., 1949) or George G. Bogert, *Cases on the Law of Sales*, 3rd Ed. (Foundation Press, 1956). The relevant statutory provisions are to be found in *The Uniform Sales Act*, *The Uniform Conditional Sales Act*, and *The Uniform Commercial Code*.

13 Negotiable Instruments

Introduction

From very early times, merchants and businessmen have sought speedier and more efficient ways to make payment for goods and services and to extend credit. The most successful means of minimizing the time, trouble, and risk involved in transferring money back and forth has been the use of negotiable instruments, which were developed centuries ago. Today it is estimated that as much as 90 per cent of the business transactions that take place every year in this country are carried out by means of checks and other types of negotiable instruments.

A negotiable instrument is simply a written obligation which calls for the payment of money and which may be transferred from one person or firm to another. In some respects, a negotiable instrument resembles an ordinary contract right to receive money. But there are two important differences: First, a negotiable instrument is more freely and easily transferable than an ordinary contract right. Second, and more important, the transferee of a negotiable instrument often acquires a better right to enforce payment than does the assignee of an ordinary contract right.[1] These special rules of law are designed to assure the free and confident transfer of negotiable instruments and to encourage their use as substitutes for money and as vehicles for creating credit.

Although there is evidence that crude forms of negotiable instruments existed in ancient times,[2] their use was not widespread. Through the Middle Ages, European courts refused to permit the negotiation (i.e., the free transfer) of such instruments from one person to another.

There were two reasons for this judicial attitude. First, the prevailing theory of law was that nothing could be legally transferred without the physical delivery of possession; and, since the right to receive money had no physical form, it was impossible to deliver it. Second, the relationship of debtor and creditor was thought by the courts to be so personal and

---

[1] At this point it would be well to review our discussion of the rights of assignees to enforce contract obligations. See pp. 303–12.

[2] Legal historians have discovered a form of negotiable note dating from approximately 2100 B.C., and negotiable instruments are known to have existed in early Rome.

private that it was considered improper for a creditor to permit someone else to take his place, especially where creditors had the power to imprison delinquent debtors.

Consequently, little use was made of negotiable instruments during the Middle Ages. As time went on, however, and as trade and commerce expanded, merchants increasingly felt the need for some legal device that would permit the free and easy transfer of money rights. Eventually the law bowed to their demands.

Italian merchants of the fourteenth century made the first major breakthrough by developing a forerunner of our modern bill of exchange. The businessmen of that period needed some means by which a debtor in one country could conveniently and safely pay a creditor in another country without actually transporting the money to the other country and having it converted into foreign currency. They hit on the idea of using middlemen who knew the relative values of foreign currencies and who specialized in exchanging money. Now a debtor could make payment to a money exchanger in his own country, and the exchanger would then correspond with an exchanger representing the creditor in another country. The creditor's exchanger would make payment to the creditor and then, later on, he would settle his account with the debtor's exchanger. These accounts were usually settled at one of the great commercial fairs that were held periodically all over Europe. In many respects these fairs were similar to our modern bank clearing houses.

In carrying out these transactions, the parties used a kind of negotiable instrument. This took the form of a letter addressed by the debtor's exchanger to the creditor's exchanger ordering the latter to pay the creditor a sum of money equal to that which the debtor had deposited with his exchanger. The debtor sent the letter to the creditor, who then presented it to his exchanger for payment. These letters were usually phrased in such a way that the creditor *or his nominee* could receive payment from the exchanger. In other words, the parties were agreeing to the free transferability of the right to receive payment. In time, the practice arose of having the creditor *indorse* the letter to his "nominee," who could then collect from the exchanger. These letters came to be known as "bills of exchange."

Eventually the money exchangers of Europe joined together in larger and more complex organizations, which ultimately evolved into our modern banking institutions. With the advent of banks came another form of negotiable instrument, the "check," which is simply a special type of bill of exchange drawn on a bank. The other principal kind of negotiable instrument—the promissory note—appeared only later.

Most of the early law of negotiable instruments was developed in the special commercial courts (the law merchant) rather than in the common-law courts. Thus it is not surprising that the first case in the reports of the English royal courts involving a bill of exchange occurred in 1602. Since the early common-law judges usually relied on the customs of merchants in deciding disputes over negotiable instruments, the influence of the law merchant was perpetuated. Indeed, by the end of the seventeenth century, most of the rules of the law merchant had been absorbed into the common law. During the eighteenth and nineteenth centuries, a period of widespread litigation in this field of law, the basic principles of negotiable-instruments law became well established.

In the American colonies, the law of negotiable instruments developed in a rather haphazard way. In the early period, most of the states incorporated the English common law into their legal systems and then enlarged upon it by their own decisions. Later on, many of the states enacted statutes on negotiable instruments—statutes that often conflicted with one another. Needless to say, these diverse approaches to the subject resulted in a great deal of chaos and confusion in the law.

By the end of the nineteenth century, lawyers and businessmen in the United States and England realized that something had to be done to make the law uniform, and in both countries the law of negotiable instruments underwent a major codification. In England, Parliament enacted the Bills of Exchange Act in 1882, and in this country the Uniform Negotiable Instruments Law (N.I.L.) was submitted to the state legislatures in 1896.

In 1891, at the prompting of the American Bar Association and several of the state legislatures, a conference had been held to discuss the problem of uniform state legislation in the various areas of commercial law. As a result of this and succeeding conferences, a committee was appointed in 1895 to draft a uniform law of negotiable instruments. The draft prepared by this committee was recommended to the states for adoption in 1896, and, within two years, fourteen states had adopted it; by 1924, the N.I.L. had been enacted, with some variations, by all the states.

Some legal scholars have criticized the speed with which the Uniform Negotiable Instruments Law was drafted and enacted, complaining that many of its provisions should have been framed more carefully and that businessmen and lawyers should have been permitted to respond to the draft before it was submitted to the states. Most experts, however, feel that the N.I.L. has worked reasonably well and has accomplished much of what it was designed to accomplish.

The Uniform Commercial Code, which has recently supplanted the N.I.L. in several jurisdictions, alters some of the N.I.L.'s more controversial sections but makes no substantial change in the law of negotiable instruments.

Since all the states have adopted one or the other of the uniform laws, we shall be mainly concerned with statutes and statutory interpretation in this chapter. But remember that the legal rules governing negotiable instruments have their roots in the law merchant and in the precedents of the common-law courts. Indeed, many judges look to these as guides in interpreting the provisions of the N.I.L.

SECTION 1

NATURE AND REQUISITES
OF NEGOTIABLE INSTRUMENTS

Classification

The N.I.L. identifies three main categories of negotiable instruments: (1) *promissory notes*, (2) *bills of exchange* (or *drafts*, as they are sometimes called), and (3) *checks*.

Promissory Notes

A *promissory note* is a written promise by one person or firm to pay a certain sum of money to another. The person who makes the promise is called the *maker;* the person to whom the note is payable is called the *payee.*

EXAMPLE

> July 1, 1962
> One year from date I promise to pay to the order of JAMES BROWN Five Hundred Dollars ($500.00), with interest at 6%.
> (signed) JOHN SMITH

Here SMITH is the maker and BROWN is the payee.

There are several different kinds of promissory note: A *mortgage note* is a note secured by a mortgage or lien on certain property.[3] A *collateral note* is also secured by property—usually stocks or bonds—which is delivered to the payee to hold until the note has been paid. An *installment note* is a note in which the maker agrees to pay the money in specified installments over a certain period of time. Although these special types of promissory note are often more complex than the one illustrated, their basic format is essentially the same.

Bills of Exchange

A *bill of exchange*, or draft, is a negotiable instrument by which one person or firm orders another to pay a sum of money to a third party. The

---

[3] In other words, the parties agree that the payee shall have the right to claim or hold certain property of the maker until the note has been paid. The maker, or debtor, is said to have given the payee, or creditor, a *mortgage* or *lien* on the property. If the money is not paid, the payee usually may have the property sold and have the proceeds applied to the payment of the debt. In short, the mortgage is given as security for the payment of the note.

person who draws up the instrument and orders payment is called the *drawer;* the person to whom it is addressed and who is ordered to pay is called the *drawee;* and the person to whom payment is to be made is called the *payee.*

EXAMPLE

> New York, N.Y.—July 1, 1962
> Sixty days after sight, pay to the order of First State Bank Five Hundred Dollars $500.00--------
>
> To: BARTHOLEMEW BUYER   (signed) SAMUEL SELLER
> 100 Main Street
> Chicago, Illinois

In this example, SAMUEL SELLER is the drawer, BARTHOLEMEW BUYER is the drawee, and First State Bank is the payee.

As we shall see later, the drawee named on a bill of exchange is not bound to pay the money unless he accepts the instrument. If he does accept it, he becomes known as the *acceptor.* For this reason bills of exchange are sometimes called *acceptances.*

Checks

A *check* is a special form of bill of exchange which, by definition, is always drawn on a bank and is always payable on demand. Again, three original parties are named on the instrument—the drawer, the drawee bank, and the payee.

EXAMPLE

> July 1, 1962
> *Merchants Bank*
> Pay to the order of WILLIAM WORKER
> One hundred dollars $100.00
>   (signed) EDGAR EMPLOYER

Here EDGAR EMPLOYER is the drawer, Merchants Bank the drawee, and WILLIAM WORKER the payee.

In addition to the ordinary check shown in the example, there are certain special types of check: A *cashier's check* is drawn by a bank on itself, usually at the request and for the use of a depositor, who designates the payee. A *bank draft* (similar to a cashier's check) is drawn by one bank on another bank.

Other Terms and Definitions

Quite often the owner of a negotiable instrument will transfer it to someone else by signing it, usually on the back, and then delivering it to the other party. Such a transfer is called a *negotiation.* When the owner writes his name on the instrument he is said to have *indorsed* it, and he is then referred to as an *indorser*. The person to whom it is negotiated is called the *indorsee*.

A person who has possession of a negotiable instrument which is payable to him is called a *holder*. A holder who has given consideration for the negotiable instrument is called a *holder for value*.

We shall discuss these terms and concepts in greater detail later on.

Requirements for Negotiable Instruments

The N.I.L. defines negotiable instruments very strictly and specifies that they must meet the following requirements:

Must Be in Writing

A negotiable instrument must be written, typewritten, printed, or set down in some legible fashion. It may, however, be in any combination of writing or printing.

Must Be Signed

To be negotiable, an instrument must be signed (1) by the drawer (in the case of a check or bill of exchange), or (2) by the maker (in the case of a promissory note).

Usually, the full name of the party is written out. If the identity of the party can be shown, however, initials or even an "x" will suffice. Moreover, the drawer or maker may sign in his representative or official capacity (e.g., "Treasurer of x CORP.") if his identity can be clearly established. A signature may be typed, printed, or stamped—so long as it can be proved that a signature was clearly intended.

As a general rule, a duly authorized representative or agent may sign for the party he represents.[4] He must, however, identify the party for whom he is acting and clearly indicate that he is signing in a representative capacity. Otherwise he alone is responsible for payment.

Must Contain Unconditional Promise or Order to Pay

To qualify as a negotiable instrument, a promissory note must contain a clear, unequivocal promise to pay. This must be more than a mere acknowledgment of a debt, such as an "I.O.U." The promise must be phrased in language that makes it unmistakably clear that the maker is committing himself to pay. For a draft or check to qualify as a negotiable instrument, it must contain an unmistakable order to pay addressed to a clearly designated drawee. The promise or order must be unconditional in nature and must not be subject to the occurrence of some event that may never occur.

In the case that follows, the Supreme Court of Michigan had to construe this provision of the Negotiable Instruments Law and decide whether cer-

---

[4] An *agent* is someone who has legal power to act on behalf of another. The person for whom he acts is called the *principal*. We shall discuss the law of agency in Chapter 14.

tain certificates were negotiable instruments within the meaning of the statute.

FIDELITY & DEPOSIT CO. OF MARYLAND v. ANDREWS et al.

Supreme Court of Michigan, 1928
244 Mich. 159, 221 N.W. 114

► WIEST, J.   During federal control of railroads, and by virtue of an act of Congress, the Pennsylvania Railroad Company, by Walker D. Hines, Director General of Railroads, caused equipment trust certificates [5] to be issued and sold by the Guaranty Trust Company of New York, as trustee. The certificates were for the sum of $1,000 each, and gave the holders an interest in the Pennsylvania Railroad Equipment Trust of 1920. The certificates were payable to bearer or to registered owner. The First Methodist Episcopal Church of Clarion, Pa., purchased two of the certificates, payable to bearer, numbered 35003 and 35004, and, for safe-keeping, placed them in the safe of the postmaster at Clarion. The night of December 27, 1924, the safe was blown open and the certificates stolen. January 12, 1925, defendant Martin purchased the certificates from Aron Rubin, a furrier of New York City. Mr. Martin, through defendant Andrews, sold the certificates to John P. Glendon & Co. of Detroit. The Glendon Company carried an indemnity bond, issued by the Fidelity & Deposit Company of Maryland. The certificates were claimed by the First Methodist Episcopal Church of Clarion, and were surrendered by the Glendon Company. Under its indemnity bond, plaintiff herein paid the Glendon Company $2,101.66, took an assignment of the right of action of that company against defendants Martin and Andrews, brought this suit,[6] and, upon trial before a jury, had verdict and judgment thereon for $2,250.49. Defendants review by writ of error.[7]

It is stated in the brief for defendants that the main issue here is the negotiability of the certificates. In behalf of plaintiff it is claimed that the certificates were non-negotiable, because they evidenced an interest in the trust, payable only from and out of rentals received from a certain lease. The question of negotiability of the certificates is to be determined from the contract they import, and application of the law on that subject in the jurisdiction where the contract was made. The contract under which the

---

[5] These certificates were similar to shares of stock in a corporation, in that they gave the owners an interest in the railroad and made them eligible for dividends. We shall discuss corporate stock in greater detail in Chapter 16.

[6] An indemnity bond is a contract whereby one party (often an insurance company, as in this case) agrees for a consideration to reimburse the other party if he suffers a certain loss. In this case, the insurance company paid Glendon Company for the loss of the bonds when the church reclaimed them. Then the company took an assignment of Glendon's rights to sue the other parties and brought this action to recover what it had paid.

[7] This is one way in which a case is appealed. In effect, it means that the appellate court, after a petition has been made, orders the lower court to transmit the record to it so that it may review the lower-court proceedings and see if any errors were committed.

certificates were issued was made in the state of New York. The New York Negotiable Instrument Law, being of the uniform series, is for all practical purposes, upon the points here involved, like our statute. C.L. 1915, 6042. Both the New York and Michigan statutes provide:

"An instrument, to be negotiable, . . . must contain an unconditional promise or order to pay a certain sum of money; . . . must be payable to order or to bearer."

Do the certificates in suit contain an unconditional promise or order to pay a sum certain in money? The answer is found upon the face of the certificates in the following language:

> Guaranty Trust Company of New York, trustee, under a certain agreement and lease, dated the 15th day of January, A.D. 1920, between Walker D. Hines, Director General of Railroads, of the first part, the Pennsylvania Railroad Company, of the second part, and the Guaranty Trust Company of New York, trustee, of the third part, hereby certifies that the bearer . . . is entitled to an interest of one thousand dollars in the Pennsylvania Railroad Equipment Trust of 1920. The principal amount represented by this certificate is payable to bearer, . . . on the 15th day of January, 1929, at the office of the trustee in the city of New York, and in the meantime dividends will be payable thereon, . . . both principal and dividends being payable in gold, . . . but only from and out of rentals received from a certain lease of railroad equipment by the Guaranty Trust Company of New York, trustee, to the Pennsylvania Railroad Company, made in and by the aforesaid agreement and lease. This certificate is one of an issue of fifty-eight thousand four hundred and twelve certificates, for $1,000 each, . . . all issued under said agreement, under which said railroad equipment and said lease thereof are held by said trustee in trust for the equal benefit of the holders of the interests represented by said certificates to which agreement and lease, filed with trustee at its office in the city of New York, reference is made for a further statement of the rights of the holder hereof thereunder.

Manifestly the certificates were not "unconditional promises or orders to pay sums certain in money." The certificates on their face stated a condition materially affecting payment, and also by apt reference constituted the agreement and lease as essential to a full understanding of the nature and extent of the promise to pay. The certificates state enough of the trust agreement and lease to render them less than unconditional promises to pay sums certain in money, for payment was expressly made contingent upon prospective receipts of rentals by the trustee. Where payment of an obligation is, by its terms made subject to the performance of a lease or receipt of funds from an underlying agreement, the promise is contingent, and, under the Negotiable Instrument Act, the obligation is non-negotiable.

In King Cattle Co. v. Joseph, 158 Minn. 481, 198 N.W. 798, bonds, by reference to a mortgage or deed of trust, made the indenture [8] a part thereof. In passing upon the question of the negotiability of such bonds, the court stated:

---

[8] An indenture is a written document in which two or more people enter into binding obligations to each other.

The mere fact that the bonds were secured by the deed did not change their character or affect their negotiability. They are deprived of negotiability because the deed is expressly made part of them. It is as though its contents were repeated in them. Negotiable paper enters the channels of commerce. It is a medium of exchange in the business world. To circulate freely it must be "a courier without luggage." Here there was "luggage," a trust deed of 89 typewritten pages incorporated in the bonds. . . .

Under the Uniform Negotiable Instrument Law the certificates were, on their face, non-negotiable. The Pennsylvania Railroad Company, in writing, unconditionally guaranteed to the holders of the certificates prompt payment thereof, and defendants contend that such guaranty rendered the certificates an unconditional promise to pay a sum certain in money at a fixed or determinable future time. The guaranty of the railroad company to unconditionally pay was not that of the maker and did not render the non-negotiable trust certificates negotiable.

We think the liability of defendant Andrews was, under the evidence showing his participation in the sale of the certificates and receipt of money thereunder a question for the jury, and the court was not in error in refusing to direct a verdict in his favor.

The judgment is affirmed, with costs to plaintiff.   ◀

COMMENTS AND QUESTIONS

1. Note that this case was decided by a Michigan court applying the law of New York. Why was that? Note also that the statutes of both jurisdictions were the same—an illustration of the benefits to be derived from the passage of uniform laws like the N.I.L.
2. Were these certificates negotiable? If not, why not? What essential ingredient of negotiability was missing?

Must Promise or Order Payment of Sum Certain in Money

A negotiable instrument must provide for payment *in money*. If it promises or orders payment of anything else (e.g., goods or other property), or if it gives the maker or drawee the option of paying in money *or* something else, it is nonnegotiable. If, however, the *holder* of the instrument has the option to demand payment in money if he so wishes, it is still negotiable.

Many instruments include provisions that make it easier for the holder or payee to collect the money that is coming to him. For example, an instrument may authorize the sale of collateral security if the money is not paid on demand. Or it may make the whole amount due and payable immediately if the maker defaults on a payment. This latter provision is known as an *acceleration clause*. If the instrument is otherwise negotiable, such provisions do not make it nonnegotiable.

The amount payable must be definitely and clearly set forth in the instrument; otherwise, there is no way of establishing the instrument's worth. This rule refers only to the principal, however; the mere fact that the amount of interest or collection charges is uncertain does not destroy negotiability. If the amount is written out both in words and in figures and there is a conflict between the two, the written words are usually held to be decisive; if the written words are unclear or ambiguous, the figures are taken as decisive.

In the New Jersey case of *Incitti v. Ferrante et al.*, the court had to decide whether a promissory note payable in Italian currency was a negotiable instrument. The decision contains an interesting discussion of the concept of "money."

INCITTI v. FERRANTE et al.

Court of Common Pleas of New Jersey, 1933
12 N.J. Misc. 840, 175 Atl. 908

▶ DEL MAR, JUDGE. This action was brought by the plaintiff against the defendants upon a promissory note alleged to have been made by the defendants for the sum of "15,400 Italian lires." The complaint does not allege any consideration for the note, and concludes with a prayer for judgment against the defendants for said sum of 15,400 Italian lires, or its equivalent in lawful money of the United States. The note is dated at Hackensack, N.J., and is made payable at the Bank Italia Company, and neither the complaint nor the note sets forth the address of said company, so that the presumption, therefore, is that the note is payable in the state of New Jersey.

Defendants moved to strike out the complaint on the ground that the same does not set forth a cause of action; and in the argument on said motion they contended that the note in question is not negotiable, and that the complaint, therefore, must allege a consideration, which it does not do.

Upon the argument the point made by defendants' counsel was that the note was not made for money, but for a commodity and that, therefore, there is no presumption that it was made upon a legal consideration. In support of this contention, counsel cites Thompson v. Sloan et al., 23 Wend. (N.Y.) 71, 35 Am. Dec. 546.

Whether the note in question is or is not negotiable must be determined by the laws of this state.

The note in question is negotiable in form unless the provision for the payment of the sum named in Italian lire makes it non-negotiable. The Uniform Negotiable Instruments Law of this state provides in title 1, art. 1, subdivision 2, that an instrument to be negotiable must contain an unconditional promise or order to pay a sum certain in money; and in section 6, subd. 5, it is provided that the negotiable character of an instrument is not affected by the fact that it "designates a particular kind of current money in which payment is to be made."

If it had been the intention of the Legislature to provide that a note in order to be negotiable must be payable in lawful money of the United States, or in legal tender, it would have been a simple matter to have used language appropriate for that purpose. The use of the words, "money and current money," indicates that such was not the purpose.

The question arises, What is money? Money is purely a legal institution; it is impossible without law. . . . Money is what the law or custom makes receivable for payments of taxes and debts. "Money by itself is but a mere device. It has value only by law and not by nature. So that a change of convention between those that use it is sufficient to deprive it of its value and of its power to purchase our requirements." Aristotle's *Politics*.

What then does our law provide? The Constitution of the United States, article 1, 8, provides that the "Congress shall have Power . . . to coin Money, regulate the value thereof, and of foreign coin," and under the power vested in it by this section of the Constitution the Congress has from time to time established the value of foreign coins. It is a matter of common knowledge that the foreign coins of various nations such as England, Spain, France, Portugal and Mexico, passed as currency in the United States prior to the civil war. (Sometimes as legal tender under Acts of Congress.) In fact, they constituted at that time, with the exception of the note issues of the state banks, the bulk of the currency then in circulation. The Congress from the earliest times has fixed the values of the various foreign coins by statute. . . .

It is well established that an instrument payable in the money of any country, that is to say in its coins, "such as guineas, ducats, Louis-d'ors, doubloons, crowns or dollars; or in the known currency of a country, as pounds sterling, lires, tournoises, francs, florins, etc., is negotiable, for in all these cases the sum of money is fixed by the par of exchange on the known denomination of the currency with reference to the par," King v. Hamilton (C.C.) 12 F. 478, the material facts of which are similar to those in the case at bar.

The law merchant is international in its character and was developed for the purpose of facilitating trade in commerce between different countries. It seems clear, therefore, that, where a note is made payable in a country in the money or coins of another country, which money or coins have a value fixed by the law or under the authority of the law of the country where the note is payable, and which value can by a simple mathematical calculation be expressed in the value of the lawful money of the latter country, such a note by the rules of the law merchant and under the Uniform Negotiable Instruments Act is negotiable. . . .

In the case of Reisfeld v. Jacobs, 107 Misc. 1, 176 N.Y.S. 223, 224, involving a contract for the purchase of Russian bank notes, it was held that such notes were not money. The court said: "In view of the fact that these notes were issued by a government now defunct, and that the United States at present has no relations with any government in Russia, the court cannot take judicial notice that these notes are backed by the credit of a responsible government, or that they even pass current anywhere as money." The court, therefore, found that the contract in question was a contract for the sale of goods.

A year prior to this decision, however, the same court, in the case of Brown v. Perera, 176 N.Y.S. 215, affirmed an opinion of a referee holding that foreign money is not, in legal contemplation, a legal commodity or article of merchandise, but that it was money, the title to which was acquired by the innocent holder, even though he purchased it from one who had no title. As was said in the former case (Reisfeld v. Jacobs) the opinion in the latter case "concerns the question whether money issued under the authority of a responsible government and used generally for the purpose of convenient transaction is negotiable, and this has no application to the question presented in the case at bar."

The contract sued on here is a contract for the payment of money and not a commodity. It is also a contract for the payment of Italian lire and, therefore, within the purview of the act of 1894, *supra,* under which act the value of this foreign coin in money of the United States is established by the Director of the Mint and proclaimed by the Secretary of the Treasury. This note was made for a sum certain, because a note for any number of Italian lire is only another form of expression for the equivalent in dollars, which equivalent is now established under the authority of the legislation previously referred to. See King v. Hamilton, *supra.*

The motion to strike out the complaint is therefore denied.   ◄

COMMENTS AND QUESTIONS

1. This case illustrates another limitation on what is and what is not "negotiable." How did the court hold? Was the note negotiable?
2. Do you think the result would have been different if this case had been tried during World War II, when this country was at war with Italy?
3. This decision seems to say that an instrument might be negotiable one day and nonnegotiable the next, depending on the stability of a particular foreign government and the convertibility of its currency. Is this a good rule?

Must Be Payable on Demand or a Time Certain to Arrive

To be negotiable, an instrument must be payable either immediately, or at some time in the future that is definitely stated or is to be fixed by some event or condition that is certain to happen. If an instrument fails to state any due date, it is regarded as payable on demand and is considered negotiable.

Occasionally, the payment date depends on some event that is certain to happen but at a time that cannot be predicted with certainty. Under the N.I.L., an instrument bearing such a due date is still negotiable. If it is uncertain that the event will ever occur, however, the instrument is not negotiable. The Uniform Commercial Code changes this rule slightly by providing that the time of payment must be "definite." Therefore, an instrument payable on some condition that is certain to occur but uncertain as to time is not negotiable under the U.C.C.

EXAMPLES

1. A note payable "60 days after my death" is negotiable under the N.I.L. but not under the U.C.C.
2. A note payable "60 days after my marriage" is nonnegotiable under both acts.

In the following case, it was contended that certain promissory notes were not negotiable because they were not payable at a fixed or determinable future time.

STATE BANK OF HALSTAD v. BILSTAD

Supreme Court of Iowa, 1912
162 Iowa 433, 136 N.W. 204

▶ SHERWIN, J. A suit to recover on three promissory notes executed by the defendant and Jon. M. Hetland. Two of the notes were drawn payable to the order of Fred B. Lawrence, and the other to the order of the plaintiff bank. No defense was interposed to the latter note, but counterclaims were pleaded as to the other two. The first question for determination is whether these two notes were negotiable. They both bore the same date, April 23, 1904, but one was due December 1, 1905, and the other December 1, 1907. Both contained the following provision, however: "It is agreed that if crop on Secs. 25 and 26 is below 8 bushels per acre (for 1905 as to one and 1907 as to the other) this note shall be extended one year." The appellant contends that the agreement for an extension of the time of payment did not make the notes non-negotiable, because they would become due in any event, although the exact time could not be determined when they were executed, while the appellee insists that the notes were non-negotiable because they were not due upon a fixed or determinable future time. Although the notes were made in Minnesota and were payable there, it is conceded that their character as to negotiability is to be determined by the law of this state.

Our negotiable instruments act says that an instrument to be negotiable must be payable on demand or at a fixed or determinable future time, and section 3060-a4 undertakes to define what is meant by a determinable future time. . . .

The notes in suit provided for an extension of time for one year on the condition herein named. The time at which they must eventually become due was therefore fixed and certain. The only uncertainty as to the time or fact of payment was whether they should be paid at a particular time in one year, or at the date named in the next year. If the crop of wheat fell below eight bushels per acre in the years named, the payee could not enforce payment until a year later, nor could the maker compel the payee to accept his money sooner than that time. A note, payable on or before a fixed date, has generally been held to be negotiable and is so declared to be by the negotiable instruments act. And we are quite confident that a note made payable at a fixed time, or at an earlier fixed time at the option of the maker, would be negotiable, because there could be no just distinction drawn between such a case and one where the instrument was to be paid on or before. And, in my judgment, the only difference between the supposed case and the case at bar is to be found in the fact that, in the former case, the maker would decide when the note was payable, while in the instant case it was to be determined by a physical fact which was certain to happen; a distinction which cannot be made unless it be said that a question might have arisen as to the fact whether the crop of wheat was more or less than eight bushels per acre. But, even then, no greater difficulty could arise than is often presented in determining whether a negotiable note is, or is not, due when suit is brought thereon. . . .

Section 3060-a4 expressly says that a note that is payable at a determinable future time, or that is payable on or before a fixed period after the occurrence of a specified event, which is certain to happen, is negotiable. These provisions clearly provide for flexibility in fixing the time of payment, provided only that there shall certainly come a time when the note is, by its terms, due. In other words, they recognize the right of the parties to an instrument to contract for their mutual benefit, and say, in effect, that, if the contract made is certainly to be performed at some definite time in the future, its negotiability is not destroyed. A determinable future time, as used in the second clause of the section, can mean nothing else than a time that can be certainly determined after the execution of the note. The contingency which will render a note non-negotiable under the last clause of the section clearly means an event which may or may not happen. A contingency is, in law, an uncertain future event, and as a contingency may never happen, a note payable only upon the happening thereof may never become due. We think this is the meaning of the language used, construed with the other provisions of the section and in the light of former rules. We reach the conclusion that the two notes in question were negotiable, and that the judgment must be reversed because the trial court did not so hold. . . .

Reversed.   ◄

COMMENTS AND QUESTIONS

1. Were these notes negotiable or nonnegotiable? For what reasons?
2. Note that counterclaims were made by the maker (i.e., the defendant). Apparently, the trial court held the notes to be nonnegotiable and permitted the maker to set up the counterclaims as a defense to avoid payment. If, however, the notes were negotiable, there was a good chance that such defense could not be used—hence the importance of determining negotiability. This point will be discussed in more detail later in the chapter (see pp. 490–506).

Must Be Payable to Order or Bearer

The maker or drawer of a negotiable instrument must indicate in some fashion that he is willing to have the instrument circulate freely after issue. Otherwise the instrument is not negotiable. This requirement is met by including the words "pay to the order of x" or "pay to x or order" or similar words that show a willingness to have x negotiate the instrument to another person who may himself demand payment.

Another way of creating negotiability is to make the instrument payable to *bearer,* or to use some other phraseology indicating a willingness to have the instrument pass freely from holder to holder. When an instrument that is otherwise negotiable is made payable to "cash," or when some other term is used that does not designate any specific person or organization as the payee, it is payable to bearer; the theory is that a negotiable instrument should be capable of being negotiated, and, if no one can indorse it, it should be negotiable without indorsement.

Sometimes the maker will name a fictitious or nonexistent person as payee, with no intention that the instrument will actually be payable to the person named. Under the N.I.L. such an instrument is deemed payable to bearer, since there is no one who can negotiate it. Under the Uniform Commercial Code, however, such an instrument is not considered payable to bearer but *is* payable to the order of the fictitious or nonexistent payee so long as it is indorsed in his name.

EXAMPLE

A treasurer of a company misappropriates company funds by making out a paycheck payable to P, who, to the treasurer's knowledge, either does not exist or, if he does exist, is not intended to receive the check. Under the N.I.L., such a check is payable to bearer and is freely transferable without indorsement. Under the U.C.C. it is payable to the order of P and must be indorsed (i.e., forged in his name, presumably by the treasurer or someone in league with him) before it may be negotiated.

The important thing to remember is that, in order to be negotiable, an instrument must be payable either (1) to the order of some specific person or (2) to the bearer. As we shall see shortly, it is essential to differentiate between these two types of instrument because an instrument payable to order must be negotiated by indorsement and delivery, whereas an instrument payable to bearer may be negotiated by delivery alone, without indorsement.

A good discussion of these points occurs in the following Kentucky case.

WETTLAUFER v. BAXTER

Court of Appeals of Kentucky, 1910
137 Ky. 362, 125 S.W. 741

► Action by the holder against the payee-indorser of the following note:

New York, N.Y. July 3, 1905

January 15, 1906, after date we promise to pay to Newton J. Baxter, two hundred fifty dollars ($250.00) at 58 Carroll St., Buffalo, N.Y.

Buffalo Carriage Top Company

Baxter wrote his name on the back of the note and discounted [9] it with Wettlaufer. The note was dishonored on presentment.[10] Due notice was sent to Baxter. Wettlaufer sued Baxter. Demurrer to the petition. Sustained. Appeal.

CARROLL, J. . . . The questions involved in the case are: Was the note before its indorsement by Baxter a negotiable instrument within the meaning of the negotiable instrument act? Or, if not, did Baxter, by signing

---

[9] This means that he negotiated it to Wettlaufer, who paid him less than the face amount for it. The deduction from the full amount is considered to be interest taken in advance. In this case, for example, the $250 note might have been discounted for $230, with the $20 being the advance payment of interest to Wettlaufer. Of course, Wettlaufer must collect the $250 from the maker of the note in order to receive the interest.

[10] This means that when Wettlaufer asked the maker to pay the note, the maker refused or was unable to do so. This subject will be discussed in detail later in the chapter (see pp. 478–88).

his name on the back of the note and selling and delivering it before maturity to Wettlaufer, convert it into a negotiable note and make all the parties to it subject to the negotiable instrument act the same as if it had been a negotiable note in the first instance?

The contention of counsel for Baxter is that the note was not a negotiable instrument. On the other hand, the contention for Wettlaufer is that, although the note may not have been negotiable when first executed and delivered, Baxter by his indorsement converted it into a negotiable note, and that, treating it as such, the liability of Baxter and the other parties must be controlled by the negotiable instrument act.

In considering the questions involved, we will for convenience refer to the negotiable instrument act adopted in this state. The sections of the act pertinent are:

"3720B. Section 1. An instrument to be negotiated must conform to the following requirements: (4) Must be payable to the order of a specified person or to bearer."

For the purpose then of ascertaining what bills and notes it was intended should be negotiable within the meaning of this act, we may with propriety inquire what words were generally considered necessary to make a note or bill negotiable before this act went into effect, with a view of noting what change if any was made in this particular. In an article in 7 Cyc., page 606, by a well-known writer on commercial paper, it is said:

> "The usual form of negotiable paper is a provision for payment to 'order' or 'bearer.' These or similar words are in general necessary to its negotiability and are often required by statute, but a note which is nonnegotiable for want of such words is still a valid note and may be declared on as such. Bills payable to bearer were formerly held to be nonnegotiable, as being without words of transfer, but they are now recognized as negotiable and transferable by delivery. Making the instrument payable 'to the order of' a person named or 'bearer' is the same in effect as to bearer. Without words of negotiability purchasers take the bill or note subject to all defenses which were available between the original parties; and if it was originally non-negotiable, as against the original parties, it will not be rendered negotiable by subsequent transfer in negotiable form."

. . . This note in our opinion, which was payable to Baxter alone, and did not contain the words "to order" or "bearer," was not a negotiable instrument. These words by section 1 and 184 are indispensable to make the paper a negotiable instrument within the meaning of the act.

But the argument is further made that as Baxter indorsed the note in blank—that is, signed his name on the back of it without any other words—he thereby converted the note into a negotiable instrument. It is true that section 9 of the act provides that "the instrument is payable to bearer . . . when the only or last indorsement is an indorsement in blank"; but this does not mean that an indorsement in blank converts a note non-negotiable on its face and by its terms into a negotiable note. . . .

In our opinion section 9 was merely intended to describe or designate the conditions under which a note negotiable on its face might become payable to bearer, and was not intended to apply to a note not on its face or by its terms negotiable.

Having this view of the matter, Baxter should be treated under our statute as merely the assignor of a non-negotiable note. *The judgment is affirmed.*   ◄

COMMENTS AND QUESTIONS

1. Summarize the court's decision. What happened in the lower court?
2. This case illustrates the very important point that the negotiability of an instrument is determined by its original form and not by subsequent indorsements. It also emphasizes the strict requirement that a negotiable instrument must be payable to the order of a specified person or bearer.

Importance of Negotiability

Why, you may ask, all this concern about whether or not an instrument is negotiable? The answer is very simple: If an instrument is *not* negotiable, its transfer is governed by the ordinary rules of contract law dealing with the assignment of rights to receive money (see Chapter 11, Section 7). You will recall that the general rule is that if the person obligated to pay has a good defense against the assignor of the right, he may use that defense to avoid paying the assignee.

EXAMPLE

As a result of PAYEE's fraudulent representation, MAKER buys a lawnmower from PAYEE and gives him a *non*-negotiable promissory note for $20. PAYEE transfers the note to INNOCENT, who presents it to MAKER for payment. Since MAKER has a good defense (i.e., fraud) against PAYEE, he may refuse to pay INNOCENT, according to the general rules of contract law governing assignment of rights.

On the other hand, if an instrument is *negotiable,* the general rules of contract law do not always apply. Provided the transferee of a negotiable instrument is a holder for value (see page 451) and receives the instrument in good faith, unaware of any defenses, he may receive better rights than would the ordinary assignee of a contract right. In other words, he may be able to demand payment of the instrument even though the person obligated to perform may have a good defense against the person who transferred the instrument to him.

EXAMPLE

If, in the example immediately preceding, MAKER had given a *negotiable* promissory note to PAYEE and PAYEE had transferred it to INNOCENT, it is very likely that INNOCENT could collect from MAKER *despite* the defense of fraud which MAKER could have used to avoid paying PAYEE.

The purpose of this rule is to encourage the transfer of negotiable instruments and thus to promote business activity. If defenses could be used to avoid payment as in the case of an ordinary assignment of contract rights, then a transferee would have to check very carefully and very cautiously before accepting any instrument. Such constraint would serve to curtail credit and restrict economic intercourse. We shall discuss this subject in some detail in Section 4 of this chapter.

SECTION 2

TRANSFER OF NEGOTIABLE INSTRUMENTS AND LIABILITY OF PARTIES

Negotiation and Transfer of Negotiable Instruments

Initial Delivery

The N.I.L. provides that until a negotiable instrument has been issued —that is, until it has been put into circulation—it is incomplete and revocable. The maker of a promissory note, or the drawer of a bill of exchange or check, is said to have issued the instrument when he delivers it to another with the intention of making it effective. Sometimes it is hard to say whether or not such a delivery has actually been made. Take, for example, the case that follows:

In re MARTENS' ESTATE

Supreme Court of Iowa, 1939
226 Iowa 162, 283 N.W. 885

▶ MILLER, JUSTICE.   Appellant, Mabel Martens Bonk, filed a claim, based on a note for $1,500, against the administrator of this estate. The claim being denied, a petition was filed to secure the allowance thereof, to which the administrator filed an answer in the form of a general denial. Various issues were presented by the evidence. We deem it necessary to consider only one of them, namely, whether or not the action of the trial court, in denying appellant's claim, was proper because of failure to establish that the note was delivered during the lifetime of the deceased.

At the trial, appellant testified that she is the daughter of the deceased. She identified Exhibit A as a note in the handwriting of her mother, dated March 1, 1930, promising to pay appellant $1,500 on December 1, 1930, signed by the decedent. On the back of the note was the endorsement: "This money is coming to her for teaching $1,000 and $500 is what the rest got also. Mother."

The decedent died January 2, 1936. The administrator qualified on

March 1, 1936. Appellant testified that, about March 11, 1936, in examining the contents of her mother's safe, she discovered an envelope on which, in her mother's handwriting, was the notation: "Please give this to S. Fisher in case of death. Mabel Martens from Mother"; she delivered the envelope to said Simon Fisher at his law office shortly after she discovered it; Fisher opened the envelope, which was sealed, in her presence and in the presence of the administrator; the note, Exhibit A, was found in the envelope, her mother had told her that, in case of death, there was a letter for her, but she knew nothing of any note; she found the envelope after the administrator had made an examination of the contents of the safe and had not discovered it; she had loaned her parents $1,000 from time to time out of money earned teaching school; her brothers, and sisters each had received $500 when they were married; she married subsequent to March 1, 1930, and did not receive her $500.

Simon Fisher testified that he first saw the envelope and the note after the death of the decedent; he opened the envelope in the presence of the appellant and the administrator; in 1930 appellant agreed to accept a note from her mother in satisfaction of $1,500 owed by her father's estate, which was not paid because of insufficient funds; the decedent told him she had executed a note in favor of appellant for $1,500 and she had placed it in a box or safe at home and for him to get it and give it to appellant any time he heard of her death; he told her to deliver it to him or leave it with him, and if she wanted to, to turn it over to appellant.

Apparently the trial court held that the claim should be denied because the record failed to establish legal delivery of the note, which formed the basis of appellant's claim. *We hold that there was no error in this decision.*

Section 9476 of the Code provides that every contract on a negotiable instrument is incomplete and revocable until delivery of the instrument for the purpose of giving effect thereto. This was the common law rule. . . .

Obviously, the note here sued upon could not be made the basis of a valid claim against the estate unless there was a legal delivery of the same, during the lifetime of the decedent. Our decisions, relative to analogous situations, are reviewed in the recent case of Orris v. Whipple, 280 N.W. 617, 623, wherein we state:

> "All there is to show delivery in the case is that the deed was prepared and executed by Miss Aken; that she told others that she wanted the plaintiffs to have the property and that she had prepared papers so providing. She put the deeds in her safety deposit box and retained the key. We do not think these admitted facts show a legal delivery of the deed in question." ◄

COMMENTS AND QUESTIONS

1. For an instrument to be negotiable, it must be put into circulation by being delivered to someone else. Was there any such delivery in this case?

2. Suppose, instead, that the deceased had given the envelope contain-

ing the note to her attorney, during her lifetime, with instructions to hand it over to the plaintiff in the event of death. Would the result have been different?

3. Do you feel that the court's construction of this provision of the N.I.L. was rather strict?

Negotiation in General

Once a negotiable instrument has been issued, it may be negotiated, or transferred, from one holder to another until it is presented for payment. The manner in which an instrument is negotiated differs according to whether it is payable to the order of a given person or to the bearer of the instrument. Generally speaking, if it is payable to order, it must be indorsed by the person to whom it is payable and delivered to the next holder. If it is payable to bearer, it may be negotiated by delivery alone, without indorsement.

Negotiation of Order Instruments

To negotiate an instrument payable to his order, a holder must use one of the following kinds of indorsement: (1) special, (2) blank, (3) restrictive, or (4) conditional.

SPECIAL INDORSEMENT. A *special indorsement* makes the instrument payable to the order of the indorsee and requires that he, in turn, indorse it if he wishes to negotiate it further.

EXAMPLE

TOM BROWN, the holder of a promissory note payable to his order, indorses it as follows and delivers it to ROBERT JONES.

> Pay to the order
> of ROBERT JONES
> (signed) TOM BROWN

This special indorsement means that the instrument is now payable to the order of ROBERT JONES, who must indorse it himself before he can negotiate it further.

BLANK INDORSEMENT. A *blank indorsement* occurs when the party to whom the instrument is payable merely signs his name, without making the instrument payable to another person. Such an indorsement makes the instrument payable to bearer; it may be transferred from one holder to another without further indorsement.

EXAMPLE

A check payable to ALBERT JOHNSON is indorsed by him as follows and is then delivered to JAMES FREEMAN.

> (signed) ALBERT JOHNSON

Since the check is now payable to bearer, FREEMAN may negotiate it further by merely delivering it to another person, who, in turn, may deliver it to yet another. The check may be negotiated any number of times until it is finally presented to the bank for payment.

RESTRICTIVE INDORSEMENT. With either a special or a blank indorsement, an instrument may be negotiated further before it is presented for payment. If, however, the holder wishes to restrict further negotiation of the instrument, he may use a so-called *restrictive indorsement*. With this indorsement, the indorsee is usually asked to collect the proceeds of the instrument for a specific purpose and is prohibited from negotiating it further. The restrictive indorsement is most commonly used when a holder deposits a check in a bank.

EXAMPLE

PETER COOPER indorses a check, drawn on Y NATIONAL BANK, payable to his order as follows; he then delivers the check to X NATIONAL BANK, where he maintains an account.

> For Deposit Only
> (signed) PETER COOPER

By indorsing the check in this manner, COOPER is ordering X BANK to collect the amount of the check from Y BANK, and to deposit that amount in his account. He does not want X BANK to negotiate or transfer the instrument except for that purpose.

CONDITIONAL INDORSEMENT. In rare cases, an indorser will, by placing a condition on his indorsement, make the negotiation of the instrument subject to some contingency. The legal effect of such an indorsement is limited, however, since the maker or the drawee of the instrument may lawfully pay any subsequent holder who presents the instrument for payment. But the person who collects the money may be forced to pay it back to the conditional indorser if the condition is not fulfilled.

EXAMPLE

A promissory note payable to HAROLD HOMEOWNER is indorsed by him as follows and is then delivered to CONRAD CONTRACTOR

> Pay to the order of
> CONRAD CONTRACTOR if
> and when he completes
> work on my garage.
> (signed) HAROLD HOMEOWNER

CONTRACTOR negotiates the note to X, who may collect the money due on the note from the maker. Once the maker has paid the money, he has no further responsibility. If CONTRACTOR fails to complete the work on the garage, however, HOMEOWNER may recover the amount of the note from X. Then X's only recourse is against CONTRACTOR.

Qualified Indorsements

Anyone who indorses a negotiable instrument without qualification commits himself to pay the instrument if the maker or drawee fails to do so and if the holder then demands payment from the indorser.[11] An indorser who does not wish to make this commitment may use a *qualified*

---

[11] This procedure will be discussed in Section 3.

indorsement. Any type of indorsement, except a restrictive one, may be qualified simply by adding the phrase "without recourse" or any other words that signify an intention not to be liable for payment in the event of a default by the maker or drawee.

EXAMPLES

1. Pay to JOHN JONES, Without Recourse
                            (signed) IVAN INDORSER
2. Without Recourse
         (signed) IVAN INDORSER

If no words of qualification are added, the indorsement is called an *unqualified indorsement.*

Negotiation of Bearer Instruments

A negotiable instrument is deemed payable to bearer when (1) it is originally made payable in that manner, or (2) when the last indorsement on the instrument is a blank indorsement. The latter rule holds good even though the instrument was originally made payable to the order of a specific person. Bearer instruments, as these are called, may be negotiated by delivery alone and need no further indorsement.

Sometimes, however, an instrument that was originally made payable to bearer is specially indorsed by the holder. The N.I.L. provides that, despite the indorsement, the instrument remains freely negotiable by delivery alone. The Uniform Commercial Code, however, provides that such an indorsement changes the instrument from a bearer instrument to an order instrument, and that it may not be negotiated further without the indorsement of the special indorsee.

EXAMPLE

HAROLD HART holds a note payable to bearer. He indorses it as follows and delivers it to WILLIAM WEBSTER.

> Pay to the order of
> WILLIAM WEBSTER
> (signed) HAROLD HART

Under the N.I.L., such an indorsement would not preclude WEBSTER from negotiating the note to x without further indorsement. Under the U.C.C., however, the instrument is now payable to WEBSTER's order, and he must indorse it if he wishes to negotiate it to x.

Transfer by Mere Assignment

Occasionally, an instrument payable to the order of a given person is transferred without the proper indorsement. The law treats this action as an assignment rather than as a negotiation, but it gives the transferee the right to demand that the transferor indorse the instrument properly; at that point, the transferee becomes a holder by a proper negotiation. This is a matter of some importance, since the time at which a person becomes a holder may have a bearing on whether he is a holder in due course; but more on this later (see Section 4).

In the case that follows, the transferee demanded an indorsement from the transferor, but an argument arose over what kind of indorsement she was entitled to.

SIMPSON v. FIRST NATIONAL BANK OF ROSEBURG

Supreme Court of Oregon, 1919
94 Ore. 147, 185 Pac. 913

► One Josephson borrowed $1,000 from the defendant bank and gave a promissory note leaving the payee blank. The proceeds of the loan were paid to Josephson out of the account of the plaintiff Grace Simpson a depositor, who had consented to let the bank loan money for her. After debiting her account, the bank delivered the note to the plaintiff who, a short time later, filled in the name of the bank as payee. The maker Josephson became bankrupt and defaulted on the note and the plaintiff brought an action against the bank on the theory that it was obligated to indorse the note to her as an unqualified indorser and thereby was liable to her for payment on the default of the maker.

HARRIS, J. . . . Inasmuch as the statute in express terms vests the transferee with the legal title and then declares that, in addition to acquiring all the title of the transferor, the transferee acquires "the right to have the indorsement of the transferor," it necessarily follows that this additional right is granted for the purpose of accomplishing some result besides the mere transfer of the title; and, since the only other reasonably assignable purposes relate to the negotiability of the paper and to the rights arising out of the contract of indorsement, it follows as another necessary conclusion that at least one of the purposes of the statute in granting the right to the indorsement was to preserve the negotiability of the paper. All will probably concede that one of the purposes was to preserve negotiability; but there may be room for debate as to whether the transferee can call for an unqualified indorsement, and thus secure the most complete rights which an indorsement can create. The next inquiry brings us to a discussion of the kind of indorsement which the transferee can call upon the transferor to make.

The statute, section 5866, names five species of indorsement: special, blank, restrictive, qualified, and conditional. For convenience, indorsements may be referred to as qualified or unqualified, and we shall confine the discussion to a consideration of whether the transferee is entitled to an unqualified indorsement, or whether he must be satisfied with a qualified indorsement. The essential difference between a qualified and unqualified indorsement is found in the extent of the liability imposed by the contract created by the indorsement. Sections 5898 and 5899, L.O.L. A qualified indorsement constitutes the indorser a mere assignor of the title to the instrument, although section 5871, L.O.L., declares that "such an indorsement does not impair the negotiable character of the instrument." If the purpose of the statute is merely to prevent the paper from permanently losing its negotiability, then that purpose is fully accomplished by a qualified indorsement. But it must be remembered that the statute does not specify the kind of indorsement. It must also be remembered that an unqualified indorsement is the one most used in the commercial world and the one which is generally expected by the transferee unless the parties have agreed to the contrary.

If an unqualified indorsement may be considered as containing within it the whole sum of the rights capable of being given by the contract which results from an indorsement, then a qualified indorsement must be deemed to confer only a portion of these rights. One embraces the whole sum; the other represents only a part of that sum. The statute gives the right to an indorsement without saying whether it shall be the whole sum or only a part; and therefore, as in the case of a contract, when the statute gives the right to an indorsement without naming the species, the law will imply an agreement for the whole sum, rather than for only a part of the rights capable of being conferred by an indorsement, and this implication will prevail unless the party claiming in the contrary submits sufficient evidence to sustain his claim. . . .

We think therefore that section 5882 gives to the transferee the right to an unqualified indorsement unless the parties agreed that the indorsement should be qualified.

According to the amended complaint, the maker of the note authorized the bank to fill the blank, and the inference is that both the maker and the bank intended that the blank should be so filled with the name of the bank, for the pleading declares that "it was intended . . . to insert the name of the defendant." The note should have been filled pursuant to the authority so given and in accordance with the intention so entertained. When the bank delivered the note to the plaintiff, it knew that she could not compel the maker to pay the note unless the name of the bank appeared as payee in the note; and hence, in these circumstances equity will hold that to be done which ought to be done, and direct the note to be completed in conformity with the intention of the original parties. . . . Treating the note as one made payable to the order of the bank and treating the note as having been in that condition at the time of the transfer, the plaintiff would then, by force of section 5882, be entitled to the indorsement of the bank, and, moreover, she would be entitled to the unqualified indorsement unless there was an agreement to the contrary. . . . ◄

COMMENTS AND QUESTIONS
1. What was the decision of the court here? Do you agree with it?
2. Do you feel that it was the bank's intention to guarantee payment of this note as an indorser? Or was the bank merely acting as the plaintiff's agent in making the loan for her?

Liability of Parties to Negotiable Instruments

Liability in General

There are two principal kinds of liability on a negotiable instrument: *primary* and *secondary*. A party is said to have primary liability when he is bound absolutely to pay the instrument. But a party has secondary liability if he is required to pay the instrument *only* in the event that it is dishonored [12] by the person who is first asked to pay.

Parties with Primary Liability

MAKER OF PROMISSORY NOTE. When a maker executes and issues a promissory note, he becomes unconditionally liable for its payment when it comes due, assuming, of course, that he does not have a valid defense. (More on defenses in Section 4.) This liability persists so long as the instrument is in circulation (even if the due date for payment has passed) until at last the statute of limitations bars an action on it. By issuing a note, the maker not only binds himself to pay it but guarantees that the payee exists and that he has proper legal capacity to indorse the instrument.

ACCEPTOR OF BILL OF EXCHANGE. When a bill of exchange is first drawn and issued, no one has primary liability for its payment. Although it is drawn on the drawee, he has no absolute obligation to pay it. In some cases, however, the holder of a bill of exchange may ask the drawee to "accept" the bill—in other words, to agree to pay it. If the drawee does accept it, he becomes known as the acceptor, and by this act he assumes primary liability for payment of the bill.

Parties with Secondary Liability

UNQUALIFIED INDORSERS. By indorsing an instrument unqualifiedly, an indorser assumes a legal obligation to pay the instrument himself in the event that it is properly presented for payment, is dishonored by nonpayment or nonacceptance, and proper notice is given to him. (What constitutes proper presentment, dishonor, and proper notice will be explained in Section 3.) Every unqualified indorser incurs this secondary liability; if such an indorser is forced to pay, however, he in turn may collect in the same way from any unqualified indorser who indorsed the instrument before him.

EXAMPLE

MAKER gives PAYEE a negotiable promissory note for $50. PAYEE indorses it and delivers it to BLACK, who in turn indorses it and delivers it to GREEN, who in turn indorses it and delivers it to WHITE, as follows:

> Pay to the order of BLACK
> (signed) PAYEE
> Pay to the order of GREEN
> (signed) BLACK
> Pay to the order of WHITE
> (signed) GREEN

WHITE presents the note to MAKER when it comes due and MAKER refuses to pay. WHITE may then notify GREEN and collect the $50 from

---

[12] As we shall see later, an instrument is said to be dishonored when it is properly presented by the holder for payment and payment is refused, or, as sometimes happens with bills of exchange, when it is presented for acceptance and the drawee refuses to accept it.

him because of GREEN's secondary liability as an indorser. GREEN may
then collect from BLACK, who in turn may collect from PAYEE (assuming
proper notice has been given). In other words, all three indorsers may
be secondarily liable on the instrument.

An unqualified indorser also makes certain warranties or guarantees
to the indorsee and to other parties who may become holders of the instrument later on. These warranties are as follows: (1) that the instrument is
genuine; (2) that the indorser has good title to it; and (3) that all parties
who signed or indorsed the instrument before he did were legally competent to act. If these requisites are not met, the unqualified indorser is
liable for any damages that may result.

The nature and extent of an unqualified indorser's liability is the subject of the following North Carolina case.

WACHOVIA BANK & TRUST CO. v. CRAFTON

Supreme Court of North Carolina, 1921
181 N.C. 404, 107 S.E. 316

► Civil action tried before his honor, B. F. LONG, judge, and a jury at
December term, 1920, of the superior court of Buncombe county.

The action is brought by an indorsee and holder in due course of a
promissory note given by one J. M. Carver to J. W. Crafton, defendant,
for money won by defendant in a game of cards, and indorsed by the defendant, the payee of the note in due course and for value to plaintiff bank.
There was denial of liability, the defendant, the indorser, alleging that the
note in question was for an amount won in a gambling transaction. The
jury rendered the following verdict.

1. Did the defendant, Crafton, indorse the note declared on for $700,
February 18, 1919, due April 8, 1919, as alleged in the complaint and before
its maturity? Answer: Yes.
2. Did the plaintiff discount and pay $690 for the note to W. E. Shuford,
in regular course, without notice that it was for gambling debt, and before
maturity, as alleged by plaintiff? Answer: Yes.
3. Was the note executed by J. M. Carver for a gambling debt to J. W.
Crafton? Answer: Yes.

On the verdict, there was judgment that defendant go without day,[13]
and plaintiff appeals.

HOKE, J. Our statute applicable to the note in question, C.S. 2142,
renders this and all notes and contracts in like cases void, and it is urged
in support of his honor's ruling that, this being true, no action thereon
can be sustained. The position as stated is undoubtedly the law in this
jurisdiction, and is in accord with well-considered authorities elsewhere. . . .

---

[13] "Without day," or "sine die," means that no future date is set for further hearings,
and the defendant is free of all the plaintiff's claims.

This principle, however, is allowed to prevail only where the action is on the note to enforce its obligations, and does not affect or extend to suits by an innocent indorsee for value and holder in due course against the indorser on his contract of indorsement. It is very generally held, uniformly, as far as examined, that this contract of indorsement is a substantive contract, separable and independent of the instrument on which it appears, and where it had been made without qualification, and for value, it guarantees to a holder in due course,[14] among other things, that the instrument, at the time of the indorsement, is a valid and subsisting obligation. It is so expressly provided in our statutes on negotiable instruments . . . and the statute in this respect as in so many of its other features, is but a codification of the general principles of this branch of the mercantile law, as established, in the better considered decisions on the subject. . . .

In Norton on Bills and Notes, it is said that "Every indorser who indorses without qualification warrants to his indorsee and to all subsequent holders," among other things, "that the bill or note is a valid and subsisting obligation."

In applying these principles, the cases hold that, on breach of the contract of indorsement, a recovery by a holder in due course will be sustained against the indorser, though the instrument is rendered void by the statute law.

In the citation to Calvert, Daniel on Negotiable Instruments, Sec. 673, the author . . . quotes from an English case in which Lee, C. J., in denying recovery on the note void for gaming, said: "The plaintiff is not without remedy, for he may sue the indorser on his indorsement." The law which renders these contracts void was enacted for the suppression of gambling, but it would tend rather to encourage the vice if a successful gambler could procure the value of such a note on his indorsement and protect himself from the obligation so incurred by pleading his own wrongdoing. On both reason and authority, therefore, the defendant should be held liable for breach of his own contract of indorsement, and, under the facts established by the verdict, there should be judgment for plaintiff.

Reversed.   ◄

COMMENTS AND QUESTIONS

1. The note in question was given for a gambling debt and was apparently indorsed by the payee, Crafton, to one Shuford, who in turn indorsed it to the plaintiff Wachovia Bank, which brought suit against Crafton on his indorsement. If Crafton had kept the note and presented it to the maker himself, could he have collected?

2. Note the special verdict rendered by the jury in the lower court. Certain specific questions were answered and then judgment was entered on the basis of the answers. For whom?

3. Why did the appellate court reverse the decision? What rule can you formulate from this case?

---

[14] A holder in due course, simply defined, is an innocent holder for value who takes the instrument before its maturity date. We will discuss this point in greater detail in Section 4.

QUALIFIED INDORSERS. As we mentioned earlier, a qualified indorser, by including such words as "without recourse" in his indorsement, relieves himself of the secondary liability to pay if the instrument is subsequently dishonored. A qualified indorsement, however, carries with it the same warranties to the indorsee and to subsequent holders as does an unqualified indorsement—namely, (1) that the instrument is genuine; (2) that the indorser has good title to it; and (3) that all prior parties were legally competent. In addition, a qualified indorser warrants (4) that he has no knowledge of any fact that might impair the validity of the instrument or render it valueless. If his warranties are false, he is liable for damages. A qualified indorser who wishes to avoid his liability under these warranties must include the words "without warranties" in addition to "without recourse" in his indorsement.

The nature of a qualified indorser's liability is discussed at some length in the following case:

LEEKLEY v. SHORT et al.

Supreme Court of Iowa, 1933
216 Iowa 376, 249 N.W. 363

▶ ANDERSON, JUSTICE. This appeal involved only issues between the plaintiff appellant, Eleanor H. Leekley, and the defendant-appellee Ella B. Ward. A demurrer or a motion to dismiss plaintiff's petition was sustained. The plaintiff refusing to plead over and electing to stand on her petition, final judgment was entered, dismissing the petition with costs. From such judgment this appeal is prosecuted.

Division 1 of plaintiff's petition is in the ordinary form of a suit in foreclosure,[15] and alleges that on the 5th day of June, 1931, the defendants I. E. and Erma Short executed and delivered to Ella B. Ward a promissory note for $10,000 due March 1, 1936; that said note was secured by mortgage upon 270 acres of farm land in Butler county, Iowa; said mortgage also pledging the rents, issues, and profits arising from said real estate; that on or about the 1st day of August, 1931, the said plaintiff purchased from the said Ella B. Ward the said note and mortgage and paid therefor in property reasonably worth $10,000, and $208 in cash. The said Ella B. Ward indorsing the said note as follows: "Without recourse on me pay to the order of _____." At the same time the said Ella B. Ward executed a written assignment to the said plaintiff, assigning the said note and mortgage; said written assignment being made "without recourse." Subsequent to the execution and delivery of the said note and mortgage and the assignment thereof, the said I. E. and Erma Short transferred the title of the real estate involved to the Iowa Auto Market. That the semi-annual installment of interest and the taxes due September 1, 1931, had become delinquent and remained unpaid; that the makers of said note and mort-

---

[15] This is the process by which the holder of a mortgage tries to force the mortgagor to pay by selling the mortgaged property. It may not be maintained unless the mortgagee fails to keep up his payments.

gage and the title holder of the real estate had failed to keep the property insured for the sum of $4,000 as provided in said mortgage, and by reason of said delinquencies, the plaintiff elected to declare the whole amount of said mortgage and note due and payable.[16] The petition further alleges that the said real estate is not worth the sum of $10,000 and is not worth more than $6,500; that the crop raised upon the premises during the year of 1931 and belonging to the landlord, or title holder, consists of 500 bushels of corn, and the rent of the pasture land for the same period amounts to $200; that the buildings and fences are in poor repair and the property will not sell at sheriff's sale for more than $6,500; that the defendants I. E. and Erma Short are insolvent and were insolvent at the time the note and mortgage were executed.

Division 2 of plaintiff's petition restates the facts contained in Division 1 and in addition thereto states that the said Ella B. Ward knew at the time she indorsed said note and assigned said mortgage to plaintiff that the Shorts were insolvent and that the note could not be collected from them, and that she further knew that the real estate was not of the value of $10,000 and was of much less value; that plaintiff relied upon the warranties provided by law that Ella B. Ward, transferring the negotiable instrument by delivery or qualified indorsement, had no knowledge of any fact that would impair the validity of the instrument or render it valueless.

Plaintiff prays for the appointment of a receiver to take charge of the real estate; asks judgment against I. E. and Erma Short and Ella B. Ward for the amount due upon said note and mortgage, and statutory attorney fees, interest, and costs and asks that said mortgage be foreclosed as by law provided.

To this petition the defendant Ella B. Ward filed a motion to dismiss upon the following grounds: (1) that the petition shows upon its face that plaintiff has no cause of action against this defendant; (2) that this defendant indorsed the note declared upon "without recourse," and assigned the mortgage securing the same "without recourse"; (3) that the petition shows that this defendant did not breach any implied or statutory warranty in that the petition fails to allege that the note is invalid or that the note is valueless, but, on the contrary, alleges that it is valuable. . . .

It will be noticed that no fraud is charged in the petition and the only proposition relied upon for reversal is the construction to be put upon section 9525 (65, N.I.L.) of the 1931 Code, which section is as follows:

"Sec. 9525. Every person negotiating an instrument by delivery or by a qualified indorsement, warrants—

1. That the instrument is genuine and in all respects what it purports to be;
2. That he has a good title to it;

---

[16] It is commonly provided in mortgages that if the mortgagor fails to keep up his payments, the mortgagee may declare the entire principal due and payable and sue for the whole amount.

3. That all prior parties had capacity to contract;
4. That he has no knowledge of any fact which would impair the validity of the instrument or render it valueless.

But when the negotiation is by delivery only, the warranty extends in favor of no holder other than the immediate transferee."

The appellant relies upon subdivision 4 of the above-quoted section, and her claim is that even though a note is transferred by a qualified indorsement, if the indorser knew that the note was of no value and that the person could not collect it, such indorser thereby perpetrated fraud upon the purchaser and obtained the money upon false pretense. The appellant contends in argument that the appellee knew she was selling a worthless note to the plaintiff, and she cannot limit plaintiff's recovery against fraud by a qualified indorsement of the note. The plaintiff's petition is a complete answer to the contention. The petition alleges that this particular note was not worth more than $6,500 and "will not sell at sheriff's sale for an amount in excess of $6,500.00." The conclusion necessarily follows that the note was not valueless and that the defendant had "no knowledge of any fact which would impair the validity of the instrument or render it valueless." It also follows that there was no breach of an implied warranty that the note was not "valueless." The fact that the note was not worth par [17] does not render it valueless or impair its validity.

The section of the statute under consideration is a part of the Negotiable Instrument Law known as chapter 424 of the 1931 Code, and the question here presented is one of first impression in this court.

The warranties implied by the statute, accompanying an indorsement without recourse, do not include the solvency of the maker, but are restricted to matters affecting the legal enforceability of the paper, and, without an allegation of fraud or deceit, there can be no recovery thereon based upon the insolvency of the maker or his inability to pay.

We hold that the Iowa statute under consideration creates no implied warranty . . . as to the solvency of the maker of a negotiable instrument, or that the instrument is worth par. An indorsement without recourse impliedly warrants that the instrument is genuine and in all respects what it purports to be; that the transferor has a good title to it; that all prior parties had capacity to contract; and that the instrument is legally enforceable. There is the additional implication that the indorser knows of no fact which would impair the validity of the instrument or render it valueless, but this provision or implication can only arise when the indorser has such knowledge and fraudulently conceals or withholds the same from the transferee. [Citing cases.] . . . All of these cases, except the early ones, arose under the Negotiable Instruments Law and hold that the word "valueless" does not refer to the value of the security nor to the solvency of the maker, but simply to some legal insufficiency. . . .

The order and judgment appealed from is therefore affirmed. ◄

---

[17] This means that the note wasn't worth its face value—i.e., the amount payable.

COMMENTS AND QUESTIONS

1. Summarize the arguments set forth by the plaintiff to support her construction of the N.I.L. provision. Why did the court reject them?
2. Suppose, instead, that the indorsement had been unqualified. Would the plaintiff have greater rights against the defendant indorser? What steps would the plaintiff have to take in that event?

TRANSFERORS OF BEARER PAPER. As you will recall, an instrument payable to bearer may be transferred freely from holder to holder without any indorsement. Although a person who transfers a bearer instrument in this manner does not guarantee its payment in the event of dishonor, he does make the same warranties to the person receiving the instrument that a qualified indorser makes; moreover, he may be liable to his transferee for damages if these warranties are not complied with.

DRAWERS OF BILLS OF EXCHANGE. A drawer of a bill of exchange is only secondarily liable for its payment. In many ways, the drawer's liability resembles that of an unqualified indorser. If the drawee accepts the bill or pays it, the drawer never becomes liable. If, however, the drawee dishonors the bill, the drawer may be held liable for payment as in the case of an indorser (assuming that the holder gives him proper notice). The drawer also guarantees that the payee actually exists and that he has legal capacity to indorse the instrument.

ACCOMMODATION PARTIES. Occasionally, a person will sign a negotiable instrument without consideration, solely for the purpose of "accommodating" another party to the instrument. This situation may arise, for example, when a bank or lending institution desires additional security for a loan, or when a person is hesitant to accept a negotiable instrument unless the holder can get another person to indorse it. Thus when a bank lends money on the strength of a promissory note, it asks the borrower to get a "co-maker," or an "accommodation maker," to sign the note. Although an accommodation party ordinarily does not acquire title to the instrument, he is liable to the holder for the value of the instrument; this is true even though the holder was aware that the co-maker was acting merely as an accommodation party. If the accommodation party is forced to pay the instrument, however, he is entitled to collect from the party he was accommodating.

In the Maine case that follows, an accommodation party denied his liability on a promissory note and the holder brought suit. Notice that the case was decided soon after Maine's enactment of the N.I.L. The court compares the new statutory provision with the old common-law rule.

INGALLS v. MARSTON et al.

Supreme Judicial Court of Maine, 1922
121 Me. 182, 116 Atl. 216

► CORNISH, C. J. This is an action of assumpsit on the first installment of a promissory note dated August 1, 1919, against Herbert L. Marston, Almeda E. Marston, Howard M. Smith, and Walter H. Foss. Herbert L. and Almeda E. Marston signed the note on its face. Howard M. Smith and

Walter H. Foss placed their signatures on the back of the note at its inception, and before the delivery to the payee, the plaintiff. The payment of the first installment was not demanded of the makers, Herbert L. and Almeda E. Marston, at maturity, and notice of dishonor was not given to Smith and Foss. The plaintiff seeks to maintain his action against all four on the ground that Smith and Foss were original promisors, while the defendants Smith and Foss claim to be merely indorsers, and therefore free from liability because of want of demand and notice. The presiding justice sustained the contention of Smith and Foss, and directed judgment in their favor. The case is before the law court on plaintiff's exception to this ruling.

Prior to the enactment of the Uniform Negotiable Instruments Act (Public Laws 1917, c. 257) the law was firmly settled in this state, as it was in many others, though not in all, by judicial decisions, that one who signed his name on the back of a note at its inception was a joint . . . maker with one who signed on the face, so far as the necessity for demand and notice of non-payment was concerned. He was not regarded as an indorser. The passage of the Negotiable Instruments Act abrogated this rule of commercial law. This act was designed to unify the law in regard to negotiable instruments in the various states adopting it, and it has been enacted by at least 43 of the states of the Union. In those states it has superseded all pre-existing contradictory rules.

We must therefore look to the provisions of that act to determine the rights of the parties in the pending case, and we find that the issue raised here is fully covered. When a person is deemed an indorser is clearly set forth as follows in Section 63:

> "A person placing his signature upon an instrument otherwise than as maker, drawer or acceptor, is deemed to be an indorser, unless he clearly indicates by appropriate words his intention to be bound in some other capacity."

Smith and Foss placed their signatures, not on the face, as makers, but on the back—that is, "otherwise than as makers"—and they did not indicate by any words, appropriate or otherwise, any intention to be bound in some other capacity. Therefore they come within this definition.

But the plaintiff seeks to distinguish between the liability of regular and irregular indorsers in this respect, and argues that, while regular indorsers are entitled to have demand made upon the maker and due notice of dishonor given to them, irregular indorsers are not so entitled. This construction would leave the legal situation the same as before the enactment of the statute, which was designed to change it, and is not borne out by the language of the statute itself.

Section 64, defining the liability of an irregular indorser, reads:

> "Where a person not otherwise a party to an instrument, places thereon his signature in blank before delivery he is liable as an indorser, in accordance with the following rules:
> "(1) If the instrument is payable to the order of a third person, he is liable to the payee and to all subsequent parties," etc.

In the pending case the note was made payable to the order of a third person, and therefore this section applies, and these irregular indorsers were made liable to the payee Ingalls and to all subsequent parties. But liable in what capacity? As makers or joint promisors? Clearly not, but "as indorsers" as the section unequivocally provides. These words are significant. They have a well-defined meaning as legal terms which cannot be ignored, and they necessarily imply, unless it is otherwise stated, the inherent elements of demand and notice or dishonor.

Section 66 prescribes the conditional liability of a general indorser, and recites, among other things, his legal obligation in case of due presentment and dishonor. But such recital of the obligations of a general indorser in this section does not change the liability of an irregular indorser under section 64, and deprive him of his rights and privileges "as an indorser." In other words, whether one be an irregular indorser under section 64 or a regular indorser under section 66, he is entitled to have due demand made upon the maker and due notice of dishonor given to himself. The irregular indorser is no longer a joint maker or an original promisor, as he was prior to the passage of the Negotiable Instruments Act, but an indorser with all that that term implies.

The precise issue here presented has been determined by the courts of several other states under identical provisions of the Negotiable Instruments Act, and without exception, so far as has come to our attention, they sustain the conclusion reached in this case. . . .

Exceptions overruled.   ◄

COMMENTS AND QUESTIONS

1. Note the discussion of the law prior to the enactment of the N.I.L. Summarize the Maine rule that was applicable to this situation before and after passage of the act.
2. This case illustrates the role of the accommodation indorser, who usually signs his name to the instrument to bolster the credit of the maker.

SECTION 3

ENFORCEMENT OF SECONDARY LIABILITY

Introduction

In the preceding section, we discussed the liabilities and obligations of the various parties to a negotiable instrument, and we distinguished the parties who are primarily liable from those who are only secondarily liable. Since the holder of a negotiable instrument is sometimes unable to collect from the parties who are primarily liable (the maker or drawee), it is important for him to preserve whatever rights he may have to sue the parties who are secondarily liable (the indorsers and drawers). In this section, we will outline the procedures that a holder must follow in order to retain those rights.

In general, the holder of a negotiable instrument must show that three requirements have been met before he can force a secondary party to make payment. First, he must properly present the instrument to the maker or drawee and request payment or acceptance. Second, the maker or drawee must refuse to pay or accept it—i.e., he must dishonor it. And third, the holder must give proper notice of the dishonor to the secondary party and demand payment from him.

Presentment for Payment

To enforce secondary liability, the holder must present the instrument for payment at the right time, at the right place, to the right person, and in the right way. If the instrument is payable at a fixed date, the holder must present it on that day. If it is payable on demand, he must present it for payment (in the case of a promissory note) within a reasonable time after issue, or (in the case of a bill of exchange) within a reasonable time after the last negotiation. If a place for payment is specified, the holder must present the instrument there; if no place is mentioned, he must present it at the usual residence or place of business of the maker or drawee.

Presentment must be made to the person named in the instrument. If more than one person is named, it must be made to all of them. When the members of a partnership are named, however, presentment to one partner is generally regarded as sufficient. Proper presentment requires that the instrument actually be shown to the maker or drawee, and that the holder offer to surrender the instrument once he has been paid. Presentment will be excused if the holder is unable to locate the proper party after making reasonable efforts to do so. If the holder is unavoidably delayed in making presentment, his delay will be excused so long as he presents the instrument just as soon as he can.

In the case that follows it was alleged that presentment of a demand note was not made within a reasonable time, and that the holder consequently lost his right to sue an indorser on his secondary liability. A request was made that the court take notice of the customs of the banking community. Note how the court dealt with that request.

MERRITT v. JACKSON

Supreme Judicial Court of Massachusetts, 1902
181 Mass. 69, 62 N.E. 987

► LATHROP, J. This is an action against the defendant, as indorser of four promissory notes made by the Jackson Typewriter Company, payable to the defendant upon demand, and indorsed by him in blank. One note is dated December 19, 1899, and the other three are dated January 5, 1900. Demand was made and notice given on April 4, 1900.

In the superior court, after the introduction of evidence not material to the exceptions, the defendant requested the judge to rule that upon all evidence the plaintiff was not entitled to recover. The judge refused so to rule, and found for the plaintiff, and the case is before us upon the defendant's exceptions. The only question in the case is whether the demand was made within a reasonable time.

The statute of 1898, c. 533, §71, is in part as follows: "Where it [the instrument] is payable on demand presentment must be made within a reasonable time after its issue."

Section 193 of the same act provides: "In determining what is a 'reasonable time' or an 'unreasonable time' regard is to be had to the nature of the instrument, the usage of trade or business, if any, with respect to such instruments, and the facts of the particular case."

Before the statute of 1898, which took effect on January 1, 1899, was passed the law applicable to notes payable on demand was regulated by St. 1839, c. 121, which was retained in substance in the subsequent compilations of the statutes. Section 1 of this statute provided in substance, that the maker should have the same defense against an indorsee as against a payee. Section 2 provided that on any promissory note, payable on demand, made after the act took effect, a demand made before the expiration of 60 days from the date thereof without grace, or at any time within that term, should be deemed to be made within a reasonable time. Section 3 provided for the liability of indorsers. . . .

Before St. 1839, c. 121, was passed, the rule was well settled that, as to a promissory note payable on demand, a demand, in order to charge an indorser, must be made within a reasonable time, and, if no such demand was made, the note was considered as overdue and dishonored. This question arose also in another class of cases, namely, as to the length of time in which a note payable on demand, and remaining unpaid, would be held to be dishonored, and subject to the grounds of defense which would be open to the maker in a suit by the payee. . . .

But while the general rule was well settled, there was found to be great difficulty in its application, and it was said to be impossible to fix any precise period, as each case depended upon its particular circumstances. In Seaver v. Lincoln, 21 Pick. 267, it was said by Chief Justice Shaw:

> "One of the most difficult questions presented for the decision of a court of law is, what shall be deemed a reasonable time within which to demand payment of the maker of a note payable on demand in order to charge the indorser. It depends upon so many circumstances to determine what is a reasonable time in a particular case that one decision goes but little way in establishing a precedent for another."

As to what has been held by this court to be a reasonable or unreasonable time, the cases are thus summed up by Mr. Justice Dewey in Ranger v. Cary, 1 Metc. 369, 374:

> "In Field v. Nickerson, 13 Mass. 131, the period of eight months was held not to be within a reasonable time to make a demand to charge the

indorser; and in Seaver v. Lincoln, 21 Pick. 267, where the demand was made in seven days after the date of the note, it was held to be within due time. In Sylvester v. Crapo, 15 Pick. 92, a note that had remained unpaid for eleven months before it was negotiated was held to be dishonored; and the shorter period of six months was, in Thompson v. Hale, 6 Pick. 259, held sufficient to subject it to the defense of a note overdue. On the other hand, a note indorsed seven days after its date was held, in Thurston v. McKown, 6 Mass. 428, to have been transferred in season to avoid any ground of defense arising from the equities between the original parties."

In Ranger v. Cary it was held that a note payable on demand was not to be regarded as overdue if indorsed within one month after its date. . . .

In the case before us no evidence was introduced of the "usage of trade or business, if any, with respect to such instruments," nor do the facts of the case appear apart from what the instrument itself shows.

We have no doubt that when the holder of such a note seeks to hold an indorser, the burden is on him to show that a demand was made upon the maker within a reasonable time; and that, if there is any usage of trade or any fact or circumstance to excuse a delay, the burden is on him to show it.

It is urged, however, that the court will take judicial notice of business in a community including the universal practice of banks, and attention is called to the fact that in the charge to the jury in Field v. Nickerson, 13 Mass. 131, 132, where the question was whether an action could be maintained by an indorsee against an indorser on a promissory note payable on demand where the demand was made on the maker eight months after the date of the note, Chief Justice Parker, after stating to the jury that the demand must be made in a reasonable time, and that what was a reasonable time was a question of law in that case, further instructed the jury "that, all the parties to the transaction living in a town where credit for loans of money among merchants is commonly given for thirty, sixty, or ninety days, the indorser must be considered as having contracted with reference to the usual period; that delay of eight months was unreasonable." The jury were directed to return a verdict for the defendant. Nothing is said on this subject in the opinion. Whether or not an analogy can be drawn from the fact that in the business community the rate of credit may be 30, 60, or 90 days, St. 1898, c. 533, 193, as we already have pointed out, limits the question of usage to that of trade or business "with respect to such instruments." The statute took effect on January 1, 1899. All but one of the notes in suit were dated early in January of the next year. We are not aware that in the interval any usage of trade or business with respect to demand notes had grown up different from that which had had the force of law for nearly 60 years.

In a case like the present . . . we are of the opinion that a demand on the maker should be made at or before the expiration of 60 days, that the demand in this case was not made within a reasonable time, and that the ruling requested should have been given.

Exceptions sustained.   ◀

COMMENTS AND QUESTIONS

1. In this case the court was grappling with the age-old legal question of "what is reasonable?" How did the court decide, and what reasons did it give for its decision? What had happened in the lower court?
2. The statute provides that "In determining what is a 'reasonable time' . . . regard is to be had to . . . the usage of trade or business, if any, with respect to such instruments. . . ." Did the plaintiff introduce any evidence of "usage"? What arguments did the plaintiff use in support of his position? How did the court answer these arguments?

Presentment for Acceptance

You will recall that the drawee of a bill of exchange does not become primarily liable for payment until he accepts the instrument. Usually, the holder of a bill of exchange is under no obligation to present it for acceptance. But if the bill is payable at a future date and the holder wishes to ascertain whether it will be honored, he would be well advised to do so. For, once the bill has been accepted, the drawee is bound absolutely to pay it. If presentment for acceptance is not required, and if the holder makes no effort to present the bill for acceptance, he should present it for payment at maturity, as described in the preceding section.

In a few cases, presentment for acceptance is required if the holder is to protect his rights to sue parties with secondary liability. These are:

1. Where presentment for acceptance is necessary to fix the maturity date of the instrument.

EXAMPLE

A bill of exchange payable "60 days after sight" (i.e., 60 days after it has been presented to the drawee and he has seen it) must be presented for acceptance in order to fix the date of payment. Until it has been presented, the 60-day period does not start to run.

2. Where the actual terms of the bill require presentment for acceptance.

3. Where the bill is made payable at some place other than the drawee's residence or place of business. If such a bill is not first presented to the drawee for acceptance, he has no way of knowing where payment is to be made, or of his obligation to be present at a certain time and place to make payment.

When presentment for acceptance is required, the holder must present the instrument within a reasonable time after he acquires it. The rules governing the time, place, and manner of presentment for acceptance are roughly the same as those governing presentment for payment.

Proper presentment requires that a bill of exchange be presented to the drawee so that he may write his acceptance on the instrument. Although the word "accepted" is commonly used, any word or phrase indicating acceptance is sufficient. The following case illustrates this point.

LAWLESS v. TEMPLE

Supreme Judicial Court of Massachusetts, 1926
254 Mass. 395, 150 N.E. 176

▶ PIERCE, J. This is an action by the payee against the drawee. The bill is as follows:

"Natick, Sept. 24, 1923

"Maurice E. Temple—Please pay to the order of Hazel Lawless $351.50, three hundred fifty one dollars and 50/100.

"Norris J. Temple
"Maurice E. Temple."

The answer raised the question of the sufficiency of the acceptance, under G.L. c. 107, 155, which reads as follows:

"The acceptance of a bill is the signification by the drawee of his assent to the order of the drawer. The acceptance must be in writing and signed by the drawee. It must not express that the drawee will perform his promise by any other means than the payment of money."

The specific contention of the defendant is that the mere signature of the name of the drawee on the bill cannot fulfill the requirements of the statute that the signification of the assent of the drawee must be in writing and must also be signed. Before the passage of the Negotiable Instruments Act, an oral acceptance of an existing bill of exchange was generally valid in this country and formerly was so in England. . . . The reason for the adoption of the rule requiring acceptance in writing, like the underlying reason for the statute of frauds and similar statutes, "is that sound policy requires some substantial and tangible evidence of the contract, and more reliable in its nature than the statement or recollection of witnesses."

The common practice before the act was to write the word "accepted" on the face of the bill, followed by the signature of the acceptor. But such was not necessary, as Sewall, J., said in Storer v. Logan, 9 Mass. 55, at page 59:

"An acceptance entered upon a bill generally, or the blank endorsement of the name of the drawee, holds him absolutely as the acceptor; and no conditions or stipulations, which he may have connected with his acceptance, unless expressed upon the bill, will avail him against an endorsee or payee, to whom the bill has been negotiated, and who had received the bill as accepted, without notice of the conditions."

It was said by Cowen, J., in Spear v. Pratt, 2 Hill (N.Y.) 582, 38 Am. Dec. 600, in considering the legal valuation of the mere signature by the drawee on the bill, under a statute of New York, which required the acceptance to be in writing and signed by the acceptor or his agent:

"The acceptance in question was, as we have seen, declared by the law merchant to be both a writing and signing. The statute contains no declaration that it should be considered less. An endorsement must be in writing and signed; yet the name alone is constantly holden to satisfy the requisition."

We are of the opinion that under G.L. c. 107, 155, a drawee may be charged as acceptor although he writes merely his name upon the bill, and that anyone taking the bill has the right to fill up a blank acceptance on the same principle that any holder may fill up a blank endorsement.

The instrument in question was legally accepted. *It follows in accordance with the terms of the stipulation that judgment is to be "entered for the plaintiff for the full amount of the bill and interest thereon from the date of demand as set forth in the second count."*

So ordered.   ◀

COMMENTS AND QUESTIONS

1. How did the court get around the statutory provision that "an acceptance must be in writing and signed by the drawee"? Should this not be interpreted to mean that something must be written by the drawee besides his mere signature?

To be effective, an acceptance must be general or unqualified—that is, the drawee must agree, without qualification, to pay the draft according to its terms. If the acceptance alters the provisions of the instrument in any significant way (by changing the time, place, or amount payable, for example, or by adding some condition that must be satisfied), it is deemed a *qualified acceptance* and may be treated as a dishonor. In that case the holder may notify parties of secondary liability and hold them to the instrument as if there had been no acceptance at all. If the holder agrees to a qualified acceptance—and he may if he wants to—the drawee is liable to pay accordingly. In that event, all secondary parties will be discharged unless they are immediately notified of the terms of the qualified acceptance and fail to object to them within a reasonable time.

EXAMPLE

DRAWER draws a bill of exchange on DRAWEE payable to PAYEE "30 days after sight." PAYEE negotiates the bill to HOLDER, who presents it to DRAWEE for acceptance. DRAWEE writes across the face of the draft, "Accepted—but payable 60 days after sight—January 15, 1963 (signed) DRAWEE." Since the acceptance alters the terms of payment, HOLDER may treat it as a dishonor and notify and hold PAYEE and/or DRAWER as secondary parties. Or else HOLDER may agree to DRAWEE's qualified acceptance and look only to him for payment, thereby losing his rights against PAYEE and DRAWER. Or, if he wishes to preserve his rights against the secondary parties, he may promptly notify PAYEE and DRAWER of the qualified acceptance; in that case they will continue to be secondarily liable unless they notify HOLDER within a reasonable time that they do not wish to be bound.

Dishonor of Instrument

The second requirement for the enforcement of secondary liability is that the instrument be dishonored. Dishonor of an instrument occurs when the maker or drawee fails or refuses to make payment after the instrument has been properly presented for payment, or when the drawee refuses to accept the instrument after it has been properly presented for acceptance.

Notice to Secondary Parties

The last step necessary to enforce secondary liability is for the holder to give proper notice of the dishonor to all the secondary parties he wishes to hold responsible. Any secondary party who is not properly notified will be released from liability to the holder. Since the rules governing notice, like those dealing with presentment, are long and involved, again we will confine ourselves to a brief discussion of the main points.

Generally speaking, the notice may be either written or oral, but it must identify the instrument and make clear that it has been dishonored. Moreover, the notice must be given promptly; if the party to be notified lives in the same place as the holder, he must be notified within one day; if he lives elsewhere and the notice has to be mailed, it must be postmarked within one day if it is possible for the holder to mail it within that time. Finally, the notice must be addressed to the proper party at his residence or place of business.

If the holder makes a reasonable effort to give notice but is unsuccessful through no fault of his own, he is still entitled to collect. Notice need not be given if the instrument itself expressly waives it. And, in the case of a bill of exchange or check, no notice to the drawer is necessary if the drawer should realize without notice that the drawee will not accept or make payment on the instrument (e.g., where the drawer of a check does not have sufficient funds on deposit to cover payment or where he stops payment).

Any secondary party who is notified of the dishonor has the right to notify any prior secondary party and hold him liable in the event the party first notified is forced to pay. Such notice must be given within the same time after notice is received as the original holder had to give notice after the dishonor.

> EXAMPLE
>
> M gives a promissory note to P, who indorses it to X, who indorses it to Y, who indorses it to H. H presents it for payment to M, who refuses to pay it. H, X, Y, and P all live in the same city. If H wishes to notify Y and hold him liable, he may call Y at his office before the close of business on the following day. If Y receives the notice on the next day, he, in turn, must call X at X's place of business not later than the following day. And X must notify P in the same way.

Once notice of dishonor is given to a secondary party by the holder, it serves as effective notice to all persons who have a right to recover from that party; a second notice is not required.

> EXAMPLE
>
> M gives P a bill of exchange drawn on D and payable to P 30 days after sight. P indorses the bill to X, who indorses it to Y, who indorses it to Z,

who indorses it to H. H presents it for acceptance to D, who refuses to honor it. H immediately gives proper notice to Z, Y, X, and P. No further notice need be given to any of the secondary parties, since all have received notice from H. Thus, if H elects to hold Z, Z in turn may collect from Y without giving him any notice. H's notice thus works to the benefit of the others. So, in turn, Y may hold X and X may hold P, without further notice.

As we have mentioned, effective notice may be either oral or written, or both—though obviously it is safer to give notice in writing before a witness. In the procedure known as *protest*, the holder goes to a Notary Public and informs him that an instrument has been dishonored. The Notary then writes out a formal notice, called a *certificate of protest*, in which he recites what has happened. The Notary signs the certificate and sends it to the secondary parties.

Notice of dishonor *may* be given by protest in any case where the holder feels it is warranted. In the case of the so-called *foreign bill of exchange*, however, notice of dishonor *must* be given by protest. This is a bill that is drawn in one state (or country) and is payable in another—for example, the drawer may draw a draft in New York on a drawee located in California. If a dishonored foreign bill is not protested, both the drawer and the indorsers are discharged (unless, as often happens, the protest requirement has been waived by express provision in the bill itself).

Where protest is required, it must be made on the day of dishonor and it must recite all the pertinent data: the time and place of presentment, the manner of presentment, the reason for dishonor, whether or not the drawee or acceptor could be located, and so forth.

In the concluding case in this section a bank is trying to collect from an indorser on a promissory note. The indorser's defense is that she did not receive proper notice of dishonor.

STATE BANK OF EAST MOLINE v. STANDAERT et al.

Appellate Court of Illinois, Second District, 1948
335 Ill. App. 519, 82 N.E. 2d 393

► BRISTOW, JUSTICE. In a proceeding instituted by the plaintiff, State Bank of East Moline, to recover payment on a note from the defendants Alfons and Lena Standaert, and Alois and Anna DeVos, makers and indorsers respectively, the Circuit Court of Rock Island County, in a trial without jury, entered a judgment in favor of the plaintiff, from which the defendant indorser, Anna DeVos, appeals. The co-indorser Alois DeVos died prior to the trial, and suit was dismissed as to him.

The sole issue presented herein is whether the plaintiff bank gave the defendant indorser notice of dishonor as required under the terms of the Negotiable Instruments Law. (Ch. 98, 110, 111, Rev. Stats. 1947.)

From the record it appears that on February 28, 1920, defendants Alfons Standaert and Lena Standaert made and delivered their promissory note to the defendants Alois DeVos and Anna DeVos, in the amount of $6,737.50

at 6% interest due 5 years after date, and payable at the office of the plaintiff bank. The note recited that it was secured by a real estate mortgage.

Before maturity the defendants Alois and Anna DeVos sold the note and mortgage to the plaintiff bank. The note was not paid, either at maturity on February 28, 1925, or during the ensuing years. Suit was instituted against the defendants in 1932, but the cause was stricken from the docket on May 28, 1941, for want of prosecution. Within a year thereafter, plaintiff commenced this proceeding.

At the trial the plaintiff bank contended that, when the note in controversy was not paid on the due date, notice of its dishonor was sent to the defendant indorsers.

In support thereof plaintiff offered the testimony of Leota Baker, who was employed as teller-bookkeeper in 1925, and charged with the duty of attending to maturing notes. She stated that it was the unswerving custom of the bank to send to the parties, 10 days prior to the due date of a note, a notice describing the note and specifying its maturity date. If the note was not paid at maturity, this same form of notice with the added notation that it had not been paid by the maker, and that the indorser should make payment thereon, was mailed by the bank at the close of the day on which the note was due.

She further testified that she did not recall preparing or sending out the particular notice of dishonor to the defendant indorsers, Alois and Anna DeVos, on February 28, 1925, when the Standaerts failed to pay the obligation, but that during her 7 years of service to the bank she knew of no instance when the bank failed to give notice of dishonor. Nor did she know who was charged with the actual mailing of the notice on February 28, 1925. With reference thereto she stated that probably Emma Callewaert mailed it since the post office was on her way home, or perhaps even she, Leota Baker, posted the bank mail. However, B. H. Ryan, who was assistant cashier in 1925, admitted in his testimony that Emma Callewaert was not in the employ of the bank on February 28, 1925. He reiterated the custom of the bank respecting notices of dishonor, and explained that some of the records of the bank pertaining to such notices, including the records in the instant case, where destroyed after 10 years.

He further explained that in 1930 a foreclosure suit was instituted by the Moline State Trust & Savings Bank which held a first mortgage on the same premises which secured the note in controversy under a second mortgage, and, inasmuch as there were insufficient funds from the sale of the property to pay the second mortgage, plaintiff's security was lost. In that foreclosure proceeding defendant, Anna DeVos, had apparently testified respecting her signature on the note and the circumstances surrounding its sale to the plaintiff bank. However, at the trial of the instant case she denied participation therein.

The defendant, Anna DeVos, contends in this proceeding that she should not be charged with the payment of the note on the ground that she did not receive notice that the instrument had been dishonored, and therefore, under the Negotiable Instruments Law she was discharged. She maintains that she did not know that the note was not paid until suit was filed in 1932, some 7 years after the obligation was due. In fact, the plaintiff bank loaned her some $19,000 in 1928 and 1929 without any reference to the note in controversy, or her liability thereon.

On the basis of the foregoing evidence, the Circuit Court entered judgment in favor of plaintiff and against the defendants, Alfons and Lena Standaert, and Anna DeVos, with the accrued interest on the note over a period of 27 years, the amount due was in excess of $11,947.83, the sum specified in the complaint, and for which judgment was entered. The defendant, Anna DeVos, contends that this judgment is contrary to the evidence and to the law.

The Negotiable Instruments Law provides that when a negotiable instrument has been dishonored by non-payment, notice of dishonor must be given to the indorser, otherwise he is discharged. (Ch. 98, 110 Ill. Rev. Stats. 1947.) Such notice may be given by mail, and where it is duly addressed and deposited in a post office, the sender is deemed to have given due notice, notwithstanding any miscarriage in the mails. (Ch. 98, 126 Ill. Rev. Stats. 1947.)

This requirement of addressing and depositing the notice in the post office does not prescribe the precise testimony to be introduced in a cause, but rather sets forth the ultimate facts to be established by the evidence. In other words, to charge an indorser with the payment of a note, the plaintiff must establish that the notice of dishonor was addressed and actually mailed . . . and these facts may be proven by direct or circumstantial evidence as any other fact in the case.

In the case at bar the only evidence of plaintiff's compliance with the statutory requirement of giving notice of dishonor to the indorser was the testimony of Leota Baker that it was the custom of the bank at the close of the business day on which a note was due and unpaid to send a notice to the parties describing the note and stating that it was not paid by the maker, and that the indorser should make payment thereon.

Although Leota Baker was charged with preparing these notices, she did not recall preparing or sending any particular notice of dishonor to the defendant, Anna DeVos, on February 28, 1925. Moreover, she did not know who was charged with posting the bank's mail on that date. She stated that perhaps Emma Callewaert did it, since the post office was on her way home, or perhaps even she, herself, posted the mail. Emma Callewaert, however, was not in the employ of the bank on the due date of the note, and there is no certainty as to who posted the mail, or whether, in fact, any mail was posted on that date. Therefore, other than the description of the general custom of the bank of notifying indorsers, the only evidence tending to prove, even circumstantially, that notice of dishonor was prepared and mailed to the defendant was the inference from Leota Baker's self-serving declaration that she always did her duty and never failed to send out a notice of dishonor.

The courts have taken cognizance of the intricacies and expansion of business enterprises, and the cases reveal a liberalizing tendency with reference to the proof required to establish the posting of a letter. . . . From a review of the cases, however, it is evident that while courts may not require the person mailing the letter for a large concern to have a distinct recollection of the particular letter, there must be some evidence on the part of the person whose general practice it was to post the mail that the custom was complied with on the date in question. . . . In Cook v. Phillips, the court stated:

> "We do not think that the mere dictation or writing of a letter, coupled with evidence of an office custom with reference to the mailing of letters, is sufficient to constitute proof of mailing the same, in the absence of some proof or corroborating circumstance sufficient to establish the fact that the custom in the particular instance had in fact been followed."

In the instant case there was not even evidence of the dictation or writing of the particular notice of dishonor. . . .

It would serve no useful purpose to analyze each case cited by the plaintiff and set forth the additional evidence of mailing presented therein supplementing the proof of the business practice. It is sufficient to point out that in the instant case there is no evidence that the particular notice was prepared, or put in an envelope, or addressed, or even deposited in a place where it would ordinarily be taken up by an employee charged with the duty of posting the bank's mail, as in the cases cited by plaintiff. Plaintiff offered no copies of the notice, or records of any kind indicating that the notice was mailed herein. Therefore, even under the most liberal interpretation of the law, plaintiff's evidence is insufficient. . . .

Under the Negotiable Instruments Law, plaintiff had a duty to establish the fact that notice of dishonor was mailed to the defendant indorser in order to impose liability on her for the payment of the note. . . .

It is the opinion of this court, in the light of the foregoing analysis, that plaintiff failed to establish, either by direct or circumstantial evidence, that it mailed the notice of dishonor to the defendant indorser, Anna DeVos, on February 28, 1925, when the obligation was due, and therefore, under the terms of the Negotiable Instruments Law, the defendant indorser was discharged. The judgment of the circuit court imposing liability upon the defendant indorser for the payment of the $6,737.50 note, together with the accrued interest, amounting to a total of $11,947.83, was therefore contrary to the law, and should properly be reversed.

Judgment reversed.

WOLFE, P. J. and DOVE, J., concur.   ◀

COMMENTS AND QUESTIONS

1. This case was finally decided twenty-three years after the due date of the note! Do you think this fact had any influence on the court's decision?

2. Note the similarities between this case and that of *Jensen v. Traders Insurance* (see page 290), where the court held that merely mailing a notice of cancellation of an insurance policy effectively canceled the policy despite the fact that the policyholder never received it. Can the two cases be distinguished?

3. The court discusses business practices with respect to the mailing of

notices and admits that it is next to impossible for the employees of a large firm to remember mailing a specific letter. Wasn't this a strong argument for the plaintiff? How could the bank protect itself in future transactions of this sort?

SECTION 4

HOLDERS IN DUE COURSE AND DEFENSES

Introduction

In Section 2, we outlined the liabilities of the various parties to negotiable instruments, and in Section 3 we reviewed the procedures necessary to enforce liability against secondary parties. In this section we shall consider the defenses that may be raised to avoid payment of a negotiable instrument when payment is demanded.

As we stated at the beginning of this chapter, the transferee or holder of a negotiable instrument often acquires a better right to enforce payment than does the assignee of an ordinary contract right to receive money. (Recall our discussion on page 462.) But to acquire this favored status, the transferee of a negotiable instrument must qualify as a *holder in due course*, or as one who is entitled to the rights of such a holder.

Holder in Due Course

To qualify as a holder in due course, a holder must be lawfully in possession of an instrument payable to himself or to bearer, and he must also (1) have given value for the instrument, (2) have purchased it before it was overdue, and (3) have received it in good faith without notice of any defect in the instrument or of any defenses that might be raised to avoid paying it. Let us examine these requirements in greater detail.

Holder for Value

Generally speaking, a holder in due course must have given some consideration for the instrument. This means that someone who receives a negotiable instrument as a gift does not qualify as a holder in due course. Nor is the holder's mere *promise* to give value regarded as sufficient; he must actually *give* value before he qualifies. This point is raised in the following case.

CITIZENS' STATE BANK v. COWLES

Court of Appeals of New York, 1905
180 N.Y. 346, 73 N.E. 33, 105

► The defendant Cowles purchased a team of horses from Miller for $600, the seller giving Cowles a warranty that the horses were sound. Cowles gave Miller a check drawn on First National Bank of Port Chester in payment. When it developed that one of the horses was sick and unsound, Cowles stopped payment on the check. Miller endorsed the check to Hoffman, the President of Citizens' State Bank, and Hoffman deposited it with that bank which credited his account. Citizens' Bank then sent the check to the First National Bank of Port Chester which dishonored it. Citizens' Bank then brought suit against the drawer Cowles who defended on the ground of breach of warranty and alleged that Citizens' was not a holder for value and therefore not a holder in due course, and subject to the personal defense.[18] The lower court found for the plaintiff and the defendant appealed.

WERNER, J. . . . It is obvious that if the evidence would support the inference that the plaintiff did not buy the check, but simply gave Hoffman credit for the amount upon its books, then plaintiff is not a holder of the check in due course, within the law merchant, as that term is now defined in the negotiable instruments law so as to render its title superior to the defenses which the drawer of the check may have against the payee. Under the negotiable instruments law four elements must concur to constitute such a title: (1) The instrument must be complete and regular on its face; (2) the holder must receive it before it is overdue, and without notice that it has been previously dishonored, if that is the fact; (3) it must have been taken in good faith and for value; (4) it must have been taken without notice of any infirmity in the instrument or defect in the title of the person negotiating it. Neg. Instruments Law, 91 (Laws 1897, p. 732, c. 612). If the plaintiff had not actually parted with value before it received notice of the dishonor of this check, it is apparent that at least one of these elements is lacking in the plaintiff's title. The authorities hold that the mere crediting to a depositor's account, on the books of a bank, of the amount of a check drawn upon another bank, where the depositor's account continues to be sufficient to pay the check in case it is dishonored, does not constitute the bank a holder in due course. . . .

The view of the evidence most favorable to the defendant would, we think, have justified a jury in finding that the amount of the check had simply been credited to Hoffman's account, and that no money was paid to him by the plaintiff upon the check before the latter had notice of its dishonor. *The judgments of the courts below should be reversed, and a new trial granted, with costs to abide the event.*   ◄

---

[18] We shall discuss personal defenses in some detail later in this section. Suffice it for the moment to say that it is the kind of defense that may not be used to avoid payment to a holder in due course.

COMMENTS AND QUESTIONS

1. Did the plaintiff qualify as a holder in due course here? If not, why not?
2. Would it have made a difference if Hoffman had actually withdrawn the funds from his account? The Uniform Commercial Code provides that a bank is deemed to have given value as soon as it has made credit available, regardless of whether the money has actually been withdrawn. If the U.C.C. had been applicable to this case, would the result have been different?

Holder Before Maturity

A holder in due course must take the instrument before it becomes overdue, or "stale." True, an instrument may always be negotiated after maturity. But if the date for payment has passed, the law considers that this suspicious circumstance should put the holder on notice. In any case, a holder who accepts an instrument after it has matured cannot become a holder in due course. When, precisely, does an instrument become overdue? Obviously, if the date for payment is fixed (e.g., "on September 15, 1959," or "60 days from date"), there is no problem. But what if the instrument is payable on demand? The courts hold that such an instrument is overdue when it has been in circulation an unreasonable length of time after being issued. What constitutes an "unreasonable" time depends on the circumstances.

Purchaser in Good Faith

A holder in due course must take the instrument in good faith—that is, he must be innocent of any knowledge of defects or irregularities in the instrument itself or of any defense that might be raised to block payment.

EXAMPLES OF DEFECTS OR IRREGULARITIES

1. The instrument contains erasures, crossed-out words, or other irregularities.
2. The holder knows or has reason to know that the instrument has been dishonored.
3. The circumstances surrounding the issuance or negotiation of the instrument are suspicious (for example, an officer of a corporation purports to pay a personal debt with a check drawn on the corporation by him).
4. The holder of a promissory note has knowledge that the payee obtained it from the maker by fraud or duress.

An interesting application of this rule occurs in the following Arkansas case. See if you agree with the decision of that state's supreme court.

COMMERCIAL CREDIT CO. v. CHILDS

Supreme Court of Arkansas, 1940
199 Ark. 1073, 137 S.W. 2d 260

▶ HUMPHREYS, J. Appellant brought suit in replevin [19] against appellee in the circuit court of Cleveland county to recover a Dodge automobile which it alleged was sold to appellee by Arkansas Motors, Inc., under a sales contract which provided that appellee would pay the sum of $26 per month on the purchase price of said car for a period of eighteen months and that the title to the car should remain in the seller until fully paid for and upon failure to make said monthly payments that the seller could retake the car and declare the contract forfeited.

It was also alleged that appellant bought said note and contract for a valuable consideration before maturity with all the rights and interest of the Arkansas Motors, Inc.; that appellee has failed to comply with the provisions of the contract and note and, under the provisions thereof, he has forfeited his right to retain possession of the automobile and that appellant is entitled under the accelerating clause in said contract and note to the immediate possession of the automobile and damages for the detention thereof. . . .

Appellee interposed several defenses, the main defense being that he exchanged an automobile of the agreed value of $175, as a down payment, for the car in question and executed a note and sales contract for the balance of the purchase money on the representation of the Arkansas Motors, Inc., through its authorized agent, that the car in question was worth $547 and that it was in first class condition or mechanical order, which representation was falsely and fraudulently made to induce him to make the exchange and sign the note and contract and believing the false and fraudulent representation was true and relying upon same as true he made the exchange and signed the note and contract.

Appellee denied that appellant was an innocent purchaser of the note and contract and alleged that he was the qualified owner of the automobile and entitled to the possession thereof on account of having put $179 in same.

The cause was submitted to a jury upon the pleadings, instructions of the court and the evidence introduced by the parties which resulted in the following verdict: "We, the jury, find for the defendant, T. F. Childs, and against the plaintiff, Commercial Credit Company, for the possession of the Dodge Coupe." Judgment was rendered in favor of appellee for the possession of the Dodge car, from which is this appeal. . . .

We must conclude that the court correctly instructed the jury as to the law applicable to the facts as revealed by the testimony introduced, leaving the only question for determination by us of . . . whether there is sufficient evidence to support the verdict and judgment. . . .

Appellant contends that it was an innocent purchaser of the note and

---

[19] Replevin is an action to recover possession of personal property (in this case, a car) which has been unlawfully taken.

contract before maturity and was entitled to take the automobile under the terms of the contract upon the failure of appellee to pay any one or more of the monthly installments of $26 and to sell same and apply the proceeds from the sale to the balance due it on the note and contract.

The note and contract are attached and constitute one instrument covering an agreement of the sale and purchase of the automobile in question. The instrument contains many provisions and conditions and there appears on the back of the contract and attached note a printed assignment to the Commercial Credit Co., appellant herein, signed by the seller, the Arkansas Motors, Inc. The note, contract and assignment were all executed and signed the same day. The instrument was prepared and delivered to the Arkansas Motors, Inc., by appellant to be used by it in the sale and purchase of cars. Appellant financed the deal.

We think appellant was so closely connected with the entire transaction or with the deal that it can not be heard to say that it, in good faith, was an innocent purchaser of the instrument for value before maturity. It financed the deal, prepared the instrument, and on the day it was executed, took an assignment of it from the Arkansas Motors, Inc. Even before it was executed, it prepared the written assignment thereon to itself. Rather than being a purchaser of the instrument after its execution it was to all intents and purposes a party to the agreement and instrument from the beginning. To say the least of it, it put the Arkansas Motors, Inc. in the position to procure appellee's signature to the instrument through fraudulent misrepresentation as to the value and condition of the automobile it was selling to appellee. There is little or no dispute in the testimony that Arkansas Motors, Inc., procured the signature of appellee to the instrument appellant has made the basis of its suit, by falsely and fraudulently representing to appellee that the car it was selling him was worth $578 and in practically perfect condition, whereas it was of little or no value and so defective that it could not be used.

Under the facts detailed above we think it was appellant's duty before taking an assignment of the instrument to inquire whether appellee's signature thereto had been obtained through fraud and misrepresentations.

This court will not disturb, on appeal, the finding of a jury that one is not an innocent purchaser of a note, if the finding is justified or warranted by any substantial evidence. . . .

It is unnecessary to decide whether the instrument in question was negotiable under our negotiable instrument act, Pope's Dig. 10152 et seq., for we have concluded under the facts and circumstances detailed above the jury was warranted in finding that appellant was not an innocent purchaser of the note sued on.

No error appearing, the judgment is affirmed.

GRIFFIN SMITH, C. J. and McHANEY, J., dissent.   ◄

COMMENTS AND QUESTIONS

1. Why did the court decide that it could not overturn the jury's finding that the plaintiff was not an innocent purchaser? Suppose the parties had agreed that the Commercial Credit Co. actually had no knowl-

edge of the fraud when it took the note. Would the court have held the same way?

2. Three judges dissented. On what grounds, do you think?

Holder Through a Holder in Due Course

Once an instrument has passed through the hands of a holder in due course, all holders who acquire it thereafter enjoy the same rights and privileges as a holder in due course. This is true even though they fail to meet the necessary qualifications, *provided* they have not been a party to any original fraud or illegality concerning the execution and issuance of the instrument. By virtue of this rule the free negotiability of an instrument is maintained; if the rule were otherwise, a holder in due course would have great difficulty negotiating the instrument further to a person who could not himself qualify as such a holder.

Defenses to Payment Generally

Two classes of defense are available to a person who is called on to pay a negotiable instrument: (1) *personal defenses* and (2) *real defenses*. *Personal defenses* may be used to avoid payment to any holder *except* a holder in due course (or a holder through a holder in due course); *real defenses* are good against all holders. To put it another way, a holder in due course (or a holder through a holder in due course) may collect on a negotiable instrument even though a personal defense has been raised, but no holder may collect if a real defense has been raised. Let us examine these classes of defense in more detail.

Personal Defenses

Lack or Failure of Consideration

Sometimes a person who is otherwise liable for the payment of an instrument may defend on the ground that he never received consideration for the instrument or that the consideration promised to him was never given. Such defenses are good against any holder except a holder in due course.

> EXAMPLE
>
> D gives P a check for $500 for painting D's house. P negotiates it to X, a holder in due course. D discovers that the work was improperly performed and stops payment on the check. Nevertheless, X, as a holder in due course, may hold D liable on the check, and D may not refuse to pay X for this reason. D's defense (failure of consideration) is personal and, therefore, not available against a holder in due course. If P had kept the check, however, D could refuse to pay P, since P is not a holder in due course.

Fraud in Inducement

Whenever a person is induced by fraud to execute a negotiable instrument, his defense is merely personal and he cannot refuse to pay a subsequent holder in due course who acquires the instrument and demands payment from him.

EXAMPLE

M gives P a promissory note in payment for a car. If M was induced to buy the car as a result of P's deceit, he has a good defense against paying the note. If, however, P negotiates the note to X, a holder in due course, and X demands payment, M may not use the personal defense of fraud against him.

Prior Payment

Occasionally, a person will pay an instrument without insisting that it be surrendered to him. If this happens before maturity, and if the instrument continues to circulate and gets into the hands of a holder in due course, such a holder may enforce payment a second time, since the defense of prior payment is only a personal one.

EXAMPLE

M gives P a promissory note payable on November 1. On October 15 M pays P the amount of the note, but P fails to surrender the note to M. Instead, P negotiates the note to X, a holder in due course, who may force M to pay again on November 1. Of course, M, having paid twice, may try to recover his loss from P.

Duress

If a person executes or signs a negotiable instrument under duress and the instrument comes into the possession of a holder in due course, payment may be enforced; duress, like fraud in inducement, is only a personal defense.

Nondelivery or Conditional Delivery of Completed Instrument

A person may fully execute an instrument without intending that it be circulated immediately, or he may deliver a completed instrument to someone else subject to the performance of some condition. If, despite his wishes or the nonperformance of the condition, the instrument gets into circulation and reaches a holder in due course, that holder may require payment, since nondelivery or conditional delivery is a personal defense only.

EXAMPLE

M makes out a note payable to P and signs it. He does not intend to give it to P, however, until P has finished a certain job for him. P, without authority, takes the instrument and negotiates it to X, a holder in due course. M must pay X, since his defense is a personal one.

Unauthorized Completion of Delivered Instrument

Occasionally, a person will sign an instrument without filling in the amount or the payee's name, and then deliver it to another person (usually an agent) with instructions to complete the instrument in a certain way. If that person makes an unauthorized completion of the instrument and negotiates it to a holder in due course, the signer of the instrument may not resist payment, since his defense is merely personal.

EXAMPLE

D signs his name to a check payable to GROCER, leaving the amount blank, and gives it to AGENT with instructions to purchase some food from GROCER and to fill in the amount necessary to pay for the food but no more. AGENT fills in twice that amount, cashes the check at GROCER's, and absconds with the proceeds. If GROCER is a holder in due course, he may enforce payment against D, since D's defense is only personal. This example also illustrates the rule that even a *payee* of an instrument (in this case, GROCER) may qualify as a holder in due course.

Real Defenses

Fraud as to the Nature of the Instrument Itself

A person who executes or signs a negotiable instrument in response to deceit as to the nature of the instrument itself has a real defense against payment. He may use this defense against any holder. The following case involved just such a situation.

C.I.T. CORPORATION v. PANAC et al.

Supreme Court of California, 1944
25 Cal. 2d 547, 154 P. 2d 710

► CARTER, JUSTICE. In this action on two negotiable promissory notes by the plaintiff, a holder in due course, against defendants as makers, the latters' defense of fraud by an agent of the payee in the execution of the notes was sustained by the trial court sitting without a jury.

The court found that defendants are husband and wife; that they are illiterate, being unable to read or write the English language, and William Hart the agent of the payee knew of that fact; that Hart gained the trust and confidence of the defendants and secured their signatures to the notes by false representations which induced the defendants to believe that they were signing a contract to repair dwelling houses and nothing else, and that defendants were ignorant of the fact that they were signing notes; that defendants relied upon such false representations and were prevented thereby from seeking independent advice although they requested that they be permitted to obtain it; that defendants were not negligent in signing the notes; and that plaintiff is a holder in due course and had no notice of any infirmities in the notes at the time they were acquired.

Turning first to the question of whether or not defendants' defense was real, and hence good against plaintiff as a holder in due course, we are satisfied that the answer must be in the affirmative. . . .

By the overwhelming weight of authority a negotiable instrument which is void under the foregoing circumstances, where there is in fact no contract or there is fraud in the execution, is not enforceable by a holder in due course in the absence of negligence on the part of the maker; that is, the maker has a real defense to an action thereon. . . .

The rule has been declared by statute in some states. . . .

It is a fundamental principle that there should be uniformity in the negotiable instruments law between states as well as within a state and the courts should have that in mind as their guiding thought in constructing the statutory law on the subject. . . . Therefore, the goal of having the law of negotiable instruments certain and uniform will best be advanced by the adoption of a rule followed by the great weight of authority.

The only case in California that has discussed the subject is Bedell v. Herring, 77 Cal. 572, 20 P. 129, 11 Am. St. Rep. 307, decided before the adoption of the negotiable instruments law. It involved an action by a holder in due course against the maker on a promissory note, the maker's defense being that he did not know he was signing a note because of the fraud of the payee. The court affirmed the judgment of the lower court based on the latter's finding that the maker was negligent. After expressly stating that it did not pass upon the question of whether the defense was real or personal, it proceeded nevertheless, to state that it was not a real defense. For the reasons appearing above that dictum is disapproved. . . .

We believe that the evidence is sufficient to support the findings. While there is some conflict in the evidence it is clearly sufficient. From an examination of the record it is apparent that the trial court could have concluded as it did, that defendants did not have an understanding of the English language. . . .

The trial court was also justified in finding that defendants were not negligent. Particular mention may be made of the illiteracy of defendants, the high pressure methods pursued by Hart, the reading of only the contract for repairs and not the notes, the insistence by Hart of an immediate execution, and Hart's brushing aside Mrs. Panac's suggestion that advice and particularly legal advice be first obtained. It is true that there were other persons present when the notes were signed but two of them were presumably friends of Hart. Krajer was also present but it is clear that Hart was using him to perpetrate the fraud through the friendship existing between defendants and him and the commission to be paid to him. The presence of Krajer and his apparent acquiescence in the transaction served to silence any apprehensions of defendants. Under all of the circumstances we cannot say as a matter of law that defendants were negligent. . . . Some cases would seem to establish the rule that one who cannot read is negligent in trusting to the representations of the other party to the transaction as to the contents of an instrument which he signs, where he can easily procure the instrument to be read by third persons who are known to him. However, a person who cannot read is not always negligent in not calling on a third person to read the instrument to him. The question as to his negligence generally being one for the jury [to decide]. . . .

For the foregoing reasons the judgment is affirmed.   ◀

COMMENTS AND QUESTIONS

1. In this case, C.I.T. Corporation was an innocent holder in due course. Why wasn't it permitted to recover on the note?

2. If the defendants had known that they were signing promissory notes but had been induced to do so by fraud, would they still have a real defense to payment?

3. Note the court's discussion of the case of *Bedell v. Herring*. What reasons did it give for not following that case as a precedent?

Forgery

A person whose name has been forged on an instrument has a real defense to payment which is good against any holder. This rule applies regardless of whether the party is a maker, drawer, or indorser. The theory is that if the signature of the maker or drawer has been forged, no valid instrument ever came into existence. If an indorser's signature is forged, no party who takes the instrument subsequently has any legal title to it, since it was never properly negotiated. Not even a holder in due course is entitled to demand payment from a person whose signature has been forged. He may, however, collect damages from the person who indorsed or passed the forged instrument to him with the warranty that the instrument was genuine. (See page 471.) The party who is ultimately responsible for a forged instrument is the one who dealt directly with the forger. That person may recover from the forger if he is able to do so.

EXAMPLE

P forges M's signature to a promissory note payable to P and then negotiates it for value to x, who in turn negotiates it to Y; both x and Y are holders in due course. Y, of course, has no right to collect from M, since M's signature was forged. However, Y may collect damages from x on x's warranty that the instrument was genuine, and x, in turn, may collect from P if he can find him. But x must bear the loss if he cannot collect from P, since it was x who dealt directly with the forger.

Lack of Capacity

Any minor, insane person, drunkard, or other person without legal capacity who executes a negotiable instrument may elect to set up his disability as a real defense against any holder. And any such person who indorses and transfers an instrument may elect to avoid the negotiation and recover the instrument from a subsequent holder. If such a person indorses an instrument and does not elect to recover it, however, good title passes to the indorsee, and the rights and liabilities of the parties other than the minor remain the same. The incapacitated person himself is not liable as an indorser, since he has a real defense to secondary liability.

EXAMPLE

M gives P a promissory note payable on demand. P indorses it and transfers it to K, a minor, who in turn indorses it and transfers it to H. If K chooses to, he may avoid his negotiation to H and recover the instrument. If K does not so choose, H may present the instrument to M for payment and recover from him, since M has no defense to payment. If M refuses or neglects to pay, H cannot look to K for payment, since K has a real defense. H could, of course, notify P and demand payment from him.

Material Alteration

If a holder makes a significant alteration in the terms of an instrument (e.g., by changing the amount payable or the due date) without permission to do so, the alteration is in no way binding on the party responsible for payment and he may raise it as a real defense. If the holder who presents the instrument for payment does not qualify as a holder in due course, payment may be refused altogether. If a holder in due course presents it for payment, however, he is entitled to recover on the instrument in accordance with its original provisions before the alteration.

The New Jersey case that follows illustrates how this rule works. Notice that the jury's verdict was logically inconsistent with the law.

SMITH, KLINE & FRENCH CO. v. FREEMAN

Supreme Court of New Jersey, 1919
93 N.J.L. 45, 106 Atl. 22

► Action by the Smith, Kline & French Company against George T. Freeman. Verdict for defendant, and plaintiff's rule to show cause why verdict should not be set aside.[20]

TRENCHARD, J.   The plaintiff sued upon a promissory note made by the defendant to the Guarantee Food Company, and by the latter transferred by indorsement to the plaintiff. The defense was that the note was made for $55, and was thereafter altered by the agent of the payee to $550 without the assent of the defendant. The verdict was for the defendant.

We are of the opinion that the verdict was contrary to the law of the case as declared in the charge of the court. The trial judge seems to have assumed that the evidence showed conclusively that the note was complete and regular on its face, and was taken by the plaintiff, before maturity, in good faith, and for value, in the regular course of business, and without notice of any infirmity in the note or defect in title of the Guarantee Food Company. Accordingly, he instructed the jury that the plaintiff was a holder in due course. Of course, if such assumption as to the facts was right, the instruction was right, for it was correct in law. (N.I.L. Sec. 52.)

The judge, however, considered that it was open to the jury to find from the evidence, if they saw fit, that the note had been altered from $55 to $550 by the agent of the payee, without the assent of the maker, before it was negotiated to the plaintiff. That question he therefore submitted to the jury, and in connection therewith charged that when a note has been materially altered, and is in the hands of a holder in due course, not a party to the alteration, he may enforce payment according to the original tenor. That was correct in law. (N.I.L. Sec. 124.)

Finally, the judge instructed the jury to determine from the evidence whether or not the note was altered from $55 to $550; that if it was altered, the plaintiff could recover $55 only; that, if not altered, the plaintiff should recover $550, with due allowance for interest.

It is therefore manifest that the verdict for the defendant was contrary to the law of the case as declared in the charge of the court, and must be set aside for that reason.

The other reasons assigned we have not considered. The rule will be made absolute.[21]   ◄

---

[20] This means that the plaintiff asked the court to set aside the verdict unless the defendant could show good cause why it shouldn't be.

[21] In other words, the defendant was unable to show cause why the verdict should not be set aside.

COMMENTS AND QUESTIONS

1. Summarize the judge's instructions to the jury in the lower court. What was the jury's verdict? Why was the verdict contrary to law?
2. If the plaintiff had not been a holder in due course, would the verdict have been allowed to stand? Why?

Nondelivery of Incomplete Instrument

In most states, a maker or drawer who partially executes an instrument but does not deliver it has a real defense to any holder if some unauthorized person subsequently completes the instrument and puts in into circulation. This situation is to be distinguished from the situation in which an instrument is completed and not delivered, and also from the situation in which an instrument is delivered but not completed; in both these latter cases the defense is personal and, consequently, is not available against a holder in due course. In other words, the instrument must be both completed without authority and delivered without authority in order for a real defense to arise.

EXAMPLE

M makes out a promissory note payable to P, without filling in the amount, and leaves it on his desk. P takes the note without M's permission, fills in the amount for $100, and negotiates it to H, a holder in due course. H may not collect, since M has the real defense of nondelivery of an incomplete instrument.

The Uniform Commercial Code changes this rule by providing that such a defense is personal rather than real. So, in the above example, H could collect from M. The theory behind this change is that if the maker or drawer is careless enough to let such an instrument get into circulation, he should not be able to defend against an innocent holder in due course. The following decision contains a good discussion of whether this defense should be real or personal.

PAVILIS v. FARMERS UNION LIVESTOCK COMMISSION

Supreme Court of South Dakota, 1941
68 S.D. 96, 298 N.W. 732

▶ ROBERTS, J. This is an action brought to recover upon an instrument alleged to be a check transferred to plaintiff for value by one C. Hoard who was named as payee therein. Defendant interposed an answer alleging, first, that plaintiff was not a holder of the check in due course, and second, that the instrument, having been signed in blank by the defendant, having been stolen from its possession prior to delivery, had no legal inception or existence as a check. The court made findings in favor of the plaintiff and from the judgment entered thereon defendant has appealed.

The case was submitted upon an agreed statement of facts. The facts material to a decision are as follows:

"It was the practice of defendant's office manager, who was authorized to sign checks, to sign a block of instruments, printed to be used as checks . . . at the beginning of the business day and deliver the same to the bookkeeper whose regular duty it was to complete the instruments as checks and deliver the same to customers during the business day and it was likewise the practice of such office manager to procure the return of such signed instruments not delivered at the close of the business day for the purpose of safekeeping and for the purpose of checking or auditing the same, which instruments were thereafter placed in a safe in defendant's office; that the office of said office manager adjoined the front office in which the bookkeepers worked and it was the practice of the office manager to personally supervise the work of the bookkeepers during the business day and during the business day such bookkeepers worked at open desks in the presence of customers at the counter, in the presence of each other and in the presence of yardmen employed by defendant, who used the office occupied by bookkeepers as their headquarters.

"That upon February 24, 1939, and for some time prior thereto, one C. Hoard was employed by defendant as a bookkeeper and clerk whose duties were particularly to prepare an account of sales from the scale tickets presented by defendant's customers, and that it was the duty of another bookkeeper in defendant's employ, . . . to prepare or complete instruments printed to be used as checks upon such shippers' proceeds account for amounts indicated by such scale ticket and account of sales which instruments had, previous to being so completed, been signed by defendant's manager or office manager, who were the only employees of defendant expressly authorized by it to sign checks; that said Hoard was expressly authorized by defendant in the absence of such other bookkeeper to complete and deliver checks . . . only during business hours and only to defendant's customers and only for amounts due them as shown by such account of sales, but said Hoard was not expressly authorized by defendant to prepare, complete or deliver checks on such account, except during business hours, or for any amount other than as indicated by such scale tickets and account of sales or to anyone other than customers for whom livestock had been sold by defendant, and said Hoard was not expressly authorized to sign or endorse checks in the name of or on behalf of defendant.

"That the said Hoard was not entrusted with a key to the defendant's office although he did have access to a key kept in a desk in the office for the purpose of unlocking the padlock on the inside of the gate across the counter between defendant's office and the hall, it being his duty to enter the office after it had been opened by one of the defendant's employees entrusted with a key to such office, and if the gate had not been previously opened to unlock the same at the opening of the business day with the key placed in such desk.

"That on or about the 24th day of February, 1939, after the close of defendant's office, said Hoard gained access thereto by unlocking the gate across the counter, presumably with the key to the lock which he had removed from the desk before leaving the office, and climbed over the counter into defendant's office, and thereafter opened the safe in defendant's office by using the combination, which he knew, and without defendant's knowledge and consent took therefrom certain instruments printed for use as checks upon such shippers' proceeds account, blank as to amount, date and payee, which had been signed by defendant's office manager authorized to sign checks, in one of which instruments said Hoard thereafter without defendant's knowledge or express consent inserted the date, amount and payee in the manner which appears more fully from such instrument. . . .

"That said Hoard thereafter on said 24th day of February, 1939, placed his name upon the back of said instrument and delivered the same to plaintiff for a consideration of the value of One Hundred Two and 85/100 Dollars ($102.85). . . ."

S.D.C. 46.0120, referring to incomplete instruments, is worded as follows:

"Where an incomplete instrument has not been delivered it will not if completed and negotiated, without authority, be a valid contract in the hands of any holder, as against any person whose signature was placed thereon before delivery."

We think it clear that the check in controversy was an incomplete instrument when stolen and cannot be enforced in the absence of conduct on the part of the drawer creating an estoppel. . . .

It is urged by counsel that defendant is chargeable with negligence and is estopped to deny liability. . . . The cases cited are those in which the party sought to be charged upon a negotiable instrument has entrusted an instrument signed in blank to an agent or some other person who has wrongfully completed and negotiated the instrument; an agency or trust was created by means of which the fraud was committed and the fact that there was no authority for completing the instrument or that the paper was otherwise wrongfully dealt with was no defense.

Plaintiff also cites the case of Phillips v. A. W. Joy Co., 114 Me. 403, 96 A. 727, 728; L.R.A. 1916 E. 690. The question of the liability of the signer of a blank check which was stolen, completed and negotiated to the plaintiff was presented. The court held that the signer of the check was liable, and referring to the negligence of the defendant said:

"It is conceded that this check was signed in blank. Was there such negligence on the part of the defendant company or its agents as will permit this plaintiff to recover? The case seems to show quite clearly that the check book was left about the office in such a way that this check was, in fact, undoubtedly stolen, and, as we have already seen according to the plaintiff's undisputed testimony, the bookkeeper admitted that it would be easy for anybody to come in and abstract one of the checks. Under all the circumstances it seems to us, in view of the character of the paper stolen, its condition as to signature when stolen, the negligence in leaving the signed checks in such environment that theft was easy, and the apparent care of the plaintiff before cashing the check, that we should apply the rule of estoppel noted in Salley v. Terrill, as well as the rule that, when one of two innocent persons must suffer by the act of a third, he who has enabled such person to occasion the loss must sustain it."

This case differs in its facts from the case at bar. Checks signed in blank by the defendant in that case and left unguarded in his office to which strangers had access rendered him liable by reason of negligence. . . .

In Linick v. A. J. Nutting & Co. a blank check signed by the plaintiff was stolen by persons who filled in the amount and a fictitious name as payee and presented it to the drawee bank to be certified. They endorsed the name of the payee and transferred the check to the defendant for value who collected the amount of the check from the bank. The drawer having taken up the check from the bank instituted action for money had and received. Defendant sought to defend on the ground that plaintiff was estopped by reason of negligence to deny liability on the check. But the court held that the check was an incomplete instrument and that negligent custody of the check was not borne out by the facts.

While there can be no question that the provisions of the Negotiable Instruments Law do not prevent an inquiry into the question of the negligent custody of an incomplete instrument, and that, if as a result of negligence such instrument comes into the hands of a holder in due course, the latter may recover, yet we cannot say under the facts and circumstances of the instant case that defendant was negligent. The loss did not result from completion and negotiation of the check by one entrusted with its possession, and we are not concerned with a breach of duty as between a depositor and drawee. It does not appear that defendant company had reason to mistrust its employee and to anticipate the wrongful taking by him of a check signed in blank and the subsequent care in the execution of checks. It does not follow as a legal conclusion that signers of checks in blank assume the risk of liability in all cases where such instruments are wrongfully taken, completed and negotiated. To hold that a person is negligent in having in his possession a check signed in blank would require something more than the exercise of ordinary care.

The judgment appealed from is reversed.

All the judges concur.   ◀

COMMENTS AND QUESTIONS

1. Summarize the rule of law applied by the court in this case. Why did the court reject the plaintiff's argument that the defendant had been negligent?
2. The Uniform Commercial Code changes the law set forth in this case. Would the result have been different if the U.C.C. rule had been applied? Which rule do you prefer? Why?
3. The court discusses the case of *Phillips v. A. W. Joy,* which the plaintiff cited. How did the court distinguish that case?

Illegality of Instrument Itself

If the law of a state specifically makes an instrument void, not even a holder in due course can demand payment on it. The instruments most commonly found in this category are instruments whose terms are usurious, and instruments used for the payment of illegal gambling debts. If the law merely makes certain transactions illegal but does not void the instrument itself, the defense is only a personal one.

This point was at issue in the following Oklahoma case, which grew out of what must have been a remarkable poker game.

HUFFMAN v. KAHN

Supreme Court of Oklahoma, 1934
167 Okla. 389, 29 P. (2d) 767

▶ Busby, Justice.   The plaintiff in error (defendant in the trial court),
C. E. Huffman, engaged in a poker game with one J. L. Jones and others
on the evening of December 19, 1927. The game was played at a residence
in Oklahoma City. At the close of the game he executed and delivered to
J. L. Jones his check in the sum of $2,902 to cover his losses. The check was
a negotiable instrument. On the following morning Jones, by delivery and
indorsement, transferred the check to B. M. Kahn, proprietor of the Broad-
way Central Hotel, where Jones owed a hotel bill. He received from Kahn
the difference in cash between the amount of the check and the hotel bill.
Jones then, according to his statement to Kahn, departed for California.

As soon as the bank opened on December 20, 1927, Huffman stopped
payment on the check.[22]

B. M. Kahn, as the owner and holder of the check in the due course
of business, then brought suit in the district court of Oklahoma county
against C. E. Huffman. During the course of the litigation B. M. Kahn
assigned his interest to his wife, Alpha U. Kahn, who was substituted as
plaintiff and who appears in this court as defendant in error.

The cause was tried to the court without the intervention of a jury.
The trial court found as a matter of fact that the check "was given in a
gambling transaction, but that the original plaintiff B. M. Kahn was an
innocent purchaser thereof in due course and for value." The trial court
then concluded as a matter of law that an innocent purchaser for value of
a negotiable instrument was entitled to recover thereon even though the
same was originally given in payment of a gambling debt. In accordance
with this conclusion judgment was rendered for the plaintiff.

It is the contention of the defendant that a negotiable instrument given
in connection with a gambling transaction is absolutely void and is therefore unenforceable even in the hands of a holder in due course.

In this jurisdiction playing poker for money is made a misdemeanor
by statute section 1939, C.O.S. 1921. However, we have no statute, as some
states have, which specifically provides that notes given in connection with
gambling transactions are void in the hands of a holder in due course.
In jurisdictions having such statutes it has been generally held that a holder
in due course is not protected by the Negotiable Instruments Law. A number of decisions based upon such statutes are cited in defendant's brief.
Such decisions are not controlling in this jurisdiction.

The general rule applicable to this situation is stated in Joyce, Defenses
to Commercial Paper, p. 378, par. 296, as follows:

> "In the absence of a statutory provision that a bill or note given for a
> wagering contract shall be void, the defense that it was for such a con-

---

[22] This is a procedure by which the drawer instructs the drawee bank not to honor
the check when it is presented for payment. We will discuss this procedure in Section 5.

sideration cannot be sustained against a bona fide holder thereof for value before maturity and without notice." . . .

Commercial paper is designed to pass freely in the course of business between individuals. Jones, the winner in the poker game, could not have enforced collection of the check as against Huffman, the loser and maker. But this personal defense does not follow where the check in due course has been properly negotiated and falls into the hands of an innocent purchaser for value. If Huffman had not desired to pay his poker debt, he should not have issued a negotiable instrument.

We find no legal reason to depart in this jurisdiction from the general rule or to create an exception in behalf of this defendant who lost in a poker game. The penalty of one's folly in engaging in a losing and illegal enterprise at cards cannot under the present state law be visited on an innocent holder in due course of commercial paper. The learned trial judge so held. *We affirm his decision.*   ◀

COMMENTS AND QUESTIONS

1. Summarize the court's decision in this case. Do you agree with it?
2. The court mentions the fact that some states have statutes providing that negotiable instruments given in payment for gambling debts are void and unenforceable, even in the hands of a holder in due course. The defendant contended that Oklahoma should follow that rule. What reasons did the court give for rejecting the defendant's contention?

SECTION 5

SPECIAL RULES FOR CHECKS AND BANKS

In General

Checks are a special form of bill of exchange in that they are always drawn on a bank and are always payable on demand. Not surprisingly, there are special rules of law that govern their issuance, transfer, and payment, as well as the liability of the parties involved.

Enforcement of Secondary Liability

In order for a holder to protect his right to sue an indorser who fails to pay a check, he must present the check for payment to the bank within a reasonable time after it has been negotiated to him. If he does not do so, he loses that right. If the check is dishonored by the bank, the holder usually has the right to recover from the drawer. The only instance in which the holder loses this right to sue the drawer is when the check circulates for an unreasonable period of time after being issued and the drawer can show that he has suffered loss as a result of the delay. About the only way in which such a loss can occur, of course, is for the bank to become insolvent between the time the check is issued and the time it is presented for payment.

These rules are discussed at some length in the Kentucky case that follows:

ARTERBURN v. WAKEFIELD et al.

Court of Appeals of Kentucky, 1949
309 Ky. 212, 217 S.W. 2d 203

▶ The defendant Arterburn made out a check payable to the plaintiffs J. H. and H. A. Wakefield who presented it to the drawee bank where it was dishonored by nonpayment. Thereupon, the payees Wakefield brought suit against the drawer Arterburn. Apparently, no notice of dishonor was given Arterburn and none was alleged in the plaintiff's complaint.

Sims, Chief Justice. The sole question for determination on this appeal is whether or not in an action on a check the petition must aver that the maker or drawer was given notice that it was dishonored by the bank. The form in which the question arises is whether the pleadings support the judgment. . . .

It is insisted by appellant that as the petition did not aver notice was given him of the nonpayment of the check when presented at the bank, no cause of action was stated, therefore the pleadings do not support the judgment. He strenuously argues that a check is a bill of exchange under KRS 356.185, and that 356.089 requires notice of dishonor must be given the drawer of a bill of exchange, otherwise he is discharged. These two sections read:

"356.185. Check defined. A check is a bill of exchange drawn on a bank payable on demand. Except as herein otherwise provided, the provisions of this chapter applicable to a bill of exchange payable on demand apply to a check.

"356.089. Notice of dishonor. Except as otherwise provided in this chapter, when a negotiable instrument has been dishonored by nonacceptance or nonpayment, notice of dishonor must be given to the drawer and to each endorser, and any drawer or endorser to whom such notice is not given is discharged."

The two sections just quoted when standing alone do imply that a failure to give notice of dishonor of a check discharges the maker. However, the several provisions of the Negotiable Instrument Act stand in *pari materia* [23]

---

[23] This means that the various sections of the statute must be construed together and be consistent with each other.

and must be so construed as to give each a field of operation to effectuate
the legislative purpose. While KRS 356.185 makes a check a bill of exchange, it does not do so unqualifiedly but only "except as herein otherwise provided." We must not lose sight of KRS 356.186, which reads:

> "356.186. Time of presenting check; effect of delay. A check must
> be presented for payment within a reasonable time after its issue, or
> the drawer will be discharged from liability thereon to the extent of
> the loss caused by the delay."

It is seen that distinction is made between a bill of exchange and a
check by sections KRS 356.089 and 356.186. When notice of dishonor of
a bill of exchange is not given the drawer, he is released by KRS 356.089;
but when there is delay in presenting a check for payment, the maker is
only released by KRS 356.186 to the extent of the loss caused by the delay.
By enacting KRS 356.186 it is clear that the Legislature intended to place
the drawer of a bill of exchange and the maker of a check on a different
plane as to notice of dishonor of the respective instruments, since the latter
is regarded as the principal debtor and the check purports to be drawn
upon a fund deposited to meet it. . . .

We have neither found nor been cited to any case of ours, decided after
the Uniform Negotiable Instrument Act was adopted in this jurisdiction in
1904, which is directly in point; thus we presume there is none. But counsel
for appellee cites Deal v. Atlantic Coast Line R. Co., 225 Ala. 533, 144 So.
81, 83; 86 A.L.R. 455, on page 459, which decides the question now before
us. It is there said:

> "But as the purpose of notice is to enable the drawer to protect his
> interest when his check has been dishonored, and since presentment may
> be made, and hence the dishonor may occur, at any time within the stat-
> ute of limitations (say, five years) subject only to the drawer's right to
> recoup his actual loss, the importance of notice seems too slight for the
> statutory penalty of complete discharge for its omission. So unreasonable
> an interpretation is to be avoided if possible. Presentment and giving of
> notice are so closely connected, in purpose and performance, that, in
> the light of the rule of Law Merchant, and of Negotiable Instrument Law,
> 186, discharging the drawer of a check only to the extent of his loss
> in case of non-presentment, the courts might well conclude that section
> 89 requiring notice to the drawer was meant to apply to the drawer of
> a bill of exchange only; and that a literal interpretation of section 89
> as applicable to the drawer of a check is not within the meaning and
> the spirit of the two sections read together. . . .
>
> "As a general rule, the drawer or indorser of a check is not discharged
> from liability by the holder's omission, delay, or laches [24] in presenting
> it for payment within a reasonable time, and in not giving notice of dis-
> honor or nonpayment, unless such drawer or indorser has suffered some
> actual loss or damage, through the failure of the bank or otherwise, and
> then he is only discharged pro tanto." [25]

---

[24] Laches refers to an unreasonable delay in pressing one's rights. It is a term most
often used in equity courts.

[25] For so much; for as much as may be shown.

There are many authorities cited in the Deal case as well as in the annotation following it in 86 A.L.R. 463, which support the principle therein stated.

Appellant cites 1 Newman's Pleading & Practice, 3rd Ed., 301e, p. 393, to the effect that the petition in an action on a bill of exchange must aver notice of dishonor was given (or else the pleading must set out some excuse why notice was not given, such as waiver, etc.). Also, he relies upon Risk v. Bridgeford & Co., 15 Ky. Law. Rep. 206 and Frazier v. Harvie, 12 Ky. 185, as supporting his position that it was necessary for the petition to aver notice of dishonor of his check was given appellant. None of these authorities strike us as being in point as none of the three deals with a check, hence they do not make the statutory distinction between a check and a bill of exchange.

Furthermore, KRS 356.114 reads:

> "356.114. When notice to drawer not required. Notice of dishonor is not required to be given to the drawer in either of the following cases: (1) Where the drawer and the drawee are the same person. (2) Where the drawee is a fictitious person or a person not having capacity to contract. (3) Where the drawer is the person to whom the instrument is presented for payment. (4) Where the drawer has no right to expect or require that the drawee or acceptor will honor the instrument. (5) Where the drawer has countermanded payment."

It is common knowledge that when a bank refuses to honor or pay a check in the vast majority of cases it is because the maker has not sufficient funds on deposit to meet it or that he has countermanded payment. If he has not sufficient funds in the bank, he has no right to expect or require the bank to pay his check; in which instance under subsection 4 of KRS 356.114 he is not entitled to notice. Of course, should he countermand payment, no notice is required. It appears to us that the failure to give notice to the maker of the nonpayment of his check should be an affirmative defense under KRS 356.186 and the maker should be required to set out in his answer the damage which has resulted to him by reason of such failure. Consequently, we hold that it is not necessary for a petition in an action on a check to aver that notice was given to the maker that the instrument was dishonored by the bank on which it was drawn. The views herein expressed are supported by the great weight of authority.

Therefore, we hold that the petition in the instant case stated a cause of action and it supports the judgment.

The judgment is affirmed.   ◀

COMMENTS AND QUESTIONS

1. For whom did the lower court find? What happened on appeal?
2. With respect to the notice requirement, the court distinguishes a bill of exchange from a check. How do the rules applicable to the two types of instrument differ? Is the distinction justified, do you think?
3. Isn't the court saying, in effect, that the drawer of a check, like the maker of a promissory note, is primarily liable?

Obligation of Bank to Pay

So long as a drawer has a sufficient balance in his checking account, his bank is obligated to honor any check he draws on that account. If the bank refuses to pay, it is liable to the depositor for any damage that may be done to his credit standing or reputation. The obligation of the drawee bank, however, extends only to the drawer; it does not extend to any other party. In other words, the holder of a check may not force the bank on which it is drawn to pay it; his only remedy is to notify the secondary parties (i.e., indorsers or the drawer) and to collect from one of them.

As a general rule, a bank has no obligation to honor a check if the amount exceeds the balance in the drawer's account. But a bank does have an obligation in certain cases to protect the credit standing of its depositors. Take, for example, the situation presented in the Massachusetts case that follows.

CASTALINE v. NATIONAL CITY BANK OF CHELSEA

Supreme Judicial Court of Massachusetts, 1923
244 Mass. 416, 138 N.E. 398

► Action of contract and tort by Sam Castaline against National City Bank of Chelsea for nonpayment of checks drawn by plaintiff, a depositor, on the defendant bank. Directed verdict for defendant, and case reported. . . .

The bank refused to pay either of two checks because the total amount exceeded the available amount to plaintiff's credit. The case was reported on an agreement that, if the order was right, the verdict was to stand, and, if wrong, the case to be remanded for new trial on the question of damages.

CARROLL, J. The plaintiff, a depositor in the defendant bank, on July 12, 1920, drew two checks—one for $100 and one for $300. They were presented to the bank for payment simultaneously on July 13, 1920, arriving with others through the mail. The available funds to the credit of the plaintiff when the checks were presented, were $379.57. The defendant refused to pay either of the checks on the ground that the total amount of both exceeded the deposit of the plaintiff. The action is in contract or tort to recover damages for injury to the plaintiff's credit. The case is here on a report from the superior court.

If the check of a depositor exceeds the amount of his deposit, the bank may decline to pay it, and is not required to apply the deposit in partial payment of the check. . . . But a bank is bound to honor the checks of its depositors, if it has sufficient funds belonging to them when a check is presented, provided the funds are not subject to some lien or claim. If a bank refuses payment of its depositor's checks when in possession of his funds, it is liable to an action by the depositor. . . .

The two checks drawn by the plaintiff were presented for payment at the same time. There were sufficient funds on deposit to pay one of them, and in our opinion, it was the duty of the bank, in the absence of custom or rule of bankers to the contrary, to honor one of the checks, the bank having the right to make payment in any order it may decide, until the deposit is exhausted. It was so decided in Reinsch v. Consolidated National Bank, 45 Pa. Super. Ct. 236. In that case the plaintiff's balance was $328. Seventeen checks aggregating $664, were presented at one time through the clearing house. Payment was refused and they were all returned. It was held that it was the duty of the bank to pay some of the checks until the balance was so reduced that it was not longer possible to pay any of the remaining checks. In the opinion of the court, there was no necessity for injuring the plaintiff's credit by dishonoring all his checks when some of them could be paid. . . .

In 1 Halsbury's Laws of England, p. 605, it said:

> "If two checks are presented simultaneously, e.g., by the same mail or through the same clearing, and there are only funds sufficient to pay one, it is doubtful whether both may be returned," and "(c) unnecessary damage would be caused to the customer's credit."

Dykers v. Leather Manufacturers' Bank, 11 Paige, Ch. (N.Y.) 612, is not in conflict. In that case the depositor directed the bank to pay none of his checks, and later, the same day, checks were presented and dishonored. The depositor then withdrew all his funds paying some of his creditors. The plaintiffs, who were payees of a check drawn by the depositor, brought a bill in equity to recover from the bank. It was held that the bank was right in obeying the order of the depositor to stop payment, and was not obliged to distribute the money among the depositor's check-holders.

The credit of a customer might be seriously harmed if all his checks presented simultaneously exceeded his deposit and payment on all of them was refused. And we know of no reason why this should be done. The banker is not injured. The payment of the checks according to his discretion imposes no hardship on him. All that he is required to do, is to pay the checks in whatever order he decides until the depositor's funds are no longer sufficient to pay any of the remaining checks. The depositor cannot complain that some of the checks have been selected for payment and some refused. He is himself responsible that his account is overdrawn, he has caused the condition, and if any damage is occasioned because some of the checks are dishonored, the loss must fall on himself.

According to the terms of the report the case is to be remanded to the superior court for a new trial upon the question of damages.

So ordered. ◄

COMMENTS AND QUESTIONS

1. This case raises an interesting question: Does the decision mean that the bank has complete freedom to select whichever check it wishes for payment and to dishonor all the others? Suppose the amounts of two checks presented for payment were quite disproportionate, say $10 and $1,000, and the drawer had only $1,005 on deposit. Could the bank elect to pay the $10 check and dishonor the $1,000 check, knowing that the choice would probably do greater harm to the depositor's credit standing than would have been done if the $1,000 had been honored?

2. This case was remanded to the lower court for a new trial on the question of damages. How do you suppose these damages were ascertained?

Right to Stop Payment

For various reasons, a drawer may wish to stop payment on a check after it has been issued. For example, the payee or a holder may have lost the check, and the drawer may be afraid that some unauthorized person will try to present it for payment. Or the payee may not have performed all the services for which the check was issued.

As a general rule, a drawer may stop payment by giving notice to the bank in sufficient time. If, after receiving a timely notice, the bank goes ahead and pays the check, it is liable to the drawer and must restore the funds to his account. Many deposit agreements between drawers and banks require that a stop-order notice must be given in writing before it is binding on the bank. It is customary, however, for banks to waive this requirement and to accept an oral notice, provided a written confirmation follows.

Certification of Checks

As we have mentioned, although the bank is liable to the drawer of a check, it is under no duty to pay the *holder* of a check even when sufficient funds are on deposit. It may, however, obligate itself to pay him by certifying the check. The certification of a check is just like the acceptance of an ordinary bill of exchange (i.e., the bank stamps "certified" on the face of the check and one of the officers of the bank signs it). Once a bank has certified a check, the bank becomes absolutely liable for payment just as the acceptor of a bill of exchange does. Upon certification, the bank sets aside funds from the depositor's account to assure payment when the check is later presented. In effect, the bank guarantees that the drawer's signature is genuine and that it has, and will maintain, sufficient funds on deposit to pay the check. For this reason, a certified check is a very reliable instrument and is often used for the payment of important obligations, such as the purchase of real estate.

Certification has certain legal consequences. In the first place, it bestows primary liability on the bank, making the bank absolutely liable for payment. Moreover, if the certification is at the request of the holder, all prior parties (i.e., the drawer and any persons who may have indorsed the instrument before the *holder* received it) are discharged from liability, on the theory that the holder could have demanded payment from the bank but chose instead to take the promise of certification. In other words, having chosen not to receive payment (as he *could* have done when he had the check certified), the holder may no longer look to the secondary parties for payment; he may sue only the bank. If, on the other hand, the *drawer* requests certification of a check, the secondary liability of the parties remains, and the holder may look to the indorsers and the drawer if the check is not paid by the bank.

Note that bank is under no *duty* to the holder or the depositor to certify a check; nor does its refusal to certify constitute a dishonor of the instrument. A check must always be presented for *payment* before it is deemed to be dishonored.

Liability of Bank for Improper Payment

In General

There are several situations in which a bank may be held liable for the improper payment of a check. We have already mentioned one of these situations: that is, where the bank pays a check after the depositor has given timely notice to stop payment. A bank is also liable if it goes ahead and pays a check after receiving sufficient notice of the drawer's death; the theory here is that the contract between bank and depositor is terminated by the depositor's death, and the bank no longer has authority to charge his account. If the bank is not aware of a depositor's death, it is usually protected for a reasonable period—that is, until it should, in the normal course, receive notice thereof. Of course, if the bank refuses payment because of the depositor's death, the holder may always notify the prior indorsers of the dishonor and recover from them.

Forgery of Drawer's Signature

A bank is liable to a depositor if it charges his account without authority. Therefore it follows that if a bank pays a check on which the drawer's signature has been forged, the bank must bear the loss and restore the funds to the depositor's account. The bank's only remedy in such a case is to try to recover from the forger; it has no right to collect from the person who receives the money or from any indorser. In other words, the bank is charged with the duty of knowing the signatures of its depositors and of detecting any forgeries.

Many states recognize two exceptions to this general rule, however. First, a depositor has the duty to review his canceled checks within a reasonable time after the bank returns them to him and to inform the bank promptly of any forgeries. If he fails to do this, he, and not the bank, is responsible for any subsequent forgeries that might have been detected by the bank had it been promptly notified of the forgeries that had already occurred. In the case that follows, the court was faced with just this type of situation; it discusses the obligations of a depositor at some length.

DETROIT PISTON RING CO.
v. WAYNE COUNTY & HOME SAVINGS BANK

Supreme Court of Michigan, 1930
252 Mich. 163, 233 N.W. 185

▶ Helen Culbert was employed as a payroll clerk of the plaintiff Detroit Piston Ring Co., it being her job to prepare the bi-weekly paychecks drawn on the defendant bank, which were then signed by a duly authorized officer of the company on the assumption that the checks represented payment for wages due. Regularly, during the period from June 1922 to January 1925, Helen Culbert fraudulently made out several checks to nonexistent employees, had them duly signed and then indorsed and cashed them herself at banks and stores. These checks totaled over $28,000 in amount and were all paid by the defendant bank as drawee. Although the company was aware of higher costs in this particular plant, periodic audit inspections failed to uncover these misappropriations since the accounts had been falsified to conceal the fraud. However, inspection of the payroll sheet by one familiar with the names of the employees would have uncovered the scheme. During this period, the company's cancelled checks were returned each month and an agent of the company signed a receipt stating, "If no error is reported in 10 days the account will be considered correct." When the fraud was finally discovered by a comparison of the payroll records with the list of employees, the plaintiff brought suit against the defendant bank to recover the amount of the checks paid plus interest. In the lower court, the judge directed a verdict for the plaintiff for $33,942.54. The defendant appealed, alleging that the plaintiff was negligent in not detecting the misappropriation and was thereby estopped from recovery.

BUTZEL, J. . . . The difficult question in this case, one on which the authorities do not agree, is whether the question of plaintiff's negligence in issuing the checks should have been submitted to the jury. The trial judge, in directing a verdict for the plaintiff, held that the negligence of the plaintiff, if it was negligence on these facts, was no bar to the action.

It is a well-settled rule that a bank is not warranted in paying out the money of its depositor except in strict accordance with his order. If payment is made on a check on which the indorsement of the payee is forged, no amount of care on the part of the bank in identifying the person receiving payment, or in examining the indorsement, will entitle it to charge the payment against the account of the depositor. The bank may justify such payment, however, by showing that the depositor was negligent in carrying out some duty which it owed the bank, in such a way as to be the cause of the improper payment. . . .

At the beginning of the period during which the fraudulent checks were issued, the only negligence on the part of the company consisted in the failure of its officers to make a thorough check of the pay roll. Each time the pay checks were issued, the officer signing them would compare the checks with the pay roll, but at no time was a complete investigation made, i.e., a comparison of the checks with the time cards, nor was an audit of the pay roll ever made. It is perfectly clear that a complete investigation would have disclosed the fraud at once.

The estoppel of the depositor, on the ground of negligence, to recover for an unauthorized payment, is based on the failure of the depositor to act as a prudent business man in issuing his checks. In the present instance, during the first months plaintiff's officers did but one thing of which complaint can be made. They relied implicitly upon the honesty and faithfulness of a clerk, whom they had no reason to suspect of dishonesty, while the means of checking the accuracy of her work were readily available. After a study of the . . . authorities, while recognizing a conflict in them, we do not think this is the sort of conduct that should operate as an estoppel of the plaintiff.

A depositor may not sit idly by, however, after knowledge has come to him that his funds seem to be disappearing or that there may be a leak in his business and refrain from taking the steps that a careful and prudent business man would take in such circumstances, and which, if taken, would result in stopping the issuance of fraudulent checks. If he fails to take such steps, the facts may establish his negligence in the eyes of a jury, and in that event he would be precluded from recovering against the bank. At some time during the period of the defalcations, in the present case, the officers of the plaintiff had a fact brought to their attention which should have given them notice that something was amiss in their accounting system. This was the fact that the cost of production of their piston rings became noticeably higher, so that it became very difficult to secure orders. When this was first realized, the officers had a check made of their accounting system, but it was a superficial one, for the accountants did not make an audit of the pay roll. Just when, if at all, sufficient knowledge was brought home to them to have caused a prudent business man to carefully check his expenditures, and whether they exercised due care in their attempt to discover possible leaks in their business, are questions for the jury. The judgment must be reversed and a new trial granted; this court cannot properly pass upon questions of negligence except when the facts are such that all reasonable men would be likely to draw the same inference from them. . . .

All courts in this country are agreed that the depositor should carefully examine the bank statement, the check stubs, and the returned checks. It is evident that this was not done in the present case, but it is also clear that, even if appellee had done this, it would not have discovered the fraud, because no discrepancy would have been found. The failure to compare the returned checks with the bank statement and the check stubs was not the proximate cause of the failure to uncover the fraud. . . .

It was also argued that plaintiff was negligent in failing to compare the returned checks with the employment cards or the time cards. This would have disclosed the forgeries, but we do not believe the depositor has a duty to compare his returned checks with any of the records of his office except his check book or register. . . . After knowledge of the increased cost of production came to the officers of the company, due care might have required such comparisons, but this is a question which must be considered on the new trial. . . .

The judgment must be reversed, with costs to appellant, and a new trial granted.

Five judges concurred with BUTZEL, J. Two judges concurred in the result. ◀

COMMENTS AND QUESTIONS

1. The judge in the lower court had directed a verdict for the plaintiff. What happened in the appellate court? Do we know from this decision how the case finally came out?
2. The court acknowledged a split of authority in the decisions of the

state courts. Summarize the arguments for and against the decision. How much of a burden should be placed on companies to discover frauds of this sort, where, as the court admits, examination of the bank statements and checks themselves would disclose nothing?

The other commonly recognized exception to the general rule that a bank is liable for payment of a forged check occurs (1) when a person negligently takes a check from the forger without checking his identity, or (2) when a person has reason to be suspicious of the circumstances but, nevertheless, takes the check without further investigation. In such cases the person who receives the check must bear the loss, rather than the drawee bank that pays it; the theory is that the check would never have been presented for payment at all were it not for that person's carelessness. The application of this rule is well illustrated in the two cases that follow. In one case, the court upheld the exception to the general rule; in the other, it refused to apply it. Can you reconcile the conflicting results?

LOUISA NATIONAL BANK v. KENTUCKY NATIONAL BANK

Court of Appeals of Kentucky, 1931
239 Ky. 302, 39 S.W. 2d 497

► RICHARDSON, J. This action is by the Kentucky National Bank, the drawee of a check of $600, against the holder, the Louisa National Bank, which paid the check to the payee, Fred Banfield, a stranger, without inquiry, and without requiring his identification. The action was tried by the court without the intervention of a jury on an agreed statement of facts. The judgment was for the Kentucky National Bank, and the Louisa National Bank appeals. . . . The rule that the drawee of a bill of exchange could not recover in an action for money had and received the amount paid out by him on the bill to which the name of the maker had been forged was first announced in 1762, in Price v. Neal, 3 Burr. 1355. . . .

The question under consideration has been presented and decided by courts of foreign jurisdictions. As usual, they are not agreed as to the effect of the Negotiable Instrument Law on the doctrine of Price v. Neal, nor as to the application of its principles. Some of them hold that the provisions of the Negotiable Instrument Law adopt the rule in Price v. Neal, free from the exception which the courts have grafted into it.

Others hold that the Uniform Negotiable Instrument Law is merely a legislative affirmation of the rule of Price v. Neal with the equitable exception. . . .

The exceptional rule to Price v. Neal is not expressly included in any provisions of the Negotiable Instrument Law. Nor is it abrogated by any of its express provisions. It is consistent, and in perfect harmony, with it. It should therefore be applied and enforced when the proven facts require it to effectuate and administer substantial justice. And, since we have recognized it in Deposit Bank of Georgetown v. Fayette National Bank and applied it in Farmers' National Bank v. Farmers' & Traders' Bank of Maysville, *supra*, it may now be regarded as the law in this state in such cases.

The appellee, on presentation for payment of the $600 check, failed to discover it was a forgery. It was bound to know the signature of its customer, Armstrong, and it was derelict in failing to give his signature to the check sufficient attention and examination to enable it to discover instantly the forgery. The appellant, when the check was presented to it by Banfield, failed to make any inquiry of or about him, and did not cause him to be identified. Its act in so paying to him the check is a degree of negligence on its part equivalent to positive negligence. It indorsed the check, and, while such indorsement may not be regarded within the meaning of the Negotiable Instrument Law as amounting to a warranty to appellee of that which it indorsed, it at least substantially served as a representation to it that it had exercised ordinary care and had complied with the rules and customs of prudent banking. Its indorsement was calculated, if it did not in fact do so, to lull the drawee bank into indifference as to the drawer's signature to it when paying the check and charging it to its customer's account and remitting its proceeds to appellant's correspondent.

If in such transaction between the drawee and the holder of a check both are without fault, no recovery may be had of the money so paid. . . .

If, on the other hand, the holder acts in bad faith, or is guilty of culpable negligence, a recovery may be had by the drawee of such holder. The negligence of the Bank of Louisa in failing to inquire of and about Banfield, and to cause or to have him identified before it parted with its money on the forged check may be regarded as the primary and proximate cause of the loss. Its negligence in this respect reached in its effect the appellee, and induced incaution on its part. In comparison of the degrees of the negligence of the two, it is apparent that of the appellant excels in culpability. . . .

The views of the trial court are in harmony herewith, and the judgment is therefore affirmed. ◄

COMMENTS AND QUESTIONS

1. The court states that it is applying an exception to the general rule of *Price v. Neal.* What facts were present in this case to justify the result?
2. Suppose the Bank of Louisa had asked Banfield for satisfactory identification and he had supplied it. Would that have changed the result?

FIDELITY & CASUALTY CO. OF NEW YORK v. PLANENSCHECK

Supreme Court of Wisconsin, 1929
200 Wisc. 304, 227 N.W. 387

► Action by the Fidelity & Casualty Company of New York, plaintiff, against J. Planenscheck, defendant, commenced on the 12th day of October, 1927, to recover from said Planenscheck the amount of two checks paid by the drawee, the Security National Bank of Sheboygan. From a judgment rendered in favor of the defendant on the 1st day of December, 1928, the plaintiff appeals.

The Kohler Company is a manufacturing concern located at Kohler, in Sheboygan county, Wis., having in its employ a large number of employees. It carried an account in the Security National Bank of Sheboygan, Wis., and customarily paid its employees by checks drawn on that bank. The defendant operates a business in the city of Sheboygan.

On or about June 30, 1926, two checks, one for $76.21 and the other for $82.43, purporting to have been drawn by the Kohler Company, were presented to the defendant. One was payable to the order of Karl Kurz. It was indorsed "Karl Kypze." The other was payable to Mike Kowalsi. and was indorsed "Mike Kowalshi." The defendant cashed these checks and deposited them in the Security National Bank, which bank gave him credit for the amounts thereof upon his account. Between the 12th and 15th of July these checks were returned and cancelled to the Kohler Company, together with many others, and, upon examination by the Kohler Company, it was discovered that these two checks, together with many others not involved herein, were forgeries. The name of V. C. Mueller, paymaster, was the only written and forged signature upon the checks.

The bank was notified of the forgery, and it credited the Kohler Company with the amount thereof. Prior to this time, the plaintiff had issued its depositors' forgery policy No. 930601 to the Kohler Company and said Security National Bank, to indemnify said Kohler Company and said bank against loss by reason of the cashing of such forged checks.

On the 4th day of October, 1926, the plaintiff company discharged its obligation under said policy by paying the amount of such forged checks, thereby becoming subrogated [26] to all of the rights and claims of said Kohler Company and said Security National Bank, or either of them, growing out of the loss of the payment of said pretended checks. On October 3, 1927, the plaintiff notified the defendant in writing that the signature of V. C. Mueller on said checks was forged, that the payees named in the checks were fictitious persons, that the names indorsed on the back of the checks were forged, and demanded of the defendant that he pay to said plaintiff the amount of said checks.

The case was tried before a jury. At the close of the evidence, both parties moved for a directed verdict, which the court treated as a stipulation waiving a jury trial and submitting the entire case to the court for decision on the facts as well as the law, and discharged the jury. The court thereafter, without filing its findings of fact or conclusions of law, rendered judgment in favor of the defendant, from which judgment the plaintiff appeals.

OWEN, J. It was early held that the drawee of a bill of exchange could not recover the amount paid out by him on a bill to which the name of the drawer had been forged, in an action for money had and received. Price v. Neal, 3 Burr. 1355. . . .

This rule has met with varying favor in this country. It has been assailed by textwriters, repudiated by some courts, and adopted with exceptions by others. Although this court has not contributed to the controversy,

---

[26] This refers to the right of an insurance company (the plaintiff, in this case), after it has paid a loss, to sue the party responsible for causing the loss.

there has been much discussion and disagreement concerning the question. . . .

The framers of the Negotiable Instruments Act resolved this controversy, and gave expression to what they presumably considered the sound and just rule in two sections of the act, which will be found in our Statutes as sections 116.67 (62) and 118.64 (188). The former provides that: "The acceptor by accepting the instrument engages that he will pay it according to the tenor of his acceptance; and admits: (1) The existence of the drawer, the genuineness of his signature, and his capacity and authority to draw the instrument; and (2) The existence of the payee and his then capacity to indorse." The latter provides that: "Where the holder of a check procures it to be accepted or certified the drawer and all indorsers are discharged from liability thereon." While the statute says nothing about the effect of payment of the instrument, this is because payment plainly constitutes an acceptance as to which all courts are in agreement. So far as these two sections have been construed, with a single exception, it has been held that they adopt the principle of Price v. Neal in its purity, free from the exceptions which many American courts grafted onto the rule. . . .

The First National Bank of Oregon v. United States National Bank of Oregon, 100 Or. 264, 197 P. 547, 14 A.L.R. 479, seems to hold that these provisions of the Uniform Negotiable Instruments Act preserved the exceptions to the rule of Price v. Neal, approved and adopted by the majority of American courts. We have considered the reasons assigned by the Oregon court for its conclusion, and do not regard them of sufficient force to justify us in dissenting from what appears to be an otherwise uniform construction of this statute.

The adoption of the Negotiable Instruments Act by nearly every state of the Union resulted from a belief that a uniform law upon the subject approximated in importance a national currency system, and it was passed for the purpose of harmonizing and making uniform the law upon a subject concerning which there was much disagreement, giving rise to embarrassment and confusion in the commercial world. The end thus attained should not be frittered away by conflicting judicial interpretations of the act. In construing the act, courts should the more readily yield to precedent in order to avoid a conflict of authority as discouraging as the situation existing prior to the adoption of the law. . . .

It is, consequently, necessary to consider whether the defendant was a holder of the instrument in due course. It is undisputed that these checks were complete and regular upon their face; that he had no notice of any infirmity in the instrument or defect in the title of the person negotiating it, and that he took it in the usual course of business. It is urged, however, that the fact that there was a discrepancy in each instance between the spelling of the name of the payee on the face of the check and of the indorser on the back of the check was sufficient to have put the defendant upon inquiry concerning the forgery, and that he should at least have required the identification of the payee. Upon this question the custom prevailing in the city of Sheboygan with reference to cashing of pay checks has a very important bearing.

The evidence shows that the Security National Bank, upon which these checks were drawn, required no identification whatever of those possessing similar pay checks. They were cashed as a matter of course. A teller of that bank testified that, if they required identification of all factory pay roll checks, they would not get through until 12 o'clock that night. It was a practical impossibility. It further appears, not only by the testimony of this teller, but by the cashier of the Farmers' & Merchants' Bank of Sheboygan and of Mr. Mueller, the paymaster of the Kohler Company, that discrepancies between the spelling of the name of a payee as it appeared on the face of a check and as indorsed on the back of a check were not uncommon on pay checks, and that the banks ascribed little, if any, importance to such discrepancies. Mr. Mueller testified that the names of the employees of the Kohler Company were not infrequently misspelled upon their records and that they used the indorsements on the returned checks to correct their own records with reference to the spelling of the names of their employees. The defendant had been in business in the city of Sheboygan for many years, and was frequently called upon to cash pay checks issued by the Kohler Company. He presumably knew of this custom on the part of the banks in paying these checks without identification and of overlooking discrepancies between the spelling of the name of the payee on the face and on the back of the check. The checks were, concededly, very good imitations of the Kohler pay checks, and, under all the circumstances, there is no room to question that he stands in the position of a bona fide holder of the checks.

Judgment affirmed.   ◄

COMMENTS AND QUESTIONS

1. Distinguish this case from the *Louisa National Bank v. Kentucky National Bank* case immediately preceding. Wasn't this case more favorable to the bank—that is, shouldn't Planenscheck have noticed the discrepancies between the payees' names and their indorsements? How can the decision for the defendant be justified here?

2. Note the court's discussion of the evidence concerning the custom of cashing employee pay checks in Sheboygan. Should the law encourage this sort of practice?

Forgery of Indorsements

Legally, a forged indorsement is a nullity; therefore, it is not considered as a valid transfer of the ownership of a negotiable instrument. It follows that a person whose indorsement has been forged may recover possession of the instrument from any person who holds it after the forgery has occurred. If a bank has already paid a forged check, the person whose signature has been forged may recover the proceeds from the person who collected them. In most states, however, he may not sue the drawee bank to recover. The bank, for its part, has no right to pay such a check, since, by paying someone who does not legally own the instrument it is not following the order of its depositor. Therefore, it must restore the funds to the depositor's account. If the bank is forced to do this, however, it may then sue any of the indorsers who indorsed after the forgery, because they have, by their indorsement, warranted the genuineness of the prior signatures. For the same reason, the bank may recover from the person to whom it has erroneously made payment.

EXAMPLE

D draws a check on B BANK payable to P. F steals the check, forges a special indorsement from P to F on it, and then negotiates the check to x. x then indorses the check and negotiates it to H, who collects the proceeds from B BANK.

> Pay to the order of F
> (signed) P *Forgery*
> Pay to the order of x
> (signed) F
> Pay to the order of H
> (signed) x

P, whose indorsement was forged, may recover the proceeds from H, but he has no right to sue B BANK. The bank would have no right to charge D's account; indeed, it must restore the funds to his account. Having done this, the bank may then recover from H (the person whom it paid) or from x (whose indorsement guaranteed the genuineness of P's signature). If H is forced to pay, he in turn may recover from x on the same warranty. In such an event, x's only recourse is to sue F, the forger.

Alteration

A drawee bank that honors a check whose amount has been improperly altered is liable to the depositor for the increased amount and must restore that amount to his account. As in the case of a forgery, the bank is responsible for detecting the alteration. By honoring an altered check, the bank is charging the depositor's account without authority. The bank may, however, recover its loss from the person who received payment, or else it may sue any secondary party who indorsed the check after it was altered, for breach of the warranty that the instrument was genuine.

Many states recognize an exception to the general rule when the drawer makes out a check so carelessly that it can easily be altered—for example, by leaving a blank space after the amount. In such cases, the bank is not liable for the overpayment; the drawer's only recourse is to the person who made the alteration.

SECTION 6

DISCHARGE OF NEGOTIABLE INSTRUMENTS

In General

A negotiable instrument is said to be discharged when the rights and liabilities of all the parties to the instrument have been terminated. In this concluding section, we shall summarize the principal methods of discharging negotiable instruments.

Discharge by Payment

Most instruments are discharged by payment, by the maker or the drawee, in the usual course of business either when the instrument matures or after it has reached maturity. If the maker of a promissory note pays the instrument and acquires it before it reaches maturity, he may negotiate it further and keep it in circulation, just as any other holder could. However, if the maker pays a note before it reaches maturity and fails to get possession of the note, it may be negotiated to a holder in due course, who can then force the maker to pay again. Witness the following case.

MANCHESTER et al. v. PARSONS

Supreme Court of Appeals of West Virginia, 1915
75 W.Va. 793, 84 S.E. 885

► The defendant Parsons executed a negotiable promissory note for $800 payable to Burton & Co. 18 months from date. Around Nov. 1, 1910, the payee negotiated the note for value to the plaintiff Manchester. On June 3, 1911, the defendant Parsons (the maker) sold and delivered some colts to Burton & Co. (the payee) for the sum of $1,675, it being understood that by means of this sale the note was to be paid off in full and the balance to be paid by Burton & Co. to Parsons. The plaintiff Manchester (the indorsee and a holder in due course) sued the defendant Parsons (the maker) on the note and the defendant offered evidence of payment to Burton & Co. as a defense. The court excluded this evidence and directed a verdict for the plaintiff.

WILLIAMS, J. . . . Counsel contends that defendant's note was thus discharged. But the uncontradicted testimony of L. A. Burton, the surviving partner, and of Lee Whorton, is that it had been indorsed to plaintiffs, for value, about the 1st of November, 1910, and therefore payment to the original holders did not discharge it. Counsel invokes subsection 4 of section

119 of the Negotiable Instruments Act as authority for his contention. Section 119 describes how a note may be discharged, and subsection 4 reads: "By any other act which will discharge a simple contract for the payment of money." This subsection must be interpreted with reference to the general purpose of the Negotiable Instruments Act. It must be read in connection with its other provisions, and made to harmonize with the general scheme and plan of the act. Thus viewing subsection 4, it is apparent that it was never the legislative intent to make so radical a change in the general law respecting negotiable instruments, as would be wrought by the literal interpretation contended for. It is clear, from other provisions of the act, as well as from the preamble thereto, that the Legislature did not contemplate making so vital and radical a change in the law, as to permit equities between the original parties to a negotiable instrument to defeat the title of an innocent holder for value in due course. That would counteract the purpose of the statute, which was not to revolutionize the law, but to amend, enlarge and re-enact certain sections of the statute law respecting negotiable instruments, and consolidate and arrange in one act the general laws on the subject, so as to make them uniform with laws of other states. The acts which will discharge a simple contract for payment of money, in order to effect a discharge of negotiable paper within the contemplation of subsection 4, must therefore necessarily be limited to such acts as relate to and affect the holder of the paper demanding payment of it. It does not include a holder for value in due course. Negotiable paper, in the hands of such holder, is not discharged by payment made to his transferor, either before or after the transfer. Such was the rule of the common law respecting negotiable paper, and it was clearly not the legislative purpose to change the rule. It would injuriously affect the value of commercial paper, by putting it on a plane with simple contracts for the payment of money. We cannot conceive that the Legislature intended any such thing, although a literal interpretation of the subsection in question might indicate otherwise. Other provisions of the statute expressly preserve the rights of holders in due course. Section 52 (sec. 4223) defines a holder in due course to be one who takes the paper in good faith for value without notice of any infirmities in it or defect in the title of the person negotiating it. And section 57 (sec. 4228) says that such a one holds it "free from any defect of title of prior parties, and free from defenses available to prior parties among themselves and may enforce payment of the instrument for the full amount thereof against all parties liable thereon." To construe subsection 4 of section 119, as contended for by counsel, would defeat section 57 and other provisions contained in the act. . . . Trust Co. v. Crawford & Ashby, 69 W. Va. 109, 70 S.E. 1089, 33 L.R.A. (N.S.) 587, holds that "the rights of a bona fide assignee of such a note, in due course, are not affected by the equities of the maker." Although that was a suit on a negotiable note, given and payable, before the passage of the negotiable instruments statute, still it does not change the general commercial law in that respect. Hence payment by defendant to Burton & Co. before the note became due, whether before or after they had negotiated it,

could not defeat collection by an innocent holder for value who acquired it in due course.

The judgment is affirmed.   ◄

COMMENTS AND QUESTIONS

1. Was the defendant justified in assuming that Burton & Co. still had the note when he sold the colts to them? Do you think Burton & Co. should have informed him that they had negotiated the note to Manchester at that time?

2. If Manchester had known of the sales transaction involving the colts at the time he took the note, would he still be entitled to recover from Parsons?

3. The court states that it was "clearly not the legislative purpose to change the [common-law] rule . . . although a literal interpretation of the subsection in question might indicate otherwise." This is an interesting illustration of statutory interpretation, which we discussed at some length in Chapter 6.

Is an instrument discharged when payment is made by a secondary party (e.g., an indorser)? Not necessarily, since the secondary party may have the right to sue a prior indorser or the maker or drawer. If he is forced to make payment, a secondary party may take possession of the instrument and, in turn, may sue other prior parties for reimbursement.

Although a negotiable instrument is always payable in money, it may be discharged, if all the parties agree, by the transfer of property or by the performance of services.

Discharge by Cancellation

The holder of an instrument may intentionally cancel it by tearing it up, crossing out its terms, burning it, or destroying it in some other way. Intentional cancellation of this sort is considered to be an effective discharge of the instrument. If, however, the holder can show that the instrument was destroyed accidentally, or without intent to cancel, or without his authority, no discharge occurs and the parties are still bound.

In the Virginia case that follows the court was asked to decide whether a promissory note had been discharged by cancellation.

JONES' ADM'RS. v. COLEMAN

Supreme Court of Appeals of Virginia, 1917
121 Va. 86, 92 S.E. 910

► PRENTIS, J. This proceeding was a motion under section 3211, of the Code, made by Kate D. Coleman against W. R. Jones and Jack Shell, administrators of Reps Jones, deceased, upon which there was a judgment in favor of the plaintiff.

The notice states that the plaintiff will move the court for judgment for the sum of $500, and then uses this language:

"... The same being evidenced by that certain promissory negotiable note, made by the said Reps Jones, deceased, bearing date on the 1st day of January, 1915, and payable to me at the Bank of Brunswick, Lawrenceville, Virginia, 365 days after date, which said note waives the benefit of the homestead exemption and was executed by the said Reps Jones, deceased, and is for the principal sum of five hundred ($500.00) dollars."

A jury was waived, and the case was submitted to the judge of the trial court. To sustain the motion, a mutilated paper was presented, upon which there was neither date nor signature: both apparently having been destroyed by burning. The paper originally was a printed blank form of a negotiable note, payable at the Bank of Lawrenceville. This mutilated remnant shows that the figures "500" (succeeding the "$" mark) and "365" (preceding the printed words "days after date"), the name "Kate D. Coleman," and the words "five hundred," had been inserted in ink. The evidence of those familiar with the handwriting of the decedent, Reps Jones, is sufficient to show that these words and figures were written by him.

The only witness introduced by the plaintiff for the purpose of proving the existence of the note described in the notice was Beverly Coleman, a brother of the plaintiff. He is an ignorant man, and his testimony is vague and unsatisfactory,[27] amounting substantially to this: That the plaintiff had been a domestic servant of the decedent for 15 or 16 years prior to his death; that some time in the year 1914 he saw in his sister's room in a sewing machine drawer a note for $500 which had Mr. Reps Jones' name on it. Upon demurrer to the evidence, his testimony may be sufficient to identify the mutilated paper as constituting the remnant of the paper which he saw; he did not, however, remember the date of the paper, which at that time was in an envelope; and after Jones' death his sister showed him a mutilated envelope and the mutilated paper above referred to, which it had been when presented as the note sued on. It will be noted that the notice alleges that this note was dated January 1, 1915, and that this date was subsequent to the time when the witness said he saw the paper with Reps Jones' name on it. This is substantially all of the testimony, and there was no attempt to explain or account for the mutilation of the paper.

In our opinion this evidence is clearly insufficient to support the judgment.

Paragraph 123, 2841a of the Code, being section 123, art. 8 of the Negotiable Instruments Law, which is in accord with an established rule of evidence, reads thus:

"A cancellation made unintentionally or under a mistake, or without the authority of the holder, is inoperative; but where an instrument or any signature thereon appears to have been canceled, the burden of

---

[27] Note the court's comments on the intelligence of the witness and the vagueness of his testimony. Perhaps, if he had been a brighter and more coherent witness, the result of the case would have been different.

proof lies on the party who alleges that the cancellation was made unintentionally or under a mistake or without authority."

The language and meaning of the statute are clear and controlling. We can only speculate as to why the date and the signature, which we may assume were originally upon the paper presented, have been destroyed by burning. The presumption is that the burning was intentional and done for the purpose of canceling the instrument. This presumption can only be overcome by evidence showing that such burning was done "unintentionally, or under a mistake, or without authority." The plaintiff has failed to sustain the burden which the statute clearly puts upon her.

For these reasons, the judgment must be reversed, and this court will enter judgment dismissing the motion.

Reversed.

Burks, J., absent.   ◄

COMMENTS AND QUESTIONS

1. Note the provision of the N.I.L. which the court is called on to interpret here. Upon whom does the court throw the burden of proof? Do you agree with the result?

2. Wouldn't it be a better rule to say that a note like this is deemed to be valid unless the other party can prove that there was an intent to cancel it?

Discharge by Renunciation

The holder of an instrument may at any time renounce his rights against any or all parties to the instrument. To be effective, either the renunciation must be set down in writing, or else the instrument itself must be surrendered to the primary party. The reason for this rule is obvious: If the renunciation were oral, and if the instrument were not delivered to the party with primary liability, the instrument might be negotiated to a holder in due course who was unaware of the renunciation. In that case, the primary party would be liable to such a holder. Finally, a renunciation must be unconditional before it constitutes an effective discharge. Notice how the court disposed of the following case, which involved an alleged renunciation.

FARMER v. FARMER

Supreme Court of Appeals of Virginia, 1953
195 Va. 92, 77 S.E. 2d 415

► On June 10, 1947, P. W. Farmer deeded land to the defendants Annie T. Farmer and D. S. Farmer in exchange for a promissory note for $12,000 executed by the defendants, payable to P. W. Farmer in 15 annual installments, to be secured by a deed of trust[28] on the property. Sometime in 1948, P. W. Farmer informed the defendants that he intended to leave his entire estate, including the note, to a college whereupon the defendants

---

[28] A deed of trust is similar to a mortgage.

suggested that P. W. Farmer leave them the property they had purchased from him free and clear of the note obligation. He said he would consider this suggestion. A few weeks later he made the following notation on the back of the note: "At death, this note is to be cancelled and not to be collected. 5/1/48 (signed) P. W. Farmer." Later that year, he noted on the deed of trust "At my death, this deed of trust is to cancel and Note not collected. Sept. 2, 1948 (signed) P. W. Farmer." He died on Sept. 1, 1949, at which time there was a balance of roughly $10,750 unpaid on the note. The administrator of his estate brought suit on the note against the defendants who alleged that P. W. Farmer had renounced his rights and the note was no longer enforceable. The trial court found in favor of the plaintiff administrator.

EGGLESTON, JUSTICE. . . .

The simple issue is whether the notations on the note and the deed of trust, or either of them, satisfy the requirements of Code, 6-475 (N.I.L. 122), so as to constitute a renunciation by the holder of his rights against the makers. That section reads:

> "Renunciation by holder.—The holder may expressly renounce his rights against any party to the instrument before, at, or after its maturity. An absolute and unconditional renunciation of his rights against the principal debtor made at or after the maturity of the instrument discharges the instrument. But a renunciation does not affect the rights of a holder in due course without notice. A renunciation must be in writing unless the instrument is delivered up to the person primarily liable thereon." . . .

The statute relates solely to the renunciation of the rights of a holder of a negotiable instrument and is complete and self-executing. It provides a method whereby the holder of a negotiable instrument may renounce his rights against any party to the instrument and effect its discharge, save as to a holder in due course without notice. . . .

Under the statute the necessary requirements of an effective renunciation are: (1) the holder must "expressly renounce" his rights, as stated in the first sentence; and (2) The renunciation "must be in writing unless the instrument is delivered up to the person primarily liable thereon," as embodied in the last sentence. Under the second sentence, a discharge of the instrument is effected by "an absolute and unconditional renunciation" of the holder's rights against the principal debtor made "at or after the maturity of the instrument." In the third sentence is the qualification that "a renunciation does not affect the rights of a holder in due course without notice."

There is no requirement that a renunciation must be made effective immediately, or provision that it cannot be made effective at a future time, or after the death of the holder of the instrument. Nor is there any requirement that a renunciation without consideration must meet the essentials of a gift *inter vivos*.[29] There is nothing in the language used to suggest

---

[29] Literally, a gift between the living. This is to be distinguished from a gift by one who feels he is about to die and wishes to dispose of certain property. The latter is called a gift *causa mortis*.

that a written renunciation may not be in the form of a will, or that if "testamentary in character," but not properly executed as a will, it must be cast aside as not constituting a valid renunciation. . . .

When we examine the writings or notations with which we are here concerned in the light of the circumstances under which they were made, we are of opinion that they clearly meet the requirements of the first sentence of the statute. The holder of the note indicated to Mrs. Farmer, one of the makers, his desire to relieve her and her husband, the co-maker, of the obligation to pay such balance as might be due on the note at the holder's death. Having made up his mind to do this he consulted his counsel as to the manner in which it could be accomplished. Following the advice of his counsel, in the presence of one of the makers, he wrote on the back of the note "At death this note is to be cancelled and not to be collected." In this manner he did "expressly renounce" his rights against the makers of the note effective at a future date, but upon the happening of his death, an event which was bound to occur. It was an express present renunciation of the holder's right to claim whatever balance might be due on the note at the date of the holder's death.

Not only does this notation satisfy the requirement of the statute that the renunciation be in writing, but it was placed on the back of the note where the person who might come into possession of the instrument was bound to see the evidence of renunciation. . . .

It is argued that the notations here do not constitute an effective renunciation under the statute, because at any time before his death the holder might have changed his mind and canceled either or both of them. There are two ready answers to this argument. In the first place, no question of the cancellation of the renunciation is here involved. The admitted fact is that the holder made no attempt to cancel the renunciation, or ever expressed an intent or desire to do so. Indeed, he delivered the note carrying the notation to Mrs. Farmer, one of the makers, and allowed her to retain it up to the time of his death, thus precluding an erasure or cancellation by him of the evidence of the renunciation.

In the next place, assuming that a valid renunciation once made may be canceled, any written renunciation, whether effective immediately or in the future, would be subject to the same infirmity so long as the holder retained possession of the note and the evidence of renunciation. Hence, the possibility of cancellation is not a determinative factor in ascertaining the validity of a renunciation effective at a future date.

Although a similar statute has been adopted by all of the States, there are few decisions as to the essential requirements of a renunciation. We have been pointed to no authority, nor have we been able to find any, which holds, as the administrator contends, that a renunciation under the statute may not be made effective at a future date. Indeed, such decisions as we have been able to find uphold renunciations of this character. . . .

We are of opinion that the notations on the note and deed of trust constitute a valid renunciation by P. W. Farmer, the holder, of his rights against the defendants under the note, and that, therefore, the note is not a valid and enforceable obligation of the defendants.

Accordingly, the decree is reversed and the cause remanded for the entry of a proper decree.

Reversed and remanded.   ◄

COMMENTS AND QUESTIONS

1. What was the appellate court's decision?
2. Note that the deceased had actually delivered the note to one of the defendants before he died. If he had kept possession of the note, would the result have been different?
3. Suppose the deceased had written nothing on the note or deed of trust but, instead, had delivered the note to the defendants with the oral statement that he was thereby renouncing all rights to collect? Would this have been a binding renunciation?

Discharge by Alteration

The material alteration of an instrument by a holder discharges all parties to the instrument, except those who know about the alteration and assent to it, and subsequent indorsers who, by their indorsement, warrant the genuineness of the instrument. An alteration is said to be "material" when it affects an important term in the instrument, such as the amount payable, the date or place of payment, or the parties. An immaterial alteration has no effect.

There is one exception to this general rule, as we have already seen (pp. 499–500): If a holder in due course subsequently acquires an altered instrument, he may enforce it according to its original terms.

EXAMPLE

M gives P a note for $500. P changes the amount of the note to $5,000 and negotiates it to H, a holder in due course. H may collect $500 (the original amount of the note) from M. To recover the rest of his loss, H must look to P.

SUMMARY OF THE LAW OF NEGOTIABLE INSTRUMENTS

Classification and Definitions

There are three main categories of negotiable instruments: (1) promissory notes, (2) bills of exchange, and (3) checks. A *promissory note* is a promise by one person (called the maker) to pay another person (called the payee) a specified sum of money. A *bill of exchange* is an order by one person (called the drawer) addressed to another person (called the drawee) directing that person to pay a specified sum of money to a third person (called the payee). A *check* is a special form of bill of exchange that is always payable on demand and in which the drawee is always a bank.

The transfer of a negotiable instrument is commonly called a negotiation. The person who transfers the instrument indorses it by signing his name to it; he then becomes known as the indorser, and the person who receives it is known as the indorsee. A person lawfully in possession of an instrument is called a holder; if he has given consideration for the instrument, he is known as a holder for value.

Requirements for Negotiable Instruments

To qualify as a negotiable instrument under the Uniform Negotiable Instruments Law, an instrument (1) must be in writing, (2) must be signed by the maker or drawer, (3) must contain an unconditional promise or order to pay a certain sum of money, (4) must be payable on demand or at a fixed or certain time in the future, and (5) must be payable to someone's order or to bearer.

An instrument that does not meet these requirements is considered non-negotiable, and the law governing its transfer and the rights and liabilities of the parties is the same as the law governing the assignment of a contract right. An instrument that does meet these standards is classified as negotiable and is governed by the rules of the N.I.L. (or, where it has been enacted, the Uniform Commercial Code).

Indorsement and Transfer

A negotiable instrument is not deemed to be in circulation until it has been issued—that is, until the maker or the drawer has delivered it to another party with the intention of making it effective. Once it has been issued, it may be negotiated from one holder to another until it is presented for payment.

In order for a holder to negotiate an instrument payable to his order, he must indorse it and deliver it to the next holder. His indorsement may be (1) special, (2) blank, (3) restrictive, or (4) conditional. A *special indorsement* makes the instrument payable to the order of the indorsee and requires that he, in turn, indorse it if he wishes to negotiate it further. A *blank indorsement* consists of a signature only and makes the instrument payable to bearer. A *restrictive indorsement* restricts the further negotiation of the instrument and usually orders the indorsee to collect the proceeds for a specific purpose. A *conditional indorsement* makes the negotiation of the instrument conditional upon the happening of some event.

A negotiable instrument payable to bearer may be negotiated by delivery alone; no indorsement is required. If an instrument originally payable to bearer is specially indorsed by a holder, the N.I.L. holds that the instrument remains negotiable by delivery alone despite the indorsement, while the U.C.C. holds that such an indorsement makes it payable to order and therefore requires an indorsement for further negotiation.

If an instrument payable to order is transferred without indorsement, it is treated the same as an assignment of a contract right. However, the transferee has a right to demand that the transferor properly indorse the instrument; once that has been done, the transferee becomes a holder by proper negotiation.

Liability of Parties

There are two principal kinds of liability on a negotiable instrument: (1) primary, and (2) secondary. A person with *primary liability* is under an absolute obligation to pay the instrument. A person with *secondary liability* is required to pay only if payment is refused by the person who is called on to pay it first.

The maker of a promissory note is primarily liable for its payment; by executing the note, he makes a warranty that the payee exists and has legal capacity to negotiate the instrument. If the drawee of a bill of exchange accepts the instrument and agrees to pay it, he becomes known as the acceptor; by the act of accepting the bill, he assumes primary liability for its payment.

Generally speaking, indorsers are only secondarily liable for payment. An ordinary, or unqualified, indorser commits himself to pay the instrument only in the event that it is properly presented for payment and is dishonored, and only if proper notice of the dishonor is given to him. An indorser who wishes to avoid this secondary liability may qualify his indorsement by adding "without recourse," or words of similar meaning. However, both qualified and unqualified indorsers guarantee to subsequent parties (1) that the instrument is genuine, (2) that they have good title to it, and (3) that all parties who previously signed the instrument were legally competent to act. In addition, a qualified indorser warrants that he has no knowledge of any fact that would impair the validity of the instrument or make it valueless. An indorser who wishes to avoid his responsibility for these warranties, as well as his secondary liability for payment, must include the words "without warranties" in addition to "without recourse."

Although a person who transfers an instrument payable to bearer without indorsement does not have secondary liability for its payment, he makes the same warranties to his transferee that a qualified indorser makes.

The drawer of a bill of exchange, like an unqualified indorser, is secondarily liable for payment if the instrument is presented for payment and is dishonored, and if he is properly notified of the dishonor. Like the maker of a promissory note, the drawer of a bill of exchange guarantees the existence and the legal capacity of the payee.

A person who signs his name to an instrument merely to give the holder additional security is known as an accommodation party. He is liable for payment to a holder for value. If he is forced to pay, however, he may recover from the party who was originally obligated to make payment.

Enforcement of Secondary Liability

In order for secondary liability to be enforced, certain conditions must exist: (1) the holder must present the instrument for payment or acceptance, (2) it must be dishonored by nonpayment or nonacceptance, and (3) notice must be given to the secondary parties against whom liability is to be enforced.

An instrument that is payable at a fixed date must be presented for payment on that date; an instrument payable on demand must be presented within a reasonable time after issue (if it is a promissory note), or within a reasonable time after the last negotiation (if it is a bill of exchange). It must be presented to the proper person at the proper place and at the proper time, it must be shown to the party to whom presentment is being made, and it must be surrendered to him if he pays it. Presentment is excused or delayed in certain cases if the circumstances warrant it.

In certain situations—for example, when it is necessary to fix a maturity date—a bill of exchange must first be presented for acceptance. The requirements for such presentment are roughly the same as for presentment for payment.

If an instrument is dishonored by nonpayment or nonacceptance, prompt notice must be given by the holder to any secondary parties he wishes to hold responsible. Such notice may generally be either oral or written (except in the case of a foreign bill of exchange, where a written notice in the form of a *protest* is required), and must meet certain requirements. A secondary party who receives notice of the dishonor may in turn send notice to prior secondary parties; if he is forced to pay, he may in turn recover from the parties he has notified.

Holders in Due Course and Defenses

To qualify as a holder in due course, a person must be lawfully in possession of an instrument payable to him or to bearer and must (1) have given value for it, (2) have purchased it before it became overdue, and (3) have received it in good faith without notice of any defects or defenses. Initially, every holder is legally presumed to be a holder in due course.

Any holder who acquires an instrument after it has been held by a holder in due course is entitled to the same rights as a holder in due course, provided he has not been a party to any fraud or illegal activity in connection with the execution and issuance of the instrument. Such a person is known as a holder through a holder in due course.

As a general rule, two kinds of defense are available to a party who is liable for the payment of a negotiable instrument: (1) *personal defenses,* and (2) *real defenses. Personal defenses* may be used to avoid liability to all persons other than holders in due course and holders through holders in due course. *Real defenses* may be used to avoid liability to any and all holders, including holders in due course.

Personal defenses include: (1) lack of consideration, or failure to perform consideration, (2) fraud in inducement, (3) prior payment, (4) duress, (5) nondelivery or conditional delivery of a completed instrument, and (6) unauthorized completion of a delivered instrument.

Real defenses include: (1) fraud as to the nature of the instrument itself, (2) forgery, (3) lack of legal capacity, (4) material alteration, (5) nondelivery of an incomplete instrument (only a personal defense under U.C.C.), and (6) illegality of the instrument itself.

Checks and Banks

So long as a drawer maintains a sufficient balance in his account, his bank is obligated to honor all checks he may draw on it. If the bank improperly dishonors a check, it is liable for any damage that results to the credit of the drawer. The holder of a check, however, may not compel the bank to pay it. If the bank refuses to pay the check, the holder's only remedy is to sue the drawer or prior indorsers.

A drawer may stop payment of a check by giving the bank notice in sufficient time. If the bank pays a check after receiving timely notice, it must restore the funds to the drawer's account.

Certification of a check, which is similar to the acceptance of an ordinary bill of exchange, makes the bank primarily liable for payment. Certification at the request of the holder releases the drawer and all prior indorsers from liability. Certification at the request of the drawer, however, releases none of the secondary parties.

If a bank honors a check on which the drawer's signature has been forged, it is charging his account improperly and must restore the funds to him. If, however, the drawer neglects to review his canceled checks and fails to detect a series of such forgeries over a period of time, some states hold that he (and not the bank) will be liable for the payment of subsequently forged checks. In addition, many states hold that a drawee bank is not liable when a prior holder takes a forged instrument without properly checking the identity of the person transferring it, or when a prior holder ignores suspicious circumstances surrounding the negotiation.

A person whose indorsement is forged on a check may recover possession of the instrument from any subsequent holder. If payment has already been made, he may recover the proceeds from the person who collected them. In such cases, the drawee bank must restore the funds to the drawer's account. In that event, however, the bank may recover from the person who received the proceeds, or it may sue any indorsers who indorsed the check after the forgery, for breach of their warranty that the instrument was genuine.

If the amount of a check has been raised by an alteration and the bank pays the altered amount, the bank is liable to the drawer for the difference and must restore it to his account. Many states recognize an exception to this rule when the drawer makes out the check in such a careless way that it is easy to alter the amount.

Discharge of Liability

Most instruments are discharged by payment at or after maturity. If payment is made before maturity, the instrument may be negotiated further.

Negotiable instruments may also be discharged by (1) intentional cancellation, (2) renunciation in writing (or orally, if the instrument is surrendered), and (3) material alteration.

Supplementary Reading:
Negotiable Instruments

Two fine textbooks on negotiable instruments are William E. Britton, *Handbook of the Law of Bills and Notes* (West Publishing Co., 1943) and Frederick K. Beutel, *Beutel's Brannan Negotiable Instruments Law,* 7th Ed. (Anderson, 1948). For cases and other materials, see Ralph W. Aigler, *Cases on the Law of Bills and Notes,* 2nd Ed. (West Publishing Co., 1955). The important statutes are *The Uniform Negotiable Instruments Law* and *The Uniform Commercial Code.*

14 Agency

Introduction

Agency is a legal relationship in which one person or organization (called the *agent*) acts on behalf of another (called the *principal*). Agency is a useful device, for it enables the individual to spread and enlarge his operations beyond the limits of his own presence. Indeed, without agency, the scope of commercial life would be confined to a few simple transactions, and whole areas of business activity would cease to exist. The corporation, for example, which is an impersonal entity, has no choice but to operate through the medium of agents; even partnerships, as we shall see in the next chapter, owe their existence largely to the fact that each partner may act as an agent for the others in transacting business.

Every day, most of us either act as agents or deal with agents. If we are employed by a firm or by an individual businessman, for example, we are usually acting as an agent in one capacity or another. If we buy something in a store, we generally deal with a clerk who is performing the duties of an agent. If we sell a house, we often hire a real estate agent; if we buy insurance, we deal with an insurance agent. Most companies employ a variety of agents to perform certain jobs and to represent them in certain capacities. A manufacturing firm, for example, employs workers to run machinery, salesmen to sell goods, truck drivers to make deliveries, buyers to purchase raw materials, and clerks to keep records and make out payroll checks. All these persons are agents acting for the company.

Agency is an ancient doctrine. Even in primitive societies, there were servants and slaves who performed services for the family unit. From very early times until comparatively recently in history, the role of the agent (often referred to in this context as a *servant*) was generally limited to the performance of routine tasks under the strict control of his principal (or *master*). Out of this master-servant relationship there grew a special body of legal rules covering the master's liability for acts and misdeeds of his servant resulting in injury or damage to others. We will discuss these rules in some detail in Section 4 of this chapter.

535

In more recent times, with the vast expansion of trade and commerce, business transactions have become increasingly more complex, and agents have been called upon to perform more varied and more responsible tasks for their principals. In the modern business world, agents often enjoy broad and sweeping powers to conduct transactions for others. Consequently, the courts have been forced to deal with many new and difficult problems of agency law.

A convenient way to classify agency law is in terms of the interrelationships among the various parties involved, and in terms of the respective rights and duties of those parties. First, there is the relationship between the principal and his agent. For the most part, this is governed by the basic rules of contract law. Since the relationship demands a great deal of mutual trust and confidence, however, the law imposes special duties on both sides. We will discuss these rules briefly in Section 3 of this chapter.

The thorniest problems in agency law arise out of the relationship between the principal and third persons who deal with him through his agent. All sorts of legal difficulties arise in this area. For example, how much power does the agent have to make contracts with others on behalf of his principal? If he has been specifically authorized by the principal, few difficulties arise. But what if he exceeds his authority and makes a contract he has no authority to make? Is the principal bound to carry out the unauthorized agreement? What happens if the agent fails to disclose the existence of his principal? What is the legal result if a person *appears* to be an agent but actually is not? The greater part of our discussion in this chapter will be devoted to these and related problems.

Lastly, there is the relationship between the agent himself and the third persons with whom he deals. In most situations, if the agent is following his principal's instructions he is in no way responsible to the third person; the theory here is that the agent is merely the tool of his principal. In certain situations, however, as we shall see, special rights and obligations do arise between the agent and third persons.

The primary purpose of agency law is to govern the relationships that prevail when persons or firms deal with one another through the medium of agents. In formulating rules in this area, the courts strive to preserve stability and security in commercial dealings. Thus, if a man chooses to do business through an agent, the law will require him to stand behind the acts of his agent, not only when the agent is carrying out his instructions but, where justice requires it, when the agent is acting without his authorization. If the law were otherwise, third persons would hesitate to deal with agents, and business activity would be severely limited.

The courts also require third persons to live up to contracts made with agents; this is true, in most cases, even though the third person has no knowledge of the principal's existence. In other words, agency has come to be an accepted way of doing business, and the law requires both sides to carry out their commitments.

Most of the rules of agency law originated in the commercial courts and the law merchant and were later absorbed into the common law. As in the case of contract law, there has been little statutory modification of agency law in most states.[1] Therefore, our main emphasis will be on judge-made law built on precedents.

SECTION 1

NATURE OF AGENCY—HOW CREATED

Purposes of Agency

A principal may appoint an agent to perform any act that the principal may legally perform himself. There are only a few exceptions to this rule: the law prohibits the delegation of authority to cast a vote in an election, to execute a will, and to sign an income tax return. Aside from these and certain other isolated cases, however, any qualified person is perfectly free to have an agent represent him and act on his behalf.

Capacity to Act as Principal or Agent

Any person with legal capacity to enter into a contract may act as a principal; a person who lacks such capacity (e.g., an insane person for whom a guardian has been appointed) may not. The courts disagree on whether or not a minor may be a principal. Earlier decisions generally held that a minor's appointment of an agent was void and that any agreement made by such an agent was of no effect. Recent decisions, however, have held that a contract of agency in which the principal is a minor is only voidable rather than void, and that it is binding on the minor until he disaffirms it.

Any person, regardless of age or mentality, who understands the nature of the transaction he is entering into and who has the physical capacity to perform may serve as an agent.[2] This means that a minor, or any other person who lacks general contractual capacity, may be an agent. The theory here is that an agent is acting, not in his own capacity, but on behalf of his principal, and that any contract or transaction into which he enters will be binding only on the principal. This point is well illustrated by the South Carolina case that follows.

---

[1] There has, of course, been a vast amount of legislation in the area of employer-employee relations, both on the federal and state levels. We have already discussed this aspect of agency law in some detail in Chapter 9.

[2] Certain types of agent, however, must be licensed before they can carry out their responsibilities—real estate agents, for example, and insurance agents, attorneys, and stockbrokers.

CHASTAIN v. BOWMAN

Supreme Court of South Carolina, 1833
1 Hill 270

► This was an action on the case,[3] against the defendants as common carriers on the Savannah River, for a loss sustained by the burning of the plaintiff's cotton, on board their boat. The boat was passing down the river when the plaintiff came to a landing and asked if it could carry his cotton. The patroon (a slave belonging to one of the defendants) answered that it could. The cotton was received, and was burnt on board the boat, before it reached Augusta. It was proved that the defendants had given general instruction to their patroons to take in freight whenever it could be had, and that in one instance, one of the defendants had received pay for freight engaged by his patroon. There was also some evidence to show the general custom of the river. Some witnesses proved, that it is the custom to allow patroons to take in freight generally, and others, that they are only allowed to receive freight, when a boat is not fully loaded.

The presiding judge charged the jury, the defendants were not liable, unless the patroon was his master's agent, and the patroon authorized to take in freight. That the authority might be proved by showing that such was the custom of boat owners, or by proving that the defendants had given such authority; that a slave might be the agent of his master, and if his agency was established, the master was bound; and whether the agency of the slave was established in this case, was a question submitted for their decision. The jury found for the plaintiff, and the defendants appealed, and move for a new trial, on the ground of error in the charge of the presiding judge.

JOHNSON, J.   From the instruction given to the jury, it is more than probable that they found the verdict on the ground that the defendants had constituted their patroon, the slave, Jack, their agent to contract with the plaintiff for carrying his cotton, and on the ground it can be well sustained.

It is not questioned that a master may constitute his slave his agent, and I cannot conceive of any distinction between the circumstances which constitute a slave and a freeman an agent. They are both the creatures of the principal, and act upon his authority. There is no condition, however degraded, which deprives one of the right to act as a private agent; the master is liable even for the act of his dog done in pursuance of his command. Two witnesses, Beck and Eaton, prove that the defendants had given general instructions to their patroons to procure freight whenever they could, and in one instance it is shown that one of the defendants received the price of freight on produce so received and carried by the patroon, a distinct recognition of their authority to contract for them; and there is not a tittle of evidence that this authority was ever rescinded. The

---

[3] "Action on the case," or "trespass on the case" as it is sometimes called, is the ancient common-law description of a suit to recover damages for injuries caused by the wrongful act of another. In many states the term is still used.

authority was general as to that particular business, and the contract to carry was directly in pursuance of it. The defendants were therefore bound. . . .

Motion dismissed. ◄

COMMENTS AND QUESTIONS

1. What was the substance of the trial judge's charge to the jury? Was it upheld on appeal?
2. This case illustrates the general rule concerning capacity to act as an agent. The court states that "There is no condition, however degraded, which deprives one of the right to act as a private agent. . . . "

Creation of Agency

By Express Appointment

Most agencies are created by a contract in which the principal expressly authorizes the agent to perform certain functions on his behalf in return for a specified compensation: a company hires a salesman to sell paint at a salary of $100 a week. As a general rule, such contracts are just like any other contract and require no particular formalities. Although an oral contract establishing agency is usually binding, most states require the contract to be in writing if (1) the agent is being given authority to buy or sell real property, or (2) the contract cannot be performed within one year. A few states insist that the agent be given written authorization if he is to execute any contract with third parties which the Statute of Frauds requires to be in writing.

The authority delegated to the agent may be spelled out in detail or stated in very general terms. In the latter case, the courts usually look to commercial customs and usages, and to the powers of other agents in similar positions, in their effort to ascertain the nature and extent of the authority that has been conferred.

Although the usual type of agency is based on a contract of employment, with a clear indication of what compensation the agent is to receive for his services, such a contract is not essential to the creation of agency. In fact, many agents agree to act gratuitously. Any promise to act as an agent which is not supported by consideration, of course, is unenforceable, and the appointment of an agent in such circumstances may always be revoked before the agent has performed. Once authority has been granted, however, and the agent has begun to exercise that authority, an agency relationship arises and the agent is bound to perform his duties.

EXAMPLE

FARMER P asks FARMER A to take one of his hogs to market the next day and sell it at the highest price possible. FARMER A agrees. He is not bound by contract, however, since FARMER P has not agreed to compensate him. Therefore, FARMER A can refuse to carry out his bargain. But if FARMER A actually takes the hog to market the next day, he becomes an agent of FARMER P. He must try to get the best price possible and he must account to FARMER P for the proceeds of the sale.

Sometimes it is hard to determine whether a person has been appointed to act as an agent or not. In the case of *McKeon v. Tyler,* which follows, the court was faced with just this problem. The situation is a common one in the business world, and the decision should encourage agents and principals to arrive at a clear understanding of their relationship.

JOHN J. McKEON v. GEORGE C. TYLER

Supreme Judicial Court of Massachusetts, 1925
254 Mass. 142

► Contract for $10,000, alleged to be a "commission due on the sale of motion picture rights of the play 'Merton of the Movies.' " Writ dated February 18, 1924.

In the Superior Court, the action was heard by McLAUGHLIN, J., without a jury. Material evidence and findings by the judge are described in the opinion. There was a finding for the plaintiff in the sum of $10,569.34. The defendant alleged exceptions.

CARROLL, J. This is an action to recover a broker's commission for the sale of a motion picture play, known as "Merton of the Movies," to the "Famous Players-Lasky Corporation." The plaintiff was a play-broker negotiating the sale of plays, spoken and pictured. The judge, sitting without a jury, found for the plaintiff. In the findings and rulings of the judge it is stated: "I have accepted the defendant's version of this matter in all material respects in which his testimony differs from that of the plaintiff, drawing such inferences therefrom as seem just and reasonable."

The plaintiff had acted for the defendant in the sale of a play for which a commission was paid to him by the defendant. At the time of the transaction in question, the plaintiff said to the defendant, "What about 'Merton of the Movies' for motion pictures?" to which the defendant replied, " 'Merton of the Movies' . . . (is) not for sale for motion pictures"; he also stated that "Merton of the Movies" was now playing to capacity; that he expected it would run in New York for two or three years; that he did not know when it would be sold. The plaintiff then asked the defendant if he would not like to meet one Lasky, representative of the "Famous Players." To this the defendant said he saw no reason for meeting Lasky, "that he had nothing to sell him." When asked if he would see Lasky if the plaintiff brought him to his office, the defendant said he would be pleased to see him whenever he called. On the next day the plaintiff brought Lasky to the defendant's office; at this interview Lasky proposed to the defendant to buy "Merton of the Movies." The defendant replied "How in the world can I sell 'Merton of the Movies'? I don't know when it could be released, I don't know when I can sell it." The defendant testified he believed that at that time it would run for five years. Lasky then suggested that if the play was in the market at any time in the future "it comes to us." The defendant in answer to this proposition said, "No, I couldn't do that." When the question of price was mentioned the defendant declared: "That wouldn't influence me at all. It is not for sale." He further stated that he had already made an arrangement with one Hunter, by which the play was not to be sold to "anyone else provided he can give me as much money as anybody else will offer when the time comes." The defendant in response to a remark by Lasky, "When the time comes to sell it let us know," said, "When the time comes to sell it I will notify you so that you get the first chance to buy it. I can't say when that will be." The plaintiff was present at this interview.

About five months after this conversation, the defendant returned from Europe and found that the attendance at "Merton of the Movies" was falling off. He decided to sell the motion picture rights and directed his manager to take up the matter with the various motion picture companies, saying to him in substance, "Don't forget one thing, I have agreed with Mr. Lasky that when the time comes to sell . . . he is to be notified . . . let him know at once." The manager informed Lasky and another person who was in the moving picture business, that the defendant was willing to sell, and shortly after, in December, 1923, the play was sold to the Famous Players-Lasky Corporation for $100,000. The judge found for the plaintiff and the defendant excepted.

The plaintiff cannot recover unless he was employed by the defendant to make the sale. This agency and authority must be shown. He did not earn his commission by merely offering his services to the defendant, even if the defendant availed himself of the information and sold the property to the broker's customer. . . .

The testimony of the defendant, which was accepted by the presiding judge as true,[4] shows that at the time, when the plaintiff suggested the sale of the play, the defendant believed that it would continue to succeed as a spoken play for an indefinite period. He had no intention of selling the moving picture rights, and he stated distinctly that it was not for sale. His willingness to meet Lasky does not contradict the fact that the defendant had no intention of selling the play at that time or at any other time in the future. There was no employment of the plaintiff in this particular transaction, and nothing appears from which it could be inferred that he was the defendant's agent. The defendant's positive and definite refusal to sell, negatives any employment of the plaintiff at that time. The fact that the defendant stated to Lasky in the plaintiff's presence that he would notify the Famous Players-Lasky Corporation and give them the first chance to buy, whenever he decided to sell, is not enough to show that the plaintiff was the defendant's agent. Nor is the circumstance that subsequently, when he sold the moving picture rights, he sold to this corporation, sufficient to give the plaintiff a right to recover against the defendant. The information furnished by a broker, who is not employed by the seller, may be availed of him without making him liable to pay a com-

---

[4] In this case both sides waived their right to a jury, so the trial judge decided both the facts and the law. When the appellate court says that the presiding judge accepted the testimony of the defendant as true, it is simply saying that, after hearing the conflicting stories, the judge believed the defendant's story and found, as a fact, that his testimony reflected the true state of affairs. Therefore, as you will remember from our previous discussion, the appellate court accepts the trial judge's finding of fact as final, and the only question to be decided on appeal is whether the correct rule of law was applied to the facts as found.

mission. Taking advantage of the services performed by the broker, without some evidence to show an original employment or subsequent ratification, does not make the defendant liable. . . .

Although the defendant knew the plaintiff was a broker, in view of the defendant's positive refusal to sell, no agency either expressed or implied was shown and there was no evidence of ratification. . . .

The transaction in question took place in New York, but there is nothing to show that the law of New York bearing on the question differs from the law of Massachusetts. (Farmers National Bank of Annapolis v. Venner, 192 Mass. 531, 535.)

As there was no evidence that the plaintiff was employed by the defendant to act as his agent, the order must be

Exceptions sustained.   ◄

COMMENTS AND QUESTIONS

1. What was the outcome of this case? Summarize the reasons given by the court for reversing the decision of the trial judge.

2. Isn't it clear that the plaintiff was the moving force in getting the buyer and seller together? Shouldn't he have been entitled to recover for his services? How can a broker protect himself in this type of situation?

3. The court notes that this was a New York contract, but apparently no New York decisions were cited by the attorneys in their arguments. Perhaps the plaintiff missed an opportunity to strengthen his case by not citing such decisions.

By Estoppel

In some situations, although there has been no express delegation of authority, the principal behaves in such a way that he gives the impression that agency exists. If a third party actually relies on what he takes to be a valid agency relationship, the principal is legally prohibited from denying the agent's authority to act on his behalf. This legal prohibition is called *estoppel*. In such cases, the agent is said to possess *apparent authority* to bind his principal. This concept will be discussed in greater detail in Section 2 of this chapter.

EXAMPLE

P, the owner of a small hotel, allows A to sit behind the desk while the regular clerk is out to lunch; P specifically instructs A not to accept any money and to call him if any guest wants to check out. Contrary to instructions, A takes money from a guest without calling P and then absconds with it. P is estopped (i.e., not permitted) to deny that A was his agent, since he allowed a situation to arise in which a third person, the guest, was justified in believing that agency existed and actually relied on that belief. Therefore the guest's payment to A constitutes good payment to P, and P's only remedy is against A.

By Ratification

As a general rule, when the principal gives no express or implied authority to an agent, and when the principal's conduct has not created agency by estoppel, the agent is powerless to act and can make no transactions or contracts that will be binding on the principal. Even in these circumstances, though, the principal may decide to affirm a transaction or be bound by a contract made on his behalf by an agent acting without authorization. If, by his words or conduct, the principal indicates his assent to be bound, he is said to have *ratified* the unauthorized act of the agent; from that point on, the agent's act is just as binding on the principal as it would have been if the agent had been authorized to act on behalf of the principal in the first place. Ratification may be express (that is, the principal makes some written or oral statement of ratification) or implied (the principal accepts the benefits of the contract or performs in accordance with it). Usually, mere silence does not constitute ratification unless, under the circumstances, it very strongly indicates a clear intention to be bound. As a general rule, ratification need not be in writing unless written au- . thorization would have been necessary had it been given originally. In other words, ratification must meet the same formal requirements as prior authorization.

EXAMPLE

Without authority, A enters into a contract on behalf of P to sell goods to T. When P learns of the unauthorized transaction, he sends the goods to T and bills him at the agreed price. Such conduct on P's part constitutes ratification of the unauthorized contract that A purported to make for him. If P does nothing, however, he is not bound by the contract, and T's only remedy is against A.

Ratification, obviously, can take place only in a situation where the agent has acted without authority to bind the principal. It is also essential that the agent has represented to the third party that he was acting for the principal and not for himself or some other person. In other words, the agent must purport to be acting on behalf of the principal, even though he has no authority to do so; otherwise, the principal may not ratify the act.

The principal must ratify the entire transaction or none of it. He cannot elect to be bound by certain portions of an agreement and reject the rest. This rule of law was relied on by the defendant in the following Missouri case, in which the plaintiff was trying to recover possession of a mule. Let's see what happened.

CRUTE v. BURCH et al.

Kansas City Court of Appeals, Missouri, 1911
154 Mo. App. 480, 135 S.W. 1004

▶ BROADDUS, P. J. This is a suit in *replevin* [5] to recover a mule. The proceeding was instituted in a justice court, where defendant prevailed. The cause was taken by plaintiff to the circuit court on appeal, and tried anew, and plaintiff recovered judgment, and defendant appealed. [6]

The facts are the plaintiff resided in Kansas City, and owned a farm

---

[5] As previously noted, replevin is a special type of action to recover possession of goods or property which have been unlawfully taken from the plaintiff.

[6] Quite a bit of litigation over a mule!

in Johnson county, on which one Sheets resided as a tenant. The plaintiff was also the owner of a certain bald-faced sorrel mare. On or about the 28th day of July, 1908, Sheets came to Kansas City and represented to plaintiff that the mare was in such a bad condition that she would not answer for work during the cropping season, and stated that he had the opportunity of selling her for $60. The plaintiff authorized him to sell her for that amount. Soon thereafter Sheets took the mare, and also a mule colt, the foal of the mare, that belonged to the plaintiff, to Harrisonville, in Cass county, and sold both to W. B. Scruggs for $115. Later, but before plaintiff learned that Sheets had sold the mule, Scruggs sold the mule and mare to the defendant. Sheets paid to plaintiff $60, the price of the mare, for which he gave his receipt.

Plaintiff made an effort to get Sheets to pay for the mule, and fixed its price at the sum of $60. He authorized his lawyer, Mr. Byram, to act for him in the matter. Sheets wrote the following letter to Byram: "Latour, Mo. Aug. 20, 1908. Mr. L. W. Byram—Dear Sir. Have been and got all the details of the law i am ready to settel with you for the mule come down. Henry Sheets." Byram replied: "The price of the mule is $65. You might send the money through your bank there. I have spent so much time and money coming to Latour, I can't get there now. I started proceedings to get the mule. I will hold that, however, until I get a letter from you. Please answer by return mail." To this letter Sheets made no answer. There was no evidence that plaintiff looked to Sheets to pay for the mule, but that he was willing for him to do so. It appeared that plaintiff did not know that the mare had a mule colt at the time he authorized Sheets to dispose of her, and that he learned of its existence after Sheets had sold it to Scruggs.

The contention of appellant is that, when plaintiff accepted from Sheets the $60 as payment for the mare, he affirmed the sale also of the mule, and that he will not be permitted to ratify that part of the contract that was beneficial to him, and repudiate that which is not. Defendant cites a great number of cases, which undoubtedly sustain his theory; but they do not help his case. Plaintiff was obligated to affirm the sale of the mare, because he could not do otherwise, as he had authorized Sheets to make it. But he did not thereby confirm the sale of the mule. The sale of the latter was without authority. In ratifying the authorized act of his agent, he did not ratify his unauthorized act.

And it is further contended that plaintiff, by entering into negotiations with Sheets for collection of the price of the mule, ratified the contract of sale. The position is equally as untenable as the first. He did not agree to take Sheets as paymaster for the price of the mule, but was willing that he should pay for it. Surely it cannot be said this can be construed as an affirmation of the theft of the mule. Had he accepted from Sheets the price of the mule, or had he agreed to look to him for its payment, that would have been an affirmation of the sale. This is not a case where an agent is acting within, but is misusing, his authority, but where he was acting wholly without any authority. The case is too plain to admit of controversy.

Affirmed. ◀

COMMENTS AND QUESTIONS

1. Do you agree that the plaintiff should get his mule back? Why not let the defendant keep the mule and require the plaintiff to recover the value of the mule from Sheets?
2. If Sheets had paid the plaintiff the price of the mule, would this have constituted a ratification of the sale?

Another requirement for ratification is that the principal be aware of all the important facts surrounding the transaction that he is ratifying. An attempt to ratify without full knowledge of the circumstances will not be binding on the principal.

EXAMPLE

A knows that P wants to sell his car but has no authority to represent him. Even so, he enters into a contract on P's behalf to sell the car to T for $400. As an inducement to the sale, A agrees to give T a ninety-day guarantee on all major repairs. When A informs P of the contract, he mentions the purchase price but fails to say anything about the guarantee. P tells T that he will go through with the contract. P is not bound by his ratification and may repudiate it when he learns of A's guarantee on repairs. If P remains silent, however, and does nothing after he is told about the guarantee, he is probably bound.

A third party who learns that an agent had no authority to bind the principal he was purporting to represent may want to repudiate the contract before it has been ratified. Most states permit him to withdraw from the contract at any time before the principal has ratified. A few states hold that a principal must be given a reasonable time in which to ratify an unauthorized contract after he has learned about it, and that the third party remains liable during that time. Most authorities reject the latter view, on the ground that it works a hardship on the third party. In all states, however, both the principal and the third party are bound as soon as the principal has ratified the contract.

If the principal does not ratify an unauthorized contract, he is not liable to the third party. The third party's only remedy is to sue the agent for any loss resulting from the agent's lack of authority.

The following case is a good illustration of the difficulties that are sometimes encountered in applying the general rules of law dealing with ratification. The court's sympathies are clear, but the court is somewhat troubled by the fact that it must disregard certain precedents to reach the desired result.

KLINE BROS. & CO. v. ROYAL INSURANCE CO.

Circuit Court of the United States, S.D. N.Y., 1911
192 F. 378

► In this case actions were brought to collect the proceeds on certain fire insurance policies issued by the defendants. One McIntosh, who had no actual authority to act for the plaintiff, purported to purchase the policies on its behalf. Subsequently, the plaintiff sustained a loss under the policies and sought to hold the defendants on the theory that after the loss occurred the plaintiffs had tendered the premium to the defendants and thus had ratified the contract which McIntosh purported to make on its behalf. The defendants argued that no ratification was possible after the loss occurred.

HAND, J. . . . There seems to be no escape from the conclusion that by his contract with the defendants McIntosh did not bind the corporation to pay the premium. Furthermore, the board of directors never learned of the policies until after the fire, and did not therefore ratify them up to that time. At least, there is no evidence upon that question, and the burden rests with the plaintiff. As I view it, no subsequent ratification was possible. After the fire McIntosh tendered the premium, and after that the defendants repudiated any liability.

The facts, therefore, raise two questions: First, whether a third party who has made a contract with an unauthorized agent on behalf of his principal is bound before the principal has ratified; and second, if not, whether the occurrence of a fire before the unauthorized application for the policy had been ratified prevents its future ratification so as to bind the company. Upon the first question, there is no doubt some division of authority. In England the law now is that the third party may not withdraw, provided the principal ratifies the contract in season. Bolton Partners v. Lambert, 41 Ch. D. 295. . . . On the other hand in Wisconsin (Dodge v. Hopkins, 14 Wis. 630; Atlee v. Bartholomew et al., 69 Wis. 43, 33 N.W. 110, 5 Am. St. Rep. 103), and apparently in Illinois (Cowan v. Curran, 215 Ill. 598, 75 N.E. 322), the whole unauthorized contract seems to amount only to an offer by the third person, which must be accepted *de novo* by the principal, a rule certainly at variance with the well established law that an uncommunicated ratification by the principal will bind him. The English case proceeds on the civil law maxim, *"Omnis ratihabito retrotrahitur,"* [7] though it by no means follows, because a ratification relates back when once a valid contract is made, that the third party is bound meanwhile, and may not withdraw while the principal remains unbound. Now, relation back is in the sense here used a fiction, and certainly should not be extended to cover unjust cases, of which this is one, as I shall show. In so far as by the maxim it is only meant to say that a ratification carries with it by implication the intention of the principal that the contract shall in fact date from the time when it was made between the agent and the third party, it is unobjectionable in principle, and accords with the facts; but, if taken in the sense that the law will regard both parties as bound from the date of the contract, it merely misstates the facts, because, by hypothesis, the principal is not bound before ratification. All that the law can do is to hold the third party bound from the outset, and that by the mere force of authority. It certainly serves no useful purpose to cloak that authority in a phrase which misstates the truth in Latin, unless it accords with the principles of the law of contracts, or at least produces just results at the expense of those principles.

Upon principle the doctrine does not appear to be correct, and it has

---

[7] "Every ratification relates back." In other words, it has the same effect as prior authority.

been criticised by text-writers. Wambaugh, 9 Harv. L.R. 60; 31 Cyc. 1291. The contract of insurance is bilateral, and, until the principal ratifies, he is by hypothesis under no obligation to pay the premium. If so, there is until then no consideration to support the counter promise of the third person, for a consideration implies a legal obligation, and his promise ought not in principle to bind him, being indeed *nudum pactum*.[8] Second, the result is unfair to the third party, since it permits the principal to speculate on the value of the contract, while he himself remains unbound. If it proves advantageous, he may ratify. If not, he may repudiate. There is no just ground for giving him such an advantage over the third party merely because of an unknown defect in the agent's powers. In view of the dearth of authority in this country and especially of any decisions binding upon me, I do not think that I should follow the rule in Bolton v. Lambert, *supra*, but rather what I cannot but believe to be the result necessary under the principles of the laws of contract. . . .

The next question is whether, if the contract was not binding upon either party until McIntosh tendered the premium, the occurrence of the fire terminated that possibility. I may assume that the tender was sufficient, even though there is no evidence that even at that time McIntosh had been authorized to make it by the other two directors. If, however, the fire, which was known to both the insured and the insurer, terminated the possibility of binding the bargain by either ratification or tender, it was nullity. An insurer's undertaking is a promise to pay upon a given event which either must happen in future, or if it have already happened must be still unknown. Were it not so, the promise would be merely to pay a large sum of money in consideration of a small one, which is an absurd intention to ascribe to any one. In the case at bar, since the loss had happened before the policy became binding, the promise could only be to pay for an existing loss. . . .

There is no difference of judicial opinion so far as I can find upon the proposition that the insurer is not bound, where the insured at the time of the binding of the bargain had learned that the loss has happened or the risk has changed since the original application. The only difference between those cases and the case at bar is this: That here the insurer likewise knew that the loss had occurred, and nevertheless did not withdraw from the contract. This fact would perhaps be irrelevant in any case, even if the insurer did not formally withdraw his offer upon learning of the loss, for it might be held that to withdraw it after a loss has occurred would be an idle ceremony; but that question is not up at present, because the defendants had no knowledge that McIntosh had not bound the plaintiff to pay the premium, and that their own undertaking had therefore been without consideration from the outset. They certainly dealt with him in good faith, and were not called upon to disaffirm a contract which, as far as they knew, was binding upon them. If, however, it be once admitted that it was not binding upon them until ratified, it could be ratified or accepted by

---

[8] This term is used to describe a voluntary promise which is not supported by consideration and, therefore, not legally binding on the promisor—literally, a naked pact.

paying a premium after the risk had ceased and the fundamental condition of the promise no longer existed. This would be quite obvious had the offer never been accepted at all, before the loss, but, if the policy was not binding while unratified, the situation was the same as though the offer had never been accepted. . . .

Judgment for defendants. ◄

COMMENTS AND QUESTIONS

1. What was the decision of the court here? Summarize the reasons given by Judge Hand in support of his position.
2. The court makes much of the fact that under the general rule the principal can sit back and "speculate on the value of the contract, while he himself remains unbound" and may ratify if it proves advantageous and repudiate if it turns out unfavorably. This situation, says the court, is unfair to the third party. Why would it be unfair to the defendants in this case if they intended all along to provide insurance coverage for the plaintiff and were paid the premium in full?
3. Notice how Judge Hand shrugs off the authority of the English case of *Bolton v. Lambert* and the general rule of law governing the principal's right to ratify contracts.
4. Do you agree or disagree with the result of this case? The state courts are divided in their approach to cases of this sort.

Agent's Right to Delegate Authority to Subagents

Since the relationship between principal and agent is one of trust and confidence, agents are usually selected on the basis of their personal qualifications. As a general rule, therefore, no agent is allowed to delegate his authority to another without the principal's permission. If an agent tries to delegate his authority without permission, the subagent usually has no authority to bind the principal. An exception to this general rule is recognized when the duties delegated are purely ministerial or technical in nature and do not involve the exercise of skill or discretion.

EXAMPLES

1. An agent for an insurance company who is authorized to adjust claims may not delegate his authority to a subagent, since his duties demand the exercise of skill and judgment.
2. An insurance agent who is authorized to accept risks and issue policies may hire a clerk to type up the policies he has approved and send them to policyholders, since such acts are purely technical in nature.

In some cases, the principal's delegation of authority is so extensive that the agent is clearly expected to appoint subagents to carry out his functions.

EXAMPLE

The general manager of a branch store is usually given implied authority, if not express permission, to hire the employees needed to carry on the business. Such employees are deemed to be subagents of the principal, and the principal is ultimately responsible for their actions.

SECTION 2

AGENT'S AUTHORITY, AND LIABILITY OF PRINCIPAL AND THIRD PARTY

Authority of Agent to Bind Principal

In General

As a general rule, a principal is liable only for those acts of an agent that come within the scope of the agent's actual or apparent authority, or for those transactions that he has ratified despite the agent's lack of original authority. If neither authority nor ratification exists, the principal is not bound. In this section we will examine the various kinds of authority that may be conferred on an agent, and the liability that results from that authority.

Actual Authority

In most agency relationships, the principal expressly confers on the agent authority to act on his behalf. If the principal spells out this authority in explicit terms, leaving little to implication, he is said to be granting *express actual authority*. But if the principal describes the agent's authority in more general terms, merely implying the agent's actual powers, he is said to be granting *implied actual authority*. In both situations the principal actually intends to confer authority on the agent. In the latter case, however, he lets it be understood that the agent will have any powers that are reasonably necessary to accomplish the principal's purpose. These powers must be inferred from custom and trade usage, from previous dealings between the parties, or from the nature of the particular situation.

EXAMPLES

1. A real estate agent is hired to sell P's house for $15,000 or better. He possesses express actual authority, for his powers are clearly delineated.
2. An agent is hired to act as general manager of P's firm. No further description of his powers is given. This agent has implied actual authority to bind his principal by exercising powers that are incidental or reasonably necessary to running the business.

It is not always easy to determine whether actual authority has been conferred. Take, for example, the case that follows.

SCHLICK v. BERG et al.

Supreme Court of Minnesota, 1939
205 Minn. 465, 286 N.W. 356

▶ STONE, J. Action for personal injury with verdict for plaintiff. Defendant, L. J. Dorenkemper, appeals from the order denying his motion in the alternative for judgment notwithstanding or a new trial.[9]

Plaintiff was injured during the remodeling of a building of which her employer was tenant and Oscar Berg owner. (He is out as defendant because of a verdict in his favor.) The contract for remodeling was made orally by Berg and Carl Dorenkemper, son of defendant. Carl supervised the work. The dominant question is whether evidence justifies the finding that the contract was made and performed by Carl as the agent of his father, so as to make the latter liable for the negligence of the employees engaged in the work. Throughout our consideration it will be convenient to refer to L. J. Dorenkemper as defendant and to his son merely as Carl.

The work was to be done for cost plus 10%. The lumber came from the Dorenkemper Lumber Company, of which defendant was sole proprietor. The contract was carried on the books of the lumber company as the "Berg Job." When Carl presented the bill for lumber to Berg, it was upon the printed statement of the lumber company and showing the company as creditor and Berg as debtor. The bill and the bills for labor Berg paid by one check to Carl, who in turn paid defendant for the lumber.

The equipment used in the work appears to have been the property of Carl. His also was the profit, the only benefit to Dorenkemper being payment for the lumber.

Such are the salient facts about the Berg contract. It is insisted for plaintiff that they are enough to show a relationship of principal and agent between defendant and Carl. Just as strongly does defendant contend that there is no evidence of agency.

There is evidence that Berg and Carl treated the contract as one on behalf of the lumber company, and that the latter acquiesced in that view by carrying the lumber as the "Berg Job." But Carl's ownership of the equipment and supervision of the work, the fact that Berg made payment to Carl and that Carl retained the profit, paying to the company only the price of the lumber, all indicate that Carl was not the agent of the defendant. The facts are equivocal. If there were evidence only of the Berg contract, we doubt that the verdict could be sustained.

But there was other evidence. Shortly after plaintiff was injured during remodeling of the Berg store, Carl entered into a contract to construct a building for one Piche, signing the contract to construct "Dorenkemper Lumber Co. C. J. Dorenkemper." Again the lumber came from defendant's yard, and was carried upon its books as the "Piche Job." Payment for lumber

---

[9] After the jury found in favor of the plaintiff, the defendant made a motion requesting the trial judge to set aside the verdict and enter judgment in his favor or, in the alternative, to set aside the verdict and order a new trial. The judge denied the motion and entered judgment for the plaintiff; the defendant appealed, saying that his motion should have been allowed.

and labor was by checks to the "Dorenkemper Lumber Company." They were indorsed for payment by Carl.

Soon after the accident to plaintiff, Piche became worried and took the contract to defendant, who, according to the testimony of Piche, assured him: "The contract is okay and you don't need to be afraid of nothing. We stand back of this contract. My son does that work for me all the time like this."

A few months prior to the Berg job, Carl and one Robinson contracted for the rebuilding of some houses. . . . Robinson received a statement "in acct with Dorenkemper Lbr. Co. Contract for repair and additions to three houses as per agreement." Despite Dorenkemper's denial of knowledge of this contract, he did in his own hand make out a deposit slip for the check in payment of the above statement, writing on it "Robinson."

There was an earlier contract to erect a schoolhouse, in respect to which the jury could easily have found that Carl was acting either as agent or partner of defendant. . . . All debits were against the "Job." Checks in payment, whether made to defendant, Carl, or the Dorenkemper Lumber Company were indorsed for payment frequently by Carl and sometimes by defendant. The latter always got payment for his lumber.

For plaintiff reliance is correctly put upon authority in fact rather than authority resulting from holding out or estoppel. That is because authority by holding out is of no importance until a third party relies thereon. [Citations omitted.] In the ordinary personal injury case the injured person does not rely upon authority of any kind in getting hurt. Proof of actual authority is therefore essential to recovery. Restatement, Agency, 265; 2 Mechem, Agency, 2d Ed., 1858, 1859. . . .

For defendant it is insisted that Carl at no time had authority to represent him in any of the contracts, and that, whatever evidence there may be of apparent, there is none of actual authority.

The argument misconceives what is meant by actual authority. Authority of this kind can, of course, be shown by express agreement between principal and agent. But it can also be inferred from the course of dealing between the two. All authority must be traced to the principal. But it may be found in his adoption of, or acquiescence in, similar acts done on other occasions by the assumed agent. It then becomes what is conveniently but inaccurately called implied authority. . . . Only the evidence of it is found in implication by conduct. . . .

. . . Knowledge was inferred from the length of time over which the acts had continued, and acquiescence from the lack of objection. Here too is evidence of the principal's knowledge and acquiescence, the former to be inferred from defendant's close contact with the other similar contracts. There is no evidence of objection. We think there was established such a course of dealing by defendant, the principal, as to make the question of agency one of fact. For all that a good cap sheaf [10] was defendant's admission to Piche that "My son does that work for me all the time like this." . . .

Order affirmed. ◄

---

[10] A good clinching point. In other words, on top of everything else, this admission conclusively establishes the correctness of the trial court's decision.

COMMENTS AND QUESTIONS

1. The decision in this case revolves around whether Carl (the son) was acting for himself or as an agent for his father (the defendant) in making and performing the remodeling contract. In the lower court, the issue was submitted to a jury. What was the jury's verdict? What happened on appeal?

2. Was there any evidence that Carl's father ever expressly authorized him to make a binding contract on his behalf? If not, how can the decision be justified?

3. In the opinion, Judge Stone refers to the "Piche Job" and certain statements of Carl's father with reference to that contract. Do you think the court should give any weight to statements made about an entirely different contract *after* the job in question had been performed? Are such statements really material?

EXTENT OF ACTUAL AUTHORITY CONFERRED. As a general rule, anyone who deals with an agent must determine for himself the extent of the agent's actual authority. A third party is not justified in relying solely on the agent's representations or assurances. If he has any doubt about the agent, he should go directly to the principal for a clarification of the situation. Once the principal states that he has indeed bestowed authority on the agent, he is usually estopped to deny its existence in the future. When the third party knows that the agent's authority has been spelled out in some written document, he should ask to examine the document before entering into any agreement with the agent, for he is bound by any limitations on authority contained in the written statement.

CUSTOMARY AUTHORITY—SECRET LIMITATIONS. A third party is ordinarily justified in assuming that an agent has the authority customarily granted to agents in similar circumstances in the community. If there is no evidence to the contrary, he may assume that the principal intends his agent to possess that authority. If the principal wishes to limit the agent's authority, he should make this limitation known, or at least available, to third parties who may be dealing with the agent. Otherwise, they may take the agent's authority at its face value.

The Illinois case of *Thurber & Co. v. Anderson* is typical of this sort of situation.

THURBER & CO. v. ANDERSON

Supreme Court of Illinois, 1878
88 Ill. 167

► SCHOLFIELD, C. J. The controversy in this case is whether appellee is liable for a bill of cigars and imported ale shipped by appellants to his address, on an order drawn in his name by his son, on them, to that effect. The son received the goods and made use of them himself, without the knowledge of appellee.

Appellee denies that his son had any authority to purchase goods for him and also denies that he ever had any knowledge of his having ordered or received these goods; but it does not appear that appellants had any reason to suspect that the goods were not ordered by him.

The goods were ordered December 4, 1875, and several witnesses testify, that at that time, and prior and subsequent thereto, appellee's son was in his grocery, and that, during the time he was there, he sold goods, gave orders to runners for goods, received money in payment for goods, sold, receipted, in his father's name for express packages, ordered goods from other houses in his father's name, and corresponded with reference thereto; and, also, that during that time, he did not profess to be doing business for himself. And of all this, the reasonable presumption, from the evidence is, appellee had full knowledge.

We do not think it important to inquire precisely what authority appellee, in fact, conferred upon his son in regard to his business, because, in our opinion, the decided preponderance of the evidence is, that he was suffered to act as a general agent both in buying and selling, and the public were therefore justified in assuming that he possessed all the powers requisite to a general agent in buying and selling. It is true, as contended by counsel for appellee, that an authority to buy can not be inferred simply from an authority to sell; yet where a clerk or shopman has been accustomed to buy as well as to sell, the presumption of full authority is equally applicable to both. Story on Agency, 89. By permitting another to hold himself out to the world as his agent, the principal adopts his acts, and will be held bound to the person who gives credit thereafter to the other, in the capacity of his agent. 2 Kent's Com. (8th ed.) 799.

It is suggested, however, that the goods here ordered were not such as were suited to the business in which appellee was engaged, and that, in no view, could the son bind appellee by contracts for goods not in the line of his trade.

The evidence fails to show that the goods ordered were not such as are within the line of business in which appellee was engaged. His evidence was: "Am in grocery; general stock; keep tobacco, etc." Another witness, Benjamin Kinkly, speaks of his having a "grocery and saloon."

No witness says that imported ale and cigars, such as were ordered, are articles not adapted to such business, and we are not warranted in so presuming in the absence of evidence.

We are of opinion that, under the evidence before us, the judgment does injustice to appellants, and that it should, therefore, be reversed. The judgment is reversed and the cause remanded.[11]

Judgment reversed.   ◀

COMMENTS AND QUESTIONS

1. The lower court presumably found that Anderson's son had no authority to order goods in his name and denied recovery against the father. What happened in the appellate court? Summarize the reasons given by the court for its decision.

---

[11] The case was sent back to the lower court with instructions to change the original decision and enter judgment for the plaintiff against Anderson, the father.

2. If Anderson was subsequently required to pay for the goods, do you think he would have had any recourse against his son?

3. Suppose, instead, that the son had ordered some furniture instead of ale and cigars. Would Anderson still have been liable? If not, why not?

4. One wonders why a case like this, involving the price of a few cigars and some imported ale, ever arrived at the Illinois Supreme Court. Surely, the cost to both parties exceeded the recovery.

IMPLIED AUTHORITY RESULTING FROM EMERGENCY. Sometimes an emergency arises that calls for an agent to take immediate action to protect his principal's interests. If the agent is unable to request and receive from his principal approval before taking action, he has implied authority to do whatever is necessary to meet the situation, even though he exceeds his express authority. This enlarged power is strictly limited to the immediate emergency, however; it does not extend any further.

EXAMPLE

A, who drives a delivery truck for P GROCERY STORE, has been instructed never to carry riders or to deviate from his prescribed route. One day, in the course of his duties, A hits X, a pedestrian, and injures him. A has implied authority to deviate from his regular route in order to take X to the hospital in the truck. On the other hand, he would not have authority to tell X, or the hospital, that P GROCERY STORE would pay X's medical bill.

Apparent Authority

As we mentioned earlier, a principal may, through his own conduct, create a situation that justifies a third party in assuming that the principal has bestowed authority on an agent. (Recall the example of the hotel clerk on page 542.) This is an agency by estoppel, and the authority that the principal appears to have given to the agent is called *apparent authority* or *ostensible authority*.

Apparent authority obviously exists only in situations where no actual authority has been given to the agent. It may adhere to a person who is in no sense an agent of the principal, or it may suggest that a proper agent has more power than he has actually been granted. In any case, the principal is bound by any contract or transaction which the agent, or the seeming agent, enters into within the scope of his apparent authority.

For apparent authority to exist, there must be (1) some conduct by the principal which creates the appearance of agency, (2) knowledge of that conduct by a third party, and (3) actual reliance by the third party on what he takes to be the agent's real authority. If the principal has not been responsible for creating the apparent authority, he is not bound by the unauthorized agent's actions.

EXAMPLES

1. P, the owner of a small store, leaves it open and unattended while he goes to lunch. S, a stranger, enters the store, goes behind the counter, and poses as a clerk. He makes several sales to customers and then leaves with the money he has taken in. Such sales are binding on P,

and he has no right to recover the goods from the customers. Although s clearly has no actual authority, either express or implied, P's carelessness has created a situation in which s has apparent authority to run the store and sell goods on P's behalf.

2. But suppose that several of P's customers have purchased goods on credit and owe him money. s, again without actual authority, calls on the customers, represents himself as P's bill collector and receives money from them. These payments are not deemed to be made to P, since he has done absolutely nothing to contribute to the appearance of agency. No apparent authority exists, and P may still recover from his customers if s does not account to him for the money collected.

In the two cases that follow, the question of apparent authority was decisive. In one case, the court held that it was present; in the other, that it did not exist. See if you can distinguish between the two situations and justify the difference in result.

LIVINGSTON v. FUHRMAN

Municipal Court of Appeals for the District of Columbia, 1944
37 A. 2d 747

► Action by Beatrice Fuhrman against Bernard Livingston, trading as Livingston & Company, for breach of warranty as to the quality of a watch purchased by plaintiff from defendant. From a judgment for plaintiff, defendant appeals.

Hood, J. The record shows that prior to the transaction in question the appellee wished to buy a diamond ring and was given the name of one Lassover. On the card appeared the name of Lassover and a telephone number and address. The number and address were that of Livingston & Company, a retail jewelry store operated by appellant.

Appellee called Lassover at Livingston's and made an appointment to see him. Pursuant to the appointment she went to the store of Livingston and was there shown diamond rings by Lassover. Later Lassover brought some rings to her home and she selected and purchased one. Thereafter appellee, desiring to purchase a waterproof wrist watch for her husband who was in the army, called Lassover at Livingston's and arranged an appointment. She went to the store and Lassover showed her some wrist watches. Afterwards Lassover brought some watches to her home and she selected and purchased the watch in question for $50. The watch was given by her to her husband who kept it for approximately six months. At the end of that time the watch was rusty and would not operate. Appellee took the watch to Livingston for repair. Livingston sent the watch to the factory but later informed appellee that the watch was in such a condition it could not be repaired. Appellee sued Livingston to recover the purchase price of the watch. She testified she thought Lassover was working for Livingston.

The testimony of appellant was that he conducted a wholesale and retail jewelry business, that Lassover was not his employee but was an independent jeweler, who purchased jewelry at wholesale from him and sold it at retail to his own customers; that appellant permitted Lassover to use the store telephone number for the purpose of receiving customers' calls and in Lassover's absence appellant would take messages for him; and that Lassover was permitted to use the store for the purpose of meeting customers and showing them merchandise. The evidence of appellant further was that Lassover was not his agent, that all merchandise received by Lassover was paid for by Lassover and appellant did not know to whom Lassover sold or for what prices and under what conditions he sold, and that appellant had nothing to do with Lassover's sales or customers.

The trial court found that appellant had "clothed Lassover with at least apparent authority to act as its agent" and that appellee "assumed she was dealing with Livingston & Co. through Lassover, its agent"; and awarded appellee judgment for the full purchase price. Appellant contends the trial court was in error in holding Lassover was the apparent agent of appellant; but we think the evidence justified this holding. The law with respect to apparent authority was well stated in Berryhill v. Ellett, 10 Cir., 64 F. 2d 253, 256, as follows:

> "Apparent authority may result from a manifestation of consent made to a third person or to third persons and inferred from words or conduct which, although ordinarily not indicating such consent, cause the third person because of facts known to both parties reasonably to believe that such consent exists, either where the apparent principal intended to cause such belief on the part of the third person, or where he ought to have anticipated that such belief would be caused."

When appellee went to appellant's retail jewelry store and was there shown jewelry by a salesman, she could reasonably assume that the salesman was the agent of the store and not acting as an independent jeweler; and appellant was bound to anticipate that the situation permitted by him might reasonably lead to such a conclusion. . . .   ◄

COMMENTS AND QUESTIONS

1. Why did the court decide that Lassover's sale of the watch was binding on Livingston & Co.? Wasn't Lassover acting independently of the store?

2. When Mrs. Fuhrman took the watch to Livingston for repairs, Livingston apparently sent the watch back to the factory and said nothing. Suppose, instead, that Livingston had refused to take the watch back and had informed her that the company was in no way responsible for the sale. Would this action have changed the result of the case?

3. How could Livingston have maintained its arrangement with Lassover but avoided responsibility in a situation of this kind?

HANSCHE v. A. J. CONROY, INC.

Supreme Court of Wisconsin, 1936
222 Wis. 553, 269 N.W. 309

► Hansche brought suit against Conroy for the sale price of onion sets which were allegedly purchased from him by Conroy through their employee Schultz. The trial court found for the plaintiff and the defendant appealed.

MARTIN, J. The appellant is engaged in the wholesale commercial produce business, dealing in fruit and produce for consumption. It never dealt in sprouted onion sets, which are sold only for planting purposes and in the trade are regarded as a specialty. Fred Schultz was in the employ of the appellant as a salesman, but occasionally made purchases of such farm produce dealt in by appellant company. He had never been authorized by his employer to buy onion sets on its behalf or to engage in that business in his own behalf or for others while working for appellant.

There is no testimony that the appellant had any knowledge that Schultz ever purchased onion sets on his own account or for anyone else while in its employ. It learned of his having purchased the sets of the plaintiff some time during April of 1935, the exact date not appearing. Prior to this time, Schultz had made a part payment on account to the plaintiff and had also given him an order on E. R. Peacock, to whom he had sold the onion sets, for the balance due plaintiff. This order was presented to Mr. Peacock, who explained to plaintiff that he was not then in a position to pay but would be in a few days. He asked plaintiff if that would be satisfactory to which he replied: "If I get the money in a few days it would be all right." It appears that Peacock sustained a fire loss on April 8, 1935, and some complications followed over the matter of insurance. It was not until after this occurrence that respondent informed Mr. Conroy of his transaction with Schultz and asserted his claim against appellant company. Respondent seeks to hold appellant liable on the basis of apparent agency. This brings us to consideration as to what is meant by apparent authority. . . .

Three elements are necessary to establish apparent agency: (1) Acts by the agent or principal justifying belief in the agency. (2) Knowledge thereof by the party sought to be held (in the present case, appellant). (3) Reliance thereon by the plaintiff, consistent with ordinary care and prudence. . . .

In Commonwealth Telephone Co. v. Paley, 203 Wis. 447, 233 N.W. 619, 620, the court said:

> "It is the rule that a person dealing with an agent known to be acting for a principal must at his peril ascertain the extent and nature of the agent's authority. . . . [Citations omitted.] However, this rule is to be read in connection with another rule stated in McDermott v. Jackson, 97 Wis. 64, 72 N.W. 375, quoted approvingly in Voell v. Klein, 184 Wis. (620), 622, 200 N.W. 364, 365, that: 'If a "third person, because of appearances for which the principal was responsible, believe, and have reasonable ground to believe, that the agent possessed power to act for the principal in the particular transaction, if such third person was, in the exercise of reasonable prudence, justified in believing that the agent possessed the necessary authority, then the principal is responsible to such third person the same as if the agent possessed all the power he assumes to possess." ' "

The apparent authority for which the principal may be liable must be traceable to him, and cannot be established by the acts and conduct of the agent. The principal is only liable for that appearance of authority caused by himself. If words or conduct of the agent are relied upon, it must be shown that the principal had knowledge of and acquiesced in them.

In the instant case, the basis of the claimed apparent authority is the introduction of Schultz to the plaintiff by a neighbor as "a man from Conroy's" and Schultz's alleged statement, "I am from Conroy," and the further statement, claimed to have been made by Schultz when there was some discussion as to paying for the onion sets, that Conroy was "good." Assuming that these statements were made, they fail to establish apparent authority. Nor does the fact that Schultz occasionally bought some farm produce in the line dealt in by appellant company create any apparent authority in him to buy the sprouted onion sets, a produce entirely foreign to his employer's business. An agent may be authorized by his principal to buy horses. The existence of such agency could not be regarded as apparent authority for the agent to buy sheep. No claim is made by the plaintiff or any of his witnesses that appellant company ever purchased sprouted onion sets or in any manner dealt in them. Plaintiff did not know Schultz until he was introduced at the time of the transaction in question. He did not become acquainted with Mr. Conroy until March 28th, or later, although he claims to have heard mention of his name, that he was located in Milwaukee, and that he was engaged in the farm produce business.

The burden of proof to establish the apparent authority of the agent was upon the plaintiff. [Citations omitted.] Upon a careful examination, we can find no competent evidence to sustain any finding of fact that Schultz had actual or apparent authority from his employer to purchase the onion sets in question. There is no liability on the part of the appellant company. *It follows that the judgment must be reversed and the action dismissed as to appellant.* ◄

COMMENTS AND QUESTIONS

1. How did the appellate court decide? Summarize the reasons for its decision.
2. Note that Schultz had resold the onion sets to Peacock, and Peacock had assured Hansche that he would pay for them. When Peacock neglected to pay, Hansche then went after Conroy. Suppose, instead, that Schultz had not sold the sets to Peacock and Hansche had billed Conroy in the first place. Would the result have been different?
3. The court, by way of example, says that the fact that an agent is authorized by his principal to buy horses could not be regarded as apparent authority to buy sheep. Why not? What if the principal had been a farmer who regularly purchased both animals?

Agent's Knowledge

As a general rule, if an agent knows or hears of any information that might affect his principal's business, the court will rule that the principal also possesses such knowledge, if any question is raised. This holds true even though the agent fails to pass the information along to the principal. If the agent is acting for another principal, however, or in collusion with a third party against the interests of his principal, the principal is not bound by the agent's knowledge; in such circumstances, it is hardly likely that the agent will communicate his knowledge to the principal.

E X A M P L E

P, the owner of an apartment house, hires A to manage it for him. T, a tenant in the apartment house, gives notice to A that he is not going to renew his lease. Even though A fails to pass this information on to P, P is bound by it and cannot claim that he did not receive proper notice from T. In other words, A's knowledge is binding on P even though it is not communicated to him.

Liability of Parties When Principal Is Not Disclosed

Frequently an agent will negotiate a contract with a third party without ever disclosing the fact that he is acting as the representative of someone else. So far as the third party is concerned, the agent is actually the principal. In a situation of this sort, the true principal is said to be *undisclosed*. If the third party knows that the agent is acting for a principal but does not know the identity of the principal, the principal is said to be *partially disclosed*.

Undisclosed Principals

As a general rule, even when the existence of the principal is completely undisclosed, the principal is, nevertheless, entitled to enforce the contract and, in turn, is liable for its performance. Since the third party assumes that he is dealing directly with the agent, however, any defenses or counterclaims he may have against the agent apply with equal force against the principal. The third party may enforce the contract against either the agent or the principal, once the latter's existence has been disclosed. Moreover, the agent, subject to the supervision and control of the principal, may enforce the contract against the third party.

EXCEPTIONS TO GENERAL RULE. There are a few important exceptions to the rule that an undisclosed principal is liable for and may enforce a contract made by his agent:

1. If an agent executes a negotiable instrument (see page 451) without indicating clearly that he is acting on behalf of a designated principal, the agent alone is liable and the principal is not bound. Conversely, in most states, the principal is not allowed to enforce the instrument. A few states also apply this exception to the execution of contracts under seal.

2. Frequently, the third person will indicate to the agent, either expressly or impliedly, that he wants to deal solely with the agent and has no intention of contracting with anyone else. If the agent then fails to disclose the existence of his principal, the third party may later claim that he has been deceived and may avoid the contract. When the contract is of a personal nature, or when it involves the skill, integrity, judgment, or credit of the parties, an undisclosed principal is usually denied the right to enforce it.

If the agent, in response to a direct question, falsely denies that he is acting as an agent, the third party may of course rescind the contract on the ground of fraud.

3. If the third party performs his part of the contract for the benefit of the agent before learning of the principal's existence, he is no longer liable to the principal. If, in such circumstances, the agent fails to account to the principal for the benefit received, the principal's only recourse is to the agent. On the other hand, once the third party learns of the principal's identity, he must deal directly with him rather than with the agent.

In the case that follows, the third party argued that the undisclosed principal had no right to enforce a contract which had been made with the agent.

SHIELDS v. COYNE

Supreme Court of Iowa, 1910
148 Iowa 313, 127 N.W. 63

► Coyne agreed to lend money to Shields to be used for the purchase of land. After the contract was made Shields' wife notified Coyne that Shields was acting as her agent and that she was an undisclosed principal. When Coyne refused to make the loan to Mrs. Shields, she brought suit against Coyne. The lower court directed a verdict for Coyne and Mrs. Shields appealed. The appellate court held that Shields was not acting as his wife's agent and then discussed the applicability of the undisclosed principal rule.

McCLAIM, J. . . . While the first of these reasons appears to us to be conclusive of the case, the argument of counsel relates to the second proposition, and we shall briefly express our views as to appellant's contentions. It is true that if one, as agent and acting for another, makes a contract in his own name for the benefit of his undisclosed principal, the principal may be sued for breach of such contract, and on the other hand may recover damages for breach thereof by the other party. But this general rule is subject to well-recognized exceptions, one of which is that if the party contracting with the agent having no knowledge of the agency may reasonably be supposed to have entered into such contract in consideration of some element of personal trust and confidence, and the contract remains wholly executory, the undisclosed principal cannot enforce the contract in his own name and right. This exception is based on the very good reason that a contracting party is not bound to accept performance of personal services from or extend confidence or credit to another person than the one with whom he supposed he was entering into the contract relation. Mechem, Agency, 769–771.

The facts of this case bring it clearly within the exception to the rule that the undisclosed principal may sue for breach of contract made by his agent. There is no evidence that Patrick Shields agreed to secure the payment of the money to be loaned by a mortgage of the land which as he represented he proposed to purchase, and even if it appeared that the loan was to be thus secured, there is no evidence the defendant relied entirely upon such security, and not to any extent upon the personal responsibility of Patrick Shields. It is clear that he was under no obligation therefore to make the loan to plaintiff, and if he were under no such obligation, he is not liable for damages to plaintiff for refusing to make it. If the contract was by Patrick Shields as agent for plaintiff, it could only be carried out by the loan of the money to plaintiff, and plaintiff cannot recover damages if the contract was only for the loan of money to her husband.

The cases relied upon for appellant are not in point. In Winchester v. Howard, 97 Mass. 303, 93 Am. Dec. 93, it is said that an agent may sell the property of his principal without disclosing the fact of his agency, or that the property is not his own, and the principal may maintain an action in his own name to recover the price. But the court follows this general proposition with the statement that, on the other hand, every man has a right to elect what parties he will deal with, and to take into account in such dealing the character, credit, and substance of the person with whom he contracts. And in Kelly v. Thuey, 143 Mo. 422, 45 S.W. 300, the court, commenting upon the case of the same title above cited, simply holds that an agent may enter into a contract for the purchase of land for an undisclosed principal, and the principal may maintain suit in his own name and enforce the contract. But it is not indicated that any credit was extended or was to be extended to the agent as supposed principal in the transaction. . . .

The judgment was correct, and it is affirmed.   ◀

COMMENTS AND QUESTIONS

1. Did the court *need* to discuss the question of undisclosed principal once it had decided that Shields was not acting as his wife's agent? Doesn't this make the quoted portion of the opinion mere dictum? If so, would the authority of this case as precedent be lessened?
2. Assume that Shields *had* been acting as his wife's agent, that he had agreed to give Coyne a mortgage on the land, and that the value of the land was more than adequate to secure repayment of the loan. Do you think the result would have been different?

THIRD PARTY'S ELECTION TO HOLD PRINCIPAL OR AGENT. As we mentioned earlier, a third party who has entered into a contract with an agent acting for an undisclosed principal may sue either the agent or the principal to enforce the contract. Since, however, he cannot hold them both liable, at some point he must choose between them. Precisely when he is deemed to have made this final election is often a hotly contested question. Obviously, no final election is possible so long as the third party is unaware of the principal's existence. In such circumstances, even though he sues the agent, he does not lose his rights against the principal. Of course, once the agent has fully performed, the third party has no further rights against either of them.

EXAMPLE

A, who is acting on behalf of P without disclosing the agency, contracts to purchase goods from T. T delivers the goods to A and brings suit against him when he fails to pay for them. T obtains a judgment against A for the price of the goods. T may still sue and collect from P if he later discovers P's existence, unless and until A pays him in full. And if A has made a part payment for the goods, T may collect the balance from P. Of course, T is entitled to collect no more than the contract price. If A pays him in full, he is not entitled to recover anything from P.

When the third party knows of the principal's existence, he must be more careful. In such situations, some states hold that he makes a final and binding choice the moment he brings suit against either the principal or the agent, and that if he is unsuccessful in getting satisfaction from the party he chooses to sue, he may not turn around and bring suit against the other. Other states hold that no binding choice is made until the third party actually pursues the case to a conclusion and obtains a judgment against the party he has sued. Still other jurisdictions are more liberal, holding that no final choice has been made in any case until either the agent or the principal, or both, complete performance of the contract. Obviously, there is a wide difference of opinion on how far a third party may move against one person before losing his rights against the other. The following case is typical of many decisions in this area of agency law.

LINDQUIST v. DICKSON

Supreme Court of Minnesota, 1906
98 Minn. 369, 107 N.W. 958

▶ START, C. J. Action to recover from the defendant, as an undisclosed principal, for labor and material performed and furnished by the plaintiff in decorating and repairing her house, pursuant to an alleged contract made for her by her husband, Joseph M. Dickson. The complaint alleged, in effect, that at the time the contract was entered into with the husband he was in fact acting as agent for his wife, the defendant, but he failed to disclose to the plaintiff the fact of such agency, or the fact that she was the real party in interest and owned the house, the decorating and improvement of which was the subject matter of the contract; that the plaintiff performed the contract on his part; that he was not paid therefor; and that he commenced an action against the husband to recover the balance due him on the contract, and on August 29, 1904, he recovered judgment against him for the sum of $273.68, no part of which has been paid; and further that thereafter (in the month of October, 1904) the plaintiff learned for the first time that the defendant was the real party in interest, and that the contract was made for her by her husband as her agent. This action was commenced in the month of June, 1905. The defendant by her answer denied that she ever made the contract alleged in the complaint, and alleged as a defense the recovery of a judgment by the plaintiff against her husband, Joseph M. Dickson. The trial resulted in a verdict in favor of the plaintiff for the amount stated, and the defendant appealed from an order denying her motion of a new trial. . . .

The general rule is that, where a simple contract, by parol or writing, is made by an authorized agent without disclosing his principal and the other contracting party subsequently discovers the real party, he may abandon his right to look to the agent personally and resort to the principal. Lindeke

Land Co. v. Levy, 76 Minn. 364, 79 N.W. 314. But whether the creditor can proceed against the undiscovered principal, after he has obtained a judgment on his claim against the agent, is a question as to which the adjudged cases are conflicting. In the case of Kingsley v. Davis, 104 Mass. 178, the creditor, after being fully informed that the party with whom he made the contract was acting for an undiscovered principal, brought an action against the agent and recovered judgment for his claim. Afterwards he brought an action against the principal to recover for the same claim, and the court held that the action against the principal could not be maintained for the reason that:

> "The general principle is undisputed that, when a person contracts with another who is in fact an agent of an undiscovered principal, he may upon the discovery of the principal resort to him or to the agent with whom he dealt at his election. But if, after having come to a knowledge of all the facts, he elects to hold the agent, he cannot resort to the principal."

In Beymer v. Bonsall, 79 Pa. 298, it was held that nothing short of satisfaction of the judgment against the agent would discharge the principal. The case of Kingsley v. Davis suggests the true basis for solving the question. It is a question of election. Election implies full knowledge of the facts necessary to enable a party to make an intelligent and deliberate choice. Perdson v. Christoperson, 97 Minn. 491, 106 N.W. 958. We therefore hold upon principle, and what seems to be the weight of judicial opinion, that: If a person contracts with another, who is in fact an agent of an undisclosed principal, and, after learning all the facts, brings an action on the contract and recovers judgment against the agent, such judgment will be a bar to an action against the principal. But an unsatisfied judgment against the agent is not a bar to an action against the undiscovered principal when discovered, if the plaintiff was ignorant of the facts as to the agency when he prosecuted his action against the agent. . . .

Order affirmed.   ◄

COMMENTS AND QUESTIONS

1. Summarize the rule of law enunciated by the Minnesota court in this case. Other state courts have followed different rules. Do you agree with this decision?
2. What if the plaintiff had become aware of the undisclosed principal after he had brought suit but before he had recovered judgment against the agent? Must he either have dropped the action against the agent and gone after the principal, or else have lost his rights? How do you think Minnesota would decide that question?

Partially Disclosed Principals

A partially disclosed principal is liable to the third party so long as the agent had authority to enter into the transaction. In most states the agent is also liable, and may be sued by the third party. What happens when an unauthorized agent acts on behalf of a partially disclosed principal? Most states will not permit the principal to ratify the resulting contract, since one of the requirements of ratification is that the agent must purport to be acting for an identified principal. A third party who enters into an agreement with an authorized agent acting for a partially disclosed principal may not avoid his obligation later on by claiming that he was unaware of the principal's identity when he made the contract. He was perfectly aware that a principal existed. And he had every right either to ascertain the principal's identity or else refuse to enter into the contract.

SECTION 3

RIGHTS AND DUTIES OF PRINCIPAL, AGENT, AND THIRD PARTY

In General

Inherent in the relationship of principal, agent, and third party are certain rights and obligations. We shall review these rights and obligations by treating each relationship separately.

Agent's Obligations to Principal

Loyalty

An agent has a strong obligation to be loyal and faithful to his principal. He is not permitted to make any personal gain or profit at the expense of his principal's interests, nor may he use his position as an agent to buy, sell, or lease property for his own advantage without getting the principal's approval. An agent is never permitted to represent both parties to a transaction without the full knowledge and assent of both. Moreover, he may not compete with his principal's business in any way, directly or indirectly, or accept gifts or payments from a third party which might tend to weaken his loyalty to his principal. In summary, an agent must serve his principal first, foremost, and exclusively, and must avoid any conduct that might tend to impair the faithful and effective performance of his duties and the furthering of his principal's interests.

The case of *Henry T. Raymond v. Anne T. Davies* well illustrates these rules of law.

HENRY T. RAYMOND v. ANNE T. DAVIES

Supreme Judicial Court of Massachusetts, 1935
293 Mass. 117

► CROSBY, J.   This is an action of contract upon an account annexed [12] to recover salary due and money lent. The case was referred to an auditor under an order that his findings of fact were to be final by agreement of the parties. The plaintiff filed a motion that the auditor's report be confirmed, and that judgment be entered for the plaintiff. . . . Upon the hearing of the motion the defendant filed the following request for rulings:

> "1. Upon all the facts found by the auditor a finding must be entered for the defendant. 2. The plaintiff having been guilty of taking a secret profit in regard to the matter in which he was employed by the defendant, the plaintiff is not entitled to recover any wages from the defendant. 3. The credits admitted by the plaintiff to have been received from the defendant more than offset the amounts claimed by the plaintiff for items other than wages, and a finding must be made for the defendant. 4. The intent of the plaintiff in taking the secret profit is immaterial, and upon all the facts a finding must be made for the defendant."

The trial judge granted the defendant's requests for rulings, denied the plaintiff's motion and "found" for the defendant. To the "rulings, orders, and judgment," the plaintiff excepted.

It appears from the facts found by the auditor that the plaintiff had been employed by the defendant as manager of her farm, known as Carver Hill Farm, in Natick in this Commonwealth; that he hired the employees and paid them and the bills generally; that he kept a bank account under the name of "Carver Hill Orchard," drew checks on the account, and made purchases of supplies for the farm, the checks being signed by him as manager; that at times he advanced his own money to pay bills, including the expense of spraying the orchards; that he rendered annually to the defendant a report which was "insufficient in detail"; that the funds were not sufficient to meet the expenses of carrying on the farm owing to the inability of the defendant to supply them, and the expenses were taken care of in part by the plaintiff, and his son, who was one of the employees on the farm. . . . The plaintiff was a stockholder in the Farmers Co-operative Exchange, and made purchases of farm supplies from this exchange. By reason of these purchases he received as a bonus or commission seven shares of stock from the exchange, which he did not disclose to the defendant. The defendant by letter sent to the plaintiff on March 26, 1934, complained of the inadequacy of his accounts, and notified him that he was discharged. The auditor further found that the plaintiff "had no right to the seven shares (of stock) which were a secret profit." . . . The auditor stated the account to be that the defendant was indebted to the plaintiff in the sum of $1,515.17 with interest thereon of $70.75, making a total of $1,585.92.

As manager of the defendant's farm the plaintiff was bound to exercise the utmost good faith in his dealings with her.

---

[12] This means that the plaintiff attached to his declaration or complaint a detailed statement of the exact amounts due him for salary, and so forth.

"If the agent does not conduct himself with entire fidelity towards his principal, but is guilty of taking a secret profit or commission in regard to the matter in which he is employed, he loses his right to compensation on the ground that he has taken a position wholly inconsistent with that of agent for his employer, and which gives his employer, upon discovering it, the right to treat him so far as compensation, at least, is concerned as if no agency had existed. This may operate to give the principal the benefit of valuable services rendered by the agent, but the agent has only himself to blame for that result." Little v. Phipps, 208 Mass. 331, 333, 334.

The auditor found that the plaintiff made purchases on behalf of the defendant from a corporation in which he was a stockholder, and that because of such purchases he received a commission of seven shares of stock from that corporation. He did not inform the defendant of the receipt of these shares of stock. They constituted a "secret" profit for which he never accounted to the defendant. As the plaintiff was guilty of taking a bonus in the form of shares of stock in a corporation in which he was a stockholder, by reason of his purchases from that corporation on behalf of his employer, he is barred from the recovery of salary or wages. . . .

No error of law appears in the rulings of the trial judge. The entry must be

Exceptions overruled.   ◀

COMMENTS AND QUESTIONS

1. The auditor found that the agent had no right to the seven shares of stock but held that he *should* be entitled to collect his back salary. What did the trial judge do? What happened on appeal?
2. Isn't this decision rather hard on the agent? Doesn't it allow the principal to receive valuable services from the agent free of charge? What is the justification, if any, for this result?

Obedience to Instructions

An agent must obey all instructions issued by the principal which fall within the scope of the duties he has been appointed to perform. The principal may not, however, compel an agent to perform duties which do not fall within the agency agreement. If the agent refuses or neglects to carry out the proper orders of his principal, he is liable for any resulting damage. He is also liable if he disobeys the principal's instructions or exceeds his actual authority in any way in good faith, with no intention of hurting his principal's interests.

Obligation to Account—Separation of Principal's Property

An agent has a strict obligation to give his principal a complete and accurate accounting of all money or property belonging to the principal which comes into his possession or control. In order to carry out this obligation, the agent must keep adequate records of receipts and expenditures and make them available for the principal's inspection.

An agent must also segregate his principal's funds from his own. He must never mingle them so that they cannot be separated and identified. If such mingling occurs, the agent is liable for any loss that results.

> EXAMPLE
>
> P hires A as an agent to collect rent from P's tenants. A deposits P's money in his own personal bank account and the bank fails. A is liable to P for the full amount, since he neglected to keep P's money separate. If A had deposited the rent money in a special bank account, set up in P's name, he would not be liable for it when the bank failed.

Duty to Convey Information

An agent has a duty to keep his principal fully informed of any facts that affect the subject matter of the agency. Since notice to the agent is deemed to be notice to the principal, the principal cannot protect his interests if the agent fails to carry out this obligation.

> EXAMPLE
>
> A is appointed by P to sell P's land for $10,000 or more. While trying to find a buyer, A comes across certain information that greatly enhances the value of the property. A has a duty to relay this information to P, since P may wish to raise the price or withdraw the property from the market. If A fails to notify P and sells the property at the original price, he will probably be liable for the loss that P sustains.

Duty to Use Reasonable Care and Diligence

An agent must perform his duties with a degree of care and diligence that seem reasonable under the circumstances. In other words, his behavior must be compatible with what is ordinarily expected of other agents in similar situations. If an agent professes to have special skills and training (e.g., a lawyer or an engineer) he must meet the commonly accepted standards of his profession. An agent who fails to use reasonable care and diligence may be held accountable for any loss or damage that his principal sustains as a result of his unsatisfactory performance.

Principal's Obligations to Agent

Duty to Employ and Compensate

If the agency relationship is based on a contract, the principal is obligated to perform according to its terms. This means that if the agent is hired for a certain period, the principal must allow him to carry out his duties during that time and to pay him accordingly. If the agent is wrongfully discharged, he may claim damages in one of the following ways:

1. He may simply sue the principal for the reasonable value of services he has performed up to the time of discharge.

2. He may sue immediately for any damages he has sustained by reason of the principal's breach of contract. The amount of damages is usually taken to be the loss the agent has sustained from his inability to complete his duties. Many states refuse to permit the agent to take immediate action,

however, on the ground that the damages are still speculative and hard to measure.

3. In all states, the agent may bring an action for breach of contract after the full term of the agency has expired. In the meantime, however, he may not simply sit back and do nothing. Instead, he must try to mitigate his losses by seeking and accepting other employment of a similar nature within the same general locality. Then, at the end of the contract period, he may sue for the loss he has actually sustained.

> E X A M P L E
>
> A is employed as a paint salesman for P at a salary of $10,000 for a one-year period. At the end of six months, A is wrongfully discharged, having been paid half of his year's salary. He must look for a similar job in roughly the same locality for the remaining six months of the contract period and thereby minimize his damages. If the best job he can find pays him only $3,000 for the remaining six months, he will be entitled to collect $2,000 in damages from P at the end of the year. If he tries in good faith but fails to find a similar position, he may recover the entire $5,000 remaining due on his contract with P.

Note that the above rules dealing with the agent's rights in the event he is discharged apply only where the agency contract is for a definite period of time, and only if it is a contract that may not be broken by either party. If it is an agreement that the principal may terminate at will, the agent is entitled only to payment for the services he has rendered before being discharged.

Duty to Reimburse Agent

The principal must reimburse the agent for any expenses that he has reasonably and necessarily incurred in performing his duties. The agent is not entitled to reimbursement for expenses caused by his own neglect, however.

Indemnification of Agent

If, in the course of carrying out his duties in good faith, the agent incurs liabilities to third persons, he is entitled to be indemnified by his principal. Again, however, if the liability results from some misconduct on the agent's part, he loses the right of indemnification.

> E X A M P L E
>
> A, without disclosing P's identity, contracts to purchase some property for P from T. P later refuses to go through with the agreement and T sues A for damages. If A is forced to pay T, he may recover the full amount from P.

Agent's Obligations to Third Party

Liability for Unauthorized Contracts

If someone without proper authority purports to act as an agent, the resulting contract is not binding on the principal unless he later ratifies it.

The third party's only recourse is against the would-be agent. The liability of the agent for such damage rests on the theory of a breach of his implied warranty of authority to represent the principal. Of course, if the third party agrees not to hold the agent liable if he lacks authority, he thereby loses his right to sue him.

In the case that follows, the court was faced with a situation in which the president of a corporation purported to act for the corporation but actually had no authority to do so.

JESSE J. MOORE v. EDWARD S. MADDOCK

New York Court of Appeals, 1929
251 N.Y. 420, 167 N.E. 572

► LEHMAN, J., delivered the opinion of the court:

The complaint herein alleges that in August, 1921, the plaintiff was in the employ of the Continental Guaranty Corporation. The defendant was the president of the corporation. He represented to the plaintiff that he was authorized as president to act as agent and representative of the corporation, and on behalf of the corporation he entered into a contract with the plaintiff for the organization and promotion of a similar corporation to engage in the same line of business, either as a subsidiary of, or in co-operation with the said Continental Guaranty Corporation, and agreed that, in consideration of the services to be rendered by the plaintiff, the plaintiff should receive a large block of stock in the new corporation, and a substantial payment in money. In pursuance of the agreement, and in reliance upon the defendant's representation that the defendant was duly authorized to act as the agent of the said Continental Guaranty Corporation in the making of the contract, the plaintiff rendered services as required by the contract. Subsequently the Continental Guaranty Corporation asserted that the defendant had no authority to act as agent for it, as president or otherwise, in the making of the above-mentioned agreement. On or about February 17th the defendant repudiated the said agreement, and notified the plaintiff that the plans for the development of the project thereunder had been abandoned by the defendant and by the said Continental Guaranty Corporation. The plaintiff has never received the agreed compensation.

The complaint is undoubtedly based upon the theory that the plaintiff has a cause of action for damages caused by the breach of defendant's alleged warranty of authority to enter into a contract binding upon the corporation. The contract was, it is alleged, made in August, 1921. The action was commenced by service of the summons on the 17th day of February, 1928. The defendant thereupon moved for an order dismissing the complaint on the ground that the cause of action did not accrue within the time limited by law for the commencement of the action. On the hearing of the motion, the plaintiff presented affidavits in accordance with the provisions of the Rules of Civil Practice, and the motion of the defendant has been denied.

The affidavits presented by the plaintiff, read with the complaint, sufficiently establish that the plaintiff believed that the defendant had authority to enter into the contract on behalf of the corporation, and that, in performing services under this contract, he acted in co-operation with the defendant, the president of the corporation. The defendant wrote to the plaintiff, a letter dated February 17th, 1922, terminating the plaintiff's services, in which he stated:

> "We have made up our minds to drop the International Equipment Corporation as a separate enterprise, and if we use that corporation at all it will merely be to clear merchandise transactions beyond our charter power."

The letter was written on the corporate letterhead, and was signed "E. S. Maddock, President." It was received a few days after its date and within six years of the bringing of this action. In March, 1923, the plaintiff brought an action against the corporation in Pennsylvania. The corporation filed an answer stating that the defendant Maddock had no authority to represent it or to enter into said contract in its behalf. Until that time the plaintiff had no knowledge or notice that defendant's representation of authority to act for the corporation was untrue. . . .

The defendant maintains that since at the time when, as the plaintiff alleges, the defendant represented and warranted that he had authority to enter into a contract binding upon the corporation, the representation was false, the warranty was broken as soon as made, and only when made. That does not follow. Before we can determine when a warranty or promise is broken, the terms of the warranty or promise must be formulated. The defendant did not, in fact, make any promise or warranty. No inference can be drawn from the allegations of the complaint or affidavits that he intended to make any promise or warranty. The only promise or warranty on the part of the defendant, alleged in the complaint, is implied by the law, regardless of the defendant's actual intent. If the defendant attempted to make a contract on behalf of the corporation without authority, then according to a long line of judicial decisions, it is but just that the loss occasioned by there being no contract with the principal should be borne by the agent who acted without authority. As a device by which that loss may be placed upon the agent, the courts have held that a promise or warranty must be implied. . . . The purpose for which the device of an implied promise has been created must dictate the terms of the promise when the courts are called upon to formulate it. . . .

Here the defendant was the president of the corporation which he assumed to represent. The contract called for the performance of services by the plaintiff in co-operation with the defendant as president of the corporation. The defendant impliedly asked the plaintiff to sign the contract with the corporation in reliance upon the defendant's authority to bind the corporation. No less did the defendant ask the plaintiff to continue to rely upon his assertion of authority when, as president of the corporation, he co-operated with the plaintiff in the organization of the corporation. Finally, the corporation repudiated the contract but in a letter which the defendant signed as president. There was no assertion in that letter that the defendant as president of the corporation had no authority to contract with the plaintiff for his services. On the contrary, it was calculated to disarm any possible suspicion that the defendant did not have such authority, and in effect constituted a renewal of his assertion that he did have authority. Our decision that the defendant's assertion of authority was a continuing warranty rests upon no fiction, but the actual intention of the parties as disclosed by their acts. We hold only that where a person makes an assertion of authority to bind a principal, which is intended and understood to be a continuing assertion, the warranty of the truth of that assertion, which the law implies, must from its nature be a continuing warranty. The plaintiff's cause of action did not accrue till after he had received the letter signed by the defendant as president of the corporation. We do not attempt to indicate what would be our decision if the circumstances presented were different.

The order should be affirmed, with costs. . . .   ◄

COMMENTS AND QUESTIONS

1. In this case an action was brought against an agent personally. What was the decision of the court?
2. The court states that the plaintiff had sued the principal (i.e., the corporation) in Pennsylvania in 1923 and that the principal had denied liability on the ground that Maddock had no authority to represent it. Apparently, the Pennsylvania case was dropped and never pursued to a conclusion. If it had been, do you think the corporation would have been liable for its president's contract? Wouldn't he have had apparent authority to bind it?
3. The defendant raised the defense that this action was barred by the Statute of Limitations, and it was conceded that more than six years had elapsed between the making of the contract and the commencement of the suit. How did the court get around this defense?

Warranty of Competent Principal

An agent who undertakes to represent a principal is implying that the principal has legal capacity to contract. If this is not true (if, for example, the principal is a minor), the agent is liable to the third party for any resulting loss.

Liability for Money Received

Sometimes a third party makes an overpayment or a mistaken payment to an agent. If the agent is aware of that fact, he must return the money to the third party; he will be liable for damages if he turns the money over to the principal. If the agent is unaware of the mistake when he receives the money but learns of it before turning it over to the principal, he must still return it to the third party. If, however, the agent receives the money in good faith, unaware that the third party is making a mistake, and then turns it over to his principal before finding out about the mistake, he is absolved from all liability to the third party. The third party's only recourse in such a situation is against the principal since the agent has acted in good faith.

Third Party's Obligations to Agent

As a general rule, a third party is not liable to an agent on contracts that the agent makes on his principal's behalf. The main exception to this rule occurs when the agent is acting for an undisclosed principal. You will recall that in such cases the agent has the right to enforce any contract he has negotiated, subject to the principal's control and supervision.

SECTION 4

LIABILITY OF PRINCIPAL FOR AGENT'S TORTS

In General

Up to now, most of our discussion has dealt with an agent's power to make contracts for and to represent his principal in business transactions. In this section, we will consider another aspect of the agency relationship: the liability of a principal for the torts of his agent. Under what circumstances is a principal responsible for wrongful acts committed by his agent which cause injury to third persons or damage to their property?

The general rule is simply stated: A principal is liable to third persons for injury or damage resulting from the tortious acts of an agent so long as the agent is acting within the scope of his employment. If the agent is acting outside the scope of his principal's business or is engaged in his own business when the tort is committed, the principal is not liable. Obviously, if the principal directs or authorizes the agent to commit a wrongful act, he is liable for the consequences. Difficult problems arise, however, when the agent's torts occur without the knowledge or consent of the principal.

In the case that follows, the person who committed the wrongful act was not even an agent at the time. The opinion, which was written by the renowned Justice Holmes, makes interesting reading.

DEMPSEY v. CHAMBERS

Supreme Judicial Court of Massachusetts, 1891
154 Mass. 330, 28 N.E. 279

► McCullock, without the authority or consent of the defendant, took it upon himself to deliver coal to the plaintiff on behalf of the defendant. While delivering the coal at the plaintiff's premises, McCullock carelessly broke one of the plaintiff's windows. After being informed of the delivery and the accident the defendant sent a bill for the coal to the plaintiff. The plaintiff brought suit for the damage to the window caused by McCullock and the defendant denied liability on the theory that McCullock was not acting as his agent.

HOLMES, J. . . . If we were contriving a new code today, we might hesitate to say that a man could make himself a party to a bare tort,[13] in any case, merely by assenting to it after it had been committed. But we are not at liberty to refuse to carry out to its consequences any principle which we believe to have been part of the common law, simply because the grounds of policy on which it must be justified seem to us to be hard to find, and probably to have belonged to a different state of society.

It is hard to explain why a master is liable to the extent that he is for the negligent acts of one who at the time really is his servant, acting within the general scope of his employment. Probably master and servant are "faimed to be all one person" by a fiction which is an echo of the *patria potestas* and of the English frankpledge.[14] Byington v. Simpson, 134 Mass. 169, 170; 45 Am. Rep. 314; Fitz, Abr. Corone, pl. 428. Possibly the doctrine of ratification is another aspect of the same tradition. The requirement that the act should be done in the name of the ratifying party looks that way. . . .

The earliest instances of liability by way of ratification in the English law, so far as we have noticed, were where a man retained property acquired through the wrongful act of another. . . . But in these cases the defendant's assent was treated as relating back to the original act, and at an early date the doctrine of relation was carried so far as to hold that, where a trespass would have been justified if it had been done by the authority by which it purported to have been done, a subsequent ratification might justify it also. . . . This decision . . . has been followed or approved so continuously . . . that it would be hard to deny that the common law was as there stated by Chief Justice Gascoigne. . . .

If we assume that an alleged principal by adopting an act which was unlawful when done can make it lawful, it follows that he adopts it at his peril, and is liable if it should turn out that his previous command would not have justified the act. It never has been doubted that a man's subsequent agreement to a trespass done in his name and for his benefit amounts to a command so far as to make him answerable. . . .

Doubts have been expressed, which we need not consider, whether this doctrine applied to the case of a bare personal tort. Adams v. Freeman, N.Y., 9 Johns 117, 118. Anderson and Warberton, JJ. in Bishop v. Montague, Cro. Eliz. 824. If a man assaulted another in the street out of his own head, it would seem rather strong to say that, if he merely called himself my servant, and I afterwards assented, without more, our mere words would make me a party to the assault, although in such cases the canon law excommunicated the principal if the assault was upon a clerk. Sext. Dec. 5,

---

[13] That is, an openly wrongful act.

[14] *Patria potestas* refers to the power that the head of a family, traditionally, held over his wife, children, and other close relatives. The "frankpledge" was a pledge taken by all the inhabitants of a village to secure one another's good behavior.

11, 23. Perhaps the application of the doctrine would be avoided on the ground that the facts did not show an act done for the defendant's benefit. . . . As in other cases it has been on the ground that they did not amount to such a ratification as was necessary. . . .

But the language generally used by judges and text-writers and such decisions as we have been able to find, is broad enough to cover a case like the present when the ratification is established.

The question remains whether the ratification is established. As we understand the bill of exceptions, McCullock took on himself to deliver the defendant's coal for his benefit and as his servant, and the defendant afterwards assented to McCullock's assumption. The ratification was not directed specifically for McCullock's trespass, and that act was not for the defendant's benefit if taken by itself, but it was so connected with McCullock's employment that the defendant would have been liable as master if McCullock really had been his servant when delivering the coal. We have found hardly anything in the books dealing with the precise case, but we are of opinion that consistency with the whole course of authority requires us to hold that the defendant's ratification of the employment established the relation of master and servant from the beginning, with all its incidents, including the anomalous liability for his negligent acts. See Coomes v. Houghton, 102 Mass. 211, 213, 214; Cooley, Torts, 128, 129. The ratification goes to the relation, and establishes it *ab initio*.[15] The relation existing, the master is answerable for torts which he has not ratified specifically, just as he is for those which he has not commanded, and as he may be for those which he has expressly forbidden. In Gibson's Case, Lane 90, it was agreed that, if strangers as servants to Gibson, but without his precedent appointment, had seized goods by color of his office and afterwards had misused the goods, and Gibson ratified the seizure, he thereby became a trespasser *ab initio,* although not privy to the misusing which made him so. . . . In Coomes v. Houghton, 102 Mass. 211, the alleged servant did not profess to act as servant to the defendant, and the decision was that a subsequent payment for his work by the defendant would not make him one. For these reasons, in the opinion of a majority of the court, the exceptions must be overruled.

Exceptions overruled.   ◀

COMMENTS AND QUESTIONS

1. On what theory did the court hold the defendant liable for the broken window? Do you agree with the decision?
2. What if McCullock had not told the defendant about the accident, but had merely informed him that the coal had been delivered? Would the defendant still be liable for the broken window if he billed the plaintiff for the coal?
3. Suppose, instead, that McCullock had assaulted and injured the plaintiff while delivering the coal. Do you think Justice Holmes would have held the defendant liable?

---

[15] That is, from the beginning.

Torts Within Scope of Employment

In determining whether the principal is liable for wrongful acts committed by his agent, the crucial question is this: Was the agent acting within the range of activities he was hired to perform, and was he acting in the course of that employment? To put it another way: At the time he committed the wrongful act, had the agent deviated from the duties he was hired to perform to such an extent that he was no longer acting for his principal? So long as the agent was acting within the scope of his employment, the principal may not excuse himself from liability simply by claiming that the agent was violating his instructions. Sometimes the answer to these questions is clear; in other situations, it is very difficult to determine.

EXAMPLES

1. A is hired to drive P's truck from Boston to New York; P instructs him to obey all traffic regulations and not to go over fifty miles an hour. Along the way, A drives through a red light while going sixty miles an hour and collides with x; he damages x's car and injures x severely. P is liable to x for the damage and injury caused by his agent's tort, since A was acting within the scope of his employment (that is, driving P's truck from Boston to New York). P may not avoid liability on the grounds that A disobeyed his instructions.
2. A is hired to drive P's truck from Boston to New York. Without permission or authority, he drives the truck to Maine to see his family. While en route to Maine, he loses control of the vehicle and strikes x, injuring him severely. x probably cannot hold P liable for A's tort, since A was not acting within the scope of his employment at the time of the accident. His trip to Maine would be a sufficient deviation from the range of duties he was hired to perform so as to absolve P from liability.

Having offered two relatively clear-cut examples, we now present two actual cases in which the results were not achieved so easily. In one, the court held the principal liable; in the other, it ruled that no liability was present. The two decisions will give you some idea of the confusion and uncertainty which pervade this area of agency law.

KOHLMAN v. HYLAND

Supreme Court of North Dakota, 1926
54 N.D. 710, 210 N.W. 643

► One Ludwig, an employee of the defendant, was instructed to drive the defendant's truck from Hillsboro due west to Carrington by way of Finley and Cooperstown. He was to perform certain work for the defendant in Carrington and to remain there over night. After reaching Finley, Ludwig deviated from the prescribed route and drove north to McVille to see the sister of one Sinner, an employee of the defendant who was a passenger in the truck. After completing his personal business in McVille, he proceeded west toward his destination Carrington. While en route from Mc-

Ville to Carrington he negligently collided with the plaintiff car. The trip from Hillsboro to Carrington over the prescribed route was about 100 miles; by way of McVille, the journey covered roughly 136 miles. The plaintiff sued the defendant for personal injuries and the defendant moved to dismiss the case on the theory that Ludwig was not in the course of his employment when the accident occurred. The trial judge directed a verdict for the defendant and the plaintiff appealed.

JOHNSON, J. . . . The rule that the master must respond in damages for injuries inflicted by his servant while within the course of the employment has been explained or rested upon a great variety of grounds. It would be neither practically possible nor substantially useful to recanvass territory which has been surveyed many times by nearly every court of last resort in the land. We have heretofore said that the underlying philosophy of the Workmen's Compensation Act is that industry, not the individual, shall bear the risk of injury to laborers engaged therein. Altman v. Comp. Bur., 50 N.D. 215, 195 N.W. 287. There is always present the possibility of injury to employees, notwithstanding every conceivable precaution may be taken to guard against it. So it is when we look at the situation from the viewpoint of the public. There is an ever-present probability that third persons will suffer injury because somebody's servant is careless, disobedient, or unfaithful to his master. This is a real, not an imaginary risk to which bear abundant witness the development of the doctrine of *respondeat superior* [16] and the myriad cases where courts have been lost in the mazes of metaphysical refinement in definition between frolic and detour. This latter risk to the public is clearly one which industry, on the analogy of the Compensation Acts, may well be required to carry, within reasonable bounds. He who employs a servant, and puts under his control an automobile must know, as every one knows, that it is not improbable that he will, on occasion, depart from strict instructions. As a fact of practical experience, this is beyond dispute; and that it does result in injury to the public the growing number of cases involving attempted distinctions between frolic and detour, clearly shows. Such a departure from the path of duty may become so great as to amount to an abandonment of the service in the minds of all reasonable men; it should then be a question of law for the court. On the other hand, there is an area, beyond and around the place within which the strict terms of the employment require the servant to remain, into which common experience with, and observation of, human nature suggest that he will, as inclination dictates, probably go, that is, a risk which properly belongs to the business, and injury to the public by the servant while within this area should ordinarily be accepted as a burden upon the industry itself. Whether the servant is within this permissible "zone" of deviation—permissible only in the sense that he is still within his employment—depends on the facts. The facts may be such that reasonable minds could draw but one conclusion; the question would then be one of law for the court. We are of the opinion in the case at bar, that reasonable

---

[16] Literally, let the master answer. This merely states the rule that the master (or principal) is liable in certain cases for the wrongful acts of his servant (or agent).

men might well reach different conclusions as to whether the servant was within the area of probable deviation, and therefore within his employment, when the accident occurred. That question should have been submitted to the jury. . . .

It may be conceded, for the sake of the argument only, that, had the injury occurred while he was on his way to McVille, and after he left the prescribed route, there would have been no liability, as a matter of law, for the reason that he embarked on an adventure of his own, and departed from his duties to such an extent as to terminate or suspend temporarily the employment. The primary question is whether the servant was, at the time of the accident, performing any act in furtherance of his master's business. He was undeniably en route back to the course from which he departed and to the designated place where he and his associates had been directed to remain for the night; in other words, he had resumed his purpose to go to McKenzie county, and was carrying equipment and passengers in the master's conveyance, and on the master's business. . . .

The judgment is reversed and a new trial ordered.

BURKE, J. (dissenting). . . . In what way could Ludwig justify the going to McVille to see Sinner's sister? Could he collect pay for extra time employed on the trip? Certainly not. Why not? Because it was no part of his journey. He did not go to McVille for the defendant. The relation of master and servant had ceased to exist between Ludwig and the defendant. Ludwig had become the servant of Sinner, and Ludwig and Sinner are alone responsible, not only to the plaintiff, but to the defendant for the destruction of the automobile. . . .

There is no conflict in the evidence, and no inference can be drawn, except that at the request of Sinner Ludwig abandoned his employment, went to McVille, and made such an unusual diversion that the trial court was justified in granting defendant's motion for a directed verdict, and the judgment should be affirmed.   ◄

COMMENTS AND QUESTIONS

1. What was the decision of the appellate court?
2. The majority opinion concedes "for the sake of argument . . . that, had the injury occurred while he was on his way to McVille . . . there would have been no liability, as a matter of law. . . ." Should it make any difference whether Ludwig was on his way to McVille or coming back from it at the time of the accident? The court seems to think so. Wasn't he on an unauthorized detour in either case?
3. Note the dissenting opinion. Do you agree with it?

HERR v. SIMPLEX PAPER BOX CORPORATION

Supreme Court of Pennsylvania, 1938
330 Pa. 129, 198 A. 309

► In the lower court there was verdict for the plaintiff and the defendant moved to have judgment entered in its favor notwithstanding the verdict. The motion was denied and defendant appealed.

SCHAFFER, J. Plaintiff was employed as a tank truck driver and salesman by an oil company. Defendant's employee, upon whose alleged-to-be negligent act liability in damages upon defendant is sought to be fixed, was employed by it as a truck driver.

Defendant is a manufacturer of paper boxes. Outside its factory is maintained an under-the-surface gasoline tank, gasoline for which was supplied by plaintiff's employer. On the morning the event occurred which gives rise to this suit, plaintiff was engaged in delivering gasoline from a truck into the underground tank. This he accomplished by drawing the gasoline from the tanks on the truck into five gallon cans, carrying it to the underground tank and pouring it through a large funnel into the orifice of the tank which protruded above the surface of the ground. Because he poured it too fast, the gasoline spurted out of the orifice into the air and onto plaintiff's clothing. As this happened, according to plaintiff's story, defendant's employee Weidner came out of the factory for the purpose of signing a receipt for the gasoline, as he had done on other occasions, and when ten feet from plaintiff struck a match to light a cigarette, thus causing the gasoline fumes in the air to ignite, seriously burning plaintiff. This theory of what brought about the firing of the gasoline was denied by Weidner, who testified that he lit his cigarette in the garage adjoining the factory, before plaintiff drove up in the gasoline truck, in so doing violating a rule of his employer against smoking; that he was eighteen feet away from plaintiff when the gasoline ignited; and that the cause of its doing so was plaintiff's violently "yanking" the large funnel out of the orifice, when the gasoline spurted up, thus causing friction and a resulting spark which set off the gasoline. For the purpose we are asked by defendant to accomplish, the entry of judgment in its favor, we accept plaintiff's version of what occurred.

We then have this situation: An employee of defendant, outside of its factory in the open air, being there for the purpose of signing a receipt in his employer's behalf, strikes a match to light a cigarette, with the result that the man delivering the gasoline is burned. Under this state of facts is the employer liable in damages to the injured man? We think it would be conceded generally as a legal proposition, as it was at bar, that if there had been no gasoline present, and if in striking the match the flaming head had flown off and injured plaintiff, or if the cigarette had been thrown upon plaintiff and he had been injured, there could be no recovery, because with such acts the employer has nothing to do, they are not an incident of, or part of, or in furtherance of, and therefore not within the scope of the employee's employment. Does the presence of the gasoline change the picture and the result so far as defendant is concerned? This is not a situation similar to one where the attendant at a garage, while engaged in putting gasoline into a customer's automobile, the better to see, would strike a match, in which case there might well be liability on his employer, because striking the match was concerned with and in aid and furtherance of the act the employee was hired to do. Here, however, in striking the match the servant was doing nothing in furtherance of or in connection with his employer's business.

The difficulty we see, if we are to sustain the recovery, is that in principle, we are going to fix a liability on employers that apparently has no limit. Thus an employer sends his employee to a store in which gasoline is kept to make a purchase and the employee strikes a match to light a cigarette, with the result of igniting the gasoline and thereby causing destruction of the store. Is responsibility to be visited on his employer? If a farmer sends his employee to his neighbor's barn on a mission, and as a result of the employee's striking a match to light his pipe, the inflammable contents of the barn is set afire and the barn destroyed, is the employer to be mulcted with damages? Approved recovery in this case would answer yes on principle in both instances.

The only filament which unites Weidner's act in lighting the match to his employer is that he was intending to sign a receipt for the gasoline. However, the delivery of the gasoline had not been completed and the receipt was not prepared when Weidner struck the match. Smoking was an act in no way connected with the business of his employer or with service to it. It was something done by Weidner for his own enjoyment and satisfaction. Had there been nothing in the case about signing the receipt, and had Weidner merely stepped out of the building to enjoy a smoke, and the accident had happened, it could not be successfully argued that his employer would be liable, nor do we think it can be with the element of the intended signing of the receipt in the case, because the striking of the match preliminary to smoking had nothing to do with the contemplated act to be performed for the employer. . . .

There is a type of case . . . in which liability of an employer was sustained because of evidence which showed that the employer had knowledge of the propensity of his servants to smoke, which habit they were likely to indulge in while at work. The question in these cases was not whether the men in smoking were acting within the scope of their employment, but whether the doing of the act was to be reasonably apprehended by defendants. In the present case the record is devoid of any evidence which would charge the defendant with knowledge that Weidner was in the habit of smoking near or around the intake pipe of the gasoline tank, and therefore these cases have no application to the controversy.

Another class of cases in which recovery has been allowed are those in which the employee is in possession of an inflammable article, and is controlling it for his employer's benefit. This was the situation presented in Jefferson v. Derbyshire Farmers, Ltd. (1921), 2 K.B. 281. There an employee of a garage keeper was drawing motor spirits from a drum into a tin, and while doing so struck a match to light a cigarette, and then threw it on the floor, causing oil thereon to ignite and consume the garage. The court in that case did not consider whether the act of throwing the lighted match on the floor was within the scope of the servant's employment, but placed liability on the ground that the servant was under an obligation to empty the motor spirits into the tins, and to do so while smoking was not doing it with reasonable care. A similar situation to that in the Jefferson case was presented in Maloney Tank Mfg. Co. v. Mid-Continent Petroleum Corporation, 10 Cir., 49 F. 2d 146, where the employee at the time was engaged in demolishing gas tanks, where danger from fire was inherent in the situation if smoking occurred, as the employees knew, and in Wood v. Saunders, 228 App. Div. 69, 238 N.Y.S. 571, where an employee of a filling station, while putting gasoline into the automobile of a customer, flipped a lighted cigarette over the open tank and caused the fire. . . .

Judgment reversed and entered for defendant.

DREW and MAXEY, JJ., dissented. . . .   ◄

COMMENTS AND QUESTIONS

1. The lower court entered judgment for the plaintiff, but the Supreme Court of Pennsylvania reversed the decision. On what grounds?
2. Note that two judges in the appellate court dissented. What arguments do you think they used to support their position?
3. The court takes pains to point out that the delivery of the gasoline had not been completed and the receipt was not prepared when the accident occurred. Do you think the court's decision would have been different if the gasoline had been delivered and Weidner had been in the process of signing a prepared receipt when he struck the match?

Willful or Intentional Acts of Agent

The principal's liability for an agent's torts is not confined to situations in which the agent inadvertently causes harm to a third party through carelessness or negligence. The principal is responsible even where the agent acts willfully or intentionally, so long as the agent is acting within the scope of his employment or is deemed to be furthering his principal's interest when the tort is committed. If it is clear that the agent has departed from his principal's business, however, or is acting solely for his own motives, the principal is not liable. Again, this test is hard to apply. Often the question becomes one of fact which is left to the jury to decide.

EXAMPLES

1. A is hired as a real estate agent to sell P's house. By making fraudulent representations concerning the house, A induces X to purchase it. Although A acted willfully and intentionally, P is responsible for his deceit, since A was acting within the scope of his employment (that is, to sell the house) and was furthering P's interest at the time he committed the tort.
2. A is hired as a floorwalker for the P DEPARTMENT STORE, with instructions to detect shoplifters. A, mistakenly suspecting that X, a customer, has stolen some merchandise, wrongfully detains him. When X resists, A assaults and injures him. P is probably liable for A's wrongful act even though it was intentional, since A would be regarded as furthering his principal's interest at the time.
3. P, a landlord, hires A to manage his property and collect rent from his tenants. A calls on X, a tenant, and demands payment. When X refuses to pay, A assaults him and beats him up. Although a much closer case than the one above (No. 2), P is probably liable for A's tort, since A was acting within the scope of his employment and was furthering his principal's interests.
4. A is hired to deliver ice for P. While on his route, A is accosted by

several youths who start teasing him and yelling at him. In a fit of
temper, A hits one of the children with his ice tongs. P is probably
not responsible for A's tortious act, since A has gone beyond the scope
of his employment.

In each of the three cases that follow, the agent acted intentionally and
deliberately, causing harm to a third party who sued the principal. Read
the cases carefully and see if you can distinguish between them. Reconcile
the different results that were reached.

SAUTER v. NEW YORK TRIBUNE, INC.

Court of Appeals of New York, 1953
305 N.Y. 442, 113 N.E. 2d 790

► A bus driven by the plaintiff collided with a truck owned by the defendant and operated by one Finnegan. Following the accident, it was
alleged that Finnegan assaulted and injured the plaintiff. The plaintiff's
version was as follows:

> "I pulled my bus to a stop as soon as possible. I got out, I asked the
> driver for his license. He said to me, 'You wise guy' and he called me
> a name. And I said, 'Well, let's stop this fooling around and give me
> your license: I want to get out of here.' And he struck me, give me a
> punch in the nose, my hands down. So I pushed him away. Some pas-
> sengers jumped off and separated us. I went back in the bus then, to
> get a piece of paper to get the license plate number of this truck. This
> truck had a tail gate on it, so I had to bend down to get the license plate,
> which was underneath the body of the truck. I got down on one knee,
> was preparing to get the number of the bus—of the truck, and this fellow
> came over and kicked me in the face."

The plaintiff sued the defendant for injuries and received judgment in the
trial court. The Appellate Division unanimously sustained the lower court's
decision and the defendant appealed to the N.Y. Court of Appeals, contending that Finnegan was not acting within the scope of his employment when
he injured the plaintiff.

LEWIS, CHIEF JUDGE. . . . In the circumstances disclosed by this record,
we do not believe it may be said that the second assault upon plaintiff by
the defendant Finnegan was an act done in the course of his employment
"in furtherance of" defendant-appellant's business or interest. This is not
a case—as are those cited by the Trial Judge and relied on by the plaintiff—
where the employee, though overly aggressive in adopting methods not
authorized by employer, was nevertheless carrying out the duties specifically enjoined upon him at the time of the wrong. In each of these cases
the ultimate result which the employee was attempting to effect by the
use of force or personal violence was an act which the employee had been
authorized to perform in furtherance of his employer's interest. Not so in
our present case where the evidence clearly demonstrates that the conduct
of the defendant Finnegan—through lack of judgment and while under the

influence of temper unprovoked by the plaintiff—went beyond the line of his duty or authority and inflicted injury upon the plaintiff which was not justified.

The assault committed by the driver Finnegan accomplished nothing which might be said to have benefited, or to have been intended to benefit his employer. Upon the facts of record, including the fact that Finnegan—having first struck the plaintiff and having been pulled away by intervening bus passengers—later sought out the plaintiff and kicked him in the face while he was kneeling on one knee, inflicting the injuries of which complaint is made, it is clear, that the sole purpose of the driver's second unprovoked assault upon the plaintiff was prompted by unrighteous anger on the part of the defendant Finnegan.

The trial court took the position that "The exchange of information upon the happening of an accident is an integral part of the operation of the truck" for which Finnegan concededly was employed by defendant-appellant. Assuming that to be true, we do not think it follows that the employer New York Tribune, Inc. can be held legally responsible for the second attack upon plaintiff by Finnegan which occurred subsequently to plaintiff's request to see Finnegan's license and at a time when plaintiff had walked away from Finnegan and had abandoned his efforts to exchange license numbers with him. If, as the Trial Judge said, "the driver . . . is engaged to submit credentials when circumstances require it," it is clear that, at the time of plaintiff's injury, the driver Finnegan was not only not pursuing the course directed by his employment, but on the contrary, he had already refused to perform the duty so imposed upon him and had chosen physical violence for purposes of his own. The assault upon plaintiff was something more than imperfect performance of the duty to submit credentials when circumstances required: it was a positive refusal to act as impliedly directed by the employer New York Tribune, Inc., thereby constituting a willful departure from the employer's business and the furthering of its interests.

Giving the plaintiff the benefit of every favorable inference which may reasonably be drawn from the facts of record, we do not believe it may be said that the assault committed upon plaintiff by the defendant Finnegan was an act within the course of driver's employment in furtherance of the interests of the employer, New York Tribune, Inc.

Accordingly, the judgments should be reversed and the complaint dismissed as to defendant New York Tribune, Inc. with costs in all courts. ◀

COMMENTS AND QUESTIONS

1. Why did the Court of Appeals reverse the decision of the two lower courts? How do you distinguish this case from the case of *Francis v. Barbazon* on page 585? In both cases, the employee clearly went beyond his instructions.

2. The court's opinion is confined to a discussion of the second assault, presumably because the plaintiff was not injured in the first altercation involving the punch in the nose. If the plaintiff *had* been injured by the first attack, do you feel he should have been entitled to recover against the New York Tribune?

3. Finnegan, of course, was personally liable for the unprovoked assault, but, apparently, was judgment-proof—i.e., lacking funds to pay any judgment against him. That fact suggests how important it is for a plaintiff to try to hold the employer liable in cases of this sort.

GILLIS v. GREAT ATLANTIC & PACIFIC TEA CO.

Supreme Court of North Carolina, 1943
223 N.C. 470, 27 S.E. 2d 283

► This was an action to recover damages for slander.[17] It was alleged that the defendant Little spoke of and concerning the plaintiff that she had stolen a bundle or package from the defendant company's store and further that the defamatory words were spoken while Little was acting within the scope of his employment by his co-defendant as manager of the store. The defendants denied that the slanderous words alleged were spoken by defendant Little, or that the corporate defendant was liable therefor.

Upon issues submitted there was verdict that defendant Little spoke of and concerning the plaintiff, in the presence and hearing of another or others besides her husband, in substance, the words alleged in the complaint, and that defendant Little was at that time acting within the course and scope of his employment. Compensatory damages in the sum of $1,400 were awarded.

From judgment on the verdict defendants appealed.

DEVIN, J. . . . We think the evidence of sufficient probative force to warrant submission to the jury the question of the corporate defendant's liability.

In Kelly v. Shoe Stores Co., 190 N.C. 406, 130 S.E. 32, 34, it was said:

"The designation 'manager' implies general power, and permits a reasonable inference that he was invested with the general conduct and control of the defendants' business centered in and about their Wilmington store, and his acts are, when committed in the line of duty and in the scope of his employment, those of the company." . . .

The principle that the employer is to be held liable for the torts of his employee when done by his authority, express or implied, or when they are within the course and scope of the employee's authority, is equally applicable to actions for slander. . . .

This principle was recently considered by this Court in case of Hammond v. Eckerd's of Asheville, 220 N.C. 596, 18 S.E. 2d 151, 155. While in that case judgment of nonsuit as to the corporate defendant was affirmed, the facts in some material respects were different from those in our case. There the clerk at the cigar counter of defendant's store followed a customer out of the store and along the street and charged him with having stolen cigars. It was said in the opinion by Winborne, J.:

"Applying these principles to the case in hand, it is manifest that the employment of Richard E. Young, Jr. (the cigar clerk), carried no im-

---

[17] Slander is the speaking of false and malicious words about another, thereby injuring his reputation in the community. Libel is the writing or printing of such statements.

plied authority to go out of the store and prefer charges against, and cause the search of, a third party, as attributed to him. . . . On the other hand, the evidence tends only to show that Richard, Jr. was employed as a mere clerk behind the cigar stand, and that he sold cigars. Furthermore, if the custody of the cigars were under his control, and, if his suspicion had been well founded, the cigars had already been stolen, and passed from his possession and out of the store. Under such circumstances the defamatory language used and the acts committed, while outside the store, and on the street, are clearly without the scope of his employment, and cannot possibly be brought within the limits of implied authority of an agent." . . .

Defendant excepted to the exclusion of the question asked defendant Little as to what instructions had been given him by the corporate defendant "relative to making any statement to people that might be interpreted as accusing them of stealing." The witness, if permitted, would have answered, "We are never to accuse anyone as to taking anything and to lay no accusation against anyone of having taken anything." While it does not appear when, how, or by or to whom the instructions referred to were given, such evidence, if properly presented, may have been competent in corroboration of the witness' testimony that he did not make the accusation charged. But private instructions of this character would not have had the effect of relieving the defendant from liability for defamation uttered by the manager if in fact he was at the time acting within the scope of his authority and in the line of his duty, in the effort to preserve and safeguard the company's property and to prevent its being carried off the premises. Otherwise an employer could avoid all liability for the torts of his employees by the simple expedient of instructing them not to commit them. It is not necessary that the employer should have known that the act complained of was to be done. It is enough if the injury is caused by the wrongful act of the employee while acting in the scope of his employment.

Where the wrong done to a third person is within the general scope of the employee's authority, is in the line of his duty, and is in furtherance of the employer's business, a deviation from actual authority will not necessarily foreclose recovery, Cole v. Motor Co., 217 N.C. 756, 9 S.E. 2d 425, though a substantial deviation from the scope of the duties imposed on the employee will relieve the employer of liability for those acts not immediately connected with his employer's business.

We do not regard the exclusion of the proffered testimony under the circumstances as prejudicial to the corporate defendant, or sufficient to overthrow the verdict and judgment in plaintiff's favor. It is only when the court's ruling on some material matter is prejudicial, amounting to the denial of a substantial right, that a new trial will be justified. . . .

Upon consideration of the entire case as it appears in the record, we conclude that the verdict and judgment should be upheld.   ◄

COMMENTS AND QUESTIONS

1. On what theory does the court base its decision in this case? Do you agree with the decision?

2. The court refers to a case of *Hammond v. Eckerd's of Asheville*, which

it had decided a year or two before. In that case, the facts were very similar, but the court found for the employer. How did the court distinguish the two cases? Do you think the distinction is sound?

3. The defendants objected to the exclusion of a question that had been asked of Little concerning the instructions he had been given. Note the answer that would have been given had he been permitted to reply. This is called an "offer of proof" by the defendant's counsel, and it goes into the record; this practice enables the appellate court to determine for itself how important the evidence would have been had it not been excluded. Did it make any difference in this case? If not, why not?

FRANCIS v. BARBAZON

Court of Appeal of Louisiana, 1931
16 La. App. 509, 134 So. 789

▶ This was a suit for damage to the plaintiff's truck which resulted from a collision with a truck owned by the defendant and operated by his employee at the time of the accident. In the lower court, there was a judgment for the plaintiff and the defendant appealed.

Higgins, J. . . . The evidence shows that the plaintiff and the defendant were engaged in the garage business and operated wrecking trucks for the purpose of salvaging and returning to their garages for repairs wrecked automobiles. On the day in question plaintiff received a telephone message that an automobile had overturned and was requested to send his service truck. He and two of his employees started out to the scene, and as they neared the place where the defendant's truck was parked, the driver of it backed out into the road and started in the same direction as plaintiff. As the plaintiff approached the defendant's truck from the rear, he sounded his horn, and the driver of defendant's truck pulled over to his right and then deliberately crossed back to the left side of the road, causing a portion of his truck to strike the right front side of the plaintiff's truck, resulting in the latter truck being overturned in the ditch beside the road. The driver of the defendant's truck continued on his way and, incidentally, his testimony was not taken.

The first defense, that the defendant's driver was an independent contractor, is clearly without merit, because that issue was not raised in defendant's answer, and evidence tending to support it, having been timely and properly objected to, it was rejected on the trial of the merits. In fact the defendant admits in his answer that the driver of the truck was his employee and was acting "within the scope of his employment." May v. Yellow Cab Co., 164 La. 920, 114 So. 836.

Passing to the second defense, that the driver of the defendant's truck acted willfully and deliberately and, therefore, out of the scope of his employment, the evidence indicates that, while the plaintiff and his two witnesses felt that the driver of the defendant's truck acted willfully and deliberately in causing the collision, this was merely a conclusion they reached because of the fact that there was no occasion for defendant's employee to have driven the truck to the left side of the road, after having pulled clear to the right. But, assuming that it was a willful and deliberate act, it appears that there had not been any previous personal difficulty or encounter between the plaintiff and the defendant's employee. There was no personal malice or hatred existing between them. Apparently the driver of the defendant's truck was determined to reach the wrecked automobile before the plaintiff, because when he heard the plaintiff sound his horn, he turned and looked, and seeing that it was the plaintiff's wrecking truck, he then deliberately pulled over, as we have described, in order to prevent it from passing, or with a view of causing it to run into the ditch, so that it could not continue on its mission. What appeared to be uppermost in the defendant's employee's mind was that plaintiff was a business rival and that if he could get to the scene of the wrecked car first, he could thereby obtain the business. We have come to the conclusion that defendant's driver acted within the scope of his employment. . . .

Affirmed.   ◄

COMMENTS AND QUESTIONS

1. What was the decision of the appellate court? Do you agree with the court's reasoning?
2. Don't you think the defendant's driver went too far here? Should the defendant reasonably expect his employee to use such tactics to get business?
3. The court notes that "there had not been any previous personal difficulty or encounter between the plaintiff and the defendant's employee." Suppose there *had* been. Would that have changed the result?

Liability of Agent for Torts

An agent is personally liable for any torts he commits, whether in the course of his employment or not. The fact that his principal may also be responsible does not affect the agent's liability in any way. Moreover, if the principal is held responsible, he may sue the agent. If the tortious act is committed at the principal's direction, however, and if the agent is ignorant of the wrongful character of the act, he may recover from the principal any damages he is required to pay to the third person.

Principal's Liability for Torts of Independent Contractor

By definition, an agent is subject to the strict supervision and control of the principal and must obey the principal's instructions while performing his duties. This right of the principal to control his agent's activities is one of the main reasons for his being held responsible for the agent's torts.

In this connection, it is important to distinguish independent contractors from agents. Whereas an agent is subject to the principal's supervision and control, an *independent contractor* is hired to bring about a certain result, and he retains full control of the means that will be employed to achieve that result. In other words, he uses his own discretion in deciding how the work should be done. As a general rule, an employer is not responsible in any way for the torts of an independent contractor, since he has no right to control the contractor's activities. If the employer himself is negligent in selecting an incompetent contractor, of course, or if the employer's own carelessness or fault helps cause injury to a third party, the employer is liable. An employer is sometimes held responsible, even in the absence of fault, if the activity being performed by the independent contractor is very dangerous or hazardous.

EXAMPLE

P hires A to paint the outside of his house. A furnishes his own men, materials, and equipment. P has no control over how the job is to be done, leaving that to A's discretion. A, while working on the job, drops a bucket of paint on X, a passer-by. P is not liable, since A is an independent con-contractor. X may, of course, recover damages from A for whatever injury he sustains.

The opinion in the following New York case contains a good discussion of this rule of law.

HEXAMER v. WEBB

Court of Appeals of New York, 1886
101 N.Y. 377, 4 N.E. 755

► MILLER, J.   This action was brought by the plaintiff to recover damages alleged to have been sustained by means of the negligence of defendant's agent and servants in making repairs and improvements upon the hotel of the defendant, situated in the city of New York. The alleged negligence consisted in fixing and securing the staging used in performing the work, and the proof showed that the ladder used as a scaffold was suspended from the roof over the eaves of the hotel, and that upon it were placed planks which were used as a platform upon which the workmen employed stood to do the work. This scaffold was moved from time to time around the bay windows from place to place. A heavy wind was blowing, and while shifting the ladder a gust came and the working of the wind and the grating against the cornice and wall cut the rope which held the planks on the ladder, and the wind turned the planks up so that they fell, and one of them falling to the sidewalk bounded and struck the plaintiff. One Burford, who was engaged in the roofing and cornice business, was employed by the defendant to do the work, which was intended to obviate a difficulty caused by pigeons making their nests under the eaves of the roof of the hotel.

At the close of the testimony, a motion was made to dismiss the complaint upon the ground, among others, that if there was proof of negligence, it was not negligence of the defendant, or his agents or servants, but of an independent contractor, and the plaintiff's counsel then asked to go to the jury upon several grounds, which were stated and refused. The motion to dismiss the complaint was granted, and the plaintiff's counsel excepted to the decision of the court.

The employment of Burford was of a general character, and the contract between him and the defendant was not restricted as to time or amount, or the specific services which were to be rendered. The accident occurred while Burford and his men were engaged in the performance of this work and this action was sought to be maintained upon the ground that the workmen employed, including Burford, were the servants of the defendant, and that the defendant as owner of the real estate was responsible to third persons for the carelessness, negligence or want of skill in those who were carrying on or conducting the business, and this whether the persons employed were working for wages or on contract. We think that the principle laid down has no application to the facts presented in the case at bar. As a general rule, where a person is employed to perform a certain kind of work, in the nature of repairs or improvements to a building by the owner thereof, which requires the exercise of skill and judgment as a mechanic, the execution of which is left entirely to his discretion, with no restriction as to its exercise and no limitation as to the authority conferred in respect to the same, and no provision is especially made as to the time in which the work is to be done, or as to the payment for the services rendered; and the compensation is dependent upon the value thereof, such person does not occupy the relation of a servant under the control of the master, but he is an independent contractor, and the owner is not liable for his acts or the acts of his workmen who are negligent and the cause of injury to another. . . . It is absolutely essential in order to establish a liability against a party for the negligence of others, that the relation of master and servant should exist. In King v. N.Y.C. & H.R.R. Co., 66 N.Y. 184, 23 Am. Rep. 37, the rule applicable to such a case is laid down by Andrews, J., as follows:

> "It is not enough in order to establish the liability of one person for the negligence of another, to show that the person whose negligence caused the injury was, at the time, acting under an employment by the person who is sought to be charged. It must be shown, in addition, that the employment created the relation of master and servant between them. Unless the relation of master and servant exists, the law will not impute to one person the negligent act of another."

In the case considered, we think that by the contract between the defendant and Burford, the relation of master and servant was not created. Burford was a mechanic engaged in a particular kind of business which qualified him for the work which he was employed to do. By the arrangement with the defendant he was an independent contractor engaged to perform the work in question. He was employed to accomplish a particular object by obviating the difficulty which he sought to remove. The mode and manner in which it was to be done and the means to be employed in its accomplishment were left entirely to his skill and judgment. Everything connected with the work was wholly under his direction and control. No right was reserved to the defendant to interfere with Burford or the conduct of the work. It was the result which was to be attained, that was provided for by the contract, without any particular method or means by which it was to be accomplished. So long as the contractor did the work the defendant had no right to interfere with his way of doing it. The fact that no price was fixed and no specifications made as to the work to be done did not render the contract one of mere hire and service, or create the relation of master and servant between the parties. It cannot, we think, be said that Burford did not agree to do the work required of him and that no contract was made because after the subject matter and the difficulties attending the work had been considered and talked about, Burford said he would try and do something, and the defendant replied he didn't care how he did it. The conversation had amounted in law to an agreement that Burford would perform all the work that was required of him according to his own judgment as to what was necessary to be done to accomplish the object intended. He was an independent contractor, and the men employed by him were his servants and had nothing to do with the defendant. Burford was not the agent of the defendant in any sense in purchasing the material or in hiring the men to do the work. That the work was charged for by the day could make no difference, and did not alter the position which Burford occupied, in reference to the defendant, as an independent contractor. It did not give the defendant control over the job, or authority to hire or discharge the men, or render him any way liable to them instead of Burford. It is very evident that the men employed were the servants of Burford, and therefore the defendant cannot be made responsible for their negligence. The test to determine whether one who renders service to another does so as a contractor or not, is to ascertain whether he renders the service in the course of an independent occupation, representing the will of his employer only as to the result of the work, and not as to the means by which it is accomplished. . . .

Judgment affirmed. ◄

COMMENTS AND QUESTIONS

1. Summarize the rule of law governing the decision in this case. What are the crucial facts which made Burford an independent contractor rather than an agent or employee of the defendant?

2. Would the result have been different if the defendant had reserved the right to supervise the work, and if Burford had agreed to report his progress daily to the defendant? In such a situation would it make any difference whether or not the defendant actually exercised his right to supervise?

3. Was Burford personally liable to the plaintiff in this case? If so, could the plaintiff have sued him after losing the present case?

SECTION 5

TERMINATION OF AGENCY

In General

Since agency is based on voluntary assent, it may be terminated at any time by either party. Neither side may compel the other to continue the relationship against his will. If there is a binding contract between agent and principal, however, the party who terminates the agency is liable for any damages resulting from the breach.

One exception to this general rule occurs in a situation where an agency is coupled with an interest. We shall discuss this exception on page 593.

Termination by Act of Parties

An agency may be terminated by: (1) the principal's discharge of the agent, (2) the agent's abandoning or renouncing the agency, (3) mutual agreement of principal and agent, (4) the expiration of the period for which the agency was to run, or (5) the achievement of the purpose for which the agency was created. When an agency is terminated in any of these ways, the agent ceases to have actual authority to bind the principal. If the principal discharges the agent, however, the termination does not become effective until the agent actually receives some notice of his discharge; until that time, he may continue to act for the principal.

In the case that follows, there was no express revocation of authority by the principal. It was argued, however, that his actions amounted to an implied revocation.

ULYSSES F. DES RIVIERES v. MARIE M. SULLIVAN

Supreme Judicial Court of Massachusetts, 1923
247 Mass. 443, 142 N.E. 111

► CARROLL, J. The defendant signed and delivered to the plaintiff, a real estate broker, this writing:

"Boston, January 18, 1923

I hereby employ U. F. Des Rivieres as exclusive agent to sell my houses at 389 and 391 Salem Street, Medford, Mass., for a price of not less than twelve thousand dollars ($12,000) and I agree to pay him a regular broker's commission, in any event, when a sale is consummated.

U. F. Des Rivieres is to do his advertising and showing of the property at his own expense.

Marie M. Sullivan."

The declaration alleges that the defendant agreed to make the plaintiff her exclusive agent, as stated in the agreement; and that the plaintiff secured a purchaser but was informed the defendant had already sold the property.

There was evidence tending to show that the plaintiff submitted several offers of less than $12,000 from prospective purchasers, which offers were refused; that on Sunday, February 25, 1923, the plaintiff submitted to the defendant an offer of $12,000 for the purchase of the property, only a few hundred dollars of which was to be paid in cash, the remainder to be on mortgage, and that this offer was refused, the defendant then informed the plaintiff "Not to bother about the property any more, I will sell it myself"; that on February 27 defendant made a written agreement to sell the real estate to her own purchaser; that on February 28 the plaintiff was notified by the defendant's attorney that a sale had been made by the defendant; that on March 1, the plaintiff was informed by the defendant's daughter that her mother had sold the property to her own purchaser. On February 27, the plaintiff secured a purchaser able, ready and willing to buy the real estate for $12,000.

The writing signed by the defendant was an offer on her part to pay the plaintiff a broker's commission when the transaction contemplated was performed by him. The defendant's promise was unilateral; it was without consideration until the performance of the condition; the promise could be revoked at any time before performance by the plaintiff.

> "Where one promises to pay another a certain sum of money for doing a particular thing, which is to be done before the money is paid, and the promisee does the thing upon the faith of the promise, the promise, which was before a mere revocable offer, thereby becomes a complete contract, upon a consideration moving from the promisee to the promisor; as in the ordinary case of an offer or reward." Cottage Street Church v. Kendall, 121 Mass. 528. . . .

It is a general rule that by employing a broker to secure a customer, the principal, in the absence of an agreement to the contrary, has the right to revoke the appointment and make the sale himself. . . .

The plaintiff was appointed the "exclusive agent" of the defendant to sell the real estate, but the term "exclusive" did not deprive the defendant of the power to revoke the agent's authority and sell the property herself without liability to pay a commission to the broker if the purchaser was not procured by him. . . .

In Wier v. American Locomotive Co., 215 Mass. 303, Randall v. Peerless Motor Car Co., 212 Mass. 352, and Garfield v. Peerless Motor Car Co., 189 Mass. 395, the agent was given the exclusive agency to sell the defendant's product in a certain territory under a contract between the parties founded upon a sufficient consideration. These decisions are not in conflict with the rule that where a unilateral promise is made to pay a broker a commission when a sale is made by him, and he is appointed the exclusive agent, a sale by the owner to a customer secured by himself revokes the authority of the agent. "A regular broker's commission" was to be paid the plaintiff "in any event, when a sale is consummated." The payment of a broker's commission "in any event" was to be made when the sale was effected by the plaintiff, but the words "in any event" did not make the defendant liable to pay the commission, unless the plaintiff was the efficient cause of the sale, and did not impose liability upon the defendant when the sale was the result of her own efforts.

There was evidence that the defendant made a written contract to sell the real estate to her own purchaser on February 27, 1923; the plaintiff was notified of this agreement on February 28. While the plaintiff had a purchaser able, ready and willing to buy the property for $12,000 on February 27, there was no evidence that the defendant knew of this, when she made the agreement to sell to the purchaser whom she procured. Assuming but not deciding that the revocation attempted on February 25, 1923, when the plaintiff was informed by the defendant "Not to bother about the property any more" was ineffectual, because made on the Lord's day . . . the owner by her sale revoked the authority of the plaintiff before she knew the plaintiff had a purchaser. The offer appointing the plaintiff to secure a customer, and giving him the exclusive agency, was revocable and was in fact revoked by the sale to one whom the plaintiff did not produce. The broker's power was not coupled with an interest, it came to an end when the subject matter of the agency was disposed of by the principal. . . .

The plaintiff had no notice of this sale by the defendant until February 28. The defendant's offer to the plaintiff was to pay the commission "when a sale is consummated." Even if this language means no more than the production of a purchaser able, ready and willing to buy, until the customer was produced or the owner had notice of the completion of the negotiations with the broker, the owner was free to sell to her own customer without liability to the plaintiff. The mere making of the contract with his customer did not entitle the plaintiff to a commission; he was required to produce the purchaser and bring the transaction to the defendant's notice. . . . Since no notice was given to the defendant that the plaintiff had secured a purchaser able, ready and willing to buy, when she had made sale of the property, the agency was revoked and notice of this revocation was not essential to bar the plaintiff's claim. . . .

The trial judge ruled that the plaintiff was entitled to his commission if the defendant sold the real estate and based his finding on the sale made by her; this was error, and it was error to refuse the defendant's requests that the defendant "was not precluded from selling property herself, without liability for commission to plaintiff. . . . Contract was terminated without liability for commission, by principal's sale of the property."

The order of the Appellate Division must be reversed and judgment entered for the defendant.   ◄

COMMENTS AND QUESTIONS

1. On what theory did the Supreme Judicial Court reverse the findings of the trial court and the Appellate Division? Do you agree with the decision?

2. The court states that since this was, in effect, a unilateral contract, the defendant's "promise could be revoked at any time before performance by the plaintiff." Assuming that the sale of the property constituted the revocation of the offer, hadn't the plaintiff actually performed prior to that time by procuring a purchaser who was ready, willing, and able? The general rule is that a unilateral contract becomes binding when the act called for is performed, and not when the offeror actually receives notice of performance (see page 221). How, then, could the court justify its decision that the contract was not binding on the defendant until she had received notice of the agent's performance?

3. The court, referring to a notice of revocation that was given on Sunday, assumes for the purpose of its decision that such revocation was not effective. If such notice had been the *only* evidence of revocation, how do you think the court would have decided? Isn't a Sunday revocation just as good as any other?

Termination by Operation of Law

Generally speaking, the death or incapacity of either party to an agency automatically terminates the relationship. If either party becomes bankrupt, the agency is terminated unless the bankruptcy has no effect on the operation of the agency. If the purpose of the agency becomes illegal, or if its subject matter is destroyed, the agency is automatically terminated. And finally, if the principal's country goes to war with the agent's country, the relationship is either terminated or suspended for the duration of the conflict.

Revocability of Agency Coupled with Interest

An *agency coupled with an interest* arises when the agent is given an interest in the subject matter of the agency itself. (In the ordinary agency relationship, the agent has no actual interest in the property he is dealing with, though he may receive a commission or some other compensation.) In most cases, such interests are given as security for the performance of an obligation by the principal.

EXAMPLES

1. P hires A to collect overdue accounts for him. He pays A a salary or, perhaps, a commission on the debts A collects. However, A has no legal interest in the proceeds he recovers for P. Here the agency is not coupled with an interest.

2. On the other hand, suppose that P owes A $100 and that x owes P $200. If P gives A authority to collect his claim against x, and instructs A to pay himself $100 out of the money collected from x and to account to him for the surplus, P has given A an interest in the subject matter of the agency itself. Here we have an agency coupled with an interest.

An agency coupled with an interest may not be terminated by the principal without the agent's consent. If the agent dies, the agency does not terminate automatically as in the usual case. His executor or other representative is generally allowed to exercise the authority in order to protect the agent's original interest in the subject matter of the agency.

EXAMPLE

Let's look back at the second example above. If A dies before collecting the debt from x, A's executor retains the authority to collect the $200 and to reimburse A's estate the $100 that P owed him.

The courts are split on the effect of the principal's death on an agency coupled with an interest. Some hold that this event terminates the agency; others hold that the agency is not terminated and that the agent may continue to exercise his authority.

In the New Mexico case that follows, the principal died and a question arose concerning the termination of the agency. Notice how the court dealt with the problem.

In re Estate of JAMES D. WARD, Deceased

New Mexico Supreme Court, 1943
47 N.M. 55, 134 P. 2d 539

► BRICE, J., delivered the opinion of the court:

The appellant filed a claim against the estate of James D. Ward, deceased, and Sadie Ward (the administratrix) individually, asserting that the deceased employed him to sell deceased's ranch properties consisting of real property, live stock and ranch equipment for the sum of $35,000; and that deceased's estate and Sadie Ward, his widow, were indebted to him in the sum of $2,000 for his services in securing a purchaser for said property.

The question is whether the appellant is entitled to a broker's commission because of the sale made by the heirs and the administratrix of the estate of his principal.

The substance of the facts found by the court necessary to a decision are as follows:

The property in question was listed with the appellant for sale at a price of $32,000, in January, 1940. Ward agreed to pay appellant a commission of $2,000 if he furnished a purchaser who would pay that price. Thereafter, on June 18, 1940, the owner Ward raised the price at which appellant was authorized to sell said property to $40,000 net to the owner. In August, 1941, John F. Callioux made inquiry of one Porterfield as to the latter's knowledge of the property. Porterfield advised him that he would secure information regarding it, and for that purpose contacted appellant and secured from him a mimeographed prospectus containing facts regarding the property and the name, address and telephone number of the owner Ward. This prospectus had been furnished to appellant to assist him in making a sale. The owner Ward died on the 11th of September thereafter, and a few days later Callioux was informed of that fact when he attempted to contact Ward in Amarillo.

In October, 1941, Callioux purchased the property from the heirs and the administratrix Sadie Ward for $35,000. At the time the sale was made Mrs. Ward owned as her separate estate 250 head of the cows sold to Callioux in addition to her community interest in the remainder of the property.

From these facts the trial court concluded . . . that the agency of claimant was revoked by the death of Ward before any liability was incurred by him. . . .

That the death of Ward revoked appellant's power to sell the property, is well settled. Unless he had earned his commission before Ward's death he is without remedy.

The case of Trickey v. Crowe, 8 Ariz. 176, 71 P. 965, is an almost identical case. The broker had secured for his client an option to purchase certain mining property and a deed was placed in escrow, to be delivered upon payment of the purchase price. If the sale was effected the owners agreed to pay the broker a commission. During the life of the option the owners of the property died. Thereafter the option lapsed and the deed was delivered to the administrators of the estate. The administrators and heirs sold the property at the same price, although on different terms to the person who had held the option. The Supreme Court of the Territory of Arizona held that as no binding contract had been made, and no purchaser furnished during the lifetime of the owners who was ready, able and willing to buy the property at the price and upon the terms specified, that notwithstanding the subsequent sale of the property at the same price to the same person by the administrators and heirs, that no commission could be recovered because the agency had been revoked by the death of the owner. This case was appealed to and affirmed by, the Supreme Court of the United States (204 U.S. 228, 27 S.Ct. 275, 51 L.Ed. 454), and that court stated that the deaths of Chaplin and Neville (the owners) terminated the authority of Crowe to sell on commission; as the power to sell was not coupled with an interest in the property on which the power was to operate. . . .

As the appellant was not the agent of the administratrix and heirs, and his agency for the sale of the property having been revoked by the death of Ward prior to any sale, or the furnishing of a client, ready, able and willing to purchase upon the terms authorized by the contract, and his power to sell not being coupled with an interest, it follows that the appellant is not entitled to a commission for the sale of the property by the heirs and administratrix. *The judgment of the district court should be affirmed and it is so ordered.* ◄

COMMENTS AND QUESTIONS

1. Do you think the court's decision is fair? Shouldn't the agent get the commission for this sale, since he furnished the prospectus to the buyer? Would it have made any difference if the administratrix, Sadie Ward, had known of the listing of the property when she sold it to Callioux?

2. Note the court's discussion of an Arizona case involving a similar fact situation which was appealed to the United States Supreme Court. Wasn't the Arizona case much more favorable to the broker, inas-

much as he had already negotiated an option for the person who ultimately purchased the property?

3. How and why did such a case ever go beyond the Arizona Supreme
Court to the United States Supreme Court? Notice the court's comment that "the power to sell was not coupled with an interest in the
property on which the power was to operate." If it *had* been, would
this fact have raised a constitutional question?

4. Can you think of any way in which an agent could protect himself
in situations where his authority is terminated by the property owner's
death?

Notice of Termination to Third Persons

Whether an agency is terminated by act of the parties or by operation of
law, the agent's *actual* authority to represent his principal obviously ceases
as soon as the relationship is dissolved. Third persons who are not informed
of the agency's termination, however, may very well continue to deal with
the agent on the assumption that he still possesses authority. How does the
law protect the interests of such innocent parties?

If a principal revokes the authority of his agent, he has a duty to inform
third parties of the termination. Otherwise, the agent will continue to enjoy *apparent* authority to represent him. The third parties who are entitled
to such notice are of two sorts: (1) those who have learned of the agency
and have dealt with the principal through his agent, and (2) those who have
learned of the agency but have had no dealings with the principal through
his agent. Third parties in the first group are entitled to actual notice of
termination, and until they receive such notice they are justified in assuming that the agent's apparent authority continues. On the other hand, third
parties in the second group need only be notified by public notice, such
as an advertisement in a widely distributed newspaper. They may not
complain if they do not receive actual notice of the termination.

As a general rule, if the agency is terminated by operation of law, the
principal is not obliged to notify third persons in either category. The theory
behind this rule is that such matters as death, insanity, bankruptcy, and
illegality are widely enough publicized so that third persons should be
aware of them. A few courts, however, have ruled that when the principal
dies, his agent continues to have apparent authority to act for him until
third parties have actually been notified or until a reasonable period of time
has elapsed. The case of *Montana Reservoir & Irrigation Co. v. Utah Junk
Co.* presents an unusual illustration of these rules of law.

MONTANA RESERVOIR & IRRIGATION CO.
v. UTAH JUNK CO.

Supreme Court of Utah, 1924
64 Utah 60, 228 P. 201

► One Rosenblatt had been employed as a purchasing agent by the defendant and, in that capacity, had often bought junk for them from the
Montana Power Company. Rosenblatt was discharged from his job but

the defendant neglected to give notice thereof to the Montana Power Co. Following his discharge and without authority Rosenblatt purported to order junk for the defendant from the plaintiff (i.e., Montana Reservoir and Irrigation Co.), which was a subsidiary of Montana Power Co., and closely connected to it by common management. The defendant received the junk and then paid Rosenblatt for it, Rosenblatt having told them that he had purchased it on his own and was the owner. The plaintiff sued the defendant for the price of the junk on the theory that Rosenblatt still had apparent authority to bind them. The lower court held for the plaintiff and the defendant appealed.

GIDEON, J. . . . There is no controversy, nor can there be, as to the general rule of law that one who has dealt with an agent in a matter within the agent's authority has the right to assume, if not otherwise informed, that such authority continues, and, unless notice of revocation of such agency is brought to his knowledge, the principal is bound, if the dealings continue after the authority is actually revoked. No citation of authority is necessary in support of that general proposition. Clearly, under that, if the purchase in this instance had been from the Montana Power Company, in the absence of any notice of the revocation of Rosenblatt's agency, the junk company would be liable, assuming, as the proof in this case shows, that Rosenblatt represented himself to be such agent, and the power company acted in good faith in dealing with him as such. As above stated, the officers of the Montana Power Company were likewise officers of the plaintiff. The agent, in transacting business with the plaintiff, was dealing with the same individuals that he had dealt with in making the purchase from the Montana Power Company. The Montana Power Company and the plaintiff company are two distinct legal entities. It does not appear that the plaintiff had ever dealt with the junk company through the agency of Rosenblatt. On the contrary, it appears that no such relationship existed.

The concrete question presented may be stated. Did the officers of the Montana Reservoir & Irrigation Company have the legal right to rely upon their knowledge gained while acting as officers of the Montana Power Company that Rosenblatt had been the agent of the junk company, and then representing himself to be such agent, and thereby bind the junk company?

I have found no case dealing with a like situation. The authorities cited by counsel do not aid in the solution of the problem here presented. Corporations act, and can act, only through and by their officers or agents designated by such officers. Knowledge imparted to the officers is generally held to be knowledge of the corporation. If the Utah Junk Company, by its acts and conduct, is estopped to deny the agency of Rosenblatt while dealing with the officers of the Montana Power Company, it would be illogical to hold that it would not be estopped while dealing with the same individuals as the officers of another or different corporation, especially so, when, as shown here, the two corporations have the same ownership. The author, in Mechem on Agency, 2d Ed., 628 says:

> "Where a general authority is once shown to have existed, it may be presumed to continue until it is shown to have been revoked, and per-

sons who have dealt with the agent as such, or who have had knowledge of his authority, and are therefore likely to deal with him may very properly expect that if the authority be withdrawn, reasonable and timely notice of that fact will be given and they may therefore lawfully presume, in the absence of such notice, that the authority still continued." . . .

The judgment of the district court is affirmed, with costs.   ◀

COMMENTS AND QUESTIONS

1. What was the decision of the Supreme Court of Utah? Do you agree with it?
2. The court admits that the plaintiff had never previously dealt with the defendant through Rosenblatt. Why, then, should the defendant have any obligation to notify the plaintiff that Rosenblatt was no longer their agent?
3. Suppose the defendant Utah Junk Co. had given proper notice of Rosenblatt's discharge to the Montana Power Co. but had failed to notify the plaintiff Montana Reservoir & Irrigation Co. Would that have affected the court's decision?

SUMMARY OF THE LAW OF AGENCY

Definitions and Classifications

Agency is a legal relationship in which one person or organization, called the agent, acts on behalf of another, called the principal. If the agent's duties are confined to the performance of routine tasks or manual labor, and if the agent is not authorized to make contractual agreements, he is usually described as a servant and the principal as a master.

Capacity to Act as Principal or Agent

A principal may appoint an agent to perform any act that the principal may legally perform himself. (There are a few exceptions to this rule, including voting, making a will, registering for the draft, and so forth.) Any person with legal capacity to enter into a contract may act as a principal. A minor may act as a principal, though he retains the right to avoid contracts made by his agent. Any person, regardless of his age, who understands the nature of the relationship and who has the physical and mental capacity to perform may serve as an agent.

Creation of Agency Relationship

Most agencies are created by a contract in which the principal expressly authorizes the agent to act on his behalf. Generally speaking, such contracts need not be in writing, except where (1) the agency is to run more than one year, or (2) the agent is authorized to buy or sell real property. Although most agencies are based on a contract, agents often agree to act gratuitously. In the latter case, the agent is under no legal obligation to perform for the principal. Once he has begun to exercise his authority, however, he must carry out his duties properly.

Sometimes, though there has been no express delegation of authority, the principal's behavior creates the impression that someone is acting as his agent. If a third party relies on that impression and acts accordingly, the principal cannot deny the agency. This is called agency by estoppel.

A third way of creating agency is by ratification. This occurs when the agent, without authorization, transacts business for the principal, and the principal then indicates, either expressly or by implication, that he is willing to honor the agent's commitment. Here the legal result is the same as if the principal had authorized the agent to act for him in the first place. As a general rule, ratification need not be in writing unless written authorization would have been necessary had it been given originally. In addition, the principal must ratify the entire transaction or none of it. Another requirement is that the principal must be aware of all the important facts surrounding the transaction that he is ratifying. Lastly, the principal must ratify the transaction before the other party repudiates it. In most states, a third party may withdraw from the contract at any time before the principal has ratified. A few states hold that a principal must be given a reasonable time in which to ratify an unauthorized contract after he has learned about it, and that the third party remains liable during that time. In all states, however, both the principal and the third party are legally bound as soon as the principal has ratified the contract.

Generally speaking, no agent is allowed to delegate his authority to another without the principal's permission. An exception to this general rule is recognized, however, when the duties delegated are purely ministerial or technical in nature and do not involve the exercise of special skill or discretion.

Authority of Agent to Bind Principal

As a general rule, a principal is liable only for those acts of an agent that come within the scope of the agent's actual or apparent authority, or for those transactions that he has ratified despite the agent's lack of original authority.

An express grant of authority may be spelled out in explicit terms; or else it may be described in more general terms, with the actual powers left to be implied from the circumstances, or from customs and trade usages. Generally speaking, anyone who deals with an agent must determine for himself the extent of the agent's actual authority. If in doubt, the third party should go directly to the principal for clarification; once the principal assures him that the agent possesses authority, the principal is estopped to deny its existence in the future. When the third party knows that the agent's authority has been spelled out in a written document, he should ask to examine it before dealing with the agent, for the agent is bound by any limitations of authority contained in the written statement. When the third party is not aware of any written statement of authority, however, he is ordinarily justified in assuming that the agent has the authority customarily granted to agents in similar circumstances in the community. If the principal wishes to limit this customary authority, he should make this limitation known to third parties who may be dealing with the agent. Otherwise, they may take the agent's authority at face value.

Apparent authority exists only in situations where no actual authority has been given to the agent. For apparent authority to exist, there must be (1) some conduct by the principal which creates the appearance of agency, (2) knowledge of that conduct by a third party, and (3) actual reliance by the third party on what he takes to be the agent's real authority.

As a general rule, if an agent has knowledge of any information relative to his principal's business, it will be assumed that the principal also possesses such knowledge. If the agent is acting for another person, however, or against the interests of his principal, the principal is not bound by the agent's knowledge.

Undisclosed Principals

Generally speaking, even though the existence of the principal is completely undisclosed to a third party, the principal is nevertheless entitled to enforce the contract and, in turn, is liable for its performance. If the third party has any defenses or counterclaims against the agent, however, he may use them against the principal. The third party may enforce the contract against either the agent or the principal. And the agent may enforce the contract against the third party, subject, of course, to the control and supervision of his principal.

The following exceptions to the general rule are recognized: (1) If an agent executes a negotiable instrument or, in some states, a contract under seal, without disclosing his principal, the agent alone is liable and the principal may not sue or be sued under the contract. (2) If a third party indicates that he wants to deal solely with the agent and with no one else, and if the agent fails to disclose the existence of his principal, the third party may avoid the contract on the grounds of fraud. (3) If the third party performs his part of the contract for the benefit of the agent before learning of the principal's existence, he is no longer liable to the principal.

When the principal is undisclosed, the third party may choose to enforce the contract against either the agent or the principal, when he learns of the principal's existence. Obviously, however, he cannot compel performance by both; at some point he must choose which one he will hold. So long as the third party is unaware of the principal's existence, no action he takes against the agent will deprive him of his rights against the principal, unless, of course, the agent has fully performed his part of the contract. After the third party has learned of the principal's existence, however, the third party must be more careful. In some states, the moment he brings suit against either the principal or the agent, he automatically loses his rights against the other. In other states, no binding election is made until he obtains a court judgment against the party sued. In still other jurisdictions, he does not lose his rights until he has obtained full performance from one or the other, or both.

If the principal is partially disclosed, he is liable to any third party who enters into a transaction with the agent that falls within the agent's authority. In most states, the agent is also liable to the third party. If the agent is not authorized to act, the principal is not liable; indeed, in most states, he may not even ratify the resulting contract. A third party who enters into a contract with an authorized agent for a partially disclosed principal is fully liable for its performance and may not avoid his obligation on the ground that he was unaware of the principal's identity.

Rights and Duties of Parties

An agent must be loyal and faithful to his principal and may not use his position as an agent for personal gain. He must not compete with his principal's business in any way, and he is never permitted to represent both parties to a transaction without their full knowledge and assent. He must obey and carry out his principal's instructions fully and must accurately account for any of his principal's money or property that comes into his possession. Moreover, he must keep the principal's funds separate from his own and never mingle the two. He has a duty to keep the principal fully informed of any facts which he acquires that affect the principal's business. Finally, he must perform his duties with reasonable care and diligence.

If the agency relationship is based on a contract, the principal is obligated to carry out its terms faithfully, to pay the agent what is due him, and not to discharge the agent wrongfully. If it is an agency that may be terminated at will, the principal may discharge the agent but must pay him for services rendered. In addition, the principal has a duty to reimburse the agent for any expenses reasonably and necessarily incurred by the agent in performing his duties. Finally, he must indemnify the agent for any liabilities to third persons incurred while the agent was acting in good faith and in accordance with his instructions.

If someone without proper authority purports to act as an agent, he is liable to the third party for any loss the third party sustains by reason of his inability to enforce the contract against the principal. Similarly, an agent who undertakes to represent a principal implies that his principal has the capacity to contract. If this is not true, the agent is liable to the third party in the event that the principal decides to repudiate the contract.

Liability of Principal for Agent's Torts

A principal is liable to third persons for injury or damage resulting from the wrongful acts of an agent so long as the agent is acting within the scope of his employment. If the agent is acting outside the scope of his principal's business when the tort is committed, the principal is not liable. In either case, of course, the agent is personally liable; the fact that the principal may also be liable does not affect the agent's liability in any way. So long as the agent is acting within the scope of his employment, the principal is liable not only for the agent's carelessness and negligence but for any intentional and willful activities that cause harm to others.

In questions of tort liability, it is important to distinguish an agent from a so-called independent contractor. Unlike an agent, an independent contractor is not subject to the principal's control and supervision; rather, he is merely hired to perform a certain job in his own way. Since the principal has no right to control the activities of an independent contractor, he is not liable for the contractor's wrongful acts unless he has in some way participated in them.

Termination of Agency

Generally speaking, an agency may be terminated at any time by either party, subject to the right of the other side to claim damages if there has been a breach of contract. Upon termination, the agent ceases to have authority. He may continue to act for the principal, however, until he has actually been notified of the termination. The death, incapacity, or bankruptcy of either party usually terminates the relationship automatically. And an agency is automatically ended if its purpose becomes illegal or if its subject matter is destroyed.

There is an exception to these rules: an agency that is coupled with an interest may not be terminated by the principal unless the agent consents. Nor is such an agency terminated by the agent's death. The courts are split on the question of whether the death of the principal terminates an agency coupled with an interest. Some hold that it does; others hold that it does not.

If a principal revokes the authority of his agent, he has a duty to inform third parties of that fact—otherwise, the agent will have apparent authority to represent him. Third parties who have previously dealt with the agent are entitled to actual notice. Third parties who have learned of the agency but have had no previous dealings with the agent need only be notified by public notice. Generally speaking, most states hold that if the agency terminates by reason of death, incapacity, bankruptcy, or illegality, notice need not be given to third parties.

Supplementary Reading: Agency

Perhaps the best-known summary of agency law is the *Restatement of Agency* (American Law Institute, 1933). For a fine textbook, see Floyd R. Mechem, *Outlines of the Law of Agency*, 4th Ed. (Callaghan, 1952). An extremely useful casebook is Warren A. Seavey and Livingston Hall, *Cases on the Law of Agency* (West Publishing Co., 1956).

15 Partnerships

Introduction

Generally speaking, there are three principal forms of business organization: (1) the sole proprietorship, (2) the partnership, and (3) the corporation. The sole proprietorship, which is the oldest and simplest of the three, involves few legal problems of a special nature. If a sole proprietor needs help in carrying on his business, he may hire agents to represent him and employees to work for him. If he needs capital, he may borrow it from a bank; if he needs property or equipment, he may buy it or rent it from others. If the enterprise is successful, he keeps the profits; if it loses money, he alone must bear the loss.

The increasing complexity of trade and commerce, however, has made it more and more difficult for a person to set up and operate a business all by himself. As a result, there has been a strong tendency toward multiple ownership and management of business enterprises.

The most complicated form of business association is the corporation (which we shall discuss in detail in the next chapter). In forming a corporation, several persons combine to invest their capital and to do business under a charter granted by the state. In exchange for their investment they receive shares of stock representing their interest in the organization. As a general rule, each stockholder is liable only up to the amount of his investment; he is not personally liable for losses which the corporation may suffer beyond that amount. Once organized, a corporation is treated as a separate and distinct entity capable of making contracts and owning property in its own right. A corporation remains in existence even though stockholders die or transfer their interest. Corporations are expensive to form and operate; moreover, they are heavily taxed and are required to keep accurate records and make extensive reports of their operations.

A partnership is far less complicated than a corporation. Its organization is more informal and, in most cases, approval of the state is not required for its formation. As a general rule, a partnership is less expensive to run, involves less paperwork, and enjoys more freedom to do business in other states than does a corporation. Its greatest drawback is that each partner is personally liable for the losses of the firm and may risk losing his own assets if the enterprise fails. In addition, a partnership is a very tenuous form of association, since it usually must be dissolved if one of the partners dies or otherwise becomes incapacitated.

It should be apparent from this brief discussion that each type of organization offers advantages and disadvantages, depending on the nature and size of the business, the number of persons involved, and many other factors. We will have more to say about this later (page 678).

Basically, a partnership is an agreement between two or more persons to carry on a business together; hence the relationship between partners is essentially contractual in nature. Since carrying on a business requires transactions with others, and since it is inconvenient for all the members of the firm to participate in and approve such dealings, each partner is usually authorized to act as an agent for the others in such matters. As we shall see, this concept of mutual agency plays an important role in partnership law.

The partnership form of business organization was well established and recognized under Roman Law. Until the seventeenth century, however, most disputes involving partnerships were brought before the special mercantile courts; hence, early partnership law was derived from the rules and customs of the law merchant. Because the early common-law judges of England refused to recognize a partnership as a separate legal entity, merchants rarely brought their cases before the English royal courts.

Starting in the seventeenth and continuing into the eighteenth century, largely as a result of the efforts of Lord Coke and Lord Mansfield, many of the rules and customs of the law merchant were absorbed into the common law of England. During this period we note a significant increase in the number of partnership cases in the official reports. Partnerships, along with other forms of business enterprise, increased in number during the nineteenth century, and it was during these years that the great bulk of the common law of partnerships was developed.

As our brief historical review indicates, the modern law of partnerships is a fusion of the strict rules of common law and the more liberal rules of the law merchant. Unfortunately, this mixture has not always been a happy one and has led to much confusion and uncertainty.

The basic conflict between the two schools of law revolves around the very nature of the partnership itself. Mercantile law treated a partnership as an entity separate and distinct from its members. The entity itself (like a corporation) could hold title to property in its own name and could acquire rights and assume obligations of its own. As an entity it could even deal with its own members (e.g., a partnership could lend money to or borrow from an individual partner).

Common law, on the other hand, refused to treat a partnership as a separate entity, looking upon it instead as an association of individuals. At common law, a partnership could not contract with its members, because a person could not contract with himself. Nor could a partnership hold title to property or acquire rights and obligations in its own name.

As the law of partnerships developed in this country, some states favored the law-merchant approach, others stuck to common-law doctrines, and still others tried to find a happy medium. Understandably, the result was chaos. By the end of the nineteenth century a strong movement for codification and uniform legislation had been launched.

In 1902 the Commissioners on Uniform State Laws [1] asked Dean James Barr Ames of the Harvard Law School to draft a Uniform Partnership Act. Dean Ames died, however, while engaged in this project, and the task of completing it was assigned to William Draper Lewis of the University of Pennsylvania Law School. The task was finally completed in 1914, and the act was submitted to the state legislatures for their consideration. Since then, almost two-thirds of the states have adopted it, including most of the large, commercially important states.

Although the U.P.A. has helped to establish uniformity, it has met with some criticism from legal experts. First, since the act does not attempt to cover all aspects of partnership law, it leaves many areas still in dispute. Second, though the act adopts, at least in a limited way, the entity concept of partnerships, the courts have not always construed its provisions in that sense.

As a result, in many states much of the law of partnerships is still governed by judicial decisions, or by a combination of decisions and statutes. As you read this chapter, you will notice that the cases cited reflect some of the old basic conflicts between mercantile law and common law.

SECTION 1

NATURE AND CREATION OF PARTNERSHIPS

Partnerships in General

The Uniform Partnership Act defines a *partnership* as "an association of two or more persons to carry on a business for profit." The persons so associated are called *partners,* and their relationship is created by a voluntary agreement. Although it is good business practice to spell out the rights and obligations of the parties in writing, ordinarily no written agreement is required in forming a partnership.

In the absence of a clearly phrased, detailed agreement, however, it is often difficult for the courts to determine whether a partnership actually exists. Lacking any other evidence, they must rely on the intention of the parties, their conduct, and the circumstances. If the parties meant to create

---

[1] This is the same group that initiated the drafting of the Uniform Sales Act and the Uniform Negotiable Instruments Law, which we discussed in earlier chapters.

a relationship with all the ingredients of a partnership, they are partners in the eyes of the law even though they might call their relationship something else. Conversely, unless the necessary legal elements are present, the parties cannot create a partnership merely by calling their relationship a partnership.

In each of the three following cases, the principal issue was whether a valid partnership had been formed. Note the various tests the courts applied in arriving at their decisions.

RUNO v. ROTHSCHILD

Supreme Court of Michigan, 1922
219 Mich. 560, 189 N.W. 183

► WIEST, J. This action was commenced by *capias ad respondendum.* Upon his arrest defendant moved to quash the writ and dismiss the suit; [2] one ground of the motion being that plaintiff's affidavit for the writ stated his claim arose out of partnership relations with defendant, and therefore his remedy is by way of an accounting, and not an action at law and the arrest of his copartner.

The motion was granted, the writ quashed, and the suit dismissed, and plaintiff has brought the case here by writ of error.

The parts of plaintiff's affidavit for the writ, bearing upon the relations of the parties, follow:

> "That prior to the 3d day of March, A.D. 1918, he had his offices at 1544 David Whitney building, and practiced his profession there as a urologist, which said offices included a suite of offices and a laboratory used in the practice of his profession. . . .
>
> "That just prior to the 3d of March, A.D. 1918, he approached the defendant herein, Dr. Douglas Rothschild, who was then his assistant, and offered to permit the said Dr. Douglas Rothschild to continue the occupation of the suite of offices aforesaid, together with the service of the laboratory and to practice his profession for the said plaintiff's patients; that the income derived from the practice of the profession from Dr. Runo's patients and from the laboratory aforesaid and would be used in the following manner:
>
> "First, to pay all the bills necessary to the maintenance of the offices, the practice and the laboratory, and that after the bills would be paid to divide the proceeds of the income share and share alike, to which agreement this deponent swears the said defendant, Dr. Douglas Rothschild, agreed to and actually commenced his services under this agreement; that the services of said Dr. Douglas Rothschild continued under this agreement from the 3d day of March, A.D. 1918, until the 31st day of October, A.D. 1921, during which time the plaintiff herein, Dr. Herman Runo, was in the service of the United States Army and traveling in the Orient.

---

[2] This suit was commenced by a *capias ad respondendum,* which means that the sheriff took the defendant into custody pending the outcome of the suit. To secure his release, the defendant is usually allowed to file a bond which guarantees payment of the plaintiff's claim if the plaintiff wins. The defendant moved to quash the writ—that is, he asked the court to dismiss the case.

"That the said Dr. Douglas Rothschild continued to receive the income, to make the disbursements, and shared in the income according to the agreement with Dr. Herman Runo until the 1st day of January, A.D. 1921, at which time he commenced to neglect the sharing of the proceeds of the income.

"That certain bills for the maintenance and upkeep of the offices and laboratory accrued which the defendant herein, Dr. Douglas Rothschild, neglected to pay and wholly refused to pay and which this plaintiff has been compelled to pay.

"That commencing with the 1st day of January, A.D. 1921, and continuing up to and including the 31st of October, A.D. 1921, the defendant herein received the entire income from the offices aforesaid, amounting to $7,093.05, and he neither paid the bills falling due during that time nor made a division of the proceeds from the income, in accordance with the agreement aforesaid, and wholly appropriated and took into his possession and expended the assets and property of this plaintiff during that time, which said amount is $2,095.28.

"That this deponent has further been compelled to expend from his own pocket large sums of money in paying the bills left unpaid by this defendant and which the defendant, Dr. Douglas Rothschild, should have paid; that after the 1st day of January, A.D., 1921, the said Dr. Douglas Rothschild well knowing that he had no interest in and to the share of the proceeds belonging to this plaintiff, and with intent to defraud this plaintiff, took and converted this plaintiff's proceeds to his own use and used and appropriated the same and expended the same to parties unknown to this deponent."

Does this state a mere hiring of defendant or a partnership between the parties?

Counsel for plaintiff insist the relation was a fiduciary [3] one, and for a fraudulent breach of the trust plaintiff was entitled to sue out the *capias.*

Plaintiff's affidavit shows an agreement under which defendant was to take charge of his offices and equipment and carry on the business for their joint benefit, pay all expenses out of the income, and divide the profits with him. This severed their previous relations under which defendant was but an employee and constituted the parties copartners.

Defendant had a right to manage and control the business, and his share of the profits was not in the nature of compensation for services rendered to plaintiff. Plaintiff did not hire defendant to carry on his practice, but entered into relations with him wholly inconsistent with those of master and servant or employer and employé. Defendant was empowered to act for both in management of the business, and both were liable for the expenses if the income was not sufficient to pay the same. This was not a mere joint adventure, but a community of interests with all the essential incidents of partnership rights and liabilities. The agreement delegated to defendant the power and authority to manage and control the same for their common benefit and profit. Plaintiff contributed toward the earning of

---

[3] A fiduciary relation is one in which the parties must have the highest mutual trust and confidence in each other and must act in good faith and complete fairness toward each other.

profits, in the practice to be conducted by defendant, his offices, laboratory and equipment, and his clientele, and defendant contributed his time, labor, and skill, and such new business as he could command, and these contributions were dedicated to the enterprise for the profits to be derived therefrom.

While the law has always considered the partnership relation one of contract and intention, it makes determination of the status of the parties from their agreement, and draws their intention from their acts.

Act No. 72, Public Acts. 1917, known as the "Uniform Partnership Act," defines a "partnership" as an association of two or more persons to carry on as co-owners a business for profit. The act also declares:

> "The receipt by a person of a share of the profits of a business is prima facie evidence that he is a partner in the business, but no such inference shall be drawn if such profits were received in payment:
> "(a) As a debt by installments or otherwise.
> "(b) As wages of an employee or rent to a landlord. . . ."

It is clear, judging from the affidavit, that the business was carried on under the agreement for the mutual pecuniary benefit of the parties, and not merely for the benefit of plaintiff with pay to defendant for services rendered. . . .

We are of opinion that the plaintiff, in his affidavit for the writ, stated an agreement between himself and the defendant constituting them copartners with reference to the subject-matter of this action.

The circuit judge was right in his holding that plaintiff was not entitled to maintain the action.

"As a rule an action at law by one partner against his copartners will not lie on a claim growing out of the partnership transactions, until the business is wound up and the accounts finally settled." . . .

The judgment is affirmed, with costs to defendant. ◄

COMMENTS AND QUESTIONS
1. Was the plaintiff alleging the existence of a partnership in this case? What defense did the defendant raise? How did the court decide?
2. Summarize the reasons for the decision. What factors caused a change in the relationship of the two doctors?
3. Does this decision mean that the plaintiff was left without any remedy against the defendant? Or does it mean that his action was brought in the wrong form?

HARVEY v. CHILDS

Supreme Court of Ohio, 1876
28 Ohio St. 319, 22 Am. Rep. 387

► Action for money. The case is sufficiently stated in the opinion of the court.

DAY, J. The original action was brought by Harvey against Childs and Potter, to recover $158.40, for seventeen hogs sold by Harvey to Potter.

Potter is in default. Childs denies his liability. His liability is claimed solely on the ground that he was a partner of Potter in the adventure for which the hogs were purchased.

The partnership claimed rests on the following state of facts: Potter went to Childs, and told him that he had contracted for about two car loads of hogs, to be delivered at Loudonville the next day, and had not the money to pay for them. He asked Childs to advance the money and take an interest in the hogs. Childs refused. Thereupon Potter proposed that if he would let him have the money to enable him to pay for the hogs he had bought, and others he might have to buy to make the two car loads, he (Childs) should take possession of the hogs when carried at Loudonville, as security for the money, take them to Pittsburgh, sell them, and take his pay from the proceeds of the sale; that he might have one-half the net profits of the adventure, and that in no event should Childs sustain any loss, but the money advanced by him should be fully paid by Potter in case the amount realized from the sale of the hogs was insufficient. Childs accepted the proposition, and it being agreed that $2,500 would be enough to pay for the two car loads he advanced that sum to Potter. Afterward without the knowledge of Childs, Potter bought the hogs in question of Harvey, on his own credit, and they made part of the two car loads of hogs which were taken possession of by Childs, sold in Pittsburgh, and the avails of the sale were appropriated in payment of the money advanced to him. No profits were made. The avails [4] of the sale were insufficient to pay the amount advanced by Childs, and Potter paid him the deficiency, and for his time and expense in the transaction.

The question to be considered, then, is, are the defendants, by construction of law, to be regarded partners as to the plaintiff, being a third person in the debt incurred to him by Potter in his own name? . . .

Although a partnership may be said to rest upon the idea of a communion of profits, nevertheless the foundation of the liability of one partner for the acts of another is the relation they sustain to each other, as being each principal and agent. That relation, it would seem then, constitutes the true test of a partnership liability, and rests upon the just foundation that the joint liability was incurred on the express or implied authority of the party sought to be charged.

But if the relation of principal and agent be regarded as the test of a partnership and consequent joint liability, the question still remains, what shall be deemed sufficient evidence of that relation, or to raise the implication of authority to incur the liability in question?

To this end numerous tests have been supposed to exist; but the best considered and least objectionable is that of a community of interest in the profits of a business or transaction as a principal or proprietor. . . .

But this test is valuable as a rule chiefly because it evinces a relation between the parties, where each may reasonably be presumed to act for himself and as agent for the others, and to that extent establishes the fact that the liability was incurred on the authority of all so participating in the profits. Participation in the profits of a business, however, cannot be

---

[4] That is, the proceeds.

regarded as a rule so universal and unrelenting as to be unjustly applied to a case where a debt is incurred by one who cannot be said to be acting, in the particular transaction, as the agent or on behalf of the party sought to be charged. Therefore, on principle, the true test of partnership, at least, is left to be that of the relation of the parties as principal and agent, to be proved by any competent evidence; for when they sustain that relation, a joint liability may be said to have been incurred by the authority, or on behalf of each of the parties so related. The tendency of the more modern authorities, both English and American, is to this conclusion. . . .

In the case before us it is obvious that it was not contemplated in the arrangement between Childs and Potter that any indebtedness should be incurred in the purchase of hogs for the contemplated adventure, to which the whole business was to be confined. There is, then, no ground for the implication of authority from Childs to incur the debt in question. On the contrary, such implication is rebutted by the advancement of money to pay for all the hogs that were to come to his hands.

Moreover, Childs had no legal interest in any of the hogs until they were delivered to him at the cars, nor had he any equitable interest in hogs, before such delivery, that were bought by Potter and not paid for by money received from Childs. He had, then, no interest whatever in the hogs bought of Harvey on credit, when the debt to him was incurred; and Potter, before delivery to Childs, might have sold them without being liable to Childs. The fact is apparent that it was the understanding of the parties that Potter had bought for himself, and, if need be, was in like manner to buy enough more hogs to make two car loads; and it cannot be doubted that, until their delivery at least, all the hogs belonged to Potter alone, and at most were only regarded as his contribution to the enterprise. . . .

But the truth is, Potter was the owner of the hogs until they were sold by Childs, for Childs declined to take any interest in the hogs other than as security for the money advanced by him to Potter. Looking to the whole matter, it is clear that the transaction was a loan of money by one party to the other, on the security afforded by the possession of the hogs. Childs, therefore, was the mere pledgee of the hogs, with a power of sale by agreement of the parties, and, as such, had only special property in the hogs. The general property in the hogs, from first to last, remained in Potter. He was the owner, and if they had died on the way to market, without the fault of Childs, the loss would have fallen upon Potter, both by the positive agreement of the parties, and the legal effect of the transaction between them as bailor and bailee.[5]

There was, then, strictly speaking, no mutuality or community of interest between them in the hogs. Childs had no interest in them other than as security for a debt, and to find in half the profits of their sale the measure of his reward for the use of his money, to be paid out of Potter's property.

The relation of the parties was that of debtor and creditor, of bailor

---

[5] In a *bailment*, possession of personal property is delivered by one party (called the bailor) to another (called the bailee) who agrees to hold it and then return it to the bailor. The bailor retains ownership of the property throughout.

and bailee, and not that of partners. They had no mutual interest in the hogs in common as principals or proprietors, nor was either acting as principal for himself and agent for the other. If, however, that relation could be said to exist after the hogs were delivered to Childs there is no ground for an inference that the debt to Harvey, previously contracted by Potter, was incurred upon the authority of Childs. . . .

Judgment accordingly.   ◄

COMMENTS AND QUESTIONS

1. What was the principal question at issue here? How did the court decide?
2. Outline the tests that were applied in determining whether a partnership existed. Was there not a joint enterprise here?
3. Note that no profits were derived from the transaction. Do you think the decision would have been different if the venture had been successful and Childs had received half of the profits? Suppose Childs had agreed to assume half of the losses. Would that have made a difference?

COMMISSIONER OF INTERNAL REVENUE v. OLDS

Circuit Court of Appeals of the United States
Sixth Circuit, 1932
60 F. 2d 252

► MOORMAN, CIRCUIT JUDGE. The question for decision in this case is whether an agreement which respondent made with his three daughters constituted a partnership within the meaning of section 218(a) of the Revenue Acts of 1918 and 1921 (40 Stat. 1070, 42 Stat. 245).

The respondent conducted a dock and timber business in Cheboygan, Mich. He had three daughters, one married and two unmarried. Desiring to train his daughters in the handling of large sums of money, and wishing to divide his property during his lifetime so as to avoid any family disputes after his death, in December of 1918 he entered into a written agreement to sell to each of them a one-fourth interest in everything he owned. Upon the execution of the agreement each of the daughters executed to the respondent her promissory note for $400,000, payable on demand without interest. It was stipulated in the agreement that the business should be conducted by the respondent "in his name" or in any other name that he might choose; that the daughters should draw out of the profits of the business only such amounts as he saw fit to pay them and as they might "need for their living and comfort during his lifetime"; that they should have "the privilege of looking over the books of the company" and "everything pertaining to the business" at all times; and that, if at any time any one of them should become dissatisfied with the way the business was being conducted or should think her interest was being impaired, he would return to her her note and take over her interest.

Upon the completion of the agreement, entries were made on the books of the business debiting the respondent and crediting the daughters with the amounts represented by the notes. During the year 1919 further entries

were made showing that a fourth interest in the business had been transferred to each of the daughters. In that year and the succeeding years
withdrawals of profits were debited to the parties receiving them, with the
result that at the close of each of these business years the books showed
net balances in favor of the parties in different amounts. Upon these facts,
found more in detail than herein stated, the Board concluded that a bona
fide partnership was entered into, and determined the taxable income of
the respondent for the years here involved—1919, 1920, and 1921—in accordance with the provisions of section 218(a) of the Revenue Acts of 1918
and 1921.

The Commissioner contends that the agreement did not constitute a
partnership within the meaning of the section of the Revenue Act referred to, and, subsidiarily, that the Board of Tax Appeals erred in receiving evidence of the purposes of the respondent in making the agreement,
the negotiations with his daughters with reference thereto, and the entries
on the books and accounts of the business after the agreement was made.

The agreement was executory in form. In order to transform it into an
executed one, and thus call the partnership into being, it was necessary
that the parties do the things that they agreed to do, that the daughters
execute and deliver to the respondent their respective notes, and that he
transfer to them the property interest he had agreed to sell. . . . The daughters evidenced their performance by executing the notes. The respondent
signalized his by causing entries to be made on the books of the business
showing that each of the daughters owned a fourth interest. This act, as
well as subsequent acts of a like nature, were plainly admissible to show
that the agreement was executed.

It is contended that the agreement is invalid because it does not permit
the daughters to withdraw their share of the profits without restraint. In
our opinion, it is not essential to the validity of a partnership agreement
that the rights of the partners as to the control of the business or the disposition of profits be equal. It is within the power of the parties entering
into a partnership agreement to restrict the rights of the several partners
to the extent of making one of them the sole agent of the others for conducting the business. . . . They may also agree that profits shall not be
distributed but put back in the business, or shall be distributed only upon
the happening of a specified event or as authorized by the partner in charge
of the business. . . .

Nor in our opinion was the agreement rendered invalid by the undertaking of the respondent to repurchase upon the dissatisfaction of the
daughters. Partnership agreements can be created only by contract, express
or implied. . . . In the absence of statutory inhibitions, they are governed,
as between the parties, by the principles applicable to other contracts.
There are many cases holding that contracts making fulfillment depend
upon the satisfaction of one of the parties are valid. Where the fulfillment is
denied in such cases, the test of its sufficiency is the good faith of the dissatisfaction. . . . The contract here under consideration is an executed contract of sale. It carries, it is true, an obligation to repurchase for a named

consideration if the buyers shall become dissatisfied, not with the contract, but with the way the business is run. Whether the buyers could defeat a suit on the notes or could compel a repurchase would depend, under the authorities cited, upon the good faith of their dissatisfaction. We know of no reason why an executed contract of sale which provides for a repurchase or the return of the purchase consideration upon the occurrence of a designated determinable event is not valid and binding as between parties, nor why it should not be binding as to third parties. Indeed, we have no doubt that, if this business should fail while the contract is in existence, the separate estates of the daughters, if they have any, could be reached by creditors.

It is not important that the respondent did not intend to require payment of the notes. They were executed and were collectible in his hands except upon a good-faith showing of dissatisfaction. Besides, he had the right to give an interest in his business to his daughters. There is no creditor attacking the transaction, and, if the gift was made in good faith, the taxing authorities cannot complain. . . . Here the respondent did not undertake to establish a joint tenancy in salaries or fees to be earned or to create a subcontract and convey a part of his earnings from the business to his daughters. He sold or gave to each of them a one-fourth interest in his business, and later, when a part of it was sold for a large sum, they received their partnership share of the proceeds. In such circumstances the Board of Tax Appeals was justified in holding that a partnership existed.

The order of the Board is affirmed.

HICKS, CIRCUIT JUDGE (dissenting). The question is well stated in the opinion of the court. . . .

During the year 1918 respondent operated a coal dock and owned certain timber properties and various bonds and stocks. He, with Mrs. Olds, lived at Cheboygan, Mich. He had two unmarried daughters, Blanche, and Gertrude, and one married daughter, Mrs. Florence Buhrman, who lived at Dayton, Ohio. During the summer of 1918 respondent conceived the idea of a general business partnership between himself and his daughters. While the family was together at the home of Mrs. Buhrman on December 31, 1918, there was a general discussion upon the subject, unimportant now in view of the written instrument above referred to which was executed by the parties on that date. At the same time the three daughters each executed a note for $400,000 in compliance with the terms of the writing. . . .

The Board decided that a partnership existed between respondent and his daughters, and upon this basis determined respondent's tax liability for the years involved in accordance with the applicable statutes above cited. The court is in accord.

I cannot accept this view.

I have briefly recited the circumstances leading to the execution of the instrument because of its very meager reference to the subject-matter, but their consideration is not required, or as I understand, allowed, in ascertaining the intention of the parties. The writing, read in connection with the notes, is unambiguous. The "Memorandum of Agreement" is between the father and his daughters. Respondent agreed to sell, and each of his daughters agreed to buy, "one quarter interest in everything he owns." Each daughter agreed to give her note for $400,000 in settlement. I need not discuss other features appearing in the second paragraph which the parties were fully competent to include if they chose to do so.

I think the weakness of respondent's contention is found in the [agreement]. Therein the makers of the notes expressly reserved the right to have them returned if at any time or in any way they should become dissatisfied with the way respondent conducted the business and should think that their interest was being impaired by his management. The exercise of this right was to be determined by the independent judgment of the makers of the notes. . . . This right imposed from the beginning an obligation upon the respondent to return the notes upon demand. The effect was to destroy the notes as enforceable obligations as between the parties and to strip the instrument of all mutuality of engagement. To promise to pay and at the same time to reserve the right to revoke reduces the promise to no promise. The obligation to hold the notes subject to the demand for their return is wholly inconsistent with the idea that the notes were either a promise to respondent or a consideration for the purchase. I think, therefore, that the agreement was void. The obligation to pay the notes was negatived by the reserved right to demand their return.

I think we are not dealing with a contract effective until terminable at will but with a contract invalid from its inception. . . .

A different situation would have arisen if the makers had paid the notes, but they have never done so. The notes were renewed on December 31, 1924, and respondent still holds them.

Section 6(1) of part 2 of the Uniform Partnership Act adopted in Michigan (Comp. Laws. Mich. 1929, 9846), where the written agreement was to be performed defines a partnership as "an association of two or more persons to carry on as co-partners a business for profit."

Upon the foregoing consideration, I think that respondent failed to establish before the Board by any substantial evidence that any partnership, as contemplated by the Partnership Act or by section 218(a) of the Revenue Acts involved, was ever effected between respondent and his daughters. The parties never became co-owners of respondent's property.

But, aside from all this, I think the matter can be brought into clearer view by the application of a very practical test. . . . Suppose we lay aside everything that was spoken or written between the parties and examine the question from the standpoint of what they really did or failed to do. In this light it appears to me that the daughters did nothing of consequence. During the six years intervening between the execution of the agreement and the bringing of this action the daughters neither invested any money in the business nor contributed any service. The record fails to disclose that they even exercised the "privilege of looking over the books." Upon the other hand, respondent managed the business for the whole period exactly as he did before the execution of the agreement, with this one difference: He distributed to them such "profits" as he chose to distribute, taking into consideration their living necessities. But there is no magic in words. Profits imply investment, and there was no investment by the daughters.   ◄

COMMENTS AND QUESTIONS

1. Summarize the decision of the court majority, and the reasons Judge Moorman gave for that decision.
2. Note the dissenting opinion of Judge Hicks. Do you agree or disagree with him? What tests did he apply?
3. Presumably, the payment of a large amount of taxes was at issue in this case. If the daughters were partners, they would each pay taxes on their individual share of the profits rather than have all the profits taxed as the father's income. In this way, great tax savings could be enjoyed, since each daughter's income would fall into a lower tax bracket than her father's.

Sharing of Profits as Test

Generally speaking, co-ownership of the business and the sharing of management responsibilities provide some evidence of the existence of a partnership, but they do not provide *conclusive* evidence. In the eyes of the law, the crucial test is usually the sharing of profits. The Uniform Partnership Act declares that, if the parties to the association share the profits, a partnership exists, unless there is strong evidence to the contrary. This rule is not applied, however, if the profits are distributed in payment of a debt, or as wages, or as rent to a landlord, or as annuity to a widow or to the representative of a deceased partner, or as interest on a loan, or as payment for the sale of good will. In these situations, it is clear that no partnership relation is intended, and that the profits are being used only as a means of paying off obligations.

EXAMPLES

1. A and B enter into an agreement whereby A is to supply the capital and B is to purchase and run a grocery store; profits are to be shared equally. Their association is probably a partnership.
2. A owns a store and leases it to B, who agrees to pay A a certain percentage of the profits as rent. In the absence of other evidence, no partnership exists. This is merely an agreement between landlord and tenant whereby the rent is to be paid from profits.

Who May Be a Partner

A partnership, as we have seen, calls for the association of two or more "persons." Although most partners are individuals, it is legally possible for a partnership itself, or for some other sort of association, to act as a partner. Even a corporation may be a partner, but only if it is so authorized by its charter or by statute. In short, the term "persons" has a broad meaning when used in this connection.

EXAMPLE

JONES, an individual, and X, Y, and Z, an existing partnership, agree to go into business together as partners. JONES is one partner and the firm of XYZ is the other partner. If, instead, X, Y, and Z have formed a corporation called "XYZ, INC.," the corporation itself could enter into the partnership, unless the state law or its own charter forbids it to do so.

As in other contractual situations, certain persons lack the capacity to enter into a partnership agreement. Thus a minor who becomes a partner may later elect to disaffirm and withdraw from the partnership without obligation to his copartners. Authorities disagree, however, on whether, in such an event, the minor may recover his capital contribution. Some states permit him to recover his full contribution, while others permit him to recover only his proportionate share of the firm's assets after its debts and losses have been paid.

Partnership by Estoppel

Frequently the circumstances surrounding a relationship give innocent third persons reason to believe that a partnership exists, where, in fact, no partnership has been established. If a person is represented to be a partner in a firm and does nothing to dispel that impression, he is liable as a partner to anyone who relies on the representation in dealing with that firm. A partner of this sort is called a *partner by estoppel*, or an *ostensible partner*. Notice, though, that the third party must actually act in reliance on the representation; otherwise no estoppel arises.

> EXAMPLE
>
> BLACK and WHITE operate, as partners, a hardware store under the name of BLACK, WHITE & BROWN CO. BROWN, a wealthy friend, is not a partner and has no interest in the business, but he permits them to use his name to enhance the store's prestige. X, a manufacturer who is ignorant of the true state of affairs, supplies goods and extends credit to the firm, relying on BROWN's participation. BLACK and WHITE fail to pay for the goods X supplies. X may hold BROWN liable as a partner by estoppel and BROWN will be forced to pay.

When a person represents himself as a partner or when the representation is made with his consent, there is little difficulty in holding him to be an ostensible partner. The situation is a little more troublesome, however, when the representation is made without his permission. Some courts hold that a person who was not responsible for the partnership representation has no duty to deny it. Other states require him to take all reasonable steps to disclaim his reputed connection with the firm; otherwise he may be estopped to deny liability as a partner.

In the following case, the plaintiff tried to show a partnership by estoppel.

STANDARD OIL CO. OF NEW YORK v. HENDERSON

Supreme Judicial Court of Massachusetts, 1928
265 Mass. 322, 163 N.E. 743

► Appeal from Third District Court of Bristol; James P. Doran, Special Judge.

Action on contract by the Standard Oil Company of New York against Thomas Henderson, Sr., for goods sold and delivered. From an order of the appellate division of the district court, dismissing report of the trial court, plaintiff appeals. Affirmed.

Plaintiff's requested rulings, denied by the trial court, are as follows:

1. If the place of business to which the plaintiff sold and delivered its gasoline and oil was conducted under the name of Thomas Henderson & Son, with the knowledge of the defendant Thomas Henderson, Sr., he would be liable to the plaintiff.

3. If the plaintiff was honestly misled by the fact that the name of the defendant Thomas Henderson, Sr., was used as owner of the business, and gave credit to the apparent partnership, the defendant would be liable for the indebtedness as if he had been a partner in fact.

4. The plaintiff and its agents were justified to interpret the appearance of the defendants' place of business as being owned and conducted by the defendants as copartners.

PIERCE, J. This case is before this court on the appeal of the plaintiff from an order, "Report dismissed," of the appellate division of the Third District Court of Bristol county. The report of the special justice of the Third District Court of Bristol to the appellate division "contains all the evidence material to the questions reported," which are: Should the special justice have ruled and should he have refused to rule, as requested by the plaintiff?

The pertinent facts disclosed in the report in substance are as follows: About November 13, 1924, one Thomas Henderson, Jr., opened a gasoline station at 660 Brock Avenue, New Bedford, and put on the window of the station the words "Henderson & Son." "This was the only name which appeared on the premises." On November 13, 1924, the plaintiff and Thomas Henderson, Jr., executed an "equipment loan agreement" for the installation of a tank, pump, and accessories for the gasoline station. The agreement recites that it is made between the Standard Oil Company of New York, by J. E. Winter, and Henderson & Son, of 688 Brock Avenue, New Bedford, and it was signed: "Standard Oil Company of New York, by J. E. Winter, Henderson & Son, by Thomas Henderson, Jr." The business was conducted by Thomas Henderson, Jr., the son of the defendant, who was a loom fixer employed in one of the local mills. His wife and daughter conducted a grocery store within a short distance of the gasoline station. Thomas Henderson, Jr., at the time the action was commenced and at the time of the trial, was in the state of California.

On the evidence the trial judge found that the plaintiff sold and delivered the items referred to in the plaintiff's declaration; that they were charged to Henderson & Son; that the delivery slips were signed by Thomas Henderson, Jr. "The plaintiff's evidence did not show that the defendant was a partner in fact." For the purposes of this case we assume the defendant was not a partner of Thomas Henderson, Jr. The record contains no direct evidence that the defendant had knowledge or notice that he was held out as a partner in the business of his son, and no circumstantial evidence to warrant a finding of such knowledge and notice, other than can logically be deduced from the evidence that he "walked past the gasoline

station almost every day: . . . that he saw the name Henderson & Son"
on a window of the premises, and knew that the business was conducted
under that name; that he made no inquiries as to whether any credit was
being extended by the plaintiff or any person or concern, relying on the
fact that his name was used in connection with the business, and he did
not tell anyone that he was not connected with the business or ask his son
to remove his name.

The trial judge specifically found "that (the defendant) was not asked
by the plaintiff concerning his responsibility." He stated that he was "unable to find . . . that the defendant ever visited the place of business of
the plaintiff." Other than as above stated, there is no evidence reported to
warrant an inference that the defendant consented to the use of the sign
"Henderson & Son" on the window of the station, and there is no affirmative
evidence reported that the plaintiff gave credit to "Henderson & Son" on
the faith that Thomas Henderson, Sr., the defendant, was a partner in the
business carried on by the son under the sign name "Henderson & Son."

St. 1922, c. 486, 16 (1), provides that:

> "When a person, by words spoken or written or by conduct, represents
> himself, or consents to another representing him to any one, as a partner
> in an existing partnership or with one or more persons not actual partners,
> he is liable to any such person to whom such representation has been
> given, who has, on the faith of such representation, given credit to the
> actual or apparent partnership, and if he has made such representation
> or consented to its being made in a public manner he is liable to such
> person, whether the representation has or has not been made or com-
> municated to such person so giving credit by or with the knowledge of
> the apparent partner making the representation or consenting to its
> being made."

On the evidence the issues which were presented at the trial were:
(1) As a matter of fact did the defendant consent to his being held out
as a partner in a public manner? . . . And (2) did the plaintiff give credit
to the apparent partnership on the faith that there was a partnership and
that the defendant was a member of it? . . . The statutory rule is an expression of the common law as recognized in this commonwealth.

The first request of the plaintiff was denied rightly. The evidence presented an issue of fact, and did not warrant the requested ruling of law
that the defendant was a partner by estoppel in the business carried on
under the style of "Henderson & Son." Bartlett v. Raymond, 139 Mass. 275,
30 N.E. 91, relied on by the plaintiff, decided merely that the evidence in
that case warranted a finding for the plaintiffs.

The third request was also denied rightly. There is no evidence reported
to warrant a finding that the plaintiff gave credit to the apparent partnership on the faith that the defendant was a partner in the partnership. The
evidence does not bring the case within Phipps v. Little, *supra*. The fourth
request was properly denied.

The second request, which was given, reads:

> "If the defendant permitted himself to be held out as a partner in the
> gasoline and oil business conducted at 660 Brock Avenue, New Bedford,

he is liable to the plaintiff as a partner whether actually a partner or not. Rice v. Barrett, 116 Mass. 312."

This request did not require that the judge should have entered judgment for the plaintiff; there remained open the issue whether the defendant consented to the holding out and whether the plaintiff gave the credit on the faith of the membership of the defendant.

The fifth request of the defendant:

> "The plaintiff cannot recover on the ground that the defendant Thomas Henderson, Sr., is liable as a partner for estoppel unless he proves by a fair preponderance of the evidence: (a) That Thomas Henderson, Sr., held himself out as a partner; (b) that such holding out was by Thomas Henderson, Sr., or his authority; (c) that the plaintiff had knowledge of such holding out; (d) that the plaintiff acted on the strength of such holding out to his prejudice,"

—correctly stated the law applicable to the evidence before the court. We find no error. The entry must be:

Order of appellate division dismissing report affirmed.
So ordered.

◀

COMMENTS AND QUESTIONS

1. Did the plaintiff contend that Henderson, Jr., and Henderson, Sr., were partners? If not, what was the basis for his suit against Henderson, Sr.? How did the court decide?
2. What necessary elements would have to be shown in order to hold Henderson, Sr., liable? Which of these were missing in the plaintiff's case?
3. Note that Henderson, Jr., had gone to California when this action was started, and that Henderson, Sr., was probably the only person the plaintiff could sue.
4. This case was heard by a trial judge alone, sitting without jury. Note the requests for rulings by each party. These requests, which are similar to the judge's instructions in a jury trial, require the trial judge to indicate the principles of law on which he bases his decision. If no requests are made in such cases, it is often impossible for the appellate court to determine the basis for the lower court's finding.

Firm Name

As a general rule, a partnership may do business under any name it chooses. The name may consist of one or more of the partners' names or it may be wholly fictitious. There are certain restrictions and limitations on this right, however:

1. The firm may not adopt the name of another organization, since this would create confusion in the mind of the public and would wrongfully take business away from the other.

2. Several states forbid the use of a name that tends to mislead third persons as to the number and identity of the partners. For example, many jurisdictions forbid the use of the phrase "and Son" or "and Company"

unless a son is actually a partner or unless there are actually other partners in the firm in addition to those named. Thus, the name "x, y AND SON" or "x, y AND CO." could not be used for a firm in which x and y were the only partners.

3. Many states require that a partnership doing business under a fictitious name must register the names and the addresses of its partners at the local city hall or in some other public place. This requirement is designed to enable third parties to ascertain the identity of the partners they are dealing with. Where such requirements exist, the penalty for failing to register is often quite severe—witness the following Michigan case.

CASHIN et al. v. PLITER

Supreme Court of Michigan, 1912
168 Mich. 386, 134 N.W. 482

► Action by McArthur Cashin and another, copartners doing business under the firm name of Flint Construction & Realty Company, against William G. Pliter. Judgment for defendant, and plaintiffs bring error.

STEERE, J.   In this case a verdict was directed in favor of defendant, for the reason that the contract sued upon was void under Act No. 101 of Public Acts of 1907; the same being entitled "An Act to regulate the carrying on of business under an assumed or fictitious name."

This act prohibits the conduct or transaction of any business in this state under an assumed name, or any other than the real name of each individual owning or conducting the same, unless such person or persons shall acknowledge and file in the office of the clerk of the county in which the business is or is to be conducted, or an office maintained, a certificate setting forth the name under which such business is or is to be conducted, and setting forth the real name of each of the owners of such business, together with the residence and post office address of each of said owners. A copy of such certificate is made evidence of the facts therein contained in courts of law in this state. Violation of the requirements of this act is declared a misdemeanor punishable by fine and imprisonment.

The declaration alleges in the first count that plaintiffs are a copartnership, doing business under the firm name of Flint Construction & Realty Company; that on March 14, 1910, plaintiffs, "under the firm name of Flint Construction & Realty Company," entered into a written contract with defendant to build him a house in the city of Flint for the sum of $825; that the same is fully performed and the house finished; that there is a balance due on said contract which defendant refuses to pay. A copy of said contract is attached to and made a part of the declaration. The declaration also contains the common counts. Defendant's plea was the general issue.

At the trial plaintiffs proved that they were engaged in the building and contracting business in the city of Flint in 1910, with offices in the National Bank building in that city, doing business as copartners under the name of the Flint Construction & Realty Company; that as such copartners, and under such name, they entered into a certain contract in writing with defendant to build a house for him. The contract was identified and offered in evidence. No proof was made or offered that plaintiffs had complied with the requirements of said Act No. 101. The contract was objected to, and timely objection was also made to all other evidence offered in support of the allegations in the declaration on the ground that plaintiffs had not complied with the requirements of said act, and had been transacting business in violation thereof; that any contract so made under an assumed name was illegal and not enforceable. The objections were sustained. The court also held that plaintiffs were not entitled to recover under the common counts for labor and material furnished in the construction of said building, and after parties had rested, directed a verdict as stated. Plaintiffs made a motion for a new trial, which was denied.

The points presented on the motion for a new trial, and upon which error is assigned, are substantially the same as those urged and argued during the trial of the cause. Briefly stated they are: That said Act No. 101 is a penal act, not implying or intending other punishment or loss to those violating it than that expressly provided by fine and imprisonment; that the act has no application in a case where defendant knows who comprise the members of the concern with which he deals, he being estopped by such knowledge, that even if the contract be void, inasmuch as the same is fully performed, and defendant has benefited thereby, plaintiffs are entitled to recover, under the common counts, the reasonable value of material furnished and labor performed; and that said act is unconstitutional under section 21, art. 5 of the Constitution of this state.

The last objection is not discussed in appellant's brief, but is presented in the record. The one object of the act is manifestly to protect the public against imposition and fraud, prohibiting persons from concealing their identity by doing business under an assumed name, making it unlawful to use other than their real names in transacting business without a public record of who they are, available for use in courts, and to punish those who violate the prohibition.

The object of this act is not limited to facilitation of the collection of debts, or the protection of those giving credit to persons doing business under an assumed name. It is not unilateral in its application. It applies to debtor and creditor, contractor and contractee, alike. Parties doing business with those acting under an assumed name, whether they buy or sell, have a right, under the law, to know who they are, and whom to hold responsible, in case the question of damages for failure to perform or breach of warranty should arise.

The general rule is well settled that, where statutes enacted to protect the public against fraud or imposition, or to safeguard the public health or morals, contain a prohibition and impose a penalty, all contracts in violation thereof are void. . . . This rule has been recognized and adopted in Shattuck v. Watson, 164 Mich. 167, 129 N.W. 196, wherein the following language is used: "It is a well-settled principle of law that all contracts which are founded on an act prohibited by statute under penalty are void, although not expressly declared to be."

. . . In interpreting the statute under consideration, it can be contended with reason, and in harmony with former decisions of this court construing acts somewhat analogous, we are inclined to the view that it is not the intent to render a contract made in violation of this act absolutely null and void for every purpose. While, as heretofore stated, the general rule is well settled that a contract made in violation of a statute is void when the statute is otherwise silent, and contains nothing from which the contrary is to be inferred, nevertheless the diversity of legislation gives rise to varying exceptions to this rule; and before applying it in full the court should carefully scrutinize the particular statute under advisement, for the purpose of ascertaining, from the subject matter and language used, the object for which it was enacted and the intent of its makers, to the end that such intent may be rendered effectual and the indicated purpose accomplished. As this act involves purely business transactions and affects only money interests, we think it should be construed as rendering contracts made in violation of it unlawful and unenforceable at the instance of the offending party only, but not as designed to take away the rights of innocent parties who may have dealt with the offenders in ignorance of their having violated the statute.

In behalf of the plaintiffs, it is urged that, the contract having been performed and labor and material having been furnished, of which defendant retains the benefit, recovery can be had therefor under the common counts, on an implied promise to pay for the same what they are reasonably worth. But they were furnished under an illegal express contract, by virtue of which there can be no recovery. It is an elementary rule that, where there is an express agreement between parties covering the subject-matter, the law will not imply one. If we say that, the contract declared on being unenforceable, there was, as a matter of law, no contract, and so seek to imply one for the labor and materials furnished, then the implied contract, under the allegations of the declaration and proof offered, is not relieved of the infirmity; for plaintiffs furnished the labor and material and transacted the business under an assumed name in violation of law. Changing the name or form of pleading does not change the character of the illegal transaction; under whatever guise the claim is presented, its ground work is a violation of the act. In such a case, the doctrine of estoppel cannot be invoked by the plaintiff; but the law leaves the parties where it finds them and refuses relief. It recognized the defense of illegality, not as a protection to the defendant, but as a disability to the plaintiff. . . .

We are constrained to hold that the contract sued upon was illegal and unenforceable as to plaintiffs for the reasons above stated. The trial court held that no recovery could be had under the special count or common counts of the declaration and the proof offered in that connection.

The judgment is affirmed.   ◄

COMMENTS AND QUESTIONS

1. Was there anything wrong with the contract itself in this case? If not, what was the court's reason for not enforcing it?
2. Does the statute in question set forth any specific prohibition against an unregistered firm's entering into contracts? If not, is the court justified in its decision?

3. Do you think it is fair for the defendant to have a house built for him and not have to pay for it? Is this not an excessive penalty to impose on the plaintiffs?
4. What is the purpose of this statute? Is it not designed to protect those who give credit to an unregistered firm, rather than to protect those who, like the defendant, *receive* credit from it? Decisions in other states have held the other way in similar situations.

Partnership as a Legal Entity

At common law, a partnership, unlike a corporation, is not deemed to be a legal entity in itself. Instead, common law looks on a partnership merely as a group of individuals doing business together. Thus, as a general rule under common law, property cannot be held in the firm name nor can suit be brought by or against a partnership.

Where it has been enacted, the Uniform Partnership Act has changed this situation somewhat by permitting a partnership to buy, hold, and sell property in its own name. In addition, many states have passed laws permitting partnerships to sue and to be sued in their firm names. Since many states still observe the common-law rules, however, the law in this area is clearly in a state of confusion.

SECTION 2

PARTNERSHIP PROPERTY

What Is Partnership Property?

In General

Often the courts must decide whether certain property used in a firm's business is partnership property, or the personal property of one of the partners, or the property of some other person or organization. The answer to this question is of great importance, for an individual partner may take his personal property with him if he withdraws from the firm or if the firm is dissolved. On the other hand, no one of the partners may withdraw partnership property, for partnership property remains subject to the claims of the firm's creditors and to the rights of the other partners.

As a general rule, the courts will accept the agreement of the partners as decisive in determining what is, and what is not, partnership property. In the absence of any express agreement among the partners, the courts will examine the conduct of the parties and the circumstances of the case in deciding the question. The mere use of property by a partnership does not necessarily make it partnership property, because one of the partners, or even a third party, may lend or lease property to the partnership while retaining full title to it.

EXAMPLE

A, B, and C form a partnership to carry on a laundry business. A, who owns a delivery truck, lends it to the firm to use temporarily while the business is getting started. Here the truck remains the individual property of A. On the other hand, if A brings the truck into the business with the understanding that it will be used permanently, it will probably be regarded as partnership property.

Sometimes, it is very difficult to determine what constitutes partnership property. The following case is a good illustration.

In re AMY

Circuit Court of Appeals of the United States
Second Circuit, 1927
21 F. 2d 301

► SWAN, CIRCUIT JUDGE. This is a contest between individual creditors of Louis H. Amy and partnership creditors of the firm of H. Amy & Co., of which he was a partner.[6] Both the firm and the partners have been adjudicated bankrupts. The dispute originated in a petition by the appellants, who claim as individual creditors of Louis H. Amy, to have the proceeds of the sale of a seat in the New York Stock Exchange, amounting to $88,918.82, allocated as an asset of his individual estate. The District Court, confirming an order of the referee in bankruptcy, held the membership, and its proceeds, to be partnership property.

Louis H. Amy purchased a membership in the New York Stock Exchange in 1888 with money given him by his father, Henry Amy. A partnership was formed between them, which continued from January 1, 1889, until the father's death in 1901. Thereupon, this partnership was liquidated, and in such liquidation and in the settlement of the father's estate, the latter was treated as having no interest in the Stock Exchange seat. It had not been carried on the books of that firm. It is clear, therefore, that the seat was the individual property of Louis H. Amy when he formed with his brother, Ernest J. H. Amy, the partnership which is now in bankruptcy. This was formed by formal articles of agreement dated December 31, 1901. After stating the purpose of the copartnership to be the carrying on of the general business of banking and brokerage under the firm name of H. Amy & Co., beginning January 1, 1902, the agreement sets forth, among others, the following provisions:

"Third. The said Louis H. Amy shall bring as his capital into the partnership the sum of thirty-seven thousand five hundred dollars

---

[6] The rules of law governing the distribution of assets in such a situation are explained on page 667.

($37,500), and the said Ernest J. H. Amy the sum of twenty-two thousand five hundred dollars ($22,500), and the said parties hereto agree to bestow all their skill, time, and attention upon the said partnership business."

"Fifth. Interest on the individual accounts of the two parties shall be charged and credited at the rate of 4 per cent, per annum; and the said Louis H. Amy shall be entitled to and interested in 62½ parts and the said Ernest J. H. Amy shall be entitled to and interested in 37½ parts of so much of the net gains and profits of said business as shall remain after the payment of the interest due on the accounts of the respective parties; and the said parties shall bear and defray all the losses and damages, which may be sustained by said copartnership in said business, in the same proportions as they are respectively entitled to in the net profits. Previous to any division of profits or losses the individual account of the said Louis H. Amy party of the first part, shall be credited with an amount equal to interest at the rate of six per cent, per annum on sixty thousand dollars ($60,000) to wit: Three thousand six hundred dollars ($3,600) as compensation for and in consideration of his contributing to the firm the entire and exclusive benefit of his membership in the New York Stock Exchange free from all taxes, fees and charges whatsoever to which the said membership may be subject.

"Whenever the capital of this business shall be increased, the present proportion of the capital put in by the parties, namely, thirty-seven thousand five hundred dollars ($37,500) and twenty-two thousand five hundred dollars ($22,500) shall remain the same, so that both the partners only can increase the capital and then only in the above-named ratio; and the respective shares of each in the profits and losses of the business shall remain the same as above stipulated."

"Eleventh. In case the said Louis H. Amy shall die during the continuance of the partnership his legal representatives shall have the right, equally with the surviving partner, to liquidate the business; and if the party of the second part shall be desirous of continuing the business the party of the second part shall pay for the good will of the business such a sum as shall be determined by three disinterested persons, each party selecting one and the two selecting a third. In case Ernest J. H. Amy should die during the continuance of the partnership then the said Louis H. Amy shall be entitled to continue the business as before without the interference of the legal representative of the deceased party and shall be entitled to the firm name and all the books, papers and good will of the business and shall pay one-third part of the moneys standing to the credit of the said Ernest J. H. Amy within three months after his death and shall pay the remaining two-thirds of such moneys within six months after his death, interest thereon to be allowed; and he shall duly pay his share of the net profits as soon as they shall have been ascertained."

Whether property owned by a partner and used in the firm business shall be deemed an asset of the firm or of the individual depends upon the intention of the partners. . . . The above-quoted provisions of the partnership articles appear to express an intention not to contribute Louis' membership as capital, but to grant the firm the use of his seat for the stipulated compensation.

The third article deals with capital contributions and specifies that

Louis shall bring as his capital $37,500 and Ernest $22,500. If the seat, apparently valued at $60,000 in the fifth article, is also to be deemed a capital contribution of the two it would be inconsistent not only with the third article, but also with the last paragraph of the fifth article, which deals with increasing the capital. Moreover, profits and losses are to be divided in the same proportion, namely, five-eighths to Louis and three-eighths to Ernest, and if the seat were included as a capital contribution, this proportional division would not be followed. It is, of course, true that the division of profits and losses need not accord with capital contributions, but these articles appear to be drafted on the theory that they shall.

The fifth article deals chiefly with the division of profits and losses, and the mention of the seat appears to come in merely as a direction how the profit or loss shall be calculated. Louis is to be credited "with an amount equal to interest at the rate of 6 per cent, per annum on $60,000 as compensation for . . . his contributing to the firm the entire and exclusive benefit of his membership." This item of $3,600 is an expense of the firm, to be deducted before profit or loss is ascertained. It is paid by the firm as compensation for its use of the seat. If the word "use" had been employed, no question could be raised. We attribute no different meaning, however, to "benefit" in the phrase "entire, and exclusive benefit." Why should the firm pay "compensation," if a seat were already contributed as firm assets? It might have allowed interest on its value as a capital contribution, before figuring profits; but it is significant that the "compensation" is not spoken of as interest, but as "an amount equal to interest." This would be an unnatural way to refer to interest on a capital contribution. Even an agreement for "interest" on a stipulated valuation for the seat would not be conclusive evidence that it was contributed as partnership assets. . . . Again, if the seat were firm assets, we should expect the firm to pay the taxes, fees, and charges assessed upon it. . . . Whereas, if it remains the property of Louis, of which the firm has only the use, the provision that he shall pay such charges is natural enough.

It is argued by the appellees that the phrase "good will" in the eleventh article includes the seat and hence indicates that it was a firm asset. We cannot accede to so strained a construction. We mention the argument merely to indicate that it has not been overlooked.

The conduct of the partners—at least, until the making of their assignment for the benefit of creditors, which will be discussed hereafter—was entirely consistent with the construction we have placed upon the partnership agreement. Ernest paid into the firm his capital contribution of $22,500. Half of this sum he obtained from the younger brother, Henry, Jr. under an agreement contemporaneous with the partnership articles, and an account was opened in his name in which he was credited or debited with three-sixteenths. Louis, as his contribution of $37,500, left in his interest in the former firm of which his father had been a member. The new firm continued in the same offices and with the same equipment as had been used by the former firm, and new books of account were not opened. No entry was made of the stock exchange seat as a capital contribution. As has been shown, Louis's seat was not a partnership asset of the former firm, although used in its business. When the new firm was formed the seat was apparently treated in the same manner; that is, it was not considered a capital contribution, but Louis granted the exclusive use of it to the firm for compensation. Such compensation was credited each year to his account in the firm books and his account was debited with the taxes, fees, and charges which the firm paid on account of his membership.

The only act of the partners which tends to show any departure from the understanding regarding the seat expressed in their formal articles of partnership occurred just before the bankruptcy. On March 5, 1919, the partners executed an assignment for the benefit of creditors to their attorney, Edward J. McGuire, who later became trustee in bankruptcy of the assets of the firm and of the individual partners. Ten days later they signed and swore to an inventory of the property of H. Amy & Co. and included as an item therein: "One seat N.Y. Stock Exchange, in name of Louis H. Amy, $70,000." This inventory in the matter of their general assignment was filed in the New York county clerk's office, March 18, 1919, one day before the filing of the petition in bankruptcy. We do not find it necessary to decide whether this inventory sworn to by Louis H. Amy, would be competent evidence to affect the relative rights of individual and firm creditors. At best it would be but an admission, and it was made under circumstances which render it insufficient to outweigh the contrary evidence found in the original contract and the long course of conduct thereunder.

The trustee in bankruptcy received the proceeds of the sale of the seat in July, 1919. Section 5d of the Bankruptcy Act (11 U.S.C.A. 23; Comp. St. 9589) makes it his duty to keep separate accounts of the partnership property and of the property belonging to the individual partners. He failed to do this, and deposited the proceeds of the seat and all other moneys collected by him in a bank account kept in the name of the firm. He also filed numerous interim reports, in which no distinction was made between firm and individual assets. Such conduct by the trustee, however, cannot affect the rights of creditors under section 5f. The issue was properly raised before distribution, and on the evidence we are compelled to hold the membership to have been an individual asset of Louis H. Amy.

The decree is reversed, with costs to the appellants. ◀

COMMENTS AND QUESTIONS

1. What was the nature of this case, and what was the main issue before the trial court? How did it decide?
2. Summarize the reasons given for the appellate court's reversal of the lower court's decision.
3. Note the carefully drafted provisions of the partnership agreement, especially those dealing with the capital contributions, the sharing of profits, and the death of either partner.

Nature and Kinds of Partnership Property; Good Will

In general, a partnership may hold any kind of property, real and personal, tangible and intangible. Moreover, in the absence of an express agreement or a statutory regulation, there is no limit on the amount of property a partnership may acquire.

Often included under partnership property is the firm name, along with the so-called *good will*, or *going-concern value*, that goes with it. The *good will* of a firm resides in the reputation it has built up in the community, and in the justifiable expectation of continued patronage by the public. Good will is often very valuable. It may even be carried on the firm's balance sheet as an asset.

As a general rule, anyone who purchases a firm's business along with its good will is entitled to advertise himself as the successor of the old firm. Authorities disagree, however, on whether he may use the name of the old firm; many states deny him that right and others grant it. Most states permit the seller of a business to start a new business of the same character, provided he does not actively solicit his old customers or advertise that he is carrying on the old firm. But some states deny him the right to compete in any way with a business he has sold. Moreover, most states prohibit the seller from using his own name in a new venture if by doing so he creates the impression that he is carrying on his old business. In other words, a seller generally has an obligation to refrain from interfering with the good will of the business he has sold.

In the following case, Judge Cardozo discusses the concept of good will at great length. The issue in the case was whether the good will of a brokerage firm was an asset which should have been accounted for when one of the partners died.

In re BROWN

Court of Appeals of New York, 1926
242 N.Y. 1, 150 N.E. 581

► CARDOZO, J. Vernon C. Brown & Co., were stockbrokers for many years in the city of New York. Stephen H. Brown, one of the partners, died. The survivors, denying that there was any good will to be accounted for, continued the business at the old stand and in the old name. The executors acquiesced. For so acquiescing, they have been held to be at fault, and their accounts have been surcharged accordingly. The question is whether the decree may be sustained.

The Browns, Vernon and Stephen, were brothers. They began business in 1895 with one Watson, under the name of Watson and Brown. In 1901, Watson withdrew, and the brothers went on and "Vernon C. Brown & Co." became the name of the continued partnership. New members were admitted from time to time, but the firm name remained unchanged. Good will was not mentioned in the partnership articles or in any books of account. Incoming members did not pay anything for it. One member, Mr. Schoonmaker, retired while Stephen Brown was alive. If good will was an asset, he was entitled to share in it. The evidence is uncontradicted that nothing was paid him. We may infer that in the thought of the partners nothing was due.

At the outset, Stephen Brown, like his brother, was active in the business. He had a seat on the Exchange, and represented the firm upon the floor. Falling ill in 1912, he sold his seat, and, though leaving his capital intact, gave no services thereafter. His share of the profits, which before his illness had been 33 per cent, was gradually reduced till at his death in July, 1917, it was only 15 per cent. The business was lucrative, though it was run, one would gather, in a more or less old-fashioned and conservative way, without advertising in newspapers or solicitation of accounts. It had four branches or departments: (1) The general commission business; (2) the so-called "odd lot" business, which proved to be the most lucrative of all; (3) the so-called "two-dollar" business; and (4) speculative business transacted for the firm itself. There is a finding that all the branches of the business, except the last, had in them an element of good will for which the survivors were accountable. The net profits of the three branches were averaged for a period of three years; allowance being made for interest on capital and for the personal services rendered by the partners. The value of the good will was fixed at two years' purchase price of the profits so computed. On this basis, the value was $103,891.60 of which 15 per cent, $15,583.74, was the share due to the estate. The surrogate, confirming the report of a referee, held that the accounts of the executors were to be surcharged for failing to collect this amount from the survivors. The Appellate Division unanimously affirmed.

The books abound in definitions of good will. . . . There is no occasion to repeat them. Men will pay for any privilege that gives a reasonable expectancy of preference in the race of competition. . . . Such expectancy may come from succession in place or name or otherwise to a business that has won the favor of its customers. It is then known as good will. Many are the degrees of value. At one extreme there are expectancies so strong that the advantage derived from economic opportunity may be said to be a certainty; at the other are expectancies so weak that for any rational mind they may be said to be illusory. We must know the facts in any case.

Good will, when it exists as incidental to the business of a partnership, is presumptively an asset to be accounted for like any other by those who liquidate the business. . . .

Assuming for present purposes that the disposition of good will has not been varied by agreement, we reach the question whether there was any good will to be disposed of upon the facts recited in the findings. To answer that question, we must consider at the outset what rights would have passed to a buyer of the good will if the surviving partners had sold it in the course of liquidation. The chief elements of value upon any sale of a good will are, first, continuity of place; and, second, continuity of name. . . . There may, indeed, at times be others, e.g., continuity of organization. That element is of value in business of a complex order. Where the business is simple, the benefits of organization are slight, and not so easily transmitted. Confining ourselves now to the two chief elements of value, we may assume that the buyer of this good will would have been reasonably assured of continuity of place. The firm offices were the same from the beginning of the business till the death of Stephen Brown and later. There is nothing to show that the survivors, genuinely endeavoring to dispose of the good will, would have been unable to deliver possession to a buyer of the lease. A more difficult question is presented when we ask to what extent there would have been continuity of name. "Vernon C. Brown & Co." was not an arbitrary symbol, like the Snyder Manufacturing Company, e.g. in Snyder Mfg. Co. v. Snyder, 54 Ohio St. 86, 43 N.E. 325, 31 L.R.A. 657. It had not gained a secondary meaning supplanting a primary meaning which had been descriptive of a man or men, and instead identifying impersonally an organization or a product. Writ large in this style or title was the name of a living man who had done nothing by word or act to give the name a reality or a significance external to himself. A buyer of the good will would gain no right to the use of any style or title whereby this man would be represented as still a partner in the business. We assume that in conducting the new business he would be privileged to describe himself, subject, however, to the rules of the Exchange, as the "successor" to the old one. . . . He would not be suffered to go farther. One who writes his name at large in the style or title of a partnership does not dedicate to the partnership, by force of that act alone without other tokens of intention, the right to sell the name at auction upon every change of membership.

We do not overlook the provisions of the statute (Partnership Law 80, subd. 1, formerly Partnership Law, 20 [Consol. Laws, c. 39]) whereby partnership names are made capable of transfer to the successors to a business. The sole effect of that provision is to give the approval of the law to a use that would otherwise be criminal though a transfer were attempted. . . . The statute tells us what the partners are at liberty to assign; it does not tell us what they are under a duty to assign. . . . Rowell v. Rowell, 122 Wis. 1, 99 N.W. 473. A name, which in popular thought is solely or predominantly the name of a living man, may not be sold against his protest as it might be if it were the impersonal symbol of an organization or a product. The objection is not merely that the partner, whose name is thus appropriated, may be exposed to the risk of liability for debts of continued business. . . . If that were all, he might be adequately protected by the certificate which his successors must file under the statute. . . . He would remain exposed to other perils though this one were averted. Business designed for him might be diverted to some one else. Worse than this he might suffer in standing or good name "by reason of inferiority of goods or dishonorable business conduct, to which he is thereby made ostensibly a party. . . . " A different situation presents itself when the name is "arbitrary or fancy." . . . The like is true when, though it may once have designated a person, it has "practically become an artificial one, designating nothing but the establishment." . . . The question in last analysis is one of probable intention. To answer it we must know whether by reasonable intendment, as gathered from the nature of the business and the course of dealing, the partner whose name is appropriated by a stranger has given consent to his associates to submit to an impersonation so disturbing and deceptive. In the record before us there is neither finding of consent nor evidence pointing to the conclusion that consent should be implied.

We have said that the members of the old firm might compete without restraint, after a sale of the good will, with the members of the new one. There are distinctions in that regard between voluntary and involuntary sales. . . . After a voluntary sale, the seller, though he may compete, may not drum up or circularize the customers of the business. After a sale *in invitum*,[7] he is not subject to a disability so heavy. For the purpose of this distinction, a sale, by surviving partners upon a liquidation of the business, is sale coerced by law. . . .

We conclude, then, that a buyer of this good will, if it had been put up for sale by the liquidating partners, would have had the benefit at most of continuity of place and of such continuity of name as would belong to a "successor." We have next to consider the relation of these benefits to the several branches or departments in which the business was conducted.

1. There is a finding unanimously affirmed, that appurtenant to the general commission branch was an element of good will not incapable of conveyance. We cannot say that this finding is qualified by others to such an extent that as a matter of law it must be disregarded as erroneous. The buyer of the good will would take over the firm records, which would give the names of the old customers. He would be in a position to notify them that he had succeeded to the business. True, the old partners might send out notices that they were still in business for themselves. None the less, some customers might wander into the old place from forgetfulness or habit. Once there, inertia might lead them to give an order to brokers whom they found established in possession. . . . The relation is not so distinctly personal or professional that good will is excluded either for reasons of public policy or as an inference of law. . . . We may doubt whether a privilege so uncertain would be worth a great deal. The surrogate would have been justified in placing the value at a much lower figure than he did, or even at a nominal amount. . . . The question is not whether the buyer would be willing to pay much or would be making a wise bargain. The question is whether a reasonable man would be willing to pay anything.

2. The odd lot business stands on a different basis. Its essential characteristics are established by the findings. There is a rule of the New York Stock Exchange by which the unit of trading on the floor of the exchange is declared to be 100 shares. Dealings in smaller numbers of shares are known as odd lot transactions. Most stockbrokers do not transact an odd lot business, but there are some that do, and Vernon C. Brown & Co. was one of them. Orders for odd lots do not come through the office. They are given on the floor of the Exchange to the individual member or members of the firm who are its floor representatives. They come invariably from other brokers communicating with fellow members of the Exchange whom they know as individuals.

A buyer of the good will would gain nothing in respect of this branch of the business from continuity of place. There was no relation between such orders and the place where the firm business was transacted. He would gain nothing from the privilege of announcing himself the successor of the business without continuity of name. The individual brokers who had been accustomed to receive these orders from fellow members of the Exchange would still be on hand to receive them as before. The findings suggest no

---

[7] That is, an involuntary sale. In other words, this sale was required by law even though the parties did not wish it to take place.

reason why business so individual and personal should be diverted or diminished. Very likely the new firm, when announcing its succession to the business, would advertise the fact that its board members, if there were any, would buy and sell odd lots. It might advertise a like readiness though the business it was starting had no relation of succession to any that had gone before. The appeal to favor would be different if the old partners had been about to withdraw from the field of competition. While they remained in the arena, the tie of succession was too attenuated to give to the buyer in transactions so individual and personal a fair promise of advantage. One cannot gain a foothold upon a ledge of opportunity so narrow. Expectancy in such conditions may be said to have reached the vanishing point at which it merges in illusion.

3. The "two-dollar" or "specialist" business is personal and individual like the department just considered. The specialist is a broker who remains at one post of the Exchange where particular stocks are dealt in, and there executes orders received from other brokers. He receives a commission of $2.50 for every 100 shares. Good will does not attach to business of this order for the same reason that none attaches to dealings in odd lots.

Mention should be made in conclusion of a provision of the will of Stephen Brown, whereby his executors are relieved of responsibility for mistakes or errors of judgment. This provision may become important upon a rehearing in determining liability for the value of the good will, if any, incidental to the commission business. In the event that the value of such good will shall be found to be doubtful or insignificant, the surrogate may properly conclude that the failure to collect it was an error of judgment and nothing more.

The order of the Appellate Division and the decree of the Surrogate's Court so far as such decree is appealed from, should be reversed, and rehearing ordered, with costs to abide in the event.

Hiscock, C. J., and Pound, McLaughlin, Crane, Andrews, JJ., concur. Order reversed, etc.   ◀

COMMENTS AND QUESTIONS

1. In the lower court, the executors of the estate of the deceased partner were held liable because they had neglected to collect money for good will from the surviving partners, who continued the business. What happened on appeal?
2. Summarize the elements that Cardozo outlines as being essential to good will. How did he apply them to the various branches of the partnership's business?

Partnership Capital Distinguished from Partnership Property

Partnership property, as we have seen, consists of all the real and personal property owned by the firm itself. The term *partnership capital*, on the other hand, refers to the permanent investment that the partners have made in the business. When a partnership is formed, each partner may contribute money, property, or services to the firm as a permanent investment. This capital contribution is carried on the books as an obligation to the partners; if the partnership is subsequently dissolved, each partner is entitled to retrieve his capital before profits and losses are computed and distributed. If property or services are contributed by a partner as capital, the partners usually agree on the value to be placed on them, and this amount is fixed as the capital contribution of that partner. During the life of the partnership no partner may alter his original capital investment without the consent of all the other partners. (Incidentally, it is not necessary for a person to invest capital in the business in order to become a partner. He may contribute his services only.)

EXAMPLE

x, y, and z form a partnership for the purpose of running a hardware store. x contributes $50,000 and receives credit for that amount as a capital investment. y contributes the store site and certain equipment which the partners value at $25,000; his capital investment is set at that figure. z contributes no capital, but he is to manage the store and share in the profits. The *partnership capital* of the firm is $75,000—that is, the amount of the permanent investment in the business. The *partnership property* consists of the store, its equipment, and any other property it may acquire in the course of its operations. z is a partner despite his lack of capital contribution.

It is possible for a partner to *lend* money to the firm without having it treated as a capital investment. The following case illustrates this point.

LESERMAN v. BERNHEIMER et al.

Court of Appeals of New York, 1889
113 N.Y. 39, 20 N.E. 869

► DANFORTH, J. The capital of the firm was $225,000, to which each partner contributed $75,000, under an agreement that each partner should share the profits and bear the losses equally with the others, *viz.*, one-third each. No time was fixed for its continuance, and November 25, 1873, Leserman elected to have the business wound up, and notice to his partners required that an account should be taken for that purpose. This was done, an account of stock taken, and balance struck as of the 31st day of December of that year; at which time the referee finds "it was distinctly known and understood by all the parties that the partnership was to be dissolved and wound up in pursuance of the notice already given by Leserman." It was not, however, formally dissolved until March 13, 1874. . . .

It was found that Leserman had drawn out of his original capital $10,499.67; that Bernheimer had increased his $56,621.39; while Goldsmith had drawn out the whole of his, and also owed the firm $897.99. After paying all the liabilities of the firm, there remained, according to the report, $128,920 in the hands of the liquidating partner. This sum is carried on to the capital account, and whether its disposition by the referee is correct presents the first important inquiry.

The interest of each partner in the partnership property is his share in the surplus after the partnership accounts are settled and all just claims satisfied. In this case, by the terms of the partnership, the partners were to contribute equally and to divide profits and share losses equally, from the beginning of the partnership to its dissolution. There is no evidence which requires or would permit any finding that this arrangement had been changed, nor are we referred to such finding. It would seem to follow that the division of profits and charges of losses should be in the proportion of one-third of each to each partner. To carry out that mode of adjustment as the one provided by the agreement of the parties the advances made by either partner beyond the capital called for by that agreement should be treated as a debt due from the firm, and paid out of the surplus before any division is made upon the partnership capital. If that advance was not in strictness to be regarded as a debt during the existence of the firm, nor until the debts of the firm to third persons were satisfied, it came into that relation the moment these debts were paid, and the concern, as regards its business and its outside obligations, wound up. This is an equitable disposition of the matter, for otherwise the larger the advances made for the firm the greater would be the share of losses, or if profits, the greater the share of profits accruing to the partner making the advance,—in either case, a result entirely opposed to the actual agreement of the parties, which exacted equality in both respects. Nor is the rule opposed to the authorities cited by the respondent. . . .

Bernheimer was a contributor to capital. He was also in advance of that contribution, and the sum advanced must be repaid before the surplus can be ascertained, and from that surplus alone can there be distribution; then to each partner equally; and, if a loss is incurred, its ratio must be ascertained, as originally agreed by the parties. The learned referee has not dealt with the appellant Bernheimer in accordance with these rules. He gives one-third only of the surplus by reason of his original capital, and in accordance with the same theory the learned referee gives one other third of the surplus to Leserman, and the remaining third to Goldsmith. This method would be well enough if the surplus was sufficient to pay all. But it is not, and, moreover, the advance made by Bernheimer is left entirely unpaid. To cover it, therefore, the sum advanced is divided into three parts and Bernheimer is given a judgment against Goldsmith for a like amount, or one-third, leaving him to bear a certain loss as to the remaining third, and imposing on him the risks of collection as against Goldsmith. We think this result inequitable, and not required by any rule or principle of law.

The sum advanced by Bernheimer over his $75,000 should be first paid from the partnership surplus, and the residue divided among the partners, according to the partnership agreement. Of course, Goldsmith, having drawn out his whole capital, could be entitled to no part of the surplus, and Leserman's share would be diminished by reason of the sum already drawn by him. The losses entailed upon the firm, by reason of Goldsmith's overdrafts of capital or otherwise, must, of course, be borne equally. . . .

Judgment reversed.   ◄

COMMENTS AND QUESTIONS

1. This case illustrates the difference between a capital contribution and a loan or advance to the firm by a partner. Explain how the court's formula would be applied in distributing the $128,920 remaining after the payment of the partnership's liabilities.

2. Note the withdrawals of capital by two of the partners. Presumably, these were made with the unanimous consent of the partners.

Title to Partnership Property

Personal Property

As a general rule, personal property may be acquired, held, and disposed of in the firm name even though that name is fictitious. On the other hand, if the partners so choose, title to personal partnership property may be taken and transferred in the name of one, or more, of the partners acting as an agent on behalf of the firm.

Real Property

Authorities disagree on whether a partnership has the right to hold title to real property in the firm name. In those states that still follow the common-law rule, a partnership is not treated as a separate legal entity, and any attempt by a partnership to take title to real property in its firm name is held to be null and void. These jurisdictions require that the title be transferred instead to one or more of the partners as individuals, who may then hold the property for the benefit of the firm.

In a majority of the states, including those which have enacted the Uniform Partnership Act, the common-law rule has been amended to permit a partnership to acquire and hold title to real property in the firm name alone. Moreover, a partner acting on behalf of the partnership may transfer title in that name.

> EXAMPLE
>
> A, B, and C form a partnership called "The Acme Shoe Repair Shop." They decide they want to buy some real estate on which to conduct their business. In a common-law state, title to the real estate would have to be acquired in the name of one or more of the partners—for example, the conveyance might be "to A, B, and C." In other jurisdictions, title could be acquired in the name of "The Acme Shoe Repair Shop."

Partner's Interest in Partnership Property

As co-owner of partnership property, each of the partners generally has an equal right to use that property in carrying on the business of the firm. No partner may use the property for any other purpose, however, without the consent of all the other partners. Since no one partner owns any of the partnership property as such, he cannot sell or transfer any interest in the property to a third party. Each partner has a right to insist that the partnership property be used solely for the business of the firm, and that it be used to pay creditors of the firm if necessary. Personal creditors of the partners may not attach partnership property to satisfy the partners' personal debts.

> EXAMPLE
>
> BLACK and WHITE are partners in a house-painting business; the partnership property consists of a truck, ladders, scaffolding, and other equipment. Neither BLACK nor WHITE personally owns any of the property,

and neither can sell it except on behalf of the firm. Nor could a personal creditor of either BLACK or WHITE attach, say, the truck or the ladders.

When one of the partners dies, his right to use the partnership property passes to the surviving partners, who must continue to use the property for partnership purposes only. If only one partner survives, he may sell the property and wind up the business.

Partner's Interest in the Partnership Itself

A partner's interest in partnership property is quite distinct from his interest in the partnership itself. His interest in the partnership consists of his right to share in the profits and, on dissolution of the firm, his right to retrieve his capital contribution and to share in the distribution of any surplus. This interest corresponds roughly to the "share" a stockholder owns in a corporation.

Under the Uniform Partnership Act, a partner may assign his interest in the partnership to someone else without dissolving the firm. The assignee then enjoys the right to receive profits and to take the partner's share on dissolution, but he is not permitted to interfere in any way with the management of the business.

The Uniform Act also permits the personal creditors of a partner to attach his interest in the partnership by means of a so-called *charging order*. When this procedure is followed, the court usually appoints a receiver to take over the partner's share of the profits and to apply them to payment of the debt. The debtor partner remains a member of the partnership, however, and the partnership itself need not be dissolved.

SECTION 3

RIGHTS AND DUTIES OF PARTNERS AMONG THEMSELVES

Fiduciary Duties and Obligations to Each Other

In a sense, a partnership is based on mutual agency—that is, each partner acts on behalf of his copartners. Thus the relationship by its very nature requires mutual good faith and trust, and the law imposes strict duties and obligations on partners in their dealings with each other.

Loyalty to Firm

A partner's first duty is to his copartners, and he must direct his best efforts toward advancing the business of the firm. He may not use his firm association or any of the firm property to secure a personal gain that is not shared with the other partners. Nor may he compete directly or indirectly with the partnership business. If he violates these duties, he is liable to the firm for damages and must account to it for any benefits he derives from his improper activities. In short, a partner must always exercise the utmost good faith in his relations with the firm.

EXAMPLE

x, y, and z are partners in a roadside restaurant business. x knows that the firm is about to move to a new location. In the name of a third party acting for him, he buys two choice parcels of land in that area for $10,000. The partnership later purchases the land for use as a restaurant site for $12,000; y and z are still unaware that x is the real owner. When and if x's role in the transaction is discovered, he will have to account to y and z for his secret profit.

The following case deals with a real estate transaction in which one partner allegedly took advantage of his associates.

HODGE v. TWITCHELL

Supreme Court of Minnesota, 1885
83 Minn. 389, 23 N.W. 547

▶ GILFILLAN, C. J. The findings of fact by the court below, so far as they are essential to the determination of the case, are justified by the evidence. The facts are substantially these:

In January, 1883, the plaintiff, the defendant Edgar A. Twitchell, and one Roby agreed that they would make joint purchases of real estate in the city of Minneapolis, each furnishing an equal amount of the purchase money for each venture; and that on a sale of any piece purchased they would divide equally the profits of the venture. In the same month said defendant called the attention of the other two to a lot which was offered for sale at the price of $2,500, and advised them that the lot was cheap, and advisable property to purchase on joint account pursuant to said agreement. While the two were considering the matter, it was agreed between the persons offering the lot for sale and said defendant that, if he would find a purchaser of the remainder of the lot at said price, they would in consideration thereof convey the north 50 feet front and rear of the lot to him or to any one he should designate. Thereupon he purposely concealing from plaintiff and Roby the agreement that he had made with the parties offering the lot for sale, misrepresented to them that the north 50 feet front and rear of the lot had been sold to some other person, so that it could not be purchased by the three, and informed them that the remainder of the lot could still be purchased at the said price of $2,500, and advised them to make such purchase; and on his recommendation it was made, each of the three paying one-third of the purchase price, and the lot was conveyed to the three; and at the request of said defendant the persons offering the lot for sale, conveyed, pursuant to their said agreement with him, the said north 50 feet to the defendant Clara S., she paying no consideration therefor, but being ignorant of the means by which he procured the same to be conveyed to her. Plaintiff had no knowledge, till after the venture was closed by a sale of the remainder of the lot, that said Edgar A., had by the transaction secured to himself any advantage in which the others did not share. The value of said north 50 feet is $1,500.

The relation of the parties, with respect to any venture they might enter upon pursuant to their agreement, was in the nature of a partnership. Each owed to the other, in their transactions, the utmost good faith and openness of dealing. Neither had the right to secure, without the consent of the others, any private advantage to himself out of such transactions, either in making the purchases or the sales, either from the money jointly contributed or from the property purchased. Securing such advantage would be a fraud upon the other parties interested with him, which equity would defeat by holding him a trustee for the others of the thing which he so secured to himself. There is no principle of equity jurisprudence better established or more rigorously enforced than this. In this case the real consideration for the entire lot was the $2,500; the thing really purchased, as between Edgar A., and the seller, with that money, was the entire lot. It was the consideration for the part conveyed to Clara S., as much as it was for the other. The thin device resorted to, of calling the conveyance of the north 50 feet a payment for services rendered the seller in procuring a purchaser, when he had no right to render such services to the seller,—for that would place him in a situation where his bias and interest would be inconsistent with the duty which he owed to his associates, to do the best he could for their common good,—did not change the real character of the transaction. It was a fraud upon his associates, by reason of which, if that part of the lot had been conveyed to him, equity would have treated him as holding it in trust for them to the extent of their agreed interest in the venture. The defendant Clara S., having paid no consideration for the conveyance to her, holds it, as he would have done, subject to the same trust.

Order affirmed.   ◄

COMMENTS AND QUESTIONS

1. What was the final outcome of this case? What happened to the fifty-foot lot that had been conveyed to Clara S.?
2. How did the court answer the defendant's argument that the conveyance of the lot was a payment for services rendered to the seller in procuring a purchaser for the land?

Although a partner must be very careful in dealing with his associates, it is perfectly possible for him to do business with the firm as a separate individual. The following case illustrates just such a situation.

FARNEY v. HAUSER

Supreme Court of Kansas, 1921
109 Kan. 75, 108 P. 178

► DAWSON, J. This action was to dissolve a partnership, and for an accounting between the partners, and it also involved the question of a liability of the partnership in certain business transactions with one of their number.

In 1915 the plaintiff J. P. Farney, and the four defendants, Hauser, Ricks, Rathgeber, and McBrayer, formed a partnership for the purpose of conducting a grain elevator business at Kiowa. The capital invested by the partners was $5,300, of which the plaintiff contributed $1,500. Hauser was chosen as president and general manager, and Ricks as secretary and treasurer, and the partnership business was placed in their charge. They purchased an elevator, and hired a manager, one Hagenmaster, to conduct it.

Under an agreement with Hagenmaster, the plaintiff placed some 10,000 bushels of wheat in the elevator to be stored, cleaned, and loaded on railway cars, at 2½ cents per bushel. This wheat was to be loaded on cars when plaintiff chose to have that done, and in May, 1916, some 1,378 bushels of plaintiff's wheat was thus loaded out of the elevator. In February, 1917, plaintiff directed Hagenmaster to load the balance of the wheat, but this was not done, for the reason, as it afterwards developed, that Hagenmaster had in some way made away with most of plaintiff's wheat; and on March 4, 1917, the elevator burned. Plaintiff took charge of the more or less damaged wheat found in the ruins of the elevator and sold it. Plaintiff then started an investigation as to the disposition of the remainder of his wheat, but this was interrupted by another fire which burned the elevator office and books of the partnership. Hagenmaster, the manager, was arrested for the crime of burning the elevator but he died before trial. The partnership collected some insurance on the elevator and sold some other assets for cash. It also held a policy of insurance for $2,000 on the contents of the elevator, whether "their own or held by them in trust or on commission but not delivered if assured is legally liable, all while contained in above described buildings." The partnership officers did not include in their claim and proofs of loss to the insurance company any item for the loss of plaintiff's wheat, and settled with the insurance company for $969, and at the same time gave a bond indemnifying the insurance company against any liability for the loss of the plaintiff's wheat.

The assets of the company were apportioned and distributed among the partners other than the plaintiff.

The plaintiff's petition narrated the pertinent facts, and defendants joined issues. The cause was tried before an advisory jury which answered many special questions which, with a minor exception, were adopted by the trial court. The trial court made an accounting which by computation showed that the partnership was indebted to plaintiff in the sum of $11,-436.59; that the net assets of the firm were $4,524.82; that each of the parties, plaintiff and defendants, must stand his respective proportionate share of the net losses and liabilities; and the plaintiff should have judgment against his defendant partners for their respective shares of the amount due him as an individual patron or customer of the partnership. The court also held the partnership liable to plaintiff for the sum which should have been collected from the insurance company for the burning of plaintiff's wheat. While the computations are somewhat complex, the defendants do not complain of the mathematics involved in the judgment.

Defendants assign error on the ruling of the trial court that plaintiff was entitled to judgment against his partners on account of the wheat misappropriated by the partnership's manager, Hagenmaster, less the proportionate share thereof which he himself must bear as a partner in the business. They contend that Hagenmaster was the agent of all the partners and that there should be no contribution between them for his tort. Such a view fails to take note of plaintiff's additional relationship to the partnership, that of customer as well as partner. Hagenmaster made away with $11,436.59 worth of plaintiff's wheat which had been placed in the elevator under a valid contract. The partnership therefore owes plaintiff that sum. But being a partner to the extent of $1,500, and the total capital of the firm being $5,300, plaintiff, as partner, must bear his proportionate share of the liability, $15/53$ of $11,436.59. The other partners must likewise bear their share of this liability according to their respective interests in the partnership. Of course, the mode by which a partner may enforce his claim as creditor is not by an ordinary lawsuit, but by an accounting and dissolution.

There was nothing illegal, or at variance with the theory of a partnership, for plaintiff to deal with it as an ordinary customer. It would be absurd to hold that in this commercial age when partnerships are so common that a man could not buy from, sell to, trade with, or patronize a business partnership as any other person might do, and with the same rights and liabilities, merely because he had a partner's interest in the firm business. If the partnership gets into financial difficulties with third parties, a partner who is a creditor of the firm may have his claim postponed until third parties are satisfied. But for nearly all practical purposes a partnership may be considered as a business entity. . . . It has its own capital, its own assets and liabilities, its own business activities, and it has a commercial life and credit of its own, virtually if not technically independent of the members comprising it. . . .

Defendants' final contention is that they should not be charged with their failure to collect insurance on plaintiff's wheat. They do not appear to question the general rule that where a warehouseman takes out a policy of insurance to protect his own interest in property and that held in trust by him, or concerning which he may have a liability, it is his duty to claim and collect such insurance not only for a fire loss on his own property but also for the loss sustained by the owner of the property intrusted or bailed to him. Such, of course, is the general rule. . . . And it is also settled that the failure of the warehouseman to collect such insurance renders him personally liable therefor to his customer or bailee. . . . But defendants resist the allowance made by the trial court for their failure to collect the insurance for plaintiff, not by taking issue with the rule just stated, but merely on the same general ground urged by them against the imposition of any liability for the loss of any part of plaintiff's grain—that the partnership was not liable to plaintiff—but that matter is already disposed of in this opinion and needs no further discussion.

The record contains no error; and the judgment is affirmed.
All the Justices concurring.   ◄

COMMENTS AND QUESTIONS

1. In this case, the plaintiff had a dual relationship to the firm. In what sense was this true? As a partner in the firm, wasn't Farney responsible for the misconduct of Hagenmaster, the firm's agent?

2. Apparently, the partnership was in the business of storing grain, and the plaintiff stored his own grain in the firm's elevator. This created a *bailment* contract—that is, an agreement whereby possession of personal property is given over to the custody of another (called the bailee), who agrees to keep it and later return it. The bailee (i.e., the partnership) had insurance protection for the type of loss sustained here. For what reasons did the court decide that the partnership was liable to Farney for the loss of his grain?

Right to Information and Inspection of Books

Each partner has a duty to inform his copartners of all matters relating to the conduct of the business, and each has a right to demand full disclosure from his copartners. Further, unless they agree to the contrary, all the partners are entitled to inspect the firm's books. Each partner has a duty to keep full and accurate records of all partnership business that he transacts and to turn those records over to the firm's bookkeeper.

Right to Accounting

Since each partner has the right of access to the firm's books and records, he can ordinarily get a clear picture of the firm's financial condition by a simple inspection. For this reason, the courts will not usually order a formal accounting to settle disputes between partners. If the partnership is dissolved, of course, each partner is then entitled to a full and formal accounting to determine his share of the profits or losses.

In the following situations, the courts make an exception to the general rule and will order an accounting if one or more of the partners request it: (1) a partner is improperly denied access to the firm's records; (2) a partner refuses to account for profits he has made from a transaction involving the firm; and (3) the firm is on the verge of insolvency and action must be taken quickly to protect the rights of the partners and to prevent further losses.

Right to Manage Business

Many partnership agreements spell out in detail just how the business is to be run. The agreement may, for example, specify that all control over the management will be exercised by a single partner or a group of partners and that the other partners will have no control over the firm's affairs. The fact that a partner has invested in the firm does not entitle him to participate in its management if the agreement denies him that right. This situation is not uncommon.

In the absence of a specific agreement, all the partners are entitled to share equally in the management, regardless of their capital contribution, and, as a general rule, all decisions are made by a majority vote. If, for one

reason or another, the partners find it impossible to reach a decision regarding management, the firm has to be dissolved.

> EXAMPLE
>
> A, B, C, and D form a partnership. A contributes $10,000; B contributes
> $5,000; C contributes only his skill and labor; and D contributes some
> real estate. They do not draw up a partnership agreement. All four share
> equally in the management, and decisions must be made by majority
> vote. If the partners deadlock two-two, no action may be taken and the
> firm will have to be dissolved.

The right of the majority to disregard the wishes of the minority is
subject to certain limitations, however. The majority may not, over the
objections of the minority, change the essential nature of the business, or
start a new business, or admit new partners, or change the capital structure
of the firm.

In the case that follows, a minority of the partners challenged the right
of the majority to run the affairs of the firm.

STAPLES v. SPRAGUE

Supreme Court of Maine, 1883
75 Me. 458

► WALTON, J. This is a suit in equity, in which Josiah M. Staples and
Marshal B. Graves, are the plaintiffs, and Thomas H. Sprague, James E.
Lilly, and Alvah J. Hildreth, are the defendants. And, by a supplementary
bill, Jeremiah Millay, Seth T. Woodward, and S. Thomas Woodward, are
also made defendants.

The prayer of the bill is for an account, and that the defendants may
stand charged with, and be required to pay over to the plaintiffs, two-fifths
of the net proceeds or value of one thousand seven hundred and twenty-five
and one-half tons of ice.

The bill states and the evidence proves that in December, 1879, the
two plaintiffs and the three first named defendants, agreed to cut and pack
for sale a quantity of ice, and that, after deducting all expenditures, the
residue of the money derived from the sale, if any, should be divided among
them in equal shares.

And the case shows that March 3, 1880, one of the defendants (Sprague)
sold the ice for one dollar and twenty-five cents a ton.

The bill charges that this sale was for less than the market value of the
ice, and that Sprague, in making the sale, acted without authority. And the
plaintiffs claim that the defendants (the last three named being the purchasers of the ice) shall be charged, not only with the price for which the
ice was actually sold by Sprague, but further, for the highest price for which
it might have been sold during that season.

We have read the evidence with care, and the impression which it makes
upon our minds is that Sprague, in selling ice, acted in perfect good faith;
that he hesitated, negotiated, consulted such of his associates as he could
reach, made every possible effort to get a better offer, and finally accepted
the offer of one dollar and twenty-five cents a ton, because he thought it

would be better for his associates as well as himself to do so, rather than to reject the offer and take the chances of getting a better one. The evidence shows that the price of ice immediately went up, but the evidence fails to show that on the day of the sale of this ice, the market price was much, if any, above what was obtained for it.

And there is no evidence of fraud or collusion on the part of the purchasers. True, they bought to sell again, and undoubtedly bought as cheaply as they could, and with the hope, and probably the expectation that ice would be higher, and that they would be able to sell at a profit. But the evidence fails to show any fraudulent practices on their part, or any collusion with Sprague or the other defendants, to defraud or injure the plaintiffs.

Having come to the conclusion that the sale was made without fraud or collusion, our next inquiry is whether Sprague had authority to make it. We think he had. The agreement to cut and store the ice created a partnership between the contracting parties. And it is familiar law that each partner is the agent of all. Story's Agency, 39. Or, as Chancellor Kent states the law, in the absence of fraud, each one has the complete *jus disponendi* [8] of the whole partnership interests, and is considered to be the authorized agent of the firm. 3 Kent, 50, 10th edition. And such ought to be the law; for when there is a community of interest, certainly it is the will of the majority, and not the will of the minority, that ought to control. If there is a fraudulent combination on the part of the majority to injure or oppress the minority, the law is otherwise. But in the absence of fraud, certainly it is the majority, and not the minority, that ought to control. In this case, the sale by Sprague was with the knowledge and consent of Lilly and Hildreth; and they three constituted a majority of the firm. If the two plaintiffs had been present, and had actually dissented, we think it was a case where the will of the majority should control, and that Sprague, Lilly and Hildreth, being a majority of the firm, could have made a valid sale of the ice, without the consent of the plaintiffs. We think the sale was valid, and being made in good faith, it is the opinion of the court that the alleged purchasers are in no way liable to the plaintiffs, and that they (Millay and the two Woodwards) must be discharged with several costs; and that the other defendants (Sprague, Lilly, and Hildreth) are to be charged with the amount for which the ice was actually sold by Sprague, and no more. With respect to the three last named defendants (Sprague, Lilly, and Hildreth) the bill must be sustained for the purpose of settling up the affairs of the firm; and for that purpose the case must go to a master.

Original bill against Sprague, Lilly, and Hildreth, sustained; the case to go to a master to take an account.

Supplementary bill against Millay, and the two Woodwards, dismissed with costs for each.   ◄

COMMENTS AND QUESTIONS

1. What relief was sought by the plaintiffs in this case? On what grounds did they base their claim? How did the court decide?

_____

[8] That is, the right to sell or dispose of property.

2. Does this decision mean that a majority of partners can override the will of the minority and make contracts for the firm without consulting the other partners? If not, what does it mean?

Sharing of Profits and Losses

So long as there is no agreement to the contrary, all the partners, regardless of their initial investment, share equally in the profits of the firm and are required to make equal contributions to its losses, if any. The partners may, however, agree to divide profits and losses in any proportion they see fit. If the agreement specifies the manner in which profits are to be shared but neglects to mention losses, any losses will be shared in the same proportion as the profits.

EXAMPLES

1. BLACK, WHITE, and GREEN form a partnership. BLACK contributes $20,000, WHITE contributes $10,000, and GREEN contributes his skill and labor. There is no partnership agreement. Each partner will receive one-third of the profits and will pay one-third of any losses, despite the difference in their initial contributions.

2. Suppose, instead, that BLACK, WHITE, and GREEN enter into an agreement providing that BLACK is to receive 60 per cent, WHITE 30 per cent, and GREEN 10 per cent of the profits. If no provision is made for sharing losses, they would be shared in the same percentages. The proportions for sharing profits and losses need not be the same, however. Therefore, it would be permissible to provide that profits will be shared on a percentage bases of 60-30-10, and that losses will be shared one-third each.

Partner's Right to Compensation for Services

In the absence of an agreement to the contrary, a partner is not entitled to compensation for his services even though he may be doing all the work or rendering more valuable services than his copartners. In other words, each partner's remuneration is usually limited to his share of the firm's profits.

Sometimes, one of the partners will incur a personal liability while acting for the partnership as a whole, or will personally discharge a debt or obligation of the firm. Then he is entitled to be reimbursed out of the partnership assets for the amount he has spent.

EXAMPLE

A, B, C, and D are partners in a hardware store. They vote to buy a delivery truck for use in the firm's business and authorize A to make the purchase. A buys the truck with his own money. He is entitled to be reimbursed by the firm.

As a general rule, if a partner incurs expenses while conducting firm business, he is entitled to be reimbursed by the partnership. In the following case, a partner sought reimbursement for legal expenses which he incurred in defending a suit brought against him. He argued that the legal action against him arose out of his conduct of partnership business and, therefore, that his copartner should share the expense.

HADLEY v. COFFIN

Supreme Court of Iowa, 1920
188 Iowa 896, 176 N.W. 885

▶ GAYNOR, J. Plaintiff alleges that during the year 1911, and up to the 28th day of October, 1914, he and defendant were partners, engaged in the real estate business in Indianola, Iowa, under the firm name of Coffin & Hadley; that in the spring of 1911, as agent for the owners, they exchanged with B. G. Clark a quarter section of land in Wyoming for Indianola, Iowa, property, and sold to J. W. Buckingham another quarter section in the same state. After these deals were completed, and after the partnership had been dissolved, the purchasers brought separate suits against him to recover damages on account of alleged false and fraudulent representations made as to the quality of the lands sold. In each of these suits he made a defense, and alleges that this defense was made in behalf of the partnership of Coffin and Hadley; that Coffin, as a member of the firm, participated in whatever false and fraudulent representations were made, and in all of the transactions leading up to the exchange and sale, and was equally active with the plaintiff in consummating the deals; that in defending said suits, brought against him personally, he was compelled to employ counsel, and incur expense in so doing, and he has paid the same. He brings this action to recover contribution from the defendant, his former partner, and demands judgment for one-half of the attorney's fees so incurred in defending said suits; that both of said suits terminated in his favor. The second count of the petition is substantially the same as the first count, except that it seeks to recover one-half of the expenses necessarily incurred in going to Wyoming and securing testimony to be used in the defense of the suits aforesaid. Defendant demurred to the several counts of plaintiff's petition, and this demurrer was sustained, and plaintiff's petition dismissed. Plaintiff appeals.

The only question here presented is: Did the court err in sustaining the demurrer? The demurrer was predicated on the thought that the expenses sought to be recovered were expenses incurred in an action against the plaintiff individually, and that the defense was made in his own behalf, and not for this defendant, or for the firm of Coffin & Hadley, who were not sued, and were not made parties. Second, that this defendant had no legal interest in these suits; that in the event judgment had been obtained against this plaintiff, this defendant could not have been required to contribute to the payment of the same for the reason that the cause of action in each of said suits was based upon alleged tort, committed by the plaintiff knowingly, and was a tort of such a nature that contribution could not have been compelled even between partners.

The Clark Case referred to in the petition came to this court, and is reported in 181 Iowa 487, 164 N.W. 757. This court affirmed the judgment of the court below in favor of Hadley.

The demurrer admits all the facts well pleaded, but not necessarily the conclusions of the pleader. The petition shows the following facts: Plaintiff and defendant entered into partnership in the year 1911, and continued until some time in October, 1914. While this partnership existed, they had certain lands in Wyoming for sale or trade. They sold or traded to Clark a certain portion of the land in Wyoming, and to Buckingham another portion. Before this deal was consummated, Hadley and Coffin both visited Wyoming in company with Clark and Buckingham. The Wyoming lands were inspected and purchased through the firm. These deals were completed, and the commission paid to the firm. Thereafter, in December, 1915, and after the firm had been dissolved, Clark and Buckingham each brought separate suits against this plaintiff, Hadley, individually alleging that he made certain false and fraudulent representations touching the land. Recovery was sought in tort on account thereof. In those suits it was not alleged that the defendant, Coffin, made any of the false representations upon which the suit was predicated, nor is it alleged that he was party in any way to the fraud upon which the suits rested. These suits were both tried, and both terminated in favor of this plaintiff, and he was exonerated from any liability on account of the alleged fraud. In defending himself against those suits, plaintiff incurred the expense for which he now sues, and it is on account of the expense so incurred that he seeks contribution from this defendant.

It will be noted that when this transaction took place out of which the Clark and Buckingham suits grew, the plaintiff and defendant were partners. It will be noted that the partnership had been dissolved, and they were no longer partners, at the time these suits were commenced. It will be noted that no claim was made there against this defendant, and it will be noted that no claim is now made that this defendant perpetrated any fraud on either Clark or Buckingham, nor was it affirmatively alleged in either of the cases that the fraud was practiced by the firm, or that this plaintiff was authorized by the firm to make any of the allegations upon which the fraud was predicated. The firm was not impleaded, and in no event could a judgment be entered against the firm, even had the plaintiffs in these suits been successful. It is not shown in this petition, or alleged, that defendant in this suit made any false or fraudulent representations for which he could be made personally liable in any suit brought by either Clark or Buckingham. The best that can be said for the petition is that plaintiff was active in consummating the deal with Clark and Buckingham. It affirmatively appears that neither the plaintiff nor the defendant practiced any fraud upon either Buckingham or Clark. It therefore appears that the plaintiff was wrongfully sued by Buckingham and Clark for a fraud that was never practiced by either the firm, Coffin or Hadley. The verdict and judgment of the court in each of said cases determined conclusively that the fraud charged was not practiced on either Buckingham or Clark. There was therefore no tort committed, either jointly or otherwise.

It appears that Hadley was unjustly charged with the commission of a tort—a tort which had not been committed by him. This unjust charge, however, called on Hadley for defense. The judgment in those cases finally and conclusively shows that the fraud charged had not been committed for which either the firm, Coffin, or Hadley could be held responsible. The record simply presents a case in which one member of a firm, transacting business for the firm, was wrongfully charged with the commission of a tort, defends against the charge, and is acquitted. The theory upon which the acquittal rests is that no tort was committed. There was therefore no liability on the part of any one. Further than that, liability for the tort, if one had been committed, was not sought in the action to be enforced against any one but Hadley. It was charged as his independent tort to which a personal liability attached. This case presents no grounds for assuming that it was a joint tort, or any tort for which either the firm, or any member of the firm, is liable. It presents, therefore, no basis for contribution.

The question here presented we do not find has ever been passed upon by this court before.

Applying general principles to the facts herein stated, we hold that the court was right in sustaining the demurrer; that the petition presented no cause of action against this defendant, and its action is therefore affirmed. ◄

COMMENTS AND QUESTIONS

1. On what basis did the court deny Hadley the right to reimbursement by his ex-partner for legal and other expenditures? Wasn't he engaged in firm business at the time of his transactions with Clark and Buckingham?
2. If Buckingham and Clark had sued the partnership in their original action and Hadley had defended the action alone, would he have been entitled to contribution from Coffin? If so, why would this factor have made a difference?
3. What pleading did the defendant file in the lower court? Was any evidence heard by that court?

Right to Interest on Capital and Loans

Unless there is a specific agreement on the point, partners are not entitled to receive interest on their capital contribution. Here again the theory is that their monetary reward should be derived exclusively from the profits of the business.

On the other hand, if a partner makes a *loan* to the partnership, over and above his capital contribution, he is entitled to interest on it, just as if he were a third party dealing with the firm.

SECTION 4

AUTHORITY OF PARTNERS
IN DEALING WITH THIRD PARTIES

Authority of Partners In General

Since much of partnership law is based on the principles of agency, each partner, as an agent of the partnership, has authority to make contracts and enter into transactions on behalf of the firm. The partnership as a whole is bound by the acts of each partner, just as any principal is bound by the acts of an authorized agent. Moreover, the partnership may ratify the unauthorized acts of a partner according to the general rules of agency law (discussed on pp. 542–43).

Extent of Partner's Apparent Authority

A great many difficult problems have arisen over the apparent authority (as distinguished from the actual authority—see page 549) of a partner to make binding contracts and commitments on behalf of the firm, and the efforts of the partnership as a whole to set limits on that authority. Section 9 of the Uniform Partnership Act deals with this situation as follows:

> Every partner is an agent of the partnership for the purpose of its business, and the act of every partner, including the execution in the partnership name of any instrument, for apparently carrying on in the usual way the business of the partnership—binds the partnership, unless the partner so acting has no authority to act for the partnership in the particular matter, and the person with whom he is dealing has knowledge of the fact that he has no such authority.

In other words, a partner has apparent authority to bind the firm to any act or transaction that comes within the usual business of the firm. True, the firm may expressly limit the authority of a partner. But unless a third party is aware of that limitation, the firm is still bound by the acts of a partner who exceeds his actual authority.

The Uniform Act goes on to say:

> An act of a partner which is not apparently for the carrying on of the business of the partnership in the usual way does not bind the partnership unless authorized by the other partners.

Notice that a crucial question arises here: Which acts fall within the category of carrying on in the usual way the business of the partnership and which do not? The answer depends on the nature of the partnership itself and on the customs and usages of the business in which it is engaged. Court decisions and statutes, however, provide us with certain general rules.

Acts Within Normal Business of Firm

POWER TO BORROW MONEY. In determining the extent of the apparent authority of partners, the courts have drawn a distinction between trading partnerships and nontrading partnerships. A *trading partnership* is one whose principal business is the buying and selling of commodities. A *nontrading partnership*, on the other hand, is one that is organized for a non-commercial purpose—a law firm, for example.

In a trading firm each partner has apparent authority to borrow money and to execute negotiable instruments for the firm in the usual course of the firm's business. He also has the power to mortgage partnership property to secure loans made to the firm. In a nontrading partnership, however, a partner does not have the power to borrow money for it unless the firm has expressly granted him that power.

EXAMPLES

1. X, Y, and Z are partners in a grocery store. They agree that no member of the firm shall borrow money for it without express authorization from the other partners. X, in violation of the agreement, borrows money for the firm. Unless the person who lent the money was actually aware of the limitation on his authority, the loan is binding on the partnership.

2. A, B, and C are doctors who form a partnership to operate a clinic. A borrows money for the clinic without authorization from his partners. Since the clinic is a nontrading partnership, none of the partners has apparent authority to borrow money, and the partnership is not bound by A's act.

CLAIMS BY AND AGAINST FIRM. Generally speaking, a partner has apparent authority to compromise or to pay any claims against the partnership. He may make the payment either with firm funds or with other firm property. Each partner also has apparent authority to adjust debts and to receive payments due the partnership. Consequently, a debtor is held to have satisfied his obligation to the firm by paying any one of the partners. This rule holds good even though the partner fails to turn the money over to his copartners.

PURCHASE AND SALE OF PROPERTY. Each partner has power to sell any personal property which the firm would normally sell in its business. This power does not extend, however, to the sale of fixtures or other equipment used by the partnership in its business. Similarly, a partner may purchase on behalf of the partnership any property that is normally used in the regular course of the firm's business.

Generally speaking, a partner does not have the power to sell any of the firm's real property unless the other partners expressly authorize him to do so. A logical exception to this rule occurs when the partnership is actually engaged in the real estate business.

Sometimes a partner will sell some of the firm's real property even though he lacks the authority. Then certain complications arise. If title to the property was in the firm name, the conveyance to the buyer may be set aside, on the theory that the purchaser should have been aware of the partner's lack of apparent authority. If the buyer, in turn, sells the property to an innocent third party, however, the firm may not recover it. On the other hand, if title to real property is in the name of one of the partners rather than in the name of the partnership itself, and if the buyer is unaware of the firm's ownership, he takes good title and the partnership may not set aside the conveyance.

In the New York case that follows, the court had to decide whether a partner in an automobile sales business had apparent authority to purchase auto supplies on behalf of the firm.

IROQUOIS RUBBER CO. v. GRIFFIN

Court of Appeals of New York, 1919
226 N.Y. 297, 123 N.E. 369

► CRANE, J. The Iroquois Rubber Company of Buffalo, N. Y., sold to Mathes & Griffin of Albion, N. Y., in 1913, auto supplies consisting of gas burners, tank washers, magneto cable, engine paint, etc., amounting to $513.67 on which has been paid $148.06, leaving a balance due of $365.61. A. Ray Griffin, one of the defendants, was in the garage business under the name of Oakland Garage of Albion. Stanley Mathes was not in the garage business or connected with the Oakland Garage. He and Griffin constituted the firm of Mathes & Griffin, agents of the Oakland automobile to sell Oakland automobiles. They also sold secondhand cars.

The plaintiff brought this action against the firm to recover for the automobile supplies furnished, and the defendant Mathes, while admitting that he and Griffin were co-agents, or partners, for the sale of automobiles, denied that they were partners for any other purpose or that the supplies were furnished to the partnership. The denial also raised the issue as to whether the special partnership or business was such as to impliedly authorize Mathes to purchase automobile supplies.

The plaintiff has recovered in the courts below, and the appeal is brought here by the defendant Mathes upon exceptions to the judge's charge.

The testimony showed that a purchase of $139.22 was made by Griffin in March of 1913 at the plaintiff's store, and that the balance of the bill, $277.79, was purchased in the following May by a written order on the letter head of the defendants. Witnesses for the plaintiff said that Mathes was with Griffin in the store at the time of the March purchase and was introduced as Griffin's partner. This was denied by the defendant.

There was no evidence as to the May order except as it appeared in the letter sent. A copy of this letter is not in the record, and the circumstances of the purchase are not given. The defendant did not sign the letter and knew nothing about these transactions, according to his testimony. He says further that none of the articles thus purchased were ever received by him or by his firm, and, if this testimony be true, the fair inference is that they went to Griffin for his personal use in the Oakland Garage.

The plaintiff says that as agents for the Oakland car the firm had no office, but had sold a few cars, both new and secondhand. The case is lacking of any evidence that the firm, as selling agents, repaired cars, had a place of business, or used automobile accessories. In the absence of any evidence as to the nature of the business, it cannot be assumed as a matter of law that a selling agent carries on repair work or has need for automobile accessories. Especially would this be so where it appears that one of the partners in the selling agency conducts a separate and distinct business of an automobile garage, and that the other partner never ordered or received the goods and, by his testimony, had no occasion for them.

These brief statements make it clear, therefore, that an issue of fact was presented for the jury as to whether they believed the testimony of Mathes, and, if they did, whether the partnership with Griffin was such as authorized him to purchase the bill of goods from the plaintiff.

Mathes would be liable if Griffin's purchases were within the scope of his partnership agency, actual or as represented by Mathes, and not otherwise. This was a question for the jury and not for the court.

In its charge, the learned court said:

> "But the only actual partnership with the plaintiff proved to exist between Mathes and Griffin was one for the handling of the Oakland automobiles. As far as their actual business between themselves was concerned it does not appear that their partnership extended any further than that. So there is no proof of a general partnership which would authorize Mr. Griffin to charge Mr. Mathes by reason of the fact that they were in a general partnership."

But the court went further and held, as a matter of law, that as the May order was sent upon a letter head reading "Mathes & Griffin, dealers in ten different makes of autos: a full line of used cars," Mathes was bound to pay for the goods so ordered.

> "I have no doubt," said the judge to the jury, "that I am justified in saying to you that from and after May 6, 1913, Mr. Mathes is chargeable for the goods purchased by Mr. Griffin in the name of Mathes & Griffin from the plaintiff in this action regardless of whether there was any partnership between Mr. Mathes and Mr. Griffin or not. . . . Your duty in this case is to find a verdict for the plaintiff, either for the full amount —$367.01 if you think that Mr. Mathes was in the store on the 13th of March 1913, and heard Mr. Griffin say that they were partners in the automobile business, or for $227.79 if you do not find that he was in the store on March 13, 1913, and heard Mr. Griffin say that he and Mr. Mathes were partners in the automobile business."

The judge, by this charge, directed a verdict for the amount of the May purchase, because it was ordered on the letter head of the defendants, and this representation of the business authorized Griffin's act.

We think that this circumstance was but evidence to be considered by the jury together with the testimony of the defendant Mathes in determining the litigated facts as above stated. The issue litigated and which should have been submitted to the jury was the scope of the partnership business as it actually existed or as represented by Mathes, and the authority of Griffin who made the purchases to bind Mathes by his acts.

Considering the nature of the agency, the letter heads, the business as previously conducted and as explained by this defendant, was the partnership merely to sell automobiles, or did it include their fixing and repair, thus requiring accessories? This was for the jury.

Another request should also have been charged. It was this:

> "I ask your honor to charge the jury that in order to hold the defendant Mathes liable on this account set up or claimed in this action, the goods delivered and the credit given must be within the scope of the business in which he was held out to be a partner."

The court ruled:

> "I decline to charge otherwise on that subject because I do not think the question is further involved in the case. It is true as an elementary proposition of law, but I do not think it affects this case in any way."

In the light of what we have here stated, the exceptions taken to this refusal and to the direction of a verdict require a reversal of this judgment.

The amount involved is not large as litigation goes; the plaintiff has waited a long time for its money, and the case is very simple, but the law still remains that a man who enters into a partnership for only one purpose is not liable for the purchase of the other partner unless used in that business or the articles are of the kind usually and customarily bought for such an undertaking existing or as represented to exist.

The judgment should be reversed, and a new trial granted; costs to abide the event.

HISCOCK, C. J., and CHASE, COLLIN, CUDDEBACK, HOGAN, and McLAUGH-LIN, JJ., concur.   ◄

COMMENTS AND QUESTIONS

1. What was the main issue here? How did the trial judge instruct the jury on that issue? Why did the appellate court rule that the charge was incorrect?

2. Note the defendant's request to the trial judge to include certain instructions to the jury. How did the judge deal with this request?

3. The court notes in passing that "the plaintiff has waited a long time for its money," and that the amount "is not large as litigation goes." And yet the case was sent back for a new trial. Presumably, both parties spent far more money litigating the case than they could have hoped to gain by winning it.

GENERAL MANAGEMENT FUNCTIONS. Each partner has apparent authority to hire a reasonable number of employees to carry on the business; he also has the power to discharge employees so long as he doesn't go so far as to cripple the firm's operations. Moreover, he may lease property or equipment for the firm and may bind the firm to any contract that appears to be necessary for the transaction of its business.

NOTICE TO INDIVIDUAL PARTNER. As a general rule, every partner is authorized to receive notice for the firm concerning any matter that falls within the scope of its business; the notice is binding on the partnership regardless of whether the partner who receives it communicates it to his copartners. This, again, as you will remember, is a general principle of agency law.

Acts Outside Normal Business of Firm

Section 9 of the Uniform Partnership Act also speaks of acts performed by partners outside of the normal business of the partnership:

> Unless authorized by the other partners or unless they have abandoned the business, one or more but less than all the partners have no author- ity to:
> a) Assign the partnership property in trust for creditors or on the assignee's promise to pay the debts of the partnership,
> b) Dispose of the goodwill of the business,
> c) Do any other act which would make it impossible to carry on the ordinary business of a partnership,
> d) Confess a judgment,
> e) Submit a partnership claim or liability to arbitration. . . .

In addition to the foregoing limitations, a partner does not have authority to commit the firm to a contract guaranteeing the payment of another party's debt (unless, of course, the partnership is in that business). Nor can a part- ner give away any assets of the firm, except, perhaps, a reasonable amount to charity.

The following case dealt with the authority of a partner to sell the firm's business and dispose of its good will. Also involved was an agreement not to compete with the buyer.

KIDDER EQUITY EXCHANGE v. NORMAN

Supreme Court of South Dakota, 1919
42 S.D. 229, 173 N.W. 728

► WHITING, J. This action was brought to enjoin defendant from engaging in the business of grain dealer at Kidder, S. D. Judgment was for plaintiff, and defendant appeals from the judgment and from an order denying a new trial.

The facts are undisputed. Defendant, together with one Johnson, under the firm name and style of Norman & Johnson Grain Company, was en- gaged in the business of buying grain at Kidder. Plaintiff, desiring to pur- chase an elevator at the said town, entered into negotiations with defendant for the purchase of the elevator wherein the above partnership was doing business, supposing the said elevator to be the property of such copartner- ship. Norman had charge of the business at Kidder. Johnson resided at and had charge of a similar business for said firm at another town. The firm had in all some four places of business at as many different towns. Plaintiff and defendant entered into an agreement, of which a memorandum was made, which memorandum was dated July 31, 1917. The substance of such memorandum was that the party of the first part, the Norman and Johnson Grain Company, agreed to sell their elevator at Kidder, S. D., for $6,500, and agreed not to enter into the buying or selling of grain in Kidder, S. D., and plaintiff agreed to pay the above amount for the elevator on or before August 4, 1917. This memorandum was signed on the part of the first party as follows: "Norman & Johnson Grain Company, by G. N. Norman, Mgr." Plaintiff had prepared a bill of sale in which the copartnership was named as grantor, which bill of sale described the said elevator and contained a clause to the effect that the grantors conveyed the good will of their business and agreed not to engage in the buying and selling of grain in and around Kidder, S. D. When this bill of sale was presented to Norman for signature, he advised plaintiff that the elevator was not the property of the partnership, but was his sole and separate property, and that therefore he could not sign the bill of sale as prepared. A new bill of sale was then prepared by Norman, which in no manner referred to the copartnership, except that in designating said elevator it was referred to as the "Norman & Johnson Grain Company." In this bill of sale there was included the following:

> "As a further consideration for the sale and purchase of the above-described property, the parties of the first part individually hereby agree not to engage in the buying and selling of grain in and around Kidder, S.D. It being agreed that all the parties of the first part hereby sell the good will of the business as well as the described property."

The above-quoted words were in substance identical with the corresponding part of the unexecuted bill of sale. While Johnson was advised by Norman that he had contracted to sell the elevator, he never was advised of, and he never knew of or gave any authority for, the sale of the business or its good will, and he never authorized an agreement not to engage in the business of buying grain at Kidder. The partnership, by Norman, afterwards entered upon the business of buying and selling grain at Kidder.

We think it perfectly clear that the trial court was in error. The memorandum and the unexecuted bill of sale were absolutely immaterial. Plaintiff knew what the true situation was before it closed the deal and took the bill of sale. The rule is that contracts in restraint of business are void as against public policy. Section 898, Rev. Code 1919. An exception is made in the case of a sale of the good will of a business. In such case there can be a valid agreement not to engage in the same business; such agreement limited as to time and place. Section 899, Rev. Code 1919. One partner, as such, has no authority to dispose of the good will of a partnership business unless his copartners have abandoned the business to him, or are incapable of acting. Section 1313, Rev. Code 1919. Johnson had not abandoned the business; neither was he incapable of acting. Therefore, if the bill of sale was subject to a construction holding it to attempt to transfer the good will in the partnership business, it was in that respect void. There can be no good will in a building; hence Norman had no good will which he, as an individual, could sell. The good will which is property, and therefore subject to sale, is the "good will of a business." Section 253, Rev. Code 1919. No "good will of a business" having been sold, the attempted agreement not to engage in business was invalid, just as much as it would have been invalid if some person other than Norman, or some firm or corporation in which Norman had no interest, had been occupying this elevator at the time Norman gave the bill of sale.

The judgment and order appealed from are reversed.   ◄

COMMENTS AND QUESTIONS

1. The plaintiff alleged that he had purchased the good will of the defendant's business at Kidder and asked the court to enjoin the defendant from competing with him in that town. What did the lower court do? What happened on appeal?
2. If the agreement had been signed by Johnson, the other partner, would it have been binding and enforceable?

Tort Liability of Partnership

A partnership, like any other principal, is liable for the tort of one of its partners if the tort is committed while the partner is acting within the scope of the firm's usual business. And a partnership is liable for the wrongdoing of any employee so long as he is engaged in his regular employment. The following case presents an example of this liability.

WOLF et al. v. MILLS

Supreme Court of Illinois, 1870
56 Ill. 360

► THORNTON, J. The appellee brought an action on the case, alleging that appellants sold him a lot of sheep pelts, having on them a large quantity of wool, and, with intent to defraud him, delivered other and inferior pelts in quality, and deficient in the quantity of wool. Appellee recovered a verdict.

Wolf & Haber jointly owned the pelts at the time of the sale. The proof is satisfactory that the pelts sold averaged about five pounds of wool per pelt, and the pelts delivered only three pounds. As to the alleged fraud, the evidence is conflicting. One witness testified positively that he saw young Haber, a son of appellant, change the pelts, and that he placed light in place of the heavy pelts, soon after the sale. This was contradicted by the son; but the weight of evidence has been determined by a jury, and we shall not disturb the finding, unless some principle of law has been violated.

Appellants urge that, as there is no evidence to prove the change, if made, was by the direction of Wolf, or by any person in his employment or under his control, therefore he is not liable. The evidence does show that Wolf and Haber were partners in the buying and selling of the sheep pelts, and that young Haber was handling them, and throwing them from one pile to the other. The jury was justified in the inference that this was in the scope of the partnership business, as it was connected with the joint property. It is improbable that the son would be thus engaged, unless directed. The father must have given him some instructions in regard to the exchange.

There was, then, no error in the following instruction given for appellee:

> "If the jury believe from the evidence that the defendants sold the plaintiff a certain lot of sheep pelts at an agreed price, and that plaintiff has paid such price, and that the defendants afterward, either in person, by their agents, servants, or employes, delivered to plaintiff a lot of sheep pelts in any respect different from and inferior to those actually sold, intending thereby to have the plaintiff believe they were the same he had purchased, and intending to deceive and defraud the plaintiff, then the jury are instructed to find defendants guilty, and to assess as damages whatever loss the evidence may show the plaintiff sustained through such fraud and deceit."

A tortious act of one partner will often create a liability against the firm. So a fraud committed by one partner in the course of the partnership business binds the firm even though the other partners have no knowledge of, or participation in, the fraud. The jury might reasonably infer all that was necessary to fix the liability of the firm.

Judgment affirmed. ◀

COMMENTS AND QUESTIONS

1. On what theory was Wolf held liable for fraud here? Was he not innocent of any wrongdoing?
2. Again, this case illustrates the importance of basic agency law in the law of partnerships. You will recall the cases in the agency chapter dealing with a principal's responsibility for his agent's torts. The same rules generally apply to a partner's liability for another partner's acts.

SECTION 5

DISSOLUTION, WINDING UP, AND TERMINATION OF PARTNERSHIPS

Termination Process in General

In many respects, the partnership is a very unstable form of business organization. It is based solely on the voluntary association of its partners, and its existence is consequently tenuous. Since the terms used to refer to the process of terminating a partnership often give rise to confusion, we shall define and distinguish them before proceeding further. A partnership comes to an end in successive stages. The first stage is *dissolution*. The Uniform Partnership Act provides that "the dissolution of a partnership is the change in the relation of the partners caused by any partner ceasing to be associated in the carrying on as distinguished from the winding up of the business." The act says further "on dissolution the partnership is not terminated but continues until the winding up of partnership affairs is completed." Dissolution, then, occurs when the partners cease to do business together; with dissolution, the firm ceases to exist as a going concern. The second stage, *winding up,* involves settling the partnership affairs, completing its operations, paying its debts, and distributing whatever property remains. The third stage, *termination,* occurs only after the winding-up period has come to an end; until that time, the firm continues to exist as a legal entity.

Causes of Dissolution

In General

The causes of dissolution are many and varied. Dissolution may come about as the result of a voluntary act of the partners, either in accordance with their agreement or contrary to it. Or it may occur by operation of law on the happening of a certain event. Or it may be decreed by a court.

Dissolution by Act of Partners

AGREEMENT. Sometimes the original partnership agreement will provide that the firm is to continue in existence for a definite period of time, or until the completion of certain business or of a certain project. Then dissolution occurs automatically at the expiration of the period specified. If all the partners consent, of course, the life of the partnership may be extended or shortened by means of a subsequent agreement.

WITHDRAWAL OF PARTNER. Since the law does not compel any person to remain in a firm, a partner may always withdraw from a partnership when he wants to. If his withdrawal is contrary to an express agreement to remain a partner for a particular period, however, he may be liable to his copartners for any damages they suffer as a result of his premature withdrawal. In the absence of such an agreement, a partner may usually withdraw without liability to his associates. In any event, the withdrawal of a partner brings about the dissolution of the firm.

SALE OR ASSIGNMENT OF INTEREST. In many of the states that have not adopted the Uniform Partnership Act, a partner's sale or assignment of his interest in the partnership to a third party or to a creditor is regarded as a withdrawal and serves to dissolve the firm. Under the Uniform Act, however, such a move on the part of one of the partners does not necessarily dissolve the partnership.

Dissolution by Operation of Law

DEATH OF A PARTNER. Even where there is an agreement to the contrary, the death of a partner brings about the dissolution of the partnership. The winding-up and termination stages may be postponed, and the surviving partners and the representative of the decreased partner may carry on the business. But then the courts hold that the old firm has been dissolved and has been replaced by a new one.

BANKRUPTCY. If one of the partners goes bankrupt, he ceases to control his property interests and the firm is automatically dissolved. Similarly, if the partnership itself goes bankrupt, dissolution inevitably occurs. On the other hand, if a partner merely becomes insolvent (unable to pay his debts) and has not been formally declared a bankrupt, dissolution does not occur automatically.

ILLEGALITY. If, during the existence of a partnership, its business or the form of its organization becomes illegal, dissolution takes place.

EXAMPLES

1. A partnership operating a liquor store is automatically dissolved when the community in which it is doing business goes "dry."
2. A and B are partners in an insurance business. The state in which they are operating passes a law requiring insurance companies to incorporate. The partnership is automatically dissolved.

Dissolution by Court Decree

There are certain other circumstances in which the courts, on the request of one or more of the partners, will declare a partnership dissolved. Under the Uniform Partnership Act, the following situations are grounds for dissolution: (1) a partner is declared to be legally insane; (2) a partner becomes physically or mentally incapable of carrying out the terms of the partnership agreement; (3) a partner is guilty of conduct that hurts the business; (4) a partner willfully and consistently commits acts that are so contrary to the partnership agreement that they make continuance of the business impracticable; (5) the business can be continued only at a loss, and there is no reasonable prospect of success; (6) fraud, duress, or other circumstances arise that call for a dissolution of the firm.

In the following case, the plaintiff requested dissolution of a partnership, alleging that one of his copartners had been guilty of misconduct. The opinion contains a good summary of the law on this point.

CASH v. EARNSHAW et al.

Supreme Court of Illinois, 1872
66 Ill. 402

► SCOTT, J. This bill was to dissolve a copartnership entered into by the parties to this suit on the 26th day of November, 1869, for the purpose of carrying on the business of quarrying stone, and was to continue through the full period of five years.

The ground set out in the bill, upon which the plaintiff seeks relief, is the misconduct of the partner Emanuel Earnshaw. No cause of complaint is alleged against any other member of the firm. He is charged with specific acts of wrongful conduct and general mismanagement of the business of the firm. On account of the charges in the bill plaintiff in error sought to have the court dissolve the copartnership, appoint a receiver, and close up the affairs of the firm. The court below denied the relief, and plaintiff brings the cause to this court on error.

It is not for every act of misconduct on the part of one partner that a court of equity, at the instance of another, will dissolve the partnership and close up the affairs of the company. The court will require a strong case to be made, and it is laid down as a general principle that a court has no jurisdiction to make a separation between partners for trifling causes or temporary grievances involving no permanent mischiefs.

Story, in his work on Partnership, states the rule to be that, to justify such an extraordinary interposition, the court always expects a strong and clear case to be made out of positive and meditated abuse. For minor misconduct or grievances, he says, if they require any redress, the court, ordinarily, will go no further than to act upon the faulty party by way of an injunction. Story on Partnership, 288, and authorities cited.

We have carefully examined the evidence in the record, and we fail to discover that clear and satisfactory proof of the allegations in the bill that the law undoubtedly requires. Indeed, so far as we can see, there is no act on the part of Emanuel Earnshaw that the plaintiff in error can have any just cause of complaint, unless it was the failure to give him a check for $500 on the 12th day of November, 1870, when requested. And, if there was no explanation of this fact, we do not think that it is of sufficient gravity to justify the use of the extraordinary power by the court of equity to put an end to the entire contract between the parties. The contract of co-partnership was deliberately entered into after mature consideration, and not without considerable knowledge of each other's characters and fitness, and it ought not to be dissolved on account of any mere trifling cause.

It is apparent, from what took place at the time, that Earnshaw did not intend any wrong to plaintiff in error by the refusal to give the check. The evidence warrants us in saying that there was an honest dispute as to the amount then due to him. Plaintiff in error, for some reason satisfactory to himself, did not choose to have the account passed upon at the time, and hence the check was not given. It turned out, however, upon subsequent investigation, that there was more than the amount demanded due him and he ought, in fact, to have the check; but Earnshaw may have been honestly in doubt as to the amount. If so, he ought not be charged with willful misconduct, and his contract for that reason alone dissolved, and his business broken up. The consequences of the dissolution of copartnership are of too serious a character to be justified by so slight a cause. Under the most unfavorable view, it would only work a temporary inconvenience, and it is not pretended that any permanent injury resulted from the refusal to give him a check for the desired amount on that day. His own conduct in the premises is not altogether blameless, and he ought not to be allowed to make the mistaken judgment of his partner the ground for the dissolution of their contract.

By the agreement of the parties, Emanuel Earnshaw was made general superintendent of the affairs of the company, and it is insisted that he made large sales on credit to the injury of plaintiff in error as a member of the firm. It was not provided by the articles of copartnership that no sales should be made on a credit. It was, however, stipulated that no sales should be made on a credit by one member "against the express wish of consent of two others." The evidence tends to show that the sales that were made on credit, of which complaint is made, were not recklessly done, but were deemed reasonable sales at the time. Certainly they were not so improvidently made as to be regarded as willful misconduct on the part of the superintendent. Losses did occur, but they were through mere error of judgment. The credits given were for short periods, and other parties, considered prudent men, engaged in the same line of business, made similar sales with like disastrous results. In making the sales on credit, he violated no express agreement of the parties, and inasmuch as it appears that it was in accordance with the custom of the trade, we see no grounds for just complaint against the action of the superintendent in this regard. He seems to have acted with reasonable prudence, and certainly no willful conduct can be imputed to him that ought to be visited with any serious consequences.

The most serious cause of complaint seems to be in regard to making the Shannon contract in the first place, and the subsequent agreement with Steele and McMahan to perform and complete his contract with them. It is alleged that by reason of the improvident contract with Shannon, and the subsequent agreement to complete the work on Lake Street, large losses were incurred through mismanagement of Emanuel Earnshaw. No doubt the contract with Shannon was an unfortunate one, but it was certainly deemed a good one by all the parties when made, and, if he had been able to perform it, it would have been in the end greatly to their interest. When Shannon failed, Earnshaw deemed it most advantageous for the interest of all concerned that the company should assume the contract and complete the work. It was thought it would be a great saving to the company. It is true that the superintendent made the contract with Steele and McMahan without having first consulted with any of the partners; but they certainly all consented to the arrangement after it was made. Plaintiff in error says that he protested against the company assuming the contract but he himself superintended the work for part of the time, and did other acts that cannot but be regarded as a ratification of the act of the superintendent in undertaking to complete the work. It does not appear but that, under all the circumstances, it was the very best thing the company could do, and perhaps prevented heavier losses than would otherwise have been sustained.

It is hardly necessary to comment separately on the other charges of misconduct. We do not find in all the record any cause of sufficient gravity, proven by clear and satisfactory evidence, that would justify a court of equity to interpose to put an end to the partnership relations between the parties. It may be that there were slight errors in judgment on the part of the superintendent; but no evidence of willful misconduct appears that would result in serious injury to plaintiff in error or any member of the firm. No reason appears that would prevent a profitable and harmonious co-operation between the several partners in the prosecution of the common business of the firm, and hence no cause for dissolution; and the decree of the superior court is affirmed.

Decree affirmed.   ◄

COMMENTS AND QUESTIONS

1. On what basis did the plaintiff Cash attempt to have the partnership dissolved? Did the court agree? Summarize the reasons for its decision.
2. This case illustrates the reluctance of courts to intervene in partnership affairs. Note that the agreement was to continue for a period of five years. This may explain why the plaintiff sought dissolution by court decree rather than by his own action. In the latter case he might have been liable to his copartners for damages, but if he could have got the court to dissolve the firm he would not have been liable.

Effect of Dissolution on Partner's Authority

Although, as we have seen, dissolution does not terminate a firm's existence, it does curtail the authority of the partners to act on behalf of the firm during the winding-up period that follows. As a general rule, on dissolution, a partner loses all authority to act as an agent for the partnership, except in settling the affairs of the firm and winding up its business.

EXAMPLE

ABBOTT, BAKER, and ZANY are partners in a retail clothing store. ZANY is declared insane, and on the application of ABBOTT and BAKER the firm is dissolved. In the winding-up period that follows, ABBOTT still has power to pay bills and dispose of the stock on hand, since these acts must be completed before the firm's affairs can be settled. He loses his authority to borrow money for the firm or acquire new merchandise, however, unless he can show that these actions are necessary in winding up the firm's business.

Notice of Dissolution to Partners and Third Parties

Agency law recognizes certain exceptions to the general rule that a partner loses his authority to represent the firm after its dissolution. These exceptions occur in situations where other partners or third persons have not received notice of the dissolution.

Notice to Partners

If a partnership is dissolved by the act of one of the partners, the other partners retain authority to bind the firm until they have been formally notified of the dissolution, or until it has been brought to their attention in some other way. Or, as it is stated in Section 34 of the Uniform Partnership Act,

> Where the dissolution is caused by the act, death or bankruptcy of a partner, each partner is liable to his copartners for his share of any liability created by any partner acting for the partnership as if the partnership had not been dissolved, unless (a) the dissolution being by the act of any partner, the partner acting for the partnership had knowledge of the dissolution, or (b) the dissolution being by the death or bankruptcy of a partner, the partner acting for the partnership had knowledge or notice of the death or bankruptcy.

EXAMPLE

WILSON, COOLIDGE, and HOOVER are partners in a trading firm. WILSON withdraws from the firm, notifying COOLIDGE but not HOOVER of his withdrawal. If, before he learns of WILSON's act, HOOVER orders certain merchandise for the firm, WILSON is liable for his share of the contract. On the other hand, if COOLIDGE contracts for the firm, WILSON is not responsible.

Notice to Third Persons

When dissolution is caused by the act of one of the partners or by a voluntary agreement among the firm members, notice must be given to third persons. Until they receive such notice, they may assume that the firm is still a going concern, and any contracts they make with a partner within the scope of the business are binding on the firm. Persons who have dealt with the firm in the past must be given actual notice. For those who have not done business with the partnership before, notice by publication (in a newspaper, for example) is sufficient.

When the firm is dissolved because its business has become illegal, no notice to third parties is necessary. The same is true when dissolution is caused by the bankruptcy of one of the partners. In both cases, the cause of dissolution is deemed to be a matter of public knowledge.

EXAMPLE

HOLMES, WARREN, and JONES are partners in a drugstore and agree to dissolve the firm. ANDERSON, who has sold goods to the store for many years, enters into a contract with HOLMES to supply certain cosmetics to the store. If ANDERSON has not personally been notified of the dissolution, the contract is binding on the firm. If ANDERSON has not previously dealt with the firm, and if notice of the dissolution has been published in a newspaper, however, the partnership is not liable. In the latter case, if ANDERSON has received neither personal nor public notice, the contract is binding on the firm. HOLMES is still personally liable to ANDERSON, of course, even if the firm is not.

In each of the two cases that follow, contracts were made with third parties following the dissolution of a partnership; the issue before the court was whether proper notice had been given to them.

SOLOMON v. KIRKWOOD et al.

Supreme Court of Michigan, 1884
55 Mich. 256, 21 N.W. 336

► COOLEY, C. J. The plaintiffs, who are in the city of Chicago dealers in jewelry, seek to charge the defendants as partners upon a promissory note for $791.92, bearing date of November 9, 1882, and signed "Hollander & Kirkwood." The note was given by the defendant Hollander, but Kirkwood denies that any partnership existed between the defendants at the date of the note.

The evidence given on the trial tends to show that on July 6, 1882, Hollander & Kirkwood entered into a written agreement for a partnership for one year from the 1st day of the next ensuing month in the business of buying and selling jewelry, clocks, watches, etc., and in repairing clocks, watches, and jewelry, at Ishpeming, Mich. Business was begun under this agreement, and continued until the latter part of October, 1882, when Kirkwood, becoming dissatisfied, locked up the goods and excluded Hollander altogether from the business. He also caused notice to be given to all persons with whom the firm had had dealings that the partnership was dissolved, and had the following inserted in the local column of the paper published at Ishpeming:

"The copartnership heretofore existing between Mr. C. H. Kirkwood and one Hollander, as jewelers, has ceased to exist; Mr. Kirkwood having purchased the interest of the latter." This was not signed by any one.

A few days later Hollander went to Chicago, and there, on November 9, 1882, he bought, in the name of Hollander & Kirkwood, of the plaintiffs goods in their line amounting to $791.92, and gave to the plaintiffs therefor the promissory note now in the suit. The note was made payable December 15, 1882, at a bank in Ishpeming. When the purchase was completed, Hollander took away the goods in his satchel. The plaintiffs had before had no dealings with Hollander & Kirkwood, but they had heard there was such a firm, and were not aware of its dissolution. They claim to have made the sale in good faith and in the belief that the firm was still in existence. . . .

The questions principally contested on trial were, first, whether the acts of Kirkwood amounted to a dissolution of the partnership; second, whether sufficient notice of dissolution was given, . . . The trial judge, in submitting the case to the jury, instructed them: That Kirkwood, notwithstanding the written agreement, had a right to withdraw from the partnership at any time, leaving matters between him and Hollander to be adjusted between them amicably or in the courts; and for the purposes of this case it made no difference whether Kirkwood was right or wrong in bringing the partnership to an end. If wrong, he might be liable to Hollander in damages for the breach of his contract. Also, that when partners are dissatisfied, or they cannot get along together, and one partner withdraws, the partnership is then at an end as to the public and parties with whom the partnership deals, and neither partner can make contracts in the future to bind the partnership, provided the retiring partner gives the proper notice. Also, that if they should find from the evidence that there was trouble between Hollander and Kirkwood prior to the sale of the goods and the giving of the note, that Kirkwood informed Hollander in substance that he would have no more dealings with him as partner, that he took possession of all the goods and locked them up, and from that time they ceased to do business, then the partnership was dissolved. Further, that whether sufficient notice had been given of the dissolution was a question for the jury. Kirkwood was not bound to publish notice in any of the Chicago papers. He was only bound to give actual notice to such parties there as had dealt with the partnership. But Kirkwood was bound to use all fair means to publish as widely as possible the fact of a dissolution. Publication in a newspaper is one of the proper means of giving notice, but it is not absolutely essential; and on this branch of the case the question for the jury was whether Kirkwood gave such notice of the dissolution as under the circumstances was fair and reasonable. If he did, then he is not liable on the note; if he did not, he would still continue liable.

We think the judge committed no error in his instructions respecting the dissolution of the partnership. The rule on this subject is thus stated in an early New York case: The right of a partner to dissolve, it is said,

> "is a right inseparably incident to every partnership. There can be no such thing as an indissoluble partnership. Every partner has an indefeasible right to dissolve the partnership as to all future contracts by publishing his own volition to that effect; and after such publication the other members of the firm have no capacity to bind him by any contract. Even where partners covenant with each other that the partnership shall continue seven years, either partner may dissolve it the next day, proclaiming his determination for that purpose; the only consequence being that he thereby subjects himself to a claim for damages for a breach of his covenant. The power given by one partner to another to make joint contracts for them both is not only a revocable power, but a man can do no act to divest himself of the capacity to revoke it." . . .

There may be cases in which equity would enjoin a dissolution for a time, when the circumstances were such as to make it specially injurious; but no question of equitable restraint arises here. When one partner becomes dissatisfied, there is commonly no legal policy to be subserved by compelling a continuance of the relation, and the fact that a contract will be broken by the dissolution is no argument against the right to dissolve. Most contracts may be broken at pleasure, subject, however, to responsibility in damages; and that responsibility would exist in breaking a contract of partnership as in other cases.

The instruction respecting notice was also correct. No court can determine for all cases what shall be sufficient notice and what shall not be. The question must necessarily be one of fact. . . .   ◄

COMMENTS AND QUESTIONS

1. Summarize the trial judge's instructions to the jury relative to Kirkwood's right to dissolve the partnership and the duty to notify third parties. Were these instructions correct?
2. If the note had been given before Kirkwood acted to dissolve the firm, would it have been binding on him? In other words, would Hollander have had authority to bind Kirkwood to the purchase of the goods from Solomon?

LYON et al. v. JOHNSON et al.

Supreme Court of Errors of Connecticut, 1859
28 Conn. 1

► Assumpsit for coal sold to the defendants as partners. It was claimed in defense that the partnership between the defendants had been previously dissolved and sufficient notice of the dissolution given.

The defendants, Johnson and Signor, previous to the 9th day of March, 1857, had been in partnership in the town of Danbury under the name of

R. Johnson & Co., and as such partners had in the fall of 1856 purchased coal of the plaintiffs, who also did business in Danbury as partners under the name of Lyon & Burr. On the 9th day of March, 1857, the firm was dissolved, and the business was thereafter carried on by Signor alone. Notice of the dissolution was published for three successive weeks in the Danbury Times, a weekly newspaper published in Danbury; but no other notice was given to the plaintiffs. In the fall of 1857 Signor bought a quantity of coal of the plaintiffs, which they sold and delivered upon the credit of the firm of R. Johnson & Co., and in the belief that he bought it for that firm. The advertisement of the dissolution of the partnership of the defendants was inserted in the newspaper next after an advertisement of the plaintiffs; but the plaintiffs did not take the paper, and had not seen the notice of the dissolution, and had no knowledge that the partnership was dissolved. The sale of coal by the plaintiffs to the defendants in 1856 was the only previous dealing of the firm of Lyon & Burr with the defendants; but for some years before the defendants had bought coal of the firm of Lyon & Bates, a firm of which the plaintiff Lyon was a member, and which was dissolved in the summer of 1856; Bates retiring from the business, and Lyon forming a new partnership with Burr, who had been a clerk of Lyon & Bates, and the new firm taking and continuing the business of the former firm.

The case was tried in the superior court. . . . The court specially found the above facts and rendered judgment thereon for the plaintiffs. The defendants thereupon filed a motion in error and brought the record before this court for revision.

BUTLER, J. There is no error in the judgment of the court below, and this will be apparent from a brief statement of the principles applicable to the case.

By the constitution of a general partnership, and as one of the elements of it, each partner is vested by his copartners with power to contract for and bind the firm within the scope of the partnership business. Each is constituted agent of all, and each is responsible for the acts of all.

Once existing, and publicly known to exist, the continuance of the connection will be presumed by the public till the contrary appears. If a dissolution takes place by operation of law, as by death or bankruptcy, no notice is required. The operations of law have a notoriety which all are bound to regard. But a dissolution by limitation, or the voluntary and mutual assent of the partners, is a matter of private arrangement, which cannot be presumed to be known to others unless they are informed of it. Until such information is given, actually or constructively, therefore, the continuance of the connection, and of the powers and liabilities of each partner, may well be presumed by every one who has occasion to deal with either on account of the firm. It follows upon the principles of justice and policy, and in conformity with the perfectly well settled rule of law, that upon such a dissolution of the partnership a retiring partner, who wishes to do justice to others and terminate his own responsibility, is under the obligation to give information of the fact to all who have dealt or are dealing with the firm, and to the public at large, with whom new attempts to deal may be made. It is equally clear that the notice so given by a retiring partner should be coextensive with the obligation assumed and as particular and specific as can be reasonably required of him under the circumstances of the case. He knows or may know who the persons are who have dealt with the firm, and he can, without unreasonable effort, give each of them actual notice, and therefore the law requires that he should do so. He cannot, without more effort or expense than can reasonably be demanded of him, give actual notice to every other member of the public, and therefore the law does not require it; but it does require him to discharge his obligation if he would terminate his liability, and to give some, and reasonable, notice to the public at large. Ordinarily a publication in one of the newspapers published in the place or county where the partnership business was conducted, as it is the customary mode of giving such information, will, as to all who have not had previous dealings with the firm, be deemed sufficient. That is the least that can be required of him in an ordinary case in respect to the public, and even that may not in all cases be sufficient, and whether it be or not will depend on the circumstances of the particular case. But in relaxing the rule as applicable to those who have not dealt with the firm, and considering a general notice, operating as a constructive notice, to be sufficient as to them, because of the difficulty of giving actual notice to everybody, the courts have not intended to relax, and have not relaxed, the rule in respect to those who have dealt with the firm. As to them there is no reason for such relaxation, and a publication is never sufficient, unless, indeed, it can be shown that the publication was seen by them, and therefore that they in fact had actual knowledge.

In this case the dissolution of the firm of R. Johnson & Co. was voluntary, and not by operation of law. The plaintiffs had previously dealt with the firm, and upon the facts found they may well be considered as regular dealers. No actual notice of the dissolution was given them, and it is found that they had no actual knowledge of it.

The publication, unless it came to their knowledge, was not as to them sufficient. The character of their previous dealing and the circumstances attending the publication of the notice, including the contiguity of the advertisements, were proper matters of evidence to be taken into consideration by the court in the question whether the plaintiffs actually knew of the dissolution or not. Doubtless the court considered them. But having found that no actual notice was given to the plaintiffs, and they did not see the publication, and had no actual knowledge of the dissolution, and that there had been previous dealing between the parties, the court correctly rendered judgment for the plaintiffs.

The judgment of the superior court is therefore affirmed.

Judgment affirmed.　◄

COMMENTS AND QUESTIONS

1. Summarize the reasons for the court's decision in this case. The opinion is a good explanation of the basic rules of law in this field.
2. Suppose, instead, that the plaintiffs had read the notice of dissolution in the paper prior to making this sale to the firm. Would the result have been the same?

Winding Up the Partnership Affairs

Following dissolution, during the period when the firm's business is being closed out, each partner's authority is limited to winding up the firm's affairs. No partner has the power to bind the partnership to new obligations.

As a general rule, each partner may participate in the winding-up process, unless his misconduct has caused the firm to dissolve. The courts will not interfere with this right unless special circumstances justify court supervision.

When dissolution is caused by the death of a partner, the surviving partner must wind up the firm's affairs and make an accounting to the estate of the deceased partner. To do this, it is often necessary for them to liquidate or dispose of partnership property. This presents few problems if title to the property is held by the firm itself. However, complications arise if title to firm property is held in the name of the deceased partner (see page 635). In that case, title technically passes to his heirs when he dies, and the surviving partners must get a court order to retrieve the property for the firm. This is sometimes a slow and complicated procedure and may delay the winding-up process.

Distribution of Assets on Termination

The final act in bringing a partnership to an end is the distribution of firm assets. Here, certain rules of priority have been established by the Uniform Partnership Act and by the courts.

As we mentioned earlier, if a partnership becomes insolvent and is dissolved, the partners are personally responsible for making up the firm's losses and paying its creditors. In such cases, a contest often develops between the personal creditors of a partner on the one hand, and the firm creditors on the other. The rule is that firm creditors have first claim on partnership assets, and personal creditors of a partner have first claim on the individual assets of the partner. If the firm creditors are not paid in full out of the firm assets, they may seek payment from the individual assets of a partner, but only *after* the personal creditors of the partner have been paid.

The following case presents an illustration of this type of situation.

RODGERS v. MERANDA et al.

Supreme Court of Ohio, 1857
7 Ohio St. 179

► The original proceeding was a petition for an order of distribution of the separate or individual assets of an insolvent debtor, as between separate and partnership creditors.

It appears from the record that about 13th of June, 1854, Peter Murray, an insolvent debtor, made an assignment of all his estate, real and personal, to the plaintiff, in trust for the payment of his individual creditors in proportion to the amount of their respective demands. Though possessed of a large and valuable estate, it had been found insufficient to pay his separate debts and liabilities in full. At the date of his failure and assignment he was a partner with John W. Dever in a mercantile firm under the name and style of Dever & Murray; which firm had also become insolvent, and likewise Dever; and the firm had made an assignment of the partnership property and assets about the same time to John Meranda, one of the defendants, in trust for the payment of the joint debts or liabilities of the firm.

In this condition of affairs the partnership creditors, although they have filed their claims with the assignee of the firm for their distributive shares out of the partnership property, claim the right to be admitted to a participation in the dividends of the separate estate of Murray, *pari passu* [9] with his individual creditors; while the latter deny the right, and insist that his separate estate shall be applied to the satisfaction of his individual debts in preference to his partnership debts.

It appears, further, that Murray, besides advancing his part of the capital of the firm, also loaned money to the firm to a large amount, for which he held the obligations of the firm, which obligations, by the assignment of Murray, came into the hands of the plaintiff, who has presented the same to the assignee of the firm, and claims to have the same paid out of the assets of the firm, *pari passu* with the other partnership debts. The other creditors resist this, and plaintiff asks an order of distribution to that effect out of partnership assets. Defendants demurred to the petition. The court below sustained the demurrer, and gave judgment in favor of the defendants; and this petition in error is filed to review and reverse that judgment.

BARTLEY, C. J. Two questions are presented for determination in this case. The first is whether, in the distribution of the assets of insolvent partners, where there are both individual and partnership assets, the individual creditors of a partner are entitled to be first paid out of the individual effects of their debtor, before the partnership creditors are entitled to any distribution therefrom. It is well settled that, in the distribution of the assets of insolvent partners, the partnership creditors are entitled to a priority in the partnership effects, so that the partnership debts must be settled before any division of the partnership funds can be made among the individual creditors of the several partners. This is incident to the nature of partnership property. It is the right of a partner to have the partnership property applied to the purposes of the firm, and the separate interest of each partner in the partnership property is his share of the surplus after the payment of the partnership debts. And this rule, which gives the partnership creditors a preference in the partnership effects, would seem to produce, in equity, a corresponding and a correlative rule, giving a preference to the individual creditors of a partner in his separate property; so that partnership creditors can, in equity, only look to the surplus of the separate property of a partner, after the payment of his individual debts, and, on the other hand, the individual creditors of a partner can in like manner only claim distribution from the debtor's interest in the surplus of the joint fund after the satisfaction of the partnership creditors. The correctness of this rule, however, has been much controverted; and there has not been always a perfect concurrence

---

[9] That is, on equal terms, without preference.

in the reasons assigned for it by those courts which have adhered to it. . . .

The remaining matter for determination in this case involves whether, in the case of an indebtedness for money lent to the partnership by a partner who afterward becomes insolvent, the separate creditors of the latter shall be entitled therefor to a pro rata distribution with the partnership creditors out of the joint fund. It is claimed that the liability of the firm to a partner for money loaned is a partnership debt, and that the individual creditors of that partner are, in equity, entitled to an equal distribution therefor out of the partnership property. On the other hand, it is claimed that as each partner is individually liable for the debts of the firm, and as no partner can be allowed to participate with his own creditors in the distribution of a fund, the separate creditors of a partner, as they can only claim through the rights of their debtor, cannot be allowed such participation with the joint creditors. . . .

The separate creditors of Murray, therefore, are not, on account of this claim for money lent by Murray to the firm, entitled to participate with the partnership creditors in the distribution of the joint effects.

Judgment of the common pleas reversed, and ordered that the separate effects of Peter Murray be distributed pro rata, first among his individual creditors, before any application thereof to be made to the payment of the partnership debts of Dever & Murray, and that the partnership effects be applied first to the payment of the partnership debts, irrespective of the claim of the partner, Peter Murray, of money loaned by him to the firm. ◄

COMMENTS AND QUESTIONS

1. Explain how the court ordered the firm's assets to be distributed between the partnership creditors and the individual creditors. Was Murray himself entitled to partial repayment of his own loan to the firm? If so, could his individual creditors then collect that payment from him?

2. This case illustrates the importance of determining what is and what is not partnership property. Obviously, the answer to this question makes a big difference to the two groups of creditors.

After the partnership creditors have been satisfied, the remaining assets, if any, are distributed in accordance with the following priorities:

1. Any loans or advances, other than capital contributions, that a partner has made to the firm are returned to him.

2. Capital contributions are then returned to each partner.

3. Any remaining assets are distributed to the partners as profits. As we have seen, both profits and losses are shared equally so long as there is no agreement to the contrary.

EXAMPLES

1. A, B, and C form a partnership, agreeing to share profits in the ratio of 60 per cent, 30 per cent and 10 per cent, respectively. A contributes $20,000 to the capital, B contributes $10,000, and C contributes his skill. The partnership is dissolved. $15,000 is owed to creditors. There is $60,000 in assets, all in cash. No profits or capital have been withdrawn.

To break even, the assets should be $45,000, exactly the amount of liabilities to creditors plus the capital contribution. However, the balance sheet is as follows:

ASSETS		LIABILITIES		
Cash	$60,000	Due Creditors		$15,000
		Net Worth		
		A's Capital	$20,000	
		B's Capital	10,000	
		Total Capital	30,000	
		Profit	15,000	
		Total Net Worth		45,000
Total Assets	$60,000	Total Liabilities & Net Worth		$60,000

After the creditors have been paid, the $45,000 remaining is distributed to the partners according to the following table:

Partner	Capital	Profit Ratio, %	Share of Profit	Sum to Partner
A	$20,000	60	$ 9,000	$29,000
B	10,000	30	4,500	14,500
C	—	10	1,500	1,500
Total	$30,000	100	$15,000	$45,000

2. A, B, C, and D are partners and have agreed to share *profits* in the ratio of 25, 25, 30, and 20 per cent, respectively. No agreement has been made on how *losses* will be shared, so losses will be borne in the same proportion. A contributes $6,000 to the capital; B, $3,000; C, $1,000; and D, his skill. The partnership is dissolved. Creditors are owed $35,000. There is $5,000 in assets, all in cash. There have been no withdrawals of profits or capital.

The assets are insufficient to pay the creditors, let alone to return any capital. The balance sheet may be drawn up as follows:

ASSETS		LIABILITIES	
Cash	$ 5,000	Due Creditors	$35,000
(Loss)	40,000	Capital	10,000
Total	$45,000		$45,000

Or it may be drawn up this way:

ASSETS		LIABILITIES		
Cash	$ 5,000	Due Creditors		$35,000
		Net Worth		
		Capital	$10,000	
		Loss	40,000	
		Negative Net Worth		30,000
Total	$ 5,000			$ 5,000

The liabilities to creditors will be adjusted as follows:

Partner	Capital	Loss Ratio, %	Share of Loss	Additional Contribution
A	$ 6,000	25	$10,000	$ 4,000
B	3,000	25	10,000	7,000
C	1,000	30	12,000	11,000
D	—	20	8,000	8,000
Total	$10,000	100	$40,000	$30,000

The $5,000 in cash plus the $30,000 in additional contributions will go to the creditors.

3. A, B, C, and D are partners and have agreed to share *profits* equally but to share losses in the ratio of 10, 20, 30, and 40 per cent, respectively. A contributes $10,000 to the capital; B, $5,000; C, $5,000; and D, his skill. When the partnership is dissolved, creditors are owed $30,000, and assets consist of $10,000 in cash. There have been no withdrawals by the partners. The balance sheet may be drawn up in either of the following ways:

ASSETS		LIABILITIES	
Cash	$10,000	Due Creditors	$30,000
Loss	40,000	Capital	20,000
Total	$50,000	Total	$50,000

ASSETS		LIABILITIES		
Cash	$10,000	Due Creditors		$30,000
		Net Worth		
		Capital	$20,000	
		Loss	40,000	
		Negative Net Worth		20,000
Total	$10,000			$10,000

ADJUSTMENT OF LIABILITIES

Partner	Capital	Loss Ratio, %	Share of Loss	Additional Contribution	Refund
A	$10,000	10	$ 4,000	—	$6,000
B	5,000	20	8,000	$ 3,000	—
C	5,000	30	12,000	7,000	—
D	—	40	16,000	16,000	—
Total	$20,000	100	$40,000	$26,000	$6,000

DISTRIBUTION OF FUNDS

Available		How Distributed	
Cash	$10,000	To Creditors	$30,000
Additional Contributions	$26,000	To A	6,000
Total	$36,000	Total	$36,000

SUMMARY OF THE LAW OF PARTNERSHIPS

Partnerships in General

A partnership is an association of two or more persons (called partners) to carry on a business for profit. The partnership relation is created by voluntary agreement of the parties; this agreement may be expressly stated or implied from the circumstances. Co-ownership of the business and the sharing of management responsibilities afford some evidence of the existence of a partnership, but a more important test is whether the parties share profits. Distribution of profits in the payment of debts, wages, rents, or similar obligations is not considered evidence of the existence of a partnership.

Although a partnership is usually composed of two or more natural persons, it is legally possible for a partnership, corporation, or other type of association to act as a partner. A minor who becomes a partner may later elect to withdraw, in which case the authorities disagree on whether or not he is entitled to the return of his entire capital contribution.

Partnership by Estoppel

A person who is represented to be a partner in a firm and does nothing to dispel that impression is liable as a partner by estoppel to any innocent third party who relies on the representation in dealing with that firm. If the representation is made without his consent, some courts hold that he has no duty to repudiate it; others require him to disclaim his reputed connection with the firm or else risk being held liable by estoppel.

Firm Name

Generally speaking, a partnership may do business under any name it chooses. The name may consist of one or more of the partners' names, or it may be wholly fictitious. However, one firm cannot adopt the name of another; nor can it adopt a name so similar to that of another as to cause confusion. Nor can it use phrases such as "and Son" if the designation is false or misleading. In addition, most states require a firm with a fictitious name to register the names and addresses of the partners at a public place.

Partnership Property

Since an individual partner may take his personal property with him if he withdraws from the firm or if the firm is dissolved, it is important to decide whether the property used in a firm's business is partnership property or the personal property of a partner or of some other person or firm. As a general rule, the courts will accept the agreement of the partners as decisive in determining what is and what is not partnership property. In the absence of any express agreement, the courts will examine the conduct of the parties and the circumstances of the case in deciding the question. Mere use of property by a partnership does not necessarily make it partnership property, since a partner or a third person may lend or lease property to the partnership while retaining ownership.

Good Will

Often included under partnership property is the good will of the firm— i.e., the reputation it has built up in the community and its expectation of continued patronage by the public. Good will is often carried as an asset on the firm's balance sheet and must be accounted for on dissolution.

Anyone who purchases a firm's business along with its good will may advertise himself as the successor of the old firm. The courts disagree, however, on whether a purchaser may use the name of the old firm. The courts also split on whether the seller of a business with its good will may start a new business of the same character and solicit his old customers.

Partnership Capital

Partnership capital is the permanent investment that the partners make in the business. It may be in the form of money, property, or services. Capital is carried on the firm's books as an obligation to the partners and will be returned to them before profits and losses are computed. It is usual, but not necessary, for a person to invest capital in the firm in order to become a partner. In addition, it is possible for a partner to lend money to a partnership and not have it treated as a capital investment.

Title to Property

Generally speaking, *personal* property may be acquired, held, and disposed of in the partnership name or in the name of one or more of the partners acting as agent for the firm. Authorities disagree, however, on whether a partnership has the right to hold title to *real* property in its firm name. States following the common law, which does not regard a partnership as a separate legal entity, insist that title to real property be held by one or more of the individual partners. Other states, including those that have enacted the Uniform Partnership Act, permit partnerships to acquire and hold real property in the firm name alone.

Nature of Partner's Interest

As co-owner of partnership property, each partner generally has the right to use that property in carrying on the business of the firm; he does not have the right to use it for any other purpose, unless the other partners agree. When one partner dies or withdraws, his right to use the partnership property passes to the remaining partners.

A partner's interest in the partnership itself consists of his right to share in the profits, and, on dissolution, his right to retrieve his capital contribution and share in the distribution of any profits.

Fiduciary Relationship of Partners

The close relationship between partners requires mutual good faith and trust. A partner's first duty is to his co-partners, and he must direct his best efforts toward advancing the firm's business. A partner may not use his firm association or any of the firm property to secure a personal gain which is not shared with his copartners. A partner may, however, do business with the firm as a separate individual if he does so without taking an unfair advantage of his association with the firm.

Partner's Right to Information and Accounting

Each partner has a duty to inform his copartners of all matters relating to the firm's business. Moreover, unless otherwise agreed, all partners are entitled to inspect the firm's books and records.

On dissolution, each partner is entitled to a full and formal accounting to determine his share of the profits or losses. While the firm is still in operation, the courts will not usually order an accounting except in the following cases: (1) where a partner is denied access to the firm's records; (2) where a partner refuses to account for profits he has made from a transaction involving the firm; and (3) where the firm is on the verge of insolvency and action must be taken quickly to prevent further losses.

Partner's Right to Manage Business

Many partnership agreements spell out in detail how the business is to be run and may provide that one or more partners will have the exclusive right to manage it. The fact that a partner has invested in the firm does not entitle him to participate in its management if the agreement denies him that right. In the absence of a specific agreement, all partners are entitled to share equally in management and all decisions must be made by majority vote. If the partners find it impossible to decide management questions in such cases, the firm must be dissolved.

Sharing of Profits and Losses

Unless agreed to the contrary, all partners, regardless of their capital investment, share equally in profits and make equal contributions to losses. The partners may, however, agree to divide profits and losses in any proportion they see fit. If the agreement specifies how profits are to be shared but is silent on losses, any losses will be shared in the same proportion as profits.

Partner's Right to Compensation and Reimbursement

Unless otherwise agreed, each partner's remuneration is limited to his share of the firm's profits; he is not entitled to additional compensation for his services even though he renders more valuable services than his copartners. Nor is a partner entitled to receive interest on his capital contribution unless there is a specific agreement on that point. On the other hand, if a partner makes a loan to the firm, he is entitled to interest on it just as if he were a third party.

A partner who incurs a personal liability while acting for the partnership, or personally discharges a debt or obligation of the firm, or incurs expenses while conducting firm business, is entitled to be reimbursed by the partnership.

Partner's Authority to Act for Firm

Generally speaking, each partner is an agent of the firm and has authority to make contracts and enter into transactions on its behalf. The partnership is bound by the acts of each partner just as any principal is bound by the acts of an authorized agent; it may ratify the unauthorized acts of a partner according to the general rules of agency law.

In addition to his actual authority, a partner has apparent authority to bind the firm to any act or transaction that comes within the usual business of the firm, unless he actually has no authority and the person with whom he is dealing is aware of that fact. On the other hand, if the act or transaction does not come within the usual business of the firm, the firm is not bound unless the partner was actually authorized by the other members of the partnership.

The following acts and transactions are usually held to be within the usual business of the firm and, thus, within the apparent authority of a partner: (1) the power to borrow money and execute negotiable instruments, provided the firm is a trading partnership; (2) the power to compromise claims, pay firm debts, and receive payments due the firm; (3) the power to buy and sell personal property normally used or sold in the firm's business (this does not apply to real property unless the firm is actually engaged in the real estate business); (4) the power to hire and fire employees to carry on the firm's business; (5) the power to make any contract that appears to be necessary for the transaction of firm business; (6) the power to receive notice for the firm concerning any matter that falls within the scope of its business.

The following acts and transactions are usually considered to be outside the normal business of the firm and, thus, not within the apparent authority of a partner: (1) the power to assign partnership property in trust for creditors; (2) the power to dispose of the good will of the business; (3) the power to confess judgment against the firm; (4) the power to submit a partnership claim to arbitration; (5) the power to do any act that would make it impossible for the firm to carry on its business; (6) the power to guarantee the payment of another party's debt—unless the firm is actually engaged in that business; and (7) the power to give away firm property, except a reasonable amount to charity.

A partnership, like any other principal, is liable for the torts of a partner if they are committed while the partner is acting within the scope of the firm's usual business.

Dissolution of Partnership

Dissolution occurs when the partners cease to do business together. It may be brought about (1) by an act of the partners, (2) by operation of law, or (3) by court decree.

As a general rule, on dissolution, each partner loses all authority to act as an agent for the firm, except in settling the affairs of the firm and winding up its business. However, the law recognizes certain exceptions to this rule where other partners or third persons have not received notice of the dissolution.

If a partnership is dissolved by an act of one of the partners, or by his death or bankruptcy, the other partners retain authority to bind the firm until they have been notified of the circumstances.

When dissolution is caused by the act of a partner, notice must be given to third parties. Until they receive such notice, any contracts they make with a partner within the scope of the firm's usual business are binding on the firm. Persons who have previously dealt with the firm must be given actual notice. For those who have not done business with the partnership before, notice by publication is sufficient.

Winding Up the Partnership Affairs

Following dissolution, each partner's authority is limited to winding up the firm's affairs; no partner has authority to bind the partnership to new obligations. As a general rule, each partner is entitled to participate in the winding-up process unless it was his misconduct that caused the firm to dissolve. When dissolution is caused by the death of a partner, the surviving partners must wind up the firm's affairs and make an accounting to the estate of the deceased partner.

Distribution of Assets on Termination

If a partnership is insolvent on dissolution, the partners are personally responsible for assuming the firm's losses and for paying its creditors. If a conflict arises between personal creditors of the partners and creditors of the firm, the rule is that firm creditors have first claim on partnership assets and that personal creditors have first claim on the individual assets of the partners. If firm creditors are not paid in full out of partnership assets, they may seek payment from the individual assets of the partners, but only after the personal creditors have been paid.

After partnership creditors have been paid, the remaining assets, if any, are distributed as follows: (1) loans that a partner has made to the firm are repaid to him; (2) capital contributions are then returned to each partner; (3) any remaining assets are distributed to the partners as profits, in proportions according to their agreement or, if no agreement was made, in equal proportions.

Supplementary Reading: Partnerships

A good text on partnership law is Judson A. Crane, *Handbook of the Law of Partnership* (West Publishing Co., 1938). For cases and other supplementary materials, see Eugene A. Gilmore, *Cases on the Law of Partnership,* 3rd Ed. (West Publishing Co., 1949) or Reuschlein, *Cases on Partnership and Unincorporated Business* (West Publishing Co., 1952). The important statute in this area is *The Uniform Partnership Act.*

16 Corporations

Introduction

The corporation is the most important form of business organization. Recent statistics released by the United States Department of Commerce show that corporations do over 90 per cent of all the business carried on by manufacturing establishments. Moreover, the 12 per cent of retail establishments that are incorporated (most of the others are sole proprietorships) account for roughly one-half of all the retail business done.

The popularity of the corporate device is understandable, for it has many attractive features. First, and perhaps most important, is the concept of limited liability. This means, in effect, that a stockholder is not personally responsible for the debts of a corporation except to the extent of his original investment in purchasing his shares of stock. (You will recall that a partner usually has unlimited personal liability for the partnership's obligations over and above his capital contribution.) Second, the corporate form is often the only vehicle, outside of government, capable of raising sufficient capital to launch and carry on large-scale enterprises. The corporation can sell stock to large numbers of people who are willing to invest not only because of the limited liability they will incur but because they know that they can transfer their interest whenever they choose. Third, a stockholder can invest in a corporation without taking any active role in its management. Finally, the corporation is a permanent form of organization that continues to exist as a legal entity despite the death of its stockholders or the transfer of their interest.

The extensive use of the corporate device is a comparatively recent development. Up to the middle of the sixteenth century it was rarely used except by nonprofit organizations such as schools, churches, and charitable institutions. The first large business corporations in England were the foreign trading companies formed during the great period of exploration and colonization in the sixteenth and seventeenth centuries. Created by royal charter or by special act of Parliament, these corporations were granted the privilege of exploring and trading with certain lands across the sea. Among them were the Russia Company, chartered in 1555; the East India Company, chartered in 1600; the Africa Company, chartered in 1619; the Hudson's

Bay Company, chartered in 1670; and the South Sea Company, chartered in 1711.

During the seventeenth and eighteenth centuries, another forerunner of the modern business corporation appeared on the scene—the unincorporated joint stock company. These companies were created merely by agreement among the interested parties. Although they issued transferable shares of stock, their shareholders were subject to unlimited liability for corporate debts; in this respect these companies resembled partnerships. Despite this unlimited liability, there was a great deal of investment and speculation in the shares of joint stock companies throughout the eighteenth and the early part of the nineteenth century. In 1844, Parliament enacted the Joint Stock Companies Registration Act, requiring joint stock companies to incorporate and file formal registration papers. Although certain corporate privileges (e.g., the right to sue and be sued as a legal entity) were granted by this act, the members of such companies were still subject to unlimited personal liability. Moreover, the rapid rise of economic activity during this period prompted more and more businessmen to press for legislation that would permit them to form companies with limited liability for shareholders.

In response to this demand, Parliament passed the Limited Liability Act of 1855, which limited the liability of members of joint stock companies to the amount they paid for their shares. The act also required that the word "Limited" be used after the company name, so that anyone dealing with the company would be on notice that its members were not personally responsible for its obligations.

In this country, somewhat similar developments were taking place during this period. Up to the end of the eighteenth century, the formation of a corporation was a privilege that was granted only by royal charter or by a special act of the legislature. Starting in the early part of the nineteenth century, the need for such special authorization was gradually eliminated by the enactment of so-called general incorporation laws which permitted any and all applicants to incorporate their businesses with limited liability, provided they complied with certain statutory requirements. The first law of this sort was passed in New York in 1811.

Although these early laws permitted corporations to be *formed* freely, they often imposed severe restrictions on corporate size and activity. Many observers were suspicious of the corporate device because they feared that too great a concentration of private wealth in such organizations was a dangerous thing. Even so, a movement sprang up in several states to liberalize and relax the statutory restrictions. In the latter part of the nineteenth century, New Jersey and Delaware took the lead by passing legislation that removed many of the limitations on the size and powers of business corporations and that permitted them to hold stock in other corporations. Following the enactment of these laws, businessmen hastened to incorporate their companies in New Jersey and Delaware to take advantage of their liberal provisions. Soon other states were obliged to relax their own requirements, until now few state restrictions on corporate size and activity survive.

Debate over the position of the corporation in our modern society persists, however. Stockholders, particularly in the larger corporations, play little part in management and have very little sense of responsibility for the manner in which corporate business is conducted. One authority has commented that shareholding no longer constitutes ownership but merely "a form of passive absentee profit sharing."

The great concentration of economic power in big corporations has also provoked comment. Mr. Justice Brandeis, in his dissent in the case of *Louis K. Liggett Co. v. Lee*, 288 U.S. 517, makes these comments:

> Able, discerning scholars have pictured for us the economic and social results of thus removing all limitations upon the size and activities of business corporations and of vesting in their managers vast powers once exercised by stockholders—results not designed by the states and long unsuspected. They show that size alone gives to giant corporations a social significance not attached ordinarily to smaller units of private enterprise. Through size, corporations, once merely an efficient tool employed by individuals in the conduct of private business, have become an institution—an institution which has brought such concentration of economic power that so-called private corporations are sometimes able to dominate the state.
>
> . . . In the United States the process of absorption has already advanced so far that perhaps two-thirds of our industrial wealth has passed from individual possession to the ownership of large corporations whose shares are dealt in on the stock exchange; that 200 nonbanking corporations, each with assets in excess of $90,000,000 control directly about one-fourth of all our national wealth, and that their influence extends far beyond the assets under their direct control; that these 200 corporations, while nominally controlled by about 2,000 directors, are actually dominated by a few hundred persons—the negation of industrial democracy. . . .

It is evident from our discussion that much of our corporation law is found in the various state statutes which control the formation of corporations and the exercise of corporate powers. Although most of these laws conform to a general pattern, there has been little uniformity of legislation among the states.

Despite the multiplicity of state legislation, however, many aspects of corporate law are not governed by statute. Decisional lawmaking still plays an important role. Moreover, since most of the larger corporations operate in interstate commerce, federal statutes and clauses in the federal Constitution are of considerable significance in corporation law. Some of these federal problems will be discussed in this chapter; others will be reserved for the final chapter, "Government Regulation of Business."

SECTION 1

NATURE AND CREATION OF CORPORATIONS

Characteristics of Corporations

The Corporation as a Separate Legal Entity

A corporation is an artificial legal being separate from the people who create and manage it. As a separate and distinct entity, it may buy and sell property, may sue and be sued, and, generally, may deal with others in its own name. Furthermore, it continues to exist despite changes in its membership.

> EXAMPLE
>
> X, Y, and Z form a corporation called "Sputnik, Inc." The three founders hold the stock and they alone manage the company's affairs. Nevertheless, since the corporation is a separate entity, all its property is held and all its contracts are made in the corporate name. X, as an individual, may make a contract with "Sputnik, Inc.," or may even bring suit against it. If Y sells his stock to A, the corporation continues to exist, with X, Z, and A as its stockholders.

A corporation is often referred to as a legal "person," and as such it is entitled to some of the constitutional protections that are afforded to natural persons. For example, the provision of the federal Constitution that prohibits the national and state governments from depriving any "person" of life, liberty, or property without due process of law applies to corporations as well as to private persons. And the Fourteenth Amendment's provision that the states may not deny to any "person" the equal protection of the laws has been construed to guarantee equality of treatment to corporations. A corporation, as a "person," is subject to criminal laws and must pay income taxes as an entity separate from its stockholders. As a practical matter, of course, a corporation cannot be a legal "person" in every sense: it cannot vote, nor can it be imprisoned for violating a criminal law. Nor does it have the constitutional right of a natural person to do business wherever it chooses.

In the United States Supreme Court case that follows, Justice Black, in a dissenting opinion, discusses the concept of the corporation as a "person" and seriously questions the interpretation which the Court has given to the

Fourteenth Amendment. His review of the historical background of the amendment is particularly interesting.

CONNECTICUT GENERAL LIFE INSURANCE CO. v. JOHNSON

Supreme Court of the United States, 1938
303 U.S. 77, 58 S.Ct. 436

▶ MR. JUSTICE STONE delivered the opinion of the Court.

Appellant is a Connecticut corporation, admitted to do an insurance business in California. In addition to its business conducted within that state it has entered into contracts with other insurance corporations likewise licensed to do business in California, reinsuring them against loss on policies of life insurance effected by them in California and issued to residents there. These reinsurance contracts were entered into in Connecticut where the premiums were paid and where the losses, if any, were payable. The question for decision is whether a tax laid by California on the receipt by appellant in Connecticut of the reinsurance premiums during the years 1930 and 1931, infringes the due process clause of the Fourteenth Amendment. . . .

All that appellant did in effecting the reinsurance was done without the state and for its transaction no privilege or license by California was needful. The tax cannot be sustained either as laid on property, business done, or transactions carried on within the state, or as a tax on a privilege granted by the state.

Reversed.

MR. JUSTICE BLACK (dissenting).

I do not believe that this California corporate franchise tax has been proved beyond all reasonable doubt to be in violation of the Federal Constitution and I believe that the judgment of the Supreme Court of California should be affirmed. Traditionally, states have been empowered to grant or deny foreign corporations the right to do business within their borders and "may exclude them arbitrarily or impose such conditions as (they) will upon their engaging in business within (their) jurisdiction." . . .

But it is contended that the due process clause of the Fourteenth Amendment prohibits California from determining what terms and conditions should be imposed upon this Connecticut corporation to promote the welfare of the people of California.

I do not believe the word "person" in the Fourteenth Amendment includes corporations. The doctrine of *stare decisis*, however appropriate and even necessary at times, has only a limited application in the field of constitutional law. This Court has many times changed its interpretations of the Constitution when the conclusion was reached that an improper construction has been adopted. Only recently the case of West Coast Hotel Company v. Parrish, 300 U.S. 379, 57 S.Ct. 578, 81 L.Ed. 703, 108 A.L.R. 1330, expressly overruled a previous interpretation of the Fourteenth Amendment which had long blocked state minimum wage legislation. When a statute is declared by this Court to be unconstitutional, the decision until reversed stands as a barrier against the adoption of similar legislation. A constitutional interpretation that is wrong should not stand. I believe this Court should now overrule previous decisions which interpreted the Fourteenth Amendment to include corporations.

Neither the history nor the language of the Fourteenth Amendment justifies the belief that corporations are included within its protection. The historical purpose of the Fourteenth Amendment was clearly set forth, when first considered by this Court in the Slaughter House Cases, 16 Wall. 36, 21 L.Ed. 394, decided April, 1873—less than five years after the proclamation of its adoption. Mr. Justice Miller, speaking for the Court said:

> "Among the first acts of legislation adopted by several of the States in the legislative bodies which claimed to be in their normal relations with the Federal government, were laws which imposed upon the colored race onerous disabilities and burdens, and curtailed their rights in the pursuit of life, liberty, and property to such an extent that their freedom was of little value, while they had lost the protection which they had received from their former owners from motives both of interest and humanity. . . .
>
> "These circumstances, whatever falsehood or misconception may have been mingled with their presentation, forced . . . the conviction that something more was necessary in the way of constitutional protection to the unfortunate race who had suffered so much. (Congressional leaders) accordingly passed through Congress the proposition for the fourteenth amendment, and . . . declined to treat as restored to their full participation in the government of the Union the States which had been in insurrection, until they ratified that article by a formal vote of their legislative bodies." 16 Wall. 36, at page 70, 21 L.Ed., 394.

Certainly, when the Fourteenth Amendment was submitted for approval, the people were not told that the states of the South were to be denied their normal relationship with the Federal Government unless they ratified an amendment granting new and revolutionary rights to corporations. This Court, when the Slaughter House Cases were decided in 1873, had apparently discovered no such purpose. The records of the time can be searched in vain for evidence that this amendment was adopted for the benefit of corporations. It is true that in 1882, twelve years after its adoption, and ten years after the Slaughter House Cases, *supra*, an argument was made in this Court that a journal of the joint Congressional Committee which framed the amendment, secret and undisclosed up to that date, indicated the committee's desire to protect corporations by the use of the word "person." Four years later, in 1886, this Court in the case of Santa Clara County v. Southern Pacific Railroad, 118 U.S. 394, 6 S.Ct. 1132, 30 L.Ed., 118, decided for the first time that the word "person" in the amendment did in some instances include corporations. A secret purpose on the part of the members of the committee, even if such be the fact, however, would not be sufficient to justify any such construction. The history of the amendment proves that the people were told that its purpose was to protect weak and helpless human beings and were not told that it was intended to remove corporations in any fashion from the control of state governments. The Fourteenth

Amendment followed the freedom of a race from slavery. Justice Swayne said in the Slaughter House Cases, *supra,* that: "By any 'person' was meant all persons within the jurisdiction of the State. No distinction is intimated on account of race or color." Corporations have neither race nor color. He knew the amendment was intended to protect the life, liberty, and property of human beings.

The language of the amendment itself does not support the theory that it was passed for the benefit of corporations.

The first clause of section 1 of the amendment reads: "All persons born or naturalized in the United States, and subject to the jurisdiction thereof, are citizens of the United States." While efforts have been made to persuade this Court to allow corporations to claim the protection of this clause, these efforts have not been successful.

The next clause of the second sentence reads: "Nor shall any State deprive any person of life, liberty, or property, without due process of law." It has not been decided that this clause prohibits a state from depriving a corporation of "life." This Court has expressly held that "the liberty guaranteed by the 14th Amendment against deprivation without due process of law is the liberty of natural, not artificial persons." Thus, the words "life" and "liberty" do not apply to corporations, and of course they could not have been so intended to apply. However, the decisions of this Court which the majority follow hold that corporations are included in this clause in so far as the word "property" is concerned. In other words, this clause is construed to mean as follows:

"Nor shall any State deprive any human being of life, liberty or property without due process of law; nor shall any State deprive any corporation of property without due process of law."

The last clause of this second sentence of section 1 reads: "Nor deny to any person within its jurisdiction the equal protection of the laws." As used here, "person" has been construed to include corporations.

Both Congress and the people were familiar with the meaning of the word "corporation" at the time the Fourteenth Amendment was submitted and adopted. The judicial inclusion of the word "corporation" in the Fourteenth Amendment has had a revolutionary effect on our form of government. The states did not adopt the amendment with knowledge of its sweeping meaning under its present construction. No section of the amendment gave notice to the people that, if adopted, it would subject every state law and municipal ordinance affecting corporations (and all administrative actions under them) to censorship of the United States courts. No word in all this amendment gave any hint that its adoption would deprive the states of their long-recognized power to regulate corporations.

The second section of the amendment informed the people that representatives would be apportioned among the several states "according to their respective numbers, counting the whole number of persons in each State, excluding Indians not taxed." No citizen could gather the impression here that while the word "persons" in the second section applied to human beings, the word "persons" in the first section in some instances applied to corporations. Section 3 of the amendment said that "no person shall be a Senator or Representative in Congress," who "engaged in insurrection." There was no intimation here that the word "person" in the first section in some instances included corporations.

This amendment sought to prevent discrimination by the states against classes or races. We are aware of this from words spoken in this Court within five years after its adoption, when the people and the courts were personally familiar with the historical background of the amendment. "We doubt very much whether any action of a State not directed by way of discrimination against the negroes as a class, or on account of their race, will ever be held to come within the purview of this provision." Yet, of the cases in this Court, in which the Fourteenth Amendment was applied during the first fifty years after its adoption, less than one-half of 1 per cent invoked it in protection of the negro race, and more than 50 per cent asked that its benefits be extended to corporations.

If the people of this nation wish to deprive the states of their sovereign rights to determine what is a fair and just tax upon corporations doing a purely local business within their own state boundaries, there is a way provided by the Constitution to accomplish this purpose. That way does not lie along the course of judicial amendment to that fundamental charter. An amendment having that purpose could be submitted by Congress as provided by the Constitution. I do not believe that the Fourteenth Amendment had that purpose, nor that the people believed it had that purpose, nor that it should be construed as having that purpose.

I believe the judgment of the Supreme Court of California should be sustained.   ◄

COMMENTS AND QUESTIONS

1. What was the decision of the majority of the Court?
2. Summarize the arguments given by Justice Black in support of his dissenting opinion.
3. Do you think the framers of the Fourteenth Amendment, or the members of Congress, had corporations in mind when they drafted and passed the amendment? If not, is there any justification for the Court's interpretation?
4. Corporations are organized, financed, and managed by natural persons. Couldn't one argue that if a corporation is deprived of property without due process of law, the stockholders are the real losers and should be entitled to protection?
5. Note the statement by Justice Black that the doctrine of *stare decisis* "has only a limited application in the field of constitutional law." Do you agree?

Wrongful Use of Corporate Entity

The courts take the separate legal identity of corporations quite literally; rarely will they try to look behind it, even though all or most of the stock of a given corporation is held by one person with absolute control over its operations. Occasionally, however, when the corporate entity is used to perpetrate a fraud, or to avoid a legal obligation, or to gain an unjust advantage, the entity is disregarded and the "corporate veil is pierced." Then the individual members are held responsible as if no corporation existed.

EXAMPLE

s sells his grocery store to B, agreeing, as part of the contract, not to compete with B in the same neighborhood for five years. s forms a corporation called "Better Food, Inc." and opens a store in the same area two years later. B may sue s for breach of contract. s may not defend on the theory that it is the corporation, not s as an individual, that is competing with B. The courts will hold s personally liable on the ground that he has wrongfully used the corporate device to avoid his legal obligation to B.

An interesting illustration of this rule occurs in the following New Jersey case, in which it was alleged that a husband had used the corporate device to defraud his wife.

TELIS v. TELIS et al.

Court of Errors and Appeals of New Jersey, 1942
132 N.J. Eq. 25, 26 A. 2d 249

► Suit by Sophie Telis against Jacob Telis and Telise's Bargain Store to attach an inchoate right of dower [1] to real estate held by corporate defendant. From an adverse decree, complainant appeals.

Reversed and remanded.

PERSKIE, JUSTICE. The question for decision in this cause, between husband and wife, is whether the Advisory Master erred in advising a decree dismissing that part of the wife's bill which sought to attach an inchoate right of dower to certain real estate, legal title to which was in a corporation formed by the husband for the alleged purpose of defrauding the wife and depriving her of her right of dower in and to the realty.

The bill of complaint filed by the wife sets forth two causes of action. The first cause of action was for support and maintenance. After hearing, an order was entered directing the payment by the husband of $15 a week to the wife. This order is not here challenged.

The second cause of action was predicated upon allegations that the husband caused real estate located at 223 South Connecticut Avenue, in Atlantic City, to be purchased in the name of a corporation owned and wholly controlled by him, solely for the purpose of defrauding his wife of her dower right in and to that real estate. Although at the hearing the husband offered to convey the property to his wife, he apparently suffered a change of heart and refused to carry out his promise. The Advisory Master then advised a decree dismissing this cause of action upon the ground that the proofs failed to disclose that any fraud was perpetrated. The wife has appealed from this decree.

Notwithstanding that there is considerable dispute over the legal effect of the proofs the basic facts are, in the main, uncontradicted. The parties were married in New York in 1921. Two children were born of the marriage,

---

[1] This refers to a wife's interest in land owned by her husband during his life. On his death, a wife's dower right entitles her to a share of his land regardless of the provisions of his will. "Dower," which provides for a widow, is to be distinguished from "dowry," which refers to a gift of property to a bride on her marriage.

a boy now nineteen years old and a girl now twelve years of age. The former is an invalid as a result of paralysis. Shortly after the marriage, the husband commenced periodically to disappear, on several occasions, taking European trips. The husband deserted his wife in New York in 1933 and did not reappear until April of 1937 when he called upon her to take her to Atlantic City to show her a store he was operating there. During the interval of his desertion, he failed to provide for his wife and children. From 1937, he contributed $40 a month for their support during winter months. In the summer months they lived in one room, provided by the husband, in a rooming house in Atlantic City. They largely depended for sustenance, raiment and medical care upon the efforts of the wife and the charity of her friends and relatives.

On March 20, 1939, the husband formed a corporation called Telise's Bargain Store and thereafter operated his business under the corporate name. The certificate of incorporation was filed in the county clerk's office on March 22, 1939 but it does not appear when, if ever, the certificate was filed with the Secretary of State. One hundred shares of stock were purportedly issued, 98 to the husband, one to his son and one retained by the husband, respondent herein. Approximately eight months later, on November 6, 1939, the corporation entered into an agreement to purchase the aforesaid property, and on December 29, 1939 a deed to this property was delivered to the corporation. The purchase price was $4,000 of which sum respondent paid in cash $1,331.41, the balance, exclusive of settlement charges, being secured by a purchase money mortgage apparently executed by the corporation. It is against this property in the name of "Telise's Bargain Store" that the wife sought to attach her inchoate right of dower. It appears that the corporation is about to sell this property but the parties have stipulated that in the event of sale the proceeds will be left in escrow pending the outcome of this appeal. . . .

Notwithstanding all of this, we are of the mind that the relief sought should be granted upon the ground that respondent is in fact the owner of the realty and, therefore, his wife is entitled to her inchoate right of dower therein. For the wife is not only entitled to dower in real estate held to the use of her husband but also in real estate the husband himself was seized of during coverture. N.J.S.A. 3:37-1. If under the dower act a wife's dower right may be secured against one who holds to the use of her husband in reason and justice she should, and we hold that she is entitled to the same relief when, as here, the husband factually is the owner of the real estate, irrespective of the corporate form employed to veil that ownership.

The right of our courts, in a proper case, to pierce the corporate veil can not be gainsaid. The common exercise of that right does not trench upon the general principle that "a corporation is not an individual even if the individual owned all the stock of the corporation." . . . Nor does it trench upon the established principle that the legality of the existence of a *de facto* corporation [2] may be attacked only by the state in a direct proceeding, by

---

[2] *De facto* corporations will be discussed in detail later in this section. In brief, they are corporations which are defectively formed but are recognized as corporations "in fact" if not "in law."

information in the nature of *quo warranto* proceedings. . . .[3] Rather is the common exercise of the right to pierce the corporate veil deeply and firmly rooted in the principle that our courts do not permit the doctrine of corporate entity to be used for the purpose of defeating justice.

The proofs in the case at bar clearly satisfy us that the corporation was never perfected: Respondent held all of the stock notwithstanding that the two shares were in the name of others; the respondent and not Telise's Bargain Store, the corporation, owns the real estate; there never was a formal meeting; no by-laws were ever adopted and corporate funds were intermingled with respondent's funds and used in payment of respondent's personal obligations. Form and not substance was effected. These and all other circumstances in the case entirely convince us that the corporate creation was, and its existence is, a mere sham, a mere subterfuge, a mere instrumentality employed for concealing the truth and, therefore, in the equitable sense, fraudulent.

The denial of the wife's statutory right of dower, under the circumstances of the case at bar, defeated the relief to which she was justly entitled and, therefore, can not be permitted. She is entitled to have her statutory right of dower in and to the premises in question secured to her. We so hold. . . .

The decree is reversed with costs.   ◄

COMMENTS AND QUESTIONS

1. What was the decision of the lower court? What happened on appeal?
2. Summarize the reasons given for the court's decision.
3. Note the court's reference to an offer by the husband at the hearing to convey the property to his wife and his subsequent "change of heart." Do you think this evidence should have been considered by the court in deciding the merits of the case?

Classification of Corporations

Corporations may be classified in several different ways. First, they may be classified as private or public. A *private corporation* is organized by private persons to serve a private interest. A *public corporation* is established for governmental purposes—many cities and towns, for example, are incorporated. Second, corporations may be classified according to their basic purposes: some are organized for *profit*, while others, such as religious and educational institutions, are formed for *charitable* or *nonprofit* purposes. Finally, corporations may be classified on the basis of whether or not they issue stock. A corporation that issues stock and is owned by shareholders is called a *stock* corporation. One that does not issue stock is referred to as a *nonstock* corporation. In our discussion, we will deal almost exclusively with private, profit, stock corporations.

---

[3] This refers to a legal action by the state to test the legality of a corporation's existence or the exercise of certain powers. Two examples occur later in this chapter, in the cases of *People v. Ford* and *Commonwealth of Pennsylvania v. Philadelphia Electric Co.*

Creation of Corporations

Procedure for Incorporation

Every state has incorporation statutes prescribing the steps that must be taken in order to form a corporation. Although there is some variation from state to state, the general pattern is much the same everywhere.

Generally speaking, three or more persons of legal capacity (called the *incorporators*) who are citizens of the United States may form a corporation and be granted a charter. First, they must sign and file an application reciting (1) the names and addresses of the incorporators; (2) the name of the proposed corporation; (3) the object or purpose of the corporation; (4) its anticipated duration; (5) the location of its principal office; (6) the amount of authorized capital stock, the number and type of shares to be issued, and the value and voting rights, if any, of each type of stock; (7) the names and addresses of subscribers to the capital stock;[4] and (8) the amount of capital stock to be issued at the inception of the corporation and whether it is to be paid for in cash or property.

The application, together with a filing fee, is then delivered to the appropriate state official (e.g., the secretary of state or the commissioner of corporations), who reviews it to see if all statutory requirements have been met. If they have, he then issues a *charter*, or *certificate of incorporation*, which outlines the powers and privileges of the corporation and the purposes for which it has been formed. In most states, a copy of the charter must be filed in the local recording office where the corporation is to have its principal place of business.

After the charter has been issued and recorded, the incorporators must hold an organization meeting to elect the board of directors (if they have not already been named in the charter), adopt the bylaws (the internal rules) of the corporation, and elect the officers of the corporation. At this same meeting, the basic operating procedures of the corporation are usually formulated and the corporate books and records are opened.

In most states, the corporation legally comes into existence as soon as the charter has been issued. In some states, however, corporate life does not commence until the organization meeting has been held, and, in a few states, not until a report of the organization meeting has been filed with the proper authority.

A corporate charter is regarded as a binding contract; it may not be repealed or altered by the state unless the state has expressly reserved the right to do so. The charter may, however, be amended by the stockholders of the corporation.

De Jure and De Facto Corporations

A corporation that has met all the requirements of incorporation law is ascribed legal existence and is known as a *corporation de jure*.

In some cases, however, a corporation fails to comply with one or more

---

[4] Capital stock will be discussed in detail in Section 3 of this chapter. Briefly, the term refers to the total amount of stock issued by the corporation.

of the statutory provisions; then a question arises as to status of the corporation. If the defect is trivial and of no consequence, it will be ignored and a *de jure* corporation is assumed to exist. But if the noncompliance is substantial, there can be no legal corporation in the true sense. Even then, however, if certain circumstances are present, the courts will recognize the organization as a corporation in fact if not in law. The necessary conditions for the existence of a so-called *de facto corporation* are: (1) a valid law authorizing the formation of such a corporation; (2) a good-faith effort to organize the corporation and to comply with all the requirements of the corporation law; and (3) some use or exercise of corporate power by the corporation. If these tests are met, the *de facto* corporation has all the powers, rights, and privileges of a *de jure* corporation, except that its existence may be challenged by the state authorities. But if the state takes no action to dissolve the corporation or to force compliance with the law, no third party may avoid his contracts with the corporation on the ground that it was improperly formed.

EXAMPLES

1. The signature of one of the incorporators on the application for a charter has not been notarized, as required by law in most states. The charter has nevertheless been issued and the corporation commences business operations. There is little doubt that the firm will be considered a corporation *de jure*, since the defect is trivial and of no major consequence.
2. Three persons make a good-faith effort to form a corporation and actually manage to secure a charter. None of the three incorporators, however, is a citizen of the state of incorporation (as is sometimes required). Moreover, they neglect to fill in the location of the principal business office in their application. When such a corporation comes into existence and starts to do business, it may be considered a *de facto* corporation, having all the rights of a legal corporation but subject to challenge by the state. The defects of incorporation are so substantial that no *de jure* corporation can be recognized. Yet the corporation may be recognized in fact, if not in law.

In the case that follows, the state of Illinois challenged the legality of a corporation on the ground that the statutory requirements had not been complied with.

PEOPLE v. FORD

Supreme Court of Illinois, 1920
293 Ill. 319, 128 N.E. 479

▶ Information in the nature of *quo warranto* by the People against E. E. Ford and others, to determine the legality of the organization of a corporation. From a judgment dismissing the information, after overruling a demurrer to the plea, the People appeal. Affirmed.

DUNN, J.   The Fifty-First General Assembly passed an act in relation to corporations for pecuniary profit, known as the General Corporation Act, which was approved on June 28, and became effective July 1, 1919. Laws of 1919, p. 316. Section 4 provides that—

> "Whenever three or more adult persons, citizens of the United States of America, at least one of whom shall be a citizen of this state, shall desire to form a corporation under this act, they shall sign, seal and acknowledge before some officer, competent to take acknowledgment of deeds, a statement of incorporation setting forth the following: [Here follow thirteen paragraphs stating the facts to be contained in the statement.]"

The section closes with the sentence that—

> "Such statement shall be filed in duplicate in the office of the secretary of state on forms prescribed and furnished by the secretary of state."

Section 5 provides that—

> "Upon the filing of such statement, the secretary of state shall examine the same, and if it is in conformity with the provisions of this act, he shall indorse thereon the word 'Filed' followed by the month, day and year of such filing. Upon such filing the corporation shall be deemed fully organized and may proceed to business."

On September 5, 1919, a certificate of incorporation of the Washer Maid Company was filed in duplicate in the office of the secretary of state. The Attorney General afterward, by leave of the court, filed in the circuit court of Cook county an information in the nature of *quo warranto* against E. E. Ford, A. J. Fisher, and C. R. Gilbert, charging them with having unlawfully usurped, intruded into, held and executed the office of directors of a pretended corporation known as the Washer Maid Company, under color of a void and illegal certificate of incorporation, and calling upon them to show by what warrant they exercised such privileges.

The respondents filed a plea showing the various steps taken for the organization of the corporation, setting forth *in haec verba* [5] the statement filed by them, alleging that it was made on forms prescribed and furnished by the secretary of state, which were executed and acknowledged by the respondents, and that the respondents had in all respects complied with the requirements of the General Corporation Act. The Attorney General demurred and for special cause of demurrer showed that the respondents in their statement of incorporation did not sign, seal and acknowledge the same, but, on the contrary failed to seal the same or to affix their seals to said statement of incorporation, as required by the General Corporation Act. The statement set forth in the plea shows the signatures of the respondents as follows:

> E. E. Ford,
> A. J. Fisher,   Incorporators.
> Charles R. Gilbert,

---

[5] In the same words. That is, the respondents quoted their statement exactly as they had filed it.

The word "seal" does not appear, nor are there any letters, scrawl, or marks which might be regarded as seal, unless it is the bracket which joins the names, and neither the statement itself nor the certificate of acknowledgment contains any reference to a seal. The court overruled the demurrer, and the Attorney General electing to stand by it, the information was dismissed. An appeal was taken, and at the June term the cause was submitted, with a request by both parties for an early decision because of the public importance of the question involved. . . .

The question presented was whether the requirement that the incorporators shall seal the statement is mandatory or directory. It was argued on behalf of the People that the requirement of the seal is a condition precedent to the legal existence of a corporation. A somewhat similar question arose early in the history of the state in the case of Cross v. Pinckneyville Mill Co., 17 Ill. 54. The act of 1849, to authorize the formation of corporations for manufacturing, agricultural, mining or mechanical purposes, provided that any three or more persons desiring to form a company for such purpose should make, sign and acknowledge, and file "in the office of the clerk in the county in which the business of the company should be carried on and a duplicate thereof in the office of the secretary of state, a certificate in writing," in which should be stated the name of the company and other facts mentioned in the statute. It was further provided that when the certificate should have been filed as aforesaid the persons who should have signed and acknowledged, and their successors, should be a body politic and corporate. In the case mentioned the duplicate certificate of organization had not been filed in the office of the secretary of state, but the court held that fact unimportant to defeat the organization or rights growing out of it: that there is a well settled distinction between mandatory and directory provisions, and that carrying out of the true intention of the Legislature and effectuating the object of the law would not be promoted by strict technical constructions, converting every direction and detail of power into a mandatory prerequisite of corporate existence.

More recently a question arose as to the effect of the failure to mail notices of the meeting of subscribers of the capital stock to elect officers, as required by section 3 of the Corporation Act of 1872 (Laws 1871-72, p. 296). We said:

> "The statute prescribes a certain course to be pursued in organizing a corporation in this state. It does not necessarily follow, however, that any departure from that course will prevent a corporation from becoming one *de jure*. Whether or not such departure will have that effect depends upon the nature of the provision which is violated. If it is a mandatory provision, a failure to substantially comply with its terms will prevent the corporation from becoming one *de jure;* but if the provision is merely directory, then a departure therefrom will not have that consequence."

It was held that it was immaterial whether or not notice had been given in the manner directed by the statute; the persons entitled to notice having waived it and actually attended the meeting, so that the purpose of the statute in requiring the notices to be given was accomplished. Butler Paper

Co. v. Cleveland, 220 Ill. 128, 77 N.E. 99, 110 Am. St. Rep. 230. . . .

The requirement of a seal in the execution of documents by individuals has become a mere formality. It means nothing. Private seals no longer exist as a means of execution of specialties, for even an individual scrawl is not required. In most deeds the word "seal" is printed on the blank form which is used, and the grantor does not know whether he has used a seal or not. It depends upon whether the word was printed on the paper or not. The solemnity of the sealed instrument is purely Pickwickian and no longer represents an idea. While courts of law in this state cannot disregard the legal quality of the sealed instrument, courts of equity frequently relieve parties from the difficulties arising from the application of the rigid rules of the common law to such instruments.

We may look to the intention of the statute in determining the effect of an omission to add the seal. The purpose is to make a public record of the corporation, the definition of its powers, the amount of its stock, the names of its stockholders, its location, and other facts in connection with it, which are of interest to the public to know, and of the state in its supervision over corporations to be acquainted with. The addition of a seal is of no importance for these purposes. It is not of the essence of the thing to be done, and no prejudice can result from its omission. The essential act of making the statement, though not in the precise manner indicated, accomplished the substantial purpose of the statute, and that is sufficient. It would not be carrying out the intention of the Legislature to hold that the addition of a scrawl by the signers of the statement is mandatory and its omission invalidates the incorporation.

For these reasons the judgment of the circuit court was affirmed.

Judgment affirmed.

FARMER, J. (dissenting). The Legislature saw fit to require the statement to be under seal. Whether this was an important requirement or not, the Legislature had the power to, and did make it. Courts cannot disregard it, on the ground that it was a useless requirement, or that the Legislature did not mean what it said.   ◀

COMMENTS AND QUESTIONS

1. Note the pleadings that were filed in the lower court. The Attorney General demurred to the defendants' answer. How was the case decided?
2. Note the court's reference to similar cases in the past. Explain the distinction between "mandatory and directory provisions," as outlined by the court.
3. One wonders why the State of Illinois took the time and trouble to challenge the legality of the corporation on this point; other circumstances may have been present that were not mentioned in the opinion.
4. Note the strict construction of the statute by the dissenting judge.

Seriously Defective Corporations

If the failure to comply with the laws governing the formation of corporations is substantial, no corporation is formed either in law or in fact. The persons who organize such a firm and hold themselves out as a corporation are usually treated as if they were partners personally liable for the obligations of the firm.

The rule of partnership liability is not always applied to seriously defective corporations, however. When a third person deals with the organization as if it were a corporation, on the assumption of corporate liability, several states have held that he is estopped from denying later on that a corporation exists. In other words, he is not permitted to hold the organizers or shareholders personally liable as partners after he has once dealt with the firm as a corporation.

EXAMPLES

1. X, Y, and Z organize and start a business which they call "XYZ DELIVERY SERVICES, INC." They apply for a charter but fail to fill out the application properly. No charter is issued. Nevertheless, they go ahead and start operations. Subsequently, A, a pedestrian, is struck and injured by one of the company's trucks. Since no corporation has ever existed, A may sue X, Y, or Z as partners and hold one or more of them individually liable for his injuries.

2. This time, B, a truck dealer, enters into a contract with the "XYZ DELIVERY SERVICE, INC." in which he agrees to sell a truck to the "corporation" for a given price. Even though he subsequently learns that no corporation exists, he may be estopped to hold X, Y, and Z liable as partners, since he originally dealt with the organization as a corporation.

The following case presents a good illustration of the application of the rules we have just discussed.

HARRILL v. DAVIS
Circuit Court of Appeals of the United States
 Eighth Circuit, 1909
 168 F. 187

► In error to the United States Court of Appeals in the Indian Territory. . . .

SANBORN, CIRCUIT JUDGE. The patent and indisputable facts in this case are that the four defendants associated themselves together, and from June, 1902, until December 22, 1902, actively engaged in purchasing lumber, material, and labor of the plaintiff, and in constructing a cotton gin under the name "The Coweta Gin Company," and in conducting the business of buying, selling and ginning cotton for profit under the name "The Coweta Cotton & Milling Company," and that during this time they incurred more than $4,700 of the indebtedness of $5,145.48 for which this action was brought. On December 22, 1902, they made their first real attempt to incorporate, and for the first time took on the color or appearance of a corporation. On that day they filed articles of incorporation with the clerk of the Court of Appeals, but they never filed any duplicate of them with the clerk of the judicial district in which their place of business was located, as required by the statutes in order to constitute them a legal corporation and to authorize them to do business as such. Act Feb. 18, 1901, c. 379, 31 Stat. 794; Mansfield's Dig. Laws Ark. 960, 968, 979.

The general rule is that parties who associate themselves together and actively engage in business for profit under any name are liable as partners for the debts they incur under that name. It is an exception to this rule that such associates may escape individual liability for such debts by a compliance with incorporation laws or by a real attempt to comply with them which gives the color of a legal corporation, and by the user of the franchise of such a corporation in the honest belief that it is duly incorporated. When the fact appears, as it does in the case at bar, by indisputable evidence that parties associated and knowingly incurred liabilities under a given name, the legal presumption is that they are governed by the general rule, and the burden is upon them to prove that they fall under some exception to it. . . . [Citing cases.] But in every one of these authorities articles of incorporation had been filed under a general enabling act, or a charter had been issued and there had been a user of the franchise of the supposed corporation which had been colorably created by the filing of the articles or the issue of the charter before the indebtedness in question was created, while nothing of this nature had been done before the debt for the $4,700 which we are now considering was incurred. The authorities which have been recited rest upon the proposition that where parties procure a charter or file articles of association under a general law, thereby secure the color of a legal incorporation, believe that they are a corporation, and use the supposed franchise of the corporation in good faith, and third parties deal with them as a corporation, they become a corporation *de facto* and exempt from individual liability to such third parties, although there are unknown defects in the proceedings for their incorporation. The statement of Morawetz on Corporations, at section 748, upon which counsel seem to rely, that:

> "If an association assumes to enter into a contract in a corporate capacity, and the party dealing with the association contracts with it as if it were a corporation, the individual members of the association cannot be charged as parties to the contract, either severally or jointly, or as partners. This is equally true whether the association was in fact a corporation or not, and whether the contract with the association in its corporate capacity was authorized by the Legislature or prohibited by law, or illegal."

—is too broad to be sound. Parties who actively engage in business for profit under the name and pretense of a corporation which they know neither exists nor has any color of existence may not escape individual liability because strangers are led by their pretense to contract with their pretended entity as a corporation. In such cases they act as the agents of a principal that they know does not exist, and they are liable under a familiar rule, because there is no responsible principal. . . . The burden is not on the strangers who deal with them as a corporation but on themselves who act under the name of a pretended corporation, to see that it is so organized that it exempts them from individual liability, and if they fail in this they must pay the liabilities they incur, even in the absence of fraud or bad faith, upon the salutary principle that where one of two parties must suffer he must bear the loss whose breach of duty caused it.

There are cases in which stockholders who took no active part in the business of a pretended corporation which was acting without any charter or filed articles, who supposed that the corporation was duly organized, have been held exempt from individual liability for the debts incurred; but if they had been actively conducting its business with knowledge of its lack of incorporation, those decisions must have been otherwise. . . .

Neither the hope, the belief, nor the statement by parties that they are incorporated nor the signing of articles of incorporation which are not filed, where filing is requisite to create the corporation, nor the user of the pretended franchise of such a nonexistent corporation, will constitute such a corporation *de facto* as will exempt those who actively and knowingly use its name to incur obligations from their individual liability to pay them. Color of legal organization as a corporation under some charter or law and user of the supposed corporate franchise in good faith are indispensable to such exemption.

Under the general law of Arkansas in force in the Indian Territory, the filing of articles of incorporation with the clerk of the Court of Appeals was a *sine qua non* of any color of a legal corporation. Without that there was not, and there could not be, an apparent corporation or the color of a corporation. Agreements to form one, statements that there was one, signed articles of association to make one, acts as one, created no color of incorporation, because there could be no incorporation or color of it under the law until the articles were filed. . . . In Finnegan v. Norenber, . . . Chief Justice Gilfilian well said:

> "To give to a body of men assuming to act as a corporation, where there has been no attempt to comply with the provisions of any law authorizing them to become such, the status of a *de facto* corporation, might open the door to frauds upon the public. It would certainly be impolitic to permit a number of men to have the status of a corporation to any extent, merely because there is a law under which they might have become incorporated, and they have agreed among themselves to act, and they have acted, as a corporation. That was the condition in Johnson v. Corser, 34 Minn. 355, 25, N.W. 799, in which it was held that what had been done was ineffectual to limit the individual liability of the associates. They had not gone far enough to become a *de facto* corporation. They had merely signed articles, but had not attempted to give them publicity by filing for record, which the statute required."

The defendants cannot escape individual liability for the $4,700 on the ground that the Coweta Cotton & Milling Company was a corporation *de facto* when that portion of the plaintiff's claim was incurred because it then had no color of incorporation, and they knew it and yet actively used its name to incur the obligation. . . .

Counsel insist that the defendants are not liable here because one who deals with a corporation *de facto* is estopped from denying its existence as a corporation; but the true meaning and legal effect of this rule is that such a dealer is estopped from denying its existence on the ground that it was not legally incorporated. One who deals with parties who masquerade under a name which represents no corporation *de facto* is no more estopped from denying that it is a corporation than he would be from denying that they constituted or acted for the Union Pacific Railroad Company, or any other well known corporation, when they did not. The fact that the plaintiff dealt with and treated the Coweta Cotton & Milling Company as a corporation did not estop it from denying that it was such before the defendants filed their articles of incorporation, because it was not a corporation *de facto* before that time and because the indispensable elements of an estoppel *in pais,*[6] ignorance of the truth and absence of equal means of knowledge of it by the party who claims the estoppel, and action by the latter induced by the misrepresentation of the party against whom the estoppel is invoked, do not exist in the case at bar. Bigelow on Estoppel (4th Ed.) p. 679. The plaintiffs did not, and the defendants did, represent that the milling company was a corporation when it was not. The defendants had better means of knowledge of the fact than the plaintiff, and they knew it was not a corporation, and they were not induced to act on any representation of the plaintiff that it was such, or by its treatment of it as such.

Nor was the plaintiff estopped by the fact that its general manager stated under oath in its claim for lien in May, 1903, that the milling company was a corporation, first, because the defendants were not induced to take any action by this statement from which they can suffer any injury by the proof of the truth, and, second, because one is not estopped from pursuing his true legal remedy by a mistaken attempt to pursue a supposed remedy that does not exist. . . .

It is said that the plaintiff is estopped from denying the existence of the defendants' supposed corporation because it was one of its promoters and stockholders, but the evidence fails to convince us that it was ever either. . . .

And our conclusion is that the defendants never became a corporation *de facto* prior to December 22, 1902, that they never became a corporation *de jure,* that the indebtedness here in question was not incurred under any promise or assurance of the defendants as promoters that it should become the obligation of a corporation to be formed, that a large part of it was incurred in the conduct of a general commercial business, and not to prepare for the commencement of such a business or for the organization of a corporation, and that the trial court below should have instructed the jury that the defendants were individually liable for that portion of the plaintiff's claim which was incurred prior to December 22, 1902. Its failure to do so was a fatal error which necessitates a reversal of the judgments below. . . .

The judgments of the courts below must be reversed, and the case must be remanded to the proper court for a new trial; and it is so ordered.   ◄

COMMENTS AND QUESTIONS

1. During the period up to December 22, 1902, was "The Coweta Gin Company" a corporation *de jure, de facto,* or neither? After that date, what was it? Summarize the reasons for the court's decision here.

---

[6] "In pais" means without legal proceedings.

2. How did the court deal with the defendants' argument that the plaintiff dealt with them as a corporation and therefore should be estopped to deny the existence of the corporation?

Promoters

Ordinarily a great deal of preliminary work must be done before a corporation formally comes into existence. Contracts must be made with banks, brokers, and suppliers; advertising must be prepared; the necessary papers must be filled out; and a host of other things must be attended to, depending on the nature and size of the enterprise. These activities are usually carried out by *promoters*.

Is a corporation liable for the pre-incorporation contracts of its promoters? Generally speaking, a promoter has no authority to bind the corporation to carry out such contracts even though he purports to be acting on its behalf. Once the corporation has actually come into existence, it is free to "adopt" or reject the contracts made by promoters. This process of adoption should not be confused with the ratification by a principal of a contract made by an agent, since the corporation does not even exist as a principal when the promoter makes contracts on its behalf. By adopting a promoter's contract, either expressly or impliedly, the corporation becomes bound by it. Unless the third party discharges the promoter by agreeing to a novation (see page 308), however, the promoter also remains personally liable. To avoid this result, promoters often include a provision in the contracts exempting themselves from personal liability.

> EXAMPLE
>
> P, a promoter, purporting to act for an organization called "Good Food, Inc.," which is about to be incorporated, enters into a two-year lease with L for a grocery store. P is personally liable on the lease. If "Good Food, Inc.," after incorporation, decides not to be bound by the lease, P alone is liable to L for damages. If the corporation assumes the obligations of the lease, however, it becomes bound together with P. L may agree to release P and substitute "Good Food, Inc." as the contracting party; then a novation occurs and P has no further liability. To protect himself, P could include a provision in the lease absolving him from liability if the contract is not adopted by the corporation.

As a general rule, a corporation is not required to reimburse a promoter for his expenses and services unless it agrees to do so after the corporation has formally come into existence. Some states, however, hold that a corporation is liable to the promoter for any expenses that were actually necessary to bring the corporation into existence, regardless of whether it chooses to pay for them.

A promoter occupies a position of trust with respect to the corporation he is helping to form. He may not use that position to win for himself any benefit or advantage at the expense of the shareholders. If he violates this fiduciary duty, he must account to the corporation for any profit he derives.

The main issue in the following case was whether a corporation had adopted a contract made by its promoters. The opinion contains a good discussion of the rules we have just outlined.

McARTHUR v. TIMES PRINTING CO.

Supreme Court of Minnesota, 1892
48 Minn. 319, 51 N.W. 216

▶ MITCHELL, J. The complaint alleges that about October 1, 1889, the defendant contracted with plaintiff for his services as advertising solicitor for one year; that in April, 1890, it discharged him, in violation of the contract. The action is to recover damages for the breach of the contract. The answer sets up two defenses: (1) That plaintiff's employment was not for any stated time, but only from week to week; (2) that he was discharged for good cause. Upon the trial there was evidence reasonably tending to prove that in September, 1889, one C. A. Nimocks and others were engaged as promoters in procuring the organization of the defendant company to publish a newspaper, that about September 12th, Nimocks, as such promoter, made a contract with plaintiff in behalf of the contemplated company, for his services as advertising solicitor for the period of one year from and after October 1st,—the date at which it was expected that the company would be organized; that the corporation was not, in fact organized until October 16th, but that the publication of the paper was commenced by the promoters October 1st, at which date plaintiff, in pursuance of his arrangement with Nimocks, entered upon the discharge of his duties as advertising solicitor for the paper; that after the organization of the company he continued in his employment in the same capacity until discharged, the following April; that defendant's board of directors never took any formal action with reference to the contract made in its behalf by Nimocks, but all of the stockholders, directors, and officers of the corporation knew of this contract at the time of its organization, or were informed of it soon afterwards, and none of them objected to or repudiated it, but, on the contrary retained plaintiff in the employment of the company without any other or new contract as to his services.

There is a line of cases which hold that where a contract is made in behalf of, and for the benefit of, a projected corporation, the corporation, after its organization, cannot become a party to the contract, either by adoption or ratification of it. . . . This, however, seems to be more a question of name than of substance; that is, whether the liability of the corporation, in such cases, is to be placed on the ground of its adoption of the contract of its promoters, or upon some other ground, such as equitable estoppel. This court, in accordance with what we deem sound reason, as well as the weight of authority, has held that, while a corporation is not bound by engagements made on its behalf by its promoters before its organization, it may, after its organization, make such engagements its own contracts. And this it may do precisely as it might make similar original contracts; formal action of its board of directors being necessary only where it would be necessary in the case of a similar original contract. That it is not requisite that such adoption or acceptance be expressed, but it may be inferred from acts or acquiescence on the part of the corporation, or its authorized agents, as any similar original contract might be shown. . . . The right of the corporate agents to adopt an agreement originally made by promoters depends upon the purposes of the corporation and the nature of the agreement. Of course, the agreement must be one which the corporation itself could make, and one which the usual agents of the company have express or implied authority to make. That the contract in this case was of that kind is very clear; and the acts and acquiescence of the corporate officers, after the organization of the company, fully justified the jury in finding that it had adopted it as its own.

The defendant, however, claims that the contract was void under the statute of frauds, because "by its terms, not to be performed within one year from the making thereof," which counsel assumes to be September 12th,—the date of the agreement between plaintiff and the promoter. This proceeds upon the erroneous theory that the act of the corporation, in such cases, is a ratification, which relates back to the date of the contract with the promoter, under the familiar maxim that "a subsequent ratification has a retroactive effect, and is equivalent to a prior command." But the liability of the corporation, under such circumstances, does not rest upon any principle of the law of agency, but upon the immediate and voluntary act of the company. Although the acts of a corporation with reference to the contracts made by promoters in its behalf before its organization are frequently loosely termed "ratification" yet a "ratification," properly so called, implies an existing person, on whose behalf the contract might have been made at the time. There cannot, in law, be a ratification of a contract which could not have been made binding on the ratifier at the time it was made, because the ratifier was not then in existence. . . . What is called "adoption," in such cases, is in legal effect, the making of a contract of the date of the adoption, and not as of some former date. The contract in this case was, therefore, not within the statute of frauds. The trial court fairly submitted to the jury all the issues of fact in this case, accompanied by instructions as to the law which were exactly in the line of the views we have expressed; and the evidence justified the verdict.

The point is made that plaintiff should have alleged that the contract was made with Nimocks, and subsequently adopted by the defendant. If we are correct in what we have said as to the legal effect of the adoption of the corporation of a contract made by a promoter in its behalf before its organization, the plaintiff properly pleaded the contract as having been made with the defendant. But we do not find that the evidence was objected to on the ground of variance between it and the complaint. The assignments of error are very numerous, but what has been already said covers all that are entitled to any special notice.

Order affirmed.   ◀

COMMENTS AND QUESTIONS

1. Summarize the decision of the court and the legal rules offered in support of that decision.
2. How did the court deal with the defendant's contention that the agreement was void and unenforceable under the Statute of Frauds?

SECTION 2

CORPORATE POWERS

Express Powers

The express powers of a corporation are usually set forth in its charter. In making out an application for a charter, the incorporators commonly describe the powers they wish in very broad language, in order not to hamper the company's operations later on. So long as the powers requested do not exceed those permitted by statute and do not conflict with the state or federal Constitution, they are usually granted as a matter of course.

Implied Powers

In addition to the powers expressly granted in the charter, a corporation also possesses certain implied powers that are necessary for carrying out the purposes for which it was organized. The following case illustrates this point.

> COMMONWEALTH OF PENNSYLVANIA et rel. THOMAS J.
> BALDRIDGE, Attorney General v. THE PHILADELPHIA
> ELECTRIC COMPANY
>
> Court of Common Pleas of Pennsylvania, Philadelphia County, 1929
> 18 Pa. Corp. Rep. 243; affirmed, 300 Pa. 557, 151 A. 344

▶ BY THE COURT, June 7, 1929:

This case was tried by the Court without a jury.

It is a *quo warranto* [7] proceeding wherein the suggestion is made that the respondent, The Philadelphia Electric Company, has exercised powers and franchises that are not within the latter's corporate powers. The Attorney General permitted the use of the name of the Commonwealth.

Findings of Fact

From the pleadings and the proofs we find the facts to be as follows:

1. The respondent, The Philadelphia Electric Company, is a corporation incorporated under the laws of the Commonwealth of Pennsylvania on

---

[7] Literally, "by what warrant." This is a proceeding in which the defendant is asked to show by what authority he exercises certain powers. In this particular case, the defendant corporation's right to sell electrical appliances was challenged by the state.

October 27, 1902, for the purpose of "supplying light, heat and power by electricity to the public in the city and county of Philadelphia, and to such persons, partnerships and corporations residing therein or adjacent thereto as may desire the same."

2. Electricity is a commodity which can only be used through the medium of some sort of an appliance and before it can be successfully sold prospective customers must necessarily be supplied with appliances which in one form or another consume electricity.

3. During the entire period of its corporate existence it has been the practice of the respondent in common with practically all other electric light, heat and power companies throughout the Commonwealth, to merchandise and sell electrical appliances as a part and branch of its business incidental to the development of its business generally, and this practice of respondent and others has always been considered to be an important and essential incident to the continued growth and success of respondent's main corporate purpose of supplying electricity to the public.

4. The appliances so merchandised and sold by the respondent include, *inter alia*, such devices as vacuum cleaners, washing machines, electric refrigerators, curling irons, heaters, sewing machines, hair dryers, heating pads, bread mixers, percolators, toasters, grills, waffle irons, dish washers, ranges, fans and radios.

5. Respondent added electrical refrigerators to its general line of appliances more than eleven years ago, and until the commencement of the present proceeding the Commonwealth never questioned respondent's corporate right to do so.

6. Respondent has eleven branch offices or places of business in its territory where these appliances are demonstrated and offered for sale in connection with the business of selling electric current at these branch offices.

7. These safe appliances, including specifically electric refrigerators, are also being continually and generally sold throughout the respondent's territory by the manufacturers thereof, as well as by department and other stores in direct competition with respondent.

8. It has been found that the efforts of the respondent in popularizing and demonstrating these appliances has resulted in a considerable benefit to other distributors and dealers in such appliances.

9. The volume of merchandising business thus done by respondent itself amounts to approximately only five per cent of respondent's entire business, and the volume of respondent's business in the sale of electric refrigerators amounts to approximately only one per cent of its said entire business.

10. The primary object of respondent in merchandising electrical appliances is to stimulate in every proper way a demand for the use and consumption of electric current which in turn promotes the respondent's business generally by increasing the sale of such current.

11. An increase in the respondent's sales of electric current is a distinct advantage to the customer because in its final effect such increase produces and makes possible a lower energy cost rate to the customer.

12. One of the duties of respondent, essential to its continued success in business, is to maintain a thoroughly satisfactory service to its customers and the nature of the commodity sold is such that this involves from a practical standpoint the maintenance in good condition of the appliances on its lines.

13. This present action was initiated by the Attorney General only after the filing with him of a petition for the institution of same by Merchant & Evans Company, a private corporation engaged in the business of manufacturing and selling a certain kind of electric refrigerator which is not one of the kinds sold by respondent.

Discussion

The plaintiff correctly states the general propositions of law which govern the case: A Pennsylvania corporation cannot engage in any business except that expressly authorized by its charter, and has no powers except those which are necessary to enable it to carry out an express grant. . . .

This being the conceded rule, the problem we face is the interpretation of the respondent's grant.

This was: That it be incorporated "for the purpose of supplying heat, light and power by electricity to the public."

This grant was made in 1902, and the phrase used was no doubt intended to include, in a general way, all of the conveniences that could be produced by the use of the electric current. The relator's objections do not raise any question arising out of any particular use, but they dispute the right of the respondent to do anything more than supply electric current, and particularly they dispute its right to engage in merchandising the devices needed for converting electricity.

This interpretation, however, runs counter to the express language of the grant, which is not a power to "supply electricity," but certain things produced by electricity. Far from preventing the Company from dealing in the converting devices needed, it would be our inclination to insist that it is part of its duty to furnish them to its customers. It is unimportant whether the converting device is supplied separately, by means of a sale or a billing and a charge specially made for it, or whether the bill rendered the customer for the service includes also the use of the converting device.

A grant very similar to the one before us was passed upon by the Supreme Court in the case of Malone v. The Lancaster Gas Light Company, 182 Pa. 309, 37, A. 932. The company in that case, as the name indicates, was a gas company. There is a close analogy between the supply of heat, light and power by electricity and their supply by means of gas. Both gas and electricity are useless until they are converted into some form of activity, and for this in both cases mechanical devices are needed. In Malone v. The Lancaster Gas Light Company, the grant was "for the purpose of manufacturing and supplying illuminating and heating gas." Plaintiff's counsel is not correct in his brief in saying that the company in the case cited "was chartered to supply light and heat." The power was to supply gas. If the Lancaster Company had been chartered to supply light and heat by means of gas, the analogy of the two charters would be complete.

Yet notwithstanding the fact that the express words of the Lancaster grant were only "to supply gas," the Supreme Court held that it "might not only supply gas itself, but may also incidentally deal in such appliances and conveniences as will induce new customers to use gas or old ones to use more." "It is argued for plaintiff," said Mr. Justice Mitchell, "that the charter purpose of the gas company is limited by the words 'manufacturing and supplying illuminating and heating gas,' and that nothing can be included which it (*sic*) not a necessary part or appliance for manufacturing or supplying. This is too narrow and literal a construction, and overlooks the fundamental object of the corporation, the manufacture and supply of gas to customers for profit. It would be no use to manufacture gas if there were not customers to buy, and hence the company may fairly supply not only the gas itself, but incidentally such appliances as will induce new customers to use gas, and old customers to use more."

It is plain that the instant case is much stronger for the respondent than the case cited, because in the latter the power was to "supply gas," while here it is to supply certain conveniences "by means of electricity." As we have pointed out, this must include the supply of any device that will be needed to turn electricity into the convenience desired.

It is not wandering too far afield to point out, and it appears in the proofs, that in 1902 the industry in which the respondent was and still is engaged was comparatively new. The public had not been educated with regard to the multitude of conveniences which the electric current will supply. To furnish the housekeeper with electric current alone would have resulted in neither profit to the company nor convenience to the customer. What the latter wanted, and what the Legislature intended to grant when it authorized the respondent to furnish light, heat and power by electricity, was something more than furnishing the customer with the end of an insulated copper wire, that he did not know how to use, or had not the appliances to use. It was intended that he should have and the company should furnish the conveniences that could be obtained by the use of the electric current.

For these reasons we come to the following

Conclusions of Law

1. The sale by respondent of electrical refrigerators and other electrical appliances is in furtherance of its main corporate purpose of "supplying light, heat, and power by electricity to the public," in the territory covered by respondent's charter.
2. *A verdict and judgment thereon should be entered in favor of the respondent.*   ◄

COMMENTS AND QUESTIONS

1. Note the formal organization of this opinion. What were the issues and how were they resolved by the court?
2. Paragraph 13 of the findings of fact indicates that the prime mover behind the state's petition was a competing appliance corporation. Do you think this fact influenced the court's decision? Is it material evidence?

Powers That Are Usually Implied

A corporation ordinarily possesses the following implied powers, which are deemed essential to the carrying on of corporate activities:

Power to Adopt Corporate Name

Generally speaking, a corporation may adopt any name it wishes, provided it is not the same as that of another firm or so similar as to deceive or confuse the public. Many states require that the name conclude with some such term as "Corporation," "Company," "Incorporated," "Inc.," or "Limited," to indicate the corporate nature of the firm.

Power to Adopt Bylaws

Most corporations have the implied power to adopt their own bylaws for the internal management of their affairs. These rules outline the powers, duties, and authority of the company officers and directors; they are binding on the stockholders unless they conflict with the charter or with state statutes.

Power to Acquire and Hold Property

Most charters expressly authorize the acquisition and holding of any real or personal property needed for corporate business. Even if this power is not granted expressly, it is implied. If the property is not to be used for authorized company business, however, its acquisition is restricted.

EXAMPLE

A corporation organized to run a chain of department stores has the implied power to purchase real estate for store sites, but it has no power to acquire real estate for resale or speculation.

Power to Acquire Stock in Other Corporations

As a general rule, a corporation may acquire and hold the stock of other corporations so long as the acquisition of that stock helps to further its own operations and does not change the basic purposes of the corporation. If the stock acquired amounts to a controlling interest, the corporation must be able to show that the acquisition is reasonably necessary to co-ordinate and further its own operations—as, for example, when a subsidiary is formed by a parent corporation. On the other hand, acquisitions whose main objective is to eliminate competition are often prohibited by the antitrust laws, as we shall see in the next chapter.

The case that follows presents an interesting illustration of the power of a corporation to purchase another corporation's stock.

JOSEPH BANCROFT & SONS CO. v. BLOEDE

Circuit Court of Appeals, Fourth Circuit, 1901
106 Fed. 396

► On September 21, 1889, Joseph Bancroft & Sons Company (hereinafter called "Bancroft Company") was incorporated under the laws of Delaware and became successor to the business of the partnership of Joseph Bancroft & Sons.

The object of the corporation was:—"the manufacturing, bleaching, dyeing and finishing of cotton and other fabrics, and every other business incident thereto or that may be combined therewith." The capital stock was fixed at $1,000,000, of which at least $500,000 was to be paid in before commencing business.

From 1874 to 1895, Victor G. Bloede, a chemist, had been in close relations with the business and had been consulting chemist of both the partnership and the corporation. He was also, on his individual account, engaged at Baltimore in the manufacture of dyes, pulp colors, finishing oils, and chemicals, in which he used secret formulae and processes of his own invention. The corporation became a large purchaser and user of dyes, colors, oil and chemicals, manufactured by Bloede.

In 1893, Bloede incorporated his business as Victor G. Bloede Company (hereinafter called "Bloede Company") under the laws of Maryland. He was largely if not wholly influenced to do so by the persuasion of the Bancroft interests. The Bloede Company had an authorized capital stock of $150,000, of the par value of $100 per share, of which $100,000 in par value or 1,000 shares were then issued. Bloede transferred his entire business assets, the formulae and processes used therein, to the Bloede Company, in payment for $99,400 par value or 994 shares of its capital stock.

Between May 5, 1893, and July 13, 1893, the following transactions took place:—

(a) On May 5, 1893, a meeting of shareholders of Bancroft Company authorized its board of directors to issue 475 shares of its capital stock of $47,500 par value, in exchange for a like number of shares of equal par value of the then proposed Bloede Company.

(b) On July 13, 1893, the board of directors of Bancroft Company adopted a resolution, which, after reciting the above shareholders' action and the incorporation of the Bloede Company, provided:

> "Be it Resolved:—First, that the president and treasurer of the Joseph Bancroft & Sons Company be, and they are hereby, authorized to issue and certify 474 shares of this company to Victor G. Bloede, to be exchanged with him for certificates of the same number of shares of the said Victor G. Bloede Company and report the same to this board after said exchange is executed; it being mutually agreed and understood between Victor G. Bloede and this company that these 474 shares will not participate in, or be entitled to any interest in the next dividend to be declared out of the earnings of this company, being No. 14, of 4 per cent., but to participate in, and be entitled to all dividends subsequent to No. 14, of 4 per cent., aforesaid."

(c) Pursuant thereto on July 13, 1893, 474 shares of Bancroft Company, as an original issue, were issued to Bloede, and Bloede transferred to Bancroft Company 474 shares of Bloede Company.

At or about the same time, some undisclosed form of arrangement was made between the two corporations by which Bloede Company should not sell colors and materials manufactured by it to anyone other than Bancroft Company for any purpose which in the judgment of the latter Company, would conflict with its interests.

Dissatisfaction arose with the intercompany arrangement, with the result that, in January 1895, Bancroft Company refused payment of further dividends on the above 474 shares of its capital stock held by Bloede, and he brought an action against it in the Baltimore City Court, *inter alia,* to recover the dividends declared by Bancroft Company, claimed to accrue to him on said 474 shares.

The case was removed to the United States Circuit Court for the District of Maryland, where it was tried without a jury. The Bancroft Company set up as its defense that the issue to Bloede of said 474 shares was *ultra vires* and void. The Circuit Court gave judgment for Bloede. A writ of error was issued, and assignments of error filed by Bancroft Company.

SIMONTON, C. J. . . . Two questions arise under these assignments of error: First, Was the issue of its paid-up stock by the Bancroft Company in purchase of or exchange for stock held by Victor G. Bloede in the Bloede Company *ultra vires?* Second, Was the circuit court in error in admitting testimony tending to show the relations between the Bancroft Company and Bloede, and the importance and necessity to the Bancroft Company of the dyes, colors and various specialties used in the production of cotton fabrics, and transferred by Bloede to the Bloede Company?

Was the issue of its paid-up stock by the Bancroft Company in purchase of or exchange for the stock held by Bloede in the Bloede Company *ultra vires?* There can be no doubt that a corporation, instituted for a specific purpose, such as banking, cannot deal in stocks—purchase them for investment or speculation. . . . And, unless there is express power given in its charter to do so, a corporation cannot purchase the stock of other corporations for the purpose of controlling their management. . . . But the purchase of stock by a corporation in other corporations, such purchase being incidental to its business, is not unlawful. . . . Indeed, the rule may be expressed more generally. A corporation can exercise no power or authority which is not granted to it by the charter under which it exists, or by some other act of the legislature to which it owes its charter. . . . To determine, therefore, the powers of this Delaware corporation, we must look to its charter and, as it was incorporated under a general law, we must take notice of the documents recorded or filed upon its application for a charter, upon which, as authorized and controlled by the general law, depend the existence of the corporation, the extent of its corporate powers, its capacity to act as a corporation. . . .

The Joseph Bancroft & Sons Company was incorporated in 1889, under the provisions of the general act of 1883. Its business, as set out in its application, was "the manufacturing, bleaching, dyeing, and finishing of cotton and other fabrics, and any other business incident thereto or that may be combined therewith." Under its charter, the directors could purchase mines, manufactories, or other property necessary for their business, and issue paid-up stock therefor. The directors, under express instructions of the stockholders, purchased shares of stock in the Bloede Company. Was this property necessary for their business,—the manufacturing, bleaching, dyeing, and finishing of cotton or other fabrics, and any other business incident thereto or that may be combined therewith?

That shares of stock are property goes without saying. They are bought, sold, taxed, bequeathed, and distributed as any other property may be. Was this property necessary for the business of the Joseph Bancroft & Sons Company? This is a question depending upon circumstances to be developed in testimony. The court below very properly permitted the introduction of such testimony. It appears that Victor G. Bloede was for many years, covering the years from 1875 to 1895, the consulting chemist of this company; that he was a man of science and invention; that he was a manufacturer of dyes, pulp colors, finishing oils, and chemicals; that the formulas of these were secret, his own discovery, to be used in secret processes of his own invention. Very many of them were not on the market, and were in use by the Bancroft Company alone. This was secured to the Bancroft Company by an agreement that during their joint relations with Bloede the colors and materials should not be sold to any one outside of themselves for any purpose, in the judgment of the company, in conflict with its interests. The lines of goods turned out by the Bancroft Company, in which these discoveries and manufactures of Bloede were used, were dependent upon their use and the processes for their application.

This being the case, it was for the interest of the Bancroft Company greatly, if not essential to its interest, to secure permanent control of these valuable aids in their business. The individual Bloede was mortal. When his life ended, these discoveries, secret formulas, and secret processes of his would pass to his legal representatives,—perhaps would be disclosed to the world at large or get into the hands of competitors. To secure the services of Bloede during his life, and to perpetuate the agreements made with him, the controlling officials in the Bancroft Company thought that an incorporation would prove effective. They felt that it was essential for their company that the relationship between Bloede and it should be cemented; that it was important that the business conducted by Bloede should be put into a condition of permanency; that such permanency could be secured and Bloede's attachment cemented by getting him a holding of some of their stock. To this end they induced him to form the Victor G. Bloede corporation, into which he should turn the whole of his plant, his discoveries, his secrets, and his business, and this was done. It may well be believed that at the time this was considered the best mode of promoting the business of the company, and to be a course necessary to its business. Carrying out this the Bancroft Company purchased from Bloede 474 shares in this corporation, so formed at their insistence, for paid-up shares of their own stock. The purchase removed all risks of the life of Bloede; gave an influential voice in the production, control, and management of materials of great value to and directly in the line of their business. It gave them an interest in a business incident with their own, and which could easily and naturally combine with their own. It would appear that this purchase was directly under the intention and within the power of its charter.

There is another point of view from which this case can be considered, and which impressed the circuit court in reaching its conclusion. In 1897 the state of Delaware adopted another constitution. Article 9 of this instrument provided for the formation of corporations under general laws, and forbade special legislation, either in the creation of corporations, or in the amendment, renewal, or revival of their charters. Section 3 of this article is in these words:

> "No corporation shall issue stock, except for money paid, labor done or personal property or real estate or leases thereof actually acquired by such corporation, and neither labor nor property shall be received in payment of stock at a greater price than the actual value at the time the said labor was done or property delivered or title acquired."

The legislature of Delaware, under the authority of this constitution, passed an act providing a general corporation law, approved 10th March 1899. The second section of that act made provision for the powers to be enjoyed by every corporation created under its provisions. The third section declares that every corporation (not confining itself to corporations created under that act) shall possess and exercise all the powers and privileges contained in this act, and the powers expressly given in its charter, so far as the same are necessary or convenient to obtain the objects of its charter, and shall be governed by the provisions, and be subject to the restrictions and liabilities in this act contained, so far as the same are appropriate to, and not inconsistent with its charter. This is clearly a general provision, applicable to all charters before as well as under this act. Section 133 gives the right to any corporation created under this act to hold stock in other corporations. Sections 139 repeals all inconsistent laws, preserving, however, all existing rights, privileges and immunities. No constitutional or statutory provision of the state of Delaware had ever forbidden a corporation from holding stock in another corporation. This act, at the least, shows such holding not to be against the public policy of the state. So when for the purposes-of its business, to promote its interests, and to secure permanency in the supply to it of important valuable material used in manufacture, the Bancroft Company purchased from Bloede his stock in the Bloede Company, the mere fact that the property purchased was stock in another corporation did not, in itself, make such purchase unlawful and against public policy. The circuit court went further than this. It held that, even were the original exchange or purchase of stock not authorized by the charter of the Bancroft Company, the passage of the act of 1899 legalized the transaction and gave it validity. For this position, Gross v. Mortgage Co., 108 U.S. 477, 2 Sup.Ct. 940, 27 L.Ed. 795, and In re Buffalo, N.Y. & E.R.R. Co. (Sup.Ct.) 37 N.Y. Supp. 1048 are cited. The last cited case seems almost on fours with the case at bar. It is, however, unnecessary to pass upon this point. *For the reasons heretofore given, the conclusion reached by the circuit court is approved, and its judgment is affirmed.* ◄

COMMENTS AND QUESTIONS

1. Note the resolution of the board of directors and the procedures used to transfer the stock between the two companies.

2. What were the issues before the court? How were they resolved? Outline the reasons for the court's decision.

Power to Acquire Own Stock

A corporation's right to acquire its own stock is usually limited by statute. Most states permit such acquisitions only if the corporation is solvent and the purchase is made from surplus.[8] The purpose of this regulation is to protect creditors by ensuring that the original investment is maintained. In some jurisdictions, a company may not purchase its own stock under any circumstances, though it may receive stock as a gift or in payment of a debt.

In the New Jersey case that follows, a corporation's right to purchase its own stock was challenged.

WOLFF v. HEIDRITTER LUMBER CO.

Court of Chancery of New Jersey, 1932
112 N.J. Eq. 34, 163 A. 140

► On appeal from receiver's disallowance of claim (of Poppenga).

BUCHANAN, V. C.   The bill in this case was filed for the appointment of a receiver and the winding up of the defendant corporation, under the statute.

Adolph U. Poppenga filed proof of claim as creditor, with the receivers, which was disallowed by them; from such disallowance the claimant has appealed.

Poppenga's claim is based upon a written agreement, dated July 9th, 1924, between himself and the defendant lumber company, whereby he agreed to sell and the lumber company agreed to buy from him one hundred and fifty shares of the capital stock of the lumber company for $40,000.

The agreement provides that Poppenga "hereby sells" "and the lumber company hereby purchases" the said stock; and that the purchase price is to be paid by the lumber company in installments of $1,000 each, every three months, commencing October 9th, 1924, together with interest on the balance unpaid from time to time; that upon final payment in full Poppenga will transfer the shares to the lumber company; that Poppenga shall have the right to repurchase the said shares "at any time during the continuance of this agreement" by repaying to the lumber company the moneys theretofore paid by it.

Prior to the appointment of the receiver in this suit, the lumber company has paid $13,500 (with interest) on account of the $40,000 purchase price. Poppenga's claim is for the balance, $25,500, together with interest from January 15th, 1931.

The receivers concluded that by reason of the determination in Hoover Steel Ball Co. v. Schaefer Ball Bearing Co., 90 N.H. Eq. 164; 106 Atl. Rep. 471, and the cases therein cited, the claim must be deemed invalid and unenforceable. The facts in the present case are different in several par-

---

[8] Surplus refers to the amount of corporate assets over and above the value of its outstanding stock. This term will be discussed in more detail in Section 3.

ticulars from those in the Hoover case, and it is contended by claimant-appellant that these differences are of such materiality as to remove the present claim from the interdiction of that decision. It is concluded that this contention is well founded; that the claim is valid and the appeal must be sustained.

The holding in the Hoover case is that a contract by a corporation with a purchaser of its stock, contemporaneously with such purchase, for the future repurchase of such stock by the corporation at the option of the purchaser, cannot be enforced against an insolvent corporation to the detriment of its creditors. In the instant case the contract was a presently operative purchase—not an executory contract to purchase *in futuro;* it gave no right to the stockholder to continue his status as a stockholder as long as he deemed it profitable and then later to convert himself into a creditor at the expense of other creditors—it converted him at once into a creditor and not a stockholder (although there was a clause giving him the option to repurchase the stock); and the corporation, at the time of making the purchase, was not insolvent but had a large net surplus.

The basic principle in the Hoover case is that the assets of a corporation are primarily liable for the payment of its debts and that the stockholders cannot take the corporate assets to repay themselves the money they invested, if such action leaves the corporation without sufficient assets to pay its creditors; they cannot do so *in praesenti* nor can they make an enforceable agreement to do so *in futuro.* On the other hand, however, the assets of a corporation over and above the amount required to pay its creditors are the property of the stockholders and can be withdrawn by them for their individual benefit in such manner as they agree on.

Suppose a corporation with assets of $100,000, debts of $10,000, and outstanding capital stock of $10,000 held in equal amounts by ten stockholders. There could be no objection if that corporation (all stockholders consenting) should reduce its capital stock by purchasing from each stockholder one-half of his holdings for $500 per share since ample assets would be left to pay all creditors; likewise there could be no objection to such a purchase from a single stockholder only—if the other stockholders all consented. And if such a purchase would be valid if the money were then and there paid out of the corporate treasury, it is not perceived why the purchase would be invalidated if the company instead of giving its check in payment gave its note or its other obligation for deferred payment. The contract would be complete; the corporate assets necessary to pay would have no greater right to complain. The stockholder would become a creditor—and an unpaid creditor instead of a paid vendor; but the debt due him being valid then, would not become invalid by reason of the company subsequently becoming insolvent before the date of the debt's maturity.

The court of errors and appeals determined in Berger v. United Steel Co., 63 N.J. Eq. 809; 53 Atl. Rep. 68, that a corporation organized under the general Corporation Act of this state has the power to purchase shares of its own stock, "for legitimate corporate purposes": that it may just as validly purchase on credit as for cash; and that it may give security for the credit extended to it. No rights of creditors were involved in that case;

the issues were raised not by or on behalf of creditors, but by stockholders. The principles therein enunciated must of course be deemed to be limited by the rights of creditors if any such are involved or affected in a given case; but both on reason and authority the conclusion seems inescapable that a corporation may purchase shares of its own stock for "legitimate corporate purposes," and may, instead of paying cash therefor, issue its obligation payable at a future date, and that the vendor holding such obligation becomes forthwith a creditor (instead of a stockholder) of the company and entitled to rank equally with other creditors in the event of subsequent insolvency of the company, provided that at the time of the purchase the company has sufficient assets to pay its creditors in full and provided the purchase is not made in disregard of the equitable rights of other stockholders.

In the instant case the company admittedly had far more than sufficient assets to pay its creditors in full, and all of the stockholders expressly consented to the purchase. Under such circumstances it may well be doubted that much, if any, consideration need be given toward the determination of what is a "legitimate corporate purpose." Aside from the rights of creditors (which in the instant case were in nowise prejudiced or infringed), and the right of the state that no criminal or fraudulent act be perpetrated (which is in nowise intimated in the present case), it would seem that the stockholders are the only ones interested, and that any purchase might be made to which all stockholders expressly assented. If, however, the "legitimate corporate purpose" be deemed a requisite even under such circumstances, no doubt is entertained as to its existence in the case at bar.

The corporation was involved in litigation wherein persons having a "life estate" in the "inchoate" dividends of certain shares of stock of the company (held by trustees, in trust to pay the income on that stock, during the life of a third party, to the litigating complainants and to transfer the stock at the death of the third party to other beneficiaries of whom Poppenga was one) sought to obtain payment of dividends to themselves out of accumulated profits of the company.

An opinion had been filed in the litigation, foreshadowing the possibility, if not the probability, of a decree that the corporation should pay such dividends out of the accumulated profits. The accumulated profits had been put back into the business, so that it would have been very difficult, if not impossible, for the corporation to have paid such dividends at that time, without liquidating its affairs, notwithstanding it was amply solvent, as has been said. . . .

The purchase by the company was therefore part of an entire transaction intended, and believed to be, and agreed upon by all stockholders as being —and which apparently in fact actually was—for the benefit not only of Poppenga but also of all the other stockholders of the company. (It does not appear that the present unfortunate financial situation of the company was in anywise attributable to this transaction, or that it could have been foreseen at that time.) The corporation is simply the stockholders in corporate form; the interests of the stockholders are the interests of the corporation; the purpose of the corporation is to benefit the interests of the stockholders. The legitimate benefit of the stockholders is therefore a legitimate corporate purpose, especially when all agree.

It is not intended by anything that has been said herein to intimate that a purchase by a corporation of shares of its own stock would be valid if the then present ability of the corporation to pay its creditors in full was in anywise open to doubt—if, for instance, although then honestly believed to be fully solvent, it should later appear doubtful that the company had, in fact, been then fully solvent. That situation does not exist here, and no opinion is expressed thereon. . . .

The appeal will be sustained and the claim allowed as that of a general creditor; but under all the circumstances costs of the appeal will be awarded against him. ◄

COMMENTS AND QUESTIONS

1. How did this case arise? What was the lower court's decision? What happened on appeal?
2. Summarize the rules of law which this case stands for.
3. How does the court distinguish this case from the *Hoover* case, which was relied on by the receiver?

Power to Borrow Money

A corporation has the implied power to borrow the money it needs to carry on authorized business. For this purpose it may issue or execute negotiable instruments, bonds, or other instruments. Generally, a corporation also has the power to mortgage, lease, or transfer its property to raise money or pay debts.

Limitations on Implied Powers

Certain powers are usually *not* implied in corporate charters. For example, a corporation may not agree to act as surety for, or guarantee the payment of, another person's debt unless the charter expressly authorizes it to enter into such transactions. Similarly, a corporation usually does not have the implied power to form a partnership with another firm or with an individual. Nor may it merge or consolidate with another firm without express authorization. Many states, however, permit such mergers provided a certain percentage of the stockholders vote their approval.

The limitations on the implied powers of a corporation are discussed at some length in the following North Carolina case. Note the broad provisions contained in the charter. These provisions are typical.

BRINSON v. MILL SUPPLY CO., INC.

Supreme Court of North Carolina, 1941
219 N.C. 408, 14 S.E. 2d 505

► Appeal from Superior Court, Craven County.
Affirmed.
Civil action instituted by W. T. Brinson in behalf of himself and all the stockholders and creditors of The Mill Supply Company against The Mill

Supply Company, alleging insolvency and seeking the appointment of a receiver and the liquidation of the corporation.

When the original action came on to be heard on the motion for the appointment of a receiver, E. F. Smallwood was appointed receiver and placed in charge of the assets of the defendant corporation to the end that the corporation might be liquidated and the assets applied to the payment of creditors.

The claimant, Laura H. Harvey, executrix of the last will and testament of Harriet L. Hyman, filed claim with the receiver in the amount of $2,318.97, representing the balance due on a note in the sum of $5,000, executed by Albert F. Patterson, who was at the time of the execution thereof, president of the defendant company. The facts in respect thereto are as follows:

On March 14, 1931, Albert F. Patterson borrowed from Harriet L. Hyman the sum of $5,000, evidenced by his note which, under the terms thereof, was payable in stipulated monthly instalments. Fifty shares of the capital stock of the Mill Supply Company was deposited with the payee as collateral security and the note contained the stipulation

> "that upon payment of the sum of $1,000 on the principal of this note that $1,000 of the par value of said stock shall be released to the maker of this note and upon payment of each subsequent $1,000 a like amount of collateral shall be released to the maker."
>
> "The payment of this note is guaranteed by the Mill Supply Company in accordance with a separate contract of guaranty of even date herewith executed by the Mill Supply Company."

On April 2, 1931, A. F. Patterson, president, and the secretary of the defendant corporation, executed in the name of the corporation, a contract of guaranty of said note, which contract of guaranty was executed pursuant to a resolution duly adopted by the executive committee, March 14, 1931. This contract contains a similar stipulation to the effect that upon the payment of $1,000 upon the principal of the note, $1,000 par value of the stock deposited as collateral is to be released to A. F. Patterson, the maker.

The executive committee in adopting the resolution authorizing the execution of the contract of guaranty acted by virtue of a resolution of the board of directors vesting it during the interim between meetings of the board, "with the same power and authority as is vested in the Board of Directors and by any act of said committee taken between the meetings of the Board of Directors shall be as equally binding on the company as though said action had been taken by the Board of Directors."

The receiver denied the claim and the claimant appealed to the Superior Court. Upon hearing in the Superior Court the Judge found the facts and concluded that the contract of guaranty was *ultra vires*. It thereupon adjudged that the claimant recover nothing of the receiver. The claimant excepted and appealed.

BARNHILL, JUSTICE. Was the act of the officers of the defendant corporation, in authorizing and executing the contract of guaranty, *ultra vires*

as contended by the receiver? The court below so concluded. In this conclusion we concur.

For a contract executed by the officer of a corporation to be binding
on the corporation it must appear that (1) it was incidental to the business
of the corporation; or (2) it was expressly authorized and (3) it was properly executed.

The charter of the defendant corporation vests it with general authority
to acquire, own, mortgage, sell and otherwise deal in real estate, chattels
and chartels real without limit as to amount; to deal in mortgages, notes,
shares of capital stock and other securities; to acquire the good will, rights,
property and assets of all kinds and to undertake the whole or any part of
the liabilities of any person, firm, association or corporation and to pay for
the same in cash, stock, bonds, debentures, notes or other securities of this
corporation or otherwise; to purchase or acquire its own capital stock from
time to time to such an extent and in such manner and upon such terms
as its board of directors shall determine; to borrow or raise money for any
purpose of its incorporation and to issue its bonds, notes or other obligations
for money so borrowed, or in payment of or in exchange for, any real or
personal property or rights of franchises acquired or other value received
by the corporation and to secure such obligations by pledge or mortgage;
and "to do all and everything necessary, suitable, convenient or proper for
the accomplishment of any of the purposes or the attainment of any one or
more of the objects herein enumerated, or incident to the power herein
named, or which shall at any time appear conducive or expedient for the
protection or benefit of the corporation, either as holders of or interest in,
any property, or otherwise; with all the powers now or hereafter conferred
by the laws of North Carolina upon corporations." There are other powers
granted which are in nowise pertinent to the question here presented.

The powers thus granted do not expressly authorize the corporation to
issue accommodation paper or to guarantee the obligations of a third party.

It is true that in a letter addressed to the payee of the note the treasurer of the defendant corporation recited the conditions of the note, including the provision in respect to the surrender of the collateral, and says in the
letter that such stock "shall be released and turned over to the Mill Supply
Company, free and discharged of the lien of said note." But this letter was
merely one of transmittal. It constitutes no part of the contract. The guaranty enclosed, as well as the note, which together form the contract, provides that such stock, on compliance with the condition, is to be surrendered
to the maker A. F. Patterson. Furthermore, there is no evidence tending to
show that any of the stock was ever delivered to the corporation. Hence the
contract was not a method adopted for the purchase by the defendant of
its own stock as authorized by its charter. Claimant's contention in that
respect cannot be sustained.

The provision in the charter authorizing the corporation "to undertake
the whole or any part of the liabilities of any person, firm, association or
corporation and to pay for the same in cash, stock, bonds, debentures, notes
or other securities of this corporation or otherwise" is in connection with,

related to and a part of the power granted "to acquire the good will, rights, property and assets of all kinds . . . of any other person," etc. The power granted is the power to assume the liabilities of such firm or corporation whose rights, property and assets are acquired by the corporation. This provision may not be construed to mean that the corporation was vested with power to issue accommodation paper or to become guarantor upon the obligation of a third party.

The contract of guaranty was no part of a transaction in which the corporation was borrowing or raising money for the purposes of its incorporation. It was clearly and exclusively an act in aid and for the accommodation of its president as an individual. From it the corporation received no benefit.

Hence, it appears that the undertaking of the corporation was not directly necessary, suitable, convenient or proper for the accomplishment of either of these or of any other purpose authorized by the charter.

Was the contract of guaranty incidental to or in furtherance of the powers expressly granted? If not, it was *ultra vires* and unenforceable.

A corporation is an artificial being, created by the State, for the attainment of certain defined purposes, and, therefore, vested with certain specific powers and others fairly and reasonably to be inferred or implied from the express powers and the object of the creation. Acts falling without that boundary are unwarranted—*ultra vires.* . . .

Ordinarily, the power to endorse or guarantee the payment of negotiable instruments for the benefit of a third party is not within the implied powers conferred upon a private business corporation.

The general rule is that no corporation has the power, by any form of contract or endorsement, to become a guarantor or surety or otherwise lend its credit to another person or corporation. 19 C.J.S. Corporations, p. 917, 1230, and numerous authorities cited in note 14; 7 Fletcher on Corps. 647; 7 R.C.L. 675.

In the absence of express statutory authorization, a corporation has no implied power to lend its credit to another by issuing or endorsing bills or notes for his accommodation, where the transaction is not related to the business activity authorized by its charter as a necessary or usual incident thereto. . . .

A corporation is without implied power to guarantee for accommodation the contract of its customers with third persons on the ground that it may thus stimulate its own business. Such use of its credit is clearly beyond the power of an ordinary business corporation. . . .

The question here presented is not whether there was sufficient consideration to support the note. The question is, was there sufficient consideration moving to the corporation to support the contract of guaranty? The liability of the individual upon the note (which was not signed by the corporation) is not contested. It is the liability of the corporation which is at issue. Hence, the rule that where the corporation has received the benefits under a contract which is not incidental, it will be held liable under the doctrine of estoppel, for the reason that it should not be permitted to accept and retain the benefits and at the same time disavow the contract on the pleas of *ultra vires* has no application. It is when the corporation has received the full benefits of the contract that it will not be relieved of liability because the contract was *ultra vires*. . . . This rule does not impose liability upon the corporation when no benefit has accrued to it by reason of the contract—here the contract of guaranty.

> "If it shall be found that the notes were executed by the president of defendant corporation, not in pursuance of or as an incident of the corporate business, wholly without consideration or benefit of any kind to the corporation, then such execution and delivery of the notes would be an *ultra vires* act." Lentz v. Johnson & Sons, Inc., 207 N.C. 614, 178 S.E. 226, 228, and cases cited. . . .

The contract of guaranty was executed for the benefit of an individual. No part of the consideration moved to the defendant corporation. It was not either expressly or impliedly authorized by its charter to enter into contracts for the accommodation of a third party. To permit the payment of the claim would clearly result in an invasion of the assets of the defendant corporation in the hands of the receiver as a trust fund for the payment of legitimate creditors. . . . The defendant's plea of *ultra vires* must be sustained.

The judgment below is affirmed.   ◄

COMMENTS AND QUESTIONS

1. Note the actual parties involved here and the nature of the proceeding. The payee of the note had died and his executrix brought suit against the receiver of the insolvent corporation to recover the proceeds for his estate. Was she successful?
2. What was the main issue before the court and how was it decided?

Ultra Vires Acts

If a corporation performs an act or enters into an agreement that is outside the scope of its express or implied powers, the act or agreement is said to be *ultra vires* [9] and may be challenged in certain cases.

Formerly, when a corporation entered into an *ultra vires* contract, either the third party or the corporation could avoid liability under the contract and refuse to carry it out. Today, however, most courts have restricted the use of this defense by adopting the following rules:

1. If the *ultra vires* contract is executed on both sides, neither party can object to it or rescind it.

2. If the *ultra vires* contract is wholly executory, neither party can enforce it or sue for damages.

3. When one side has performed an *ultra vires* contract and the other has not, the authorities disagree. A majority of states hold that the contract should be rescinded and both sides restored to their original position—by the payment of damages, if necessary. Other states, however, reject this solution and require that the contract be completed.

---

[9] That is, beyond the powers granted.

Although the use of the *ultra vires* defense has been severely restricted, *ultra vires* acts are still open to challenge in many cases. For example, if it is known that a corporation is contemplating an *ultra vires* act, a shareholder may procure an injunction to restrain the officers or directors from going ahead. If such an act has already been performed, and if it causes loss to the corporation, a suit for damages may be brought against those responsible; the money recovered goes back into the corporate treasury. If the wrongful act is of a serious nature, the attorney general of the incorporating state may take steps to have the corporation's charter revoked.

Right to Do Business in Other States

A corporation is known as a *domestic corporation* in the state in which it is incorporated. In any other jurisdiction, it is known as a *foreign corporation*. As a general rule, no foreign corporation has a constitutional right to do business in a state that wishes to exclude it. If it does business without permission, it may be punished by fine, by the arrest of its officers and agents, or by the denial of its right to sue in court.

A state may also insist that any foreign corporation desiring to do business within its borders must first comply with special rules and regulations. Many states, for example, require that a foreign corporation, before it can do business, pay special entrance fees and taxes, file copies of its charter, appoint a resident agent, designate its principal office within the state, and appoint someone within the state as its agent to receive summonses in case a third person wishes to sue it. Once a corporation has been admitted to do business in a state, however, the state may not discriminate against it in favor of domestic corporations. Moreover, the federal Constitution prohibits the states from imposing restrictions or levying taxes on foreign corporations engaged exclusively in interstate commerce if the effect is to interfere substantially with the free flow of goods between states. Regulation of that sort is reserved to the federal government.

It is not always easy to determine whether or not a corporation is "doing business" within a given state to such an extent as to fall within the regulatory power of that state. As a general rule, it may be said that a company is "doing business" in a state when it transacts a substantial and continuous part of its business in the state, as distinguished from business transactions which are merely casual or occasional. But there are many borderline cases in this area of the law.

EXAMPLES

1. An insurance company incorporated in Connecticut has no right to do business in any other state, and, theoretically, may be excluded from every other state. Most states, however, will admit the company after it has complied with certain entrance requirements. If it opens an office and starts to sell insurance in, say, New York, without first qualifying to do business there, the New York authorities may impose criminal penalties on it.
2. Suppose, however, that the Connecticut company merely solicits mail-order business in New York. It receives applications and premiums

and mails policies from its Connecticut office and maintains no office or place of business in New York. Is the company actually "doing business" in New York to such an extent that it is subject to that state's regulations and controls? The answer is probably no.

SECTION 3

CORPORATE STOCK

Corporate Membership

Anyone who owns one or more shares of the stock of a stock corporation is a member of that corporation. Each share represents a part interest in the assets of the corporation; it confers the right to share in profits, to participate to a limited extent in management, and to receive a pro rata share of the corporation's capital if and when the corporation is dissolved. A stockholder does not, however, acquire any interest in or control over corporate property—that is, property which is held in the name of the corporation.

Stock Certificates

As evidence of corporate membership, most corporations issue stock certificates. Although there is no prescribed form for these certificates, they usually name the corporation and the state in which it was incorporated, identify the registered owner, indicate the number and type of shares held, specify the par value, if any, of the stock, and summarize the voting and dividend rights to which the stockholder is entitled.

Kinds of Stock

Common Stock

Common stock, the ordinary stock of the corporation, usually entitles the owner to a vote for each share held, the right to receive dividends, and a share in the corporate assets on dissolution. Common stock ordinarily bestows on the holder no special rights or privileges and no preference or priority in the distribution of dividends.

Preferred Stock

Preferred stock confers on its owner certain preferential rights in the disbursement of dividends and in the distribution of corporate assets on dissolution. For example, the holder of preferred stock is usually entitled to a certain specified dividend before any dividends are paid to the holders of common stock. In other words, he is assured of a certain return on his investment so long as the corporate earnings are sufficient for any dividends to be declared at all.

Preferred stock may be created only if it is expressly provided for in the corporate charter, or, in the absence of such a provision, only if the common stockholders give their unanimous consent. The preferential rights that go with the stock must be clearly stated on the stock certificate in order to be effective.

CUMULATIVE PREFERRED. Although a preferred stockholder is entitled to receive a specified dividend before the common stockholders receive anything, there is no guarantee that any dividend at all will be declared in a given year or over a period of years. The corporate earnings may not be sufficient, or the directors may, in their discretion, refuse to declare a dividend even when the company makes a profit. May a preferred stockholder whose dividend has been "passed" in a given year carry his claim over to the next year? Yes, if the stock he holds is *cumulative* preferred. No, if it is *noncumulative* preferred. In a corporation that issues noncumulative preferred stock, the directors are in a position to defeat the rights of the preferred stockholders by refusing to declare any dividends for a number of years, thus building up a surplus for a larger dividend to the common stockholders. For this reason, unless there is a clear indication to the contrary, preferred stock is always deemed to be cumulative, and back dividends must be paid on it before any dividend is declared on common stock. A few states hold that preferred stock is cumulative even though it is issued as noncumulative.

PARTICIPATING PREFERRED. Sometimes preferred stock carries the right of participation. This means that if a dividend of a certain amount is paid to the preferred stockholders, an equal amount of dividends may then be paid to the common stockholders; then, if the directors wish to pay any additional dividends, they must apportion the remainder equally between the two classes of shareholders. In other words, the preferred stockholders have a right to participate in any additional dividends which may be declared after both classes of stockholders have received an amount equal to that guaranteed to the preferred stockholders. The right to participate must, however, be expressly stated in the charter or in the stock certificate; otherwise, all the preferred stock of a corporation is deemed to be nonparticipating.

The three cases that follow provide examples of the various kinds of stock we have just described and the rights of the different classes of shareholders to receive dividends. Note the struggle in each case between the common stockholders and the preferred stockholders.

WABASH RAILWAY COMPANY et al. v. BARCLAY et al.
AUSTIN v. SAME

Supreme Court of the United States, 1930
280 U.S. 197, 50 S.Ct. 106

► Suit by John C. Barclay against the Wabash Railway Company and others. Decree for defendant (23 F. 2d 691) was reversed by the Circuit Court of Appeals (30 F. 2d 260), and the Wabash Railway Company and others and Shirley P. Austin separately bring certiorari. Reversed.

MR. JUSTICE HOLMES delivered the opinion of the Court.

This is a bill by holders of first preferred stock (called Class A) of the Wabash Railway Company, to have it declared that holders of such stock are entitled to receive preferential dividends up to five per cent. for each fiscal year from 1915 to 1926 inclusive to the extent that such dividends were earned in such fiscal years but were unpaid, before any dividends are paid upon other stock; and that the Company may be enjoined from paying dividends upon preferred stock B or common stock unless it shall have first paid such preferential dividends of five per cent. to the extent that the Company has had net earnings available for the payment and that such dividends remain unpaid. The case was heard upon bill and answer. The bill was dismissed by the District Court but the decree was reversed by the Circuit Court of Appeals, one of the Judges dissenting, 30 F. 2d 260, and a writ of certiorari was granted by this Court. Wabash R. Co. v. Barclay, 279 U.S. 828, 49 S.Ct. 265, 73 L.Ed. 979.

The railway company was organized in 1915 under the laws of Indiana with three classes of capital stock: Shares of the par value of $100, of Five Per Cent. Profit Sharing Preferred Stock A; shares of the same par value of Five Per Cent. Convertible Preferred Stock B; and shares of the same par value of Common Stock. At the date of the bill there were 693,330.50 shares of A, 24,211.42 B and 666,977.75 common. From 1915 to 1926 there were net earnings on most of the years but for a number of years no dividend, or less than five per cent. was paid on Class A while $16,000.00 net earnings that could have been used for the payment were expended upon improvements and additions to the property and equipment of the Road. It is not denied that the latter expenditures were proper and were made in good faith, or that the money could not have been applied to dividends consistently with the duties of the Road. The Company now is more prosperous and proposes to pay dividends not only upon A but also on B and the common stock, but the plaintiffs say that it is not entitled to do so until it has paid to them unpaid preferential dividends for prior fiscal years in which it had net earnings that might have been applied to them but were not.

The obligations assumed by the Company appear in its instrument of incorporation and in the certificates of Preferred Stock A in substantially the same words,

> "The holders of the Five Per Cent. Profit Sharing Preferred Stock A of the Company shall be entitled to receive preferential dividends in each

fiscal year up to the amount of five per cent. before any dividends shall be paid upon any other stock of the company, but such preferential dividends shall be non-cumulative."

In the event of a liquidation the holders shall be entitled to be paid in full out of the assets of the Company the par amount of their stock and all dividends thereon declared and unpaid before any amount shall be paid out of said assets to the holders of any other stock of the Company. By the plain meaning of the words the holders "are not entitled, of right, to dividends, payable out of the net profits accruing in any particular year, unless the directors of the Company formally declare, or ought to declare, a dividend payable out of such profits": in the first instance at least a matter for the directors to determine.

We believe that it has been the common understanding of lawyers and businessmen that in the case of non-cumulative stock entitled only to a dividend if declared out of annual profits, if those profits are justifiably applied by the directors to capital improvements and no dividend is declared within the year, the claim for that year is gone and cannot be asserted at a later date. But recently doubts have been raised that seem to have affected the minds of the majority below. We suppose the ground for the doubts is the probability that the directors will be tempted to abuse their power, in the usual case of a corporation controlled by the holders of the common stock. Their interest would lead them to apply earnings to improvement of the capital rather than to make avoidable payments of dividends which they do not share. But whether the remedies available in case of such a breach of duty are adequate or not, and apart from the fact that the control of the Wabash seems to have been in Class A, the class to which the plaintiffs belong, the law, as remarked by the dissenting Judge below, "has long advised them that their rights depend upon the judgment of men subject to just that possible bias."

When a man buys stock instead of bonds he takes a greater risk in the business. No one suggests that he has a right to dividends if there are no net earnings. But the investment presupposes that the business go on, and therefore even if there are net earnings, the holder of stock, preferred as well as common, is entitled to have a dividend declared only out of such part of them as can be applied to dividends consistently with a wise administration of a going concern. When, as was the case here, the dividends in each fiscal year were declared to be non-cumulative and no net income could be so applied within the fiscal year referred to in the certificate, the right for that year was gone. If the right is extended further upon some conception of policy, it is enlarged beyond the meaning of the contract and the common and reasonable understanding of men.

Decree reversed.   ◀

COMMENTS AND QUESTIONS

1. What relief were the preferred stockholders seeking in this action? Did the Supreme Court go along with their argument?
2. Summarize the reasons given by Justice Holmes for the decision. Do you agree with it or do you feel the result is unfair?

MORAN v. UNITED STATES CAST IRON PIPE
AND FOUNDRY COMPANY
DAY v. SAME

Court of Chancery of New Jersey, 1924
95 N.J. Eq. 389, 123 A. 546

▶ Bills by Anson B. Moran and John Day against the United States Cast
Iron Pipe & Foundry Company. Bill of first complainant dismissed, and
decree for other complainant advised.

BACKERS, V. C.   There has been no material change in the subject-
matter of this litigation since the decision in 1908 in Bassett v. U.S. Cast
Iron Pipe & Foundry Co., 74 N.J. Eq. 668, 70 A. 929, affirmed 75 N.J. Eq.
539, 73 A. 514.

It will be recalled that at that time the company had a reserve fund,
accumulated by withholding dividends from its preferred and common
stockholders, which, though listed on the books as "Reserve for Additional
Working Capital," was held to be surplus profits and not working capital
in the statutory sense of section 47 of the Corporation Act (2 Comp. St.
1910, p. 1629), and that so much thereof as was derived from withholding
dividends from the preferred stockholders was held to be available for
division among them; that is to say, whenever in the opinion of the directors
it was no longer needed for the purpose for which it was reserved and they
in their discretion saw fit to divide it. The character of that fund remains
the same, except that its book title is now "Working Capital Reserve," and
the respective amounts composing the fund withheld from the two classes
of stock have changed. At the end of the fiscal year 1922, the amount of
dividends withheld from preferred stock was $700,000; from common stock
$1,800,000 in round figures. The outstanding capital stock is now $12,-
000,000 preferred, 7 per centum, noncumulative dividends, and $12,000,000
common.

The company's earnings during the year 1922 were over a million
dollars, and after paying a dividend of 5 per cent. ($600,000) on the pre-
ferred stock the balance ($559,595.75) was transferred to the working
capital reserve. Later a further dividend of 2 per cent. was declared for
the year 1922, and the amount of ($240,000) was withdrawn from the
working capital reserve to pay it. On November 16, 1923, the company
resolved to pay to the preferred stockholders an additional dividend of
one-half of 1 per cent., and a like dividend of one-half of 1 per cent. to the
common stockholders, and drew upon the working capital reserve for the
amount ($120,000). The resolution declaring the dividend on the pre-
ferred stock recites that it was out of earnings withheld from the preferred
stockholders in previous years and was no longer needed as working capital,
and the one declaring the dividend on the common stock, after setting forth
the fact that a dividend of 7 per cent. had been paid to the preferred stockholders for the year 1922 out of the profits of that year, states that it is out
of the net earnings for the year 1922. At this juncture the complainant
Moran, a common stockholder, filed his bill to enjoin the payment of the
additional dividend to the preferred stockholders, and the complainant Day,

a preferred stockholder, filed his bill to prevent the payment of the dividend declared on the common stock.

The Moran bill:—The complainant, a common stockholder, contends that the company having paid 7 per cent. in dividends on the preferred stock for the year 1922—the yearly maximum fixed by its charter—it was unlawful to declare the extra dividend of one-half of 1 per cent. out of withheld dividends of prior years because the charter limits the payment of dividends in any one year to 7 per cent. The certificate of incorporation fixes the yearly dividend at not to exceed 7 per centum.

Section 18 of the Corporation Act of 1896 (P.L. p. 283) provides as to preferred stock, that—

> "The holders thereof shall be entitled to receive, and the corporation shall be bound to pay thereon, a fixed yearly dividend, to be expressed in the certificate, not exceeding eight per centum, payable quarterly, half yearly or yearly, before any dividend shall be set apart or paid on the common stock."

This obviously means, as to noncumulative dividends, that out of the profits of any fiscal year not more than the percentage fixed by the charter shall be paid on such stock for such year, but it does not prohibit the company, after having paid the fixed yearly dividend, from, in the same year, declaring and paying additional dividends out of profits earned in prior years applicable to dividends for such years, and which for holding them in reserve for economic reasons, would have been distributed in dividends in those years. These profits belong primarily to the preferred stockholders, and the directors are in no wise restricted either as to amount, time, or occasion when distribution shall be made.

It has been suggested that the withheld profits are available only for dividends in lean years to make up deficiencies, and that was the effect of the opinion in the Bassett case. That situation was involved, but the point was not.

The resolution declaring the dividend is lawful, and the bill will be dismissed.

The Day bill:—This bill is by a preferred stockholder to prevent the payment of the dividend declared on the common stock "out of the profits of 1922." The dividend was declared after the company had paid 7 per cent on the preferred stock for that year. The point made is that no dividend can be declared on the common stock until all the withheld profits applicable to dividends on the preferred stock have first been divided and paid.

It will be observed that section 18 provides not only that preferred stockholders shall be entitled to receive, and the corporation shall be bound to pay, a fixed yearly dividend, but also declares that such dividend shall be paid "before any dividend shall be set apart or paid to the common stock." The quoted language is unmistakable and the reason for it is aptly demonstrated in the present effort of the board of directors to favor the common stock at the expense of the preferred stockholders. While the statute says that the preferred stockholders shall be entitled to receive and the company shall be bound to pay a fixed yearly dividend out of the profits, when that obligation is to be performed is largely a matter of discretion with the directors. They are at liberty to pass dividends year after year and pile up profits if in their opinion it is for the welfare of the company that this be done—as was done here—and in the absence of fraud, actual or constructive, their judgment is controlling. But once having decided to divide the profits, duty supplants discretion, and it becomes incumbent upon the directors to discharge the company's obligation to pay the fixed yearly dividends, and this before any dividend shall be set apart or paid on the common stock, *viz.:* To holders of cumulative dividend shares, all arrearages; to holders of noncumulative dividend stock, the dividends withheld. Otherwise, if the action of the defendant company were sanctioned and the directors pursued the course they have outlined, the rights of the preferred stockholders in the reserve profits could be indefinitely ignored and altogether subordinated to those of the common stock. Although each class had a definite sum in the reserve and one cannot encroach on the others for dividends, the preferential right of payment of dividends assured by the statute cannot be disregarded. The statutory design was to meet just such a situation as here confronts the preferred stockholders. The legislative scheme was to protect them in their priority rights to dividends over the common stock in all events, and where, as here, profits of past years applicable to dividends on both preferred and common stock, it was conceived that this protection would be afforded for forbidding the payment of any dividends on the common stock until the amount due the preferred stockholders was first paid. The statute in this respect is nothing more or less than a definition of the equitable rights of the preferred stockholders arising out of the company's obligation to pay the yearly fixed dividend, for if the company had profits not needed in its business, and was about to distribute them among the common stockholders when it owed dividends on the preferred stock, a court of equity would enjoin the division, just as it would intervene in behalf of creditors of a corporation when dividends are in derogation of their rights.

The fact that the dividend was declared out of the profits of 1922 adds no merit. The profits of that year had been in fact transferred to the working capital reserve, and the amount of the dividend was later withdrawn to meet it; but that is unimportant. The profits of 1922 were bulk surplus profits by whatever name, and, as Vice Chancellor Howell observed, mere bookkeeping entries cannot change their character. The dividend cannot be differentiated because it was out of the profits of the last fiscal year any more than if it had been declared out of the profits of any preceding year and carried in the working capital reserve.

The defendant company's conception of section 18 is illustrated by the stock preference clauses contained in the certificate of incorporation, which read as follows:

> "The preferred stock shall be entitled out of any and all surplus net profits, whenever declared by the board of directors, to noncumulative dividends at a rate not to exceed seven per cent (7%) per annum for the fiscal year beginning on the first day of June, 1899, and for each and every other fiscal year thereafter, payable in preference and priority

to any payment of any dividend on the common stock for such fiscal year. In the event of the dissolution of the corporation the holders of the preferred stock shall be entitled to receive par value of their preferred shares out of the surplus funds of the corporation remaining after the payment of its debts, before any payment shall be made therefrom to the holders of the common stock. The common stock shall be subject to prior rights of the holders of the preferred stock as herein declared. If after providing for the payment of full dividends for any fiscal year on the preferred stock there shall remain any surplus net profits for such year, any of such net profits of such year and of any other fiscal year, after full dividends shall have been paid on the preferred stock, shall be applicable to such dividends upon the common stock as from time to time shall be declared by the board of directors; and out of any such surplus net profits, after the closing of any fiscal year, the board of directors may pay dividends upon the common stock of the corporation for such fiscal year, but not until the dividends upon the preferred stock for such fiscal year shall have been actually paid or provided for and set apart."

This interpretation, if such it be, is, in effect, that noncumulative dividends are entitled to precedence only in years for which dividends are declared on the common stock out of profits of such years sufficient to pay dividends on both preferred and common stock, and not for years when applicable profits are available but undivided. The view is manifestly too narrow, for in the favored circumstances the preferred stock would be, as a matter of course, entitled to priority because of, as has already been pointed out, the company's bounden duty to pay the preferred stockholder a fixed yearly dividend. The fixed yearly dividend is the measure of their income per year out of profits per year, and the obligation of lean years is not met by preferential payments in fat years. Sight is lost entirely of the specific subordination of all dividends on the common stock.

Section 18 was amended in 1901 (P.L. 1901, p. 245, 1), and in respect of dividends on preferred stock it provides:

"And such dividends may be made payable before any dividends shall be set apart or paid on the common stock, and such dividends may be made cumulative; provided, the corporations shall set apart or pay the said dividends to the holders of noncumulative preferred stock before any dividends shall be paid on the common stock."

The preservation of the priority right of noncumulative dividends, it would seem, emphasizes the view here entertained that the Legislature intended that no profits were to be divided among common stockholders, whatever may have been their origin or however applicable, unless the company's obligation to the preferred stockholders was first discharged.

The statutory ban on payments of dividends on the common stock until the preferred stockholders have been awarded their just due is explicit and imperative. The preference clauses in the certificate of incorporation in so far as they are thus inconsistent with the statute are invalid. Section 8, par. 7. C.S. 1910, p. 1604.

The dividend under consideration is without warrant in law and will be enjoined.   ◄

COMMENTS AND QUESTIONS

1. In this case, the provision for noncumulative dividends was about the same as in the *Wabash Railway* case immediately preceding. What was the court's decision in this action?

2. Note the provisions of the New Jersey Corporation Act. Do you think the result would have been different if this statute had not been in force?

3. Can you reconcile this case with the *Wabash Railway* case? Or do the two cases represent conflicting views of the rights of preferred stockholders?

LOCKWOOD v. GENERAL ABRASIVE COMPANY

Supreme Court of New York, Appellate Division
    Fourth Department, 1924
210 App. Div. 141, 205 N.Y.S. 511

► Appeal by defendant, General Abrasive Company, from a judgment by the Supreme Court in favor of plaintiffs, upon the decision of the court rendered after a trial at Erie Special Term.

CLARK, J. This action was brought for a declaratory judgment. (See Civil Practice Act., 473; Rules Civil Practice, rule 210 et seq.) The controversy is between the common and preferred stockholders of the General Abrasive Company, a domestic corporation.

The certificate of incorporation of the company is the contract between the two classes of stockholders, and their rights must be determined by the language of that instrument.

The real question to be determined here is: Are the common stockholders entitled to cumulative dividends? If they are, the authority to pay them must be found in the certificate of incorporation.

We may not read into that instrument words which it does not contain.

The dispute here is over the distribution of dividends. The defendant company proposes to distribute its surplus profits for the year 1923 by paying a seven per cent dividend to owners of preferred stock and seven per cent to owners of the common stock, and the remainder, if any, between the owners of the two classes of stock, in the ratio of their respective shares.

Plaintiffs contend that the provisions of the certificate of incorporation will not permit distribution of surplus earnings in this way. They contend that seven per cent should be paid on the preferred stock and seven per cent on the common stock and the remainder of the surplus to be applied in payments of dividends in arrears on the common stock, and after that is done the remainder, if any, to be distributed equally between the holders of the preferred stock and the holders of the common stock.

Defendant claims that after seven per cent. has been paid to the owners of the preferred stock and a like amount to the owners of the common stock, the remainder of the surplus should be divided pro rata between the holders of the preferred and the holders of the common stock, without first paying to the owners of the common stock amounts that would have been paid in former years if the surplus earnings in those years had justified it.

The learned court below was of the opinion that after the payment of seven dollars per share on the preferred stock, and seven dollars per share on the common stock, the common stockholders were next entitled to a payment of thirty-one per cent. on their shares to make up for dividends not earned or paid in former years, and that the surplus, if any, should be divided equally between the preferred and common shareholders.

I think the learned court adopted an erroneous construction of the certificate of incorporation with reference to dividends.

The clauses of the certificate of incorporation affecting the right of stockholders to dividends are as follows:

> "Fourth. Dividends upon the preferred stock of the company at the rate of seven per centum (7%) per annum, cumulative after July first, one thousand nine hundred sixteen, may be declared and paid out of the surplus profits, and no dividend in excess thereof shall be declared upon said preferred stock until dividends at a rate of seven dollars ($7.00) per annum shall have been declared and paid upon each share of the common stock.
>
> "Whenever, after the declaration or payment of all accumulated dividends upon the preferred stock, any surplus profits shall remain the same may be paid in dividends declared upon the common stock of the company up to the amount at the rate of seven dollars ($7.00) per annum upon each share of the common stock. Any surplus profits over and above said cumulative dividends upon preferred stock, and seven dollars ($7.00) per share per annum upon the common stock, may be paid in dividends in equal amounts upon each share of preferred stock and upon each share of common stock of the company."

It will be noticed that the certificate expressly provides that dividends upon the preferred stock shall be cumulative after July 1, 1916.

There is nothing in the certificate which says that the common stock shall be entitled to cumulative dividends, and inasmuch as the certificate is the contract between the shareholders, it must be presumed that it represented what they intended at the time of its execution, and we may not read into the instrument words which were not used, and evidently not intended to be used when the certificate was made and executed.

The words of the certificate must be given their usual and ordinary meaning, and when it says that owners of common stock, after the declaration or payment of all accumulated dividends upon the preferred stock, may be paid dividends on common stock at the rate of seven per cent per annum, it meant that they were to be paid such dividends yearly, or by the year, dividends that were earned, and paid in any particular year, but that they could not out of a present surplus be paid dividends for former years which had never been declared or earned.

A cumulative dividend is one "With regard to which it is agreed that if at any time it is not paid in full the difference shall be added to the following payment." Cent. Dict. "A dividend . . . which is not paid or received when due is added to what is to be paid in the future." Webster International Dict. The idea being that arrearages of one year are payable out of the surplus earnings for subsequent years.

No such dividend distribution was contemplated by the certificate of incorporation in the instant case. If it had been the intention of the incorporators that the owners of common stock should be entitled to cumulative dividends it is fair to assume that they would have provided for such payments in so many words in the certificate of incorporation, as they did with reference to cumulative dividends for the preferred shareholders. If there were not profits to be divided in any year after making payments to preferred stockholders in accordance with the terms of the certificate of incorporation, they were lost forever, for each new year would mark the beginning of a new dividend period. . . .

There is no justification for holding that the owners of the common stock are entitled to go back of the current year and claim to be reimbursed for unearned dividends of former years. To do so would make dividends cumulative in behalf of the owners of the common stock, and that was not expressed or contemplated by the certificate of incorporation.

In the absence of an agreement, expressed or implied, that dividends shall be cumulative, unpaid dividends in the past cannot be claimed. 10 Cyc. 573; 14 C.J. 421.

Since the incorporation of defendant company in 1916 the preferred stockholders have received dividends amounting to forty-five and one-half per cent. That would be seven per cent per annum. The common stockholders have received dividends amounting to fourteen and one-half per cent. The reason that the holders of the common stock did not receive larger returns in years gone by is because the dividends were not earned and declared.

If the certificate of incorporation had provided in terms that they were to receive cumulative dividends, as it did in the case of the owners of preferred stock, plaintiffs' position here would be unassailable, but in the absence of such provision in the certificate, to say that the owners of common stock are entitled to cumulative dividends, is to put a construction upon the certificates which, to my mind, would be unjustified.

The owners of the common stock, after provision was made for payment of dividends to the owners of the preferred stock, were entitled to seven per cent per annum if it was earned in any one year, but I can see no justification in the language of the certificate itself for holding that out of the surplus earnings of 1923 the common stockholders have a preferential right to be paid dividends not earned and declared in former years so as to make their dividend payments since the organization of the company correspond with the payments that have been made to preferred stockholders. To adopt plaintiffs' theory would be to make the owners of common stock actually preferred stockholders, and that was not within the contemplation of the parties who organized the company.

The judgment should be modified by providing that any dividends in excess of cumulative dividends of seven per cent upon the preferred stock of the defendant company and seven per cent, per share upon the common stock of defendant in any year shall be paid in equal amounts upon each share of preferred and common stock and as so modified the judgment should be affirmed, without costs of this appeal to either party.

The first conclusion of law is disapproved and reversed.

HUBBS, P. J. and DAVIS, J. concur; SEARS and CROUCH, JJ. dissent and vote for affirmance.

Judgment modified . . . any dividend in excess of cumulative dividends of 7% per share upon the common stock of defendant in any year shall be paid in equal amounts upon each share of preferred and common stock, and as so modified, judgment affirmed.   ◄

COMMENTS AND QUESTIONS

1. This was a controversy between the common and preferred stock-holders of a corporation. Summarize the contentions of each side.
2. What was the decision of the lower court? On what ground did the Appellate Division reverse that decision?
3. Note the citation of Webster's International Dictionary in defining a "cumulative dividend." Do you think this is good legal authority?

Voting Rights of Preferred Stockholders

A preferred stockholder does not ordinarily have a vote in the management of the corporation. This privilege is usually reserved for the common stockholders. Sometimes, however, the charter provides that if the corporation fails to pay dividends to the preferred stockholders for a certain period, the common stockholders may lose their voting right to the preferred holders. Such was the situation in the case that follows; as you will see, the preferred stockholders took full advantage of their position.

ELLINGWOOD v. WOLF'S HEAD OIL REFINING COMPANY, INC. et al.

Supreme Court, Delaware, 1944
27 Del. Ch. 356, 38 A. 2d 743

► Appeal from Court of Chancery.

Proceeding under Revised Code 1935, 2063, by Charles H. Ellingwood against Wolf's Head Oil Refining Company, Incorporated, and others, to determine the validity of election of directors of the corporation. From an adverse decree, 33 A. 2d 409, the complainant appeals.

Affirmed.

In the Supreme Court of the State of Delaware, No. 1 November Term, 1943, session Appeal from a decision of the Court of Chancery reviewing the corporate election of directors of Wolf's Head Oil Refining Company, Incorporated, held on May 3, 1943, under Section 31 of the General Corporation Law, Rev. Code 1935, 2063.

This case was originally brought in the Court of Chancery by the complainant below, appellant in his capacity as a common stockholder of Wolf's Head Oil Refining Company, Incorporated, which was originally incorporated in this State in October, 1929, under the corporate name of Wolverine-Empire Refining Co. The present name having been acquired by an amendment to its charter in November 1940.

The charter provided for both preferred and common stock. The authorized number of shares of preferred stock being 50,000, of which

46,100 are outstanding, and the authorized number of shares of common stock being 30,000, all of which are outstanding.

The right of the corporation to redeem the preferred stock, and the respective rights of both the preferred and common stock in the event of any liquidation, dissolution or wind up of the affairs of the corporation are set forth in Article 4 of the Certificate of Incorporation. Likewise, the dividend and voting rights of both the preferred and common stock are set forth in Article 5 of the Certificate of Incorporation. . . .

> Article 5. "The holders of preferred stock shall be entitled to cumulative dividends thereon at the rate of six per cent. for each and every fiscal year of the company, and no more, payable out of any and all surplus or net profits quarterly, half-yearly or yearly, when and as declared by the Board of Directors. Such dividends on the preferred stock shall be payable in any fiscal year before any dividends shall be paid or set aside for the common stock in that year, and the preferred stock shall not be entitled to participation in any other or additional profits. Out of any surplus or net profits of the corporation remaining after the full dividend of six per cent. on the preferred stock then outstanding shall have been declared and paid, or provided for in any year, dividends may be declared on the common stock for such year. . . .
>
> "Except as otherwise required by the statutes of the State of Delaware, or as herein otherwise provided, the holders of the common stock shall exclusively possess voting power for the election of directors, and for all other purposes, and the holders of the preferred stock shall have no voting power; provided however, that if at any time the corporation shall be in default in respect to the declaration and payment of dividends in the amount of two years' dividends on the preferred stock, then the holders of a majority of the preferred stock shall have an election to exercise the sole right to vote for the election of directors and for all other purposes, to the exclusion of any such right on the part of the holders of the common stock until the corporation shall have declared and paid for a period of a full year a 6% dividend on the preferred stock, when the right to vote for the election of directors, and for all other purposes, shall revert to the holders of the common stock. The election on the part of the holders of the preferred stock shall be consummated and effectuated by a notice to the corporation of their decision to exercise such right by holders of a majority of the preferred stock. During the time within which the holders of the preferred stock are exercising under this election the right to vote upon their stock, the holders of the common stock shall have no right to vote upon their stock. The said right of the preferred stock and its holders to exercise an election to vote shall survive any exercise of such election and a subsequent reversion of the right to vote to the common stock and its holders, and shall be a continuing privilege and right of said preferred stock; and the subsequent right to a reversion of the voting power to the common stock in the event of the payment of a full year's 6% dividend shall be a continuing privilege and right of said common stock and its holders."

The By-laws of said corporation fix its fiscal year as the calendar year, and further provide that it shall be managed by a Board of Directors consisting of seven who are to be elected at the annual meeting of the stockholders to be held on the first Monday of May of each year, and to serve for one year or until their successors shall be elected and qualified.

The bill discloses that at the closing of the year 1934, the respondent corporation, the appellee, had defaulted in the declaration and payment of dividends in the amount of two years' dividends, on its outstanding preferred stock; but that regardless of said default, the preferred stockholders of said corporation did not elect to exercise the sole right to vote for the election of directors at the annual stockholders meeting on May 6, 1935. But at the annual meeting of the stockholders held on May 4, 1936, said holders of the preferred stock of the corporation did assume to exercise the sole voting rights claimed by them under the above-quoted provisions of Section 5 of the Certificate of Incorporation and continued to exercise such voting rights down to and including the year 1942.

From the time of the organization of the said corporation in 1929, various arrearages of dividends accrued on the preferred stock. When a majority of the preferred stockholders finally decided to exercise their sole right to vote for the election of directors and for all other purposes, by giving a notice to the corporation of their decision to exercise such right, dividends had accrued on the preferred stock in the amount of 37½% of the par value. Dividends paid on the preferred stock during the same period, however, amounted to 15% of the par value, leaving accrued and unpaid dividends on said preferred stock in May 1936, when said preferred stockholders first gave notice to the corporation of their election to exercise the sole right to vote for the election of directors and for all other purposes, amounting to 22½% of the par value.

After the preferred stockholders acquired the sole right to vote for the election of directors and for all other purposes in May 1936, they continued to exercise that right until May 1943, at which time the common stockholders claimed that the sole right to vote for the election of directors and for all other purposes had reverted to them under the provisions of Article 5 of the Certificate of Incorporation above set forth. In support of this contention they relied upon the fact that during the year 1942, and for the period of a full year prior to May 3, 1943, a six per cent dividend had been paid on the preferred stock.

In April 1943, the holders of a majority of the preferred stock again gave notice to the corporation of their election to exercise the sole right to vote for the election of directors and for all other purposes, giving as their reason therefor, that the corporation was in default in regard to the declaration and payment of dividends in the amount of two years' dividends on the preferred stock. Consequently at the annual meeting on May 3, 1943, a majority of the preferred stockholders, claiming their right to vote for the election of directors and for all other purposes, elected a board of seven directors. Likewise certain common stockholders, including the appellant, claiming their right to vote for the election of directors and for all other purposes, at said annual meeting on May 3, 1943, elected a board of seven directors. The appellant instituted this proceeding before the Chancellor to determine which of said elections was valid and who constituted the Board of Directors of the corporation.

The Chancellor held that the preferred stockholders were entitled to vote for the election of directors and for all other purposes at the annual meeting held on May 3, 1943, and that the persons whose names were contained on the ticket for which they voted were the legally elected directors of the corporation.

This appeal was taken to review this decision and four assignments of error were filed. These assignments of error are all embraced in the first, which is as follows:

> "That the Chancellor erred in declaring that the persons owning the preferred stock of Wolf's Head Oil Refining Company, Incorporated, had the sole right and power to vote at the meeting of stockholders of the corporation on May 3, 1943, for the election of directors and for all other purposes."

RICHARDS, JUDGE. There is no dispute between the parties interested in this proceeding, that when the preferred stockholders and the common stockholders met at the annual meeting held on May 3, 1943, the corporation was in default in respect to the declaration and payment of dividends in the amount of two years' dividends on the preferred stock. All of said arrearages of dividends having accrued prior to 1942, and that during said year 1942, the corporation declared and paid a full six per cent dividend on the preferred stock.

This being the situation the Court is called upon to determine the voting rights of the two classes of stock under the pertinent charter provisions.

It is well recognized that a certificate of incorporation may contain any provision with respect to the stock to be issued by the corporation, and the voting rights to be exercised by said stock, that is agreed upon by the stockholders, provided that the provision agreed to is not against public policy. Thompson on Corporation, 3d Ed., Sec. 989. . . .

Nothing is to be presumed in favor of preferences attached to stock, and when a corporate charter attempts to confer preferences upon any class of stock provided for by it the same should be expressed in clear language. In interpreting the meaning of charter provisions the same method is applied as that which is followed in interpreting written contracts generally. The instrument should be considered in its entirety, and all of the language reviewed together in order to determine the meaning intended to be given to any portion of it. . . .

The charter of Wolf's Head Oil Refining Company, Incorporated, evidences an intention on the part of the incorporators to make provision for the protection of the preferred stockholders.

It is specified in article four of the charter, that in case of "liquidation, dissolution or winding up of the affairs of the corporation," said preferred stockholders shall be entitled to full payment of the par value of their shares, and all unpaid dividends accrued thereon, before any of the assets shall be distributed to the common stockholders. This same article gives to the Board of Directors the optional right to redeem the preferred stock in whole or in part, at any time before January first, 1940, but requires said Board of Directors to give sixty days' notice to all record holders of said preferred stock; and in addition thereto to pay in cash to each holder of preferred stock to be redeemed one hundred and ten per cent of the par value thereof.

Now we come to article five of the charter which guarantees to the holders of the preferred stock "Cumulative dividends thereon at the rate of six per cent for each and every fiscal year of the company." This same article gives to the holders of the common stock exclusive "voting power for the election of directors, and for all other purposes." This is followed by the provision that the preferred stockholders shall have no voting power. Then comes the proviso,

> "that if at any time the corporation shall be in default in respect to the declaration and payment of dividends in the amount of two years' dividends on the preferred stock, then the holders of a majority of the preferred shall have an election to exercise the sole right to vote for the election of directors and for all other purposes, to the exclusion of any such right on the part of the holders of the common stock until the corporation shall have declared and paid for a period of a full year a 6% dividend on the preferred stock, when the right to vote for the election of directors, and for all other purposes, shall revert to the holders of the common stock."

We desire to emphasize the fact that the wording of the above-quoted article is, "if at any time the corporation shall be in default in respect to the declaration and payment of dividends in the amount of two years' dividends on the preferred stock."

The appellant contends that the subsequent wording of the article "until the corporation shall have declared and paid for a period of a full year a 6% dividend on the preferred stock," restricts the above-quoted language of the article with respect to the duration of the time when the preferred stockholders have the right to elect to exercise the sole right to vote for the election of directors and for all other purposes. If this be true, it likewise takes from the preferred stockholders a portion of the protection which we have pointed out was conferred upon them by the charter.

The appellant takes the position that after the preferred stockholders have elected to exercise the sole right to vote for the election of directors and for all other purposes, and have actually exercised said right to vote in pursuance of the election to do so, the payment of a six per cent dividend for the period of a full year causes said sole right to vote by the preferred stockholders, to revert to the common stockholders until the corporation shall again default in respect to the declaration and payment of dividends in the amount of two years' dividends. This also loses sight of the fact that the plain words of the charter are, "if at any time the corporation shall be in default"; and the further plain provision that "the said right of the preferred stock and its holders to exercise an election to vote shall survive any exercise of such election and a subsequent reversion of the right to vote to the common stock and its holders, and shall be a continuing privilege and right of said preferred stock." We agree that when a six per cent dividend for a period of a full year is paid on the preferred stock, the sole right to vote for directors and for all other purposes reverts to the common stockholders, notwithstanding the fact that dividends in the amount of two years are due on the preferred stock. If the preferred stockholders failed to again elect to exercise the sole right to vote, by giving notice to the corporation of their decision to exercise such right as the charter requires them to do, the common stockholders would be entitled to exercise the right to vote for the election of directors and for all other purposes. But if the corporation is still in default in the declaration and payment of dividends in the amount of two years' dividends on the preferred stock, when a six per cent dividend is paid on preferred stock for the period of a full year, said preferred stockholders can still avail themselves of the right to vote for the election of directors and for all other purposes, if they comply with the condition of the charter by giving notice to the corporation of their decision to exercise such right to vote.

The language used in the charter describing the conditions under which the preferred stockholders obtain the right to vote has nothing to say about the time when the arrearage in dividends on said stock shall have accrued. If the position is taken that the arrearage in dividends must have accrued after the right to vote had reverted to the common stock, the preferred stockholders would be deprived of the right to vote for the election of directors no matter how great the arrearage in dividends might be, until additional dividends in the amount of two years' dividends should accrue. This construction would take from the preferred stockholders the benefit which we think the charter intended to confer upon them.

It is not denied that when a majority of the preferred stockholders first elected to exercise their right to vote for the election of directors and for all other purposes in 1936, the dividends accrued and unpaid on the preferred stock amounted to 22½%, of that said accrued and unpaid dividends was more than two years' dividends.

Neither is it denied that from 1936 to May 3, 1943, additional dividends accrued on the preferred stock amounting to 40½%, and that the dividends paid on said stock during that period amounted to 25½%.

Therefore it clearly appears that when the annual meeting of the corporation was held on May 3, 1943, dividends amounting to 37½% were accrued and unpaid on the preferred stock. Thus it appears that the corporation was in default in respect to the declaration and payment of dividends in the amount of two years' dividends.

In view of this situation we are of the opinion that the preferred stockholders were entitled to vote for the election of directors and for all other purposes, at the annual meeting of the corporation held on May 3, 1943, and that the persons whose names appeared on the ticket nominated and voted for by them are the legally elected directors of the corporation.

The decree of the Chancellor is affirmed.   ◄

COMMENTS AND QUESTIONS

1. What was the issue before the court in this case? How was it decided?

2. Summarize the provisions of the Certificate of Incorporation dealing with voting rights and dividends. What was the contention of the common stockholders? Did the court agree?

3. Do you think the court's interpretation of the voting-rights provisions reflects the true intention of the parties who drafted them?

Valuation of Stock

When a corporation issues stock, it is customary for the directors to place a valuation on it. This is commonly done by giving the stock a so-called *par value*, which represents the amount a subscriber must pay to acquire it. If, as frequently happens, the stock is issued with no par value, the amount that must be paid for it is determined by the directors.

Capital Stock and Surplus

The *capital stock* of a corporation is the declared value of its outstanding stock. If the stock has a par value, the amount of capital stock is the number of shares outstanding multiplied by the par value. If the stock has no par value, the amount of capital stock is the number of shares outstanding multiplied by the declared value of each share as determined by the directors.

EXAMPLES

1. A corporation issues 50,000 shares of stock with a par value of $5. The capital stock of the corporation is $250,000.
2. A corporation issues 1,000 shares of stock with no par value. The directors value the stock at $50 a share. The capital stock of the corporation is $50,000.

Any net assets of a corporation over and above the value of its capital stock are referred to as *surplus*. In other words, the amount by which the total net assets exceed the capital stock constitutes the surplus.

EXAMPLE

On incorporation, the xyz co. issues 10,000 shares of common stock with a par value of $5.00 a share. In the first year of operations it makes a profit of $20,000. Its total net assets are $70,000: $50,000 in capital stock and a $20,000 surplus.

As we shall see later, these concepts and valuations are very important, since many states permit dividends to be paid only out of surplus. Thus the capital stock of a corporation serves as a kind of buffer for the protection of creditors, and many states require the approval of two-thirds of the stockholders before the amount of capital stock may be reduced. We will discuss these points in greater detail in the section on dividend declaration (page 756).

Stock Subscriptions

In General

A stock subscription is a commitment by a prospective stockholder to purchase a given number of a certain kind of share when those shares are issued. The legal effect of a subscription depends on whether it is made before or after incorporation.

Subscriptions Before Incorporation

Most states treat a prior subscription—that is, a subscription made before incorporation—merely as an offer to purchase stock; it does not become binding on the prospective stockholder until the corporation has actually been formed and has formally accepted the subscription. At any time before acceptance, the offer may either lapse or be withdrawn, according to the usual rules of contract law. Some states modify the rule by providing that the subscription is automatically accepted and becomes binding the moment the corporation is formed, without the necessity for any formal acceptance. Still other jurisdictions hold that prior subscriptions are irrevocable for a certain period (usually one year).

In the following case, which involved a subscription prior to incorporation, the court had to decide which of these rules to apply.

COLLINS v. MORGAN GRAIN COMPANY

Circuit Court of Appeals of the United States
   Ninth Circuit, 1926
16 F. 2d 253

► Action at law by the Morgan Grain Company, Inc., against H. W. Collins. Judgment for plaintiff, and defendant brings error. Reversed, and cause remanded for a new trial.

RUDKIN, CIRCUIT JUDGE. This was an action by a corporation to recover a balance due on a stock subscription. There is little controversy over the facts. In the latter part of 1920, one Morgan, a grain dealer of San Francisco, conceived the idea of forming a corporation to take over the grain business then conducted by certain operators on the Pacific Coast. With this object in view, he consulted Collins, a grain operator in Oregon and the Pacific Northwest, and Sibley and Anderson, American managers for Wills & Sons of London, and proposed that Wills & Sons, Sibley, Anderson, Collins, and himself take stock in the proposed corporation. The proposition was looked upon with favor by Wills & Sons, and they directed the American managers to proceed to New York and meet one of their directors, to discuss the matter with Morgan. A conference was held in New York, attended by Morgan, Sibley, Anderson, and a director of Wills & Sons and as a result of this conference Morgan wired Collins concerning the matter. The telegram is not in the record, but in response thereto Collins wired Morgan, agreeing to take $25,000 in stock in the proposed corporation, payable in installments.

Upon receipt of this message, Wills & Sons agreed to subscribe for 1,260 shares, Anderson and Sibley for 10 shares each, and Morgan for 625 shares, of the par value of $100 each. Sibley and Morgan then returned to San Francisco, and while at Chicago on their return, two additional subscriptions were taken, one for 50 shares, the other for 25 shares. After the return of the parties to San Francisco, the Morgan Grain Company was organized under the laws of the state of Delaware, and Morgan became president of the company. Morgan reported to the board of directors that he had secured subscriptions to the capital stock as above detailed. The subscriptions were accepted by the board and a call of 25 per cent was made. The call was paid, and certificates issued to the several stockholders for the number of shares paid in full. Thereafter a certificate for the remaining shares subscribed by Collins was tendered, but he refused to accept the certificate or to pay the additional subscription. This action followed.

Upon the trial in the court below the defendant offered to prove that, before the organization of the corporation or the acceptance of his offer to subscribe, he met Morgan and Sibley in San Francisco and informed Morgan that he withdrew his subscription, that if Morgan would consent to its cancellation he would subscribe for and take $5,000 of stock in the corporation, and that Morgan agreed to this. The court below ruled that this evidence was incompetent, and directed a verdict for the plaintiff. The judgment on the verdict is now before us for review.

The principal assignment of error is based on the ruling of the court excluding testimony tending to prove a revocation or cancellation of the subscription before the corporation was formed, and before the offer was accepted. Agreements to subscribe for stock of corporations to be formed in the future may assume different forms, with different results. For example, if an individual, acting singly and without co-operation with others, offers to take stock in such a corporation, all the authorities agree that the offer may be rescinded or revoked at any time before the corporation is formed and the offer accepted; this upon the familiar principle that it takes two parties to make a contract, and that, if one is not bound, the other is not—in other words, that a mere unaccepted offer cannot in the nature of things constitute a binding contract.

Again, such an agreement may assume a double aspect, as where a number of persons agree to form a corporation and to subscribe to its capital stock. Such an agreement constitutes a contract as between the subscribers themselves, operative at once, and it likewise constitutes a continuing offer to the proposed corporation, which, upon acceptance, becomes as to each subscriber a contract between him and the corporation. Some of the authorities hold that contracts of the latter class are irrevocable without the consent of all the parties thereto; but there is usually found in such cases some element of estoppel, which does not exist in the case at bar. But, without attempting to distinguish the present case from the cases so holding, we deem it sufficient to say that the cases relied on are not supported by the weight of authority.

> "According to the weight of authority, a subscription may be withdrawn at any time before it is accepted by the corporation, whether made before or after the formation of the corporation, for the reason that until such acceptance there is no binding contract, because, until then, there is no agreement and no mutuality of object, and hence no consideration, and, in the case of subscriptions made before the corporation is formed, for the additional reason that, until it is formed, the other contemplated party to the contract is not yet in existence; nor, where this rule obtains, is a subscriber deprived of the right to withdraw

under such circumstances because other subscribers have acted upon the strength of his subscription, nor because he has induced others to subscribe" 2 Fletcher, Cyc. Corp. 1225. [Citing cases.]

The reason for the majority rule is well stated in Hudson Real Estate Co. v. Tower, 156 Mass. 82, 30 N.E. 465, 32 Am. St. Rep. 434:

> "At the time when the defendant signed the subscription paper declared on, it was not a contract, for want of a contracting party on the other side; but it has now been established that a subscription of this sort becomes a contract with the corporation when the corporation has been organized, and in this way the objection of the want of a proper contracting party is finally avoided, provided everything goes on as contemplated without any interruption. Until the organization of the corporation, the subscription is a mere proposition or offer, which may be withdrawn, like any other unaccepted offer. Unless the signer is bound upon a contract, he is not bound at all. It is open to him to withdraw. It is not on the ground that there was no sufficient consideration. The seal would do away with any doubt. But it is on the ground that for the time being, and until the corporation is organized, the writing does not take effect as a contract, because the contemplated party to the contract, on the other side, is not yet in existence, and for this reason, there being no contract, the whole undertaking is inchoate and incomplete, and since there is no contract the party may withdraw."

Again in Bryant's Pond Steam-Mill Co. v. Felt, 87 Me. 234, 32 A. 888, . . . in reference to the minority rule, the court added:

> "It is urged by the counsel for the plaintiff corporation that such subscriptions create binding and enforceable contracts between the subscribers themselves, and are therefore irrevocable, except with the consent of all the subscribers, and some of the authorities cited by him seem to sustain that view. But we find on examination that such views, when expressed, are in most cases mere dicta, and that the cases are very few in which such a doctrine has been acted upon. Reason and the weight of authority are opposed to such a view. Of course, subscription papers may be so worded as to create binding contracts between the subscribers themselves. But we are not now speaking of such subscription, or of voluntary and gratuitous subscriptions to public or charitable objects, which, when accepted and acted upon, become binding. We are now speaking only of subscriptions to the capital stock of proposed business corporations. With regard to such subscriptions, we regard it as settled law that they do not become binding upon the subscribers till the corporations have been organized, and the subscriptions accepted, and that till then the subscribers have a right to revoke their subscriptions. And in view of the fact that such subscriptions are often obtained by overpersuasion, and upon sudden and hasty impulses, we are not prepared to say that the rule of law which allows such a revocation is not bounded in wisdom. We think it is."

We give adherence to the majority rule, not only because it is best supported by authority, but because it is supported by the sounder reasoning as well. It is contended by the defendant in error that the ruling of the court below rejecting the testimony was not excepted to, or that the exception was insufficient, but with that contention we are unable to agree. The court below treated the exception as sufficient and gave full consideration to the case on the merits, on the hearing of the motion for a new trial, and this court will follow the same course. . . .

For the foregoing reasons, we are of opinion that the court below erred in excluding the testimony tending to show a revocation or cancellation of the subscription before the corporation was formed and before the offer was accepted, and for this error *the judgment is reversed, and the cause is remanded for a new trial.*   ◄

COMMENTS AND QUESTIONS

1. Summarize the facts in this case. How was it decided in the lower court? What happened on appeal?
2. The court refers to the majority and minority rules governing stock subscriptions. How do they differ? Which rule was followed in this case?
3. Note the procedural point raised by the defendant in the next-to-last paragraph of the opinion. What was his contention?

Subscriptions After Incorporation

Post-incorporation subscriptions are treated just like any other contract. The offer may be made either by the corporation or by the prospective stockholder, and there must be a valid acceptance before the contract becomes binding. Once the subscription contract has been made, the subscriber immediately becomes a stockholder of the corporation.

Transfers of Stock

Right of Transfer

As a general rule, a stockholder may transfer his shares to any person or organization he chooses. So-called "closely held" corporations often impose restrictions on this right of transfer, however, and the courts will enforce these restrictions if they do not seem to be unreasonable. For example, it is often provided in the charter or the certificate that a stockholder must first give the corporation, or its principal shareholders, an option to purchase his stock before selling it to someone else. If the restriction further provides that he is free to sell his stock to another party in the event that the corporation refuses to meet his price, then the courts will probably uphold the restriction. Similarly, an agreement that an employee stockholder will sell his shares back to the corporation at a stipulated price if he leaves its employment is usually enforceable. No restriction, incidentally, even though it is perfectly reasonable and valid, is binding on an innocent purchaser of stock unless it is expressly set forth in the stock certificate.

Method of Transfer

In most states, the methods of transferring stock are prescribed by the Uniform Stock Transfer Act. This statute provides that "title to a certificate and to the shares represented thereby can be transferred only (a) by a delivery of the certificate, indorsed either in blank or to a specified person, by the person appearing by the certificate to be the owner of the shares represented thereby, or (b) by a delivery of the certificate and a separate document containing a written assignment of the certificate or a power of attorney to sell, assign, or transfer the same or the shares represented thereby, signed by the person appearing by the certificate to be the owner of the shares represented thereby. Such assignment or power of attorney may either be in blank or to a specified person."

Notice that, under the Uniform Act, no legal transfer is possible without the physical delivery of the certificate itself either properly indorsed or accompanied by a written assignment executed by the transferor. Once delivery has been made, the transfer is effective even though no record of it has been entered in the books of the corporation.

The Uniform Act also provides that, if a creditor wants to attach a stockholder's shares in order to satisfy a debt, he must take physical possession of the stock certificate before the attachment becomes binding. At common law, the attachment could be made without seizure of the certificate, on the theory that the certificate was merely evidence of the shares and nothing more. But this practice meant that the certificate could still be transferred to an innocent third party who had no notice of the attachment. It is generally agreed that the Uniform Act has improved the law in this respect.

Negotiability of Stock Certificates

At common law, which holds that a stock certificate is nonnegotiable, a transferee receives no greater rights to the stock than those possessed by the transferor. The Uniform Stock Transfer Act has changed this rule by ascribing to stock certificates many of the attributes of negotiable instruments. The act holds that if a person purchases stock in good faith and for value, he takes good title to the stock free and clear of any defenses or claims that may be raised by former owners or other claimants. The act also holds that a good-faith transferee is not bound by any restrictions imposed by the corporation on the transfer of the stock certificate unless the restrictions are clearly stated on the certificate.

> EXAMPLE
>
> A, who holds stock in X CORPORATION, is induced to sell it to B as a result of B's fraudulent misrepresentation. B, in turn, transfers the stock to C, an innocent purchaser for value. Under the Uniform Act, C would take the stock free and clear of any claim by A.

A similar situation arises when a stockholder who owes the corporation money for his stock transfers it to an innocent third party. Under the Uniform Act, the transferee does not become responsible to the corporation for the transferor's debt; at common law, he would become responsible. If the certificate clearly states that money is still due, however, the act holds that the transferee must pay it, since he has been notified of the corporation's claim.

Recording Transfers—Right to Dividends

Until the corporation has been notified that a transfer of stock has taken place, it is entitled to assume that the transferor is still the legal owner of the stock. Consequently it may continue to pay dividends to the transferor and recognize his right to vote.

How are dividends paid when shares of stock are transferred? As a general rule, if the dividend is declared *before* the transfer takes place, it belongs to the transferor, even though actual payment is to be made after the transfer occurs. If the dividend is declared *after* the transfer takes place, it belongs to the transferee. Often a dividend is declared as of a given date and is made payable to holders of record as of a later date; if, in this situation, a transfer occurs between the two dates, the dividend goes to the transferee. The parties themselves, of course, may agree on some other arrangement. If the corporation is not notified of the transfer of stock, it is always justified in paying dividends to the transferor, since he is still the holder of record. A transferor who wrongfully receives a dividend, of course, must account for it to the transferee.

SECTION 4

RIGHTS AND LIABILITIES OF STOCKHOLDERS

Rights of Stockholders

In General

By electing the board of directors, the stockholders of a corporation have the power to control—at least indirectly—the operations and destiny of their firm. But they seldom participate directly in the management of the corporation. Usually their main interest is in receiving some share of the profits, by way of dividends; they may know little, if anything, about the directors and officers of the company. Nevertheless, a stockholder does have certain legal rights and privileges.

Right to Vote

Although not every class of stock is voting stock (preferred stock, for example, is frequently nonvoting stock), every stock corporation has at least one class of stock which carries with it the right to attend stockholders' meetings, to participate in the election of directors, and to vote on other matters. Such meetings are normally held at least once a year.

As a general rule, only those stockholders who appear on the corporate books are entitled to vote. Thus, a transferee of stock may not vote the shares he has acquired until the corporation has been informed of the transfer and has recorded it.

Ordinarily, a stockholder may authorize someone else to cast his vote for him by means of a *proxy* (an instrument signed by the stockholder delegating his voting right to another). Since most shareholders do not attend meetings, proxies are frequently the only means of gathering enough votes to constitute a quorum.

As a general rule, stockholders are allowed to enter into agreements to pool their voting strength for the purpose of controlling the management, provided the agreement does not go too far. Sometimes these agreements take the form of a *voting trust*, whereby a group of stockholders agree to transfer their shares to a trustee who is authorized to vote all of their combined holdings. In some states, voting trusts are strictly regulated, and a few states have outlawed them entirely. Most jurisdictions, however, permit them if they are reasonable.

In each of the two New York cases that follow, a group of stockholders agreed to pool their votes to keep a certain management group in power. The Court of Appeals upheld the agreement in one case but refused to enforce it in the other. See if you can distinguish the two cases.

McQUADE v. STONEHAM et al.

Court of Appeals of New York, 1934
263 N.Y. 323, 189 N.E. 234

► Action by Francis X. McQuade against Charles A. Stoneham and another. Judgment for plaintiff for $42,827.38, and other relief (142 Misc. 842, 256 N.Y.S. 431) was unanimously affirmed by the Appellate Division (238 App. Div. 827, 262 N.Y.S. 966), and plaintiff appeals by permission. Reversed and complaint dismissed.

POUND, CHIEF JUDGE. The action is brought to compel specific performance of an agreement between the parties entered into to secure the control of National Exhibition Company, also called the Baseball Club (New York Nationals or "Giants"). This was one of Stoneham's enterprises which used the New York Polo Grounds for its home games. McGraw was manager of the Giants. McQuade was at the time the contract was entered into a city magistrate. He resigned December 8, 1930.

Defendant Stoneham became the owner of 1,306 shares or a majority of the stock of National Exhibition Company. Plaintiff and defendant McGraw each purchased 70 shares of his stock. Plaintiff paid Stoneham $50,338.10 for the stock he purchased. As a part of the transaction, the agreement in question was entered into. It was dated May 21, 1919. Some of its pertinent provisions are:

> "VIII. The parties hereto will use their best endeavors for the purpose of continuing as directors of said Company and as officers thereof the following:

"Directors:
"Charles A. Stoneham,
"John J. McGraw,
"Francis X. McQuade
"—with the right to the party of the first part (Stoneham) to name all additional directors as he sees fit:
"Officers:
"Charles A. Stoneham, President,
"John J. McGraw, Vice-President,
"Francis X. McQuade, Treasurer.
"IX. No salaries are to be paid to any of the above officers or directors, except as follows:

"President $45,000
"Vice-President 7,500
"Treasurer 7,500

"X. There shall be no change in said salaries, no change in the amount of the capital, or the number of shares, no change or amendment of the by-laws of the corporation or any matters regarding the policy of the business of the corporation or any matters which may in anywise affect, endanger or interfere with the right of minority stockholders, excepting upon the mutual and unanimous consent of all of the parties hereto. . . .

"XIV. This agreement shall continue and remain in force so long as the parties or any of them or the representative of any, own the stock referred to in this agreement, to wit, the party of the first part, 1,166 shares, the party of the second part 70 shares and the party of the third part 70 shares, except as may otherwise appear by this agreement." . . .

In pursuance of this contract Stoneham became president and McGraw vice-president of the corporation. McQuade became treasurer. In June, 1925, his salary was increased to $10,000 a year. He continued to act until May 2, 1928 when Leo J. Bondy was elected to succeed him. The board of directors consisted of seven men. The four outside of the parties hereto were selected by Stoneham, and he had complete control over them. At the meeting of May 2, 1928, Stoneham and McGraw refrained from voting, McQuade voted for himself, and the other four voted for Bondy. Defendants did not keep their agreement with McQuade to use their best efforts to continue him as treasurer. On the contrary, he was dropped with their entire acquiescence. At the next stockholders' meeting he was dropped as a director although they might have elected him.

The courts below have refused to order the reinstatement of McQuade, but have given him damages for wrongful discharge, with a right to sue for future damages.

The cause for dropping McQuade was due to the falling out of friends. McQuade and Stoneham had disagreed. The trial court has found in substance that their numerous quarrels and disputes did not affect the orderly and efficient administration of the business of the corporation; that plaintiff was removed because he had antagonized the dominant Stoneham by persisting in challenging his power over the corporate treasury and for no misconduct on his part. The court also finds that plaintiff was removed by Stoneham for protecting the corporation and its minority stockholders. We will assume that Stoneham put him out when he might have retained him, merely in order to get rid of him.

Defendants say that the contract in suit was void because the directors held their office charged with the duty to act for the corporation according to their best judgment and that any contract which compels a director to vote to keep any particular person in office and at a stated salary is illegal. Directors are the exclusive executive representatives of the corporation, charged with administration of its internal affairs and the management and use of its assets. They manage the business of the corporation. (General Corporation Law, Consol. Laws, c. 23, 27.) "An agreement to continue a man as president is dependent upon his continued loyalty to the interest of the corporation." Fells v. Katz, 256 N.Y. 67, 72; 175 N.E. 516, 517. So much is undisputed.

Plaintiff contends that the converse of this proposition is true and that an agreement among directors to continue a man as an officer of a corporation is not to be broken so long as such officer is loyal to the interests of the corporation and that, as plaintiff has been found loyal to the corporation, the agreement of defendants is enforceable.

Although it has been held that an agreement among stockholders whereby it is attempted to divest the directors of their power to discharge an unfaithful employee of the corporation is illegal as against public policy (Fells v. Katz, *supra*), it must be equally true that the stockholders may not, by agreement among themselves, control the directors in the exercise of the judgment vested in them by virtue of their office to elect officers and fix salaries. Their motives may not be questioned so long as their acts are legal. The bad faith or the improper motives of the parties does not change the rule. . . .

Stockholders may, of course, combine to elect directors. That rule is well settled. As Holmes, C. J. pointedly said (Brightman v. Bates, 175 Mass. 105, 111; 55 N.E. 809, 811): "If stockholders want to make their power felt, they must unite. There is no reason why a majority should not agree to keep together." The power to unite is, however, limited to the election of directors and is not extended to contracts whereby limitations are placed on the power of directors to manage the business of the corporation by the selection of agents at defined salaries.

The minority shareholders whose interest McQuade says he has been punished for protecting are not, aside from himself, complaining about his discharge. He is not acting for the corporation or for them in this action. It is impossible to see how the corporation has been injured by the substitution of Bondy as treasurer in place of McQuade. As McQuade represents himself in this action and seeks redress for his own wrongs, "we prefer to listen to [the corporation and the minority stockholders] before any decision as to their wrongs." Faulds v. Yates, 57 Ill. 416, 417; 11 Am. Rep. 24.

It is urged that we should pay heed to the morals and manners of the market place to sustain this agreement and that we should hold that its violation gives rise to a cause of action for damages rather than base our decision on any outworn notions of public policy. Public policy is a dangerous guide in determining the validity of a contract and courts should not interfere lightly with the freedom of competent parties to make their own contracts. We do not close our eyes to the fact that such agreements, tacitly or openly arrived at, are not uncommon, especially in close corporations [10] where the stockholders are doing business for convenience under a corporate organization. We know that majority stockholders, united in voting trusts, effectively manage the business of a corporation by choosing trustworthy directors to reflect their policies in the corporate management. Nor are we unmindful that McQuade has, so the court has found, been shabbily treated as a purchaser of stock from Stoneham. We have said: "A trustee is held to something stricter than the morals of the market place" (Meinhard v. Salmon, 249 N.Y. 458, 464; 164 N.E. 545, 546; 62 A.L.R. 1) but Stoneham and McGraw were not trustees for McQuade as an individual. Their duty was to the corporation and its stockholders, to be exercised according to their unrestricted lawful judgment. They were under no legal obligation to deal righteously with McQuade if it was against public policy to do so.

The courts do not enforce mere moral obligations, nor legal ones either, unless someone seeks to establish rights which may be waived by custom and for convenience. We are constrained by authority to hold that a contract is illegal and void so far as it precludes the board of directors, at the risk of incurring legal liability, from changing officers, salaries, or policies or retaining individuals in office, except by consent of the contracting parties. On the whole, such a holding is probably preferable to one which would open the courts to pass on the motives of directors in the lawful exercise of their trust. . . .

The judgment of the Appellate Division and that of the Trial Term should be reversed and the complaint dismissed, with costs in all courts. ◄

COMMENTS AND QUESTIONS

1. What was the issue in this case? How was it decided in the lower court? What happened in the Court of Appeals?
2. McQuade urged the court to "pay heed to the morals and manners of the market place," and the court acknowledged that such agreements are common in close corporations. How, then, did the court justify its decision?

CLARK v. DODGE

Court of Appeals of New York, 1936
269 N.Y. 410, 199 N.E. 641

► Action by David H. Clark against John L. Dodge and others, wherein defendants filed a counterclaim. From an order of the Appellate Division, Second Department, entered on October 10, 1934, dismissing the complaint (242 App. Div. 728, 274 N.Y.S. 677), plaintiff appeals.

---

[10] A close corporation is one in which all, or a large part, of the stock is held by its officers and directors, who thus have complete control over its operations. This type of corporation is often found in small business establishments, especially in so-called "family" corporations.

Judgment of Appellate Division reversed and order of Special Term affirmed.

CROUCH, JUDGE. The action is for the specific performance of a contract between the plaintiff Clark, and the defendant Dodge, relating to the affairs of the two defendant corporations. To the complaint a joint answer by the three defendants was interposed, consisting of denials and a separate defense and counterclaim. To the separate defense and counterclaim a reply was made. The defendant then moved under rule 112 of the Rules of Civil Practice, and under sections 476, 96, and 279 of the Civil Practice Act, to dismiss the complaint. The motion was made "on the pleadings in this action and the admissions of the plaintiff" in two affidavits submitted by him on a prior motion in the action. The alleged admissions are equivocal at best, and clearly were not "intended to be treated as a part of a pleading or made to avoid some question arising on the pleadings." Lloyd v. R.S.M. Corporation, 251 N.Y. 318, 320; 167 N.E. 456. We shall deal therefore, with the questions here presented in the light of the facts most favorable to plaintiff appearing in the pleadings only.

Those facts, briefly stated, are as follows: The two corporate defendants are New Jersey corporations manufacturing medicinal preparations by secret formulae. The main office, factory, and assets of both corporations are located in the state of New York. In 1921, and at all times since, Clark owned 25 per cent and Dodge 75 per cent of the stock of each corporation. Dodge took no active part in the business, although he was a director, and through ownership of their qualifying shares, controlled the other directors of both corporations. He was the president of Bell & Co., Inc., and nominally general manager of Hollings-Smith Company, Inc. The plaintiff Clark was a director and held the offices of treasurer and general manager of Bell & Co., Inc., and also had charge of the major portion of the business of Hollings-Smith Company, Inc. The formulae and methods of manufacture of the medicinal preparations were known to him alone. Under date of February 15, 1921, Dodge and Clark, the sole owners of the stock of both corporations, entered into a written agreement under seal, which after reciting the stock ownership of both parties, the desire of Dodge that Clark should continue in the efficient management and control of the business of Bell & Co., Inc., so long as he should "remain faithful, efficient and competent to so manage and control the said business"; and his further desire that Clark should not be the sole custodian of a specified formula, but should share his knowledge thereof and of the method of manufacture with a son of Dodge, provided, in substance, as follows: That Dodge during his lifetime and after his death, a trustee to be appointed by his will, would so vote his stock and so vote as a director that the plaintiff (a) should continue to be a director of Bell & Co., Inc.; and (b) should continue as its general manager so long as he should be "faithful, efficient, and competent"; (c) should during his life receive one-fourth of the net income of the corporations either by way of salary or dividends; and (d) that no unreasonable or incommensurate salaries should be paid to other officers or agents which would so reduce the net income as materially to affect Clark's profits.

Clark on his part agreed to disclose the specified formula to the son and to instruct him in the details and methods of manufacture; and, further, at the end of his life to bequeath his stock—if no issue survived him—to the wife and children of Dodge.

It was further provided that the provisions in regard to the division of net profits and the regulation of salaries should also apply to the Hollings-Smith Company.

The complaint alleges due performance of the contract by Clark and breach thereof by Dodge in that he has failed to use his stock control to continue Clark as a director and as general manager, and has prevented Clark from receiving his proportion of the income, while taking his own, by causing the employment of incompetent persons at excessive salaries, and otherwise.

The relief sought is reinstatement as director and general manager and an accounting by Dodge and by the corporations for waste and for the proportion of net income due the plaintiff, with an injunction against further violations.

The only question which need be discussed is whether the contract is illegal as against public policy within the decision in McQuade v. Stoneham, 263 N.Y. 323, 189 N.E. 234, upon the authority of which the complaint was dismissed by the Appellate Division.

"The business of a corporation shall be managed by its board of directors." General Corporation Law (Consol. Laws. c. 23). That is the statutory norm. Are we committed by the McQuade Case to the doctrine that there may be no variation, however slight or innocuous, from that norm, where salaries or policies or the retention of individuals in the office are concerned? There is ample authority supporting that doctrine and something may be said for it, since it furnishes a simple, if arbitrary test. Apart from its practical administrative convenience, the reasons upon which it is said to rest are more or less nebulous. Public policy, the intention of the Legislature, detriment to the corporation, are phrases which in this connection mean little. Possible harm to bona fide purchasers of stock or to creditors or to stockholding minorities have more substance; but such harms are absent in many instances. If the enforcement of a particular contract damages nobody—not even, in any perceptible degree, the public—one sees no reason for holding it illegal, even though it impinges slightly upon the broad provisions of section 27. Damage suffered or threatened is a logical and practical test, and has come to be the one generally adopted by the courts. Where the directors are the sole stockholders, there seems to be no objection to enforcing an agreement among them to vote for certain people as officers. There is no direct decision to that effect in this court, yet there are strong indications that such a rule has long been recognized. The opinion in Manson v. Curtis, 223 N.Y. 313, 325; 119 N.E. 559, 562. Ann. Cas. 1918E., 247, closed its discussion by saying:

> "The rule that all the stockholders by their universal consent may do so as they choose with the corporate concerns and assets, provided the interests of creditors are not affected, because they are the complete owners of the corporation, cannot be invoked here."

That was because all the stockholders were not affected, "the parties in interest, might, by their original agreement of incorporation, limit their respective rights and powers," even where there was a conflicting statutory standard. . . .

Except for the broad dicta in the McQuade opinion, we think there can be no doubt that the agreement here in question was legal and that the complaint states a cause of action. There was no attempt to sterilize the board of directors, as in the Manson and McQuade Cases. The only restrictions on Dodge were (a) that as a stockholder he should vote for Clark as a director—a perfectly legal contract; (b) that as director he should continue Clark as general manager, so long as he proved faithful, efficient, and competent—an agreement which could harm nobody; (c) that Clark should always receive as salary or dividends one-fourth of the "net income." For the purposes of this motion it is only just to construe that phrase as meaning whatever was left for distribution after the directors had in good faith set aside whatever they deemed wise; (d) that no salaries to other officers should be paid, unreasonable in amount or incommensurate with services rendered—a beneficial and not a harmful agreement.

If there was any invasion of the powers of the directorate under that agreement, it is so slight as to be negligible; and certainly there is no damage suffered by or threatened to anybody. The broad statements in the McQuade opinion, applicable to the facts there, should be confined to those facts.

The judgment of the Appellate Division should be reversed and the order of the Special Term affirmed, with costs in this court and in the Appellate Division.

Judgment accordingly.   ◄

COMMENTS AND QUESTIONS

1. Summarize the provisions of the contract between Dodge and Clark. Did the court hold this agreement to be enforceable?
2. How does the agreement here differ from that in the *McQuade* case immediately preceding? Why did the court in this case not follow the decision handed down in that case? Are the two decisions consistent?

Pre-emptive Right to New Stock

The amount of capital stock issued by a corporation is usually fixed by the corporate charter and may be increased only with the approval of the stockholders. An increase in the amount of capital stock necessarily changes the percentage of stock held by each stockholder, perhaps even to the point of destroying or endangering a controlling interest. Consequently, each stockholder ordinarily is given a *pre-emptive right* to subscribe to the same percentage of the new stock as he holds of the old.

EXAMPLE

x holds 600 shares of stock of $10 par value out of a total capital stock of 1,000 shares. The capital stock of the corporation is $10,000. If the corporation, after proper authorization, decides to issue 1,000 more shares, thereby increasing its total capital stock to $20,000, it must give x a chance to buy 600 of the new shares.

Pre-emptive rights are not always granted, however. Nonvoting stock, for example, carries with it no measure of corporate control; consequently a holder of such stock ordinarily has no guaranteed right to subscribe to a new issue. Similarly, pre-emptive rights are generally not extended when treasury stock is reissued.

The following case presents an interesting example of this doctrine.

ROSS TRANSPORT, INCORPORATED et al. v. CROTHERS et al.

Court of Appeals of Maryland, 1946
185 Md. 573, 45 A. 2d 267

▶ Stockholders' derivative suit by Charles T. Crothers, for himself and for other stockholders who might join and be made parties, against Ross Transport, Inc., and Wallace Williams, and others to set aside the issuance of shares of stock to defendants, Elizabeth B. Williams, Corrine Williams, Lois Williams Young, and William B. Ross, wherein Edmund W. Crothers joined as a party plaintiff. Decree for plaintiffs, and defendants appeal. Affirmed.

MARBURY, CHIEF JUDGE. . . . It appears from the record that the corporation was organized on January 19, 1942 to operate a fleet of buses to transport employees of Triumph Explosives, Inc. to and from its plant at Elkton, Maryland. The incorporators were Wallace Williams, William B. Ross and Gervase R. Sinclair who later died. These three and F. DuPont Thomson and James W. Hughes were the directors. At the organization meeting of the directors, Williams was named as President and Ross as General Manager. The authorized stock was 5000 shares of no par value. At the organization meeting a resolution was passed authorizing the sale of this stock at $20 a share, and providing that stock to the value of $30,000 be offered for sale. This limited the stock to be issued to 1500 shares. . . . (The total original amount of stock issued was 1035 shares.)

In the latter part of July 1942, after the death of Mr. Sinclair, Charles T. Crothers purchased the Sinclair stock, 200 shares, at $20 and 5% interest from the date of issuance. This did not, of course, increase the amount of stock outstanding. On August 26, 1942, the stock complained of was issued to the wife and daughters of Wallace Williams and to William B. Ross, totaling 365 shares in all, and increasing the outstanding stock to 1400 shares. All of this stock was issued at the set price of $20.00 a share. The stock issued to the Williams family was paid by Mr. Williams' check for $4800. Mr. Ross paid the company $2500 for his stock. . . .

Williams and Ross, therefore, had the controlling interest in the company. Mr. Williams testified that all of the stock in the company was sold by him personally under the directors' resolution. . . .

The sale of this additional stock to a director and to the family of the president and director without any further authority than the original resolution, and without opportunity to buy given to other stockholders, is sought to be justified on the ground that it was originally planned, and that the money was needed to purchase additional buses at a cost of about

$16,000. The facts, however, show no such need. The company was an immediate financial success. It was engaged in a special business, of which it had a monopoly, and in which it could not help making money so long as Triumph Explosives continued to operate its large plant, employing the workmen the Transport Corporation hauled. . . . On November 27, 1942, a dividend of $5 a share was declared. On December 17, 1942, one of $15 (called a return of capital, but not authorized by the stockholders, Code, Article 23, Sec. 32). On the same date, another dividend of $5 a share was declared payable June 30, 1943. The defendants, Williams and Ross, who were operating the company, knew on August 26, 1942, that they were about to receive large sums in dividends in addition to the salaries they were getting. The benefit of these dividends would not only increase the value of the stock, but the first two would pay back all the subscribers had invested, leaving any future earnings and distributions pure profit. Under these circumstances, they took the opportunity they thought they had to increase their investment, and in fact received in December the full amount they invested in August, leaving them with the additional stock on which to receive such further dividends as were obviously in sight.

The appellants contend that the company was not in the claimed good financial condition in August, because no allowance had been made for income and profits taxes. But if we reduce the book surplus of $25,000 on August 16, 1942, by allowing for a 40% tax (the limit unless the earnings increased), we still find the company with a net surplus of $15,000, 75% of the original investment. The stock had no "market value" but it must be obvious that it was worth much more than $20 a share on August 26th.

The appellees gave two reasons for their contention that the stock sales of August 26th were void: First because they deprive them and the other original stockholders of their pre-emptive rights to purchase a proportionate amount of the remaining shares, and second, because in selling to themselves and their nominees, Williams and Ross have abused their trust as officers and directors. They claim to be injured in two ways. Their voting powers have been proportionately lessened, and the control of the company has passed to Williams and Ross. And the amount paid in dividends has to be divided among 365 more shares of stock to the consequent financial loss of the holders of the original shares. . . . The doctrine known as the pre-emptive right of shareholders is a judicial interpretation of general principles of corporation law. Existing stockholders are the owners of the business, and are entitled to have that ownership continued in the same proportion. Therefore, when additional stock is issued, those already having shares are held to have the first right to buy the new stock in proportion to their holdings. This doctrine was first promulgated in 1807 in the case of Gray v. Portland Bank, 3 Mass. 364, 3 Am. Dec. 156. At that time, corporations were small and closely held, much like the one before us in this case. But in the succeeding years, corporations grew and expanded. New capital was frequently required. New properties had to be acquired for which it was desirable to issue stock. Companies merged, and new stock in the consolidation was issued. Stock was issued for services. Different kinds of stock were authorized—preferred without voting power but with prior dividend rights—preferred with the right to convert into common— several classes of both common and preferred with different rights. Some stock had voting rights. All of these changes in the corporate structure made it impossible always to follow the simple doctrines earlier decided. Exceptions grew, and were noted in the decisions.

Only one of these exceptions is involved in the present case. It has been held that pre-emptive rights do not exist where the stock about to be issued is part of the original issue. This exception is based upon the fact that the original subscribers took their stock on the implied understanding that the incorporators could complete the sale of the remaining stock to obtain the capital thought necessary to start the business. But this gives rise to an exception to the exception, where conditions have changed since the original issue. The stock sold the Williams family and Ross was part of the original issue, and it is claimed by the applicants that it comes within the exception, and the appellees and the other stockholders have no pre-emptive rights. . . . The appellees, on the other hand, contend, and the chancellor found, that changed conditions made it unnecessary to use the remaining unsold stock to obtain capital, and pre-emptive rights exist in it just as they would exist in newly authorized stock. . . .

It is unnecessary for us to decide which of these two conflicting points of view applies to this case, because another controlling consideration enters. The doctrine of pre-emptive right is not affected by the identity of the purchasers of the issued stock. What it is concerned with is who did not get it. But when officers and directors sell to themselves, and thereby gain an advantage, both in value and in voting power, another situation arises, which it does not require the assertion of a pre-emptive right to deal with. . . .

Decree affirmed with costs.   ◄

COMMENTS AND QUESTIONS

1. Outline the facts that gave rise to this litigation and the contentions of each side. How did the court decide?
2. The court speaks of "an exception to the exception" to the doctrine of pre-emptive rights. Explain.

Right to Inspect Books

Every stockholder has the right to inspect the books of the corporation, so long as his examination is for a reasonable purpose and so long as he gives reasonable notice. Since few stockholders know very much about bookkeeping, the right to inspect may be deputized to an accountant or to some other agent.

In the case that follows, the defendant corporation refused to permit the plaintiff stockholder to examine its books. The plaintiff then brought a writ of mandamus to compel the defendant to permit inspection.

SLAY v. POLONIA PUBLISHING CO.

Supreme Court of Michigan, 1930
249 Mich. 609, 229 N.W. 434

▶ SHARPE, J.   Plaintiff, the owner of one share of stock in the defendant company, petitioned for mandamus to compel its officers to permit him to inspect and examine the books and statements of the corporation. Defendant seeks review by certiorari of the order of the trial court granting the writ.

Plaintiff's right thereto is based upon the following provision in section 11, chap. 1, pt. 2, Act No. 84, Pub. Acts 1921 (Comp. Laws Supp. 1922, sec. 9053 [50]):

> "The books of every corporation containing its accounts shall be kept, and shall at all reasonable times be open in the city, village or town where such corporation is located, or at the office of the treasurer of such corporation within this State, for inspection by any of the stockholders of said corporation, and said stockholders shall have access to the books and statements of said corporation and shall have the right to examine the same in the said city, village or town or at said office."

Before its enactment, this court had held that, under the common law, a stockholder in a corporation had the right in a proper case and for a proper purpose, to inspect the corporate records. . . . But such right was a qualified, and not an absolute, one. The duty devolved upon the stockholder to make it appear to the officers that he was actuated by motives that were lawful and proper, and that his purpose in securing the information was to subserve the interest of the corporation or his personal interest as a holder of corporate stock.

The provision in the statute above quoted contains no such limitation. This court must assume that the legislature was aware of the rights of the stockholder under the common law, and that its purpose in including this provision in the corporation act was to make some change therein. It cannot be said to be merely declaratory of the common law, for the reason that it omits the requirement in that law as to the duty devolving on the stockholder, as above stated, when making his request.

It is to be assumed that the request is made for a proper purpose; that the stockholder is acting in good faith and seeking thereby to protect his own interest or that of the corporation, and therefore his request therefor need not be accompanied by any statement of his purpose. The statute accords the right to him, and he is entitled to the privilege for the asking. . . .

Thus far it may fairly be said there is substantial uniformity in the holdings of the courts. But when his request is denied and he seeks mandatory relief, and the answer of the corporation sets up facts from which it appears that his purpose is not as above stated, but is inimical to the best interests of the corporation and its other stockholders, and these facts are conceded, or established by proofs, the authorities are much at variance as to the duty of the court to issue the writ.

The supreme court of Wisconsin (State ex rel. Dempsey v. Werra Aluminum Foundry Co., 173 Wis. 651, 182 N.W. 354, 22 A.L.R. 1) has held that the writ will issue as a matter of course, but intimates that the stockholder may be prevented from using the information thus secured for an unlawful purpose. In Johnson v. Langlon, 135 Cal. 624, 67 Pac. 1050, 87 Am. St. Rep. 156, the right of the stockholder is held to be absolute, and that he cannot "be met with the defense that his motives are improper." In Wilson v. Mackinaw State Bank, 217 Ill. App. 494, it was said that the right was absolute and did not depend upon any circumstance or condition except the ownership of stock. There are other decisions of similar import, although later cases in some of the same courts qualify the language used.

But the great weight of authority sustains the rule that, while the right given by the statute is absolute, mandamus is a discretionary writ, which will not be issued to enforce such right except for a just cause, and a proper purpose. In Guthrie v. Harkness, 199 U.S. 148, 156; 26 Sup.Ct. 4, 4 Ann. Cas. 433, it was said:

> "It does not follow that the courts will compel the inspection of the bank's books under all circumstances. In issuing the writ of mandamus the court will exercise a sound discretion and grant the right under proper safeguards to protect the interests of all concerned. The writ should not be granted for speculative purposes or to gratify idle curiosity or to aid a blackmailer, but it may not be denied to the stockholder who seeks the information for legitimate purposes."

. . . Mandamus is the proper remedy of a stockholder to secure such right. . . . It is "not a writ of right . . . and will not issue to compel an unlawful act or to work an injustice." Johnson v. Board of Supervisors, 202 Mich. 597, 600; 168 N.W. 421. The question presented, then, is this, Under the facts appearing in this record, was the plaintiff entitled to the writ?

The defendant in its answer to the order to show cause, verified by its vice-president and general manager, averred that the real owner of the share of stock assigned to plaintiff was one Louis Wojcik. The seventh paragraph thereof reads as follows:

> "That as to the matters alleged in paragraph seven of said petition, this respondent says that one Louis Wojcik is, and had been for some time past, the principal owner and the editor of the Polish Daily News, the sole competitor of this respondent in publishing a Polish daily newspaper in the city of Detroit. That the said Louis Wojcik has interviewed numerous of the advertisers, whose advertisements appear in the issues of this respondent's paper, and falsely stated to them that this respondent did not have the circulation it claimed to have; that it was losing money and it would only be a matter of time when he, the said Louis Wojcik, would own this respondent or put it out of business; and that they, the advertisers, were foolish in wasting their time in advertising in respondent's paper, and made divers and false statements relative to this respondent corporation, to its paper, and to its business, and made threats to divers persons that he would ruin this respondent, and as a part of his scheme so to do this, respondent shows that in the month of

June or July in the year 1927, he induced one Anthony Glowczewski to buy one share of this respondent's capital stock, and to that end the said Anthony Glowczewski approached one Dr. Lazowski and purchased from the said Dr. Lazowski one share of stock, and that the consideration therefor was paid to the said Anthony Glowczewski by the said Louis Wojcik.

"This respondent further shows that the said Louis C. Slay, alleged petitioner herein, was and is an employee of the said Louis Wojcik, and has been associated with him in business for some years in the Detroit Commerce Corporation and in other enterprises; and avers and charges the truth to be, that the said Louis C. Slay is merely a figurehead for the said Louis Wojcik, and that the said Louis Wojcik is desirous of obtaining the information sought by the said Louis C. Slay for the purpose of using the same against the best interest of this respondent and of the stockholders, and of distorting the information obtained thereby for the purpose of unfair competition with this respondent and with its business, and for the purpose of attempting to cripple this respondent and its stockholders, and that the information sought by this alleged petitioner is not sought in good faith, nor for the personal use of said petitioner, and that the furnishing of such information would be detrimental to the interests of all the stockholders of this respondent, but, as aforesaid, it is merely a blind to obtain such information to use in an unjust and unfair attempt to injure and damage this respondent and its stockholders."

At the opening of the hearing, counsel for the defendant said: "If the relator is willing to make it the sole issue, that is, that the motive for the obtainance of information is not relevant to the issue and that he has a right of inspection irrespective of motives or desires, then I am willing to proceed. If he is willing to admit that it does not make any difference what a man's motives are, but that he has a right to inspect the books irrespective of any ulterior or improper motive."

After some discussion, he further said: "Your proposition is that no matter how detrimental to the Polonia Publishing Company your desire may be, it is absolutely immaterial."

To which counsel for the plaintiff replied: "Absolute, unless it appears we are going to perpetrate a criminal act."

We must, therefore, accept the statements in the answer above quoted as expressive of the purpose of the plaintiff in seeking the inspection. It needs no analysis of the language used to conclude that such purpose was entirely foreign to his status as a stockholder; that the privilege of inspection by him was not sought in good faith for the protection of the interests of the corporation, or of his own interests as a stockholder; and that he was not entitled to the writ.

The order reviewed is reversed and set aside and the petition dismissed, with costs to appellant.

WIEST, C. J. and BUTZEL, CLARK, McDONALD, POTTER, NORTH, and FEAD, JJ., concurred.   ◄

COMMENTS AND QUESTIONS

1. What was the issue before the court here? How did the lower court rule? What happened on appeal?

2. Note, toward the end of the opinion, the quoted exchange between defendant's and plaintiff's counsel. Do you think the argument of the plaintiff's counsel was a good one? Did he have any choice?

3. The court notes that the statute puts no condition on the right to inspect, whereas the common-law right was conditional; the court then assumes that the purpose of the legislature was to make some change in the common-law right. Does the court's decision carry out that legislative purpose?

Right to Dividends

IN GENERAL. Each stockholder has the right to receive his proportionate share of any dividends declared by the corporation, subject, of course, to the rights of any preferred stockholders. He has no absolute right to receive dividends even when the corporation has earned a profit, however. Except in certain rare cases (to be discussed shortly), the directors have sole discretion in deciding whether or not a dividend will be declared.

KINDS OF DIVIDEND. Customarily, a certain dividend is declared for each share held, according to its class and preference, and that amount is paid in cash. Dividends may, however, be paid in property, as, for example, in some amount of the goods manufactured by the corporation (e.g., a whiskey company might give each of its stockholders a bottle of bourbon for each share held). Dividends may also be paid in the form of stock held in other corporations, or in stock of the corporation itself. The latter type of dividend is referred to as a *stock dividend.* Although such a dividend increases the number of outstanding shares, the proportionate interest of each stockholder remains unchanged.

EXAMPLE

A corporation has 1,000 shares of stock outstanding, of which x owns 550. The directors declare a stock dividend of one share for each share held. As a result, x receives a dividend of 550 additional shares, so that he now holds 1,100 shares out of a total of 2,000 issued. His controlling interest in the corporation is still 55 per cent.

WHEN DIVIDENDS MAY BE DECLARED. In a majority of states, dividends may be declared only out of surplus—that is, only out of that portion of the net assets of the corporation in excess of its capital stock. If no surplus exists, no dividends may be declared. Other jurisdictions have liberalized this rule to permit dividends to be declared out of current net profits, even though such profits are not great enough to create a surplus.

EXAMPLE

A corporation has 100,000 shares of $5 par value stock outstanding—that is, capital stock of $500,000. In its first year of operations, it loses $50,000. No dividends may be declared. In its second year, it has a $25,000 net profit; its net assets amount to $475,000. In a majority of states, no dividend could be declared at the end of the second year, since there is as yet no surplus. However, in some states, dividends could be paid out of the $25,000 net profits if the directors chose to do so. If in the third year a $50,000 net profit is made, giving total net assets of $525,000, a majority of states would then permit a dividend to be paid out of the $25,000 surplus (i.e., the excess over the capital stock) which now exists. In other states, the directors could declare dividends up to $50,000, the amount of the current net profits.

Clearly, a corporation might decide to create a surplus or to increase the amount of any existing surplus by the simple expedient of placing a higher value on its corporate assets (e.g., its building or equipment), or by decreasing the amount of its capital stock. Many states do not permit dividends of any kind to be paid out of such "paper" surpluses, however. Other states permit only stock dividends to be declared.

If a corporation wrongfully declares a dividend and later becomes insolvent, many jurisdictions hold the directors personally liable to the corporate creditors. If a corporation is contemplating the improper declaration of dividends, an injunction may be obtained prohibiting them from doing so.

The two cases that follow illustrate some of the difficulties involved in determining whether a dividend may be lawfully declared. Note carefully the discussion of the definitions of capital stock, surplus, and net profits.

GOODNOW v. AMERICAN WRITING PAPER COMPANY

Court of Errors and Appeals of New Jersey, 1908
73 N.J. Eq. 692, 69 Atl. 1014

► SWAYZE, J. The appellant filed his bill to have a resolution for the payment of a dividend upon the preferred stock of the defendant declared unlawful, null and void, and to restrain payment thereof. The bill charges that the capital stock of the company was for the most part issued for property purchased, which included trade-marks and good will taken at a grossly excessive valuation, and that whatever the value of the property given in exchange for the stock may have been at the time of purchase, it now falls short of the aggregate of the debts and the par value of the stock; that the operations of the company have been successful, and to some extent profitable, a considerable sum of money having been earned in excess of the interest upon the mortgage, and of the $100,000 required annually to be set aside as a sinking fund for the mortgage bonds, and of the cost of operating the company and keeping up its manufacturing plant; that the net annual gains as reported by the directors to the stockholders prior to 1906 were used in part to purchase the company's own bonds for its treasury and for the sinking fund, and in part were set aside for working capital; and that on July 1st, 1906, the balance sheet of the company showed accumulated profits to an amount several times the amount required to pay the proposed dividend; that the dividend was authorized by resolution of October 2d, 1906 (1905 in the printed case seems to be a clerical error), which directed the treasurer to pay the dividend out of net profits on April 1st, 1907. The gravamen [11] of the bill is that the payment of this dividend would constitute a division and withdrawal and payment to the holders of preferred shares of a part of the capital stock of the company, and would con-

---

[11] That is, the gist of the plaintiff's allegations.

stitute an unlawful reduction of the capital stock in violation of the Corporation Act.

To this bill the defendant demurred, and the court of chancery allowed the demurrer.

We think it unnecessary to discuss the question dealt with by the learned vice-chancellor as to the right of the stockholders to raise this question, or the question so thoroughly discussed at the bar as to the meaning of net profits under our Corporation Act as it stood prior to the enactment of chapter 143 of the Laws of 1904. The question seems to us to involve only the construction of that act, and to turn upon the change introduced thereby. Cases cited from other jurisdictions are therefore of little assistance.

The material language in the Act of 1896 (P.L. 1896, p. 286) is as follows:

> "No corporation shall make dividends, except from the surplus or net profits arising from its business, nor divide, withdraw, or in any way pay to the stockholders, or any of them, any part of its capital stock, or reduce its capital stock, except according to this act."

In the Act of 1904 this section is changed so as to read as follows:

> "The directors of a corporation shall not make dividends except from its surplus, or from the net profits arising from the business of such corporation, nor shall it divide, withdraw, or in any way pay to the stockholders, or any of them, any part of the capital stock of such corporation, or reduce its capital stock except as authorized by law."

Under the Act of 1896 there was room to contend that the words "net profits" were intended to be synonymous with the word "Surplus"; the language used was "from the surplus or net profits." Under the Act of 1904, this contention is no longer possible; the language used is "from its surplus, or from the net profits." The evident intent of the change is to point out two funds from which dividends may be made.

Although the change in language indicates that the legislature made a distinction between surplus and net profits, it does not necessarily follow that net profits mean the difference between gross earnings and what may be called operating expenses. Such profits may be called annual profits upon the whole of the company's business from its organization. If either of these meanings is adopted, the declaration of the present dividend is justified. There was an excess of gross earnings over the operating expenses of the current year, and the value of the present assets exceeded the value of the actual assets with which the company began business.

The complainant contends, however, that the term "net profits" is used in neither of these senses, but in the sense of an excess of the value of the present assets over the par value of the capital stock issued and outstanding; and the claim is that since that stock was issued for property at a gross overvaluation, there can be no dividend until the difference between the actual value of the property, and the value at which it was taken over is made up. The argument is that the intent of section 30 is to prevent the capital stock being distributed in the form of dividends, and the words "capital stock" are supposed to be used in that section as synonymous with "share capital."

The ambiguity on the term "capital stock" was noticed by this court in Wetherbee v. Baker, 35 N.J. Eq. (8 Stew.) 501. It may mean either the capital subscribed (the share capital) or the capital paid in, the actual assets with which the company does business. It seems to be used in both senses in this very section. When the legislature forbids the dividing, withdrawing or paying to the stockholders any part of the capital stock it means the capital actually invested; when it forbids the reduction of capital stock it means the share capital subscribed, or the authorized capital.

We are led to the conclusion that the words "capital stock" in the first instance mean capital actually invested, by the fact that it is only actual assets that can be divided, withdrawn, or paid over. These words are not apt words to apply to nominal or share capital, which may be reduced, but can hardly be withdrawn, divided, or paid over. Thus, capital actually invested does not include net profits arising from the business of the company, for the reasons that the language of the section itself makes a distinction between the declaration of dividends of profits and the withdrawing of capital; that another method of securing payment of the par value of the stock is provided in other sections of the act; that the policy to be served by the prohibition of section 30 is to prevent the frittering away of the actual assets with which the company is to do business, not the nominal assets which it has never received and for which it still has a claim against the subscribers for unpaid stock. The section distinguishes between surplus and net profits; but if the complainant is correct in his contention that net profits mean only the excess above the share capital, we see no distinction in fact, but only in bookkeeping entries.

It may not infrequently happen that stock is issued on which avowedly only a partial payment is made of the amount subscribed, which is therefore subject to further calls. We cannot think that in such a case, where the company prospers, there are no net profits available for dividends until the earnings accumulate to an amount equal to the par value of the shares. The complainant's brief concedes this, and the concession seems quite fatal to his argument.

The language of section 47 supports this view. It requires the directors, after reserving over and above its capital stock paid in such sum, as shall have been fixed as a working capital, to declare a dividend of the whole accumulated profits. Here the profits are clearly to be ascertained by reference to the capital stock paid in, and not to the nominal share capital. It would be quite inconsistent to require by section 47, a dividend out of profits to be ascertained with reference to capital stock paid in, and to forbid by section 30, a dividend, unless there were net profits over and above the amount of the nominal share capital. . . .

The decree is affirmed with costs.

For affirmance—THE CHANCELLOR, CHIEF JUSTICE, GARRISON, SWAYZE, REED, PARKER, BERGEN, VOORHEES, MINTURN, BOGERT, VREDENBURGH, VROOM, GREEN, GRAL, DILL—15.

For reversal—None.   ◄

1. What was the plaintiff trying to accomplish in this case? Did he succeed?

2. The Act of 1904 provided that dividends could be declared out of "surplus" or "net profits" and that the "capital stock" should not be impaired. What was the plaintiff's contention on the manner in which this statute should be interpreted? How did the court construe these terms?

BERKS BROADCASTING COMPANY, Appellant
v. CRAUMER et al.

Supreme Court of Pennsylvania, 1947
356 Pa. 620, 52 A. 2d 571

► Appeal, No. 21, Jan. T., 1947, from judgment of C. P. Berks Co., May T., 1945, No. 95, in case of Berks Broadcasting Company v. Harry S. Craumer et al. Judgment reversed; reargument refused May 26, 1947.

Assumpsit. Before MAYS, P. J., without a jury.

Adjudication filed. Finding for defendants. Plaintiff appealed.

Opinion by MR. JUSTICE HORACE STERN, May 7, 1947: The determinant of this litigation is the provision of the Business Corporation Law of May 5, 1933, P.L. 364, section 701, that a corporation, in computing a surplus from which cash dividends may lawfully be paid, must not include as an asset any unrealized appreciation in the value of its fixed assets. The application of that mandate to the uncontroverted facts in this case compels a reversal of the judgment for defendants which was entered by the court below.

The circumstances underlying the controversy, though intricate in detail, are simple in substance. Briefly stated they are as follows:

In 1931 the three defendants, together with one Landis, incorporated and organized the plaintiff company, Berks Broadcasting Company, under the Corporation Act of 1874, for the purpose of constructing and operating a radio broadcasting station in Reading. The authorized capital was $100,000, consisting of 1,000 shares, each of a par value of $100, and stock in that amount was issued to the four incorporators, who thereupon became the directors of the company. According to the book entries of the corporation the stock was fully paid for by the receipt from each of the shareholders of $5,000, and by the fixing of a value of $80,000 upon an asset denominated "Franchise and Promotion Expense."

A year later this latter item was written off the books and in its place were substituted entries (1) of $50,000 as an amount "due on Unpaid Stock Subscriptions" and (2) of the following "write-ups" or increases in the valuations of fixed assets of the company over and above the cost of those assets less depreciation: Land $7,000, Building $9,000, Transmitter and Equipment $7,000, Furniture and Fixtures $3,000, and Building Improvements $4,000,—a total of $30,000. It was stated that these "write-ups" were "to record re-appraisal of Fixed Assets as of 8/31/32 by officers of Corporation." As against the $50,000 entry of unpaid stock subscriptions each of the shareholders paid the sum of $4,200, thus reducing that item to

$33,200, and in 1933 it was cancelled altogether and in lieu thereof an item in the same amount was entered as an asset under the designation of "Good Will and Promotion Expense." This was reduced in 1935 by the sum of $20,000, and $4,000 was eliminated from the "write-ups."

As of December 31, 1943, the balance sheet of the company showed assets in excess of the liabilities, and the issued capital stock in the amount of $2,545.94. However, the existence of that alleged surplus depended on the inclusion in the assets of the "write-ups" of $26,000 which still remained on the balance sheet, for, if that amount were eliminated, so far from there being a surplus there would have been a deficiency to the extent of $23,454.06.

In June 1944 the four shareholders entered into an agreement for the sale of their stock to certain parties for $210,000, subject to the approval of the Federal Communications Commission. Until that approval was forthcoming and final settlement for the stock was made the sellers were to continue in control of the company. In April, two months before the making of the agreement, defendants had declared and paid a dividend of $4,000. The approval by the Commission being delayed for a considerable period, settlement for the stock was not made until January 1945, and meanwhile the directors declared and paid further dividends of $4,000 in July, $2,000 in October and $3,000 in December, which, with the April payment, made a total during 1944 of $13,000. These dividends were declared on the basis of earnings of the company during that year of $12,309.78, which, together with the alleged surplus of $2,545.94 as of the end of the year 1943, made a surplus of $14,855.72; that amount, being $1,855.72 in excess of the dividends paid during 1944, would have justified those payments, but it would be far short of requirements if the $26,000 "write-ups" were to be excluded from the balance sheet. The corporation, now under the control of the new shareholders, brought the present action to recover for its treasury the $13,000 which it alleged defendants had unlawfully declared and paid out as dividends.

One of the basic principles of corporation law is that the capital of a corporation must not be impaired in any manner, except, of course, as such an impairment may involuntarily occur through losses resulting from the operation of the company's business. It is illegal to declare and pay dividends from other than a surplus consisting of an excess in the value of the assets over the aggregate of the liabilities and the issued capital stock. The object of this prohibition is to afford a margin of protection for creditors in view of the limited liability of the shareholders, and also to protect the interest of the shareholders themselves by preserving the capital so that the purposes for which the corporation was formed may be carried out.

The real problem that arises in the implementation of this legal principle is in regard to the computation of the surplus from which dividends may properly be declared and paid, and, in that connection one of the rules which has been generally recognized and adopted is that such a surplus must be a bona fide and not an artificial or fictitious one; it must be founded upon actual earnings or profits and not be dependent for its existence upon a theoretical estimate of an appreciation in the value of the company's assets. The reason why a purely conjectural increase in valuations cannot be considered for the purpose of dividends is because such re-appraisals, however apparently justified and accurate for the time being, are subject to market fluctuations, are merely anticipatory of future profit, and may never be actually realized as an asset of the company.

The rule thus stated is expressly embodied as a categorical imperative, in the Business Corporation Law of 1933. Section 701 A provides that

> "no corporation shall pay dividends: (1) In cash or property, except from the surplus of the aggregate of its assets over the aggregate of its liabilities, including in the latter the amount of its stated capital after deducting from such aggregate of its assets the amount by which such aggregate was increased by unrealized appreciation in value or revaluation of fixed assets."

Section 707 provides that

> "if any dividend shall be paid, or if any withdrawal or distribution of the corporate assets shall be made, except as provided in this act, the directors under whose administration the same were made . . . (with an exception not here relevant) shall be jointly and severally liable to the corporation in an amount equal to the amount of the unlawful dividend or the unlawful withdrawal or distribution of assets."

It is clear, therefore, from these express provisions that since the "write-ups" of $26,000 represented an unrealized appreciation in value of the plaintiff company's fixed assets, their inclusion in determining the existence of a surplus from which dividends might be declared was unlawful, and since, when eliminated, there would be, not a surplus, but a revealed deficiency in capital, it would follow that the corporation is now entitled to recover from these defendants the amount improperly distributed by them as dividends.

What are the defenses sought to be interposed to the corporation's right of recovery? Defendants apparently place chief reliance upon the Act of July 17, 1935, P.L. 1123, which amends Section 701 of the Business Corporation Law by adding to the words "after deducting from such aggregate of its assets the amount by which such aggregate was increased by unrealized appreciation in value or revaluation of fixed assets," the words "unless the amount thereof shall have been transferred to, or included in, its stated capital."

But defendants seem to be confused in regard to the meaning of the term "stated capital." The "write-ups" in valuation of the plaintiff company's fixed assets were not transferred to, or included in, its stated capital. "Stated capital" is defined in Section 2 of the Corporation Business [sic] Law as meaning "at any particular time, the sum of the par value of all shares then issued . . . and such other amounts as may have been transferred to the stated capital account of the corporation, whether from the issue of shares, as a share dividend, or otherwise, . . ." What obviously was designed, therefore, by the words: "unless the amount thereof shall have been transferred to, or included in, its stated capital," was that the amount of un-realized appreciation or "write-ups" was not to be included among the assets of the corporation for dividend purposes unless the stated capital was increased to the same extent—an increase that might be effected by the issue of additional stock in the amount, as by a stock dividend. The pro-hibition against declaring and paying a dividend based on unrealized appreciation in value or revaluation of fixed assets is confined by Section 701 of the Business Corporation Law to dividends "in cash or property"; there is no such prohibition against declaring a stock dividend to represent the alleged increases in value. The reason for this distinction is that a stock dividend cannot affect creditors or shareholders adversely since, unlike a cash or property dividend, it does not decrease the company's assets.

Defendants assert that even with the "write-ups" of $26,000 eliminated from the company's balance sheet there would have been enough assets to warrant the declaration of the dividends if, instead of the reduced "Good Will and Promotion Expense" item of $13,200, there were restored the original "Franchise and Promotion Expense" item of $80,000. This conten-tion apparently rests upon the proposition that the original value of the franchise, on the basis of which the stock was issued, still exists, even though defendants saw fit from time to time to reduce its valuation and to substi-tute other items in its place. Aside from the fact that they never actually attempted to reinstate the original valuation on their books, they did noth-ing more, in making such successive reductions, than what is quite usually done by corporations, namely, the gradual elimination of such intangibles from the balance sheet. The present record does not disclose the nature or the terms of the "franchise" which the company acquired,—whether it was perpetual, limited, or indeterminate; if limited, it would naturally have to be amortized over its term; if indeterminate, and subject to revocation at the pleasure of the Commission which had granted it, proper accounting would require that it be written off as quickly as possible. As to defendants' argument that the high price paid for the stock indicates that a surplus must have existed, it is sufficient to say that the market price, being de-pendent, as it undoubtedly was, upon speculative consideration of future possibilities, has no relation whatever to the factors which the law prescribed as determinative of the right of a corporation to declare divi-dends.

Since, therefore, the general principles of corporation law, the rules of accounting and the express mandate of the Business Corporation Law, all alike prescribe that the items representing unrealized appreciation in the valuation of the company's assets cannot be included in computing a sur-plus from which dividends may lawfully be paid, the court below errone-ously entered judgment for defendants. On the contrary, there being no factual issue, the court should have entered judgment for the plaintiff cor-poration.

Judgment reversed, and record remanded with direction to enter judg-ment for plaintiff and against defendants in the sum of $13,000 with interest as set forth in the statement claimed. ◀

COMMENTS AND QUESTIONS

1. Summarize the facts that gave rise to this litigation. Note the many and varied accounting and bookkeeping transactions involved.
2. What happened in the lower court? Why did the Supreme Court of Pennsylvania reverse the judgment of that court?
3. The court draws a distinction between cash and stock dividends in these circumstances. Explain.

RIGHT TO COMPEL DIVIDEND. As a general rule, the directors of a corporation have sole authority to determine whether a dividend will be declared. They may decide not to do so even when ample funds are available, since the mere fact that a surplus is available does not mean that a dividend must be declared. The theory is that such decisions should be based on good business judgment, and if the directors decide that the profits should be left in the business rather than distributed, they have a perfect right to do so. If the stockholders are aggrieved, they have the right to elect a different board of directors at their next meeting.

In rare cases, however, the courts will intercede to compel the directors of a corporation to declare a dividend. If it is clear that a huge surplus has been accumulated which far exceeds any foreseeable business needs of the corporation, the directors may be required to distribute at least part of it to the stockholders. This power is seldom exercised, however.

The famous case of *Dodge v. Ford Motor Co.* is, without doubt, the finest illustration of a situation in which the court stepped in to compel the declaration of a dividend. Mr. Henry Ford's testimony, which is quoted in the opinion, has long been a subject of heated controversy, since it questioned the traditional view that the first duty of a corporation is to its stockholders.

DODGE v. FORD MOTOR CO.

Supreme Court of Michigan, 1919
204 Mich. 459, 170 N.W. 668

► The Ford Motor Company was incorporated in 1903 under the laws of Michigan with authorized capital stock of $150,000 of which $100,000 was then issued, $49,000 for cash, $40,000 for patents and $11,000 for other property. In 1908, the authorized and issued capital stock was increased to $2,000,000 by the declaration of a stock dividend out of accumulated profits. Thereafter its directors regularly declared cash dividends at the rate of 60 per cent per year on the increased capital of $2,000,000 and between December, 1911, and October, 1915, also declared additional special cash dividends from time to time amounting in all to $41,000,000. Thereafter no special dividends were declared except one of $2,000,000 declared on November 9, 1916, before the answers in the present case were filed, and Henry Ford, who controlled the board of directors, had stated that no more special dividends would be declared at present and that the greater portion of the profits should be put back into the business in order to expand it, thereby increasing employment and selling a larger number of cars at a lower price per car. The surplus of the corporation at July 31, 1916, was $112,000,000 and it had cash and municipal bonds amounting to nearly $54,000,000. On November 2, 1916, the directors voted to expend $11,325,000 to erect blast furnaces and other plant in which to manufacture iron and other products for use in the manufacture of cars, and also $5,150,000 out of a program calling for $9,895,000 for a substantial duplication of existing plant. Thereupon, two minority stockholders, owning one tenth of the company's stock, brought suit to compel the declaration of an additional dividend of not less than 75 per cent of the accumulated cash surplus. The court ordered the declaration of a dividend of $19,275,385.96. Defendants appealed.

OSTRANDER, J. . . . When plaintiffs made their complaint and demand for further dividends the Ford Motor Company had concluded its most prosperous year of business. The demand for its cars at the price of the preceding year continued. It could make and could market in the year beginning August 1, 1916, more than 500,000 cars. Sales of parts and repairs would necessarily increase. The cost of materials was likely to advance, and perhaps the price of labor, but it reasonably might have expected a profit for the year of upwards of $60,000,000. It had assets of more than $132,000,000, a surplus of almost $112,000,000, and its cash on hand and municipal bonds were nearly $54,000,000. Its total liabilities, including capital stock, was a little over $20,000,000. It had declared no special dividend during the business year except the October, 1915 dividend. It had been the practice, under similar circumstances, to declare larger dividends. Considering only these facts, a refusal to declare and pay further dividends appears to be not an exercise of discretion on the part of the directors, but an arbitrary refusal to do what the circumstances required to be done. These facts and others call upon the directors to justify their action, or failure or refusal to act.

In justification, the defendants have offered testimony tending to prove, and which does prove, the following facts. It had been the policy of the corporation for a considerable time to annually reduce the selling price of cars, while keeping up, or improving, their quality. As early as in June, 1915, a general plan for the expansion of the productive capacity of the concern by a practical duplication of its plant had been talked over by the executive officers and directors and agreed upon, not all of the details having been settled and no formal action of directors having been taken. The erection of a smelter was considered, and engineering, and other data in connection therewith secured. In consequence, it was determined not to reduce the selling price of cars for the year beginning August 1, 1915, but to maintain the price and to accumulate a large surplus to pay for the proposed expansion of plant and equipment, and perhaps to build a plant for smelting ore. It is hoped, by Mr. Ford, that eventually 1,000,000 cars will be annually produced. The contemplated changes will permit the increased output.

The plan, as affecting the profits of the business for the year beginning

August 1, 1916, and thereafter, calls for a reduction in the selling price of the cars. It is true that this price might be at any time increased, but the plan called for the reduction in price of $80 a car. The capacity of the plant, without the additions thereto voted to be made (without a part of them at least), would produce more than 600,000 cars annually. This number, and more, could have been sold for $440 instead of $360, a difference in the return for capital, labor and materials employed of at least $48,000,000. In short, the plan does not call for and is not intended to produce immediately a more profitable business but a less profitable one; not only less profitable than formerly but less profitable than it is admitted it might be made. The apparent immediate effect will be to diminish the value of shares and the returns to shareholders.

It is the contention of plaintiffs that the apparent effect of the plan is intended to be the continued and continuing effect of it and that it is deliberately proposed, not of record and not by official corporate declaration, but nevertheless proposed to continue the corporation henceforth as a semi-eleemosynary institution and not as a business institution. In support of this contention they point to the attitude and to the expressions of Mr. Henry Ford.

Mr. Henry Ford is the dominant force in the business of the Ford Motor Company. No plan of operations could be adopted unless he consented, and no board of directors can be elected whom he does not favor. One of the directors of the company has no stock. One share was assigned to him to qualify him for the position, but it is not claimed that he owns it. A business, one of the largest in the world, and one of the most profitable, has been built up. It employs many men, at good pay.

> "My ambition," said Mr. Ford, "is to employ still more men, to spread the benefits of this industrial system to the greatest possible number, to help them build up their lives and their homes. To do this we are putting the greatest share of our profits back in the business."

> "With regard to dividends, the company paid sixty per cent, on its capitalization of two million dollars, or $1,200,000, leaving $58,000,000 to reinvest for the growth of the company. This is Mr. Ford's policy at present, and it is understood that the other stockholders cheerfully accede to this plan."

He had made up his mind in the summer of 1916 that no dividends other than the regular dividends should be paid, "for the present."

> "Q. For how long? Had you fixed in your mind any time in the future, when you were going to pay—
> "A. No.
> "Q. That was indefinite in the future?
> "A. That was indefinite, yes sir."

The record, and especially the testimony of Mr. Ford, convinces us that he has to some extent the attitude towards shareholders of one who has dispensed and distributed to them large gains and that they should be content to take what he chooses to give. His testimony creates the impression, also, that he thinks the Ford Motor Company has made too much money, has had too large profits, and that although large profits might be still earned, a sharing of them with the public, by reducing the price of the output of the company, ought to be undertaken. We have no doubt that certain sentiments, philanthropic and altruistic, creditable to Mr. Ford, had large influence in determining the policy to be pursued by the Ford Motor Company—the policy which has been herein referred to.

It is said by his counsel that—

> "Although a manufacturing corporation cannot engage in humanitarian works as its principal business, the fact that it is organized for profit does not prevent the existence of implied powers to carry on with humanitarian motives such charitable works as are incidental to the main business of the corporation."

And again:

> "As the expenditures complained of are being made in an expansion of the business which the company is organized to carry on, and for purposes within the powers of the corporation as hereinbefore shown, the question is as to whether such expenditures are rendered illegal because influenced to some extent by humanitarian motives and purposes on the part of the members of the board of directors."

In discussing this proposition, counsel have referred to decisions such as Hawes v. Oakland, 104 U.S. 450; Taunton v. Royal Ins. Co., 2 Hem & Miller, 135; Henderson v. Bank of Australia, L.R. 50 Ch. Div. 170; Steinway v. Steinway & Sons, 40 N.Y. Supp. 718; People ex rel. Metropolitan Life Ins. Co. v. Hotchkiss, 136 App. Div. 150 (120 N.Y. Supp. 649). These cases, after all, like all others in which the subject is treated turn finally upon the question whether it appears that the directors were not acting for the best interest of the corporation. We do not draw in question, nor do counsel for the plaintiffs do so, the validity of the general propositions stated by counsel nor the soundness of the opinions delivered in the cases cited. The case presented here is not like any of them. The difference between an incidental humanitarian expenditure of corporate funds for the benefit of the employees, like the building of hospitals for their use and the employment of agencies for the betterment of their condition, and a general purpose and plan to benefit mankind at the expense of others, is obvious. There should be no confusion (of which there is evidence) of the duties which Mr. Ford conceives that he and the stockholders owe to the general public and the duties which in law he and his codirectors owe to protesting, minority stockholders. A business corporation is organized and carried on primarily for the profit of the stockholders. The powers of the directors are to be employed for that end. The discretion of directors is to be exercised in the choice of means to attain that end and does not extend to change in the end itself, to the reduction of profits or to the nondistribution of profits among stockholders in order to devote them to other purposes.

There is committed to the discretion of directors, a discretion to be exercised in good faith, the infinite details of business, including the wages which shall be paid to employees, the number of hours they shall work, the conditions under which labor shall be carried on, and the prices for which products shall be offered to the public. It is said by appellants that the motives of the board members are not material and will not be inquired into by the court so long as their acts are within their lawful powers. As we have pointed out, and the proposition does not require argument to sustain it, it is not within the lawful powers of a board of directors to shape and conduct the affairs of a corporation for the merely incidental benefit of shareholders and for the primary purpose of benefiting others, and no one will contend that if the avowed purpose of the defendant directors was to sacrifice the interests of shareholders it would not be the duty of the courts to interfere.

We are not, however, persuaded that we should interfere with the proposed expansion of the business of the Ford Motor Company. In view of the fact that the selling price of products may be increased at any time, the ultimate results of the larger business cannot be certainly estimated. The judges are not business experts. It is recognized that plans must often be made for a long future, for expected competition, for a continuing as well as an immediately profitable venture. The experience of the Ford Motor Company is evidence of capable management of its affairs. It may be noticed, incidentally, that it took from the public the money required for the execution of this plan and that the very considerable salaries paid to Mr. Ford and to certain executive officers and employees were not diminished. We are not satisfied that the alleged motives of the directors, in so far as they are reflected in the conduct of the business, menace the interests of shareholders. It is enough to say, perhaps, that the court of equity is at all times open to complaining shareholders having a just grievance.

Assuming the general plan and policy of expansion and the details of it to have been sufficiently, formally approved at the October and November, 1917 meetings of directors, and assuming further that the plan and policy and the details agreed upon were for the best ultimate interest of the company and therefore of its shareholders, what does it amount to in justification of a refusal to declare and pay a special dividend, or dividends? The Ford Motor Company was able to estimate with nicety its income and profit. It could sell more cars than it could make. Having ascertained what it would cost to produce a car and to sell it, the profit upon each car depended upon the selling price. That being fixed, the yearly income and profit was determinable, and, within slight variations, was certain.

There was appropriated—voted—for the smelter $11,325,000. As to the remainder voted there is no available way for determining how much had been paid before the action of directors was taken and how much was paid thereafter, but assuming that the plans required an expenditure sooner or later of $9,985,000 for duplication of the plant, and for land and other expenditures $3,000,000, the total is $24,220,000. The company was continuing business at a profit—a cash business. If the total cost of proposed expenditures had been immediately withdrawn in cash from the cash surplus (money and bonds) on hand August 1, 1916, there would have remained nearly $30,000,000.

Defendants say, and it is true, that a considerable cash balance must be at all times carried by such a concern. But, as has been stated, there was a large daily, weekly, monthly, receipt of cash. The output was practically continuous and was continuously, and within a few days, turned into cash. Moreover, the contemplated expenditures were not to be immediately made. The large sum appropriated for the smelter plant was payable over a considerable period of time. So that, without going further, it would appear that accepting and approving the plan of the directors, it was their duty to distribute on or near the first of August, 1916, a very large sum of money to stockholders.

In reaching this conclusion, we do not ignore, but recognize the validity of the proposition that plaintiffs have from the beginning profited by, if they have not lately officially, participated in the general policy of expansion pursued by the corporation. We do not lose sight of the fact that it had been, upon one occasion, agreeable to the plaintiffs to increase the capital stock to $100,000,000 by a stock dividend of $98,000,000. These things go only to answer other contentions now made by plaintiffs and do not and cannot operate to estop them to demand proper dividends upon the stock they own. It is obvious that an annual dividend of sixty per cent upon $2,000,000 or $1,200,000 is the equivalent of a very small dividend upon $100,000,000, or more.

The decree of the court below fixing and determining the specific amount to be distributed to stockholders is affirmed. In other respects except as to the allowance of costs, the said decree is reversed. Plaintiffs will recover interest at five per cent per annum upon their proportional share of said dividend from the date of the decree of the lower court. Appellants will tax the costs of their appeal, and two thirds of the amount thereof will be paid by plaintiffs. No other costs are allowed.

STEERE, FELLOWS, BROOKE, and STONE, JJ., concurred with OSTRAN-
DER, J.   ◀

COMMENTS AND QUESTIONS

1. What was the principal issue before the court? How was it resolved?
2. Summarize the position taken by Henry Ford relative to the corporation's duties to its stockholders and the public. What were the contentions of the minority stockholders?
3. The lower court issued an injunction prohibiting the company from owning, holding, or operating any smelting plant or blast furnace. What happened on appeal?
4. It is interesting to note that the minority stockholders sold out right after the decision in this case, leaving Henry and Edsel Ford as sole owners of the company.

Liabilities of Stockholders

As a general rule, the liability of each stockholder is strictly limited to the amount of his original capital investment (i.e., the amount he paid for his stock). Unlike a partner, who is personally responsible if the assets of the partnership prove insufficient to pay creditors, a stockholder is not liable for the debts and liabilities of the corporation. The theory behind this rule is that a corporation is a distinct legal entity, separate and apart from its stockholders, and people who deal with it should realize that its obligations may be satisfied only out of corporate assets.

There are one or two exceptions to this rule of limited liability, however. In most jurisdictions, if a dividend is improperly declared, and if the capital stock of the corporation is so depleted that creditors cannot be paid, the stockholders may be held liable to the creditors for the dividends they have wrongfully received. In some states, the application of this rule depends on whether the corporation was insolvent at the time of the dividend declaration and on whether the creditors' claims were then in existence.

Several states also hold that stockholders may be personally liable for the payment of wages and salaries to employees of the corporation when the corporate assets are insufficient to meet the payroll. This situation frequently arises when a corporation goes out of business and is dissolved.

SECTION 5

MANAGEMENT OF CORPORATIONS

Management in General

Most corporations are managed by three groups of people: (1) the stockholders, (2) the directors, and (3) the officers. The powers and functions of these groups are defined and limited by the corporate charter and its bylaws, and by state statute. In spite of the resulting variation in managerial responsibility from corporation to corporation, certain general rules may be formulated.

Management by Stockholders

Although stockholders rarely play a direct role in corporate management, they normally have the right to select the board of directors and to vote on major issues that affect the business of the corporation and their interest in it. For example, a corporation ordinarily may not change the basic nature of its business operations or the amount of its capital stock without the approval of its stockholders.

Action by stockholders is not binding on the corporation unless it is taken at a meeting that has been properly called. Most corporate charters or bylaws provide that a regular meeting be held at least once a year. Although most states do not insist that notice of these meetings be given to stockholders, that is the usual practice. Special meetings, in addition to the annual meeting, may be called by the directors or by a specified percentage of the stockholders. Reasonable notice of such meetings, together with a statement of the business to be transacted, must be given to all the stockholders. Ordinarily, a *quorum* (i.e., a certain percentage or number of stockholders) must be present at a meeting before any proposal may be officially acted on.

Management by Directors

Most corporations entrust the broad powers of management to a board of directors. The number of directors, the length of their terms, and the qualifications necessary for election are generally set down in the charter or bylaws. As a general rule, no director is entitled to compensation for his services unless it is expressly provided for.

Directors' Meetings

The board of directors functions as a unit. It may take action only when the members are assembled at a meeting that has been duly called. The time and place of the board's regular meetings are usually prescribed in the bylaws or charter; generally, provision is also made for calling special meetings. A director who actually attends a meeting cannot later object on the ground that he did not receive notice.

Ordinarily, a majority of the directors constitutes a quorum; if a quorum is not present, no binding action may be taken. No director may cast his vote by proxy; in order to vote, he must be present in person.

In the Connecticut case that follows, a decision taken by a board of directors was challenged on the ground that some of the directors did not receive proper notice of the meeting.

CHASE et al. v. TUTTLE et al.

Supreme Court of Errors of Connecticut, 1888
55 Conn. 455, 12 A. 874

▶ LOOMIS, J. This is an action of replevin, brought by the trustee of Brown & Bros., an insolvent corporation, for certain goods that were on the 4th of January, 1886, attached by the defendant, as a deputy-sheriff, on the suit of the National Shoe & Leather Bank of New York against the corporation. On the evening of the same day an assignment for the benefit of all the creditors of the corporation was made, pursuant to a vote of a majority of its directors, as is claimed, which was lodged on file in the probate court, and subsequently accepted, approved, and recorded by that court; and the plaintiffs were appointed and qualified as trustees. The sole defense against this action is that the assignment was invalid and of no effect. The claimed illegality of the assignment is based upon three objections only: (1) That two of the five directors being out of the state at the time, did not receive any notice of the meeting; . . . (3) that the notices of the meeting sent to the directors did not specify the object of the meeting, as required by statute.

1. We do not think the assignment invalid for want of actual notice to the two directors who were at the time absent from the state. Notice was sent by telegram to them, as to the others, at their address in this state; but one being in the territory of Montana, and the other in South Carolina, they failed to receive the notices. Under these circumstances, it would seem unreasonable to hold that a majority of the whole number, being present, could not do a legal act binding the corporation. The exigency demanded immediate action to save the property and to save expense. It is easy to see how disastrous might be the consequences were we to adopt the principle contended for by the defendants. The situation of the absent directors might be much more remote and inaccessible than in the present case, requiring many months, or even years, to reach them by actual notice. Must the corporation remain paralyzed all this time, without ability to protect itself?

But the suggestion was made, in the argument in behalf of the defendants, that it might be treated as a case of vacancy, which the remaining directors could fill, pursuant to the act of 1880 (Sess. Laws 1880, p. 5617). If, however, the office was vacant as to the two absent directors, then surely the remaining directors could lawfully represent the corporation; for there is no general law or principle requiring vacancies in the board of directors to be filled before the remaining directors can act in the business of the corporation; provided, of course, the number left is sufficient to constitute a legal quorum. Under our General Statutes, p. 279, 12, "a majority of the directors of any corporation, convened according to the by-laws, shall constitute a quorum for the transaction of business." In order, probably, to avoid a doubt that might arise whether a general assignment was such business as was contemplated under the above statute, the legislature, by the act of 1885 (Sess. Laws, 1885, p. 493), provided that the assignment of any corporation may be made by the directors in legal meeting called for such purpose. This, however, was not intended to change the rules as to a quorum under the preceding statute. There can be no doubt that a majority of the directors could make a valid assignment. . . .

3. The only remaining objection is that the meeting of the directors for the making of the assignment was illegal for defects in the notice. The only by-law or rule adopted relative to the matter, prescribed simply that "meetings of directors may be held as often, at such place, and in such manner, as they may from time to time determine." No formality whatever is prescribed; and if all the directors happened to be together, and agreed to hold a meeting immediately for a particular object within their jurisdiction, we do not see how their action could be impeached on that ground. As the want of actual notice to the two directors who were absent from the state, at places so remote that they could not be reached, has been excused in this case, all the directors capable of acting under the circumstances were present. But it is said that the statute which empowers directors to make an assignment requires that "the meeting be called for such purpose," and, in this connection, the defendants rely on the finding, which says that there was no evidence that the telegram contained any notification as to the purpose of the proposed meeting. It will be observed that this is not a finding that the purpose was not specified, but only that the contents of

the telegram had not been proved by either party; but, under the circumstances we are about to mention, the burden of showing that the object was not specified was on the defendants. The record of this meeting is annexed as part of the finding, and it says: "At a special meeting of the directors of Brown & Bros., called for the purpose of making an assignment of its estate in insolvency for the benefit of all the creditors, pursuant to the statutes," etc. Upon this record, until the contrary is found, it must be presumed that the purpose was specified in the call. This principle is sustained by the case of Sargent v. Webster, 13 Metc. 504, where the validity of an assignment by a corporation for the benefit of creditors was sought to be impeached for want of notice to all the directors. Chief Justice Shaw disposed of the objections as follows:

> "Another objection of the same kind is that it does not appear that notice of the meeting was given to all directors. But the contrary does not appear; and it would be hazardous to decide that every vote passed by an aggregate body is void, if it does not appear by the record that all were notified. We believe it not usual in corporate records to state how the members were notified. The presumption, *omnia rite acta*,[12] covers multitudes of defects in such cases, and throws the burden on those who would deny the regularity of a meeting, for want of due notice to establish it by proof."

Our own court in Lane v. Brainerd, 30 Conn. 565, applied the same principle both to directors' and to stockholders' meetings. The mere record of the meeting in the former case was presumptive proof that all the directors had been duly notified; and in the latter case the mere record of the organization of a corporation was presumptive evidence of a fact which was an indispensable condition precedent to its lawful organization.

We advise judgment for the plaintiffs.   ◀

COMMENTS AND QUESTIONS

1. What was the main issue in this case? How did the court decide?
2. Summarize the defenses raised by the attaching creditors. For what reasons did the court reject them?

Powers of Directors

The board of directors enjoys broad discretionary powers to manage the corporation. The directors may take any action and enter into any contracts that are reasonably necessary to the conduct of the business for which the corporation was formed. To carry out this responsibility, the board may appoint officers and employees and delegate authority to them. Moreover, it may delegate certain of its functions to a committee of its own members so that action may be taken promptly without a meeting of the full board.

Liability of Directors

Directors must exercise their managerial powers with the utmost good faith and diligence; they are not permitted to use their position to gain a secret profit or advantage at the expense of the corporation. If a director

---

12 That is, all things are presumed to have been done rightly.

deals with the corporation, he must fully disclose his interest in the negotiations; no director may vote on any personal matter. An interesting example of this rule is offered in the case that follows.

GLOBE WOOLEN CO. v. UTICA GAS AND ELECTRIC CO.

Court of Appeals of New York, 1918
224 N.Y. 483, 121 N.E. 378

▶ CARDOZO, J.   The plaintiff, a corporation, sues to compel the specific performance of contracts to supply electric current to its mills. The defendant, also a corporation, answers that the contracts were made under the dominating influence of a common director; that their terms are unfair, and their consequences oppressive; and that hence they may not stand. A referee has sustained the defense; and the Appellate Division, with some modification, has affirmed his judgment.

The plaintiff is the owner of two mills in the city of Utica. One is for the manufacture of worsteds and the other for that of woolens. The defendant generates and sells electricity for light and power. For many years John F. Maynard has been the plaintiff's chief stockholder, its president, and a member of its board of directors. He has also been a director of the defendant, and chairman of its executive committee. He received a single share of the defendant's stock to qualify him for office. He returned the share at once, and he has never held another. His property interest in the plaintiff is large. In the defendant he has none.

The history of the transaction may be briefly stated. At the beginning, the mills were run by steam, and the plant was antiquated and inadequate. As early as 1903, one Greenridge, then the superintendent and later the general manager of the defendant's electrical department, suggested to Mr. Maynard the substitution of electric power. Nothing came of the suggestion then. Mr. Maynard was fearful that the cost of equipment would be too great unless the defendant would guarantee a saving in the cost of operation. None the less, a change was felt to be important, and from time to time the subject was taken up anew. In 1904, there was an investigation of the power plant by Greenridge and a written report of its condition. For this service, though he was still in the defendant's employ, he was paid by Mr. Maynard. In 1905, the substitution of electricity was again considered, but dismissed as impracticable because of the plaintiff's continued insistence upon a guarantee of saving. In the fall of 1906, the project was renewed. It was renewed by Maynard and Greenridge, who debated it between themselves. There were other officers of the defendant who knew that the project was afoot, but they took no part in formulating it. Maynard still insisted on a guarantee of saving. The plaintiff's books were thrown open to Greenridge, who calculated for himself the cost of operation with steam and the probable cost with electricity. When the investigation was over, a contract was closed. It took the form of letters exchanged between Greenridge and Maynard. In the letter signed by Maynard on October 22, 1906, the plaintiff accepted the proposal. At once the defendant made preparations to install the new equipment. Six weeks later, on December 1, 1906, Mr. Maynard laid the contract before the defendant's executive committee. He went to the meeting with Mr. Greenridge. The contract was read. Mr. Lewis the vice-president, asked Mr. Greenridge what the rate would be and was told about $.0104 per kilowatt hour. Mr. Beardsley, another director, asked whether the contract was a profitable one for the company, and was told by Mr. Greenridge that it was. Mr. Maynard kept silent. A resolution was moved and carried that the contract be ratified. Mr. Maynard presided at the meeting, and put the resolution, but was excused from voting.

This settled the problem of power for the worsted mill. Attention was next directed to the woolen mill. Again, Mr. Maynard and Mr. Greenridge put the project through, unaided. In February, 1907, letters, similar in most things to the earlier ones, were exchanged. The guarantee of saving for this mill as for the other was to be $300 a month. There were, however, new provisions to the effect that the contract should apply to "current used for any purposes in any extensions or additions to the mills," and that in case of shortage of electricity the plaintiff should be preferred in service over all other customers except the city of Utica. At a meeting of the executive committee, held February 11, 1907, this contract was ratified. The statement was made by Mr. Greenridge in the presence of Mr. Maynard, that it was practically a duplicate of the first contract, except that it related to another mill. Nothing was said about the new provisions. Mr. Maynard presided and put the resolution, but did not vote.

At a cost to the plaintiff of more than $21,000, the requisite changes in the mills were made, and the new power was supplied. It quickly appeared that the defendant had made a losing contract; but only gradually did the extent of the loss, its permanence and its causes unfold themselves. Greenridge had miscalculated the amount of steam that would be required to heat the dye houses. The expenditure for coal mounted by leaps and bounds. The plaintiff dyed more yarn and less slubbing than before. But the dyeing of yarn takes twice as much heat as that of slubbing and thus doubles the cost of fuel. These and like changes in the output of the mills had not been foreseen by Greenridge, and Maynard had not warned of them. In 1909, the defendant became alarmed at the mounting loss. Various tests and palliatives were suggested and adopted, but there was no change in the result. Finally, in February, 1911, the defendant gave notice of rescission. At that time, it had supplied the plaintiff with electricity worth $69,500.75 if paid for at the maximum rate fixed by the contract and $60,000 if paid for at the lowest rate charged to any customer in Utica. Yet not only had it received nothing, but it owed the plaintiff under its guarantee $11,721.41. The finding is that a like loss prolonged to the end of the term would amount to $300,000.

These are the contracts which the courts below have annulled. The referee annulled them absolutely. The Appellate Division imposed the condition that the defendant reimburse the plaintiff for the cost of installation. The defendant makes no complaint of the condition. The plaintiff, appealing, stands upon its bargain.

We think the evidence supports the conclusion that the contracts are voidable at the election of the defendant. The plaintiff does not deny that

this would be true if the dual director had voted for their adoption. . . .
But the argument is that by refusing to vote, he shifted the responsibility
of his associates, and may reap a profit from their errors. One does not
divest oneself so readily of one's duties as trustee. The refusal to vote has,
indeed, this importance; it gives to the transaction the form and presumption of propriety, and requires one who would invalidate it to probe beneath the surface. . . . But "the great rule of law . . . which holds a trustee
to the duty of constant and unqualified fidelity, is not a thing of form and
phrases. A dominating influence may be exerted in other ways than by a
vote. . . . A beneficiary, about to plunge into a ruinous course of dealing,
may be betrayed by silence as well as by the spoken word. The trustee is
free to stand aloof, while others act, if all is equitable and fair. He cannot
rid himself of the duty to warn and to denounce, if there is improvidence
or oppression, either apparent on the surface, or lurking beneath the surface, but visible to his practiced eye. . . .

There was an influence here, dominating perhaps, and surely potent
and persuasive, which was exerted by Mr. Maynard from the beginning to
the end. In all the stages of preliminary treaty, he dealt with a subordinate,
who looked up to him as to a superior, and was alert to serve his pleasure.
There was no clean-cut cleavage in those stages between his conflicting
offices and agencies. . . . No label identified the request of Mr. Maynard,
the plaintiff's president, as something separate from the advice of Mr.
Maynard, the defendant's chairman. Superior and subordinate together
framed a contract, and together closed it. It came before the executive
committee as an accomplished fact. The letters had been signed and delivered. Work had been begun. All that remained was a ratification, which
may have been needless, and which even if needful took the aspect of a
mere formality. There was some attempt to show that Mr. Lewis, the vice-
president, had seen the letters before. The testimony of Mr. Greenridge
indicates the contrary. In support of the judgment, we accept his testimony
as true. That the letters had been seen by others, there is not even a pretense. The members of the committee, hearing the contract for the first time,
knew that it had been framed by the chairman of the meeting. They were
assured in his presence that it was just and equitable. Faith in his loyalty
disarmed suspicion.

There was, then, a relation of trust reposed, of influence exerted, of
superior knowledge on the one side, and legitimate dependence on the
other. . . . At least a finding that there was this relation has evidence to
sustain it. A trustee may not cling to contracts thus won, unless their terms
are fair and just. . . . His dealings with his beneficiary are "viewed with
jealousy by the courts, and may be set aside on slight grounds." He takes
the risk of an enforced surrender of his bargain if it turns out to be improvident. There must be candor and equity in the transaction, and some
reasonable proportion between benefits and burdens.

The contracts before us do not survive these tests. The unfairness is
startling, and the consequences have been disastrous. The mischief consists in this: that the guarantee has not been limited by a statement of the

conditions under which the mills are to be run. No matter how large the business, no matter how great the increase in the price of labor or of fuel, no matter what the changes in the nature or the proportion of the products, no matter even though there be extensions of the plant, the defendant has pledged its word that for ten years there will be a saving of $600 a month, $300 for each mill, $7,200 a year. As a result of that pledge it has supplied the plaintiff with electric current for nothing, and owes, if the contract stands, about $11,000 for the privilege. These elements of unfairness, Mr. Maynard must have known, if, indeed, his knowledge be material. He may not have known how great the loss would be. He may have trusted to the superior technical skill of Mr. Greenridge to compute with approximate accuracy the comparative cost of steam and electricity. But he cannot have failed to know that he held a one-sided contract, which left the defendant at his mercy. He was not blind to the likelihood that in a term of ten years there would be changes in the business. The swiftness with which some of the changes followed permits the inference that they were premeditated. There was a prompt increase in the proportion of yarns as compared with slubbing when the guarantee of saving charged the defendant with the greater cost of fuel. But whether these and other changes were premeditated or not, at least they were recognized as possible. With that recognition, no word of warning was uttered to Greenridge or to any of the defendant's officers. There slumbered within these contracts a potency of profit which the plaintiff neither ignored in their making nor forgot in their enforcement.

It is no answer to say that this potency, if obvious to Maynard, ought also to have been obvious to other members of the committee. They did not know, as he did, the likelihood or the significance of changes in the business. There was need, too, of reflection and analysis before the dangers stood revealed. For the man who framed the contracts there was opportunity to consider and to judge. His fellow members, hearing them for the first time, and trustful of his loyalty, would have no thought of latent peril. That they had none is sufficiently attested by the fact that the contracts were approved. There was inequality, therefore, both in knowledge and in the opportunity for knowledge. It is not important in such circumstances whether the trustee foresaw the precise evils that developed. The inference that he did, might not be unsupported by the evidence. But the indefinite possibilities of hardship, the opportunity in changing circumstances to wrest unlooked for profits and impose unlooked for losses, these must have been foreseen. Foreseen or not, they were there, and their presence permeates the contracts with oppression and inequity.

We hold, therefore, that the refusal to vote does not nullify as of course an influence and predominance exerted without a vote. We hold that the constant duty rests on a trustee to seek no harsh advantage to the detriment of his trust, but rather to protest and renounce if through the blindness of those who treat with him he gains what is unfair. And because there is evidence that in the making of these contracts, that duty was ignored, the power of equity was fittingly exercised to bring them to an end.

The judgment should be affirmed with costs.

HISCOCK, C. J., CHASE, COLLIN, CUDDEBACK and POUND, JJ. concur; ANDREWS, J. absent.

Judgment affirmed.   ◄

COMMENTS AND QUESTIONS

1. Summarize the provisions of the contracts which the defendant sought to rescind in this case. What was the decision of the court?
2. What arguments were raised by the plaintiff in support of its position? How did Cardozo deal with them?

A director is personally liable for any misapplication or misappropriation of corporate assets. For example, if a dividend is improperly declared, the directors who vote for it may be held responsible. Directors are not, however, liable for losses resulting from their management if they have acted in good faith and with reasonable care. Generally speaking, before a director can be held personally responsible, there must be some evidence of a willful or negligent misuse of power.

In each of the two cases that follow, an effort was made to hold a director liable for losses incurred by the corporation. In one instance, the effort was successful; in the other, it failed.

BATES v. DRESSER et al.

Supreme Court of the United States, 1920
251 U.S. 524, 40 S.Ct. 247

► Appeal from the United States Circuit Court of Appeals for the First Circuit.

Suit by John L. Bates, receiver of the National City Bank of Cambridge, Mass., against Sumner Dresser, administrator of Edwin Dresser, deceased, and others. From a decree of the Circuit Court of Appeals (250 F. 525, 162 C.C.A. 541), reversing a decree of the District Court (229 F. 772), and dismissing the bill against some of the defendants, the receiver and certain defendants appeal. Modified and affirmed.

MR. JUSTICE HOLMES delivered the opinion of the Court.

This is a bill in equity brought by the receiver of a national bank to charge its former president and directors with the loss of a great part of its assets through the thefts of an employee of the bank while they were in power. The case was sent to a master who found for the defendant; but the District Court entered a decree against all of them. 229 F. 772. The Circuit Court of Appeals reversed this decree, dismissed the bill as against all except the administrator of Edwin Dresser, the president, cut down the amount with which he was charged and refused to add interest from the date of the decree of the District Court. Dresser v. Bates, 250 F. 525, 162 C.C.A. 541. Dresser's administrator and the receiver both appeal, the latter contending that the decree of the District Court should be affirmed with interest and costs.

The bank was a small bank at Cambridge with a capital of $100,000 and average deposits of somewhere about $300,000. It had a cashier, a bookkeeper, a teller and a messenger. Before and during the time of the losses, Dresser was its president and executive officer, a large stockholder, with an inactive deposit of from $35,000 to $50,000. From July, 1903, to the end, Frank L. Earl was cashier. Coleman, who made the trouble, entered the service of the bank as messenger in September, 1903. In January, 1904, he was promoted to be bookkeeper, being then not quite eighteen but having studied bookkeeping. In the previous August an auditor employed on the retirement of a cashier had reported that the daily balance book was very much behind, that it was impossible to prove the deposits, and that a competent bookkeeper should be employed upon the work immediately. Coleman kept the deposit ledger and this was the work that fell into his hands. There was no cage in the bank, and in 1904 and 1905 there were some small shortages in the accounts of three successive tellers that were not accounted for, and the last of them, Cutting, was asked by Dresser to resign on that ground. Before doing so he told Dresser that someone had taken the money and that if he might be allowed to stay he would set a trap and catch the man, but Dresser did not care to do that and thought that there was nothing wrong. From Cutting's resignation on October 7, 1905, Coleman acted as paying and receiving teller, in addition to his other duty, until November, 1907. During this time there were no shortages disclosed in the teller's accounts. In May, 1906, Coleman took $2,000 cash from the vaults of the bank, but restored it the next morning. In November of the same year he began the thefts that came into question here. Perhaps in the beginning he took the money directly. But as he ceased to have charge of the cash in November, 1907, he invented another way. Having a small account at the bank he would draw checks for the amount he wanted, exchange checks with a Boston broker, get cash for the broker's check, and when his own check came to the bank through the clearing house, would abstract it from the envelope, enter the others on his book and conceal the difference by a charge to some other account or a false addition in the column of drafts or deposits in the depositors' ledger. He handed to the cashier only the slip from the clearing house that showed the totals. The cashier paid whatever appeared to be due and thus Coleman's checks were honored. So far as Coleman thought it necessary, in view of the absolute trust in him on the part of all concerned, he took care that his balances should agree with those in the cashier's book.

By May 1, 1907, Coleman had abstracted, $17,000, concealing the fact by false additions in the column of total checks, and false balances in the deposit ledger. Then for the moment a safer concealment was effected by charging the whole to Dresser's account. Coleman adopted this method when a bank examiner was expected. Of course when the fraud was disguised by overcharging a depositor it could not be discovered except by calling in the passbooks or taking all the deposit slips and comparing them with the depositors' ledger in detail. By November, 1907, the amount taken by Coleman was $30,100 and the charge on Dresser's account was $20,000. In 1908 the sum was raised from $33,000 to $49,671. In 1909 Coleman's activity began to increase. In January he took $6,829.26; in March, $10,-833.73; in June, his previous stealings amounting to $83,390.94, he took

$5,152.06; in July, $18,050; in August, $6,250; in September, $17,350; in October, $47,277.08; in November, $51,847; in December, $46,956.44; in January, 1910, $27,395.53; in February, $6,473.97; making a total of $310,-143.02, when the bank closed on February 21, 1910. As a result of this the amount of the monthly deposits seemed to decline noticeably and the directors considered the matter in September, but concluded that the falling off was due in part to the springing up of rivals, whose deposits were increasing, but was parallel to a similar decrease in New York. An examination by a bank examiner in December, 1909, disclosed nothing wrong to him.

In this connection it should be mentioned that in the previous semi-annual examinations by national bank examiners nothing was discovered pointing to malfeasance. The cashier was honest and everybody believed that they could rely upon him, although in fact he relied too much upon Coleman, who also was unsuspected by all. If Earl had opened the envelopes from the clearing house, and had seen the checks, or had examined the deposit ledger with any care he would have found out what was going on. The scrutiny of anyone accustomed to such details would have discovered the false additions and other indications of fraud that were on the face of the book. But it may be doubted whether anything less than a continuous pursuit of the figures through many pages would have done so except by a lucky chance.

The question of the liability of the directors in this case is the question whether they neglected their duty by accepting the cashier's statement of liabilities and failing to inspect the depositors' ledger. The statements of assets always were correct. A by-law that had been allowed to become obsolete or nearly so is invoked as establishing their own standard of conduct. By that, a committee was to be appointed every six months

> "to examine into the affairs of the bank, to count its cash, and compare its assets and liabilities with the balances on the general ledger, for the purpose of ascertaining whether or not the books are correctly kept, and the condition of the bank in a sound and solvent condition."

Of course liabilities as well as assets must be known to know the condition, and, as this case shows, peculations may be concealed as well by a false understatement of liabilities as by a false show of assets. But the former is not the direction in which fraud would have been looked for, especially on the part of one who at the time of his principal abstractions was not in contact with the funds. A debtor hardly expects to have its liability understated. Some animals must have given at least one exhibition of dangerous propensities before the owner can be held. This fraud was a novelty in the way of swindling a bank so far as the knowledge of any experience had reached Cambridge before 1910. We are not prepared to reverse the finding of the master and the Circuit Court of Appeals that the directors should not be held answerable for taking the cashier's statement of liabilities to be as correct as the statement of assets always was. Their confidence seemed warranted by the semi-annual examinations by the Government examiner and they were encouraged in their belief that all was well by the president, whose responsibility, as executive officer; interest, as large stockholder and depositor; and knowledge, from long daily presence in the bank, were greater than theirs. They were not bound by virtue of the office gratuitously assumed by them to call in the passbooks and compare them with the ledger, and until the event showed the possibility they hardly could have seen that their failure to look at the ledger opened a way to fraud. See Briggs v. Spaulding, 141 U.S. 132, 11 S.Ct. 924, 35 L.Ed. 662; Warner v. Penoyer, 91 F. 587, 33 C.C.A. 222, 44 L.R.A. 761. We are not laying down general principles, however, but confine our decision to the circumstances of the particular case.

The position of the president is different. Practically he was the master of the situation. He was daily at the bank for hours, he had the deposit ledger in his hands at times and might have had it any time. He had had hints and warnings in addition to those that we have mentioned, warnings that should not be magnified unduly, but still that taken with the auditor's report of 1903, the unexplained shortages, the suggestion of the teller, Cutting, in 1905, and the final seeming rapid decline in deposits, would have induced scrutiny but for an invincible repose upon the status quo. In 1908 one Filimore learned that a package containing $150 left with the bank for safe keeping was not to be found, told Dresser of the loss, wrote to him that he could but conclude that the package had been destroyed or removed by someone connected with the bank, and in later conversation said that it was evident that there was a thief in the bank. He added that he would advise the president to look after Coleman, that he believed he was living at a pretty fast pace, and that he had pretty good authority for thinking that he was supporting a woman. In the same year or the year before, Coleman, whose pay was never more than twelve dollars a week, bought an automobile (as was known to Dresser and commented on unfavorably to him). There was also some evidence of notice to Dresser that Coleman was dealing in copper stocks. In 1909 came the great and inadequately explained seeming shrinkage in the deposits. No doubt plausible explanations of his conduct came from Coleman and the notice as to speculations may have been slight, but taking the whole story of the relations of the parties, we are not ready to say that the two courts below erred in finding that Dresser had been put upon his guard. However little the warnings may have pointed to the specific facts, had they been accepted they would have led to an examination of the depositors' ledger, a discovery of past and prevention of future thefts. . . .

Decree modified by charging the estate of Dresser with interest from February 1, 1916 to June 1, 1918, upon the sum found to be due, and affirmed.

Mr. Justice McKenna and Mr. Justice Putney dissent, upon the ground that not only the administrator or the president of the bank but the other directors ought to be held liable to the extent to which they were held by the District Court. 229 F. 772.

Mr. Justice Van Devanter and Mr. Justice Brandeis took no part in the decision.   ◄

1. In this action to charge the former president and directors of the bank, the lower court found all the defendants liable. What happened on appeal to the Circuit Court of Appeals? What was the final outcome in the Supreme Court?
2. On what ground did two of the justices dissent? Do you agree with their views?
3. The opinion makes interesting reading; one is astounded that such thefts could have gone on so long undetected. Justice Holmes obviously relishes his job as storyteller.

BARNES v. ANDREWS

District Court of the United States
Southern District of New York, 1924
298 Fed. 614

► In Equity. Suit by Earl B. Barnes, as receiver of the Liberty Starters Corporation against Charles Lee Andrews. Decree for defendant.

Final hearing on a bill of equity, under section 91a of the General Corporation Law of New York (Consol. Laws. c. 23), to hold liable the defendant as director for misprision of office. The corporation was organized under the laws of that state to manufacture starters for Ford Motors and aeroplanes. On October 9, 1919, about a year after its organization, the defendant took office as a director, and served until he resigned on June 21, 1920. During that period over $500,000 was raised by the sales of stock of the company, made through an agent working on commission. A force of officers and employees was hired at substantial salaries, and the factory, already erected when the defendant took office, was equipped with machinery. Starter parts were made in quantity, but delays were experienced in the production of starters as a whole and the funds of the company were steadily depleted by the running charges.

After the defendant resigned, the company continued business until the spring of 1921, when the plaintiff was appointed receiver, found the company without funds, and realized only a small amount on the sale of its assets. During the incumbency of the defendant there had been only two meetings of directors, one of which (i.e., that of October 9, 1919) he attended; the other happening at a day when he was forced to be absent because of his mother's death. He was a friend of the president, who had induced him as the largest stockholder to become a director, and his only attention to the affairs of the company consisted of talks with the president as they met from time to time.

The theory of the bill was that the defendant had failed to give adequate attention to the affairs of the company, which had been conducted incompetently and without regard to the waste in salaries during the period before production was possible. This period was unduly prolonged by the incompetence of the factory manager, and disagreements between him and the engineer upon whose patents the company depended. The officers were unable to induce these men to compose their differences, and the work languished from incompetence and extravagance. More money was paid the engineer than his royalty contracts justified, and money was spent upon fraudulent circulars to induce the purchase of stock.

LEARNED HAND, D. J. (after stating the facts as above). This cause may be divided into three parts: First, the defendant's general liability for the collapse of the enterprise; second, his specific liability for overpayments made to Delano; third, his specific liability for the expenses of printing pamphlets and circulars used in selling the corporate shares.

The first liability must rest upon the defendant's general inattention to his duties as a director. He cannot be charged with neglect in attending directors' meetings, because there were only two during his incumbency, and of these he was present at one and had an adequate excuse for his absence from the other. His liability must therefore depend upon his failure in general to keep advised of the conduct of the corporate affairs. The measure of a director's duties in this regard is uncertain; the courts contenting themselves with vague declarations, such as that a director must give reasonable attention to the corporate business. While directors are collectively the managers of the company they are not expected to interfere individually in the actual conduct of its affairs. To do so would disturb the authority of the officers and destroy their individual responsibility, without which no proper discipline is possible. To them must be left the initiative and the immediate direction of the business; the directors can act individually only by counsel and advice to them. Yet they have an individual duty to keep themselves informed in some detail, and it is this duty which the defendant in my judgment failed adequately to perform.

All he did was to talk with Maynard as they met, while commuting from Flushing, or at their homes. That, indeed, might be enough, because Andrews had no reason to suspect Maynard's candor, nor had any reason to question it been yet disclosed. But it is plain that he did not press him for details, as he should. It is not enough to content oneself with general answers that the business looks promising and that all seems prosperous. Andrews was bound, certainly as the months wore on, to inform himself of what was going on with some particularity, and if he had done so, he would have learned that there were delays in getting into production which were putting the enterprise in most serious peril. It is entirely clear from his letters of April 14, 1920, and June 21, 1920, that he had made no effort to keep advised of the actual conduct of the corporate affairs, but had allowed himself to be carried along as a figurehead, in complete reliance upon Maynard. In spite of his own substantial investment in the company, which I must assume was as dear to him as it would be to other men, his position required of him more than this. Having accepted a post of confidence he was charged with an active duty to learn whether the company was moving to production, and why it was not, and to consider, as best he might, what could be done to avoid the conflicts among the personnel, or their incompetence, which was slowly bleeding it to death.

Therefore I cannot acquit Andrews of misprision in his office, though his integrity is unquestioned. The plaintiff must, however, go further than to show that he should have been more active in his duties. This cause of action rests upon a tort, as much though it be a tort of omission as though it had rested upon a positive act. The plaintiff must accept the burden of showing that the performance of the defendant's duties would have avoided loss, and what loss it would have avoided. I pressed Mr. Alger to show me a case in which the courts have held that a director could be charged generally with the collapse of a business in respect of which he had been inattentive, and I am not aware that he found one. In Bowerman v. Hammer, 250 U.S. 504, 39 Sup.Ct. 549, 63 L.Ed. 1113 the defendant was held for specific illegal loans, made by the president; so also in Kavanaugh v. Commonwealth Trust Co., 223 N.Y. 103, 119 N.E. 237. In Briggs v. Spaulding, 141 U.S. 132, 11 Sup.Ct. 924, 35 L.Ed. 662, a case decided by a narrow margin, which today would probably have gone the other way, the only attempt to charge the defendant was upon specific loans. Even in Hun v. Cary, 82 N.Y. 65, 37 Am. Rep. 546, it was for a single foolish investment that the defendant was held. The report of Allen v. Roydhouse (D.C.E.D. Pa.) 232 Fed. 1010 is not full enough to ascertain just what the verdict included, but apparently it too was for specific losses due to improper investments, and the same was true in Robinson v. Smith, 3 Paige (N.Y.) 222, 24 Am. Dec. 212.

When the corporate funds have been illegally lent, it is a fair inference that a protest would have stopped the loan, and that the directors' neglect caused the loss. But when a business fails from general mismanagement, business incapacity, or bad judgment, how is it possible to say that a single director could have made the company successful, or how much in dollars he could have saved? Before this cause can go to a master, the plaintiff must show that, had Andrews done his full duty, he could have made the company prosper, or at least could have broken its fall. He must show what sum he could have saved the company. Neither of these has he made any effort to do.

The defendant is not subject to the burden of proving that the loss would have happened, whether he had done his duty or not. If he were it would come to this: That if a director were once shown slack in his duties, he would stand charged prima facie with the difference between the corporate treasury as it was, and as it would be, judged by a hypothetical standard of success. How could such a standard be determined? How could any one guess how far a director's skill and judgment would have prevailed upon his fellows, and what would have been the ultimate fate of the business, if they had? How is it possible to set any measure of liability, or to tell what he would have contributed to the event? Men's fortunes may not be subjected to such uncertain and speculative conjectures. It is hard to see how there can be any remedy, except one can put one's finger on a definite loss and say with reasonable assurance that protest would have deterred, or counsel persuaded, the managers who caused it. No men of sense would take the office, if the law imposed upon them a guaranty of the general success of their companies as a penalty for any negligence.

It is, indeed, hard to determine just what went wrong in the management of this company. Any conclusion is little better than a guess. Still some discussion of the facts is necessary, and I shall discuss them. The claim that there were too many general employees turned out to be true, but, so far as I can see, only because of the delay in turning out the finished product. Had the factory gone into production in the spring of 1920, I cannot say, and the plaintiff cannot prove, that the selling department would have been prematurely or extravagantly organized. The expense of the stock sales was apparently not undue, and in any event Andrews was helpless to prevent it, because he found the contract an existing obligation of the company. So far as I can judge, the company had a fair chance of life, if the factory could have begun to turn out starters at the time expected. Whether this was the fault of Delano, as I suspect, is now too uncertain to say. It seems to me to make no difference in the result whether Delano, through inattention, or through sickness, or through Taylor, or for all three reasons, did not send along "Van Dycks" or whether Taylor should have got along without them, or should have shown more initiative and competence than he did. Between them the production lagged, until it was too late to resuscitate the dying company; its funds had oozed out in fixed payments, till there was nothing left with which to continue the business.

Suppose I charge Andrews with a complete knowledge of all that we have now learned? What action should he have taken, and how can I say that it would have stopped the losses? The plaintiff gives no definite answer to that question. Certainly he had no right to interject himself personally into the tangle; that was for Maynard to unravel. He would scarcely have helped to a solution by adding another cook to the broth. What suggestion could he have made to Maynard, or to his colleagues? The trouble arose either from an indifferent engineer, on whom the company was entirely dependent, or from an incompetent factory manager, who should have been discharged, or because the executives were themselves inefficient. Is Andrews to be charged for not insisting upon Taylor's discharge, or for not suggesting it? Suppose he did suggest it; have I the slightest reason for saying that the directors would have discharged him? Or, had they discharged him, is it certain that a substitute employed in *medias res* would have speeded up production? Was there not as fair a chance that Delano and Taylor might be brought to an accommodation as there was in putting in a green man at that juncture? How can I, sitting here, lay it down that Andrews' intervention would have brought order out of this chaos, or how can I measure in dollars the losses he would have saved? Or am I to hold Andrews because he did not move to discharge Maynard? How can I know that a better man was available? It is easy to say that he should have done something, but that will not serve to harness upon him the whole loss, or is it the equivalent of saying that, had he acted, the company would now flourish.

True, he was not very well-suited by experience for the job he had undertaken, but I cannot hold him on that account. After all, it is the same corporation that chose him which now seeks to charge him. I cannot agree with the language of Hun v. Cary, *supra*, that in effect he gave an implied warranty of any special fitness. Directors are not specialists, like lawyers or doctors. They must have good sense; perhaps, they must have acquaintance with affairs; but they need not, indeed, have any technical talent. They are the general advisers of the business, and if they faithfully give such ability as they have to their charge, it would not be lawful to hold them liable. Must a director guarantee that his judgment is good? Can shareholders call him to account for deficiencies which their votes assured him did not disqualify him for his office? While he may not have been the Cromwell for that Civil War, Andrews did not engage to play any such role.

I conclude, therefore, as to this first claim that there is no evidence that the defendant's neglect caused any losses to the company, and that, if there were, that loss cannot be ascertained. . . .

[The defendant was held not to be liable for the payments to Delano, it being found that they were not in fact overpayments. He was also held to be without liability for the cost of printing fraudulent circulars used to sell the company's stock, the court finding that he was not chargeable with knowledge of their falsity, and, further, that the circulars had caused no damage to the company since no stockholders had attempted to rescind their stock purchases on the ground of fraud. The bill was accordingly dismissed.]   ◄

COMMENTS AND QUESTIONS

1. What was the issue before the court? How did Judge Hand resolve it?
2. Summarize the principal points made by the court in support of its decision.
3. Note Judge Hand's statement, "I pressed Mr. Alger to show me a case in which the courts have held that a director could be charged generally with the collapse of a business in respect of which he had been inattentive, and I am not aware that he found one." Do you think his decision would have been different if the attorney had cited such a case? What if the attorney had cited the case of *Bates v. Dresser et al.,* immediately preceding?

In spite of this position of trust with respect to the corporation, however, directors are often permitted to deal with individual stockholders on a less straightforward basis. For example, in most states, a director who purchases stock from a stockholder is not required to tell the stockholder everything he knows about the stock's value. Some jurisdictions, however, hold the other way. Notice how the Massachusetts court dealt with this problem in the case that follows.

GOODWIN v. AGASSIZ et al.

Supreme Judicial Court of Massachusetts, 1933
283 Mass. 358, 186 N.E. 659

► Suit by Homer Goodwin against Rodolphe L. Agassiz and another. From a decree dismissing plaintiff's bill plaintiff appeals.

RUGG, CHIEF JUSTICE. A stockholder in a corporation seeks in this suit relief for losses suffered by him in selling shares of stock in Cliff Mining Company by way of accounting, rescission of sales, or redelivery of shares. The named defendants are MacNaughton, a resident of Michigan not served or appearing, and Agassiz, a resident of the Commonwealth, the active party defendant. . . . The facts thus displayed are these: The defendants, in May, 1926, purchased through brokers on the Boston stock exchange seven hundred shares of stock of the Cliff Mining Company which up to that time the plaintiff had owned. Agassiz was president and director and MacNaughton a director and general manager of the company. They had certain knowledge, material as to the value of the stock, which the plaintiff did not have. The plaintiff contends that such purchase in all the circumstances without disclosure to him of that knowledge was a wrong against him. That knowledge was that an experienced geologist had formulated in writing in March 1926, a theory as to the possible existence of copper deposits under conditions prevailing in the region where the property of the company was located. That region was known as the mineral belt in Northern Michigan, where are located mines of several copper mining companies. Another such company, of which the defendants were officers, had made extensive geological surveys of its lands. In consequence of recommendations resulting from that survey, exploration was started on property of the Cliff Mining Company in 1925. That exploration was ended in May, 1926, because completed unsuccessfully, and the equipment was removed. The defendants discussed the geologist's theory shortly after it was formulated. Both felt that the theory had value and should be tested but they agreed that before starting to test it, options should be obtained by another copper company of which they were officers on land adjacent to or nearby in the copper belt, that if the geologist's theory were known to the owners of such other land there might be difficulty in securing options, and that that theory should not be communicated to any one unless it became absolutely necessary. Thereafter options were secured which, if taken up, would involve a large expenditure by the other company. The defendants both thought, also, that, if there was any merit in the geologist's theory, the price of Cliff Mining Company stock in the market would go up. Its stock was quoted and bought and sold on the Boston Stock Exchange. Pursuant to agreement, they bought many shares of that stock through agents on joint account. The plaintiff first learned of the closing of exploratory operations on property of the Cliff Mining Company from an article in a paper on May 15, 1926, and immediately sold his shares of stock through brokers. It does not appear that the defendants were in any way responsible for the publication of that article. The plaintiff did not know that the purchase was made for the defendants and they did not know that his stock was being bought for them. There was no communication between them touching the subject. The plaintiff would not have sold his stock if he had known of the geologist's theory. The finding is express that the defendants were not guilty of fraud, that they committed no breach of duty owed by them to the Cliff Mining Company, and that that company was not harmed by the non-disclosure of the geologist's theory, or by their purchases of its stock, or by shutting down the exploratory operations.

The contention of the plaintiff is that the purchase of his stock in the company by the defendants without disclosing to him as a stockholder their knowledge of the geologist's theory, their belief that the theory was true, had value, the keeping secret the existence of the theory, discontinuance by the defendants of exploratory operations begun in 1925 on property of the Cliff Mining Company and their plan ultimately to test the value of the theory, constitute actionable wrong for which he as stockholder can recover.

The trial judge ruled that conditions may exist which would make it the duty of an officer of a corporation purchasing its stock from a stockholder to inform him as to knowledge possessed by the buyer and not by the seller, but found, on all the circumstances developed by the trial and set out at some length by him in his decision, that there was no fiduciary relation requiring such disclosure by the defendants to the plaintiff before buying his stock in the manner in which they did.

The question presented is whether the decree dismissing the bill rightly was entered on the facts found.

The directors of a commercial corporation stand in a relation of trust to the corporation and are bound to exercise the strictest good faith in respect to its property and business. . . . The contention that directors also occupy the position of trustee toward individual stockholders in the corporation is plainly contrary to repeated decisions of this court and cannot be supported. In Smith v. Hurd, 12 Metc. 371, 384; 46 Am. Dec. 690, it was said by Chief Justice Shaw:

> "There is no legal privity, relation, or immediate connexion between the holders of shares in a bank in their individual capacity, on the one side, and the directors of the bank on the other. The directors are not the bailees, the factors, agents or trustees of such individual stockholders."

In Stewart v. Joyce, 201 Mass. 301, 311, 312; 87 N.E. 268, 271, occurs this language with reference to sale of stock in a corporation by a stockholder to two of its directors: "The fact that the defendants were directors created no fiduciary relation between them and the plaintiff in the matter of the sale of his stock."

The principle thus established is supported by an imposing weight of authority in other jurisdictions. . . . A rule holding that directors are trustees for individual stockholders with respect to their stock prevails in comparatively few states; but in view of our own adjudications it is not necessary to review decisions to that effect. . . .

While the general principle is as stated, circumstances may exist requiring that transactions between a director and a stockholder as to stock in the corporation be set aside. The knowledge naturally in the possession of a director as to the condition of a corporation places upon him a peculiar obligation to observe every requirement of fair dealing when directly buying or selling its stock. Mere silence does not usually amount to a breach of duty, but parties may stand in such relation to each other that an equitable responsibility arises to communicate facts. . . . Purchases and sales of stock dealt in on the stock exchange are commonly impersonal affairs. An honest director would be in a difficult situation if he could neither buy nor sell on the stock exchange shares of stock in his corporation without first seeking out the other actual ultimate party to the transaction and disclosing to him everything which a court or jury might later find that he then knew affecting the real or speculative value of such shares. Business of that nature is a matter to be governed by practical rules. Fiduciary obligations of directors ought not to be made so onerous that men of experience and ability will be deterred from accepting such office. Law in its sanctions is not coextensive with morality. It cannot undertake to put all parties to every contract on an equality as to knowledge, experience, skill and shrewdness. It cannot undertake to relieve against hard bargains made between competent parties without fraud. On the other hand, directors cannot rightly be allowed to indulge with impunity in practices which do violence to prevailing standards of upright businessmen. Therefore, where a director personally seeks a stockholder for the purpose of buying his shares without making disclosure of material facts within his peculiar knowledge and not within reach of the stockholder, the transaction will be closely scrutinized and relief may be granted in appropriate instances. [Citing cases.] The applicable legal principles "have almost always been the fundamental ethical rules of right and wrong."

The precise question to be decided in the case at bar is whether on the facts found the defendants as directors had a right to buy stock of the plaintiff, a stockholder. Every element of actual fraud or misdoing by the defendants is negatived by the findings. Fraud cannot be presumed; it must be proved. . . . The facts found afford no ground for inferring fraud or conspiracy. The only knowledge possessed by the defendants not open to the plaintiff was the existence of a theory formulated in a thesis by a geologist as to the possible existence of copper deposits where certain geological conditions existed common to the property of the Cliff Mining Company and that of other mining companies in its neighborhood. This thesis did not express an opinion that copper deposits would be found any way in a particular spot or on property of any specified owner. Whether that theory was sound or fallacious, no one knew, and so far as appears has never been demonstrated. The defendants made no representations to anybody about the theory. No facts found placed upon them any obligation to disclose the theory. A few days after the thesis expounding the theory was brought to the attention of the defendants, the annual report by the directors of the Cliff Mining Company for the calendar year 1925, signed by Agassiz for the directors, was issued. It did not cover the time when the theory was formulated. The report described the status of the operations under the exploration which had been begun in 1925. At the annual meeting of the stockholders of the company held early in April, 1926, no reference was made to the theory. It was then, at most, a hope, possibly an expectation. It had not passed the nebulous stage. No disclosure was made of it. The Cliff Mining Company was not harmed by the nondisclosure. There would have been no advantage to it, so far as appears, from a disclosure. The disclosure would have been detrimental to the interest of another mining corporation in which the defendants were directors. In the circumstances there was no duty on the part of the defendants to set forth to the stockholders at annual meeting their faith, aspirations and plans for the future. Events as they developed might render advisable radical changes in such views. Disclosure of the theory, if it ultimately was proved to be erroneous or without foundation in fact, might involve the defendants in litigation with those who might act on the hypothesis that it was correct. The stock of the Cliff Mining Company was bought and sold on the stock exchange. The identity of buyers and seller of the stock in question in fact was not known to the parties and perhaps could not readily have been ascertained. The defendants caused the shares to be bought through brokers on the stock exchange. They said nothing to anybody as to the reasons actuating them. The plaintiff was no novice. He was a member of the Boston stock exchange and had kept a record of sale of Cliff Mining Company stock. He acted upon his own judgment in selling his stock. He made no inquiries of the defendants or of other officers of the company. The result is that plaintiff cannot prevail.

Decree dismissing bill affirmed with costs.   ◄

COMMENTS AND QUESTIONS

1. What was the plaintiff trying to accomplish in this lawsuit? Did he succeed?
2. Summarize the reasons for the court's decision.
3. Suppose, instead, that the defendants had purchased the stock personally from the plaintiff and had denied any knowledge of the copper deposits when the plaintiff inquired about the company's plans. Would this have changed the result?

Action Against Directors

A corporation that sustains injury as a result of the negligent or wrongful activities of one or more of its directors must itself bring suit in order to recover damages. If the corporation fails to act, any stockholder may bring action on the corporation's behalf. First, however, the stockholder must show that he has made a reasonable effort to induce the corporation itself to act. If the stockholder's suit is successful, whatever he recovers goes into the corporate treasury to be used solely for the benefit of the corporation. The stockholder is entitled to reimbursement for whatever he spent in prosecuting the action.

Management by Officers

Corporate charters or bylaws normally provide for the election or appointment of certain officers, such as president, vice-president, secretary, and treasurer. As a general rule, these officers are appointed by the board of directors, but sometimes they are elected by the stockholders. Frequently, a director will also serve as an officer; there is rarely any prohibition against such dual service.

The officers of a corporation, who are in charge of its day-to-day operations, also have the authority and the responsibility for carrying out the long-range policies of the board of directors. The authority of corporate officers is defined by the rules of agency law. Thus, for example, the top management positions usually carry broad authority, both real and apparent, to act on behalf of the corporation.

Officers, like directors, occupy positions of great trust and responsibility.

They are liable to the corporation for any damage resulting from their willful, negligent, or improper acts, and they must exercise reasonable prudence in carrying out their duties. They may be sued by the corporation, or, if the corporation fails to take action, by an individual stockholder.

In the concluding case in this section, a stockholder challenged the right of a corporate officer to receive a certain salary, on the ground that the salary was excessive.

ROGERS v. HILL et al.

Supreme Court of the United States, 1933
289 U.S. 582, 53 S.Ct. 731

► On Writ of Certiorari to the United States Circuit Court of Appeals for the Second Circuit.

Consolidated suits by Richard Reid Rogers against George W. Hill and others and against Thomas R. Taylor and another. An order granting a temporary injunction having been reversed by the Circuit Court of Appeals (60 F. 2d 109), the District Court vacated the temporary injunction and dismissed the bills of complaint upon the merits, which decree was affirmed by the Circuit Court of Appeals (62 F. 2d 1079) and plaintiffs bring certiorari (289 U.S. 716, 53 S.Ct. 593, 77 L.Ed. 1469).

Decree of the Circuit Court of Appeals reversed, decree of the District Court dismissing the bills on the merits vacated, and case remanded to the District Court with directions.

Mr. Justice Butler delivered the opinion of the Court.

The American Tobacco Company is a corporation organized under the laws of New Jersey. The petitioner, plaintiff below, acquired in 1916 and has since been the owner of 200 shares of its common stock. He also has 400 shares of common stock B. In accordance with bylaw XII, adopted by the stockholders at their annual meeting, March 13, 1912, the company for many years has annually paid its president and vice-presidents large amounts in addition to their fixed salaries and other sums allowed them as compensation for services.

Plaintiff maintains that the by-law is invalid and that, even if valid, the amounts paid under it are unreasonably large and therefore subject to revision by the courts. In March, 1931, he demanded that the company bring suit against the officers who have received such payments to compel them to account to the company for all or such part thereof as the court may hold illegal. The company, insisting that such a suit would be without basis in law or fact, refused to comply with his demand. He brought suit in the Supreme Court of New York against the president and some of the vice-presidents to require them so to account, and joined the company as defendant. The case was removed to the federal court for the Southern District of New York. In May, 1931, plaintiff brought suit in that court against Taylor, a vice-president, not a defendant in the earlier suit, to require him to account and made the company defendant. The cases were consolidated, plaintiff filed an amended complaint and defendants answered.

The officers of the company now before the court are Hill, the president, Neiley, Riggio, and Taylor, vice-presidents. . . .

The plaintiff alleges that the measure of compensation fixed by it is not now equitable or fair. And he prays that the court fix and determine the fair and reasonable compensation of the individual defendants, respectively, for each of the years in question. The allegations of the complaint are not sufficient to permit consideration by the court of the validity or reasonableness of any of the payments on account of fixed salaries or of special credits or of the allotments of stock therein mentioned. Indeed, plaintiff alleges that other proceedings have been instituted for the restoration of special credits and his suits to invalidate the stock allotments were recently considered here. . . . The only payments that plaintiff by this suit seeks to have restored to the company are the payments made to the individual defendants under the by-law.

We come to consider whether these amounts are subject to examination and revision in the District Court. As the amounts payable depend upon the gains of the business, the specified percentages are not per se unreasonable. The by-law was adopted in 1912 by an almost unanimous vote of the shares represented at the annual meeting and presumably the stockholders supporting the measure acted in good faith and according to their best judgment. Plaintiff does not complain of any [payment] made prior to 1921. Regard is to be had to the enormous increase of the company's profits in recent years. The 2½ per cent. yielded President Hill $447,870.30 in 1929 and $842,507.72 in 1930. The 1½ per cent. yielded to each of the vice-presidents, Neiley and Riggio, $115,141.86, in 1929 and $409,495.25 in 1930 and for these years payments under the by-law were in addition to the cash credits and fixed salaries shown in the statement.

While the amounts produced by the application of the prescribed percentages give rise to no inference of actual or constructive fraud, the payments under the by-law have by reason of increase of profits become so large as to warrant investigation in equity in the interest of the company. Much weight is to be given to the action of the stockholders, and the by-law is supported by the presumption of regularity and continuity. But the rule prescribed by it cannot, against the protest of a shareholder, be used to justify payments of sums as salaries so large as in substance and effect to amount to spoliation or waste of corporate property. The dissenting opinion of Judge Swan indicates the applicable rule: "If a bonus payment has no relation to the value of services for which it is given, it is in reality a gift in part and the majority stockholders have no power to give away corporate property against the protest of the minority." 60 F. (2d) 109, 113. The facts alleged by plaintiff are sufficient to require that the District Court, upon a consideration of all the relevant facts brought forward by the parties, determine whether and to what extent payments to the individual defendants under the by-laws constitute misuse and waste of the money of the corporation. [Citing cases.]

The decree of the Circuit Court of Appeals is reversed, the decree of the District Court dismissing the bills on the merits is vacated, and the case is remanded to the District Court with directions to reinstate its decree granting injunction pendente lite [13] *and for further proceedings in conformity with this opinion.*

It is so ordered.   ◄

COMMENTS AND QUESTIONS

1. Trace the history of this litigation from the original suit in the New York lower court to the United States Supreme Court. What was the final decision?
2. Doesn't this case penalize success? How does the court justify its ruling? Do you agree?

SECTION 6

DISSOLUTION AND TERMINATION OF CORPORATIONS

Voluntary Dissolution

Expiration of Charter

If a corporation's charter is of limited duration, the corporation's existence is automatically terminated at the end of the stated period. Ordinarily, however, the life of a corporation may be extended on application to the proper state authorities.

Surrender of Charter

So long as the stockholders consent, a corporation may be dissolved by the voluntary surrender of its charter. Dissolution does not occur, however, until the state actually accepts the charter. And this is usually not done until the corporate creditors have been paid in full.

Consolidation and Merger

A *consolidation* occurs when two or more corporations combine their entities and assets to form a new corporation. The old corporations are dissolved, and the consolidated corporation assumes all their rights, powers, and liabilities.

A *merger* differs from a consolidation in that one of the corporations continues to exist and absorbs the other corporation, which is dissolved. In a merger, the surviving corporation usually takes over all the rights, duties, and liabilities of the merged corporation.

---

[13] That is, pending the suit, or until the outcome of the case is finally determined.

Mergers and consolidations are generally subject to statutory regulation and are closely scrutinized and supervised by the courts. The following case is typical.

COLE et al. v. NATIONAL CASH CREDIT ASS'N. JOURNAL SQUARE BANK BUILDING CO. v. NATIONAL CASH CREDIT ASS'N. et al.

Court of Chancery of Delaware, 1931
18 Del. Ch. 47, 156 A. 183

► Two bills, one by Frank H. Cole and others against the National Cash Credit Association, and the other by the Journal Square Bank Building Company against the National Cash Credit Association and another. Rules for preliminary injunction were issued in both causes and were heard together.

Rules discharged.

Bills to enjoin the defendant from proceeding with a merger agreement, by which it, contemporaneously with Franklin Plan Company, Franklin Thrift and Loan Association and American Cash Credit Corporation, all Delaware corporations, will merge with another existing Delaware corporation called Franklin Plan Corporation.

The Cole bill was filed by a holder of preferred stock of the National Cash Credit Association in behalf of himself and other preferred stockholders. . . . The complainants in the Cole bill object to the merger of their corporation with the Franklin Plan Corporation on the ground that if all the mergers, which are mutually dependent for completion on the carrying through of each, are effected, the asset security underlying the preferred stock of the absorbing company which is to be given in exchange for their present preferred stock will be less in value than that which underlies their present National Cash Credit Association stock; and that this reduction in value is due to the fact that in estimating the asset contribution which each of the merging companies makes to the common pool, the National Cash Credit Association assets are underappraised in comparison with the assets of the other merging companies, whereby the stockholders of the latter are given an advantage over them and other stockholders of the National Cash Credit Association similarly situated. The result, say the complainants, will be that their present stock will, if converted into the proposed new stock, suffer not only in security value but also in market value. . . .

The bill of the Journal Square Bank Building Company assails the proposed merger on the additional ground that if it is consummated as planned, the liabilities of the absorbing company will be greatly increased without any commensurate increase in the quick assets available for debts, that the financial condition of the defendant is more sound than will be that of the corporation into which it is proposed to be merged, and that as a consequence the security which the complainant now has in the assets of its debtor will be greatly impaired.

Rules for preliminary injunction were issued in both causes. They now come on to be heard together upon bills and affidavits.

THE CHANCELLOR. The rules for preliminary injunction in these two cases were heard together. In disposing of the rules, I shall first take notice of the suit filed by the Journal Square Bank Building Company.

Bill of Journal Square Bank Building Company.

The complainant in this suit is a creditor of the defendant. As a general proposition, it is not permitted to a creditor of a corporation to prevent its merger or consolidation with another if the statutory law of its creation authorized it. . . .

If creditors are in no position to object to a proposed consolidation of their debtor with another corporation because resort to equity against the debtor's assets affords them protection, then *a fortiori* the express conference upon them by statute of a right of action generally by which not only the assets of their debtor but as well the entire assets of the consolidated company, whether derived from the debtor constituent or not, may be seized in satisfaction, would render less defensible the right of creditors to prevent a consolidation.

The statute of Delaware, under which the corporations here involved were created, expressly provides that in case of merger or consolidation, the rights of creditors of the constituent corporations shall be preserved unimpaired, and all debts, etc., of the constituent companies shall thenceforth, after the merger of consolidation, attach to the consolidated corporation and be enforceable against it to the same extent as if said debts, etc., had been incurred or contracted by it. Section 60, General Corporation Law (35 Del. Laws, c. 85, 19). . . .

The complainant as creditor, as now appears, will have all the security it now has and considerably more besides. It is difficult then to see how the consolidation can possibly injure it.

But the Journal Square Bank Building Company objects further that it now has the right and, so long as its claim lives, will continue to have the right, by reason of its debtor's having qualified by license to do business in New Jersey, to sue it in that State, a condition on which its license to do business in that State was granted being that, even though it should withdraw from the State, process might still be served upon it through the Secretary of State of New Jersey; and that this remedy of suit in New Jersey will be lost to the complainant if the merger goes through, because in that event the life of the defendant will be terminated (section 60, Delaware General Corporation Law), and hence the complainant could no longer sue it in New Jersey. Thus, argues the complainant, a "remedy" belonging to it as a creditor will be taken from it, in violation of section 63 of the Delaware act (Rev. Code 1915, 1977) which provides that the "rights or remedies" of creditors of a Delaware corporation "shall not in any way be lessened or impaired . . . by the consolidation of two or more corporations. . . ."

In the first place I very much doubt that the act of merging would deprive the complainant of its right to a remedy in New Jersey. . . .

But, if the consolidated company could not be sued in New Jersey as an alter ego of the defendant, I still think the complainant has no ground of complaint. The "remedy" of suit somewhere will not be taken from it by the merger. It is expressly reserved to it by statute. I conceive that the word "remedies" as used in the statute refers to those recognized forms of redress which law and equity afford for the securing of rights, without regard to the situs of the jurisdictions, in which they may be asserted. The statute makes lawful and authorized the merger here under contemplation. If, as a result of the statute's operation, a preserved remedy could no longer be asserted in a particular foreign jurisdiction, it would be a strange result if by reason of that fact the statutory authority would be nullified. The right to sue the defendant in New Jersey after it has withdrawn therefrom is a right which the New Jersey law attaches to the granting of a license to do business in that State. If that New Jersey right is in a substantial sense lost by reason of Delaware legislation, a question which as before indicated is doubtful, I think nevertheless that so far as the Delaware law is concerned the remedy in New Jersey is gone. When our statute preserves remedies generally to creditors in consolidation and merger cases, it does not undertake to guarantee to them jurisdictions in which to assert the remedies.

Bill of Cole, et al.

I now take up the case of the preferred stockholders who seek to enjoin the merger. The crucial point on which their complaint turns is one of value—whether or not they as stockholders in one of the constituents are to receive, in exchange for their present holdings, stock which has a value commensurate with the asset contribution which their company is making to the common pool.

This is a question in the last analysis of what are the fair values to be ascribed to the assets of the defendant company in the merger plan.

The statute under which the contemplated merger is proposed to be put through does not compel an objecting minority of stockholders to submit to the compulsion of the majority to the extent of being forced into the status of stockholders in the consolidated enterprise. The option is given to each dissenting stockholder to elect whether he will take his allotment of stock in the consolidated company. If he prefers to disassociate himself from the consolidation, he may, by following the procedure laid down in section 61 of the General Corporation Law (35 Del. Laws, c. 85, 20), secure a valuation of his stock in money and collect the same as a debt due.

As a general proposition dissenting stockholders are thus put to an election by the statute. There may be circumstances, however, under which a court of equity will say that the duty to make the election does not arise. For instance where the merger is not authorized by law, a dissenting stockholder is under no duty to make his election. He may enjoin its consummation. . . . Furthermore, if consent to the merger is induced by fraud practiced upon a consenting company, a stockholder is under no duty to elect whether he will abide by a merger so induced or take his money. In such a case equity holds that no just alternatives are presented to him for a choice. . . . Where also the merger proposes illegally to wipe out a right to accumulated dividends on preferred stock, a court of equity will enjoin it on the application of a preferred stockholder. In such a case the stockholder's election is invited between two alternatives one of which is highly unfair. . . . From these and other cases which may be cited it thus appears that the election which is given to the stockholder is one that he is not under any and all circumstances required to exercise. The exercise of the statutory right of merger is always subject to nullification for fraud. The cases so hold.

In the instant case fraud on the complainants is the ground on which their claimed right to an injunction is based. The fraud charged, however, is not actual fraud on the part of the directors and majority stockholders. It is constructive fraud based on an alleged discriminatory undervaluation of assets of the National Cash Credit Association on the one hand and an overvaluation of the assets of Franklin Plan Corporation, the consolidated company, on the other. When the fraud charged is of this nature, it must be so plainly made out as to disclose a breach of trust or such maladministration as works a manifest wrong to the dissentients. . . . The overvaluation or undervaluation, as the case may be, must be such as to show a conscious abuse of discretion before fraud in law can be made out. Such is the tenor of the opinion of the Vice-Chancellor in Donald v. American Smelting & Refining Co., 61 N.J. Eq. 458, 48 A. 786, 788, reversed on other grounds, 62 N.J. Eq. 729, 48 A. 771. In Jones v. Missouri-Edison Electric Co. (C.C.A.), 199 F. 64, relief was granted because it was shown that the distribution of the stock of the merged company among the stockholders of the merging companies was "grossly unjust." This circumstance, combined with the fact that the dominating interests in the merger were the beneficiaries of the inequality, moved the court to grant the relief prayed for by the protesting minority.

In the case *sub judice*, if there is an inequality as between the merging companies, it is not coupled with any showing, or even intimation, that those who have engineered the merger or whose voting influence is great enough to accomplish it, are themselves beneficiaries of the alleged inequality. The case therefore is one that rests on the sole fact of alleged undervaluation and overvaluation of the assets of two of the merging companies.

Where that is the case the rule adopted by this court as applicable to the sale of corporate assets would seem by analogy to supply a sound basis for guidance. While a consolidation is quite distinct from a sale, yet, from the viewpoint of the constituent companies, a sale of assets is in substance involved. Here it is the sole feature of the merger and that alone with which we are concerned. Looking then at the transaction as one where the stockholders of the defendant are in substance selling its assets to another in exchange for securities issued by the latter, what is the rule by which the value derived in exchange for the assets is to be tested for the purpose of discovering whether or not fraud can be said to have been shown? This question is answered by the case of Allied Chemical & Dye Corp. v. Steel & Tube Co., 14 Del. Ch. 1, 120 A. 486. The rule there laid down was that mere inadequacy of price will not reveal fraud. The inadequacy must be so gross as to lead the court to conclude that it was due not to an honest error of judgment but rather to bad faith, or to a reckless indifference to the rights of others interested. There is a presumption that the judgment of the governing body of a corporation, whether at the time it consists of directors or majority stockholders, is formed in good faith and inspired by a bona fides of purpose. . . .

I come now to the question of fact—*viz.:* was there an undervaluation of the defendant's assets, and if so, was it so gross as to indicate bad faith towards the opposing minority? It is significant, that if there was such a grossly unfair discrimination against the class of stockholders among whom the complainants are numbered, only 40,000 shares out of the total of 327,324 are protesting. Apparently about eighty-eight per cent. of the preferred stock outstanding is satisfied with the terms proposed. I do not mean to speak slightingly of forty thousand shares as a negligible number. The figures are given merely to point out that in the judgment of an overwhelming majority of the stock in the interest of which this suit was filed, there is nothing in the situation which warrants a protest. . . .

The complainants, speaking for themselves and others, vigorously complain because the stock which they bought has suffered a great market loss. That is unfortunate. It has however nothing to do with the merits or demerits of the proposed merger, which is to be judged in the light of values without reference to prices paid by investors.

After a rather painstaking study of the evidence before me, I fail to see anything in the proposed plan of merger which reveals any fraud, actual or constructive. The complainants therefore are not entitled to be relieved of exercising the election given to them by the statute of choosing whether they will accept stock under the merger or take the necessary steps to secure a valuation and payment in money.

The rules in both cases will be discharged. ◄

COMMENTS AND QUESTIONS

1. What were the allegations of the plaintiff here? Did the court agree?
2. What was the basis of Cole's complaint? How did the court decide?
3. This case illustrates the care with which courts scrutinize proposed mergers and consolidations to make sure that stockholders and creditors are protected.

Involuntary Dissolution

Forfeiture of Charter

Each state has the power, through its attorney general, to dissolve a corporation by requiring it to forfeit its charter. Generally speaking, this step is taken only if the corporation is found to have misused its power or to have acted illegally. A corporation that fails to use its powers or ceases to operate may also be dissolved by forfeiture.

Insolvency

The existence of a corporation is not automatically terminated when the corporation becomes insolvent. Upon the application of its creditors, a receiver may be appointed to liquidate the corporation's assets and distribute them to the creditors to pay off the corporate debts. Until it is actually dissolved (an action that often requires a court order), the corporation continues to exist; during that time its creditors may pursue their usual remedies, such as the attachment of corporate property.

Distribution of Assets on Dissolution

On the dissolution of a corporation, its assets are first used to pay all its outstanding debts and obligations. The remaining funds are distributed to the stockholders in accordance with the amount of capital stock each of them holds. As in the distribution of dividends, preferred stockholders are often entitled to preference in the distribution of the remaining assets.

SUMMARY OF THE LAW OF CORPORATIONS

Characteristics of Corporations

A corporation is a legal entity separate and distinct from the people who create and manage it; it continues to exist despite changes in its membership. As a separate legal "person," a corporation is entitled to certain constitutional protections; it may not be deprived of property without due process of law, nor may it be denied the equal protection of the laws. Unlike a natural person, however, it does not have a constitutional right to do business wherever it chooses.

Generally speaking, the courts will not look behind the corporate identity even though most of the corporation's stock is held by one person. If a corporation is used unjustly to perpetrate a fraud or to avoid a legal obligation, however, the entity may be disregarded and the individual members held responsible.

Creation of Corporations

Each state has incorporation statutes prescribing the steps that must be taken to form a corporation. As a general rule, three or more persons of legal capacity must file, with the proper state official, an application containing certain basic information about the proposed corporation. If the application is in order, the state then issues a charter outlining the powers of the corporation and the purposes for which it has been formed. After the charter has been issued, an organization meeting is held at which officers and directors are elected, bylaws are adopted, and the books and records are opened. In most states, the corporation legally comes into existence as soon as the charter has been issued, but in some jurisdictions corporate life does not start until the organization meeting has been held.

A corporation that has met all the requirements of the incorporation laws is known as a corporation *de jure*. Even though all the requirements have not been met, a corporation may be recognized as a *de facto* corporation if it has made a good-faith effort to comply with the requirements and if it has made some use or exercise of its corporate power. The existence of a *de facto* corporation may be challenged only by the state authorities; no third party may avoid his obligations to the corporation on the ground that it was improperly formed. If there is a substantial failure to comply with the incorporation laws, no corporation exists either in law or in fact. In such cases, the persons who organized the firm are usually treated as if they were partners and are personally liable for the firm's obligations. Some states, however, hold that a third person who deals with such a firm as a corporation is estopped from denying its corporate existence and may not hold the members personally liable.

Promoters

A promoter is a person who does the preliminary work before a corporation formally comes into existence. As a general rule, a promoter has no authority to bind the corporation to pre-incorporation contracts; once the corporation has been formed, it is free to adopt or reject such contracts. Even though the corporation chooses to adopt a contract, the promoter remains personally liable unless the other contracting party agrees to discharge him. Generally speaking, a corporation is not required to reimburse a promoter for his services and expenses unless it agrees to pay for them after it has formally come into existence. Some states, however, hold that a promoter is entitled to recover any expenses that were actually necessary to bring the corporation into existence.

Corporate Powers

The express powers of a corporation are usually set forth in its charter. They are commonly phrased in broad terms, to avoid hampering the corporation's future activities. In addition to its express powers, a corporation also possesses implied powers that are necessary for carrying out the purposes for which it was organized. Generally speaking, a corporation has the implied power: (1) to adopt a corporate name, provided it is not too similar to that of another firm; (2) to adopt bylaws; (3) to acquire and hold property; (4) to acquire stock in other corporations, so long as such acquisitions help to further its own operations and do not violate the antitrust laws; (5) to acquire its own stock, provided the corporation is solvent and its creditors are protected; (6) to borrow money to carry out its authorized business. As a general rule, a corporation does *not* have implied power: (1) to guarantee payment of another person's debt; (2) to form a partnership with another firm or individual; or (3) to merge or consolidate with another firm without express authorization.

Ultra Vires Acts

An act or agreement is said to be *ultra vires* if it is outside the scope of a corporation's express or implied powers. Formerly, if a corporation entered into an *ultra vires* contract, either side could avoid its obligations. Today, however, the following rules are generally accepted: (1) if the *ultra vires* contract is executed on both sides, neither party can avoid it; (2) if the *ultra vires* contract is wholly executory, neither party can enforce it; (3) if only one side has performed, most states hold that the contract should be rescinded, though some states require that the contract be completed by the other party. If a corporation is contemplating an *ultra vires* act, a stockholder may enjoin the management from going ahead; or, if the act has already been performed, he may sue for damages and reimburse the corporate treasury. If the *ultra vires* act is serious enough, the state may revoke the corporation's charter.

Right to Do Business in Other States

As a general rule, no foreign corporation has a constitutional right to do business in a state that wishes to exclude it. If it does so without permission, the corporation and its officers may be subject to criminal penalties. Most states permit a foreign corporation to do business within its borders provided the corporation complies with certain rules and regulations and pays certain entrance fees and taxes. Once a foreign corporation has been admitted to do business, however, the state may not discriminate against it in favor of domestic corporations. In addition, the federal Constitution prohibits a state from imposing overly harsh restrictions on corporations engaged exclusively in interstate commerce.

Corporate Membership

Anyone who owns one or more shares of stock is a member of the corporation that issued the stock. Each share represents a part interest in the corporation's assets and entitles the stockholder to share in profits, to participate in management, and to receive a pro rata share of the corporate assets on dissolution. As evidence of corporate membership, most corporations issue stock certificates outlining the rights and privileges to which the stockholders are entitled.

Kinds of Stock

Common stock, the ordinary stock of the corporation, usually entitles the owner to a vote for each share held, the right to receive dividends, and a share in assets on dissolution. However, common stock ordinarily bestows on the holder no special preferences or priority in the distribution of dividends or the sharing of assets on dissolution.

Preferred stock, on the other hand, confers certain preferential rights in the disbursement of dividends and in the distribution of assets on dissolution. Ordinarily, the holder of preferred stock is entitled to a certain specified dividend before any dividends are paid to the holders of common stock.

Preferred stock may be either cumulative or noncumulative. The holder of cumulative preferred may carry over his priority claim to dividends during those years when no dividends are declared; he is entitled to receive the accumulated back dividends before any dividends are paid on common stock. If his stock is noncumulative preferred, however, the holder is not entitled to back dividends for those years when no dividends are declared. Unless there is a clear indication to the contrary, preferred stock is always deemed to be cumulative.

Preferred stock may also be classified as participating or nonparticipating. Participating preferred stock gives the holder the right to share equally with the common stockholders in any additional dividend distribution after the common stockholders have been paid an amount equal to the amount paid to the preferred stockholders. In the absence of an express provision in the charter or stock certificate, all preferred stock is deemed to be nonparticipating.

A preferred stockholder does not ordinarily have a vote in the management of the corporation. However, in some cases, the charter provides that if the corporation fails to pay dividends to the preferred holders for a certain period, they may take over voting rights from the common stockholders.

Capital Stock and Surplus

The capital stock of a corporation is the declared value of its outstanding stock. Any net assets of a corporation over and above the value of its capital stock are referred to as surplus.

Stock Subscriptions

In most states, a subscription for stock made before incorporation is treated merely as an offer to purchase stock; the subscriber is not bound until the corporation has been formed and has formally accepted the subscription. Like any other offer, it may lapse or be withdrawn before acceptance occurs. Some states, however, hold that a subscription is automatically accepted when the corporation is formed; another group of states hold that prior subscriptions are irrevocable for a certain period (usually one year).

Post-incorporation subscriptions are treated just like any other contract; they are not binding until there has been a formal acceptance of the offer.

Transfer of Stock

Generally speaking, a stockholder may transfer his shares to any person or organization he chooses. Restrictions on this right will usually be upheld, however, if they are reasonable and if the stockholder is left free to sell to others if the corporation, or its principal shareholders, do not exercise their option to purchase the stock. No restriction on this right is binding on innocent purchasers of stock, however, unless it is expressly set forth in the stock certificate.

In most states, the methods of transferring stock are prescribed by the Uniform Stock Transfer Act. This statute ordinarily requires actual delivery of the stock certificate, together with an indorsement or a written assignment. It also holds that if a person purchases stock in good faith and for value, he takes good title free and clear of any defenses or claims that may be raised by former owners or other claimants.

Until a corporation has been notified that a transfer of stock has taken place, it may continue to pay dividends to the transferor and recognize his right to vote. Generally speaking, if a dividend is declared before a transfer takes place, the dividend belongs to the transferor. If it is declared after the transfer takes place, it belongs to the transferee. The parties themselves, of course, may agree on some other arrangement. A transferor who wrongfully receives a dividend must account for it to the transferee.

Rights of Stockholders

Every stock corporation has at least one class of stock (usually common) which carries with it the right to attend stockholders' meetings, to participate in the election of directors, and to vote on other matters. Ordinarily, a stockholder may authorize someone else to cast his vote for him by means of a proxy. As a general rule, stockholders are allowed to enter into agreements or voting trusts to pool their voting strength for the purpose of controlling the management, provided the agreement or trust is reasonable and for a lawful purpose.

Whenever the amount of a corporation's capital stock is increased, each stockholder is ordinarily given a pre-emptive right to subscribe to the same percentage of the new stock as he holds of the old, so that his percentage of the total stock remains constant. Pre-emptive rights are not granted on a new issue of nonvoting stock, however, since no measure of corporate control is involved. Similarly, pre-emptive rights are generally not extended when treasury stock is reissued.

Every stockholder has the right to inspect the books of the corporation so long as his examination is for a reasonable purpose and so long as he gives reasonable notice.

Stockholder's Right to Dividends

Each stockholder has the right to receive his proportionate share of any dividends declared, subject, of course, to the rights of any preferred stockholders. Although dividends are normally paid in cash, they are sometimes paid in property or goods. Stock dividends may be declared so long as the proportional share of each holder is not affected.

In a majority of states, dividends may be declared only out of surplus. In some jurisdictions, however, dividends may be declared out of current net profits even though no surplus actually exists. If a corporation wrongfully declares a dividend and later becomes insolvent, the directors may be held personally liable to the corporate creditors.

As a general rule, the directors of a corporation have sole discretion to determine whether a dividend will be declared; the courts will not compel them to do so even if ample funds are available. In rare cases, however, when it is clear that a huge surplus has been accumulated which far exceeds any foreseeable needs of the corporation, the directors may be required to distribute at least part of it to the stockholders.

Liabilities of Stockholders

As a general rule, the liability of each stockholder is limited to the amount he paid for his stock; if the assets of the corporation prove insufficient to pay creditors, he is not personally responsible for the deficit. There are two principal exceptions to this rule, however: (1) if a dividend is improperly declared and, as a result, creditors cannot be paid, the stockholders may be held liable to the creditors for dividends they have wrongfully received; (2) if corporate assets are insufficient to pay the wages and salaries of its employees, the stockholders may be held personally liable for paying them.

Management by Stockholders

Although stockholders rarely play a direct role in corporate management, they normally have the right to select the board of directors and to vote on major issues that affect the business of the corporation. Action by stockholders is not binding unless it is taken at a meeting that has been properly called. Generally speaking, reasonable notice of a meeting must be given and a quorum must be present before any proposal may be officially acted on.

Management by Directors

Most corporations entrust the broad powers of management to a board of directors. The board may appoint officers and employees and delegate authority to them. The board functions as a unit and may take action only at a meeting that has been duly called and at which a quorum is present. No director may cast his vote by proxy; in order to vote, he must be present in person.

Directors must exercise their managerial powers with the utmost good faith and may not use their position to gain a secret profit or an unjust advantage at the expense of the corporation. A director is personally liable for any misappropriation of corporate assets. Directors are not, however, liable for losses resulting from poor management if they have acted in good faith and with reasonable care.

A corporation that sustains injury as the result of a director's wrongful activities must itself bring suit against him in order to recover damages. If the corporation fails to act, however, any stockholder may bring an action on the corporation's behalf.

Management by Officers

As a general rule, the principal officers of a corporation are appointed by the board of directors, though sometimes they are elected by the stockholders. The officers are in charge of the day-to-day operations of the corporation and usually have broad authority to carry out the long-range policies of the board of directors. Like directors, they occupy positions of great trust and are liable to the corporation for any damage resulting from their negligent or wrongful acts.

Dissolution and Termination of Corporations

A corporation may be voluntarily dissolved: (1) by the expiration or surrender of its charter, or (2) by a merger or consolidation with one or more other corporations. A corporation may be dissolved involuntarily: (1) by forfeiture of its charter at the request of the state when the corporation has acted wrongfully or illegally, or (2) by becoming insolvent.

On the dissolution of a corporation, its assets are first used to pay all its outstanding debts and obligations. The remaining funds are then distributed to the stockholders in accordance with the amount of stock each of them holds. As in the distribution of dividends, preferred stockholders are often entitled to preference in the distribution of the assets remaining on dissolution.

Supplementary Reading: Corporations

The best basic textbook in this field is Henry W. Ballantine, *Corporations*, Rev. Ed. (Callaghan, 1946). For an excellent analysis of the role of the corporation in our society see A. A. Berle and G. C. Means, *The Modern Corporation and Private Property* (Macmillan, 1933). For case materials, see E. Merrick Dodd and Ralph J. Baker, *Cases and Materials on Corporations*, 2nd Ed. (Foundation Press, 1951) and A. A. Berle and William C. Warren, *Cases and Materials on the Law of Business Organization (Corporations)* (Foundation Press, 1948).

17 Government Regulation of Business

Introduction

There was a time, in the not too distant past, when a businessman could organize and finance a business, hire employees, and sell his goods with little or no interference from the state or federal government. Not so today. At almost every turn the businessman is confronted with some form of government regulation. Let us pause for a moment to review the extent of government's role in business.

In earlier chapters we mentioned some of the restrictions that have been imposed on the formation and operation of business enterprises: licensing statutes must be complied with, fees must be paid, statements must be filed. Securities must be registered with the Securities and Exchange Commission, and the company issuing them must make a full disclosure of all material facts about its operations. In labor-management relations, a multitude of laws and regulations govern the hiring and firing of employees, wages, hours, working conditions, workmen's compensation, unemployment compensation, and the like. Companies must comply with local building and zoning codes and with board-of-health regulations. Manufacturing firms must submit to periodic inspections of plant machinery and working conditions. Public utilities, common carriers, banks, and insurance companies are subject to strict supervision by state and federal regulatory bodies that control the nature and extent of their operations and the rates they may charge for their services.

In recent years, government has taken vigorous action to outlaw unfair and improper business practices. The Federal Trade Commission, for example, curbs such activities as the use by one firm of another's trade-mark or trade name, the packaging or wrapping of goods in a manner that confuses the public or trades on a competitor's reputation, and the disparaging of the products of a competitor. In addition, new regulations have been adopted to protect the public by restricting false and misleading advertising, exaggerated or deceptive claims, improperly labeled goods, and incorrectly stated weights and measures; also measures have been taken against manufacturers who fail to reveal harmful ingredients in products.

Most of these regulations have been accepted by the business community as necessary to the maintenance of a free and healthy economy. In some areas, however, as we shall see, government regulation has met with strong opposition.

In this chapter, we shall confine our discussion to that area of government regulation which has met with the most resistance from the business world and which continues to be the subject of heated controversy. We refer to the federal antitrust laws,[1] designed to outlaw or control business practices that tend to restrain trade and impair free competition.

Competition has not always been the guiding principle of business activity. Indeed, throughout most of early history, competition was actually suppressed as an undesirable practice. During the Middle Ages and afterward, most economic activity was conducted within the framework of legalized monopolies.[2] Even the commercial markets and fairs, where most of the buying and selling took place, were controlled by royal franchises granting the exclusive right to conduct trade and commerce in a particular geographic area. Since sales outside the prescribed market area were generally prohibited, little competition was possible.

During the seventeenth century, however, as trade and commerce expanded, the system of local monopolies proved inadequate and began to break down. Moreover, there was widespread opposition to the royal practice of raising revenue by selling monopoly privileges to private businessmen. Finally, in 1624, the Parliament of England enacted the Statute of Monopolies, which prohibited the granting of monopolies by the king. But this law did not outlaw monopolies arising from the agreement of private individuals, nor did it forbid monopolies that controlled a large part, but not all, of a given market.

It was not until the advent of the Industrial Revolution in the late eighteenth century that competition came to be accepted as a desirable means of regulating business activity. With the general acceptance of the economic philosophy of *laissez faire*, freedom of economic activity (i.e., free competition) became the guiding principle of commercial life.

In the United States, during the latter part of the nineteenth century, business activity underwent a tremendous growth. Encouraged by the almost total absence of governmental controls, industrialists threw together great empires and engaged in unrestrained monopolistic practices. Convinced that this behavior threatened to destroy our competitive system, observers began to clamor for corrective legislation. In response, Congress passed the Sherman Act in 1890 and the Clayton Act and other federal antitrust laws in subsequent years.

---

[1] The "trust" was originally a device by which several corporations in the same general business combined to eliminate competition, to control output, and to maintain and regulate prices. Often a voting trust (see page 743) was set up to ensure that the stock of all the participating companies would be voted the same way. The trust has now given way to the holding company, and the term "trust" is rarely used in this context. However, the first laws were designed to control trusts—hence, the term "antitrust."

[2] A monopoly, generally speaking, signifies ownership or control of so large a part of the supply or output of a given commodity as to eliminate any effective competition and give the monopolist power to fix prices at whatever level he desires.

The goals of the antitrust laws have been summarized as follows:

> The general objective of the antitrust laws is promotion of competition in open markets. This policy is a primary feature of private enterprise. Most Americans have long recognized that opportunity for market access and fostering of market rivalry are basic tenets of our faith in competition as a form of economic organization. . . .
>
> Antitrust is a distinctive American means for assuring the competitive economy on which our political and social freedom under representative government in part depend. These laws have helped release energies essential to our leadership in industrial productivity and technological development. They reinforce our ideal of careers open to superior skills and talent, a crucial index of a free society. As a result, the essentials of antitrust are today proclaimed by both political parties as necessary to assure economic opportunity and some limitation on economic power incompatible with the maintenance of competitive conditions.[3]

Why is it, then, that the antitrust laws have met with so much opposition? There are several reasons. First, businessmen complain that the language of the statutes is too vague, and that the courts have never interpreted that language in a clear and consistent way. Conflicting decisions by the courts leave the businessman without guidance in planning his operations; he is never sure whether or not his activities will provoke a criminal prosecution. Critics also complain that the strictness with which the laws have been interpreted and enforced has shackled business, destroyed incentive, and penalized success. They argue that no firm should be penalized for achieving a dominant position in an industry, even a monopoly position, provided it does so by lawful means. Still another criticism is that most antitrust problems involve economic and social questions which should be decided outside the courts. These critics contend that the Supreme Court has been given too much power to shape the economic and social structure of the nation. Lastly, many authorities feel that the laws are unrealistic, that "pure" competition is often a destructive force, and, therefore, that a certain amount of co-operation between businessmen (e.g., in setting prices) is inevitable and desirable. As you read this chapter, notice how often these criticisms crop up in the decisions cited, and notice how much disagreement there is within the Supreme Court itself over their validity.

The following sections deal mainly with statutory interpretation. And, since the principal antitrust laws are federal statutes, most of the decisions are those of the United States Supreme Court. The cases will give you some idea of the conflicting views of the justices (note the vigorous dissents to some of the majority opinions!) on how certain economic problems should be dealt with. They also illustrate the major role that administrative agencies, particularly the Federal Trade Commission, play in lawmaking.

---

[3] *The Report of the Attorney General's National Committee to Study the Antitrust Laws* (1955).

SECTION 1

GOVERNMENT REGULATION OF BUSINESS

Restraint of Trade and Monopoly Defined

The term restraint of trade refers to business practices or activities that tend to interfere with free competition. Restraint of trade is said to exist, for example, when a person or a firm agrees with another firm not to continue in a present business or not to enter a new business, when competitors agree to fix prices or divide up markets, when a firm, or a group of firms, restricts competitors from gaining access to goods or supplies, or when a dealer agrees with a supplier not to handle the products of the supplier's competitors. The degree of restraint differs from case to case, and, as we shall see, not all restraints are illegal.

Frequently, restraint of trade takes the form of a *monopoly*, the elimination of all effective competition. When this occurs, commerce is stifled and prices may be fixed at whatever level the traffic will bear. A monopoly arises when one person or firm buys up or wins control of the entire supply of a needed product, or when enough competing companies merge or consolidate under one management to seize control of a given market. Another form of monopoly is the cartel—an agreement among firms to fix prices at an arbitrary level or to divide a market in order to eliminate competition. Every monopoly produces some restraint of trade, but not every restraint of trade amounts to a monopoly.

Common-Law Rules

At common law, contracts or agreements that created monopolies or led to an unreasonable restraint of trade were void and unenforceable. Usually, however, they were not punished by criminal penalties. As a result, by the end of the nineteenth century, such practices had become so widespread and uncontrolled that many observers feared for the future of the whole competitive system. It was at that time that both the federal and state governments passed corrective legislation.

Federal Antitrust Legislation

Scope and Coverage

Congress, exercising its power to regulate interstate commerce, has taken steps to curb monopolistic practices in firms engaged in interstate business.

Many state legislatures have enacted similar laws to control domestic concerns. We shall limit our discussion to the interpretation and enforcement of federal statutes.

The Sherman Antitrust Act

The basic federal antitrust law is the Sherman Act, which was passed by Congress in 1890. The most important provisions of this act appear in its first two sections, which read as follows:

> Every contract, combination in the form of a trust or otherwise, or conspiracy, in restraint of trade or commerce among the several states, or with foreign nations, is declared to be illegal.
>
> Every person who shall monopolize, or attempt to monopolize, or combine or conspire with any other person or persons to monopolize any part of the trade or commerce among the several states or with foreign countries, shall be deemed guilty of a misdemeanor.

The penalty for violating these provisions is a fine up to $5,000 or imprisonment up to one year, or both. Moreover, the act authorizes the federal government to ask for an injunction to stop unlawful practices and, in addition, provides that any person who suffers loss or damage by reason of such practices may sue the wrongdoer and recover three times the amount of his actual damages, plus attorney's fees.

The Clayton Act

It soon became clear that the Sherman Act would not bring about the reforms that had been hoped for. Its vague language gave rise to a variety of judicial interpretations, and many critics argued that it created more problems than it solved, that it left businessmen confused about what they could and could not do.

In an attempt to dispel this confusion and to put an effective check on monopolistic practices and restraint of trade, Congress enacted the Clayton Act in 1914. This statute was a comprehensive effort to outlaw practices such as price discrimination, exclusive-dealing contracts,[4] stock acquisitions, and interlocking directorates that tend to lessen competition.

The Robinson-Patman Act

Although the Clayton Act did succeed in curbing certain monopolistic practices, it was not effective in controlling discriminatory pricing practices. To help remedy this situation, Congress passed the Robinson-Patman Act in 1936. This statute, which contained specific prohibitions against certain activities, has been at least partially successful. We shall discuss it in detail later in the chapter (see pp. 853–54).

The Federal Trade Commission Act

The Federal Trade Commission Act, which was passed in 1914 (the same year as the Clayton Act), was an attempt by Congress to establish an

---

[4] We will discuss exclusive-dealing contracts at some length later in this chapter (see page 854).

administrative agency that would administer the antitrust laws effectively. The act set up the Federal Trade Commission with broad powers to interpret and enforce the provisions of the Sherman and Clayton Acts. The Commission's jurisdiction was subsequently extended to include the Robinson-Patman Act and other antitrust laws, as well as various federal statutes regulating false advertising, the mislabeling of products, the infringement of trade-marks, and other unfair methods of competition. Again, we shall have more to say about the Federal Trade Commission later on (see page 863).

Coverage and Interpretation of Antitrust Laws

In General

As we have already noted in the introduction to this chapter, there has been a great deal of confusion in interpreting and enforcing the antitrust laws. Changing economic conditions and shifting public attitudes have been reflected in what seem to be inconsistent judicial decisions in several areas. In any case, the issues are complicated and the solutions difficult— a point that the following rough classification of the major problems in antitrust law makes clear.

Interpreting the Sherman Act—The "Rule of Reason"

In the first two decades following its enactment, the Sherman Act was interpreted very strictly. It provided that "every contract, combination . . . or conspiracy in restraint of trade . . . is . . . illegal," and the Supreme Court originally held that any and every restraint of trade, whether substantial or minimal, violated the law. In 1911, the Supreme Court reversed its position by establishing the so-called "rule of reason" as its guiding principle in deciding cases brought under the Sherman Act. According to this doctrine a contract or combination is not unlawful unless it unreasonably restricts trade or competition; reasonableness is to be determined by the nature of the transaction and the surrounding circumstances. Although this vague test has produced a series of decisions that seem somewhat conflicting, it has also served to crystallize judicial attitudes toward certain practices. The two cases that follow will give you some idea of the approach the Supreme Court has taken in interpreting the Sherman Act.

UNITED STATES v. TRENTON POTTERIES CO.

Supreme Court of the United States, 1927
273 U.S. 392, 47 S.Ct. 377

► Mr. Justice Stone delivered the opinion of the Court. Respondents, 20 individuals and 23 corporations, were convicted in the District Court for Southern New York of violating the Sherman Antitrust Law. . . . The indictment was in two counts. The first charged a combination to fix and maintain the uniform prices for the sale of sanitary pottery, in restraint of interstate commerce; the second, a combination to restrain interstate commerce by limiting sales of pottery to a special group known to respondents as "legitimate jobbers." On appeal, the Circuit Court of Appeals for the Second Circuit reversed the judgment of conviction on both counts on the ground that there were errors in the conduct of the trial. 300 F. 350. This court granted certiorari. . . .

Respondents, engaged in the manufacture or distribution of 82 per cent of the vitreous pottery fixtures produced in the United States for use in bathrooms and lavatories, were members of a trade organization known as the Sanitary Potters' Association. Twelve of the corporate respondents had their factories and chief places of business in New Jersey, one was located in California, and the others were situated in Illinois, Michigan, West Virginia, Indiana, Ohio, and Pennsylvania. Many of them sold and delivered their product within the Southern District of New York, and some maintained sales offices and agents there.

There is no contention here that the verdict was not supported by sufficient evidence that respondents, controlling some 82 per cent of the business of manufacturing and distributing in the United States vitreous pottery of the type described, combined to fix prices and to limit sales in interstate commerce to jobbers.

The issues raised here by the government's specification of errors relate only to the decision of the Circuit Court of Appeals upon its review of certain rulings of the District Court made in the course of the trial. It is urged that the court below erred in holding in effect . . . that the trial court should have submitted to the jury the question whether the price agreement complained of constituted an unreasonable restraint of trade. . . .

The trial court charged, in submitting the case to the jury that, if it found the agreements or combination complained of, it might return a verdict of guilty without regard to the reasonableness of the prices fixed, or the good intentions of the combining units, whether prices were actually lowered or raised or whether sales were restricted to the special jobbers, since both agreements of themselves were unreasonable restraints. These instructions repeated in various forms applied to both counts of the indictment. The trial court refused various requests to charge that both the agreement to fix prices and the agreement to limit sales to a particular group, if found, did not in themselves constitute violations of law, unless it was also found that they unreasonably restrained interstate commerce. In particular the court refused the request to charge the following:

> "The essence of the law is injury to the public. It is not every restraint of competition and not every restraint of trade that works an injury to the public; it is only an undue and unreasonable restraint of trade that has such an effect and is deemed to be unlawful."

. . . The question therefore to be considered here is whether the trial judge correctly withdrew from the jury the consideration of the reasonableness of the particular restraints charged.

That only those restraints upon interstate commerce which are unreasonable are prohibited by the Sherman Law was the rule laid down by the opinions of this court in the Standard Oil and Tobacco cases. But it does not follow that agreements to fix or maintain prices are reasonable restraints and therefore permitted by the statute, merely because the prices themselves are reasonable. Reasonableness is not a concept of definite and unchanging content. Its meaning necessarily varies in the different fields of the law, because it is used as a convenient summary of the dominant considerations which control in the application of legal doctrines. Our view of what is a reasonable restraint of commerce is controlled by the recognized purpose of the Sherman Law itself. Whether this type of restraint is reasonable or not must be judged in part at least, in the light of its effect on competition, for whatever difference of opinion there may be among economists as to the social and economic desirability of an unrestrained competitive system, it cannot be doubted that the Sherman Law and the judicial decisions interpreting it are based upon the assumption that the public interest is best protected from the evils of monopoly and price control by the maintenance of competition. . . .

The aim and result of every price-fixing agreement, if effective, is the elimination of one form of competition. The power to fix prices, whether reasonably exercised or not, involves power to control the market and to fix arbitrary and unreasonable prices. The reasonable price fixed today may through economic and business changes become the unreasonable price of tomorrow. Once established, it may be maintained unchanged because of the absence of competition secured by the agreement for a price reasonable when fixed. Agreements which create such potential power may well be held to be in themselves unreasonable or unlawful restraints, without the necessity of minute inquiry whether a particular price is reasonable or unreasonable as fixed and without placing on the government in enforcing the Sherman Law the burden of ascertaining from day to day whether it has become unreasonable through the mere variation of economic conditions. Moreover, in the absence of express legislation requiring it, we should hesitate to adopt a construction making the difference between legal and illegal conduct in the field of business relations depend upon so uncertain a test as whether prices are reasonable—a determination which can be satisfactorily made only after a complete survey of our economic organization and a choice between rival philosophies. . . .

Cases in both the federal and state courts have generally proceeded on a like assumption, and in the Second Circuit the view maintained below that the reasonableness or unreasonableness of the prices fixed must be submitted to the jury has apparently been abandoned. See Poultry Dealers' Association v. United States (C.C.A.) 4 F. 2d 840. While not necessarily controlling, the decisions of this court denying the validity of resale price agreements, regardless of the reasonableness of the price, are persuasive. . . .

Respondents rely upon Chicago Board of Trade v. United States [246 U.S. 231, 238; 38 S.Ct. 242, 62 L.Ed. 683 (1918)], in which an agreement by the members of the Chicago Board of Trade controlling prices during certain hours of the day in a special class of grain contracts and affecting only a small proportion of the commerce in question was upheld. The purpose and effect of the agreement there was to maintain for a part of each business day the price which has been that day determined by open competition on the floor of the exchange. That decision, dealing as it did with a regulation of a board of trade, does not sanction a price agreement among competitors in an open market such as is presented here.

The charge of the trial court, viewed as a whole, fairly submitted to the jury the question whether a price-fixing agreement as described in the first count was entered into by the respondents. Whether the prices actually agreed upon were reasonable or unreasonable was immaterial in the circumstances charged in the indictment and necessarily found by the verdict. The requested charge which we have quoted, and others of similar tenor, while true as abstract propositions, were inapplicable to the case in hand and rightly refused. . . .

It follows that the judgment of the Circuit Court of Appeals must be reversed and the judgment of the District Court reinstated.

MR. JUSTICE VAN DEVANTER, MR. JUSTICE SUTHERLAND and MR. JUSTICE BUTLER dissent.   ◄

COMMENTS AND QUESTIONS

1. What was the substance of the trial judge's charge to the jury? What happened in the Circuit Court of Appeals? In the Supreme Court?
2. Summarize the reasons given by the Court in support of its decision.
3. Does this ruling mean that any and *every* agreement to fix prices is unlawful? We shall discuss this question in more detail later in the chapter.

APPALACHIAN COALS, INC. et al. v. UNITED STATES

Supreme Court of the United States, 1933
288 U.S. 344, 53 S.Ct. 471

► MR. CHIEF JUSTICE HUGHES delivered the opinion of the Court.

This suit was brought to enjoin a combination alleged to be in restraint of interstate commerce in bituminous coal and in attempted monopolization of part of that commerce, in violation of sections 1 and 2 of the Sherman Antitrust Act. . . . The District Court, composed of three Circuit Judges, made detailed findings of fact and entered final decree granting the injunction. 1 F. Supp. 339. The case comes here on appeal. . . .

Defendants, other than Appalachian Coals, Inc., are 137 producers of bituminous coal in eight districts (called for convenience Appalachian territory) lying in Virginia, West Virginia, Kentucky, and Tennessee. These districts, described as the Southern High Volatile Field, form part of the coal bearing area stretching from central and western Pennsylvania through eastern Ohio, western Maryland, eastern Kentucky, eastern Tennessee, and northeastern Alabama. In 1929 (the last available) the total production of bituminous coal east of the Mississippi River was 484,786,000 tons, of which defendants mined 58,011,367 tons or 11.96 per cent. In the so-called Appalachian territory and the immediately surrounding area, the total production was 107,008,209 tons, of which defendants' production was 54.21 per cent, or 64 per cent, if the output of "captive" mines (16,445,001 tons) be deducted. With a further deduction of 12,000,000 tons of coal produced in the immediately surrounding territory, which, however, is not essentially different from the particular area described in these proceedings as Appalachian territory, defendants' production in the latter region was found to amount to 74.4 per cent.

The challenged combination lies in the creation by the defendant producers of an exclusive selling agency. This agency is the defendant Appalachian Coals, Inc., which may be designated as the Company. Defendant producers own all its capital stock, their holdings being in proportion to their production. The majority of the common stock, which has exclusive voting rights, is held by seventeen defendants. By uniform contracts, separately made, each defendant producer constitutes the Company an exclusive agent for the sale of all coal (with certain exceptions) which the mines produce in the Appalachian territory. The Company agrees to establish standard classifications, to sell all the coal of all its principals at the best prices obtainable and, if all cannot be sold, it apportions orders upon a stated basis. The plan contemplates that prices are to be fixed by the officers of the Company at its central office, save that, upon contracts calling for future deliveries after sixty days, the Company must obtain the producer's consent. The Company is to be paid a commission of 10 per cent, of the gross selling prices f.o.b. at the mines, and guarantees accounts. In order to preserve their existing sales outlets, the producers may designate subagents, according to an agreed form of contract, who are to sell upon the terms and prices established by the Company and are to be allowed by the Company commissions of eight per cent. The Company has not yet begun to operate as selling agent; the contracts with it run to April 1, 1935, and from year to year thereafter unless terminated by either party on six months' notice.

The Government contention, which the District Court sustained, is that the plan violates the Sherman Antitrust Act—in the view that it eliminates competition among the defendants themselves and also gives the selling agent power substantially to affect and control the price of bituminous coal in many interstate markets. On the latter point the District Court made the general finding that this elimination of competition and concerted action will affect market conditions, and have a tendency to stabilize prices and to raise prices to a higher level than would prevail under conditions of free competition. The court added that the selling agency "will not have monopoly control of any market nor the power to fix monopoly prices."

Defendants insist that the primary purpose of the formation of the selling agency was to increase the sale, and thus the production, of Appalachian coal through better methods of distribution, intensive advertising and research to achieve economies in marketing, and to eliminate abnormal, deceptive and destructive trade practices. They disclaim any intent to restrain or monopolize interstate commerce, and in justification of their design they point to the statement of the District Court that

> "it is but due to defendants to say that the evidence in the case clearly shows that they have been acting fairly and openly in an attempt to organize the coal industry and to relieve the deplorable conditions resulting from overexpansion, destructive competition, wasteful trade practices, and the inroads of competing industries." 1 F. Supp. page 341.

Defendants contend that the evidence establishes that the selling agency will not have the power to dominate or fix the price of coal in any consuming market, that the price of coal will continue to be set in an open competitive market, and that their plan by increasing the sale of bituminous coal from Appalachian territory will promote, rather than restrain, interstate commerce.

First. There is no question as to the test to be applied in determining the legality of the defendants' conduct. The purpose of the Sherman Antitrust Act is to prevent undue restraints of interstate commerce, to maintain its appropriate freedom in the public interest, to afford protection from the subversive or coercive influences of monopolistic endeavor. As a charter of freedom, the act has a generality and adaptability comparable to that found to be desirable in constitutional provisions. It does not go into detailed definitions which might either work injury to legitimate enterprise or through particularization defeat its purposes by providing loopholes for escape. The restrictions the act imposes are not mechanical or artificial. Its general phrases, interpreted to attain its fundamental objects, set up the essential standard of reasonableness. They call for vigilance in the detection and frustration of all efforts unduly to restrain the free course of interstate commerce, but they do not seek to establish a mere delusive liberty either by making impossible the normal and fair expansion of that commerce or the adoption of reasonable measures to protect it from injurious and destructive practices and to promote competition upon a sound basis. . . .

In applying this test, a close and objective scrutiny of particular conditions and purposes is necessary in each case. Realities must dominate the judgment. The mere fact that the parties to an agreement eliminate competition between themselves is not enough to condemn it. . . . The familiar illustrations of partnerships, and enterprises fairly integrated in the interest of the promotion of commerce, at once occur. The question of the application of the statute is one of intent and effect, and is not to be determined by arbitrary assumptions. It is therefore necessary in this instance to consider the economic conditions peculiar to the coal industry, the practices which have obtained, the nature of defendants' plan of making sales, the reasons which led to its adoption and the probable consequences of the carrying out of that plan in relation to market prices and other matters affecting the public interest in interstate commerce in bituminous coal.

Second. The findings of the District Court, upon abundant evidence, leave no room for doubt as to the economic condition of the coal industry. That condition, as the District Court states, for many years has been indeed "deplorable." Due largely to the expansion under the stimulus of the Great War, "the bituminous mines of the country have a developed capacity exceeding 700,000,000 tons to meet a demand of less than 500,000,000 tons." In connection with this increase in surplus production, the consumption of coal in all the industries which are its largest users has shown a substantial relative decline. The actual decrease is partly due to the industrial condition but the relative decrease is progressing, due entirely to other causes. Coal has been losing markets to oil, natural gas and water power and has also been losing ground due to greater efficiency in the use of coal. . . .

In addition to these factors, the District Court found that organized buying agencies, and large consumers purchasing substantial tonnages, "constitute unfavorable forces." "The highly organized and concentrated buying power which they control and the great abundance of coal available have contributed to make the market for coal a buyers' market for many years past."

It also appears that the "unprofitable condition" of the industry has existed particularly in the Appalachian territory where there is little local consumption as the region is not industrialized.

> "The great bulk of the coal there produced is sold in the highly competitive region east of the Mississippi river and north of the Ohio river under an adverse freight rate which imposes an unfavorable differential from 35 cents to 50 cents per ton."

And in a graphic summary of the economic situation, the court found that

> "numerous producing companies have gone into bankruptcy or into the hands of receivers, many mines have been shut down, the number of days of operation per week have been greatly curtailed, wages to labor have been substantially lessened, and the states in which coal producing companies are located have found it increasingly difficult to collect taxes." . . .

Fourth. Voluminous evidence was received with respect to the effect of the defendants' plan upon market prices. As the plan has not gone into operation there are no actual results upon which to base conclusions. The question is necessarily one of prediction. The court below found that, as between defendants themselves, competition would be eliminated. This was deemed to be the necessary consequence of a common selling agency with power to fix the prices at which it would make sales for its principals. Defendants insist that the finding is too broad and that the differences in grades of coal of the same sizes and the market demands at different times would induce competition between the coals sold by the agency "depending upon the use and the quality of the coals."

The more serious question relates to the effect of the plan upon competition between defendants and other producers. As already noted, the District Court found that "the great bulk" of the coal produced in Appalachian territory is sold "in the highly competitive region east of the Mississippi river and north of the Ohio river under an adverse freight rate." Elaborate statistics were introduced with respect to the production and distribution of bituminous coal and the transportation rates from the different producing sections to the consuming markets, as bearing upon defendants' competitive position, together with evidence as to the requirements of various sections and consumers and the relative advantages possessed by reason of the different qualities and uses of the coals produced. It would be impossible to make even a condensed statement of this evidence (which has been carefully analyzed by both parties), but an examination of it fails to disclose an adequate basis for the conclusion that the operators of the defendants' plan would produce an injurious effect upon competitive conditions, in view of the vast volume of coal available, the conditions of production, and the network of transportation facilities at immediate command. While strikes and

interruptions of transportation may create temporary and abnormal dislo-
cations, the bituminous coal industry under normal conditions affords most
exceptional competitive opportunities. Figures as to developed and potential productive capacity (as found by the court below) are impressive. . . .
"Conditions in the coal industry are such that new companies are free to
enter the business of producing and marketing coal in competition with
existing companies." In connection with this proof of developed and potential capacity, the "highly organized and concentrated buying power" that
can be exerted must also have appropriate consideration.

Consumers testified that defendants' plan will be a benefit to the coal
industry and will not restrain competition. . . . There was similar testimony by wholesale and retail dealers in coal. There are 130 producers of
coal other than defendants in the Appalachian territory who sell coal commercially. There are also "a large number of mines that have been shut down
and could be opened up by the owners on short notice." Competing producers testified that the operation of the selling agency, as proposed by
defendants, would not restrain competition and would not hurt their business. Producers in western Pennsylvania, Alabama, Ohio, and Illinois testified to like effect. Referring to this testimony, the court below added,

> "The small producer can, to some extent, and for the purpose of pro-
> ducing and marketing coal, produce coal more cheaply than many of the
> larger companies and is not prevented by higher cost of operation from
> being a competitor in the market." . . .

Fifth. We think that the evidence requires the following conclusion:

1. With respect to defendants' purposes, we find no warrant for determining that they were other than those they declared. Good intentions will
not save a plan otherwise objectionable, but knowledge of actual intent is
an aid in the interpretation of facts and prediction of consequences. . . .
The evidence leaves no doubt of the existence of the evils at which defendants' plan was aimed. The industry was in distress. It suffered from
overexpansion and from a serious relative decline through the growing use
of substitute fuels. It was afflicted by injurious practices within itself—
practices which demanded correction. If evil conditions could not be entirely cured, they at least might be alleviated. The unfortunate state of the
industry would not justify any attempt unduly to restrain competition or to
monopolize, but the existing situation prompted defendants to make, and
the statute did not preclude them from making an honest effort to remove
abuses, to make competition fairer, and thus to promote the essential interests of commerce. The interests of producers and consumers are interlinked.
When industry is grievously hurt, when producing concerns fail, when
unemployment mounts and communities dependent upon profitable production are prostrated, the wells of commerce go dry. So far as actual purposes
are concerned, the conclusion of the court below was amply supported that
defendants were engaged in a fair open endeavor to aid the industry in a
measurable recovery from its plight. The inquiry, then, must be whether in
spite of this objective the inherent nature of their plan was such as to create
an undue restraint upon interstate commerce.

2. The question thus presented chiefly concerns the effect upon prices. The evidence as to the conditions of the production and distribution of bituminous coal, the available facilities for its transportation, the extent of developed mining capacity, and the vast potential undeveloped capacity, makes it impossible to conclude that defendants through the operation of their plan will be able to fix the price of coal in the consuming markets. . . . While conditions are more favorable to the position of defendants' group in some markets than in others, we think that the proof clearly shows that, wherever their selling agency operates, it will find itself confronted by effective competition backed by virtually inexhaustive sources of supply, and will also be compelled to cope with the organized buying power of large consumers. The plan cannot be said either to contemplate or to involve the fixing of market prices.

The contention is, and the court below found, that while defendants could not fix market prices, the concerted action would "affect" them, that is, that it would have a tendency to stabilize market prices and to raise them to a higher level than would otherwise obtain. But the facts found do not establish, and the evidence fails to show, that any effect will be produced which in the circumstances of this industry will be detrimental to fair competition. A cooperative enterprise, otherwise free from objection, which carries with it no monopolistic menace, is not to be condemned as an undue restraint merely because it may effect a change in market conditions, where the change would be in mitigation of recognized evils and would not impair, but rather foster fair competitive opportunities. Voluntary action to rescue and preserve these opportunities, and thus to aid in relieving a depressed industry and in reviving commerce by placing competition upon a sounder basis, may be more efficient than an attempt to provide remedies through legal processes. The fact that the correction of abuses may tend to stabilize a business or to produce fairer price levels, does not mean that the abuses should go uncorrected or that cooperative endeavor to correct them necessarily constitutes an unreasonable restraint of trade. The intelligent conduct of commerce through the acquisition of full information of all relevant facts may properly be sought by the cooperation of those engaged in trade, although stabilization of trade and more reasonable prices may be the result. . . . Putting an end to injurious practices, and the consequent improvement of the competitive position of a group of producers is not a less worthy aim and may be entirely consonant with the public interest, where the group must still meet effective competition in a fair market and neither seeks nor is able to effect a domination of prices.

Decisions cited in support of a contrary view were addressed to very different circumstances from those presented here. They dealt with combinations which on the particular facts were found to impose unreasonable restraints through the suppression of competition, and in actual operation had that effect. . . .

3. The question remains, whether despite the foregoing conclusions the fact that the defendants' plan eliminates competition between themselves is alone sufficient to condemn it. Emphasis is placed upon defendants' control of about 73 per cent of the commercial production in Appalachian

territory. But only a small percentage of that production is sold in that territory. . . . Even in Appalachian territory it appears that the developed and potential capacity of other producers will afford effective competition. Defendants insist that on the evidence adduced as to their competitive position in the consuming markets, and in the absence of proof of actual operation showing injurious effect upon competition, either through possession or abuse of power, no valid objection could have been interposed under the Sherman Act if the defendants had eliminated competition between themselves by a complete integration of their mining properties in a single ownership. . . . We agree that there is no ground for holding defendants' plan illegal merely because they have not integrated their properties and have chosen to maintain their independent plants, seeking not to limit but rather to facilitate the production. We know of no public policy, and none is suggested by the terms of the Sherman Act, that in order to comply with the law those engaged in industry should be driven to unify their properties and businesses in order to correct abuses which may be corrected by less drastic measures. Public policy might indeed be deemed to point in a different direction. If the mere size of a single embracing entity is not enough to bring a combination in corporate form within the statutory inhibition, the mere number and extent of the production of those engaged in a cooperative endeavor to remedy evils which may exist in an industry, and to improve competitive conditions, should not be regarded as producing illegality. The argument that integration may be considered a normal expansion of business, while a combination of independent producers in a common selling agency should be treated as abnormal—that one is a legitimate enterprise and the other is not—makes but an artificial distinction. The Antitrust Act aims at substance. Nothing in theory or experience indicates that the selection of a common selling agency to represent a number of producers should be deemed to be more abnormal than the formation of a huge corporation bringing various independent units into one ownership. Either may be prompted by business exigencies and the statute gives to neither a special privilege. The question in either case is whether there is an unreasonable restraint of trade or an attempt to monopolize. If there is, the combination cannot escape because it has chosen corporate form, and, if there is not, it is not to be condemned because of the absence of corporate integration. As we stated at the outset, the question under the act is not simply whether the parties have restrained competition between themselves but as to the nature and effect of that restraint. . . .

The fact that the suit is brought under the Sherman Act does not change the principles which govern the granting of equitable relief. There must be "a definite factual showing of illegality." Standard Oil Company v. United States, 283 U.S. page 179, 51 S.Ct. 421, 427; 75 L.Ed. 926. We think that the Government has failed to show adequate grounds for an injunction in this case. We recognize, however, that the case has been tried in advance of the operation of defendants' plan, and that it has been necessary to test that plan with reference to purposes and anticipated consequences without the advantage of the demonstrations of experience. If in actual operation it should prove to be an undue restraint upon interstate commerce, if it should appear that the plan is used to the impairment of fair competitive opportunities, the decision upon the present record should not preclude the Government from seeking the remedy which would be suited to such a state of facts. We think also that in the event of future controversy arising from the actual operation of the plan the results of the labor of both parties in this litigation in presenting the voluminous evidence as to the industry, market conditions and transportation facilities and rates, should continue to be available, without the necessity of reproducing that evidence.

The decree will be reversed, and the cause will be remanded to the District Court with instructions to enter a decree dismissing the bill of complaint without prejudice and with the provision that the court shall retain jurisdiction of the cause and may set aside the decree and take further proceedings if future developments justify that course in the appropriate enforcement of the Antitrust Act.

It is so ordered.

MR. JUSTICE MCREYNOLDS thinks that the court below reached the proper conclusion and that its decree should be affirmed.   ◄

COMMENTS AND QUESTIONS

1. Describe the arrangement that was challenged by the government in this case. What was the decision of the lower court?
2. What happened on appeal to the Supreme Court? Summarize the reasons for the Court's decision.
3. Wasn't this a price-fixing agreement just as much as the agreement in the *Trenton Potteries* case? How can the two cases be distinguished?
4. The Court puts great stress on the economic conditions existing at the time. Does this mean that the antitrust laws are to be interpreted according to whether the country as a whole, or one industry in particular, is in a period of prosperity or depression?
5. Note that, since the government was seeking an injunction to prevent the coal producers from putting their plan into operation, the actual effects of the plan were unknown at the time of the decision. This was why the Supreme Court ordered the District Court to retain jurisdiction over the case. Explain.

Business Expansion by Integration of Firms

In order to expand its operations, a company may decide to merge or consolidate with another firm, or else to acquire the stock or assets of another firm or several other firms. Although such activities are not illegal in themselves, they are closely scrutinized by the authorities and may well be viewed as violations of the antitrust laws if certain factors are present.

Originally, Section 7 of the Clayton Act provided that

> "No corporation . . . shall acquire, directly or indirectly, the whole or any part of the stock of another corporation where the effect . . . may be to substantially lessen competition between the corporation whose stock is so acquired and the corporation making the acquisition, or to restrain . . . commerce in any section or community, or tend to create a monopoly of any line of commerce. . . ."

This provision was not particularly effective, however, for it soon became clear that a corporation wishing to gain control over another corporation could do so simply by acquiring its assets rather than its stock. To plug this loophole, Section 7 was amended in 1950 to provide that

> "No corporation . . . shall acquire, directly or indirectly, the whole or any part of the stock . . . and no corporation . . . shall acquire the whole or any part of the assets of another corporation where in any line of commerce in any section of the country, the effect of such acquisition may be substantially to lessen competition, or to tend to create a monopoly."

The Clayton Act goes on to provide (in Section 8) that

> "no person at the same time shall be a director of any two or more corporations, any one of which has capital, surplus and undivided surplus aggregating more than $1,000,000 . . . if such corporations are or shall have been theretofore . . . competitors, so that the elimination of competition between them would constitute a violation of any of the antitrust laws."

Since this provision has been hard to enforce and easy to circumvent, however, it has been of little effect in preventing combinations and mergers in restraint of trade.

The integration of firms may be regarded as either horizontal or vertical. *Horizontal integration* occurs when two or more companies in direct competition with each other on the same level of business activity combine their operations under one management. *Vertical integration* occurs when two companies that operate on different levels of business activity, and that do not compete directly, combine their operations.

EXAMPLES

1. Two steel-producing companies in direct competition with each other decide to merge. This is horizontal integration, since both are operating on the same level of business activity.
2. A steel company purchases a controlling interest in a railroad that it can use to transport raw materials and finished products to and from its mills. This is vertical integration, since the two firms are not in direct competition and are operating on different levels of business activity (i.e., one is engaged in producing and selling while the other is engaged in transportation).

Generally speaking, the courts are more likely to condemn horizontal combinations, since integration of this sort often produces a substantial lessening of competition between the acquired and acquiring companies. Vertical integration, on the other hand, is usually permitted unless it is accomplished in an unlawful way (e.g., by boycotts, price discrimination, threats, or force) or unless the vertically integrated firm that results from the combination is so large and powerful that it promises to reduce competition substantially.

The following case, which was decided shortly after the 1950 amendment to Section 7 of the Clayton Act was passed, presents an interesting illustration of horizontal integration.

HAMILTON WATCH CO. v. BENRUS WATCH CO.

District Court of the U.S., District of Conn., 1953
114 F. Supp. 307

▶ HINCKS, CHIEF JUDGE.

Hamilton is engaged in the business of manufacturing jeweled lever escapement watches and selling the same under the trade name "Hamilton" directly to over 12,000 retail jewelers throughout the country.

Hamilton's dollar volume in these watches amounted in 1950 to $18,-719,000, in 1951 to approximately $16,000,000, and in 1952 approximately $14,000,000.

Hamilton's sales in 1950 accounted for at least 11% of the dollar volume of the aggregate sales of branded jeweled watches in the United States by firms having any nation-wide advertising. Hamilton's sales of jeweled watches in 1950 constituted about 6% of the unit sales of all jeweled watches in the United States in that year. In 1950 Hamilton's sales were the fourth largest in the industry in dollar volume. In 1951 and 1952 Hamilton sold somewhat lesser percentages than in 1950.

Benrus is engaged in the business of importing jeweled watch movements, which it manufactures in Switzerland. . . . The majority of Benrus' watches are sold to retail jewelry stores, including many who also purchase and sell Hamilton watches. . . .

Benrus' sales in 1950 accounted for 9½% of the dollar volume in nationally advertised branded watches sold in the United States. Benrus' sales of jeweled watches constituted about 9% of the unit sales of all jeweled watches in the United States in 1950 and were the fifth largest in the industry in dollar volume. In 1951 and 1952 Benrus' sales (in dollars) exceeded the dollar volume of Hamilton's sales.

The leading companies selling jeweled lever watches in the United States are Elgin National Watch Company and Bulova Watch Company, each of which in 1951 and 1952 sold in the United States more jeweled lever watches than Hamilton and Benrus combined as measured both by number of units and by dollar amount. The "Bix Six" of the watch industry (Elgin, Bulova, Benrus, Longine-Wittnauer, Hamilton and Gruen) account for about 90% of the sales of nationally advertised branded jeweled watches.

Hamilton watches are superior in quality to Benrus watches, and are in part distributed in different trade channels and in different manner from Benrus watches. . . . In the eyes of the public the watches of both companies compete.

Hamilton and Benrus compete actively with one another in interstate commerce in the sale of nationally advertised branded jeweled watches and with all other companies selling jeweled watches.

The effect of a merger of Hamilton and Benrus may be substantially to lessen the active competition now existing between the two in the sale of jeweled watches in the United States. By the same token such a merger would substantially lessen competition in the sale of jeweled watches in the United States. The control of Hamilton by Benrus or even Benrus' representation on Hamilton's board through its stock ownership would afford an opportunity not otherwise present for collaboration tending to lessen competition.

Before purchasing Hamilton stock Benrus ascertained that a considerable amount of Hamilton stock was available, that the directors and management of Hamilton controlled only a small portion of this stock, and that there were no other large stockholders.

On March 17, 1952, when Hamilton stock had a book value in excess of $20, Benrus began to purchase Hamilton stock in substantial quantities, all on the New York Stock Exchange. . . .

In June 1952, after Benrus had acquired approximately 10% of the voting stock of Hamilton, Benrus advised the president of Hamilton of this fact and stated that the purchase had been made as an investment. . . .

Under agreement dated July 23, 1952, certain of Hamilton's stockholders organized a 10-year voting trust and solicited deposits of stock therein. Under the terms of the trust the stockholders participating have no rights to vote or in any way to control the action of the voting trustees. A S.E.C. prospectus dated August 1, 1952 reveals that nineteen stockholders had agreed to deposit 45,578 shares in the trust, and that a stock purchase syndicate was contemplated. According to the report of the S.E.C. dated November 19, 1952, 154,908 shares had already been deposited with, or pledged to, the voting trust. This amounts to 40% of Hamilton's common stock.

The express purpose of the voting trust was to prevent Benrus from gaining control over the policies or management of Hamilton through merger, consolidation or otherwise. This purpose was achieved at least for an indefinite period. The voting trust has effective working control and the management has been assured of support from additional stockholders to give it an absolute majority of the outstanding voting stock. . . .

Benrus owns at the present time 92,200 shares of Hamilton's outstanding common stock or about 24%. . . .

The business of Benrus is dependent on the importation of watch movements into the United States from Switzerland and on the existence of tariffs permitting such importation. Were tariffs to be greatly increased, or were war or similar conditions in Europe to block importation of Swiss watch movements, the business and income of Hamilton and Elgin, which manufacture watch movements only in the United States, would be favorably affected. . . .

An investment in a company manufacturing watch movements in the United States would be, at least to a certain extent, a hedge for Benrus against the danger of reduction in its income through the impact of increased tariffs or of world conditions cutting off Swiss imports, for Benrus would to a substantial extent be compensated by the correspondingly increased value of the stock of the domestic watch manufacturing company in which it invested. . . .

On January 5, 1953, Benrus' president advised officers of Hamilton that as a hedge against possible future difficulties in importing watch movements from Switzerland there were two alternatives: (1) to acquire facilities and trained technicians in the United States, which would have been prohibitive in cost and time; or (2) to acquire a substantial financial interest in an existing company which manufactured movements in the United States. He stated further that it was in line with the second alternative that Benrus bought the Hamilton stock. . . .

On January 23, 1953, the president of Benrus offered to refrain from voting Benrus' 92,200 shares of stock for one year if Hamilton's management would bring about a dissolution of the voting trust.

Benrus insists upon its right to vote its shares of stock in Hamilton and will do so at the Hamilton stockholders' meeting on April 14, 1953, unless enjoined.

By letter dated December 9, 1952, Benrus' president stated that as of that time Benrus had no intention to solicit proxies.

By cumulative voting under Pennsylvania law Benrus will be able to elect for a term of three years at least one director at the meeting of stockholders on April 14, 1953.

Benrus purchased the Hamilton stock for the purpose of obtaining collaboration from Hamilton advantageous to Benrus by acquiring stock control or by merger. Benrus did not purchase the stock solely for investment.

Prior to the consolidation of control in the voting trust it was probable that the acquisitions of Hamilton stock by Benrus would give Benrus control of Hamilton or failing that, at least collaboration brought about through representation on the Hamilton board accomplished by the exercise of its right to cumulative voting provided by Pennsylvania corporation law. The effect of control or collaboration thus obtained would probably have been to lessen competition in the sale of jeweled watches in the United States.

Benrus now has no control or power to control Hamilton and while the voting trust remains in effect cannot by its efforts alone obtain control. However, if allowed representation on the Hamilton board and thus to participate in Hamilton's management, it will be afforded opportunity not now available to it to bring about collaboration. . . .

A director on Hamilton's board elected by Benrus would be in a position to obtain confidential information of value to Benrus as a competitor, the disclosure of which would be harmful to Hamilton and would materially impair its competitive position. In participating in the management, such a director would be subject to frequent conflicts of loyalties involving decisions dependent upon the exercise of his judgment faculties, many of which would be of such a nature that it would be impossible to demonstrate the presence or extent of the Benrus influence if that had been a factor. Common experience has demonstrated that stockholders' suits, as a remedy for grievances growing out of such situations, are expensive and of doubtful efficacy. The Benrus stake in Benrus is many times greater than its stake in Hamilton. The presence of such a director on the Hamilton board would create a situation in which Benrus would have power to discourage the vigor of competition by Hamilton and so to embarrass and impede Hamilton's management that it might well be driven to unwanted collaboration or to a merger as the least of two evils. Such a situation would constitute irreparable harm to Hamilton.

Hamilton will be irreparably damaged if Benrus shall exercise its electoral rights by voting its Benrus stock at the April 14th stockholders' meeting.

The granting of a preliminary injunction will not seriously impair the pecuniary value of Benrus' stock holding as an investment only.

Conclusions of Law

. . . The language of Section 7 of the Clayton Act as amended forbidding acquisitions of "all or any part of the stock" of a competitor was intended if in other respects applicable to include within its ban not only acquisitions of a majority interest and an interest effective to carry control but also an interest carrying an electoral right large enough to enable the competing holder to elect its nominee to the board.

A purchase in contravention of Section 7 of the Clayton Act is illegal not only when made but also remains illegal even if the purchaser's purpose to obtain control or collaboration through the purchase fails of achievement. . . .

The defendant's present purpose to vote its Hamilton stock in Hamilton's forthcoming annual meeting, if accomplished, will probably be effective substantially to lessen competition. . . .

That stock was acquired by a competitor in violation of the Clayton Act is a fact which may be considered together with other pertinent evidence in determining whether an inference is warranted that a director elected by that stock will probably not abstain from efforts the effect of which may be substantially to lessen competition. . . .

A preliminary injunction should be granted to prevent irreparable damage to the plaintiff which plainly outweighs any foreseeable harm to the defendant. . . .

The threatened harm to the plaintiff is enjoinable under Section 16 of the Clayton Act. . . .

Opinion

It is plain that the preliminary injunction sought should not have been granted unless there was a sufficient showing that the defendant in acquiring its Hamilton stock violated Section 7 of the Clayton Act, as amended. It is equally plain, and I think also undisputed, that there would be a violation of Section 7 here only if the situation was such that an acquisition of control of Hamilton by Benrus would have constituted a violation. I found myself persuaded by the reasoning and citations appearing in plaintiff's briefs and have nothing now to add. Its position on the several factors involved in this question is sustained by my findings and conclusions.

Next arises a question of law. May the acquisition of a competitor's stock insufficient to carry control constitute a violation? On this point, too, the plaintiff's briefs satisfied me that its position is sound even though there appears as yet to be no precedent directly in point under Section 7 as amended by the Act of December 29, 1950. 64 Stat. 1125. My answer is "yes," in cases in which there is a showing that the acquisitions were made pursuant to a plan or to obtain control the achievement of which, at the time the acquisitions were made, was reasonably probable and which, if achieved, would probably have had the effect to substantially lessen the competition which the amended Act sought to preserve. Whether this stated condition of the answer has been satisfied is essentially a question of fact and in so far as the question depends upon the defendant's plan or purpose a further discussion of the underlying facts may serve a useful purpose.

Were the acquisitions made for investment purposes only as Benrus contends? In my judgment such a finding would have been naive. The underlying facts rather require an inference that the purchases were made with a purpose to obtain control. Benrus spent over $1,300,000 for the stock, much of which appears to have been borrowed. Although less than 40,000 shares per year of Hamilton stock were previously traded, Benrus bought 92,200 shares in six months undeterred by a rising market. The market price returned to normal soon after Benrus ceased buying. This suggests that a pure investment policy would have been pursued with more patience. The holding is obviously of limited liquidity. Benrus made no offer to show that its Hamilton stock was but one item in a diversified investment portfolio or to justify the soundness of an investment precept of diversification. I think it of considerable significance that Benrus ceased purchasing almost as soon as it had become apparent that the voting trust had at least for the time being consolidated control. Even if it be so that the Hamilton stock was at normal dividend rates a good buy at the average price paid, this does not require a finding that the purpose of the acquisition was investment only. However, the condition of Hamilton was not good in most of 1952. For the first time since the war dividends were being passed and sales had been declining for two years. On the other hand, Elgin sales were booming; yet Benrus had just disposed of a sizable "investment" in the stock of that company. Benrus' claim that its Hamilton holding was intended merely as an investment hedge against a possible raising of the tariff wall, all of Benrus' manufacturing facilities being in Switzerland, is not inconsistent with a finding that control of Hamilton was an objective in the Benrus policy. For if Benrus should suffer by inability to continue its Swiss imports its control of Hamilton would greatly facilitate its use of Hamilton as a source of supply for its movements. Furthermore, Elgin like Hamilton was a company which had manufacturing facilities only in the United States, yet Benrus sold all its recently acquired Elgin stock and concentrated entirely on Hamilton. And the very size of Elgin might have obstructed acquisition of a controlling interest by Benrus. Lastly, Benrus' plainly evidenced hostility to Hamilton's voting trust, the effect of which was to consolidate control in the management, is not plausibly explained if its purchases were merely for investment.

Even if, contrary to any inference, the acquisitions were made without a formulated purpose to obtain control, there was at least a purpose to obtain minority representation on the Hamilton Board. Benrus was chargeable with knowledge of the Pennsylvania Corporation law providing for cumulative voting. It acquired a sufficient amount of stock to enable it under that law to elect each year at least one director for a three-year term, and an intent to hold the stock without exercise of the appurtenant electoral right is highly improbable and completely refuted by its subsequent conduct. It must be deemed to have intended the natural consequences of its own act in acquiring the stock.

In the situation here, I incline to the view that the acquisition if made only with intent to obtain minority representation constituted a violation of Section 7. Having in mind the probable effect on the relevant "line of commerce" of the competitive practices of these two competitors and the practical considerations that confront the board of directors of any corporation in a competitive enterprise, I think it fairly inferable that minority representation, because of the opportunity thereby afforded to persuade or to compel a relaxation of the full vigor of Hamilton's competitive effort, would come within the ban of Section 7. In Chesapeake & Ohio Railway Company Purchase, 271 I.C.C. 5, it was held that even minority representation by a petitioning railroad on the board of a competitor would probably so disturb the competitive situation that the petitioner was restricted in the exercise of the electoral right appurtenant to its stock.

The plaintiff, of course, to prevail must prove not only a violation of Section 7 of the Clayton Act but also that it is in immediate danger of "irreparable loss or damage," and hence qualified for injunctive relief under Section 16 of the Clayton Act. 15 U.S.C.A. 26. As to this, beyond dispute there was immediate danger that Benrus if allowed to vote its stock at the April, 1953, annual meeting would obtain a minority representation on the Hamilton board. And the immediate effect of such representation would be . . . as between Hamilton and Benrus to improve the competitive position of Benrus with a reciprocal impairment of Hamilton's position. This, I think, is a sufficient showing of immediately threatened irreparable damage to bring the case within Section 16. . . .   ◄

COMMENTS AND QUESTIONS

1. What was the outcome of this case? Summarize the reasons given by Judge Hincks for his decision.
2. Note the voting trust which the Hamilton stockholders organized to prevent Benrus from gaining control of Hamilton's management. In view of this and the fact that Benrus had not acquired a controlling interest, how did the court justify its interference in this matter?
3. Do you think the result would have been different if the stock held by Benrus had been nonvoting?

Internal Business Expansion Without Integration

Some firms, without ever resorting to mergers or other forms of integration, grow so large that they acquire overwhelming power or outright monopoly contol over a given industry. This gives rise to a question that has perplexed the Supreme Court ever since the passage of the Sherman Act: Is mere size illegal in itself?

For many years after the act was passed, the Court refused to break up an industrial giant unless it was using its bigness to exercise monopolistic powers, or unless it threatened to exercise such powers. More recent decisions, however, suggest that bigness, regardless of how it is achieved, automatically becomes illegal once a corporation has grown so powerful that effective competition ceases to exist. Apparently the fact that such a firm has not abused its powers is of no consequence. The point at which size and domination will be declared illegal per se is hard to predict and seems to depend to a large extent on the nature of the industry and the market conditions. The following case contains the best-known and most persuasive dissertation on this aspect of antitrust law, *despite* the fact that it was not decided by the Supreme Court.

UNITED STATES v. ALUMINUM CO. OF AMERICA

Circuit Court of Appeals of the United States
Second Circuit, 1945
148 F. 2d 416

► Before L. HAND, SWAN and AUGUSTUS N. HAND, CIRCUIT JUDGES.

L. HAND, CIRCUIT JUDGE. This appeal comes to us by virtue of a certificate of the Supreme Court, under the amendment of 1944 to 29 of 15 U.S.C.A. The action was brought under 4 of that title, praying the district court to adjudge that the defendant, Aluminum Company of America, was monopolizing interstate and foreign commerce, particularly in the manufacture and sale of "virgin" aluminum ingot, and that it be dissolved, and further adjudge that the company and the defendant, Aluminum Limited, had entered into a conspiracy in restraint of such commerce. It also asked incidental relief. The plaintiff filed its complaint on April 23, 1937, naming sixty-three defendants. . . . At the date of judgment there were fifty-one defendants who had been served and against whom the action was pending. We may divide these, as the district judge did, into four classes: Aluminum Company of America, with its wholly owned subsidiaries, directors, officers, and shareholders. (For convenience we shall speak of these defendants collectively as "Alcoa," that being the name by which the company has become almost universally known.) Next, Aluminum Limited, with its directors, officers and shareholders. (For the same reason we shall speak of this group as "Limited.") Third: the defendant, Aluminum Manufacturers, Inc., which may be treated as a subsidiary of "Alcoa." Fourth: the defendant Aluminum Goods Manufacturing Company, which is independent of "Alcoa" as will appear. The action came to trial on June 1, 1938, and proceeded without much interruption until August 14, 1940, when the case was closed after more than 40,000 pages of testimony had been taken. The judge took time to consider the evidence, and delivered an oral opinion which occupied him from September 30 to October 9, 1941. Again he took time to prepare findings of fact and conclusions of law which he filed on July 14, 1942; and he entered final judgment dismissing the complaint on July 23rd of that year. The petition for an appeal, and assignments of error, were filed on September 14, 1942, and the petition was allowed on the next day. On June 12, 1944, the Supreme Court, declaring that a quorum of six justices qualified to hear the case was wanting, referred the appeal to this court under 29 of Title 15, already mentioned. The district judge's opinion, reported in 44 F. Supp. 97, discussed the evidence with the utmost particularity; it took up every phase and every issue with the arguments of both parties, and provided a reasoned basis for the subsequent findings of fact and conclusions of law. For the purposes of this appeal we need not repeat the greater part of the facts; so far as it is necessary, we do so, leaving acquaintance with the remainder to the opinion itself. Although the plaintiff challenged nearly all of the 407 findings of fact, with negligible exceptions these challenges were directed not to misstatements of the evidence, but to the judge's inferences—alleged to be "clearly erroneous." . . .

I.
Alcoa's Monopoly of "Virgin" Ingot.

"Alcoa" is a corporation, organized under the laws of Pennsylvania on September 18, 1888; its original name, "Pittsburgh Reduction Company," was changed to its present one on January 1, 1907. It has always been engaged in the production and sale of "ingot" aluminum, and since 1895 also in the fabrication of the metal into many finished and semifinished articles. It has proliferated into a great number of subsidiaries, created at various times between the years 1900 and 1929, as the business expanded. Aluminum is a chemical element; it is never found in a free state, being always in chemical combination with oxygen. One form of this combination is known as alumina; and for practical purposes the most available material from which alumina can be extracted is an ore, called "bauxite." Aluminum was isolated as a metal more than a century ago, but not until about 1886 did it become commercially practicable to eliminate the oxygen, so that it could be exploited industrially. One Hall discovered a process by which this could be done in that year, and got a patent on April 2, 1889, which he assigned to "Alcoa," which thus secured a legal monopoly of the manufacture of the pure aluminum until April 2, 1906, when this patent expired. Meanwhile Bradley had invented a process by which the smelting could be carried on without the use of external heat, as had theretofore been thought necessary; and for this improvement he too got a patent on February 2, 1892. Bradley's improvement resulted in great economy in manufacture, so that, although after April 2, 1906, anyone could manufacture aluminum by the Hall process, for practical purposes no one could compete with Bradley or with his licensees until February 2, 1909, when Bradley's patent also expired. On October 31, 1903, "Alcoa" and the assignee of the Bradley patent entered into a contract by which "Alcoa" was granted an exclusive license under that patent, in exchange for "Alcoa's" promise to sell to the assignee a stated amount of aluminum at a discount of ten per cent below "Alcoa's" published list price, and always to sell at a discount of five per cent greater than that which "Alcoa" gave to any other jobber. Thus until February 2, 1909, "Alcoa" had either a monopoly of the manufacture of "virgin" aluminum ingot or the monopoly of a process which eliminated all competition.

The extraction of aluminum from alumina requires a very large amount of electrical energy, which is ordinarily, though not always, most cheaply obtained from water power. Beginning at least as early as 1895, "Alcoa" secured such power from several companies by contracts, containing in at least three instances, covenants binding the power companies not to sell or let power to anyone else for the manufacture of aluminum. "Alcoa"— either itself or by a subsidiary—also entered into four successive "cartels" with foreign manufacturers of aluminum by which, in exchange for certain limitations upon its import into foreign countries, it secured covenants from the foreign producers, either not to import into the United States at all, or to do so under restrictions, which in some cases involved the fixing of prices. These "cartels" and restrictive covenants and certain other practices were the subject of a suit filed by the United States against "Alcoa" on May 16, 1912, in which a decree was entered by consent on June 7, 1912, declaring several of these covenants unlawful and enjoining their performance; and also declaring invalid other restrictive covenants obtained before 1903 relating to the sale of alumina ("Alcoa" failed at this time to inform the United States of several restrictive covenants in water-power contracts; its justification—which the judge accepted—being that they had been forgotten). "Alcoa" did not begin to manufacture alumina on its own behalf until the expiration of a dominant patent in 1903. In that year it built a very large alumina plant at East St. Louis, where all of its alumina was made until 1939, when it opened another plant in Mobile, Alabama.

None of the foregoing facts are in dispute, and the most important question in the case, is whether the monopoly in "Alcoa's" production of "virgin" ingot, secured by the two patents until 1909, and in part perpetuated between 1909 and 1912 by the unlawful practices, forbidden by the decree of 1912, continued for the ensuing twenty-eight years; and whether, if it did, it was unlawful under 2 of the Sherman Act, 15 U.S.C.A. 2. It is undisputed that throughout this period "Alcoa" continued to be the single producer of "virgin" ingot in the United States; and the plaintiff argues that this without more was enough to make it an unlawful monopoly. It also takes an alternative position: that in any event during this period "Alcoa" consistently pursued unlawful exclusionary practices, which made its dominant position certainly unlawful, even though it would not have been had it been retained only by "natural growth." Finally, it asserts that many of these practices were of themselves unlawful, as contracts in restraint of trade under 1 of the Act, 15 U.S.C.A. 1. "Alcoa's" position is that the fact that it alone continued to make "virgin" ingot in this country did not, and does not, give it a monopoly of the market; that it was always subject to the competition of imported "virgin" ingot, and of what is called "secondary" ingot; and that even if it had not been, its monopoly would not have been retained by unlawful means but would have been the result of a growth which the Act does not forbid, even when it results in a monopoly. We shall first consider the amount and character of this competition; next, how far it established a monopoly; and finally if it did, whether that monopoly was unlawful under 2 of the Act.

From 1902 onward until 1928 "Alcoa" was making ingot in Canada through a wholly owned subsidiary; so much of this as it imported into the United States it is proper to include with what it produced here. In the year 1912, the sum of these two items represented nearly ninety-one per cent of the total amount of "virgin" ingot available for sale in this country. This percentage varied year by year up to and including 1938; in 1913 it was about seventy-two per cent; in 1921 about sixty-eight per cent; in 1922 about seventy-two; with these exceptions it was always over eighty per cent of the total and for the last five years 1934–1938 inclusive it averaged over ninety per cent. The effect of such a proportion of the production upon the market we reserve for the time being, for it will be necessary first to consider the nature and uses of "secondary" ingot, the name by which industry knows ingot made from aluminum scrap. This is of two sorts though for our purposes it is not important to distinguish between them. One of these is the clippings and trimmings of "sheet" aluminum, when patterns are cut out of it, as a suit is cut from a bolt of cloth. The chemical composition of these is obviously the same as that of the sheet from which they come, and, although they are likely to accumulate dust or other dirt in the factory, this may be removed by well known processes. . . . Nevertheless, there is an appreciable "sales resistance" even to this kind of scrap, and for some uses (airplanes and cables among them), fabricators absolutely insist upon "virgin"; just why is not altogether clear. The other source of scrap is aluminum which has once been fabricated and the article, after being used, is discarded and sent to the junk heap, as for example, cooking utensils, like kettles and pans, and the pistons or crank cases of motorcars. These are made with a substantial alloy and to restore the metal to its original purity costs more than it is worth. However, if the alloy is known both in quality and amount, scrap, when remelted, can be used again for the same purposes as before. In spite of this, as in the case of clippings and trimmings, the industry will ordinarily not accept ingot so salvaged upon the same terms as "virgin." There are some seventeen companies which scavenge scrap of all sorts, clean it, remelt it, test it for its composition, make it into ingots and sell it regularly to the trade. There is in all these salvage operations some inevitable waste of actual material; not only does a certain amount of aluminum escape altogether, but in the salvaging process itself some is skimmed off as scum and thrown away. The judge found that the return of fabricated products to the market as "secondary" varied from five to twenty-five years, depending upon the article; but he did not, and no doubt could not, find how many times the cycle could be repeated before the metal was finally used up.

There are various ways of computing "Alcoa's" control of the aluminum market as distinct from its production—depending upon what one regards as competing in that market. The judge figured its share—during the years 1929–1938, inclusive—as only about thirty-three per cent; to do so he included "secondary," and excluded that part of "Alcoa's" own production which it fabricated and did not therefore sell as ingot. If, on the other hand, "Alcoa's" total production, fabricated and sold, be included, and balanced against the sum of imported "virgin" and "secondary," its share of the market was in the neighborhood of sixty-four per cent for that period. The percentage we already mentioned—over ninety—results only if we both include all "Alcoa's" production and exclude "secondary." That percentage is enough to constitute a monopoly; it is doubtful whether sixty or sixty-four per cent would be enough; and certainly thirty-three per cent is not. Hence it is necessary to settle what we shall treat as competing in the ingot market. That part of its production which "Alcoa" itself fabricates, does not of course ever reach the market as ingot; and we recognize that it is only when a restriction of production either inevitably affects prices, or is intended to do so, that it violates section 1 of the Act. . . . However, even though we were to assume that a monopoly is unlawful under section 2 only in case it controls prices, the ingot fabricated by "Alcoa" necessarily had a direct effect on the ingot market. All ingot—with trifling exceptions— is used to fabricate intermediate, or end, products; and therefore all intermediate, or end, products which "Alcoa" fabricates and sells, *pro tanto* reduce the demand for ingot itself. . . . We therefore cannot agree that the computation of the percentage of "Alcoa's" control over the ingot market should not include the whole of its ingot production.

As to "secondary," as we have said, for certain purposes the industry will not accept it at all; but for those for which it will, the difference in price is ordinarily not very great; the judge found that it was between one and two cents a pound—hardly enough margin on which to base a monopoly. Indeed, there are times when all differential disappears, and "secondary" will actually sell at a higher price; e.g., when there is a supply available which contains just the alloy that a fabricator needs for the article which he proposes to make. Taking the industry as a whole, we can say nothing more definite than that, although "secondary" does not compete at all in some uses (whether because of "sales resistance" only, or because of actual metallurgical inferiority), for most purposes it competes upon a substantial equality with "virgin." On these facts the judge found that "every pound of secondary or scrap aluminum which is sold in commerce displaces a pound of virgin aluminum which otherwise would, or might have been, sold." We agree; so far as "secondary" supplies the demand of such fabricators as will accept it, it increases the amount of "virgin" which must seek sale elsewhere; and it therefore results that the supply of that part of the demand which will accept only "virgin" becomes greater in proportion as "secondary" drives away "virgin" from the demand which will accept "secondary." . . . At any given moment therefore "secondary" competes with "virgin" in the ingot market; further, it can, and probably does, set a limit or "ceiling" beyond which the price of "virgin" cannot go, for the cost of its production will in the end depend only upon the expense of scavenging and reconditioning. It might seem for this reason that in estimating "Alcoa's" control over the ingot market, we ought to include the supply of "secondary," as the judge did. Indeed it may be thought a paradox to say that anyone has the monopoly of a market in which at all times he must meet a competition that limits his price. We shall show that it is not.

In the case of a monopoly of any commodity which does not disappear in use and which can be salvaged, the supply seeking sale at any moment will be made up of two components; (1) the part which the putative monopolist can immediately produce and sell; and (2) the part which has been, or can be, reclaimed out of what he has produced and sold in the past. By hypothesis he presently controls the first of these components; the second he has controlled in the past, although he no longer does. During the period when he did control the second, if he was aware of his interest, he was guided not alone by its effect at that time upon the market, but by his knowledge that some part of it was likely to be reclaimed and seek the future market. That consideration will to some extent always affect his production until he decides to abandon the business or for some other reason ceases to be concerned with the future market. Thus, in the case at bar "Alcoa" always knew that the future supply of ingot would be made up in part of what it produced at the time, and, if it was as farsighted as it proclaims itself, that consideration must have had its share in determining how much to produce. How that accurately it could forecast the effect of present production upon the future market is another matter. Experience, no doubt, would help, but it makes no difference that it had to guess; it is enough that it had an inducement to make the best guess it could, and that it would regulate that part of the future supply, so far as it should turn out to have guessed right. The competition of "secondary" must therefore be disregarded as soon as we consider the position of "Alcoa" over a period of years; it was as much within "Alcoa's" control as was the production of the "virgin" from which it had been derived. This can be well illustrated by the case of a lawful monopoly; e.g., a patent or a copyright. The monopolist cannot prevent those to whom he sells from reselling at whatever prices they please. . . . Nor can he prevent their reconditioning articles worn by use, unless they in fact make a new article. . . . At any moment his control over the market will therefore be limited by that part of what he has formerly sold. Yet no one would think of saying that for this reason the patent or the copyright did not confer a monopoly. Again, consider the situation of the owner of the only supply of some raw material like iron ore. Scrap iron is a constant factor in the iron market; it is scavenged, remelted into pig, and sold in competition with newly smelted pig; an owner of the sole supply of ore must also always face that competition and it will serve to put a "ceiling" upon his price, so far as there is enough of it. Nevertheless, no one would say that, even during the period while the pig which he has sold in the past can so return to the market, he does not have a natural monopoly. Finally, if "Alcoa" is right, precisely the same reasoning ought to lead us to include that part of clippings and trimmings which a fabricator himself saves and remelts—"process scrap"—for that too *pro tanto* reduces the market for "virgin." It can make no difference whether the original buyer reclaims, or a professional scavenger. Yet "Alcoa" itself does not assert that such "process scrap" competes; indeed it was at pains to prove that this scrap was not included in its computation of "secondary."

We conclude therefore that "Alcoa's" control over the ingot market must be reckoned at over ninety per cent; that being the proportion which its production bears to imported "virgin" ingot. The producer of so large a proportion of the supply has complete control within certain limits. It is true that, if by raising the price he reduces the amount which can be marketed—as always, or almost always, happens—he may invite the expansion of the small producers who will try to fill the place left open. Nevertheless, not only is there an inevitable lag in this, but the large producer is in a strong position to check such competition; and, indeed, if he has retained his old plant and personnel, he can inevitably do so. There are indeed limits to his power; substitutes are available for almost all commodities, and to raise the price enough is to evoke them. . . . Moreover, it is difficult and expensive to keep idle any part of a plant or of personnel; and any drastic contraction of the market will offer increasing temptation to the small producers to expand. But these limitations also exist when a single producer occupies the whole market; even then, his hold will depend upon his moderation in exerting his immediate power.

The case at bar is, however, different, because, for aught that appears there may well have been a practically unlimited supply of imports as the price of ingot rose. Assuming that there was no agreement between "Alcoa" and foreign producers not to import, they sold what could bear the handicap of the tariff and the cost of transportation. For the period of eighteen years—1920–1937—they sold at times a little under; but there was substantially no gross difference between what they received and what they would have received, had they sold uniformly at "Alcoa's" prices. While the record is silent, we may therefore assume—the plaintiff having the burden—that had "Alcoa" raised its prices, more ingot would have been imported. Thus there is a distinction between domestic and foreign competition; the first is limited in quantity, and can increase only by an increase in plant and personnel; the second is of producers who, we must assume, produce much more than they import, and whom a rise in price will presumably induce immediately to divert to the American market what they have been selling elsewhere. It is entirely consistent with the evidence that it was the threat of greater foreign imports which kept "Alcoa's" prices where they were and prevented it from exploiting its advantage as sole domestic producer; indeed, it is hard to resist the conclusion that potential imports did not put a "ceiling" upon those prices. Nevertheless, within the limits afforded by the tariff and the cost of transportation, "Alcoa" was free to raise its prices, as it chose, since it was free from domestic competition, save as it drew other metals into the market as substitutes. Was this a monopoly within the meaning of 2? The judge found that, over the whole half century of its existence, "Alcoa's" profits upon capital invested, after payment of income taxes, had been only about ten per cent, and, although the plaintiff puts this figure a little higher, the difference is negligible. . . .

. . . It is no excuse for "monopolizing" a market that the monopoly has not been used to extract from the consumer more than a "fair" profit. The Act has wider purposes. Indeed, even though we disregarded all but economic considerations, it would by no means follow that such concentration of producing power is to be desired, when it has not been used extortionately. Many people believe that possession of unchallenged economic power deadens initiative, discourages thrift and depresses energy; that immunity from competition is a narcotic, and rivalry is a stimulant, to industrial progress; that the spur of constant stress is necessary to counteract an inevitable disposition to let well enough alone. Such people believe that competitors, versed in the craft as no consumer can be, will be quick to detect opportunities for saving and new shifts in production, and be eager to profit by them. In any event the mere fact that a producer, having command of the domestic market, has not been able to make more than a "fair" profit, is no evidence that a "fair" profit could not have been made at lower prices. . . . True, it might have been thought adequate to condemn only those monopolies which could not show that they had exercised the highest possible ingenuity, had adopted every possible economy, had anticipated every conceivable improvement, stimulated every possible demand. No doubt, that would be one way of dealing with the matter although it would imply constant scrutiny and constant supervision, such as courts are unable to provide. Be that as it may, that was not the way that Congress chose; it did not condone "good trusts" and condemn "bad" ones; it forbade all. Moreover, in so doing it was not necessarily actuated by economic motives alone. It is possible, because of its indirect social or moral effect, to prefer a system of small producers, each dependent for his success upon his own skill and character, to one in which the great mass of those engaged must accept the direction of a few. These considerations, which we have suggested only as possible purposes of the Act, we think the decisions prove to have been in fact its purposes.

It is settled, at least as to section 1, that there are some contracts restricting competition which are unlawful, no matter how beneficent they may be; no industrial exigency will justify them; they are absolutely forbidden. . . . Starting . . . with the authoritative premise that all contracts fixing prices are unconditionally prohibited, the only possible difference between them and a monopoly is that while a monopoly necessarily involves an equal or even greater power to fix prices, its mere existence might be thought not to constitute an exercise of that power. That distinction is nevertheless purely formal; it would be valid only so long as the monopoly remained wholly inert; it would disappear as soon as the monopoly began to operate; for, when it did—that is, as soon as it began to sell at all—it must sell at some price and the only price at which it could sell is a price which it itself fixed. Thereafter the power and its exercise must needs coalesce. Indeed, it would be absurd to condemn such contracts unconditionally, and not to extend the condemnation to monopolies; for the contracts are only steps toward that entire control which monopoly confers; they are really partial monopolies.

But we are not left to deductive reasoning. Although in many settings it may be proper to weigh the extent and effect of restrictions in a contract against its industrial or commercial advantages, this is never to be done when the contract is made with intent to set up a monopoly. . . . Perhaps, it has been idle to labor the point at length; there can be no doubt that the vice of restrictive contracts and of monopoly is really one, it is the denial to commerce of the supposed protection of competition. To repeat, if the earlier stages are proscribed, when they are parts of a plan, the mere projecting of which condemns them unconditionally, the realization of the plan itself must be proscribed.

We have been speaking only of the economic reasons which forbid monopoly; but as we have already implied, there are others, based upon the belief that great industrial consolidations are inherently undesirable, regardless of their economic results. In the debates in Congress Senator Sherman himself, in the passage quoted in the margin, showed that among the purposes of Congress in 1890 was a desire to put an end to great aggregations of capital because of the helplessness of the individual before them. . . . Throughout the history of these statutes it has been constantly assumed that one of their purposes was to perpetuate and preserve for its own sake, and in spite of possible cost, an organization of industry in small units which can effectively compete with each other. We hold that "Alcoa's" monopoly of ingot was of the kind covered by 2.

It does not follow, because "Alcoa" had such a monopoly, that it "monopolized" the ingot market; it may not have achieved monopoly; monopoly may have been thrust upon it. If it had been a combination of existing smelters which united the whole industry and controlled the production of all aluminum ingot, it would certainly have "monopolized" the market. In several decisions the Supreme Court has decreed the dissolution of such combinations, although they had engaged in no unlawful trade practices. . . . We may start therefore with the premise that to have combined ninety per cent of the producers of ingot would have been to "monopolize" the ingot market; and, so far as concerns the public interest, it can make no difference whether an existing competition is put an end to, or whether prospective competition is prevented. The Clayton Act itself speaks in that alternative: "to injure, destroy, or prevent competition." 13 (a) 15 U.S.C.A. Nevertheless, it is unquestionably true that from the very outset the courts have at least kept in reserve the possibility that the origin of a monopoly may be critical in determining its legality; and for this they had warrant in some of the congressional debates which accompanied the passage of this act. . . . This notion has usually been expressed by saying that size does not determine guilt; that there must be some "exclusion" of competitors; that the growth must be something else than "natural" or "normal"; that there must be a "wrongful intent," or some other specific intent; or that some "unduly" coercive means must be used. At times there has been emphasis upon the use of the active verb, "monopolize," as the judge noted in the case at bar. . . . What engendered these compunctions is reasonably plain; persons may unwittingly find themselves in possession of a monopoly, automatically so to say; that is, without having intended either to put an end to existing competition, or to prevent competition from arising when none had existed; they may become monopolists by force of accident. Since the Act makes "monopolizing" a crime, as well as a civil wrong, it would be not only unfair but presumably contrary to the intent of Congress to include such instances. A market may, for example, be so limited that it is impossible to produce at all and meet the cost of production except by a plant large enough to supply the whole demand. Or there may be changes in taste or in cost which drive out all but one purveyor. A single producer may be the survivor out of a group of active competitors, merely by virtue of his superior skill, foresight and industry. In such cases a strong argument can be made that, although the result may expose the public to the evils of monopoly, the Act does not mean to condemn the resultant of those very forces which it is its prime object to foster. . . . The successful competitor, having been urged to compete, must not be turned upon when he wins. The most extreme expression of this view is in United States v. United States Steel Corporation, 251 U.S. 417, 40 S.Ct. 293, 64 L.Ed. 343, 8 A.L.R. 1121, which Sanford, J., in part repeated in United States v. International Harvester Corporation, 274 U.S. 693, 708; 47 S.Ct. 748, 71 L.Ed. 1302. It so chances that in both instances the corporation had less than two-thirds of the production in its hands, and the language quoted was not necessary to the decision; so that even if it had not later been modified, it has not the authority of an actual decision. But, whatever authority it does have was modified by the gloss of Cardozo, J., in United States v. Swift & Co., 286 U.S. 106, 116; 52 S.Ct. 460, 463; 76 L.Ed. 999, when he said,

> "Mere size . . . is not an offense against the Sherman Act unless magnified to the point at which it amounts to a monopoly . . . but size carries with it an opportunity for abuse that is not to be ignored when the opportunity is proved to have been utilized in the past."

"Alcoa's" size was "magnified" to make it a "monopoly"; indeed, it has never been anything else; and its size not only offered it an "opportunity for abuse," but it "utilized" its size for "abuse," as can easily be shown.

It would completely misconstrue "Alcoa's" position in 1940 to hold that it was the passive beneficiary of a monopoly following upon an involuntary elimination of competitors by automatically operative economic forces. Already in 1909, when its last lawful monopoly ended, it sought to strengthen its position by unlawful practices, and these concededly continued until 1912. In that year it had two plants in New York, at which it produced less than 42 million pounds of ingot; in 1934 it had five plants (the original two, enlarged; one in Tennessee; one in North Carolina; one in Washington), and its production had risen to about 327 million pounds, an increase of almost eight-fold. Meanwhile not a pound of ingot had been produced by anyone else in the United States. This increase and this continued and undisturbed control did not fall undesigned into "Alcoa's" lap; obviously it could not have done so. It could only have resulted, as it did result, from a persistent determination to maintain the control, with which it found itself vested in 1912. There were at least one or two abortive attempts to enter the industry, but "Alcoa" effectively anticipated and forestalled all competition, and succeeded in holding the field alone. True, it stimulated demand and opened new uses for the metal, but not without making sure that it could supply what it had evoked. There is no dispute as to this. "Alcoa" avows it as evidence of the skill, energy and initiative with which it has always conducted its business; as a reason why, having won its way by fair means, it should be commended, and not dismembered. We need charge it with no moral derelictions after 1912; we assume that all it claims for itself is true. The only question is whether it falls within the exception established in favor of those who do not seek, but cannot avoid the control of a market. It seems to us that question scarcely survives its statement. It was not inevitable that it should always anticipate increases in the demand for ingot and be prepared to supply them. Nothing compelled it to keep doubling and redoubling its capacity before others entered the field. It insists that it never excluded competitors; but we can think of no more effective exclusion than progressively to embrace each new opportunity as it opened, and to face every newcomer with new capacity already geared into a great organization, having the advantage of experience, trade connections and the elite of personnel. Only in case we interpret "exclusion" as limited to maneuvers not honestly industrial, but actuated solely by a desire to prevent competition, can such a course, indefatigably pursued, be deemed not "exclusionary." So to limit it would in our judgment emasculate the Act; would permit just such consolidations as it was designed to prevent.

"Alcoa" answers that it positively assisted competitors, instead of discouraging them. That may be true as to fabricators of ingot; but what of that? They were its market for ingot, and it is charged only with a monopoly of ingot. We can find no instance of its helping prospective ingot manufacturers. We do not forget the Southern Aluminum Company in whose origin it did have some part; though that was over before the end of 1914 and was in any event scarcely late enough to count. We are speaking not of its purchase of the remains of the plant in 1915; we are not suggesting—as the plaintiff argues—that that was a move to keep the plant out of the ingot market; we are speaking of the original venture. . . .

We disregard any question of "intent." Relatively early in the history of the Act—1905—Holmes, J., in Swift & Co. v. United States, *supra* (196 U.S. 375, 396; 25 S.Ct. 276, 49 L.Ed. 518), explained this aspect of the Act in a passage often quoted. Although the primary evil was monopoly, the Act also covered preliminary steps, which, if continued, would lead to it. These may do no harm of themselves; but if they are initial moves in a plan or scheme which, carried out, will result in monopoly, they are dangerous and the law will nip them in the bud. For this reason conduct falling short of monopoly is not illegal unless it is part of a plan to monopolize, or to gain such other control of a market as is equally forbidden. To make it so, the plaintiff must prove what in the criminal law is known as a "specific intent"; an intent which goes beyond the mere intent to do the act. By far the greatest part of the fabulous record piled up in the case at bar, was concerned with proving such an intent. The plaintiff was seeking to show that many transactions, neutral on their face, were not in fact necessary to the development of "Alcoa's" business, and had no motive except to exclude others and perpetuate its hold upon the ingot market. Upon that effort success depended in case the plaintiff failed to satisfy the court that it was unnecessary under 2 to convict "Alcoa" of practices unlawful of themselves. The plaintiff has so satisfied us, and the issue of intent ceases to have any importance; no intent is relevant except that which is relevant to any liability, criminal or civil: i.e., an intent to bring about the forbidden act. Note 59 of United States v. Socony-Vacuum Oil Co., *supra*, 310 U.S. 150, on page 226, 60 S.Ct. 811, on page 845, 84 L.Ed. 1129, on which "Alcoa" appears so much to rely, is in no sense to the contrary. Douglas, J., was answering the defendants' argument that, assuming that a combination had attempted to fix prices, it had never had the power to do so, for there was too much competing oil. His answer was that the plan was unlawful, even if the parties did not have the power to fix prices, provided that they intended to do so; and it was to drive home this that he contrasted the case then before the court with monopoly, where power was a necessary element. In so doing he said: "An intent and a power . . . are then necessary," which he at once followed by quoting the passage we have just mentioned from Swift & Co. v. United States, *supra*, 196 U.S. 375, 25 S.Ct. 276, 49 L.Ed. 518. To read the passage as demanding any "specific" intent makes nonsense of it, for no monopolist monopolizes unconscious of what he is doing. So here, "Alcoa" meant to keep, and did keep, that complete and exclusive hold upon the ingot market with which it started. That was to "monopolize" that market, however innocently it otherwise proceeded. *So far as the judgment held that it was not within 2, it must be reversed.* [Parts II–IV of opinion omitted. Case remanded to the district court.]   ◄

COMMENTS AND QUESTIONS

1. Judge Hand goes to great lengths to ascertain the percentage of the market controlled by Alcoa. Summarize his findings on this point.
2. The court states that control of 90 per cent of the market is enough to constitute monopoly; that it is doubtful whether 60 per cent or 64 per cent would be enough; and that 33 per cent would certainly not be. Do you think it a wise precedent to set forth these conclusions in terms of percentages?
3. Note the time and expense that went into this case. The trial in the lower court lasted more than two years; 40,000 pages of testimony were taken; the lower-court judge took nine days to read his opinion. Such painstaking, time-consuming proceedings are not unusual in antitrust litigation.
4. Why was this appeal not decided by the Supreme Court?

Loose-Knit Combinations and Associations

Business firms commonly join together in trade associations in order to control and organize their markets. Even though no actual merger of enterprises takes place, such co-operative ventures often tend or aim toward a genuine restraint of trade. Consequently many of them are struck down by the courts.

If such associations undertake to fix prices, allocate or split markets, control output or production, or boycott certain customers, they are almost always deemed illegal; it is no defense for them to say, for example, that the prices they set are reasonable in themselves. On the other hand, associations that are formed merely for the purpose of exchanging information on prices, production costs, market conditions, and the like, with no effort to fix prices, control production, or allocate markets, are usually not held to be in violation of the Sherman Act. Clearly, the line between lawful and unlawful concert of action is hard to draw. The following case illustrates the difficulties faced by the Court in drawing this line.

AMERICAN COLUMN & LUMBER CO. v. UNITED STATES

Supreme Court of the United States, 1921
257 U.S. 377, 42 S.Ct. 114

▶ MR. JUSTICE CLARKE delivered the opinion of the Court.

The unincorporated "American Hardwood Manufacturers' Association" was formed in December, 1918, by the consolidation of two similar associations, from one of which it took over a department of activity designated the "Open Competition Plan," and hereinafter referred to as the "Plan."

Participation in the Plan was optional with the members of the Association but, at the time this suit was commenced, of its 400 members, 365, operating 465 mills, were members of the Plan. The importance and strength of the Association is shown by the admission in the joint answer that, while the defendants operated only 5 per cent of the number of mills engaged in hardwood manufacture in the country, they produced one-third of the total production of the United States. The places of business of the corporations and partnerships, members of the Plan, were located in many states from New York to Texas, but chiefly in the hardwood producing territory of the Southwest. The defendants are the members of the Plan, their personal representatives, and F. R. Gadd, its "Manager of Statistics."

The bill alleged in substance that the Plan constituted a combination and conspiracy to restrain interstate commerce in hardwood lumber by restricting competition and maintaining and increasing prices, in violation of the Antitrust Act of 1890.

The answer denied that the Plan had any such purpose and effect as charged and averred that it promoted competition, especially among its own members.

A temporary injunction, granted by the District Court, restricting the activities of the Plan in specified respects, by consent of the parties, was made permanent (263 Fed. 147), and a direct appeal brings the case here for review.

The activities which we shall see were comprehended within the "Open Competition Plan" (which is sometimes called the "New Competition") have come to be widely adopted in our country, and, as this is the first time their legality has been before this court for decision, some detail of statement with respect to them is necessary.

There is very little dispute as to the facts. The testimony of the government consists of various documents and excerpts from others, obtained from the files of the Plan, and the testimony of the defendants consists of like documents and excerpts from other documents, also from the same files, supplemented by affidavits of a number of persons, members and nonmembers, chiefly to the point that the confessedly great increases of prices during 1919 were due to natural trade and weather conditions and not to the influence of the Plan.

The record shows that the Plan was evolved by a committee, which, in recommending its adoption, said:

"The purpose of the plan is to disseminate among members accurate knowledge of production and market conditions so that each member may gauge the market intelligently instead of guessing at it; to make competition open and above board instead of secret and concealed; to substitute, in estimating market conditions, frank and full statements of our competitors for the frequently misleading and colored statements of the buyer." . . .

Not long after the consolidation, a further explanation of the objects and purposes of the Plan was made in an appeal to members to join it, in which it is said:

"The theoretical proposition at the basis of the Open Competition Plan is that knowledge regarding prices actually made is all that is necessary to keep prices at reasonably stable and normal levels.

"The Open Competition Plan is a central clearing house for information on prices, trade statistics and practices. By keeping all members fully and quickly informed of what the others have done, the work of the Plan results in a certain uniformity of trade practice. There is no agreement to follow the practice of others, although members do follow their most intelligent competitors, if they know what these competitors have been actually doing.

"The monthly meetings held in various sections of the country each month have improved the human relations existing between the members before the organization of this Plan."

And in another later and somewhat similar appeal sent to all the members, this is found. . . .

"The keynote to modern business success is mutual confidence and cooperation. Co-operative competition, not cutthroat competition. Co-operation is a matter of business, because it pays, because it enables you to get the best price for your product, because you come into closer personal contact with the market. . . ."

Thus, the Plan proposed a system of cooperation among the members, consisting of the interchange of reports of sales, prices, production, and practices, and in meetings of the members for discussion, for the avowed purpose of substituting "co-operative competition" for "cutthroat competition," of keeping "prices at reasonably stable and normal levels," and of improving the "human relations" among the members. But the purpose to agree upon prices or production was always disclaimed.

[The Plan required each member to make six reports to the secretary: (1) A daily report of all sales, "the reports to be exact copies of orders taken." (2) A daily shipping report, with exact copies of the invoices. (3) A monthly production report. (4) A monthly stock report (inventory at first of month). (5) Pricelists, to be filed as soon as made. (6) Inspection reports—to be made out by a service of the association. The Plan provided for inspectors to examine stocks of the members from time to time.

All reports were subject to audit, and penalties resulted from failure to report.

In turn, the secretary was required to send each member the following:

(1) A monthly summary showing the production of each member. (2) A weekly report giving every sale, the price, and the name of the purchaser. (3) A weekly report of all shipments. (4) A monthly report showing the inventory of a stock on hand of each member. (5) A monthly summary of the pricelists received from the members (and immediate transmittals of any changes). (6) A market report letter giving an "analysis of the market conditions."

Meetings were to be held monthly at Cincinnati or other points agreed upon, and defendant F. R. Gadd was selected as "Manager of Statistics."]

Such, in outline, was the paper plan adopted by the association, but elaborate though it was, in practice three important additions were made to it.

First of all, the Southwestern territory for meeting purposes was divided into four districts, and instead of the monthly meeting provided for in the Plan, "in order that members could more conveniently attend," the record shows that 49 of these meetings were held between January 31, 1919 and February 19, 1920—approximately one for each week, in some part of the territory.

Second. Before each of these meetings a questionnaire was sent out to the members, and from the replies received, supplementing the other reports, the statistician compiled an estimate of the condition of the market, actual and prospective, which was distributed to the members attending each meeting, and was mailed to those not present. There were 11 questions on this list, of which the most important were:

> "(4) What was your total production of hardwood during the last month? What do you estimate your production will probably be for the next two months?
> "(10) Do you expect to shut down within the next few months on account of shortage of logs or for any other reason? If so, please state how long you will be idle.
> "(11) What is your view of market conditions for the next few months and what is the general outlook for business? State the reasons for your conclusion."

The Plan on paper provided only for reports of past transactions and much is made of this in the record and in argument—that reporting to one another past transactions cannot fix prices for the future. But each of these three questions plainly invited an estimate and discussion of future market conditions by each member, and a coordination of them by an expert analyst could readily evolve an attractive basis for cooperative, even if unexpressed, "harmony" with respect to future prices.

Third. The Plan provided for a monthly "market report letter" to go to all members of the association. In practice this market report letter was prepared by F. R. Gadd, manager of statistics, but his review of the market and forecast for the future were contained, almost from the beginning, not only in these market letters, but also in the weekly sales reports so that they were sent out to all of the members 19 times between February 1 and December 6, 1919, and they were discussed at all but one or two of the 49 meetings which were held. All the activities of the Plan plainly culminated in the counsels contained in these letters and reports.

This elaborate plan for the interchange of reports does not simply supply to each member the amount of stock held, the sales made and the prices received, by every other member of the group, thereby furnishing the data for judging the market, on the basis of supply and demand and current prices. It goes much farther. It not only furnishes such information, with respect to stock, sales and prices, but also reports, giving the views of each member as to "market conditions for the next few months"; what the production of each will be for the next "two months"; frequent analyses of the reports by an expert, with, we shall see, significant suggestions as to both future prices and production; and opportunities for future meetings for the interchange of views, which the record shows were very important. It is plain that the only element lacking in this scheme to make it a familiar type of the competition suppressing organization is a definite agreement as to production and prices. But this is supplied: by the disposition of men "to follow their most intelligent competitors," especially when powerful; by the inherent disposition to make all the money possible, joined with the steady cultivation of the value of "harmony" of action; and by the system of reports, which makes the discovery of price reductions inevitable and immediate. The sanctions of the Plan obviously are financial interest, intimate personal contact, and business honor, all operating under the restraint of exposure of what would be deemed bad faith and of trade punishment by powerful rivals. . . .

It has been repeatedly held by this court that the purpose of the statute is to maintain free competition in interstate commerce and that any concerted action by any combination of men or corporations to cause, or which in fact does cause, direct and undue restraint of competition in such commerce, falls within the condemnation of the act and is unlawful. . . .

These quotations are sufficient to show beyond discussion that the purpose of the organization, and especially of the frequent meetings, was to bring about a concerted effort to raise prices regardless of cost or merit, and so was unlawful, and that the members were soon entirely satisfied that the Plan was "carrying out the purpose for which it was intended."

As to the price conditions during the year; without going into detail the record shows that the prices of the grades of hardwood in most general use were increased to an unprecedented extent during the year. Thus, the increases in prices of varieties of oak range from 33.3 per cent to 296 per cent, during the year; of gum, 60 per cent to 343 per cent, and of ash, from 55 per cent to 181 per cent. While it is true that 1919 was a year of high and increasing prices generally, and that wet weather may have restricted production to some extent, we cannot but agree with the members of the Plan themselves, as we have quoted them, and with the District Court, in the conclusion that the united action of the large and influential membership of dealers contributed greatly to this extraordinary price increase.

Such close cooperation, between many persons, firms, and corporations controlling a large volume of interstate commerce, as is provided for in this Plan, is plainly in theory, as it proved to be in fact, inconsistent with that free and unrestricted trade which the statute contemplates shall be maintained. . . .

To call the activities of the defendants, as they are proved in this record, an "Open Competition Plan" of action is plainly a misleading misnomer.

Genuine competitors do not make daily, weekly, and monthly reports of the minutest details of their business to their rivals, as the defendants did; they do not contract, as was done here, to submit their books to the discretionary audit, and their stocks to the discretionary inspection, of their rivals, for the purpose of successfully competing with them; and they do not submit the details of their business to the analysis of an expert, jointly employed, and obtain from a "harmonized" estimate of the market as it is, and as, in his specially and confidentially informed judgment, it promises to be. This is not the conduct of competitors, but is so clearly that of men united in an agreement, express or implied, to act together and pursue a common purpose under a common guide that, if it did not stand confessed, a combination to restrict production and increase prices in interstate commerce, and as, therefore, a direct restraint upon that commerce, as we have seen that it is, that conclusion must inevitably have been inferred from the facts which were proved. To pronounce such abnormal conduct on the part of 365 natural competitors, controlling one-third of the trade of the country in an article of prime necessity, a "new form of competition," and not an old form of combination in restraint of trade, as it so plainly is, would be for this court to confess itself blinded by words and forms to realities which men in general very plainly see, and understand and condemn, as an old evil in a new dress and with a new name.

The Plan is, essentially, simply an expansion of the gentlemen's agreement of former days, skillfully devised to evade the law. To call it open competition, because the meetings were nominally open to the public, or because some voluminous reports were transmitted to the Department of Justice, or because no specific agreement to restrict trade or fix prices is proved, cannot conceal the fact that the fundamental purpose of the Plan was to procure "harmonious" individual action among a large number of naturally competing dealers with respect to the volume of production and prices, without having any specific agreement with respect to them, and to rely for maintenance of concerted action in both respects, not upon fines and forfeitures as in earlier days but upon what experience has shown to be the most potent and dependable restraints, of business honor and social penalties—cautiously reinforced by many and elaborate reports, which would promptly expose to his associates any disposition in any member to deviate from the tacit understanding that all were to act together under the subtle direction of a single interpreter of their common purposes, as evidenced in the minute reports of what they had done and in their expressed purposes as to what they intended to do.

In the presence of this record it is futile to argue that the purpose of the Plan was simply to furnish those engaged in this industry, with widely scattered units, the equivalent of such information as is contained in the newspaper and government publications with respect to the market for commodities sold on Board of Trade or Stock Exchanges. One distinguish-

ing and sufficient difference is that the published reports go to the seller
and buyer, but these reports go to the seller only; another is that there is
no skilled interpreter of the published reports, such as we have in this case,
to insistently recommend harmony of action likely to prove profitable in
proportion as it is unitedly pursued.

Convinced, as we are, that the purpose and effect of the activities of
the Open Competition Plan, here under discussion, were to restrict competition, and thereby restrain interstate commerce in the manufacture and sale
of hardwood lumber, by concerted action in curtailing production and in
increasing prices, we agree with the District Court that it constituted a
combination and conspiracy in restraint of interstate commerce within the
meaning of the Antitrust Act of 1890 . . . *and the decree of that court must
be affirmed.*

MR. JUSTICE HOLMES, dissenting.

MR. JUSTICE BRANDEIS, dissenting, with whom MR. JUSTICE McKENNA
concurs.

. . . The Plan provides for cooperation in collecting and distributing
information concerning the business of members and generally in regard
to the trade. . . . But the decree below should, in my opinion, be reversed,
because the Plan is not inherently a restraint of trade, and the record is
barren of evidence to support a finding that it has been used, or was intended to be used, as an instrument to restrain trade. . . .

In the case before us there was clearly no coercion. There is no claim
that a monopoly was sought or created. There is no claim that division of
territory was planned or secured. There is no claim that uniform prices were
established or desired. There is no claim that by agreement, force or fraud,
any producer, dealer or consumer was to be or has in fact been controlled
or coerced. The Plan is a voluntary system for collecting from these independent concerns detailed information concerning the business operations
of each, and its opinions as to trade conditions, prospects, and policy, and
of collating, interpreting, and distributing the data so received among the
members of the Association and others. No information gathered under the
Plan was kept secret from any producer, any buyer, or the public. Ever
since its inception in 1917, a copy of every report made and of every market
letter published has been filed with the Department of Justice, and with
the Federal Trade Commission. The district meetings were open to the
public. Dealers and consumers were invited to participate in the discussions,
and to some extent have done so.

It is claimed that the purpose of the Open Competition Plan was to
lessen competition. Competition among members was contemplated and
was in vigorous operation. The Sherman Law does not prohibit every lessening of competition; and it certainly does not command that competition
shall be pursued blindly, or that business rivals shall remain ignorant of
trade facts or be denied aid in weighing their significance. It is lawful to
regulate competition in some degree. . . . But it was neither the aim of
the Plan, nor the practice under it, to regulate competition in any way. Its
purpose was to make rational competition possible, by supplying data not

otherwise available, and without which most of those engaged in the trade would be unable to trade intelligently.

The hardwood lumber mills are widely scattered. The principal area of production is the Southern States. But there are mills in Minnesota, New York, New England, and the Middle States. Most plants are located near the sources of supply, isolated, remote from the larger cities and from the principal markets. No official, or other public, means have been established for collecting from these mills and from dealers data as to current production, stocks on hand, and market prices. Concerning grain, cotton, coal, and oil, the government collects and publishes regularly, at frequent intervals, current information on production, consumption, and stocks on hand; and Boards of Trade furnish freely to the public details of current market prices of those commodities, the volume of sales, and even individual sales, as recorded in daily transactions. Persons interested in such commodities are enabled through this information to deal with one another on an equal footing. The absence of such information in the hardwood lumber trade enables dealers in the large centers more readily to secure advantage over the isolated producer. And the large concerns, which are able to establish their own bureaus of statistics, secure an advantage over smaller concerns. Surely it is not against the public interest to distribute knowledge of trade facts, however detailed. Nor are the other features of the Plan—the market letters and the regional conferences—an unreasonable interference with freedom in trade. Intelligent conduct of business implies, not only knowledge of trade facts but an understanding of them. To this understanding editorial comment and free discussion by those engaged in the business and by others interested are aids. Opinions expressed may be unsound; predictions may be unfounded; but there is nothing in the Sherman Law which should limit freedom of discussion, even among traders.

It is insisted that there was a purpose to curtail production. No evidence of any such purpose was introduced. . . . The purpose of the warnings was to induce mill owners to curb their greed—lest both they and others suffer from the crushing evils of overproduction. Such warning or advice, whether given by individuals or the representatives of an association, presents no element of illegality.

It is urged that this was a concerted effort to enhance prices. There was at no time uniformity in prices. So far as appears, every mill charged for its product as much as it could get. There is evidence that the hardwood mills expected, by adopting the Plan, to earn more in profits, and to do so, at least in part, by getting higher prices for their product. It may be that the distribution of the trade data, the editorial comment, and the conferences enabled the producers to obtain, on the average, higher prices than would otherwise have been possible. But there is nothing in the Sherman Law to indicate that Congress intended to condemn cooperative action in the exchange of information, merely because prophecy resulting from comment on the data collected may lead, for a period, to higher market prices. Congress assumed that the desire to acquire and to enjoy property is the safest and most promising basis for society, and to that end it sought, among other things, to protect the pursuit of business for private profit. Its purpose, obviously, was not to prevent the making of profits, or to counteract the operation of the law of supply and demand. Its purpose was merely to prevent restraint. The illegality of a combination under the Sherman Law lies, not in its effect upon the price level, but in the coercion thereby affected. . . .

The cooperation which is incident to this plan does not suppress competition. On the contrary, it tends to promote all in competition which is desirable. By substituting knowledge for ignorance, rumor, guess, and suspicion, it tends also to substitute research and reasoning for gambling and piracy, without closing the door to adventure, or lessening the value of prophetic wisdom. In making such knowledge available to the smallest concern, it creates among producers equality of opportunity. In making it available, also, to purchasers and the general public, it does all that can actually be done to protect the community from extortion. If, as is alleged, the Plan tends to substitute stability in prices for violent fluctuations, its influence, in this respect, is not against the public interest. . . .

The refusal to permit a multitude of small rivals to cooperate, as they have done here, in order to protect themselves and the public from the chaos and havoc wrought in their trade by ignorance, may result in suppressing competition in the hardwood industry. . . . This court held in United States v. U.S. Steel Corporation, 251 U.S. 417, 40 S.Ct. 293, 64 L.Ed. 343, 8 A.L.R. 1121, that it was not unlawful to vest in a single corporation control of 50 per cent of the steel industry of the country; and in United States v. United Shoe Machinery Co., 247 U.S. 32, 38 S.Ct. 473, 62 L.Ed. 968, the court held that it was not unlawful to vest in a single corporation control of practically the whole shoe machinery industry. May not these hardwood lumber concerns, frustrated in their efforts to rationalize competition, be led to enter the inviting field of consolidation? And, if they do, may not another huge trust, with highly centralized control over vast resources, natural, manufacturing, and financial, become so powerful as to dominate competitors, wholesalers, retailers, consumers, employees, and in large measure the community? ◄

COMMENTS AND QUESTIONS

1. What were the principal reasons given in the majority opinion for declaring the activities of this trade association to be an unlawful restraint of trade?
2. Summarize the economic and social arguments made by Brandeis in the last paragraph of his dissenting opinion. Do you feel they have merit?

Price-Fixing

Under ordinary circumstances, a firm may sell its product at any price it chooses. But if the firm fixes a price artificially in agreement or in conspiracy with others, the courts will usually hold that the action is a violation of the antitrust laws.

A distinction is usually made between horizontal and vertical price-fixing. In *horizontal price-fixing* two or more companies operating on the same level of competition agree to fix their prices at a certain figure. Such arrangements are almost always looked upon as an unlawful restraint of trade, regardless of the circumstances.

EXAMPLE

Two manufacturers of electrical products agree to fix and maintain uniform prices on certain appliances. This is horizontal price-fixing, since both manufacturers are competing on the same level. Such an arrangement would undoubtedly be ruled illegal.

In *vertical price-fixing,* an agreement to maintain prices is made between manufacturers and dealers, or between wholesalers and retailers—in other words, between two persons or firms operating on different levels of competition. At common law, such agreements were unenforceable on the ground that they were in restraint of trade; after the passage of the Sherman Act, the Supreme Court declared that such agreements were in violation of that statute. In the 1930's, however, a demand arose for a change in the law. Manufacturers of trade-mark and trade-name goods argued that the law gave them no protection against dealers who cut prices on such goods, thereby damaging the reputation of the product. They pointed out that when unscrupulous dealers, trying to encourage buyers to purchase more profitable items, sell such goods below cost, other dealers cannot compete and stop handling the goods. As a result, manufacturers are deprived of their retail outlets and the benefits of their national advertising programs.

In response to this pressure, almost every state passed so-called "fair trade laws" permitting resale price maintenance agreements in which dealers agreed to sell brand-name products at a minimum fixed price. Many of the laws went a step further by providing that such agreements are binding on all retailers of the articles who are given notice of the fixed price, even though they have not signed the agreement themselves.

Following this rash of state statutes, Congress enacted the Miller-Tydings Act in 1937, which provided that the manufacturers or distributors of trade-mark or brand-name articles sold in interstate commerce may, by contract, prescribe a minimum resale price, so long as such contracts are legal in the state where the products are to be resold. In 1951, the Supreme Court, by holding that this act did not authorize the enforcement of contracts of this sort against nonsigners, destroyed much of the effectiveness of fair-trade agreements. In 1952, however, Congress passed the McGuire Act, which provided that such contracts are binding on nonsigners as well as on signers.

Except where vertical price-fixing agreements are specifically authorized by statute, they are generally regarded as illegal. Another exception to the rule is recognized, however, in vertical arrangements that permit the dealer some discretion in fixing the ultimate price he charges the consumer. For example, a manufacturer may establish suggested list prices for goods without violating the law, provided he leaves dealers free to disregard the suggested price if they so choose.

The following case presents an illustration of vertical price-fixing. The government contended that the agreement in question violated the Sherman Act; the manufacturer claimed that the agreement was permitted by the

Miller-Tydings Act. The Supreme Court, as you will see, disagreed on how the two statutes should be applied.

UNITED STATES v. McKESSON AND ROBBINS, INC.

Supreme Court of the United States, 1956
351 U.S. 305, 76 S.Ct. 937

► MR. CHIEF JUSTICE WARREN delivered the opinion of the Court.

Defendant (appellee) is the largest drug wholesaler in the United States and also manufactures its own branded drug products. Both the wholesale and manufacturing divisions, though separately staffed, are component parts of the same corporation, neither being separately incorporated.

The major portion of appellee's brand products is distributed to retailers through its own wholesale divisions, but appellee also makes direct sales to important retailers through its manufacturing division. Both divisions also sell to independent wholesalers who are in competition with the appellee's wholesale division (or manufacturing division in the case of direct sales) for the retail trade.

The Government sought an injunction under Section 4 of the Sherman Act against appellee's "fair trade" agreements with independent wholesalers with whom it was competing, charging that such agreements constituted illegal price fixing violating Section 1 of the Sherman Act. Appellee claimed the agreements were within the exemptions of the Miller-Tydings and McGuire Acts. The District Court first denied the Government's motion for summary judgment and subsequently dismissed the complaint. . . .

The issue presented is a narrow one of statutory interpretation. The Government does not question the so-called vertical "fair trade" agreements between McKesson and retailers of McKesson brand products. It challenges only appellee's price-fixing agreements with independent wholesalers with whom it is in competition. . . .

In the Miller-Tydings Act, passed as a rider to a District of Columbia revenue bill, Congress was careful to state that its exemption of certain resale price maintenance contracts from the prohibitions of the antitrust laws "shall not make lawful any contract or agreement, providing for the establishment or maintenance of minimum resale prices on any commodity herein involved, between manufacturers, or between producers, or between wholesalers, or between brokers, or between factors, or between retailers, or between persons, firms, or corporations in competition with each other."

Fifteen years later, Congress attached an almost identical proviso to the McGuire Act. . . .

Appellee is admittedly a wholesaler with resale price maintenance contracts with 94 other wholesalers who are in competition with it. Thus, even if we read the proviso so that the words "in competition with each other" modify "between wholesalers," the agreements in question would seem clearly to be outside the statutory exemption. Appellee concedes that the proviso does not exempt a contract between two competing independent wholesalers fixing the price of a brand product produced by neither of them. Yet it urges that what would be illegal if done between competing independent wholesalers becomes legal if done between an independent wholesaler and a competing wholesaler who is also the manufacturer of the brand product. This is so, appellee maintains, because in contracting with independent wholesalers it acted solely as a manufacturer selling to buyers rather than as a competitor of these buyers. But the statutes provide no basis for sanctioning the fiction of McKesson, the country's largest drug wholesaler, acting only as a manufacturer when it concludes "fair trade" agreements with competing wholesalers. These were agreements "between wholesalers."

Any doubts which might otherwise be raised as to the propriety of considering a manufacturer-wholesaler as a "wholesaler" are dispelled by the last phrase of the proviso in question, which continues the proscription against price-fixing agreements "between persons, firms, or corporations in competition with each other." Congress thus made as plain as words can make it that, without regard to categories or labels, the crucial inquiry is whether the contracting parties compete with each other. If they do, the Miller-Tydings and McGuire Acts do not permit them to fix resale prices. The Court stated in Schwegmann Bros. v. Calvert Corp., 341 U.S. 384, 389; 71 S.Ct. 745, 748, that this proviso "expressly continues the prohibitions of the Sherman Act against 'horizontal' price fixing by those in competition with each other at the same functional level." Since appellee competes "at the same functional level" with each of the 94 wholesalers with whom it has price-fixing agreements, the proviso prevents these agreements from falling within the statutory exemption. . . .

The court below did not rely on the legislative history, finding it to be "unedifying and unilluminating." We agree with this appraisal, but are not troubled by it since the language of the proviso in question in unambiguous. It excludes from the exemption from the *per se* rule of illegality resale price maintenance contracts between firms competing on the same functional level.

Both the Government and appellee press upon us economic arguments which could reasonably have caused Congress to support their respective positions. We need not concern ourselves with such speculation. Congress has marked the limitations beyond which price fixing cannot go. We are not only bound by those limitations but we are bound to construe them strictly, since resale price maintenance is a privilege restrictive of a free economy. . . .

Reversed and remanded.

MR. JUSTICE HARLAN, whom MR. JUSTICE FRANKFURTER and MR. JUSTICE BURTON join, dissenting.

Lack of sympathy with an Act of Congress does not justify giving to it a construction that cannot be rationalized in terms of any policy reasonably attributable to Congress. Rather our duty, as always, is to seek out the policy underlying the Act and, if possible, give effect to it. In this instance, I think the Court has departed from that rule by giving the Miller-Tydings and McGuire Acts an artificial construction which produces results that could hardly have been intended by Congress.

The purpose of the state fair-trade laws is to allow the manufacturer of a brand-named product to protect the good will his name enjoys by controlling the prices at which his branded products are resold. . . . The necessary result—indeed, the very object—is to permit the elimination of price competition in the branded product among those who sell it. Congress has sanctioned those laws in the Miller-Tydings and McGuire Acts, considering them not to be offensive to federal antitrust policy. Sufficient protection to the public interest was deemed to be afforded by the competition in the branded product among those who sell it. Congress has sanctioned those laws in the Miller-Tydings and McGuire Acts denying fair-trade contracts exemption from the antitrust laws unless the fair-traded product is "in free and open competition with commodities of the same general class." In short, the very purpose of the Acts is to permit a manufacturer to set the resale price for his own products while preserving competition between brands—that is, between the fair-traded item and similar items produced by other manufacturers.

If we accept the legislative judgment implicit in the Acts that resale price maintenance is necessary and desirable to protect the good will attached to a brand name, there is no meaningful distinction between the fair-trade contracts of integrated and non-integrated manufacturers. Certainly the integrated manufacturer has as strong a claim to protection of his good will as a non-integrated manufacturer, and the economic effect of the contracts is the same. In both cases price competition in the resale of the branded product is eliminated, and in neither case does the price fixing extend beyond the manufacturer's own product. While the Government concedes the right of a non-integrated manufacturer to eliminate price competition in his products between wholesalers, it finds a vice not contemplated by the Acts when one of the "wholesalers" is also the manufacturer, for then the contracts eliminate competition between the very parties to the contracts. But, in either case, all price competition is eliminated, and I am unable to see what difference it makes between whom the eliminated competition would have existed had it not been eliminated. The other bases of distinction suggested by the Government are equally tenuous and reflect a subtlety of analysis for which there is no support in either the Acts or their history.

So unsatisfactory, indeed, are the Government's attempts to rationalize the result contended for, that the Court chooses not to rely upon them, finding the language of the provisos so clear as to make it unnecessary even to hypothesize a consistent rationale attributable to Congress that might justify the discrimination against integrated producers. Indeed, not even the fact that the only legislative history directly in point is squarely opposed to the Court's reading of the statute . . . prompts enough doubt in the Court to require an inquiry into the purpose of the Acts. The Court's reasoning is this: the provisos except from the Acts contracts "between wholesalers" or "between persons, firms, or corporations in competition with each other"; McKesson is a "wholesaler" as well as a manufacturer and is also "in competition with" independent wholesalers; its contracts with independent wholesalers are therefore forbidden contracts "between wholesalers" and "between corporations in competition with each other." This verbalistic argument can be answered by the equally verbalistic one that the fair trade contracts, being made in connection with the sale of its own branded products, were made by McKesson in its capacity as a "manufacturer" rather than as a competing "wholesaler." Neither argument being more conclusive than the other, the answer to the problem can be found only by looking to the purpose of the provisos and its relation to the basic policy of permitting resale price maintenance of branded goods.   ◄

COMMENTS AND QUESTIONS

1. The majority opinion states that the issue "is a narrow one of statutory interpretation." What *was* the issue, and how did the majority of the Court decide it? Do you agree that "the language of the proviso in question is unambiguous"?
2. The dissenting opinion stresses the underlying purposes that the Miller-Tydings Act was designed to accomplish. What conclusions does Justice Harlan reach?

Price Discrimination

Section 2 of the Clayton Act forbids price discrimination between purchasers "where the effect . . . may be to substantially lessen competition or to tend to create a monopoly in any line of commerce." The main purpose of this provision was to eliminate price-cutting in highly competitive areas in an effort to kill off competitors, while keeping prices high in noncompetitive areas. The effectiveness of this section was seriously weakened, however, by the proviso "that nothing herein contained shall prevent discrimination in price between purchases of commodities on account of difference in the grade, quality, or quantity of the commodity sold, or that makes due allowance for difference in the cost of selling or transportation, or discrimination in price and in the same or different communities made in good faith to meet competition." (In other words, a seller could justify discrimination between buyers on the ground that his selling or transportation expenses were greater for one than for the other; or that one buyer was entitled to a lower price because he purchased a greater quantity of goods; or that the seller was forced to lower his prices for some buyers in order to meet competition.) Nor did the framers of the act make any attempt to regulate indirect price discrimination in the form of rebates, allowances to customers, or the furnishing of free advertising and demonstrators. These inadequacies soon made it apparent that the Clayton Act would not be effective in controlling discriminatory pricing practices, and there was spirited agitation for a stronger law.

Congress responded to these demands by enacting the Robinson-Patman Act in 1936. This statute made several important changes in this area of the law. The old law, for example, placed few restrictions on a manufacturer's right to charge a lower price to a buyer who purchased goods in quantity. The amended act permits quantity discounts only to the extent that they can be justified by actual economies in the seller's costs of manufacture, sales, or delivery. On the other hand, the Robinson-Patman Act clarifies the law by spelling out certain conditions under which price discrimination *will* be permitted. For example, a seller may charge different prices to different buyers for perishable goods that may deteriorate if not sold quickly. (A similar rule applies to seasonal goods—bathing suits, for example—which can be sold only during certain times of the year.) In addition, a seller is permitted to discriminate in prices if he is, in good faith, discontinuing his business and selling all his merchandise. Further, the act subjects buyers as well as sellers to penalties for violation, a belated recognition that price discrimination is often induced or initiated by the purchasers of goods.

Perhaps the most important provisions of the Robinson-Patman Act were those that were specifically aimed at indirect price discrimination. Sections 2(c), (d), and (e) of the act were designed to curb certain practices that had been devised in an effort to circumvent the provisions of the original Clayton Act. Section 2(c) prohibits the payment of commissions or other fees, allowances, or discounts except for services actually rendered. Sections 2(d) and (e) forbid discrimination in the furnishing of advertising, merchandising services, and demonstrations unless such services are offered to all competing customers on substantially the same terms.

Exclusive-Dealing and Tying Arrangements

Section 3 of the Clayton Act prohibits a firm from selling or leasing goods to another firm under an arrangement whereby the buyer or lessee is forced to agree not to buy or use the goods of any of the seller's (or lessor's) competitors where the effect of such an agreement "may be to substantially lessen competition or tend to create a monopoly. . . ." Such arrangements take many different forms, and some are looked on with more favor by the Court than others.

An *exclusive-dealing* contract is an agreement between a manufacturer and a retailer in which the retailer agrees not to deal with any of the manufacturer's competitors and the manufacturer promises to supply the retailer with his products. Such an arrangement is to be distinguished from an *exclusive-representation* contract, in which the manufacturer agrees not to sell his products to any of the retailer's competitors and, in return, the retailer promises to deal in the manufacturer's products. The latter type of agreement is not prohibited by the Clayton Act and is usually held to be legal.

The courts have been relatively lenient in enforcing the Clayton Act's provisions against exclusive-dealing agreements. As a general rule, they regard such contracts as unlawful only if the manufacturer holds a dominant position in the market and seeks to maintain or enlarge that position by the use of such devices. Many authorities feel that exclusive-dealing contracts are actually beneficial to the economy.

The courts are not quite so lenient, however, when *several* manufacturers combine to impose exclusive-dealing conditions on retailers. The following case presents a good illustration of such an effort.

FASHION ORIGINATORS' GUILD OF AMERICA, INC.
v. FEDERAL TRADE COMMISSION

Supreme Court of the United States, 1941
312 U.S. 457, 61 S.Ct. 703

▶ MR. JUSTICE BLACK delivered the opinion of the Court.

The Circuit Court of Appeals, with modifications not here challenged, affirmed a Federal Trade Commission decree ordering petitioners to cease and desist from certain practices found to have been done in combination and to constitute "unfair methods of competition" tending to monopoly (114 F. 2d 80). Determination of the correctness of the decision below requires consideration of the Sherman, Clayton, and Federal Trade Commission Acts.

Some of the members of the combination design, manufacture, sell and distribute women's garments—chiefly dresses. Others are manufacturers, converters or dyers of textiles from which these garments are made. Fashion Originators' Guild of America (FOGA), an organization controlled by these groups, is the instrument through which petitioners work to accomplish the purposes condemned by the Commission. The garment manufacturers claim to be creators of original and distinctive designs of fashionable clothes for women, and the textile manufacturers claim to be creators of similar original fabric designs. After these designs enter the channels of trade, other manufacturers systematically make and sell copies of them, the copies usually selling at prices lower than the garments copied. Petitioners call this practice of copying unethical and immoral and give it the name of "style piracy." And although they admit that their "original creations" are neither copyrighted nor patented, and indeed assert that existing legislation affords them no protection against copyists, they nevertheless urge that sale of copied designs constitutes an unfair trade practice and a tortious invasion of their rights. Because of these alleged wrongs, petitioners, while continuing to compete with one another in many respects, combined among themselves to combat, and, if possible, destroy all competition from the sale of garments which are copies of their "original creations." They admit that to destroy such competition they have in combination purposely boycotted and declined to sell their products to retailers who follow a policy of selling garments copied by other manufacturers from designs put out by Guild members. As a result of their efforts, approximately 12,000 retailers throughout the country have signed agreements to "cooperate" with the Guild boycott program, but more than half of these signed the agreements only because constrained by threats that Guild members would not sell to retailers who failed to yield to their demands—threats that have been carried out by the Guild practice of placing on red cards the names of non-cooperators (to whom no sales are to be made), placing on white cards the names of cooperators (to whom sales are to be made), and then distributing both sets of cards to the manufacturers.

The one hundred and seventy-six manufacturers of women's garments who are members of the Guild occupy a commanding position in their line of business. In 1936, they sold in the United States more than 38% of all women's garments wholesaling at $6.75 and up, and more than 60% of those at $10.75 and above. The power of the combination is great; competition and the demand of the consuming public make it necessary for most retail dealers to stock some of the products of these manufacturers. And the power of the combination is made even greater by reason of the affiliation of some members of the National Federation of Textiles, Inc.—being an organization composed of about one hundred textile manufacturers, converters, dyers, and printers of silk and rayon used in making women's garments. Those members of the Federation who are affiliated with the Guild have agreed to sell their products only to those garment manufacturers who have in turn agreed to sell only to cooperating retailers.

The Guild maintains a Design Registration Bureau for garments, and the Textile Federation maintains a similar Bureau for textiles. The Guild employs "shoppers" to visit the stores of both cooperating and non-cooperating retailers, "for the purpose of examining their stocks, to determine and report as to whether they contain . . . copies of registered designs. . . ." An elaborate system of trial and appellate tribunals exists for the determination of whether a given garment is in fact a copy of a Guild member's design. In order to assure the success of its plan of registration and restraint, and to ascertain whether Guild regulations are being violated, the Guild audits its members' books. And if violations of Guild requirements are discovered, as, for example, to red-carded retailers, the violators are subject to heavy fines.

In addition to the elements of the agreement set out above, all of which relate more or less closely to competition by so-called style copyists, the Guild has undertaken to do many things, apparently independent of and distinct from the fight against copying. Among them are the following: the combination prohibits its members from participating in retail advertising; regulates the discount they may allow; prohibits their selling at retail; cooperates with local guilds in regulating days upon which special sales shall be held; prohibits its members from selling women's garments to persons who conduct businesses in residences, residential quarters, hotels or apartment houses; and denies the benefits of membership to retailers who participate with dress manufacturers in promoting fashion shows unless the merchandise used is actually purchased and delivered.

If the purpose and practice of the combination of garment manufacturers and affiliates runs counter to the public policy declared in the Sherman and Clayton Acts, the Federal Trade Commission has the power to suppress it as an unfair method of competition. From its findings the Commission concluded that the petitioners, "pursuant to understandings, arrangements, agreements, combinations and conspiracies entered into jointly and severally," had prevented sales in interstate commerce, had "substantially lessened, hindered and suppressed" competition, and had tended "to create in themselves a monopoly. . . ." The relevance of [Section 3] of the Clayton Act to petitioners' scheme is shown by the fact that the scheme is bottomed upon a system of sale under which (1) textiles shall be sold to garment manufacturers only upon the condition and understanding that the buyers will not use or deal in textiles which are copied from the designs of textile manufacturing Guild members; (2) garment manufacturers shall sell to retailers only upon the condition and understanding that the retailers shall not use or deal in such copied designs. And the Federal Trade Commission concluded in the language of the Clayton Act that these understandings substantially lessened competition and tended to create a monopoly. We hold that the combination, upon adequate and unchallenged findings, constituted an unfair method of competition.

Not only does the plan in the respects above discussed thus conflict with the principles of the Clayton Act; the findings of the Commission bring petitioners' combination in its entirety well within the inhibition of the policies declared by the Sherman Act itself. Section 1 of that Act makes illegal every contract, combination or conspiracy in restraint of trade or commerce among the several states; Section 2 makes illegal every combination or conspiracy which monopolizes or attempts to monopolize any part of that trade or commerce. Under the Sherman Act "competition, not combination, should be the law of trade." National Cotton Oil Co. v. Texas, 197 U.S. 115, 129; 25 S.Ct. 379, 381, 382; 49 L.Ed. 689. And among the many respects in which the Guild's plan runs contrary to the policy of the Sherman Act are these: it narrows the outlets to which garment and textile manufacturers can sell and the sources from which retailers can buy . . . , subjects all retailers and manufacturers who decline to comply with the Guild's program to an organized boycott . . . , takes away the freedom of action of members by requiring each to reveal to the Guild the intimate details of their individual affairs . . . , and has both as its necessary tendency and as its purpose and effect the direct suppression of competition from the sale of unregistered textiles and copied designs. . . . In addition to all this, the combination is in reality an extra-governmental agency, which prescribes rules for the regulation and restraint of interstate commerce, and provides extra-judicial tribunals for determination and punishment of violations, and thus "trenches upon the power of the national legislature and violates the statute." Addyston Pipe & Steel Co. v. United States, 175 U.S. 211, 242; 20 S.Ct. 96, 107; 44 L.Ed. 136.

Nor is it determinative in considering the policy of the Sherman Act that petitioners may not yet have achieved a complete monopoly. For "it is sufficient if it really tends to that end, and to deprive the public of the advantages which flow from free competition." . . . It was, in fact, one of the hopes of those who sponsored the Federal Trade Commission Act that its effect might be prophylactic and through it attempts to bring about complete monopolization of an industry might be stopped in their incipiency.

Petitioners, however, argue that the combination cannot be contrary to the policy of the Sherman and Clayton Acts since the Federal Trade Commission did not find that the combination fixed or regulated prices, parcelled out or limited production, or brought about a deterioration in quality. But action falling into these three categories does not exhaust the types of conduct banned by the Sherman and Clayton Acts. And as previously pointed out, it was the object of the Federal Trade Commission Act to reach not merely in their fruition but also in their incipiency combinations which would lead to these and other trade restraints and practices deemed undesirable. In this case, the Commission found that the combination exercised sufficient control and power in the women's garments and textiles businesses "to exclude from the industry those manufacturers and distributors who do not conform to the rules and regulations of said industries." While a conspiracy to fix prices is illegal, an intent to increase prices is not an ever-present essential of conduct amounting to a violation of the policy of the Sherman and Clayton Acts; a monopoly contrary to their policies can exist even though a combination may temporarily or even permanently reduce the price of the articles manufactured or sold. For as this Court has said,

> "Trade or commerce under those circumstances may nevertheless be badly and unfortunately restrained by driving out of business the small dealers and worthy men whose lives have been spent therein, and who might be unable to readjust themselves to their altered surroundings. Mere reduction in the price of the commodity dealt in might be dearly paid for by the ruin of such a class and the absorption of control over one commodity by an all-powerful combination of capital."

But petitioners further argue that their boycott and restraint of interstate trade is not within the ban of the policies of the Sherman and Clayton Acts because "the practices of FOGA were reasonable and necessary to protect the manufacturer, laborer, retailer and consumer against the devastating evils growing from the pricing of original designs and had in fact benefited all four." The Commission declined to hear much of the evidence that petitioners desired to offer on this subject. As we have pointed out, however, the aim of petitioners' combination was the intentional destruction of one type of manufacture and sale which competed with Guild members. The purpose and object of this combination, its potential power, its tendency to monopoly, the coercion it could and did practice upon a rival method of competition, all brought it within the policy of the prohibition declared by the Sherman and Clayton Acts. For this reason, the principles announced in Appalachian Coals, Inc. v. United States, 288 U.S. 344, 53 S.Ct. 471, 77 L.Ed. 825, and Sugar Institute v. United States, 288 U.S. 553, 56 S.Ct. 629, 80 L.Ed. 859, have no application here. Under these circumstances it was not error to refuse to hear the evidence offered, for the reasonableness of the methods pursued by the combination to accomplish its unlawful object is no more material than would be the reasonableness of the prices fixed by unlawful combination. . . .

Affirmed.   ◄

COMMENTS AND QUESTIONS

1. This case illustrates the power of the Federal Trade Commission to suppress unfair methods of competition. What were the practices complained of? What action did the F.T.C. take? What happened on appeal?

2. Summarize the arguments of the petitioners in support of their position. How did the Court deal with them?

In so-called *tying contracts,* the buyer or lessee of certain products agrees to use other products made by the manufacturer, or else *not* to use the products of the manufacturer's competitors. In a similar arrangement, known as *full-line forcing,* the manufacturer requires the dealer to carry either his entire line of products or none at all.

The courts have been quite severe in their attitude toward tying contracts. After all, a manufacturer can hardly resort to such devices unless he has already achieved a dominant or monopolistic position in the market; the effect, then, is almost always to stifle whatever competition remains. Consequently, the courts have regarded almost all tying contracts as an unlawful restraint of trade. Witness, for example, the following case.

INTERNATIONAL BUSINESS MACHINES CORPORATION v. UNITED STATES

Supreme Court of the United States, 1936
288 U.S. 131. 56 S.Ct. 701

▶ MR. JUSTICE STONE delivered the opinion of the Court.

This is an appeal from so much of a decree of the District Court for Southern New York as enjoins the appellant from leasing its tabulating and other machines upon the condition that the lessees shall use with such machines only tabulating cards manufactured by appellant, as a violation of 3 of the Clayton Act.

The government brought this suit against three other defendants, two of whom were eliminated from the proceedings. The third, Remington Rand, Inc., stipulated that the decree to be entered against it shall conform to that entered against appellant upon this appeal.

Appellant's machines and those of Remington Rand, Inc., are now the only ones on the market which perform certain mechanical tabulations and computations, without any intervening manual operations, by the use in them of cards upon which are recorded data which are the subject of tabulation or computation. Appellant manufactures three types of machines, known as punching machines, sorters, and tabulators. The punching machines are used to perforate cards, called tabulating cards, in such manner that the positions of the perforations indicate numerical or other data. When the cards are passed through the sorter or tabulator, control of its mechanism is effected by electrical circuits established by contacts through the perforations. The cards are thus made permanent records of information, and by the perforations are given such form that they may be used as often as required, to control the function of the machines through which they are passed. The sorting machines are used to sort the perforated cards so as to classify them by the selection and segregation, in the desired manner, of those signifying any particular type of information. The tabulating machines are used to record the information denoted by the perforated cards or to make computations based upon it. In the Remington Rand machines the control is not electrical, but is accomplished by the use of cards which admit of the movement, into the perforations, of small pins which, by linkage, guide the mechanical operation of the machine so as to effect the desired result.

To insure satisfactory performance by appellant's machines it is necessary that the cards used in them conform to precise specifications as to size and thickness and that they be free from defects due to slime or carbon spots, which cause unintended electrical contacts and consequent inaccurate results. The cards manufactured by appellant are electrically tested for such defects.

Appellant leases its machines for a specified rental and period, upon condition that the lease shall terminate in case any cards not manufactured by the lessor are used in the leased machine. A special form of lease has been granted to the government by which it is permitted to use cards of its own manufacture upon paying a 15% increase in the rental of the leased machines, but upon condition that the lease shall be terminable if the Government uses such cards without payment of the additional rental.

Appellant insists that the condition of its leases is not within the prohibition of the Clayton Act, and it has assigned as error the conclusion of the district court that the condition tends to create monopoly. But its principal contentions are that its leases are lawful because the protection secured by the condition does not extend beyond the monopoly which it has acquired by patents on the cards and on the machines in which they are used, and that in any case the condition is permissible under 3 of the Clayton Act because its purpose and effect are only to preserve to appellant the good will of its patrons by preventing the use of unsuitable cards which would interfere with successful performance of its machines.

1. Section 3 of the Clayton Act . . . in precise terms makes unlawful a condition that the lessee shall not use the supplies or commodities of a competitor of the lessor if the effect of the condition "may be" to lessen competition substantially or if it tends to create a monopoly.

Little need be said of the contention that the condition of appellant's leases does not infringe these prohibitions. It is true that the condition is not in so many words against the use of the cards of a competitor, but is affirmative in form, that the lessee can make no use of the cards except with the leased machines. But the specified use of appellant's cards precludes the use of the cards of any competitor, and the condition operates in the manner forbidden by the statute. See United Shoe Machinery Co. v. United States, 258 U.S. 451, 457, 458; 42 S.Ct. 363, 66 L.Ed. 708; compare Federal Trade Commission v. Sinclair Ref. Co., 261 U.S. 463, 473; 43 S.Ct. 450, 67 L.Ed. 746. A different question is presented from that in the Sinclair Case, where a wholesale distributor of gasoline leased gasoline pumps to retail dealers with the stipulation that they should not be used for the pumping of gasoline of the lessor's competitors. As the only use made of the gasoline was to sell it, and as there was no restraint upon the purchase and sale of competing gasoline, there was no violation of the Clayton Act.

The conclusion of the trial court that appellant's leases infringe the monopoly provisions of the section does not want for support in the record. The agreed use of the "tying clause" by appellant and its only competitors, and the agreement by each of them to restrict its competition in the sale of cards to the lessees of the others, have operated to prevent competition and to create a monopoly in the production and sale of tabulating cards suitable for appellant's machines, as the district court found. The commerce in tabulating cards is substantial. Appellant makes and sells 3,000,000,000 cards annually, 81% of the total, indicating that the sales by the Remington Rand company, its only competitor, representing the remaining 19%, are approximately 600,000,000. It is stipulated that appellant derives a "substantial" profit from its card sales. Its gross receipts from its entire business during the past ten years have averaged $9,710,389 a year, of which approximately one-third, or $3,192,700, has been derived from the sale of its cards. These facts, and others, which we do not stop to enumerate, can leave no doubt that the effect of the condition in appellant's leases "may be to substantially lessen competition," and that it tends to create monopoly, and has in fact been an important and effective step in the creation of monopoly.

2. At the trial appellant offered to prove its ownership of patents which, it asserts, give it a monopoly of the right to manufacture, use and vend the cards, separately, and in a combination with its sorting and tabulating machines, of which, it insists, they are a part. It argues that the condition of its leases is lawful because it does not enlarge the monopoly secured by the patents, and that the trial court erred in refusing to consider the appellant's patent monopoly as a defense to the suit.

Appellant's patents appear to extend only to the cards when perforated, and to have no application to those which the lessees purchase before they are punched. The contention is thus reduced to the dubious claim that the sale of the unpunched cards is a contributory infringement of the patents covering the use of perforated cards separately and in combination with the machines. . . .

But we do not place our decision on this narrow ground. We rest it rather on the language of 3 of the Clayton Act which expressly makes tying clauses unlawful, whether the machine leased is "patented or unpatented." The section does not purport to curtail the patent monopoly of the lessor or to restrict its protection by suit for infringement. But it does in terms deny to the lessor of a patented, as well as of an unpatented, machine the benefit of any condition or agreement that the lessee shall not use the supplies of a competitor. The only purpose or effect of the tying clause, so far as it could be effectively applied to patented articles, is either to prevent the use, by a lessee, of the product of a competitor of the lessor, where the lessor's patent, prima facie, embraces that product, and thus avoid judicial review of the patent, or else to compel its examination in every suit brought to set aside the tying clause, although the suit could usually result in no binding adjudication as to the validity of the patent, since infringement would not be in issue. The phrase "whether patented or unpatented" would seem well chosen to foreclose the possibility of either alternative.

When Congress had before it the bill which became 3 of the Clayton Act, it was familiar with the decision of this Court in Henry v. A. B. Dick Co., 224 U.S. 1, 32 S.Ct. 364, 56 L.Ed. 645, Ann. Cas. 1913, D, 880, and with the contentions made in United States v. United Shoe Mach. Co., 247 U.S. 32, 33; 38 S.Ct. 473, 62 L.Ed. 968, then pending before this Court—cases in which it was held that a tying clause could lawfully be extended to unpatented supplies for a leased patented machine. . . . One purpose of 3 undoubtedly was to prevent such use of the tying clause. . . . But the debates on 3, on the floor of the Senate, disclose that it was well known to that body that one of the contentions in the pending cause, United States v. United Shoe Mach. Co., 247 U.S. 32, 33; 38 S.Ct. 473, 62 L.Ed. 968, was that it was permissible, in any circumstances, for a lessor to tie several patented articles together. They show that the proponents of the bill were as much concerned that the practice should be prohibited as that the tying of non-patented to patented articles should be ended. Cong. Rec., Vol. 51, Part 14, 63rd Cong., 3rd Sess., 14275. The phrase, "whether patented or unpatented," as used in 3 is as applicable to the one practice as to the other. It would fail of the purpose which it plainly expresses if it did not operate to preclude the possibility of both, and to make the validity of the tying clause a matter to be determined independently of the protection afforded by any monopoly of the lessor. Such, we think, must be taken to be the effect of the section unless its language and history are to be disregarded. Under its provisions the lawfulness of the tying clause must be ascertained by applying to it the standards prescribed by 3 as though the leased article and its parts were unpatented.

3. Despite the plain language of 3, making unlawful the tying clause when it tends to create a monopoly, appellant insists that it does not forbid tying clauses whose purpose and effect are to protect the good will of the lessor in the leased machines, even though monopoly ensues. In support of this contention appellant places great emphasis on the admitted fact that it is essential to the successful performance of the leased machines that the cards used in them conform, with relatively minute tolerances, to specifications as to size, thickness and freedom from defects which would affect adversely the electrical circuits indispensable to the proper operation of the machines. The point is stressed that failure, even though occasional, to conform to these requirements, causes inaccuracies in the functioning of the machine, serious in their consequences and difficult to trace to their source, with consequent injury to the reputation of the machines and the good will of the lessors.

There is no contention that others than appellant cannot meet these requirements. It affirmatively appears, by stipulation, that others are capable of manufacturing cards suitable for use in appellant's machines, and that paper required for that purpose may be obtained from the manufacturers who supply appellant. The Remington Rand company manufactures cards suitable for its own machines, but since it has been barred by the agreement with appellant from selling its cards for use in appellant's machines, its cards are not electrically tested. The Government, under the provisions of its lease, following its own methods, has made large quantities of the cards, which are in successful use with the appellant's machines. The suggestion that without the tying clause an adequate supply of cards would not be forthcoming from competitive sources is not supported by the evidence. "The very existence of such restrictions suggests that in its absence a competing article of equal or better quality would be offered at the same or at a lower price." Cabrice Corporation v. American Patents Development Corp., 283 U.S. 27, at page 32, 51 S.Ct. 334, 335; 75 L.Ed. 819, 822, note 2, quoting Vaughan, Economics of Our Patent System, 125, 127. Appellant's sale of cards returns a substantial profit and the Government's payment of

15% increase in rental to secure the privilege of making its own cards is profitable only if it produces the cards at a cost less than 55% of the price charged by appellant.

Appellant is not prevented from proclaiming the virtues of its own cards or warning against the danger of using in its machines, cards which do not conform to the necessary specifications, or even from making its leases conditional upon the use of cards which conform to them. For aught that appears such measures would protect its good will, without the creation of monopoly or resort to the suppression of competition.

The Clayton Act names no exception to its prohibition of monopolistic tying clauses. Even if we are free to make an exception to its unambiguous command . . . we can perceive no tenable basis for an exception in favor of a condition whose substantial benefit to the lessor is the elimination of business competition and the creation of monopoly, rather than the protection of its good will, and where it does not appear that the latter can not be achieved by methods which do not tend to monopoly and are not otherwise unlawful.

Affirmed.   ◀

COMMENTS AND QUESTIONS

1. What was the issue before the Court here? How was it decided? Summarize the reasons given in support of the decision.
2. How did the Court distinguish this case from the *Sinclair Refining Co.* case, in which a distributor of gasoline was permitted to lease gas pumps to retail dealers, provided they were not used to pump gasoline of the distributor's competitors? Do you feel the distinction is valid?
3. In the next to last paragraph, the Court suggests certain legal measures that a manufacturer may take to protect himself in this kind of situation. What are they?

Remedies and Enforcement Proceedings Under Federal Antitrust Statutes

As we noted earlier (pp. 810–11), the responsibility for administering and enforcing the antitrust laws rests with the Federal Trade Commission and the Department of Justice.

The Federal Trade Commission may investigate and issue complaints when it has reason to believe that unfair trade practices are being carried on. After a complaint has been issued, the Commission may direct the alleged wrongdoer to appear at a hearing and show cause why he should not stop such practices. After the hearing, the Commission may decide to issue a cease and desist order. If the wrongdoer fails to comply with the order, the Commission may ask the federal court of appeals to enforce it. The party against whom the complaint is directed may appeal to the same court if he feels the order is unjust. Failure to comply with a final order of the Commission is punishable by fine or imprisonment.

The following case illustrates the procedure we have just outlined. A majority of the Supreme Court upheld the findings of the Commission, but the dissenting justices strongly disagreed and criticized the manner in which the Commission arrived at its decision.

FEDERAL TRADE COMMISSION
v. MOTION PICTURE ADVERTISING SERVICE CO., INC.

Supreme Court of the United States, 1953
344 U.S. 392, 73 S.Ct. 361

▶ Mr. Justice Douglas delivered the opinion of the Court.

Respondent is a producer and distributor of advertising motion pictures which depict and describe commodities offered for sale by commercial establishments. Respondent contracts with theatre owners for the display of these advertising films and ships the films from its place of business in Louisiana to theatres in twenty-seven states and the District of Columbia. These contracts run for terms up to five years, the majority being for one or two years. A substantial number of them contains a provision that the theatre owner will display only advertising films furnished by respondent, with the exception of films for charities or for governmental organizations, or announcements of coming attractions. Respondent and three other companies in the same business (against which proceedings were also brought) together had exclusive arrangements for advertising films with approximately three-fourths of the total number of theatres in the United States which display advertising films for compensation. Respondent had exclusive contracts with almost 40 per cent of the theatres in the area where it operates.

The Federal Trade Commission, the petitioner, filed a complaint charging respondent with the use of "Unfair methods of competition" in violation of Section 5 of the Federal Trade Commission Act, 38 Stat. 717, 719; 52 Stat. 111, 15 U.S.C. 45, 15 U.S.C.A. 45. The Commission found that respondent was in substantial competition with other companies engaged in the business of distributing advertising films, that its exclusive contracts have limited the outlets for films of competitors and has forced some competitors out of business because of their inability to obtain outlets for their advertising films. It held by a divided vote that the exclusive contracts are unduly restrictive of competition when they extend for periods in excess of one year. It accordingly entered a cease and desist order which prohibits respondent from entering into any such contract that grants an exclusive privilege for more than a year or from continuing in effect any exclusive provision of an existing contract longer than a year after the date of service in the Commission's order. 47 F.T.C. 378. The Court of Appeals reversed, holding that the exclusive contracts are not unfair methods of competition and that their prohibition would not be in the public interest. (5 Cir.) 194 F. 2d 633.

The "Unfair methods of competition," which are condemned by 5(a) of the Act, are not confined to those that were illegal at common law or that were condemned by the Sherman Act, 15 U.S.C.A. 1–7, 15 note. . . . Congress advisedly left the concept flexible to be defined with particularity by the myriad of cases from the field of business. . . . It is also clear that the Federal Trade Commission Act was designed to supplement and bolster the Sherman Act and the Clayton Act . . . to stop in their incipiency acts and practices which, when full blown, would violate those Acts, . . . as well as to condemn as "unfair methods of competition" existing violations of them. . . .

The Commission found in the present case that respondent's exclusive contracts unreasonably restrain competition and tend to monopoly. Those findings are supported by substantial evidence. This is not a situation where by the nature of the market there is room for newcomers, irrespective of the existing restrictive practices. The number of outlets for the films is quite limited. And due to the exclusive contracts, respondent and the three other major companies have foreclosed to competitors 75 per cent of all available outlets for this business throughout the United States. It is, we think, plain from the Commission's findings that a device which has sewed up a market so tightly for the benefit of a few falls within the prohibitions of the Sherman Act and is therefore an "unfair method of competition" within the meaning of 5(a) of the Federal Trade Commission Act.

An attack is made on that part of the order which restricts the exclusive contracts to one-year terms. It is argued that one-year contracts will not be practicable. It is said that the expenses of securing these screening contracts do not warrant one-year agreements, that investment of capital in the business would not be justified without assurance of a market for more than one year, that theatres frequently demand guarantees for more than a year or otherwise refuse to exhibit advertising films. These and other business requirements are the basis of the argument that exclusive contracts of a duration in excess of a year are necessary for the conduct of the business of the distributors. The Commission considered this argument and concluded that, although the exclusive contracts were beneficial to the distributor and preferred by the theatre owners, their use should be restricted in the public interest. The Commission found that the term of one year had become a standard practice and that the continuance of exclusive contracts so limited would not be an undue restraint upon competition, in view of the compelling business reasons for some exclusive arrangement. The precise impact of a particular practice on the trade is for the Commission, not the courts, to determine. The point where a method of competition becomes "unfair" within the meaning of the Act will often turn on the exigencies of a particular situation, trade practices, or the practical requirements of the business in question. Certainly we cannot say that exclusive contracts in this field should have been banned in their entirety or not at all, that the Commission exceeded the limits of its allowable judgment . . . in limiting their term to one year.

The vice of the exclusive contract in this particular field is in its tendency to restrain competition and to develop a monopoly in violation of the Sherman Act. And when the Sherman Act is involved the crucial fact is the impact of the particular practice on competition, not the label that it carries.

Reversed.

MR. JUSTICE FRANKFURTER, whom MR. JUSTICE BURTON joins, dissenting.

My doubts that the Commission has adequately shown that it has been guided by relevant criteria in dealing with its findings under 5 of the Federal Trade Commission Act are dispelled neither by those findings nor by the opinion of the Court. The Commission has not explained its conclusion with the "simplicity and clearness" necessary to tell us "what a decision means before the duty becomes ours to say whether it is right or wrong." . . .

My primary concern is that the Commission has not related its analysis of this industry to the standards of illegality in 5 with sufficient clarity to enable this Court to review the order. Although we are told that respondent and three other companies have exclusive exhibition contracts with three-quarters of the theatres in the country that accept advertising, there are no findings indicating how many of these contracts extend beyond the one-year period which the Commission finds not unduly restrictive. We do have an indication from the record that more than half of respondent's exclusive contracts run for only one year; if that is so, that part of respondent's hold on the market found unreasonable by the Commission boils down to exclusion of other competitors from something like 1,250 theaters, or about 6%, of the same 20,000 theaters in the country. The hold is on about 10% of the theaters that accept advertising.

Apart from uncritical citations in the brief here, the Commission merely states a dogmatic conclusion that the use of these contracts constitutes an "unreasonable restraint and restriction of competition." In re Motion Picture Advertising Service Co., 47 F.T.C. 378, 389. The Court's opinion is merely an echo of this conclusion and states without discussion that such exclusion from a market without more "falls within the prohibition of the Sherman Act" because, taken with exclusive contracts of other competitors, 75% of the market is shut off. But there is no reliance here on conspiracy or concerted action to foreclose the market, a charge that would of course warrant action under the Sherman Law. . . . If other factors pertinent to a Sherman Law violation were present here, the Commission could not leave such factors unmentioned and simply ask us to review a broad unexplained finding that there is such a violation. In any event, the Commission has not found any Sherman Law violation.

But we are told, as is of course true, that 5 of the Federal Trade Commission Act comprehends more than violations of the Sherman Law. The Federal Trade Commission Act was designed, doubtless, to enable the Commission to nip in the bud practices which, when full blown, would violate the Sherman or Clayton Act. But this record does not explain to us how these practices, if full blown, would violate one of those Acts. The Commission has been content to rest on its conclusion that respondent's exclusive contracts unreasonably restrain competition and tend to monopoly. If judicial review is to have a basis for functioning, the Commission must do more than pronounce a conclusion by way of fiat and without explication. This is not a tribunal for investigating an industry. Analysis of practices in the light of definable standards of illegality is for the Commission. It is for us to determine whether the Commission has correctly applied the proper standards and thus exhibited that familiarity with competitive problems which the Congress anticipated the Commission would achieve from its experience. . . .

It is of great importance to bear in mind that the determination of the scope of the prohibition of "unfair methods of competition" has not been left to the administrative agency as part of its fact finding authority but is a matter of law to be defined by the courts. . . . The significance of such judicial review may be indicated by the dissimilar treatment of comparable standards entrusted to the enforcement of the Interstate Commerce Commission. In dealing with the provisions of the Interstate Commerce Act requiring reasonableness in rates and practices from carriers subject to the control of the Commerce Commission, we read the Act as making the application of standards of reasonableness a determination of fact by that Commission and not an issue of law for the courts. Unlike the Federal Trade Commission Act, the Interstate Commerce Act dealt with governmental regulation not only of a limited sector of the economy but of economic enterprises that had long been singled out for public control. The range within which the broadly stated concepts of reasonableness moved was confined as well as defined by experience, and application of the concepts was necessarily limited to easily comparable economic activity. On the other hand, the Federal Trade Commission Act gave an administrative agency authority over economic controls of a different sort that began with the Sherman Law—restrictions upon the whole domain of economic enterprise engaged in interstate commerce. The content of the prohibition of "unfair methods of competition," to be applied to widely diverse business practices, was not entrusted to the Commission for *ad hoc* determination within the interstices of individualized records but was left for ascertainment by this Court.

The vagueness of the Sherman Law was saved by imparting to it the gloss of history. . . . Difficulties with this inherent uncertainty in the Sherman Law led to the Clayton Act. 38 Stat. 730. The creation of the Federal Trade Commission, 38 Stat. 717, made available a continuous administrative process by which fruition of Sherman Law violations could be aborted. But it is another thing to suggest that anything in business activity that may, if unchecked, offend the particularizations of the Clayton Act may now be reached by the Federal Trade Commission Act. The curb on the Commission's power, as expressed by the series of cases beginning with the Gratz case *supra*, so as to leave to the courts rather than the Commission the final authority in determining what is an unfair method of competition, would be relaxed, and unbridled intervention into business practices encouraged.

I am not unaware that the policies directed at maintaining effective competition, as expressed in the Sherman Law, the Clayton Act, as amended by the Robinson-Patman Act, and the Federal Trade Commission Act, are difficult to formulate and not altogether harmonious. Therefore, the interpretation of the Acts by the agency which is constantly engaged in construing them should carry considerable weight with courts even in the solution of the legal puzzles these statutes raise. But he is no friend of administrative law who thinks that the Commission should be left at large. In any event, whatever problems would be raised by withholding judicial review from determinations of the Commission are for Congress to face, at least in the first instance. . . . Until Congress chooses to do so, we cannot shirk our duty by leaving determinations of law to the discretion of the Federal Trade Commission. Not only must we abstain from approving a mere say so of the Commission and thus fail to discharge the task implied by judicial review. It is also incumbent upon us to seek to rationalize the four statutes directed toward a common end and make of them, to the extent that what Congress has written permits, a harmonious body of law. This opinion is an attempt, at least by way of adumbration, to carry out this aim.

I would have the Court of Appeals remand this case to the Commission. ◄

COMMENTS AND QUESTIONS

1. Summarize the provisions of the cease and desist order of the Federal Trade Commission in this case. What happened in the Court of Appeals? In the Supreme Court?
2. Justice Frankfurter's dissent is something of an essay on administrative law. What main points does he raise? Do you agree with his criticisms?

Since violation of the Sherman Act and other antitrust statutes is a federal crime, the Attorney General, acting through the Antitrust Division of the Justice Department, may bring a criminal prosecution against the alleged wrongdoers. Although fines are frequently imposed on guilty parties, imprisonment has rarely been ordered.[5]

Another course open to the government is to seek an injunction to prevent violations of the antitrust laws. When such proceedings are brought, the courts may order the dissolution of unlawful combinations or associations or require a firm to divest itself of stock or assets in other companies. Many such proceedings are finally settled by so-called *consent decrees*, under which the government and the offending firm agree on the facts of the case and on what steps should be taken to eliminate existing restraints on competition. Such decrees are not binding, however, until they have been approved by the court in which the suit was brought.

Private persons or firms may resort to two remedies if they are damaged by an antitrust violation. First, the Sherman Act, as we have seen, provides that an injured party may bring a civil action for triple the amount of his actual loss. In many cases, however, this remedy is not very effective, since it is exceedingly difficult to prove the amount of damages sustained. Second, the Clayton Act permits a private party to seek an injunction to prevent a firm from violating the antitrust laws.

In the case that follows, the government sought to enjoin certain violations of the Sherman Act. The case also suggests the difficulties faced by the Court in framing a suitable decree in such cases. Notice the several conflicting viewpoints expressed by the members of the Supreme Court.

---

[5] A notable exception took place in 1961, when a federal district court judge sentenced a number of corporate executives to jail for price-fixing activities. This action, which shocked and surprised many businessmen, may indicate a stiffer judicial attitude toward violations of the antitrust laws.

TIMKEN ROLLER BEARING CO. v. UNITED STATES

Supreme Court of the United States, 1950
341 U.S. 593, 71 S.Ct. 971

► Mr. Justice Black delivered the opinion of the Court.

The United States brought this civil action to prevent and restrain violations of the Sherman Act by appellant, Timken Roller Bearing Co., an Ohio corporation. The complaint charged that appellant, in violation of 1 and 3 of the Act combined, conspired and acted with British Timken Ltd. (British Timken), and Société Anonyme Française Timken (French Timken) to restrain interstate and foreign commerce by eliminating competition in the manufacture and sale of antifriction bearings in the markets of the world. After a trial of more than a month the District Court made detailed findings of fact which may be summarized as follows:

As early as 1909 appellant and British Timken's predecessor had made comprehensive agreements providing for a territorial division of the world markets for antifriction bearings. These arrangements were somewhat modified and extended in 1920, 1924, and 1925. Again in 1927 the agreements were substantially renewed in connection with a transaction by which appellant and one Devar, an English businessman, cooperated in purchasing all the stock of British Timken. Later some British Timken stock was sold to the public with the result that appellant now holds about 30% of the outstanding shares while Devar owns about 24%. In 1928 appellant and Devar organized French Timken and since that date have together owned all the stock in the French company. Beginning in that year, appellant, British Timken and French Timken have continuously kept operative "business agreements" regulating the manufacture and sale of antifriction bearings by the three companies and providing for the use by the British and French corporations of the trade-mark "Timken." Under these agreements the contracting parties have (1) allocated trade territories among themselves; (2) fixed prices on products of one sold in the territory of the others; (3) cooperated to protect each other's markets and to eliminate outside competition; and (4) participated in cartels to restrict imports to, and exports from, the United States.

On these findings, the District Court concluded that appellant had violated the Sherman Act as charged, and entered a comprehensive decree designed to bar future violation. 83 F. Supp. 284. The case is before us on appellant's direct appeal under 15 U.S.C. 29, 15 U.S.C.A. 29.

Although appellant has indiscriminately challenged the District Court's judgment and decree in over 200 separate assignments of error, the real grounds relied on for reversal are only a few in number. In the first place, appellant contends that most of the District Court's material findings of fact are without evidential support, that they "ignore or fail properly to evaluate" evidence supporting appellant's position, and that it was error for the court to refuse to make additional findings. For the most part this shotgun approach is actually only a dispute as to the proper inferences to be drawn from the evidence in the record, in effect, it is an invitation for us to try the case de novo. This Court must decline such an invitation just as it does when the Government makes the same request. . . . In the present case, the trial judge after a patient hearing carefully analyzed the evidence in an opinion prepared with obvious care. Appellant's lengthy brief has failed to establish that there was error in making any crucial or even important ultimate or subsidiary finding. Since we cannot say the findings are "clearly erroneous," we accept them. Fed. Rules Civ. Proc. 52(a), 28 U.S.C.A.

Appellant next contends that the restraints of trade so clearly revealed by the District Court's findings can be justified as "reasonable," and therefore, not in violation of the Sherman Act, because they are "ancillary" to allegedly "legal main transactions," namely, (1) a "joint venture" between appellant and Devar, and (2) an exercise of appellant's right to license the trade-mark "Timken."

We cannot accept the "joint venture" contention. That the trade restraints were merely incidental to an otherwise legitimate "joint venture" is to say the least doubtful. The District Court found that the dominant purpose of the restrictive agreements into which appellant, British Timken and French Timken entered was to avoid all competition either among themselves or with others. Regardless of this, however, appellant's argument must be rejected. Our prior decisions plainly establish that agreements providing for an aggregation of trade restraints such as those existing in this case are illegal under the Act. . . . The fact that there is common ownership or control of the contracting corporations does not liberate them from the impact of the antitrust laws. . . . Nor do we find any support in reason or authority for the proposition that agreements between legally separate persons and companies to suppress competition among themselves and others can be justified by labeling the project a "joint venture." Perhaps every agreement and combination to restrain trade could be so labeled.

Nor can the restraints of trade be justified as reasonable steps taken to implement a valid trade-mark licensing system, even if we assume with appellant that it is the owner of the trade-mark "Timken" in the trade areas allocated to the British and French corporations. Appellant's premise that the trade restraints are only incidental to the trade-mark contracts is refuted by the District Court's finding that the "trade mark provisions (in the agreements) were subsidiary and secondary to the central purpose of allocating trade territory." Furthermore, while a trade-mark merely affords protection to a name, the agreements in the present case went far beyond protection of the name "Timken" and provided for control of the manufacture and sale of antifriction bearings whether carrying the mark or not. A trade-mark cannot be legally used as a device for Sherman Act violation. Indeed, the Trade Mark Act of 1946 itself penalizes use of a mark "to violate the antitrust laws of the United States."

We also reject the suggestion that the Sherman Act should not be enforced in this case because what appellant has done is reasonable in view of current foreign trade conditions. The argument in this regard seems to be that tariffs, quota restrictions and the like are now such that the export and import of antifriction bearings can no longer be expected as a practical matter; that appellant cannot successfully sell its American made goods abroad; and that the only way it can profit from business in England, France and other countries is through the ownership of stock in companies organized and manufacturing there. This position ignores the fact that the provisions in the Sherman Act against restraints of foreign trade are based on the assumption, and reflect the policy, that export and import trade in commodities is both possible and desirable. Those provisions of the Act are wholly inconsistent with appellant's argument that American business must be left free to participate in international cartels, that free foreign commerce in goods must be sacrificed in order to foster export of American dollars for investment in foreign factories which sell abroad. Acceptance of appellant's view would make the Sherman Act a dead letter insofar as it prohibits contracts and conspiracies in restraint of foreign trade. If such a drastic change is to be made in the statute, Congress is the one to do it.

Finally, appellant attacks the District Court's decree as being too broad in scope. The decree enjoins continuation or repetition of the conduct found illegal. This is clearly correct. . . . It also contains certain other restraining provisions which were within the court's discretion because "relief, to be effective, must go beyond the narrow limits of the proven violation." . . . The most vigorous objection, however, is made to those portions of the decree relating to divestiture of appellant's stockholdings and other financial interest in British and French Timken.

MR. JUSTICE DOUGLAS, MR. JUSTICE MINTON and I believe that the decree properly ordered divestiture. Our views on this point are as follows: Appellant's interests in the British and French companies were obtained as part of a plan to promote the illegal trade restraints. If not severed, the intercompany relationships will provide in the future, as they have in the past, the temptation and means to engage in the prohibited conduct. These considerations alone should be enough to support the divestiture order. . . . But there are other considerations as well. The decree should not be overturned unless we can say that the District Court abused its discretion. Absent divestiture, it is difficult to see where other parts of the decree forbidding trade restraints would add much to what the Sherman Act by itself already prohibits. And, obviously, the most effective way to suppress further Sherman Act violations is to end the intercorporate relationship which has been the core of the conspiracy. For these reasons, MR. JUSTICE DOUGLAS, MR. JUSTICE MINTON and I cannot say that the District Court abused its discretion in ordering divestiture.

Nevertheless, a majority of this Court, for reasons set forth in other opinions filed in this case, believe that divestiture should not have been ordered by the District Court. Therefore, it becomes necessary to strike from the decree VIII, IVB, and the phrase "or B" in IVC. As so modified, the judgment of the District Court is affirmed.

It is so ordered.

Judgment modified and affirmed.

MR. JUSTICE BURTON and MR. JUSTICE CLARK took no part in the consideration or decision of this case.

MR. JUSTICE REED, with whom the CHIEF JUSTICE joins, concurring.

It seems to me there can be no valid objection to that part of the opinion which approves the finding of the District Court that the Timken Roller Bearing Company has violated 1 and 3 of the Sherman Act. It may seem strange to have a conspiracy for the division of territory for marketing between one corporation and another in which it has a large or even a major interest but any other conclusion would open wide the doors for violation of the Sherman Act at home and in foreign fields. My disagreement with the opinion is based on the suggested requirement that American Timken divest itself of all interest in British Timken and French Timken as required by paragraph VIII of the decree set out below.

There are no specific statutory provisions authorizing courts to employ the harsh remedy of divestiture in civil proceedings to restrain violations of the Sherman Act. Fines and imprisonment may follow criminal convictions. 15 U.S.C. 1, 15 U.S.C.A. 1, and divestiture of property has been used in decrees, not as punishment, but to assure effective enforcement of the laws against restraint of trade.

Since divestiture is a remedy to restore competition and not to punish those who restrain trade, it is not to be used indiscriminately, without regard to the type of violation or whether other effective methods, less harsh, are available. That judicial restraint should follow such lines is exemplified by our recent rulings in United States v. National Lead Co., 332 U.S. 319, pages 348, 353; 67 S.Ct. 1634, pages 1647–1650; 91 L.Ed. 2077, where we approved divestiture of some of the properties belonging to the conspirators and denied it as to others. While the decree here does not call for confiscation, it does call for divestiture. I think that requirement is unnecessary.

In this case the prohibited plan grew out of the effort to implement a patent monopoly. The difficulties of cultivating a foreign market for our manufactured goods obviously entered into creation of the British and French companies so as to enjoy a right of distribution into areas where otherwise restrictions, because of tariffs, quotas and exchange, might be expected. We fail to see such propensity toward restraint of trade as is evidenced in the Crescent case.

What we have is an American corporation, dominant in the field of tapered roller bearings, producing between 70 and 80 per cent of the American output. In 1947 it did over $77,000,000 gross sales. This is a distinctive type of bearing, competing successfully for adoption by industry with other antifriction bearings. Timken produces about 25% of all United States antifriction bearings. As there were no findings of facts tending to show violation of the Sherman Act otherwise than through formal agreements for partition of territory, we assume appellant's conduct was otherwise lawful.

In such circumstances, there was, of course, no occasion for the lower court to order any splitting up of a consolidated entity. . . . There has been no effort to create numerous smaller companies out of Timken so that there will be no dominant individual in the tapered roller bearing field. The American company had had a normal growth and development. Its relations with English and French Timken were close and American Timken had stock and contracts for further stock in both foreign companies of value in the development of its foreign business. Such business arrangements should not be destroyed unless necessary to do away with the prohibited evil.

An injunction was entered by the District Court to prohibit the continuation of the objectionable contracts. Violation of that injunction would threaten the appellant and its officers with civil and criminal contempt. . . . The paucity of cases dealing with contempt of Sherman Act injunctions is, I think, an indication of how carefully the decrees are obeyed. The injunction is a far stronger sanction against further violation than the Sherman Act alone. Once in possession of facts showing violation, the Government would obtain a quick and summary punishment of the violator. Furthermore this case remains on the docket for the purpose of "enforcement of compliance" and "punishment of violations." This provision should leave power in the court to enforce divestiture, if the injunction alone fails. Prompt and full compliance with the decree should be anticipated.

This Court is hesitant, always, to interfere with the scope of the trial court's decree. However, in this case, it seems appropriate to indicate my disapproval of the requirement of divestiture and to suggest a direction to the District Court that provisions leading to that result be eliminated from the decree. Such remand would also give opportunity for reconsideration of the changes necessary in the decree because of the remand and the death of Mr. Devar.

In my view such an order should be entered.

Mr. Justice Frankfurter, dissenting.

The force of the reasoning against divestiture in this case fortifies the doubts which I felt about the Government's position at the close of argument and persuades me to associate myself, in substance, with the dissenting views expressed by Mr. Justice Jackson. Even "cartel" is not a talismanic word, so as to displace the rule of reason by which breaches of the Sherman Law are determined. Nor is "division of territory" so self-operating a category of Sherman Law violations as to dispense with analysis of the practical consequences of what on paper is a geographic division of territory.

While American Banana Co. v. United Fruit Co., 213 U.S. 347, 29 S.Ct. 511, 53 L.Ed. 826, presented a wholly different set of facts from those before us, the decision in that case does point to the fact that the circumstances of foreign trade may alter the incidence of what in the setting of domestic commerce would be a clear case of unreasonable restraint of trade.

Of course, it is not for this Court to formulate economic policy as to foreign commerce. But the conditions controlling foreign commerce may be relevant here. When as a matter of cold fact the legal, financial, and governmental policies deny opportunities for exportation from this country and importation into it, arrangements that afford such opportunities to American enterprise may not fall under the ban of fair construction of the Sherman Law because comparable arrangements regarding domestic commerce come within its condemnation.

Mr. Justice Jackson, dissenting.

I doubt that it should be regarded as an unreasonable restraint of trade for an American industrial concern to organize foreign subsidiaries, each limited to serving a particular market area. If so, it seems to preclude the only practical means of reaching foreign markets by many American industries.

The fundamental issue here concerns a severely technical application to foreign commerce of the concept of conspiracy. It is admitted that if Timken had, within its own corporate organization, set up separate departments to operate plants in France and Great Britain, as well as in the United States, that would not be a conspiracy; we must have two entities to have a conspiracy. Thus, although a single American producer, of course, would not compete with itself, either abroad or at home, and could determine prices and allot territories with the same effect as here, that would not be a violation of the Act, because a corporation cannot conspire with itself. Government counsel answered affirmatively the question of the Chief Justice: "Your theory is that if you have a separate corporation that makes the difference?" Thus, the Court applies the well established conspiracy doctrine that what it would not be illegal for Timken to do alone may be illegal as a conspiracy when done by two legally separate persons. The doctrine now applied to foreign commerce is that foreign subsidiaries organized by an American corporation are "separate persons," and any arrangement between them and the parent corporation to do that which is legal for the parent alone is an unlawful conspiracy. I think that result places too much weight on labels.

But if we apply the most strict conspiracy doctrine, we still have the question whether the arrangement is an unreasonable restraint of trade or a method and means of carrying on competition in trade. Timken did not sit down with competitors and divide an existing market between them. It has at all times in all places had powerful rivals. It was not effectively meeting their competition in foreign markets, and so it joined others in creating a British subsidiary to go after business best reachable through such a concern and a French one to exploit French markets. Of course, in doing so, it allotted appropriate territory to each and none was to enter into competition with the other or with the parent. Since many foreign governments prohibit or handicap American corporations from owning plants, entering into contracts, or engaging in business directly, this seems the only practical way of waging competition in those areas.

The philosophy of the Government, adopted by the Court, is that Timken's conduct is conspiracy to restrain trade solely because the venture made use of subsidiaries. It is forbidden thus to deal with and utilize subsidiaries to exploit foreign territories, because "parent and subsidiary corporations must accept the consequences of maintaining separate corporate entities," and that consequence is conspiracy to restrain trade. But not all agreements are conspiracies and not all restraints of trade are unlawful. In a world of tariffs, trade barriers, empire or domestic preferences, and various forms of parochialism from which we are by no means free, I think a rule that it is restraint of trade to enter a foreign market through a separate subsidiary of limited scope is virtually to foreclose foreign commerce of many kinds. It is one thing for competitors or a parent and its subsidiaries to divide the United States domestic market which is an economic and legal unit; it is another for an industry to recognize that foreign markets consist of many legal and economic units and to go after each through separate means. I think this decision will restrain more trade than it will make free. ◄

SUMMARY OF GOVERNMENT REGULATION OF BUSINESS

Restraint of Trade and Monopoly

The term restraint of trade refers to business practices that tend to interfere with free competition. Restraint of trade often takes the form of monopoly—that is, the elimination of all effective competition.

At common law, contracts or agreements that created monopolies or led to an unreasonable restraint of trade were void and unenforceable. Usually, however, they were not punished by criminal penalties.

Federal Antitrust Legislation

The basic federal antitrust law is the Sherman Act, which was passed in 1890. This act declares that contracts and combinations in restraint of trade are illegal and that persons who monopolize or attempt to monopolize trade are guilty of a misdemeanor and subject to fine and imprisonment.

Another important antitrust statute is the Clayton Act, passed in 1914, which outlaws practices such as price discrimination, exclusive-dealing contracts, and stock acquisitions and interlocking directorates that tend to restrain trade and lessen competition. The provisions of the Clayton Act dealing with price discrimination were somewhat ineffective; the Robinson-Patman Act was enacted in 1936 in an effort to strengthen them.

The Federal Trade Commission Act of 1914 established the Federal

Trade Commission and gave it broad powers to interpret and enforce the antitrust laws as well as other federal statutes dealing with unfair and improper methods of competition.

Interpreting the Sherman Act

In the period immediately following its enactment, the Sherman Act was interpreted very strictly; the Supreme Court held that any restraint of trade, no matter how small, violated the law. The Court reversed this position later on, however, in favor of the so-called "rule of reason," which holds that a contract or combination is not unlawful unless it unreasonably restrains trade; here reasonableness is determined by the nature of the transaction and the surrounding circumstances.

Business Expansion by Integration of Firms

The Clayton Act prohibits a company from acquiring the stock or assets of another company if the effect is substantially to lessen competition or to tend to create a monopoly. The act also prohibits a person from being a director of two or more competing companies if competition is substantially lessened as a result.

Integration of firms may be either horizontal or vertical. Horizontal integration occurs when two or more companies competing with each other on the same level of business activity combine under one management; it is usually prohibited by the courts if it produces a substantial lessening of competition. Vertical integration occurs when two companies operating on different levels of business activity and not in direct competition combine their operations. Such integration is usually permitted unless it is accomplished by unlawful means or unless the resulting combination is so large and powerful that it promises to reduce competition substantially.

Internal Expansion Without Integration

Early decisions interpreting the Sherman Act held that mere size in itself was not illegal unless a company used its bigness to exercise monopolistic powers. More recent decisions, however, suggest that bigness automatically becomes illegal once a company has grown so powerful that effective competition ceases to exist, *regardless* of whether the company has abused its power.

Loose-Knit Combinations and Associations

Trade associations that undertake to fix prices, allocate or split markets, control output or production, or boycott certain customers are almost always deemed illegal; it is no defense for them to say that the prices they set are reasonable in themselves. On the other hand, associations that merely exchange information on prices, production costs, and so forth, and do not attempt to fix prices or control markets, are generally permitted.

Price-Fixing

Price-fixing may be classified as either horizontal or vertical. In horizontal price-fixing, two or more companies operating on the same level of competition agree to fix their prices at a certain figure. Such arrangements are almost always looked upon as an unlawful restraint of trade.

In vertical price-fixing, an agreement to maintain prices is made between manufacturers and dealers, or between wholesalers and retailers—i.e., between two firms operating on different levels of competition. Such agreements have generally been held to be in violation of the Sherman Act. However, the Miller-Tydings Act of 1937 specifically permits resale price maintenance agreements between manufacturers and dealers so long as such agreements are legal in the state where the products are to be resold. In addition, the McGuire Act of 1952 provides that such contracts are binding even on nonsigners, provided they are given notice of the fixed price.

Vertical price-fixing agreements are also held to be legal if they permit the dealer some discretion in fixing the ultimate price he charges the consumer.

Price Discrimination

The Clayton Act forbids price discrimination between purchasers if the effect is to lessen competition substantially. The act permits discrimination, however, if the seller can justify it in terms of differences in the quality or quantity of the goods sold or in terms of genuine differences in selling or transportation costs, or if he can show that the discrimination is a good-faith attempt to meet competition.

The Robinson-Patman Act strengthens the Clayton Act by providing that quantity discounts shall be permitted only to the extent that they can be justified by actual economies in the seller's costs of manufacture, sales, or delivery. The act *permits* price discrimination on goods that are perishable or seasonal, or in the case of close-out sales made in good faith. Further, the act subjects *buyers* as well as sellers to penalties if they are responsible for the discrimination. Other provisions of the Robinson-Patman Act prohibit certain indirect price-discrimination practices, such as (1) the payment of commissions, fees, or discounts when no services are rendered in exchange, and (2) the furnishing of advertising or merchandising services unless they are offered to all competing customers on the same basis.

Exclusive-Dealing and Tying Arrangements

The Clayton Act prohibits exclusive-dealing and tying agreements whose effect is to lessen competition substantially. An exclusive-dealing contract is an agreement between a manufacturer and a retailer in which the manufacturer agrees to supply the retailer with his products in exchange for the retailer's promise not to deal with any of the manufacturer's competitors. As a general rule, the courts have taken a lenient view of such agreements, holding them unlawful only if the manufacturer commands a dominant position in the market and seeks to maintain or enlarge that position by the use of such devices.

In tying contracts, the buyer or lessee of certain products agrees to use other products made by the manufacturer, or else not to use the products of the manufacturer's competitors. Since contracts of this sort usually produce a substantial lessening of competition, they are almost always regarded as an unlawful restraint of trade.

Remedies and Enforcement Proceedings

The responsibility for administering and enforcing the antitrust laws rests with the Federal Trade Commission and the Department of Justice. The Federal Trade Commission may investigate business practices, issue complaints, hold hearings, and issue cease and desist orders. Either the Commission or the party named in the action may appeal to the federal court of appeals for a review of the ultimate disposition of the case.

The government, acting through the Department of Justice, may bring a criminal prosecution against any person or firm that violates the antitrust laws; the court that hears the case may impose a fine or imprisonment as penalty. Another course open to the government is to seek an injunction to prevent violations of the antitrust laws. In such cases, the court often orders the dissolution of unlawful combinations or the divestiture of controlling stock interests. Frequently, such proceedings may be settled by consent decrees, which must, however, be approved by the court.

Private persons or firms harmed by a violation of the antitrust laws may also seek an injunction. In most cases, however, the amount of damages incurred as a result of such violations is very difficult to prove.

Supplementary Reading:
Government Regulation of Business

S. Chester Oppenheim, *Cases on Federal Antitrust Laws*, 2nd Ed. (West Publishing Co., 1959) is comprehensive, extremely useful, and highly recommended. Another valuable casebook is Milton Handler, *Cases on Trade Regulation*, 2nd Ed. (Foundation Press, 1951). An interesting analysis and criticism of the antitrust laws is *The Report of the Attorney General's National Committee to Study the Antitrust Laws*, 1955. See also G. W. Stocking and M. W. Watkins, *Monopoly and Free Enterprise* (Twentieth Century Fund, 1951).

Glossary
of Selected Terms

This Glossary contains a selection of the more important legal terms used in the book. Other legal terms are listed in the Index.

A number in roman type indicates a page in the *text* on which the term is explained or used illustratively. A number in italics indicates the first page of a *case* in which the meaning of a term is illustrated.

An asterisk following a term used in a definition indicates that that term is itself defined in the Glossary.

Actual authority. In agency law, the authority that is expressly or impliedly conferred on an agent by the principal. 549, 550.

Adjudication. The process by which impartial arbiters settle disputes—namely, by appraising the evidence and arguments presented by the parties and then applying legal (or other) principles to their findings of fact. The term usually refers to proceedings before courts of law, but it sometimes refers to administrative and arbitration proceedings. A distinction is drawn between the *adjudicative* (case-deciding) consequences and the *lawmaking* (precedent-creating) consequences of such proceedings, although the two are obviously intertwined. A related distinction is drawn between *adjudicative* and *legislative* facts. 13, 22n.; 159.

Administrative law. The body of legal rules that delimit the powers of executive and administrative officials and agencies, including their power to issue *regulations°* and to adjudicate cases. 149, 864.

Adversary system. The system of administering justice used in American courts, based on the principle that justice is best achieved in an adjudicative proceeding by making each party responsible for presenting factual evidence and legal arguments to support his position. 39, 40.

Agency. A legal relationship in which one person or organization (called the *agent*) acts on behalf of another (called the *principal*). 535, 538, 540.

879

Agency coupled with an interest. An agency in which the agent is given an interest in the subject matter of the agency itself, usually as security for the performance of an obligation by the principal. 593, 594.

Antitrust laws. Statutes designed to outlaw or control business practices that tend to restrain trade and impair free competition. 807, 809, 811.

Apparent authority. In agency law, the authority that exists when a principal, through his conduct, creates a situation that justifies a third party in assuming that the principal has bestowed authority on an agent despite the fact that the principal has bestowed no such authority. Apparent authority, also known as *ostensible authority* or *agency by estoppel,* is to be distinguished from *actual authority.*° 554, 555, 556.

Appellate court. A court that hears appeals from the decisions of lower courts. An appeal is based on an assertion that the lower court has made errors in applying the law. (The appealing party is known as the *appellant;* the other party is known as the *appellee.*) 14, 16, 28.

Arbitration. A method of settling a controversy outside the courts by submitting it to nonofficial persons known as arbitrators, who are chosen by the contending parties. The parties agree in advance that they will accept the arbitral decision. 181, 186.

Assignment. The transfer of a contract or a property right from one person (the *assignor*) to another (the *assignee*). It is to be distinguished from a *delegation°* and a *novation.*° 303, 310.

Bankruptcy. A procedure by which a person who is unable to pay his debts is permitted to have all his available assets distributed *pro rata* to his creditors, thereby releasing him from any further obligation. This is one method by which a party may discharge a contractual obligation to pay money. 332, 423.

Bilateral contract. A contract in which the offeror requests the offeree to indicate acceptance by making a promise in return; both sides are obligated once the mutual promises have been exchanged. 211, 223.

Breach of contract. The failure, without legal excuse, to perform a promise which forms the whole or a part of a contract. Normally, breaches occur only after the time for performance has arrived. An *anticipatory breach* occurs when a party repudiates his contractual obligation prior to the time when he is required to perform. 203n., 323.

Capacity. In contract law, the competence to enter into binding contractual relationships. A minor or an insane person, for example, is said to lack legal capacity. 265, 266, 270.

Capital. In partnership law, the permanent investment that the partners make in the business. On *dissolution,*° each partner's capital investment is returned to him before profits are computed. 632, 633.

Capital stock. The declared money value of the outstanding stock of a corporation. 736, 757.

Civil law. 1. The body of legal rules governing private rights and remedies, used in contradistinction to the rules of *criminal* law. 2. Roman law, or, more generally, the legal system of countries whose legal traditions stem from Roman law; used in this sense in contradistinction to the *common law.*° 10, 58n., 59n.

Civil wrong. An act (or an omission to act) which violates a legal *duty** owed to another, and which gives the person wronged the right to bring a lawsuit (sometimes called a *civil action*). It is to be distinguished from a *criminal wrong*, or *crime.** 10.

Code. A rationally organized compilation of legislative enactments. In Civil Law* countries, codes are the principal embodiments of law. (The process of collecting rules of law and embodying them in a code is known as *codification*.) 59n., 94, 103.

Collective bargaining. The process of negotiation between an employer and the union that represents his employees. A major aim of such bargaining is to arrive at a *collective bargaining agreement*. There is also continuous bargaining over employee *grievances*. Federal law requires employers and unions under its authority to bargain collectively in good faith. 162, 174.

Common law. It is used variously to mean: 1. The legal tradition of the English-speaking world. 2. The body of rules originally administered by the royal courts of law, as distinguished from *equity.** 3. All judge-made, *decisional law** which emerges from the application of principles and precedents, and not from the interpretation of *legislative law.** 4. The body of English legal rules transplanted to the American colonies and in force there in 1776. 58n., 80g.

Common stock. The ordinary stock of a corporation. Common stock usually gives the holder the right to vote on corporate matters and to share in dividends, but it does not entitle him to any priority as to dividends or the distribution of corporate assets on dissolution. 719, 727.

Conditional sale. A sales transaction in which the buyer is given the possession and use of the goods and agrees to pay the seller (usually in installments) at some future date. The seller retains title to the goods until he has been fully paid and may retake possession of them if he is not paid. 429, 430.

Conflict of laws. The name given to the body of rules that determine which set of laws will actually govern a case that might possibly be governed by the laws of several jurisdictions. 20, 270.

Consideration. An act or a promise to act which is offered by one party to a contract and which is accepted by the other party as an inducement to act or to promise to act. To furnish consideration, a party must do, or agree to do, something that he is otherwise not legally obligated to do. As a general rule, one party to an agreement cannot require the other party to perform unless he can show that he has furnished consideration for the other party's promise. 247, 248, 258.

Constitution. 1. A document which enunciates the principles that establish the structure and organization of the major branches and levels of government, and which allocates and limits the powers of those branches and levels. 2. More broadly, the body of *decisional law** which has elaborated the principles embodied in the basic document, and the generally accepted arrangements and understandings which have developed as problems of government have been resolved. 127, 143.

Corporation. A legal entity created by one or more individuals under authority granted by the state for the purpose of conducting a business or other enterprise. 681, 686.

Crime. A violation of a legal *duty** that is considered to affect the public interest and therefore leads to intervention by officials (e.g., the police and the public prosecutor). It is to be distinguished from a *civil wrong.** 10, 379.

Damages. The money compensation that A must pay to B when the court has ruled that A, by violating a legal *duty** owed to B, has caused B to suffer an injury. 333, 334.

De facto corporation. A corporation that fails to comply with one or more requirements of the incorporation law, but is nevertheless recognized as a corporation in fact if not in law. As a general rule, the legality of such a corporation may be challenged only by the state authorities; it may not be challenged by a party who contracts with or otherwise deals with the corporation. 690, 694.

De jure corporation. A corporation that has been formed in full compliance with the incorporation law and other legal requirements. 689, 690.

Decisional law. Rules of law that emerge from the decision of particular cases. These rules may result from the application of *precedents** and principles of *common law** or from the interpretation and application of the provisions of *statutes** and *constitutions.** While the term usually refers to the rules created by courts, it is sometimes extended to include the rules created by the adjudicative decisions of administrative agencies. It is to be distinguished from *legislative law.** 12, 66, 88, 161.

Delegation. The transfer of an obligation to perform some contractual duty. It is to be distinguished from an *assignment.** 304, 305.

Demurrer. A *pleading** in which the demurring party in effect says, "Even if the facts alleged by my adversary were true, they would fail to provide the basis for a legal claim (or a legal defense)." A demurrer raises a *question of law.** (A defendant's demurrer is sometimes known as a "motion to dismiss for failure to state a cause of action.") 24, 26, 73.

Dictum. A statement in a judicial opinion concerning some hypothetical legal question that the court does not have to answer in order to decide the case at hand. *Dicta* have some influence on the development of *decisional law,** but they tend to be less influential than the court's actual *holding* in the case. 63, 746.

Dishonor. The neglect or refusal to pay a negotiable instrument when it is properly presented for payment. (The term also refers to a refusal to accept a bill of exchange when it is presented for acceptance.) 484, 486.

Dissolution. In partnership law, the stage at which a firm ceases to exist as a going concern and the partners cease to do business together. In corporation law, the stage at which a corporation ceases to exist as a legal entity. 656, 658, 662, 793.

Diversity of citizenship. The term used to describe that category of cases over which federal courts have jurisdiction (concurrently with state courts) because the parties are citizens of different states. (The other major category of cases over which federal courts have jurisdiction are the so-called "federal-question" cases.) 20, 223.

Due process of law. The constitutional guarantee, embodied in the Fifth and Fourteenth Amendments of the federal Constitution, that no person shall be deprived of "life, liberty, or property without due process of law." Among the many applications that the Supreme Court has given the term, perhaps the most significant has been the insistence on strict adherence to fair procedures whenever official action affects individual rights. 129, 140, *682.*

Duty. The obligation imposed on the addressees of a legal rule that commands or prohibits a certain type of action. A violation of a duty is a legal *wrong.* Those for whose benefit the duty is imposed are sometimes said to have a legal *right.* 8, 66.

Equal protection of the laws. The constitutional guarantee, embodied in the Fourteenth Amendment of the federal Constitution, that no state "shall deny to any person within its jurisdiction the equal protection of the laws." This is a guarantee against invidious and unwarranted discrimination by state officials. 129.

Equity. A body of legal rules and remedies originally developed in England in response to the growing rigidity of the rules and remedies of the *common law.*° Many of the American states originally followed the British practice of assigning equity jurisdiction to special courts (chancery courts), but nowadays both common-law and equity cases are handled by the same courts in virtually all American jurisdictions. Among the equitable remedies are the *injunction*° and the decree of *specific performance;* ° these remedies are granted, however, only when the plaintiff has satisfied the court that the common-law remedy of *damages*° is inadequate. 58, 267n., *435.*

Estoppel. The legal principle which holds that a party is legally barred, because of his prior conduct, from asserting certain facts or doing certain acts. The doctrine of estoppel originated in equity and is used to avoid an unjust result in certain special situations. 252n., *258.*

Evidence. Any factual data which the parties present to a trial court—whether through the medium of witnesses, records, documents, or objects—for the purpose of inducing the judge or jury to believe their contentions. The "rules of evidence" set limits to the kinds and sources of data which may be introduced. 35, *829.*

Fiduciary relationship. A relationship involving a high degree of trust and confidence. One who has a *fiduciary duty* to another must perform it with scrupulous good faith and candor. 606, 607n.

Fraud. In contract law, the making of false or misleading statements or representations to another to induce him to enter into a contract. 241, *243.*

Good will. The value that attaches to the name of a business firm as a result of the firm's reputation in the community and its justifiable expectation of continued patronage by the public. *628.*

Holder in due course. A person in possession of a negotiable instrument who enjoys certain preferential rights because of the circumstances under which he acquired the instrument. Such a holder is immune from certain defenses that might otherwise be used to avoid payment of the instrument. 490, *491, 493.*

Injunction. A remedy of *equity*° consisting of a court order that requires the addressee to do or to refrain from doing certain acts. Noncompliance may result in a citation for contempt of court. 39, *283.*

Instruction. A statement made by the judge to the jury, after both sides have presented their cases, in which he summarizes the evidence, outlines the applicable rules of law, and instructs the jurors on how they must go about applying the rules to the facts they find. (Sometimes called the *charge.*) 37, *218.*

Issue. Any matter on which the parties in a case take opposite positions. When the case is before an *appellate court,*° the issues still to be settled normally involve *questions of law.*° 21, 25.

Judgment. The decision that the trial judge orders entered on the court record at the end of a lawsuit. It should not be confused with the *verdict,*° which is the decision reached by a jury on the matters put before it. When a judgment follows a jury trial, however, it normally (but not necessarily) confirms the verdict. On appeal, a judgment may be *affirmed* or *reversed.* 38, 39, 80.

Judicial review. The function performed by a court when, during the course of a legal proceeding, it reviews the validity of an official act; this act may be a legislative enactment, an executive order, or the act or decision of an administrative official or body. The issue is often whether or not the official act meets constitutional requirements. Whether or not a particular party is entitled to judicial review depends on a variety of statutory and constitutional rules. 130, *143,* 160, *864.*

Jurisdiction. The authority of a court to hear and decide a case. Among the considerations affecting a court's jurisdiction are: its authority in relation to particular geographical areas; its authority over particular subject matter, persons, and property; its authority to grant particular types of remedy; and its authority to hear cases either originally or on appeal. 18, *794, 811.*

Law merchant. A body of rules and precedents originally developed as a system of private law or *quasi-law*° by the merchants and financiers of Medieval Europe; eventually much of it was absorbed into the *common law.*° 169, 447.

Legal entity. The concept that permits an organization to be treated as separate and distinct from the persons who compose it. In corporation and partnership law, this concept is important in determining in whose name property is to be held, in whose name suit is to be brought, and who is liable for the obligations of the organization. See also *Limited liability.*° 681, 686.

Legislative history. Evidence of the purposes of a statute as recorded in the legislature's deliberations before the statute was enacted. 114, *117.*

Legislative law. Written law; that part of the law which is formally enacted in the form of an official text. It is to be distinguished from *decisional law,*° which consists of the rules that emerge from the decision of particular cases. Legislative law includes *statutes,*° *constitutions,*° and, sometimes, executive orders and administrative *regulations.*° 12, 88, 152.

Liability. Broadly, any obligation one may incur for having violated some legal *duty.*° 66, 71, 782.

Liberty. The legal position of a person with respect to actions permitted by the law. A *liberty* (also sometimes called a "privilege") exists when there is no *duty*° to act or to refrain from acting. 8.

Liberty (freedom) of contract. The doctrine that the constitutional guarantee of *due process*° bars government interference with private contractual relations—e.g., between employer and employee—unless such interference can be justified as a "reasonable" exercise of the government's regulatory power. 141, *143,* 205.

Lien. A right or claim which one person has on the property of another as security for the payment of a debt or the performance of an obligation. 449n.

Limited liability. In corporation law, the doctrine that a stockholder shall not be individually liable for the debts of the corporation over and above the amount he has paid, or has agreed to pay, for his shares of stock. 678.

Mixed question of law and fact. An issue to be resolved in an adjudicative proceeding involving elements of fact and law so intertwined that the question cannot be classified either as a *question of fact** or a *question of law.** 23, 100n., 165.

Negligence. Failure to act with the care that a reasonable, prudent person would show under like circumstances. If the defendant and plaintiff in a lawsuit have both been negligent, the plaintiff's negligence is described as *contributory*. 46–47, 65, 513.

Negotiable instruments. Promissory notes, bills of exchange, or checks evidencing an obligation to pay a sum of money. Negotiable instruments may be transferred freely from one person to another by indorsement and delivery or, in some cases, by delivery alone. To be negotiable, an instrument must meet certain prerequisites set by the Uniform Negotiable Instruments Law (N.I.L.). The transferee of a negotiable instrument often acquires greater rights than does an assignee of an ordinary contract right to recover money. See *Holder in due course.** 449, 458, 460.

Novation. An agreement between two contracting parties that a third party shall be substituted for one of the original parties, who is thereby released from further obligation. It is to be distinguished from an *assignment.** 308.

Parol evidence rule. The rule that prohibits the introduction in evidence of written or oral statements or agreements made by the contracting parties before or at the time they entered into a written contract. 287, 289.

Partnership. An association of two or more persons (called *partners*) to carry on a business together. As a general rule, partners share in the profits of the business and are personally responsible for its losses. 605, 606, 608.

Personal property. All property other than *real property.** *Tangible personal property* is property that can be touched or felt and has physical existence. *Intangible personal property* consists of legal rights that do not have any physical form. 351.

Plain meaning rule. A rule of statutory interpretation holding that, when the language of a statutory provision appears to be clear and unambiguous, its "plain meaning" will be applied and no effort need be made to ascertain the probable purpose underlying the provision. *103*, 106.

Pleadings. The exchange of legal documents by which the parties to a lawsuit seek to define the issues in dispute. The basic pleadings in modern practice are the plaintiff's *complaint* and the defendant's *answer*. Another important pleading is the *demurrer.** 26–27.

Power. The legal position of a person with respect to actions that the law not only permits (cf. *liberty**) but endows with certain legal consequences. For instance, a person has a *power* to make a will: if he executes the will properly, the state will see to it that his property is distributed at his death according to the provisions of the will. 9, 193.

Precedent. The decision in an adjudicative proceeding viewed as an authoritative determination to be relied on in deciding similar or analogous cases arising later. The doctrine that precedents, and the reasoning that supports them, should normally control the decision of later cases is known as *stare decisis.** 60, 61, 66, 73.

Preferred stock. Stock that confers on its owner certain preferential rights in the disbursement of dividends or in the distribution of corporate assets on dissolution, or both. *719, 721.*

Quasi-contract. An obligation imposed by law on a party who has benefited from the act of another, requiring him to return the fair value of the benefit he has received on the theory that it would be unjust for him to retain it. *230.*

Quasi-law. A system of private rules resembling law (in the traditional sense) in that it channels the behavior and relationships of some considerable number of persons, but differing from law in that it has been created by private groups. The so-called *law merchant*° of England was quasi-law until it was absorbed into the common law during the eighteenth century. The formal agreement arising out of *collective bargaining*° is quasi-law governing the relations between employer and employees. *170.*

Question of fact. An issue to be resolved in an adjudicative proceeding involving differing allegations as to "what happened" in the particular case. It is to be distinguished from a *question of law.*° *21–22, 794.*

Question of law. An issue to be resolved in an adjudicative proceeding involving differing assertions as to the content and scope of the rule of law that is applicable to the case at hand and similar cases. It is to be distinguished from a *question of fact.*° *21–22, 823.*

Ratification. The affirmation or confirmation by a person of a previous act or contract that would not otherwise be binding on him in the absence of such confirmation. In contract law, the term usually refers to the affirmation of a contractual obligation by a minor after he attains majority. In agency law, the term refers to the confirmation of an unauthorized act by an agent, or by one who purports to act as an agent. *269, 542, 543, 545.*

Real property. Land, and the buildings and vegetation on land. It is to be distinguished from *personal property.*° *351n.*

Regulations. A set of rules promulgated by an administrative agency. Regulations are sometimes classed as either *interpretive* or *legislative.* The former are merely interpretations by the agency of the law it is administering. If, however, the agency has been expressly authorized by the legislature to issue regulations, its regulations are a form of *legislative law,*° and have the same force as other embodiments of law. *152, 154.*

Remedies. The means by which the violation of a right is prevented, redressed, or indemnified. The term most often refers to *judicial* remedies (money damages, injunctions, and so forth) that may be granted at the end of a civil suit, and the sanctions (fine, imprisonment, and so forth) that may result from a criminal prosecution. *5, 333, 794, 869.*

Res judicata. The principle which holds that once a controversy has been adjudged on its merits, and all allowable appeals have been taken, the issues involved may not be raised again in a subsequent lawsuit between the parties, since they are considered to have had their "day in court." *29, 38.*

Rescission. The cancellation of a contract and the restoration of each party to his original position prior to the making of the contract. *331, 426.*

Respondeat superior. The doctrine that a principal or an employer is liable for wrongful acts committed by an agent or an employee in the course of his employment even though the acts were not authorized. *575, 576, 577.*

Restraint of trade. Business practices or activities that tend to interfere with free competition. When restraint of trade reaches the point where all effective competition is eliminated, it becomes a *monopoly*. 809, 841.

Specific performance. In contract law, a remedy of *equity*° consisting of a court order directing a party actually to perform his contractual obligation instead of just paying damages. Generally speaking, *specific performance* will not be ordered unless the court feels that the award of money damages would not be adequate compensation. Noncompliance may result in a citation for contempt of court. 342, 746.

Stare decisis. The doctrine that courts should ordinarily follow the *precedents*° established by earlier decisions in like cases, so as to give continuity and predictability to the law. 60, 243.

Statute. Any law enacted by a legislative body. This generic term comprehends such terms as "acts" (e.g., of Congress), "laws" (e.g., of Massachusetts), and "ordinances" (e.g., of the city council). 86n., 110.

Statute of frauds. A statute providing that certain kinds of contract are not enforceable unless there is a written memorandum or other written document signed by the party who is being asked to carry out its terms. 294, 300, 364.

Statute of limitations. A statute restricting the period of time within which a party may sue for breach of contract or for other legal wrongs. 332.

Tort. Any *civil wrong*° other than a breach of contract. Whenever a person violates a legal *duty*° to which he is subject, unless it is a duty imposed by criminal law or by contractual commitments, he has committed a tort. 10, 267n.

Ultra vires. In corporation law, a phrase referring to an act or contract that a corporation has no legal power to do or make. 713, 717.

Unilateral contract. A contract in which one party makes an offer to another without receiving any promise or commitment in return. The offeror requests the offeree to indicate his acceptance by performing some act; neither side is obligated unless and until the offeree has actually performed the act requested. It is to be distinguished from a *bilateral contract*.° 212.

Verdict. The formal and usually unanimous findings of a jury on questions submitted to it during a trial. When the jury is asked for a *special verdict*, it is required merely to resolve disputed questions of fact; when, however, it is asked for a *general verdict*, it must both resolve the questions of fact and apply the rules of law (on which the judge has instructed it) to its findings of fact. 37–38, 471.

Void contract. An agreement that has no legal effect whatsoever. It is to be distinguished from a *voidable contract*.° 208, 278, 283, 284.

Voidable contract. An agreement that, because of special circumstances surrounding the making of the agreement or because one party lacks legal capacity, is binding on one side but not on the other. If the party having the right to avoid the contract does not choose to do so, however, both sides are bound to perform. It is to be distinguished from a *void contract*.° 207, 232, 239, 270.

Warranty. A guarantee by a seller of goods that the goods meet certain standards. *Express warranties* are affirmative representations by the seller in the form of written or oral statements. *Implied warranties* are warranties imposed by law in the absence of any express warranty. 384, 388, 390, 395.

Table
of Cases

When the court's opinion in a case is quoted at length in the text, the case title is italicized; the page reference on which the opinion begins is also in italics. The titles of cases merely cited or discussed in the text, and all references to pages on which cases are merely cited or discussed, are in roman type.

Index

(Note: Items followed by an asterisk are defined in the Glossary.)